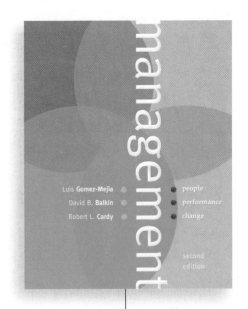

Management
SECOND EDITION

people

performance

change

Luis R. Gomez-Mejia
Arizona State University

David B. Balkin
University of Colorado

Robert L. Cardy
Arizona State University

McGraw-Hill
Irwin

Boston   Burr Ridge, IL   Dubuque, IA   Madison, WI   New York   San Francisco   St. Louis
Bangkok   Bogotá   Caracas   Kuala Lumpur   Lisbon   London   Madrid   Mexico City
Milan   Montreal   New Delhi   Santiago   Seoul   Singapore   Sydney   Taipei   Toronto

The McGraw-Hill Companies

McGraw-Hill
Irwin

MANAGEMENT: PEOPLE, PERFORMANCE, CHANGE
Published by McGraw-Hill/Irwin, a business unit of The McGraw-Hill Companies, Inc., 1221
Avenue of the Americas, New York, NY, 10020. Copyright © 2005, 2002 by The McGraw-Hill
Companies, Inc. All rights reserved. No part of this publication may be reproduced or
distributed in any form or by any means, or stored in a database or retrieval system, without
the prior written consent of The McGraw-Hill Companies, Inc., including, but not limited to, in
any network or other electronic storage or transmission, or broadcast for distance learning.
Some ancillaries, including electronic and print components, may not be available to
customers outside the United States.

This book is printed on acid-free paper.

1 2 3 4 5 6 7 8 9 0 VNH/VNH 0 9 8 7 6 5 4

ISBN 0-07-284697-6

Editorial director: *John E. Biernat*
Sponsoring editor: *Ryan Blankenship*
Senior developmental manager: *Christine Scheid*
Executive marketing manager: *Ellen Cleary*
Producer, Media technology: *Mark Molsky*
Project manager: *Jim Labeots*
Production supervisor: *Gina Hangos*
Designer: *Adam Rooke*
Photo research coordinator: *Jeremy Cheshareck*
Photo researcher: *Jennifer Blankenship*
Supplement producer: *Betty Hadala*
Senior digital content specialist: *Brian Nacik*
Cover design: *Adam Rooke*
Interior design: *Adam Rooke/Kaye Farmer*
Typeface: *10.5/13 Palatino*
Compositor: *Carlisle Communications, Ltd.*
Printer: *Von Hoffmann Corporation*

Library of Congress Cataloging-in-Publication Data

Gomez-Mejia, Luis R.
    Management : people, performance, change / Luis R. Gomez-Mejia, David B. Balkin,
Robert L. Cardy.--2nd ed.
        p. cm.
    Includes bibliographical references and index.
    ISBN 0-07-284697-6 (alk. paper) -- ISBN 0-07-111131-X (international : alk. paper)
    1. Management.   I. Balkin, David B., 1948–   II. Cardy, Robert L., 1955–   III. Title.
HD31.G58955 2005
658--dc22

2003066595

INTERNATIONAL EDITION ISBN 0-07-111131-X
Copyright © 2005. Exclusive rights by The McGraw-Hill Companies, Inc. for manufacture and
export. This book cannot be re-exported from the country to which it is sold by McGraw-Hill.
The International Edition is not available in North America.

www.mhhe.com

dedicated

to my sons, Vince and Alex, my daughter Dulce Maria, and my wife Ana—LG-M

to my parents, Daniel and Jeanne—DBB

to my wife and daughters, Laurel, Lara, and Emery—RLC

Luis R. Gomez-Mejia is a full professor of management in the College of Business at Arizona State University. Before joining ASU, he taught at the University of Colorado and the University of Florida. He has also been on the faculty at Universidad Carlos III de Madrid and Instituto de Empresas and has offered seminars in both Spanish and English in many countries and universities around the world.

He received his Ph.D. and M.A. in industrial relations from the College of Business at the University of Minnesota and a B.A. (summa cum laude) in economics from the University of Minnesota. Prior to entering academia, Professor Gomez-Mejia worked in human resources for the City of Minneapolis and Control Data Corporation and served as consultant to numerous organizations.

He has served two terms on the editorial board of the *Academy of Management Journal* and is editor and co-founder of two journals: *Journal of High Technology Management Research* and *Management Research*. Dr. Gomez-Mejia has published more than 100 articles in the most prestigious management journals including the *Academy of Management Journal, Academy of Management Review, Administrative Science Quarterly, Strategic Management Journal, Industrial Relations,* and *Personnel Psychology.* He has also written and edited a dozen management books.

Dr. Gomez-Mejia has received numerous awards including "best article" in the *Academy of Management Journal* and the Outstanding Alumni Award at University of Minnesota. He has been named a Dean's Council of 100 Distinguished Scholar at Arizona State University every year since 1994, holds the Horace Steel Chair at Arizona State University, is a member of the Academy of Management's Journals Hall of Fame, and is a Fellow of the Academy of Management.

He is also president of the Iberoamerican Academy of Management (an affiliate of the Academy of Management), which covers Spain and Portugal, all of Latin America, and Hispanic faculty in U.S. universities.

David B. Balkin   is the chair of the Management Division and is a full professor in the College of Business and Administration at the University of Colorado. Previously he was an associate professor at the university. Before joining the University of Colorado in 1988, he taught at Louisiana State University and Northeastern University. He served as a visiting professor for the University of Toulouse in France and the University of Montreal in Quebec, Canada, and has also taught courses in Norway, Spain, Israel, and Santo Domingo, Dominican Republic.

He received his Ph.D. in industrial relations from the University of Minnesota Graduate School of Business, where he specialized in human resources management. He earned a master's degree in industrial relations at the University of Minnesota Graduate School of Business and a bachelor's degree in political science at the University of California at Los Angeles. Dr. Balkin has been a management consultant for Control Data Corporation, a personnel analyst for Honeywell Corporation, and a marketing research associate for National Broadcasting Company. He also serves as an expert witness in cases involving pay and employment discrimination.

Professor Balkin has served as associate editor for *Human Resource Management Review* since 1997 and as a member of the editorial review board for the *Journal of High Technology Management Research* since 1990. He has also been a member of the editorial review board for the *Academy of Management Journal* and serves as a reviewer for several publications. He is widely published in the professional literature, most recently in the Academy of *Management Journal, Journal of Business and Psychology, Group and Organization Management, Human Resource Management Review, Journal of Compensation and Benefits, Journal of Occupational and Organizational Psychology,* and *HR Magazine.*

He is the author and editor of several books on human resources, the management of innovation, compensation, and other topics. He has received the North American Case Research Association's Curtis E. Tate Jr. Outstanding Case Writer award, the National Academy of Management's Best Article of the Year award, and the Western Academy of Management's Outstanding Paper award.

Robert L. Cardy is a full professor of management in the W. P. Carey School of Business at Arizona State University. Before joining ASU, he taught at the State University of New York at Buffalo.

He received his Ph.D. in industrial/organizational psychology from Virginia Tech. His masters and undergraduate degrees are from Central Michigan University. Dr. Cardy has consulted with a variety of organizations, particularly in the areas of performance appraisal and competency model development and implementation.

Professor Cardy has served multiple terms as a member of the executive committee of the Human Resource Management Division of the Academy of Management. He has regularly written columns for the *HR Division Newsletter* on new and innovative issues since 1991. Dr. Cardy was the co-founder and editor of the former *Journal of Quality Management.* He has been a member of the editorial review boards for the *Journal of Applied Psychology* and the *Journal of Organizational Behavior* and serves as a reviewer for several publications. He has published articles in a variety of journals including *Journal of Applied Psychology, Organizational Behavior and Human Decision Processes, Journal of Management, Management Communication Quarterly*, and *HR Magazine.*

Dr. Cardy has authored or edited several books on human resource management and performance management. He has twice received a "best paper" award from the Human Resource Management Division of the Academy of Management. He has received a "University Mentor Award" for his work with doctoral students at Arizona State University. He is also an honors Fellow of the W. P. Carey School of Business for which he is a faculty mentor to teams of honors students working on community development projects.

About the Authors

brief contents

Gomez-Mejia/Balkin/Cardy:

Ask your incoming students what "management" is, and they'll talk about the kind of management they know from their own (limited) work experience. Managers assign people their hours, give raises or promotions, tell people what job to do—the manager, in other words, is "the boss."

In most other work settings, however, management means something far more important and complex. In addition to people, managers also manage performance, processes, relationships, and more increasingly in today's world, deal with the pressure and flux of constant change. This, coupled with the fact that workplaces have steadily become less hierarchical and more team- and group-driven, means the traditional responsibilities of the manager have gradually been dispersed throughout the organization. Students preparing to work in today's business environment may not start in a corner office with an assistant, but they still need to *think like* managers and understand the strategic goals of the organization.

Management prepares your students to join a new kind of workplace, one where management is *everyone's* business.

In order to prepare your students for a rapidly changing workplace, *Management* seeks to go beyond the scope of other management textbooks in our approach and our content. It does this in three key aspects:

Management Is Everyone's Business

Beyond the **ordinary.** Your students start the course thinking of managers as little more than traditional "bosses." *Management* helps your students to move beyond this perception by offering coverage and exercises that emphasize the multifaceted nature of modern management. In particular, the "Management Close-Up" boxed feature offers unique perspectives. Each close-up has a theme of either **Ethics, Customer Focus,** and/or **Dealing With Change** to illustrate contemporary issues that managers and organizations confront that go beyond merely "being the boss."

Beyond theory. Nothing as complex as management can be understood merely by reading the theory. While *Management* is careful to ground students in the relevant theories, it gives your students numerous opportunities to apply their learning to real-world management situations. More than **40 interactive exercises** on the **student CD-ROM**—and highlighted with a CD icon throughout the book—put your students in the manager's chair to deal with important and complex issues. Additionally, the **end-of-chapter material** provides a variety of exercises, including mini-cases, collaborative learning exercises, Internet exercises, and skill-building exercises.

Beyond your **expectations.** We've worked hard to make the *Management* textbook package more comprehensive, more useful, and more flexible than any other on the market. Our ancillaries will open whole new avenues of teaching for you - from our impressive range of video cases and our new "Manager's Hot Seat" videos which put real managers in the hot seat of a sticky management issue to a Test Bank that's unmatched by any other book.

GOMEZ-MEJIA | BALKIN | CARDY

MANAGEMENT IS EVERYONE'S BUSINESS

Management is full of innovative chapter features to make studying productive and hassle-free. The following pages show the kind of engaging, helpful pedagogical features that make up Management's powerful approach.

Organizational Culture as Competitive Tool: Some Tips

4.2 **MANAGER'S NOTES**

1. Check whether your culture is strong or weak.
   - Do employees agree on the core values?
   - Do ceremonies, stories, and so on present a coherent and consistent message?
   - A strong culture should lead to greater cohesiveness and higher performance.
2. Is the culture consistent with the objectives of the organization?
   - Do the policies, practices, and employee beliefs and values line up with the strategy?
   - Does everyone know the mission of the organization?
     - A culture that is compatible with the strategy can reinforce the strategy and help to get everyone working together for the same purpose.

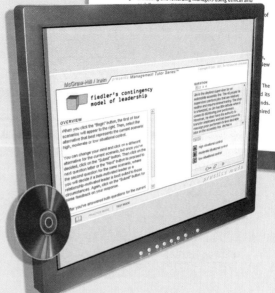

No Sweat for Levi Strauss

Few companies take ethics and social responsibility as seriously as Levi Strauss and Co. In 1992 the values of this clothing manufacturer were put to the test by two sewing subcontractors in Bangladesh that were using child labor. Child labor was unacceptable to the company, but without jobs, some of the children would be forced into prostitution to support their families. The management team at Levi Strauss devised a unique solution: they took the children out of the factory, continued to pay their wages so long as they attended school full time, and guaranteed the children factory jobs when they reached age 14, the local age of maturity.

Levi Strauss began finding ways to blend profitability and social responsibility during the Great Depression. Instead of firing employees when demand for products decreased, the company kept workers busy laying new floors in its San Francisco offices until business improved. Levi Strauss sustains its corporate goals by encouraging both employees and managers to make ethical and socially responsible business decisions. Strategies that are used include:

1. Donations of 2.5 percent of pretax profits to the Levi Strauss Foundation, which supports charitable organizations in the communities in which the company operates.
2. A week-long ethical decision-making course that is a requirement for every employee. Managers learn to consider ethical challenges when making decisions.
3. Evaluating and rewarding managers using ethical and

www.levistrauss.com

101

Manager's Notebook

These features supplement chapter content with a practicing manager's perspective. Manager's Notebooks provide valuable insider tips to dealing with common situations and are an ideal jumping-off point for classroom discussion.

Opening Vignettes

These vignettes neatly encapsulate actual business issues students will encounter as they read the chapter. The vignettes in the 2nd edition include critical thinking questions that are answered at the end of the chapter.

Interactive Exercises

What is a SWOT Analysis? Who is Fiedler and why is his model important? Part of studying management is learning new terminology and theories, but students want to know how they apply. Over 40 topics can be explored more thoroughly with the Interactive Exercises included on the student CD-ROM. These topics are marked in the text with a convenient CD icon and help students apply management theory to everyday situations.

GOMEZ-MEJIA | BALKIN | CARDY

2.b management close-up

A New Round of Globalization Is Sending Upscale Jobs Offshore

THEME: DEALING WITH CHANGE

"The handwriting is on the wall," writes a veteran information-technology specialist in an internal e-mail. This sense of resignation arose from the changing world surrounding the company. Just three years ago, the Charlotte (N.C.) banking operation needed IT talent so badly that the company was forced to outbid rivals. However, in recent months the entire 15-member engineering team had been told their jobs "wouldn't last through September."

Recently, Bank of America had reduced domestic operations by eliminating 3,700 of its 25,000 tech and back-office employees. These layoffs were not the result of declining demand. Instead, former company employees and contractors charged that nearly one-third of the jobs (about 1,100) were simply being relocated to India, where work which costs $100 per hour is completed for less than $20 per hour.

Cut to India: In dazzling new technology parks rising on the dusty outskirts of the nation's major cities, no one is talking about downsizing. Inside Infosys Technologies Ltd.'s impeccably landscaped 55-acre campus in Bangalore, 250 engineers develop IT applications for the Bank of America. Elsewhere, Infosys staffers process home loans for Greenpoint Mortgage of Novato, California. Near Bangalore's airport, at the offices of Wipro Ltd., five radiologists

These New Delhi white collar workers at Wipro Spetramind are 60 percent cheaper than their U.S. counterparts.

new world of globalization includes finding locations where both cost and quality goals can be met, a ... lesson fo...

6.a management close-up

How UPS Managed to Deliver During the 9/11 Crisis

THEME: CUSTOMER FOCUS Many crisis decisions were made following the September 11, 2001, terrorist attacks at the World Trade Center in New York City and at the Pentagon in Washington DC. As the attacks took place, airborne aircraft were advised to land at the nearest airport and subway trains that were headed toward the World Trade Center were halted, thereby saving thousands of lives. Thousands of people were evacuated from buildings close to ground zero. United Parcel Service (UPS), the package delivery service company, went into crisis management mode shortly after the attack. With all air traffic grounded, Joe Liana, UPS's Manhattan district manager, called in all employees to report to UPS's package sorting facility to identify high-priority packages such as medical supplies that were ...

truck because air travel was prohibited, and nobody knew when air transportation would resume. UPS vice chairman Michael L. Eskew decided to transfer packages designated for aircraft to trucks when they met certain criteria. A package needed to be able to be delivered within three days by truck in order to avoid overwhelming the truck operations' ability to deliver. Eskew gambled that aircraft operations would be resumed within one week. This turned out to be a correct assumption. As a result of UPS's crisis management decisions, the company was able to resume package delivery operations quickly, without losing market share.

The key decisions made at UPS were: (1) empowering local district managers to handle a crisis on their own, and (2) holding back from the ground delivery system any air ... ken more th... ... days to ...

2.g management close-up

Competition to Make Products for Western Companies Has Received an Old Form of Abuse: Debt Bondage

THEME: ETHICS Debt bondage means it is impossible to "get ahead" financially, because you owe too much money to others. There are many forms. In the U.S. it wasn't long ago that coal miners were forced to buy overpriced food from "company stores." Sharecroppers were trapped by their debts to landowners. Even today, many illegal Mexican immigrants are working to pay off debts to the so-called "coyotes" who smuggle them across the Rio Grande.

Unlike the coyotes, the Asian labor brokers to whom many workers are indebted operate in the open. Their services ... ... the factories

Management Close-Ups

To help students look up-close at the issues real managers deal with, *Management* includes "Management Close-Up" boxes. Ethics, Customer Focus, or Dealing With Change subtitle these boxes and highlight aspects of management particularly important today.

Dealing With Change

New technology or new CEOs, globalization and the information economy, regulatory changes: all of these factors constantly conspire to reshape the contemporary business workplace or a particular organization. The successful manager needs to be able to anticipate and adapt to change, and these boxes illustrate how a particular change can impact the successful functioning of a firm.

Customer Focus

In today's hyper-competitive world, relationships and trust are increasingly important. For the manager, everyone is a customer, whether they are *internal* or *external*. Within their organizations, managers rely on maintaining good relationships with managers and employees in other departments to get things done. Just as important are relationships with external customers, potential partnerships, and alliances. The Customer Focus boxes offer real-world examples of how relationships play crucial roles in the success of organizations.

Ethics

Ethical conduct in business has become an increasingly public issue. Whether the issue is recognizing the importance of stakeholders, a regulatory issue, or issues with employees, ethical behavior and policies cut across all management issues. Nearly every chapter of *Management* includes these special illustrations of how ethics and trust play an important role in all aspects of business.

PEDAGOGY

END OF CHAPTER EXERCISES AND APPLICATIONS

Applications for Managers

Falling at the end of the chapter but before the Summary, this unique pedagogical tool helps students see how the information from the chapter applies to managers, teams, and individuals.

Skill Building Exercises

Most chapters now include skill-building exercises that summarize management skills crucial to workplace effectiveness. "Manager's Check-Up" exercises provide students a fun and interesting way to practice and refine those skills, and are found with the End-of-Chapter material.

Individual/Collaborative Learning Case/Exercises

Each chapter includes an in-class exercise designed to be completed in teams. Teams read the case and then recommend a course of action for the issue or problem presented in the exercise.

Management Mini-Cases

These popular exercises have been completely revamped for the 2nd edition. At least half of the cases have been replaced by newer ones, and many have been expanded to provide a more comprehensive approach to the issue. Each chapter has two Management Mini-Cases.

Internet Exercises

One of the most popular features of the 1st edition, the Internet Exercises have been rewritten or updated for the 2nd edition.

APPLICATIONS: MANAGEMENT IS EVERYONE'S BUSINESS

Applications for the Manager Certain types of organizational changes routinely provoke strong employee resistance because they can negatively affect employees' status or quality of life. By becoming aware of these sources of resistance, managers can better apply tactics that will make these changes more palatable for employees. Resistance most frequently arises in response to:

- *Changes that affect skill requirements.* Employees are likely to resist changes that will make their skills obsolete or their work more routine.

- *Changes that represent economic or status loss.* Employees are likely to resist a change that demotes them to a less significant role or decreases their earnings. For example, when a company's

What are Your Ethical Beliefs?

MANAGER'S CHECKUP 3.1

Instructions: Answer the following questions as honestly as you can. Circle the number between 1 and 5 that best represents your own beliefs about business.

	Strongly Disagree				Strongly Agree
1. Financial gain is all that counts in business.	1	2	3	4	5
2. Ethical standards must sometimes be compromised in business practice.	1	2	3	4	5
3. The more financially successful the businessperson, the more unethical the behavior.	1	2	3	4	5
4. Moral values are irrelevant in business.	1	2	3	4	5

Enterprise Resource Planning: An Example of Organizational Change

INDIVIDUAL/ COLLABORATIVE LEARNING CASE 4.1

Being the champion of a change, or a change agent, isn't always easy. Enterprise Resource Planning (ERP), software that integrates information from accounting, manufacturing, distribution, and human resource departments, can give management a unified view of these processes in an organization. Unfortunately, the ERP software began gaining a reputation for being difficult to implement and often failing. The majority of these failures were attributed to software performance problems, but the reality was that in most of these situations the failure was due to inadequate attention to change. In other words, technology was not usually the problem; rather it was a lack of management recognition of ERP as an organizational change. An ERP system can add administrative tasks that may not seem needed, but without an overall understanding of the system, workers may not complete these tasks. Further, an ERP implementation may require a change in roles and increased technical expertise. The implementation of an ERP system at SI Corporation, a small manufacturer of industrial textiles is an example of an ERP success story. SI expected the implementation of ... to have ... impact on its organizational cult...

Should Job Seekers Stretch the Truth to Get a Job?

MANAGEMENT MINICASE 3.1

In a competitive job market, some people stretch the truth about themselves in order to obtain an advantage over others who are applying for the same job. Austin McGregor International, a Dallas-based search firm, has compiled a list of the top five fibs that job seekers tell:

Pay. People exaggerate their salary histories in order to obtain higher pay, since employers try to match or exceed the pay an applicant received from a former employer.

Job tenure. Some job applicants *reduce* the number of years of tenure with a former employer to appear to be risk takers. Others *add* years of tenure with a former employer to avoid the appearance of being job hoppers.

PART TWO

Integrated Case

Bribery: A Global Custom?

Since 1993, Lee Raymond has served as the chairman and CEO of Exxon. In 1999, he was responsible for the $81 billion merger of Exxon and Mobil that created a new entity Exxon-Mobil, one of the largest global corporations, ranking third after Microsoft (No. 1) and General Electric (No. 2) with a market value of $241,036.50 in millions. Exxon-Mobil is the world's leading oil corporation. In 2001, Exxon-Mobil's return on capital was nearly 18 percent, some 7 percent better than industry results. In 2002, Exxon-Mobil earned more than $9 billion after taxes from its oil

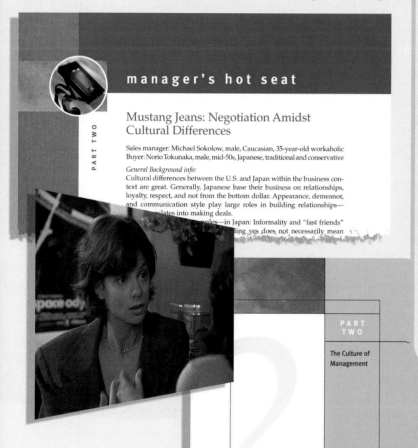

manager's hot seat

Mustang Jeans: Negotiation Amidst Cultural Differences

Sales manager: Michael Sokolow, male, Caucasian, 35-year-old workaholic
Buyer: Norio Tokunaka, male, mid-50s, Japanese, traditional and conservative

General Background info:
Cultural differences between the U.S. and Japan within the business context are great. Generally, Japanese base their business on relationships, loyalty, respect, and not from the bottom dollar. Appearance, demeanor, and communication style play large roles in building relationships— translates into making deals.

...examples—in Japan: Informality and "fast friends" ...ding yes does not necessarily mean

PART TWO

2

The Culture of Management

Each of the book's six parts begin and end with special exercises that make reinforcing the material even easier.

An opening **introduction** provides a broad overview of the skills and issues that the student will learn in the ensuing chapters.

The **Integrative Cases** combine all the concepts from the part's chapters into one comprehensive case exercise, providing a great opportunity for students to assimilate what they've read and absorbed.

Finally, **Management Hotseat Cases** are video-based cases used to present stimulating, real-world management situations in the classroom. Focusing on tough issues and sensitive topics, the scenarios include:

- **Negotiation amidst cultural differences**
- **Group dynamics**
- **Conflict management**
- **Personal disclosure**
- **Working in teams**
- **HR issues**

In Part Two we will begin by examining threats and opportunities firms face in the global environment. This will lead to a discussion of global business strategies and advantageous ways to enter foreign markets given a firm's unique characteristics. Next we analyze the nature of business ethics and the basis of ethical decisions. Then we present the broader context of social responsibility and identify key stakeholders and ways to manage relationships with them. Finally, we examine organizational culture and how it helps an organization achieve its objectives. In Part Two we also explain the forces that drive organizational change and describe ways to manage and counsel employees who resist the need for change.

What's NEW in the 2nd Edition

Chapter 1 – Management and Its Evolution

Coverage of the evolution of management thought has been expanded, with emphasis on "old" management theories that still provide valuable insights today.

New management close-ups have been added describing how scientific management has revolutionized industry, the problem of hierarchical organizational structures, contingency theory in action, and other topics.

Chapter 2 – Managing in a Global Environment

Coverage on the expanded European Union and what it will mean to American firms has been improved.

A new section has been added on entry strategies into foreign markets and strategic alliances (including how to choose foreign countries, when to enter foreign countries, the scale of involvement, and the like).

Several new features explore how globalization is sending upscale jobs offshore.

New country profiles are included for China, Japan, Mexico, and other emerging markets.

New coverage of ethical responsibility for multinationals has been added.

Chapter 3 – Managing Social Responsibility and Ethics

Coverage of the recent financial scandals at Enron has been added, along with a new case that looks at the impact of Enron's collapse on its employees' retirement savings.

A new section examines managing ethical behavior in the workplace, with applications related to managing performance appraisals, employee discipline, office romance and exchange of gifts.

Chapter 4 – Managing Organizational Culture and Change

New Manager Notebooks focus on measuring culture, approaching culture as a management tool for competitiveness, and managing resistance to change.

Various types of culture are addressed and the competing values framework for identifying types of cultures is now included.

Change, varying from planned events to a dynamic condition is addressed and the star model is presented as a means for implementing change efforts.

New management close-ups and cases are included, covering topics such as taking a customer focus in a health care setting and approaching enterprise resource planning as an example of organizational change.

Chapter 5 – Managing the Planning Process

This chapter has been extensively revised to cover a variety of critical issues that affect planning effectiveness, such as encouraging employee participation, focusing attention on different time horizons, the link between planning and organizational control systems, contingency planning, implementation of standing versus single use plans, and more.

New management close-ups cover how General Electric successfully used short- and long-term planning to enter China's market, how Southwest Airlines responded to the 9/11 crisis, and how quantifiable objectives may lead to ethical lapses.

The chapter now includes exercises for students to practice contingency planning.

Chapter 6 – Decision Making

New topics include decision making in a crisis requiring a rapid response and non-rational models of decision making.

Chapter 7 – Strategic Management

New sections analyze the external and internal environments, with special emphasis on demographic changes, the economic context, political/legal forces, socio-cultural conditions, technological changes, and globalization.

Corporate diversification strategies and corporate governance are now discussed, including coverage of the 2002 Sarbanes-Oxley Act.

The revised chapter now includes numerous new features and company examples concerning applications of the SWOT model, rebounding of e-commerce, strategic implications of an increasingly older population, adaptation of product offering to fit diverse socio-cultural conditions world-wide, impact on strategy formulation and implementation of an interdependent global economy, and other topics.

Chapter 8 – Entrepreneurship and Innovation

Examples of new start-up ventures, ranging from a trip-planning service to electronic paper, have been added.

New section on innovation.

Chapter 9 – Managing the Structure and Design of Organizations

New topics added to this chapter include explanations of customer-based divisions and informal organizations.

Expanded coverage of environmental turbulence and boundaryless designs has also been added.

Chapter 10 – Human Resource Management

New material added to this chapter concerns legal changes, labor relations, behavioral selection approaches, and ethics training, among others.

Several new features have been added covering changes in interviewing practice, considering external customers in designing selection programs, and executive development.

Chapter 11 – Managing Employee Diversity

This chapter has been revised to incorporate most recent demographic data in the USA and foreign countries.

New subjects covered include diversity vs. affirmative action, the role of religious diversity, special problems faced by older workers, differences in communication styles between men and women, and potential value and downside of company sponsored support groups representing a variety of constituencies.

New features discuss how organizations meet the needs of minority customers and make money in the process, how successful business leaders see diversity as a source of competitive advantage, and the challenges faced by many countries (particularly in Europe) who are rapidly becoming very diverse, after centuries of high homogeneity and minimal immigration.

Chapter 12 – Motivation NEW!

A new opening case based on Shell Oil company's Ursa project provides an example of how motivation can have significant performance effects.

Motivation models are now divided into content and process approaches.

Cases and exercises include linking employee motivation to the customer and considering whether removing bonuses or taking a negative approach to motivation are good management practices.

Using organizational design characteristics as motivational tools is now included in the chapter, and the application of the manufacturing cell concept to the office environment is addressed.

Chapter 13 – Leadership NEW!

The categories of person, situation, dispersed, and exchange are used to organize and present the major approaches to leadership.

The chapter includes authentic leadership as an emerging approach and emphasizes ethical issues in management close-ups, cases, and exercises.

Chapter 14 – Managing Teams

A new topic added to this chapter covers the three types of interdependence that affect team behavior: pooled, sequential and reciprocal.

Expanded coverage of conflict management skills and negotiation skills has been added to this chapter.

Chapter 15 – Managing Communication

New topics added to this chapter cover assertive communication skills and perception barriers to communication.

Expanded coverage of presentation skills, nonverbal communication skills, and listening skills have been added.

Chapter 16 – Control NEW!

This new chapter organizes various control approaches using a categorization scheme of focus (either outcomes or processes) and type (either informal or formal). Some of the issues addressed in the management close-ups, cases, and exercises include hand-washing control systems, identifying causes for accidents, value-stream mapping, controlling employee theft and tying finances to the work process though the use of profit velocity.

Chapter 17 – Operations Management

New cases and exercises address issues such as avoiding counterfeit parts, flexible production processes, quality in service settings, and the impact of security requirements on the efficiency of operations.

Chapter 18 – Managing Information Systems

New topics added to this chapter include the six functions of information technology, the types of e-commerce applications, and human resource information systems.

Expanded coverage of computer ethics and computer security have been added.

An applications of Management Perspectives has been placed at the end of the chapter which provides practical advice on the use of outsourcing arrangements for information technology and groupware for team project collaboration, as well as emphasizing the need for employees to continuously upgrade their computer skills to keep up with changes in business application software.

WHAT'S NEW

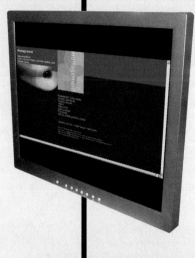

The Management Student CD-ROM

By now your students may be used to getting free CDs bundled with their textbooks. But we're willing to bet they have yet to see a CD-ROM like the one we've prepared for *Management*.

The *Management* Student CD-ROM has been assembled with the very latest multimedia creation tools to give your students a digital learning environment like no other. With a mix of video, flashcards, Web links, and interactive exercises, the *Management* Student CD-ROM is sure to become your students' favorite study partner.

Videos offer a stimulating mix of topical reinforcement and real-world insight to help students master the most challenging management topics.

Chapter Quizzes give your students the means to test themselves on important concepts and terminology.

Interactive Exercises let your students work hands-on with text concepts in a state-of-the-art multimedia environment. Students take these exercises on their own and receive instant, comprehensive feedback to their responses. These exercises coordinate with each text chapter and are highlighted with a distinctive CD icon next to the corresponding discussion. There are nearly 50 exercises on the CD covering many topics, including:

- **Management's Historical Figures**
- **Maslow's Hierarchy of Needs**
- **Comparing Affirmative Action, Valuing Diversity, and Managing Diversity**
- **SWOT Analysis**
- **Characteristics of Successful Entrepreneurs**
- **Categories of Managerial Control**
- **What Is Your Primary Conflict-Handling Style?**
- **Assessing Your Emotional Intelligence**

GOMEZ-MEJIA | BALKIN | CARDY

STUDENT CD-ROM

Creating an Online Course

For the instructor needing to educate students online, we offer *Management* content for complete online courses. To make this possible, we have joined forces with the most popular delivery platforms currently available. These platforms are designed for instructors who want complete control over course content and how it is presented to students. You can customize the *Management* Online Learning Center content and author your own course materials. It's entirely up to you.

Products like WebCT, Blackboard, and eCollege all expand the reach of your course. Online discussion and message boards will now complement your office hours. Thanks to a sophisticated tracking system, you will know which students need more attention — even if they don't ask for help. That's because online testing scores are recorded and automatically placed in your grade book, and if a student is struggling with coursework, a special alert message lets you know.

Remember, *Management's* content is flexible enough to use with any platform currently available. If your department or school is already using a platform, we can help. For information on McGraw-Hill/Irwin's course management supplements, including Instructor Advantage and Knowledge Gateway, see "Knowledge Gateway" on page xx.

PageOut - McGraw-Hill's Course Management System

PageOut is the easiest way to create a Website for your accounting course.

There's no need for HTML coding, graphic design, or a thick how-to book. Just fill in a series of boxes with simple English and click on one of our professional designs. In no time, your course is online with a Website that contains your syllabus!

Should you need assistance in preparing your Website, we can help. Our team of product specialists is ready to take your course materials and build a custom Website to your specifications. You simply need to call a McGraw-Hill/Irwin PageOut specialist to start the process. (For information on how to do this, see "Superior Service" on the next page.) Best of all, PageOut is free when you adopt *Management*! To learn more, please visit **www.pageout.net**.

Today, nearly 200,000 college instructors

use the Internet in their respective courses. Some are just getting started, while others are ready to embrace the very latest advances in educational content delivery and course management.

That's why we at McGraw-Hill/Irwin offer you a complete range of digital solutions. Your students can use Management's complete Online Learning Center and PowerWeb on their own, or we can help you create your own course Website using McGraw-Hill's PageOut.

In addition to Web-based assets, Management boasts the Presentation Manager CD-ROM, which gives instructors access to nearly every crucial supplement, from the Resource Manual to the Test Bank, in both print and electronic media.

McGraw-Hill is a leader in bringing helpful technology into the classroom. And with Management, your class gets all the benefits of the digital age.

Online Learning Center (OLC)

www.mhhe.com/gomez2e

More and more students are studying online. That's why we offer an Online Learning Center (OLC) that follows Management chapter by chapter. It doesn't require any building or maintenance on your part. It's ready to go the moment you and your students type in the URL.

As your students study, they can refer to the OLC Website for such benefits as:

- **Internet-based activities**
- **Self-grading quizzes**
- **Learning objectives**
- **Extended chapter summaries**
- **Video exercises**

A secured Instructor Resource Center stores your essential course materials to save you prep time before class. The Instructor's Manual, Solutions, PowerPoint®, and sample syllabi are now just a couple of clicks away. You will also find useful packaging information and notes.

PowerWeb provides high quality, peer-reviewed content including up-to-date articles from leading periodicals and journals, current news, weekly updates with assessment, interactive exercises, Web research guide, study tips, and much more. PowerWeb is free with your Management adoption.

The OLC Website also serves as a doorway to other technology solutions like PageOut which is free to Management adopters.

PowerWeb

Keeping your course current can be a job in itself, and now McGraw-Hill does that job for you. PowerWeb extends the learning experience beyond the core textbook by offering all of the latest news and developments pertinent to your course, brought to you via the internet without all the clutter and dead links of a typical online search

PowerWeb is a robust Website that offers these *course-specific* features:

- current articles related to managerial accounting
- daily *and* weekly updates with assessment tools
- informative and timely world news culled by a managerial accoutant in academia,
- refereed web links
- online handbook to researching, evaluating and citing online sources

In addition, PowerWeb provides a trove of helpful learning aids, including self-grading quizzes and interactive glossaries and exercises. Students may also access study tips, conduct online research, and learn about different career paths.

Visit the PowerWeb site at **www.dushkin.com/powerweb.**

Knowledge Gateway

Knowledge Gateway

Developed with the help of our partner, Eduprise, the McGraw-Hill Knowledge Gateway is an all-purpose service and resource center for instructors teaching online. While training programs from WebCT and Blackboard will help teach you their software, only McGraw-Hill has services to help you actually *manage and teach* your online course, as well as run and maintain the software. Knowledge Gateway offers an online library full of articles and insights that focus on how online learning differs from a traditional class environment.

The First Level of Knowledge Gateway is available to all professors browsing the McGraw-Hill Higher Education Website, and consists of an introduction to OLC content, access to the first level of the Resource Library, technical support, and information on Instructional Design Services available through Eduprise.

The Second Level is password-protected and provides access to the expanded Resource Library, technical and pedagogical support for WebCT, Blackboard, and TopClass, the online Instructional Design helpdesk and an online discussion forum for users. The Knowledge Gateway provides a considerable advantage for teaching online—and it's only available through McGraw-Hill.

To see how these platforms can assist your online course, visit **www.mhhe.com/solutions**.

Superior Service

No matter which online course solution you choose, you can count on the highest level of service. That's what sets McGraw-Hill apart. Once you choose *Management,* our specialists offer free training and answer any question you have through the life of your adoption.

PageOut

PageOut is McGraw-Hill/Irwin's custom Website service. Now you can put your course online without knowing a word of HTML, selecting from a variety of prebuilt Website templates. And if none of our ideas suit you, we'll be happy to work with your ideas.

If you want a custom site but don't have time to build it yourself, we offer a team of product specialists ready to help. Just call 1-800-634-3963, press 0 to get the receptionist, and ask to speak with a PageOut specialist. You will be asked to send in your course materials and then participate in a brief telephone consultation. Once we have your information, we build your Website for you, from scratch.

Instructor Advantage and *Instructor Advantage Plus*

Instructor Advantage is a special level of service McGraw-Hill offers in conjunction with WebCT and Blackboard. A team of platform specialists is always available, either by toll-free phone or e-mail, to ensure everything runs smoothly through the life of your adoption. Instructor Advantage is available free to all McGraw-Hill customers.

Instructor Advantage Plus is available to qualifying McGraw-Hill adopters (see your representative for details). IA Plus guarantees you a full day of on-site training by a Blackboard or WebCT specialist, for yourself and up to nine colleagues. Thereafter, you will enjoy the benefits of unlimited telephone and e-mail support throughout the life of your adoption. IA Plus users also have the opportunity to access the McGraw-Hill Knowledge Gateway.

Supplements

Instructor Supplements

Instructor's Resource CD-ROM

ISBN 0072847026

Allowing instructors to create a customized multimedia presentation, this all-in-one resource incorporates the Computerized Test Bank, PowerPoint® Slides, Instructor's Resource Guide, additional Videos not part of the VHS series, downloaded figures from the text, and links to the Online Learning Center and PageOut.

Instructor's Resource Guide and Video Manual

To help with organizing your classroom presentation, this supplement contains extensive chapter-by-chapter lecture outline notes, chapter overviews, tips for teaching difficult topics, and highlighted key terms. It also includes embedded powerpoint slide notations, alternative examples for difficult topics, answers to the box questions and end-of-chapter material, and a guide to using the videos.

Test Bank

Nearly 3,600 questions are organized by chapter and include true/false, multiple-choice, and essay.

PowerPoint slides

Organized in an outline format, and containing additional material, the powerpoint presentation slides number 20-25 per chapter.

VHS format Videos

0072846992

Each chapter will have a corresponding video that will tie in with chapter topics, supplemented with notes and information in the Instructor's Resource Guide. Additional digital video footage will be found on the Instructor's Resource CD and Student CD-ROM.

DVD format Videos

Get all of the video footage available with MANAGEMENT in one DVD package – including the VHS chapter videos, footage found on the Instructor's Resource CD-ROM, and the Student CD-ROM.

Student Supplements

Student CD-ROM

Along with the Interactive Exercises discussed earlier, the Student CD will have chapter quizzes for students to review material, and video exercises.

OLC with PowerWeb

More and more students are studying online. That's why we offer an Online Learning Center (OLC) that follows Management chapter by chapter. It doesn't require any building or maintenance on your part. It's ready to go the moment you and your students type in the URL.

As your students study, they can refer to the OLC Website for such benefits as:

- Internet-based activities
- Self-grading quizzes
- Learning objectives
- Extended chapter summaries
- Video exercises

Powerweb provides high quality, peer-reviewed content including up-to-date articles from leading periodicals and journals, current news, weekly updates with assessment, interactive exercises, Web research guide, study tips, and much more. PowerWeb is free with your Management adoption.

SUPPLEMENTS

Reviewers

We are very grateful to Ryan Blankenship, Sponsoring Editor, and John Biernat, Editorial Director, at McGraw-Hill/Irwin for their continuing commitment to our book and making it a reality. We also appreciate the efforts of Christine Scheid, Senior Developmental Editor; Ellen Cleary, Executive Marketing Manager; James Labeots, Project Manager; Gina Hangos, Production Supervisor; Adam Rooke, designer; Jeremy Chesharek, photo research coordinator; and Dan Wiencek and Erwin Llereza, advertising. Thanks also to Don Baake of Pittsburgh State for his keen eye and insight into all chapters.

1st Edition Reviewers

Charles Beavin, Miami-Dade Community College

Gunther S. Boroschek, University of Massachusetts—Boston

Ken Dunegan, Cleveland State University

Janice M. Feldbauer, Austin Community College

William Jedlicka, Harper College

Jon Kalinowski, Mankato State University

Joan Keeley, Washington State University

Stephen T. Margulis, Grand Valley State University

J. L. Morrow, Jr., Mississippi State University

Nga T. Nguyen, Temple University

Carl L. Swanson, University of North Texas

James R. Terborg, University of Oregon

Kenneth R. Thompson, DePaul University

Walter Wheatley, University of West Florida

2nd Edition Reviewers

Dave Adams, Manhattanville College

Cheryl Adkins, Longwood University

Baltasar Allende, Sul Ross State University—Alpine

Joseph Anderson, Northern Arizona University

Allen Amason, University of Georgia

M Ruhul Amin, Bloomsburg University of Pennsylvania

Michael Avery, Northwestern College

Barry Axe, Florida Atlantic University—Boca Raton

Harold Babson, Columbus State Community College

Richard Bacha, Pennsylvania State University—York

Kristin Backhaus, State University College—New Paltz

Mark Bagshaw, Marietta College

Kevin Baker, Roanoke College

Mark Baker, Illinois State University

John Bedient, Albion College

James Bell, SouthweSt Texas State University

Toni Bell, Williston State College

Richard Benedetto, Merrimack College

Ellen Benowitz, Mercer Co Community College

Dan Benson, Kutztown University of Pennsylvania

Bill Bergman, California State University—Chico

Sharon Berner, Manhattan Christian College

Danielle Beu, Louisiana Tech University

Wesley Bitters, Utah Valley State College—Orem

Don Boyer, Jefferson College

Bill Brown, Montana State University—Bozeman

James Browne, University of Southern Colorado

Rochelle Brunson, Alvin Community College

Diane Caggiano, Fitchburg State College

Elizabeth Cameron, Alma College

Anthony Cantarella, Murray State University

James Carlson, Manatee Community College—Bradenton

Nancy Carr, Community College of Philadelphia

Lesley Casula, Lord Fairfax Community College

Denise Chachere, St. Louis University

Aruna Chandra, Indiana State University—Terre Haute

Bruce Charnov, Hofstra University

Walter Childs, Pennsylvania State University—Abington

Jack Chirch, Hampton University

Janet Ciccarelli, Herkimer County Community College—Herkimer

Tony Cioffi, Lorain County Community College

Alfred Colonies, Community College of Rhode Island—Flanagan

Dennis Conley, University of Nebraska—Lincoln

Suzanne Crampton, Grand Valley State University

Barbara Dalby, University of Mary Hardin Baylor

David Danforth, Bethel College

Ajay Das, Bernard M. Baruch College

Miles Davis, Shenandoah University

Dave Day, Columbia College—Columbia

Gita De Souza, Pennsylvania State University—Delaware Campus

Tom Deckelman, Owens Community College

Paul Dellinger, Western Piedmont Community College

Kate Demarest, Carroll Community College

Mike Drafke, College of Dupage

Sally Dresdow, University of Wisconsin—Green Bay

Linda Duncan, Arkansas State University—Newport

Wendy Eager, Eastern Washington University

Ellen Fagenson Eland, George Mason University

Ray Eldridge, Freed—Hardeman University

Elizabeth Evans, Concordia University

Steve Farner, Bellevue University

Judson Faurer, Metro State College of Denver

Lou Firenze, Northwood University

Paul Fisher, Rogue Community College

David Foote, Middle Tennessee State University

Monique Forte, Stetson University

Mark Fox, Indiana University—South Bend

William Fox, Brenau University

Jennifer Frazier, James Madison University

Pat Fuller, Brevard Community College—Titusville

Richard Gayer, Antelope Valley College

Peter Georgelas, Bridgewater State College

Carmine Gibaldi, St. John's University—Jamaica

Carol Gilmore, University of Maine

Catherine Giunta, Seton Hill College

Norma Givens, Fort Valley State University

Connie Golden, Lakeland Community College

Luis Gonzalez, Bloomfield College

Hugh Graham, Loras College

Wesley Green, Lindsey Wilson College

Mark Grimes, Georgia Southwestern State University

Allison Grindle, Messiah College

Douglas Guthe, University of North Carolina—Chapel Hill

Dave Hall, Saginaw Valley State University

Robert Hanna, California State University—Northridge

Roberta Hanson, Metro State College of Denver

James Harbin, Texas A & M University—Texarkana

Bob Hatfield, Morehead State University

Carolyn Hatton, Cincinnati State Tech & Community College

Ellis Hayes, Wingate University

Brad Hays, North Central State College Ot112

Samuel Hazen, Tarleton State University

Jeff Hefel, St. Mary's University

Gary Hensel, Mc Henry County College

James Herbert, Kennesaw State University

Ronald Herrick, Mesa Community College

David Herzog, St. Louis Community College—Flors Valley

James Hess, Ivy Tech State College—Fort Wayne

Dorothy Hetmer-Hinds, Trinity Valley Community College

Bob Hoerber, Westminster College

David Holloman, Victor Valley College

John Howery, Lindsey Wilson College

Fred Hughes, Faulkner University

Alvin Hwang, Pace University

Lynn Isvik, Upper Iowa Unive—Fayette

Joe Izzo, Alderson—Broaddus College

Elizabeth Jackson, Keystone College

Donna Jarrell, WeSt Virginia State College

Tom Jay, Flathead Valley Community College—Kalispell

Velma Jesser, Lane Community College

Jack Johnson, Cosumnes River College

Sharon Johnson, Cedarville University

Jordan Kaplan, Long Island University—Brooklyn

Joseph Kavanaugh, Sam Houston State University

George Kelley, Erie Community College City Campus—Buffalo

Claire Kent, Mary Baldwin College

Sara Kiser, Alabama State University

Judith Kizzie, Clinton Community College

Tom Knapke, Wright State University—Celina

Margareta Knopik, College of St. Mary

Reviewers

Dennis Kovach, Community College Allegheny City N—Pittsburgh

Kenneth Kovach, University of Maryland—College Park

Subodh Kulkarni, Howard University

Doug Laher, Whitworth College

Lowell Lamberton, Central Oregon Community College

Patrick Langan, Wartburg College

John Leblanc, Cedarville University

Martin Lecker, Rockland Community College

Robert Leonard, Lebanon Valley College

Andrea Licari, St. John's University—Jamaica

Benyamin Lichtenstein, University of Hartford

Meilee Lin, State University College—Potsdam

Tom List, Finlandia University

Paul Lister, Eureka College

Woody Liswood, Sierra Nevada College

Thomas Lloyd, Westmoreland Community College—Youngwood

Bruce Locker, Southwestern Oregon Community College

Victor Lopez, SUNY—Delhi

Tom Loughman, Columbus State University

Richard Lowery, Bowie State University

Barbara Luck, Jackson Community College

William Lyke, Webster University—375 Mssq/Mse

Cheryl Macon, Butler County Community College

Zam Malik, Governors State University

Joseph Manno, Montgomery College—Rockville

Santo Marabella, Moravian College

Michel Marette, Northern Virginia Community College—Loudon Campus

Jackie Mayfield, Texas A & M University International

Martha Mc Creery, Rend Lake College

Loretta McAdam, Seminole Community College—Sanford

Tom McFarland, Mt. San Antonio College

Michael Messina, Gannon University—Erie

Stuart Milne, Georgia Institute of Technology

Barbara Minsky, Troy State University—Dothan

Carol Moore, California State University – Hayward

Mark Moore, St. Cloud State University

Bill Morgan, Felician College

Jaideep Motwani, Grand Valley State University

Peter Moutsatson, Montcalm Community College

Carolyn Mueller, Stetson University

David Murphy, Madisonville Community College

Tom Murphy, Ozarks Technical Community College

Brian Murray, University of Dallas

Robert Nale, Coastal Carolina University

Maria Nathan, Lynchburg College

Chris Neck, Virginia Polytechnic Institute

Albert Novak, St. Vincent College

John O'Brian, Adams State College

Ronald O'Neal, Camden County College

David Olson, California State University—Bakersfield

Floyd Ormsbee, State University College—Potsdam

Pam Pack, Pikeville College

Ranjna Patel, Bethune Cookman College

John Paxton, Wayne State College

Michael Pepper, Transylvania University

Nicholas Peppes, St. Louis Community College—Forest Park

Donna Perkins, University of Wisconsin—Platteville

Sheila Petcavage, Cuyahoga Community College Western—Parma

Barbara Petzall, Maryville University

Jim Pfister, St. Petersburg College—Clearwater

Eustace Phillip, Emmanuel College

Jeff Phillips, Thomas College

Allayne Pizzolato, Nicholls State University

Carl Poch, Northern Illinois University

Brian Porter, Hope College

Larry Potter, University of Maine—Presque Isle

Paula Potter, Western Kentucky University

James Powell, Chaffey College

Michael Provitera, St. Peters College

Richard Raspen, Wilkes University

Nancy Ray-Mitchell, McLennan Community College

Doug Reed, University of Pittsburg—Johnstown

Bob Reese, Illinois Valley Community College

Erella Regev, Montclair State University

Clint Relyea, Arkansas State University—State University

Danny Rhodes, Anderson College

Shelton Rhodes, Bowie State University

Rick Ringer, Illinois State University

Orlando Roybal, Northern New Mexico Community College—Español

Terry Rumker, Ashland University

Cyndy Ruszkowski, Illinois State University

Tracey Ryan, Longwood University

James Salvucci, Curry College

Hindy Schachter, New Jersey Institute of Technology

Rebecca Schaupp, Fairmont State College

Gerald Schoenfeld, Florida Gulf Coast University

Shirley Schooley, Birmingham Southern College

Greg Schultz, Carroll College

Marian Schultz, The University of West Florida

Michael Schultz, Menlo College

Connie Schwass, West Shore Community College

Mark Seabright, Western Oregon University

Pat Setlik, William Rainey Harper College

Richard Shapiro, Cuyahoga Community College—Metro—Cleveland

Paul Shibelski, Trinity College

Ted Shore, Kennesaw State University

Marion Sillah, South Carolina State University

Cynthia Simerly, Lakeland Community College

Roy Simerly, East Carolina University

Richard Slovacek, North Central College

James Smith, Rocky Mountain College

Nellie Smith, Rust College

Paul Smith, Mars Hill College

Andrea Smith-Hunter, Siena College

R. Spear, University of Idaho

Vernon Stauble, California State Polytechnic University—Pomona

Jeff Strom, Va Western Community College

Mary Kay Sullivan, Maryville College

Harry Sweet, University of Mary Hardin Baylor

James Swenson, Minnesota State University Moorhead

Sarina Swindell, Tarleton State University

Patricia Tadlock, Horry Georgetown Tech Col

Robert Tansky, St. Clair County Community College

Virginia Taylor, William Paterson University

Ira Teich, Yeshiva University

Frank Titlow, St. Petersburg College

Ricardo Trujillo, Red Rocks Community College

Richard Tyler, Anne Arundel Community College—Arnold

Anthony Urbaniak, Northern State University

Matthew Valle, Elon University

Barry Vanhook, Arizona State University—Tempe

Gina Vega, Merrimack College

Roger Volkema, American University

Cheryl Waddington, Wayne State College

Betty Wanielista, Valencia Community College—East Campus

Gary Ward, Reedley Community College

William Ward, Susquehanna University

John Washbush, University of Wisconsin—Whitewater

Harry Waters, California State University—Hayward

William Waxman, Edison Community College

Mark Weber, University of Minn/3—150 Carsmgmt

Steve Welch, West Chester University of Pennsylvania

Richard Wertz, Concordia University

Kenneth Wheeler, University of Texas – Arlinton

David White, Southwest Missouri State University—West Plains

Kathleen White, Macmurray College

Sam White, University of Colorado—Colorado Springs

Ellen Whitener, University of Virginia—Charlottesville

Timothy Wiedman, Thomas Nelson Community College

Dave Wilderman, Wabash Valley College

Ethlyn Williams, University of South Florida

Kathy Wilson, North Carolina Wesleyan College

Laura Wolfe, Louisiana State University—Baton Rouge

Colette Wolfson, Ivy Tech State College—South Bend

Michael Yahr, Robert Morris College

Ray Zagorski, Kenai Peninsula Community College

Austin Zekeri, Lane College

Jason Zimmerman, South Dakota State University

Chapter 3
Managing Social Responsibility and Ethics   *100*

Chapter 4

Managing Organizational Culture and Change *142*

table of contents

table of contents

Chapter 10

Chapter 11

Managing Employee Diversity   *456*

table of contents

Chapter 14

Managing Teams *574*

table of contents

Chapter 17

Operations Management   *696*

Chapter 18

Managing Information Systems *728*

Management

SECOND EDITION

people

performance

change

1

Overview

Welcome to the exciting world of management! A rapidly accelerating trend in recent years has seen management become a significant part of everyone's job duties, from front-line employees serving customers to the executives who are at the top of the organization hierarchy. The increasing competitive pressures on companies to make decisions rapidly and to delegate more responsibilities to employees closest to customers, along with wide accessibility of massive amounts of information provided by the Internet, have given rise to a need for everyone to develop management skills—individuals and teams as well as managers. At minimum, employees now have responsibilities for managing information in addition to managing their relationships with customers both internal and external to the organization and with organizational peers, subordinates, and managers. How well employees can manage these relationships and the information for which they are responsible will have a critical impact on their success or failure.

In this section we will provide an overview of the four functions of management: planning and strategizing, organizing, leading, and controlling. These functions are what the work of management is about. Then we will explore the evolution of management ideas from their earliest origins to the most recent thinking that influences managers in the 21st century.

Management and Its Evolution

chapter 1

After reading this chapter, you should be able to:

- Understand the roles played by individuals, teams, and managers in carrying out company activities.

- Practice the four major functions of management.

- Recognize the interpersonal, informational, and decisional roles played by top-level managers.

- Apply the general skills needed to carry out managerial responsibilities.

- Integrate the major elements from the various perspectives of management theory.

Lincoln Electric Finds One "Best Way"

The Lincoln Electric Company of Cleveland, Ohio, is a leading producer of arc-welding products. Lincoln dominated its markets by utilizing a management philosophy that is similar to the early twentieth-century ideas of Frederick Winslow Taylor, the father of scientific management. Few companies today give much credence to Taylor's principles, which assume there is one "best way" to do a job (see page 17), but Lincoln Electric put those ideas into practice with great success.

Lincoln Electric's key strategy is to reduce costs. Currently, the company is the low-cost producer in the arc-welding equipment industry. These savings are passed along to consumers in the form of lower prices.

Lincoln's employee incentive system rewards productivity improvements, cost reduction ideas, high quality, and individual contributions to the company. Between 1934 and 1994, Lincoln paid profit-sharing bonuses that averaged 90 percent of base wages, making Lincoln employees the highest paid in the industry. Despite company setbacks in the mid-1990s, Lincoln employees still earned substantial bonuses. The year 2003 marked the 70th consecutive year the bonuses had been paid. Lincoln chairman, president, and chief executive officer Anthony A. Massaro describes the reward system as "a competitive advantage, and that is something we take very seriously."

Lincoln employees work hard to earn these generous bonuses. The climate has been described as a pressure cooker, with constant peer pressure to produce. Lincoln uses a piecework system, which ties the worker's pay to the amount and quality of output. Production quotas are based on time studies developed by industrial engineers, with a base wage comparable to the average for Cleveland area manufacturing employees if the quota is reached. Quotas are revised when new production methods are introduced.

In return, Lincoln has a guaranteed-employment policy where employees with more than three years of service can keep their jobs until they retire. In return, they agree to accept pay cuts or reassignments. They may be asked to work overtime or to cut back on their hours, and may be assigned to jobs with different levels of pay depending on demand. "We believe in adjusting the workforce to put

5

people where we need to if the economy goes a different way," says Lincoln's Roy Morrow. Lincoln's policies strengthen the organization in hard times. Management experts believe employees who know the company will preserve their jobs will be more loyal and will be more likely to help develop new ways to save money knowing their bonuses will benefit as a result.

Lincoln's production incentives illustrate Frederick W. Taylor's *scientific management* principles, which assumed that workers are trained by experts to do their jobs in the most efficient manner and paid on a piecework basis; workers would agree to these conditions because they could earn additional pay. By the 1930s, most companies had moved to standardized hourly wage scales guaranteed in labor contracts. Lincoln Electric's management avoided unionization and sustained its "high-performance" culture by remaining profitable and sharing the profits with employees.

Sources: P. Hyde, "Timesizing: Less Work and More Pay," www.timesaving.com, January 22, 2003; E. Wahlgren, "Alternatives to the Ax," *Business Week,* February 19, 2001; N. Fast, "The Lincoln Electric Company," in F. K. Foulkes (Ed.), *Human Resources Management.* Englewood Cliffs, NJ: Prentice Hall, 1982; B. J. Feder, "Rethinking a Model Incentive Plan," *The New York Times,* September 5, 1995, section 1, p 33; www.lincolnelectric.com.

CRITICAL THINKING QUESTIONS

1. *Why could Lincoln Electric successfully apply the principles of scientific management throughout the twentieth century and well into the twenty-first century?*

2. *Why has Lincoln Electric been able to offer generous bonuses for seven decades in a row?*

3. *How has Lincoln Electric been able to maintain a "guarantee of employment policy" throughout the years even during the first decade of the twenty-first century when layoffs are commonplace across most industries?*

This chapter provides the "big picture," or an overview, of the field of management. First, we explain what management is, including presentations about the different types of managers, the functions that managers perform, and the skills needed to successfully carry out managerial activities. Next, the history and evolution of the field is described, along with ideas about how they have affected the practice of management. Some ideas, such as bureaucratic management, were in vogue and then fell out of favor, while other ideas have withstood the test of time and continue to be used by managers today.

James Parker, CEO and Colleen Barrett, President have kept Southwest in the air by sticking to the company's mantra of low fares and low costs. Southwest has turned a profit and protected its employees from layoffs, while the industry itself lost billions during 2001–2004 and laid off thousands.

Management in the New Millennium

Organizational performance depends, to a large extent, on how resources are allocated and management's ability to adapt to changing conditions. In successful organizations, people are managed wisely and resources are used efficiently and effectively. This helps managers reach key organizational goals, such as keeping the company functioning in a changing external environment in which technology, governmental activities, and competition create constant challenges.

To be successful, a company must be both efficient and effective. A firm is *efficient* when it makes the best possible use of people, money, the physical plant, and technology. It is *effective* when goals are met which sustain a company's competitive advantage. A firm with excellent goals could still fail miserably by being *inefficient,* meaning that the company hired the wrong people, lost key contributors, relied on outdated technology, and made poor investment decisions. A firm is *ineffective* when it fails to reach goals that sustain a company's competitive advantage. High quality companies do things right (they are efficient) and do the right things (they are effective).

The twenty-first century world of business is strongly influenced by three issues. The first is the *management of change.* Organizational leaders must cope with and adapt to rapid change on a daily basis. Change creates uncertainty and risk. The number of competitors and product offerings is greater than ever before. Globalization means that most firms are exposed to competitive challenges both domestically and internationally. Many products (such as software) become obsolete in a matter of a few years or even months, forcing the firm to continuously innovate or die. Today's managers must effectively deal with a host of technological, legal, cultural, and organizational changes, such as downsizing, restructuring, and mergers.

The second is an increasing emphasis on *customer service*. The company must satisfy the needs of customers in ways that contribute to long-term loyalty. The term *customer* is now used in a broader sense. It refers to anyone who receives a service from an employee. Customers are both external (current or prospective consumers of the firm's products or service) and internal (other managers or employees who depend on the manager's performance or inputs in some capacity). For most successful operations, the customer represents the starting point and an ending point for almost every activity.

The third critical issue affecting the management profession in the twenty-first century is the need for higher *business ethics*. Ethics are the standards and values which are considered necessary for the collective interests of employees, shareholders, and society. Recently, several well-publicized examples of cheating, dishonesty, and use of the firm's resources for personal gain have emerged in firms such as WorldCom, Tyco, General Dynamics, Enron, and Arthur Andersen. In the long run, these violations will have a negative impact on those who are influenced by such managers' decisions, including employees, other managers, and customers.

In this book, we will deal with managing change and improving customer service, along with various ethical concerns as various topics are discussed. We will provide examples of what we consider to be both good and bad management practices.

Traditionally, the term *manager* referred only to individuals responsible for making resource allocation decisions and with the formal authority to direct others. There are three levels of management: **strategic managers,** the senior executives with overall responsibility for the firm; **tactical managers** responsible for implementing the directives of strategic managers; and **operational managers** responsible for day-to-day supervision. Table 1.1 describes different management levels.

Managers still have authority over people and financial resources, but today's organizations are more decentralized than ever before, and employees have more autonomy to define their jobs, prioritize tasks, allocate time, monitor their own work, and set their own objectives. By being *empowered* to make these important choices, employees are less dependent on superiors to tell them what to do and are encouraged to use their own expertise and ideas. In a very real sense, employees are increasingly being asked to manage themselves.

Barriers between departments are also breaking down. Functional areas, rivalries and divisions cause people to develop narrow, parochial views of their jobs and to discourage innovation. Departmentalization prevents employees from understanding corporatewide objectives and promotes interunit conflict rather than cooperation, so the organization loses flexibility and is unable to respond to competitive challenges in a more integrated, cohesive fashion. For this reason, firms are increasingly relying on employee *teams* that form to work on common projects. When these teams are composed of individuals from different parts of the organization, they are referred to as *cross-functional teams;* when team mem-

strategic managers

The firm's senior executives who are responsible for overall management.

tactical managers

The firm's management staff who are responsible for translating the general goals and plan developed by strategic managers into specific objectives and activities.

operational managers

The firm's lower-level managers who supervise the operations of the organization.

TABLE 1.1

Management Levels

Strategic Managers

Strategic managers are the senior executives of an organization and are responsible for overall management. Their major activities include developing the company's goals, and typically strategic managers focus on long-term issues. The growth and overall effectiveness of the organization is the primary responsibility of the strategic management team.

The chair of the board, president, chief executive, and vice president and other top managers are concerned primarily with the interaction between the organization and its external environment. This interaction often requires them to work extensively with outside individuals and organizations.

Tactical Managers

Tactical managers are responsible for translating the general goals and plans developed by strategic managers into specific objectives and activities. These decisions, or tactics, involve both a shorter time horizon and the coordination of resources. Tactical managers are often called middle managers, because in large organizations they are located between the strategic and operational managers.

Operational Managers

Operational managers are lower-level managers who supervise the operations of the organization. These managers often have titles such as supervisor or sales manager. They are directly involved with nonmanagement employees, implementing the specific plans developed with tactical managers. This role is critical in the organization, because operational managers are the link between management and nonmanagement personnel. Your first management position probably will fit into this category.

Source: Adapted from T. S. Bateman and S. A. Snell, *Management: Competing in the New Era,* 5th ed. New York: McGraw-Hill/Irwin, 2002.

bers have diverse backgrounds, the teams are *cross-disciplinary.* Teams are asked to perform many of the managerial roles of traditional managers. That is, rather than relying on a superior for direction, a team often defines the problem, sets objectives, establishes priorities, proposes new ways of doing things, and assigns members to different tasks. Teams fulfill important managerial roles by linking various parts of the organization to focus on common problems, issues, and complex tasks that require integration and concerted actions by dissimilar individuals.

The Four Management Functions

More than once the question has been posed, "What do managers do?" Or perhaps more precisely, "What *should* they do?" Whether at the managerial, individual, or team level, the management process should include planning and strategizing, organizing, leading, and controlling. Some of these activities are typically performed at particular organizational levels; for example, planning and strategy-making are core activities for senior executives. However, in most contemporary organizations, all employees are responsible for at least some aspects of the various management functions.

The four management functions are closely linked. For instance, the control system warns the organization when plans and strategies are not working and should be reconsidered. Inspiring leadership would quickly lead to frustration if people didn't know what their roles were or if there were no procedures to guide their actions. Grouping employees into

Coca-Cola Isn't Sugarcoating Things

THEME: RESPONDING TO CHANGES IN CONSUMER DEMAND
In the late 1990s, Coca-Cola embarked on an ambitious program to increase the consumption of its products in the United States from 400 to 500 annual per capita servings. Coca-Cola's chief executive officer at the time, M. Douglas Ivester, launched a major production and distribution buildup, spending lavishly as the company raced to meet the expected demand. Ivester also pushed bottlers to buy new trucks, vending machines, and coolers. His theory was that Coca-Cola's brand recognition (considered a key company strength) and increased consumer demand would lead the firm to its goal.

These assumptions proved wrong, and Ivester was fired shortly before Christmas in 1999. After considering the threats facing Coca-Cola (more competitors dividing up its stable "market pie") and its weaknesses (overcapacity and too much centralization of power in Coca-Cola's corporate headquarters), new CEO Douglas Daft launched the most sweeping shake-up in the firm's 114-year history, including the elimination of 6,000 jobs—about 20 percent of the company's 29,000-employee payroll.

Daft decentralized operations in more than 200 global markets. To get closer to local markets, he reassigned hundreds of headquarters staffers to far-flung outposts. He rolled back the ambitious expansion plans of his predecessor, biting the bullet on poorly performing investments. In 2004, Coca-Cola sells about 300 drink brands, including coffees, juices, sport drinks and teas, commanding about 50% of the global soft-drink market in some 200 nations.

Sources: Adapted from R. O. Crockett and S. Rosenbuch, "Doug Daft Isn't Sugarcoating Things," *Business Week*, February 7, 2000, pp. 36–38; P. Simao, "Coke Q2 Net Rises, Volume Trails Estimates," *Reuters*, July 18, 2001; Hoover's Company and Industry Publications (January 31, 2003), The Coca-Cola Companies, www.hoovers.com.

teams may lead to much wasted time and confusion unless there is an overarching plan for unifying their efforts.

planning

The management function that assesses the management environment to set future objectives and map out activities necessary to achieve those objectives.

PLANNING AND STRATEGIZING   Planning and strategizing are designed to lead the company to fulfill its mission. **Planning** includes setting future objectives and mapping out the activities necessary to achieve those objectives. To be effective, the objectives of individuals, teams, and management should be carefully coordinated.

Because no firm operates in a vacuum, reaching the firm's mission in spite of changes in the environment and competitive landscape is difficult. It involves a continuing assessment of the firm's strengths, weaknesses, opportunities, and threats (referred to as SWOT, to be discussed in detail in Chapter 7), so that appropriate strategies may be taken. Management Close-Up 1.a shows how Coca-Cola took its strengths, weaknesses, opportunities, and threats into account in order to respond to disappointing results during the late 1990s. Chapter 2, Managing in a Global Environment; Chapter 5, Managing the Planning Process; Chapter 7, Strategic Management; and Chapter 8, Entrepreneurship, focus on issues related to planning and strategizing.

organizing

The management function that determines how the firm's human, financial, physical, informational, and technical resources are arranged and coordinated to perform tasks to achieve desired goals; the deployment of resources to achieve strategic goals.

ORGANIZING   Specifying how the firm's human, financial, physical, informational, and technical resources are to be arranged and coordinated is the process of **organizing**. This includes defining roles for all players, delegating tasks, marshalling and allocating resources, clarifying procedures, and determining priorities. Chapter 4, Managing Organizational Culture and Change; Chapter 9, Managing the Structure and Design of Organizations; Chapter 10, Human Resource Management; and Chapter 14, Managing Teams, describe various aspects of organizing.

LEADING   Energizing people to contribute their best individually and in cooperation with other people is the **leading** function. This involves clearly communicating organizational goals, inspiring and motivating employees, providing an example for others to follow, guiding people, and creating conditions that encourage people from diverse backgrounds to work well together. Chapter 3, Managing Social Responsibility and Ethics; Chapter 6, Decision Making; Chapter 11, Managing Employee Diversity; Chapter 12, Motivation; Chapter 13, Leadership; and Chapter 15, Managing Communication, focus on various aspects of leadership.

leading
The management function that energizes people to contribute their best individually and in cooperation with other people.

CONTROLLING   Measuring performance, comparing it to objectives, implementing necessary changes, and monitoring progress are the functions of **control.** Collecting quality feedback, identifying potential problems, and taking corrective action are crucial to long-term success. Organizations should use many approaches to detect and correct significant variations or discrepancies in the results of planned activities designed to meet the specific challenge of those activities. Chapter 16, Control; Chapter 17, Operations Management; and Chapter 18, Managing Information Systems, deal with specialized issues related to control.

controlling
The management function that measures performance, compares it to objectives, implements necessary changes, and monitors progress.

Managerial Roles

The traditional management functions described above may give the false impression that day-to-day management activities are routine, orderly, and rational. A researcher named Henry Mintzberg studied a group of managers and came to the conclusion that the typical manager is not a systematic person who carefully decides how to plan, organize, lead, and control. Rather, managers face constant interruptions, make decisions based on limited data, change tasks frequently depending on shifting priorities, spend most of their time in meetings and informal discussions, and experience a hectic work pace that leaves little room for reflection. Using a method called "structured observation" that involved keeping track of the activities of top-level executives, Mintzberg summarized what managers do on a day-to-day basis by identifying a set of specific roles. A role consists of the behaviors expected of people who hold certain positions. These roles have been grouped by Mintzberg into three major categories, although managers often perform several of them simultaneously.

INTERPERSONAL ROLES   Managers engage in a great deal of interaction, continually communicating with superiors, peers, subordinates and people from outside the organization. In doing so, a manager serves

When the father and son team of Cablevision Systems Corporation, Chairman Charles F. Dolan and CEO James L. Dolan, decided not to include the new Yankees Entertainment & Sports Network as part of its basic offerings, diehard Yankee fans said, "Na na na na, hey hey hey, goodbye."

as a *figurehead,* or the visible personality representing an organization, department or work unit; a *leader* who energizes others to get the job done properly; and a *liaison* who links together the activities of people from both inside and outside the organization.

INFORMATION ROLES   Managers obtain, interpret, and give out a great deal of information. These roles include being a *monitor* and *disseminator,* as well as the organization's *spokesperson.*

DECISIONAL ROLES   Managers are also asked to choose among competing alternatives. This includes balancing the interests of the various parties who have a stake in a decision. Four decisional roles include that of *entrepreneur,* who introduces changes into the organization; *disturbance handler,* who takes corrective action, provides damage control, and responds to unexpected situations or crises; *resource allocator,* responsible for assigning people and other resources to best meet organizational needs; and *negotiator,* reaching agreements and making compromises. These activities occur within and outside the firm when working with parties who control valuable resources, such as other organizational managers, suppliers, and members of various financial institutions.

Management as a Set of Skills

The basic functions of management and the managerial roles just discussed require a distinct set of skills. Most managerial tasks are unique, ambiguous, and situation-specific. Consequently, there is seldom one best way to approach them, or if there is, it is not obvious to everybody. For example, while Amazon.com saw the Internet as a great opportunity, Barnes & Noble saw it as a major threat, even though both firms are in the

SKILLS FOR MANAGERIAL SUCCESS

Strategic Skills

- Environmental assessment scanning.
- Strategy formulation.
- Mapping strategic intent and defining mission.
- Strategy implementation.
- Human resource congruency.

Task Skills

- Setting and prioritizing objectives.
- Developing plan of action and implementation.
- Responding in a flexible manner.
- Creating value.
- Working through the organizational structure.
- Allocating human resources.
- Managing time efficiently.

People Skills

- Delegating.
- Influencing.
- Motivating.
- Handling conflict.
- Win–win negotiating.
- Networking.
- Presentation.
- Nonverbal communication.
- Listening.
- Cross-cultural management.
- Heterogeneous teamwork.

Self-Awareness Skills

- Personal adaptability.
- Understanding personal biases.
- Internal locus of control.

business of selling books. For years, Barnes & Noble focused on expanding its "bricks-and-mortar" stores around the country and believed that it would be undermining its business if it sold books over the Internet. Not until Barnes & Noble began to feel pressure from Amazon.com did the company enter the Internet world, but by then significant market opportunities had already been lost. There is usually more than one reasonable way to do something, and the challenge is to use informed judgment "to call the shots" in a timely fashion.

Success in carrying out the four management functions and the set of roles discussed above depends on the ability to appropriately define and deal with the managerial problems at hand and successfully applying various management skills. This book emphasizes the skills or talents that will make you a better manager, individual contributor, and member of a team. Practicing the skills provides valuable preparation and will allow you to learn from your experiences more quickly.

Four major categories of skills will help you become a good manager. They are strategizing skills, task-related skills, people-related skills, and self-awareness skills. Skills for Managing 1.1 lists these skills.

STRATEGIZING SKILLS   The ability to see "the big picture" and to focus on key objectives without getting mired in details, as well as to sense and understand what is happening inside and outside the company, is **strategizing.** Top executives are usually responsible for making the major strategic decisions that affect the organization. Successful firms, however, instill a strategic mentality and develop the strategic skills of individuals and teams from all levels. The interaction between the inputs provided by individuals and teams and the corporatewide perspective of senior executives greatly enhances the odds of success of major strategic decisions.

TASK-RELATED SKILLS   The ability to define the best approach to accomplish personal and organizational objectives means utilizing task-related skills. These include consideration of all resources, including time, organizational structure, financial resources, and people. They also involve the ability to prioritize, remain flexible to make changes if necessary, and ensure that value is being created. In contemporary organizations, task-related skills are required for most employees from factory workers to top executives.

Active Listening
Skills Inventory

PEOPLE-RELATED SKILLS   Getting work done through others and with others requires people-related skills. Accomplishing tasks over the long haul requires more than a boss giving orders and supervising employees. People skills include the ability to delegate tasks, share information, resolve conflicts, be a team player, and work with people from different backgrounds.

Often, managers fail not because they lack technical knowledge or motivation but rather because they lack people skills. This is a serious problem because managers are in the position to have a direct negative effect on the behaviors of employees in other units as well as in their own departments.

Assessing
Emotional
Intelligence

SELF-AWARENESS SKILLS   The Greek philosopher Socrates pointed out that to be successful in life, you first need to "know yourself." We all have special talents, weaknesses, biases, and needs. Being aware of your personal characteristics can help you adapt to others or at least understand why you react to them the way you do. You can then be more appreciative of the nuances of situations confronting you, avoid rushed judgments, size up opportunities, capitalize on your personal strengths, avoid situations in which you are likely to fail, and influence other people.

The Evolution of Management Thought

Many of the key management ideas that blossomed in the nineteenth and twentieth centuries are practiced by managers to this day. This section examines these early management ideas, from the operational perspective, the bureaucratic management approach, the administrative management approach, the behavioral perspective, and contemporary management approaches. Systems theory, contingency theory, and the learning organization are part of the contemporary management perspective. These contemporary ideas represent the most recent thinking on sound management practices in the twenty-first century.

The following section is a rough chronology of the time period in which each particular management perspective occurred. It is important to keep in mind that some of the "old" views are still being applied in varying degrees today. For instance, the operational approach with an emphasis on scientific management is still alive and well at Lincoln Electric (see introductory vignette). Many of the principles of bureaucratic management, with its emphasis on rules and procedures, still ring true in the U.S. Post Office and most government agencies. The military is still largely organized following the prescriptions of the administrative management school. You may find many of the ideas of the behavioral perspective, with its emphasis on human relations, present in "high-tech" firms such as Tandem and Intel. And you may even think of some modern organizations that follow a Machiavellian leadership style, in which tight control through fear and punishment is the norm.

Early Management Thought

The art and practice of management have been present for many centuries. Designing and building such huge public works projects as the Great Wall of China, the pyramids of Egypt, and the aqueducts that provided water to cities in the Roman Empire required an understanding of management. For many years management was viewed as an art and was verbally passed on without documenting theoretical principles that could be used by future generations of managers. However, a few early thinkers laid the foundation for the classical and behavioral schools of management thought that arose during the last century. These thinkers included Sun Tzu in China, Niccolò Machiavelli in Italy, and Adam Smith in Great Britain.

EARLY IDEAS ABOUT MANAGEMENT STRATEGY Some of our earliest management concepts are found in *The Art of War,* written about 2,500 years ago by Sun Tzu, a Chinese general. Sun Tzu's ideas focus on developing military strategies that can lead to victory in battle. For example, he recognized that it is better to use intelligence and cunning to subdue an enemy than to rely on violence and destruction. Alliances and negotiated settlements allow a military leader to expand his empire without sacrificing soldiers or resources or destroying cities. Sun Tzu recognized that strategy involved a long-term perspective. He recommended attacking the enemy's weak points and taking advantage of one's own army's strengths. Sun Tzu's insights about dispassionately taking stock of strengths and weaknesses are still prominent features of strategic management.

Niccolò Machiavelli (1469–1527) was imprisoned, tortured, and banished from Florence by the ruling Medici family, who believed he had conspired against them. While in exile he wrote *The Prince*, hoping it would win favor with the Medicis. Although Machiavelli eventually regained some prestige with them, *The Prince* was not published until 1532, five years after Machiavelli's death.

Adam Smith (1723–1770), today regarded as the founder of classical economics, wrote during the earliest years of the Industrial Revolution. He regarded the personal interest of the individual and the human urge to seek advantage as the source of wealth and social progress.

division of labor

The production process in which each worker repeats one step over and over, achieving greater efficiencies in the use of time and knowledge.

operational perspective

The management perspective formed during the nineteenth and early twentieth centuries when the factory system and modern corporations evolved to meet the challenges of managing large, complex organizations.

EARLY IDEAS ABOUT LEADERSHIP   Niccolò Machiavelli wrote *The Prince* during the Renaissance in sixteenth-century Florence, Italy. It was one of the first books that described leadership. Machiavelli was a government official during a period of warfare and political intrigue between city-states vying for control of the region, and he had a cynical view of human nature, believing that people were motivated by very narrow self-interests.

Machiavelli advised the leader or prince that it was better to be feared than to be loved. Love is a fickle emotion, whereas fear is constant. In other words, survival is a basic human instinct that dominates other emotions. Machiavelli also suggested that a leader may engage in lies or deceptions for the good of society, as long as he appears to be virtuous to the people. The leader should be fair yet tough, harshly punishing disloyal subjects to discourage others from engaging in treason. Machiavelli believed that the aristocrats close in stature to the prince posed the greatest threat to his welfare and that the prince had to use cunning and intrigue to keep them off balance. Thus, he warned the leader not to trust his peers. He believed that an effective leader forms alliances of convenience with some enemies to keep the more powerful ones off balance.

Machiavelli's leadership philosophy was that "the end justified the means." Contemporary leaders are called Machiavellian if they engage in manipulative and self-serving tactics. Although many contemporary executives and leaders might judge Machiavelli's advice to be extreme and unrealistic, even today rivals fight behind the scenes in highly politicized corporations, and sibling rivalry runs rampant in some family businesses.

EARLY IDEAS ABOUT THE DESIGN AND ORGANIZATION OF WORK   The efficient organization of work has its roots in the classic eighteenth-century book *The Wealth of Nations*, written in 1776 by Adam Smith. As a professor of logic and moral philosophy at Glasgow University in Scotland, Smith was the first to recognize the principle of the **division of labor** in a manufacturing process. Division of labor converted production by craftsmen or artisans who were generalists into simple steps. Each worker became a specialist who repeated one step over and over, thereby achieving greater efficiencies in the use of time and knowledge. Smith showed how the manufacture of pins could be reduced to 18 steps done by 10 specialists who each performed one or two steps. Organizing the 10 laborers in a small factory made it possible to produce 48,000 pins in one day. When the pin makers operated independently as generalists, the total daily output was 200 pins. Smith observed that the division of labor was responsible for revolutionary gains in factory output. His work laid the theoretical groundwork for scientific management.

The Operational Perspective

The **operational perspective** on management thought originated in the nineteenth and early twentieth centuries. It coincided with the rise of the factory system and the formation of modern corporations, both of which provided challenges in efficiently operating and coordinating large, complex organizations. The operational perspective attempted to apply logic and the scientific method to management so as to discover and practice the one best way of doing a job.

Some of the legacy of the operational perspective is found today in a subfield called "productions and operations management" (see Chapter 17), although most contemporary management thinkers note the crucial role played by the human element of an organization. Three approaches fall into the operational perspective: scientific management, quantitative management, and quality management.

SCIENTIFIC MANAGEMENT   In the last half of the nineteenth century, organizations were unable to obtain increased productivity from employees despite making large investments in new technologies. Frederick Winslow Taylor (1856–1915) believed his life's calling was to change this situation. Born to a Philadelphia lawyer in 1856, Taylor learned the trades of common laborer and machinist in a small Philadelphia machine shop where he worked for four years. He was then hired by the Midvale Steel Company in Pennsylvania, where he moved quickly through the ranks while studying for a mechanical engineering degree at night. At Midvale, Taylor carefully documented the large amount of time that was wasted by workers who were ill equipped and poorly trained to perform the simplest tasks. Even shoveling coal was inefficient, because workers brought their own shovels with differing weights, sizes, and sharpness. No one had any idea which type of shovel worked best.

Taylor discovered that workers sometimes avoided doing their best work, a practice called *soldiering,* because they feared that management might raise quotas without increasing pay or that some employees would lose their jobs. Complicating the situation, there were no systematic rules to serve as guidelines for doing the jobs most efficiently. Workers learned their jobs by the use of rules of thumb and trial-and-error processes.

In response to the inefficiencies he observed in the steel industry, Taylor developed **scientific management,** which is summarized in Table 1.2. The scientific method should be applied to determining the one best way to do a particular job. This optimal approach to work spares the worker from management criticism and provides managers and owners with the most output from each worker. Taylor encouraged management to share productivity gains with employees by using a piecework production system in which each worker's output would be measured against standardized productivity quotas. When workers reached or exceeded the quota, the financial gains would be shared. The result would be that workers could earn more by cooperating with management.

Next, Taylor supported the use of scientific selection methods to make the best matches between workers and jobs. At the time, seniority or the boss's preference was used to match workers with jobs. Taylor

scientific management

A management method that applies the principles of the scientific method to the management process: determining the one best way to do a job and sharing the rewards with the workers.

TABLE 1.2

Taylor's Four Principles of Scientific Management

1. Scientifically study each part of a task and develop the best method of performing the task.
2. Carefully select workers and train them to perform the task by using the scientifically developed method.
3. Cooperate fully with workers to ensure that they use the proper method.
4. Divide work and responsibility so that management is responsible for planning work methods using scientific principles and workers are responsible for executing the work accordingly.

Source: F. W. Taylor, *The Principles of Scientific Management*, New York: Harper, 1911.

Frederick Winslow Taylor (1856–1915), although born to a wealthy Philadelphia family, began his career as a machinist in a metal products factory. His observations there led to his 1911 work, *The Principles of Scientific Management*. His method timed tasks for both machines and workers—who often resented being treated as machines.

found this approach inefficient, and he suggested using measures of worker aptitudes, traits, and performance to scientifically determine the fit between person and job.

Finally, Taylor perceived a clear separation between the work of employees and managers. In Taylor's view, employees did the physical work, and managers planned, directed, and coordinated employees' efforts so that the goals would be reached. He believed that managers and employees should be dependent on each other to achieve desired output, which would encourage cooperation and result in fewer conflicts or strikes. Taylor also believed that the job of management was to inspire and motivate workers to fully cooperate and learn the scientific management principles applied to their job. Until his death in 1915, Taylor committed himself to what he termed a "mental revolution" in the practice of industrial management.

Following Taylor's footsteps Frank Gilbreth and Lillian Gilbreth introduced the idea of time and motion studies using the stopwatch and motion picture camera to improve workplace efficiencies. The Gilbreths analyzed each movement a worker performed during a particular task by filming the task actions and observing the film frame by frame. They then looked for better ways to perform each step to ensure that all the steps could be performed more efficiently with less time and effort.

Henry Gantt was a school teacher who felt that Taylor's piece rate incentive system placed employees under a great deal of stress. He introduced the notion of a "guaranteed day rate," in which employees knew the minimum income they would receive. When employees exceeded certain standards they were paid bonuses. Gantt also developed work scheduling charts which are still used today.

Scientific management had a profound effect on the captains of American industry. In one of the most famous applications, Henry Ford utilized scientific management in the production process of the factory that manufactured the Model-T Ford (see Management Close-Up 1.b). The lasting contribution of scientific management was to transform man-

How Scientific Management Revolutionized Industry: The Case of Model T

Prior to 1900, workers worked in small groups, cooperating to hand-build cars with parts that often had to be altered and modified to fit together. This system, a type of small-batch production, was expensive. Assembling just one car took considerable time and effort and workers could produce only a few cars per day. To reduce costs and sell more cars, managers of early car companies needed better techniques to increase efficiency.

Henry Ford revolutionized the car industry. In 1913, Ford opened the Highland Park car plant in Detroit to produce the Model T. Ford and his team of manufacturing managers pioneered the development of mass production manufacturing, a system that made the small-batch system obsolete almost overnight. In mass production, moving conveyor belts bring the car to the workers. Each individual worker performs a single assigned task along a production line, and the speed of the conveyor belt is the primary means of controlling employee activities. Ford experimented to discover the most efficient way for each individual worker to perform an assigned task. The result was that each worker performed one specialized task, such as bolting on the door or attaching the door handle, and jobs in the Ford car plant became very repetitive.

Ford's management approach increased efficiency and reduced costs by so much that by 1920 he was able to reduce the price of a car by two-thirds and sell over 2 million cars a year. At the same time, Ford doubled worker pay, reducing employee turnover and attracting a large number of applicants who were willing to work on his assembly lines. Ford Motor Company (*www.ford.com*) became the leading car company in the world, and many competitors rushed to adopt the new mass-production techniques. Two of these companies, General Motors (GM) (*www.gm.com*) and Chrysler (*www.chryslercorp.com*), eventually emerged as Ford's major competitors.

Source: Adapted from G. R. Jones, J. M. George, and C. W. Hill, *Contemporary Management.* New York: Irwin/McGraw-Hill, 2000, pp. 37–38.

agement into a more objective, systematic body of knowledge in which best practices can be discovered for different jobs. It also gave managers and supervisors more active and clearly defined roles.

Despite these noteworthy contributions, scientific management had shortcomings. It did not appreciate the social context of work and the needs (beyond pay) of workers. It often led to dehumanizing working conditions in which every aspect of a worker's effort was measured, prohibiting employee initiative. Scientific management also assumed that workers had no useful ideas, and that only managers and experts were capable of coming up with good ideas or innovations.

A major problem that Taylor, the Gilbreths, and Gantt did not anticipate was that many firms would "pick and choose" what they wanted from scientific management while ignoring worker interests. For example, "some managers using scientific management obtained increases in performance, but rather than sharing performance gains with workers through bonuses as Taylor had advocated, they simply increased the amount of work that each worker was expected to do. Many workers experiencing the reorganized work system found that as their performance increased, managers required them to do more work for the same pay.

Workers also learned that increases in performance often meant fewer jobs and a greater threat of layoffs, because fewer workers were needed."[1]

These problems have given scientific management a "bad name" in some circles, which continues to this day. They were at least in part responsible for the rapid rise in legislation designed to protect labor unions in the 1930s. They still provide some of the rationale for unions' existence in the twenty-first century. Workers continue to join together to defend their interests collectively as well as to prevent employers' abuses. Employment in manufacturing, where scientific management is most appropriate, as a percentage of the labor force has declined steadily over the years. The percentage of unionized workers has also been dropping, from about 35 percent of the workforce in the mid-1940s to less than 15 percent at the beginning of the twenty-first century.[2] In general, unions have not been able to repeat their success in organizing "blue collar" workers when they have tried to organize "white collar" workers in the service sector, containing retail stores, banks, schools, and governmental agencies, which is where most new jobs are located.

QUANTITATIVE MANAGEMENT   The scientific management perspective later became known as the "quantitative management" school. The focus is on the development of various statistical tools and techniques to improve efficiency and allow management to make informed decisions regarding the costs and benefits of alternative courses of action. Four of these quantitative methods, which are still widely used today, include: (1) break-even analysis, (2) basic economic order quantity (EOQ) model, (3) material requirements planning (MRP), and (4) quality management. These are briefly described below and will be revisited in greater detail in Chapter 17, Operations Management.

Break-even analysis provides formulas which assess the total fixed costs associated with producing a product, the variable costs for each unit, and the contribution made by the sale of each unit to recovering both fixed and variable costs. The break-even point is the number of units which must be sold at a given price to recover all fixed and variable costs. At that point there is neither a profit nor a loss, but rather the company "breaks even." Additional sales result in profits and fewer sales result in losses.

The *economic order quantity (EOQ) model* dates back to 1915. The formula is generally credited to Ford W. Harris, who argued in his book *Operations and Cost* that effective management of inventories is critical to sustained profitability.[3] EOQ's objective is to minimize the total costs of inventory. The inventory holding costs include housing costs (building rent, taxes, and insurance), investment costs (interest payments), material handling costs (equipment and labor costs) and other miscellaneous expenses (pilferage, scrap, and obsolescence). The holding cost increases as the order quantity increases, because larger average inventories need to be maintained. On the other hand, as the quantity ordered increases, the annual set up or ordering cost per unit decreases (for instance, material handling and tooling may be made more efficient as the quantity purchased increases). Mathematically, the EOQ model demonstrates that the optimal reorder point occurs when the total set up cost is equal to the total holding cost.

Material requirements planning (MRP) is a set of tools designed to manage components where the demand for the items is linked to another demand. For example, the demand for TV antennas is linked to the demand for TVs. To determine the number of antennas needed, a TV manufacturer starts by determining the number of TVs that will be built and when. Once management forecasts the demand for TVs, quantities required for all other components such as antennas, knobs, and screens can be computed, because all components are dependent items. MRP helps a company reduce inventory costs and ensures that all items will be available when needed. Consider the following example: "Nancy Mueller turns quiche into cash. Her firm, Nancy's Specialty Foods, is designed for today's busy lifestyle, producing 750,000 prepackaged, frozen quiche hors d'ouvres each month. Material requirements planning (MRP) software has been key to her growing success. MRP is the primary management tool that keeps the ingredients and labor coming at the proper times and the schedule firm. Once Nancy's Specialty Foods knows the demand for her crabmeat quiche, she knows the demand for all of the ingredients from dough, to cheese, to crab meat, because all of the ingredients are dependent."[4]

QUALITY MANAGEMENT   The need for improved product quality emerged in the 1980s, when it became apparent that the United States was lagging behind some industrialized countries, most notably Japan, in the area of product quality. Many of the tools and techniques that were used to identify quality problems and take corrective action date back decades earlier. For instance, Walter A. Shewhart, a Bell Labs statistician, developed a set of methods in the 1920s that were designed to ensure standardization and reduce quality defects. His book *Economic Control of Quality,* published in 1931, is still considered a classic. Joseph M. Juran was a statistician who in the 1940s introduced the concept of "pareto analysis," which argues that 80 percent of all quality problems may be traced to a relatively small number of causes. Phillip Crosby spent his entire career at International Telephone and Telegraph. While there, Crosby documented the enormous costs of having to fix something that was not done right the first time. His ideas were later published in the 1970s in the business best seller *Quality Is Free.* Arnand V. Feigenbaum developed the concept of *total quality control* in the 1940s, which argued for an integrated quality improvement effort across all functional areas (e.g., purchasing, finance, marketing) and not only in production and manufacturing. These ideas were later published in his 1951 book, *Total Quality Control.*

By now, most people are familiar with the concept "total quality management" popularized by W. Edwards Deming. Deming was an American statistician who advanced the use of statistics for constant quality improvement. Deming assisted many Japanese business leaders after World War II. His approach was to put quality first. Ironically, he

TABLE 1.3

Deming's 14 Points of Total Quality Management

1. Create constancy of purpose toward improvement of product and service, with the aim to become competitive and to stay in business, and to provide jobs.

2. Adopt the new philosophy. We are in a new economic age. Western management must awaken to the challenge, must learn their responsibilities, and take on leadership for change.

3. Cease dependence on inspection to achieve quality. Eliminate the need for inspection on a mass basis by building quality into the product in the first place.

4. End the practice of awarding business on the basis of price tag. Instead, minimize total cost. Move toward a single supplier for any one item, on a long-term relationship of loyalty and trust.

5. Improve constantly and forever the system of production and service, to improve quality and productivity, and thus constantly decrease costs.

6. Institute training on the job.

7. Institute leadership. The aim of supervision should be to help people and machines and gadgets to do a better job. Supervision of management is in need of overhaul as well as supervision of production workers.

8. Drive out fear, so that everyone may work effectively for the company.

9. Break down barriers between departments. People in research, design, sales, and production must work as a team, to foresee problems of production and in use that may be encountered with the product or service.

10. Eliminate slogans, exhortations, and targets for the work force asking for zero defects and new levels of productivity. Such exhortations only create adversarial relationships, as the bulk of the causes of low quality and low productivity belong to the system and thus lie beyond the power of the work force.

    a. Eliminate work standards (quotas) on the factory floor. Substitute leadership.

    b. Eliminate management by objective. Eliminate management by numbers, numerical goals. Substitute leadership.

11. Remove barriers that rob the hourly worker of his right to pride of workmanship. The responsibility of supervisors must be changed from sheer numbers to quality.

12. Remove barriers that rob people in management and in engineering of their right to pride of workmanship. This means, *inter alia,* abolishment of the annual merit rating and of management by objective.

13. Institute a vigorous program of education and self-improvement.

14. Put everybody in the company to work to accomplish the transformation. The transformation is everybody's job.

Source: From W. Edwards Deming, *Out of the Crisis,* MIT Press, 1986. Reprinted with permission of the MIT Press.

---

total quality management (TQM)

An organizationwide management approach that focuses on quality as an overarching goal. The basis of this approach is the understanding that all employees and organizational units should be working harmoniously to satisfy the customer.

was largely ignored in the United States for most of his professional life. Deming finally achieved recognition as a quality guru in the United States when he was well into his eighties, following the publication of his book *Out of the Crisis* in 1986. (See Table 1.3)

Total quality management (TQM) is an organizationwide approach that focuses on quality as an overarching goal. The basis of this approach is the understanding that all employees and organizational units should be working harmoniously to satisfy the customer. Since the customer's needs are in constant flux, the organization must strive to continuously improve its systems and practices. The TQM perspective views quality as the central purpose of the organization, in contrast to the focus on efficiency advocated by the operational perspective. In TQM, quality is viewed as everybody's job, not just the role of quality control specialists, as in bureaucratic management (to be discussed below).

TQM reflects the thinking and practice of management in many of the world's most admired companies, including Toyota, Motorola, Xerox, and Ford. The key elements of the TQM approach are

- *Focus on the customer.* It is important to identify the organization's customers. External customers consume the organization's product or service. Internal customers are employees who receive the output of other employees.

- *Employee involvement.* Since quality is considered the job of all employees, employees should be involved in quality initiatives. Front-line employees are likely to have the closest contact with external customers and thus can make the most valuable contributions to quality. Therefore, employees must have the authority to innovate and improve quality. In TQM workers are often organized into empowered teams that have the authority to make quality improvements.

- *Continuous improvement.* The quest for quality is a never-ending process in which people are continuously working to improve the performance, speed, and number of features of the product or service. Continuous improvement means that small, incremental improvements that occur on a regular basis will eventually add up to vast improvements in quality.

W. Edwards Deming, considered the father of TQM, outlined 14 points of quality, as listed in Table 1.3.

Bureaucratic Management

Another traditional perspective is **bureaucratic management,** which examines the entire organization as a rational entity. Max Weber (1864–1920), a German sociologist, introduced the concept of bureaucratic management as an "ideal" model that managers should try to emulate in order to operate an organization on a fair, rational, and efficient basis. According to Weber, the ideal bureaucracy should use impersonal rules and procedures for decision making rather than custom, family connections, or social class. Bureaucratic management challenged the aristocratic notion that authority should be based on birth and divine right. Instead, competence should be the criterion. For example, in the Germany of Weber's day only men of aristocratic birth could become officers in the Prussian army.

Table 1.4 summarizes the important principles of Weber's bureaucratic management. Building on Adam Smith's early work on the division of labor, the ideal bureaucracy uses the principle of *specialization of labor* to break jobs down into well-defined tasks at which a person can become very competent. Formal rules and procedures are applied consistently and uniformly so that employees and customers can count on a rational and

bureaucratic management

The management approach that examines the entire organization as a rational entity, using impersonal rules and procedures for decision making.

TABLE 1.4

Key Characteristics of Weber's Ideal Bureaucracy

1. *Specialization of labor.*	Jobs are broken down into routine, well-defined tasks so that members know what is expected of them and can become extremely competent at their particular subset of tasks.
2. *Formal rules and procedures.*	Written rules and procedures specifying the behaviors desired from members facilitate coordination and ensure uniformity.
3. *Impersonality.*	Rules, procedures, and sanctions are applied uniformly regardless of individual personalities and personal considerations.
4. *Well-defined hierarchy.*	Multiple levels of positions, with carefully determined reporting relationships among levels, provide supervision of lower offices by higher ones, a means of handling exceptions, and the ability to establish accountability of actions.
5. *Career advancement based on merit.*	Selection and promotion are based on the qualifications and performance of members.

Source: M. Weber, *The Theory of Social and Economic Organizations,* ed. and trans. A. M. Henderson and T. Parsons. New York: Free Press, 1947, pp. 328–337.

predictable environment. Weber opposed the idiosyncratic management style of bosses who lorded over underlings in an unpredictable and arbitrary manner. He suggested that a well-defined hierarchy with clearly delineated reporting relationships was an effective way to maintain accountability. Thus the most appropriate organizational form was a pyramid structure with many reporting levels and a vertical downward chain of command. Finally, Weber strongly believed in career advancement based on merit, which stressed competency over nepotism and family connections.

Today bureaucracy is often associated with meaningless rules and red tape, but in fact Weber's bureaucratic management made positive contributions to management thought. The use of impersonal rules and procedures provides a fair and consistent way to deal with employee relations; for example, an employee handbook spells out the rules for employee discipline, performance appraisal, and work schedules rather than allowing management to handle employment policies in an arbitrary manner. Similarly, Weber's emphasis on merit as the basis of career advancement is now deeply embedded into the business culture of the United States and many other countries.

Other aspects of bureaucratic management are open to criticism. In particular, the need for a well-defined hierarchy has been challenged by the quality management viewpoint, which argues that hierarchies form barriers between employees and customers and result in reductions in quality and customer satisfaction. Current practice suggests that for firms facing rapid change and competing in markets that require constant innovation (for instance, the software industry) hierarchies should be minimized, moving away from a pyramid structure toward one that is flatter, with less

TABLE 1.5

Fayol's 14 Principles of Management

1.	*Division of work.*	Work should be divided into specialized tasks with responsibility for each task assigned to specific individuals.
2.	*Authority.*	Authority should be delegated along with responsibility.
3.	*Discipline.*	Clarify expectations and provide consequences for not meeting them.
4.	*Unity of command.*	Each employee should report directly to one supervisor.
5.	*Unity of direction.*	The organization's objectives should be the focus of the employee's work.
6.	*Subordination of individual interest to the general interest.*	The organization's interests should take precedence over individual interests.
7.	*Remuneration.*	Efforts that support the organization's objectives should be compensated.
8.	*Centralization.*	Superior and subordinate roles should be determined and their relative importance clarified.
9.	*Scalar chain.*	Communications among organizational areas should follow the chain of command.
10.	*Order.*	The organization of materials and jobs should support the goals of the organization.
11.	*Equity.*	Treat all employees the same, with justice and respect.
12.	*Stability and tenure.*	Employee loyalty and continuing service should be encouraged.
13.	*Initiative.*	Individual initiative of employees that supports the organization's objectives should be encouraged.
14.	*Esprit de corps.*	Employees and management should be encouraged to share the goal of achieving the organization's objectives.

Source: H. Fayol, *General and Industrial Management*, trans. C. Storres. Marshfield, MA: Pitman Publishing, 1949.

direct supervision and more cooperation between workers and managers. On the other hand, the bureaucratic model developed by Weber still applies to organizations seeking to minimize deviations from standard procedures and norms. In other words, the bureaucratic approach to organizing is still advisable when reliability and efficiency are paramount.

Administrative Management

The **administrative management** approach examines an organization from the perspective of the managers and executives responsible for coordinating the activities of diverse groups and units across the entire organization. It views management as a profession that can be learned by understanding basic principles. The key advocate was Henri Fayol (1841–1925), a French mining engineer and industrialist. In 1916, he wrote a book entitled *Administration Industrialle et Generalle* featuring what he considered to be practical guidelines for effective management based on his administrative experiences. Even though the book was not translated into English until almost four decades later, it had a significant impact on management thought and teaching.

Fayol identified five functions generic to all management activities: planning, organizing, commanding, coordinating, and controlling. He codified general principles of management that he thought could be applied to the management of any organization, as shown in Table 1.5. Conceiving of management as being made up of diverse functions is known as the *functional approach* to management.

administrative management

The management approach that examines an organization from the perspective of the managers and executives responsible for coordinating the activities of diverse groups and units across the entire organization.

Today, most organizations try to incorporate the following principles into policies and procedures:

- *Unity of command.* Each employee should be assigned to only one supervisor.
- *Unity of direction.* The employees' efforts should be focused on achieving organizational objectives.
- *Equity.* Employees should be treated with justice and respect.

Some other principles advocated by Fayol have not held up as well over time. For example, his principle that the *scalar chain of command* should define the path of communication in a top-down direction has been challenged. Both upward and horizontal communication can be equally important ways of communicating in organizations. In some situations, poor communication flows through the ranks have led to major mistakes, as documented in Management Close-Up 1.c. Fayol could not have foreseen the revolution that has made the knowledge worker, who may be located at the base of the organization, a source of critical information and competitive advantage for organizational decision makers.

Still, as was the case for Weber's bureaucratic model, there may be some situations (such as the military) in which Fayol's administrative principles are still applicable. In general Fayol's main contribution to management was to specify the "best universal" way to organize by separating managerial tasks into interdependent areas of responsibilities or functions. Fayol's contention that these functions should flow in a logical manner from planning to controlling is still reflected in many modern management texts, even though they are often criticized for being too orderly and rigid to help the company adapt to a changing environment.

Behavioral Perspective

behavioral perspective

The management view that knowledge of the psychological and social processes of human behavior can result in improvements in productivity and work satisfaction.

The **behavioral perspective** incorporates psychological and social processes of human behavior to improve productivity and work satisfaction. Operational theorists view management as a mechanical process in which employees would fit into any job or organization designed for optimum efficiency if given monetary incentives to do so. The behavioral perspective argues that human factors alone may affect workplace efficiency. The behavioral perspective traces its roots to the work of Mary Parker Follett and the Hawthorne studies, a series of long-term behavioral research experiments performed in an industrial setting. These works led to the human relations approach to management, which stresses the need for managers to understand the dynamics of the work group so as to positively influence employee motivation and satisfaction.

Management's Historical Figures

The Problem of Hierarchical Organizational Structures: How the FBI Missed the Boat

THEME: ETHICS In 2003, a 48-year-old Coleen Rowley, a 20-year veteran FBI agent, was chosen as person of the year by *Time Magazine*. She had written a 13-page secret memo to a congressional committee which eventually landed on front pages of many newspapers. The memo described how the FBI's upper echelons ignored pleas from her office to investigate some of the terrorists involved in the 9/11 attacks months before they actually occurred. In her memo, she issued damning indictments—agents were drowning in paperwork and lived in fear of offending the higher-ups. "There's a certain pecking order, and it's pretty strong," she said. "It's very rare that someone picks up the phone and calls a rank or two above themselves."

Rowley has been stung by a nasty backlash within the FBI. For example, there was the statement on loyalty from an old Elbert Hubbard essay, which Rowley received from a number of retired agents. A paraphrased version of Hubbard's words used to hang on the walls of FBI headquarters, when J. Edgar Hoover was director. It read, in part: "If you work for a man, in heaven's name work for him; speak well of him and stand by the institution he represents. Remember—an ounce of loyalty is worth a pound of cleverness . . . If you must growl, condemn, and eternally find fault, why—resign your position and when you are on the outside, damn to your heart's content."

The copies she received had "resign your position" heavily underlined. "It wasn't even anonymous!" she says. "They signed their names!" Even though that statement is not on the FBI's walls anymore, it is still in the hearts and minds of many agents.

Source: Adapted from A. Ripley & M. Sieger, "The Special Agent," *Time*, January 6, 2003, pp. 34–40.

MARY PARKER FOLLETT Questioning much of the wisdom of scientific management, because it ignored the many ways in which employees could contribute ideas and exercise initiative, was Follett's primary contribution. She advocated increased employee participation, greater employee autonomy, and organizing the enterprise into "cross-functional" teams, composed of members of different departments working together on common projects. This would, in turn, foster upward and downward communication across various units. She also proposed that authority should rest with knowledge and expertise rather than with one's position in the hierarchy. "In other words, if workers have the relevant knowledge, then workers, rather than managers, should be in control of the work process itself, and managers should behave as coaches and facilitators—not as monitors and supervisors."[5]

Although individual workers perform specialized tasks on an assembly line, they work as a group rather than as individuals.

THE HAWTHORNE STUDIES The Hawthorne studies were performed at the Western Electric Company's Hawthorne plant near Chicago from 1924 to 1932 under the direction of Harvard University researchers Elton Mayo and Fritz Roethlisberger. Their original purpose was to study the effects of physical working conditions on employee productivity and fatigue.

In the first set of studies, light was steadily decreased for an experimental group of employees, while illumination remained constant for the control group of employees working in a different area. Despite the different levels of illumination, the performance of both groups of employees rose consistently. This result surprised the researchers, who expected the control group to outperform its experimental counterpart. They concluded that the special attention paid to the employees in the studies motivated them to put greater effort into their jobs. They labelled the phenomenon the **Hawthorne effect,** and suggested that when a manager or leader shows concern for employees, their motivation and productivity levels are likely to improve.

Later studies at Hawthorne revealed that the informal organization had a profound effect on group productivity. Mayo and Roethlisberger discovered that a work group would establish its own informal group performance norm, which represented what it considered to be a fair level of performance. Individuals who exceeded the group performance norm were considered "ratebusters," and those who performed below the

Hawthorne effect

The finding that paying special attention to employees motivates them to put greater effort into their jobs (from the Hawthorne management studies, performed from 1924 through 1932 at Western Electric Company's plant near Chicago).

part one   Overview

norm were viewed as "chiselers." The work group disciplined both types of norm violations because ratebusters could speed up the pace of work beyond what was considered fair, while chiselers avoided doing their fair share of the work. The work group was likely to convince rate-busters to slow down and chiselers to work faster. These findings suggest that the influence of the work group may be as significant as the influence of the supervisor. Thus supervisors need the support of group members in establishing performance norms that converge with the work expectations of management.

The Hawthorne studies provided evidence that employee attitudes significantly affect performance in a manner which differs from the financial incentives championed by advocates of scientific management. Understanding the informal work organization made it possible to create cooperation between employees and management that resulted in a more productive organization.

HUMAN RELATIONS   The Hawthorne studies generated intense interest in the human side of various companies. Managers who previously concentrated on job design, work methods, or applications of technology to the task environment turned their attention to group behaviors, leadership, and employee attitudes. The **human relations approach** to management made relationships between employees and supervisors a vital aspect of management. Its advocates were people trained in the behavioral sciences, such as clinical and social psychologists, who emphasized building collaborative and cooperative relationships between supervisors and workers. Two key aspects of the human relations approach are focused on employee motivation and leadership style.

human relations approach

A management approach that views the relationships between employees and supervisors as the most salient aspect of management.

Employee Motivation   Abraham Maslow (1908–1970), a clinical psychologist who developed a theory of motivation based on a *hierarchy of needs,* assumed that unsatisfied human needs motivate behavior. The underlying assumption in Maslow's work was *humanism,* or the belief that the basic inner natures of people are good. This represented a stark contrast to Freudian psychology, which assumed the inner nature of personality was destructive, violent, and evil. This new, more positive view of human nature had a substantial impact on the fields of both psychology and management.

The hierarchy of needs model, explained in greater detail in Chapter 12, suggests that managers can motivate employees by providing an environment in which the employees can satisfy their most pressing needs. From a human relations perspective, this suggests that managers must develop positive relationships with subordinates in order to discover what their motivational needs are. For example, a manager who knows that employees are motivated by social relationships may be able to facilitate good coworker relations that will be nurturing to work group productivity. Maslow's ideas suggest that employee motivation is more

TABLE 1.6

McGregor's Theory X and Theory Y Assumptions

Assumptions of Theory X

1. The average human being has an inherent dislike of work and will avoid it if he or she can.
2. People need to be coerced, controlled, directed, and threatened with punishment to get them to put forward adequate effort toward the organization's ends.
3. The average person prefers to be directed, wants to avoid responsibility, has relatively little ambition, and wants security above all.

Assumptions of Theory Y

1. The expenditure of physical and mental effort in work is as natural as in play or rest—the typical human being does not inherently dislike work.
2. External control and threat of punishment are not the only means for bringing about effort toward a company's goals. A person will exercise self-direction and self-control in the pursuit of the objective to which he is committed.
3. The average person learns, under the right conditions, not only to accept but to seek responsibility.
4. The capacity to exercise a relatively high degree of imagination, ingenuity, and creativity in the solution of organizational problems is widely, not narrowly, distributed in the population.
5. The intellectual potential of most people is only partially utilized in most organizations.

Source: Adapted from D. McGregor, *The Human Side of Enterprise.* New York: McGraw-Hill, 1960, pp. 33–48.

complex than was assumed by the scientific management approach, which focused strictly on pay. Maslow assumed that pay can motivate only lower level needs, and once those are satisfied it loses its power to shape employee behavior. Instead, nonmonetary factors such as praise, recognition, and job characteristics motivate human behavior.

Leadership Style   Douglas McGregor (1908–1964), a professor at MIT, used a human relations perspective to compare the assumptions leaders make about employees. He called them Theory X and Theory Y (see Table 1.6).

Leaders and managers who operate under Theory X assumptions believe that employees are inherently lazy and lack ambition, and these managers use the external controls of punishments and rewards to drive employees to achieve organizational goals. They tend to supervise subordinates closely and deprive them of opportunities to show individual initiative and creativity. McGregor believed that highly controlling and autocratic supervisory styles based on Theory X assumptions would most likely be inefficient because they waste the human potential that could make substantial contributions to the organization.

According to McGregor, leaders who hold Theory Y assumptions believe that most employees enjoy work and seek to make useful contributions to the organization. Employees are looking for ways to exercise creativity and initiative, and will most likely perform up to or even exceed

Human Relations at Work: The New Face of Air Rage

THEME: DEALING WITH CHANGE Jamy Owens was expecting a quiet flight home to Seattle when she suddenly heard a commotion. But it wasn't an unruly passenger—it was a flight attendant. According to Ms. Owens, the attendant started berating a man across the aisle. Pretty soon the attendant was making a scene, even shouting at the confused passenger. His mistake—leaving a beeping cell-phone in the overhead bin.

"I about jumped out of my skin," says Ms. Owens, a retail consultant. "I'm thinking the guy's going to be duct-taped to his seat."

In case you hadn't noticed, there's a new kind of air rage out there—but it's the crew, not the passengers, who seem to be losing their cool. Stressed out by layoffs, extra security duties, and now two big airline bankruptcies, pilots and flight attendants may have reached a boiling point. While no one keeps hard numbers on angry outbursts aloft, in a first-of-its-kind survey American Express found that 55 percent of fliers have seen a "noticeable decline" in cabin service. One flight attendant union hired a psychologist to study job stress. Even the airlines acknowledge a frazzled workforce. "As human beings we can only take so much," a United spokesman says.

Of course, most flight attendants still do their jobs without blowing their stacks. However, the past few months have witnessed a host of new pressures, from pay cuts big and small, to a 20 percent reduction in the number of attendants on some flights. The list of 9/11-related security duties keeps growing as well. "A lot of us are in a terrible mood before we even set foot on the plane," says Glenda Talley, a US Airways flight attendant who just took a pay cut.

How bad is it? In one widely reported case, an American pilot went so far as to throw a balky steward off the plane. According to an airline spokesman, the attendant started "exhibiting rude behavior" so bad the pilot had to make an emergency stop in Dallas. (Both the airline and the flight attendants' union declined to comment further.) In another case, Josh Holdeman says he couldn't believe it when a stewardess turned him down for pretzels—and told him to watch his waistline. "I'm still furious," says the New York art expert, adding he works out three times a week. The airline, which happened to be American, says his experience was "very unfortunate."

Source: Adapted from B. Barnes, "The New Face of Air Rage," *Wall Street Journal*, January 3, 2003, p. w-1.

---

job expectations when given responsibility. McGregor believed that managing on the basis of Theory Y assumptions allows the organization to utilize the human potential of all employees and become more productive. Sharing power and responsibilities with employees will make them more committed to organizational goals. McGregor's Theory Y assumptions fit with contemporary leadership styles that stress employee participation and empowerment, and they are often used in knowledge-based organizations where employee knowledge is a source of competitive advantage. Management Close-Up 1.d deals with how negative employee behavior results from poor working conditions, stress, and insecurity.

Contemporary Management Perspectives

Contemporary management perspectives include systems theory, contingency theory, and the learning organization perspective. Each of these contemporary viewpoints builds on the work of earlier management thinkers.

THE SYSTEMS APPROACH   The operational, bureaucratic, administrative, and behavioral approaches studied management by dividing it into elements or components such as work scheduling, motions, and functions, or employee needs and attitudes. While taking things apart is useful for analytical purposes, in reality all relevant parts of organizational activity interact with each other. System theorists warn us that "reductionism" in management thought may lead to simplistic prescriptions and may not help us understand why some firms perform at higher levels than others. In other words, system theorists believe that the whole is greater than the sum of the parts.

Chester I. Barnard's Early Systems Perspective   Barnard was a former president of New Jersey Bell Telephone Company. Based on his experience as a practicing executive, he believed that isolating specific management functions and principles may lead to the proverbial failing to see the forest for the trees. In his classic book, *The Functions of the Executive* (1938), Barnard depicted organizations as cooperative systems: "A cooperative system is a complex of physical, biological, personal, and social components which are in a specific systematic relationship by reason of the cooperation of two or more persons for at least one definite end."[6] He viewed organizations as complex, dynamic wholes where willingness to serve, common purpose, and communication are critical.

General Systems Theory   This perspective views an organization as a *system* consisting of interrelated parts that function in a holistic way to achieve a common purpose. The system takes *inputs* (resources) from the external environment and puts them through a *transformation process* (a technology) that converts them to *outputs* (finished products and services). The outputs are then put into the external environment.

The *environment* is comprised of the market, technological, social, and political forces that surround the system, and is a critical factor that managers must consider in order to achieve organizational goals and objectives. The manner in which the outputs are received determines organization survival. If the environment rejects the outputs because quality is too low, the organization is likely to perish. The system receives **feedback,** information about how well the outputs were received, and uses the feedback to adjust the selection of inputs and the transformation process.

Systems theory has contributed some important concepts that affect management thinking. These include open and closed systems, subsystems, synergy, and equifinality.

Open and closed systems. Open systems interact with the environment in order to survive. Closed systems do not need to interact with the envi-

part one   Overview

ronment. In reality, all organizations depend on the environment for inputs and for the purchase of outputs. The operational and bureaucratic perspectives on management treated the organization as if it were a closed system by overlooking the effect of the environment on management practice. Systems theory argues that the environment must always be taken into consideration in management decision making.

Subsystems. Subsystems are interdependent parts of a system. A change in one subsystem affects the other subsystems. For example, when a company changes its reward system for sales representatives from salary to commission, the volume of sales revenues is likely to increase. This would, in turn, increase the level of output required from the manufacturing system. If the manufacturing system is operating at full capacity, an improved manufacturing process may be needed in order to satisfy the increased demand.

Synergy. When the whole is greater than the sum of its parts, a synergism exists. Management of organizational subsystems can result in synergies. For example, Microsoft sells more business applications software because all its applications software products are compatible with the Windows operating system. In other words, Microsoft's Windows operating system unit provides synergy for its business applications unit because the compatible products create value for the customer. Without the operating system unit, Microsoft would sell less business applications software.

Equifinality. In an open system, equifinality means that an organization can reach the same goal though a number of different routes. Also, not every organization must begin from the same place or use the same tactics to achieve success. Advocates of scientific management and human relations believed that management can be reduced to "one best way." By contrast, systems theory suggests that different inputs, subsystems, and transformation processes can lead to a similar outcome.

CONTINGENCY THEORY   What works for one organization may not work for another, because situational characteristics differ. The situational characteristics are called *contingencies.* Managers need to understand the key contingencies that determine the most effective management practices in a given situation. Thus, whether application of a management principle or rule (such as division of work and a well-defined hierarchy) leads to positive results "depends" on the particular conditions. Each situation has its own nuances and presents to the manager a unique set of problems. Lack of "fit," or a mismatch between management practice and what the situation calls for, leads to poor performance (see Management Close-Up 1.e, "What Worked at GE Isn't Working at Home Depot"). Alternatively, high performance results when

contingency theory

The management theory that there is no "one best way" to manage and organize an organization because situational characteristics, called contingencies, differ; also, the view that no HR strategy is "good" or "bad" in and of itself but rather depends on the situation or context in which it is used.

Contingency Theory in Action: What Worked at GE Isn't Working at Home Depot

THEME: CUSTOMER FOCUS When Home Depot Inc. landed Robert L. Nardelli as CEO at the end of 2000, it was hailed as a coup for the nation's second-largest retailer. Nardelli was a manufacturing star at General Electric Co.'s Power Systems unit but was new to the area of retailing. Home Depot's board bet that the company would benefit from his operational savvy. But by 2003, sales at Home Depot were down by 10 percent and its share value had dropped by 50 percent. Analysts and investors now believe that his management philosophy that worked so well at GE did not fit the business context of Home Depot. There appears to be a customer backlash against Nardelli's ambitious inventory and staffing initiatives, which badly disrupted service and sales. "I think there are people on Wall Street who are questioning his ability to make the change and run a retail organization," says Erik Becker, an analyst at Waddell & Reed Financial Inc.

Nardelli dismisses the skeptics, insisting that the transition from turbines to tools has been relatively smooth. "Is retail different? Sure it is," he admits. "But there are certain fundamentals in running a business that are pretty portable." Critics argue, however, that Home Depot's woes stem from Nardelli's efforts to force manufacturing-like processes onto retailing. In his GE days, he was able to shave inventory even as he pushed managers to move products out the door quicker. Unfortunately, efforts to do the same at Home Depot have simply slowed reorders, leaving stores out of stock in such key areas as electronics. Meanwhile, following previous practices at GE's factories, Nardelli has shaken up the workforce in order to save on labor costs. The share of part-time sales clerks has gone from 26 percent to as high as 50 percent during his tenure—even as rival Lowe's with a staff that's 80 percent full-time is garnering a reputation for better service.

Source: Adapted from D. Foust, "What Worked at GE Isn't Working at Home Depot," *Business Week,* January 27, 2003, p. 40.

management practice is attuned to or congruent with the demands of the particular context being faced. Contingency theory strongly warns that managers must be flexible in order to apply those practices and techniques that are most appropriate to specific situations.

An example of an important contingency is the degree of change in the environment. Change can include the development of new technologies or the entry of new competitors to the market. When the environment is turbulent, managers are likely to select a *decentralized organization structure* in which authority is pushed to lower levels so that decisions can be made rapidly and flexibly. When the environment is stable and predictable, managers select a *centralized organization structure* in which decisions are made on a top-down basis to exercise more control and efficiency over resources. Contingency theory suggests that a manager should first identify and understand the contingency, then select the management practice that best fits the situation. Other contingencies include organization cultures, industry structures, and products and process or manufacturing technologies.

THE LEARNING ORGANIZATION The **learning organization** approach suggests that organizations that can "learn" faster than their counterparts have an advantage over competitors in the marketplace. Rather than *reacting* to change, which is a normal part of the business landscape, organizations need to *anticipate* change so they are well positioned to satisfy their customers' future needs with the most satisfying products and services. Therefore, a learning organization attempts to institutionalize continuous learning. This means that knowledge and information will be shared between employees and teams rather than controlled by an elite group of technocrats. Organizational structures should facilitate the sharing and transfer of information as broadly and quickly as possible. Flat structures with few management layers and cross-functional teams that bring together people from different business or scientific disciplines are examples of ways to break down barriers that keep people from sharing information and learning from each other.

Organizations learn in two ways. With *experimental* learning, an organization learns from its own experiences. For example, a fast-food chain can test market a new item in a few restaurants on a trial basis to determine whether to retain or change its menu. With *external* learning, an organization can learn from the experiences of other organizations and the environment. External learning occurs when an organization scans the environment and learns about competitor successes and failures, new technologies, and changes in the legal system. While external learning offers the greater potential, it is often underutilized because organizations may unconsciously impose barriers to inhibit the understanding and utilization of outside knowledge. Companies that become too insular and reject external knowledge by favoring internally developed solutions over potentially superior quality parts or products from outside sources are usually penalized in the marketplace for their limited vision. For example, IBM in the 1980s tried to manufacture all of its computer hardware and software within the company. In many cases the company rejected using superior components available from outside suppliers, which would have forced IBM to alter its computer designs and learn how to best use those components. The result? IBM was slow to bring new computer models to market and lost customers to competing firms that had adapted their products and applied the superior components to them.

learning organization
The management approach based on an organization anticipating change faster than its counterparts to have an advantage in the market over its competitors.

In the introductory vignette, we posed some critical thinking questions regarding Lincoln Electric. Now that you have had the opportunity to learn about different management perspectives, try to deal with the questions that were raised there. First, Lincoln Electric has been able to apply scientific management successfully for almost 80 years, because it is appropriate to its situation. The company has been a low-cost producer of a relatively narrow product line with a stable technology, a stable market, and relatively few competitors. For Lincoln Electric efficiency rather than innovation provides the competitive advantage. Contingency theory suggests that scientific management techniques fit well in that context. Imagine trying to use the same approach at a company such as 3M, where more than one-fourth of its revenues come from new products that were introduced in the last five years!

Second, the incentive system works nicely in Lincoln's context. The same incentive system would be unlikely to work for a pharmaceutical firm, because in that situation much of the work is carried out by teams, technology changes quickly, it may take 10 years to develop a new product, and only a small percentage of projects lead to profitable products. Therefore it would take far too long to receive rewards for performance results.

Finally, Lincoln has not had a layoff for almost half a century as a result of successfully implementing a combination of operational management and behavioral management policies. The work week is adjusted to production needs, which may range from 55 hours a week to 32 hours a week, depending on production demand. Thus, rather than laying off workers, the company simply cuts back on the number of hours worked. Even in the worst case scenario (such as a two-year period in the early 1980s when the work week dropped to 32 hours), Lincoln employees continued to earn the highest pay of any rust-belt employees in the world. Lincoln asks three things from employees in return for their lifetime employment guarantee: (1) complete cooperation, (2) the willingness to accept job reassignment, and (3) acceptance of the principle that everyone benefits and sacrifices together from the CEO to the lowest-paid worker.

Managerial activities are carried out not only by managers who have the formal authority to command others and to allocate resources, but also by employees and teams. Each has a role in planning and strategizing, organizing, leading, and controlling. Successful accomplishment of these management functions requires strategizing skills, task-related skills, people-related skills, and self-awareness skills.

The earliest management thinkers include Sun Tzu, an early Chinese general who recognized that management strategy meant taking a long-term perspective; Niccolò Machiavelli, a Renaissance Italian who advised leaders to be cunning and crafty in order to survive against ambitious rivals; and Adam Smith, an eighteenth-century philosopher who recognized that the division of labor could have a powerful effect on an organization's productivity.

The **operational perspective** of management thought was developed during the late nineteenth and early twentieth centuries and represented an attempt to apply logic and the scientific method to management. The operational perspective consists of scientific management, quantitative management, and quality management.

Scientific management, represented by the ideas of Frederick Winslow Taylor, focuses on using experts to teach workers the best methods and techniques to do their jobs. Employees do the physical labor and managers provide the planning and organizing. It was assumed that employees would be willing to cooperate with managers, since employees were to be paid according to their level of output, and they could earn more pay this way.

Quantitative management emphasizes the development of statistical tools and techniques to improve efficiency. *Quality management* focuses on approaches that may be used to improve quality and reduce the time and effort devoted to replacing what was done wrong in the first place.

Bureaucratic management was developed by Max Weber, a German sociologist. Bureaucratic management is an "ideal model" of an organization that is governed by a set of impersonal rules and policies, including merit as a basis for career advancement. Weber believed that bureaucratic management was the most efficient way to organize and govern an enterprise.

The **administrative management** perspective, advocated by Henri Fayol, assumes that general principles of management can be applied to any situation or circumstance. Fayol divided the activities of management into five functions: planning, organizing, commanding, coordinating, and controlling.

The **behavioral perspective** of management thought focuses on understanding how to manage human factors to improve workplace productivity. It traces its roots to the works of Mary Parker Follett and the *Hawthorne studies* performed at the Western Electric Company. These studies suggested that leaders are able to positively influence employee motivation and productivity by showing concern for employee relationships.

Inspired by the works of Follett and the Hawthorne studies, the *human relations approach* to management emphasized work relationships as the key to a productive workplace. Abraham Maslow developed a theory of employee motivation based on a hierarchy of human needs. Maslow believed that managers need to view employees from a humanistic perspective, identify unfulfilled employee needs, and then show employees how these needs may be satisfied in the context of the workplace. The result should be a higher level of employee motivation and productivity.

Douglas McGregor, another advocate of the human relations approach, examined the assumptions made by leaders. *Theory X* leaders assume that subordinates avoid work, whereas *Theory Y* leaders assume that subordinates want to do good work and are interested in taking on more job responsibilities. McGregor believed that Theory Y assumptions are more desirable because they encourage employees to utilize more of their human potential for the good of the organization.

Contemporary management perspectives build on the operational and behavioral perspectives and go beyond them. They include **systems theory, contingency theory,** and the **learning organization.** According to these perspectives, it is futile to search for "one best way" to manage an organization. Instead, managers must take into account the external environment so as to match the appropriate management practices to the surrounding circumstances for an effective outcome.

DISCUSSION QUESTIONS

1. Think of any organizations with which you are intimately familiar—an educational institution, a business, a student association, or the like. How does this organization carry out the four management functions? Based on your observations, how do the managerial skills discussed in this chapter help in the effective execution of the four management functions? How does their absence hinder it? Explain.

2. Explain Machiavelli's advice to leaders that "it is better to be feared than loved." In the context of contemporary management, consider this modification of Machiavelli's advice: "It is better for a leader to be *respected* than loved." Would you agree or disagree with this statement? Discuss its implications.

3. What were the important contributions of scientific management? What were its limitations?

4. Examine the list of Fayol's 14 principles of management in Table 1.5. Which principles are still useful today? Which principles appear to be obsolete, according to contemporary management thinking?

5. Compare the behavioral management perspective to the operational perspective. What are their similarities and differences?

6. According to the human relations perspective, leaders can influence certain factors within work groups that can result in improved performance and satisfaction. Describe how a leader would be likely to put knowledge of this perspective into practice and obtain increased performance from his or her subordinates.

7. Within the context of systems theory, what is the significance of an open system? What is the significance of equifinality?

8. Think of an example that illustrates an application of the following contemporary theories:

    a. Systems theory.

    b. Contingency theory.

9. From the learning organization perspective, compare and contrast experimental and external learning. What are the barriers to learning for organizations? Are there some circumstances in which it would be desirable to have such barriers? Describe a situation where learning in an organization would be dysfunctional.

Are Job Descriptions Always Necessary?

One rule of thumb that generations of U.S. managers have assumed to be true is that *job descriptions* must be used for all jobs in an organization. Job descriptions are summary statements of important job duties and responsibilities and also contain the important knowledge, skills, and abilities (KSAs) to perform the job competently.

The practice of using job descriptions traces its roots to the scientific management approach that Frederick Taylor developed in the early part of the twentieth century. Taylor believed jobs should be measured very precisely so that employees could be taught the "one best way" to do the job. Job descriptions were adopted by followers of scientific management to document the most important elements of employees' jobs, making it possible to hold employees accountable for doing exactly the duties and responsibilities that are listed in the description.

In recent years, however, some managers have avoided using job descriptions in their organizations, believing that the practice encourages employees to behave as if the job were their personal property, thus limiting management's ability to deploy workers flexibly in different work roles according to need. In addition, critics of job descriptions claim that is almost impossible to provide an accurate job description, since many jobs are in a state of continuous flux as technologies and market conditions change. As one manager put it, "Job descriptions are obsolete in my company before they are even written."

On the other hand, the majority of companies in the United States still use job descriptions for all their jobs without questioning the practice. The legal staffs of many U.S. corporations advise managers to require job descriptions, in order to provide a defense against a host of legal challenges that more and more companies face from disgruntled employees. Job descriptions allow companies to provide documented evidence admissible in court for disputes over contested job duties and responsibilities that entail hiring, firing, promotion, or pay decisions.

Discussion Questions

1. Apply contingency theory to the practice of job descriptions. How can contingency theory explain the current situation in which some organizations use job descriptions and others choose not to use them?

2. Which contingencies might affect the use of job descriptions? Describe a specific situation that would be favorable for the use of job descriptions. Now describe another situation that would be unfavorable for the effective use of job descriptions.

3. Do you think job descriptions support or hinder the goals of the learning organization approach?

Having Fun Is a Top Priority at PeopleSoft

Self-made multibillionaire and PeopleSoft CEO Dave Duffield prides himself on his company's crazy corporate culture, where "having fun" is an official goal. The firm's quarterly meetings are run as if they were Letterman shows. Jumbo-sized employee pictures grin down from the hallways at corporate headquarters in Pleasanton, California. Duffield even took the entire company to Lake Tahoe.

In the midst of all the antics, Duffield has built a phenomenally successful company. PeopleSoft sells enterprise resource planning (ERP) software, which automates manufacturing processes, organizes human resource files, and crunches accountants' numbers. Sales practically doubled in each of six years, and in one recent two-year period PeopleSoft's stock was up 280 percent. In this rapidly growing market, the firm moved into second place, behind Germany's SAP.

In 1997 PeopleSoft earned $108 million in profits on $816 million worth of revenues, which greatly pleased its shareholders. Despite its success through 1997, PeopleSoft experienced some setbacks in 1999, when it declared a loss of $178 million on annual revenues of $1.43 billion. Its stock also experienced considerable volatility during this period. By 2004, however, the company continued to show a strong earnings trend that started about three years earlier.

Dave Duffield considers PeopleSoft's culture an important reason for its current success. Software industry analysts agree that PeopleSoft has risen as much on the strength of its personality as on the high quality of its software, and customers give PeopleSoft rave reviews for its excellent service.

Discussion Questions

1. Apply the human relations approach to management to explain the success of PeopleSoft.

2. What other explanations may account for this company's incredible success?

3. Do you think PeopleSoft's special culture would translate well to other kinds of business, such as a bank or a large accounting firm? Why or why not?

Sources: A. Stone, "PeopleSoft: No Need for the Hard Sell," *Business Week,* May 10, 2001; adapted from E. Brown, "PeopleSoft: Tech's Latest Publicly Traded Cult," *Fortune,* May 25, 1998, pp. 155–156; B. Bacheldor, "PeopleSoft Earnings," www.peoplesoft.com, January 22, 2003.

What Can a Company Do to Change Employees' Bad Habits?

Union Pacific Railroad (UP) has long known that many of its 48,000 employees—mostly middle-aged men—are overweight. Excess weight can also be a dangerous problem for people who ply the rails and may cost the company up to $50 million per year in medical expenses. Consequently, 16 years ago the Omaha-based company began a massive program designed to help workers improve their health and shed pounds. UP has devoted so much time and money to this effort (about $2 million a year) that the company has won several national health awards. The result? Employee smoking rates, cholesterol levels, and blood pressure levels are down. Still, the workforce is fatter than ever. UP's story illustrates how hard it is for any employer to help employees to lose weight.

In the late 1980s, UP's medical costs per employee were almost double the national average. Lack of fitness, the company concluded, was the major reason. A 1995 survey by UP showed that 40 percent of its employees were obese, which was well above that year's national average of 15 percent. Helping employees lose weight "wasn't just something good to do," says CEO Dick Davidson. "It also became good business."

In 1987, UP opened an 8,000-square-foot gym at headquarters offering everything from treadmills to advice from exercise specialists. Later, the railroad made arrangements with 450 gyms across the country, in order to provide free access to employees scattered across 23 states. Meanwhile, Dennis Richling, a staff physician UP had asked to head its health-improvement program, devised other ways to help employees lighten up. One program involved peer-to-peer mentoring for overweight employees.

Sadly, from 1995 to 2003, the percentage of obese UP employees rose from 40 percent to 52 percent. How is that possible? First, no company can insulate its workers from the pervasive temptations of fast food and other high-fat, high-calorie treats. Second, no company can force an employee to embark on a weight-loss program. According to marketing studies, 10 percent to 20 percent of any group are "resisters." UP reluctantly gave up trying to convert those people. Says Richling: "It just isn't cost-effective."

Critical Thinking Questions

1. Based on the management perspectives discussed in this chapter, what do you think accounts for UP's level of success in the attempt to help employees slim down? Explain.

2. What are advantages and disadvantages for a firm trying to influence employee behaviors, such as overeating, which only indirectly may be work-related (for instance an obese person may have less stamina)? Is it the company business to get involved in what may be considered a personal matter? Explain.

3. If you were asked to redesign UP's program, how would you proceed and what features would you include to ensure success? Explain.

Source: Adapted from J. Schlosser, "Uphill Battle," *Fortune*, February 3, 2003, p. 64.

INTERNET EXERCISE 1.1

www.lincolnelectric.com.

Lincoln Electric

Explore the website of Lincoln Electric, the company that was featured in the opening vignette of this chapter. Use the site's map feature to locate and read about the history of Lincoln Electric ("our history") and also learn what it is like to work at Lincoln Electric ("career opportunities"). Then answer the following questions:

1. What are the important features of the Lincoln Electric Performance System?
2. What do you think it would be like to work at Lincoln Electric? Would you enjoy working there? Why or why not?
3. What are Lincoln Electric's mission and vision? How does its Incentive Performance System support them?
4. Do you think Lincoln Electric is a well-managed company based on what you have read about it? On what information do you base your conclusion? Explain.

MANAGER'S CHECKUP 1.1

Do You Fit In A Bureaucratic Organization?

Many organizations still exhibit the characteristics of a bureaucracy as described by Weber. Some people fit in well with highly bureaucratic organizations; others feel stifled and cramped by a bureaucratic organization. What is your preference? To determine your level of comfort with bureaucratic organizations, try the following exercise.

Instructions: For each statement, check the response that best represents your feelings.

		Mostly Agree	Mostly Disagree
1.	I value stability in my job.	____	____
2.	I like a predictable organization.	____	____
3.	The best job for me would be one in which the future is relatively certain.	____	____
4.	The federal government would be a nice place to work.	____	____
5.	Rules, policies, and procedures tend to frustrate me.	____	____
6.	I would enjoy working for a company that employed 85,000 people worldwide.	____	____
7.	Being self-employed would involve more risk than I'm willing to take.	____	____
8.	Before accepting a job, I would like to see an exact job description.	____	____
9.	I would prefer a job as a freelance house painter to one as a clerk for the department of motor vehicles.	____	____
10.	Seniority should be as important as performance in determining pay increases and job promotion.	____	____
11.	It would give me a feeling of pride to work for the largest and most successful company in its field.	____	____

12. Given a choice, I would prefer to make $40,000 per year as vice president in a small company to $45,000 as a staff specialist in a large company. ____ ____

13. I would regard wearing an employee badge with a number on it as a degrading experience. ____ ____

14. Parking spaces in a company lot should be assigned on the basis of job level. ____ ____

15. If an accountant works for a large firm, he or she cannot be a true professional. ____ ____

16. Before accepting a job (given a choice), I would want to make sure that the company had a fine program of employee benefits. ____ ____

17. A company will probably not be successful unless it establishes a clear set of rules and procedures. ____ ____

18. Regular working hours and vacations are more important to me than finding thrills on the job. ____ ____

19. You should respect people according to their rank. ____ ____

20. Rules are meant to be broken. ____ ____

Scoring and Interpretation

If you mostly agree with items 1–4, 6–8, 10–11, 14, and 16–19 that would mean that you have a high level of comfort with bureaucratic organizations. The opposite would be true if you mostly disagree with those items yet mostly agree with items 5, 9, 12–13, 15, and 20.

Sources: From *Human Relations: A Job Oriented Approach* by DuBrin, Copyright © 1978. Reprinted by permission of Pearson Education, Inc., Upper Saddle River, NJ.

Are You a Theory X or a Theory Y Manager?

Instructions: Circle the level of agreement or disagreement that you personally feel toward each of the following 10 statements.

SA = Strongly Agree
A = Agree
U = Uncertain
D = Disagree
SD = Strongly Disagree

1. People need to know that the boss is in charge. SA A U D SD

2. Employees will rise to the occasion when an extra effort is needed. SA A U D SD

3. Employees need direction and control or they will not work hard. SA A U D SD

4. People naturally want to work. SA A U D SD

5. A manager should be a decisive, no-nonsense leader. SA A U D SD

6. Employees should not be involved in making decisions that concern them.   SA   A   U   D   SD

7. A manager has to be tough-minded and hard-nosed.   SA   A   U   D   SD

8. A manager should build a climate of trust in the work unit.   SA   A   U   D   SD

9. If a unit is to be productive, employees need to be pushed.   SA   A   U   D   SD

10. Employees need the freedom to innovate.   SA   A   U   D   SD

Scoring and Interpretation

Items	SA	A	U	D	SD
1, 3, 5, 7, 9	1 point	2 points	3 points	4 points	5 points
2, 4, 6, 8, 10	5 points	4 points	3 points	2 points	1 point

To determine your score, add up your total points for all 10 items. High scores suggest managerial attitudes in line with Theory Y. Low scores indicate attitudes that fit with Theory X.

Source: Adapted from R. E. Quinn, S. R. Faerman, M. P. Thompson, and M. R. McGrath, *Becoming a Master Manager,* 2nd ed., New York: John Wiley.

Anne Mulcahy: New Managerial Challenges at Xerox

The name Xerox has always been synonymous with copiers. How many times have you asked someone to "please, make me a Xerox of this letter" instead of saying "please make me a copy of this letter"? In recent years, the good name and image of Xerox have become seriously tarnished and the company has been in some very deep financial trouble, teetering on the edge of bankruptcy, with weak sales, high costs, troubled employee morale, customer dissatisfaction, and increasing debt. In addition, the Securities & Exchange Commission (SEC) has investigated the company for possible accounting irregularities.

In May 2000, the board of directors dismissed G. Richard Thomas, president of Xerox, after only a little more than a year in office. The same month the board of directors turned to Anne Mulcahy, a long-time Xerox insider, and appointed her president. At first blush, Mulcahy seemed an unlikely candidate to lead Xerox from its deep financial and legal abyss. True, she did have various-level job experiences during her past 25 years at Xerox, but she had not been part of a deliberate corporate succession planning model where she was taken "under the wing" of the CEO and "groomed" for the presidency. Moreover, her work experiences did not seem to put her on the prospective high flyer CEO track. More than half of her work experience at Xerox was in sales and her most recent leadership experience was as vice president of human resources and chief staff officer to then company CEO Paul Allaire.

Mulcahy's educational background was different from most aspiring CEOs. She was not an attorney, nor a Ph.D. in the sciences or technology field, nor was she a holder of an undergraduate business degree or an MBA. Rather she attended Marymount College (NY) and graduated with a degree in English/journalism, and she possessed some unique personal traits. One incident early in her tenure as president suggests that she may be too frank. On October 3, 2000, in a meeting she stated that Xerox had an "unsustainable business model." Her remarks caused Xerox stock to drop more than 20 percent. In retrospect, she believes that she probably

This case was prepared by Joseph C. Santora, who is professor of business at Essex County College, Newark, New Jersey.

should have couched her statement more cautiously—"The company has recognized that changes have to take place in the business model"—which would have caused less stir.

Colleagues and underlings alike have remarked at the variety of her personal traits. She is very focused and very decisive. She is also open to criticism, but more important than her openness to criticism is her ability to listen carefully and attentively to what various stakeholders are saying. She is a person of polarities—both compassionate and tough. Her tenacity is legendary and her competitiveness has been attributed to her parents, who encouraged her to compete with four brothers. Finally, she combines a "can-do" attitude with a fierce company loyalty and strong customer focus.

Despite these appealing characteristics, some outsiders believed that her appointment as president of Xerox was a problem: an insider and not up to the task at hand. As an insider with 25 years of experience would her management of Xerox be business as usual? Family members including her husband (retired from sales) and her brother (head of Global Solutions Division) have worked for the company. So could Mulcahy cut $1 billion from Xerox costs? In addition, Mulcahy had a limited understanding of accounting and finance. But here too, she was different. What would a person of Mulcahy's caliber and traits do about this limitation? She brought in an expert in finance to tutor her to bring her up to speed.

People should always work from their strengths. And that's exactly what Mulcahy did. She began to turn the company around by doing what she does best: She used her popularity and experience with customers to get them on board; she began changing the image of company from "just a copier company" to a company that offered varied customer services similar to IBM model. Within her first year in office, to assuage employee morale problems, she created and circulated a memo, "Turnaround Talk," held dozens of meetings with employees, and traveled more than 100,000 miles to meet with employees. As part of her corporate persona, she adopted the military mantra of "anywhere, anytime" to help close a deal with CEO's of client companies. In her first two years in office, she dealt with the unpleasant task of reducing management staff (14,200 employees) to cut $1 billion. She outsourced many functions that existed outside Xerox's core business, eliminated low-end product lines (ink jet copiers)

part one Overview

and focused on the high-end product lines (color/commercial copying/printing), and sold business operations in China (for $550 million in 2000) as well as half interest in Fuji Xerox (for $1.3 billion in 2001). Finally, she was able to eliminate the SEC accounting problem. Overall, she reduced product prices, cut expenses by $1.7 billion, and sold (noncore) businesses to the tune of $2.7 billion.

As a result of her management and leadership, Mulcahy has increased market share, created a more stable management, and developed a stronger customer focus. On July 26, 2001, Mulcahy, president of Xerox, added the title of CEO and in January 2002 she added the title of chairman. She is the first woman to hold these positions at Xerox. Today, Mulcahy, chairman and CEO, ranks sixth on *Fortune*'s list of the most powerful businesswomen. She shares the limelight with superstars Carly Fiorina (#1), CEO/chair, Hewlett-Packard; Meg Whitman (#3), president and CEO, eBay; and Andrea Jung (#5), chair and CEO, Avon Products. Her back-to-basics management approach and her strong desire to change the image of the company may allow Xerox to live another day.

Discussion Questions

1. What do Mulcahy's initial successes at Xerox tell you about her management philosophy?

2. What traits do leaders/managers need to turn their companies around? For success?

3. Do you think Mulcahy will be able to lead Xerox completely out of harm's way? Why? Why not?

Sources: "CEOs under Fire. Voices from the Front: The Day I Was Too Candid," *Fortune*, November 18, 2002 (online); O. Kharif, "Anne Mulcahy Has Xerox by the Horns," *Business Week Online*, May 29, 2003; O. Kharif, "Xerox: So Far, So Good," *Business Week Online*, January 9, 2002; G. Marcial, "Xerox's Image Is Getting Crisper," *Business Week Online*, December 2, 2002; P. L. Moore, "Anne Mulcahy: She's Here to Fix the Xerox," *Business Week Online* August 6, 2001; B. Morris, "The Accidental CEO," *Fortune*, June 9, 2003 (online).

The Culture of Management

An organization's external and internal environments are the context in which the practice of management takes place. Managers and nonmanagers alike must understand that effective business decisions take into consideration pressures from the external environment such as from global markets, technological changes, and the requirement to behave and be perceived as a socially responsible member of the community, as well as from internal factors within an organization such as the organizational culture and the expectation of ethical business conduct.

In Part Two we will begin by examining threats and opportunities firms face in the global environment. This will lead to a discussion of global business strategies and advantageous ways to enter foreign markets given a firm's unique characteristics. Next we analyze the nature of business ethics and the basis of ethical decisions. Then, we present the broader context of social responsibility and identify key stakeholders and ways to manage relationships with them. Finally, we examine organizational culture and how it helps an organization achieve its objectives. In Part Two, we also explain the forces that drive organizational change and describe ways to manage and counsel employees who resist the need for change.

Managing in a Global Environment

chapter 2

After reading this chapter, you should be able to:

- Understand the landscape of the global market.

- Develop an awareness of the role of culture in international management.

- Recognize the major options firms face when they choose a global strategy and the conditions that make each strategic choice most appropriate.

- Determine the best mode of entry into foreign markets given a firm's unique characteristics.

- Develop effective human resource practices for managing international subsidiaries.

- Become aware of ethical issues in international operations.

Toyota Goes Local for Growth

Seventy-four-year-old George Taylor fought the Japanese in World War II, and he still has bitter memories. As mayor of Princeton, Indiana, population 8,100, he gladly put his feelings aside, however, when Toyota unveiled plans to build a $700 million pickup-truck plant in the economically sagging town.

"I've changed my mind a little bit," Taylor says. "The way I look at it, the Japanese are coming over here and giving American workers good jobs, while American companies are closing factories and taking work overseas for low wages." As a sign of appreciation, Taylor traded his Chrysler Fifth Avenue for a new Camry sedan built just down Interstate 64 at the Toyota plant in Georgetown, Kentucky. Avalon (Toyota's flagship car) and the Sienna minivan are also manufactured there.

The 500-mile stretch of Interstate 64 that winds past Georgetown and Princeton on its way from West Virginia to Missouri could be renamed "Toyota Road." The world's third-largest automaker after General Motors and Ford, Toyota is investing at least $10 billion to build a vast industrial empire in the center of America's heartland. The investment includes expanding Toyota's facilities two miles south of Princeton so that it can build 50,000 sport utility vehicles and up to 100,000 Tundra pickup trucks annually.

Japan's largest industrial corporation, with sales around $101 billion per year, Toyota already has more than 20,000 U.S. employees. The company holds a 6.9 percent share of the U.S. car and truck market, which puts it in fourth place, ahead of Honda (4.8 percent), though still well behind Chrysler (16.6 percent). About 75 percent of the cars the company sells in the United States are also assembled in the United States. With the expansion along Interstate 64, Toyota plans to boost its U.S. output by at least a third.

"We can now do everything the Big Three do," says Yale Gieszl, Toyota's American-born executive vice president for U.S. sales and marketing. "The flag of the parent company is really irrelevant."

According to Gary Convis, a Michigan native who is president of the Georgetown, Kentucky, manufacturing plant, "This plant is Toyota's largest operation outside of Japan, and plays a key role in the company's success globally." By 2004, the plant had produced more than five million vehicles. Toyota has

also made major commitments to the community, giving large monetary contributions to about 20 organizations, including Project One (serving the needs of inner-city, at-risk youngsters), the Lexington Philharmonic, the Lexington and Louisville Urban League, and the Georgetown United Child Development Center. The company is also deeply involved in programs to enhance employee and community welfare. Toyota established scholarship funds for the children of company employees, has hired minorities at a rate that is twice the percentage of the Kentucky population, and assigns priority to purchasing raw materials, parts and components from companies within the state. Toyota helped open a new fire station and supports the Georgetown Main Street Revitalization Project.

Sources: Toyota Motor Manufacturing Kentucky Newsletter, "Toyota's Commitment to Good Corporate Citizenship," January 25, 2003, www.toyotageorgetown.com; W. A. McWhirter and J. R. Szczesny, "Toyota Road U.S.A.," *Time,* October 7, 1996, pp. 73–76; T. Raithel, "Toyota Expansion 'Makes Sense,' " *Evansville Courier and Press,* July 2, 1999, pp. 1–2; T. Raithel, "Panel to Look at Changes Brought by Toyota," *Evansville Courier and Press,* July 2, 1999, pp. 3–4; R. Brim, "Toyota Plant Has New President," *Lexington Herald,* March 30, 2001; A. Berstein, L. Woellert, and P. Magnusson, "Time to Regroup," *Business Week,* August 6, 2001.

CRITICAL THINKING QUESTIONS

1. *What international trends are exemplified by Toyota's move to Kentucky?*

2. *Why is Toyota so deeply involved in the local community?*

3. *Why does Toyota staff its plant with American citizens, including all of its top management positions?*

The Environment of International Business

global shift

A term used to characterize the effects of changes in the competitive landscape prompted by worldwide competition.

The world of international competition is one which eliminates companies that fail to adapt. The term **global shift** characterizes the effects of changes in the competitive landscape prompted by worldwide competition. Global shift means the international business environment is changing faster than ever. In industries ranging from automobile to steel, banking to financial services, airlines to shipping, and low-technology manufacturing to R&D-intensive firms, each individual company faces a growing number of competitors for whom national barriers are almost irrelevant. In other words, the international business environment is forcing many firms to see the entire world as the stage for manufacturing, production,[1] and marketing. Old animosities must be replaced by a new, more global view, as described in the opening vignette about Toyota. According to one observer, "We are moving away from an economic system in which national markets are distinct entities, isolated from each other by trade barriers and barriers of distance, time and culture, and toward a system in which national markets are merging into one huge global mar-

Perhaps the single most important innovation affecting globalization has been the development of the microprocessor, shown here being manufactured by two technicians. Not only has it enabled the explosive growth of high-power, low-cost computing, but it has vastly increased the amount of information that can be processed by individuals and firms.

ketplace. . . . In many industries it is no longer meaningful to talk about the 'German market,' the 'American market,' or the 'Japanese market'; there is only the 'global market.' "[2]

The Changing Pattern of International Business

International competition is fierce in this new millennium. Successful firms survive by creating high-quality, competitively priced products and services. These goods must be well received both locally and globally. Some of the major developments in the global business community are a changing world output and world trade picture; lower trade barriers; integrated economic markets; global consumer preferences; technological innovation; globalized production; and management across cultures.

CHANGING WORLD OUTPUT AND WORLD TRADE PICTURE
Four major changes in the world output and world trade picture occurred during the last few decades. This period corresponds to the time when most of the senior executives now in charge of major corporations were in low- to mid-level management positions.

First, the United States no longer dominates the world economy. World output attributed to the United States was almost 40 percent lower at the start of the new century than in the 1960s. Similarly, the percentage of world exports of manufactured goods represented by goods from the United States in the 1990s was about half what it had been in the 1960s.[3] In the first decade of this century, this trend seems to be accelerating. Since the U.S. economy grew at an average of approximately 3 percent annually during this period, this decline means that other economies, such as Germany's and those in Asia, grew even faster. While powerhouses such as Japan and Germany have not done as well in the 2000s, China has been making enormous strides and is likely to become a major economic world player by 2010.

Second, large U.S. multinationals no longer dominate international business. In the mid-1970s, U.S. firms made up almost half of the largest multinationals, while Japanese firms accounted for only 3.5 percent of them. By the mid-1990s, Japan and the United States were nearly even, with Japanese firms accounting for 29.8 percent and U.S. firms for 30.2 percent.[4] Small and medium-sized businesses, many of them in rapidly industrializing Asian countries, are becoming "mini-multinationals" in the mid-2000s. This trend is opening the door to greater participation in the world economy for countries that traditionally remained on the sidelines. For instance, Sainco is a relatively small high-technology firm focusing on electronic control devices. Located in Seville, Spain, Sainco was started from scratch about 30 years ago. Today, the company has facilities in more than 10 developing countries and does close to 70 percent of its business internationally.

Third, the centrally planned communist economies that made up roughly half the world suddenly became accessible to Western businesses during the late 1980s. Before that, their international dealings were often guided by political rather than economic considerations. Although the economies of formerly communist nations and the few remaining communist enclaves are not robust, most of these countries are committed to free market economics. Over time, they are likely to have a major effect on international trade. For instance, Shanghai and other Chinese provinces and cities have the fastest growing economies in the world and, if current trends continue, China's per capita income could approach that of southern European countries by the year 2020. China has almost a third of the world's population, so the global economic consequences would be enormous. In Europe, eight of the 10 new members that entered the European Union in 2004 (discussed in some detail below) are formerly communist countries that used to have tightly controlled economies (Latvia, Estonia, Lithuania, Poland, Hungary, Czech Republic, Slovakia, and Slovenia). Most Europeans that form part of the 25-nation bloc of 450 million people also expect to expand the European Union by the end of the decade to include Russia and Romania, which were previous hard core communist nations.[5]

Finally, the global economy has become more knowledge-intensive and national barriers to labor markets are falling. This means that a growing number of firms consider the entire world their labor market, and companies now hire talent wherever it may be found, as shown in Management Close-Ups 2a, 2b, and 2e.

CHANGING DEMOGRAPHICS   In general, the population is getting older in the industrialized countries. Western Europe would have actually dropped in population during the past two decades had it not re-

NAFTA's Ripple Effect

When NAFTA, the North American Free Trade Agreement, was enacted in 1994, then-presidential candidate Ross Perot said we would soon hear the "giant sucking sound" of U.S. jobs moving to Mexico and Canada. Three years after the agreement was signed, a report to Congress stated that 2.2 million jobs had actually been added each year to the U.S. labor force. Commerce secretary William Daley noted, "People were screaming that the sky was going to fall, and that hasn't happened."

Although some lower-paying jobs have shifted to Mexico, the United States has benefited from the reverse migration of jobs from Asia as a result of NAFTA. One example is Lucent Technologies, which set up a plant in Guadalajara in 1991, with 7,000 employees, to manufacture almost all of Lucent's telephones and answering machines. Their Guadalajara plant buys more components from U.S. suppliers and less from Asian subcontractors. Orders for the Guadalajara plant to Miles Press, a $2 million supplier of directory cards based in Indianapolis, grew by 20 percent in the past few months. Berg Electronics in St. Louis expected to triple its sales to Guadalajara.

Service sector jobs were affected favorably as well. When Fisher-Price Inc., based in East Aurora, New York, shifted production from Hong Kong to Monterrey, Mexico, the result was 800 new jobs for Celadon Trucking of Indianapolis, which transports goods for Fisher-Price from Monterrey.

Roy Strickland's Texas-based transportation brokerage, Canusamex, was launched in 1994, in the wake of NAFTA. Since then, trade between the United States and Mexico has jumped more than 200 percent. There may be some dark clouds on the horizon. At the time of this writing

Assembly-line workers today make up the majority of the labor force in Mexico.

(2004), farm leaders in Mexico have been putting pressure on the Mexican government to renegotiate NAFTA in order to grant greater tariff protection for farmers. Mexican farmers argue that they cannot compete with larger U.S. operations and government-sponsored farm subsidy programs. Most Mexican farms are tiny by U.S. standards, with less than 12 acres each on average.

Sources: P. Magnusson, E. Malkin, and B. Vlasic, "NAFTA: Where Is That 'Giant Sucking Sound'?" *Business Week,* July 7, 1997; G. Smith and E. Malkin, "Mexican Makeover," *Business Week,* December 21, 1998, pp. 50–52; J. H. Coplan, "Border Crossing? No Problema," *Business Week,* July 16, 2001; C. J. Whalen, P. Magnusson, and G. Smith, "NAFTA's Scorecard: So Far, So Good," *Business Week,* July 9, 2001, pp. 54–60; and M. Stevenson, "Mexican Farmers Renew NAFTA Protests," Yahoo! News, www.yahoo.com, January 20, 2003.

---

ceived several dozen millions of immigrants, mostly from prior colonies (it is estimated that approximately 200 million people now live in countries other than their place of birth). On January 1, 2003, Estonia's president sounded an unusual warning to his 1.4 million countrymen: "Let us remember," said Arnold Ruutel in a live TV address, "that in just a couple of decades the number of Estonians seeing the New Year will be one-fifth less than today".[6]

That same downward trend in birth rates is apparently taking place in other parts of the world, although it is not as severe (see Table 2.1). This

TABLE 2.1

Malthus May Have Been Wrong

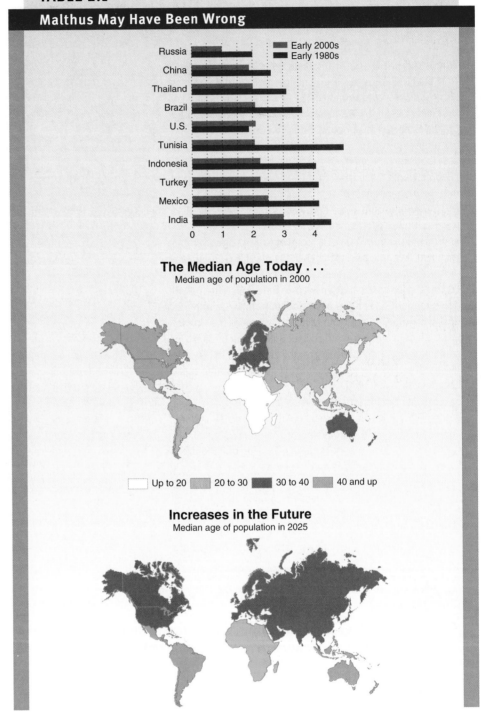

The Median Age Today . . .
Median age of population in 2000

Legend: Up to 20 | 20 to 30 | 30 to 40 | 40 and up

Increases in the Future
Median age of population in 2025

Source: From G. Naik et al., "Malthus May Have Been Wrong," *The Wall Street Journal,* January 24, 2003, p. B-1. Copyright © 2003 by Dow Jones & Co., Inc. Reproduced with permission of Dow Jones & Co., Inc. via Copyright Clearance Center.

A New Round of Globalization Is Sending Upscale Jobs Offshore

"The handwriting is on the wall," writes a veteran information-technology specialist from the Bank of America in an internal e-mail. This sense of resignation arose from the changing world surrounding the company. Just three years ago, the Charlotte (N.C.) banking operation needed IT talent so badly that the company was forced to outbid rivals. However, in recent months the entire 15-member engineering team had been told their jobs "wouldn't last through September."

Recently, Bank of America had reduced domestic operations by eliminating 3,700 of its 25,000 tech and back-office employees. These layoffs were not the result of declining demand. Instead, former company employees and contractors charged that nearly one-third of the jobs (about 1,100) were simply being relocated to India, where work which costs $100 per hour is completed for less than $20 per hour.

Cut to India: In dazzling new technology parks rising on the dusty outskirts of the nation's major cities, no one is talking about downsizing. Inside Infosys Technologies Ltd.'s impeccably landscaped 55-acre campus in Bangalore, 250 engineers develop IT applications for the Bank of America. Elsewhere, Infosys staffers process home loans for Greenpoint Mortgage of Novato, California. Near Bangalore's airport, at the offices of Wipro Ltd., five radiologists interpret 30 CT scans a day for Massachusetts General Hospital. Not far away, 26-year-old engineer Dharin Shah talks excitedly about his $10,000-a-year job designing third-generation mobile-phone chips, as sun pours through a skylight at the Texas Instruments Inc. research center. The

These New Delhi white collar workers at Wipro Spetramind are 60 percent cheaper than their U.S. counterparts.

new world of globalization includes finding locations where both cost and quality goals can be met, a hard lesson for employees in some of the more industrialized countries.

Source: Adapted from P. Engardio, A. Bernstein, & M. Kripalani, "Is Your Job Next?" *Business Week,* February 3, 2003, pp. 52–60

means that both the business and government sectors must be more attuned to the needs of older people. It also means that the management of diversity (see Chapter 11) is likely to become more important in the future as richer countries experience rising levels of both legal and illegal immigration from poorer countries.

LOWER TRADE BARRIERS   For many years, most industrialized countries placed high tariffs on foreign goods in order to protect domestic producers. Countries such as West Germany, Italy, and Great Britain imposed tariffs that averaged about 25 percent of the value of the goods in the 1950s. Developing countries followed a policy of "import substitution" designed to stimulate domestic industry by establishing artificially high prices for foreign producers. These tariffs often exceeded 100 percent of the value of the product.

Most countries now realize that nationalistic trade policies do not work. Consumers pay higher prices for lower-quality goods when competition is curtailed. Also, countries are tempted to progressively raise trade barriers against each other, depressing world demand. This was a major factor behind the worldwide depression of the 1930s. As firms disperse production around the globe in search of cost efficiencies, identifying a product with a particular country has become increasingly difficult. A tariff on "foreign" products harms domestic firms and the citizens of the country that imposes the tariff because companies within that country miss out on global business opportunities. A University of Kentucky study credits Toyota's Georgetown presence with creating 22,000 jobs in the state, of which 6,500 were in the plant itself, and adding $1.5 billion to Kentucky's economy during its first eight years in operation.[7] Lower trade restrictions led to this economic windfall for the state.

Although protectionism is still popular in some quarters—including some U.S. politicians, industry associations, and union leaders who advocate "buy American" legislation—trade barriers continue their downward trend. In the 2000s, tariff rates imposed by various countries are generally three to five times lower than in the 1950s. The goal of removing tariffs is embodied in the comprehensive **General Agreement on Tariffs and Trade (GATT)** treaty signed by 120 nations. Under GATT there have been eight rounds of negotiations, resulting in a lowering of trade barriers for manufactured goods and services. In 1993, the GATT negotiations in Uruguay, known as the Uruguay Round, created a **World Trade Organization (WTO)** to ensure compliance by member nations.

INTEGRATED ECONOMIC MARKETS Economic integration between groups of countries in a particular geographical area is gaining momentum, and today there are 33 such agreements, compared to 11 in the 1980s. The objective of economic integration is to reduce or eliminate barriers to the free flow of goods, services, labor, capital, and other inputs of production between member nations.

Figure 2.1*a* shows the major economic communities in Europe and the Americas. Of these, the 25-member European Union (EU) has achieved the highest level of political and economic integration, allowing unrestricted movement of merchandise, people, and capital among member countries. The EU has also established a uniform set of product standards and financial regulations, a common central bank, and monetary union, although some management issues still remain unresolved. In 2004, the EU expanded by incorporating eastern European countries that

General Agreement on Tariffs and Trade (GATT)

A treaty signed by 120 nations to lower trade barriers for manufactured goods and services.

World Trade Organization (WTO)

Organization created in 1993 to ensure compliance with GATT.

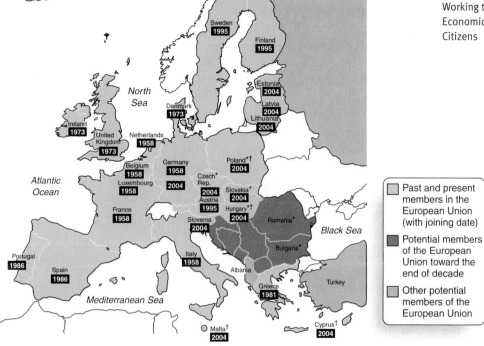

FIGURE 2.1*a*

Economic Communities:
Selected Economic
Partnerships That Are
Working to Improve the
Economic Conditions of
Citizens

Past and present
members in the
European Union
(with joining date)

Potential members
of the European
Union toward the
end of decade

Other potential
members of the
European Union

FIGURE 2.1*b*

NAFTA
Central America
Andean Pact
MERCOSUR
★ G-3

Source: Adapted from *International Business*, by C. W. Hill. Copyright The McGraw Hill Companies, Inc.,
2003. Reprinted with permission.

were once behind the "iron curtain" as well as such "fringe" countries as Malta and Cyprus. Turkey is currently negotiating with the EU for future membership. One of the challenges facing the EU in the future is how to manage an increasingly diverse group of countries, some whose economies (such as Poland and Lithuania) are far behind those 15 EU members that formed the union up to 2004.

Figure 2.1*b* represents a second major economic alliance, the North American Free Trade Act (NAFTA). Ratified in 1994 by the United States, Mexico, and Canada, NAFTA eliminated tariff and most nontariff barriers among member nations in 2004. It also allows for the free flow of agricultural products between the United States and Mexico by 2009. Most experts agree that NAFTA has confounded many predictions by increasing U.S. employment rather than moving U.S. jobs to Mexico.

Two major regional economic groups are present in Asia. The oldest is the Association of Southeast Asian Nations, or ASEAN, formed in 1967. It includes Brunei, Indonesia, Laos, Malaysia, Myanmar, Philippines, Singapore, Thailand, and Vietnam. While its intent is to foster trade among its members and achieve greater economic cooperation, progress has been slow.

The second is the Asia Pacific Economic Cooperation (APEC) group, founded in 1990. This group of countries has the potential to become highly influential if it were to turn itself into a free trade area. Doing so would make it the world's largest trade bloc, because the 18 member states account for more than half of the world's GNP. The APEC group consists of countries such as China, Japan, and the United States (see Table 2.2). Several well-publicized meetings have been held among the heads of state with the intent of removing their trade and investment barriers by 2010 for the richest members and by 2020 for the poorest members. However, some members complain that the plan is vague and commits APEC members to doing little more than holding additional meetings.[8]

GLOBAL CONSUMER PREFERENCES Consumer tastes and preferences are converging, even though some national differences persist. The success of such firms as Coca-Cola, Levi Strauss, Taco Bell, Sony, and McDonald's illustrates this trend. Part of the reason for the development of worldwide tastes and preferences is the presence of the mass media, exposure to goods from various countries, and marketing strategies of multinational firms that tend to offer standardized products worldwide, because doing so costs less than customizing goods to local conditions.

GLOBALIZED PRODUCTION To be cost efficient, firms are increasingly splitting up production around the world to take advantage of other countries' ability to perform parts of the process better for less money. By establishing a global web of production activities, firms hope to achieve

TABLE 2.2

Asia Pacific Economic Cooperation

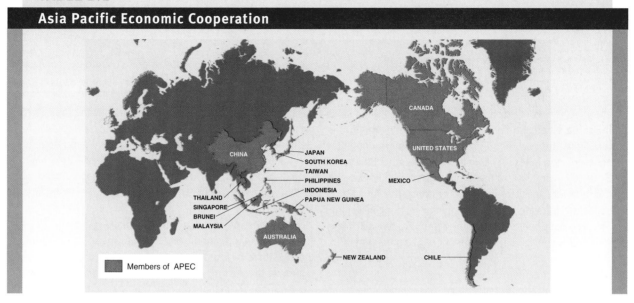

Source: Reprinted with permission from C. W. Hill, *International Business*. New York: Mc-Graw-Hill/Irwin, 2003, p. 282.

the highest quality standards at the lowest possible cost. For instance, of the $20,000 sticker price of a General Motors Chevrolet LeMans,

- $6,000 goes to South Korea, where the car is assembled.
- $3,000 goes to Japan for sophisticated high-tech parts, including engines, transaxles, and electronics.
- $800 goes to Taiwan, Singapore, and Japan for small parts.
- $500 goes to Great Britain to cover advertising and marketing services.
- $1,000 goes to Ireland for data processing.
- About $7,600 goes to GM and to the lawyers, bankers, insurance agents, and consultants that GM uses in the United States.[9]

TECHNOLOGICAL INNOVATIONS   Technology has made what was once impossible possible. In 1990, it would have been a logistical nightmare to build the Boeing 777 by outsourcing 132,500 parts to suppliers around the world. Now, Boeing outsources most of the components for the Boeing 777 commercial jet aircraft to 545 of the best suppliers around the world, and these companies produce the 132,500 engineered parts.[10]

Advances in communications, information processing, and transportation technology have made today's large international business feasible. Fiber optics, wireless technology, and the Internet and World Wide

| *Global Is Local in a New World Order of Business*

THEME: DEALING WITH CHANGE
A group of IBM computer programmers at Tsinghua University in Beijing writes software using Java technology. At the end of each day, the work is sent via the Internet to an IBM facility in Seattle, where programmers build on it during their workday. Then, the Seattle programmers send the working files another 5,222 miles to the Institute of Computer Science in Belarus and Software House Group in Latvia, which work on it and send it east to India's Tata Group. The Tata Group sends the software back to Tsinghua by morning in Beijing. The cycle continues until the project is done. "We call it Java Around the Clock," says John Patrick, vice president of Internet technology for IBM. "It's like we've created a 48-hour day through the Internet."

Communications technology has transformed the world into a single work place. As in the IBM programming cycle, workers collaborate in different locations using a computer network in ways they never could before. Caterpillar's global engineers in different countries simultaneously collaborate on tractor designs with a 3-D model over a computer network. ParaGraph International, a software company started by a Russian, Stepan Pachikov, links product development in Moscow and Campbell, California. The 50,000 employees at Schlumberger, a technology services company, work around the world but stay connected through the Schlumberger Information Network.

The Internet creates possibilities far beyond the phone or private data networks that used to be the backbone of international business. The Web is inexpensive and open to customers and suppliers worldwide, not just to the company's workers. Says Irving Wladawsky-Berger, head of IBM's Internet division, "The difference between Peoria and Romania on the Web is not very large."

The cost of doing business globally has also diminished thanks to technology. Eastman Chemical found the cost of three or four managers in the United States is the same as the cost of stationing one U.S. manager abroad; its U.S.-based managers can now use communication technology to manage by long distances. Of the company's 1,500 employees who work outside the United States, only 130 are Americans.

Sources: Adapted from K. Maney, "Technology Is Demolishing Time, Distance," *USA Today,* February 28, 1999, p. A1; D. Jones, "Costs Force Companies to Cut Foreign Posts," *USA Today,* February 26, 1997, p. A1. See also special issue of *Business Week* on the Internet Age, October 4, 1999, and special issue of *Business Week* on globalization, February 3, 2003.

Web make it possible to process a vast amount of information at very low cost. For example, the cost of a three-minute phone call from London to New York fell from $13.73 in 1973 to about $4.30 by the late 1990s. By 2004 the cost had fallen to less than 50 cents.

Many firms depend on satellite technology to link worldwide operations and integrate plants and activities. Texas Instruments uses satellite technology to link 50 plants in 19 countries and to coordinate production planning, cost accounting, financial planning, marketing, customer service, and the personnel function.[11] Management Close-Up 2.c provides other examples of how "global is local," with technology diminishing both time and distance challenges. Management Close-Up 2.d shows how Wal-Mart's amazing international success would not have been possible without recent technological developments.

MANAGEMENT ACROSS CULTURES   Culture still plays a major role in shaping consumer preferences and tastes. For instance, "Mattel's Barbie doll was a faltering product in Japan until marketing research de-

Wal-Mart's Miracle Overseas

Compared with other U.S. brands like Coca-Cola or McDonald's, Wal-Mart has been slow to go global. Although it is the world's largest retailer with more than 3,100 stores and almost $200 billion in revenue, Wal-Mart did not open its first foreign store (in Mexico) until 1991. Over 90 percent of the company's sales and profits still come from the United States, yet this balance is changing quickly.

Having succeeded in Mexico and Canada—where Wal-Mart has become the top retailer in less than a decade—Bobby Martin, head of Wal-Mart's international division, now has his sights set on other targets: Asia (where Wal-Mart has stores in China and Korea), Latin America, and most notably Europe, home to 500 million potential customers. This growth is occurring with amazing speed. At least one new store opens every week overseas. Two years after entering the German market in 1997, Wal-Mart had become the fourth-largest retailer there; its annual revenue of about $3.1 billion was equivalent to a 15 percent market share. The firm already has 499 stores in Mexico, 20 in Brazil, 11 in Argentina, 11 in China, and 6 in South Korea. Wal-Mart's purchase of Britain's 231-store Asda chain in July 1999 doubled the firm's international sales overnight.

Along with large amounts of capital readily available for investment overseas, Wal-Mart has several other advantages. One of them is a technology that allows distant subsidiaries to send scanner data via satellite to company headquarters in Bentonville, Arkansas, which has the capacity to store 43 terabytes of purchasing information. These data are critical to much of Wal-Mart's success worldwide. They allow the company to manage its supply chain, automatically reordering goods as stocks run low. Technology also enables Wal-Mart to discover new marketing opportunities by analyzing purchasing patterns across different markets.

The firm has also made accommodations to the local culture as it expands to new markets. For instance, abroad there is no "10-foot rule"—U.S. Wal-Marts mandate that every Wal-Mart employee must speak with any customer standing within 10 feet. Instead, employees abroad are merely encouraged to be customer-friendly. However, Wal-Mart is democratizing the shop floor the same way it did in the United States, by flattening hierarchies and giving employees (called "associates") the information and power necessary to make decisions. By 2004 Wal-Mart had stores on most continents and its online sales program had increased dramatically now that its offerings are available from almost all corners of the world.

Sources: Adapted from J. Kahn, "Wal-Mart Goes Shopping in Europe," *Fortune,* June 27, 1999, pp. 105–110; K. Capell and H. Dawley, "Wal-Mart's Not-So-Secret British Weapon," *Business Week,* January 24, 2000; and B. Saponto, "Can Wal-Mart Get Any Bigger?" *Time,* January 13, 2003, pp. 38–43.

termined that few Japanese identified with the Americanized doll. For the Japanese, Barbie was too tall, too long legged, and her blue eyes were the wrong color. Mattel produced a Japanized Barbie—shorter, with brown eyes, and a more Asian figure. Not surprisingly, 2 million Barbies were sold in two years."[12]

International firms often respond to local needs by customizing products and the marketing strategies which are designed to meet different consumer tastes. Likewise, firms establishing ventures overseas may need to adapt business strategies, structures, operational policies, and human resource programs to the culture. For instance, nepotism, or the hiring of relatives, is discouraged in Anglo-Saxon countries, but it is a common practice in many southern European, South American, and Asian countries.

Major Factors Affecting International Business

As firms internationalize to take advantage of global opportunities and to meet the competition, they need to consider factors that vary across countries and that are often very different from the familiar domestic setting. These factors include the general business environment, the legal system, economic conditions, and cultural norms.

GENERAL BUSINESS ENVIRONMENT   The general business environment of a country consists of all the factors that combine to affect the benefits, costs, and risks of conducting business in that country. Benefits are affected by the size of the market, the purchasing power of the population, and most important, the likely future wealth of consumers. Sometimes these factors can change unexpectedly. For example, Argentina was one of the eight wealthiest countries in the world until the 1940s, then fell below the top 40 by 2004 in part due to political instability, mismanagement of the economy, and widespread corruption. South Korea, on the other hand, was a very poor third-world nation in 1960. It is currently one of the 10 largest economies in the world and the fourth largest trading nation after Japan, the United States, and Germany.

The cost of doing business varies greatly from country to country. It may be necessary to make payments to the government or the political elite, or there may not be an appropriate infrastructure, or adherence to regulations may involve a major financial commitment. In some European countries, for example, it is necessary to give employees a month's paid vacation, numerous government-mandated holidays, and double pay for Christmas. McDonald's discovered that it had to develop dairy and vegetable farms, cattle ranches, and food-processing plants in Russia in order to serve food that met its quality standards in its Moscow outlet.

Operating in a foreign country also involves risk. Risks come in three forms and vary dramatically from nation to nation. *Political risk*, which is common in developing countries, may involve government changes (often by force), social unrest, strikes, terrorism, and violent conflict. There are several well-known consulting and publishing firms that provide up-to-date information on political risks country by country. These include:[13]

- Bank of America World Information Services
- Business Environment Risk Intelligence (BERI) S.A.
- Control Risks Information Services
- Economist Intelligence Unit (EIU)
- Euromoney
- Institutional Investor
- Standard and Poor's Rating Group
- Moody's Investor Services

A firm may also be exposed to *economic risk.* Some countries, such as Bolivia, have experienced annual inflation rates exceeding 26,000 percent, while others, such as Russia, make it difficult for foreign firms to get paid in hard currency (such as U.S. dollars) that can be repatriated to corporate headquarters, or may be riddled with corruption. Finally, firms may incur *legal risks.* For instance, some governments insist on local or government ownership of a percentage of equity of foreign firms. In other countries, intellectual property rights are not adequately protected. The illegal reproduction of CDs and software is a booming business in some Asian countries, and estimated annual losses exceed $2.2 billion.[14]

LEGAL SYSTEMS The legal system of a nation consists of the rules defining what is permissible or illegal, the process for enforcing the laws, and the procedures available to redress grievances. A country's legal system reflects its culture, religion, and traditions. A firm must comply with the host country's legal system.

In general, there are three major types of legal systems. Countries with an Anglo-Saxon background or influence rely on **common law,** in which precedents based on past court decisions play a key role in interpreting the meaning and intent of legal statutes. This legal system is used in the United States and 26 other countries. **Civil law** relies on a comprehensive set of rules that form part of a highly structured code, and enforcement and interpretation of laws are made in reference to this code. About 70 countries, including most European nations and Japan, use a civil law system. **Muslim law,** based on religious beliefs, regulates behavior in approximately 27 Islamic countries, although interpretations and levels of enforcement vary significantly from country to country.

ECONOMIC ENVIRONMENT Firms entering international markets are subject to unpredictable economic shifts that may have major effects on earnings. High inflation is one example, as in the Bolivian case noted above. The *exchange rate,* or the rate at which the market converts one currency into another, may also fluctuate. A devaluation occurs when more local currency is necessary to obtain a given amount of foreign currency, in effect making the local currency worth less outside the country. Companies are normally paid in local currency and later convert it into the currencies of their home countries. If the local currency is devalued relative to the company's domestic currency, the firm may receive less value for its products or services than was expected. To maintain profit levels, the firm must raise its prices, which may lead to fewer sales in the future.

Between late December 1994 and mid-January 1995, the value of the Mexican peso dropped 40 percent relative to the dollar, and U.S. firms in Mexico experienced an abrupt decline in revenues. Wal-Mart's Mexican stores were selling merchandise purchased with American dollars prior to the devaluation. Chrysler, Ford, and General Motors had imported parts from the United States and Canada to use in Mexican plants, and

> **common law**
>
> The legal system in which precedents based on past court decisions play a key role in interpreting the meaning and intent of legal statutes.

> **civil law**
>
> The legal system that relies on a comprehensive set of rules that form part of a highly structured code; enforcement and interpretation of laws are made in reference to this code.

> **Muslim law**
>
> The legal system based on religious Muslim beliefs that regulates behavior; strict interpretation and enforcement varies significantly from country to country.

this caused the price of their automobiles to increase by 40 percent in early 1995, causing demand to drop between 30 percent and 50 percent below the levels attained in 1994.[15] Although the peso continued to fluctuate, by 2000 Mexico's car prices had recovered and demand had risen to almost their precrisis levels. As another example of the effect of devaluation, the French tourism industry suffered a 30 percent decrease in profits as the value of the dollar dropped up to 35 percent relative to the euro during 2002–2004 (which kept many American tourists home).

Taxation represents another economic factor. Variations in tax policies are a major challenge to firms trying to minimize global tax liabilities. In Europe, the top corporate income tax rate ranges from 25 percent in Finland to 60 percent in Germany. An American manager sent to a subsidiary in Norway is exempted from domestic taxes for two years, but one sent to Spain must pay domestic taxes, which are far higher than in the United States, after a six-month stay. *Forbes* conducts an annual analysis of the tax burden in 47 countries (including corporate income tax, personal income tax, wealth tax, social security, and sales tax); this annual report can be found on the Web at www.forbes.com/misery.

Also, firms that rely on technological innovations as a source of competitive advantage may have to deal with complicated licensing agreements and royalties. In Germany, royalties on patents are limited to 10 percent of sales, with the duration of patents and trademarks set at 20 years and 10 years, respectively. Egypt, on the other hand, places no limits on royalties, but only production processes may be patented and only for a maximum of 15 years.

More than 80 countries adhere to the International Convention for the Protection of Industrial Property (often referred to as the Paris Union), but the rules may be interpreted differently. What constitutes industrial espionage may also differ among countries, and firms face major risks in protecting their technology. A firm may find that its proprietary technology is copied by joint-venture partners, franchisees, licensees, and former employees who are hired by other firms, encouraged in part by lax enforcement of so-called intellectual property laws.

culture shock

The reaction when exposed to other cultures with different norms, customs, and expectations.

power distance

The extent to which individuals expect a hierarchical structure that emphasizes status differences between subordinates and superiors.

Hofstede's Model of National Culture

CULTURAL ENVIRONMENTS   *Culture* is the "collective programming of the mind which distinguishes the members of one group from another . . . Culture, in this sense, includes systems of values; and values are among the building blocks of culture."[16] Culture reflects differences in the social structures, religions, languages, and historical backgrounds of various countries. **Culture shock** occurs when a person is exposed to a new culture with different norms, customs, and expectations and has difficulty adjusting.

To succeed internationally, businesses need to understand and be willing to make accommodations for cultural differences. Five dimensions summarize different cultures:

1. **Power distance** is the extent to which individuals expect a hierarchical structure that emphasizes status differences between subordinates and superiors. For example, in countries that are high in

Going Abroad for Better Customer Service at Lower Cost

THEME: CUSTOMER FOCUS Drop by the Manila offices of Source 1 Asia at two or three in the morning, and you might think you've stumbled into some late-night college cram session. Some 750 men and women in their early 20s, jazzed on cappuccino and junk food, are pulling all-nighters in front of computers. The walls of the cavernous room are painted hot pink, purple, and lime green. It's not Calculus 101 that has these Filipinos burning the midnight oil. They're busy handling credit card queries from Chevron Texaco Corp. customers and walking users through the intricacies of Microsoft Corp. software.

Most Americans think of a call center as a tedious, low-paid, dead-end job where employees resolve complaints about phone bills or bank statements. In the Philippines, call centers are viewed as a gateway to exciting careers working on behalf of the best service companies in the world. Some 10,000 Filipinos, almost all with college degrees, staff 45 such centers around the clock, seven days a week. Companies like American Express, Eastman Kodak, Intel, Microsoft, and Dell Computer are flocking to the Philippines, lured by the country's low wages, generous tax breaks, and ample supply of English speakers. The call-center staff consists of "a very, very talented pool of people," says Arun Khanna, Procter & Gamble's Manila-based accounting director. "They're committed, and comfortable with being trained and taking on responsibility."

Philip Sy is a typical call-center worker. After graduating in 1998 from the University of the Philippines with a degree in German and Italian, Sy took a $250-per-month job at Source 1 providing assistance to people installing software on their computers. Now 28, Sy is a Source 1 operations manager overseeing 150 people and earning $13,000 a year, a small fortune in a country where 40 percent of the population lives on less than a dollar a day. "Considering the career growth opportunities, a job here is pretty desirable," says Sy, practicing yo-yo tricks as he wanders the floor monitoring calls. Another Source 1 employee, Karen Betita, 25, is the daughter of a diplomat and has a college degree in communications. She says she views her job as a good starting place for a marketing career.

It's that kind of attitude—and the fact that good jobs are scarce in the Philippines—that helps keep turnover at call centers under 10 percent per year, compared with upwards of 70 percent in the United States. Indeed, Nathan Shapiro, Source 1's director of Asian operations, says he has just one headache: Filipino employees are often too polite, leading to longer and more costly phone chats. "We have to teach them to be more rude," says Shapiro, which may be one area in which U.S. service providers can't be beaten.

Source: Adapted from F. Balfour, "The Way Back Office," *Business Week,* February 3, 2003, p. 60.

---

power distance, such as the Philippines, Mexico, and most Arab nations, employees expect visible rewards that project power for people higher up in the organizational pyramid, such as a large office or an elegant company car.

2. **Individualism** is the degree to which a society values personal goals, autonomy, and privacy over group loyalty, commitment to group norms, involvement in collective activities, social cohesiveness, and intense socialization. In countries that are high in individualism, such as the United States, Great Britain, and New Zealand, employees believe they should look after their own interests.

3. **Uncertainty avoidance** is the extent to which a society places a high value on reducing risk and instability. Greece, Portugal, Italy, and other countries with high uncertainty avoidance have organizations with extensive rules and procedures and careful delineation of the work each individual is supposed to do.

individualism

The degree to which a society values personal goals, autonomy, and privacy over group loyalty, group norms, collective activities, social cohesiveness, and intense socialization.

uncertainty avoidance

The extent to which a society places a high value on reducing risk and instability.

4. **Masculinity/femininity** is the degree to which a society views assertive or "masculine" behavior as important to success and encourages rigidly stereotyped gender roles. Countries that are high in masculinity, such as Austria, Mexico, and the United States, value stereotypically male traits such as aggressiveness, initiative, and leadership.

5. **Long-term/short-term orientation** is the extent to which values are oriented toward the future (saving, persistence) as opposed to the past or present (respect for tradition, fulfilling social obligations). Japan and China value employee seniority and believe that wisdom increases with age, which reflects a longer-term orientation.[17]

Figure 2.2 shows the alignment of countries in terms of power distance and uncertainty avoidance. Latin, Mediterranean, and Far Eastern countries with relatively high masculinity and strong uncertainty avoidance make up the largest cluster, in the bottom right corner. The other clear cluster, in the top left corner, groups countries with low masculinity and weak uncertainty avoidance and includes mostly Anglo countries.

As a general principle, management practices that conform to prevailing societal norms are more likely to succeed, and those that do not are more likely to fail. A firm with operations in two or more countries should carefully consider how management practices are likely to mesh with the other countries' cultural values. Table 2.3 summarizes the organizational features and human resource management policies that work best in countries with high and low individualism.

Entry Strategy

A firm contemplating foreign expansion faces three key entry decisions: (1) which countries to enter, (2) when to enter, and (3) scale of involvement. Each of these decisions is described in turn.

Choosing Foreign Countries

There are more than 180 countries in the world. Not all of them are equally attractive. Ultimately, the decision to sell products in a new country should be based on long-term profit potential considerations. While profit potential depends on the type of firm and what it looks for (for instance, a mining company may be most interested in the existence of certain minerals while a high technology firm may be more interested in the availability of scientific talent), in general there are some factors that most companies would consider. Other things being equal, the appeal of a particular country is likely to be greater when:

1. The size of the domestic market is large. For instance, Starbuck's has chosen China as a foreign location, even though the president

FIGURE 2.2

Alignment of Countries in Terms of Power Distance and Masculinity

Source: From Gert Hofstede, *Cultures and Organizations: Software of the Mind.* Copyright © 1991. Reprinted with permission of author and rights holder.

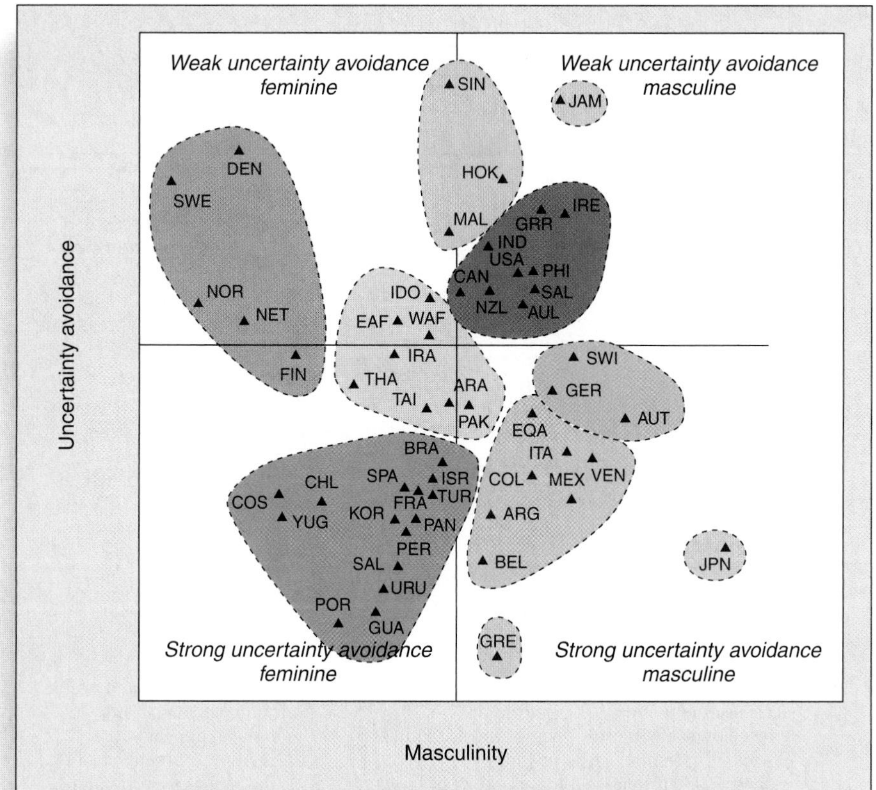

Source: From Gert Hofstede, *Cultures and Organizations: Software of the Mind.* Reprinted with permission of author and rights holder.

Abbreviations for Countries and Regions

ARA	Arab countries (Egypt, Lebanon, Libya, Kuwait, Iraq, Saudi Arabia, U.A.E.)	JAM	Jamaica
		JPN	Japan
ARG	Argentina	KOR	South Korea
AUL	Australia	MAL	Malaysia
AUT	Austria	MEX	Mexico
BRA	Brazil	NET	Netherlands
CAN	Canada	NZL	New Zealand
CHL	Chile	PAK	Pakistan
COL	Colombia	PAN	Panama
COS	Costa Rica	PER	Peru
DEN	Denmark	PHI	Philippines
EAF	East Africa (Kenya, Ethiopia, Zambia)	POR	Portugal
EQA	Equador	SAF	South Africa
FIN	Finland	SAL	El Salvador
FRA	France	SIN	Singapore
GBR	Great Britain	SPA	Spain
GER	Germany	SWE	Sweden
GRE	Greece	SWI	Switzerland
GUA	Guatemala	TAI	Taiwan
HOK	Hong Kong	THA	Thailand
IDO	Indonesia	TUR	Turkey
IND	India	URU	Uruguay
IRA	Iran	USA	United States
IRE	Ireland	VEN	Venezuela
ISR	Israel	WAF	West Africa (Nigeria, Ghana, Sierra Leone)
ITA	Italy	YUG	Yugoslavia

TABLE 2.3

Cultural Characteristics and Dominant Values (Individualism, Organizational Characteristics, and Selected HR Practices)

DOMINANT VALUES	SAMPLE COUNTRIES	ORGANIZATIONAL FEATURES	REWARD PRACTICES	STAFFING/APPRAISAL PRACTICES
High Individualism				
Personal accomplishment Selfishness Independence Belief in individual control and responsibility Belief in creating one's own destiny Business relationship between employer and employee	United States Great Britain Canada New Zealand	Organizations not compelled to care for employees' total well-being Employees look after their own individual interests Explicit systems of control necessary to ensure compliance and prevent wide deviation from organizational norms	Performance-based pay Individual achievement rewarded External equity emphasized Extrinsic rewards are important indicators of personal success Attempts made to isolate individual contributions (i.e., who did what) Emphasis on short-term objectives	Emphasis on credentials and visible performance outcomes attributed to individual High turnover; commitment to organization for career reasons Performance rather than seniority as criterion for advancement "Fitting in" deemphasized; belief in performance as independent of personal likes and dislikes Attempts at ascertaining individual strengths and weaknesses and providing frequent feedback to employee
Low Individualism				
Team accomplishment Sacrifice for others Dependence on social unit Belief in group control and responsibility Belief in the hand of fate Moral relationship between employer and employee	Singapore South Korea Indonesia Japan Taiwan	Organizations committed to high-level involvement in workers' personal lives Loyalty to the firm is critical Normative, rather than formal, systems of control to ensure compliance	Group-based performance is important criterion for rewards Seniority-based pay utilized Intrinsic rewards essential Internal equity guides pay policies Personal needs (such as number of children) affect pay received	Value of credentials and visible performance outcomes depends on perceived contributions to team efforts Low turnover; commitment to organization as "family" Seniority plays an important role in personnel decisions "Fitting in" with work group crucial; belief that interpersonal relations are important performance dimension Limited or no performance feedback to individual to prevent conflict and defensive reactions

Source: From *Managing Human Resources* by Gomez-Mejia, et al. Copyright © 2001. Reprinted by permission of Pearson Education, Inc., Upper Saddle River, NJ.

 International Cultural Diversity

of Starbuck's admits that "per capita consumption of coffee in China is very small." He quickly adds, however, that "what you have is a tremendous amount of people, so the market will grow".[18]

2. The present wealth (purchasing power) of consumers in the market is high and projected to grow in the future. For instance, only about 40,000 people in the world can afford to buy a $300,000 Rolls Royce. Almost all of them are found in about 12 countries.[19]

3. The needed resources are readily available. "British entrepreneur Richard Branson opened several of his Virgin Megastores in Japan despite its reputation as a tough market to crack. One reason for Branson's initial attraction to Japan was a cost of capital of only 2.5 percent—roughly one-third its cost in Britain."[20] For many firms, as shown in Management Close-Ups 2.a and 2.d, a key factor is the availability of qualified labor at a cost that is lower than the firm would pay in the domestic labor market.

4. The firm's product offerings are suitable to a particular market. For instance, a sports firm specializing in baseball paraphernalia is likely to face an uphill battle in countries such as France and Italy, where baseball is practically unknown.

5. A positive business climate exists. Political risks, laws, business practices, and cultural norms all have a profound effect on the appeal of a particular location. A sudden change in a government may mean that contracts signed under a prior government may no longer be enforceable. Government regulations can restrict international firms from withdrawing profits. Cultural norms may influence the kinds of products that are sold and the extent to which they need to be adapted to suit local preferences. An accurate assessment of a nation's business climate is crucial when considering an international opportunity. While in the end there is some subjectivity involved in assessing the degree to which a business climate is favorable or not, firms have access to a great deal of information that can help them make this judgment. For instance, worldatlas.com (www.worldatlas.com) and the *World Factbook* (published by the CIA) provide detailed data on the sociopolitical and economic situations of most countries around the world, which is continually updated. Table 2.4 shows a recent summary profile obtained from these sources of Mexico, China, and Japan, countries that are important to keep an eye on for many American firms competing in international markets.

When to Enter Foreign Countries

The timing of entry into a foreign market is a key consideration. Being the first to enter a market offers a *first-mover advantage* by preempting rivals, capturing demand by establishing a strong brand name, and in general making it difficult for later entrants to win business. For example, Gillette controls a large market segment in Latin America for razor blades, in part because it was the first international shaving company to move aggressively into that market. On the other hand, these advantages also have a downside. First movers face higher *pioneering costs,* such as the effort, time, and expense of entering a national market and educating consumers (particularly when the product or service is unfamiliar to local consumers). Late entrants may also learn from the experience of the

TABLE 2.4

Select Country Profiles: The Cases of Mexico, China and Japan

Mexico

Mexico has a population of approximately 102 million. A third of the population is under the age of 14. Almost 90 percent of Mexico's exports go to the United States, and 75 percent of its imports come from the United States. Mexico is the largest U.S. trading partner. Gross domestic product per capita is $9,100 a year. Spanish is the official language but various Mayan, Nahuatl, and other indigenous languages are also spoken. Approximately 60 percent of the population is mestizo (Native American–Spanish), 30 percent Native American, 9 percent of European origin, and 1 percent from other ethnic groups.

The site of advanced Amerindian civilizations, Mexico was under Spanish rule for three centuries before achieving independence early in the nineteenth century. Ongoing economic and social concerns include low real wages, underemployment for a large segment of the population, inequitable income distribution, and few advancement opportunities for the largely Amerindian population in the impoverished southern states.

Mexico has a free market economy with a mixture of modern and outmoded industry and agriculture, increasingly dominated by the private sector. The number of state-owned enterprises in Mexico has fallen from more than 1,000 in 1982 to fewer than 200 in 2004. In recent years, the government has privatized and expanded competition in seaports, railroads, telecommunications, electricity, natural gas distribution, and airports. Mexico still needs to overcome many structural problems while striving to modernize the economy and to raise living standards. Income distribution is unequal. The top 20 percent of income earners account for 55 percent of income. Trade with the United States and Canada has tripled since NAFTA was implemented in 1994. Mexico completed free trade agreements with the EU, Israel, El Salvador, Honduras, and Guatemala in 2000, and is pursuing additional trade agreements with countries in Latin America and Asia to lessen its dependence on the United States. Current president Vicente Fox Quesada has made a top priority of his administration to improve treatment of the millions of Mexican nationals in the United States, most of whom live and work in a legal limbo.

China

China's population is almost five times greater than that of the United States even though its territory is slightly smaller (close to 1.3 billion inhabitants). Mandarin is the official language of business, though there are many dialects. Twenty-one percent of China's exports are to the United States, while 10 percent of its imports come from the United States. Gross domestic product per capita is $3,600 a year.

In late 1978, the Chinese leadership began moving the economy from a sluggish Soviet-style centrally planned economy to a more market-oriented system. The system operates within a political framework of strict communist control; however, the economic influence of non-state managers and enterprises has been steadily increasing. China's authorities have switched to a system of household responsibility in agriculture in place of the old collectivization. The government has increased the authority of local officials and plant managers in industry, permitted a wide variety of small-scale enterprise in services and light manufacturing, and opened the economy to increased foreign trade and investment. The result has been a quadrupling of GDP since 1978. With its 1.3 billion people in 2004 but a GDP of just $3,600 per capita, China stands as the second largest economy in the world after the United States. Agricultural output doubled in the 1980s, and industry also posted major gains, especially in coastal areas near Hong Kong and opposite Taiwan, where foreign investment helped spur output of both domestic and export goods. On the darker side, the leadership has often experienced in its hybrid system the worst results of socialism (bureaucracy and lassitude) and of capitalism (windfall gains and stepped-up inflation). Beijing thus has periodically backtracked, retightening central controls at intervals. The government has struggled to: (a) collect revenues due from provinces, businesses, and individuals; (b) reduce corruption and other economic crimes; and (c) keep afloat the large state-owned enterprises many of which had been shielded from competition by subsidies and had been losing the ability to pay full wages and pensions. 80 to 120 million surplus rural workers are adrift between the villages and the cities. Many subsist through part-time low-paying jobs. Popular resistance, changes in central policy, and loss of authority by rural cadres have weakened China's population control program, which is essential to maintaining growing living standards. Another long-term threat to continued rapid economic growth is the deterioration of the environment, notably air pollution, soil erosion, and the steady fall of the water table, especially in the north. China continues to lose arable land due to erosion and economic development.

Japan

Japan's population consists of approximately 127 million inhabitants living in an area slightly smaller than California. Japan is a homogeneous country, with 99.4 percent of the population speaking Japanese, and little ethnic diversity. A third of Japan's exports are to the United States while 19 percent of its imports come from the United States. Gross domestic product per capita is $24,900 a year.

Government-industry cooperation, a strong work ethic, mastery of high technology, and a comparatively small defense allocation (1 percent of GDP) have helped Japan expand economically. Japan holds the rank of the second most technologically powerful economy in the world after the United States and has the third largest economy in the world after the United States and China. One notable characteristic of the economy is the cooperation between manufacturers, suppliers, and distributors in closely-knit groups called Keiretsu. A second feature has been the guarantee of lifetime employment for a substantial portion of the urban labor force. Both of these features are now eroding.

TABLE 2.4

Select Country Profiles: The Cases of Mexico, China and Japan (Continued)

Japanese industry, the most important sector of the economy, is heavily dependent on imported raw materials and fuels. The much smaller agricultural sector is highly subsidized and protected. Crop yields in Japan are among the highest in the world. Usually self-sufficient in rice, Japan imports about 50 percent of its requirements of other grain and fodder crops. Japan maintains one of the world's largest fishing fleets and accounts for nearly 15 percent of the global catch.

For three decades, overall real economic growth had been spectacular: a 10 percent average in the 1960s, a 5 percent average in the 1970s, and a 4 percent average in the 1980s. Growth slowed markedly in the 1990s largely due to the aftereffects of overinvestment during the late 1980s along with contractionary domestic policies designed to wring speculative excesses from the stock and real estate markets. Government efforts to revive economic growth have met little success. They were further hampered in late 2000 by the slowing of the U.S. and Asian economies. During 2001–2004 Japan is the only industrialized nation since the Great Depression that has experienced a sustained period of declining prices, or deflation. The crowding of habitable land area and the aging of the population are two major long-run problems. Robotics constitutes a key long-term economic strength, with Japan possessing 410,000 of the world's 720,000 "working robots."

Source: Adapted from www.worldatlas.com, January 28, 2003, with further statistical updates by the authors.

Motorola is taking advantage of the opportunities in China with their two plants that manufacture mobile phone handsets, cellular networks, and semiconductors—and turning a profit.

first movers and perform better as a result. Kentucky Fried Chicken is generally credited with creating a market in China for American-style fast food, yet it was latecomer McDonald's which became most profitable in that market.[21] As can be seen in Management Close-Up 2.f, Motorola has been able to achieve some first-mover advantages in China, but still faces the risk that latecomers may take over the Chinese market for cell phones in the future, a market that Motorola helped create in the first place.

management close-up

First Mover Advantage, but How Long Will It Last?
The Case of Motorola in China

THEME: DEALING WITH CHANGE As the world's largest cellular market with over 200 million subscribers, China is the marketing fixation of every company in the industry. The Motorola company was a pioneer in China. Current Chairman Christopher B. Galvin first visited Shanghai as a rising exec and met with Jiang Zemin—then a little-known local party functionary, later to become China's president—in 1986. The U.S. giant has been nurturing the Chinese market ever since, investing $3.4 billion in manufacturing and research and development facilities there, more than any other Western company.

The commitment paid off. Motorola sells more cell phones than anyone else in China: nearly 17 million a year. Recently, Motorola manufactured telecom and other equipment valued at $5.7 billion in China, selling roughly $2 billion worth abroad, making it one of China's top exporters. Some 20 percent of the company's $26.2 billion annual revenue came from China, according to brokerage Bear, Stearns & Co. Motorola executives confidently predict sales will continue to increase at double-digit rates.

Even more important, analysts say Motorola is profitable in China. And it's growing faster there than anywhere else—big news for a company that had been languishing in the red and was expected to eke out just a small profit globally. "China has been great for Motorola," says Mike S. Zafirovski, the company's president and chief operating officer. "It's very much a bright spot."

Unfortunately the bright spot may soon start to dim. Archrival Nokia has poured $2.4 billion into China and has a giant complex producing cell phones and components near Beijing. Korea's Samsung Electronics is benefiting from looser regulations following China's 2001 entry into the World Trade Organization. Even more ominous for Motorola is new competition from local Chinese handset makers. These companies held less than 35 percent of the market as late as 1999, but today control some 26 percent.

Motorola is in little immediate danger of losing its lead in China, but there is little doubt that local rivals are gaining ground. Many Chinese companies plan to double or triple current capacities, flooding the market with handsets and driving down prices. "If the local guys get too much market share, that could put huge pressure on Motorola," says Bear, Stearns analyst Wojtek Uzdelewicz, which is a pressure the company can't afford.

Source: Adapted from B. Einhorn, D. Roberts, & R. Crockett, "Winning in China." *Business Week,* January 27, 2003, pp. 98–100.

Scale of Involvement

The firm must consider not only where and when to enter but also the magnitude of its commitment to the foreign location. In the example shown in Management Close-Up 2.f, Motorola has recently made some huge investments in China, a country company leaders consider to be crucial to future profitability. Motorola opened a $1.5 billion semiconductor plant in Tianjin in 2003 to make phone-handset chips, and has announced investment plans in China for year-end 2006 reaching $30 billion dollars.[22] The decision to enter a foreign market on such a large scale is a major strategic commitment with long-term consequences for the corporation. It is also difficult to reverse. The scale of involvement decision is closely tied to mode of entry, to be discussed next. In general, scale of involvement is lowest if the firm simply decides to export

TABLE 2.5

Advantages and Disadvantages of Various Modes of Entry Choices

MODE OF ENTRY	ADVANTAGES	DISADVANTAGES
Exporting	• Economies of scale • Lower foreign expenses	• No low cost sales • High transportation costs • Potential tariffs
Turnkey Project	• Access to closed markets	• Competition from local client • Loss of competitive advantage
Licensing	• Quick expansion • Lower expenses and risks • Lower political risk	• Loss of competitive advantage • Limited ability to use profits in one country to increase competition in another
Franchising	• Quick expansion • Lower development costs and risks • Lower political risk	• Loss of competitive advantage • Potential quality control problems • Limited ability to use profits in one country to increase competition in another country
Joint Venture	• Knowledge of local markets • Lower development costs and risk • Access to closed markets	• Potential for conflict of interest • Loss of competitive advantage
Strategic Alliance	• Access to closed markets • Pooled resources increase partner firm's capabilities • Benefit from complementary skills and assets	• Loss of competitive advantage • Potential overestimation of partner's capabilities
Wholly Owned Subsidiary	• Maximum control over proprietary knowledge/technology • Greater strategic flexibility • Efficiencies of global production system	• Large capital outlay • Lack of local knowledge • Increased risk

Source: T. S. Bateman and S. A. Snell, *Management: Competing in the New Era*, 5th ed. New York: McGraw-Hill/Irwin, 2002.

its products to the foreign location and highest if the firm decides to have a wholly owned subsidiary in the foreign country (as in the case of Motorola in China; see Management Close-Up 2.f).

Mode of Entry

The seven ways to enter foreign markets are exporting, turnkey projects, licensing, franchising, joint ventures, wholly owned subsidiaries, and strategic alliances. The advantages and disadvantages associated with each entry mode are summarized in Table 2.5.

Exporting

Manufacturing firms typically begin globalization by **exporting** products to other countries and retaining production facilities within domestic borders. Exporting has two advantages. First, the firm may realize substantial savings through economies of scale. In other words, expanding the market creates greater demand, which requires increasing production,

exporting

A means of entering new markets by sending products to other countries and retaining production facilities within domestic borders.

which results in fuller use of plant and equipment and improved learning as a result of practice, so unit costs tend to go down. Second, the firm avoids the expenses of establishing, controlling, and coordinating manufacturing operations on foreign soil. Japanese firms that have used this entry mode successfully, particularly in U.S. markets, include Sony, Matsushita, Honda, and Toyota.

The most obvious limitation of exporting is that foreign competitors may enjoy a cost advantage that far exceeds the economies of scale the company realizes. For instance, unskilled and semiskilled labor in most less-developed countries may be hired at a fraction of the cost of comparable labor in the domestic market. This is one reason why established and relatively simple products like bicycles, irons, and small domestic appliances are no longer manufactured in the United States. Moreover, bulk products, such as chemicals, may be expensive to transport from the home country to distant locations. Finally, imports are a politically sensitive issue in many countries, including the United States, and tariffs may be imposed on imported goods.

Turnkey Projects

Turnkey projects are a specialized type of exporting. The selling firm handles the design, construction, start-up operations, and workforce training of a foreign plant, and a local client is handed the key to a plant that is fully operational. Turnkey projects are most often used in newly developed and less-developed countries. Limited access to complex, expensive production process technologies such as chemical production, pharmaceutical production, petroleum refining, and metal refining makes them more viable. A turnkey project allows a company to use its know-how to earn a profit in a foreign country without making a major, long-term investment. Some host countries, including many oil-rich nations, prohibit foreign ownership of an asset such as a petroleum refinery. In such cases, a turnkey deal may be the most attractive business option available.

Turnkey projects also have potential disadvantages. For one, the selling firm may be creating a competitor by giving away its technological superiority. For example, Saudi Arabia, Kuwait, and other Persian Gulf nations are using turnkey-built petroleum plants to directly compete with the Western firms that built those facilities. Also, the selling firm may lose a source of competitive advantage by transferring complex know-how to actual or potential competitors.

Licensing

In **licensing,** a company transfers the rights to produce and sell its products overseas to a foreign firm. In return, the licensing company receives a negotiated fee, normally in the form of a royalty. The typical licensing arrangement involves intangible property, such as patents, inventions, formulas, trademarks, designs, and copyrights. For instance, Xerox receives 5 percent of net revenues from Fuji-Xerox for allowing Fuji-Xerox to sell Xerox's photocopying technology in the Asian Pacific region.

An advantage of licensing is that the firm does not have to incur the expense and risk of opening a facility overseas. Instead, the licensee puts up most of or all of the capital necessary to start production. When a local government will not allow a firm to set up a wholly owned subsidiary, licensing may be the best alternative. This was why Xerox set up a joint venture with Fuji and licensed its technology to Fuji-Xerox. Also, a firm may own intangible property that has commercial value but may not wish to engage in manufacturing activities. For example, Bell Laboratories at AT&T invented the transistor in the 1950s but licensed the technology to other firms for manufacture.

A disadvantage of licensing is that the foreign firm may build on the technology and use an enhanced version to compete in global markets against the licensing firm that invented it. This happened to RCA when it licensed its color television technology to several Japanese firms, including Matsushita and Sony. Licensing also imposes constraints on the firm, limiting strategic flexibility on a global scale. Because each licensee establishes its own manufacturing operations, costs will go up, and increased prices will reduce demand for products using that technology (which would have an adverse effect on royalties). Licensing also greatly limits a firm's ability to use profits earned in one country to make bold competitive moves in other countries.

Franchising

Franchising is similar to licensing, except that it is mainly used by service companies, whereas licensing is primarily used by manufacturing firms. The franchisee pays a fee for using the brand name and agrees to strictly follow the standards and abide by the rules set by the franchise. McDonald's, for example, has approximately 3,000 locally owned franchises around the world. The menu, cooking methods, ingredients, and physical appearance of these restaurants must comply with McDonald's standards. McDonald's helps the stores obtain supplies and is closely involved in training managers to ensure that uniform quality standards are met.

Like licensing, franchising allows a firm to expand rapidly with relatively small capital investment and little risk exposure. The main drawback of franchising is that the firm depends on franchisees for quality control, and there is a risk that standards followed by the different stores may not be uniformly met by all the stores. Since the franchise name is intended to guarantee consistent product quality, a lack of uniformity hurts the reputation of the franchise.

franchising

A means of entering new markets similar to licensing, mainly used by service companies, in which the franchisee pays a fee for using the brand name and agrees to strictly follow the standards and abide by the rules set by the franchise.

McDonald's restaurants serve a varied, yet limited, value-priced menu in 120 countries around the world. Franchisees are independent entrepreneurs, typically local businesspeople.

Joint Ventures and Strategic Alliances

joint venture

A means of entering new markets where two or more independent firms agree to establish a separate firm; the firms normally own equivalent shares of the joint venture and contribute a corresponding proportion of the management team.

In a **joint venture,** two or more independent firms agree to establish a separate firm that is owned by the participating companies. The firms normally own equivalent shares of the joint venture and contribute a corresponding proportion of the management team.

Joint ventures are increasing in popularity. One major advantage is that foreign firms benefit by establishing a working relationship with a domestic firm that is familiar with the local labor market, political environment, competitive landscape, tastes and preferences, cultural norms, language, and legal systems. In return, the local partner receives access to the know-how, technology, and capital of the foreign firm. Further, the two firms gain by sharing development costs and risks, reducing the potential of unacceptably large losses in the case of poor results or business failure. Also, local equity partners may discourage a government from interfering with a multinational. Joint ventures are another way for companies to do business in countries that do not allow foreign firms to maintain fully owned subsidiaries.

Joint ventures have two serious drawbacks. First, the goals, strategies, culture, and personalities of the firms may conflict. Unless it is successfully resolved, conflict may lead to a dissolution of the union, with considerable cost to all involved. Second, the local partner may use the foreign firm's technology for its own competitive advantage.

strategic alliances

Cooperative arrangements between competitors or potential competitors from different countries, possibly to establish a formal joint venture or collaboration between firms on specific projects.

International **strategic alliances** are cooperative arrangements between competitors or potential competitors from different countries.

They may involve establishment of a formal joint venture as discussed above, such as the case of Fuji-Xerox, or collaboration between firms on specific projects. Strategic alliances have become extremely popular in recent years. Among the firms involved in these arrangements are

- *General Electric Snecma of France.* Joint venture to develop and manufacture a variety of low-thrust commercial aircraft engines.

- *Toshiba-IBM.* Sharing the $1 billion cost of developing a 64-megabyte and 256-megabyte memory chip facility, technology that will be transferred to a new IBM plant in Virginia.

- *Mitsui-General Electric.* GE's power-systems unit has picked up Asian contracts with Mitsui's well-connected bank. GE has the technology; Mitsui has the contacts and deep pockets.

- *Toyota-GM, TRW.* GM's parts division, Delphi, supplies components to Toyota and participates in Toyota's Keiretsu strategy meetings. TRW says it has become part of the Toyota group.

- *Canon–Hewlett Packard.* The two share laser printer technology. Hewlett-Packard buys engines from Canon, but they compete with end products around the world.

- *Mitsubishi-Caterpillar.* A long-time joint venture has become Cat's primary Asian manufacturing source. American and Japanese staff jointly designed a successful excavator line made in Japan, the United States, Indonesia, and China.[23]

Several advantages account for the recent growth of strategic alliances. First, "keeping pace with technological change and competing globally have stretched the resources of even the richest companies."[24] Pooling resources enables firms to accomplish tasks that neither can afford to do alone. Strategic alliances also allow firms to enter relatively closed foreign markets.

A strategic alliance means that firms can utilize complementary skills and assets. This was the case, for instance, in the alliance between Mitsui and GE noted above. Sharing core competencies can create synergies that enhance the competitive positions of both companies. Strategic alliances may result in the creation of technological standards for the industry, which would simplify the manufacturing process for the firms involved and also benefit the end user.

Strategic alliances have drawbacks similar to those of joint ventures. Most notably, the firm runs the risk of losing its competitive advantage by "giving away" proprietary know-how to the partner. The firm may also misjudge the partner's capabilities. The success of any strategic alliance depends on the interpersonal relationship between the managers of the firms. Lack of trust, misunderstandings, and opportunistic behaviors may cause the alliance to dissolve, which may result in writing off millions of investment dollars.

OPENING A FACILITY ABROAD

AACC is a U.S. manufacturer of prosthetic devices, including canes, crutches, walkers, and other devices that help partially disabled people maintain some independence. All of AACC's management functions are located in the United States. Domestic sales account for 85 percent of its revenues, with the remaining 15 percent originating mostly in Canada and Mexico. AACC has decided to expand its international operations in order to remain competitive and increase its market share. CEO Ralph Solomon met with the firm's top executives and set up a committee within AACC to develop concrete proposals for internationalizing the company. Solomon has prepared the following memo that lists four areas that should be covered as part of the committee's recommendations.

TO: Members of AACC International Task Force
FROM: Mr. Ralph Solomon
SUBJECT: International Task Force

If we are to remain a strong and competitive firm, AACC must begin to exploit opportunities abroad. Several task forces will study alternative means of internationalizing AACC, including opening a manufacturing site abroad and moving aggressively into international markets.

I have appointed you to a task force to provide recommendations to guide future actions. Your analysis and recommendations must be clearly supported by facts. Any reasonable assumptions you make as part of your analysis should be justified in a clear and logical manner.

I am counting on you to develop a high-quality proposal, covering the following areas:

1. If AACC should be involved in overseas production, indicate where plants should be located and why.

2. AACC will entertain any of the following alternatives:
   - *Licensing of AACC Technology and Patents:* In this option, AACC would license its technology and patents to a foreign producer who would then produce products for AACC at a contracted price. AACC could purchase all or part of this producer's total output under this arrangement.
   - *Joint Venture:* AACC could invest funds in a new or existing company within a country with a partner in that country.
   - *Wholly Owned Facility:* Instead of having a host country partner, AACC could build or buy a production facility on a wholly owned basis.
   - *Strategic Alliance:* In this option AACC may develop a partnership with a foreign firm to conduct R&D on prosthetic devices and manufacture a variety of such products without formally setting up a joint venture.

   Analyze the pros and cons of each option. What alternative should be used for foreign manufacturing in the country you have selected? Justify your choice.

3. Develop a plan outlining how the foreign venture will be managed and the steps that should be taken to minimize potential problems that may emerge.

Wholly Owned Subsidiaries

wholly owned subsidiary

A means of entering new markets in which a firm fully owns its subsidiary in foreign countries.

When a multinational firm fully owns a company in a foreign country, the local company is a **wholly owned subsidiary** of the multinational. Wal-Mart owns all of its stores worldwide. This arrangement has several advantages. A wholly owned subsidiary offers a firm maximum control

Exercise

Form committees, each consisting of four students, with the following roles assigned:

Chairperson

- Coordinates team members' activities.
- Monitors team members' progress.
- Acts as a clearinghouse for information from various functional areas so that it can be easily understood and used by the entire team.
- Develops, proposes, and evaluates various scenarios, in close collaboration with other team members.
- Establishes agendas and protocol for team meetings, and controls any dysfunctional behavior, such as long monologues, personality clashes, and unfocused argumentation.
- Develops implementation and corporate strategy plans that integrate the team's functional areas.

Political/Legal Adviser

- Conducts political risk analysis for various countries under consideration.
- Provides legal support to the team including judicial interpretation of issues being discussed.
- Makes recommendations regarding the legal and political ramifications of various manufacturing arrangements overseas, such as joint venture versus wholly owned subsidiary.
- Analyzes government policies that may have an effect on AACC's operation, such as laws controlling profit repatriation to the United States.

Financial/Economic Adviser

- Provides the team with relevant data and recommendations concerning the general economic conditions of countries under consideration.
- Conducts research on the tax advantages and disadvantages in various countries.
- Analyzes business factors that may affect AACC's operations, such as inflation, devaluation, and convertibility of local currency into dollars.

Human Resources Adviser

- Analyzes human resources of those countries under consideration
- Works with the political/legal adviser in evaluating legal restrictions concerning expatriates.
- Estimates labor costs for AACC's foreign operation.
- Develops a resource plan for managing AACC's international venture.

Each committee will prepare a written report and make an oral presentation of an independent proposal covering the areas noted in the memo. The instructor will play the role of CEO and may ask questions of committee members to assess the soundness of the recommendations being offered.

Source: This exercise builds on an earlier simulation by L. R. Gomez-Mejia and J. E. McCann, *Meeting the Challenges of Foreign Expansion: An International Business Simulation*, Columbus, OH: Grid Publishing Co., 1985.

over proprietary knowledge and technology, so that competitors cannot gain access. In addition, the foreign company retains full discretion to move resources to other countries and thereby enjoys greater strategic flexibility. For instance, it may use profits from one country to move aggressively into other countries. A global production system may provide efficiencies because "the various operations must be prepared to accept centrally determined decisions as to how they will produce, how much they will produce, and how output will be priced for transfer to the next operation."[25]

On the other hand, wholly owned subsidiaries require large capital outlays, and ownership is thus the most expensive method of operating in foreign markets. The firm bears the full brunt of business risks, since these are not shared with a local partner. Corporate managers of a wholly owned subsidiary may not sufficiently understand local conditions. A firm that exclusively relies on wholly owned subsidiaries may be unable to operate in markets where legal or political imperatives require foreign firms to establish joint ventures with local partners.

Managing the Global Firm

ethnocentric approach

An approach to managing an international subsidiary that involves filling top management and other key positions with people from the home country (expatriates).

polycentric approach

An approach to managing an international subsidiary in which subsidiaries are managed and staffed by personnel from the host country (local nationals).

geocentric approach

An approach to managing an international subsidiary in which nationality is deliberately downplayed, and the firm actively searches on a worldwide or regional basis for the best people to fill key positions.

third-country nationals

Citizens of countries other than the host nation or the firm's home country.

The success of a foreign venture depends on who is in charge. If a manager does not perform up to par in a domestic unit, others can fill in. This is not the case in an overseas operation. The importance of choosing the right managers was underlined by CEOs of U.S. companies with revenues in the $300 million to $1 billion range who identified the choice of management for overseas units as one of their most crucial business decisions.[26]

There are three basic approaches to managing an international subsidiary: the ethnocentric, polycentric, and geocentric approaches. The **ethnocentric approach** involves filling top management and other key positions with people from the home country. These managers are known as *expatriates.* In the **polycentric approach,** international subsidiaries are managed and staffed by personnel from the host country, or local nationals. Nationality is deliberately downplayed in the **geocentric approach** as the firm actively searches on a worldwide or regional basis for the best people to fill key positions. Many of these individuals are likely to be **third-country nationals**—citizens of countries other than the host nation or the firm's home country.

Table 2.6 summarizes the pros and cons of using local nationals and expatriates in foreign operations. It costs firms more than a third of a million dollars annually to transfer and compensate expatriates. Consequently, firms use them only for key positions, such as senior managers, high-level professionals, and technical specialists.

Twenty percent to 40 percent of expatriates return before completing their assignments, compared with fewer than 5 percent of Japanese expatriates.[27] Premature returnees cost $85,000 to $260,000 each, and the costs of business disruptions, lost opportunities, a leadership vacuum, and family hardships are probably many times greater. Six factors, which are summarized in Table 2.7, account for most failures, although their relative importance varies by firm. Selection, training, career development, and compensation practices can deal with the factors that lead to failure.

TABLE 2.6

Advantages and Disadvantages of Using Local and Expatriate Employees to Staff International Subsidiaries

ADVANTAGES	DISADVANTAGES
Locals	
• Lowers labor costs	• Makes it difficult to balance local demand and global priorities
• Demonstrates trust in local citizenry	
• Increases acceptance of the company by the local community	• Leads to postponement of difficult local decisions (such as layoffs) until they are unavoidable, when they are more difficult, costly, and painful than they would have been if implemented earlier
• Maximizes the number of options available in the local environment	
• Leads to recognition of the company as a legitimate participant in the local economy	• May make it difficult to recruit qualified personnel
• Effectively represents local considerations and constraints in the decision-making process	• May reduce the amount of control exercised by headquarters
Expatriates	
• Cultural similarity with parent company ensures transfer of business/management practices	• Creates problems of adaptability to foreign environment and culture
• Permits closer control and coordination of international subsidiaries	• Increases the "foreignness" of the subsidiary
• Gives employees a multinational orientation through experience at parent company	• May involve high transfer, salary, and other costs
• Establishes a pool of internationally experienced executives	• May result in personal and family problems
• Local talent may not yet be able to deliver as much value as expatriates can	• Has disincentive effect on local-management morale and motivation
	• May be subject to local government restrictions

Source: From *Managing Human Resources* by Gomez-Mejia, et al., Copyright © 2001. Reprinted by permission of Pearson Education, Inc., Upper Saddle River, NJ.

Selection

Choosing expatriate managers with the best odds of success means utilizing an effective selection process. Selection criteria should include cultural sensitivity. The selection board should have some expatriates. The company should require previous international experience and verify that the candidate's spouse and family are flexible, patient, and adaptable.

Training

Cross-cultural training sensitizes candidates to the local culture, customs, language, and government. Table 2.8 summarizes three approaches to cross-cultural training. More rigorous and lengthy training is generally reserved for key executives and those expected to be overseas for an extended period of time. Skills for Managing 2.2, "How Would You Train Expatriates to Go Overseas?" asks you to develop such a program.

TABLE 2.7

Why International Assignments End in Failure

Career blockage	Initially, many employees see the opportunity to work and travel abroad as exciting. But once the initial rush wears off, many feel that the home office has forgotten them and that their career has been sidetracked while their counterparts at home are climbing the corporate ladder.
Culture shock	Many people who take international assignments cannot adjust to a different cultural environment, a phenomenon called culture shock. Instead of learning to work within the new culture, the expatriate tries to impose the home office's or home country's values on the host country's employees, tending to internal conflict.
Lack of predeparture cross-cultural training	Surprisingly, only about one-third of multinationals provide any cross-cultural training to expatriates, and those that do tend to offer rather cursory programs.
Overemphasis on technical qualifications	The person chosen to go abroad may have impressive credentials and an excellent reputation in the home office for getting things done. Yet this person may lack cultural adaptability as an important trait to be effective overseas.
Getting rid of a troublesome employee	International assignments may seem to be a convenient way of dealing with managers who are having problems in the home office. By sending these managers abroad, the organization is able to resolve difficult interpersonal situations or political conflicts at the home office, but at a significant cost to its international operations.
Family problems	The inability or unwillingness of the expatriate's spouse and children to adapt to life in another country is one of the most important reasons for failure. In fact, more than half of all early returns can be attributed to family problems.

Source: From *Managing Human Resources* by Gomez-Mejia, et al. Copyright © 2001. Reprinted by permission of Pearson Education, Inc., Upper Saddle River, NJ.

Career Development

Expatriates are more likely to complete foreign assignments and to be highly motivated to succeed when they believe that the assignments are instrumental to their future career opportunities. Unfortunately, this has not always been the case. Only 15 percent of the top 50 executives in U.S. corporations have worked abroad as compared with 35 percent of European executives and 27 percent of Japanese executives.[28] About 80 percent of executives posted abroad feel that employers do not value their international experience. Although 75 percent expect the move to benefit their careers, only 10 percent receive promotions when they return to the home office.[29] Female executives have less access to opportunities overseas than male executives, and the perceived value of international experience in their careers is also lower.[30]

At a minimum, successful career planning for expatriates requires firms to position international assignments as a step toward advancement

TABLE 2.8

Three Approaches to Cross-Cultural Training

LENGTH OF STAY	LENGTH AND LEVEL OF TRAINING	CHARACTERISTICS
Impression Approach		
1–3 years	1–2 months + High	Assessment center Field experiences Simulations Sensitivity training Extensive language training
Affective Approach		
2–12 months	1–4 weeks Moderate	Language training Role-playing Critical incidents Cases Stress-reduction training Moderate language training
Information-Giving Approach		
1 month or less	Less than a week Low	Area briefings Cultural briefings Films/books Use of interpreters "Survival-level" language training

Source: Adapted from M. Mendenhall and G. Oddou, "Acculturation Profiles of Expatriate Managers: Implication for Cross-Cultural Training," *Columbia Journal of World Business* 21, no. 4 (1986), p. 78.

within the firm. In addition, the home office should provide continued support to expatriates, such as by appointing a senior executive as a mentor, offering short sabbaticals in the home office, and bringing expatriates back to the home office occasionally.

Manager's Notes 2.1 lists the key management skills for managing a global firm.

Compensation

In the international management setting, money makes the world go around. When salaries are inappropriately low, misgivings that the expatriate manager and spouse may have about foreign assignment rise. The cost of housing, food, and other consumer goods is far higher in many foreign locations than in the United States. For example, a survey conducted in 2001 indicates that the same standard of living costs three times more in Seoul and Tokyo than in Bombay or Toronto, and a third more than in New York City.[31]

HOW WOULD YOU TRAIN EXPATRIATES TO GO OVERSEAS?

Assume that you are a human resource manager for a large energy firm with facilities in Colombia, Norway, Nigeria, and Saudi Arabia. In five months or so the company intends to send approximately 10 American expatriate managers to each of those locations. They are expected to stay at least a year.

You have been asked to develop a training program to help those expatriates and their families to adjust. Provide an outline of a training program, with key features that may be more appropriate for each of these countries such as security concerns and language training. (The instructor may decide to make this a team project by dividing the class into teams of five.)

Planning expatriate compensation should follow two guidelines. First, the firm should provide the expatriate with a disposable income that is equivalent to what he or she would earn in the home office. This may require special allowances for housing, children's education, medical care, and so on. Second, the firm should provide an explicit "add-on" incentive, such as a sign-on bonus and a bonus at the end of the assignment for going overseas, and the bonus should be larger for less desirable locations.

Ethics and Social Responsibility

Globalization greatly increases the possibility that a manager will face an ethical dilemma. Different cultures have different notions of right and wrong. A firm may lose business if it applies a stricter code of ethics than foreign competitors follow. A transaction that an American might perceive as bribery could be construed by others as a commission or as an incentive necessary to conduct business in a foreign country. While many Americans were disgusted by news reports in 1999 that Salt Lake City officials had bribed the Olympic Commission to select Salt Lake City as a future Olympic site, several of the officials defended the practice on the grounds that gifts were expected in that situation.

The U.S. Foreign Corrupt Practices Act of 1977 is a tough anticorruption law governing international business. The Act was passed as a re-

Skills for Managing in the International Environment

- *International assessment skills.* Develop an appreciation and awareness of global forces that should be tracked because they may have an effect on your firm.

- *Cross-cultural sensitivity skills.* To succeed in the international arena, you must be able to deal with people from different cultural backgrounds. Since many of the common bonds that people share domestically, such as operating under the same legal system, do not exist beyond national borders, the effect of cultural diversity tends to be magnified the more countries a firm operates in, and the challenge for managers increases accordingly.

- *Global strategy formulation and implementation skills.* The manager of a firm operating in more than one country needs to develop special skills to make the appropriate strategic choices about entering and competing successfully in the international arena. Standards of what is good or bad can vary dramatically from country to country, and you will also need to consider the ethical implications of your choices, which may be less apparent internationally.

sult of United Brands's $2.5 million bribe to Honduran government officials to reduce the banana tax. The law expressly forbids substantial payments by American firms to foreign officials to influence decisions. Many businesspeople believed that the act would put U.S. firms at a disadvantage overseas, but there is little evidence that this has occurred. It is possible that the legislation created a better image for American firms internationally, counterbalancing any losses.

Many firms and industry groups have developed their own code of conduct for foreign operations. For example, the American Apparel Manufacturers Association (AAMA), whose members include Sara Lee, Jockey International, and VF, requires members to pay the existing minimum wage, maintain certain minimum safety standards, and avoid the use of child labor. Nevertheless, as shown in Management Close-Up 2.g, many ethical issues remain uresolved when a firm goes overseas in search of cheaper labor. At the same time that globalization continues to increase dramatically, abuses by some multinational firms and governments have given globalization a bad name for many, even though it has improved the economic conditions of many countries around the world.

Competition to Make Products for Western Companies Has Revived an Old Form of Abuse: Debt Bondage

THEME: ETHICS Debt bondage means it is impossible to "get ahead" financially, because you owe too much money to others. There are many forms. In the U.S. it wasn't long ago that coal miners were forced to buy overpriced food from "company stores." Sharecroppers were trapped by their debts to landowners. Even today, many illegal Mexican immigrants are working to pay off debts to the so-called "coyotes" who smuggle them across the Rio Grande.

Unlike the coyotes, the Asian labor brokers to whom many workers are indebted operate in the open. Their services are sought by the factories importing foreign workers and are sanctioned by the governments that send and receive them. The labor trade they facilitate functions in the name of global competition. When Motorola, Ericsson, Nike, and other Western companies contract with Asian factories to produce cell phones and modems, sew clothes, or prepare leather for shoes, cost is a major factor. The globalization of manufacturing has been a tremendous boon to corporations, allowing them to seek the lowest-cost suppliers, wherever they may be.

Today the vast majority of suppliers reside in Asia, and the lowest costs on the continent are found in the new manufacturing mecca: China. What does that have to do with the labor trade? Everything. With its vast pool of cheap labor, China has proven to be irresistible to Western manufacturers, which have been flocking there since liberalization in the mid-1990s. As a result, factories that operate in countries such as Taiwan, South Korea, and Malaysia, which have higher labor costs, have been forced to scramble to compete. The solution they devised was to import workers from poor neighbors—Vietnam, Thailand, the Philippines—and sign them up for two- or three-year contracts. The cost savings are real: In Taiwan, for example, native factory workers earn between $600 and $850 a month, while their foreign co-workers get the minimum wage of $450 and are ineligible for raises and promotions. More-

Most foreign contract workers live in factory dorms near their jobs. Many suffer abuse, and the breakup of families left behind.

over, because they need the job to pay off labor brokers, overseas workers are less likely to complain about long hours or abusive supervisors. The logic has caught on: The number of foreign contract workers in Taiwan alone has doubled, to 316,000, in the past seven years.

Five years ago, the chief labor issue for American companies like Nike, Liz Claiborne, and Gap was the sweatshop conditions in supplier factories. In response to protests and boycotts, U.S. companies began to demand that factories meet basic health and safety standards and provide workers with facemasks, bathroom breaks, and well-ventilated workspaces. The debt bondage ensnaring many foreign workers in those factories may be creating an even larger ethical dilemma. In theory, engaging foreign contract workers is a solution that should benefit all parties: Poor countries reduce their unemployment; wealthy countries get cheaper labor; and the workers earn far more abroad than they could at home. In practice, however, the labor brokers have every incentive and opportunity to gouge the workers under their control.

Source: Adapted from N. Stein, "No Way Out," *Fortune,* January 20, 2003, pp. 102–108.

Applications for the Manager   Two major barriers preventing firms from capitalizing on business opportunities overseas are: (1) a lack of awareness about how to enter foreign markets and (2) how to operate in diverse national settings. Managers can learn how to function well in foreign lands by developing a better appreciation of the unique challenges that may confront them. Few firms today have the luxury of avoiding globalization. New managers should be groomed to play a key role in internationalization.

Applications for Managing Teams   Many firms are entering joint ventures with companies in other countries. Joint ventures usually require that employees from different nations work in teams. The success of joint ventures largely depends on the ability of international teams to work together in a climate of mutual respect. This requires not only a great deal of cross-cultural sensitivity but also an understanding of the international context in which the firm operates.

Applications for Individuals   The career mobility of an employee is likely to be enhanced if the individual has international skills. International savvy is increasingly valued, particularly by medium-sized to large firms that are expanding their foreign operations or that face foreign competition. Many firms require employees to have international experience before they can move into the upper management ranks. Your ability to function well internationally should improve your chances of assuming an important managerial role. Although some firms have not valued international experience in the past, its importance is rapidly increasing.

At the beginning of the chapter we posed some questions pertaining to Toyota's investments in the United States. Now that you had the opportunity to read the chapter, it is time to revisit those questions. Toyota's example shows that the distinction between domestic and foreign firms is increasingly becoming obsolete as firms capitalize on market and production opportunities beyond their home countries. Firms without a global vision are more likely to experience a major competitive disadvantage. In the case of Toyota, most of its market is in the United States. To compete effectively against domestic producers such as Chrysler and General Motors, Toyota considers that it is necessary to manufacture cars in the United States. This globalization of business is fueling unprecedented economic growth in many parts of the world.

The competitive landscape is more complex than ever, and globalization presents many additional challenges. This chapter has dealt with the unique issues and problems firms face in the global environment. Toyota has chosen to enter the United States as a wholly owned subsidiary. To gain the goodwill of the local population and ensure acceptance by American citizens, some of whom may react negatively to a foreign firm "taking over the town," Toyota spent an enormous amount of time and energy to support worthy causes and the local community. In this manner, the company can protect itself against potential backlash and the political risk that may ensue, such as higher taxes, difficulty in obtaining permits, restrictions to imported parts, and closer government supervision.

Finally, by hiring locally at all levels, Toyota has better information about local conditions. This works to reduce the costs associated with bringing Japanese employees to the United States, and to reduce potential culture clashes. The goal is to be perceived as a domestic firm that happens to have a foreign name.

Firms increasingly compete in a global market characterized by high uncertainty, many players, and great complexity. A lessening of U.S. dominance in the world economy and U.S. multinationals no longer controlling international business activities has created a global shift. Trade barriers are being dramatically reduced, economic markets are more integrated than ever, consumer preferences are becoming more uniform, and production of most commodities is spread out across many countries. Technological innovations fuel the internationalization process by expediting communications and decreasing the cost of managing across domestic boundaries. As internationalization increases, firms must deal effectively with cultural differences in order to remain competitive. Company leaders also need to develop a greater understanding of international differences in political economies, legal systems, and the economic environments because these can all affect the benefits, costs, and risks of operating in various countries.

There are several different ways firms can enter international markets. Each has advantages and disadvantages. The appropriateness of each depends on the overall business strategies of the firm and the nature of the business. An **exporting** mode is primarily used by firms entering international markets for the first time. In this mode, all manufacturing takes place within the domestic borders, which may result in foreign competitors enjoying significant cost advantages. The **turnkey** mode is used by firms that prefer to receive payment for designing and building a plant that is then handed over to locals. The **licensing** mode generates profits in the form of a fee or royalty by granting rights to manufacture and sell a product in another country. **Franchises** are similar to licensing, except that franchising is used primarily for services. **Joint ventures** and strategic alliances allow quick access to international markets by establishing new entities in conjunction with local firms. **Wholly owned subsidiaries** give a firm maximum control over the foreign facility, but the firm also incurs all the costs and risks of the foreign venture.

Firms can manage foreign subsidiaries by using personnel from the home office or expatriates (the **ethnocentric approach**), hiring individuals from each country in which subsidiaries are located (the **polycentric approach**), or recruiting personnel regardless of nationality (the **geocentric approach**). A problem with using expatriates is that the failure rate for foreign assignment can be high. Firms can develop human resource policies that help expatriates succeed.

Norms vary by country, and a major concern for firms operating internationally is defining ethical behavior. Although competitors may abide by a different set of rules, U.S. firms must comply with regulations that prohibit the payment of bribes. They may develop their own codes of conduct or may follow codes drawn up by international organizations.

1. If you were CEO of a medium-sized U.S. manufacturing firm, which of the changing patterns of international business identified in this chapter would concern you most? Explain.

2. Do you think there should be a large common market from Alaska to Tierra del Fuego, similar to the European Union? Why or why not?

3. Some observers note that the world's industrialized areas are becoming more alike every day. Do you agree? Why or why not?

4. What potential problems do you see in applying a power distance–uncertainty or similar framework to developing management programs that "fit" the cultural profile of particular countries?

5. If you were the owner of a small but rapidly growing high-tech firm making sophisticated computer chips for medical equipment, which mode of entry would you prefer for entering foreign markets? Explain.

6. Do you think an international firm should have local managers in all important posts? Why or why not?

7. Is a firm justified in paying a bribe if it believes a competitor will do so to win an important contract? Explain.

Kickbacks in Germany Spotlight U.S. Complaints

Swiss electrical-engineering company ABB AG filed a criminal complaint against Volkswagen officials over VW's alleged extortion of suppliers in exchange for lucrative contracts. VW says its internal auditors have found no evidence of a criminal conspiracy. The allegations arose as the United States attempted to end bribery. German authorities say they are generally unable to prevent business bribes, as their economy nurtures a culture of corruption. "The German criminal-justice system is kaput," says General Motors Corp. subcontractor Rolf Lagrange, who had blown the whistle on earlier extortion at GM's Adam Opel AG unit in 1995. As in the Opel investigation, flaws in Germany's legal system seem to support the practice:

> Demanding and accepting kickbacks is illegal, but paying them is considered a business expense and German companies can deduct this payment on their tax bills. In 1996 Germany changed the law, making the payments taxable as soon as they are part of a criminal complaint.

> Prosecutors can act on anonymous tips to investigate public officials, but a formal complaint (which companies prefer to avoid because of the resulting adverse publicity) must be lodged before they can investigate private-sector kickbacks.

> Public-sector corruption carries stiff penalties and is given a high priority; private-sector corruption is perceived as a problem that companies should deal with privately. Penalties for private-sector corruption, if they are assessed, are light.

Private-sector corruption cases are rarely uncovered and often dismissed or result in a plea bargain. Only if contracts are padded to cover the cost of kickbacks or bribes, resulting in fraud, will the penalties be more severe. In the sweeping 1995 Opel probe, 81 cases of 174 investigated were dropped for lack of evidence, 13 fines were assessed, and only 9 indictments resulted.

Discussion Questions

1. Do you think it is appropriate for a firm to pay bribes in a foreign country if it believes that is the only way to meet the competition on a level playing field? Explain.

2. Do you think it is important to draw the line between a business practice's being unethical and being illegal? Is this distinction more important in international business? Explain.

3. How can an international company protect itself against corruption of its employees overseas, when the definition of corruption may vary significantly from country to country?

Source: Adapted from B. Mitchener, "Germany Says Business Bribes on the Rise," *The Wall Street Journal,* April 14, 1997, p. A12.

What Ethical Responsibility Does a Multinational Company Have?

Li Tung International, one of Taiwan's largest labor brokerages, occupies the fifth floor of a low-rise building on the industrial outskirts of Taipei. The firm's general manager, Eric Chiang, has been in the business for 10 years. He has a fleet of luxury automobiles to show for his efforts, including a Porsche Boxster, a Lotus Elise, and a chauffeur-driven BMW sedan. Sitting in his well-appointed office one December afternoon, surrounded by fine art and antiques, Chiang acknowledges that other Taiwanese labor brokers may take advantage of foreign workers. He insists, however, that his firm charges only the legal limit. "We sign contracts with the Thai and Philippine governments," he says. "It is impossible that we charge higher than what the law requires." For a worker on a three-year contract, that limit is $1,725, about 10 percent of a worker's gross pay, collected in monthly installments.

The foreign workers under contract to Li Tung, however, tell a different story. *Fortune Magazine* spoke to more than a dozen, some in the company of their factory managers and others in the privacy of their dorms. All cited payments far in excess of the legal limit. At a tannery that provides leather to Nike for its athletic shoes, a young worker from Thailand says he is paying $2,100 for his three-year contract. At the plastics factory producing parts destined for Motorola, General Motors, Mercedes Benz, and others, a Thai worker says he is paying $2,900 on a two-year contract. And at a garment factory that supplies brassieres to the underwear giant Wacoal, a Filipina worker tells *Fortune* that she paid $2,900, all of it in the first 15 months, which meant monthly payments four times the legal limit. A Li Tung spokesman would not confirm these fees but says many workers return to the agency for a second contract, so they must find the terms acceptable.

Overcharging, it turns out, is an accepted business practice for labor brokers, and some are not afraid to admit it. In Manila, a labor broker from the D.A. Rodrigo agency said that her firm charges Taiwan-bound workers a $1,600 fee, equivalent to more than three months' salary, even though Philippine law prohibits a broker's fee from exceeding one month's wages. The laws are simply not enforced. In fact, the broker admitted overcharging during an interview that took place while she was waiting to file papers inside the Philippine Overseas Employment Administration, the government branch charged with protecting the interests of workers who go abroad. "One month's salary is not enough to maintain a business like this," says Salvador Curameng, a Manila labor broker who presides over the profession's trade association, the Asian Recruitment Council. "Once you dip your fingers into this market, you are committing to do something illegal."

Governments of nations importing labor are willing to look the other way because of what they get in return: The labor trade means that jobs and capital will stay in their countries and not get shipped to China. Nations that import labor also tailor their laws to keep local factories happy. To hold turnover to a minimum, governments allow factories to retain workers' passports, impose curfews, and deduct compulsory savings bonds—or "run-away insurance"—which workers get back only when they have completed their contract. In South Korea, which limits foreign laborers to a single three-year visit, workers are considered trainees their first two years, so they are exempt from most of the country's labor laws, including minimum wage and overtime. In an effort to aid Taiwan's slumping manufacturing sector, the government last year passed a law allowing factories to charge foreign workers for room and board.

Stranded in a foreign country with no knowledge of the local language or labor laws, lacking government protection, and restrained by debt, foreign contract workers are especially vulnerable to mistreatment. Unfortunately, this segment of the labor force is growing rapidly in many countries whose own people don't want to do the jobs that foreigners from poor nations are eager to take.

Discussion Questions

1. Do you think U.S. companies have the moral responsibility to fight exploitative practices in foreign countries, even if doing so means putting the company at a competitive disadvantage?

2. Many workers from poor countries continue to go to Taiwan and other countries as long as jobs remain scarce at home, even if they owe nearly everything to the labor brokers. If workers are eager to work abroad, and they believe that debt burdens and abuses are "lesser evils," are companies such as Nike, Motorola, and Ericsson (whose subcontractors rely on overseas contract workers) acting in a fair manner? Why or why not?

3. Some believe that the United States is hypocritical in its treatment of illegal immigrants. On the one hand, the economy needs cheap foreign labor, particularly in such sectors as hotels, restaurants, agriculture, and construction, which often means that immigration laws are laxly enforced. On the other hand, these foreign workers enjoy little legal protection. Explain your views on this matter.

Source: Adapted from N. Stein, "No Way Out," *Fortune*, January 20, 2003, pp. 102–108.

The New Cold War at Boeing

As the Soviet Union collapsed more than 12 years ago, Boeing started recruiting out-of-work Russian aerospace engineers to collaborate on space and commercial-airplane projects. At first, their numbers were small. The Russians did high quality work for as little as $5,400 a year which caused Boeing to begin to view its Russian staff as the vanguard of a new push into the European market. In 1998, Boeing opened its Moscow Design Center, which now boasts nearly 700 engineers. From the day the center opened, engineers at Boeing's Seattle hub voiced concerns. These fears are now boiling over.

Boeing's 22,000 engineers in Seattle, represented by the Society of Professional Engineering Employees in Aerospace (SPEEA), threatened to walk out in 2003 if the Russian venture wasn't cut back. Partly as a result, Boeing reduced its corps of Moscow engineers to about 350, though the company will not state the precise number. "The underlying fear is that we're giving away our technology and our competitive advantage, and we're losing jobs," says Dave Landress, a test engineer and union representative. The union has good reason for concern: Struggling to reduce costs to cope with the sharp falloff in orders from the ailing airline industry, Boeing had laid off 5,000 engineers in the prior two years. Still, Boeing has refused to yield entirely to the union's demands. It declined, for instance, to adopt tough new job-security language. The best the union could muster: a nonbinding letter acknowledging the concerns of both sides. And Boeing still plans to shift jobs to Russia in the future, company insiders say.

The strategy is to integrate the cheaper Russian engineers into the design process for everything Boeing makes. The Russian staff—spread over seven cities—already works on everything from redesigning jet-wing parts to designing components for the International Space Station. Boeing's other goal is to develop a 24-hour global workforce, made possible by satellite link from Russia to Boeing's Seattle office. "We have achieved substantial cost reductions on every airplane we deliver with the help of our Moscow team," Hank Queen, Boeing vice president for engineering, told SPEEA members recently.

It's not just lower pay that makes Russia so attractive. The company hopes a local presence will help to win Russian orders, although it hasn't thus far. Aeroflot recently weighed the pros and cons of the Boeing 737 versus the Airbus A320 and picked Airbus, which opened its own Russian design center last year and plans to hire 50 engineers. Still, given the savings, Boeing is likely to keep shifting work to Russia. This is certain to keep some engineers sleepless in Seattle.

Critical Thinking Questions

1. How does a multinational firm benefit from seeing the entire world as its labor pool? Do you see any potential problems with this vision? Why or why not?

2. Does a firm have a moral responsibility to support its domestic employees even if it is less expensive to rely on foreign labor? Why or why not?

3. If you were an employee such as Dave Landress in the case, what would you do to avoid being replaced by foreign labor?

Collaborative Learning Exercise

You have been appointed to a task force that advises the president of the United States on whether restrictions should be placed on U.S. firms' ability to outsource work abroad, replacing American workers. The task force (composed of three to five students) will provide its recommendations and reasoning to the president (played by the instructor).

Source: Reprinted with permission from S. Holmes and S. Ostrovsky, "The New Cold War at Boeing," *Business Week*, February 3, 2003, pp. 58–59.

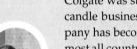

Colgate's Clean Sweep

Colgate was started in 1806 by an English immigrant who set up a starch, soap, and candle business on Dutch Street in New York. Form these humble origins the company has become one of the largest multinational corporations with operations in almost all countries of the world, despite its "low-tech" product line of toothpaste, razor blades, soaps, and shaving creams. Visit Colgate's website as well as other related Internet sites to answer the following questions:

1. What accounts for Colgate's international success, despite the potential for intense competition in most markets?

2. Colgate boasts that its "Colgate Culture" has a worldwide basis. How can a company create such a culture despite operating in many different cultural milieus? What are the advantages and disadvantages of a company culture that transcends national culture?

3. Compare and contrast the structure of Colgate's executive team with another company's, which you can research on the Internet. Analyze the implications of your comparison from an international perspective.

4. After researching Colgate, would you advise the company to engage in licensing patents, joint ventures, or strategic alliances, or to establish wholly owned subsidiaries? Explain your answer.

Careers in Global Management

Given the substantial increases in global business over the last decade, it has become increasingly important for managers and companies to understand the career aspirations of young managers. This questionnaire allows you to increase your understanding of your own career aspirations.

What Are Your Career Plans?
The following section asks you a number of questions about your career plans. In the questions:

Home country is your country of citizenship.

An *international assignment* is one in which the company sends an employee for a single assignment of a year or more to another country.

A *global career* is a series of international assignments in various countries.

International travel is a business trip to another country without the employee moving there.

An *expatriate* is an employee who is sent by the company to live and work in another country.

For each of the following items, rate the extent to which you agree:

1 = Disagree

2 = Don't have an opinion

3 = Agree

How true is each of the following statements for you?

1. I am seriously considering pursuing a global career. ____

2. I would like my first job after school to be in another country. ____

3. If offered an equivalent position in my home country or in the foreign country of my choice, I would rather work at home. ____

4. While continuing to live in my home country, I would like to travel internationally more than 40 percent (approximately 20 weeks/year) of my time. ____

5. I would like to have an international assignment at some time in my career. ____

6. I would like to follow a global career in which I have a series of international assignments. ____

7. I had never thought about taking an international assignment until I read this questionnaire. ____

There are many reasons why people choose not to pursue a global career. Which of the following would discourage you from pursuing a global career or taking an international assignment?

8. I like living in my home country. ____

9. I do not want to learn another language. ____

10. I do not want to adjust to another culture. ____

11. My spouse or significant other would not want to move to another country. ____

12. It is not good to move children. ____

13. I want my children to be educated in my home country. ____

14. I do not want to live in:

    a. A country outside my home country. ____

    b. North America. ____

    c. Europe. ____

    d. Latin or South America. ____

    e. Asia. ____

    f. Africa. ____

    g. The Middle East. ____

    h. My home country. ____

    i. Other (specify). ____

15. International jobs involve too much travel. ____

16. If I live in an another country, my children will not gain a sense of national identity. ____

17. My spouse or significant other would not want to interrupt his or her career. ____

18. I will lose my sense of identity, my roots. ____

19. International assignments put too much strain on a marriage. ____

20. When you are on an international assignment you become "invisible" to the company and tend to be forgotten for promotions. ____

21. It would be difficult to come back home after having lived and worked for a long time in another country. ____

22. I do not want to be exposed to political instability in some parts of the world. ____

23. I would be more socially isolated and lonely in another country. ____

24. I would be exposed to more personal danger in another country. ____

In comparing potential domestic and global careers, which do you think could give you the greatest professional opportunities? (Mark one)

	Domestic Career	About Same	Global Career
25. I could succeed faster in	____	____	____
26. I could earn a higher salary in	____	____	____
27. I could have greater status in	____	____	____
28. I could be more recognized for my work in	____	____	____
29. I could have a more interesting professional life in	____	____	____
30. I could have a more satisfying personal life in	____	____	____

In comparing women and men, who do you think will have the greater chance of being (Mark one)

	Women	Equal Chances	Men
31. Selected for an international assignment?	____	____	____
32. Effective on an international assignment?	____	____	____
33. Successful in advancing in a global career?	____	____	____
34. Effective on domestic assignments?	____	____	____
35. Successful in advancing in a domestic career?	____	____	____
36. Socially isolated and lonely in another country?	____	____	____
37. Exposed to personal danger in another country?	____	____	____

In Your Opinion

1. What are the main reasons that would lead you to accept an international assignment? List three.

2. What are the main reasons why you would turn down an international assignment? List three.

3. What, if any, are the major challenges for women successfully pursuing global careers that include international assignments (which do not exist for men)?

Source: From *International Dimensions of Organizational Behavior*, 3rd edition, by N. J. Adler © 1997. Reprinted with permission of South-Western College Publishing, a division of Thompson Learning.

THREE

Managing Social Responsibility and Ethics

chapter 3

After reading this chapter, you should be able to:

- Apply the four key ethical criteria that managers and employees should use when making business decisions.

- Understand why businesses establish codes of ethics as a method of guiding employee conduct.

- Recognize ways to encourage ethical behavior in business.

- Make ethical decisions in morally challenging situations.

- Value corporate social responsibility.

- Understand the influence of various stakeholders on a company's priorities, policies, plans and goals.

No Sweat for Levi Strauss

Few companies take ethics and social responsibility as seriously as Levi Strauss and Co. In 1992 the values of this clothing manufacturer were put to the test by two sewing subcontractors in Bangladesh that were using child labor. Child labor was unacceptable to the company, but without jobs, some of the children would be forced into prostitution to support their families. The management team at Levi Strauss devised a unique solution: they took the children out of the factory, continued to pay their wages so long as they attended school full time, and guaranteed the children factory jobs when they reached age 14, the local age of maturity.

Levi Strauss began finding ways to blend profitability and social responsibility during the Great Depression. Instead of firing employees when demand for products decreased, the company kept workers busy laying new floors in its San Francisco offices until business improved. Levi Strauss sustains its corporate goals by encouraging both employees and managers to make ethical and socially responsible business decisions. Strategies that are used include:

1. Donations of 2.5 percent of pretax profits to the Levi Strauss Foundation, which supports charitable organizations in the communities in which the company operates.

2. A week-long ethical decision-making course that is a requirement for every employee. Managers learn to consider ethical challenges when making decisions.

3. Evaluating and rewarding managers using ethical and socially responsible criteria. Peers, subordinates, and customers provide input into the performance evaluations of managers.

4. The company founded and continues to be closely associated with Project Change, an independent nonprofit organization that combats racism in Albuquerque, New Mexico, El Paso, Texas, Knoxville, Tennessee, and Valdosta, Georgia. Project Change includes Fair Lending Centers in New Mexico and Georgia.

These actions have not kept Levi Strauss from being profitable. The company remains a global leader in the apparel industry, and its blue jeans and Dockers line are among the best-recognized brands. The company has consistently been one of the most admired

www.levistrauss.com

corporations in *Fortune* magazine's poll of top executives and was ranked second in the magazine's list of the 50 best companies for minorities in 2000.

Eric Frumin, health and safety director for the Union of Needletrades, Industrial and Textiles Employees, notes that Levi Strauss has developed an ergonomics program that reduced injuries while saving money. "These employers are already dealing with workers' injuries, quickly and effectively. They are not fighting over the definition," said Frumin.

Sources: S. Sherman, "Levi's: As Ye Sew, So Shall Ye Reap," *Fortune,* May 12, 1997, pp. 104–116: Natasha Sharpley, "Levi's Mends the Social Fabric," *Fortune,* July 10, 2000, p. 194; L. Strope, "Forum Addresses Workplace Safety," Associated Press, July 16, 2001.

CRITICAL THINKING QUESTIONS

1. *What benefits does Levi Strauss receive by focusing attention on corporate social responsibility?*

2. *Organizational stakeholders are groups that have an interest in how a company performs or uses its resources. Which organizational strategy most closely corresponds to how Levi Strauss manages relationships with diverse stakeholder groups? Is it a proactive approach or an accommodation approach?*

It's a tricky world out there. Consequently, ethics and social responsibility should be a high priority for every member of an organization. This chapter examines the nature of business ethics and the basis of ethical decisions. It presents codes of ethics and provides examples of ethical challenges you are likely to encounter as an employee or a manager in a business setting. Skills for Managing 3.1 lists the management skills related to business ethics and social responsibility.

Next, the broader context of corporate social responsibility as well as the key stakeholders involved are examined. The goal is to help you gain a heightened awareness of the many ethical challenges that are present in the new millennium.

What Are Business Ethics?

Ethics are principles that explain what is right or wrong, good or bad, and what is appropriate or inappropriate in various settings. These ideas make it possible to prescribe a code of behavior for both work and one's personal life. **Business ethics** provide standards or guidelines for the conduct and decision making of employees and managers. Without a code of

ethics

Principles that explain what is good and right and what is bad and wrong and that prescribe a code of behavior based on these definitions.

business ethics

Standards or guidelines for the conduct and decision making of employees and managers.

SKILLS FOR MANAGING ETHICS AND SOCIAL RESPONSIBILITY

What management skills are needed to make ethical decisions and to deal with the concerns of stakeholders with diverse interests in the company?

- *Ethical decision-making skills.* From time to time, every businessperson faces an ethical dilemma that is difficult to solve. Your solution may cause other people to become angry or resentful. You will need to be able to see beyond your own self-interest. One decision can enhance your reputation as a manager or detract from it. Even if you do not engage in unethical practices, a coworker or a subordinate may. How you deal with unethical behavior will be likely to influence your reputation.

In this chapter, guidelines for ethical decision making are discussed. You can practice these skills in various situations.

- *Analyzing stakeholder concerns.* Stakeholders are people with interests in how a company performs and how it uses its resources. It is important to be proactive in dealing with stakeholder issues. First, identify who the stakeholders are along with how they are affected by company policies, how they have been treated in the past, and then you will know how they can affect your ability to pursue business goals.

ethics, there is usually no consensus regarding ethical principles. Different people will use different ethical criteria in determining whether a practice or behavior is ethical or unethical. For example, it is not unusual for a manager to exaggerate the positive accomplishments of an employee in order to promote the employee or provide a big salary increase. Another manager may consider inflating an employee's performance record a distortion of the truth, and thus unethical conduct.

Business ethics are not the same thing as laws. Law and ethics are in agreement in some situations but not in others. For example, it is both illegal and unethical to steal merchandise from an employer, but often it is not illegal to engage in conduct that is unethical. While it may not be illegal to take credit for the work of a colleague, it is highly unethical. Unfortunately, more than a few individuals have engaged in such tactics in order to advance in their careers. When an organization does not condemn this behavior, others are encouraged to imitate them. Soon the organization develops a culture of political back-stabbing that drives away the most talented people and drains the energies of those who remain.

Nearly half the workers surveyed in a recent study admitted to engaging in at least one unethical act during the previous year. The most frequent unethical behaviors included cutting corners on quality, covering up potentially damaging incidents, abusing or lying about sick days, and lying to or deceiving customers. The workers blamed such daily pressures as trying to balance work and family, being forced to work longer hours due to layoffs, and poor communications for their behavior. They felt that ethical dilemmas could be reduced by better communication and a serious commitment by managers to establishing ethical standards of conduct.[1]

Ethics Approaches

People utilize different ethical value systems. These systems are based on personal experiences along with religious, educational, and family training. One manager might consider it beneficial to downsize a company's workforce because the surviving employees, who make up the majority, will be employed by a more effective and efficient firm. Another manager might view a downsizing decision as being unethical because the employees who lose their jobs are deprived of economic opportunities simply because it is cost effective. The different ethical value systems of the two managers lead them to place different judgments on the attractiveness or repulsiveness of downsizing.

Managers typically use one of four key ethical approaches when making business decisions. They are utilitarianism, individualism, the rights approach, and the justice approach. Each involves a different view of what is most important to individuals and society.

Utilitarianism

utilitarianism

A means of making decisions based on what is good for the greatest number of people.

Decisions should be made on the basis of what is good for the greatest number of people from a **utilitarian** perspective. To apply the utilitarian criterion, one would examine all the people affected by a decision and choose the solution that satisfies the most people. Utilitarianism is sometimes referred to as the "calculus of pain," because it tries to minimize pain and maximize pleasure for the greatest number of people. Although utilitarianism strives to attain the ideal of democracy by promoting good for the majority, it may overlook the rights or needs of a minority of individuals.

Individualism

individualism

The degree to which a society values personal goals, autonomy, and privacy over group loyalty, commitment to group norms, involvement in collective activities, social cohesiveness, and intense socialization; ethical decisions based on individualism promote individual self-interest as long as it does not harm others.

People who base ethical decisions on **individualism** believe that personal self-interests should be promoted as long as they do not harm others. Individualism as a basis for making business decisions is derived from the principles of capitalism first expressed in the eighteenth century by Adam Smith. In *The Wealth of Nations,* Smith wrote that markets should be free, that they should be the basis of all transactions, and that they should be subject to a minimum of interference by other forces such as governments. All available information is utilized when individuals make economic choices. Lying and other unethical behavior are penalized because it is in people's self-interest to do business with ethical firms and individuals rather than with liars and cheats.

At the same time, the costs of obtaining information about individuals' or firms' motives may be steep, and there are differences in power between individuals bargaining in the market. In such cases, some individuals can take advantage of their power or access to information to the detriment of others. For example, American consumers of health care have less power than insurance companies and have little access to specific information on the implications of choosing one policy or one doctor over another. Citizens of France, Germany, and Sweden believe individualism has resulted in the lack of a national health care plan for U.S. citizens. Consequently, they believe, the weakest members of society are the ones who suffer the most.

Rights Approach

The belief that each person has fundamental human rights that should be respected and protected is the **rights approach.** People have the rights of freedom of speech, privacy, and due process when charged with a crime or rule infraction. They also have the right to a safe and healthy environment. These rights make it possible for them to act in their own best interests, which in turn benefits society. According to the rights approach, a decision is unethical if it deprives an individual of fundamental human rights.

rights approach

A means of making decisions based on the belief that each person has fundamental human rights that should be respected and protected.

The rights approach provides specific criteria for judging the ethics of a decision; however, conflicting rights must often be sorted out when making business decisions. For example, a manager who shares negative information about personal problems experienced by a former employee with another employer who is considering hiring that individual, exercises the right of free speech but may also have violated the employee's right to privacy. Whose rights should have priority?

Justice Approach

Treating all people fairly and consistently when making decisions is the basis of the **justice approach.** This includes considering both distributive and procedural justice. *Distributive justice* examines the fairness of rewards, punishments, and outcomes in an organization. It asks whether an employee received compensation equitable with performance or whether the employee was overpaid or underpaid. *Procedural justice* involves the fair and consistent application of rules and procedures. When an employee is disciplined for a safety rule infraction, the procedural justice standard would be violated if other employees who broke the rule were not similarly disciplined.

justice approach

An approach to decision making based on treating all people fairly and consistently when making business decisions.

The justice approach is more flexible than other ethical approaches, because it recognizes that standards of fairness vary depending on the individuals involved in the decision. For example, unionized auto workers see equal raises for all workers as the fair way to distribute salary increases.

After working at Andersen his entire life, Joseph Berardino, former CEO of Andersen Worldwide, found himself in the midst of 2002's biggest accounting scandal. His focus on revenue growth, and his auditors' stamp of approval on the cooked books of Enron, Qwest Communications, and WorldCom, caused the crumbling of the partnership.

Equality raises union solidarity. Managers consider rewarding people on the basis of individual performance as fair, because they believe rewards should be based on the workers' contributions to profitability.

Applications of Ethics Approaches

To see how the four approaches to ethical decision making differ, consider the policy of random drug testing. A utilitarian sees random drug testing as ethical because more employees and customers are protected from accidents caused by drug-using employees than are angered by having to submit to random drug tests. Random drug testing would also be perceived as ethical when applying the criterion of individualism: owners are free to enact policies that make the company more efficient, and employees are free to exercise their disapproval by quitting and seeking employment at a firm that does not require random drug testing.

On the other hand, a manager who applies the rights approach may consider random drug testing unethical because it violates an employee's right to privacy and the right of protection from searches without probable cause to justify the test. Similarly, random drug testing would be seen as unethical in the justice approach because it presumes that an employee is guilty of using drugs and makes employees prove that they are innocent based on the chemical analysis of body fluids. In American justice, a person is innocent unless proven guilty.

Codes of Ethics

When there is a void of ethical guidelines in a company, employees rely on personal value systems. Creating a more standardized approach can be accomplished by developing a code of ethics.

A **code of ethics** is a formal statement of ethics and values that is designed to guide employee conduct in a variety of business situations. It is particularly useful for giving employees ways to deal with conflicts of interest, gift giving and receiving, communicating with competitors, and making political contributions. More than 90 percent of large U.S. companies and almost half of smaller firms have established codes of ethics.[2] Codes are typically published as either corporate credos or ethical policy statements. Also, many professions, such as doctors, lawyers, engineers, literary agents, and college professors, have codes of ethics.

code of ethics

A formal statement of ethics and values that is designed to guide employee conduct in a variety of business situations.

Corporate Credos

A **corporate credo** details a company's responsibility to its stakeholders. *Stakeholders* are groups or individuals with vested interests in the performance of the enterprise, including how managers distribute company resources. Stakeholders include employees, customers, and shareholders. The corporate credo focuses on principles and beliefs that can provide direction in a variety of ethically challenging situations.

corporate credo

A formal statement focusing on principles and beliefs, indicating the company's responsibility to its stakeholders.

The credo of Johnson & Johnson is reproduced in Figure 3.1 As shown, the company identifies its responsibilities to consumers, employees, communities, and stockholders. This led to an extraordinary response to a difficult situation in the 1980s. When a criminal put capsules laced with cyanide in Tylenol bottles and some customers died as a result of taking the tainted medicine, Johnson & Johnson immediately took Tylenol off the market until it could be reissued in tamper-proof packaging. The credo was one factor that helped Johnson & Johnson effectively handle the crisis.

Ethical Policy Statements

Sometimes a credo is not specific enough for a large company that faces complex ethical challenges in many different markets and cultures. In such situations, more concrete guidelines on ethical conduct are needed. **Ethical policy statements** provide specific formulas for employee conduct. They answer such questions as whether a salesperson may offer a gift to a good customer, how much technical information can be shared with a competitor, whether an executive may purchase company stock in advance of a proposed merger, and whether the company can award a franchise to a relative of an employee.

ethical policy statements

A firm's formal guidelines that provide specific formulas for employees' ethical conduct.

Numerous companies have adopted ethical policy statements that inform employees of acceptable standards of conduct. Examples of such employers include:

1. St. Paul Companies, which specializes in commercial and personal insurance, and states that employees may accept gifts of inexpensive pens or appointment diaries, but not liquor, lavish entertainment, travel, or clothing.[3]

FIGURE 3.1

Johnson & Johnson Corporate
Credo

Source: Reprinted with
permission of Johnson & Johnson,
www.jnj.com.

Our Credo

We believe our first responsibility is to the doctors, nurses, and patients,
to mothers and fathers and all others who use our products and services.
In meeting their needs everything we do must be of high quality.
We must constantly strive to reduce our costs in order to maintain reasonable prices.
Customers' orders must be serviced promptly and accurately.
Our suppliers and distributors must have an opportunity to make a fair profit.

We are responsible to our employees,
the men and women who work with us throughout the world.
Everyone must be considered as an individual.
We must respect their dignity and recognize their merit.
They must have a sense of security in their jobs.
Compensation must be fair and adequate, and working conditions clean, orderly and safe.
We must be mindful of ways to help our employees fulfill their family responsibilities.
Employees must feel free to make suggestions and complaints.
There must be equal opportunity for employment, development
and advancement for those qualified.
We must provide competent management, and their actions must be just and ethical.

We are responsible to the communities in which we live and work
and to the world community as well.
We must be good citizens – support good works and charities and bear our fair share of taxes.
We must encourage civic improvements and better health and education.
We must maintain in good order the property we are privileged to use,
protecting the environment and natural resources.

Our final responsibility is to our stockholders.
Business must make a sound profit.
We must experiment with new ideas.
Research must be carried on, innovative programs developed and mistakes paid for.
New equipment must be purchased, new facilities provided and new products launched.
Reserves must be created to provide for adverse times.
When we operate according to these principles, the stockholders should realize a fair return.

Johnson & Johnson

2. Eli Lilly and Company, a pharmaceutical firm, in which employees may not conduct business with a company with which they or their relatives are associated, unless Eli Lilly has given specific approval and authorization.[4]

3. General Dynamics Corporation, a defense-industry contractor, where employees may not use or share inside information that is not available to the general public for personal gain.[5]

4. J. D. Edwards and Company, a software firm, which prohibits profanity, as well as racial and sexual slurs. Instead, language should convey a loving, caring, and sensitive attitude toward other people.[6]

Managing Ethics

Is it possible to actually change the ways in which employees behave? Many organizational leaders, who are interested in creating more ethical climates, believe the answer is "yes." To do so means establishing a corporate culture in which ethical behavior is the norm. Among the approaches that are available are ethics training, ethical structures, and whistleblower policies.

Ethics Training

Ethics training gives employees and managers the opportunity to actually practice handling the ethical dilemmas they are likely to experience. More than 40 percent of large U.S. companies provide **ethics training** to their employees. Most courses contain the following elements:

1. Messages from top executives emphasizing ethical business practices.
2. Discussion of codes of ethics.
3. Procedures for discussing or reporting unethical behavior.

Ethics training at aircraft manufacturer Boeing provides an excellent model for other firms. Led by the business ethics adviser of the division involved, it includes a customized videotape with an opening message by the division's general manager and the presentation of dramatic and routine situations.

At Matsushita, a large Japanese consumer electronics company, ethics training emphasizes treating customers with dignity and respect. Manager's Notes 3.1 on business ethics in Japan provides examples of ethical values instilled in Japanese employees at Matsushita.

ethics training

A means of providing employees and managers practice in handling ethical dilemmas that they are likely to experience.

Ethical Structures

Ethical guidelines are one component of an **ethical structure.** The other is the division or department that is assigned the responsibility of overseeing those guidelines. These two elements must be carefully coordinated.

One type of ethical structure uses an *ethics officer* with a title like "director of ethics compliance." This individual deals with potential ethical violations and advises decision makers regarding ways to comply with the company's code of ethics. This is the case at General Dynamics Corporation, which established an ethical structure in the 1980s after being sanctioned for overcharging the military for defense contract work. Currently 40 divisional ethics program directors report to the corporate director of ethics, and they operate 30 hotlines over which employees can request information or counsel and report incidents of potential misconduct.

ethical structure

The procedures and the division or department within a company that promotes and advocates ethical behavior.

Business Ethics in Japan: The Case of Matsushita

Business ethics have international dimensions. In large Japanese firms, business ethics blend Confucian philosophy—the basis of Asian values—with capitalist values. Here are some examples of ethical principles taught to employees at Matsushita, the world's largest consumer electronics company, with headquarters in Osaka, Japan.

- Treat people you do business with as if they were part of your family. Prosperity depends on how much understanding one receives from the people with whom one conducts business.

- After-sales service is more important than assistance before sales. It is through such service that one gets permanent customers.

- Don't sell customers goods that they are attracted to. Sell them goods that will benefit them.

- To be out of stock is careless. If this happens, apologize to the customers, ask for their address, and tell them that you will deliver the goods immediately.

- It is not enough to work conscientiously. No matter what kind of job, you should think of yourself as being completely in charge of and responsible for your own work.

- If we cannot make a profit, that means we are committing a sort of crime against society. We take society's capital, we take their people, we take their materials, yet without a good profit, we are using precious resources that could be better used elsewhere.

Source: Adapted from J. P. Kotter, "Matsushita: The World's Greatest Entrepreneur," *Fortune,* March 31, 1997, pp. 105–110.

Another ethical structure approach is to have senior-level managers from different functions and units serve on an *ethics committee* that provides ethical oversight and policy guidance for management decisions. Dow Corning's business conduct committee conducts ethical audits of company plants on a worldwide basis. An auditor from the committee interviews managers and other employees to determine whether the ethical code is being followed and the kinds of violations that are occurring. The auditor of a sales unit, for example, looks for kickbacks or inappropriate gifts given or received, while the auditor of a manufacturing unit focuses on environmental pollution. Universities also use ethics committees, which focus on allegations of such unethical conduct as faking research data and situations in which a faculty member plagiarizes the work of students or colleagues.

Whistleblower Policies

Employees who are willing to disclose illegal, immoral, or illegitimate practices by their employer require the protection of a **whistleblower policy**.[7] Companies with whistleblower policies rely on individual employees to report unethical activities to the ethics officer or committee, which then gathers facts and investigates the situation in a fair and impartial manner. Whistleblower policies protect these individuals from retaliation by executives or coworkers whose practices have been exposed. In situations in which whistleblower policies are not present, employees face many obstacles. For example, the quality control officers for the Trans Alaska Pipeline were threatened with actual physical harm and demotion, and were victims of spying, as other employees attempted to keep them from reporting problems that might lead to oil spills.[8]

While the federal government and some states have enacted laws to protect whistleblowers from retaliation, there is scant protection for those who report unethical activities that are not specified in the laws. A whistleblower policy provides a communication channel to report unethical activities. Whistleblower policies should include the following key features:

1. The policy encourages reporting unethical conduct and sets up meaningful procedures to deal fairly with reported violations.

2. Those who report violations are protected from retaliation. Even if an informant is incorrect about the alleged wrongdoing, the protection is extended as long as the informant acted in good faith in making the complaint.

3. Alternative reporting procedures are provided in cases where those to whom the report must be given are involved in the wrongdoing.

4. A provision is made for anonymous reporting to an ethics officer or committee.

5. Feedback on ethics violations is provided to employees so that they are aware that the policy is being taken seriously and that complaints are being investigated.

6. Top management supports and is involved in the whistleblower policy.[9]

The recent financial scandals at Enron and WorldCom have put the whistleblowers, who tried to report the misconduct of executives at these firms, in the limelight.[10] In 2001, Enron executive Sherron Watkins wrote a blunt memo to Enron CEO Kenneth Lay warning him that the company might "implode in a wave of accounting scandals." Instead of thanking her, management factions tried to squelch the bad news and intimidate her for not being a team player. After the financial scandal broke and became a media event, Watkins was congratulated for her

whistleblower policies
A method by which employees who disclose their employer's illegal, immoral, or illegitimate practices can be protected; companies with whistleblower policies rely on whistleblowers to report unethical activities to the ethics officer or committee, which will then gather facts and investigate the situation in a fair and impartial way.

 What is Your Primary Conflict-Handling Style?

Enron Executive Sherron Watkins reported financial misconduct as a whistle-blower.

courage in confronting a CEO about Enron's controversial off-the-books partnerships and shaky finances. She serves as a positive role model for whistleblowers.[11]

Personal Ethics

Ethical decisions are among the most difficult decisions you will ever have to make. When one presents itself, allow yourself plenty of time to consider the alternatives. Examine the consequences as well as the proposed procedures established to arrive at the outcome. Think about how the decision would look if it were made public in the company newsletter. Make sure you consider all the people who are directly or indirectly affected by the decision. It is a good idea to get feedback from a trusted friend or colleague before you act.

Manager's Notes 3.2 lists eight steps you can take to make sound ethical business decisions.

The U.S. military has recognized the importance of having officers set examples for enlisted personnel and holds officers to a higher standard of conduct. Officers who disobey a command or act unethically face

Eight Steps to Sound Ethical Decision Making in Business

1. *Gather the facts.* Avoid jumping to conclusions without having the facts available to you. Consider the following questions: How did the situation occur? Are there historical facts I should know? Are there facts concerning the current situation I should know?

2. *Define the ethical issues.* Identify the ethical values at stake in this problem. Sometimes two important values are in conflict. For example, the right to privacy may conflict with the right to expect a safe workplace. Is there a code of ethics that suggests which values have the highest priority?

3. *Identify the affected parties.* Start with the parties directly affected by the outcome of the decision. Next, think broadly and include other parties who may also be affected, such as employees in other units, people in the community, or customers. How would your decision affect all these parties?

4. *Identify the consequences.* Think about the consequences for all the parties that you have identified. What is the probability of each different consequence for each party? Do you see any highly negative consequences that must be avoided? What are the short-term and long-term consequences of the decision?

5. *Identify your obligations.* Identify the obligations you feel and the reasons for each. For example, did you make a promise to another employee that you could be in jeopardy of breaking? Is your duty at odds with keeping your word to this person? Can you justify making an exception for this decision? Since we each enact numerous roles (as employee, leader, parent, spouse, volunteer, etc.), we are bound to have role conflicts that force us to favor one role over another for a given situation. It is important to be aware of all our obligations when considering a decision.

6. *Consider your character and integrity.* How would others judge your character and integrity if they knew all the facts about the decision that you were about to make? Would you feel good about disclosing your decision to a newspaper that would be read by the members of your community? If you would be ashamed of disclosing your decision to others, perhaps you should rethink your decision so that you feel more comfortable with it when scrutinized by others.

7. *Think creatively about potential actions.* Perhaps there are limitations on your ability to develop good alternatives to your ethical problem. Are they caused by your own personal interest in the outcome of the decision, such as ego or the possibility of a reward? Are your motives honorable? Get the input of others when you perceive such limitations.

8. *Check your gut feelings.* After you make a decision, check your gut feelings. Intuition can be very useful in sorting out problematic decision alternatives. If you are uncomfortable, something is probably not right. Check your responses to the earlier steps in the decision process to make sure you did not skip a step or ignore some important information.

Source: Adapted from L. K. Trevino and K. A. Nelson, *Managing Business Ethics,* 2nd ed. New York: John Wiley & Sons, 1999, pp. 71–75.

harsh sanctions. Managers set the tone for employees through their actions and by their examples. If a manager's behavior conflicts with the company's code of ethics, employees may decide to disregard the code of ethics.

 Ethics

Managers can influence the ethical behavior of those within their units in the following ways:

1. Take actions that develop trust, such as sharing useful information and making good on commitments.
2. Act consistently, so that employees are not surprised by unexpected management actions or decisions.
3. Be truthful and avoid white lies and other actions designed to manipulate people by giving a false impression.
4. Demonstrate integrity by keeping confidences and showing concern for others.
5. Meet with employees to discuss and define what is expected of them.
6. Ensure that employees are treated equitably, giving equivalent rewards for similar performance and avoiding actual or apparent special treatment of favorites.
7. Adhere to clear standards that are seen as just and reasonable—for example, neither praising accomplishments out of proportion nor imposing penalties disproportionate to offenses.
8. Respect employees, showing openly that you care about employees and recognize their strengths and contributions.[12]

In addition, Manager's Notes 3.3 includes approaches for ensuring that a climate for ethical conduct is maintained on your team.

Ethical Dilemmas in the Workplace

The workplace presents a variety of ethical challenges to managers, teams, and employees. Four examples of ethical dilemmas at work are: (1) performance appraisals, (2) employee discipline, (3) romantic relationships, and (4) gift giving.

Performance Appraisal

Performance appraisal is a formal evaluation of an employee's performance provided on a recurring basis. Typically, an employee receives feedback regarding his or her strengths and weaknesses in a document summarizing the employee's performance over the period of evaluation, which is usually one year. In most cases, the individual providing the performance appraisal is the supervisor. More specific information about performance appraisals is presented in Chapter 10 (Human Resource Management).

Tips for Managing the Ethical Climate of Teams

Here are some practical ways for improving the ethical climate governing the conduct of employees on your team:

1. Agree on a code of ethical conduct that the team expects from all members.
2. Require that all new team members learn the code of ethical conduct.
3. Integrate ethics into the team performance evaluations so that there is accountability for ethical conduct.
4. Recognize and reward ethical behavior in team members.
5. Ensure that unethical behavior is not tolerated by the team.
6. From time to time let team members explain how they handled an ethical dilemma so that others can benefit from this experience.
7. Use surveys to find out the ethical concerns of customers that the team serves.
8. Find the ethical concerns of other teams and units of your organization and share this information with your team members.

Source: Adapted From R. L. Daft, *Leadership: Theory and Practice:* Fort Worth: Dryden Press, 1999, p. 379.

In order to do an effective job at evaluation, the supervisor should devote substantial time to collecting accurate performance information. This feedback will be used to let employees know which skills they have mastered and those which require improvement. Performance ratings are also used as the basis for pay increases, future work assignments, promotions, and sometimes layoffs. So it is crucial to collect accurate and fair information. Managers who deliberately provide false or misleading information for reasons of vengeance, dislike of a subordinate, or racial or sexual discrimination are violating ethical and legal standards.

Employee Discipline

One tool that managers use to change an employee's behavior when it does not meet expectations or when it is inappropriate is the discipline system. An example of a behavior that fails to meet expectations is when an employee arrives late to work without a reasonable excuse. An illustration of inappropriate employee conduct requiring immediate intervention would be when a server in a restaurant uses profanity or verbally attacks a customer.

Supervisors can misuse discipline by making it a way to intimidate employees they do not like or for retribution when an employee makes a mistake. When a supervisor uses employee discipline for purposes of revenge rather than to correct an inappropriate behavior, the abuse of power is of course unethical. The following are examples of unethical employee discipline.

- Closely monitoring the behavior of a disliked employee, looking for the opportunity to use discipline to punish the employee, while giving more slack to employees who are not on the supervisor's "hit list."
- Using rumors and unsubstantiated evidence as a basis to apply discipline to a targeted employee without giving the employee an opportunity to defend his or her conduct.

Such examples suggest that the application of employee discipline requires some basic guidelines to protect employees from being victimized by supervisors. Here are some basic guidelines for giving employee discipline in a fair and impartial way.

1. *Notify* employees in advance of a company's work rules and the consequences for violating them. An employee who violates a work rule should be given the opportunity to correct the behavior without being punished.

2. *Investigate* the facts of an employee's misconduct before applying discipline. Give an employee the opportunity to give his or her side of the story before a decision is made about whether the misconduct actually took place.

3. *Be consistent* in the response to rule violations. Discipline should be administered consistently without favoritism or discrimination.

Office Romance

Romance often blossoms in the workplace. People who spend time together are likely to develop romantic feelings. Unfortunately, when a romantic relationship ends, as many of them do, one partner may feel angry and abandoned. A broken relationship can be highly disruptive to people who are simply trying to focus on work. Co-workers may even be drawn into the conflict which can strain working relations if the unit requires a high degree of collaboration between employees.

Further, when romantic partners are publicly affectionate in front of customers or other employees, it makes some people uncomfortable. Public displays of affection are almost always inappropriate. Jealousy or suspicion may result, if someone else has romantic intentions toward the co-worker involved, or if it is a boss involved in the romance. Subordinates may suspect that the boss is being manipulated by his or her romantic partner and showing favoritism as a result. The supervisor's credibility may be undermined in the eyes of subordinates.

Few companies actually ban romantic relationships in the workplace. However, many try to provide basic rules of conduct regarding office romances. Employees should be sensitive not only to the feelings of the partner in the relationship but also to co-workers and customers who may be affected by the couple's behavior. Here are two basic suggestions for ethical employee conduct in a romantic relationship at the workplace.

- Public displays of affection at the workplace should be discouraged.
- Employees should be prohibited from dating people they directly supervise. If a romance begins, one or the other partner should be transferred.

Giving Gifts in the Workplace

Gift giving routinely occurs in the workplace. Employees often exchange gifts with each other during the Christmas holidays, managers give flowers to their secretaries on special occasions, and vendors customarily give merchandise such as coffee mugs or pens to prospective customers. These situations represent constructive gift giving to build relationships between people by letting them know they are appreciated.

Sometimes, however, by accepting a gift from a vendor or employee a person faces an ethical dilemma. A test of the ethical appropriateness of accepting the gift would be to first think about how a manager or co-worker would perceive the gift and the person who gave it. If you would feel uncomfortable explaining the gift, the discomfort probably means it would be ethically problematic. Here are some examples of situations where it would be clearly unethical to give or accept gifts:

- A vendor seeking to develop a business relationship with a company may offer to provide lucrative financial opportunities to the executive in charge of purchasing, expecting to influence the executive to buy the vendor's product. The vendor is, in fact, using the gift as a bribe. The executive may be unduly influenced to purchase inferior goods. Closing deals with bribes probably means the products cannot compete in the marketplace. For example, several executives at Qwest, one of the major U.S. telecommunications companies, received valuable stock options from some smaller suppliers of Internet gear, and later steered large contracts to those companies. After the financial scandal was exposed, it became clear that Qwest executives made purchasing decisions based on who gave them stock options, not on the best equipment. One of the former members of Qwest's board of directors called the practice of suppliers giving stock options as an enticement an "ethical nightmare."[13]
- In part of a larger investigation of employee misconduct at A. T. Kearney Inc., a management consulting firm, it was revealed that CEO Fred Steingraber used funds from his personal expense account to purchase gifts for family members. Steingraber used

company funds to purchase a laptop computer for his son, and paid $37,000 for a lavish 50th birthday party for his wife, complete with a magician and surprise visits from her sisters, who were flown in from Germany. In defense of his spending for his wife's birthday, Steingraber stated that the party was also attended by executives from A. T. Kearney customers who would later purchase consulting services from the firm.[14] Inviting potential customers to a birthday party for the CEO's wife in order to influence their purchasing decisions is probably more than merely inappropriate. It may have been criminal.

A common approach companies use to avoid conflicts of interest in gift giving is to have a gift policy that limits the dollar value to a modest amount, such as $25 dollars. The policy may also require that each employee fully disclose each gift that is given and received along with its dollar value.

In cultures outside the United States, especially in developing economies, the laws and ethics related to giving gifts between parties as a business practice are highly diverse. In the African nation of Senegal, 40 percent of executives were reported to believe that bribery was necessary to obtain a public contract.[15] Managers seeking to do business within foreign cultures that are more tolerant of bribery and kickbacks may wish to avoid the temptation of using these practices, even if it means losing some business. Companies in countries with laws against giving bribes still face ethical challenges related to gift giving. For example, there is a tradition in the pharmaceutical industry of allowing sales representatives to give free samples of drugs to doctors. Police in Verona, Italy, opened an investigation of this practice by GlaxoSmithKline. They discovered a scheme that went beyond giving free samples to doctors. Company sales representatives gave gifts such as computers and lavish trips to doctors in exchange for writing of prescriptions for the company's drugs.[16] Such a "race to the bottom" of the ethical yardstick in order to win a foreign business contract is not worth the price, because public disclosure of this form of gift giving harms a company's reputation. A tarnished company reputation is nearly impossible to repair.

The Corruption Perceptions Index for 2002 displayed in Table 3.1 indicates the perceptions of corruption that occur in the 10 least corrupt (with high index numbers) and the 10 most corrupt countries (with low index numbers). It was based on a survey of international managers and academics. As shown, the United States is ranked as the 16th least corrupt country, behind countries with "cleaner" business practices such as Finland, Sweden, and Canada. There are a total of 102 countries ranked on corruption in the total survey. Countries ranked low on the Corruption Perceptions Index (most corrupt) are more likely to tolerate bribery as a business practice than countries with a high rank.

TABLE 3.1

The Corruption Perceptions Index 2002

LEAST CORRUPT COUNTRIES			MOST CORRUPT COUNTRIES		
COUNTRY	SCORE	RANKING	COUNTRY	SCORE	RANKING
Finland	9.7	1	Moldova	2.1	93
Denmark	9.5	2	Uganda	2.1	93
New Zealand	9.5	2	Azerbaijan	2.0	95
Iceland	9.4	4	Indonesia	1.9	96
Singapore	9.3	5	Kenya	1.9	96
Sweden	9.3	5	Angola	1.7	98
Canada	9.0	7	Madagascar	1.7	98
Luxembourg	9.0	7	Paraguay	1.7	98
Netherlands	9.0	7	Nigeria	1.6	101
United Kingdom	8.7	10	Bangladesh	1.2	102
United States	7.7	16			

Source: From Transparency International, www.transparency.org. Reprinted with permission.

Social Responsibility

Do corporations have a responsibility to conduct their affairs ethically and to be judged by the same standards as individuals? Should a business be concerned with more than the pursuit of profits for its shareholders? **Social responsibility** is the duty a company has to conduct its affairs ethically in a manner that benefits both employees and the larger society. There are both benefits and costs associated with acting in a socially responsible manner.

The Benefits of Social Responsibility

As mentioned at the beginning of this chapter, Levi Strauss devotes a portion of its profits to charitable organizations in the communities in which it does business. Levi Strauss discovered that it is good business to give back to the community because doing so also nurtures the business.

Caring for the natural environment is one of several dimensions of social responsibility that must be considered in the allocation of a firm's resources. Companies that pollute the air, water, and land must consider the rights of people in the community to breathe clean air and drink clean water and must pay to help clean up the pollution or face government penalties. Companies spend billions of dollars each year in order to comply with laws that protect the environment.

Social responsibility ultimately leads to improved odds of long-term survival for the organization. A narrow focus on producing goods

social responsibility

The belief that corporations have a responsibility to conduct their affairs ethically to benefit both employees and the larger society.

Cleaning up the *Exxon Valdez* oil spill in Alaska.

and services for profit only, without considering the ramifications of company activities may impair company performance in the long run and result in a failure to survive. In fact, social responsibility can have a positive effect on company performance. Research indicates that it is related to higher financial performance and the ability to recruit better quality job applicants.[17]

Some recent examples of the problems that corporations have faced as a result of failing to address social responsibility include the following:

1. In 1999 the courts determined that tobacco companies had purposefully withheld from the public knowledge that nicotine in tobacco is an addictive drug. Phillip Morris, R. J. Reynolds, and other large U.S. tobacco manufacturers agreed to pay $246 billion over a period of 25 years to compensate victims of lung cancer and other fatal illnesses related to cigarette smoking.[18]

2. Class action lawsuits from women injured by defective breast implants forced Dow Corning, the largest breast implant manufacturer, to pledge a $3.2 billion settlement.[19]

3. In 1989 the *Exxon Valdez* spilled 11 million gallons of oil and polluted 2,600 miles of shoreline along Alaska's Prince William Sound. Environmentalists, consumers, and local businesses mobilized and forced Exxon to pay $3 billion in damages and for the cleanup.[20]

4. Drexel Burnham Lambert, an investment bank that made huge profits financing junk bonds in the 1980s, pleaded guilty to six felony counts involving mail, wire, and securities fraud in 1989.

part two   The Culture of Management

The bank's officers, one of whom was Michael Milken, were singled out for their lack of concern for other stakeholders and Securities and Exchange Commission (SEC) regulations. The firm paid $650 million in penalties to the government and to the victims; Milken went to jail; and Drexel Burnham went out of business.[21]

5. Executives at Enron, a Houston-based energy company, approved risky financial investments with company resources in off-balance-sheet financial deals that lost billions of dollars. When these losses were disclosed in 2001, Enron stock suddenly collapsed. The stock lost 99 percent of its value within a few months, putting the company into bankruptcy, and forcing the layoff of thousands of employees as the company struggled to survive the scandal that followed. The lack of transparency of the financial dealings of Enron meant that the company did not give an important stakeholder group, shareholders, the opportunity to know about how funds were invested.[22]

As these examples indicate, actions by such stakeholder groups as environmentalists, consumers, and the government may threaten the stability and existence of a company. When the management team takes the interests of key stakeholders into consideration, the threat of dealing with hostile interest groups is reduced. When a company's executives adopt a socially responsible approach that is aligned with the goals of an important stakeholder group, the stakeholder may reciprocate and influence its members to patronize the products of the company. For example, Anheuser-Busch, the largest brewer of beer, has worked hard to cultivate positive labor relations with its unionized workforce, an important stakeholder group. In return, the unions have encouraged their membership to drink Budweiser and Busch brands of beer made by Anheuser-Busch, rather than consume the beer of companies that treat unions harshly.

The Costs of Social Responsibility

There are essentially two aspects of being socially responsible. The first is avoiding illegal and unethical activities, such as discrimination, sexual harassment, pollution, and tax evasion. These negative activities should be avoided as part of the ethical structure of a company. Other activities associated with social responsibility have costs, because the company spends money to support a social good, such as a neighborhood cleanup program, giving money to the United Way, and other beneficial activities.

In these circumstances, social responsibility may be viewed by some as counter to the ethics of individualism, which suggest that individuals and companies should be able to pursue their own self-interests. Economist Milton Friedman argues that most managers do not own the businesses they operate and should act in the best interests of the stockholders, who are primarily interested in financial returns. Corporations should deploy resources to produce goods and services as efficiently as possible. Socially responsible firms that are less efficient may be driven out of business by more efficient competitors willing to singlemindedly pursue profits. These profit-maximizing firms are able to charge lower prices because social costs are not added to the cost of production.

Firms that give profits a low priority are more likely to fail and become a detriment to society because jobs and stockholders' investments are lost. In the late 1990s, when Levi Strauss lost market share to competitors Lee and Wrangler and profits decreased, some shareholders blamed the company's CEO, Robert Haas, for giving too high a priority to corporate social responsibility.[23]

The airline industry provides another example of how the pursuit of socially responsible goals can dilute a firm's viability. Air France and Iberia Airlines are the government-owned national airlines of France and Spain, respectively (a minority ownership of Air France has been recently privatized). During the past several years, each has operated at an annual loss of several billion dollars, and the governments of France and Spain have had to bail them out, which contributed to an increase of the national debt in each country. To operate efficiently and compete effectively with more nimble and profitable private competitors, each airline needs to downsize its workforce. However, the protection of employees' jobs is a higher priority than the need to make a profit. All taxpayers in France and Spain are therefore paying higher taxes to protect the jobs of a few. Critics would argue that it is wrong to support inefficient firms in order to protect jobs, because costs increase.

A U.S. firm that has let social responsibility dominate its business strategy in a way that distracted management's attention from earning profits is Ben & Jerry's Ice Cream. Management Close-Up 3.a discusses some of the factors that have resulted in reduced profits for this company.

Rather than making social responsibility the top priority or ignoring it altogether, management should give corporate social responsibility a high priority without neglecting other important priorities, such as competing successfully in its markets. A thriving organization will have resources to support its social responsibility goals, while a failing organization is too involved in trying to survive and meet its basic business obligations. The challenge for managers is to strike a balance that responds to the concerns of both stakeholders and the general society, bearing in mind that responsible behavior is linked to long-term survival.

The benefits and costs of corporate social responsibility are summarized in Table 3.2. As Table 3.2 suggests, in most cases the advantages of working toward the realization of corporate social responsibility goals outweigh the possible disadvantages.

Ben & Jerry Did Good While Their Business Didn't

THEME: ETHICS   Ben & Jerry's Ice Cream, founded in 1978 by two former Vermont hippies, Ben Cohen and Jerry Greenfield, had always given a high priority to integrating socially beneficial actions into the business. In 1993, it came out with a new flavor called Wavy Gravy, named after the musician who, according to Cohen, "symbolizes taking Sixties values, peace and love, and turning them into action in the Nineties." The company turned the proceeds from the flavor into action, too, by donating some of the proceeds to the musician's work with children.

The company gave away 7.5 percent of its pretax profits (three times the rate of the average U.S. corporation). For its brownie ice cream, it bought brownies that cost a little higher than average from a New York bakery that employed disadvantaged workers. The company had a pay policy that limited its CEO's salary to five times what the lowest-paid employee earned, a reflection of the founders' egalitarian philosophy. They stopped making Oreo Mint ice cream because the Oreo brand is part of tobacco giant RJR Nabisco. Ben & Jerry's paid Vermont dairy farmers extra for hormone-free milk, which cost the company $375,000 over other sources of milk.

The company profits declined and the stock price decreased, but the company continued its socially responsible style. In February 1995, the company moved from being founder-led to professional management when it hired Robert Holland as its CEO. Holland resigned less than two years later, following rumors that the co-founders opposed his support of the company's fat-free (and milk-free) sorbet products. Five years later the company became part of Unilever, a major multinational, which pledged to pursue and expand Ben & Jerry's social mission. Unilever paid $365 million and kept Cohen and Greenfield with the company, although they were not involved in the day-to-day operations.

In November 2000 Unilever ice cream veteran Yves Couette was appointed Ben & Jerry's CEO and vowed to build on Ben & Jerry's social mission. "Business has an important role to play in achieving social progress," said Couette, citing his earlier work for Unilever in Guadalajara, Mexico, where the company established an ice cream shop, run by a not-for-profit organization, to support disabled children. Perhaps more pragmatic than Cohen and Greenfield in viewing how a firm's social and economic missions need to work together, Couette said: "I firmly believe that the least socially responsible business is one that's out of business."

Couette's promises weren't enough for Cohen, who had wanted a long-time Ben & Jerry's director put in the top post. Cohen's threat to quit the company unless a co-CEO steeped in the company's social mission was appointed was followed by a consumer group's boycott of Unilever products in support of Cohen's position.

Sources: Adapted from A. Taylor, "Yo, Ben! Yo, Jerry! It's Just Ice Cream!" *Fortune,* April 28, 1997, p. 374; www.benjerry.com; "Consumer Group to Boycott Unilever Products," Reuters, December 6, 2000, available at http://dailynews.yahoo.com/h/nm/20001206/bs/unilever_benjerrys_dc_2.html.

Organizational Stakeholders

Organizations are, in many ways, political arenas in which various forces and coalitions compete. Organizational **stakeholders** are individuals or groups that have an interest in or are affected by a company's performance and the way it uses its resources. Stakeholders may be part of either the internal or external environment of an organization. The female employees of a company are an internal stakeholder group, for example, and an organization of consumers is an external stakeholder group.

stakeholders

The groups or individuals who have an interest in the performance of the enterprise and how it uses its resources, including employees, customers, and shareholders.

TABLE 3.2

Benefits and Costs of Corporate Social Responsibility

SOCIAL RESPONSIBILITY BENEFITS	SOCIAL RESPONSIBILITY COSTS
1. Socially responsible companies are good corporate citizens to the community and to the environment.	1. Socially responsible companies may lose focus on the business goals while focusing on goals related to good corporate citizenship.
2. Socially responsible company policies can enhance the image of a company as well as its product brands from the perspective of the consumers.	2. Socially responsible companies may divert needed resources for improving the business into social responsibility projects, which could put a company at a competitive disadvantage.
3. Socially responsible companies have fewer conflicts with stakeholder groups who disagree with the company over how it uses its resources.	
4. Socially responsible companies are more likely to influence stakeholders to become loyal customers and become advocates of the company's products.	
5. Research shows that corporate social responsibility is related to higher financial performance and the ability to recruit better quality job applicants.	

Stakeholder groups tend to have more specific interests that may not always be in agreement with the interests of management or of other stakeholder groups. For example, shareholders may want a poorly performing company to close inefficient manufacturing plants and focus on more profitable product lines, while the labor union wants to protect worker jobs in all manufacturing plants. The management team must balance the interests of clashing stakeholder groups with its own interests. Compromises are necessary when important stakeholders have legitimate concerns that should be addressed. Management may decide to close some inefficient plants to satisfy the shareholders and invest resources in retraining displaced workers to satisfy the labor union.

A large company will have dozens of stakeholder groups exerting pressure on management. Table 3.3 lists categories of stakeholders with whom a large firm is likely to deal. They are owners, employees, governments, customers, the community, competitors, and social activist groups.

Owners

Owners who have invested a portion of their wealth in shares of company stock want a reasonable financial return on their investment. If small investors are not satisfied with the financial performance of the company, they are likely to sell their stock. Large individual investors, mutual funds, and pension funds are more likely to be actively involved in influencing management through the board of directors or by voicing their concerns at meetings of shareholders. The CEOs of WorldCom, Enron, General Motors, IBM, and American Express lost their jobs when activist investor groups put pressure on the boards of directors to dismiss them because of disappointing financial performance.

Employees

Employees are largely focused on their jobs. They want to be treated fairly and with respect by the company. New employees are likely to want challenging work assignments that will advance their careers, while senior employees may be more interested in job security and retirement benefits.

Firms that neglect employee stakeholders may have to deal with angry labor unions, which can disrupt output through work stoppages or loss of the most valuable and marketable employees to competitors. This can disrupt the firm's ability to compete in its markets. In 1997 the truck drivers represented by the Teamsters Union organized a strike against United Parcel Service (UPS) because management refused to create full-time jobs for the part-time truck drivers represented by the union. More than half of all truck drivers at UPS were part-time employees, and the wait to become a full-time driver was about 10 years. UPS settled the strike with the Teamsters after losing about $700 million in revenues and some of its market share to its competitors. UPS agreed to create 10,000 new full-time jobs over a five-year period.

Governments

The primary role played by the government is to make sure each company complies with regulations and laws. For example, automobiles must comply with Environmental Protection Agency (EPA) regulations that govern exhaust emissions. These regulations require auto manufacturers to invest in technologies such as catalytic converters to meet pollution regulations even though these investments add to the cost of manufacturing a car.

Companies' leaders will object when they believe that a proposed law will be detrimental. For example, McDonald's and other fast-food companies oppose hikes in the minimum wage because the cost structure of fast-food restaurants is highly sensitive to such increases. They may hire lobbyists to try to influence legislators to defeat proposed minimum wage increase legislation as a way of dealing with the threats in the political environment.

TABLE 3.3

Some Categories and Specific Stakeholders of a Large Firm

OWNERS	EMPLOYEES	GOVERNMENTS	CUSTOMERS
Trusts	New employees	Federal	Business purchasers
Foundations	Senior employees	EPA	Government purchasers
Board members	Retirees	FTC	Educational institutions
Management owners	Female employees	OSHA	Consumers
Mutual funds	Minority employees	State	
Employee pension funds	Labor unions	Local	
Individual owners		Foreign governments	

Source: Adapted from A. B. Carroll and A. K. Buchholtz, *Business and Society,* 5th ed., Cincinnati: South-Western Publishing, 2002.

Customers

Many firms sell products to two types of customers: (1) individuals making purchases and (2) other businesses. Both types of customers are interested in purchasing quality products that are reasonably priced and safe to use. Customer groups sometimes organize to boycott companies that behave unethically or irresponsibly. Consumer pressure has protected old-growth forests from the timber industry's chainsaws, forced cigarette manufacturers to discontinue advertising on television, and generated international guidelines to reduce the production of ozone layer–depleting chlorofluorocarbons. On U.S. airlines, smoking is banned on domestic flights because of complaints from individual consumers and consumer groups. Consumer groups put market pressure on Volkswagen, the manufacturer of the Audi line of cars, to redesign the car's power train and transmission after a number of fatal accidents. Consumer opinion is influenced by periodicals such as *Consumer Reports* that judge the performance and reliability of consumer products and identify those that offer the best value and quality.

Community

There are local, national, and global communities. All types of communities expect corporations to be good citizens and to contribute to the quality of life. Firms that neglect or degrade their communities may be subject to pressure. When citizens in several communities in Maine opposed new Wal-Mart stores because of fears that they would hurt downtown businesses as they had done in other communities, Wal-Mart decided not to build the stores.

A business that operates in a local community pays taxes that support public services such as schools, police, and fire protection. It also cre-

TABLE 3.3

Some Categories and Specific Stakeholders of a Large Firm (continued)

COMMUNITY	COMPETITORS	SOCIAL ACTIVIST GROUPS
United Way	Domestic competitor	Sierra Club
Public schools	International competitor	American Civil Liberties Union
Residents in community		NOW (National Organization of Women)
Local media		MADD (Mothers against Drunk Driving)
		Consumers Union

ates jobs that may employ local people. Businesses can give the local community funds or equipment or can encourage employees to volunteer at community nonprofit organizations. IBM provides computer equipment to local colleges and encourages executives who qualify for sabbaticals (paid time off to pursue other interests) to teach in local public schools and to work with disadvantaged children. These investments in the community should pay off for IBM in the future because students trained on IBM equipment are more likely to purchase IBM products when they graduate from college.

StorageTek, a Colorado-based electronics company, focuses its community stakeholder assistance on nonprofit organizations that provide health and human services, community services, and cultural programs. It committed funds to help the YMCA build a new community center; it provides a match of 50 cents on each dollar employees raise for the United Way; and it encourages employees to volunteer with organizations such as Meals on Wheels and Adopt-a-Road.[24]

A global community example is Levi Strauss's funding of Bangladeshi schoolchildren discussed at the beginning of the chapter.

Competitors

Competitors expect a corporation to compete fairly in the market without engaging in such unethical business practices as industrial espionage, dumping products on the market at a below-cost price, and receiving unfair government subsidies. Competitor stakeholders can form economic coalitions to put pressure on any company that violates the principles of fair competition. They can also use the courts or the legislative branch of government to punish a corporate rule breaker. For example, competitors have charged Microsoft with unfair practices and have used the courts to break Microsoft into separate operating system

SOCIALLY RESPONSIBLE INVESTING

Suppose you recently inherited $50,000 from a relative and are considering some different stock-based mutual funds in which to invest it. You are thinking about (1) mutual funds that offer the best financial return overall, or (2) mutual funds that buy stock only in socially responsible companies and offer the best financial return within this subset of funds. Socially responsible mutual funds avoid purchases of stock of manufacturers of alcohol or tobacco products, weapons, and nuclear energy; companies involved in promoting gambling; companies with poor pollution or discrimination records; and companies that test products on animals. Some socially responsible mutual funds also screen for consumer and employee policies, environmental performance, product quality, and workplace diversity.

Form groups of four to five. Each person should explain his or her own choice of investment strategy to the others. One member of the group is assigned to take notes and make a list of the advantages and disadvantages of investing money in socially responsible mutual funds. The members of the group should then work together to answer the following questions.

Discussion Questions

1. Do you think individual investors are able to put pressure on companies that engage in activities such as the manufacture of tobacco or animal testing?

2. Is it inevitable for mutual funds that invest in socially responsible companies to underperform funds that do not screen stocks for social responsibility?

3. Would you invest in socially responsible mutual funds if you knew that your investment might thereby be significantly less profitable?

4. Would it be more effective to invest your money for maximum return and then donate the extra profits directly to the social causes of your choice?

5. What alternative ways could individual investors voice their disapproval of a company's lack of socially responsible corporate behavior than by avoiding investments in that company's stock?

and applications companies. Microsoft won its appeal of the court ruling to divide the company.

Globally, Airbus, the European manufacturer of commercial jets, threatened to lobby the European Union to boycott Boeing aircraft and successfully influenced Boeing to stop signing customers such as Delta, Continental, and American Airlines to 20-year exclusive contracts.[25]

Social Activist Groups

A business practice that runs counter to an important goal of a social activist group may result in negative media attention for the company or even a product boycott orchestrated by the social activist group. Although corporations cannot always satisfy such groups, it is often in their best interests to compromise with social activist groups to avoid being the focus of a campaign that can badly damage their reputation. Nestlé was the target of a national boycott led by the National Council of Churches because the infant baby formula it marketed to developing nations caused the sickness and death of thousands of babies. After seven years and millions of dollars unsuccessfully trying to resist the boycott, Nestlé altered some of its business practices.[26] People for the Ethical Treatment of Animals (PETA) organized a boycott against L'Oreal and other cosmetics companies that tested their products on animals. After four years of futile resistance, L'Oreal promised that it would no longer conduct animal testing.

This is not to say that social activist groups prevail in all situations. For example, when the Florida Citrus Commission hired conservative talk show host Rush Limbaugh as a spokesperson, the National Organization for Women (NOW) and the National Education Association (NEA) asked consumers to avoid purchasing Florida orange juice. The boycott had no effect.[27]

Strategies for Managing Stakeholders

Balancing the interests of a variety of groups is the managerial form of a juggling act. Managers must consider various stakeholder groups while preparing an overall business strategy. The approaches stakeholders use to get their point across to management range from making suggestions at shareholder meetings to threatening to withhold resources from the firm. The latter approach was used by consumer groups that threatened a boycott of StarKist products unless the company stopped purchasing tuna from foreign fishing fleets that caught and killed thousands of dolphins in their tuna nets.

When a stakeholder group makes demands on a firm, management should first perform an analysis by answering the following questions:

1. Who are the stakeholders?
2. How are the stakeholders affected by the company policies?
3. What are the stakeholders' interests in the business?
4. How have the stakeholders behaved in the past, and what coalitions are they likely to form around their issue?
5. How effective have the company's strategies been in dealing with these and other stakeholders?
6. What new strategies and action plans need to be formulated to deal effectively with the stakeholders?[28]

Once an analysis of the stakeholders has been accomplished the management team can develop strategies for dealing with the stakeholders by selecting one of the following four general approaches: confrontation, damage control, accommodation, or being proactive.

Confrontation

confrontation strategy

One means a firm may use to deal with a stakeholder group whose goals are perceived to threaten company performance; the firm may use the courts, engage in public relations, or lobby against legislation.

Management may select a **confrontation strategy** to deal with a stakeholder group whose goals are perceived to threaten company performance. This includes using the courts, engaging in public relations, and lobbying against legislation. For many years, the tobacco companies used a confrontation strategy to deal with antismoking groups and individuals who sued them. For example, tobacco companies spent millions of dollars lobbying state legislatures to pass "smokers' rights" laws. United Parcel Service selected a confrontation strategy to deal with the Teamsters Union when contract negotiations failed, and the confrontation resulted in the costly labor strike mentioned earlier.

Management must be very careful when it chooses to use a confrontation strategy. Typically, the company spends considerable time and money fighting a stakeholder group rather than focusing on more positive outcomes. The long-term outcome may be a negative image for the company unless it is able to mend its relations with its stakeholders and with customers critical of the company's actions.

Damage Control

damage control strategy

A means a firm may use to deal with a stakeholder group when it decides that it may have made mistakes and wants to improve its relationship with the stakeholders and to elevate its public image.

The **damage control strategy** is often used when a company decides that it may have made mistakes and wants to elevate its public image and improve its relationship with the stakeholder. In 1999, after years of confrontation, the tobacco companies admitted to having deceived the public and paid $246 billion to settle the claims of people who contracted fatal illnesses related to tobacco smoking. Similarly, when a leak of poisonous gas resulted in the death of more than 2,000 people and serious injuries to 200,000 in Bhopal, India, in 1984, Union Carbide used a damage control strategy and initiated a settlement with the Indian government for $470 million to be divided among victims and their families.

Accommodation

accommodation strategy

A means of dealing with stakeholder groups when a firm decides to accept social responsibility for its business decisions after pressure has been exerted by stakeholder groups.

The **accommodation strategy** is used when management decides to accept social responsibility for business decisions after pressure has been exerted by stakeholder groups. It may require changing business practices to better align with stakeholder goals. Long the target of environmental groups, McDonald's used the accommodation strategy when it changed its packaging from polystyrene foam to paper, which is less damaging to the environment. General Motors voluntarily recognized the United Auto Workers (UAW) union in the Spring Hill, Tennessee, Saturn manufacturing plant instead of forcing the union to undergo a formal election procedure. In return, General Motors obtained a labor agreement that allowed it to deploy its workforce more flexibly than is possible in other unionized auto plants.

Proactive

A company chooses a **proactive strategy** when it determines that it wants to go beyond stakeholder expectations. Proactive companies form partnerships with stakeholders and cooperate with them. These partnerships increase management's ability to predict and control the stakeholder environment and fewer crises emerge. For example:

- The Colgate-Palmolive Company "adopted" a failing junior high school in Harlem that needed its buildings and curriculum modernized. Colgate-Palmolive contributed funds and personnel for the renovation and restructuring of the school. Company personnel worked with school staff on budgeting, strategic planning, and management. Student reading levels and math competencies improved dramatically in the renovated school.

- The Coca-Cola Company sets ambitious goals for purchasing goods and services from minority- and female-owned vendors and puts a high priority on recruiting and developing minority and female employees. One woman and two members of minorities sit on the 14-member board of directors, and there are seven women and six minority members among the top 57 corporate executives. Coca-Cola also encourages its employees to volunteer in community programs such as Adopt-a-School and provides assistance to the United Negro College Fund and the National Hispanic Scholarship Fund.

- Merck, the pharmaceutical company, formed a partnership with the Costa Rican National Institute of Biodiversity. The institute provides Merck with plant and insect samples that may become the basis for new medicines, and Merck shares its pharmaceutical product royalties with the Costa Rican institute. Merck also provides funds for conservation efforts to preserve the Costa Rican rain forest.[29]

proactive strategy
A means of dealing with stakeholders when a firm determines that it wants to go beyond stakeholder expectations.

Applications for the Manager It is critical for a manager to be seen as an ethical person. Managers are role models for other employees and consequently are held to a higher standard of personal conduct. A tarnished moral reputation interferes with a manager's ability to influence employees and makes it difficult to serve as a communication link between executives and front-line employees.

Managers are responsible for creating an environment that supports ethical behavior and discourages unethical behavior. A manager should set ethical conduct goals. For example, a financial securities manager may set a goal of zero tolerance for dishonesty among stockbrokers.

Applications for Managing Teams Teams must place a high priority on behaving ethically. If a team tolerates unethical conduct from one member, others may also try to get away with unethical conduct. Tolerance of such unethical activities as inflating an expense account can lead to more serious breaches of conduct that can damage the reputation of the entire team.

When teams or groups tolerate unethical conduct, it can be very difficult to extinguish this norm. Members of highly cohesive teams may find it distasteful to inform on unethical members for fear of being shunned by the team. Sometimes an appropriate reward can expose unethical behavior so that it can be changed.

Applications for Individuals Suppose you are facing a dilemma that is putting your personal values to the test. It can be useful to check your choices against some ethical tests:

- *Front-page test*. How would I feel if my decision became a headline in a local newspaper? Would I feel comfortable describing my actions or decision to a customer or stockholder?

- *Golden rule test*. Would I be willing to be treated in the same manner?

- *Personal gain test*. Is an opportunity for personal gain clouding my judgment? Would I make the same decision if the outcome did not benefit me in any way?[30]

In the introductory vignette we presented some critical thinking questions regarding Levi Strauss. Now that you have had the opportunity to study ethical and social responsibility issues, you can reexamine the questions that were raised in the vignette. First, one benefit that Levi Strauss derives from the attention it gives to social responsibility is its high visibility as an admired company, as reflected in a poll of executives published in *Fortune* magazine. This recognition could help Levi Strauss attract high-quality applicants for employment opportunities. The charitable activities that Levi Strauss supports in the community also produce consumer goodwill that is likely to encourage people to purchase the products made by the company.

Second, the organizational stakeholder strategy that Levi Strauss selected is the proactive approach—proactive because Levi Strauss went out into the community on its own initiative to use some of its resources to give back to worthy social causes. Levi Strauss gives to local charitable organizations within the communities where it does business and supports a nonprofit organization that fights racism. Levi Strauss underwrites the education of children in less developed countries such as Bangladesh and provides guaranteed factory jobs for the children upon completion of their education at age 14.

SUMMARY

Business ethics are principles prescribing a code of behavior that explains what is good and right and what is bad and wrong. They provide standards for conduct and decision making of employees and managers. The four key ethical approaches used to make business decisions are (1) **utilitarianism,** which looks at what is good for the greatest number of people; (2) **individualism,** which sees individual self-interest as the basis of the greatest good as long as it does not harm others; (3) the **rights approach,** which represents and protects fundamental human rights; and (4) the **justice approach,** which emphasizes treating all people fairly and consistently. Companies must find a common set of ethical values and make them known to all employees.

A **code of ethics** is a formal statement of a company's ethics and values, which guides employee conduct in a variety of business situations. The code can be a **corporate credo,** which focuses on general values and beliefs, or an **ethical policy statement,** which provides specific rules for employee conduct.

To implement the code of ethics, a company can provide **ethics training** to its employees. An **ethical structure** can be developed to monitor and audit ethical behavior. A company can have a **whistleblower policy** that encourages employees to disclose illegal or unethical practices of coworkers without fearing retaliation.

Corporate social responsibility means that a company has a duty to use some of its resources to promote the interest of various elements of society. Companies should respond to the concerns of **stakeholders,** the individuals or groups with an interest in the performance of the business and the way it uses its resources. Important categories of stakeholders are owners, employees, governments, customers, the community, competitors, and social activist groups.

Companies develop strategies for managing stakeholder demands after analyzing the nature of the stakeholders' interests and the threats or opportunities that may result. The key approaches companies use to manage stakeholder demands are (1) the **confrontation strategy,** which challenges the stakeholder; (2) the **damage control strategy,** used when management decides it made a mistake and wants to minimize the damage to the company's reputation; (3) the **accommodation strategy,** which is used when the company decides that it is in its best interest to accept social responsibility; and (4) the **proactive strategy,** used by companies that want to go beyond meeting stakeholders' expectations. Companies with proactive strategies are leaders in social responsibility.

1. Compare and contrast the four ethics approaches used for ethical decision making that are discussed in this chapter. Which criterion do you think is the best one? Which one would be the least useful? What is the basis for your selection? Now, suppose you were going to work at a business in China. Which of the four criteria would you be most likely to apply to an ethical business decision in China?

2. Why do you think companies invest resources in training their managers and employees in business ethics? Some people think that ethics should be learned within the family and by the time a person is a mature adult it is too late to learn about ethics. Do you agree or disagree with this statement? Explain.

3. Some sales organizations like to put their sales representatives on a straight commission pay plan, which means that they must successfully sell the product in order to receive any money at the end of the month. What type of ethical dilemmas or problems are likely to happen when the salespeople must operate under a straight commission plan? How might these ethical problems be managed?

4. Suppose you discover that your boss is embezzling funds from the company. Which of the policies described in this chapter would you use in deciding to disclose this situation to company officials who could take care of the problem before it becomes more serious? What kind of preparation should you make before you decide to disclose your boss's unethical conduct to the company authorities?

5. Is it possible for a business to do good for society and still make a reasonable profit? Explain.

6. In Germany, under the model of "stakeholder capitalism," employee representatives sit on company boards of directors. In the German model of business it is assumed that both labor (employee representatives) and capital (shareholder representatives) have important stakes in the enterprise and should work in harmony with each other. In the United States, the board of directors usually represents only the owners of the business. What advantages to employees as stakeholders are available in Germany that are not provided to employees in U.S. companies? In the United States, how do employees let management know their stakeholder concerns?

7. What does it mean to be a socially responsible employer? What are the benefits for a company that decides to give a high priority to its social responsibility?

8. Is it possible for a small business to take an active role in social responsibility? What are some ways that a small business (for example, a family business or a local business you are familiar with) can be socially responsible?

9. Have you ever faced an ethical dilemma in school or on the job? Which people were affected by the decision you were struggling with? How did you resolve the problem? Was there any ethical training that you could have had to better prepare you for deciding how to handle this problem? Would you handle the problem the same or differently now? Why?

Should Job Seekers Stretch the Truth to Get a Job?

In a competitive job market, some people stretch the truth about themselves in order to obtain an advantage over others who are applying for the same job. Austin McGregor International, a Dallas-based search firm, has compiled a list of the top five fibs that job seekers tell:

Pay. People exaggerate their salary histories in order to obtain higher pay, since employers try to match or exceed the pay an applicant received from a former employer.

Job tenure. Some job applicants *reduce* the number of years of tenure with a former employer to appear to be risk takers. Others *add* years of tenure with a former employer to avoid the appearance of being job hoppers.

Reason for separation from former employer. Some employees have been known to suggest that they quit for "personal reasons," when in reality they were fired or laid off.

Age. Some people try to give the impression that they are younger or older than they are in reality (even though age discrimination by employers is illegal). For example, an executive may purposely withhold the date of college graduation from a job application and select clothes and styles that project a youthful appearance in hopes of appearing younger.

Company rank. Some job seekers claim they reported to the company president, when in reality they may have had limited contact with the president from a position several levels lower in the hierarchy.

Suppose it has just been brought to your attention that one of the members of your project team exaggerated several factors like those above during the hiring process. This individual has been with your company for about one year now and appears to be performing the job satisfactorily.

Discussion Questions

1. You are the manager of the team. What will you do about the fact that one of your team members stretched the truth to get the job offer? What would be the consequences if you decided to do nothing? Does it make a difference to your decision if you are the only one aware of the truth?

2. You are not the manager but a member of the team. Will you blow the whistle on your teammate? What will happen if you do? What will happen if you don't?

Source: Adapted from L. Grant, "The Whoppers Job Seekers Tell," *Fortune*, March 31, 1997, p. 123.

Employees' Retirement Savings Disappear in the Aftermath of the Enron Scandal

Shareholders were not the only stakeholder group that suffered as a result of the dramatic collapse of Enron's stock price when its shady off-the-books financial dealings became public. Thousands of Enron employees experienced the nightmare of losing a large portion of their retirement savings. The average Enron employee had 62 percent of his or her retirement plan savings invested in Enron stock. Marie Thibaut, a 61-year-old Enron employee, saw her retirement savings in her employee retirement benefits go from $500,000 to $22,000 in the months following the Enron scandal. To make matters worse, Enron did not permit its employees to sell its Enron stock in retirement plans until they reached the age of 50.

Many companies, such as Enron, encourage employees to invest a significant portion of their retirement savings in company stock. It is common practice to give employees a 15 percent discount on the purchase of company stock when it is put into an employee's retirement savings plan. One of the motives used by a company that encourages its employees to own significant amounts of company stock is to give employees the "feel" of ownership by having a stake in the long-term performance of the company. Employees may also believe that the company stock is a good investment for their retirement because they have a long-term investment horizon of many years before retirement and expect the stock to be more valuable at the time of their retirement despite short-term variations in the price of the stock. At present there are no laws preventing employers from letting employees buy as much company stock as they want as a retirement savings investment. The question remains as to whether or not an employer is being socially responsible when employees are encouraged to buy large amounts of company stock as a retirement savings investment.

One common practice is to match an employee's retirement contribution to the plan with the employer's matching contribution made in the form of company stock. Procter & Gamble, Pfizer, General Electric, and McDonald's use company stock to match an employee's contribution to the 401(k) retirement plan in those companies. At other companies, the company stock is viewed as a "blue chip" stock, and employees are proud of the company and view the purchase of the stock as a valuable investment and a good way to show loyalty to company management. At Coca-Cola 81 percent of employees' retirement funds in the 401(k) retirement plan are in company stock.

Most students who have taken a course in business finance know that it is extremely risky to allocate a large portion of one's retirement funds to just one stock. A diversified portfolio of investments in a variety of different stocks representing different industries, as well as a portfolio containing a variety of different asset classes including bonds, cash, and real estate, help preserve the investment funds over the long run and minimize investment risk. With this insight, one wonders why so many companies continue the practice of letting their employees purchase large amounts of company stock to fund their retirement savings plans.

Discussion Questions

1. What are some possible approaches that a socially responsible employer could use with regard to the use of company stock as an investment for an employee's retirement plan? Do you think there should be a limit on the amount of stock as a percentage of overall retirement savings? Should the employer contribution match be made only in cash instead of stock? Should employees have more flexibility to reallocate their funds into different asset classes or stocks, rather than have long holding periods of many years when they are not permitted to sell their company stock within their retirement plans? Should the employer provide outside financial advice to an employee for making retirement plan investments that are neither too conservative nor too risky?

2. Why do you think so many Enron employees bought large amounts of Enron stock to fund their retirement? Do you think employees thought they knew something that other nonemployee investors were not aware of when they decided to buy large quantities of Enron stock?

Sources: C. Cropper, "The Ins and Outs of the New Tax Law: The Golden Years Get More Golden," *Business Week,* January 28, 2002, pp. 110–111; J. Quinn, "401(k)s and the Enron Mess," *Newsweek,* January 21, 2002, p. 25; "When Labor and Capital Don't Mix: Enron's Demise Unmasks Conflicts in Company Pension Plans," *The Economist,* December 15, 2001, p. 60.

**INDIVIDUAL/
COLLABORATIVE
LEARNING
CASE 3.1**

Do Sales Commissions Cause Sales Representatives to Behave Unethically?

Baker Electronics is an electronics appliance store in Columbus, Ohio, that puts its sales staff on a modest salary plus a commission based on the value of the electronics products sold in the store. The top salespeople at Baker generate about three-quarters of their take-home pay from sales commissions—only one-quarter comes from salary.

Baker frequently advertises specials on certain television models in the local Columbus newspaper, drawing people into the store asking about these models. Because these sale items have lower profit margins, the store also lowers the commission the sales staff receives on these models. The company prefers to sell higher-priced models but advertises the lower-priced ones to get customers into the store.

Baker offers little sales training. New salespeople spend a day or so working with the store manager and then are left to operate on their own. The store manager does not seem to care how sales are made as long as sales goals are achieved. The manager receives a significant bonus (as much as 100 percent of salary) based on the level of store sales.

Tom Pierce, one of the most successful salespeople at Baker Electronics, has developed some effective sales techniques that provide him a very good income on commissions. He is viewed as a role model by other salespeople at the store. Here are some examples of Tom's sales tactics:

Tom points out to all customers the special features on the higher-priced televisions, and many go along with his advice and buy the more expensive model.

When customers are more interested in the sale-priced televisions, Tom will try to convince them that the added features on the more expensive models are very important, and some customers will buy a television with more features than they really need.

When a customer rejects Tom's advice and insists on purchasing a less expensive television, Tom adjusts some of the picture control switches when he demonstrates the model so that its picture is altered and appears fuzzier than the more expensive televisions. This tactic almost always results in the sale of a more expensive television.

Critical Thinking Questions

1. Do you think Tom's conduct toward the customers at Baker Electronics is unethical? Why or why not?

2. How do you think the sales commission policy influences Tom's treatment of customers? How might Tom behave differently if he were paid on a straight salary basis, with no sales commissions?

3. Will sales commissions always motivate salespeople to act in a greedy way and take advantage of customers? Can you think of examples of salespeople who received a sales commission but treated customers with respect and catered to their needs?

Collaborative Learning Exercise

With a partner or small group, assume you are marketing consultants brought into Baker Electronics to improve the sales process so that customers are treated ethically and responsibly by the sales staff. First diagnose what is wrong with the current reward system for sales staff, and then develop a recommendation for a new plan that should result in higher levels of customer satisfaction. Be prepared to present your analysis to the instructor and other members of your class.

Source: Adapted from L. K. Trevino and K. A. Nelson, *Managing Business Ethics*, 2nd ed. New York: John Wiley & Sons, 1999.

Social Responsibility at Levi Strauss

Visit the website of Levi Strauss, the clothing company that was featured in the opening vignette of this chapter, and find its "Social Responsibility" section. Answer the following questions:

1. How do the giving programs support the social responsibility goals of Levi Strauss?

2. Some of the Levi Strauss giving programs might be considered controversial by some people, such as providing resources to fight AIDS or to achieve social justice. Why would Levi Strauss support programs that some of its customers may not agree with?

3. How can Levi Strauss employees become involved with the giving programs? Provide an example. If you were an employee at Levi Strauss, which giving program would you like to become involved with? Why?

What Are Your Ethical Beliefs?

Instructions: Answer the following questions as honestly as you can. Circle the number between 1 and 5 that best represents your own beliefs about business.

		Strongly Disagree				Strongly Agree
1.	Financial gain is all that counts in business.	1	2	3	4	5
2.	Ethical standards must sometimes be compromised in business practice.	1	2	3	4	5
3.	The more financially successful the businessperson, the more unethical the behavior.	1	2	3	4	5
4.	Moral values are irrelevant in business.	1	2	3	4	5
5.	The business world has its own rules.	1	2	3	4	5
6.	Businesspersons care only about making profits.	1	2	3	4	5
7.	Business is like a game—one plays to win.	1	2	3	4	5
8.	In business, people will do anything to further their own interest.	1	2	3	4	5
9.	Competition forces business managers to resort to shady practices.	1	2	3	4	5
10.	The profit motive pressures managers to compromise their ethical concerns.	1	2	3	4	5

Scoring: Add the total number of points. The higher your score, the more cynical you are about ethical business practice.

Think about the reasons for your responses. Be prepared to discuss them in class.

Source: Adapted from L. K. Trevino and K. A. Nelson, *Managing Business Ethics,* 2nd ed., New York: John Wiley & Sons, 1999, pp. 20–21.

FOUR

Managing Organizational Culture and Change

chapter 4

After reading this chapter, you should be able to:

- Build and maintain an appropriate company culture.
- Understand the roles of symbols, rites, ceremonies, heroes, and stories in an organization's culture.
- Identify the various categories of organizational cultures and the characteristics of people who fit best with them.
- Adapt to organizational change and the forces that drive change.
- Work with employees who resist change.
- Use tools to help implement change, including Lewin's three-step model of change and force-field analysis.

SAS: A Worker-Friendly Culture in a High-Tech World

A positive company culture is a long-term asset that solves a variety of shorter-term problems. Statistical Analysis Software, or SAS, is a privately held data analysis software company with 1,500 employees in 53 countries. The company specializes in providing software to millions of users for the purposes of combining and analyzing data collected from a variety of sources such as human resource management, finance, and sales that are not integrated into a single database. The company is noted for a worker-friendly culture that has been carefully cultivated by CEO Jim Goodnight. While many CEOs have been the subjects of media attention for unethical behaviors, Jim Goodnight was the focus of a *60 Minutes* television show in October 2002 because of his company's positive treatment of employees. Consider the following characteristics of the workplace at SAS:

- 35-hour work week.
- Free on-site health care center.
- On-site child care.
- Flexible work schedules.
- Extensive recreational and wellness opportunities.
- Artist-in-residence who oversees the installation of art on every floor in every building.

Among other workplace activities, Goodnight maintains a ritual in which M&M candies are delivered to every area of the workplace on Wednesdays. It is not a reward that is contingent upon performance. The company distributes 22.5 tons of M&Ms per year. The ritual signals the care and regard SAS has for its employees. While it may seem like a small thing, the costs of such practices do add up. Goodnight contends, however, that the benefits far exceed the costs and claims that the worker-friendly culture saves SAS $70 million per year in hiring costs. He credits SAS's culture with being the major factor in retaining employees. SAS enjoys an employee turnover rate of less than 5 percent in an industry with typical turnover rates of nearly 20 percent.

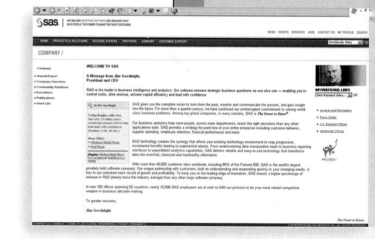

The philosophy underlying Goodnight's approach is, fundamentally, that employees are long-term investments, not short-term expenses. This view is critical to establishing and maintaining long-term customer relationships and to retaining knowledge in the organization. Many organizations pay headhunters to replace overworked and stressed employees who leave every year. For Goodnight, this short-term approach to employees makes no sense. Instead, putting money and effort into keeping workers happy and productive is a much better choice.

Sources: T. Watson, "Goodnight, Sweet Prince," *Canadian Business* (2002), pp. 77–78; J. Wiscombe, "CEO Takes HR to Prime Time," *Workforce* (2002), p. 10. *Screenshot source:* Copyright 2003, SAS Institute Inc., Cary NC, USA. All rights reserved. Reproduced with permission of SAS Institute, Inc.

CRITICAL THINKING QUESTIONS

1. *An organizational culture, such as the one at SAS, may not be a good fit for everyone. Some people may prefer less of a family-friendly atmosphere and more of a higher paying and harder-hitting environment. These people may not be hired or may leave an organization because of the misfit with the culture. Do you think this is a problem for the organization? Why or why not? What, if anything, should be done to lessen any "misfit" problem?*

2. *Jim Goodnight defends his company's worker-friendly culture as an approach that is linked to a positive bottom-line. Is this link necessary? If not, should other companies embrace this type of culture?*

3. *SAS has a very strong culture that has proven to be effective. However, environments change and Jim Goodnight will not be CEO forever. What steps would you recommend to help SAS maintain its culture in the face of changing times and changing personnel?*

4. *Do you think that a culture, such as the one at SAS, should be maintained (as assumed in the previous question), or would it be best to allow the culture to evolve with the changes that occur internally and externally to the organization? Defend your judgment.*

SAS exemplifies how an organizational culture can become a competitive advantage. SAS is known as a great place to work. The company enjoys the benefits of a low turnover rate and high levels of employee commitment. Employees, potential employees, and customers have a common understanding of what SAS is about and what behaviors are desirable and supported. For example, an SAS employee with a child in an elementary school play enjoys a flexible work schedule, which means the employee will be able to attend the play. Likewise, an SAS employee who becomes ill receives extra sick time and wishes for a speedy recovery from management. At the same time, an SAS employee who habitually takes extended weekends by not showing up for work on Fridays or Mondays quickly becomes a former SAS employee. The SAS culture supports work/life balance, not excessive weekend partying. Successful company leadership includes understanding the role of organizational culture, its determinants, and consequences.

part two   The Culture of Management

Understanding the Nature of Culture and Change

The relationship between a culture and a company is complex. When trying to understand the impact of a culture on a firm, consider the many levels at which it operates. First, the physical location of the company plays a role. In the United States, company leaders are more likely to value risk taking, encourage competition, and exhibit several more individualistic tendencies. In contrast, managers in Japan and Mexico, in which cultures are more collectivist, tend to reward risk avoidance and cooperation. The second level is the company level. The culture at Microsoft, for example, is quite different from the culture in the Marine Corps. Even individual departments display cultural characteristics. In other words, computer operators live in a world that is different from the one in the marketing department. This chapter focuses on the middle-level, companywide culture. It is designed to help you discover the nature of a culture and the impact the culture has on both individual employees and organizational performance.

In addition, this chapter examines the nature of organizational change. Change is addressed from two perspectives: (1) when it is a planned event, and (2) as an ongoing and dynamic environmental characteristic. When change is a planned event, such as when a company implements a new strategy, managers should expect resistance to change and find ways to overcome that resistance. In the case of ongoing and dynamic changes which routinely occur within and outside the organization, managers should develop approaches that are effective and offer employees a sense of stability. Both culture and change are important topics to explore and manage in order to cope effectively with the turbulent world surrounding various organizations.

Organizational Culture

Organizational culture is a system of shared values, assumptions, beliefs, and norms that unite the members of an organization. Organizational culture reflects employees' views about "the way things are done around here." In short, corporate culture may be considered to be the personality of the organization.[1] The culture specific to each firm affects how employees feel and act as well as the type of employee hired and retained by the company.

There are three aspects of an organization's culture, as shown in Figure 4.1. The most obvious is the **visible culture** that an observer can hear, feel, or see. Aspects of visible culture include how people dress, how fast people walk and talk, whether there is an open floor plan without office doors or managers have private offices, and the extent to which status and power symbols are conspicuous. Assigned parking spots based on rank, differing cafeteria or eating arrangements based on organizational level, and the degree to which furnishings are plush and conservative versus simple and modern indicates the nature of power and status differentials.

organizational culture

A system of shared values, assumptions, beliefs, and norms that unite the members of an organization.

visible culture

The aspects of culture that an observer can hear, feel, or see.

FIGURE 4.1

Levels of Corporate Culture

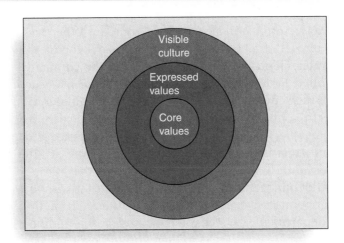

The signs of a visible culture make it possible to study dominant cultural characteristics, such as whether the organization is competitive or easygoing, formal or informal, hierarchical or egalitarian, liberal or conservative. Firms with controlling cultures often record and review their employees' communications, including telephone calls, e-mail, and Internet connections. About 40 percent of companies use software that allows managers "to record an employee's every digital move, including thoughts that she types on her keyboard and then erases as well as web sites visited and e-mails sent and received."[2]

espoused values

The aspects of corporate culture that are not readily observed, but instead can be perceived from the way managers and employees explain and justify their actions and decisions.

At a deeper level, **espoused values** cannot be readily observed but instead are the ways managers and employees explain and justify actions and decisions. For example, managers may justify layoffs primarily on the basis of a need to cut costs or to expedite decision making and improve response time by streamlining organizational levels. Other managers may say they tolerate mistakes because employees need to be encouraged to take risks or because it is better to treat workers with respect and provide them with second chances when necessary.

People may not always give the real reason behind their actions. Employees are quick to spot hypocrisy. Managers who are not honest about why actions were taken may create an organizational culture full of cynicism, dishonesty, lack of credibility, and poor ethics, all of which eventually translate into poor firm performance.

Espoused values may vary substantially from firm to firm within the same industry. For example, United Airlines's management believed that its happy workers were a competitive advantage, "even casting its employees in a series of ads trumpeting what happens when workers become their own masters."[3] On the other hand, the belief that workers are greedy and want more than they deserve is widely held by management

You wouldn't say "The Gap" and "Brooks Brothers" in the same breath when shopping for apparel. The Gap is able to differentiate not only the culture of its customers, but also its salespeople. In fact, this culture became famous (or infamous) as a skit on "Saturday Night Live."

at Northwest and American Airlines; pilot strikes and sickouts often reinforce this assumption.

Espoused values are generally consciously and explicitly communicated. At the center of organizational culture are **core beliefs** that are widely shared, operate unconsciously, and are considered nonnegotiable. In some organizations, such as SAS in the introductory vignette, a basic assumption may be that stability and commitment of the workforce are critical for success. Consequently, employees are well treated and receive liberal fringe benefits, including an on-site laundry service for clothes worn while exercising at the on-site fitness center. In addition, employees enjoy flexible work schedules and other family-friendly policies. At the other extreme, a basic assumption may be that employees are commodities and an expense that should be minimized in the business process, rather than an investment. Thus employees are tightly controlled, exceptions to established policy are kept to a minimum, there are detailed rules and procedures about what employees can and cannot do, and managers believe it is their duty to prevent deviations from the norms. Employees may be watching one another to ensure that no one breaks the rules, and people are trained to check with their superiors before making most decisions.

The basic underlying cultural assumptions create the lenses through which people perceive and interpret events. Someone sitting motionless may be seen as loafing in some firms, while at others, the employee would be perceived as pondering an important problem. When employees are absent from work, the organization's culture may lead managers to conclude they are shirking, and if an employee requests permission to perform some tasks at home, the request will probably be denied because the supervisor expects the employee will "goof off" rather than work. A simple and quick way of getting a handle on the type of culture that is operating in an organization is presented in Manager's Notes 4.1.

core beliefs

A firm's principles that are widely shared, that operate unconsciously, and that are considered nonnegotiable.

1. *What do we measure?*
   When performance is assessed, whatever is measured is what is truly important. Understanding what is actually measured reveals what the organization values. While there may be many statements about the importance of quality and customer service, if amount of sales is the only aspect of performance that is measured, the culture in the organization is more oriented to quantity than quality or customer service.

2. *What is celebrated, recognized, or rewarded?*
   What is held out in the organization as something to be celebrated or recognized? These things are the key to what is valued. Employees will be quick to pick up on this key to the culture in the organization.

3. *What data is used to assess the effectiveness of the organization?*
   Is productivity or amount of sales the sole measure focused on when making overall assessments of how well the organization is functioning? Or, are measures such as employee and customer satisfaction and loyalty also considered to be the most crucial? The data that is used as the principal means for taking the pulse of the organization reveals what is at the heart of the culture.

Source: Adapted from L. Larson, "A New Attitude: Changing Organization Culture," *Trustee* 55 (2002), pp. 8–14.

The Importance of Culture

Organization culture can be a critical factor in determining the competitiveness of an organization. While culture may seem more of a concept than something that is physically real, the potential impact of culture can be very real and merits careful attention. Results from workplace studies indicate that organizational culture can be an even more important determinant of worker commitment and loyalty than pay.[4] Culture can also differentiate an organization in the labor market. For example, SAS, the organization featured at the beginning of this chapter, is a company that many people seek out as a preferred employer. The employee- and family-friendly culture that has been carefully cultivated at SAS sets it apart and gives the organization a competitive advantage in the struggle to attract and keep the best workers. There are many ways in which organizational culture can be a key positive force in achieving organizational objectives. Manager's Notes 4.2 offers some tips to make sure the culture in your organization is a competitive asset.

Organizational culture can help managers achieve organizational objectives in several ways. In this section, key functions performed by culture, including employee self-management, continuity, employee socialization, and supporting a firm's strategies are described.

Employee Self-Management

"Keeping workers in line" consists of a variety of rational means to coordinate and control employees. Defining jobs with job descriptions; creating vertical levels and reporting relationships; drawing organizational charts; establishing departments, business units, and divisions; and developing work schedules are examples of rational controls. Still, no firm can function effectively unless employees choose to behave in the way the firm desires.

Organizational culture can induce employees to behave in a particular way without close supervision or formal control mechanisms. Most people like to feel that they belong; fitting into the culture and acting accordingly make it more likely that employees will be accepted by others. Conversely, failure to comply with cultural norms generates social pressures to conform; thus the individuals would either align with the cultural expectations or face ostracism and ridicule by their peers. Much of this process occurs informally and in an unspecified manner, filling in the gaps left by rational control systems.

Culture creates a sense of shared identity and facilitates commitment to something larger than individual self-interests. For instance, French biologist Nicolas Taquet left a state-controlled medical research lab in France because it was bureaucratic and constraining. Taquet immigrated to the United States to work as a researcher at the Baylor Institute for Immunology Research, where he was given the autonomy and the resources to pursue the development of anticancer compounds. He compared the two environments by noting that "I am so motivated here that I work weekends and nights. That wasn't the case back home."[5]

Stability

Culture provides a sense of continuity in the midst of rapid change and intense competitive pressure. In industries with "hyperturbulent environments" such as high technology, culture fulfills an important human need for predictability, security, and comfort. It can take the edge off the stress caused by projects that change overnight, products that become obsolete in a matter of months, changeable work teams and reporting relationships, and frequent shifts in work methods and operations. The continuity provided by organizational culture has become increasingly valuable in the new millennium, as most organizations are faced with a rapid rate of change. Likewise, as virtual connections and temporary alliances become commonplace, organizational culture can be the common understanding that both binds people together and facilitates their operations as a cohesive unit.[6]

Some organizations start socializing people to their culture when they recruit. Scottsdale, Arizona–based Cold Stone Creamery conveys their culture of fun and performing for customers by holding "auditions" for new workers.

Socialization

One key hurdle new employees face is finding out how to "fit in." Organizational culture subtly teaches employees the values of the organization. The process of internalizing or taking organizational values as one's own is called **socialization.** For example, the Marine Corps uses boot camps to socialize new recruits in "the Marine way." Sanyo requires new employees to live and eat together for five months at a company-paid resort to learn "how to speak to superiors [and acquire] proper grooming and dress. The company considers this program essential for transforming young employees, fresh out of school, into dedicated Kaisha Senshi, or corporate warriors."[7] Once accomplished, socialization helps the new individual feel he or she is part of the organization.

Socialization is a three-stage process. The first stage, **prearrival,** consists of the values, attitudes, biases, and expectations the employee brings to the organization when first hired. These may have been learned in the family, at school, in other organizations, or as members of a profession or discipline. Most organizations, some more deliberately than others, attempt to select employees who are most likely to fit into the company's culture. Even if the firm succeeds in hiring "the right type," however, the employee still has to learn the culture.

As the employee moves into the organization, the individual reaches the **encounter stage.** At this point, the individual begins to com-

socialization

The process of internalizing or taking organizational values as one's own.

prearrival

The first stage of socialization, consisting of the values, attitudes, biases, and expectations the employee brings to the organization when first hired.

encounter stage

The stage of socialization at which the individual begins to compare expectations about the firm's culture with reality.

TABLE 4.1

Entry Socialization Options

Formal socialization occurs when an employee's newcomer status is made obvious, through separate training or orientation away from the job.

Individual socialization occurs when the new employee is trained or receives orientation individually.

Fixed advancement socialization happens when new employees undergo the same time period for each stage of training and are expected to spend the same amount of time in the position before being considered for the next level.

Serial socialization takes place in firms that assign new employees to other staff members for specific training and mentoring in different areas.

Divestiture socialization removes new employees' individual characteristics so that the employees will fit into their roles and the company as it exists.

Informal socialization happens when the new employee receives little special attention and begins working right away.

Collective socialization occurs when a group of new employees receive training or go through orientation together.

Variable advancement socialization occurs when the next stage of training or career advancement within a company is flexible and based on the employee's development.

Random socialization occurs when new employees are not expected to resort to specific staff members but determine how to handle things themselves.

Investiture socialization assumes the new employees' individual traits and characteristics are valuable to the employees' and the firm's success.

Sources: J. Van Maanen, "People Processing: Strategies of Organizational Socialization," *Organizational Dynamics,* Summer 1978, pp. 19–36; E. H. Schein, "Organizational Culture," *American Psychologist,*" February 1990, p. 116.

pare expectations about the firm's culture with reality. To the extent that there are discrepancies between cultural expectations and reality, the employee is induced to bring his or her values and ways of doing things closer to those of the organization during the **metamorphosis stage.** Unfortunately, in their rush to fill positions, companies often do not pay enough attention to this stage. Jeffrey Pfeffer, a noted management scholar, writes that a common myth is that "you build a great and effective company by hiring only great people. . . . I hate the 'war for people' imagery. It's a trend the companies have brought on themselves. They're paying people to switch jobs and wondering why they switch jobs so much."[8]

Table 4.1 lists ways firms create a closer alignment between an employee's values and expectations and those of the firm. An organization can choose from among formal or informal, individual or collective, fixed or variable, serial or random, and investiture or divestiture socialization. Not all people are readily socialized. In extreme cases, an employee will feel disillusioned and decide that he or she is in the wrong place. Such an employee is likely to become disgruntled and/or leave the firm. Proper selection should reduce the probability of this happening.

Firms should also be wary of turning employees into conformists. A healthy organization tries to accommodate and take advantage of employee diversity, as discussed in Chapter 11, while maintaining cultural uniqueness.

metamorphosis stage

The stage of socialization at which the employee is induced to bring his or her values and ways of doing things closer to those of the organization.

Organizational Culture as Competitive Tool: Some Tips

1. Check whether your culture is strong or weak.

- Do employees agree on the core values?
- Do ceremonies, stories, and so on present a coherent and consistent message?
  - A strong culture should lead to greater cohesiveness and higher performance.

2. Is the culture consistent with the objectives of the organization?

- Do the policies, practices, and employee beliefs and values line up with the strategy?
- Does everyone know the mission of the organization?
  - A culture that is compatible with the strategy can reinforce the strategy and help to get everyone working together for the same purpose.

3. Want stability?

- Emphasize trust, fairness, and personal development in the culture.
- Offer public recognition of achievement.
- Provide opportunities for personal growth and support for work/life balance.
  - An atmosphere of trust and opportunity for personal growth can be key to retaining and attracting the best workers.

4. Manage the culture!

- Do you know what the culture is and what you want it to be?
- What are the levers by which you can influence the culture?
  - If you don't manage the culture, it will evolve on its own (and in ways you may not want). If culture isn't managed, you will have lost a potentially important tool for achieving competitive advantage.

5. Analyze the cultures of other organizations before working with them.

- Does a potential project with another organization make sense from a cultural perspective? Are the cultures compatible?
  - Incompatible cultures can lead to conflict and performance difficulty on joint projects. Also, to the extent that you are known by the company you keep, teaming with an organization with an incompatible culture could damage your own.

Source: Adapted from M. A. Mitchell and D. Yates, "How to Use Your Organizational Culture as a Competitive Tool," *Nonprofit World* 20 (2002), pp. 33–34.

Implementation of the Organization's Strategy

Organizational culture may contribute to firm performance by supporting implementation of the organization's strategy as well as desired changes in that strategy. In other words, if the firm's strategy and its culture reinforce each other, employees find it natural to be committed to the strategy. These shared values and norms make it easier for them to rally behind the chosen strategy.

Beware the Darkside

Very few things in management are absolute. While a company's culture can be a major advantage in the marketplace, there is also the potential for negative outcomes. For instance, a firmly entrenched set of cultural values and norms may cause employees to resist any change, even one that is vital for survival. Further, a strong culture may appear to some to be more like an exclusive club, causing valuable new employees or customers to feel like outsiders. Eventually these individuals may seek to work with other organizations. At the other end of the spectrum, there may be managers who neglect or fail to reinforce the key values present in a culture. This can lead to disregard for personal safety or little understanding and support for the firm's strategic efforts. Consequently, organizational leaders must continually assess the nature of an organization's culture, including what is valued and reinforced, or the problems associated with a culture that is too strong or too weak may emerge.

Managing Cultural Processes

The culture of an organization evolves gradually over time. It is normally strongly influenced by the beliefs and philosophy of the organization's founder. A firm's founder transmits his or her beliefs to a small group of close associates, often family members who already share the same values or at least know each other well. As the firm grows, the founder's values determine who is hired and who is retained and promoted. Selection and socialization processes tend to reinforce the founder's values. These values become firmly entrenched even after the founder is long gone. The Disney Company remains a close reflection of Walt Disney, even though he died four decades ago. Walt Disney strongly believed that every employee should present an ideal image to the public. This meant being impeccably groomed, cheerful, and friendly. Men were required to have no facial hair and to wear short hair.

Similarly, Jim Henson, creator of the Muppets, espoused beliefs that live on in his company. Henson "always wanted people to be creatively and emotionally invested in what they did. . . . He believed that projects worked best if they were a team effort. . . . He wanted people who were wildly and eccentrically different from himself at the company. He loved seeing what they could do and how they would surprise him."[9] "For many years, IBM was a reflection of J. Watson's personality. Southwest Airlines is made in Herb Kelleher's image. Mary Kay Cosmetics' culture reflects its founder's faith and beliefs. Microsoft's culture represents Bill Gates' intellectual, demanding, and perfectionist personality. Oprah Winfrey, the first African-American and the third woman to own a TV and film production studio, runs an organization that reflects her high-energy, nurturing style."[10]

A variety of things maintain and reinforce culture over time. Some may be deliberately imposed by management, as in the case of cultural symbols, rituals, and the choice of company heroes who best embody the firm's values. Others may be largely unconscious processes, such as the use of stories, language, and employee perceptions of the company's leadership style.

Cultural Symbols

People find it relatively easy to relate to or at least understand symbols or icons, such as flags, crosses, uniforms, or various logos (e.g., the Playboy Bunny). **Cultural symbols** are the icons and objects that communicate organizational values. Management uses them to convey and sustain shared meaning among employees. For example,

cultural symbols

The icons and objects that communicate organizational values, used by management to convey and sustain shared meaning among employees.

- Tandem Computers' corporate headquarters in Cupertino, California, looks and feels more like a college campus than a business facility. Small buildings are separated by green space. Jogging trails, a basketball court, a large swimming pool, a dance hall, and other amenities are provided on site. These symbols reinforce a company culture characterized by openness, participation, informality, and equality.

- The president of Nashville's Centennial Medical Center dramatically conveyed an open-door policy by removing the door to his office and hanging it from the lobby ceiling.

- To change their "stiff," conservative culture in order to attract new talent from freewheeling Silicon Valley firms and to appear more friendly to apprehensive customers, several leading brokerage houses, including Morgan Stanley Dean Witter, Lehman Brothers, and Goldman Sachs, introduced a policy of casual attire in 2000.

Company Rituals and Ceremonies

Organizations plan activities and events that offer all employees an opportunity to share cultural meanings. One example of a dramatic ritual occurs when police departments conduct ceremonies to honor bravery, community dedication, or acts of heroism. Ceremonies convey organizational values and display examples of outstanding performance. Medtronic, a producer of high-tech implantable medical products, holds an annual service day during which the production facility is shut down.[11] The purpose of the ritual is to provide Medtronic employees with the opportunity to contribute time and effort to a charitable cause for one day. The ritual helps to make real to employees the community-based values that are part of the Medtronic culture. Another example of a company that uses an annual event to underscore their culture is Johnson Controls. The company holds an annual meeting, called Team Rally, in which employee teams present how they improved a work process.[12] The presentations use skits and teams include how the improvements are disseminated to the rest of the organization. From a cultural standpoint, the Team Rally is a vehicle for Johnson Controls to emphasize the values of teamwork, continuous improvement, and sharing knowledge throughout the organization. Mary Kay Cosmetics Company bestows awards to high-achieving sales consultants in an auditorium filled with sales agents and their families. Glamorously dressed, they cheer as their most successful peers receive gold and diamond pins, furs, and pink Cadillacs.

Company Heroes

Organizations effectively communicate values by identifying individuals whose deeds best reflect what the organization believes in, so that other people can emulate their behavior. The police officers and firefighters who died at the World Trade Center on September 11, 2001, will long be remembered as organizational heroes.

Stories

Organizational culture is sustained by the narratives and legends that vividly capture the organization's values. At 3M, a commonly told story involves a worker who was fired for pursuing an idea that his boss asked him to drop. The former employee continued working on the idea without pay in an unused office. According to the legend, the product idea eventually became a big success, and the worker was rehired at the vice-president level. This story is used to communicate 3M's belief that perseverance is crucial to success.

Language

The language used by managerial employees may serve as a constant reminder of the organization's values. Language promotes both positive and negative values. For instance, the use of sexist language and ethnic jokes communicates to current and prospective workers that the company does not value diversity. Reliance on such euphemisms as "future enhancements" for "need to change a failing course of action," "reengineering efforts" instead of "layoffs," and "dehiring" for "termination" suggests the absence of an open, honest atmosphere in which issues can be discussed in a frank and candid fashion.

Firms often use slogans to succinctly express cultural values. For example, PepsiCo communicates the value of hiring the best people and teaching them to work together in its slogan, "We take eagles and teach them to fly in formation." Sequins International, a manufacturer of sequined fabrics and trimming, points out that "you don't have to please the boss; you have to please the customer."

Leadership

Employees infer a great deal about the organization from the leader styles they encounter. Effective leaders articulate a vision for the organization that employees find exciting and worth striving for. In addition, an effective leader provides a daily example of what the organization deems to be important. Employees make judgments about the underlying values of the organization not by what executives say, but by what they do. Many people attribute the survival of Chrysler in the early 1980s to its colorful CEO, Lee Iacocca. Iacocca negotiated a large loan from the federal government to save the company. He also served as an example by working for $1 a year plus Chrysler stock, which many analysts viewed as worthless. Within two years, Chrysler repaid the federal loan, and the value of its stock had skyrocketed. Iacocca showed Chrysler employees that perseverance, sacrifice, and commitment can overcome daunting challenges and can lead to personal success.

To reinforce an egalitarian and frugal image, Andrew Grove, CEO of Intel, the Silicon Valley manufacturer of computer chips, worked out of a cubicle similar in size to those of other engineers. Groves's cubicle was located on the main floor of the building for all to see. Grove insisted that all top managers fly coach class, rent subcompact cars, and avoid using company resources to bolster personal prestige. At Intel, offices were not to be elegantly furnished, and business meetings were not to take place at fancy restaurants.

Southwest Airlines has been profitable year after year, while most airlines struggle to survive and many have disappeared. Southwest's former CEO Herb Kelleher reinforced a culture of "be happy, enjoy your work, and make customers smile" through employee videos, "winning spirit" ceremonies, and speeches, and by serving as inspirational leader, kindly uncle, cheerleader, and clown.

Organizational Policies and Decision Making

Performance appraisals, budgets, new plans, and other policies and decisions clearly communicate company values, and therefore the company's culture. The criteria used for measuring success and the way they are used for control purposes tell employees what the organizational culture considers to be most important. For instance, some pharmaceutical firms measure innovation by the number of new patents, while others prefer to rely on the commercial value of existing or prospective patents. The former companies are signaling that they value many projects with small incremental changes to technology, risk aversion, a short-term orientation, and greater quantity. In the latter case, the signal is that focusing on fewer projects involving more radical technological changes and higher probability of large payoffs is preferred. This is more likely to lead to fewer patents, greater risk taking, a long-term orientation, and a search for one home run rather than four singles.

Employees learn what the company truly values by watching where scarce resources are spent. For instance, the word *innovation* may be used repeatedly in speeches, in company brochures, and on plaques positioned next to each elevator. But if research and development expenditures are the first thing to be cut during hard times, employees receive the opposite message.

Cultural values are also communicated by the ways people are rewarded. For instance, despite lip service to the value of effective teaching, many universities determine faculty salaries and promotions largely on research productivity. This sends a strong message to faculty that what the university values are publications, not student success stories.

Characteristics and Types of Organizational Culture

Cultural uniformity, the strength of a firm's culture, the degree of formalization, and the extent to which organizational culture differs from national culture vary from one firm to another, and can determine the extent to which organizational culture influences employees. In addition to these various external characteristics, the nature or type of culture varies widely across organizations. There are numerous typologies of culture. It is useful to be familiar with the types in order to recognize the type of culture that is present. In this section some of the characteristics along which cultures in organizations differ as well as individual types of cultures are identified.

Cultural Uniformity versus Heterogeneity

Organizations vary in the extent to which a uniform culture permeates the entire organization. In some large corporations, different subcultures may be found in different parts of the firm. This is the case at Motorola, where the culture varies among divisions. Some divisions are conservative, bureaucratic, and risk-averse and value seniority, while others are entrepreneurial, freewheeling, innovative, and risk-seeking and place little value on seniority. At 3M, on the other hand, the dominant culture, which emphasizes innovation, a focus on related products, and tolerance for failure, is evident in all parts of the corporation.

Neither uniformity nor heterogeneity is right or wrong. When divisions are largely autonomous and each has a different strategy for its own unique products or services, it makes sense for each division to have a different culture. On the other hand, subcultures could be problematic for a firm where all units are interdependent and employees must work closely together to implement the overall corporate strategy.

Strong versus Weak Cultures

The more employees believe in the espoused values, the more they act in accordance with those values and the more the culture plays a boundary-defining role, creating a distinction between the organization and others. A strong culture pressures people to do what the organization wants with less reliance on formal control mechanisms such as close supervision, hierarchies, rules, and procedures. It may also increase the level of intrinsic motivation because employees work hard for the right thing. On the other hand, a strong culture may become a liability if it presents a barrier to adaptation in a rapidly changing environment, makes some groups of employees feel unwelcome, or makes it difficult for the firm to work cooperatively with other firms.

Culture versus Formalization

In varying degrees, organizational culture can substitute for such formal systems of control and decision making as organizational structures, rules, procedures, policies, and direct supervision. A common destiny and shared meanings make it less necessary to create mechanisms to ensure compliance, predictability, orderliness, and consistency. To the extent that organizational culture increases trust among employees, it reduces the need for written documentation and monitoring of organization members.

National versus Organizational Culture

There are times when organizations use employee selection and socialization to develop cultures that are significantly different from a specific national culture. Some multinational firms, such as Colgate, deliberately attempt to create a "global company culture" to circumvent the barriers to communication and understanding present in many multinational operations.

In most countries, there is a great deal of diversity in the workforce, and most cultural traits overlap across countries. For instance, while the typical U.S. worker may be an individualistic risk seeker and the typical Japanese worker may be team and security oriented, numerous people in both countries are more like the typical person in the other country than the typical person in their own country. Thus, a firm is able to attract and retain the type of employee that fits into its culture regardless of where it is located.

Types

An increasing number of culture typologies are being used to identify various kinds of cultures. No one typology is better or more correct than the others. Regardless of which is utilized, classifying the type of culture in an organization can be useful for identifying the kind of employees and the management characteristics that are present in a culture. For example, knowing the type of culture indicates whether or not employees who are risk takers are hired. Further, the type of culture present has implications for how people should be managed. Some of the basic types of organizational culture along with implications for employees and management are described next.

One simple but powerful classification differentiates between two basic organization culture types: (1) traditional control or (2) employee involvement.[13] A traditional control culture emphasizes the chain of command and relies on top-down control and orders. Control systems are put in place so that management can be assured that assigned projects and goals are being attained. In contrast, an employee involvement culture emphasizes participation and involvement. People work together to attain goals, not because they are externally coerced by rules and control systems, but because they are internally motivated. Table 4.2 summarizes the key characteristics of these two basic types of organizational culture.

The traditional and involvement cultures have distinct differences in terms of understanding what types of employees are recruited and how the work environment should be managed. For example, employees that would be expected to be most successful in the traditional environment are more task and rule oriented. In contrast, the best performers in an employee involvement culture would be risk takers with strong

TABLE 4.2

Traditional Control and Employee Involvement Cultures

TRADITIONAL CONTROL: KEY CHARACTERISTICS	EMPLOYEE INVOLVEMENT: KEY CHARACTERISTICS
• Narrowly defined job duties	• Broadly defined job duties
• Top-down communication	• Lateral communication
• Centralized decision making	• Participative decision making
• Control systems	• Feedback systems

Source: Adapted from R. L. Heneman, M. M. Fisher, and K. E. Dixon, "Reward and Organizational Systems Alignment: An Expert System," *Compensation and Benefits Review* 33 (2001), pp. 18–29.

interpersonal skills. Effective management in a traditional culture would emphasize task performance and careful measurement and control. Effective management in an employee involvement culture would need to be much "looser," and reward people for commitment and for taking risks, even though some of them may have failed.

A second approach identifies four types of cultures based on their similarities using terms with which you are already familiar: teams, clubs, academies, and fortresses. Each type calls for a particular kind of employee. A quality match increases the odds that an employee will be successful. Having employees whose personalities match the organizational culture tends to enhance the overall performance of a firm by reducing disruptive internal friction and employee turnover.[14]

A **baseball team culture** is present in an organization facing a rapidly changing environment, with short product life cycles, high-risk decision making, and dependence on continuous innovation for survival. Organizations like this are typically in such fast-paced, competitive, high-risk industries as advertising, software development, movie production, and biotechnology. The employee who best fits this culture tends to be a risk-taker, enjoys being a "free agent," shows little commitment to one employer, and thrives on time pressure and stress.

The **club culture** seeks people who are loyal, committed to one organization, and need to fit into a group. Organization members prefer to spend their entire careers in one organization. The organization, in turn, rewards them with job security, promotes from within, and allows them to prove their competence at each level. Employees in firms with club cultures grant "bonus points" for age and experience. Club cultures are present in companies such as United Parcel Service, Delta Airlines, the "Baby Bell" telephone companies, government agencies, and the military.

Like club cultures, an organization with **academy culture** prefers to hire individuals who are interested in a long-term association and a slow, steady climb up the organization ladder. Employees in academy cultures tend to be confined to a set of jobs within a particular function, so they should be people who enjoy becoming expert in one area. They should not expect broad individual development and intense networking with

---

baseball team culture

The fast-paced, competitive, high-risk form of corporate culture typically found in organizations in rapidly changing environments, with short product life cycles, with high-risk decision making, and dependent on continuous innovation for survival.

club culture

A type of organizational culture that seeks people who are loyal, committed to one organization, and need to fit into a group, and rewards them with job security, promotion from within, and slow progress.

 Corporate Culture Preferences Scale

academy culture

A type of organization culture that seeks to hire people with specialties and technical mastery who will be confined to a set of jobs within a particular function and be rewarded by long-term association and a slow, steady climb up the organization ladder.

part two The Culture of Management

FIGURE 4.2

Competing Values Framework

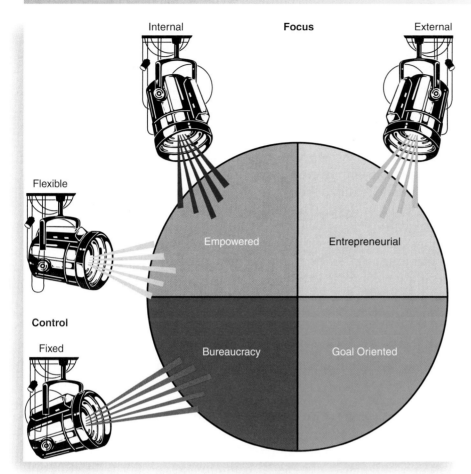

people from other areas. Specialization and technical mastery are the basis for rewards and advancement. Organizations that fit this mold include IBM, Coca-Cola, Procter & Gamble, General Motors, and Ford.

Fortress cultures are obsessed with surviving and reversing sagging fortunes. These companies restructure and downsize to cope with the challenges of economic decline or a hostile competitive environment. Textile firms, savings and loans, large retailers, forest product companies, and natural gas exploration firms are found in this group. Fortress-type firms attract confident individuals who enjoy the excitement, challenge, and opportunities of a turnaround.

A final organizational culture typology is known as the competing values framework.[15] This framework is presented in Figure 4.2. As shown, the competing values framework is based on two dimensions: focus and control. The focus dimension refers to whether the primary attention of the organization is directed toward internal dynamics or directed outward toward the external environment. The control dimension represents the extent to which the organization is flexible or fixed

fortress culture

An organizational culture with the primary goal of surviving and reversing business problems, including economic decline and hostile competitors.

in how it coordinates and controls activity. As depicted in the figure, the two ends of each continuum can be viewed as different colored spotlights. When the spotlights cross they form four unique colors that represent the four organizational culture models that make up the competing values framework. The purple spot depicts a bureaucratic culture which focuses internally and has a fixed approach to controlling the work process. A bureaucratic culture is concerned with maintaining stability and tries to achieve it with hierarchical control. The pink spot represents an empowered culture. The focus is internal, as it is with a bureaucracy, but the approach to control is looser and more flexible. The emphasis of an empowered culture is high morale and cohesiveness and it attempts to achieve these outcomes through development and support of the workforce. The light yellow quadrant depicts an entrepreneurial culture in which the organization is externally focused but flexible. The entrepreneurial organization seeks growth through being adaptable and agile. The green spot represents a goal oriented culture in which a focus on the external environment is paired with a fixed approach to control. A goal-oriented organization is paired with a fixed approach to control. A goal-oriented organization is focused on productivity and competing in the marketplace and it achieves this through careful planning and goal setting. Combining the types of focus and control leads to four unique organizational cultures. Which type of culture is best depends upon the environmental situation and management's purpose for the organization. There is evidence, however, that the type of culture that is dominant in an organization can influence how effectively the organization performs. For example, it has been found that hospitals that maintain a more empowered culture for nurses tend to have nurses with greater commitment and job satisfaction and lower tendency to quit.[16] While an empowered culture may not work in all types of business, treating professionals, such as nurses, in a flexible and supportive manner makes sense and leads to improved patient care and lower turnover costs.

The competing values framework and the other typologies are useful for evaluating organizational cultures. These models help us to rationally think through and identify the employee and management practices that match a culture and lead to improved organizational performance. It is important to recognize that these frameworks depict pure types of culture. The reality is that most organizations do not have such coherent and internally consistent cultures.

Managing Organizational Change

One of the more fixed aspects of a company is its culture. Employees tend to rely on the longstanding symbols, rituals, language, and values that provide a sense of continuity and stability. Unfortunately, the world surrounding the organization (and even the world inside the organization) is nowhere near as stable. In other words: Change happens! The second half of this chapter is devoted to the process of understanding and managing change. Only when managers effectively anticipate and execute change can the firm survive and succeed in the long term.

Types of Change

Change can be viewed as a planned event or as an unplanned and dynamic condition.[17] A planned change occurs when a change in an organization is anticipated and allows for advance preparation. In contrast, dynamic change refers to change that is ongoing or happens so quickly, such as with a crisis, that the impact on the organization cannot be anticipated and specific preparations cannot be made. For example, one organization may be in an industry in which government regulations will soon change. The change is known and can be anticipated and planned for. In contrast, a second organization may be in a field in which the market is volatile and fiercely competitive. Technological changes are the norm and difficult to anticipate. The change that this organization must contend with is dynamic and a continuous part of the organization's existence, rather than a discrete event, as with a planned change.

Whether facing a methodical shift required in a planned change or confronting a more dynamic change, many organizations have difficulty dealing with the need for change. AT&T was a regulated monopoly provider of local and long-distance telephone service for many years. When competition heated up due to government deregulation of the industry and the development of cellular phone technology, AT&T management decided to move away from its "monopoly culture," which valued security, to a "market culture," which valued high performance. Despite its efforts, AT&T management has struggled to make this cultural change a reality, with only mixed results. One major reason for its struggle was that many senior and middle managers had been promoted through the ranks under a set of rules based on the culture of a monopoly. For many of these managers, embracing the new culture that challenges the values that led to their success proved difficult.

Management Close-Up 4.a shows how an executive changed company culture from a top-down control environment to a decentralized, empowered, and energized team environment.

Forces for Change

Contrary to what many employees believe, companies simply do not make changes, "just for the heck of it." Numerous internal and external forces can cause companies to make changes. In the case of Axiom, which is featured in Management Close-Up 4.a, the driving force for change was the need to maximize corporate goals. In this section, an overview of the causes of change is provided.

The Line Stops Here: The Axciom Experience

THEME: DEALING WITH CHANGE As CEO, Charles Morgan was used to being asked for his opinions and judgments. While it is flattering to be constantly asked for your opinion, it can also be extremely time-consuming. Charles Morgan recognized the need for change in 1990. He gathered his management team and told them that people were lined up outside his door early each morning. And, as each day wore on, the line got longer. Why? Because Axciom used a traditional top-down hierarchical approach. The company is in the technology field of data mining, a technique used by many businesses to improve marketing and customer service. Morgan realized that if everyone wanted him involved in every decision, no matter how small, the company would never reach its full potential. The CEO insisted that the organization had to change.

The management team took the directive seriously and engineered massive changes. The old hierarchical structure, which employed chain-of-command and corporate titles, was replaced by a flattened, decentralized, and results-oriented environment. The new hierarchy was composed of only four levels: company, division, group, and business unit. All employees, including the CEO, were assigned the same size office space, and most of the spaces were cubicles. In this new system work is approached as a team issue and employees may be on multiple teams, playing different roles in each. Team members discuss projects and make decisions about how to best accomplish goals and serve the clients. These changes successfully transformed Axciom into a more flexible and empowered organization. The emphasis shifted from relying on the chain-of-command, which wasted time as employees presented their cases at each level. The new company structure places an emphasis on adding value and getting things done.

Did the changes at Axciom work? Charles Morgan no longer has long lines of employees waiting to have an audience with him. While that might be nice for Mr. Morgan, you are probably wondering about the impact on the business. On a variety of dimensions, it appears that the Axciom change was an effective one. The company has become a dominant force in its industry with many Fortune 500 organizations as clients. Productivity improved, and voluntary turnover, or quit rates, is below the industry's average. *Fortune Magazine* often includes Axciom in its lists of best places to work. In short, the change at Axciom appears to have been a change for the better.

Source: P. J. Kiger, "Axciom Rebuilds from Scratch," *Workforce 81* (2002), pp. 52–55.

ENVIRONMENTAL FORCES A great deal of pressure on a company can emerge from relationships with customers, suppliers, and employees. Environmental forces include these business relationships as well as changes in technology, market forces, political and regulatory agencies and laws, and social trends.

Both technology and market forces were pressuring Merrill Lynch, the financial brokerage firm, to make changes. The pressure resulted from the low-cost online trading that was pioneered by the discount broker Charles Schwab. Customers grew to prefer using the Internet to do their own research rather than paying brokers for advice about financial investments. Unfortunately, Merrill Lynch's commissioned brokers feared losing profitable commissions from clients. Consequently, the management team resisted offering online trading for several years, resulting in large losses of clients and market share to Charles Schwab. Finally, when it was evident that the market for financial services had permanently changed, Merrill Lynch management offered online trading service to

Barnes & Noble started barnes&noble.com in 1997 to compete with online booksellers. By 2001 barnes&noble.com was ranked among the top five Web properties in the world and as the number one site among brick-and-mortar brands.

customers for fees similar to those charged by Charles Schwab. Lynch was then able to curtail its loss of market share and maintain a client base.

Barnes & Noble, the large bookstore chain, faced a similar technological threat. The company was losing market share to Amazon.com, which offered books on the Internet rather than in brick-and-mortar stores. Barnes & Noble effectively responded by changing its market distribution policy to include a website to distribute books.

Political and regulatory forces for change include local, state, and national laws and court decisions that affect business relationships. For example, the 1997 change in the minimum wage, increasing it from $4.75 to $5.15 per hour, meant that firms paying the minimum wage would see an increase of 40 cents an hour in those wages. Low-wage employers, such as fast-food restaurants, had to change both wage structures and use of labor to comply with the law.

Not all political forces that cause companies to change their work cultures are legally mandated. For example, after Supreme Court nominee Clarence Thomas was accused of sexual harassment, many companies added an explicit sexual harassment policy to employment policies to protect against allegations of harassment that could wind up in court. Similarly, as more women enter the workforce, companies have been changing rigid employment policies governing work schedules. More flexible work schedules enable employees who have dependent children at home to better juggle work and family responsibilities without neglecting either. The payoff is a more satisfied workforce with better morale, which translates into improved employee retention.

INTERNAL FORCES Internal forces for change arise from events within the company. They may originate with top executives and managers and travel in a top-down direction or with front-line employees or labor unions and travel in a bottom-up direction.

In 1980, Jack Welch, CEO of General Electric (GE), decided to turn a mediocre collection of diverse and unrelated businesses into a world leader. He made each business-unit manager responsible for meeting high performance standards and reaching the ranking of first or second in market performance within the industry sector. Managers who failed to achieve this ambitious goal would lose their jobs, and their business units would be downsized or sold off. In the next several years, 100,000 of 400,000 jobs were eliminated. GE had the highest market valuation in the world by the year 2000.[18]

Employees who demand amendment of policies that affect the way they are treated can also be internal forces for change. For example, physicians have recently begun forming labor unions. They want to protect the ability to practice medicine and treat patients as they see fit rather than as managed care organizations dictate. Doctors are counting on the new unions to provide them with bargaining power to regain decision-making authority in areas such as patient loads, prescription choices, and treatment options for their patients.

Resistance to Change

When change occurs, managers routinely encounter coalitions of employees or other managers who resist the proposed change. New work routines cause short-term anxiety as employees learn new ways of doing their jobs. Employees who thrived under one set of rules governing rewards have to adjust their efforts in order to meet a new set of performance expectations. Some of the reasons employees resist change include self-interest, lack of trust and understanding, uncertainty, different perspectives and goals, and cultures that value tradition.

Resistance to some changes is based on legitimate concerns. Consequently, these changes will be modified so that the concerns are dealt with.

Resistance to change can, in the extreme, involve acts of sabotage meant to undermine the change and to send a clear signal of firm resistance. For example, a large Massachusetts warehouse recently installed an automated conveyor system.[19] The project should have substantially improved company productivity. Instead, management encountered endless headaches and *reduced* productivity. Why? The workers feared that the change might cause them to lose their jobs. Various employees

Managing Resistance to Change

Effective managers recognize that the natural human response to change is resistance. Even when individuals, teams, and even entire organizations understand that a change will be for the better, they may still resist the change, for a number of reasons.

1. The change may require an investment of time and effort that people don't want to make.

2. The change may mean giving up something that is comfortable.

3. A change may be resisted because it is externally imposed.

Resistance to change can be, to some extent, a good thing. Signs of resistance mean that the change process is proceeding. If there is no resistance people are either ignoring the change or hoping that if they wait long enough, it will go away.

You need to recognize resistance as part of the change process. It is possible to take steps to try to help people work through their resistance. Here are some tactics for managing resistance for you to consider.

- *Lead by Doing.* Managers can help overcome resistance by being a model for the change. Bill Gates, in an effort to overcome resistance within Microsoft to the tablet PC, began bringing an early model to all meetings and using it to take notes.

- *Offer Support.* People want to talk and express concerns. An effective manager provides the opportunities and helps constructively guide the discussions, rather than letting resistance develop and take hold.

- *Start the Commitment Bandwagon Early.* Don't wait for resistance to surface before taking steps to deal with it. It can be much more effective and easier to develop understanding and commitment to the change early on in the process.

- *Take It Easy.* There may be a temptation to try to implement a change as quickly as possible. Instead, starting slow can lead to achieving the change more quickly since you are giving people a chance to understand and adapt to the transformation.

Source: Adapted from J. Davidson, "Overcoming Resistance to Change," *Public Management 84* (2002), pp. 20–23.

started jamming broomsticks into the conveyor system, an action that would shut the system down until a manager could track down the problem. If concern is great enough, resistance to a change can be fairly dramatic.

Some of the reasons for resistance to change are described next. Also, Manager's Notes 4.3 identifies steps that can be taken to manage resistance to change.

SELF-INTEREST   Employees resist change when they fear losing something they value, such as economic benefits, status, or influence in the organization. Production employees may resist change in manufacturing technology because they fear having their jobs simplified and made more

New IBM CEO Sam Palmisano, who took the reins in 2002, has offered a good chunk of his own bonus to stake a performance-based bonus for 20 top executives, dissolved a committee consisting of 300 members that had been in place for generations, and placed a new emphasis on teams with his "on-demand" strategy. All with visions of remaking IBM into the powerhouse it once was.

repetitive. A plant relocation from the city to the suburbs may mean that employees have a longer commute. As mentioned earlier, commissioned financial brokers at Merrill Lynch resisted online trading services because they would lose lucrative commissions from clients who switched to online trading.

LACK OF TRUST AND UNDERSTANDING   Employees may not trust the intentions behind a proposed change, or they may misunderstand its purpose. This type of resistance is most likely when previous changes were not well understood by employees or resulted in negative consequences. For example, some organizations have launched Total Quality Management initiatives by telling employees that the objective of the quality initiative was to provide better service or product quality to the customer. The real goal was to use the quality gains to reduce the size of the workforce, but this was not disclosed to employees until later. Employees who embraced the initiative felt betrayed when the improved level of productivity was translated into layoffs. This deception has remained in the collective memory of the workforce, making it more difficult for management to obtain employee agreement to new changes.

UNCERTAINTY   Uncertainty results from fear of the unknown and lack of information about the future. It can be particularly threatening when employees' fears are based on negative consequences of previous changes in the organization. Between 1991 and 1997, employees at Apple Computer experienced three major layoffs that reduced the size of the workforce by more than a third. Many amenities that made working at the company special, such as wine and cheese parties on Friday afternoons and free bagels and cream cheese in the mornings, were also discontinued. As a result, employees feared losing jobs when projects ended, and many people substantially slowed their progress in anticipation of being discharged. Key technical and marketing personnel left for greener pastures, preferring to be in charge of their own destinies rather than waiting for the ax to fall. The uncertainty of continuing layoffs at Apple, coupled with changes that reduced the pleasant working conditions at the company, made employees more likely to demonstrate their resistance to change by quitting rather than resolving to cope with the change and uncertainty.

Assessing Your Flexibility

DIFFERENT PERSPECTIVES AND GOALS   A proposed change may be viewed through different lenses by employees with differing goals and perspectives. Even if a change is perceived as helping the organization, resistance may occur among employees who believe it will diminish the welfare of the unit to which they are attached. For example, the Saturn Division of General Motors in rural Tennessee represented a change from the way GM made automobiles in Detroit. Saturn was established to more closely follow the way the Japanese produced quality automobiles, and the improved manufacturing techniques perfected at Saturn were to be transferred to all other GM divisions to improve product quality and efficiency. Managers in the Chevrolet, Pontiac, and Oldsmobile divisions saw the Saturn Division as a rival that could threaten the flow of resources to their divisions. A coalition of division managers "ganged up" on the Saturn Division to ensure it would remain in the small-car niche, which began to shrink in the 1990s when customers switched their preferences to larger vehicles. Consequently, Saturn began to operate at a loss.

CULTURES THAT VALUE TRADITION   Some organizational cultures are not supportive of change, valuing tradition and customary ways of doing things instead. Two organizations with strong cultures that resist change are the Catholic Church and the U.S. military. For years, the Catholic Church has refused to allow women to enter the priesthood despite the fact that there are not enough men entering seminaries to fill open positions. U.S. military leaders have resisted allowing openly gay and lesbian soldiers to serve in the military. Under the "don't ask, don't tell" policy, homosexual soldiers may serve only if they keep their orientation to themselves.

Models of Organizational Change

Whatever the reason for change, an organization that effectively·responds has a competitive advantage. The process begins when management recognizes and accepts the need for change. Once this is accomplished, other

FIGURE 4.3

Star Model

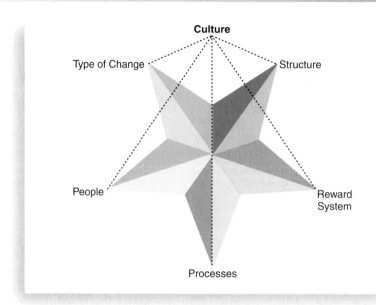

factors must be considered and possibly altered. There are three approaches which can help managers to effectively implement change and anticipate and deal with potential problems and resistance. These include the Star model, Lewin's three-step model, and the force-field analysis model.

THE STAR MODEL The Star model[20] identifies five factors that can be key to implementing a change. Further, the model is also a tool that can be used to help build and maintain an organization that is ready for change. The model was developed by noted management scholar Ed Lawler.

A five-pointed star, with each point representing a factor important to change, represents the model. Each of the five factors are briefly considered below.

1. *Type of change.* What type of change, *evolutionary,* or *transformational,* is needed? Is the change an evolutionary progression of continuous improvements or alterations? Or is transformational change needed in which more dramatic alterations are needed, such as major changes in products or business models?

   A transformational change may require alteration in the remaining factors in the star model.

2. *Structure.* How are people grouped together and decisions made? Does the structure support the change or impede it?

3. *Reward systems.* What do people get paid and rewarded for? If team effort is needed, a reward system that recognizes individual performance isn't going to motivate people toward a team approach.

BE A STAR! APPLYING THE STAR MODEL

The Star model of organizational change focuses management attention on various factors that can be critical to a change effort. It is a tool that can help you identify key issues and determine where the organization needs to be in order for a change to be successful. The following exercises provide you the opportunity to use the Star model as a tool for effective change management.

1. Select an organization of your choice. It could be a real organization, one that you work for, or one that is fictional.

2. As an individual or team, identify a change that may need to take place in the organization that is of a transformational nature. Describe the forces leading to this need for change.

3. What should be done in order to adequately prepare the organization for change? Specifically use the Star model to identify the relevant areas. For each factor included in the Star model, assess where the organization is currently and the conditions that must exist in order for the change to be successful.

4. How would you propose to make the shift in each of the factors?

5. Share with the rest of the class:

   a. The need for change you focused on (and where it came from).

   b. Your assessment of the current status of the five star factors and where each needs to be.

   c. How you would propose to make the shifts on each factor.

Further Discussion Questions

1. How would you evaluate the Star model as a tool for identifying what needs to be done in order to successfully implement a change? Is the model too complex? Does it leave anything out?

2. Are there examples of transformational change in organizations that you are familiar with or have experienced? Were the factors of the Star model in place for the change to be implemented? Was the change attempt successful? Why, or why not?

4. *Processes.* How is information communicated and behavior controlled in the organization? If the need for change is not well communicated and decisions are made in a hierarchical fashion, a change may be very difficult to implement.

5. *People.* What people skills and capabilities are needed? Are the needed skills within the organization, or do they need to be trained or brought in from outside the organization?

In addition to the five factors, the Star model includes organizational culture. However, culture is portrayed as something that is derived from and influenced by the five factors. In other words, an organization doesn't simply have a culture that values employees; it develops that type of culture through the underlying factors. The challenge is to determine the mix of the factors that will create the culture needed to successfully implement and maintain the needed change. Skills for Managing 4.1

FIGURE 4.4

Lewin's Three-Step Model of Organizational Change

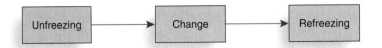

provides you with the opportunity to apply the Star model and see if you think it is an effective change management tool.

LEWIN'S THREE-STEP MODEL Kurt Lewin, a noted social psychologist, developed the **three-step model** of organizational change shown in Figure 4.4. The three steps are unfreezing, change (also called movement or transformation), and refreezing.

Unfreezing involves melting resistance to change by dealing with people's fears and anxieties so they can be more open to the change. People are given new information that makes them aware that the status quo is unacceptable and that some type of change is required.

The second step is the *change* itself, which is a departure from the status quo. Change can involve technology, people, products, services, or management policies and administration. It may be embodied in a new leader hired from outside the company to champion policies that were effective in another organization. Or, it may be represented by a new product that serves different customers and that requires new ways of selling and marketing.

The final step is *refreezing*, in which new management practices and employee behaviors become part of employees' routine activities. Coaching, training, and adopting appropriate reward systems facilitate the refreezing step.

For example, suppose management decides to change its corporate communication policy so that all company announcements are posted on a website instead of being distributed on paper. Step one would be to mobilize data to show employees that Internet communication is faster and more efficient than sending paper documents. Then the change would be made by setting up a website accessible to all employees (step two). In step three, employees who do not know how to read or post messages on the company website would receive training.

FORCE-FIELD ANALYSIS The **force-field analysis** model of change, also developed by Kurt Lewin, states that two sets of opposing forces are at equilibrium before a change takes place. The forces consist of *driving forces*, which are pushing for change, and *restraining forces*, which are opposed to change. When the two forces are evenly balanced, the organization is in a status quo state and does not change.[21] Figure 4.5 shows the restraining and driving forces when an organization is at status quo.

three-step model

A model of organizational change that features the three steps of unfreezing, change, and refreezing.

force-field analysis

A model of organizational change that states that two sets of opposing forces are at equilibrium before a change takes place and put at disequilibrium to make change come about: the driving forces, which are pushing for change, and the restraining forces, which are opposed to change.

172   **part two**   The Culture of Management

FIGURE 4.5

Force Field Model of Change

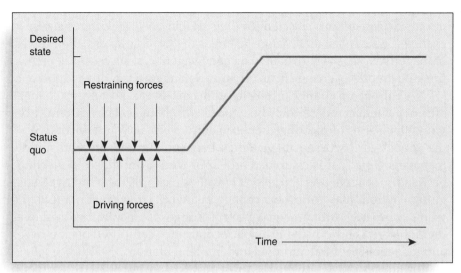

To implement change, the force-field model of change suggests that management can choose from one of three change strategies. Management can (1) *increase* the driving forces that drive the change, relative to the restraining forces; (2) *reduce* the restraining forces that oppose the change, relative to the driving forces, or (3) do both.

Implementing Organizational Change

Practically every successful management activity requires someone to take charge. This is undoubtedly true when implementing change. In most cases, a change is led by the manager or executive who introduced it. Change that is initiated by executives is called **top-down change.** Top-down change can be implemented rapidly. It is often used to respond to a crisis. For example, when data were released in 2000 showing that the Bridgestone/Firestone tires used on Ford Explorers in the United States fell apart at freeway speeds, resulting in scores of fatal traffic accidents, Ford executives decided to absorb the cost of replacing the more than 6 million tires on vehicles that were still on the road. Some of the cost was to be reimbursed by Bridgestone/Firestone. Although they blamed Bridgestone/Firestone for supplying faulty tires, Ford executives acted proactively to manage the crisis. Unfortunately, later information indicated that Ford should have changed its dealings with the people to whom they sold Ford Explorers earlier; an investigation revealed that Ford executives were aware that design flaws in Bridgestone/Firestone tires had caused fatal accidents in Venezuela and Saudi Arabia, among other countries, prior to the publicity about accidents in the United States.

top-down change

Organizational change that is initiated by managers.

People who act as catalysts and assume responsibility for managing change are called **change agents.** Change agents can be internal managers or outside consultants selected for their skill in dealing with resistance to change. Sometimes the change agents are the employees themselves. Manager's Notes 4.4 shows how a change agent can successfully orchestrate the process of change in an organization using a top-down approach.

A **bottom-up change** originates with employees. Bottom-up changes are put into effect more slowly than top-down changes. They generally begin with a series of meetings between employees and supervisors. Next, the change is discussed in meetings between supervisors and middle managers. Finally it is examined and approved or modified in meetings between managers and top executives. For example, an employee suggestion system may propose a change in a work practice that affects the whole company. After an employee-run suggestion committee approves the change, it is introduced to a policy committee composed of employees and managers for final approval and implementation.

Management Close-Up 4.b presents an example of an organization that proactively dealt with change. The approach used both top-down and bottom-up approaches in developing a new and better organizational culture.

Tactics for Introducing Change

When a major organizational change occurs, it is advisable to expect both skepticism and resistance. Advance preparation is often the key to successfully making a change. The tactics for bringing about change in an organization include communication and education, employee involvement, negotiation, coercion, and top-management support.

COMMUNICATION AND EDUCATION   One of the most effective ways to overcome resistance to change is to educate employees about why the change is needed. Information should flow in both directions. The individuals in charge should become aware of why people fear the change and provide information that eliminates some of the uncertainty. For example, Sun Microsystems, a California-based high-tech company, strives to be on the cutting edge of information systems technology by developing a steady stream of new software and hardware for its customers. Consequently, customer service managers must continually upgrade their technical skills in order to understand clients' problems and educate them about the latest product and service technologies. The company provides excellent educational support, so Sun employees are less likely to resist the relentless change that accompanies being a cutting-edge technology company.

Eight Steps to a Planned Organizational Change

Change agents should take the following steps to obtain a successful change outcome in their organizations.

1. *Establish a sense of urgency.* To thaw resistance to change, identify and discuss crises, threats, or potential opportunities.

2. *Form a powerful coalition of supporters of change.* Establish a group of people with enough power to guide the change process in order to create a broader commitment to making the change a reality. The change agent should encourage the group to work together as a team.

3. *Create a vision of change.* Create a vision of a highly desirable future state in the organization to motivate people to want to change. Then facilitate the formulation of strategies that make the vision take shape.

4. *Communicate the vision of change.* Widely communicate the vision and strategies for change. The group of change supporters can facilitate the change by modeling new behaviors needed from employees.

5. *Empower others to act on the vision.* Empower people with knowledge, resources, and discretion to move in the direction of the change. Remove obstacles to the change, such as structures, systems, or procedures that hinder the change effort.

6. *Plan and create short-term wins.* Plan for visible performance improvements, help them to happen, and then celebrate the employees who succeed. A major change takes time; sustain employee motivation by recognizing and rewarding designated milestones that pave the way to the planned change.

7. *Consolidate improvements and produce still more change.* Build on the short-term wins by using their momentum to attack larger problems or obstacles to change. Systems or procedures that hinder change but had not yet been confronted may now be changed. Hiring, promoting, and developing employees who embrace the change concept can strengthen the support for change.

8. *Institutionalize new approaches in the organizational structure.* Embed the changes into the fabric of the organizational culture to make them more stable and to permanently replace old habits, values, procedures, and mind-sets. Instill new values, beliefs, rites, rituals, and role models into the culture so that employees will view the change as a normal way that things are done in the organization.

Sources: Adapted from R. L. Daft, *Leadership.* Fort Worth: Dryden Press, 1999, pp. 430–432; J. P. Kotter, *Leading Change.* Boston: Harvard Business School Press, 1996, p. 21.

Taking Care of Patients and Your People Too!

　Mercy Health System of Owensboro, Kentucky, was created by the merger between two hospitals. However, there was more involved than changing titles on two buildings. The change meant fear, resistance, and combining two distinct cultures. Rather than stating that one culture was correct and the model to follow, a 10-person "cultural design team" made up of hospital managers and staff was formed to help develop a new culture. The basic thrust of this effort was to develop a culture that got back to the basics of healthcare—helping people get better and stay well. The team surveyed over 1,000 employees regarding their perceptions of current practices, such as the hospital's reward system. Four groups were formed to follow up on the survey findings. Focus group members helped the culture team to identify core values of the organization: integrity, respect, service, teamwork, excellence, and innovation. A group of 50 employees from across the hospital was then formed. This group generated 100 behavioral examples of how those values could be demonstrated in the hospital. Each department then chose five or six of the behaviors as a basis for a cultural action plan for that department.

Next, an annual President's Award was instituted to recognize outstanding employees. An employee is nominated for this award by his or her coworkers through a report which describes how the person makes a difference in the hospital. An average of 15 staff members and three doctors, from a pool of 2,500 employees, win the award each year. Prizes include vacations, computers, and a month off with pay. CEO Greg Carlson shrugs off the cost of the program by pointing out that the gifts cost less than one-tenth of 1 percent of the $60 million dollar payroll. Further, it is an important tool that emphasizes the culture and increased loyalty.

Other features of the culture developed at Mercy Health System include empowering workers with unilateral control over a service-related budget. Specifically, employees can solve a patient problem by spending up to $200.00 without management approval. Nurses have, for example, chosen to use their budgets to purchase hats for chemotherapy patients and plane tickets for family members. The CEO stresses aligning personal values with the values of the Mercy culture. He has borrowed a framework from General Electric to send this message. As presented in Table 4.3, the framework applied at Mercy Health System identifies four types of employees: (1) those who are committed to the organization's values and perform well, (2) those who are committed to the organization's values but don't perform well, (3) those who aren't committed to the cultural values but perform their tasks very well, and (4) those who aren't committed and don't perform well. As CEO Carlson points out, the workers who are aligned with the values but aren't performing at the desired level should be given additional chances. The tough group to deal with are those who perform well but aren't aligned with the organization's culture. Carlson's approach is that removing a person like that from the payroll sends an unmistakable message to everyone that the values of the organization are critically important.

Source: L. Larson, "A New Attitude: Changing Organizational Culture," *Trustee* 55 (2002), pp. 8–14.

EMPLOYEE INVOLVEMENT　Involving potential resistors in the design and implementation of change can often help diffuse resistance. Employees who are active in a change process become more committed to the change. A common approach is to organize employees into teams that focus on providing solutions to change issues. To deal with the need to improve service to customers, the GTE unit of Verizon, a large U.S. telecommunications company, organized its employees into quality-improvement teams that design and implement changes in work processes. Employees receive recognition and rewards for changes that are successfully implemented by the teams. In a recent year, 90 percent of GTE employees participated in at least one such team.[22]

TABLE 4.3

Four Types of Employees

		ALIGNMENT WITH CULTURE	
		NO	YES
Performance	Low	Worst	Give Another Chance
	High	Make The Tough Choice	Best

NEGOTIATION   Many times a manager is in a situation where bargaining is involved in implementing a change. Negotiation includes making concessions and giving resources or rewards to resistors in exchange for their cooperation. Individuals who have strong negative attitudes toward a change may be given the opportunity to take early retirement or to transfer elsewhere. In other cases, unions negotiate a labor contract to make trade-offs with management for their willingness to accept a proposed change. The negotiations could result in provisions that establish higher pay rates or more job security for union employees in exchange for their cooperation in plant closings, use of new technology, or mandatory overtime.

COERCION   Confronting and forcing resisting employees to change is the use of coercion. Resistors may be threatened with loss of jobs or rewards if they continue to hinder the implementation of a change. Coercion may be necessary in a crisis, when speed is essential, or changes will not be popular. For example, any employee who resists efforts to improve diversity and cultural tolerance will probably face termination.

TOP-MANAGEMENT SUPPORT   The support of top management helps discourage resistance because it signals that the change is important. Change can require the collaboration of several organization units or departments, and some units may fare better than others, creating the potential for conflict over resources. In such cases, top-management support can facilitate cooperation. For example, at Navistar International, a truck and heavy equipment manufacturer, top management supported the implementation of a new requisition process that affected maintenance, repair, and purchases of supplies and equipment. The goal was to reduce paperwork and increase the speed of purchasing of supplies while saving money by streamlining inventories. The change involved a redesigned requisition process, a computerized inventory control system, and a new procedure for analyzing vendor capability. An important reason for the success of the new requisition process was the support of top management.

Applications for the Manager   Certain types of organizational changes routinely provoke strong employee resistance because they can negatively affect employees' status or quality of life. By becoming aware of these sources of resistance, managers can better apply tactics that will make these changes more palatable for employees. Resistance most frequently arises in response to:

- *Changes that affect skill requirements.* Employees are likely to resist changes that will make their skills obsolete or their work more routine.

- *Changes that represent economic or status loss.* Employees are likely to resist a change that demotes them to a less significant role or decreases their earnings. For example, when a company's marketing strategy changes to deemphasize direct selling, commissioned sales representatives strongly resist attempts to lower sales commission rates.

- *Changes that involve disruption of social relationships.* Work is a primary source of social interaction for many people. When patterns of social interaction are disrupted, people often resist change. For example, the elimination of coffee break privileges may be met with employee resistance.

Applications for Managing Teams   Teams can help test the waters for a proposed change. For example, various employee teams can serve as focus groups (such as those used in marketing to gather consumer reactions to new products or product improvements) in order to find ways to make a change in policy more acceptable to other employees.

Applications for Individuals   When deciding whether to accept a position, learning the specifics about the company culture can help you determine your fit with the organization and the possibility of succeeding. Ask questions and gather information during the recruiting process to get a handle on the company culture and assess whether you will function comfortably in it. If you value job security, for example, you may not want to work for a company that values risk-taking and encourages people to take chances that can result in highly visible failures.

A set of critical thinking questions regarding SAS was presented in the introductory vignette. First, the issue of possible "misfit" with a culture, such as the one at SAS, was raised. It is probably a good thing if an organization's culture is distinctive enough to lead someone to conclude they would not or do not fit. A culture that stands out will attract some people to the organization and give them a reason to stay. Of course, the potential "misfit" problem could be lessened by actively recruiting and selecting the type of people who fit with the culture.

The second critical thinking issue was the extent to which an organization's culture should be justified by a link to the bottom line. Certainly, most organizations are in business to make a profit. However, directly linking everything that is done to the effect on the bottom line can be problematic. Where, for example, would ethical concerns fit into the decision-making process? Further, some organizations do things and develop a culture, not because it is instrumental in achieving greater profit, but because it is important in its own right. It is the values that the programs or rituals represent that justify the investment, not the immediate impact on profit. While this can be a controversial issue, you should determine where you stand on it. You might ask yourself how far you would go in supporting a program, such as literacy training for workers, even if there wasn't evidence of an immediate influence on the bottom line. Further, how far would you go in order to achieve greater bottom-line results? Would you cut safety corners?

The final critical thinking issue was concerned with maintaining a culture, such as the one at SAS, and whether it should be maintained or allowed to change or evolve. The maintenance of a culture requires understanding the organization and the underlying values that drive the culture. Thus, organizational culture is often associated with leaders. However, Southwest Airlines is an example of an organization that has been able to maintain its upbeat and zany culture even after a change in top leadership. The influence of a culture can be just too great to leave it to change or evolve as forces dictate. The informal connections and sense of common purpose among workers is simply too critical to not actively manage.

SUMMARY **Organizational culture** is a system of shared values, assumptions, beliefs, and norms that unite the members of an organization. Organizational culture reflects employees' views about "the way things are done around here."

The three levels of culture are **visible culture,** which includes things people can hear, see, or feel, such as formality or informality of employee dress; **espoused values,** which represent a rationale for how decisions are made; and basic **core beliefs,** which represent such fundamental values as an assumption that employee diversity matters and is important.

Organizational culture performs several important roles in organizations, including:

- Encouraging employee self-management by defining roles and expectations so employees know what to do without having to be closely supervised.

- Promoting stability by providing a sense of continuity in the midst of rapid change.

- Furthering **socialization** by teaching employees the values of the organization and what is special about it.

- Fostering strategy implementation by making it possible for employees to commit to a change of strategy when the change is linked to the organization's cultural values.

Organizational culture is sustained through the use of:

- *Cultural symbols*—icons or objects that communicate organizational values, such as uniforms, logos, and the design of an office.

- *Company rituals and ceremonies*—activities or events that provide dramatic examples of company values, such as a reward and recognition dinner for top sales performers.

- *Company heroes*—role models who reflect what an organization believes in, such as Sam Walton, the founder of Wal-Mart.

- *Stories*—legends and narratives that capture an organization's values, such as the story of the chemical engineer at 3M who persisted in developing Post-it Notes from a project that failed to produce a new adhesive product.

- *Language*—the use of slogans or special vocabulary to remind employees of the organization's values, such as, "Always put the needs of your customer first."

- *Leadership*—provided by individuals who best represent the values of the culture, such as Steve Jobs, the founder of Apple Computer, a leader who passionately focuses on building "insanely great products" for the customer.

Managers sense a need for organizational change when there is a gap between desired and actual levels of performance. Forces for change originate from the *environment,* including technology, market or legal forces, and social trends, and from sources *internal* to the organization, including decisions made by managers in the firm.

Managers who advocate change must deal with sources of resistance, which include employee self-interest, fear of uncertainty, opposing goals and perspectives on change, and a culture that opposes the change.

Models of organizational change can help managers successfully implement change efforts. The Star model identifies factors that are key to the success of a change effort.

Lewin's **three-step model** of organizational change involves (1) *unfreezing* the resistance to change by dealing with people's fears and anxieties; (2) *making the change;* and (3) *refreezing,* that is, encouraging new management practices and employee behaviors until they become routine.

Managers can implement change by communication and education, employee involvement, negotiation, coercion, and top-management support.

DISCUSSION QUESTIONS

1. What are the four main functions that organizational culture provides for an organization?

2. Name and define the three levels of organizational culture.

3. Think of a company you have worked at recently, either on a job or as an intern. What are the espoused values of this company? Did the managers or employees at this company behave consistently with those values? Give some examples if possible.

4. Pick one or more well-known companies that you are familiar with from media stories or firms that were discussed in some of your classes, such as Disney, General Motors, Microsoft, Apple Computer, Wal-Mart, Coca-Cola, or McDonald's. Give examples for each of the following approaches to sustain organizational culture for the company or companies that you have selected: (a) company rituals or ceremonies; (b) company heroes; (c) language; and (d) leadership. Does knowledge of these cultural activities reveal to you what it would be like to work at the company or companies you have selected? How might you use this information?

5. Compare and contrast strong and weak company cultures. What are the advantages of a strong company culture? What are the disadvantages of a strong company culture? In what circumstances is it preferable to have a weak culture?

6. Why do some people strongly resist change, a normal part of life in organizations?

7. What are the steps in Lewin's three-step model of organizational change? How can managers make use of this model?

8. Suppose you are a change agent and are planning to introduce a bottom-up change in an organization. Which implementation tactics are likely to give you the most effective results, with less resistance and better commitment to change? Justify your choices. Answer the same question for a top-down change. Again, justify your choices.

9. Under what circumstances would a coercive tactic to manage change be the most effective? Give an example. Which circumstances are more likely to produce strong resistance to change when a coercive tactic to change is attempted? If you can, give an example.

10. Consider the description of the actions taken at Mercy Health System to establish a new culture. How does the new culture lead to improved customer service? Identify the elements that contribute to the new culture (such as celebrations and stories). What other tactic might you recommend to Mercy Health Systems to further strengthen and maintain its culture?

How Is the Digital Age Changing Organizational Culture in Asia?

Thailand's Lamsam family maintained its business empire in a traditional way. The family kept a firm grip on its operations and discouraged taking risks that could rock the family business. For four generations, the clan elders—ethnic Chinese who own Thai Farmers Bank and the Loxley industrial group—had called the shots without much input from others.

Today Loxley's new philosophy is "try ten ideas and fail at seven—that's no problem," says executive vice president Chatikavanij Vasant, 43, who helped spearhead the change after studying and working for 14 years in the United States. "We have to make sure we are not dead." Nonfamily employees, for example, used to have to write deferential memos full of flowery Thai phrases if they wanted to be able to communicate with family members in the company's hierarchy. Since the company's massive overhaul, Loxley employees contact Vasant and his cousin, chief executive Dhongehai Lamsam, on the group's intranet.

Old-line family business dynasties across East Asia have come to the same conclusion. As one observer noted, "The Internet has become the answer for oligarchs who are questioning their business models as never before."

Discussion Questions

1. How do you think the Internet is affecting organizational culture? Explain.

2. Do you believe that a firm should actively promote open communication across management levels through the e-mail system? Why or why not?

3. Some people argue that the Internet is making it more difficult for firms to retain their own unique culture, forcing them to be more alike as information flows freely across organizational boundaries and even across national lines. Do you agree? Explain.

Source: Adapted with permission from B. Einhorn, "Look Who's Taking Asia Digital," *Business Week*, February 21, 2000, p. 102.

How Jack Welch Changed Culture at General Electric

One way CEO Jack Welch reshaped and changed General Electric's (GE) culture was the Work Out program. Welch wanted to reach and motivate 300,000 employees and insisted that the people on the front lines, where change had to happen, should be empowered to create that change.

The Work Out began in large-scale offsite meetings. A combination of top leaders, outside consultants, and human resources specialists led them. Work Outs for each business unit followed the same basic pattern: hourly and salaried workers came together from many different parts of the organization in an informal three- to five-day meeting to discuss and solve problems. The events evolved to include suppliers and customers as well as employees. Work Out is no longer an event today but instead is the process by which work is done and problems are solved at GE.

The format for Work Out follows seven steps:

Choose a work process or problem for discussion.

Select an appropriate cross-functional team of 30 to 50 people, which may also include external stakeholders.

Assign a "champion" to follow through on recommendations.

Meet for several days and come up with recommendations to improve work processes and solve problems.

Meet with leaders, who are required to respond to recommendations on the spot.

Hold additional meetings as needed to implement the recommendations.

Start the process all over again with a new process or problem.

GE's Work Out process solves problems and improves productivity for the company, but the benefits go beyond these goals. Employees are able to openly and honestly interact with each other without regard to vertical or horizontal boundaries. Work Out is one of the foundations of what Welch called the "culture of boundarylessness" that is critical for continuous learning and improvement.

Discussion Questions

1. Which types of change implementation tactics did Jack Welch apply to the Work Out program at General Electric? Do you think coercion would have been an effective tactic? Why or why not?

2. Describe what the "culture of boundarylessness" at General Electric might be like. What might company rituals and ceremonies look like? How do you envision a company hero behaving in this kind of a culture? What do you think are the key cultural values in this changed culture at GE?

Sources: Adapted from R. L. Daft, *Leadership.* Fort Worth: Dryden Press, 1999, pp. 444–445; J. Quinn, "What a Work-Out!" *Performance*, November 1994, pp. 58–63; www.ge.com/news/leadership.html, accessed July 25, 2001.

Enterprise Resource Planning: An Example of Organizational Change

INDIVIDUAL/ COLLABORATIVE LEARNING CASE 4.1

Being the champion of a change, or a change agent, isn't always easy. Enterprise Resource Planning (ERP), software that integrates information from accounting, manufacturing, distribution, and human resource departments, can give management a unified view of these processes in an organization. Unfortunately, the ERP software began gaining a reputation for being difficult to implement and often failing. The majority of these failures were attributed to software performance problems, but the reality was that in most of these situations the failure was due to inadequate attention to change. In other words, technology was not usually the problem; rather it was a lack of management recognition of ERP as an organizational change. An ERP system can add administrative tasks that may not seem needed, but without an overall understanding of the system, workers may not complete these tasks. Further, an ERP implementation may require a change in roles and increased technical expertise. The implementation of an ERP system at SI Corporation, a small manufacturer of industrial textiles, is an example of an ERP success story. SI expected the implementation of ERP to have a serious impact on its organizational culture.

After deciding to implement an ERP system, SI management created the position of "change management leader" with the responsibility of managing the human element of the implementation. The person hired for this new job, Patrick Keebler, started by assessing the environment for potential problem areas. He considered the levels of workers' computer skills and whether there were areas with a history of resistance to change. Keebler developed a change management strategy that focused on communication and training. As Keebler stated, if you unilaterally "announce that you've launched a new system, you'll get a lot of push back, but if you share your strategy and why it's important early on, people will embrace it."

Communication regarding the ERP implementation at SI included frequent meetings with departments and with shifts of workers. Surveys were also conducted. Based on the feedback at meetings and surveys, Keebler distributed a monthly newsletter about the ERP initiative. He provided information on why the company had chosen this tool and how it would work. Changes in the roles played in various positions were described. The flow of information reduced the amount of stress regarding the change and, argues Keebler, prepared the employees for the training that was needed.

After the ERP system was successfully launched, employees were offered refresher courses and self-paced tutorials on the Web. As the change manager noted "People will embrace a new system if you give them the skills and support to use it. Otherwise, you are just leaving it to chance!"

Critical Thinking Questions

1. Do you agree with the SI Corporation that implementing software such as ERP should be treated as an organizational change? Why or why not?

2. Assess what Keebler did regarding the implementation process. Do you think it was a good job or overkill? Support your judgment.

3. What other activities or approaches might you recommend to SI Corporation? (Hint: Revisit the models of organizational change described in this chapter.)

Collaborative Learning Exercise

Form a group with four or five of your classmates. Select a model of organizational change and describe how you would apply it to the issue of implementing an ERP system. Share your descriptions with the rest of the class. As a class, do you think there is one model that would seem to work best?

Source: Adapted from S. F. Gale, "For ERP Success, Create a Culture Change," *Workforce*, September, 2002, pp. 88–94.

Charles Schwab: Recommending Change as a Customer

Discount broker Charles Schwab provides online investing services and is an example of how the Internet has changed the way businesses provide services to their customers. Visit Charles Schwab's website and examine its features. Answer the following questions:

www.schwab.com

1. What features of Schwab's site do you like? Be specific.

2. Describe the advantages of making investments using the website of a company such as Schwab over the traditional method of working with a financial broker.

3. Describe the disadvantages of using the online investing services on the Schwab website. What improvements to its website would you recommend to Schwab for reducing them?

part two The Culture of Management

Assessing Personal Acceptance of Change

How well do you personally accept change? Consider the following list of changes, and include others that are applicable. Which changes occurred in your life over the past five years? As you consider each change, recall your resistance to it when it happened. In column A, write the number that reflects your level of acceptance of the change at the time it occurred. In column B, write the number that reflects your current level of acceptance of that change. (If you did not experience the change, write "0" in both blanks.)

No resistance = 1

Strong resistance = 5

		A	B
1.	You were married or engaged.	___	___
2.	There was a death in your family.	___	___
3.	You moved to a new location.	___	___
4.	You enrolled in a college or university.	___	___
5.	You had a serious health problem.	___	___
6.	You began work at a new job.	___	___
7.	You lost your job.	___	___
8.	An important relationship changed or ended.	___	___
9.	Your parents were divorced or separated.	___	___
10.	You were divorced or separated.	___	___
11.	A parent remarried with or without stepsiblings.	___	___
12.	You were rejected by your first-choice university.	___	___
13.	Other (list).	___	___

Interpretation: Note the difference between the number you wrote in column A (resistance to change) and in column B (acceptance of change). The maximum difference for each item is 4. A large difference indicates that your ability to accept change over time is strong.

1. Which changes did you strongly resist at first but now accept? Think of as many reasons as possible why you now accept these changes. Identifying these reasons may help you identify your strengths in acceptance of change.

2. Based on your responses, do you consider yourself to be open to change, or do you find change difficult to deal with? If you find change difficult, what things might others—your parents, teachers, or supervisors, for example—have done differently that would have made it easier for you to accept change? (See the section on change in this chapter to answer this question.)

3. What, if any, events did you strongly resist when they occurred and still have difficulty accepting? Identify the reasons for your continued resistance. Compare strongly resisted events that you now accept with those you do not. Can you find clues to your ability to cope with change in your life?

Source: Adapted from R. Quinn, S. Faerman, M. Thompson, and M. McGrath, *Becoming a Master Manager*, 2nd ed., New York: John Wiley & Sons, 1996, pp. 337–338.

Mustang Jeans: Negotiation Amidst Cultural Differences

Sales manager: Michael Sokolow, male, Caucasian, 35-year-old workaholic
Buyer: Norio Tokunaka, male, mid-50s, Japanese, traditional and conservative

General Background Info:
Cultural differences between the U.S. and Japan within the business context are great. Generally, Japanese base their business on relationships, loyalty, respect, and not from the bottom dollar. Appearance, demeanor, and communication style play large roles in building relationships—which translates into making deals.

A few concrete examples—in Japan: Informality and "fast friends" are considered inappropriate; nodding yes does not necessarily mean agreement but rather indicates acknowledgement; titles, status, and hierarchy are taken very seriously; "saving face" for yourself and those you work with is both standard and expected—one would never embarrass, disappoint, contradict, or overly reject another businessman or associate.

"Documents":

- Details about the "Tokunaka Account".
- Company profiles for both Pop-Wear and Mustang Jeans (company size/production, sales volumes, product line, etc.).
- The deal terms thus far—quantities/styles, price point, volume, distribution/shipping schedules, payment plans, etc.

Pre-viewing Class Questions

1. What information should Michael possess prior to his meeting with Tokunaka?
2. How should Michael approach Tokunaka at their first meeting?
3. Why is Tokunaka acting somewhat evasive with his responses?

Scene One: First Contact

Location: Michael's office at Mustang Jeans Corporate Headquarters

Backstory:
Michael Sokolow has been a sales manager at Mustang Jeans for two years. He was "recruited" or "wooed away" from a competing company.

He was given "an offer you can't refuse," an indication of his stellar reputation. Sokolow is very much a no-nonsense straight-ahead kind of guy. He is friendly, but not big on small talk. He fits the stereotypical American businessman in many ways—informal, a little loud, all about money, very direct and forthright. Michael's career has focused in national sales—this is his first foray into international business. Mustang Jeans is reorganizing to increase efficiency—all managers are now assuming larger territories.

Tokunaka has been with Pop Wear for his entire career. He has been working with American companies for many years, importing a variety of products. Most of these American companies are alliances that were formed by Tokunaka's superiors, many years before. All of Tokunaka's accounts are pre-existing accounts as opposed to newly created accounts. This year, Pop Wear is expanding their contemporary clothing line, which includes adding new suppliers and new brands.

Tokunaka has been working on a deal with Michael's associate for a very long time. Michael has just taken over this region. The prior associate's report indicates that the Tokunaka account is a done deal, with only logistics and details remaining. Sokolow and Tokunaka are having their first meeting. The deal is over the purchase of Mustang Jeans & Sportswear merchandise—the selling point: getting American clothes in Japan that are less expensive than the huge brands such as Levi's/Calvin Klein, but still offering high quality product.

Break for Manager Questions & Analysis
Transition
Discuss acceptable international business protocol.

Scene Two: Keep on Smiling
Location: Michael's office at Mustang Jeans Corporate Headquarters
Tokunaka and Sokolow have another meeting the following week, right before Tokunaka returns to Japan. Michael has decided he will revise his approach. Meanwhile, Tokunaka has returned only out of politeness and respect. He indicates that a deal between the two companies is very likely to occur—in the future. Michael tries to find out what has happened, but Tokunaka remains vague, only hinting at the issues.

Post-viewing Class Questions

1. How effective was Michael's new approach to the situation?

2. What specific things should Michael have done to bring about a successful resolution to the situation?

3. How well did Michael handle this situation? What could or should have been done differently?

PART TWO

Bribery: A Global Custom?

Since 1993, Lee Raymond has served as the chairman and CEO of Exxon. In 1999, he was responsible for the $81 billion merger of Exxon and Mobil that created a new entity Exxon-Mobil, one of the largest global corporations, ranking third after Microsoft (No. 1) and General Electric (No. 2) with a market value of $241,036.50 in millions. Exxon-Mobil is the world's leading oil corporation. In 2001, Exxon-Mobil's return on capital was nearly 18 percent, some 7 percent better than industry results. In 2002, Exxon-Mobil earned more than $9 billion after taxes from its oil dealings. For the past 19 years, Exxon has increased its dividends and its credit rating is AAA. The Exxon-Mobil merger has also generated a cost saving of $8 billion for the companies. Exxon-Mobil continuously seeks to maintain its position as number 1 in the oil industry. It allocates some $600 million annually for research and development (R&D) and boasts some 4,000 patents and 3,000 pending patents. It participates in oil exploration and drilling in nearly 50 countries.

Exxon-Mobil constantly seeks to locate and drill for oil throughout the world. Industry projections indicate that only about half of the oil and gas needed for consumption by the end of 2010 are currently in production, as it takes years before exploration and drilling leads to actual production. For example, the company's 1993 purchase of drilling rights off the coast of Angola will begin to actually produce oil only some time next year.

Conducting global business in the oil industry is not easy. It can be compared to a game of high stakes poker. There are many high rollers all vying for the same commodity and competition for oil has caused a number of problems for oil companies including Exxon-Mobil. For example, there are many serious risks when conducting business in the volatile Middle East. Then, there is the reduced demand for jet fuel as a result of terrorism associated with 9/11, and finally there are federal inquiries about pricing policies in the United States. Now Exxon-Mobil is facing

This case was prepared by Joseph C. Santora, who is professor of business at Essex County College, Newark, New Jersey.

some serious allegations from U.S. federal authorities about bribery when conducting business in certain parts of the world.

It appears that bribery has become a way of life, a rule rather than an exception, according to some, when conducting business in the oil industry, because of greedy and unscrupulous government leaders and because of the hundreds of billions of dollars at stake. Furthermore, many oil companies have sought to get "an edge" on the oil market because having access to oil can turn company liabilities into assets, can wreck or bolster executives' careers, and can have a major impact on executive compensation and shareholder earnings. As a result of consumer dependence on oil, many oil companies have been forced "to explore and drill in the most remote areas of the world" and to work cooperatively with government-controlled companies in Asia, Latin America, and Africa where corruption and bribery are common.

Exxon-Mobil has allegedly been involved in a number of "bribery" cases in an attempt to secure contracts for oil drilling and production rights over the last 30 years. Some say that Exxon-Mobil has bargained with the devil through bid-rigging and bribery schemes to level the playing field where other companies seeking oil rights willingly bribe government officials in oil-rich countries. To support this allegation, some recent covert financial dealings with foreign despots have been made public despite the fact that "oil companies generally decline to reveal payments to foreign governments, saying it would violate confidentiality clauses in their contracts."

The most recent Exxon-Mobil case allegedly involving bribery occurred in 1996. The U.S. Department of Justice is now asking the following question: To what degree did Exxon-Mobil participate in the $78 million bribery of Caspian Sea Republic of Kazakhstan's president Nursultan Nazarbayez to secure the rights for 25 percent of oil exploration and drilling contracts at Tengiz, Kazakhstan? American businessman James Giffen, who served as a special advisor to Nazarbayez, and former Mobil senior vice president J. Byron William have both been indicted in New York federal court for their alleged respective roles in the scheme.

Exxon-Mobil denies the accusation, saying through a spokesperson that "Exxon-Mobil has no knowledge of any illegal payments made to Kazakh officials by any current or former Mobil employee. We also have no knowledge of any illegal payment received by any current or former Mobil employees." However, according to one businessperson, "everyone paid fees in (Kazakhstan). It was just standard."

CEO Raymond views dealing with despots as the price of securing oil for consumers. He has publicly stated, "To explore and drill in these places (remote areas of the world) Exxon-Mobil teams up with state-run companies in corruption-plagued countries in Asia, Africa, and Latin America." However, Raymond believes that the culture of Exxon-Mobil "is very straightforward," and he has maintained the following position on corruption: "Resisting corruption at all levels and in every country is the standard of this outfit (Exxon-Mobil), and once people understand that, it's amazing how you don't have to deal with it very much." He also believes that alternatives to oil are not financially realistic.

There have been attempts by the U.S. government and several international organizations to stop bribery in global business. In 1977, the U.S. government enacted the Foreign Corrupt Practices Act (FCPA), which banned bribing foreign officials for contracts. FCPA calls for fining companies, sending oil executives to prison for a maximum of five years, prohibiting companies from receiving public contracts and withdrawing export privileges and temporarily stopping investment protection abroad. Despite its desire to keep the international business community free of bribery, the FCPA has been circumvented by companies awarding millions of dollars in the form of "signature bonuses" to middlemen and to London-based law firms who direct monies to those individuals who steer contracts to one company or another. In 1999, companies such as TotalFina Elf, BP, and Exxon-Mobil gave nearly $900 million in special bonuses called "signature bonuses" for rights to drill off the coast of Angola. President Jose Eduardo dos Santos and some of his top officials are allegedly responsible for taking $1 billion per year from the sale of oil reserves. Oil companies have also agreed to support the Organization for Economic Cooperation and Development (OECD), along with the Organization of American States (OAS), European Union (EU), Council on Europe (CE) and the United Nations (UN), to ban bribery. However, many U.S. companies believe they are at a disadvantage since companies who pay bribes are awarded contracts. Their claim has been supported by the U.S. Department of Commerce, which found that over an eight-year period nearly 500 contracts worth some $240 billion were the result of bribes and U.S. companies lost more than 100 of these contracts worth more than $35 million.

Perhaps oil is a dirty business and in order to play, oil companies must pay. Maybe Juan Pablo Perez Alfonzo, the former Venezuela Oil Minister and co-founder of the Organization of Petroleum Exporting Countries (OPEC), had it right when he called oil or "black gold" by a less endearing name—"The Devil's Excrement."

Discussion Questions

1. Should U.S. companies be restricted from conducting business in foreign countries that have corrupt regimes?
2. If bribery is a way of doing business in other countries, then is it wrong for U.S. companies to offer bribes to receive contracts from foreign governments?

3. What actions should Exxon-Mobil take regarding the Kazakhstan case?

4. If guilty of making illicit payments in Kazakhstan, should Exxon-Mobil be penalized by the U.S. government? If so, how?

5. How can Exxon-Mobil develop a culture that does not accept bribery as a part of doing business? Should the organization pursue this goal? Why or why not? Using a tool, such as the Star Model, identify how Exxon-Mobil could make this change in its culture.

Sources: "Big Oil's Dirty Secret," *The Economist,* May 10, 2003; T. Catan and J. Chaffin, "Bribery Has Long Been Used to Land International Contracts. New Laws Will Make That Tougher," *Financial Times,* May 8, 2003, p. 11; D. Fisher, "Dangerous Liaisons," *Forbes,* April 28, 2003, pp. 84–86, 88; *FT Special Report Global 500,* May 28, 2003; S. LeVine et al., "U.S. Bribery Probe Looks at Mobil," *Wall Street Journal,* April 23, 2003, p. 2A; S. Sansoni, "Dirty Oil," *Forbes,* April 28, 2003, p. 92; "The Man Who Will Lead Exxon Mobil: Can One of America's Most Controversial CEOs Be Cloned? Some Shareholders Hope So; Activists Pray Not," *Chief Executive* (US), October 2003; J. Useem, "The Devil's Excrement," *Fortune,* February 2, 2003, p. 96.

3

Management
Strategy and
Decision
Making

3

Planning and the formulation of strategy establish broad objectives for an organization so that managers can set priorities and deadlines and marshall resources—people, financial, and physical—to accomplish short- and long-term goals. To think strategically, managers must scan the business environment for threats and opportunities. An important aspect of strategy formulation is being cognizant of the strengths and weaknesses of one's own organization. Then action must be taken based on the information gathered. The goal is to develop a competitive strategy in the market in light of the internal and environmental factors that anticipates the responses of one's competitors.

In Part Three we begin by examining the planning process. This leads us to the topic of decision making. The stages of decision making are presented followed by an analysis of two critical decision-making skills—time management and delegation. Next, we look at ways to formulate and implement a business strategy, including how to evaluate a firm's internal resources and capabilities. Part Three concludes with a discussion of entrepreneurship and one of the greatest management challenges—creating a new enterprise.

FIVE

Managing the Planning Process

chapter 5

After reading this chapter, you should be able to:

- Take advantage of the benefits of planning at every level of the organization.

- Recognize major planning pitfalls and develop quality planning programs.

- Balance formal planning with opportunistic planning.

- Establish objectives to drive the entire planning process.

- Prepare action plans at the strategic, tactical, and operational levels.

- Learn how to implement plans successfully.

How Coke Rebounded

When Roberto C. Goizueta was named president of Coca-Cola in 1980, the giant firm had moved into unrelated ventures from shrimp farming to wine making, its crucial bottling system was falling apart, and major markets were being headed by underperforming operators. The firm had no strategic vision, and a corporate refusal to take risks was crippling any creativity in the firm. Coke's stock had fallen by half, with the company barely turning a profit.

Within a year, Goizueta had begun a planning process that would guide the firm for the next 17 years. During his 18-year tenure, which ended with his death in 1997, Goizueta's initiatives resulted in Coke's sales increasing by over 400 percent from $4 billion to $18 billion, and an incredible 3,500 percent increase in its market capitalization, from $4.3 billion to $180 billion. Goizueta had created the outline that resulted in that growth during his first six months as Coke's president.

Within a few weeks of becoming president, Goizueta had set up a dramatic plan for revamping Coke's network of bottlers. The franchise system of independent bottlers created almost a hundred years earlier had resulted in its nationwide expansion. Those bottling operations were now being run by third-generation owners, many of them complacent and without the capital they needed to invest in technology and to cope with changes in their markets.

Six weeks after being named Coke's president, Goizueta presented his plan to 15 of Coke's top domestic bottlers at an all-day meeting in Atlanta. The firm's recent purchase of its Atlanta bottler and investment in its New York bottler were just the start of a broader program of investment, he said, which would weed out weak operators by buying weak franchises, refurbishing them, and then offering them for sale to stronger operators. The resulting stronger bottling system would help Coke battle Pepsi with more effective distribution, and it would increase the value of the bottlers' businesses as well.

Goizueta's plan, labeled "the Spanish Inquisition," started innocently enough. Coke executives from around the world typically went to Atlanta each fall for a pro forma review of their five-year plans. This year was different. In an adversarial atmosphere, Goizueta demanded three-year plans and expected his executives to be accountable for meeting their targets. He demanded that these plans be given to him early so that he could dissect them and then confront the executives about them. Instead of waiting passively for headquarters to dictate the year's goals, each division chief now had to present his or her own brief and to defend it.

"I want you to tell me what you need to do to expand your business, what kind of capital you need to do it, and what kind of net return you're going to get," Goizueta ordered the firm's division heads. Most found they had to revise their plans to satisfy Goizueta's demands that they justify future performance targets and clearly outline how they planned to achieve them.

Seven years after Goizueta's death, Coca-Cola has continued to do well, mainly because of the long-range plans laid out during his tenure. This has occurred despite missteps by some of his successors. For instance, former CEO M. Douglas Ivester lasted just 28 months on the job. The board fired him for exercising poor judgment such as demoting Coke's highest-ranking African-American even as the company was losing a $20-million racial discrimination suit.

Coca-Cola's success in recent years has been particularly strong in global markets, which were dear to Goizueta's heart. Goizueta envisioned that India, with soft-drink consumption of just a few 8-oz servings per capita annually, had more potential for growth than any other market on the planet. "The country has a billion plus consumers, a growing middle class, and the climate is hot, hot, hot". By 2004, Coca-Cola's overall sales in India had increased by 24 percent, and the goal is to double that growth by 2010. This follows Coca-Cola's success in mainland China, where it has had a dominant market position since the mid-1990s. The blueprint for this international expansion can be found in long range plans developed by Coca-Cola more than 15 years ago.

Sources: Adapted with permission from D. Greising, "I'd Like the World to Buy a Coke: The Life and Leadership of Roberto Goizueta," *Business Week,* April 13, 1998, pp. 70–76; D. Foust and G. Khermouch "Repairing the Coke Machine." *Business Week,* March 19, 2001, pp. 86–88; G. Khermouch, S. Holmes and M. Ihlwan, "The Best Global Brands," *Business Week,* August 6, 2001, pp. 50–57; M. Kripalani and M. L. Clifford, "Finally, Coke Gets It Right," *Business Week,* February 10, 2003, p. 47; J. A. Byrne, "Leaders Are Made, Not Born," *Business Week,* February 17, 2003, p. 16; and B. McKay and S. Vranica, "Cracking the China Market," *The Wall Street Journal,* January 9, 2003, pp. B1–B2.

CRITICAL THINKING QUESTIONS

1. *What accounts for Coca-Cola's amazing success record during the years following the death of long-time CEO Roberto Goizueta?*

2. *How many years should a company's plan encompass? Three years? Five? Ten?*

3. *What are some of the advantages and disadvantages a company may face when establishing long-term performance objectives?*

What Is Planning?

Does it make sense to plan in a world typified by rapid and dramatic change? The answer is a resounding "yes!" Planning programs identify what the organization wants to accomplish and how. **Planning** is a process that helps managers set objectives for the future and map out the activities and means that will make it possible to achieve those objectives.

There are both formal and informal planning processes. Most organizational leaders prefer to develop a formal written statement of future objectives and the approaches to reach them. The document can then be shared with those responsible for the execution of the plan, thereby reducing ambiguities and creating a common understanding. The written plan can be adjusted as necessary. As shown in Figure 5.1, there are four key elements to a plan: objectives, actions, resources, and implementation.

Objectives are goals or targets that the firm wishes to reach within a stated amount of time. One firm may wish to increase its return on investment from 8 to 14 percent in the next three years. Another may seek to increase market share from 5 to 10 percent over the course of five years. Setting objectives requires the firm to anticipate what is likely to happen in the future. A reasonable forecast allows a firm to set objectives that are both challenging and realistic. For instance, if a downturn is expected in the economy, ambitious profit objectives are less likely to be met. Likewise, if major players are entering the market, it will be more difficult to expand market share. A poor forecast may lead to objectives that are overly optimistic or that fall short of what the firm is capable of achieving.

Actions are the specific steps the firm intends to take to achieve the desired objectives. For instance, return on investment may be increased by downsizing, subcontracting some of the work, decreasing inventories, using technology to increase productivity, or developing new products. Company managers may also decide to increase advertising expenditures to expand its market share. Alternatively, it may be more efficient to undercut competitors by decreasing prices.

Planned actions cannot be carried out effectively without careful **resource allocation.** A quality plan states where resources will come from (for instance, borrowed versus internally generated funds) and how they will be deployed. The management team should be aware of the resource constraints the company faces so they can decide whether the company's goals can be realistically accomplished. As discussed later in this chapter, budgets are a way to allocate and control the resources committed to each step.

Finally, plans must be accompanied by **implementation guidelines** that show how the intended actions will be carried out. Implementation involves dividing tasks among the different actors, specifying reporting relationships, and establishing timelines.

planning

The management function that assesses the management environment to set future objectives and map out the activities necessary to achieve those objectives.

objectives

The goals or targets that the firm wishes to accomplish within a stated amount of time.

Elements of the Planning Process

actions

The specific steps the firm intends to take to achieve the desired objectives.

resource allocation

The planning step that determines where the resources will come from (for instance, borrowing versus internally generated funds) and how the resources will be deployed to achieve the agreed-on objectives.

implementation guidelines

The planning step that shows how the intended actions will be carried out.

FIGURE 5.1

Key Elements to a Plan

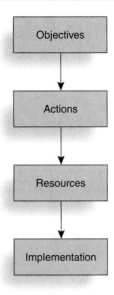

For the sake of clarity, the four elements of planning are discussed individually in this chapter. In reality, they are closely intertwined. Objectives are not meaningful unless the firm can carry out the activities to achieve them and devote resources to support their implementation. An accurate assessment of the firm's resources provides an excellent starting point. Taking advantage of the firm's **core competencies** such as know-how, skills, brand recognition, and/or the company's reputation should clearly be considered in setting objectives and laying out action plans.

Planning occurs at every level within the organization. The plans made at higher levels direct and constrain the planning that takes place at lower levels. In general, planning at the top of the pyramid focuses on broad, long-term issues. For instance, a firm may decide to focus on a particular market segment, divesting itself of products or units that are unrelated to that market segment. Planning at lower levels tends to be primarily concerned with the operational details of the overall plan. Before going into details about the four elements of planning, it is important to keep in mind both the potential benefits and pitfalls of the planning process, to be discussed next.

core competencies

The unique skills and/or knowledge an organization possesses that give it an edge over competitors.

The Benefits of Planning

Several important benefits are associated with planning. To begin with, planning requires managers to assess the external forces that affect the company. This helps the company respond to challenges present in the environment. The goals that are established as part of the plan give company members a sense of direction and purpose in that environment. Further, when planning is properly conducted, it helps the management team to establish priorities, coordinate activities, develop standards, and clarify forces that will contribute to success. Effective planning processes result in increased participation by lower-level members. This, in turn, leads to improved managerial skills for all of the members of the company. Next, planning is the basis of control. A well-designed plan sets the standards that will be used to assess performance at every level in the organizational hierarchy, both in the short term and over time. And finally, planning may help a firm reduce future uncertainty by anticipating what may happen in the future, forcing managers to think long term. These advantages are described in greater detail below.

Assessment of External Forces

One of the key aspects of planning is examining various environmental factors. This helps the firm deal with environmental uncertainty and identify both opportunities and threats present in the environment. Then, the management team can mobilize resources to neutralize potential threats as well as take advantage of opportunities.

For example, video stores, such as Blockbuster, have been forced to adjust to the beta format, VHS format, DVD format, and now the threat from direct pay-per-view delivery systems. Each time, the company has responded, most recently by creating a cooperative agreement with Direct TV to provide pay-per-view movies.

Developing a Sense of Direction and Purpose

A well-designed plan helps both managers and employees to understand what the organization is trying to achieve as well as the role that each plays in accomplishing those goals. Without a plan, managers and employees may not recognize how they share a common fate, even if they carry out the tasks they think are important. The lack of a clear sense of direction leads to multiple and often conflicting goals, and the ineffective use of resources.

Identifying the Factors That Affect the Organization

Properly conducted planning helps the organization focus on factors related to growth, renewal, and survival. Managers are able to reflect on issues that may not be obvious in the midst of day-to-day work pressures. For example, Pfizer is a leader in the development of new drugs, with some 60 drugs, for conditions ranging from diabetes to anxiety, in early stages of development. In its planning process Pfizer realized that it could take advantage of the opportunity to partner with the industry's smaller players to help them realize the potential of their own new medications.

Consequently, Pfizer co-launched Lipitor, a cholesterol-lowering pill, in conjunction with Warner-Lambert. Pfizer's potent sales force, ranked no. 1 in physician surveys, helped the drug's sales smash an industry record in the late 1990s.[1]

Encouraging Participation

When workers participate in managerial activities, they tend to "buy in" and work much harder to see an effort succeed. They also experience stronger feelings of commitment to the organization. The planning process is an excellent place to encourage managers and employees to share inputs about the goals of the organization, and to find the best ways to achieve those goals. Participation is likely to strengthen the efforts dedicated to attaining those goals and increase goodwill toward their immediate supervisors and the overall company.

Coordination of Efforts

Managers who operate independently may not be aware of what other managers are doing. The planning process may help them coordinate efforts more effectively. For example, DaimlerChrysler Corporation created a joint German (Daimler is headquartered in Germany) and U.S. (where Chrysler is based) planning team of top executives during 2001–2004 to try to help Chrysler reduce its billion-dollar losses. One of the executives in the team is Dieter Zetsche, a German who is credited with Daimler's success in restructuring Mercedes-Benz and making it profitable again. In this manner DaimlerChrysler is trying to apply valuable expertise from one part of the organization in another.[2]

In companies in which operations are decentralized, each unit may use different performance criteria and resource allocation priorities. This became a major problem at Motorola in the late 1990s, leading to a significant decline in overall firm performance. A centralized planning process can help managers understand how actions or decisions in one area have consequences for other units as well as for the entire firm.

Establishment of Priorities

Planning can help a firm prioritize its major problems or issues. Lack of priorities can dilute the organization's efforts or make it susceptible to managers who take advantage of the confusion to impose their own agendas. Also, the failure to define priorities causes the firm to drift and prevents it from developing a clear strategic focus. This was a primary reason why Pepsi lost the "war" against Coke during the 1980s. Coke focused its energies on its core product, while Pepsi's efforts were dispersed across a variety of unrelated products such as restaurants, hotels, and retail outlets.

Planning for Changes in the Short and the Long Term:
How General Electric Successfully Focused on Both

THEME: DEALING WITH CHANGE When China opened bids for plane engines to build a fleet of 500 regional jets in time for the 2008 Beijing Olympics, Rolls-Royce, Pratt & Whitney, Snecma (a French government-owned engine shop) and General Electric (GE) all competed for the $3 billion contract. General Electric won, in large measure because the company began to plan for the design and production of regional jet engines in the 1990s. GE anticipated that the demand for regional jets—those with up to 100 seats and a range of up to 1,500 miles—would grow rapidly in the future. Few rivals cared about small commercial jets in the early 1990s. GE's foresight and willingness to devote resources to a product market that competitors first ignored helped the company to capture a major share of this growing market segment. GE now holds close to three-fourths of the market share, far more than that of all competitors combined.

The GE management team's belief that regional jets would be the future of the world market for commercial jet engines, and subsequent plans to make those engines, proved to be correct. The number of regional jets in service has swelled to 1,300 from 85 in 1993. And with airlines mothballing big planes in the desert, that number is expected to grow. Air carriers increasingly appreciate their lower operating costs. Bankrupt airlines such as US Airways Group Inc. and United Airlines Inc. are replacing many big jets with the smaller, cheaper ones. The 9/11 attacks, of course, could not be foreseen a decade earlier but helped accelerate this trend. Consumers prefer small jets to propeller planes. Foreign market opportunities in commercial aviation lie primarily in up-and-coming developing nations (such as China and India) that can ill afford the expenses of large planes such as Boeing Co.'s 737 and 777.

The story behind GE's successful gamble on regional-jet engines illustrates one of the primary benefits of effective planning: responding to future changes while taking advantage of current opportunities. With both short-cycle businesses, which pay off quickly, and long-cycle ones, whose payoffs are years down the road, GE can invest heavily in new technologies it believes in, even when the payoff is not imminent. In the 90s, GE could afford to invest in new jet-engine technologies because of the strong performance by some of its shorter-cycle businesses such as NBC and GE Plastics.

Source: Adapted from S. Holmes, "GE: Little Engines That Could," *Business Week,* January 20, 2003, pp. 62–64.

Focusing Attention on Different Time Horizons

Many business programs may take years to complete. Steps can be taken to achieve long-term objectives by balancing them with short-term goals. Management Close-Up 5.a illustrates how General Electric was able to successfully plan for both short- and long-term opportunities, even those with payoffs that were years down the road.

Understanding Circumstances Contributing to Past Success or Failure

It is vital for managers to learn from past successes and failures. Planning can bring the reasons for poor and good performance into sharper view, enabling the firm to draw on experience. For example, in 1997 Kodak lost $100 million when it introduced an advanced-photo-system camera and film, only to find that it did not have enough stock on hand to meet the

Kodak's decision to revamp its original advanced film imaging camera, although costly, resulted in a much more profitable product.

demand. The company could not process the new film at enough locations. It finally responded by spending another $100 million on the system in a more focused approach. The management team also learned that most customers preferred less expensive models. As a result, Kodak introduced a new camera for under $50 that was a hybrid between digital and analog cameras. The new camera was soon responsible for 20 percent of Kodak's camera sales.[3]

Ensuring the Availability of Adequate Resources

A well-designed plan leads to identifying the resources needed for the future. These resources may come from several sources. For example, as seen in Management Close-Up 5.b, the biotechnology firm Genentech reallocated 25 percent of its research staff to developing multiple products to achieve its new business objectives.

Establishing Performance Standards

The end result of any planning process is a series of statements regarding objectives to be met along with expected activities. These criteria define expected behaviors for organizational members and allow for the assessment of progress. As time passes, the relative contributions of individuals and groups can be assessed and rewarded.

A few years ago, General Electric (GE) established a tough quality standard called six sigma. Six sigma is equivalent to generating fewer than 3.4 defects per million manufacturing or service operations. To attain this goal, GE trained tens of thousands of employees in quality techniques. A reward system to support this quality initiative was also estab-

Genentech's New Business Objectives

Biofirm Genentech had focused its efforts on developing single products, such as Pulmozyne, an enzyme to relieve lung congestion caused by cystic fibrosis. In 1998, the firm sought to expand its market share and reduce dependence on a handful of blockbuster drugs. Genentech changed business objectives to develop multiple products. The implementation plan to accomplish these objectives involved several major initiatives.

One new project, called "Speedy" by company insiders, immediately generated five product leads, including a surprising antiviral molecule, and was expected to result in 20 more within two years. The project required an overhaul of the biotechnology company's traditional approach to research. Instead of Genentech's scientists working alone or in tiny teams, the firm implemented almost an assembly line of 80 scientists researching massive gene-data warehouses.

An incentive system was also put in place to expedite drug development. Two dozen employees worked 80 hours a week to develop a marketing application for Herceptin, a breast cancer drug, to present to the Food and Drug Administration, which approved it, three months ahead of schedule. Their reward for beating their deadline by three months

(and potentially saving lives earlier)? "Genenchex" of $3,000 or more.

Genentech's planning and implementation of new objectives were likened by some to those of big pharmaceutical companies, which caused worry about stifling firm creativity and hurting morale. Genentech CEO Arthur Levinson defended his implementation direction by arguing that "there is no guarantee we'll find the Next Great Molecule, and it's not a style of science that appeals to everyone. But if we had waited two or more years, someone would have eaten our lunch."

By 2003, Genentech had been named to *Fortune's* "100 Best Companies to Work For" five years in a row. And by 2004, Genentech's development pipeline had never been more productive and promising, with a large number of antibody therapies being tried in the areas of oncology, vascular medicine, immunological disease, and biotherapeutics. Much of this success may be attributed to Genentech's ability to take advantage of a changing knowledge base in its business plans.

Sources: Adapted from R. T. King. " 'Assembly Line' Revs Up Genentech." *The Wall Street Journal,* March 12, 1998, p. B3; Genentech website, www.gene.com (2003), and updates by author (2004).

lished. GE managers and employees who meet objectives may receive as much as a 25 percent increase in their annual base salaries without a promotion; cash bonuses can increase as much as 150 percent in a year to between 20 percent and 70 percent of base pay; and generous stock options are provided to 27,000 employees. More than 1,200 employees, including 800 below the level of senior management, have received stock options totaling over $1 million.[4]

Supporting Organizational Control Systems

Organizations cannot be successful unless control systems are in place to ensure that objectives are being attained and that resources are being used appropriately. A *control* is "any process that helps align the actions of individuals with the interests of their employing firms".[5] A *control system* is "the knowledge that someone who knows and cares is paying attention to what we do and can tell us when deviations are occurring".[6]

Effective planning improves a company's control system by making it possible to compare target versus actual results. When a gap is detected between company goals and observed results, corrective actions are taken to modify activities for the future. In a few extreme cases, the existing plan may be completely abandoned. When company executives fail to abandon a plan after large resources have been spent on it even though all available evidence suggests that the plan is not working, the problem is called *escalation of commitment*. Some people believe, for instance, that the space shuttle disasters may be attributed to escalation of commitment to a space program that was doomed to failure from the beginning (see the Individual/Collaborative Learning Case at the end of this chapter entitled "Why Did NASA Stick with the Space Shuttle So Long?").

Developing "What If" Scenarios

Long ago, Ben Franklin suggested that "the only sure things in life are death and taxes." Organizations, like individuals, face a great deal of uncertainty. Planning can help managers deal with uncertainty by anticipating what may happen in the future. No firm has a crystal ball to accurately forecast the future. Planning can help identify different future scenarios and spell out what to do in each scenario. This is known as *contingency planning*. Ben Franklin recognized that uncertainty is inevitable but is still manageable. Another of his famous proverbs states that "chance favors the prepared mind." The Skills for Managing 5.1 box is designed to help you develop a contingency plan.

Management Development

Individual managers should play a major role in focusing the organization on the future. Planning helps managers to be proactive and forward-thinking rather than being reactive and just letting things happen. By considering future possibilities and developing a long-term vision, managers can become more committed to the firm and learn to convert abstract ideas or objectives into concrete actions. Including managers from every level of the organization in company planning processes is an effective form of "on the job" training. These planning experiences "season" managers, so they are able to move into more responsible roles in the future.

The Pitfalls of Planning

Company leaders will not realize the benefits of planning if the planning process itself is flawed. Future conditions can be forecasted incorrectly, reporting relationships can become overly hierarchical, planning

DESIGN YOUR OWN CONTINGENCY PLAN

You are part of a five-member group of students planning to study in France two years from now. The five of you are planning to travel together and to save on housing costs by renting a three-bedroom apartment. Your plans call for a six-month stay. Let's assume that the current exchange rate is 0.85 euro per dollar, so it will cost each of you approximately 10,000 euros (or $8,500). You plan to save this amount of money by working in the evenings and during summers, although it will require a great deal of sacrifice (skipping movies, eating at home, not buying new clothes, and so on). At a typical student wage rate of $6.00 per hour, this will require 2,125 hours of work (at $4 per hour after taxes and transportation costs) exclusively devoted to save the $8,500. Of course, you will need money in the meantime to cover your daily expenses in addition to the money you are saving for the trip.

Engage in a contingency planning exercise under the following assumptions:

1. Two years from now the euro will be .95 on the dollar, meaning the cost will be $9,500.

2. Two years from now the euro will be 1.05 on the dollar, so the cost will be $10,000.

3. Two years from now the euro will be 1.15 on the dollar, making the cost $11,500.

4. Two years from now, the euro will be 1.25 on the dollar, or a total cost of $12,500.

The team (appointed by instructor) will develop a contingency plan to deal with each of the possible scenarios above. Keep in mind that this is a problem similar to what firms face in international markets when they engage in contingency planning for the future based on the strength of the dollar (see Chapter 2, Managing in a Global Environment). Note: During the period 2001–2004, the exchange rate has oscillated between 0.80 euro per dollar and 1.20 euro per dollar.

can become a self-contained activity, bureaucratization can become oppressive, and objectives and processes that are no longer optimal for the firm may be used. Each of these problems is described in greater detail in this section.

Poor Forecasts of Future Conditions

As you have seen, the business environment is changing faster than ever. Even the most sophisticated planning techniques may not predict accurately what is likely to happen in the future. The longer the time frame, the more likely that unforeseen circumstances will occur. This is one reason many firms became skeptical of the value of strategic planning in the 1980s. Major corporations such as the Adolph Coors Company, Campbell Soup, Exxon, General Motors, Oak Industries, Shaklee, Toro, and Wang Laboratories, among others, reported poor strategic decisions driven by inaccurate forecasts. Common problems included poor estimates of the demand for new products, miscalculation of the effect of international competition on main product lines, the inability to predict technological innovations, and changes in the economic and legal systems.[7] More recently,

- An "Asian economic miracle" was predicated based on the assumption of ever-rising exports. For a long time, export-led economies like Japan and South Korea were few and relatively small compared with importing economies such as the United States. Consequently, the export strategy worked well. As exporting economies grew and proliferated, however, the sheer volume of exports began to shake the foundation of the Asian miracle. In the face of competition from Japan and China, export growth in the rest of Asia fell from a peak of 30 percent in early 1995 to zero by the late 1990s.

- Amway invested heavily in China between 1992 and 1998. In 1998, Beijing suddenly banned direct marketing, shutting down the $178 million-a-year China business of Amway Asia Pacific.

- Production costs for the movie *A.I.* reportedly were $100 million, but when it was introduced in movie theaters in the summer of 2001, attendance ran 15 percent behind forecasts.

- Valueamerica.com was able to raise more than $125 million dollars in 1999 to create a "Price Club of the Web," to sell discount products online. By 2001 the company was bankrupt, as consumers did not flock to buy its merchandise. At least 100 other e-companies that received large investment capital in the late 1990s went bust during the first years of the new millennium, not long after many investors firmly believed forecasts stating that electronic commerce was the wave of the future.[8]

Plans Imposed from Above

The traditional approach to planning is from the top down, with the CEO and senior executives, and perhaps a planning department, establishing organizational objectives and laying out general business strategies. Managers at lower organizational levels then devise implementation methods and operational plans to support the objectives and strategies set at the top. Separating the plan generators from the plan implementers often leads to the development of plans that lower level managers begrudgingly try to put into practice. Such plans often do not benefit from the wisdom and experience of those at lower levels within the firm. Many "reengineering" plans have failed in part because they were imposed on the rest of the firm by the top of the hierarchy.

Planning as a Self-Contained Activity

There is a danger that the people engaged in planning will become so enamored with the process that they become a close-knit group di-

McDonald's past planning efforts in branching out to a more diversified menu caused the worst performance ever for the once steadfast fast food giant. Poor planning in the design of a pizza that didn't fit through drive-through windows, and salad shakers that were packed so tightly the dressing wouldn't flow through them, has led McDonald's to revamp and return to basics.

vorced from the rest of the organization. Managers and employees may be cynical about objectives and suggestions for action emanating from specialized planning departments or units. Reflecting on this, one well-known consultant noted that "planning staff groups may gain much power and authority in organizations . . . [where they are] thrust into the role of proponent and doer of plans—too often, the real doers are pushed aside."[9]

Extensive Bureaucratization

When planning is conducted by specialists without the participation of other managers, there may be a tendency to generate volumes of paperwork accompanied by fancy oral presentations. In other instances, planning becomes overly quantitative and formula driven. As a result, the logic behind the recommendations may be difficult to understand and may lack common sense. In addition, the predictions of elegant mathematical models succeed or fail on the data and assumptions employed. Formulas that work relatively well in stable conditions may totally miss the mark in turbulent times.

For example, keeping Lou Neve's family-run nursery's greenhouses warm is critical to maintaining roses in good shape. The Petaluma, California, nursery based its cost calculations for 2001 on the relatively stable price of gas since the early 1990s. Unfortunately, the season immediately preceding Valentine's Day 2001 found Neve's gas bill increasing fivefold over previous years, severely affecting the bottom line. While the causes behind this huge increase in gas prices in a single year are complex, including electricity deregulation in the late 1990s, the situation illustrates how historical data used for planning purposes may be completely off the mark as the environment changes.[10]

Inflexible Adherence to Objectives and Processes

A firm may become overly committed to an outdated plan, ignoring clues that it is time to change direction. People tend to justify "sunk costs" by continuing to defend objectives in spite of disappointing results. For instance, for years Apple was obstinate in producing its Macintosh computers for loyal users in spite of continuing drops in sales that occurred largely because its software was incompatible with IBM, the market leader.

In another case, Detroit's Big Three automobile firms in the early 2000s continued their investment in SUVs, which fueled much of their earning growth during the 1990s, even though the market had become saturated over the preceding years. To spur sales the auto firms had to offer incentives; after five years of steadily increasing SUV incentive packages profit margins had disappeared in 2004. Nevertheless, the auto firms have continued pouring more resources into a dwindling market, ignoring the data showing that previously established objectives were no longer viable.[11]

Keys to Successful Planning

The planning pitfalls described above can be avoided. Successful planning includes involving managers at different levels, using a combination of numerical and judgmental methods, viewing planning as a continuous activity capable of adapting to change, avoiding paralysis of the analysis, and concentrating planning efforts on a manageable set of issues.

Involving Different Organizational Levels

To one degree or another, every level of management should be involved in planning. Planning cannot be viewed as the province of staff specialists or senior managers living in ivory towers. In general, both the quality of the plan and commitment to it are likely to increase when key managers and employees at various organizational levels contribute to its formulation and implementation.

Using Both Numerical and Judgmental Methods

Planning is as much an art as a science. An effective planning process requires a thorough understanding of interrelated environmental and organizational factors. These factors provide clues about where the firm should be moving in the future, the resources it has at its disposal, and the constraints it faces. While numerical data can be helpful, the numbers need to be carefully interpreted. There are situations in which numerical approaches are not suitable. Systematically tapping the knowledge of employees at different levels in the organization allows the firm to benefit

part three   Management Strategy and Decision Making

from their experiences and to profit from the collective judgment of company employees.

Viewing Planning as Continuous and Capable of Adapting to Change

Company leaders must be flexible enough to respond to changes in technology, competitors' reactions, international trends, and industry conditions if the planning process is to be successful. Almost any objective and the steps to accomplish it are likely to become obsolete relatively quickly unless there are built-in mechanisms to consider and respond to change. Results should be monitored continuously to detect major deviations from initial assumptions and expectations. Planning should question future directions, chosen alternatives, and priorities. In particular, the firm needs to guard against escalation of a failing course of action, as noted earlier. Past choices and sunk costs should not entice the firm to continue investing in a plan when there is sufficient evidence to question the wisdom of that plan.

Firms use a variety of approaches to keep objectives and action plans attuned to changes in internal and external environments. These include scheduled retreats of key managers and employees, workshops led by consultants, environmental scanning (see Chapter 7 on strategic management), the use of two-way feedback between managers and employees in the performance appraisal process (see Chapter 10 on human resource management), and the creation of standing cross-functional committees composed of executives and key employees to monitor progress, identify current or emerging problems, and recommend corrective actions.

In some cases the firm must react quickly to deal with unforeseen circumstances. Even with the best-made plans, managers of successful firms are often called to act by "the seat of their pants" to confront crisis situations that seem to come from nowhere (see Management Close-Up 5.c, "How Southwest Airlines Responds on the Spot").

Avoiding Paralysis of the Analysis

An obsession with paperwork, technical reports, statistical tables, and other supporting documentation causes paralysis by analysis. Plans only succeed when those responsible accept the plan and become devoted to seeing it implemented effectively. The key to successful planning is action, not becoming bogged down in overanalyzing every detail.

Concentrating on a Manageable Set of Issues

It is important to limit planning to key priority areas. As discussed in Chapter 7, a good way to identify these key areas is to focus on the firm's core competence or the resources that enable it to do things better than

How Southwest Airlines Responds on the Spot

THEME: CUSTOMER FOCUS The Executive Planning Committee of Southwest Airlines Co. meets every three weeks to decide on pricing, ticket restrictions, new routes, and other company issues. At the same time, it is embedded in the company's culture that policies and rules should not get in the way of customer service. Managers are given a great deal of discretion to handle everyday problems.

In the hours immediately after the terrorist attacks on September 11, 2001, two newly promoted executives at Southwest Airlines Co. made a bold decision. Without even consulting the legendary cofounder and current chairman Herbert D. Kelleher nor the Executive Planning Committee, Chief Executive James F. Parker and President Colleen C. Barrett swiftly agreed to grant refunds to all customers who asked for them, regardless of any ticket restrictions. Only later did they discover that the airline could have been ob-

ligated to pay several hundred million dollars, an unsettling prospect, given the uncertainty of the times and a $187 million profit-sharing payment that was due. "Fortunately, the potential flood of refund claims never came," says Parker, in his typically understated style. Quite the opposite: One devoted customer even sent $1,000 to support Southwest after the attacks.

Southwest is the only major carrier to remain profitable in every quarter since September 11, 2001. While its six biggest rivals have grounded 240 aircraft and laid off more than 70,000 workers, Southwest—which has never laid off a soul in its 31 years—has kept all of its 375 planes and 35,000 people flying.

Source: Adapted from W. Zellner & M. Arndt, "Holding Steady: As Rivals Sputter, Can Southwest Stay on Top?" *Business Week*, February 3, 2003, pp. 66–68.

competitors. This keeps planning from being a "pie in the sky" exercise and anchors it to the firm's strengths. Beside simplifying the planning task, it will make plans easier to explain, since managers and employees will be cognizant of the problems, challenges, alternatives, and priorities being addressed. Moreover, the levels of risk and uncertainty are lowered since the plan is confined to areas about which the firm has information and experience, reducing the probability of unpleasant surprises. Management Close-Up 5.d illustrates how Apple successfully capitalized on its core competence to launch a highly profitable product ahead of its time.

Formal Planning and Opportunistic Planning

A dynamic world requires dynamic planning programs. **Formal planning** systems are designed to identify objectives and to structure the major tasks of the organization to accomplish them. Formal planning is what has been described thus far in this chapter. No matter how careful the formal planning process is, however, unexpected events can derail the plan. A second type of planning, referred to as **opportunistic planning,** should coexist with formal planning and can help the formal plan function more smoothly.

As its name implies, opportunistic planning refers to programmatic actions triggered by unforeseen circumstances. Resources that are not to-

formal planning

A system designed to identify objectives and to structure the major tasks of the organization to accomplish them.

opportunistic planning

A type of planning that involves programmatic actions triggered by unforeseen circumstances; it can coexist with formal planning and can help the formal plan function more smoothly.

Apple Creates a Product Before Its Time

THEME: CUSTOMER FOCUS Personal digital assistants—calculator-sized electronic computers that allow users to track their lives merely by entering information with a stylus—are ubiquitous in the corporate world. Their prevalence today makes it seem as if Apple Computer would have been the early victor of the market when it began the Newton project way back in 1987. The company's focus on the far-sighted idea of inputting data without a keyboard was seen by John Sculley. Apple CEO at the time, as a symbol of Apple's vision and industry influence. Apple's "personal digital assistant," as Sculley termed the Newton, would be the next step in merging the computing, communications, and entertainment industries.

What happened to the Newton is a lesson in how timing—for better or worse—can affect a company's planning. The Newton, a portable multipurpose PDA packed with features, was developed before the software that could read the user's handwriting had been refined enough to make it practical. The original Newton was hit with bad publicity about flaws in its ability to recognize users' handwriting, and the brand never recovered. Although Newton's electronic mail and messaging capability was publicized, e-mail and the Internet had yet to make an impact on modern culture. The ideas for the Newton overpowered the available technology for making them happen. In fact, Sculley's successor, Steve Jobs, told Apple developers he had tried the Newton but "threw it away."

Jobs rang the death knell for the product, which never earned a profit. By the late 1990s, although the company had spend at least $500 million on Newton, Apple had stopped working on developing Newton-based products such as the handheld MessagePad and eMate.

The time was certainly ripe for the concept at the turn of the century, however, when both the consumer and the

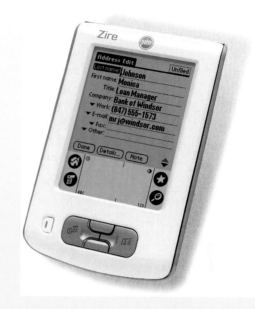

technology had caught up with the idea. Pilot (now Palm Pilot) began creating its solutions for handheld information management. By 2001 Palm Pilot products, such as the Palm III, were the industry standard.

By 2004, the Palm Zire handheld computer introduced on October 7, 2002, was the best-selling handheld information management tool of its kind. It was also very affordable, with an estimated U.S. street price under $100. Apple's story illustrates how a planning process that takes advantage of the firm's core competence is more likely to succeed in the long run.

Source: Adapted from J. Carlton, "Apple Drops Newton, an Idea ahead of Its Time," *The Wall Street Journal,* March 2, 1998, p. B1; www.palm.com (2003).

---

tally committed as part of the formal planning process may be used at the discretion of managers to deal with unexpected events. For example, since its inception Federal Express has viewed the U.S. Postal Service (USPS) as a direct competitor, predicating its growth on stealing market share from USPS by sending materials faster with almost perfect reliability. FedEx marketing and delivery plans quickly changed in 2001 when FedEx and the USPS became partners. The U.S. Postal Service now allows consumers to send FedEx packages directly from any U.S. Post Office using newly installed drop boxes, and FedEx now flies most of the Priority and Express packages for the Postal Service. This type of action as a result of "opportunistic planning" would have been unthinkable just a few months before.[12]

It is important to strike the proper balance between these two types of planning. Organizations that rely exclusively on formal planning can become too rigid, whereas firms that use only opportunistic schemes will be constantly reacting to external forces and will have no clear sense of direction. Formal planning should provide a structured framework without binding every action of the enterprise, while opportunistic planning should allow for creative responses within that organized framework. GE has a formal planning process, and its longtime CEO, Jack Welch, strongly promoted opportunistic planning during his tenure:

> The story about GE that hasn't been told is the value of an informal place. . . . I don't think people have ever figured out that being informal is a big deal. . . . Making the company "informal" means violating the chain of command, communicating across layers, paying people as if they worked not for a big company but for a demanding entrepreneur where nearly everyone knows the boss.[13]

The Formal Planning Process

As indicated earlier, the four elements of the formal planning process involve setting objectives, charting a course of action to meet the objectives, allocating resources to carry out the planned activities, and implementing the activities (see Figure 5.1). Each of these steps is discussed in turn.

Setting Objectives

Objectives are the performance targets set during the planning cycle. Objectives provide the answer to the question: What are we trying to accomplish? Inappropriate or poorly defined objectives invalidate the rest of the planning process since there is no clear guide for organizational efforts.

Objectives are set at every level in an organization. The goals established at higher levels direct and constrain the objectives set at lower levels. In general, objectives are more general at the top and become more specific at lower organizational levels. Some people refer to this as a *cascading of objectives*. DuPont stated an overall corporate objective from 2003 to 2005 in which one-third of sales would come from products introduced in the last five years (up from 24 percent in 2003). To achieve this goal, DuPont's finance department set as its objective to increase the research and development (R&D) budget by 10 percent and to devote 65 percent of this budget to new product development (up from 33 percent in recent years). The objective of DuPont's 75 R&D centers distributed across 12 countries was to identify 75 projects (an average of one per center) to launch new products that have the highest revenue potential. For one particular team, called the Suprel Group, the objective became much more specific: to develop a lightweight and puncture-resistant fabric to be used in gowns for surgeons and nurses.[14] In other words, DuPont's product introduction goal that began at the top of the organizational pyramid filtered down to lower echelons, where they became more specific. The goals at each level should support the goals established at the next higher level.

The overall objectives of the organization reflect its *mission,* which is a statement of the organization's reason to exist (more on this in Chapter 7 regarding strategic management). DuPont's objectives for 2003–2005 were consistent with the mission of being "a science company, delivering science-based solutions in markets such as food and nutrition, health care, apparel, home and construction, electronics, and transportation" (www.Dupont.com).

Specific and measurable objectives motivate behavior more than general and ambiguous ones. It is important to give employees a clear sense of direction. Unambiguous objectives allow managers to determine whether key outcomes are being reached and to take corrective action if they are not. By knowing exactly where the firm is trying to go, managers and employees can focus on the most important activities, thereby concentrating on achieving the best results. Worthwhile objectives include:

- Profitability targets, such as return on investment, return on assets, and earnings per share.

- Quality goals such as percentage of rejects, customer complaints relative to number of orders, or quality certification standards.

- Marketing objectives, such as market growth, market share, and international sales.

- Innovation outcomes, such as number of patents, percentage of sales attributed to new products, and return on R&D investments.

Further, managers should make sure that objectives are *challenging* and will "stretch" employees to work harder to use their full potential. Difficult goals must be achievable; otherwise employees will not believe that their efforts will lead to success.

Objectives should specify a *timetable* or *deadline.* This can serve to motivate individuals. A timetable can cause individuals to organize tasks, prompting them to monitor work to ensure that completion is on time. It also helps management evaluate individuals or units on the extent to which work was done in a timely fashion.

Finally, managers and employees are more likely to devote time and effort to the accomplishment of objectives that they perceive as more critical and whose achievement is associated with greater prestige, rewards, and future career opportunities. Deciding which objectives should have highest *priority* is an integral part of the planning process.

When firms have multiple objectives, scarce resources preclude pursuing them all with the same zeal. Frequently, desired objectives may work at cross purposes. For example,

- Managers may increase short-term profits by cutting back on capital expenditures, reducing R&D investments, and laying off employees. This may decrease future profits because of lost technological superiority, the introduction of fewer products into the market, and less employee commitment.

- A firm may reduce its overall level of risk by diversifying into different market areas so that downturns in one market segment may be counterbalanced by upturns in other segments. However, the overall profitability of the firm is likely to be lower, because it loses the competitive advantage of applying a core set of knowledge and skills to a focused product niche. For example, in the mid-1990s, Altavista began as an Internet search engine. By the late 1990s the company had decided to diversify its scope and to explore new market segments. Company executives invested $100 million to build the site into a multifaceted portal along the lines of Yahoo!. By 2000 Altavista realized that expanding beyond its core knowledge had been a mistake and decided to return to its original mission in 2001.[15]

- A firm may pursue rapid growth to expand market share overseas, but company profits may suffer because it has to contend with diverse cultural milieus, is exposed to currency fluctuations, and is required to develop a management structure to deal with the complexities of a global operation (see Chapter 2).

- A firm may reduce costs by moving its manufacturing operations to a developing country where environmental regulations are lax. This would conflict with corporate social responsibility objectives.

As discussed in Chapter 3, a firm has many stakeholders, including employees, shareholders, consumers, and regulatory bodies. Each group may have different objectives. The planning process should identify the wishes of each of these groups and develop objectives that are clear, achievable, measurable, and prioritized so that they contribute to overall organizational performance.

One planning technique that is widely used in the United States and abroad is *Management by Objectives* (MBO). MBO is a program in which objectives are mutually set between the employee and supervisor. The employee is held accountable for the accomplishment of those objectives at various intervals which are normally part of an annual performance appraisal. MBO programs are popular because they combine planning (through participatively set objectives) and control (employees are responsible for the attainment of measurable goals).

FIGURE 5.2

Key Steps of the Typical Management by Objectives Cycle

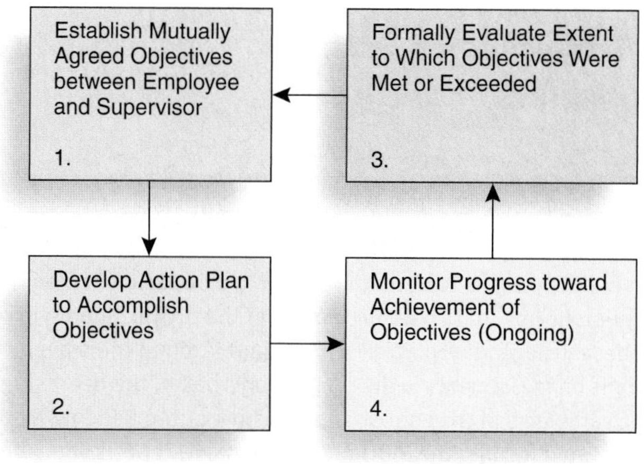

Figure 5.2 shows the key steps of a typical annual MBO cycle. In step 1, objectives are agreed to between the superior and subordinate, and put in writing. Objectives such as companywide profitability targets are first established at the top of the organizational pyramid. These more general objectives then filter down through successively lower layers. For instance, overall profitability targets are broken down into objectives for divisions and product lines. While normally these objectives are established annually, it is possible to use a longer or shorter time horizon. In step 2, managers at each level develop action plans to accomplish the objectives set for them by their immediate superiors in step 1. As the plans are implemented in step 3, there are frequent checkups to ensure that things are on track and make any necessary adjustments. In step 4 (which normally takes place a year after objectives were set in step 1), the pairs of superior and subordinate who established the mutually agreed-upon objectives in step 1 meet to discuss the extent to which objectives were met. This feedback is normally put in writing in a formal document called the *performance appraisal form.* In the words of a human resource planning consultant, "many managers struggle with feedback precisely because of a lack of planning. Without front-end planning, feedback has no context . . . the outcome of effective feedback is clarity—clarity regarding the performer's recent performance against previously agreed-upon criteria".[16]

Employees are usually rewarded with cash bonuses, stocks, promotions, and other suitable benefits when they accomplish or exceed the performance targets set in step 1. This performance information is then used as part of goal-setting for the next review cycle. Targets may be revised downward if they were deemed to be unrealistic in the prior MBO cycle, or made more difficult if the employee is ready for greater challenges.

Unfortunately, the very strength of MBO—measurability—often becomes its major weakness. Managers can manipulate the system to choose easier-to-reach targets and ignore intangible things that may be

Too Good to Be True: How Quantifiable Objectives May Lead to Ethical Lapses

THEME: ETHICS Goal-setting programs such as an MBO program can become a two-edged sword. In the mid-1990s, Tenet Health Care developed an aggressive MBO program featuring challenging profitability targets to be met each year. The second largest for-profit hospital chain in America, Tenet Health Care Corp. became legendary on Wall Street for posting the highest returns on investments in the industry during the 1990s and the early years of the 2000s. In order to achieve these unprecedented results, the MBO plan called for hospital CEOs to receive cash bonuses largely tied to exceeding ambitious profit and revenue growth targets. Most CEOs were able to deliver. Consequently, the cash bonuses represented approximately half of all the compensation hospital executives earned.

By 2003, it became apparent that these impressive results may have included a darker side. Among Tenet's raft of problems: The hospital billed some $763 million in Medicare "outlier" payments employing a loophole that boosted total profits 20 percent. Outlier payments became 17 percent of Tenet's total Medicare payments, which was far greater than the national average of 5 percent. An "outlier" billing system is meant to reimburse hospitals for excessive expenses incurred during complex procedures, such as a heart bypass surgery, that lead to complications. The system is intended to protect hospitals from having to shoulder too much of the cost for treating very sick, elderly patients. Unfortunately, outlier payments can also be easily abused, since hospitals determine the charges used to calculate payments. Tenet's Redding Medical Center in Redding, California, for example, charged 40 percent more for outlier payments than the seven other major hospitals within 200 miles. In 2003, the Justice Department filed a lawsuit against Tenet alleging that the organization had overcharged and defrauded Medicare. Around the same time, the FBI announced that up to one-half of the heart surgeries performed by the two physicians at the Redding Medical Center may have been unnecessary. Reports indicate that 167 patients treated during a 42-month period died.

The hospital was also accused of performing unnecessary medical procedures such as angioplasties, coronary bypasses, and heart catheterizations in order to meet or exceed rising profitability objectives. Furthermore, the California Public Employees' Retirement System (also known as Calpers) said that it paid nearly 50 percent more for insured members at Tenet hospitals in comparison to hospitals elsewhere in the state. This further enhanced suspicions that Tenet hospitals were manipulating billing procedures in order to beat ambitious profitability objectives. While these cases are still pending, they illustrate the potential ethical problems that emerge when managers are held accountable for meeting or exceeding tough quantitative objectives.

Source: Adapted from A. Weintraub, "A Scandal-Ridden Tenet Stands by Its Man," *Business Week,* November 25, 2002, p. 46. See also Associated Press, "Tenet's Bills to Calpers 50 Percent More than Other Hospitals," *Sacramento Bee,* February 3, 2003, p. A-1; and Redding Medical Center Net, "Half of Heart Patients May Not Have Needed Surgery," (www.reddingmedicalcenternet.com), February 6, 2003.

more difficult to measure, such as customer goodwill. They may also become reluctant to change priorities for fear of not achieving the agreed-upon objectives when the situation demands it. Worse yet, the setting of numerical objectives may lead to gaming on the part of managers to reach or exceed the quantitative targets set in step 1 (see Figure 5.2), tempting them to engage in unethical behaviors. This is exemplified in the case of Tenet Health Care, where hospital executives allegedly encouraged aggressive medical treatments in order to receive bonuses tied to ambitious growth and revenue targets (see Management Close-Up 5.e, "Too Good to Be True"). This means that for an MBO system to be effective in the long run, the system must be flexible and allow for subjective judgments when assessing whether or not objectives are being achieved. The greater the volatility of conditions faced by the firm (rapid changes in technology, markets, competitors and the like) and the more its products and services change frequently, the greater the need for flexibility in the MBO system.

Charting a Course of Action

Once objectives have been established, the next step in the planning process (see Figure 5.1) is to determine the actions necessary for producing orderly results. Three types of actions are normally planned: strategic, tactical, and operational.

STRATEGIC ACTION PLANS   Top executives are normally responsible for developing strategic action plans. At times divisional managers and the board of directors are also involved. **Strategic action plans** are based on overall organizational features, resources, and the environment. They establish long-term, corporatewide actions designed to accomplish the company's mission and major objectives. An important emphasis at this level is linking the action plans of different organizational functions and units so that they reinforce the strategies adopted by the entire organization.

To be effective, a strategic action plan should meet the following criteria:

1. *Proactivity,* which is the degree to which the strategic action plan takes a long-term view of the future and actively moves the company forward in the desired direction.
2. *Congruency,* or the extent to which the strategic action plan fits with organizational characteristics and the external environment (see Chapter 7).
3. *Synergy,* or the integration of the efforts of various organizational subunits to better accomplish corporatewide business objectives.

TACTICAL ACTION PLANS   **Tactical action plans** are developed at the division or department level. They specify the activities that must be performed, when they must be completed, and the resources a division or department will need to complete the portions of the strategic action plan under its purview. The primary criterion of effectiveness for tactical action plans is the extent to which they contribute to the achievement of the company's strategic objectives. In general, tactical action plans cover a period of one to two years. Two important aspects of tactical action plans are division of labor and budgeting.

The formal assignment of authority and responsibility to job holders is referred to as **division of labor.** This helps ensure that tasks of job

strategic action plans

Management plans based on macro approaches for analyzing organizational features, resources, and the environment and establishing long-term corporatewide action programs to accomplish the stated objectives in light of that analysis.

tactical action plans

Management action plans at the division or department level that indicate what activities must be performed, when they must be completed, and what resources will be needed at the division or departmental level to complete the portions of the strategic action plan that fall under the purview of that particular organizational subunit.

division of labor

The production process in which each worker repeats one step over and over, achieving greater efficiencies in the use of time and knowledge; also, the formal assignment of authority and responsibility to job holders.

holders are appropriate for accomplishing the overall plan of the division or the department, which in turn should support the organization's strategic action plans. Common ways to change organizational design to achieve strategic action plans include:

- Assigning more job positions in the organization to work crucial to the attainment of strategic objectives.

- Creating specialized job positions that emphasize work crucial to the attainment of strategic objectives.

- Assigning work crucial to the attainment of strategic objectives to high-level job positions.[17]

budgeting

Controlling and allocating the firm's funds; *variable budgeting* allows for deviations between planned output and actual output by considering the fact that variable costs depend on the level of output, whereas fixed costs do not; *moving budgeting* creates a tentative budget for a fixed period of time and then revises and updates it on a periodic basis to take changes into account.

By controlling and allocating funds, **budgeting** becomes an integral part of tactical action plans. As seen in Skills for Managing 5.2, budgeting provides information about the strategic direction of the firm, makes clear the contribution to strategic objectives, forces budget committees to carefully ponder strategic perspectives to decide whether to accept or reject each proposal, and creates monitoring devices to examine the extent to which the projected contribution to strategic objectives is actually realized.

Managers and/or employees may also be asked to participate in the budget-setting process. Involving them promotes better understanding of the tactical action plan by those who will be carrying it out. It can also improve acceptance of decisions and commitment to them. Employee involvement may take a variety of forms, including:

- Creating budget forecasts.
- Preparing budget proposals.
- Allocating the overall budget to various activities.
- Developing significant rewards for reaching budgetary targets, such as bonuses, pay increases, and recognition at special events.
- Transferring resources from one activity to another in the event of unforeseen circumstances.

Budgets are based on forecasts, which in turn depend on assumptions about the future. For example, a production budget for a two-year period is projected by estimating the costs of materials, labor, and capital equipment required to produce an expected sales level. The assumptions made about both sales levels and the required resources could be wrong. The sales volume could be higher or lower than expected. Market demand, competitors' pricing, shifts in consumer tastes, and interest rates all affect sales. The resources needed depend on such factors as economies of scale, efficiency of production, introduction of new technology, and the cost of supplies. For instance, using copper instead of aluminum to make microchips cut IBM's and Intel's production costs of microchips almost in half in the late 1990s. On the other hand, the cost of wood almost doubled in 1995 and 1996, greatly increasing construction costs for home builders.

BUDGETING SKILLS

- *Informing*. If most persons in the organization understand clearly the strategic directions of the organization, constructive ideas for the use of financial resources will result and unrealistic proposals should be reduced to a minimum.

- *Proposing*. Standardized guides and forms should require information that will make clear the contribution to strategic objectives of the activity to be financed.

- *Selecting*. Each proposal must be weighed by comparing its strategic value with its cost. The budget committee should be able to explain in tactical terms why each proposal is accepted or rejected.

- *Monitoring*. Proposal effectiveness should be evaluated periodically to determine whether the projected contribution of the activity financed to strategic objectives actually is realized. The learning that occurs as a result of evaluation should be used to improve the budgeting process and should affect how each step of the process is carried out in the future.

Source: Adapted from D. W. Jarrell, *Human Resource Planning.* Englewood Cliffs, NJ: Prentice Hall, 1993, p. 50.

Two budgeting techniques are designed to be more flexible: variable budgeting and moving budgeting. *Variable budgeting* accounts for deviations between planned output and actual output because variable costs depend on the level of output, whereas fixed costs do not. For instance, plant and equipment are fixed costs, because the firm pays principal, interest, and maintenance on those assets even when they are not being utilized at full capacity.

Variable budgets take into account the dependance of anticipated profits on the expected relationship between costs and output. A variable budget recognizes that planned profit and total costs do not vary proportionately with sales. The hypothetical variable budget in Table 5.1 shows how an increase in output of 30 percent, from 2,000 units to 2,600 units, can produce an increase in profits of 40 percent. To be accurate, variable budgeting also needs to consider how the cost of different inputs co-vary as a function of output level. For example, as output increases, administrative office support decreases as a percentage of total operating costs.

In contrast to variable budgeting, *moving budgeting* creates a tentative budget for a fixed period of time, normally a year. The budget is then revised and updated on a periodic basis to take changes into account. Reexamining the premises, assumptions, and estimates made when the tentative budget was initially created allows the budget to be a living, flexible document.

TABLE 5.1

An Example of a Variable Budget

Output (units)	2,000	2,200	2,400	2,600
Sales (at $10.00 per unit)	$20,000	$22,000	$24,000	$26,000
Variable costs (at $6.00 per unit)	12,000	13,200	14,400	15,600
Fixed costs	2,000	2,000	2,000	2,000
Total costs	14,000	15,200	16,400	17,600
Planned profit	$ 6,000	$ 6,800	$ 7,600	$ 8,400

One downside of moving budgets is that they demand frequent revisions, requiring employees to spend additional time on the budgeting process. Also, some managers attempt to secure more resources by arguing that the financial resources originally received were inadequate.

Firms need to be careful that managers do not become obsessed with numbers and dollars, ignoring more "intangible" aspects of performance that in the long run are critical for financial success. For example, quality, customer service, employee commitment, innovation and creativity, reputation, consumer loyalty, and ability to attract and retain top talent may suffer if managers only receive pay raises and positive performance evaluations for strictly adhering to the budget.

OPERATIONAL ACTION PLANS Line managers and employees directly responsible for individual tasks or activities are the ones who create **operational action plans.** These plans tend to be narrowly focused on resources, methods, timelines, and quality control issues for a particular kind of operation. In general, the time frame for operational action plans is shorter than for tactical action plans.

Figure 5.3 illustrates a typical operation. Inputs (human, financial, raw materials, and other resources) are transformed (through assembly, chemical treatment, combination with other elements) into outcomes (products or services). The control component includes information about the required characteristics of inputs and outputs and how inputs must be modified to produce outputs. It ensures that the quantity and quality of inputs and outputs fall within certain parameters and that costs remain within a stipulated budget. Feedback is returned from output to transformation and input, so that continuing improvement may be achieved by using resources more efficiently. Any activity creating an output that affects tactical action plans and that uses significant resources can be analyzed using this general model.

The main challenge of operational planning is using resources most efficiently. For instance, when the primary resource of an operation such as an R&D facility is people's know-how, operational plans may focus on how to transform employees' knowledge to produce an innovation (out-

---

operational action plan

A management plan normally created by line managers and employees directly responsible for carrying out certain tasks or activities.

FIGURE 5.3

A Typical Operating System

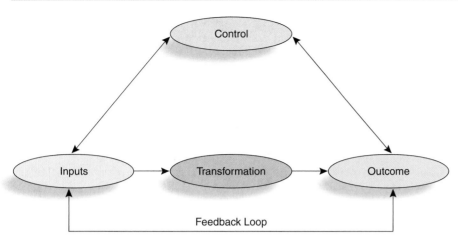

come). The goal should be to use these resources efficiently to generate innovations that add value to the company's overall operation.

When the relationship between resources and outcomes is uncertain, the control function must allow substantial latitude for failure. This is the case, for instance, in most pharmaceutical firms. There is typically less than a 10 percent chance of getting a therapeutic protein that works in the animal-disease model to market. The human testing required for approval takes at least six to eight years to complete. A particular drug may be dropped out during any of the three phases of clinical trials for reasons ranging from lack of efficacy to high toxicity.[18]

If property conducted, operational planning offers several benefits to organizations, including:

- The opportunity to use feedback for continued incremental learning.

- The ability to visualize alternative types of operations—that is, alternative ways to use resources to create a product or service.

- The ability to predict the effects of modifications in operations on the efficiency of operations.

- The ability to evaluate the effectiveness of operations.

 Project Planning

A more specific set of operational planning techniques have been developed in an area called *project management*. As the name implies, a project is a set of tasks designed to achieve certain objectives. In most cases, projects are completed by teams. Project management planning techniques allow one to identify specific tasks to be done, when they need to be completed, the resources required, and to document what has been accomplished so far. There are now many powerful Web-based programs that managers and team members can use to schedule project tasks, monitor them from start to finish, and report variances from expected results. Figure 5.4 shows a description of one program, called Intuit QuickBase.

FIGURE 5.4

Intuit QuickBase

Source: www.quickbase.com/.

"With our company, 'QuickBase' has crossed over from a noun to a verb."
—Dr. Scott Friedman

Got a vital project? Now you can QuickBase it.

Project managers—those busy conductors of the office orchestra—now have a powerful Web-based solution that is simple enough for the whole team to use. QuickBase lets managers create a central online home for all their project data: project schedules, documents, issue lists, team rosters, information of all kinds. Everyone on the team can see and update current versions, so they're always on task and in sync.

Now you can manage your project to success with our dedicated <u>Project Manager</u> application, which puts all the tools you need in one simple-to-use solution. Suddenly, life for the project manager just got easier.

With <u>Project Manager,</u> you get:

- **True accountability.** Everyone can see what's due and when. Updates and changes are available immediately. No more excuses.

- **Better collaboration.** Critical documents are never trapped on anyone's hard drive. Since QuickBase is Web-based, everyone on your team can use it anytime and anywhere they have Web access.

- **More time saved.** The familiar Web interface makes using QuickBase as easy as clicking a mouse. Your team spends less time e-mailing documents and more time on the job.

- **Immediate results.** Get your team up and running in minutes—no need to order, distribute and install new software. With QuickBase, everything you and your team need is instantly available on the Web.

Implementation

Planning is meaningless unless it can be carried out successfully. The implementation phase is a critical part of the planning process. Implementation involves defining tasks to be accomplished, assigning individual responsibilities for those tasks, and managing individuals to ensure that the tasks are appropriately completed.

One distinction that is often made is between standing plans and single-use plans. *Standing plans* regulate situations that occur repeatedly. That is, they are plans created to help the organization deal with issues that come up on a regular basis. Organizations implement standing plans using a programmed approach that includes policies, rules, and standard operating procedures. A *policy* is a general guide for managers and employees to follow. For instance, an organization with a flexible work hours policy provides employees with the opportunity to choose when to come to work and when to go home. A *rule* is a formal, written statement that states the general permissible bounds for the application of particular policies. For instance, a rule might be that employees need to arrive at work between the hours of 7 and 9 in the morning and work for nine consecutive hours, including a half-hour lunch and two 15-minute breaks. A standard operating procedure (SOP) describes in detail the precise steps to be followed in a specific situation. For instance, an SOP may specify that each employee must punch a time clock upon arriving at work, check with the supervisor, file a work plan for the day, and complete a computerized report at the end of the day that documents the percentage of time devoted to each major task and what he or she accomplished. In other words, employees are expected to show up for work regularly so standing plans may be developed to provide work scheduling flexibility and ensure that employees are there when they are supposed to be, do what they are supposed to do, and provide enough information to others so that supervisors and co-workers know the status of various tasks assigned to them.

Single-use plans are implemented for unusual or one-of-a-kind situations. For example, one of NASA's major goals was to reach the moon, which involved the design and construction of a lunar module to take astronauts to the moon and bring them back to earth safely.

In the end, all plans must be implemented by people. Plan implementation requires thinking about four major issues: the means of implementation, a process for organizational problems solving, the linking of planning with organizational control systems, and mechanisms for dealing with organizational change.

MEANS OF IMPLEMENTATION   Managers must find a way to induce people to take the necessary steps to accomplish the planned actions. Four major approaches may be used: authority, persuasion, policy, and feedback mechanism.

Authority   Authority is formal power. It is accorded to the position rather than the person. As part of plan implementation, the employee at each position is vested with the authority to make certain decisions and is held accountable for those decisions. Subordinates are expected to comply with the requests of people in positions of authority unless they are asked to do something that is unethical or illegal.

Persuasion   While most firms rely on some form of authority structure to ensure employee compliance with planned actions, a plan that is acceptable to employees increases commitment to that plan. Persuasion is an important aspect of effectively implementing plans. Employees who are convinced of the merits of a plan are more likely to respond enthusiastically to directives of managers who have formal authority and to "go beyond the call of duty" in finding better ways to effectively execute the plan.

Persuasion in most companies requires employee involvement rather than a manager simply making a speech extolling the virtues of a particular plan. For example, to become a change agent during Kellogg's conversion from cereal company to snack-foods company in the first decade of the century, CEO Carlos Gutierrez encouraged communication instead of Kellogg's traditional top-down approach. Previously, new product ideas had been presented only at monthly meetings and only by

In late 2002–2003, major airlines were still trying to recover from economic pressures and 9/11. Don Carty, then CEO of American, called on the unions of employees to accept annual concessions in pay and benefits in order to keep American afloat. However, after revealing the details of executive-retention bonuses and pension protections, he lost not only his authority and persuasion with union leaders, but his job as well.

the head of research and development. Gutierrez opened himself up to hearing from people, and now technicians from the company's three-year-old, $75 million W. K. Kellogg Institute for Food and Nutritional Research can bring their ideas directly to him.[19]

Policy Both formal authority and persuasion must operate within a general institutional context that governs the relations and actions of individuals responsible for implementing the plan. To this end, organizations develop policies that define appropriate and inappropriate behavior. These guidelines usually appear in a formal document to ensure that relevant policy information is communicated to all individuals involved. Effective policies are flexible, comprehensive, coordinated with subunits whose actions are interrelated, ethical, and written clearly and logically.

Feedback Mechanism Successful plan implementation requires a continuous flow of information that is used to determine to what extent the plan is being carried out as expected. It is also important to assess how and why individual activities are helping attain company objectives. If the information sought is threatening to people, then knowledge sharing, constructive analysis, and a spirit of open inquiry are inhibited. Active employee involvement includes initiative, honest discussion of ideas, and generation of inputs or suggestions from the "bottom up." The learning that occurs is a crucial part of problem solving during the plan implementation phase.

A PROCESS FOR ORGANIZATIONAL PROBLEM SOLVING Plan implementation seldom, if ever, occurs smoothly. Many unknowns must be dealt with. Part of an effective implementation program is establishment of a system that allows for a careful diagnosis of problems so that individuals responsible for carrying out the plan can learn from their mistakes. A six-stage approach may be used to facilitate this problem-solving process:[20]

1. *Identify performance gaps.* A diagnosis begins with a manager and a team defining the difference or shortfall between objectives and achievements. This step must not become part of such personnel decisions as merit pay, performance appraisal, and promotion. Doing so dampens people's willingness to be self-critical and openly share information.

2. *Identify tasks and work processes necessary for accomplishing the plan.* This requires defining what each individual is expected to do, the sequence of tasks, and the degree of interdependence or integration among the critical tasks needed to ensure successful execution of the plan. For instance, some key managers faced the following tasks:

PLANNING AND PERFORMANCE

Browse through several issues of major financial news-papers or business periodicals that provide in-depth coverage of firms, such as *The Wall Street Journal*, *Business Week*, *Fortune*, or *Forbes*. Select five to ten firms that are in the news. Research these firms' recent activities and answer the following questions.

1. How did the planning process affect these companies' performance?

2. How could better planning have helped their performance?

At Medtek, Torrance realized that if he were to be successful at developing innovative new products, his laboratory would have to be world-class in chemical and hydraulic technologies and be able to link these technologies to manufacturing and marketing requirements. For Chow at BOC, a critical task identified for delivering customized service to global customers was close integration across geographically dispersed organizations. With the Grenzach team's goal of reducing costs, the critical tasks were to maintain the functional excellence within the plant as well as to increase integration across the functional areas.[21]

3. *Check for organizational congruence.* Once the tasks and work processes have been identified, it is necessary to determine the extent to which other organizational elements support or hinder their attainment. In other words, it is important to know if the planned activity is aligned or fits with organizational structure, culture, human resource policies, and individual competencies and motives. If these organizational building blocks are incongruent with task requirements, the planned activities are likely to fail.

4. *If any incongruencies or inconsistencies are found, intervene to create alignment in order to effectively implement the plan.* In general, incremental changes, such as modifying the incentive system, can be accomplished without actually reconsidering the feasibility of the plan itself. But if there is systemwide lack of congruence that requires extensive changes in formal organizational arrangements, culture, and people, it probably means that the plan is impractical. In such a case, the entire plan needs to be reconsidered and better adjusted to organizational realities.

5. *Execute the plan.* At this stage, managers and employees take actions targeted at achieving the key milestones of the plan, ideally

reinforced by congruent organizational arrangements, culture, and people who facilitate the execution of those actions.

6. *Learn from the consequences.* This is an ongoing process during plan implementation. It is used to diagnose the causes of performance gaps, anticipate what may cause problems in the future, and reveal better ways of doing things. Skills for Managing Box 5.3 asks you to select five to ten firms that are in the news and analyze how the planning process may have affected their performance and how their planning process may have been improved.

LINKING OF PLANNING WITH ORGANIZATIONAL CONTROL SYSTEMS   Planning and the organizational control system should go hand in hand. As noted above in the section regarding operational action plans, an effective control system alerts managers when something is going wrong and provides them the opportunity to respond. Once plans are formulated and carried out, an effective control system allows the organization to compare planned objectives with observed results. If there is a significant discrepancy between expected and actual results, then managers should take corrective action in order to improve future plans and make modifications to those plans being implemented. It is wise to leave open the possibility of abandoning existing plans and replacing them with new ones when the control system indicates that there is a high deviation of expected versus actual results.

MECHANISMS TO DEAL WITH ORGANIZATIONAL CHANGE   Most plans require changes in the way things are currently done. This is particularly true if the firm is attempting to shift direction or is operating in a turbulent environment. There are three major challenges in trying to simultaneously implement a plan and manage change associated with its implementation: (1) dealing with power and politics, (2) reducing individual anxiety and resistance, and (3) maintaining control during the transition period. If managers can successfully handle these challenges, employees are likely to be eager to implement the plan and to make accommodations to ensure a smooth transition. If ignored, these three factors can stop the successful implementation of even the most carefully drawn plans.

Managing the Political Dynamics of Change   Practically every significant change results in politics and resistance. Managing politics can be accomplished in a number of ways, including enlisting the support of key players, being consistent, and ensuring stability.

It is important for managers to mobilize the support of key players. First, the manager must identify the people who have the power to make or break the change and who control critical resources or expertise. Once the pivotal individuals are identified, it is necessary to ascertain how the change will likely affect each of them, how each is likely to react to the

How to Influence Key Players

- *Participation involvement co-optation.* The most positive method of getting powerful individuals on board is to solicit their involvement in planning and directing the change effort. The greater their degree of involvement, the more chance they have to put their own stamp on the change, and the more they own and become committed to it.

- *Incentives.* Rewards and punishments are another powerful way to shape desired behaviors. To the extent that participants see no incentive (or worse, are penalized) for supporting the change, it is reasonable for them to resist. So it is critical to be clear about current versus future rewards.

- *Exchange.* Like political systems, organizations are filled with exchange relationships: I do you a favor, you do me a favor. Indeed, reciprocity exists worldwide and tends to balance out over time. All managers need to have a bank account of favors owed them. These favors can be called in during times of change.

- *Isolation.* To the extent that key individuals continue to resist the change, they can be either socially or physically isolated.

- *Removal or transfer.* Key antagonists who cannot be converted to supporters may have to be removed. If politically powerful opponents are permitted to actively or passively resist the change, they may encourage others to resist and form coalitions to blunt the change.

Source: Adapted from M. L. Tushman and C. A. O'Reilly III, *Winning through Innovation: A Practical Guide to Leading Organizational Change and Renewal.* Boston: Harvard Business School Press, 1997.

change, and the methods available to influence them. As shown in Manager's Notebook 5.1, managers can use a variety of approaches to influence key players. In descending order of desirability, these include active participation of all affected by the changes, rewards and punishment, reciprocity, and isolation and/or removal of those who continue to resist the change.

In managing the dynamics of change, managers must attempt to ensure consistency in words and actions. To prevent cynicism among those responsible for implementing the plan, what managers say is important must be congruent with the actions taken or being reinforced. If a plan calls for close cooperation among individuals and units, rewarding only individual actions would generate mixed messages, and employees might resist the change. Managers can use a number of symbolic activities and mechanisms to influence planned actions, including how they spend their time, the types of questions they ask, what they follow up on, what they discuss at meetings, the types of things they choose to summarize, how they use language, the type of special events they provide, and the new heroes and myths they create to illustrate the change in standards and direction.[22]

Finally, managers must build in stability. People can absorb only so much change at once, and it is necessary to create stability during the implementation. This requires sending consistent messages—signals—to lessen uncertainty:

> *Part of this signaling is to be clear about what is not changing—what people can hold onto in the future. If some aspects of culture, physical location, and staffing patterns will not change, these anchors to the past need to be communicated and reinforced early on. At Alcoa, even in the context of wholesale change, managers made it clear that the glorious Alcoa engineering heritage and its commitment to high-quality aluminum would not change. As Kodak [has refocused], George Fisher has reemphasized the firm's commitment to the photographic market and signaled an end to diversification. Clarity about what will not change helps moderate fears of the future.*[23]

Managing Individual Resistance   Organizational change can generate individual anxiety and stress. Up to a point this energizes employees, and their attentiveness and motivation increase. Too much stress, however, causes individuals to oppose change, leading them to try to block the plan or to leave in search of better employment prospects elsewhere. Dysfunctional anxiety can be reduced by showing people why the change needs to occur, making them stakeholders in the change effort through active participation, recognizing and rewarding the new behaviors required by the plan, and providing opportunities to disengage from the past at public events such as lunches, ceremonies, and employee skits.

Maintaining Control during the Transition   The turbulence and uncertainty associated with the change should not be allowed to result in chaos. Both for operational and political reasons, it is important for managers to convey the idea that the situation is under control during the transition period. This can be done by communicating a clear idea of the future state, using multiple methods to promote change, designing transition management structures, setting transition milestones, and measuring progress on a continuing basis.[24]

Applications for the Manager   Managers are expected to collaborate with employees to define objectives for their units and to clearly communicate the relative importance of those objectives. Once the objectives are established, managers need to develop a plan to accomplish them and lay out the steps of implementation. This process provides a frame of reference that can facilitate orderly change and avoid unnecessary disruptions and turmoil when unexpected changes occur. In other words, a quality planning process is useful to the manager precisely because it smooths the way change is conducted and gives employees a sense of confidence and continuity even in the midst of rapid change.

Applications for Managing Teams   Teams require a great deal of coordination and integration to function effectively. Otherwise, many hours may be lost in activities, meetings, and communication that lead nowhere. This not only wastes time, but it can also result in frustration, poor morale, lack of credibility, and high employee turnover. A sound planning process can help teams define what they are trying to accomplish and develop mechanisms to achieve objectives in a more efficient manner, keeping confusion to a minimum.

Applications for Individuals   An old adage maintains that while we all have the same amount of time, successful people know how to allocate their time efficiently. Efficient time allocation requires setting personal objectives and determining the best way to accomplish them. It is also important to periodically reassess objectives, redefining or changing them as needed and adjusting implementation plans accordingly. This planning process may be learned with practice, greatly improving your use of time and talents.

CONCLUDING THOUGHTS

Now that you have had the opportunity to learn about the benefits and pitfalls of planning as well as the elements that contribute to a successful plan, let's revisit the critical thinking questions raised at the opening of this chapter. Coca-Cola's amazing success under CEO Goizueta's guidance—still a corporate U.S. record—was largely a result of the planning process started during his first six months in office. Coke's record shows how clear organizational objectives accompanied by a well-thought-out approach to reaching them can help a firm become an industry leader. Coca-Cola's case illustrates how planning is a tool to achieve a sustainable competitive advantage. Planning requires that both the short and long term be considered. In the short term (three years or less) it is important to establish objectives that can be realistically met in the near future and specific action steps to accomplish them. The longer the time period involved, the greater the uncertainty. Promising opportunities today may dry up in a few years. For instance, competitors may quickly move in and the market for a new product will quickly become saturated. For this reason, company leaders must anticipate future opportunities so that the organization can take advantage of them when the time comes. Coca-Cola's aggressive moves to capture India's market provided impressive payoffs years after Goizueta's death. The setting of objectives gives the firm concrete targets that outline the steps needed to accomplish them. Objectives also provide criteria against which to assess whether or not actual performance was satisfactory or unsatisfactory so that corrective steps (and perhaps a redefinition of objectives) may be undertaken. On the other hand, the setting of objectives may be dangerous if they rob the firm of flexibility to make necessary changes and if managers believe that to succeed they need to play a "numbers game" to meet numerical targets.

Planning is intended to help managers set future **objectives** for the organization and to develop the means necessary to reach those objectives. If properly conducted, the planning process can offer many benefits to the firm. These include the identification of factors that affect the growth, renewal, and survival of the firm, improved coordination of efforts across different organizational subunits, establishment of priorities, better understanding of the firm's environment and the factors that contributed to past success or failure, identification of resources to meet future business requirements, establishment of performance standards to measure progress toward the achievement of objectives, and skill development.

At the same time, however, there are a number of serious pitfalls to be avoided. The firm may develop a false sense that it can predict what will happen in the environment; planning may become a specialized function in a corporate ivory tower; the planning process may become a bureaucratic exercise with a lot of paperwork and little action; and the plan may result in commitment to objectives that are not current or valuable to the firm. These pitfalls can be prevented by **involving a cross section of managers** from different organizational levels in the planning process, using a combination of **numerical and judgment methods,** imbuing **flexibility** in the plans, portraying the plans as a **means to an end** rather than an end in themselves, focusing planning efforts on a **manageable set of issues,** and allowing for a combination of **formal and opportunistic planning** so that there is proper balance between long-term direction and spontaneity.

The planning process includes several steps. The first is the **establishment of objectives.** Ideally, objectives should be concrete and measurable, challenging, with specific timetables or deadlines for accomplishment, and clearly prioritized in terms of importance. The second step is to chart a **course of action** and secure necessary **resources.** At the **strategic level,** the primary purpose is to link the action plans of different organizational functions and units so that they can help support the business strategy adopted by the entire corporation. At the **tactical level,** divisions or department leaders must decide what activities should be performed, when those activities should be completed, and what resources to allocate to accomplish them. This involves defining the responsibilities of jobholders and controlling and allocating resources through the budgeting process. At the **operational level,** employees directly responsible for carrying out activities should develop systems to transform resources into products or services, including a control component to ensure that quantity and quality of inputs and outputs meet established criteria within budget constraints.

Successful plan implementation requires three things. First, managers must find the means to accomplish the planned actions. This may be done through authority structures, persuasion, policy guidelines, and feedback mechanisms. Second, the firm has to develop a system for organizational problem solving. A six-stage approach to facilitate problem solving includes identifying performance gaps, identifying tasks and work processes to accomplish the plan, determining the extent to which organizational elements support or hinder task attainment, creating alignment between the plan and other organizational elements, executing the plan, and learning the causes of performance gaps and adjusting the plan. Third, the firm needs to establish mechanisms to facilitate organizational change. This involves managing the political dynamics of change, managing individual resistance, and maintaining control during the transition period.

1. What types of firms are most likely to benefit from a formal planning process? What types are most likely to face the planning misfires discussed in this chapter?

2. Of all the planning benefits discussed in this chapter, which ones do you think are most important? Why?

3. How would you rank the relative difficulty of carrying out the five approaches to successful planning discussed in this chapter? Explain your choices.

4. Some people argue that the best planning occurs spontaneously at lower levels in the firm, and that planning processes generated at the top of the organization stifle creativity. Do you agree? Why or why not?

5. What are the main challenges of strategic, tactical, and operational action plans? Describe them.

6. Among the four means of implementation discussed in this chapter, which are easiest to use? Which are most difficult? Why?

7. Which of the six steps in the organizational problem-solving scheme presented in this chapter is most likely to fail? Why? What should a firm do to prevent this potential failure?

8. Some people argue that managing the political dynamics of change is likely to backfire, since employees may see it as an attempt to manipulate. Do you agree? Why or why not?

The Pitfalls of Top-Down Planning

Corporations ran leaner in the mid-1990s as companies tried to enhance their bottom line, an effort brought about by mergers, increased competition, and shareholder demands. They redesigned jobs and organization structure to save money. This reengineering often was difficult to pull off; many firms that attempted to downsize their operations found that ultimately these efforts were unsuccessful.

Why did downsizing often fail? Reengineering, or downsizing, typically was orchestrated by consultants or executives not involved in the firm's actual operations. These top-down overhauls demoralize the remaining workers and hurt productivity. One example is Bell Atlantic North, formerly called Nynex. The firm projected how many workers it would need in the future and created a reengineering plan based on this projection. The company planned to reengineer work assignments in anticipation of a slowdown in demand for new lines. Instead of terminating employees, the firm offered them a generous severance plan. Although the firm was able to reduce the number of employees, the productivity improvements were never achieved, leaving Bell Atlantic with too few workers and too many jobs. It was faced with losing up to 14,000 line installers and clerical staffers—almost a third of its unionized workforce.

The Boeing Co. overhauled its manufacturing process as it faced a flood of orders. The company put off hiring workers to be able to fill the orders in the hope that its reengineering would be successful enough to handle the overload. Finally forced to look for more workers, it found that the available labor pool was dry.

Aetna merged with U.S. Healthcare and slashed 5,000 workers in an effort to make claims processing more productive. The result? Customers and providers faced lengthy delays, customers looked elsewhere for health providers, and Aetna suffered a flood of complaints.

Discussion Questions

1. Why do you think top-down planning failed in these instances?
2. Can reengineering ever be a bottom-up process? Why or why not?
3. What should firms do when they realize their downsizing efforts have gone too far?

Source: Adapted from A. Berstein, "Oops, That's Too Much Downsizing," *Business Week,* June 8, 1998, p. 38. See also J. Reingold and D. Brody, "Brain Drain," *Business Week,* September 20, 1999, pp. 113–122; J. Sadener, "Motorola to Trim Temporary Positions," *Arizona Republic,* January 12, 2001, p. D1; and J. Revell, "Can Home Depot Get Its Groove Back?" *Fortune,* February 3, 2003, pp. 110–112.

Drug Manufacturers Broad-Sided by Globalization and Internet Technology Struggle with the "Old" Planning Model

Drug manufacturers spend billions of dollars on drug development. Ninety percent of these investments have no payoff, mainly because there is a lot of uncertainty as to whether or not a particular project will lead to successful results. Still, those drug discoveries which are proven effective for certain conditions can be highly profitable. For example, the so called "blockbuster drugs" such as Viagra (for sexual dysfunction) or Propecia (for hair loss) resulted in substantial revenues. Pharmaceutical firms recover much of their sunken research expenses in drug development by charging high prices in U.S. markets. Much of this premium has been covered by rising health insurance cost in the United States. The Internet and globalization are making it increasingly difficult for drug manufacturers to continue using this "old" planning model, whereby tons of money are devoted to trial-and-error drug discovery projects, waiting for a winner to pop up that would make the billions devoted to research worthwhile.

A cup of hot cocoa may go for $5 in Lausanne, Switzerland, but Lipitor is only $1.50 a pill and Zyrtec just $1. Consequently, every time Steven Peterson, a management consultant from Petaluma, California, is there on business, he fills a pocket of his suitcase with bottles of these popular medications (along with Propranolol, an incontinence drug for the family dog), and saves about $200 a year. New York graphic designer John Dixon buys his allergy drugs online from a pharmacy in New Zealand by simply filling out a 10-question form, which results in a six-month supply arriving on his doorstep a week later for $70. The price is about 30 percent less than he would pay after going through the process of having a doctor write out a prescription and then traveling to a local pharmacy. John Mulhall, a urologist at Manhattan's New York Hospital, has lately been tipping off some of his patients to the imminent arrival of Cialis, a new, longer-lasting Viagra-like pill that has been approved in Europe. It is slated for distribution by European websites, months before it will be available at U.S. pharmacies. "You're really not supposed to buy drugs that aren't approved here yet," Mulhall confesses. "But these guys are very eager to try the latest thing. They're the same guys who buy the Sony Clie PDA as soon as it's out, too."

Frustrated by a drug-delivery system famous for red tape and huge markups, more and more Americans are taking matters into their own hands and are turning to the global marketplace. Why pay $750 for a bottle of Lamisil nail-fungus pills at your local Rite Aid when you can get it from the Canadian website Doctorsolve.com for $200? Technically, private citizens who import any prescription drug—approved or not—into this country are violating a federal law. However, the Food and Drug Administration almost never enforces the law, and Customs has its own official policy, which actually allows the practice. With the exception of hardcore controlled substances such as morphine, virtually every drug you can think of is now sold online at a discount. If the savings are impressive at online pharmacies, they may even justify a trip abroad. For example, a growing number of intrepid Americans are willing to make the trip south to Tijuana's Farmacia El Fenix, right across the California border. The same Cipro antibiotic pill that costs $3.50 at Medsmex.com (which is still a big bargain as compared to the $5.70 price in San Diego or Los Angeles) costs only $2.06 at El Fenix. This means that drug manufacturers are now finding themselves in a catch-22 situation. They have raised prices faster in the U.S. market to make up for these "losses," hoping that rising insurance premiums will cover the price increase. Insurance companies are transferring more of the cost to consumers, who in turn have greater incentives to seek alternative, low-cost suppliers.

Discussion Questions

1. Do you think drug manufacturers in the United States could have anticipated these problems just a few years ago as they planned their long-term research and development investments? Explain your answer.

2. What can pharmaceutical firms do in their planning process to deal with the trends discussed in the case above? Do you think these trends will taper off or become worse in the future? Why or why not?

3. How should corporate planners account for globalization and Internet technology as they move through the planning process? Explain.

Source: Adapted with permission from P. Jaret, "A Prescription for Savings," *Men's Journal*, February 2003, pp. 30–33.

Why Did NASA Stick with the Space Shuttle So Long?

The core problem that lay at the heart of the Challenger tragedy in the mid-1980s applies to the Columbia tragedy in 2003 as well. That core problem may be the original plan for the space shuttle itself. For 20 years, the American space program has been wedded to a space-shuttle system that is expensive, risky, and too big for most of the ways it is used, with budgets that monopolize funds that could be invested in an alternative system that would make space flight cheaper and safer.

The space shuttle is three decades old. The shuttle's main engines, first tested in the late 1970s, use significantly more moving parts than do new rocket-motor designs. The fragile heat-dissipating tiles were designed before breakthroughs in materials science. Until recently, the flight-deck computers on the space shuttle used 8086 chips from the early 1980s, the sort of pre-Pentium electronics no self-respecting teenager would dream of using for a video game.

More important, the space shuttle was designed under the highly unrealistic assumption that the fleet would fly to space once a week and that each shuttle would need to be big enough to carry a 50,000 lb payload. In actual use, the shuttle fleet has averaged five flights a year; in the year of the Columbia's disaster (2003), flights were to be cut back to four. The maximum payload is almost never carried. Yet to accommodate the highly unrealistic initial goals, engineers made the shuttle huge and expensive. The Soviet space program also built a shuttle, called Buran, with almost exactly the same dimensions and capacities as its American counterpart. Buran flew to orbit once and was canceled, as it was judged to be expensive and impractical. Originally projected to cost $5 million per flight in today's dollars, each shuttle launch instead runs to around $500 million.

In two decades of use, shuttles have experienced an array of problems—engine malfunctions, damage to the heat-shielding tiles, and other difficulties that have nearly produced other disasters. Seeing this, some analysts proposed that the shuttle be phased out, that cargo launches be carried aboard by far cheaper, unmanned, throwaway rockets and that NASA build a small "space plane" solely for people, to be used on those occasions when men and women are truly needed in space. NASA, however, has remained faithful to the original plan of using the shuttle to send people into space even though in financial terms and safety terms the results have been disappointing, to say the least. The more money that has been invested in the shuttle, the harder it has been for NASA to walk away from it.

Critical Thinking Questions

1. Why do you think NASA has been staunchly committed to the space shuttle program, more than three decades after the initial plans were drawn up, with a technology that had its origins in the 1960s? Was NASA justified in this long-term commitment to the space shuttle program, even after the Challenger disaster in the mid-1980s? Explain your answer.

2. Based on what you have learned in this chapter, what does the space shuttle program tell us about the pitfalls of planning? In retrospect, what should NASA have done differently in its planning process to prevent the problems discussed in this case? Explain.

3. Can planning help an organization better deal with uncertainty? What does the space shuttle case discussed above teach us about the difficulties of dealing with uncertainty? Explain.

Collaborative Learning Exercise

You have been appointed as part of a five-member independent panel to determine why the results of the space shuttle program differed from the objectives that were established in the original plans drawn up decades ago. Using the materials you have learned in this chapter, analyze whether the gap between objectives and results may be attributed to faulty objectives, or problems with the actions, resources, and implementation used to achieve the objectives. Based on this analysis, develop the outline of a plan to prevent past problems from happening again in the future. Carefully justify your recommendations.

Source: Adapted from C. Easterbrook, "The Space Shuttle Must Be Stopped," *Time*, February 10, 2003, pp. 46–47.

E-Business Goes E-Bankrupt but Survivors Are Doing Well

The so called "dot-com" firms were supposed to be the wave of the future in the late 1990s until the bubble burst in early 2000. Hardly any dot-com firms made any money, meaning investors had received little, if any, returns. The website F**Kedcompany. com keeps track of the death struggles of troubled dot-com companies. Very few of them have survived. Surprisingly, four years later, most of those that survived are showing healthy profits. These include the autoshopping website Autobytel Inc., financial news site Marketwatch.com, Web search site Ask Jeeves, online loan site Lendingtree, software management firm Digital River Inc., bookseller Amazon.com, jewelry retailer Blue Nile Inc., and E-Bay Inc. Research some of the dot-com firm successes and failures on the Internet and answer the following questions using the materials discussed in this chapter:

1. What reasons can you find for their success or failure? Is there a pattern? Explain.

2. Would better planning have averted the demise of those which failed? Why or why not?

3. Should the planning process be different for brick and mortar companies vis-à-vis dot-com firms?

SIX

Decision Making

chapter 6

After reading this chapter, you should be able to:

- Utilize the six steps of decision making.

- Apply the criteria of quality and acceptance to a decision.

- Recognize the nature of management decisions: programmability, uncertainty, risk, conflict, decision scope, and crisis situations.

- Reap the benefits and avoid the problems of group decision making.

- Develop time management skills to generate adequate time to make decisions.

- Know when to delegate, and how to do so wisely.

Decisions, Decisions, Decisions

www.intel.com

Management decisions make all the difference when it comes to company success. Intel, located in Silicon Valley, California, was founded in 1968 to manufacture memory and microprocessor chips to process information and drive personal computer software. By the mid-1980s, Japanese companies were selling memory chips at prices that made it difficult for U.S. firms to compete. In 1984, cofounder Andrew Grove, Intel's president, decided that the company should concentrate its resources on microprocessor chips, leaving the memory chip market. His plan proceeded over the objections of some Intel executives. Grove's decision served Intel well. Intel garnered a 90 percent share of the world market for microprocessor chips, sales of $26.3 billion, and profits of $6.1 billion. Intel is now one of the most profitable and admired companies in the United States. The memory chips that other Intel executives wanted to continue making became a commodity business, with much lower profit margins than microprocessor chips. Grove's decision to "bet the company" on microprocessors turned out to be a winning choice, resulting in fabulous success for Intel.

In 1985, Roberto Goizueta, the CEO of Coca-Cola, decided to make Coke sweeter and rename it to counter Pepsi-Cola's aggressive claims that its product tasted better than Coke in consumer taste tests. Within a month of its introduction, sales of the sweet New Coke plunged. Goizueta acted decisively and publicly admitted that he had made a mistake. The company immediately launched Coca-Cola Classic, made with the original formula. Consumers once again began buying Coke. In spite of the debacle of New Coke, Goizueta increased the firm's market value from $4.3 billion in 1981 to $180 billion by 1997. Although Goizueta made a poor decision, his rapid recovery from his mistake minimized the damage to the company and resulted in a successful outcome.

When Lou Gerstner became CEO of IBM in April 1993, the computer giant had one foot in the grave. IBM's mix of products was highly dependent on the declining mainframe computer technology business. The company had declared a loss of billions of dollars the previous year and was on the verge of a breakup. Gerstner made two key decisions to turn the company around. First, he reversed the decision to break up the company. Second, he focused the company on service businesses, which shifted IBM away from its roots as a manufacturer of computer hardware. By 2001, services were the largest and fastest growing part of IBM with 43 percent of sales. The company reported

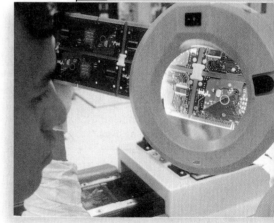

profits of $7.7 billion on sales of $87.4 billion in 2001. Gerstner's willingness to make bold decisions under risk paid off for IBM as the company by 2002 regained its position as one of the leaders in the global technology industry.

Sources: A. Grove, *Only the Paranoid Survive,* New York: Currency Doubleday, 1996; J. Huey, "In Search of Roberto's Secret Formula," *Fortune,* December 29, 1997, pp. 230–234; and "The Top Managers of the Year," *Business Week,* January 14, 2002, p. 54.

CRITICAL THINKING QUESTIONS

1. *What was the major crisis facing Coca-Cola? What evidence would indicate that such a crisis was taking place?*

2. *Would you consider that Gerstner's decisions were made at the strategic, tactical or operational level? How would you justify your choice of a decision level?*

The world of management in the new millennium is filled with risk and uncertainty. Most of the time, there is a lack of information and a limited amount of time available for managers to make decisions. In some cases, procrastinating and not making a decision (thus sustaining the status quo) takes on greater risk than a proactive change. Each management decision can contribute to or hinder the success of an enterprise. This chapter examines the characteristics of managerial decisions. It identifies the stages that decision makers move through from the beginning to the implementation of the decision. An explanation of group decision making is also provided. Finally, the chapter examines time management and delegation, two skills helpful in the decision-making process. Skills for Managing 6.1 lists the skills managers need to develop for the decision-making process.

Characteristics of Management Decision Making

decision making

The process of identifying problems and opportunities and resolving them.

Decision making is a process of identifying problems and opportunities and resolving them. Company decisions are made by managers, teams, and individual employees, depending on the scope of the decision and the design and structure of the organization. Organizations with decentralized structures delegate more decisions to teams and front-line employees.

This definition of *decision making* involves both identifying and resolving a problem. At Intel, for example, Andy Grove determined that the problem was that competing in the memory chip market was draining re-

DECISION MAKING

- *Time management skills.* To make good decisions, managers need time to understand the problem and develop creative solutions. They need to be proactive by planning activities and priorities so that enough time is budgeted for the important decisions to be made, and also to become aware of activities that waste time.

- *Delegation skills.* Managers who know how to delegate are able to accomplish more than those who feel the need to be involved in every decision, no matter how trivial. Many managers mistakenly believe that subordinates are not able to make effective decisions. Managers unable to delegate find themselves with too many tasks and decisions and too little time to do everything well.

sources that could be better deployed in the microprocessor chip market. He made the decision to withdraw from the memory chip market, which entailed closing plants and selling off assets, and to concentrate on microprocessors, which involved investing in expanded facilities.

The characteristics of management decision making include programmability, uncertainty, risk, conflict, scope, and crisis.

Programmability

Many times, there are established routines and procedures for resolving company problems. These are **programmed decisions.** For example, the job of a retail sales clerk consists primarily of making programmed decisions about stocking shelves, taking sales orders, operating a cash register, and constructing sales displays that attract customers. Well-developed procedures are established for each of these tasks in sales policy and procedure manuals developed by the marketing unit.

A **nonprogrammed decision** occurs when the situation is unique and there are no previously established routines or procedures that can be used. Situations that require nonprogrammed decisions are poorly defined and unstructured, yet they have important consequences for the organization. Managers and professionals who have more knowledge and experience make most nonprogrammed decisions. For example, an outside sales representative with a sales territory and the responsibility for calling on new and continuing customers has a job that requires nonprogrammed decision making. The sales representative must find and call on potential customers, develop rapport with them, determine whether they need the product, and close the sale. Since each customer's needs and financial situation are different, the sales representative must make a series of nonprogrammed decisions.

programmed decision

Identifying a problem and matching the problem with established routines and procedures for resolving it.

nonprogrammed decision

The process of identifying and solving a problem when a situation is unique and there are not previously established routines or procedures that can be used as guides.

Nonprogrammed decisions tend to be more important than programmed ones because they are more complicated and difficult to make and are likely to have a greater effect on organization performance. Managers are likely to delegate programmed decisions to subordinates, which frees up more time to make the more difficult nonprogrammed decisions.

Uncertainty

If all the information needed is available, a decision may be made under a condition of **certainty.** An automobile manufacturer plans for annual employee labor costs because the company has a contract with a labor union and knows with complete certainty what employee wage rates will be. Of course, not all the factors affecting businesses can be controlled by a contract. And when contracts expire, there will be uncertainty until the terms of the new contract are finalized.

Most management decisions are made under varying levels of uncertainty. **Uncertainty** means that incomplete information is available to make a management decision. Many important management decisions must be made under high levels of uncertainty. When a company launches a new product, there is uncertainty about whether consumers will buy it. New Coke was rejected by consumers, even though market research gathered prior to the decision revealed that most consumers liked cola that tasted sweeter than traditional Coke.

In the network television industry, there is about a one in ten chance that a new prime-time television program will generate sufficient viewer ratings to make a profit. Sometimes television executives must rely on gut instincts because there is little information available. The situation comedy *Seinfeld* generated poor ratings in its first two seasons, but a few executives championed the show and ultimately it became one of NBC's profitable programs.

Risk

The degree of uncertainty about the outcome of a management decision is the degree of **risk.** Risk has both positive and negative aspects. When a manager of mutual funds tries to maximize the profit potential of the fund stock portfolio and minimize the loss potential when the market is falling, the manager copes with both aspects of risk. Many mutual fund managers select some stocks from countercyclical industries, which move in opposite directions in response to market fluctuations, in order to balance the risk by ensuring that all the fund's stocks do not lose value when the economy is declining.

Decision environments for risk vary depending on company culture and size. People who work in entrepreneurial firms must be more comfortable with making risky decisions than people who work in large corporations with established procedures. A high-technology company that must deliver cutting-edge products is likely to promote a culture of risk taking, while a U.S. government agency that can plan cash flow for 25 years into the future based on demographic forecasts, such as the Social Security Administration, is more likely to support a culture of risk avoidance. Companies with risk-taking cultures encourage decision makers to take moderate risks. Such companies even tolerate some failures as part of the learning process. Organizations with risk-avoidance cultures are less tolerant of decision outcomes that result in failure.

Conflict

It is always difficult to get everyone to agree about what to do. Management decision making is often characterized by conflict over opposing goals, utilization of scarce resources, and other priorities. To ensure that the implementation of the decision will go smoothly, effective managers consider many different stakeholders. Otherwise, individuals or groups who are forced to accept a choice they oppose will not be committed to the decision and may even try to undermine it. An important criterion for choosing a decision alternative is its acceptance by key employee groups such as executives, managers, and front-line employees. This is discussed later in the chapter.

Conflict can enhance the quality of a decision by sharply focusing attention on diverse ways of thinking about the consequences of the decision from diverse agendas of the people involved. In other words, various people consider how the decision will affect them. Conflict is managed when individual perspectives are taken into consideration in fashioning the solution. Conflict is examined in greater detail in Chapter 14.

When a decision is being made about research and development funding, the chief financial officer may favor reducing funding because basic research is not expected to produce profits for the firm for six to eight years. At the same time, this executive may prefer to fund applied research that will pay off in two or three years. The chief technical officer in charge of research may strongly disagree with this "short-term" investment perspective and may seek to sustain funding for basic research so that the research pipeline for new products will not dry up. The conflict in this decision is over short-term versus long-term profits.

People who have different stakes and perspectives in a decision related to the expenditure of scarce resources should have a voice in the decision process. In most cases, involving them in the process and working through the differences makes it more likely that they will be committed to the decision outcome, even if it is not one they favored.

Decision Scope

The effect and time horizon of the decision are what is meant by the **decision scope.** The effect of a decision includes who is involved in

strategic decision

Decisions that have long-term perspective of two to five years and affect the entire organization.

tactical decisions

Decisions that have a short-term perspective of one year or less and focus on subunits of the organization, such as departments or project teams.

operational decisions

Decisions with a short time perspective, generally less than a year, and that often are measured on a daily or weekly basis.

making the decision and who is affected by it. The time horizon of a decision may range from a single day to five years or more. **Strategic decisions** encompass a long-term perspective of two to five years and affect the entire organization. They include decisions about which product markets should be entered and left, as well as determinations of appropriate firm growth and profitability goals. Top executives are responsible for making strategic decisions.

Tactical decisions have a short-term perspective of one year or less and focus on subunits of the organization, such as departments or project teams. They include determining the distribution of departmental resources for various activities in the departmental budget. Middle managers are most likely to make tactical decisions. Tactical decisions should take into consideration the broader, strategic direction of the firm and be supportive of it.

Operational decisions cover the shortest time perspective, generally less than a year. They are often made on a daily or weekly basis and focus on the routine activities of the firm such as production, customer service, and handling parts and supplies. Supervisors, teams, and frontline employees are involved in operational decisions. Operational decisions must take into consideration both the long-term perspective of the strategic decisions and the shorter-term perspective of tactical decisions.

Crisis Situations

Decision making during crisis is more challenging and difficult than under ordinary conditions. Crisis situations include: (1) highly ambiguous circumstances in which causes and effects are not known, (2) rare and extraordinary events that can threaten the survival of an organization, (3) an event in which there is a small amount of time to respond, (4) a surprise to organizational members that takes place, or (5) dilemmas in need of decisions that will result in change for better or worse.[1] A decision during crisis is likely to have the characteristics of risk, uncertainty, and nonprogrammability. Examples of crisis would include a hostile takeover of a company, a product defect discovered that is harmful to consumers, a work stoppage by organized labor, a natural disaster that disrupts the company's ability to provide service to customers, or a terrorist attack— such as what happened in New York City on September 11, 2001. See Management Close-Up 6.a for a description of decisions made by UPS after 9/11.

Making a decision in a crisis situation can make or break the career of a manager. As we saw in the opening vignette, the CEO of IBM, Lou Gerstner, decided to focus IBM on providing services to customers at a time of crisis when the survival of the company was at stake. The decision to change IBM's strategic focus by shifting its emphasis from making hardware to delivering services proved to be successful and a career-making move for Gerstner.

How UPS Managed to Deliver During the 9/11 Crisis

THEME: CUSTOMER FOCUS Many crisis decisions were made following the September 11, 2001, terrorist attacks at the World Trade Center in New York City and at the Pentagon in Arlington, VA. As the attacks took place, airborne aircraft were advised to land at the nearest airport and subway trains that were headed toward the World Trade Center were halted, thereby saving thousands of lives. Thousands of people were evacuated from buildings close to ground zero. United Parcel Service (UPS), the package delivery service company, went into crisis management mode shortly after the attack. With all air traffic grounded, Joe Liana, UPS's Manhattan district manager, called in all employees to report to UPS's package sorting facility to identify high-priority packages such as medical supplies that were time sensitive. He ordered drivers to make 200 truck deliveries to hospitals, doctors, and pharmacies. Joe and other district managers had been given a great deal of autonomy to make decisions in their districts by UPS top management.

During the days immediately after the attacks UPS set up a crisis management plan to deliver more packages by truck because air travel was prohibited, and nobody knew when air transportation would resume. UPS vice chairman Michael L. Eskew decided to transfer packages designated for aircraft to trucks when they met certain criteria. A package needed to be able to be delivered within three days by truck in order to avoid overwhelming the truck operations' ability to deliver. Eskew gambled that aircraft operations would be resumed within one week. This turned out to be a correct assumption. As a result of UPS's crisis management decisions, the company was able to resume package delivery operations quickly, without losing market share.

The key decisions made at UPS were: (1) empowering local district managers to handle a crisis on their own, and (2) holding back from the ground delivery system any air packages that would have taken more than three days to deliver.

Sources: Adapted from C. Haddad, "How UPS Delivered through the Disaster," *Business Week,* October 1, 2001, p. 66; J. Bram, J. Orr, and C. Rappaport, "Measuring the September 11 Attack on New York City," *Economic Policy Review,* November 2002, pp. 5–20.

During the 9/11 crisis, UPS diverted some of its packages designated for aircraft to ground transportation in order to maintain service to its customers.

Stages of Decision Making

Decision making is a six-step process. The stages, which are summarized in Figure 6.1, are (1) identifying and diagnosing the problem; (2) generating alternative solutions; (3) evaluating alternatives; (4) choosing the best alternative; (5) implementing the decision; and (6) evaluating the results.

Identifying and Diagnosing the Problem

The first stage of decision making is identifying and diagnosing a problem or opportunity. An *opportunity* is a special type of problem that requires committing resources in order to improve company performance. A *problem* occurs when performance is below expected or desired levels of performance. Typical problems include:

- A high level of employee turnover.
- A reduction in firm profits.
- Unacceptable levels of "shrinkage" in a store (employee theft).
- Low-quality finished goods.
- An increase in workplace injuries.
- The invention of a new technology that would increase the productivity of the workforce.

Once a problem has been recognized, the decision maker begins to look for the causes of the problem. This requires gathering information, exploring possible causes, eliminating as many causes as possible, and then focusing on the most probable causes. For example, a manager who observes a high level of employee turnover first gathers information to diagnose the problem and then attempts to understand why the turnover is occurring. Some possible causes of turnover are job dissatisfaction with unchallenging and repetitive work, below-market pay rates, job stress, opportunities for better jobs in the labor market, and conflicts between work and family obligations. It is important to fully diagnose the problem before attempting to solve it. If the real cause of turnover is work and family conflicts due to inflexible work schedules and the manager assumes that it was caused by inadequate compensation and raised employee pay as a solution, the manager may not have solved the problem.

Generating Alternative Solutions

The second step is to generate possible solutions to the problem based on the perceived causes. Some problems can be solved using programmed solutions, when there are ready-made answers. Novel situations require nonprogrammed decisions because there are no policies or procedures available to provide direction.

FIGURE 6.1

The Stages of Decision Making

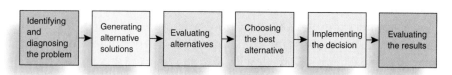

In the case of nonprogrammed decision making, it is important to come up with creative alternative solutions and to suspend judgment of their worth until all possible alternatives have been developed. If solutions are evaluated too soon during the second stage of decision making, creativity can be stifled, resulting in lower-quality solutions. Many companies use groups to generate solutions for nonprogrammed decisions because they provide a greater diversity of opinions and more innovative solutions than do people working individually. Consequently, group decision making is often used to develop continuous improvements in customer service to generate novel solutions to customer needs.

Evaluating Alternatives

The third stage requires the decision maker to examine the alternative solutions using a set of decision criteria. The decision criteria should be related to the performance goals of the organization and its subunits and can include costs, profits, timeliness, whether the decision will work, and fairness.

A practical way to apply decision criteria is to consider quality and acceptance. **Decision quality** is based on such facts as costs, revenues, and product design specifications. For example, a technical engineering problem can be solved by gathering data and using mathematical techniques. **Decision acceptance** is based on people's feelings. Decision acceptance happens when people who are affected by a decision agree with what is to be done.[2]

Decisions can be classified by how important quality and acceptance are to their effectiveness. Some technical decisions require a high degree of quality but low acceptance, since people may be indifferent to the outcome. Buying raw materials at the best price is an example of a decision where quality is important but acceptance is not. An expert buyer of raw materials can make this decision. Other decisions place a high emphasis on acceptance, while quality is not important. High-acceptance, low-quality decisions involve fairness issues, such as: Who will work the overtime hours? Who gets the office with the window? The important point in such decisions is not who gets to work overtime, but how people feel about the outcome and if they are willing to accept it.

decision quality

The aspect of decision making that is based on such facts as costs, revenues, and product design specifications.

decision acceptance

The aspect of decision making that is based on people's feelings; decision acceptance happens when people who are affected by a decision agree with what is to be done.

The most difficult decisions require high quality and high acceptance. The decision to close an automobile assembly plant and lay off employees is an example. Decision quality requires a reduction of labor costs, but acceptance requires the support of the labor union so that it will not call a strike to protest the layoff, resulting in even greater losses to the firm. The decision maker must find ways to balance conflicting goals in this type of problem.

Choosing the Best Alternative

optimizing

Selecting the best alternative from among multiple criteria.

The next stage of decision making is the selection of the best alternative by either optimizing or satisficing. **Optimizing** involves selecting the best alternative from among multiple criteria. For example, assume the decision criteria used to select an individual to fill a vacancy consists of technical job knowledge, previous work experience, and leadership skills. Further, assume that it will take six months to be able to generate a large enough applicant pool to be able to find the best person to fill the job. The optimizing solution is available when the benefits of reaching the solution outweigh the costs. However, most of the time, the costs of keeping a job vacant for six months to find the optimizing solution are not worth the effort. Therefore, the optimizing approach would not be applied. Also, many important decisions must be made under conditions of risk, which constrain the ability of the decision maker to optimize.

satisficing

Selecting the first alternative solution that meets a minimum criterion.

Satisficing involves selecting the first alternative solution that meets a minimum criterion. Decision makers satisfice when complete information is not available or gathering it is too expensive. Satisficing means that the decision maker has found an acceptable if not optimal solution. For example, when selecting a new employee to fill a job vacancy, many organizations make a job offer to the first person who meets the basic selection criteria, rather than engaging in an extensive search for the best possible candidate, which takes more time and money.

Implementing the Decision

Putting the alternative solution into practice and making sure it works is the next step of decision making. Implementation requires the decision maker to put the solution into practice. Decision making without implementation is simply an intellectual exercise.

Implementation is a critical step because it requires the support and cooperation of executives, managers, and employees who may have different interests and goals. For example, a manager's decision to hire a minority group employee to fill a job vacancy under a corporate diversity plan may not be effectively implemented if other employees resent and avoid working with the employee. An important aspect of managing and implementing diversity is to train employees to value diversity so they are supportive of the plan's goals. The omission of training could lead to

Nokia's decision to segment its mobile phone business into nine units responsible for different market opportunities has been a good one. It outsold its rivals (Motorola, Samsung, Sony Ericsson) in 2002. Taking big risks with its new 6800, a phone designed with a keyboard for those who can't get enough of text messaging, Nokia hopes to be on top of the next mobile phone craze. You can read more about Nokia in the Opening Case of Chapter 9.

poor implementation. (See Chapter 11 for more information on implementing a corporate diversity plan.)

Several factors help make implementation successful. They include:

- Providing resources, such as staff, budgets, and office space, that will be needed for successful implementation.

- Exercising leadership to persuade others to move the implementation forward.

- Developing communication and information systems that enable management to know if the decision alternative is meeting its planned objectives.

- Considering ways to recognize and reward individuals and teams that successfully put the decision alternative into practice.[3]

Evaluating the Results

The final stage in the decision-making process is to evaluate the results. Decision makers gather information and try to learn if the implemented decision achieved its goals. The availability of accurate and timely information and feedback permits the decision maker to make a thorough evaluation and to determine whether modifications are needed.

Decision makers need to establish reasonable goals and benchmarks to make sound judgments about the effectiveness of the decision. It is also important to allow enough time for a decision to take effect. An executive collecting productivity data on a new manufacturing plant would be foolish to immediately judge its effectiveness without giving plant management time to eliminate the production bottlenecks that are typical in new manufacturing plants. It would be better to suspend judgment until plant personnel learn the best ways to operate the equipment and develop routines to work well together. The pitfalls associated with decision making are summarized in Manager's Notes 6.1.

Here are some pitfalls that decision makers need to know about. These pitfalls can result in low-quality decisions or poor implementation of the decision alternative. By following each stage of decision making in the correct sequence, managers can avoid many of them.

1. *Solution focus.* Time pressures often lead decision makers to shoot from the hip without taking enough time to thoroughly diagnose and understand the management problem in all its complexity. Unless all factors causing a system to be out of control are identified, proposed solutions to the problem are not likely to be responsive to the true problem.

2. *Premature evaluation.* The temptation is always present to evaluate and judge alternatives as they are being developed and expressed by peers, subordinates, or the decision maker. Idea generation is a creative process that can be stifled and frustrated by managers who pronounce early judgment when an alternative solution is suggested. A deeply flawed idea can inspire others to come up with novel solutions that may not be expressed unless people feel free to think creatively, without worrying about others judging them for their creative ideas.

3. *The "If it isn't broke, don't fix it" syndrome.* This bias favors programmed solutions based on what worked in the past, even though that may no longer be relevant to the present or future. In a business environment of changing customer needs, decisions that favor what satisfied customers in the past are not likely to meet current and future customer expectations.

4. *Bias toward objective data.* In environments of high uncertainty, decision makers may give a high priority to objective data. For example, data on viewer behavior is collected by market research analysts for a pilot television program. Such data, however, are not likely to be useful for making accurate predictions of program success when the new program is very different from others, such as *Seinfeld* and *The Sopranos*.

5. *Overlooking important constituencies.* The decision maker should identify the diverse groups within (and sometimes outside) the organization that are likely to have strong feelings about the decision outcome and solicit their input.

The Limits of Rational Decision Making

It is a major leap of faith to assume that all decision making is rational. It is not. This is because rational decision making is based on the following assumptions:

- The problem is clear and unambiguous.
- There is a single, well-defined goal that all parties agree to.
- Full information is available.
- All the alternatives and their consequences are known.

- The decision preferences are clear.
- The decision preferences are constant and stable over time.
- There are no time and cost constraints affecting the decision.
- The decision solution will maximize the economic payoff.[4]

Many decisions are complex and are made in situations where these assumptions do not apply. There are several factors that limit rational decision making. They include organization politics, emotions and personal preferences, and the illusion of control. By being aware of these biases, decision makers can improve the quality of their decisions.

Organization Politics

Organizations are likely to have **coalitions,** which are political alliances between employees who agree on goals and priorities. Various coalitions may disagree about alternatives for a decision, and an executive or leader may need to exercise power and influence to build a consensus between diverse coalitions. **Organization politics** involves the exercise of power in an organization to control resources and influence policy. Organization politics is more likely to be present in firms with democratic cultures where power is decentralized and decisions are made through consensus.

Decisions based on political coalitions do not always favor the most rational solution. Sometimes they favor the solution that sustains the power of the top executive or dominant individual or group. For example, an executive may provide resources to a coalition of managers to obtain their support on an important decision. Still, there are times in which organization politics can lead to a successful decision, as shown in Management Close-Up 6.b.

coalitions

Political alliances between managers who agree on goals and priorities.

organization politics

The exercise of power in an organization to control resources and influence policy.

Emotions and Personal Preferences

Decision makers are not robots choosing alternatives without emotion or passion. Many times a poor decision is reached because the decision maker is having a bad day. The two emotions which are the most disruptive to quality decision making are anger and depression. An angry person is not going to look at an issue clearly, nor is someone who is depressed.

Personal preferences include a variety of individual quirks. For example, a manager who hates the idea of going into debt, both personally and in his or her company, will make decisions which may or may not benefit the company. Or the opposite may be true. The same is true for someone who enjoys taking risks as opposed to someone who is risk-averse. It is vital to make certain the person or group making a decision is not swayed by an individual agenda or pattern of decision making.

The Decision to Build the Sensor Razor at Gillette

THEME: CUSTOMER FOCUS Organization politics can influence key company decisions and affect a firm's welfare, for better or worse, as in Gillette's development of its Sensor razor. Although the Sensor was fabulously successful when it was released to the market, it came close to being a very different product due to a disagreement over its product design.

The Gillette Company's British research facility spent 13 years developing the idea behind the Sensor razor. The idea was to create a thinner razor blade that would make Gillette cartridges easier to clean. The cost for the product's research and development reached $200 million.

The technical demands of building a razor with thin blades and floating parts that could follow the contours of a man's face led researchers up several blind alleys. They tried established techniques, but none filled the bill. They tried innovative ideas, such as setting the blades on tiny rubber tubes, perhaps filled with fluid, but these ideas proved too costly and complicated to manufacture. Eventually Gillette came up with a prototype. The 500 men who tested it liked it, and the product was put into production.

The Sensor's next problems involved manufacturing and product placement. Because of the razor's innovative design, an entirely new manufacturing process was needed to laser-weld each blade to a support. Gillette management approved developing the new manufacturing equipment, but two groups of executives disagreed on the final product. One group wanted to produce and market a razor that was lightweight, expensive, and disposable; the other faction thought the product should be a heavier, more permanent razor with replaceable blades. When Gillette was threatened by an outside takeover, it reduced the resources allocated to the Sensor project. A new executive vice president made the decision to deemphasize razors that were disposable, so the Sensor's final form was determined.

The Sensor razor has been an unqualified success. It was quickly embraced by consumers, and Gillette recovered its huge investment in record time.

Gillette's decision process for the Sensor began because executives became aware of the potential for a new razor with floating, thin blades. Leaders proceeded with a trial-and-error custom design. When some alternatives were found unacceptable, Gillette returned to earlier steps until a workable product was created.

At Gillette, there is no such thing as getting ahead of oneself. New products go on the drawing board as much as a decade before they are introduced. Months before the Sensor was launched in 1994, the company already was working on its successor: the Mach 3 shaving system, a blend of leading-edge technology and relentless consumer testing, took seven years and $750 million to develop.

Sources: Adapted from R. L. Daft, *Leadership: Theory and Practice,* Fort Worth: Dryden Press, 1999, pp. 467–468; G. Rifkin, "Mach 3: Anatomy of Gillette's Latest Global Launch," *Journal of Strategy and Business,* 2nd quarter, 1999, www.strategy-business.com.

Illusion of Control

illusion of control

The tendency for decision makers to be overconfident of their ability to control activities and events.

Another limitation of rational decision making results from the **illusion of control,** which is the tendency for a decision maker to be overconfident of his or her ability to control activities and events. Top executives are especially susceptible to this problem, because they can be isolated from the rank and file employees and may be surrounded with "yes men."

A good example of the illusion of control was the decision by President Richard Nixon to cover up a break-in of Democratic party headquarters in the Watergate building by Republican party operatives during the 1972 presidential election. Nixon assumed he could control public perception of the incident because he was the president. The cover-up turned out to be a disastrous error and ultimately led to talk of impeachment and Nixon's resignation from office in 1974.

Nonrational Decision-Making Models

The actual conditions for most decisions tend to be complex and most decisions occur under conditions of uncertainty, often falling short of satisfying the assumptions of rational decision making. *Nonrational decision-making* models have been developed for these situations. Nonrational decision-making models assume that information-gathering and processing limitations make it difficult for managers to make optimal decisions. Two nonrational decision-making approaches are the satisficing model and the garbage can model.

Satisficing Model

Herbert Simon, a Nobel prize–winning economist, points out that even if all the necessary information is available to make a decision, many managers cannot completely absorb and evaluate the information appropriately.[5] This insight led to his concept of *bounded rationality*. Bounded rationality means that the ability of a manager to be perfectly rational is limited by factors such as cognitive capacity and time constraints. A decision maker's perceptions about the relative importance of various aspects of data may cause him or her to overlook or ignore some important information. Moreover, the human memory can retain and process only a limited amount of information at one time. Consequently, decision makers apply *heuristics,* or decision rules, that quickly eliminate alternatives. For example, when a manager says, "We can't afford to hire any more people," that manager has applied a decision rule that eliminates a variety of options.

As a result, managers do not assess every potential alternative. Instead, by using the heuristic known as *satisficing,* a manager seeks out the first decision alternative that appears to be *satisfactory*. Satisficing is an accurate model of many management decisions. This is because the cost of delaying a decision or searching for a better solution is outweighed by the benefits of quickly finding a satisfactory solution. For example, a home owner is satisficing when she makes a decision to sign a contract with a company to paint her house after taking only three bids. The decision rule is to consider only the quality of materials, cost, and time needed to complete the job. Choosing a satisfactory bid to paint the house without seeking the optimal solution (the best of all possible painters), is satisficing.

Garbage Can Model

Managers often behave in a random pattern when making decisions. The *garbage can* model suggests that managers have a set of preestablished solutions to problems located in "garbage cans."[6] If such a solution to a problem appears to be satisfactory or appropriate, it is applied to the problem.[7] This means that managers have some preselected solutions or skills for which they are searching for problems to "fix."

The garbage can model is likely to be used when decision makers are undisciplined and have no clear immediate goals. As a result, the decision-making process lacks structure. While the garbage can model can sometimes result in a desirable outcome, it can also lead to serious difficulties. For example, for several generations the Bronfman family owned and managed Seagram's, a highly profitable manufacturer and distributor of whiskies and other alcoholic drinks. Edgar Bronfman, the son of Seagram's CEO, persuaded his father to buy Universal Pictures, a Hollywood movie studio, because Edgar had previously financed and produced a few independent movies and had friends in the entertainment industry. Bronfman assumed he possessed the skills to run a major studio. Ultimately, neither Edgar Bronfman nor Seagram's management displayed the ability needed to effectively operate a movie business. The company was forced to sell the studio while taking a huge loss which resulted in a dramatic reversal of fortune for the Bronfman family.

Decision Making in Groups

When employee acceptance of a decision is important, it is usually necessary to involve a group of employees in the decision-making process. For example, the department chair organizes a recruitment committee to participate in the decision to hire a new professor in a university department. This is done because acceptance by colleagues is critical; all promotions and performance evaluations are performed by committees of peers in universities. Hiring decisions at law, accounting, and consulting firms also require input from groups of junior and senior colleagues. These professionals often work in cooperative teams to serve clients and expect to have a voice in selecting new organizational members. Committees, task forces, or teams can be the basis for a group decision.

The Benefits and Problems of Group Decision Making

Group decision making has several advantages, which are displayed in Table 6.1. Group decisions can improve both the quality and the acceptance of a decision. By involving people in the process, management allows them to examine all the alternatives and criteria, opening the door for deeper understanding of the rationale for the alternative that was se-

TABLE 6.1

Benefits and Problems of Group Decision Making

BENEFITS	PROBLEMS
Increased acceptance. Those who play an active role in group decision making and problem solving tend to view the outcome as "ours" rather than "theirs."	*Social pressure.* Unwillingness to "rock the boat" and pressure to conform may combine to stifle the creativity of individual contributors.
Greater pool of knowledge. A group can bring much more information and experience to bear on a decision or problem than an individual acting alone.	*Minority domination.* Sometimes the quality of group action is reduced when the group gives in to those who talk the loudest and longest.
Different perspectives. Individuals with varied experience and interests help the group see decision situations and problems from different angles.	*Logrolling.* Political wheeling and dealing can displace sound thinking when an individual's pet project or vested interest is at stake.
Greater comprehension. Those who personally experience the give-and-take of group discussion about alternative courses of action tend to understand the rationale behind the final decision.	*Goal displacement.* Sometimes secondary considerations such as winning an argument, making a point, or getting back at a rival displace the primary task of making a sound decision or solving a problem.
Training ground. Less experienced participants in group action learn how to cope with group dynamics by actually being involved.	*"Groupthink."* Sometimes cohesive "in-groups" let the desire for unanimity override sound judgment when generating and evaluating alternative courses of action.

Source: From *Organizational Behavior* by R. Kreitner and A. Kinicki. Copyright © 1995. The McGraw-Hill Companies, Inc. Reprinted with permission.

lected, and increasing the likelihood that they will accept and be committed to the decision. Groups tap a greater pool of knowledge and provide more diverse perspectives than any single individual could generate acting alone. Group decision making is also beneficial because it provides the opportunity for employees with less experience with group activities to learn how to cope with group dynamics by actually being involved.

The problems associated with group decision making arise from bringing people with different interests together. Dominant individuals or factions may intimidate others into agreeing with their goals. The group may be unwilling to deal with conflict and come to a quick settlement in order to keep the peace. Hidden agendas (such as self-promoting individual's using the group as a captive audience), political deal making, and **groupthink** (valuing social harmony over doing a thorough job) can all lead to low-quality decision outcomes unless the group decision process is managed by a leader who can protect the group from these problems.

groupthink

Valuing social harmony over doing a thorough job.

One of the limiting factors in group decision making is time. The group requires sufficient time to go through all six stages of decision making in sequence. If time for decision making is limited, it may be better for a manager to make the decision alone and then attempt to persuade others to abide by it.

Managing Group Decision Making

A leader must work to minimize the potential problems listed in Table 6.1. Some ways to ensure that quality decisions are made by groups include adapting leadership style, assuming the devil's advocate role, and using various decision-making techniques to stimulate creativity.

LEADERSHIP STYLE   A group leader can adapt his or her style to the requirements of the problem. Table 6.2 shows five different decision-making styles that leaders may select from, depending on the need for decision quality and acceptance, the time available, and leader and subordinate skills and competencies.

When a manager places a high priority on agreement among the group members about what is fair, the leader should focus on allowing each person to voice an opinion. The leader should try to involve all group members and discourage dominating individuals from monopolizing the discussion.

A manager who places a high priority on quality and acceptance must manage the decision process by carefully framing the problem and putting constraints on decision alternatives that are too risky or uncertain. In such cases, the leader may allow for some participation by group members but reserves the right to make the decision. A leader can frame the same problem as either a threat or an opportunity, which can influence how the group perceives the problem.

Research in the social sciences has shown that groups tend to take greater risks than individuals because responsibility for the outcome can be diffused over the entire group. The leader can remind the group to avoid considering decision alternatives that could lead to disastrous results. For example, the group responsible for deciding whether to go ahead with the launch of the *Challenger* space shuttle in 1986 would have made a different decision if NASA's leadership had examined the risk that a critical component would shrink when exposed to cold temperatures and cause the space shuttle to explode immediately after the launch.

Problems that involve technical or specialized knowledge are best solved alone by the decision maker. For example, if an important instrument malfunctions in the middle of an intercontinental flight, a commercial aircraft pilot may decide to land the plane at the nearest airport rather than continue to the original destination. Obviously, time is a critical factor in this situation, and the decision is best handled by the captain of the aircraft.

devil's advocate

The role of criticizing and challenging decision alternatives that are agreed on by other members of the group, to induce creative conflict and possible alternative better solutions.

DEVIL'S ADVOCATE ROLE   Social pressures to conform in groups can lead to the problem of groupthink, in which group members withhold critical comments or unpopular views in order to sustain social harmony in the group. If groupthink is not managed, it can reduce decision quality.

One way to reduce the threat of groupthink is to assign a group member the role of **devil's advocate.** The devil's advocate is expected to

TABLE 6.2

Leader Decision-Making Styles

DECISION-MAKING STYLE	CHARACTERISTICS	AMOUNT OF SUBORDINATE PARTICIPATION
Decide and persuade	Leader solves the problem and makes decision with available information	None
Discover facts and decide	Leader gathers facts from subordinates and then makes the decision	Very little; indirect involvement
Consult and decide	Leader consults with individual subordinates, obtaining their ideas and opinions, and then makes the decision	Modest amount of participation through being presented with the problem by the leader
Consult with group and decide	Leader consults with group of subordinates, gathering their collective ideas, and then makes the decision	Substantial amount of participation by being engaged in the group discussion of the problem
Group decision	Leader shares problem with group and accepts the decision made by the group, acting as a coach to the group decision-making process	High involvement of subordinates in the decision-making process

Sources: Adapted from V. H. Vroom and A. G. Jago, *The New Leadership: Managing Participation in Organizations,* Englewood Cliffs, NJ: Prentice Hall, 1988; R. L. Daft, *Management,* 4th ed., Fort Worth: Dryden Press, 1997, p. 295.

criticize and challenge decision alternatives that are agreed on by other members of the group. This person may (1) develop scenarios in which the majority-sponsored decision alternative could fail or (2) promote alternative solutions that challenge the one supported by the group. In this way, the devil's advocate introduces creative conflict and tension into the group decision-making process. This may ultimately lead to a better solution or one that is more deeply understood by members of the group. The payoff is likely to be stronger group commitment to the decision.

DECISION-MAKING TECHNIQUES TO STIMULATE CREATIVITY

Introducing criticism into the group decision-making process too early can stifle creativity. **Brainstorming** is a technique that is designed to generate creative decision alternatives verbally by interacting with members of a group. Critical and judgmental reactions to ideas from group members are not allowed during a brainstorming session. Instead, the group is encouraged to come up with the greatest number of ideas, and especially ideas that are wild and unusual. Group members are also asked to build on and extend earlier ideas, to increase the possibility of a truly innovative solution. The rules of brainstorming prohibit criticism of any ideas until all the ideas have been expressed. In the entertainment industry, teams of writers and other content creators make widespread use of brainstorming sessions. For example, brainstorming is used by the group of comedy writers who develop jokes for the "Tonight Show with Jay Leno."

brainstorming

A technique to generate creative ideas for solving problems by reducing critical and judgmental reactions to ideas from group members.

storyboarding

A variation of brainstorming in which group members jot down ideas on cards and then can shuffle, rewrite, or even eliminate cards to examine complex processes.

nominal group technique (NGT)

A decision-making technique that helps a group generate and select solutions while letting group members think independently; group members are given the problem and each presents one solution without discussion; then all solutions are discussed, evaluated, and ranked to determine the best alternative.

Assessing Your Creativity Quotient

Delphi technique

A decision-making technique in which group members are presented with a problem and complete an anonymous questionnaire soliciting solutions; the results are tabulated, summarized, and returned to the group members, and each is asked again for solutions; the process continues until a consensus decision is reached.

For more complex problems, a variation of brainstorming called **storyboarding** is used. Storyboarding begins with group members jotting down ideas on index cards and posting them on a bulletin board or on conference room walls. Group members can shuffle, rewrite, or even eliminate cards. The technique is useful for examining complex processes involving technology in order to improve efficiency. At the Xerox corporate research laboratory in California's Silicon Valley, researchers sketch ideas onto a large white wall to begin discussions of ideas with other researchers.

The **nominal group technique (NGT)** helps a group generate and select solutions while letting group members think independently. NGT is a structured group meeting in which the following steps take place:

1. Group members meet and are presented with a problem. Prior to any discussion, each member independently writes down solutions to the problem.

2. Next, each group member presents one of his or her ideas to the group. The idea is listened to and recorded on a flip chart or blackboard without any discussion or criticism.

3. After all the ideas have been presented and posted, discussion and evaluation begin.

4. At the conclusion of the evaluation, the group members anonymously vote and rank their top choices. The decision alternative that receives the highest ranking from the group is selected.[8]

NGT allows the group to discuss alternatives without inhibiting group members from engaging in independent critical thinking. NGT is often used in the strategic planning process, such as in the development of the corporate mission statement.

Another approach to group decision making is called the **Delphi technique,** which was originally developed by the RAND Corporation for technological forecasting. The Delphi technique is similar to NGT, but it does not involve face-to-face meetings of group members. Group members are presented with a problem and receive a questionnaire soliciting solutions. Each group member anonymously completes the questionnaire and sends it to a central location, where responses are tabulated and summarized. The results are then returned to the group members, and each is asked again for solutions. Having the input of all the other group members may inspire some group members to modify their positions or develop new ideas, while others may stick with their original ideas. Questionnaires are completed a second time and tabulated. The cycle of giving and receiving anonymous feedback continues until a consensus is reached on the best decision alternative.

The application of computer software provides for an electronic approach to the Delphi technique. The Leeds School of Business at the Uni-

Creativity in solving problems often is fostered in a group situation, where members can build on each others' ideas and solutions by *brainstorming*.

versity of Colorado uses an electronic meeting room with 20 computer terminals with software that allows each person in a group to view his or her input to a decision posted anonymously on the computer screen along with all the other inputs from other group members. The software handles the complexity of bringing ideas together quickly, displaying them, and helping groups analyze them. The software lets the group go through several rounds of generating and evaluating decision alternatives until a consensus is reached. The electronic meeting room is useful for making controversial decisions when highly opinionated or high-status individuals should be kept from dominating the decision process, which means shy people are better able to participate in the process.

The Delphi technique is particularly useful when experts who are geographically separated need to make a decision. For example, a Wall Street investment bank may select a panel of 30 economists from different universities around the world to use the Delphi technique to forecast macroeconomic indicators such as interest rates, growth in the economy, and rate of inflation as a basis for thinking about future investment opportunities.

Decision-Making Skills

Effective managers know one of the most important things they will be asked to do is make quality decisions. Time management skills and delegation skills can improve the quality of those decisions. These skills are described next.

Time Management

A decision maker must have enough time to make effective decisions. Adequate time makes it possible to understand the problem, develop several suitable alternatives, evaluate the decision in light of goals and priorities, and establish a workable approach to implement the decision.

Not having enough time is stressful and puts the decision maker in a reactive mode. A **reactive manager** is always dealing with the most urgent problem and putting out fires. Decisions made this way are likely to be haphazard and to have major flaws in either quality or execution. For example, it may be necessary to have employees work overtime to satisfy an urgent customer demand. The reactive manager may feel pressured to randomly assign employees to work overtime, rather than involving the group in the decision. It is likely that working overtime will conflict with family or personal plans of at least some of the employees, which leads to resentment and resistance.

Reactive managers tend to lose control of their time and lose sight of the "big picture." Always dealing with crises means living on an emotional roller coaster. Those who skip planning their daily and weekly schedules because of looming crises have no time to think about goals and priorities.

Crises can be avoided by anticipating and dealing with problems when they are smaller and more manageable. A **proactive manager** anticipates problems before they become pervasive and "works smarter, not harder." Proactive people manage time. Time is set aside on both a daily and weekly basis to set goals and priorities. Proactive managers jealously protect this time from interruptions. This way, they can complete their work, deal with important decisions, and enjoy life outside of work with family and friends. They are able to lead more balanced and less stressful lives than reactive managers.

One way to manage time is to eliminate or minimize "time wasters," activities that squander time. These include

- Television (the average American watches about four hours of television per day).
- Internet and e-mail messages.
- Lengthy telephone conversations.
- Random errands and waiting in lines.
- Interruptions by people who stop in to chat.
- Meetings (managers are often expected to attend many meetings to coordinate activities of their units).

Manager's Notes 6.2 lists helpful ways to avoid time wasters and practice effective time management.

Effective Time Management Practices

The following practices help managers eliminate or reduce time-wasting behavior and allow them to be more proactive.

1. *Make a list of things that need to be done today.* Write your daily plan during quiet time the night before, rather than at the office in the morning when urgent matters may get in the way of writing your list.

2. *Plan weekly, monthly, and annual schedules of activities.* Weekly schedules allow you to organize work, school, personal, and family activities. Longer term schedules let you plan time for nonwork facets of your life. For example, monthly plans may include travel that requires advance purchase of tickets. Annual plans also give an opportunity to consider your values and long-term objectives.

3. *Schedule difficult and challenging activities when you are at your highest level of energy and alertness.* For example, if you are a "morning person," schedule demanding activities in the morning and reserve afternoons for less difficult things such as returning phone calls or doing routine record keeping.

4. *Set deadlines.* Deadlines improve your use of time. Work always expands to fill the time available—if you don't specify a termination time, tasks tend to continue longer than they need to.

5. *Answer phone messages and e-mail in batches during a lull in your work schedule.* Phone calls and e-mail can interrupt your train of thought on important projects. Returning them all at one time allows you to use your time more efficiently.

6. *Have a place to work uninterrupted.* When a deadline is near, you can concentrate on the task at hand. Trying to refocus on a task or project after interruptions wastes a lot of time.

7. *Do something productive during nonproductive activities.* Try to multitask (accomplish multiple tasks at the same time). Listen to educational or personal improvement tapes while driving to and from work or class. Read the newspaper or balance your checking account while you're waiting in line. When watching television, take care of household tasks such as cooking, cleaning, and doing laundry.

Source: Adapted from D. A. Whetten and K. S. Cameron, *Developing Management Skills,* 4th ed., Upper Saddle River, NJ: Prentice Hall, 1998.

Delegation

The transfer of decision-making authority from a manager to a subordinate or a team at a lower level in the organization is **delegation.** It should not be confused with participation, in which the group *shares* decision-making authority with management. When a manager delegates decision-making authority, the subordinate makes the decision.

> **delegation**
>
> The transfer of decision-making authority from a manager to a subordinate or a team at a lower level in the organization.

Delegating the responsibility for resolving customer complaints to the front desk staff has resulted in satisfied customers and empowered employees for the Hampton Inn firm.

Managers delegate decisions for several reasons. The most important is that delegation gives the manager more time to spend on the most important tasks and decisions. For example, the chief executive officer (CEO) of a large corporation can focus on the overall direction and coordination of the corporation and delegate operational responsibilities for profits and losses to the general managers who report to him or her. Another reason to delegate is that it teaches subordinates how to make their own decisions and to deal with the consequences of those decisions. The subordinates receive feedback on the quality of their decision making and develop new skills that prepare them for future promotions. Finally, delegation may lead to higher quality decisions that result in greater customer satisfaction, because lower-level employees are closer to actual customers and therefore are more aware of their needs.

During the past decade, many corporations have relieved middle management of decision-making authority and have given it to teams of front-line employees, attempting to eliminate unnecessary layers of management in the process. Hampton Inn, a national hotel chain, has delegated authority to deal with customer complaints to desk clerks and housekeepers. Desk clerks can decide whether a complaint is justified and provide an immediate refund to a dissatisfied customer. This delegation of authority is part of Hampton Inn's "100% Satisfaction Guarantee," developed to gain a distinctive advantage in the highly competitive hotel industry, and it has resulted in higher levels of both customer and employee satisfaction, since Hampton employees feel more committed and motivated by being trusted to make important decisions involving guests.

Effective delegation involves the following steps:

1. Determine what you want done. Writing it down can be helpful.

2. Match the desired task with the most appropriate employee.

3. Be sure you communicate clearly when assigning the task. Follow up to make sure the task is fully understood. Set clear deadlines.

4. Keep communication channels open. Make it clear that you are available for consultation and discussion.

5. Allow employees to do the task the way they feel comfortable doing it.

6. Trust employees' capabilities. Do not hold such high expectations that they can only fail.

7. Check on the progress of the assignment, but do not rush to rescue the employee at the first sign of failure.

8. Hold the employee responsible for the work and any difficulties that may emerge, but do so as a teacher, not a police officer. Explore what is going wrong, and help employees develop their own solutions.

9. Recognize what the employee has done, and show appropriate appreciation.[9]

Some *barriers* to delegation of responsibilities by managers and ways to surmount these barriers are shown in Skills for Managing 6.2.

BARRIERS TO EFFECTIVE DELEGATION

How do barriers keep managers from effectively delegating responsibilities to their subordinates and using their full capabilities? This exercise presents some ways managers can avoid these barriers.

After reading the following justifications managers use to explain why they have not delegated responsibilities to subordinates in their work units, form groups of four or five people to discuss them.

Discuss each justification and consider what you believe are the underlying causes for a failure to delegate. Finally, work together to answer the group discussion questions that appear at the end of the exercise.

1. I feel uncomfortable asking subordinates to do some of the tasks I normally do.

2. My subordinates lack the appropriate knowledge to do the task I would like to delegate to them.

3. I can do some tasks more quickly than I can explain them to my subordinates.

4. My subordinates lack the appropriate skills and experience, so I can do the task better than they can.

5. My subordinates are already too busy.

6. If someone else does a task, it may weaken my control.

7. If someone else makes a mistake, I am responsible.

8. I feel better if people see me as an extraordinarily hard worker.

9. I feel uncomfortable relying on the judgment of subordinates around delegated tasks.

10. I no longer know what is going on.

Discussion Questions

1. What reasons or arguments could you give to counter each of the ten objections to delegation that are listed above? Is failure to delegate a symptom of a more fundamental management problem? Why or why not?

2. How could you get a manager to overcome the fear of delegating work to subordinates?

3. Are there some tasks that cannot be delegated to subordinates? If so, give some examples. Is there any type of work that you would recommend that managers not delegate? Explain.

4. Describe a situation that would be highly favorable to delegating work to subordinates. Describe a highly unfavorable situation.

Source: From *Becoming a Master Manager,* 2nd ed., by R. E. Quinn et al. Copyright © 1996 John Wiley & Sons, Inc. This material is used by permission of John Wiley & Sons, Inc.

APPLICATIONS: MANAGEMENT IS EVERYONE'S BUSINESS

Applications for the Manager   A major barrier to making effective decisions is procrastination. Managers wait until the last minute to make decisions because of inertia, too many interruptions, improperly classifying a decision as simple and low priority, hoping that the need for the decision will go away, or having insufficient information and being afraid of deciding to do the wrong thing. Managers need to establish clear priorities, and determine which activities produce the greatest value. They should then set dates for the completion of these activities. Setting priorities forces managers to make decisions and helps control procrastination.

Applications for Managing Teams   Overly relying on team meetings is a barrier to making effective team decisions. Although meetings are important for building trust in the early stages of team formation, they can waste a lot of time and frustrate people if they are used indiscriminately. By assigning tasks to subgroups or individual team members and giving them responsibility for decision making associated with these tasks, a team should be able to manage its workflow so that meetings are reserved for critical decisions or events that genuinely require the presence of all members.

Applications for Individuals   When you feel depressed, angry, anxious, or frustrated, you are not likely to be able to think clearly and focus on the problem, and it is not a good time to make a decision. It is better to postpone the decision until after you have coped with the source of stress and are in a more comfortable emotional state.

CONCLUDING THOUGHTS

After the introductory vignette we presented some critical thinking questions regarding decisions made by top executives in three different organizations. Now that you have had the opportunity to learn about decision making in the chapter, consider those critical thinking questions. First, Coca-Cola was facing a crisis situation. The CEO decided to admit that the New Coke product, which replaced the original Coca-Cola, was a mistake, and the CEO decided to return to marketing a product that was similar to the original formula of Coca-Cola, which was renamed "Coke Classic." While there were high stakes in all three decision-making examples, each CEO experienced a strong sense of urgency and had a short time span to work within. For instance, the CEO at Coca-Cola needed to control the potential damage to the brand identity of Coca-Cola. The Coca-Cola brand was and continues to be the world's most recognized brand name. An inferior product would badly hurt the value of the brand. Thus, there was a need for the CEO to act quickly and decisively to control the damage to the company's most valued asset, the brand itself.

Second, the decisions described at Intel, Coca-Cola, and IBM, were all made at a strategic level. The reasons that these decisions should be considered strategic are: (1) all three would have a high impact on the performance and survival of their respective companies; (2) all three involved selecting either the type or mix of products that each company would have in the market; and (3) all three would affect the level of future profits and company market value. These are all characteristics of strategic decisions.

Decision making is the process of identifying and resolving problems and opportunities. It involves understanding the underlying causes of a problem and implementing an effective solution. There are six characteristics of decision making:

- Programmability is the determination of whether the problem is well defined based on past experience or whether there are no established procedures for making a decision.

- **Uncertainty** involves how complete the information is that is available with which to make the decision.

- **Risk** varies with the level of uncertainty associated with the decision outcome.

- Conflict occurs when there are disagreements about goals and priorities that affect the selection of the solution. Conflict is a normal part of the decision-making process when diverse interests are competing to control the outcome.

- **Decision scope** involves the effect and time horizon of the decision.

- A crisis situation involves small amounts of time to make a decision that can impact the survival of the organization.

Strategic decisions have the largest effect and longest time horizon, while **operational decisions** are narrower in scope and time horizon. **Tactical decisions** lie between these two points.

Decision making involves a step-by-step process that unfolds in sequential stages:

1. Identify and diagnose the problem. Understand the underlying causes of the problem before attempting to form possible solutions.

2. Generate alternative solutions.

3. Evaluate the alternative solutions in light of the decision criteria. The decision criteria should be related to performance goals.

4. Choose the best alternative solution by either **optimizing** (selecting the optimally best solution) or **satisficing** (selecting the first alternative that meets minimum criteria).

5. Implement the decision. This means putting the solution into practice and establishing controls to make sure it works the way it is expected to work.

6. Evaluate the results. Decision evaluation involves gathering information and learning if the decision is on target to reach its goals. If not, modifications should be made to ensure the goals are reached.

The decision-making process is likely to reside within a group when employee commitment to the decision outcome is critical to successful implementation. Group decision making can be beneficial to the quality of the decision by involving more people who have a greater diversity of ideas and opinions, and it can enhance decision acceptance by giving more people a voice in the decision. Disadvantages of group decision making are having to deal with dominant individuals or forceful factions and **groupthink,** where the group avoids meaningful critical evaluation of solutions in favor of maintaining social harmony and cohesion.

Lower quality decisions are likely to result if the group decision-making process is not managed. Ways to increase the effectiveness of group decision making include selecting an appropriate leadership style, assigning the **devil's advocate** role to stimulate critical thinking, and using special techniques such as **brainstorming** and **storyboarding** to stimulate creative thinking.

1. What is the difference between a programmed and nonprogrammed decision? Consider a programmed decision and a nonprogrammed decision you have made recently. Compare and contrast the approaches you used to make these two decisions.

2. Can you teach people to make decisions? What types of decisions are useful for giving people experience in decision making? What types of decisions should be avoided in teaching trainees about decision making?

3. What are the advantages of delegating decision making to front-line employees and teams? Are there any disadvantages to this approach to decision making?

4. Should only top executives, such as the CEO, be involved in making strategic decisions? Can you think of a tactical or operational decision that could benefit from the involvement of the CEO or another top executive? What are the drawbacks of involving CEOs in tactical and operational decision making?

5. How can electronic communications such as the Internet and e-mail be used to improve the decision-making process? Give some examples.

6. Define the following decision-making errors and identify ways to correct for them:
   a. Poor problem identification.
   b. Solution focus.
   c. Premature evaluation.
   d. Groupthink.
   e. Overemphasis on objective data without considering gut feelings.
   f. Omission of a way to monitor and control the decision.

7. Think of a decision in which you used an optimizing criterion for selecting the best decision alternative, and another decision in which you used a satisficing criterion. What factors influenced you to optimize instead of satisfice? Which ones affected your choice to satisfice instead of optimize?

8. Under what conditions is it better to involve a group of employees in decision making, rather than an individual manager? What roles should a manager or leader take in the group decision-making process?

9. Group decision making has several pitfalls that can result in poor-quality decisions. Describe some approaches to improving the quality of group decision making so that these threats to decision quality are reduced.

10. Why is time management considered a critical skill for the process of decision making? Why do you think that managers known for their excellent decisions are also experts in the art of delegation?

US Airways Escapes a Near Death Experience

US Airways hit a double whammy in 2001 when the Justice Department rejected its proposed merger with the larger United Airlines and travel declined following the September 11 terrorist attacks. In the spring of 2002, US Airways filed for Chapter 11 bankruptcy protection, which gave the company protection from its creditors while it restructured its debt and tried to attract new capital. By the spring of 2003, US Airways was ready to emerge from bankruptcy as a viable airline. Much of the credit for this amazing escape from a near death experience should be given to the crisis management skills of David Siegel, the CEO. Siegel was a seasoned veteran airline executive who had most recently worked at Continental Airlines during its turnaround.

Shortly after Siegel was hired, he quickly implemented a new strategy at US Airways. First, he refocused the airline route structure so that the profitable short-hop routes between major East Coast cities were retained, while some of the longer routes between smaller, second-tier cities were abandoned. This route reconfiguration allowed the company to get rid of some larger jet aircraft with more expensive operational costs and replace them with cheaper and smaller regional jets.

Next, Siegel forged new ties with the pilots. His "jobs for jets" program (he let displaced pilots of large aircraft have first chance to fly regional jets) and his willingness to open the company's books induced pilots to agree to pay cuts of at least 26 percent. That cut in labor costs helped the company win conditional approval of $900 million in federal loan guarantees.

When the airline's mechanics wouldn't join other unions in making voluntary sacrifices, Siegel took the carrier into Chapter 11—a status that gives companies the ability to void labor contracts with a judge's approval. That leverage helped Siegel bring the unionized mechanics around. Siegel also got the unionized pilots to agree to major work-rule changes that increased labor cost efficiency. Finally, Siegel terminated the pilots' pension plan which eliminated a $2 billion shortfall and cleared the final hurdle for the company to move out of Chapter 11. While the pilots were grumbling about the loss of their pension plan many others were cheering. "David Siegel knows where he's going, and he's tough," says Frank Jay, a Houston-based executive recruiter for the airline industry.

Discussion Questions

1. David Siegel made some critical decisions to turn US Airways around under conditions of risk. What are the sources of risk with respect to the decisions made by Siegel? For example, what are the risks associated with taking the company into Chapter 11 bankruptcy? What are the risks of taking away benefits from the unionized pilots and mechanics?

2. David Siegel was an "outsider" who was hired to take US Airways out of a difficult financial situation that was threatening its survival. What decision-making advantages does an "outsider" such as Siegel have over an "insider" who is promoted from within to be the new CEO, when it comes to making tough decisions that can improve a distressed company's ability to survive?

Source: Adapted from J. Helyar. "A Tale of Two Bankruptcies," *Fortune,* February 17, 2003, pp. 68–69.

A Blockbuster Turnaround Decision

John Antioco, previously a CEO at convenience store chain Circle K and Mexican fast-food franchise Taco Bell, had recently been hired as CEO of Blockbuster, the world's largest video rental company. Blockbuster is part of Viacom, a diversified media corporation, with other units that are growing rapidly and with much greater profitability such as the Paramount film studios, Nickelodeon and MTV cable channels, and Simon and Schuster book publishing.

Antioco, the third CEO hired in less than two years, needed to somehow engineer a turnaround for the firm to reduce its flat growth and a 33 percent decline in cash flow compared to the previous year. Over the past two years Blockbuster had been rocked by management turmoil, strategic missteps, a slowdown in the rental business, and a troubled adoption of a new distribution system.

Part of the challenge was Blockbuster's declining industry. Video rental industry growth was flat in 1998 and declined in 1999 and 2000. Movies were starting to be available in the DVD (digital video disk) format that offered better viewing quality than the older analog video tape technology. At present, movies recorded in the DVD format are much more expensive to rent than video tape movies, but the cost gap between the two technologies is expected to decline. The video rental industry faced competition from pay-per-view television services, new premium channels being added to cable and satellite dish television providers, and video and multimedia content on the Internet. Customers now had the choice of either driving to the retail video outlets to pick up and return videos or having film content electronically delivered to their televisions and computers.

There was also competition to the video rental industry from the video game industry. Video games are sold and rented in retail malls and arcades. High-quality video games played on new platforms such as Sony's Playstation compete for customers with the Hollywood movie products offered by Blockbuster. In addition, some of Blockbuster's competitors in the video rental industry were starting to sell video movies as well as rent them as the costs of both tapes and DVDs were declining.

Antioco wasted no time before making key decisions to improve company performance at Blockbuster. He focused his turnaround strategy on a back-to-basics approach to the core operations of the business, including tighter inventory control and cost controls. Some of his actions were:

Visiting with Hollywood executives to negotiate deals for buying videotapes at lower cost from the studios.

Organizing large group meetings of demoralized store managers, where he delivered passionate motivational speeches indicating that Blockbuster was an underdog and would come back stronger and more aggressive than ever.

Lowering prices and extending rental periods for new and older video films in an effort to improve customer satisfaction.

Slowing the rate of store expansions and closing stores in poorly performing markets.

Changing the product mix between the rental and sale of video movies offered to customers.

Discussion Questions

1. What made Blockbuster's turnaround decision so important? Why do you think CEO Antioco acted so quickly and decisively when he arrived at Blockbuster from his previous job at Taco Bell? What are the upside and downside risks of taking this urgent approach to decision making?

2. How do you think the CEO perceived the problem at Blockbuster? Do you think his earlier experiences in convenience stores and fast-food franchises influenced his problem-solving approach to decision making? What do you think he viewed as the causes of the poor performance?

3. Is there another way to view Blockbuster's problem, such as the fact that it is part of a declining industry facing technological threats from competitors? How might this frame of reference influence the type of solutions that you would propose to improve the performance of Blockbuster?

Sources: Adapted from S. Forest, "Blockbuster's Fired-Up Mr. Fixit," *Business Week,* February 9, 1998, pp. 100–101; L. Stevens, "The Entertainment Glut," *Business Week,* February 16, 1998, pp. 88–95; S. Forest, "Blockbuster: The Sequel," *Business Week,* September 16, 2002, pp. 52–53.

Intel Recalls the Pentium Chip

In the fall of 1994, cofounder Andrew Grove was riding high as CEO of Intel, the largest and most profitable semiconductor company in the world. Intel's chips were found in 80 percent of the personal computers in the world. In its twenty-sixth year of making computer chips, it was anticipating a record $10 billion dollars in sales and 30 percent growth.

Intel was beginning full-scale production of the Pentium, its newest microprocessor chip. This chip's superior performance promised a bright future for the company. In the previous year, Grove began a massive advertising campaign for Intel chips, which elevated public awareness of Intel and differentiated the products that contained its chips.

In the midst of these positive circumstances, a troubling event occurred. A bug was discovered in the Pentium chip that could cause mathematical errors during processing. The bug caused a division error once every 9 billion times. At this rate a typical user of spreadsheet software on a Pentium-controlled computer would run into the problem once every 27,000 years of use. Intel scientists were aware of this error in June 1994, but because it would cause an error so infrequently, they did not consider it to be a material flaw and put the problem on the back burner, while the company continued to ship the Pentium chip.

When individual users encountered the error and turned to Intel for help, however, they were not happy with Intel's response to the problem or to their requests for replacement chips. The company's policy was to replace chips only after assessing each individual's problem. Customers who claimed their computers handled a lot of division functions were given replacement chips, while others might or might not have their chips replaced.

Users affected by the chip's flaw began posting information about the error on the Internet in late October; it was picked up by a trade newspaper, which ran a story about it on the front page; other trade papers ran the story as well. Three weeks later when CNN, the cable news network, wanted to question Intel executives about the bug on television, a media frenzy occurred. Stories appeared in major newspapers with headlines such as, "Flaw Undermines Accuracy of Pentium Chips."

The crisis mushroomed in mid-December, when IBM announced that it would stop shipments of all Pentium-based computers. Because IBM was a key player in the computer industry, its action attracted a lot of attention. Intel customers clamored to find out what Intel was going to do with the Pentium chips that it had already sold to them.

After the events of the fall, Grove knew he had to make a decision on the Pentium chip. Should Intel spend millions of dollars to replace the flawed chip for all users, or should it counter what the company felt were overly negative reports from the media with a more moderate response?

Critical Thinking Questions

1. Why do you think the media paid so much attention to the error in the Pentium chip, which occurred only once in every 9 billion divisions? Was the margin for accuracy high enough for the typical customer of a personal computer? Explain.

2. Why would Intel release the flawed Pentium chip to the market instead of delaying its introduction until the flaw was fixed?

3. Why do you think Intel treated early customer complaints about the Pentium error by relying on standard Intel customer complaint procedures—a programmed approach to decision making?

Collaborative Learning Exercise

Assume it is 1994. With a partner or small group, identify the true nature of the problem Intel CEO Andrew Grove faced. Recommend a course of action to Grove, considering the following alternatives. Should all the Pentium chips be replaced at a cost of $500 million? Or should he run an aggressive media campaign to tell Intel's side of the story, spelling out how trivial the flaw is and trying to convince customers that they are highly unlikely to be affected by it? Support your recommendation.

Source: Adapted from A. Grove, *Only the Paranoid Survive.* New York: Currency Doubleday, 1996, pp. 11–16.

Decision Making at Coca-Cola

www.cocacola.com

The opening vignette outlined how Coca-Cola CEO Roberto Goizueta acted decisively after making a mistake with the launch of the New Coke product. In this exercise you will learn more about the Coca-Cola Company and what it stands for. Visit the Coca-Cola website and explore the "About the Company" and "Investor Relations" areas there, and then answer the following questions:

1. What are the five key beliefs at Coca-Cola? What do these beliefs reveal about the Coca-Cola Company?

2. Coke sponsors many sporting events, such as World Cup Soccer, National Football League, National Basketball Association, Tour de France bicycle race, Rugby World Cup, and the Olympic Games. Why is Coke so involved with sponsoring these events? What benefits do you think Coke receives from these sponsorships?

3. Sadly, CEO Roberto Goizueta died in 1997. Who is the current CEO of Coke? How has Coke's market valuation changed since then, when it was valued at $180 billion?

Determining Decision Risk and Uncertainty Preferences

How likely are you to take risks in making decisions? Consider the following statements and mark each "True" or "False" to indicate whether you agree or disagree.

_____ 1. I get my hair cut at the same place every month because I know it will always be cut the same way.

_____ 2. If I needed to hire an engineer, I know that if I hire the job candidate who has a master's degree in engineering she'll have the knowledge to do the job.

_____ 3. With the growing consumer market in China, products should sell well there.

_____ 4. A new computer is expensive, but it will help generate enough business to cover the cost in just four months.

_____ 5. If two auto shops are equally reliable and say they can repair my car tomorrow, I'll take my car to the one that says it can do the same repairs for $25 less.

_____ 6. If a company doesn't jump into the service sector of its market, it will miss a golden opportunity.

_____ 7. If I know someone always gets to the office by 8:30 in the morning, I know I can call him there at 8:45.

_____ 8. One health-insurance policy would cost me less in premiums but charges a higher deductible; another policy has higher premiums but a lower deductible. Since I'm generally healthy, I'll buy the first policy.

_____ 9. Switching to environmentally responsible packaging will appeal to our customers, even though the packaging is not as attractive, so we should switch.

_____ 10. One hardware store opens at 7:00 in the morning and another at 9:00, but only the latter store carries the brand of batteries I prefer. I can go to either store. Since I don't need the batteries first thing in the morning, I'll wait until the second store opens.

Scoring: "True" answers to statements 1, 5, 7, and 10 indicate a preference for certainty. "True" answers to statements 2, 4, and 8 indicate an acceptance for risk. "True" answers to statements 3, 6, and 9 indicate an acceptance of uncertainty.

Source: From *Management of Organizations*, by P. M. Wright and R. A. Noe: Copyright © 1996 The McGraw-Hill Companies, Inc. Reprinted with permission.

SEVEN

Strategic Management

chapter 7

After reading this chapter, you should be able to:

- Implement the steps in the strategic management process.
- Conduct an analysis of the firm's strengths, weaknesses, opportunities, and threats.
- Identify the factors that create a sustained competitive advantage.
- Link external and internal environment data to determine a firm's strategic intent and mission.
- Choose appropriate business strategies at the corporate and business-unit levels.

Canon Climbs to the Top

Canon continues to be a standout performer, one of the few companies today that has transcended Japan's long economic malaise. In 1975 the company had sales of $400 million; by the end of the century its sales exceeded $25 billion, and Canon had jumped ahead of rivals Eastman Kodak and Xerox on *Fortune's* Global 500 list. During the 1990s, Canon's net profits grew an average of 20 percent per year. Over the same period, return on equity more than doubled to 9.6 percent—far above the 5.6 percent average annual return posted by Japan's major companies. Even during the Asian economic downturn of the late 1990s, Canon's earnings grew at a healthy rate, a remarkable achievement considering that most other Japanese firms were experiencing flat growth or declines in profits.

By 2004 Canon was earning a higher return on investments and profits than all of its major global competitors. In contrast, most other icons of Japanese high technology (Hitachi, Matsushita, Toshiba, NEC, and Fujitsu) continue to report losses.

For years Canon thrived by challenging and beating other technology leaders at their own game, such as Leica in cameras and Xerox in photocopiers. Today, Canon is the technology leader in many fields. Says Canon director of product development Ichiro Endo: "Now we have reached a point when we have to set our own targets. There is no one else to follow."

Technology is Canon's strong suit; few Japanese companies can equal it. For the most part, the company has stuck to patentable, category-killer technology in high-margin areas that it knows well, including optics, imaging, and printing. Because each of its researchers is required to file for at least four patents a year, Canon had almost 75,000 U.S. patents by 2004, second only to IBM. Its emphasis on research and development translates into revolutionary products, such as professional-quality autofocus cameras, miniature laser printer motors, and photo-quality inkjet printers.

Innovation keeps Canon moving forward. Many of its business lines are first in their category, and most are in the top three. For example, Canon's original product line is cameras, which these days account for just over 10 percent of sales—the company is first in both single-lens reflexes (34 percent of the U.S. market) and compacts (16 percent of the U.S. market). In the copier business, which accounts for about a third of sales, Canon is the leader in both color and black-and-white midrange business machines. When it comes to the printer business, which accounts for about 30 percent of Canon's sales, the company is second only to Hewlett-Packard. Canon has recently introduced several new photographic products that were immediate successes, including a digital x-ray camera and the compact, lightweight Elura digital video camcorder that records and plays back high-quality still and motion pictures.

To keep results like these rolling, Canon has adopted a two-pronged strategy. It maintains close attention to its core business by cutting costs, making its suppliers more efficient, and speeding up its product development. At the same time, Canon moved into the digital age by establishing alliances with companies that know the networking and computer worlds better than Canon. The company's vastly successful alliance with Hewlett-Packard—Canon makes the motors for HP laser printers—stands as a model. By 2004 Canon had become the world's no. 1 copier company, with almost a one-third market share. Between now and 2010, the company will be moving into enterprisewide document and image management—copiers, printers, faxes, scanners, all networked together—in other words, Xerox territory. This will put added pressure on Xerox, which 20 years earlier had almost complete dominance of the copier market. Since then, Xerox's market position has eroded down to 38.3 percent in 1998, and 14.2 percent in 2003.

Sources: Adapted with permission from E. W. Desmond, "Can Canon Keep Clicking?" *Fortune,* February 2, 1998, pp. 98–103. Updated information from www.canon.com; W. J. Holstein, "Canon Takes Aim at Xerox," *Fortune,* October 14, 2002, pp. 215–220; and I. M. Kunii, "Making Canon Click," *Business Week,* September 16, 2002, pp. 40–42.

CRITICAL THINKING QUESTIONS

1. *How has Canon been able to be highly profitable over many years in spite of an unfavorable external environment?*

2. *What is the role of strategic management in the relative success of an organization such as Canon?*

The Strategic Management Process

It is the job of top-level management to chart the course of the entire enterprise. The strategic management process includes analysis of the internal and external environment of the firm, definition of the firm's mission, and formulation and implementation of strategies to create or continue a competitive advantage. These efforts steer the organization in a particular direction and require large resource commitments, which is why strategic management is generally the responsibility of top executives.

Reversing strategic decisions can be costly, so most firms take a long-term perspective when making these choices. For instance, in the mid-1990s, Ford CEO Alex Trotman announced "Ford 2000," a new strategic direction for the firm. The strategy spelled out all the new cars and trucks Ford would manufacture in the following 10 years and the resources required to produce them. It called for reducing the number of basic designs or platforms from 24 to 16 and increasing the number of models produced from them by 50 percent. To save on costs and increase quality, Ford would revamp its design and manufacturing process on a worldwide basis. All North American and European engineering operations were consolidated in five vehicle development centers, each of which had a global mission.

Five years later, Ford realized that although centralized worldwide responsibility for functions such as product development, purchasing, design, and manufacturing generated significant cost savings, it also resulted in less customer responsiveness at the local level. Jacques A. Nasser, who became CEO following Trotman, made significant adjustments to Trotman's plan by restoring much of the power that was stripped away from regional Ford managers: "The central idea is to create bite-size, highly accountable regional brand units that can get to their target customers' tastes and needs."

Yet Nasser lasted only two years on the job. According to his successor, Bill Ford (whose great-grandfather was Henry Ford), Nasser was fired by the Ford family (which still controls one-third of Ford's shares) for "pursuing strategies that were either poorly conceived or poorly timed" (www.ford.com). Bill Ford decided to centralize many of Ford's activities in order to avoid duplication and focus the company's attention on launching new products, saving on costs, and eliminating low-margin vehicles—to "improve our quality and rationalize our capacity." Ford's strategic objective is to introduce 10 new and 10 freshened models annually in North America until 2006 (www.ford.com). It remains to be seen as of the time of this writing (2004) if results are as promising as Bill Ford thought; if not Ford may need to once again revise its strategic plans.[1]

The experience at Ford demonstrates another key attribute of strategic management: For a strategy to be successful, a firm must be flexible and make changes to the plan based on experience. Strategic management involves both long-range thinking and adaptation to changing conditions. Some of these issues are explored in greater detail in Chapter 8.

Strategies should be designed to generate a sustainable competitive advantage. This means that competitors will be unable to duplicate what the firm has done or will find it too difficult or expensive. When competitors ultimately learn how to copy the strategy, the firm should modify or reformulate the strategy to stay ahead. American Express was a pioneer in the credit card business in the 1950s. The card charged an annual fee and all purchases had to be repaid within a month of billing.

In December 1998, Ken Chenault's success at American Express made him the *Business Week* cover story.

For almost 25 years, the American Express card was a worldwide symbol of prestige. American Express posted high earnings year after year. Soon, competitors such as Visa and MasterCard entered the industry with card features that were more convenient to customers, such as no annual fees, installment payment plans, air travel insurance, and extended warranties on purchases. These cards were also differentiated based on prestige, with different-colored cards for varying credit limits. American Express began to lose its competitive advantage. In the late 1990s, American Express's CEO, Harvey Golub, and president, Kenneth Chenault, launched a fierce counterattack against Visa and MasterCard, introducing a wide variety of cards for different market segments with many features that matched or surpassed those of the competitors. In 1997, American Express kicked off 17 new cards, and in 2000 it introduced a consumer-friendly "Blue Card" with an electronic "smart" chip embedded within it that could contain account information. American Express earnings rose more than 35 percent between 1996 and 1999, and the company's stock price went up 400 percent.[2]

In the automotive sector, the truck and SUV segments were General Motors' golden goose, bringing in almost twice as much profit per vehi-

FIGURE 7.1

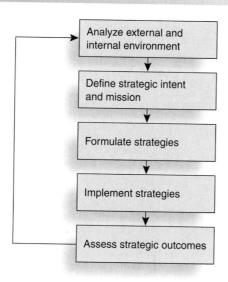

cle as compared to cars. Asian manufacturers such as Nissan and Honda quickly entered this attractive market and have already conquered about one-fourth of the light truck and SUV market in the United States. If this trend continues they will own half of this market by 2010. As noted by Van Bussman, senior vice president of Global Forecasting for J. D. Power & Associates and a former chief economist at Chrysler, "high returns attract more imitators. And guess what? Everybody and his brother is entering the SUV segment—some are even entering the hallowed pickup segment".[3] General Motors' major strategic challenge will be finding ways to effectively respond to these competitors.

By successfully exploiting its competitive advantage, a firm can earn above-average returns or returns in excess of alternative investment opportunities with a similar level of risk. In the long run, a firm must earn at least average returns if it hopes to stay in business. Investors are likely to withdraw their funds from firms with below-average earnings.

In this chapter, we discuss the major aspects of the strategic management process and how this process affects the firm's competitive advantage. Figure 7.1 shows the interdependent parts of the strategic management process that firms must manage to win battles in a global marketplace that grows more ferocious every year. First, the firm needs to analyze the external and internal environment. Second, information gathered from this analysis serves as a basis of a statement of strategic intent and mission. Next, company leaders formulate and implement strategies that will allow the firm to achieve sustained superior performance in light of its strategic intent and mission. Last, the executive team should periodically assess the outcomes of strategic plans. *Strategic outcomes* refer to intended and unintended results. Intended results can include higher

CONDUCTING A SWOT ANALYSIS

A commonly used strategy tool is a SWOT (strengths-weaknesses-opportunities-threats) analysis, which is accomplished in three steps:

Step 1: Analyze the organization's internal environment, identifying its strengths and weaknesses.

Step 2: Analyze the organization's external environment, identifying its opportunities and threats.

Step 3: Crossmatch strengths with opportunities, weaknesses with threats, strengths with threats, and weaknesses with opportunities.

Once the analysis is complete, the firm can develop strategies for the matches that appear to be of greatest importance to the organization. Most organizations give top priority to strategies that match strengths with opportunities and second priority to strategies that match weaknesses with threats. The key is to exploit opportunities in areas of organizational strength and to defend against threats in areas of organizational weakness.

In this exercise, the class forms small groups. Each group chooses a well-known firm for analysis, or the instructor may assign a firm to each group.

1. Each group researches its firm in the business press (*Business Week, Fortune, The Wall Street Journal,* etc.), conducts interviews, and searches the Internet to determine its strengths, weaknesses, opportunities, and threats.

2. Each group completes the following SWOT Worksheet. A spokesperson for the group presents the group's findings to the class.

Source: From *Management: Building Competitive Advantage,* 3rd ed., by I. Bateman and S. Snell. Copyright © 2002 The McGraw Hill Companies, Inc. Reprinted with permission.

profits, more focus on products or services, and increased stock price; unintended results can be lower customer responsiveness, higher cost, and improved productivity. The strategic outcome information in turn feeds into the analysis of the internal and external environment, which may lead to redefinition of strategic intent and mission, strategy formulation, and implementation.

As indicated in the case of Ford Motor Company, strategic management is a dynamic process. Adjustments may be necessary after examining strategic outcomes. For the sake of clarity, each step in Figure 7.1 is discussed separately, but it is important to remember that the various components of the strategic management process are closely linked to one another.

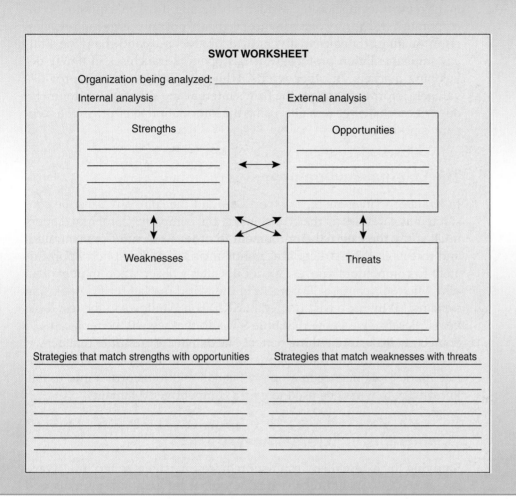

SWOT WORKSHEET

Organization being analyzed: _____

Internal analysis   External analysis

Strengths   Opportunities

Weaknesses   Threats

Strategies that match strengths with opportunities   Strategies that match weaknesses with threats

Analyzing External and Internal Environments

One commonly used strategic tool is a **SWOT (strengths–weaknesses–opportunities–threats) analysis.** The objective is to analyze factors from both within and outside the organization that may influence success. The external and internal factors to be considered in the SWOT analysis are discussed next. SWOT enables managers to identify organizational strengths (S) and weaknesses (W), and environmental opportunities (O) and threats (T). A properly conducted SWOT analysis generates information which helps a firm respond to various strategic challenges. (See Skills for Managing 7.1.) SWOT does not tell the firm what strategies to pursue;

SWOT analysis

A strategic management tool to evaluate the firm, which is accomplished by identifying its strengths and weaknesses and identifying its opportunities and threats.

instead it provides input for strategic decisions. Management Close-Up 7.a, "Will Harley-Davidson Hit the Wall?" shows a summary of a SWOT analysis for the motorcycle manufacturer. Based on this SWOT information, executives at Harley-Davidson must consider whether or not to redefine the company's strategic intent and mission. For instance, the management team should consider broadening the firm's mission to incorporate a wide array of two-wheel vehicles, not only large motorcycles, reformulating strategies to diversify its product mix, and changing strategy implementation protocols such as opening franchises in newly developing markets. In other words, while the SWOT analysis provides valuable information about the firm's internal and external environment, one critical challenge remains: using the information to improve the company's position.

The External Environment

In strategic management, the world around the company must be considered as carefully as the world inside the company. Company leaders must study the external environment in order to identify opportunities and threats in the marketplace, avoid surprises, and respond appropriately to competitors' moves. CEO Bill Gates's observation may explain why Microsoft controls 93 percent of the world market for PC operating systems: "Why have we doubled our R&D on Windows in the last three years? Because we know that unless we do that we will be replaced. . . . Somebody makes something better? The demand can shift to that person overnight."[4] A major challenge for company executives is to gather accurate market intelligence in a timely fashion and transform it into usable knowledge that may be used to gain a competitive advantage.

Components of External Analysis

Studying the external environment requires managers to tap into a variety of sources, including the media, online information, journals and trade magazines, and other sources. There are four components of an external analysis: scanning, monitoring, forecasting, and assessing.

scanning

The analysis of general environmental factors that may directly or indirectly be relevant to the firm's future.

SCANNING Analysis of general environmental factors that may be relevant to the firm's future is referred to as **scanning.** The primary objective is to identify early signs of emerging trends and changes in the environment that may result in an opportunity or a threat. For instance, when there were fewer college-age students, many private universities stayed afloat by targeting senior citizens, foreign students, and working adults. Colgate-Palmolive also looked at changing demographics before launching a new product, as Management Close-Up 7.b illustrates. Also, many corporations have adapted products and marketing campaigns to segmented markets

Will Harley-Davidson Hit the Wall? Identifying Strengths, Weaknesses, Opportunities and Threats

Wearing black leather and riding huge Harleys, a motorcycle gang thunders through northern Georgia as if on the way to a rumble. But the only rumble for this gang—the Atlanta Harley Owners Group (HOG)—is the one in their stomachs. It's another Sunday ride in the country for the group, and as usual it ends with a feast. "We live to ride, and we ride to eat," says club assistant director B. K. Ellis, a systems analyst.

Ellis is one of 55 HOG members on the outing, mostly white-collar types with secret lives as bikers—and total devotion to their Harleys. "It's the imagery, the mystique," says Ellis. The group was gearing up for a huge national rally of HOG chapters in 2003: 20,000 owners were expected to ride into Atlanta for a three-day party to mark the start of Harley-Davidson's 100th anniversary celebration. Some would be hard-core guys with big tattoos and bad tempers, the sort who once typified the Harley customer. But most would be playing hooky from $78,000-per-year jobs (the average salary of today's Harley customer), riding $16,000 motorcycles (the typical cost of Harley's biggest bike, a cruiser), and pledging fealty to an open-road cult that doubles as a highly profitable $4 billion-a-year company.

This is the motorcycle world that Harley-Davidson has reinvented, one that seems—and is—a century removed from the Milwaukee shed where William Harley and Andrew Davidson first collaborated in 1903. To continue riding this success in the new millennium, top executives at Harley-Davidson believe that the time has come to analyze the company's strengths, weaknesses, opportunities, and threats (SWOT) in order to formulate and implement future strategies. The results of the SWOT analysis are summarized below.

Strengths

- *Customer Loyalty.* Harley today is more of a fraternity than a producer of machinery. Buying a Harley makes you part of a ready-made motorcycle gang consisting of 600 U.S. HOG chapters, operated under the dealers' aegis. Style is as important as speed. On dealer floors, leather-draped mannequins outnumber the bikes. Harley has artfully parlayed the romance of the road and the independence of the biker to capture baby-boomers. The company's core customers have reprised their 1960s rebelliousness through a product that bespeaks their middle-aged success.

- *Brand Recognition.* Even though it sells a niche product, Harley consistently ranks among the 10 best-known American brands, in the company of Coca-Cola and Disney.

- *Top Growth Stocks.* Harley ranks among America's top growth stocks since its 1986 IPO. Its 37 percent average annual gain runs just behind the 42 percent pace of another 1986 debutant: Microsoft.

- *Strong Dealer Networks.* The people who catch Harley fever will be directed to a hometown dealer. A Harley dealer is never too far away. Many offer "Rider's Edge" courses for novices.

Weaknesses

- *Limited Product Line.* Most of the company's revenues are tied to the big cruiser bike.

- *Quality.* Harley hasn't built better bikes than its four main Japanese competitors and the company once had persistent quality problems. There is still room for improvements in quality.

- *Limited Cross-Cultural Appeal.* The firm has been primarily USA-centric and is strongly associated with the American culture. This has limited its international sales.

Opportunities

- *International Markets.* As foreign markets continue to expand, primarily in developing countries such as India and China with a growing middle class, there may be an excellent outlet for the firm's products.

- *Youth Market.* Harley-Davidson appeals primarily to those over 45. Thus, there is an excellent market opportunity if the firm can develop products that appeal to prospective younger buyers.

Threats

- *Narrow Market Niche.* As the customer base has grayed, the average age of a Harley rider has risen from 38 to 46. Yet, the prime age for motorcycle customers is 35 to 44. In addition, 91 percent of buyers are males, further limiting the customer base.

- *Generation Gap.* Harley's appeal still lies more in image than in performance, but fashion-driven companies are vulnerable to changes of fashion and generation. The future of Harely's business is in the new generations, not exactly the forte of a company attuned to baby-boomer rhythms and values. Naturally the boomers' kids want to ride anything but the old man's model. They may be drawn to machines that are the anti-Harley.

- *Customer Resistance to Change.* Making changes is tricky for a company with Harley's cult following: They risk alienating current customers. The V-Rod's water-cooled engine is a big departure from Harley's traditional air-cooled one, and to some uneasy riders a portent of additional unwelcome changes to come. "If they ever do anything with that [roaring] sound, they've lost their customer base," according to an industry consultant.

- *Strong Signs of Weakening Demand.* The customer waiting list for new motorcycles has shrunk from as much as two years to a matter of months. Dealer premiums that used to range between $2,000 and $4,000 have disappeared for most models.

Source: Adapted with permission from J. Helyar, "Will Harley-Davidson Hit the Wall?" *Fortune,* August 12, 2003, pp. 120–124.

to take advantage of ethnic diversity. The Internet is having a major effect on the way firms sell their products and services worldwide. It can also change the competitive landscape almost overnight.

monitoring

Observing environmental changes on a continuous basis to determine whether a clear trend is emerging.

MONITORING   Observing environmental changes on a continuous basis to determine whether a clear trend is emerging is referred to as **monitoring.** For example, many American firms are investing in Latin America and the Caribbean because they have detected strong pressures for economic liberalization and privatization in countries that formerly were closely regulated. These investments involve some risk. Monitoring can reduce the level of uncertainty by keeping them aware of such events as elections, currency stability, lower inflation, and savings rates.

Scanning and monitoring are used to interpret current or past environmental information that is consequential to strategic decisions and that requires a response. For instance, when California passed legislation requiring a certain percentage of cars sold to be nonpolluting or electric; the proportion was set at 2 percent for 1998. In the late 1990s, GM invested $350 million dollars to develop electric vehicles to comply with the law. The company also expected other jurisdictions, including some foreign countries, to pass similar legislation.

forecasting

Predicting what is likely to happen in the future, the intensity of the anticipated event, its importance to the firm, and the pace or time frame in which it may occur.

FORECASTING   In **forecasting,** the firm attempts to predict what is likely to happen in the future, the intensity of the anticipated event, its importance to the firm, and the pace or time frame in which it may occur. Some firms routinely delay investing in new information technology based on forecasts of lower costs relative to the amount of computer power that may be purchased. However, these investments can only be

Colgate Brushes Up on Demographics

THEME: CUSTOMER FOCUS Colgate-Palmolive occupies the top spot in the oral care market, unseating Procter & Gamble, maker of Crest, for the first time in 35 years. Even though its market is a mature, slow-growth market filled with approximately 131 competing toothpastes, Colgate, the almost 200-year-old producer of toothpaste, deodorant, and soap, made impressive gains in market share during 1994–1998.

How did Colgate do it? Company leaders considered the maturing population when creating a new product. In 1998 Colgate began marketing a new toothpaste called Total throughout the United States, spending $100 million to promote it. Total was already racking up sales in most of the 103 countries where it was sold. What was so different about Total? It's not just toothpaste—it's the first "oral pharmaceutical" approved by the Food and Drug Administration after years of scrutiny, and it contains triclosan. Triclosan, a broad-spectrum antibiotic, is used to fight gingivitis, a bleeding-gum disease that people are prone to as they age. Colgate's vice president for advanced technology, Abdul Gaffar, notes that treatment of diseases like gingivitis, which cause gums to bleed from a buildup of plaque and tartar, costs some $40 billion per year around the world. Total gives consumers a preventive approach against these diseases, which could save them a lot of money—a key selling point in foreign markets.

The product was developed by a Colgate team of 200 that spent 10 years and some $35 million in the process. They worked closely with dental schools in the United States and Europe, to figure out how to embed triclosan in teeth and gums for 14 hours so that two daily brushings would be effective. Fluoride to prevent cavities and a whitening substance round out the mint-flavored paste.

Five years after it was first introduced in the late 1990s, Total is now available in a variety of forms which are designed to appeal to different consumer tastes, including "Colgate Total—Fresh Stripe," "Colgate Total plus Whitening Gel," and "Colgate Total plus Whitening Paste." Several independent studies have revealed that by 2003 Colgate Total was the top-selling toothpaste in the United States, and was ranked number one by dental professionals, hygienists, and pharmacists.

Source: Adapted from L. Grant, "Outmarketing P&G," *Fortune*, January 12, 1998, p. 150. Updated in 2004 (www.colgate.com).

---

postponed for so long before the firm is at a disadvantage. As discussed in Chapter 2, firms that expand internationally attempt to predict a host of variables that may have a direct effect on return on investments. These variables include political and legal change, economic conditions, and currency convertibility.

Forecasts can be wrong, so a firm needs to retain strategic flexibility to make necessary adjustments. Continuous scanning and monitoring of the environment can provide valuable feedback about whether a firm needs to reconsider its position.

ASSESSING Evaluation of environmental data received to study the implications for the firm is the process of **assessing.** Without an accurate assessment of consequences, the firm can make major blunders. For instance, when the cost of resin, a key raw material, increased, the management team at Rubbermaid thought that the company's well-recognized brand name and strong market presence would allow it to pass the

assessing

Evaluating the environmental data received to study the implications for the firm.

increased costs on to customers. To their surprise, relatively unknown competitors such as Sterilite did not increase prices and quickly took away some of Rubbermaid's market share. Wal-Mart, which accounted for more than 15 percent of Rubbermaid's total household product sales, deleted Rubbermaid from its promotional materials and replaced it with Sterilite.

Rubbermaid was not alone. Wal-Mart, with $240 billion plus in sales in 2004 and 1.3 million employees, is the biggest employer in 21 states, with more people in uniform than the U.S. Army. And Wal-Mart "is pressuring everyone from Bloomingdale's to Banana Republic to compete on price as well as image".[5] If its present growth rate continues by 2006, Wal-Mart's share of the gross domestic product will be the largest ever for any company. This means that as Wal-Mart continues to flex its retailing muscle, other companies must find effective ways to respond, or they will suffer the same fate as Montgomery Ward or Kmart.[6]

Scope of the External Analysis

Analysis of the environment requires thinking on several levels. Managers can examine the environment at four different levels, including the general environment, the industry, strategic groups, and direct competitors.

THE GENERAL ENVIRONMENT   Broad environmental forces may have an impact on a firm even though their consequences may not be apparent or the effect may not be immediate. For instance, most population growth is occurring in third world countries. This means that a huge middle class is developing in such poor countries as India and China. This may represent a market opportunity for some Western firms. The population of the United States and many Western countries is aging rapidly as a result of increasing life expectancies and declining birth rates. Some automobile manufacturers anticipate that the demand for trucks, sport utility vehicles, and vans has peaked, because older people prefer more comfortable cars with a plush feel to them. This has implications for R&D investments, car design, and manufacturing processes.

Sometimes changes in the general environment may be abrupt and unpredictable. For instance, Boeing expected to earn $2.6 billion on sales of $47 billion by the end of 1997. Boeing ended up losing $348 million, in large measure because of a sudden economic crisis in Asia, where it had 35 percent of its backlogged orders. A few years later, Boeing had almost recovered. Then came the terrorist attacks of September 11. Once again, profits plummeted as most airlines in the United States and abroad were faced with empty flights.

The general environment may be broken down into individual segments. These segments include demographic trends, economic conditions, political/legal forces, socio-cultural conditions, technological

Subway's "Eat Fresh" and dieter Jared Fogle help propel the fast food restaurant past the big guys—namely McDonald's and Burger King. By recognizing the changing environment of its consumer—the desire for healthier fast food—Subway became the number one franchise of 2003.

changes, and globalization. Each of these is discussed next. They are not independent segments. A change in one, such as globalization, is likely to affect others, especially socio-cultural conditions.

Demographic Trends The study of population characteristics and trends is demographics. Some may have a direct impact on both current and future business opportunities. These include population size, age distribution, ethnic mix, levels of labor force participation by women and the size and composition of families. A full chapter in the book (11) is devoted to population diversity issues both in the United States and overseas. Demographic information can be useful when formulating strategies. For instance, electronic commerce was touted by many as the wave of the future in the late 1990s. Numerous investors rushed to pump money into Internet stores only to see the majority of them go bankrupt in less than two years. Surprisingly, by the middle of this decade electronic commerce is flourishing despite a weak economy. As described in Management Close-Up 7.c, a major reason for this turnaround is that the demographic characteristics of those using the Internet have changed considerably in the past five years. There are now more women who are Internet users than men. This trend is relevant for e-commerce because, as noted in Management Close-Up 7.c, women do most of the household shopping. The Skills for Managing box 7.2, "Business Implications of an Increasingly Older Population," challenges you to assess the effects of a rapidly aging population on business and the strategies firms may adopt to deal with that demographic change.

The Masses Have Arrived . . . and E-Commerce Will Never Be the Same

THEME: CUSTOMER FOCUS   In the early days of e-commerce, online shoppers were an elite bunch. As a group, they were generally wealthier, younger, and more tech-savvy than the average shopper, and they were predominantly men. The title of the first book sold online by bookseller Amazon.com says a lot about the early Web shopper: *Fluid Concepts and Creative Analogies* is a book about artificial intelligence.

That was then. In 1999, less than a quarter of U.S. households made an online purchase; now, more than a third visit Internet stores. Also the newcomers tend to be older people with lower incomes and less experience with technology. Many are women. In short, the online marketplace is looking like the rest of the marketplace.

This long-awaited maturing of e-commerce holds tremendous implications for online retailing. For one, expect a boost to mainstream retailers like Wal-Mart Stores Inc. and Sears, Roebuck & Co., whose Web stores have gotten off to sluggish starts. At the same time, if e-commerce companies that are already well-established want to continue to compete for the loyalties of these new shoppers, they will have to adjust, offering different products and modifying their delivery policies to include such features as free shipping. Stores also are going to have to be better integrated with online operations to make it easy to research products online and buy them offline.

"This group is different from the first group of customers that came to your site," says Kate Delhagen, retail research director for Forrester Research Inc. in Cambridge, Massachusetts. "Ignore them at your peril."

Shoppers who have been buying online for more than six years have average incomes of $79,300 and 57 percent have college degrees. Only 34 percent were women. In contrast, those who have shopped online for less than one year have average incomes of $52,300 and about 57 percent are women and 39 percent have college degrees.

The appearance online of more women—who directly influence more than 80 percent of all retail spending, according to BIGresearch LLC, a market-research firm in Worthington, Ohio—is a boom for e-commerce. When New York–based Bluefly Inc., a retailer of upscale closeout clothing, was launched in mid-1998, the e-commerce market was still a predominantly male place, and an apparel start-up looked like a sure loser. But the company looked ahead to the day the Internet would attract more women. "We went after this particular category based on the expected shifts," says Jonathan Morris, executive vice-president. "We think that's one of the reasons that we're still here."

The big payoff from e-commerce is probably going to go to bricks-and-mortar retailers that target mainstream shoppers in their offline businesses, such as Sears. Ironically, almost a century ago Sears grew thanks to its mail catalogue sales targeting a rural American with very limited access to shopping centers. Sears suspended catalogue operations in the early 1990s as demographic changes (the rural population is now under 6 percent in comparison to 70 percent a century ago) made them obsolete. Now Sears is quickly gaining ground with "off-premise shoppers" in what may be considered an online version of the old catalogue approach.

Source: Adapted with permission from M. Totty, "The Masses Have Arrived," *Wall Street Journal,* January 27, 2003, p. R-8.

Economic Conditions   The economy of a region surrounding a company has a major impact on the strategic success of that company. Local companies are affected by local economic conditions, regional firms by regional conditions, and national companies by both national and international economic concerns. A sharp economic downturn in Asia during 1999–2003, for instance, had a major negative effect on financial institutions in the United States as well as most larger American manufacturing

BUSINESS IMPLICATIONS OF AN INCREASINGLY OLDER POPULATION

In the richest countries of the world such as in North America and Western Europe, the population is aging rapidly. By 2020, it is estimated that approximately 35 percent of the population will be over 65, and about half will be 50 and older. A recent survey (Wiles, 2003) shows that various age groups have different attitudes toward life, including the willingness to take risks with investments or try new things. While 43 percent of those under 40 are willing to take substantial or above average risk, only 18 percent of those 58 or older are willing to do so.

In this exercise, the class is divided into groups of five. Each group chooses a well-known firm for analysis. It could be an investment bank, a brokerage house, a re-tailer, an educational institution, or a high-technology organization, for example.

1. Each group should first assess how the aging of the population is going to affect the business in the next 20 years.

2. Then each group must provide recommendations for dealing with any anticipated population effects they have identified.

3. A spokesperson from each group should then present the results of the group deliberations to the entire class.

firms. Also, the 20 percent rise of the euro currency against the U.S. dollar between 2002 and 2003 created a substantial hardship for European exporters because it meant that their products had become much more expensive for Americans to buy.

In the modern world, most firms are highly interdependent. The ups and downs in one economic sector are likely to have a ripple effect on other sectors. For this reason, company leaders should be attuned to changes and trends in the economic environment. Management Close-Up 7.d illustrates how the dramatic ripple effects from one economic sector, aerospace, moved to another, machine shops.

Political/Legal Forces   The segment of the environment in which government policies and actions take place also has major effects on firms. Local, state, and federal governments along with the judicial system constantly issue a flurry of new regulations or reinterpretations of past regulations. Some of these produce dramatic effects. Regulatory changes introduced by sovereign governments overseas compound the complexity of political/legal forces. When President George Bush decided to impose a 30 percent tariff on imported steel, other countries quickly responded with a tariff of their own on select American products. Mexican truck drivers are unable to enter the lucrative U.S. transportation market (as stipulated in the NAFTA accords drawn up about a decade

management close-up

Economy Guts Machine Shops

Machinists set up and operate a variety of high-tech machine tools to cut or grind metal, plastic, and other raw materials into parts or products with precise dimensions. Just a few years ago, Stewart Manufacturing was so desperate for machinists that Patrick Stewart recruited kids straight out of high school and searched for do-it-yourselfers at Checker Auto Parts. "If a guy was at all mechanical, I offered him a job and trained him," he said. Recruiting is the furthest thing from Stewart's mind today. The 57-year-old Deer Valley machine shop, which crafts metal into a range of aircraft parts, struggles to keep employees busy in the face of a plunge in aerospace orders. The company has cut 15 percent of its workforce and looked for savings everywhere possible. "It's been pretty brutal," the 33-year-old manager said. "Anybody non-military has just been hit with staggering losses due to the lack of stimulus in the economy and the lack of people flying on airplanes."

The downturn has been well chronicled, headlined by layoffs, losses, and cost-cutting at giant manufacturers like Boeing and Honeywell and their major customers, the airlines. Largely lost in the shuffle has been the hit to the little guys, the suppliers who help keep those businesses humming. In metropolitan Phoenix, small machine shops such as Stewart Manufacturing are hurting like never before. Many shops have closed or scaled back significantly, so much so that one survivor said most of his new work is from competitors that folded. One Tempe firm recently ran a classified ad looking for machining work—not workers—in a bid to save five jobs. Approximately 25 percent of the jobs in the machinery sector disappeared from 2001–2003. "When you dance with the gorilla, the gorilla leads," said veteran Valley machinist Mike Kapel of American Precision Machining, who has hung onto his job. "It's good in good times, but it's dangerous. Everybody has known that for years."

Source: Adapted from D. Gilbertson, "Economy Guts Machine Shops," *Arizona Republic,* February 9, 2003, p. D-1.

---

ago; see Chapter 2) mainly due to political pressure on the part of the American Teamsters Union, which claims that Mexican trucks are unsafe.

Technological changes are occurring so fast that the legal system is having a hard time keeping up. Company leaders seek to develop political strategies to influence evolving legislation that covers new technologies. For instance, there is still no answer to a seemingly simple question: If a consumer buys an item on the Internet, which government entity has the right to collect a sales tax on that item, the state government, local government, or perhaps even a foreign government? As another example, a 120-year-old body of antitrust legislation, including the Sherman Act, designed to prevent monopolies, seems to be outmoded in the Digital Age. This became clear when Microsoft was charged with antitrust violations in the late 1990s under the Sherman Act for monopolizing computer operating systems, thereby engaging in unfair competition against competitors such as Netscape Communication Corp. and Intuit. By 2003 it had become apparent that at least for now Microsoft had won the legal battle, and its dominant position in the operating systems arena had strengthened considerably. Microsoft now controls 93 percent of new PC operating systems, up from 86 percent in 1997, and 96 percent of browsers, up from 67 percent in 1999. As noted by one observer, "From its inception, this case was supposed to prove that trustbusting is still relevant in the

What's This? The French Love McDonald's?

THEME: CUSTOMER FOCUS After teaching the world about haute cuisine, France is ready to offer another culinary lesson: how to sell "le fast food." McDonald's Corp.'s French subsidiary is booming even as the parent company is struggling. The Oak Brook, Illinois, company has been losing both customers and revenues. Yet, as the parent closes 175 outlets worldwide, a new McDonald's opens in France every six days, and the typical French customer spends $9 per visit, versus only $4 in the United States, even though a Big Mac costs about the same in Paris as it does in New York.

Just as remarkably, McDonald's France appears to be breaking every rule in an efficiency-obsessed industry. It's spending lavishly to refit restaurants with chic interiors and extras such as music videos that entice customers to linger over their meals. And while McDonald's in the United States has tried to speed up service by streamlining menus, France has gone in the opposite direction, adding items such as a hot ham-and-cheese sandwich dubbed the Croque McDo. "We are upgrading the experience, making

McDonald's a destination restaurant," says Denis Hennequin, the French unit's chief executive.

McDonald's France also has defused criticism by adapting its restaurant designs to blend with local architecture. Some outlets in the Alps now boast wood-and-stone interiors reminiscent of a chalet. "The atmosphere is friendly," says Marie Schwinnt, a 16-year-old eating lunch at a McDonald's in a 19th-century building in Mulhouse, in eastern France.

The updated styling, now found in about half of McDonald's 950 French outlets, doesn't come cheap. Michel Reglat, a Toulouse franchisee, redid the interiors of 12 of his 14 restaurants, including one with barstools made from bicycle seats. Reglat figures he spent 20 percent more than if he'd used McDonald's standard designs. Sales at these spruced-up outlets, however, have soared as much as 20 percent.

Source: Adapted with permission from L. Matlock and G. Pallavi, "What's This? The French Love McDonald's?" *Business Week,* January 13, 2003, p. 50. See also M. Gogoi and M. Arndt, "Hamburger Hell," *Business Week,* March 3, 2003, pp. 104–108.

Digital Age. When the Justice Department sued the company in 1998, it argued that the century-old Sherman Antitrust Act could be applied swiftly and predictably to police high-tech monopolies. These claims now look pretty dubious."[7]

Part of the reason Microsoft was able to influence the court was a strong consumer preference for a common operating system. In other words, isn't it nice to send and open an attachment in the same manner in Washington, D.C., as you would in Moscow? As the digital economy evolves, antitrust legislation may need to change accordingly in order to accommodate these "natural monopolies" in which consumers have reasons to prefer unified technical standards.

Socio-cultural Conditions This part of the environment consists of the norms, values, and preferences of a society. These change over time, and vary by country or even by geographical area within a country. In general, firms are more likely to succeed if they can adapt products and services to prevalent socio-cultural conditions. For instance, McDonald's has recently surprised many of its competitors by being able to crack the fastidious French market (see Management Close-Up 7.e "What's This? The French Love McDonald's?"). Ironically, McDonald's has suffered declining sales in the United States, because many people are leery of unhealthy fried fast food.

Barbie Dolls, which are produced by Mattel, became a hit in the 1950s by capturing children's imaginations through what American society considered universal signs of beauty at the time: blond hair, blue eyes, large breasts, pale white skin, long legs. As the civil rights movement took hold in the 1960s, large number of non-European immigrants entered the United States, and international markets became more diverse, Mattel had little choice but to change Barbie or see its market slowly disappear. Barbie now comes in all colors and ethnic types, appealing to a wider variety of prospective buyers.

Technological Changes   The segment of the environment in which new knowledge is created and transformed into innovative products, services, or inputs is the technological environment. As the knowledge base increases, it is easier to create new knowledge or recombine existing knowledge to develop new products, processes, and materials. It took society thousands of years to create the first computer. Yet, it wasn't long ago when mainframe computers in 4,000 square feet of floor space could do less than a contemporary 2×2, one-pound personal computer can do now. In some product lines, such as software, the life cycle is measured in months, because new software quickly makes prior software obsolete.

By increasing productivity, technology can greatly decrease production costs. This, in turn, is reflected in product prices. DVD players were considered a luxury around the year 2000 with prices generally exceeding $1,000 dollars each. They now are priced at about $80, and many have better features than their more expensive predecessors. A similar downward price trend is expected for the flat, widescreen TVs which currently sell in the $3,000–$12,000 range.

More than ever before, firms must keep abreast of technological changes to remain competitive. Bill Gates, the founder of what is possibly the most economically powerful business organization in history, is fond of saying that "Microsoft is three months away from bankruptcy." As noted earlier, he is referring to the constant fear that a competitor will develop a better and cheaper technology that will quickly replace Microsoft's market dominance. While this is unlikely to happen any time soon, it is not as farfetched as it may seem. For instance, the free Linux operating system, an alternative to Microsoft's software, is rapidly catching on and threatening Microsoft as a result.[8]

Globalization   In a world that continues to get smaller, firms are becoming increasingly dependent on foreign markets for raw materials as well as for processing and the sale of products and services (see Chapter 2). In many cases, it is difficult to define what is "domestic" and what is "foreign," as companies divvy up production processes and other essential activities, such as R&D and marketing, across different countries. These

By opening franchises around the world, McDonald's has been successful in its global expansion strategy, but can it continue to guarantee (relatively) that a Big Mac anywhere in Russia, is the same as a Big Mac in the United States?

borderless strategic alliances and joint ventures with various ownership configurations are increasingly more common. For instance, is Mazda a Japanese firm even though Ford Motor Company is its major shareholder and Ford's executives play an active role in managing the company? Did DaimlerChrysler become a German or an American firm after Daimler from Germany bought Chrysler, even though most of Chrysler's facilities are in the United States and Mexico? Should Toyota's plants in Kentucky be considered Japanese or American even though they are completely staffed by Americans?

As boundaries between domestic and foreign markets are becoming blurred, company leaders must be aware of the impact of the global environment. There may be little choice but to draw needed resources from foreign sources, which means that they need to effectively manage the degree of resource dependence. Lack of preparation or overindulgence may spell disaster. This is illustrated in the case of chocolate manufacturers whose sales and profits took a sudden drop in 2003. The reason, as noted in Management Close-Up 7.f ("This Year, Say It with Flowers"), was a civil war in a distant country, Ivory Coast.

THE INDUSTRY ENVIRONMENT An industry is composed of a group of firms with products that can substitute for one another. In the computer industry, the consumer may substitute an IBM PC for an Apple Macintosh. The industry environment has a direct effect on a firm's strategic competitiveness. This input is greater than the general environment, because firms within an industry are competing for a share of the same market.

 Porter's Five Forces

The best-known framework for analyzing the industry environment was developed by Harvard professor Michael Porter.[9] According to this framework, the five forces within an industry are: the threat of new entrants, the threat of substitutes, suppliers, customers, and intensity of rivalry among competitors.

This Year, Say It With Flowers

THEME: DEALING WITH CHANGE   Slipping your sweetheart some chocolates on Valentine's Day may leave you with a bitter aftertaste. A civil war in Ivory Coast, the world's largest producer of cocoa, is making chocolate more expensive. One-third of the African coastal nation's cocoa crop has been blocked from harvest and export by rebel fighting after a September 2002 coup. Cocoa prices on New York and London markets have risen to $2,354 per metric ton, up 76 percent from a year earlier and up nearly 350 percent from the December 2000 price of $674.

Chocolate producers Nestlé and Lindt have been forced to increase retail prices to recover some of these costs. Still, it is clear that they can pass down only a small portion of the increased cost to consumers. After all, consumers might shift to chocolate substitutes or simply stop making purchases. Staggering losses may be the result unless the civil war subsides or a cheaper alternative can be found.

Source: Adapted with permission from N. Majidi, "This Year, Say It with Flowers," *Business Week*, February 17, 2003, p. 10.

The Threat of New Entrants   New competitors can change an industry overnight. Unless product demand is increasing, a new entrant is likely to take away part of the market and earnings enjoyed by existing firms.

The threat of new entrants decreases as barriers to entry and fear of retaliation by current industry participants increase. Obstacles that serve as roadblocks to prevent new companies from becoming part of an industry are called *barriers to entry*. Examples include the following.

- The government can restrict entry. For instance, trucking and liquor retailing are regulated. The costs of complying with government regulations discourages some potential entrants, and requirements such as liquor licenses may serve to limit the number of operating establishments a governmental body will allow.

- Intellectual property that is legally protected may keep firms out of the industry. For instance, Kodak could not enter the field of instant photography until the basic patents held by Polaroid had expired.

- Capital requirements may be so high that few firms have the resources to enter and few, if any, financial institutions are willing to lend them money. This would be the case for a new firm trying to enter the automobile manufacturing industry.

- If strong brand identification already exists within the industry, prospective entrants would have to spend heavily in marketing to overcome a consumer's natural inclination to purchase familiar brands.

- New entrants may not enjoy the cost advantages that help existing firms remain profitable. These include economies of scale from large size, favorable locations, and existing plants and equipment.

- New entrants may find it difficult to enter established distribution channels. For instance, they may have to use costly marketing campaigns, price breaks, and easy credit to get space on super-market shelves.

Competitors may also be reluctant to enter a market if they believe that existing firms will react strongly. For instance, a new airline has low probability of surviving for very long because existing airlines use fare wars, premiums for passengers flying certain routes, and easy up-grades to first class to beat the competition. New airlines still enter the market from time to time, but many entrepreneurs and investors have probably been dissuaded from launching a new carrier because of fears of retaliation.

At the same time, the Internet is eroding barriers to entry by allow-ing new firms access to a global customer base. One observer notes that the Web is making high-end fashion as accessible to shoppers in Peoria as to those in Paris.[10]

The Threat of Substitutes Technological changes may lead to the dis-covery and manufacturing of new products that supplant existing prod-ucts. Higher quality, lower costs, more features, and safety considerations may induce consumers to shift preferences from the old to the new. For instance, cheaper hardened plastics can now be used for automobile chas-sis in place of metal, posing a major threat to steel and aluminum compa-nies that depend on the automobile industry for a substantial portion of their revenues. Likewise, cellulose, Styrofoam, and rock wool are increas-ingly replacing traditional fiberglass as insulation.

Suppliers It is almost impossible to find a self-sufficient firm. Firms purchase inputs from suppliers and transform them to create products or services. Human resources are supplied by universities, trade schools, and other firms; raw materials are obtained from distributors, whole-salers, trading houses, and mining companies; and capital is supplied by banks, individual investors, and venture capitalists.

Suppliers can affect the cost of inputs, such as when a strong union sets a high wage for a particular craft. Dependence may pose a major threat to the firm if the skills are essential to the firm's production process. In other words, greater dependence on a particular supplier increases the power of that supplier to impose terms on the buyer. This dependence in-creases if the buyer has few other sources of supply, the supplier has many other buyers, satisfactory substitutes for the input are not available, or the cost of changing suppliers is significant.

Customers Another major force in the industry is customers, who look for higher quality and the best service at the lowest price. Customers en-joy more bargaining power and negotiate better terms when they pur-chase a large portion of the firm's output, the product is important to

Actions and Counteractions of Competitors: The Case of AT&T

THEME: DEALING WITH CHANGE Telecommunications giant AT&T entered the credit card business with a bang in the 1990s. The firm blanketed the United States with card offers and promised no annual fees for life to consumers who signed up for the card. The AT&T Universal Card turned a profit ahead of plan and snagged a Malcolm Baldrige National Quality Award in 1992.

AT&T's venture into the credit card business started a continuing brutal competition. The aggressive marketing "changed the future landscape of the credit-card industry," says Visa U.S.A. CEO Carl F. Pascarella. Consumers hold a record amount of bad debt, having signed up for record numbers of credit cards, "maxing out" one card as they signed up for the next one. Delinquencies on credit card accounts continue to rise, while the top bank issuers have seen their return on assets halved since 1990, with average returns on assets currently at 1 percent or less. Consolidation among credit card issuers is rampant as banks try to build sufficient scale to survive on thinning margins.

AT&T Universal was the biggest victim of its own price war. Other card issuers not only matched AT&T's no-fee offer—they also began offering below-prime teaser rates to attract new customers. When AT&T Universal scrambled to keep up, it was forced to target riskier customers and to use even more aggressive solicitation techniques. The resulting losses decimated the unit's profits and its return on assets fell well below the industry average. In 1998 Citicorp acquired AT&T's Universal Card services.

"This company could be a Harvard business school case study on how to build the most successful business in the country and then just as quickly how to destroy it," says one former AT&T Universal senior executive.

Sources: Adapted with permission from D. Sparks, A. Barrett, and P. Elstrom, "The Bitter Legacy of the AT&T Card," *Business Week,* December 29, 1997, pp. 32–34; A. Kupfer, "AT&T: Will the Pieces Come Together?" *Fortune,* April 26, 1999, pp. 82–86; *Citicorp Annual Report 1998.*

them, close substitutes are easily available, and the products are relatively standardized or undifferentiated.

Intensity of Rivalry among Competitors Firms use price, product differentiation, and product innovation to improve their market positions. Product differentiation includes extended warranties, "free" options, customer service, and user friendliness. Product innovations are new features that competitors don't yet offer. Typically one firm's action causes a reaction from other firms, as illustrated in Management Close-Up 7.g. A firm that makes a bold move to capture more of the market can expect retaliation from other players in the industry. For instance, airlines almost always match the price cuts of competitors, and they are quick to imitate any differentiating features of competitors. When Continental credited triple miles rather than actual miles flown as part of its frequent-flyer program, most major airlines promptly followed suit. Robert Crandall, CEO of American Airlines, summarized the competitive environment of the industry as "intensely, vigorously, bitterly, savagely competitive."[11]

The intensity of competitive rivalry increases with the number of competitors. Other factors that cause competitive rivalry to increase are slow industry growth, unused productive capacity, undifferentiated services, and high exit barriers, such as major costs incurred by a firm in purchasing specialized plant and equipment.

STRATEGIC GROUPS The management team must also examine the opportunities and threats in the external environment by focusing on the moves of competitors that follow similar strategies. A *strategic group* consists of a cluster of firms within an industry that tend to adopt common strategies of technological leadership, quality standards, prices, distribution channels, and customer service.[12] Ford, Chevrolet, and Toyota are in a different cluster than Mercedes, BMW, and Rolls-Royce. Similarly, Wal-Mart and Target are more likely competitors to Kmart than to Dillard's and Macy's. Such groups may be difficult to identify, and firms may have products that could belong to different strategic groups. However, many managers find it useful to closely track the behaviors of their closest competitors within the industry.

COMPETITOR ANALYSIS It is helpful to conduct a detailed study of each company that management considers a major competitor. Company leaders obtain data from a variety of sources including trade fairs, court records, annual reports, and competitor brochures. These data may be used to make educated inferences about competitor's goals and objectives, current strategies, strengths and weaknesses, and possible competitive moves. Deloitte & Touche estimates that 58 percent of firms have a formal process for obtaining competitor intelligence information, and that the rest use informal methods.[13]

The Skills for Managing Box 7.3, "Conducting an Environmental Analysis," challenges you to identify the external factors that are most likely to impact the success of a business of your choice.

The Internal Environment

Every company has something that it does well. These are called "core competencies." Along with an analysis of the external environment, company executives should identify the resources, capabilities, and knowledge the firm has that may be used to exploit market opportunities and avoid potential threats. The **resource-based view** argues that basing a business strategy on what the firm is capable of doing provides a more sustainable competitive advantage than basing it on external opportunities. This is so because "customer preferences are volatile, the identity of customers is changing, and the technologies for serving customer requirements are developing rapidly, [so] an externally focused orientation does not provide the constancy of direction to act as a secure foundation for formulating long-term strategy."[14]

Since 1948 Honda has successfully used its expertise in the design and development of engines to manufacture and sell motorcycles, cars, and such gasoline-based engines as ground tillers, lawn mowers, pumps,

> **resource-based view**
> A strategic management viewpoint that basing business strategy on what the firm is capable of doing provides a more sustainable competitive advantage than basing it on external opportunities.

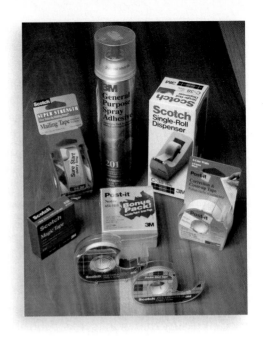

Some of 3M's products, built from the firm's development of its adhesive and thin-film technology.

and chainsaws. Likewise, 3M has used its knowledge of adhesive and thin-film technology for more than three generations to produce a broad range of successful products including Scotch Tape, magnetic tape, Post-it Notes, and adhesives that help heal minor cuts.

While a thorough understanding of company resources and capabilities can help the management team select a strategy that exploits these internal assets, no company can remain in business for very long unless there is a market for its products and services. Thus, even firms that base strategies on the internal environment must continuously monitor the external environment to devise appropriate responses to external opportunities and threats. Firms such as Sony, Black & Decker, Marks & Spencer, BMW, Motorola, and Intel attribute much of their long-term success to the ability to link information from the external environment, such as changing consumer tastes, shifting demographics, competitor's intelligence information, and new technologies, to internal resources and capabilities.

The model shown in Figure 7.2 summarizes much of this process. First, management needs to identify resources that provide the company with greater strength than competitors. Second, they should define company capabilities, or what it can do better than competitors. Third, it is important to ascertain what can be done to provide a sound basis for creating, sustaining, and exploiting a competitive advantage. Fourth, choose a strategy that best exploits the company's capabilities relative to external opportunities. Finally, delineate resource gaps that need to be filled to successfully carry out the chosen strategy. Sony is an excellent example of a firm that has been able to achieve this with great success, as shown in Management Close-Up 7.h.

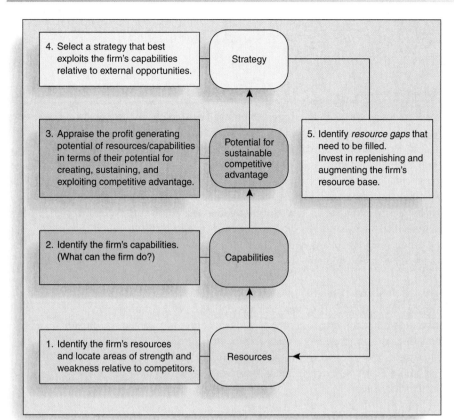

FIGURE 7.2

Core Competencies and
Market Opportunities

Source: From R. M. Grant,
Contemporary Strategy Analysis.
Copyright © 2001 Blackwell
Publishers. Reprinted with
permission of Blackwell
Publishers, Malden, MA.

Resource Types

Many ingredients must be combined effectively to create an advantage for the company. These resources include a wide spectrum of inputs that firms use to deliver products and services. Capital, equipment, talents of employees and managers, patents, and brand names are key resources that may be tangible or intangible.

TANGIBLE RESOURCES   Financial resources, physical assets, and workers are all **tangible resources** which can be observed and quantified. A strategic assessment of tangible resources should enable management to efficiently use them to support the company and to expand the volume of business. The management team may also be able to find more profitable uses for tangible resources.

INTANGIBLE RESOURCES   Items which are difficult to quantify and include on a balance sheet often provide the firm with the strongest competitive advantage. These **intangible assets** are invisible and not obvious,

tangible resources

Assets that can be quantified and observed, including financial resources, physical assets, and manpower.

intangible resources

Resources that are difficult to quantify and include on a balance sheet, which often provide the firm with the strongest competitive advantage.

Using Internal Resources and Capabilities to Remain on Top

THEME: DEALING WITH CHANGE Sony has become one of the most respected brands in the United States and one of the most profitable large corporations in the world by using its core competency in multimedia technology to capture the market through continuous innovation. The company's original success came from products like transistor radios, the Walkman personal stereo, and Trinitron televisions, which took advantage of unique technological advances such as miniaturization. Sony's competitive edge in such stand-alone products as Walkmans diminished, however, as music and video were rendered digitally on computers.

In the late 1990s, Sony took advantage of its technological resources to move into the digital world. The firm began producing digital products such as videogame machines, high-resolution videodiscs, and passport-size videocameras and still cameras that plug into personal computers. Sony also collaborated on personal computers with Intel, netsurfing hardware with Microsoft, and telephones and pagers with San Diego-based Qualcomm.

Sony's goal of dominating the global multimedia entertainment and electronics industries was summed up in its *Annual Report 2000* letter to shareholders: "During the year ended March 31, 2000, Sony began to take major steps to refashion itself as a company that can continue to grow in the network era of the 21st century." Sony chairman and CEO Nobuyuki Idei also outlined the company's strategy. "While accelerating strategies aimed at the broadband network era, we are striving to reinvigorate and to strengthen the fundamentals of the core electronics business by applying information technologies to product design, production, distribution, and sales."

Says Idei, "Convergence is happening not only between audio and video but between computers and communication. There is a fundamental change in society, and this is our opportunity." When it comes to winning the world's admiration, Sony has managed to stay ahead of the pack. A 2003 poll of 10,000 executives, directors, and analysts in 25 countries shows that Sony, along with Toyota Motor and BMW, is ranked in the top three of the world's most admired companies.[15]

Sources: Adapted with permission from F. Gibney, "A New World at Sony," *Time,* November 17, 1997, pp. 56–57; I. M. Kunii, "Sony's Shake Up," *Business Week,* March 22, 1999, pp. 52–54; B. Schlender, "Sony's New Game," *Fortune,* April 12, 1999, pp. 30–31; *Sony Annual Report 2000,* year ended March 31, 2000; and N. Stein, "America's Most Admired Companies," *Fortune,* March 3, 2003, pp. 81–98.

and are difficult for competitors to purchase or imitate. The three most strategically important intangible resources are the firm's reputation, technology, and human capital.

Reputation   Other things being equal, consumers tend to buy products or services from a firm that is held in high regard. Many customers are even willing to pay more for that firm's recognizable brand. Reputation reduces uncertainty and risk. For years, IBM was able to sell personal computers at prices which were 50 percent more than competitors because the IBM name was synonymous with reliability and excellent customer service. When Nestlé acquired the British chocolate manufacturer Rowntree in the late 1980s, the bid price exceeded the book value of Rowntree's assets by more than 500 percent, an indication of the value of Rowntree's brand names Kit Kat and After Eights. Harley-Davidson stock went up faster than competitors' during the 1990s because the Harley name supported a price premium of about 40 percent above that of comparable motorcycles. A recent worldwide survey found that the most valuable brands include Coca-Cola, Microsoft, IBM, GE, and Nokia.[16]

Technology   Valuable patents, copyrights, and trade secrets that competitors don't have are all examples of the various technological advantages companies can enjoy. Also, the ability to create new technology faster than competitors or to make more efficient use of existing technology creates a sustained advantage. For example, Affymetrix, Inc., based in Santa Clara, California, recently pioneered a technology that allows up to 60,000 gene sequences to be scanned in one step. Licensing this technology to pharmaceutical companies enables them to more precisely target certain drugs to meet the needs of the patient; and it may fundamentally alter the treatment of many types of cancer.[17]

Human Capital   The skills, knowledge, reasoning, and decision-making abilities of the workforce which support a firm's innovation and productivity reflect the value of the human capital present in the company. Human capital can provide a very strong core competence that other firms cannot imitate in the following ways:

- Knowledge resides in people's minds, so it is unique to the employees in each firm.
- The ability to harness human resources depends on the integrated achievement of interdependent individual employees and their willingness to collaboratively use their talents to support the firm's mission. That is, capabilities are created from teams of people working together, which represents an asset that is specific to the firm.
- It takes a long time to develop a core competence. Competitors are unlikely to assume the cost and risk of trying to duplicate it.
- The organization's culture may play a key role in how well people work together to achieve organizational objectives. Culture is idiosyncratic to each organization, which means it is a unique competitive factor.

Analyzing the Firm's Capabilities

Successful organizations excel or have the potential to excel in a specific activity. The Federal Express guarantee of next-day delivery anywhere within the United States is such a competitive advantage. British retailer Marks & Spencer ensures a high and consistent level of product quality across a wide range of merchandise through meticulously managed supplier relationships. General Electric reconciles control, coordination, flexibility, and innovation in one of the world's largest and most diversified corporations.

TABLE 7.1

Analyzing Capabilities by Functional Areas

FUNCTIONAL AREA	CAPABILITY	EXAMPLES
Corporate management	Effective financial control systems	Hanson, Exxon
	Expertise in strategic control of diversified corporation	General Electric, ABB
	Effectiveness in motivating and coordinating divisional and business-unit management	Shell
	Management of acquisitions	ConAgra, BTR
	Values-driven, in-touch corporate leadership	Wal-Mart, FedEx
Information management	Comprehensive and effective MIS network, with strong central coordination	American Airlines, L. L. Bean
Research and development	Capability in basic research	Merck, AT&T
	Ability to develop innovative new products	Sony, 3M
	Speed of new product development	Canon, Mazda
Manufacturing	Efficiency in volume manufacturing	Briggs & Stratton
	Capacity for continual improvements in production processes	Toyota, Nucor
	Flexibility and speed of response	Benetton, Worthington Industries
Product design	Design capability	Pinifarini, Apple
Marketing	Brand management and brand promotion	Procter & Gamble, PepsiCo
	Promoting and exploiting reputation for quality	American Express, DaimlerChrysler
	Responsive to market trends	The Gap, Campbell Soup
Sales and distribution	Effectiveness in promoting and executing sales	Microsoft, Glaxo
	Efficiency and speed of distribution	FedEx, The Limited
	Quality and effectiveness of customer service	Walt Disney Co., Marks & Spencer

Source: From R. M. Grant, *Contemporary Strategy Analysis,* copyright © 2001 Blackwell Publishers. Reprinted with permission of Blackwell Publishers, Malden, MA: Blackwell, 2001, p. 129.

functional analysis

A strategic management approach that establishes organizational capabilities for each of the major functional areas of the business.

value-chain analysis

Strategic management analysis that breaks the firm down into a sequential series of activities and attempts to identify the value-added of each activity.

Company leaders can choose from three approaches to examine their capabilities. The first analyzes organizational capabilities for each of the major functional areas of the business. Table 7.1 is an example of how a **functional analysis** is conducted. This type of approach is easy for most people to understand, and provides the basis for meaningful discussion of the firm's strategy.

The second method breaks the firm down into a sequential series of activities and attempts to identify the value-added of each activity. It is normally referred to as a **value-chain analysis.** Figure 7.3 shows the categories that may be used to analyze the value chain of a manufacturing company. Michael Porter developed a more elaborate model for an-

part three Management Strategy and Decision Making

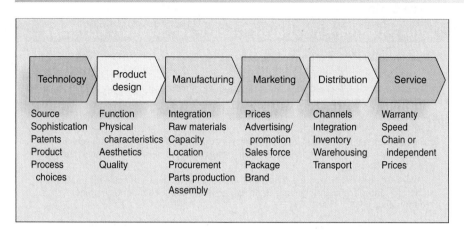

FIGURE 7.3

A Simple Value Chain: McKinsey & Company's "Business System"

Source: From R. M. Grant, *Contemporary Strategy Analysis*, copyright © 2001 Blackwell Publishers. Reprinted with permission of Blackwell Publishers.

alyzing the value chain. He distinguishes between primary activities, concerned with the transformation of inputs and outputs, and direct customer contact and support activities, which make it possible to effectively carry out the primary activities. In other words, rather than analyzing the firm's capabilities in terms of what different functions contribute, Porter suggests that it is better to identify those activities that create value and those that do not. This approach has the distinct advantage of focusing the analysis on value creation. That is, it can help managers determine the extent to which the value created by a particular activity is greater than the cost incurred to create that value. This is referred to as "margin." The greater the margin, the better. Table 7.2 lists the items Porter suggests should be studied to assess the margin (net value creation) of primary and support activities. To be a source of competitive advantage, the firm must be able to obtain a margin from the activity that is superior to that of competitors. Thus, a value chain analysis requires an examination of each activity relative to each competitor's abilities. In the long run, the firm will lose market share to competitors if the company routinely extracts a lower margin from primary and support activities.

While theoretically useful for understanding competitive advantage, the value chain concept is difficult to apply in practice. For one thing, it may be impossible to meaningfully assess the net value added (margin) of singular primary or support activity. Company activities tend to be so intertwined that they are seldom carried out in isolation. For instance, customer service, which is a primary activity, is unlikely to be superior if product quality is deficient (a production issue, which is also a primary activity) or if recruits are poorly trained (a human resource issue, a support activity). Making those comparisons in relation to competitors is even more difficult because this information is very hard to obtain.

TABLE 7.2

Value-Creating Potential of Primary and Support Activities

Primary Activities. These are related to physical conversion of raw inputs into final product form, sale, and distribution to buyers and service after sale, including:

- Inbound logistics. This includes materials handling, purchasing, inventory holding, and scheduling of reorders.
- Production. This includes machining, packaging, assembly, quality control, and equipment maintenance.
- Sales and marketing. This includes advertising and promotional campaigns, selection of appropriate distribution channels, the training and development of sales force, and public relations efforts.
- Dealer support and customer service. This includes the full range of activities related to customer interface including supplies to dealer, installation repair, and customer information.

Support Activities. These facilitate, expedite, or make possible the execution of primary activities, and consist of:

- Administrative infrastructure. This includes such activities as accounting, legal support, financial planning and budgeting, and documentation.
- Technology, research, development and design. This includes such activities as process equipment, project management, information technology, and product or service innovation.
- Procurement. This includes the acquisition of inputs needed to produce the firm's products and services such as raw material and supplies, laboratory equipment, and office equipment.
- Human resource management and development. This includes recruitment, selection, training, performance, appraisal, and compensation of the workforce.

Source: Adapted with permission from M. E. Porter, (1988). *Competitive Advantage: Creating and Sustaining Superior Performance.* Boston: The Free Press, pp. 39–43.

A third approach assesses capabilities by comparing the firm's activities or functions with those of other firms. This approach, normally referred to as **benchmarking,** has four stages:

benchmarking

A strategic management approach that assesses capabilities by comparing the firm's activities or functions with those of other firms.

1. Identifying activities or functions that are weak and need improvement.
2. Identifying firms that are known to be at the leading edge of each of these activities or functions.
3. Studying the leading-edge firms by visiting them, talking to managers and employees, and reading trade publications to ascertain how and why they perform so well.
4. Using the information gathered to redefine goals, modify processes, acquire new resources, and engage in other activities to improve the firm's functions.

Benchmarking has been used as an important strategic tool by a number of well-known companies. It played a central role in the revitalization of Xerox during the 1980s. Detailed comparisons of Xerox copiers and those of competing manufacturers revealed that Japanese rivals made copiers at half the cost in half the time and with half as many workers. Xerox's defects per thousand in assembly were 10 to 30 times greater than those of Japanese competitors. The result was the establishment of a continuous program of benchmarking in which every Xerox department is encouraged to look globally to identify "best in class" companies against which to benchmark. Similarly, ICL, the British computer subsidiary of Fujitsu, benchmarks against the manufacturing processes of Sun Microsystems and the distribution system of the retailer Marks & Spencer.

In the end, all approaches used to analyze the firm's capabilities have advantages as well as disadvantages. And while there is no model or rule that is clearly best for every situation, having an understanding of all of these perspectives (functional, value chain or benchmarking) can help strategists make better decisions and form higher quality strategies.

Strategic Intent and Mission

The second component of the strategic management process (following the analysis of the external and internal environment) consists of formal statements of strategic intent and mission (refer back to Figure 7.1). **Strategic intent** is internally focused, indicating how the firm will use its resources, capabilities, and core competencies. It guides future actions and focuses employee attention on using their talents to outdo competitors. Several large firms express their strategic intent as follows:

strategic intent

The firm's internally focused definition of how the firm intends to use its resources, capabilities, and core competencies to win competitive battles.

- Unocal Corporation: "To become a high performance multinational energy company—not the biggest, but the best."

- Eli Lilly and Company: "It is our strategic intent that customers worldwide view us as their most valued pharmaceutical partner."

- Intel: "We intend to become the premier building block supplier to the computer industry."

- Microsoft: "To provide the Yellow Pages for an electronic marketplace of on-line information systems."[18]

A firm's **strategic mission** flows from its strategic intent, defining the company's external focus in terms of what will be produced and marketed, utilizing the firm's internally based core competence. Figure 7.4 reproduces ChevronTexaco's strategic mission statement, which is distributed to all employees.

This is a good point to remind you again that even though the components of the strategic management process have been presented one at a time (following the model in Figure 7.1), they are not completely separate from each other nor do they cover every element. This is particularly true in the case of the firm's strategic intent and mission. For a brand new entrepreneurial firm being built from the ground up the strategic management process is fairly straightforward. First, the entrepreneur looks

strategic mission

The firm's externally focused definition of what it plans to produce and market, utilizing its internally based core competence.

CONDUCTING AN ENVIRONMENTAL ANALYSIS

A firm uses an environmental analysis to explore the nature of the environment relevant to the firm and to relate the characteristics of the external environment to the firm's internal environment.

Assume you are about to start a new business that will offer a wide range of products and services to clients around the globe. You are in the process of putting together your business plan and are thinking about the challenges that your business will face. The better prepared you are for the competitive challenges, the more likely your business will succeed.

You have just read that organizations are open systems, which means that they are affected by the characteristics of their business environment. This makes sense to you, but you aren't quite sure with which characteristics of the environment you should be concerned.

Form groups of three to five members. Each group chooses a particular type of business that it would like to start. Be as specific as possible about the business; for example, a fast-food restaurant selling Mexican food, or a retailer of imported boutique clothing. Team members work together on the following questions:

1. Discuss your perceptions of the business environment for your business. Determine environmental characteristics you believe will have an impact on it. Consider the business environment with respect to these characteristics, how these areas are changing, and how they affect the way your group would manage the business. The characteristics might include (but aren't limited to)

   a. Competition (e.g., intensity, competitors, tactics).

   b. Customers (e.g., demands, needs, loyalty, location).

   c. Events that affect your business (e.g., predictability, certainty, obviousness).

   d. Political/technological forces.

   e. Knowledge (e.g., pace of obsolescence, complexity, requirements, learning).

   f. Change (e.g., pace, controllability, predictability, obsolescence).

2. Determine the four environmental characteristics that your group feels will have the most impact on the success of the business. List each characteristic, explain why your group believes it is an important force affecting your business, and describe how the internal environment should be molded to deal effectively with those forces (such as its resources, capabilities, core competencies, control mechanism).

Source: Janet Wohlberg, Gail Gilmore, and Steven Wolff, *OB in Action: Cases and Exercises,* 5th Ed. Copyright © 1998 by Houghton Mifflin Company. Used with permission.

for opportunities in the environment, and then defines strategic intent and mission to take advantage of those opportunities. For instance, according to legend, Kenmons Wilson became irate at shoddy accommodations during a family vacation in the early 1950s, and sitting at night in a hotel room he dreamed up a new business whose mission would be "to provide comfortable, child-friendly, inexpensive lodging." This led to a motel chain offering customers high-quality accommodations anywhere in the world. Wilson built the first Holiday Inn in Memphis in 1952. At the time of his death in 2003 there were 3,000 motels worldwide bearing the Holiday Inn name.[19]

FIGURE 7.4

The ChevronTexaco Way

The ChevronTexaco Way explains who we are, what we do, what we believe and what we plan to accomplish.

It establishes a common understanding not only for those of us who work here, but for all who interact with us.

VISION

At the heart of the ChevronTexaco Way is our vision . . . to be the global energy company most admired for its people, partnership and performance.

Our vision means

- Providing energy products and services that are vital to society's quality of life
- Being known as people with superior capabilites and commitment, both as individuals and as an organization
- Thinking and behaving globally, and valuing the positive influence this has on our company
- Being the partner of choice because we best exemplify collaboration
- Delivering world-class performance
- Earning the admiration of all stakeholders— investors, customers, host governments, local communities and our employees—not only for the goals we achieve but how we achieve them

A Strategic Mission Statement: The ChevronTexaco Way

Source: Reprinted with permission of Chevron Texaco Corporation, 2003. All rights reserved.

As firms mature, the strategic management process is not as clear-cut. Why? Very few firms can radically change their strategic intent and mission in search for new opportunities in the external and internal environment. Most established companies have invested large sums of money in plant, equipment, and human resources to accomplish a mission. Thus, they are more likely to focus on those aspects of the environment that are relevant to their already existing strategic intent and mission. Another way of looking at it is that the firm's strategic intent and mission restrict how managers view the environment. Over the long term, however, a firm whose strategic intent and mission are incongruent with the environment is unlikely to continue to be successful, and may face extinction. Think of what would have happened to DuPont had it remained faithful to its original mission in the 19th century: the production of dynamite for use in coal mines. Instead, by diversifying into a variety of chemicals, DuPont seized on new opportunities as they became available and grew and prospered as a result.

Examples of Poor Strategy Formulation

THEME: CUSTOMER FOCUS Korean automaker Daewoo formulated a low-cost strategy to increase its market share in the automobile industry. In Britain it offered its first 1,000 customers trade-ins after six months for new models at no charge. Customers in the United States were offered three cut-rate models, starting with the $9,000 Lanos hatchback, aimed at college students. Korean customers were offered car loans with no interest for up to 30 months. In India Daewoo offered $2,500 discounts per car. Misjudging how the market would react to such low prices for automobiles in the late 1990s resulted in great losses and little increase in sales. Car sales plunged and losses mounted; in late 2000 the firm was undergoing restructuring after declaring bankruptcy, and General Motors was contemplating purchasing the company.

Quaker Oats divested itself of its pet food businesses to focus on beverages, paying $1.7 billion in 1994 to acquire Snapple Beverages, a move that seemed logical but that ultimately led to the downfall of Quaker. Not only did the firm overestimate the synergy among its beverages, it found that managing Snapple and its distribution system was different from managing Gatorade. The firm was also faced with unexpected aggressive competition from Coca-Cola's Fruitopia and PepsiCo's Lipton Tea. As a result, Quaker's overall performance suffered significantly. In 1997 Quaker sold Snapple for $300 million to Triarc Restaurant Group (three years later Triarc's Snapple Beverage Group was sold to Cadbury Schweppes for $910 million), and in late 2000 PepsiCo was in the preliminary stages of buying Quaker.

Car rental companies neglected their core business until they achieved independence from the major automakers. General Motors, Ford, and Chrysler each owned at least part of car rental companies. In the early 1990s, the car rental companies received so many incentives to take new cars from the Detroit automakers' unsold inventories that the rental companies made more money actually buying and selling cars than renting them. Many of the rental car companies lost the focus of their business and did not see the need to update technology and reservation systems. In the mid-1990s, the automakers' cash incentives to rental car companies dried up; the car rental companies ended up with too many cars and began to lose money. Only by splitting away from the automakers could the car rental companies reestablish profitability.

The above examples illustrate how losing track of the firm's primary customer focus leads to major problems in strategy formulation.

Sources: J. Veale, "How Daewoo Ran Itself Off the Road," *Business Week,* August 30, 1999, p. 48; M. A. Hitt, D. R. Ireland, and R. E. Hoskisson, *Strategic Management,* Cincinnati, OH: South-Western Publishing, 2002; *Triarc Annual Report 1997;* Alex Taylor III, "Back in the Driver's Seat," *Fortune,* May 25, 1998, p. 212; www.cadburyschweppes.com; www.pepsico.com; www.quakeroats.com.

Strategy Formulation

strategy formulation

The design of an approach to achieve the firm's mission.

Strategy formulation, the third component of the strategic management process (see Figure 7.1), is the design of an approach to achieve the firm's mission. An effectively formulated strategy integrates, marshals, and allocates the firm's internal resources and makes appropriate use of external environmental information. The idea is to formulate a mission-consistent strategy that will lead to sustained superior performance. Strategy formulation, which is the design of an approach to achieve a firm's mission, takes place at the corporate and business-unit levels. Poor strategy formulation can result in costly business failures, as Management Close-Up 7.i illustrates.

Corporate-Level Strategy

Strategy formulation begins with an overall approach to the direction of the organization. A **corporate-level strategy** encompasses the number of businesses the corporation holds, the variety of markets or industries it serves, and the distribution of resources among those businesses. For instance, the Wm. Wrigley Jr. Company focused almost exclusively on the chewing gum market. Seagram, on the other hand, diversified from its core beverage business by acquiring MCA in the entertainment industry. This is called a **diversification strategy.**

Corporate diversification strategy addresses two questions: (1) What business are we in? (2) What businesses should we be in? Corporate diversification may be analyzed in terms of portfolio mix, diversification type, and diversification process. Each of these is discussed in turn.

PORTFOLIO ANALYSIS   The basic idea of portfolio analysis is to classify the businesses of a diversified company within a single framework or taxonomy. Two of the most widely applied techniques are the McKinsey–General Electric Portfolio Analysis Matrix and the Boston Consulting Group's Growth Share Matrix.

McKinsey–General Electric Portfolio Analysis Matrix   This model has two sides, and classifies all businesses held by a diversified corporation (see Figure 7.5). The horizontal side refers to the health of the business unit in terms of markets (using indicators such as the domestic or global market share of the business, its competitive situation, and its level of profitability). The vertical side reflects the attractiveness of the industry of the business unit along the dimensions of market size, market growth, and industry profitability. This two-dimensional matrix is used to classify all the business units of a diversified corporation. Then the matrix is used as a diagnostic tool to make recommendations, such as:

- When a business unit ranks high on both dimensions (see quadrant 9), it means that it has an excellent future and should be "grown" (i.e., more resources should be allocated to it).

- When a business unit ranks low on both dimensions (see quadrant 11), it means that future prospects are poor and should be "harvested" (i.e., the corporation should squeeze all the possible profits out of it without doing much in terms of additional resources devoted to it).

- When a business unit falls in the middle (see quadrants 3, 5, 7), it becomes a candidate for a "hold" strategy (corporation adopts a "wait and see" attitude, but continues to allocate sufficient resources to maintain current level of activity).

Boston Consulting Group's Growth-Share Matrix   This approach (also known as the BCG Matrix) applies a similar method to that of the McKinsey–General Electric Portfolio Analysis Matrix except that the

---

corporate-level strategy

The corporation's overall plan concerning the number of businesses the corporation holds, the variety of markets or industries it serves, and the distribution of resources among those businesses.

diversification strategy

A firm's strategic plan to create and manage a mix of businesses owned by the firm.

portfolio analysis

An approach to classify the processes of a diversified company within a single framework or taxonomy.

FIGURE 7.5

The McKinsey–General
Electric Portfolio Analysis
Matrix

Source: From R. M. Grant,
Contemporary Strategy Analysis,
copyright 2001, Blackwell
Publishers. Reprinted with
permission.

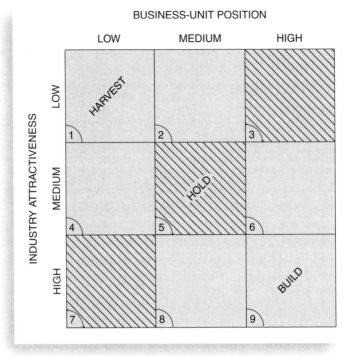

horizontal axis refers to the business unit's market share and the vertical
axis refers to the annual real rate of market growth (see Figure 7.6). The
strategic recommendations of the BCG Matrix approach are also quite direct and simple:

- A business unit that is both low in market share and low in market
  growth (a "dog") should be divested as soon as possible.

- If a business unit has a high market share in a market with low
  growth potential (a "cow"), it should be "milked" as much as
  possible with only limited additional resources devoted to it.

- If a business unit has both a high market share and operates in a
  growing market (a "star"), the corporation should greatly invest in
  it to fuel additional growth.

- If a business unit has a low market share but operates in a growing
  market (a question mark), additional analysis is necessary to decide
  whether or not more responses should be channeled its way.

The main advantage of the portfolio approach (which includes both the
McKinsey–GE Matrix and the BCG Matrix) to examine the businesses a
diversified corporation holds is that it can combine several elements of
strategically useful information in a single framework. This simplicity also
has its downside. Portfolio models assume that each business unit operates independently. Often business units are not "stand-alone" profit centers. Many do (or should) share valuable resources. Corporate executives

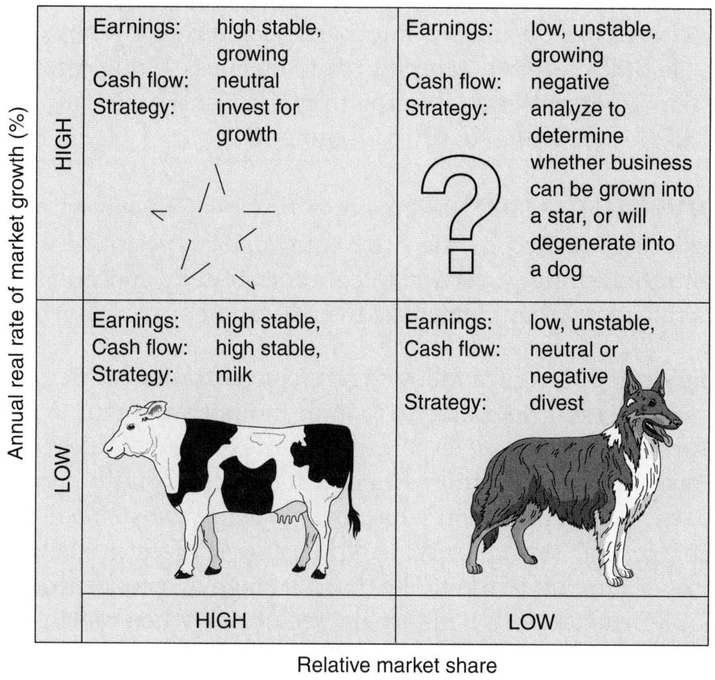

FIGURE 7.6

The Boston Consulting Group's Growth-Share Matrix

Source: From R. M. Grant, *Contemporary Strategy Analysis*, copyright 2001, Blackwell Publishers. Reprinted with permission.

Annual real rate of market growth (%)

HIGH:
- Earnings: high stable, growing; Cash flow: neutral; Strategy: invest for growth
- Earnings: low, unstable, growing; Cash flow: negative; Strategy: analyze to determine whether business can be grown into a star, or will degenerate into a dog

LOW:
- Earnings: high stable; Cash flow: high stable; Strategy: milk
- Earnings: low, unstable; Cash flow: neutral or negative; Strategy: divest

Relative market share — HIGH | LOW

may also acquire or sell business units without considering the effects this may have on the rest of the corporation's core business. Within each business unit, managers may have an incentive to "play by the numbers" to avoid their unit's being placed in the "harvest" or the "dog" categories.

Going back to the vignette at the start of this chapter, Canon suffered from most of the problems noted in the previous paragraph. The company was managed with a typical corporate portfolio mentality. Canon had a dozen major independent divisions, or profit centers with a great deal of duplication of activities that could have been shared (such as R&D and purchasing). Canon divisions "operated like individual fiefdoms, obsessed with building sales numbers at any costs".[20] Fujio Mitarai decided to change this portfolio scheme upon taking over as CEO in 1997. Since then Canon has done remarkably well. Now, there are four key divisions: copiers, printers, cameras, and optical equipment. Each cooperates rather than competes with the others. To underscore that all divisions are part of one company, Mitarai introduced consolidated balance sheets, in which profits and losses are reported at the corporate level, not at the business unit or divisional level. To keep communication flowing across divisions and reinforce a sense that all divisions are part of one company, Mitarai frequently holds an informal board meeting at 7:45 A.M. to have division executives debate the company's direction. He also holds daily lunch meetings with senior managers of various divisions and monthly meetings for 800 lower-level managers.

As a final comment, portfolio matrices may create the illusion of objectivity when in fact a considerable amount of personal judgment is involved when classifying businesses into particular boxes. As noted by one observer, "Is BMW's North American auto business a 'dog' because it holds less than 1 percent of a low-growth market or a cash 'cow' because it is market leader in the luxury car segment?".[21]

TYPES OF DIVERSIFICATION   Firms may be classified according to the mix of businesses owned by the firm. Four major types of business mix are concentration strategy, vertical integration strategy, concentric diversification strategy, and conglomerate diversification.

concentration strategy

A form of diversification strategy that focuses on a single business operating in a single industry segment.

Concentration Strategy   A firm following the **concentration strategy** focuses on a simple business operating in a single industry segment. A firm is classified as a single business if 95 percent or more of its total sales come from that business. A concentration strategy allows the firm to become the best at a particular competency, which may provide a sustained competitive advantage. For example, Wm. Wrigley specializes in chewing gum and is a leader in that market. The disadvantage of a concentration strategy is that a firm assumes a higher degree of risk when most earnings come from a single source.

vertical integration strategy

A form of diversification strategy in which a firm integrates vertically by acquiring businesses that are supply channels or distributors to the primary business; producing its own inputs is backward integration, and distributing its own outputs is forward integration.

Vertical Integration Strategy   Another method to grow quickly is to buy the company that sells you supplies. Or set up retail outlets to sell your own goods and services, rather than going through others. In **vertical integration,** a firm acquires businesses that are supply channels or distributors to the primary business. Producing its own inputs is called *backward integration,* and distributing its own outputs is *forward integration.* Either may give the firm greater control and allow it to reduce costs and uncertainty. For instance, Time Warner acquired Turner Broadcasting in part to help distribute Turner's classic movies and also so that the Turner cartoon network would show Warner Brothers cartoons. A potential disadvantage of a vertical integration strategy is that the firm may be unfamiliar with the business of suppliers or distributors, and make mistakes as a result.

concentric diversification strategy

A form of diversification strategy in which the firm expands by creating or acquiring new businesses that are related to the firm's core business.

Concentric Diversification Strategy   In **concentric diversification,** the firm expands by creating or acquiring new businesses related to the firm's core business. This would be the case, for instance, in the recent purchase of Compaq by Hewlett-Packard. Concentric diversification strategies offer two advantages. First, it may be possible to reduce costs, because two similar businesses may share HR departments, shipping processes, inventory systems, or other activities. Second, the core competency of the original company can be transferred to the newly acquired company. Two potential disadvantages of this strategy are that business-unit managers do not always cooperate with one another and that corporate headquarters may not be able to effectively manage the interrelationships among the business units.

Conglomerate Diversification   **Conglomerate diversification** involves managing a portfolio of businesses that are unrelated to each other. For instance, Union Pacific Corporation's original focus was building and managing railroads. It has now expanded into oil and gas exploration, mining, microwave technology, fiber optic systems, waste disposal, trucking, and real estate. One advantage of conglomerate diversification is that risks are spread across different markets and industries so that potential downturns in one business segment may be offset by higher earnings from other business units.

Research suggests that as a whole conglomerates are not as profitable as the other types of corporate diversification strategies.[22] The main problems appear to be that conglomerate diversification does not build on a firm's core competencies and that corporate executives do not have sufficient knowledge to effectively manage disparate business units.

PROCESS OF DIVERSIFICATION   A firm's corporate diversification strategy may also be examined in terms of the way it diversifies. Diversification occurs by acquisition and restructuring, and by internationalization.

Acquisition and Restructuring Strategies   The primary means for conducting a diversification strategy are through **acquisition**—purchasing other firms—and **merger**—integrating two firms. Firms engage in mergers and acquisitions to gain greater market power, move into new markets, avoid the cost of new product development, and spread business risks. Among the problems that can arise are failure to integrate different corporate cultures, overvaluation of the target firm, inability to achieve successful synergies between the firms, and increased inefficiencies and poor cost controls attributed to large size. For example, a recent survey suggests that companies that are merging often focus on cost-cutting, not consumer service.[23]

International Strategy   Firms are increasingly moving some manufacturing operations overseas. Even small companies seek to secure access to markets outside domestic borders. Firms internationalize for a variety of reasons, including a desire to increase market size, share resources and knowledge between units, lower costs, and spread business risks across diverse markets. Internationalization issues were discussed at length in Chapter 2.

Business-Level Strategy

Once company leaders determine a diversification strategy, they must decide how to compete in each business area or market segment. This is referred to as *business-level strategy*. For instance, Kmart and Wal-Mart have traditionally emphasized the low-cost end of the retail market while Dillard's and Dayton's have focused on high-quality, higher-priced leading-edge fashion.

> **conglomerate diversification**
>
> A form of diversification strategy that involves managing a portfolio of businesses that are unrelated to each other.

> **acquisition**
>
> The process of purchasing other firms.

> **merger**
>
> The process of integrating two firms.

There are two basic choices when selecting an industry position. One is to try to achieve lower cost than rivals. The other is to try to differentiate products and command a premium price. Providing products and services that are less expensive than those of competitors is referred to as **cost-leadership strategy.** Delivering products and services that customers perceive to be different and better is a **differentiation strategy.**

A cost-leadership strategy requires the firm to carry out its activities more efficiently than competitors, passing along cost savings to consumers in the form of lower prices. Firms may reduce costs through large-scale efficient facilities, low overhead, fast turnover of inventories, volume buying of needed inputs, state of the art technology, plants located in low-wage countries, and "build to order systems." Because their profit margins are low, such firms need to sell large volumes to earn acceptable returns. For example,

- Toys 'R' Us secured a large market share in the toy retailing industry in the United States and overseas by charging 10 percent to 15 percent less than competitors. Its efficient distribution system, volume purchasing, and large stores have given the firm the necessary cost advantage to undercut the competition.

- Unifi, Inc., one of the most efficient producers of filament polyester and nylon fiber, dominated its market by being a leader in manufacturing technologies, allowing it to underprice its competitors.

- Southwest Airlines was able to maintain high profitability in an industry where being in the red is not uncommon. It specializes in no-frills, low-price fares on selected "short-hop" routes and a highly versatile workforce willing to perform multiple jobs. A single employee may serve as a bag handler, front desk representative, ticket collector, and steward. Southwest maintains its low-cost strategy while outperforming all other U.S. carriers in terms of on-time performance, baggage handling, and number of complaints.

A differentiation strategy requires a firm to continuously invest in the creation of new products or add new features to existing products so that customers believe the products are different and better than those offered by competitors. The challenge for these firms lies in selling products at a price that customers are willing to pay. Commonly recognized differentiated products include:

- Toyota's Lexus: "the relentless pursuit of perfection."
- Ralph Lauren's and Tommy Hilfiger's clothing lines: image.
- Caterpillar: a heavy equipment manufacturing firm committed to providing rapid delivery of spare parts to any location in the world.
- Maytag appliances: product reliability.
- McKinsey & Co: the highest priced and most prestigious consulting firm in the world.

cost-leadership strategy

Providing products and services that are less expensive than those of competitors.

differentiation strategy

Delivering products and services that customers perceive as unique.

As you read in your text, Southwest Airlines has been able to successfully differentiate itself from its competitors by way of no-frills, low-price fares, and a highly diversified workforce. But Southwest also is known for its humorous flight crews, who often crack jokes and pull gags on passengers.

- Rolex watches: prestige and image.
- Gateway: low-cost PCs for home use.
- Yahoo: comprehensive Web surfing.

The term **competitive dynamic** refers to the actions and counteractions of firms competing in a particular industry segment. For instance, when a market leader decreases prices, other firms in the market are likely to follow.

competitive dynamic

The actions and counteractions of firms competing in a particular industry segment.

Firms in all kinds of industries are reacting to each other to gain a competitive advantage on the Internet. For example, Universal Music, the music label, developed piracy safeguards, supported online CD sellers, and joined in a lawsuit against Napster, the Internet music swapping firm, to protect itself and to be able to compete against smaller music labels already selling online. Merrill Lynch set up online trading to combine its traditional financial activities with the type of Internet trading capabilities offered by discount online leaders such as Charles Schwab. NBC merged several individual NBC websites (excluding MSNBC.com) into NBC Internet, Inc. (NBCi.com), a global integrated media company delivering access across all major platforms and offering users free e-mail, search, find, and buy capabilities, as well as entertainment.

Strategy Implementation

An idea is nothing until it becomes an action. The fourth key component of the strategic management process is strategy implementation (see Figure 7.1). Even the best conceived strategies are of little value if they are not implemented effectively. It is easy to think of strategy formulation and implementation as being separate activities. In reality both take place at the same time. Management will not choose a strategy unless they believe it can be implemented effectively.

Consider again AT&T's Universal Card experience as detailed in Management Close-Up 7.g. Although it was disastrous for AT&T, Charles M. Cawley, president of MBNA, the world's largest credit card issuer, pushed net income to an estimated $1.2 billion in 2000. Cawley built his success with customized group cards, offered to everyone from university alumni to members of a duck-hunting club. MBNA's entire strategic plan is summarized in nine words: "Success is getting the right customers and keeping them." The company had learned that it is difficult to make money in the industry by offering lower interest rates or fees to attract customers away from competitors. The customized group card has been an immense success as an alternative implementation strategy.[24]

In other words, a firm that is clear about where it wants to go (effective strategy formulation), how to get there (effective strategy implementation), and what works (feedback from implementation used in strategy formulation) is more likely to achieve strategic competitiveness and sustained superior performance. To implement formulated strategies successfully, company executives must consider organizational structure and controls, cooperative strategies, human resource strategies, strategic leadership, and corporate entrepreneurship and innovation.

Organizational Structure and Controls

A company's board of directors is expected to monitor the actions and decisions of top executives to ensure that they act in the best interest of the firm. Until recently, boards of directors operated freely, with little government supervision. While its interpretation by the courts is still evolving, the Sarbanes-Oxley Act of 2002 promises to change that. Crafted by Congress in the aftermath of financial collapses at corporations like Enron, Global Crossing, and WorldCom, the 2002 law outlines a set of accountability standards by public companies in the areas of financial reporting and disclosure, audits, conflict of interest, and governance. Below the top-executive level, firms have many choices for organizing the work that needs to be done to implement a particular strategy. Implementation begins with defining roles for different individuals and establishing procedures, reporting structures, chains of command, decision-making processes, and organizational forms.

Organizational structure is critical to strategy implementation because "through structure, managers largely determine what a firm does and how it completes that work, given its chosen strategies. Strategic competitiveness can be attained only when the firm's selected structure is congruent with its formulated strategy."[25]

cooperative strategies

Establishing partnerships or strategic alliances with other firms.

Cooperative Strategies

Cooperative strategies involve establishing partnerships or strategic alliances with other firms. For instance, Procter & Gamble and General Electric cooperated to develop a jet engine for Boeing's new jumbo jet. Although the companies were fierce competitors over the years, senior executives indicated that "neither of us [was] prepared to make the enormous financial, personnel, and technical investment required to develop an all-new engine in an uncertain environment." Additionally, according to a Boeing executive, "using our complementary skills and resources we can produce an engine that meets the requirements of Boeing and our airline customers in a more timely fashion and at lower cost and risk."[26] Recently many major airlines have been sharing ticket sales to make travel easier.

Strategic alliances can serve a number of purposes. Firms may combine resources, capabilities, and core competencies to gain market power, overcome trade barriers, learn from each other, pool resources for expensive and risky projects, compete more effectively in a particular industry, and speed up entry into new markets. Strategic alliances also allow a firm to create and disband projects with minimal paperwork.

Human Resource Strategies

The policies and practices of the human resource department should also support the firm's overall strategy (see Chapter 10 on human resource management). Who gets recruited, how performance is evaluated and rewarded, how training is conducted, and how career advancement is managed should be consistent with the strategic mission of the firm. For example, a company that wants to be innovative in various markets would want to develop human resource policies that stimulate rather than dissuade employees from taking risks. This may require greater tolerance for failure, more subjective assessment of performance, more incentives for taking risks, and the hiring of managers with track records of making risky but prudent decisions.

Strategic Leadership

Effective leadership plays a fundamental role in the relative success or failure of a firm (see Chapter 13 on leadership). This is particularly true for top executives who are responsible for charting general implementation plans, making key resource allocation decisions, and delegating day-to-day operations. In the opinion of three well-known management authors, "By word and/or personal example and through their ability to dream pragmatically, effective strategic leaders meaningfully influence the behaviors, thoughts, and feelings of those with whom they work."[27]

Corporate Entrepreneurship and Innovation

Competitive pressures require firms to be innovative (see Chapter 8 on entrepreneurship and innovation). High returns and investments in innovation tend to go hand in hand. Innovation contributes to a sustainable competitive advantage if (1) it is difficult or costly for competitors to imitate, (2) customers can see a value in the innovation, (3) the firm enjoys a time advantage over the other company, and (4) the firm is capable of commercializing the innovation.

Research and development is necessary for firms in high-technology markets such as computers, electronics, and pharmaceuticals. However, firms also need to encourage entrepreneurship, supporting employees who are willing to take risks and be aggressive, proactive, and creative and can see opportunities where others perceive problems.

Strategic Outcomes

The fifth and final step of the strategic management process is an analysis of the strategic outcomes, or the end result of the entire process (see Figure 7.1). Company leaders should periodically assess whether the outcomes meet expectations. This information should be used to determine whether or not company strategies are successful.

A firm must first and foremost cater to the desires of its primary stakeholders. **Stakeholders** are the individuals and institutions who have vested interests in the performance of the firm. In a capitalist system, the main stakeholders are the people who own stock in the company and who are the major suppliers of the firm's capital. These stakeholders expect to earn at least an average return on their investment, although they would prefer the return to be as high as possible. If lenders are dissatisfied, they can make it more costly for the firm to raise capital and may increase the number of restrictions on the company's borrowing. Shareholders who are unhappy with the firm's stock performance can sell stock and invest their money in other firms. Because the firm depends on investors and stockholders, its highest priority when analyzing strategic outcomes is the needs of those constituencies.

At the same time, the firm's managers should consider the desires of other people who are affected by a firm's performance. At times, the interests of these other stakeholders may conflict with those of shareholders. For instance, customers prefer products with great reliability, more features, and low price. Employees would like a greater share of the company's profits. The community may want the firm to invest in projects of social interest. Politicians and pressure groups may take advantage of popular support for particular causes, as was the case with the immigration issues in Table 7.3. The firm should try to find win–win situations for as many stakeholders as possible. For instance, higher quality products at a lower price may benefit investors if the firm's market share increases. Employees may also benefit if the company enjoys greater ability to pay and offers them greater job security.

stakeholders

The groups or individuals who have an interest in the performance of the enterprise and how it uses its resources, including employees, customers, and shareholders.

TABLE 7.3

Multiple Stakeholders in Immigration Issues

STAKEHOLDER GROUP	GROUP'S GOAL	METHODS
Social agencies/Religious organizations	Protect Immigrants from abuse	Public support/ Appeal to moral principles
Private firms	Access to low-cost labor supply	Put pressure on Congress to increase immigration quotas
Congress/President	Orderly immigration and prevention of voters' backlash	Legislation
Unions	Prevent wage erosion and loss of jobs	Negotiation/political action
Mexico	Economic safety valve	Diplomacy/international pressure
INS	Enforce immigration laws without angering employers and minority groups	Increased border patrols rather than internal surveillance groups

Source: Adapted from "The New Immigrants," *Business Week,* June 18, 2001, pp. 16–22; A. Borrus, "Land of Shrinking Opportunity," *Business Week,* August 27, 2001, pp. 124–125; R. S. Dunham, "Governing a Nation Divided," *Business Week,* August 27, 2001, pp. 128–130; D. Foust, "The Changing Heartland," *Business Week,* September 9, 2002, pp. 80–83; H. Fineman and T. Lipper, "Spinning Race," *Business Week,* January 27, 2003, pp. 25–30; and R. O. Crockett, "Diversity Is a Good Business," *Business Week,* January 27, 2003, p. 96.

Some of the standard measures of strategic success include:

- Profits
- Growth of sales/market share
- Growth of corporate assets
- Reduced competitive threats
- Innovations that fuel future success

It is vital for the executive team to assess both the short term and long range when assessing strategic outcomes. Long-term survival may be the ultimate criterion when studying strategic outcomes.

APPLICATIONS: MANAGEMENT IS EVERYONE'S BUSINESS

Applications for the Manager   An effective manager must be proactive in responding to evolving challenges and opportunities rather than being overtaken by events. Learning to think strategically forces managers to be on the alert for changes in the external and internal environments, to modify the firm's strategic intent, mission, and formulated strategy when necessary, and to effectively implement the new or redefined strategies.

Applications for Managing Teams   The strategic management process generally involves teams of managers and employees from different areas who bring their perspectives and expertise to bear on the issues facing the firm. An important factor in the success of the strategic management process is how well the firm can mobilize and integrate the efforts of manager and employees to identify relevant environmental trends, define or redefine firm strategies, and support the successful implementation of those strategies.

Applications for Individuals   Individual employees are more likely to make greater contributions to the firm if they engage in activities that have strategic value. If the firm's strategic objective is to increase market share by underpricing competitors, the employee can suggest ways to cut costs or reduce inefficiencies. The employee can also be attuned to changes in his or her areas of expertise and advise management on the strategic implications of those changes. Lastly, employee success depends on the ability to adapt to the firm's strategic change.

CONCLUDING THOUGHTS

As you will recall from the introductory vignette, Canon has been able to outperform most of its competitors during the past decade and remain highly profitable in spite of the Asian economic crisis since the late 1990s and world recession during the first years of this decade. In addition, its future looks bright based on the large number of patents it holds and the many new products it has coming down its pipeline. Canon has achieved its success by developing a strong competence in particular areas, investing in technology innovation, and creating synergies through the development, manufacturing, and marketing of related products. This business strategy has given Canon a sustained competitive advantage, or the ability to enjoy higher than average returns in the industry year after year. A well-formulated strategic management process is crucial to guiding management decisions and marshaling organizational resources to establish and sustain competitive advantage. Canon has been able to capitalize on its resources and capabilities to be number one in a related line of products (copier and photographic equipment).

This chapter is concerned with the set of business decisions and actions required to achieve long-term competitive advantage and earn above-average returns. The strategic management process involves several steps. First, the firm needs to examine opportunities and threats in the external environment and to identify internal resources, capabilities, and knowledge that can be used to take advantage of the opportunities and to deal with the threats. **Analysis of the external and internal environment** provides information the firm needs to decide its strategic intent (what it plans to do) and mission (how it will use its core competence to meet external challenges).

All firms depend to some extent on what happens in the external environment. Analyzing the external environment involves **scanning** (identifying early signals of emerging trends and changes that may affect the firm), **monitoring** (keeping a close eye on environmental changes), **forecasting** (predicting what is likely to happen in the future), and **assessing** (evaluating environmental data to determine implications for the firm). Environmental forces may be examined at four different levels of specificity: the general environment, the industry, strategic groups, and direct competitors.

Company leaders must assess the firm's internal resources and capabilities in order to take advantage of environmental opportunities and neutralize external threats. A resource analysis focuses on the internal environment of the firm, identifying tangible and intangible resources that provide the firm with capabilities that are difficult for competitors to imitate. The firm's capabilities may be analyzed by function (such as marketing and human resources), value added of various activities (**value-chain analysis**), and **benchmarking** (comparing the firm's activities and/or functions with those of firms known for best practices).

Business strategies are formulated at two levels. At the **corporate level,** managers should decide on a mix of businesses or the number of industries to compete in. The company may choose to hold a single business competing in one industry segment (**concentration strategy**), diversify by setting up or acquiring firms that serve the primary business (**vertical integration strategy**), create or purchase new businesses related to the core business (**concentric diversification**), or manage a portfolio of unrelated businesses (**conglomerate diversification**).

A **business-level** strategy involves decisions about how the firm will compete in a given industry. The two major choices are competing with price (by being a low-cost producer) and on special features that command a price premium (differentiation).

The formulated strategy must be implemented effectively, and feedback from the implementation process should be used to adjust the formulated strategy. Effective **strategy implementation** requires a corporate governance system (to ensure that executives make decisions that are most beneficial to the firm), a system for completing the necessary work (organizational structure and controls), functional strategies (to support the overall strategy), and strong leadership at the top as well as entrepreneurial activities at lower organizational levels.

1. Some argue that the business environment changes so quickly that we are entering a period of "hypercompetition," which will make it difficult to establish long-term strategic objectives. Do you agree? Identify five major forces that accelerated environmental change at the turn of the century.

2. Going back to Management Close-Up 7.e, do you think that McDonald's á la francaise will fail or succeed in the United States? Explain your answer.

3. Why should most firms develop their strategic mission following a rational process that incorporates internal and external environmental data? Explain.

4. Going back to the SWOT analysis of Harley-Davidson in Management Close-Up 7.a, what future strategies would you formulate for the company and how would you implement these strategies? Explain.

5. In what situations do you believe that strategy formulation leads to strategy implementation? In what situations do you believe that strategy implementation plays an equal role with strategy formulation as a source of competitive advantage? Explain.

6. In what situations do you believe that the external environment of the firm is more important than the internal environment as a determinant of the firm's profitability? Explain.

7. Scan business publications such as *Business Week, The Wall Street Journal,* and *Fortune.* From these publications' articles, select a firm that has been affected by each of the following: the general environment, the industry, strategic groups, and direct competitors. Explain the reason for your choice and show how that particular segment of the environment affects the firm you have chosen.

Where Has Kodak Gone Wrong?

Eastman Kodak made much of its money in the 20th century through the sale of its color films, regarded as the best in the world. Yet, as the past century came to an end Kodak encountered rough waters as foreign manufacturers such as Fuji flooded the market with picture films of comparable quality at prices substantially below those of Kodak. As Kodak film sales continue to drop by approximately 3–5 percent a year, CEO Daniel Carp (a 30-year veteran at Kodak) told investors in 2003 that Kodak is under pressure like never before. This is because a new foe has appeared on the horizon. Film sales continue to suffer as more consumers buy digital cameras. Although Kodak introduced its EasyShare digital camera, competitors have copied it and prices have fallen. Carp has tried to control what he can: costs. Kodak said it would cut up to 2,200 jobs, or 3 percent of its workforce, and it's moving more manufacturing to China.

Discussion Questions

1. Based on what you have learned in this chapter, do you think that Kodak's problems may be attributed to failures in its strategic management process? Explain.

2. What can a company such as Kodak do to prevent competitors from undercutting its market share? Explain.

3. Do you believe that Kodak's cost-cutting moves are a good way to deal with the strategic challenges it faces? Explain.

Source: Adapted with permission from F. Keenan, "Kodak: Not a Pretty Picture," *Business Week,* February 3, 2003, p. 46.

A Miracle Turnaround in a Very Tough Industry: The Case of Hyundai

In the late 1990s, the wheels were coming off at Hyundai. Jay Leno and David Letterman regularly used the shoddy Korean car as a punch line for jokes. Profits were plummeting and Hyundai's quality and brand image reputation had reached bottom. The home office in Seoul couldn't even recruit a seasoned American to jump-start the faltering company. As a last resort, just as Hyundai was facing bankruptcy, the Korean bosses turned to their corporate lawyer, Finbarr O'Neill, an affable Irishman with no experience running a car company. "We were a company looking over the precipice," says O'Neill. "I kept my law license intact as my insurance policy." O'Neill won't have to hang out his shingle any time soon. He has engineered an extraordinary turnaround at Hyundai, where sales have roared ahead 400 percent and now outpace Volkswagen and BMW since he became CEO four years ago. How did O'Neill turn Hyundai around? First, the company offered a 10-year, 100,000 mile warranty to reduce the firm's reputation of poor quality. Next, O'Neill prodded the Koreans to focus on what Americans want; inexpensive, reliable, stylish cars. Hyundai invested heavily in quality improvements. Hyundai now offers the most improved car line in J. D. Power's quality survey. Models such as the $18,000 Santa Fe SUV and $16,000 Tiburon sports car are becoming the ride of choice for those under 30.

The other major players are beginning to take notice. Chrysler, Mazda, and others have followed Hyundai's lead and extended their warranties. GM execs are grumbling that Hyundai is succeeding because of the weak Korean currency. Detroit made similar complaints when the Japanese cars entered U.S. markets in the early 1980s.

O'Neill, 50, is about to give the auto establishment even more anxiety. Hyundai just broke ground on a $1 billion Alabama factory, and a new $25 million California studio is about to start crafting designs tailored to Americans' tastes. Those moves, says O'Neill, will allow Hyundai to sell 1 million cars per year by 2010, a nearly threefold jump from 2003's 375,000 cars. That would push Hyundai into the ranks of Toyota and Honda. Transforming the Korean car maker from being the joke of the industry to a formidable player in less than five years is truly a remarkable strategic feat.

Discussion Questions

1. Using the material presented in this chapter, how would you explain Hyundai's success story? Explain your answer.

2. Would it be easy for other automobile manufacturers to successfully imitate Hyundai's business strategy? Explain your answer.

3. Based on the discussion concerning segments of the general environment in this chapter, if you were an executive of Ford or General Motors, how would you analyze the competitive challenges posed by Hyundai?

Source: Adapted with permission from K. Naughton, "Kicking Hyundai into High Gear," *Newsweek,* January 3, 2003, p. 73.

The (Fat) Wages of Scandal

The years 1999–2003 witnessed an explosion of corporate scandals. A study of CEO pay at 23 companies under investigation for accounting irregularities revealed this startling statistic: CEOs at scandal-ridden companies earned 70 percent more than the typical CEO of a large company—specifically, an average of $62 million from 1999 to 2001, compared with $36 million for the remaining 300-some CEOs in the survey. Conducted by United for a Fair Economy, a Boston nonprofit group, and the Washington-based Institute for Policy Studies, the study used data from *Business Week*'s annual Executive Pay Scoreboard.

In all, the 23 CEO's of the companies under investigation took home $1.4 billion in a three-year period during which the value of their companies plunged by $530 billion and 162,000 of their employees lost their jobs. The highest-paid CEO was Tyco's Dennis Kozlowski, who took home $466.7 million for the period in pay and perks before he quit amid tax-evasion charges. He's followed by Qwest Communications' Joseph Nacchio ($266 million), Enron's Kenneth Lay ($251 million), and AOL-Time Warner's Gerald Levin ($178.4 million), all of whom have since left their companies.

Critical Thinking Questions

1. Top executives play a key role in strategy formulation and implementation as they sit at the apex of the organizational pyramid and enjoy a great deal of power and influence. What can explain the fact that so many executives were able to take advantage of their privileged position at the expense of shareholders? Explain.

2. What types of controls would you impose on executives to make sure that these types of abuses do not happen? How would you make top executives accountable?

3. Even in firms without reported scandals, executives may earn 300–500 times more then the lowest-paid workers. Some people believe that executives deserve every nickel they get given the complexities of the job and the pressures of the position. Do you agree? Explain.

Collaborative Learning Exercise

You have been appointed to an advisory task force of the board of directors at Tyco to provide a set of recommendations for holding future executives accountable for their actions, and to ensure that their strategic decisions are consistent with the best interest of the firm. Be sure to justify your recommendations to the chairman of the board (represented by the instructor of your class).

Source: Adapted with permission from L. Lavelle, "Honchos: The Fat Wages of Scandal," *Business Week,* September 9, 2002, p. 8; see also L. Lavelle, "CEO Pay: Pain, but Still Plenty of Gain," *Business Week,* February 24, 2003, p. 16.

Internet Strategies

Dot-com firms and an increasing number of bricks-and-mortar companies rely on the Internet as a normal part of their operations. Many of these have discovered, however, that the Internet is no panacea. Choose any five firms and analyze how they use the Internet to achieve their strategic objectives. Answer the following questions:

1. After comparing and contrasting the different firms, how effectively do you think they use the Internet from a strategic perspective?

2. Is the Internet an appropriate medium to achieve a sustainable competitive advantage? Support your conclusions using the materials discussed in this chapter.

EIGHT

Entrepreneurship and Innovation

chapter **8**

After reading this chapter, you should be able to:

- Distinguish between an entrepreneurship and a small business.

- Develop the negotiation, networking, and leadership skills needed to be a successful entrepreneur.

- Recognize why entrepreneurships fail.

- Analyze the advantages and disadvantages of the legal forms of enterprises: proprietorships, partnerships, and corporations.

- Know how to raise capital through debt and equity financing and recognize the merits of each approach.

- Note the alternative forms of entrepreneurship, such as franchising, spin-offs, and intrapreneurships.

- Find ways to encourage innovation in any organization.

Entrepreneurs: Some Success Stories!

Arthur Blank and Bernard Marcus were fired from their positions in the Handy Dan home improvement chain in 1978. In response, they opened their own home improvement stores in Atlanta in 1979. The three stores lost nearly $1 million that year, but turned a profit in 1980. Those stores were the beginning of the Home Depot chain, which now employs approximately 157,000 people.

Lillian Vernon was a new bride and four months pregnant in the early 1950s, looking for a way to help support her family. Since pregnant women working outside the home were almost unheard of at the time, she decided to sell monogrammed purses and belts, manufactured by her father's leather goods company, through the mail. Vernon started the company with $2,000 that she and her husband had received as wedding gifts. She designed a bag-and-belt set for high school girls and spent $495 on a small ad in an issue of *Seventeen* magazine. By the end of the year, she was receiving $32,000 worth of orders each week, filling them at her kitchen table. By 2000 Lillian Vernon Corp. was processing more than 4 million orders annually, employing 4,000 people, and posting sales of more than $241 million.

Michael Dell went to college to become a doctor. His hobby, however, was computers. Soon he began selling them out of his dorm room. In 1984 and with $1,000, Dell founded the Dell Computer Corporation. The essence of the business was taken straight from his dorm room experience: sell directly to consumers without going through retailers. Today, Dell has offices in 34 countries and employs approximately 36,000 people. Michael Dell has been named "Entrepreneur of the Year" by *Inc.* magazine and "Man of the Year" by *PC* magazine.

Sources: National Commission on Entrepreneurship: "Stories of Entrepreneurs," www.ncoe.org/toolkit/stories_dell.html and www.ncoe.org/toolkit/stories_blank.html, accessed February 19, 2003; www.lillianvernon.com, accessed July 25, 2001.

Creating a new enterprise can be one of the most exciting management challenges. Numerous entrepreneurs have built successful companies by discovering and meeting unmet needs. Many kinds of people start businesses. Men, women, minorities, immigrants—all can and do become entrepreneurs. As a result, entrepreneurship is becoming a popular field of study for many university business students.

Like Lillian Vernon, Arthur Blank, Bernard Marcus, and Michael Dell, today's entrepreneurs face a variety of challenges. They must find answers to such questions as: Do I have the right skills and abilities to become a successful entrepreneur? What type of business should I start? How can I raise capital to grow the business? Which markets should my business compete in? How much growth and what rate of growth is desirable? Manager's Notes 8.1 presents the basic entrepreneurial skills needed to successfully launch a new business venture. This chapter explores questions and issues about starting and growing a business. The first issue is describing what entrepreneurship is and is not.

What Is Entrepreneurship?

entrepreneurship

The process of creating a business enterprise capable of entering new or established markets by deploying resources and people in a unique way to develop a new organization.

The process of creating a business enterprise capable of entering new or established markets is **entrepreneurship.** Successful entrepreneurship requires deploying resources and people in unique ways to develop a new organization. An **entrepreneur** is an individual who creates an enterprise that becomes a new entry to a market. Broadly stated, an entrepreneur is anyone who undertakes some project and bears some risk.[1]

Entrepreneurship Myths

entrepreneur

An individual who creates an enterprise that becomes a new entry to a market.

Entrepreneurs have received considerable attention from the business and popular press in recent years. Still, many misconceptions remain concerning entrepreneurs and what they do in order to succeed. We next consider some of these myths and contrast with those the common reality faced by most entrepreneurs.[2]

So, You Want to Become an Entrepreneur?
Key Skills for Entrepreneurial Success

- *Opportunity Recognition Skills.* Entrepreneurs are able to identify opportunities when they develop or exist. To be successful, an entrepreneur must scan the environment, searching for opportunities and ideas. Sometimes an entrepreneur may discover a problem to be solved or find a market need that is not being filled. Other times, a person may be committed to becoming an entrepreneur and then looks for a potential business opportunity. In either case, the entrepreneur must be aware that an opportunity exists and be able to take advantage of the situation.

- *Opportunity Fit Assessment.* Not everyone can succeed at everything. To be successful, an entrepreneur must be able to evaluate whether or not his or her personality, skills, and leadership style match with the opportunity. This includes the technical and business skills that are required in addition to personal preferences and needs.

- *Implementation Skills.* Successful entrepreneurs tend to have a high need for achievement, have an internal locus of control, be risk takers, and be confident in their ability to master unforeseen challenges.

- *Networking Skills.* Networking skills are critical to obtaining financial capital, business and technical knowledge, retail shelf space, and other resources required to start a business.

Source: N. Lindsay and J. Craig, "A Framework for Understanding Opportunity Recognition: Entrepreneurs versus Private Equity Financiers," *Journal of Private Equity* 6 (2002), pp. 13–24.

MYTH 1: ENTREPRENEURS ARE BORN, NOT MADE One common belief is that entrepreneurs possess certain innate traits that are different from regular people. In fact, many types of people with different personality characteristics have become successful entrepreneurs. Many of them studied entrepreneurship as a discipline before launching a business. Business schools offer courses in entrepreneurship that provide opportunities to learn and practice skills that are useful to entrepreneurs.

MYTH 2: IT IS NECESSARY TO HAVE ACCESS TO MONEY TO BECOME AN ENTREPRENEUR A second common myth is that only wealthy people, or those who have access to wealthy people, can start businesses. The truth is, however, that many companies have been started by people with few resources. These entrepreneurs accumulated capital by putting in long hours without pay and reinvesting the profits of the business into expansion. For example, Hewlett-Packard, the giant electronics company, was started in a Palo Alto, California, garage in 1940 by two Stanford University students with a few hundred dollars and an order for sound equipment from the Walt Disney Company.

MYTH 3: AN ENTREPRENEUR TAKES A LARGE OR IRRATIONAL RISK IN STARTING A BUSINESS Risk is part of any business venture and this reality certainly applies to entrepreneurial ventures. The costs of embracing an entrepreneurial vision in terms of personal funds and family relationships can be tremendous. However, in terms of absolute amount of financial risk, most entrepreneurs have little to risk at the outset of a new business venture. It is usually later, when trying to grow the business into a larger enterprise, that the entrepreneur can face larger risk. At this later time, the business may have developed substantial value, which means there is more to lose.

MYTH 4: MOST SUCCESSFUL ENTREPRENEURS START WITH A BREAKTHROUGH INVENTION Contrary to the idea that entrepreneurs capitalize on revolutionary change, most entrepreneurs start a new business with only a moderate or incremental change that is designed to serve a market need. Certainly, innovation and being able to distinguish your product or service from others in the marketplace is important for a start-up business. Rather than revolutionary change, however, great execution, being first in a market, or a small innovation/improvement is often enough for an entrepreneur to be successful. As an example of an entrepreneurial venture based on incremental change, see Management Close-Up 8.a.

MYTH 5: ENTREPRENEURS BECOME SUCCESSFUL ON THEIR FIRST VENTURE People tend to remember entrepreneurial successes. Many times, however, failure is a key part of the learning process. By failing, entrepreneurs learn lessons that eventually lead to the creation of successful ventures. Nolan Bushnell, the entrepreneur who is best remembered for starting the videogame company Atari, failed at several different businesses but he persisted and learned from his mistakes. Likewise, initial business ventures of Richard Branson, founder of Virgin Records, include a failed magazine launch.[3]

A Distinction between an Entrepreneurial Venture and a Small Business

small business

Any business that is independently owned and operated, that is small in size, and that is not dominant in its markets.

A **small business** is any company that is independently owned and operated, is small in size, and does not dominate its markets. According to the U.S. Small Business Administration, a small business employs fewer than 100 employees. Small businesses do not always grow into medium-sized or large businesses. Some small-business owners prefer to keep their operations modest.

Trip Planning: The Market Niche for a New Business?

THEME: CUSTOMER FOCUS Planning a trip? Looking for a hotel? You have probably already searched the Internet and possibly scanned through a guidebook for the area you are planning to visit. Are those sources of information enough and is the information you want easily accessible? An entrepreneurial business is betting it can offer better information in a format that travelers will prefer. Jeremy Simmons, co-founder of Equator Creative Media, is producing a line of CD-ROM destination guides. In Simmons's judgment, travel destination information on the Internet is scattered and limited in scope. Video is hard to come by and cumbersome to download. On the other hand, guidebooks offer a great deal of general information but can be slim on details and pictures.

In order to better serve the travel market, Equator Creative Media offers CD-ROMs that provide detailed pictures and videos. The goal is to let you see exactly where you'll be staying before you book a hotel or make a restaurant reservation. The business is just getting started. Thus far, only CD-ROM travel guides for Coronado and San Diego in California and for Rocky Point, in Mexico, are available. The Rocky Point guide contains 30 videos and hundreds of color photos of hotels, condos, and beachfront home rentals, as well as maps and information on the area.

Source: "Mexico: New Travel Resource Provides Insights into Rocky Point," *Arizona Republic*, February 23, 2003, p. T10.

One of the most important goals of an entrepreneur, on the other hand, is growth. An entrepreneurial venture may be small during its early stages, but the goal may be to become a medium-sized firm of 100 to 499 employees or a large firm with 500 or more employees. Giant firms like Wal-Mart, Home Depot, Microsoft, and Intel started as entrepreneurships with the goal of becoming dominant companies in their markets. At the start, however, a small business and an entrepreneurial venture may be hard to tell apart. For a small business owner, stability and profitability are the ideal situation. For the entrepreneur, growth and a greater presence in the market are important objectives.

The Importance of Entrepreneurship

Between 1994 and 1998, almost 500,000 new firms were formed in the United States, and 898,000 new firms were incorporated in 1998. The economies of the United States and many other countries depend on the creation of new enterprises. Entrepreneurship creates jobs, stimulates innovation, and provides opportunities for diverse people in society.

Job Creation

Small businesses accounted for 8.4 million, or 76 percent, of the 11.1 million new jobs created between 1994 and 1998.[4] Start-up companies less than four years old accounted for 75 percent of the new jobs in the small-business sector. Firms with 5,000 or more employees lost 2.1 million jobs during this same period. This pattern of job creation suggests that entrepreneurship accounts for most of the new jobs in the U.S. economy. According to U.S. government statistics (Small Business Administration, 2002), small businesses, those with fewer than 500 employees, represent 99 percent of all employers and provide two-thirds to three-quarters of the net new jobs.

Innovation

Entrepreneurships are responsible for introducing a major proportion of new and innovative products and services that reach the market. They are often started by visionary people who develop an innovative way to do something faster, better, cheaper, or with improved features. Entrepreneurships often pioneer new technologies designed to make older technologies obsolete. This was the case when Apple Computer pioneered the first commercial personal computer and challenged the computing technology of the 1970s, which was based on centralized, mainframe computers. Eventually, the personal computer became the dominant technology and spawned a huge market for computer components, software, systems, and services.

Opportunities for Diverse People

People of diverse backgrounds who have experienced frustration and blocked career paths in large corporations can improve their economic status and develop interesting careers by becoming entrepreneurs. Entrepreneurship provides an attractive alternative for women who bump up against the glass ceiling in male-dominated firms. Many female corporate executives have left their firms to become entrepreneurs to: (1) balance work and family responsibilities; (2) obtain more challenge and autonomy; and (3) avoid unpleasant organization politics.

Similarly, increasing numbers of blacks, Hispanics, and Asian Americans have launched successful entrepreneurial efforts. Entrepreneurship can provide anyone, particularly in the United States, an alternative to the corporate career path. Currently, nearly 40 percent of small businesses are owned by women and 15 percent are owned by minorities (White House, 2003).

Entrepreneurial Characteristics and Skills

There are many motives for starting a new business. Some entrepreneurs learn from successful family role models. A few stumble onto an entrepreneurial career path by inventing a new product and building a busi-

Earl G. Graves, Sr., chief executive officer of Earl G. Graves Ltd., founded Black Enterprise in 1970. His vision was to create a link of commerce and communication between the black professional class and American industry.

ness around it, as did Steven Jobs and Steve Wozniak with the first prototype of the Apple computer. Others become dissatisfied with corporate careers and discover that entrepreneurship provides an attractive set of challenges and rewards.

Manager's Notes 8.2 presents basic categories that have been used to segment entrepreneurs into various types. Whatever the type of entrepreneur, there appear to be common characteristics important for success, which we discuss next.

 Characteristics of Successful Entrepreneurs

Characteristics of Entrepreneurs

Some key characteristics associated with entrepreneurship are a high need for achievement, an internal locus of control, the willingness to take risks, and self-confidence.

People with a *high need for achievement* have a strong desire to solve problems on their own. They enjoy setting goals and achieving them through their own efforts, and like receiving feedback on how they are doing. These characteristics help entrepreneurs to be more proactive and anticipate future problems, needs, or changes.

An entrepreneur is likely to have an **internal locus of control,** with a strong belief in his or her ability to succeed. When a person with an internal locus of control fails or makes a mistake, the individual is likely to accept responsibility for the outcome and try harder, rather than searching for external reasons to explain the failure. Entrepreneurs are persistent and motivated to overcome barriers that would deter others. People with an **external locus of control** believe that what happens to them is due to luck, fate, or factors beyond their control. When people with an ex-

internal locus of control

A strong belief in one's own ability to succeed, so that one accepts responsibility for outcomes and tries harder after making mistakes.

external locus of control

A strong belief that luck, fate, or factors beyond one's control determine one's progress, causing feelings of helplessness and decreasing intensity of goal-seeking efforts in the face of failure.

- *The Craftsperson*—has trade or skill or overwhelming desire to do a craft.
- *The Opportunist*—commits to the entrepreneurial effort because it makes business sense.
- *The Inventor*—likes to create and bring new products to market.

These categories are not always mutually exclusive. Many entrepreneurs fit into more than one category. These general categories can still be useful for understanding the basic motives and approaches used by entrepreneurs. A craftsperson may not have a good handle on the financial realities of his/her new business venture. Likewise, an opportunist may have little understanding or concern for the skill and care that might be needed to produce the product or provide the service. Still, both have certain drives which may enable them to succeed.

Source: R. J. Kuntze, "The Dark Side of Multilevel Marketing: Appeals to the Symbolically Incomplete." Dissertation at Arizona State University, 2001.

ternal locus of control fail, they are more likely to feel helpless and are less likely to sustain or intensify their goal-seeking efforts.

An entrepreneur takes on some level of risk when trying to start a new venture. In some cases, entrepreneurs may risk a substantial portion of their own capital as well as funds contributed by family, friends, and other investors. The entrepreneur may leave the security of a corporate career and still be uncertain that the new venture presents a better opportunity. However, entrepreneurs, as a group, may not face quite as much risk of failure as previously thought. A widely held belief has been that 90 percent of entrepreneurial efforts fail in the first year of operation. Current data indicates that 67 percent of new ventures are successful after four years.[5] While this percentage is certainly far from a guarantee, it is not nearly as gloomy as the high 90 percent failure rate that had been previously suggested.

Entrepreneurs feel certain they can master the skills needed to run a business and that they can overcome unforeseen obstacles. This self-confidence can be used to energize and motivate others. Self-confidence enables entrepreneurs to improvise and find novel solutions to business problems that might discourage people who are more self-critical.

Michael Dell, the entrepreneur who founded Dell Computer, exhibits all of these characteristics. His background and reasons for launching his company are described in Management Close-Up 8.b.

Entrepreneurs acquire these characteristics in various ways. Some learn them from family role models. Others are exposed to entrepreneurs in school, work, or social activities. Most people have opportunities to develop entrepreneurial characteristics by imitating others who have these characteristics.

Michael Dell, Founder and CEO, Dell Computer Corporation

THEME: CUSTOMER FOCUS Michael Dell is founder and CEO of Austin-based Dell Computer Corporation, which was the third largest U.S. computer company ($32 billion in sales) in 2000. With a net worth of $17 billion, he is the wealthiest person in Texas. Dell's idea was to sell computers directly to the customer by telephone, avoiding costly middlemen and saving the customer money. Rather than building computers to distribute to retail outlets and carrying large inventories of finished computers and parts to build them, he built computers to order. The company saved money by having a lean, just-in-time inventory of parts from suppliers. Michael Dell pioneered the use of the Internet as a distribution channel for selling computers, and Dell now sells more computers on the Internet than any other company.

Dell was born into a Houston family of high achievers. His father was an orthodontist, his mother a stockbroker. When Michael was 8 years old he applied for a high school equivalency exam, and by age 13 he started a mail order stamp-trading business. When Dell was 16 he started selling subscriptions to the *Houston Post* by phone and became salesman of the month shortly after. A year later he was earning $18,000 annually supervising fellow high school students as they sold subscriptions.

At a young age Dell became very interested in computers. While spending a lot of time around computer retail stores, he realized that these stores were charging up to a 40 percent markup on their products. Even though these stores were charging a high amount for their computers, their service was not very good. Dell realized that he could buy the products directly from the manufacturer, sell them cheaply to the customer, provide better service, and completely eliminate the retail store.

Dell decided to start his computer business when he was just a freshman at the University of Texas at Austin. Working out of his dorm room, Dell sold computers built to order to interested buyers. Three months later, Dell had racked up sales of $181,000. Two years later, when Dell turned 20, the company reached $34 million in sales.

Michael Dell has remained at the helm of Dell Computer from the start, becoming one of the youngest CEOs of a major U.S. corporation while still in his twenties.

Sources: A. Serwer, "Michael Dell Rocks," *Fortune,* May 11, 1998, pp. 59–70; A. Serwer, "Michael Dell Turns the PC World Inside Out," *Fortune,* September 8, 1997, pp. 76–86; D. F. Kuratko and R. M. Hodgetts, *Entrepreneurship,* 2nd ed., Fort Worth: Dryden Press, 1992, p. 72; www.dell.com.

Entrepreneurial Skills

Just as there are certain characteristics that are likely to be found in entrepreneurs, there are also skills which are related to success. An entrepreneur utilizes a variety of business skills to create and operate an enterprise. Among these are negotiation skills, networking skills, and leadership skills.

NEGOTIATION SKILLS Whenever an exchange of goods or services between two or more parties takes place, quality negotiation skills are helpful. A party who applies negotiation skills effectively ensures favorable terms for both parties by finding common ground. This problem-solving style of negotiation, also referred to as *win–win* negotiating, requires the individual to act in good faith to forge a relationship based on trust and cooperation. This makes it easier to discover a basis of exchange that is attractive to both parties. More information on negotiation skills is provided in Chapter 14.

Entrepreneurs use negotiation skills to obtain resources needed to launch and maintain a company. Among the situations that require negotiation skills are:

- Borrowing money from a bank at good terms to finance business expansion.
- Locking into an attractive, long-term lease to control office space expenses.
- Obtaining a low price on raw materials from a supplier to gain a cost advantage over competitors.
- Negotiating employment contracts to attract and retain key executives.

NETWORKING SKILLS Gathering information and building alliances requires quality networking skills. These are applied to both personal and business networks.

A **personal network** is based on relationships between the entrepreneur and other entrepreneurs, suppliers, creditors, investors, friends, former professors, and others. These personal contacts can help an entrepreneur make effective decisions by providing information that reduces uncertainty for the business. For example,

- A fellow entrepreneur can help locate a wealthy interested private investor (sometimes referred to as a "business angel") to provide scarce capital.
- A former professor may provide free technical consulting advice and student volunteers to help develop a marketing strategy for the new venture.
- A banker may be able to locate a skilled executive who could provide complementary management skills to the entrepreneurship at a critical stage of growth.
- Talks with fellow entrepreneurs who have been through the process of building a business from the ground up can provide invaluable feedback and emotional support.

Entrepreneurs build personal networks by actively seeking out individuals with similar interests, staying in touch with them, and looking for opportunities to make the relationship mutually satisfying. Manager's Notes 8.3 presents some key suggestions for effective networking. By being responsive to the needs and interests of the people in their personal networks, entrepreneurs build trust and goodwill. A personal network can be formed through participation in professional societies, business clubs, charitable organizations, trade fairs, and networks of entrepreneurs.

Networking skills can come in handy in developing useful business alliances. A **business network** is a set of alliances forged with other businesses to achieve mutually beneficial goals. A larger company may enter

---

personal network

The relationships between an entrepreneur and other parties, including other entrepreneurs, suppliers, creditors, investors, friends, former colleagues, and others.

Jo Mei Chang left Taiwan for the U.S. in 1974 to get a PhD in computer management systems. By 1994, she was CEO of one of the hottest companies in Silicon Valley—Vitria Technology, Inc. Vitria makes software, "Businessware®" that allows old, hard-to-replace systems to accommodate newer Internet software. In 2000, Vitria grew more than 400%, and Chang was named "Entrepreneur of the Year" by BusinessWeek Magazine.

business network

A firm's alliances formed with other businesses to achieve mutually beneficial goals.

Keith Ferrazi, CEO of YaYa, a company that creates online games as customer marketing vehicles, has strong networking skills. He credits networking as being the tool he used to develop YaYa into a viable business. When Ferrazi became CEO, YaYa had technical capabilities but not customers. Ferrazi identified the most important players in the industry, including CEOs, programmers, journalists, and academics. He established relationships with many of them, and within a year in 2002 YaYa went from no revenue to $8 million in sales.

The following are some of the recommendations from Ferrazi regarding networking. While few of us may be CEOs, they also apply to other situations.

- *Know What You Want*
  Networking should have a purpose: Don't just network to network. What is your goal? Company objectives should drive who is on your networking list. A goal of shifting to a new area of business would probably lead to networking with different people than the goal of entering a new market.

- *Keep a Database of Key Names*
  Ferrazi keeps two Palm Pilots that contain over 5,000 contacts. While that is a far larger number of contacts than most people would need, a great deal can be learned from Ferrazi's system. First, he maintains two sets of contacts, one personal and the other for business. Second, he keeps a list of people he knows as well as people he would like to know. He also looks for lists of notable or up-and-coming people to add to the databases.

- *Build Relationships before You Need Them*
  Networking might be considered the cultivating groundwork that is needed before anything can be harvested. If you wait to develop your network until you need it, it will be too late. Connecting with others to find a job may look like a desperate move to use others. However, if a network is already established, a tip or good word about a job opportunity is simply another exchange in a history of exchanges.

- *It Isn't a Win/Lose Game*
  Successful networking is based on win/win exchanges. It is not just about getting what you want. Networking is about long-term relationships. A good networker helps people get in touch with each other. If you put two people together that prove useful to each other for business reasons, they will be better off, but so will you. Your network will be stronger because of the exchange and the people you helped to bring together will likely remember who facilitated the new relationship.

Source: Adapted from T. Raz, "The 10 Secrets of a Master Networker," *Inc.*, January 2003, pp. 90–99.

a partnership with a small entrepreneurship in order to gain some of the benefits of the new and innovative product or service the entrepreneurship is developing. Through licensing agreements that provide limited access to the technology or strategic alliances to pool resources, a new company may gain access to a larger corporation's marketing and finance professionals or may obtain capital to help enter markets that are difficult to reach. This includes acquiring shelf space in Wal-Mart or having a national direct sales force call on customers.

Microsoft entered a strategic alliance with IBM in 1980 to provide DOS-based operating systems for the new IBM personal computer. This strategic alliance ensured the success of Microsoft and greatly enabled it to set the technology standard for personal computer operating systems, which resulted in huge profits for Microsoft.

LEADERSHIP SKILLS   Quality leaders provide a shared vision for others to work toward common goals. As leaders, entrepreneurs inspire and motivate employees to do what is good for the enterprise, even when it is not in their short-term interests. For example, employees in a start-up company are likely to work extremely long hours for modest pay. The entrepreneur depends on leadership skills to bolster employee morale and guide the enterprise toward the objectives, overcoming obstacles that stand in the way.

Starting and Managing an Entrepreneurial Venture

An entrepreneurial venture begins with an idea. The next steps are developing a business plan, selecting the most appropriate type of legal structure to operate under, obtaining financing, and dealing with growth and expansion. Many entrepreneurial ventures are new businesses, rather than being franchises or spin-offs.

New Business Ideas

Entrepreneurs get ideas for new businesses from many different sources, including

- Newspapers, magazines, and trade journals that identify market trends.

- Inventions or discoveries that provide products or services faster, better, cheaper, or with more features. Corporations like the 3M Company give technologists unstructured time to experiment, hoping for the discovery of the next Post-it Notes.

- Trade shows and exhibitions, where new products and innovations are displayed.

- Hobbies, such as jogging, bicycling, or skiing, as was the case with new companies that marketed running shoes (Nike), mountain bicycles (Cannondale), and snowboards (Burton).

- Family members, including children, such as in the design of video games, educational toys, and the baby jogger that lets people combine jogging with taking the baby out. (See Management

NETWORKING SKILLS

Reflect on a meeting of a professional student club or organization that you have recently attended.

1. What was your purpose for attending this meeting?

2. Did you have any specific goals in mind in terms of the kinds of people you hoped to meet and how you hoped to benefit from the meeting?

3. How many people did you meet at the meeting?

4. How many of these new acquaintances did you connect with so that there was a possibility for a relationship to emerge?

5. How many people did you follow up with a phone call after the meeting?

6. What was the basis of your relationship with these new contacts?

7. Have you continued to keep in touch with these new contacts? If not, why not?

Instructions: Answer the preceding questions individually. Then form small groups of four to five students. Share your experiences in networking with each other. Then work together to answer the following questions. If time permits, attend a professional meeting after developing some network strategies and report back to the group with your experiences.

Discussion Questions

1. What are some effective practices that can be used to network with other people?

2. How can you avoid getting entangled in too many fruitless network relationships that are not mutually beneficial?

3. What are some ways to keep your network vital so that you can feel free to tap your network for opportunities when the time comes and you are in need of help?

Source: From *Entrepreneurship*, by M. J. Dollinger. Copyright © 1995 The McGraw-Hill Companies, Inc. Reprinted with permission.

Close-Up 8.c for an example of an entrepreneur whose business was inspired by her children.)

- Entrepreneurship courses in business schools. Babson University in Wellesley, Massachusetts, sponsors a business plan contest between teams of business students who compete for prize money. Student entrepreneurs with promising business plans are likely to attract the attention of investors.

Why Entrepreneurs Fail

Entrepreneurial ventures can fail if the business idea is poorly implemented. The most common reasons for business failure include:

- *Lack of capital.* When an entrepreneur underestimates the need for capital and assumes more debt than can be repaid, the new business is in trouble. Many businesses fail because investors do not purchase enough stock during the initial public offering to cover accumulated debts.

Of Kids and Mice: Making Mice Work for Children

THEME: CUSTOMER FOCUS Many kids are being exposed to computers at a very young age. Unfortunately their fine motor skills aren't always up to the task. Moving around a mouse that is too big for your hand can be very frustrating. Why not make a mouse that fits a child's hand and is cute and engaging at the same time? That's exactly what Susan Giles thought when she saw the frustration of her 4-year-old granddaughter trying to operate a computer. Giles created a rounder and smaller mouse. She decorated each one to look like a cute bug or dinosaur and gave them cute names. The venture turned out to be so successful that she devoted herself full time to running Kidz Mouse. How successful is the company? Giles keeps numbers concerning the business to herself. She did however recently sign a contract with Nickelodeon to make mice based on network characters such as SpongeBob Square Pants and Blues Clues. Another indicator of success is that the mice can now be found at outlets such as CompUSA and Best Buy, among others.

Source: M. Cassidy, "Creative Marketing: The Mouse Tap," *Detroit Free Press*, December 5, 2002, accessed February 19, 2003, at www.freep.com/money/tech/mice5_20021205.htm.

- *Poor knowledge of the market.* An entrepreneur can miscalculate the appeal of the product or service. This often occurs when an inventor "falls in love" with an invention and expects consumers to do so as well.

- *Faulty product design.* Design or other features of a product can be rejected by consumers. This was the case with word processing products sold by Wang Computer, which were linked to mainframe computers and were much more expensive than rival products that were driven by personal computers. Wang was unable to sell enough of its products and went out of business.

- *Human resource problems.* Entrepreneurs may select employees who do not support the goals of the business. In a family business, there is the potential for divorce or sibling rivalry to divide workers into feuding factions.

- *Poor understanding of the competition.* Entrepreneurs should study their competitors and try to understand their interests. Firmly entrenched businesses may react aggressively and use price cuts or special discounts to try to drive new competitors out of business. Any time a new grocery store opens, local competitors will make dramatic efforts to keep customers.

Sometimes businesses exit the market for reasons other than failure. An entrepreneur may sell the business to a competitor for a good price or close it because a more attractive business opportunity has come along.

Business Plan

Once an entrepreneur develops an idea for a new business venture, the next critical step is to prepare a **business plan,** which is a blueprint that

business plan

The business's blueprint that maps out its business strategy for entering markets and that explains the business to potential investors.

FIGURE 8.1

Outline of a Business Plan

Source: From *Entrepreneurship*, 4th ed., by R. Hisrich and M. Peters. Copyright © 1998 The McGraw-Hill Companies, Inc. Reprinted with permission.

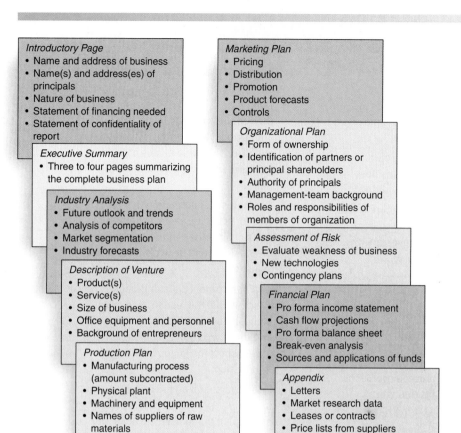

maps out the business strategy for entering markets and explains the business to potential investors. A business plan details the strategies and tactics needed to minimize the enterprise's risk of failure, which is highest during the early stages.

Key components of the business plan include:

- A description of the product or service.
- An analysis of market trends and potential competitors.
- An estimated price for the product or service.
- An estimate of the time it will take to generate profits.
- A plan for manufacturing the product.
- A plan for growth and expansion of the business.
- Sources of funding.
- A plan for obtaining financing.
- An approach for putting an effective management team in place.

A detailed outline for creating a business plan appears in Figure 8.1.

Business Plan Do's and Don'ts

- *Do* create a logical, comprehensive, and readable business plan: make it clear and to the point.

- *Do* spend time and money on preparing a professional business plan: both show your commitment.

- *Do* spell out clearly the venture's risks and the plan's assumptions about them: demonstrate to investors why these risks are acceptable.

- *Do* clarify problems in the venture: a realistic plan will present all problems the venture may encounter and your solutions to them.

- *Do* propose several sources of financing for the operation: spell out how the firm can proceed even if the initial financing falls through.

- *Do* target the investors you are approaching: banks and venture capitalists, for example, will likely look for different types of information. Create a version of your plan based on a particular audience.

- *Do* focus on realistic market and sales projections as the basis of your financial spreadsheets: your plan should reflect accurate projections, not skew the projections to make the plan "work."

- *Don't* hide the proposed members of the venture's management team: anonymous descriptions will seem suspicious. Provide names and affiliations separately, on a confidential basis.

- *Don't* present information that isn't clear or accurate: vague estimates of sales against the venture's possible production won't be acceptable to the investor.

- *Don't* use product jargon in your descriptions: the readers who understand it may not be potential investors, and those who don't understand it may suspect the jargon is hiding information.

- *Don't* overspend on the business plan and your presentation of it: a professional plan that presents a need and that details how the venture will satisfy it and earn a profit for the investors will be taken more seriously than the "bells and whistles" of an expensive marketing effort to sell the plan.

Source: Adapted from J. A. Timmons, *New Venture Creation,* 4th ed., New York: Irwin/McGraw-Hill, 1994, p. 383.

Business plans are often designed to interest potential investors. Manager's Notes 8.4 lists things to do and things to avoid in writing a business plan.

Legal Forms

Entrepreneurs can select from three different legal forms when launching a new enterprise. The legal forms are a proprietorship, a partnership, and a corporation. An entrepreneur should consider tax implications, willingness to accept personal liability, and the ease of raising capital for the business before making this important decision.

PROPRIETORSHIP   Many new businesses are owned by single individuals. **Proprietorships** are easy to form and require a minimum of paperwork. The owner keeps all of the profits and makes all of the important decisions without having to get the approval of co-owners.

A proprietorship is limited to one person, which restricts the owner from obtaining more than limited amounts of credit and capital. Another drawback is that the sole owner has unlimited liability, which means that the personal assets of the owner may be at stake in a lawsuit. About 74 percent of all U.S. businesses are proprietorships, though revenues and profits are relatively small compared to other forms of ownership.

PARTNERSHIP   An association of two or more persons acting as co-owners of a business creates a **partnership.** Each partner provides resources and skills and shares in the profits. A partnership can raise more capital than a proprietorship and can provide complementary skills that can create more opportunity for the enterprise. For example, one partner of a small Los Angeles law firm is skillful at generating new clients from his extensive networks in the local bar association, while the other is skilled at providing meticulous legal research that results in a high court success rate. The synergy between these two law partners results in more profits than would be possible if each were operating alone.

While partnerships are easy to start and are subject to few government regulations, they do have some drawbacks. Each partner is responsible for the acts of the other partners. If one partner makes a bad business decision, the other partners are liable. In other words, each owner's personal assets are at risk in a lawsuit or to pay off debts. If the partners disagree about important goals of the business, the firm may become paralyzed or fail. If one of the partners dies, a partnership will be in jeopardy unless provisions for the other partners to buy out the deceased partner's share have been made. Nonetheless, some large and successful businesses use the partnership legal structure. Large accounting firms such as Arthur Andersen have more than 1,000 partners in offices around the globe.

CORPORATION   A **corporation** is a legal entity separate from the individuals who own it. A corporation receives limited rights to operate from the state or government that provides its charter. A corporation is more complex and costly to form and operate than a proprietorship or a partnership. Since its activities are regulated by the government, many records must be kept and regularly filed with the government.

The benefit of forming a corporation is limited liability. If the corporation is sued, corporate assets are at risk, but the personal assets of the

proprietorship

A form of business that is owned by one person.

partnership

A form of business that is an association of two or more persons acting as co-owners of a business.

corporation

A form of business that is a legal entity separate from the individuals who own it.

TABLE 8.1

Partnership and Corporation Forms of Ownership

ADVANTAGES	DISADVANTAGES
Partnership	
Ease of formation	Unlimited liability for firm's debt
Direct share of profits	Limited continuity of life of enterprise
Division of labor and management responsibility	Difficulty in obtaining capital
More capital available than in a sole proprietorship	Partners share responsibility for other partners' actions
Less governmental control and regulation	
Corporation	
Owners' liability for the firm's debt limited to their investment	Extensive government regulation of activities
Ease of raising large amounts of capital	High incorporation fees
Ease of transfer of ownership through sales of stock	Corporate capital, profits, dividends and salaries double-taxed
Life of enterprise distinct from owners	Activities limited to those stated in charter

Sources: Adapted from W. Megginson et al., *Small Business Management,* 2nd ed., New York: Irwin/McGraw-Hill, 1997, pp. 74, 78; D. F. Kuratko and R. M. Hodgetts, *Entrepreneurship,* 2nd ed., Fort Worth: Dryden Press, 1992, p. 208.

owners are not. A corporation is separate from the owner. When the owner dies, the corporation continues. Corporations are able to raise more capital than any of the other legal forms of enterprise. Corporations are able to raise capital through the sale of shares of stock to the public or through loans and bonds.

Besides incorporation fees and the additional recordkeeping expenses, many corporations are doubly taxed by the government. The corporation pays taxes on its profits, and the owners pay taxes on their dividends. Some other countries do not have this double taxation system, and some firms find it attractive to incorporate in countries that offer advantageous tax treatment. The advantages and disadvantages of partnerships and corporations are summarized in Table 8.1.

Sources of Financial Resources

Entrepreneurships require capital to get started. The two principal means of obtaining the resources to fund a new business are debt financing and equity financing. Factors favoring one type of financing over the other include the value of the firm's assets, the interest rate, and the availability of investor funds.

DEBT FINANCING   Commercial loans are a common form of **debt financing.** Company leaders must set up a plan to repay the principal and interest. The schedule to repay the loan may be short term, lasting less

debt financing

A means of obtaining financial resources that involves obtaining a commercial loan and setting up a plan to repay the principal and interest.

than one year, or long term. Commercial banks are the principal source of debt financing.

The bank establishes a repayment schedule for the loan and secures the loan with company assets such as inventories, equipment, and machines or real estate. Failure to make the scheduled loan repayments can lead to **bankruptcy,** a legal procedure that distributes company assets to creditors and protects the debtor from unfair demands of creditors. Bankruptcy can hurt the reputation of an entrepreneur and make it difficult to obtain future business loans.

An entrepreneur must be careful not to take on too much debt. Excessive debt will result in most of the company's positive cash flow going to retiring the debt rather than growing the business. New ventures that have uncertain cash flows during start-up may not be able to qualify for debt financing.

Other sources of debt financing for more specific purchases are:

- Equipment manufacturers (for example, a computer firm may debt finance a computer system).
- Suppliers (credit may be given on supplies for a fee).
- Credit cards (some businesses were started by overextending several of an owner's credit cards, an expensive way to obtain financing).

EQUITY FINANCING   As a business grows, an entrepreneur will most likely combine a mix of debt and equity sources of capital. **Equity financing** is raising money by selling part of the ownership of the business to investors. In equity financing, the entrepreneur shares control of the business with the investors. Equity financing does not require collateral. Sources of equity financing include private investors, venture capitalists, and public offerings in which shares of stock are sold.

Early in the growth of a business, the risk of failure may be great. At this stage, private investors and venture capitalists may be willing to provide equity financing. **Venture capitalists** specialize in making loans to entrepreneurships that have the potential for rapid growth but are in high-risk situations with few assets and would therefore not qualify for commercial bank loans. Venture capitalists manage pools of money provided by wealthy individuals and institutions seeking to invest in entrepreneurships. High-technology businesses such as software, telecommunications, and biotechnology are particularly attractive to venture capitalists because they anticipate high financial returns from their investment. Microsoft, Compaq Computer, and Intel were started with venture capital financing and made fabulous returns for early investors. Venture capitalists also provide management knowledge, contacts to hire key employees, and financial advice.

Public offerings raise capital by selling securities in public markets such as the New York Stock Exchange and NASDAQ. A public offering

bankruptcy

A legal procedure that distributes company assets to creditors and protects the debtor from unfair demands of creditors when the debtor fails to make scheduled loan repayments.

equity financing

A means of obtaining financial resources that involves the sale of part of the ownership of the business to investors.

venture capitalists

Financial investors who specialize in making loans to entrepreneurships that have the potential for rapid growth but are in high-risk situations with few assets and would therefore not qualify for commercial bank loans.

public offerings

A means of raising capital by the sale of securities in public markets such as the New York Stock Exchange and NASDAQ.

The Kauffman Entrepreneurship Internship Program at *www.keip.org* offers real world experience for students, and the chance to work side-by-side with successful entrepreneurs in new or emerging firms. Check to see if your school participates in the internship program—over 100 U.S. colleges and universities did in 2002.

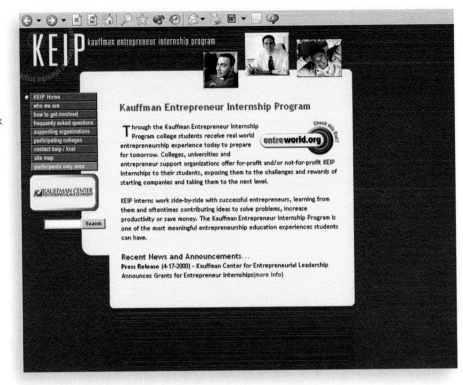

can provide large infusions of cash to fuel rapid internal growth or to finance a merger or acquisition. One drawback of a public offering is that publicly traded companies must disclose a great deal of information, including quarterly reports on income, balance sheet assets, and use of funds. Competitors can exploit weaknesses that are disclosed in these reports. After a public offering, management decisions are under a higher level of public scrutiny. There is a lower tolerance for management mistakes, and there is increased shareholder pressure for dividends and predictable quarterly profits. Unhappy shareholders can sell their shares, driving down the value of the company. Public offerings generally do not take place until an entrepreneurship achieves a critical mass of about $10 million to $20 million in annual revenue.

Managing Growth

Entrepreneurs manage business growth by establishing benchmarks based on market data and a thorough analysis of the firm's ability to handle increased demand without sacrificing quality. A business plan is an invaluable tool for planning growth targets. These milestones can be used to pace company expansion. Too much growth can put an unbearable strain on the operations of a business. A company that grows too quickly may experience the following:

- The company spends most of its available cash on expansion and has difficulty meeting obligations to creditors. The result is a cash flow crisis.

- Employees are likely to experience stress from such rapid changes as moving to new jobs without training, adjusting to new supervisors and colleagues, and making frequent changes in office locations.

- Accounting and information systems that worked well when the firm was smaller must be replaced with more complicated and sophisticated systems. Current personnel may not be capable of operating these systems, and information may not be available when it is needed.

- Management may no longer be competent to manage a larger or more diverse portfolio of business units or product lines. The board of directors may replace the chief executive officer or other key executives with more experienced managers. To make matters worse, the founder may resist stepping down. In 1985 Steve Jobs, the founder of Apple Computer, was asked to leave by its board, which felt his leadership style was not appropriate for the large company that Apple had become. (Jobs, always the entrepreneur, started another company. In 1997 he returned to Apple—by then under different leadership—with the technology he had developed in the interim and sold it to Apple for $400 million.)

Unchecked growth can threaten the survival of a business venture. For example, James L. Bildner, the founder of J. Bildner & Sons Inc., a specialty food business, expanded rapidly from a single store to a chain of 20 stores after a public offering in 1986. The company ran out of cash because it had built too many stores. Employees started leaving and operations became chaotic. Too many new stores, ineffective new products, attempts to hire too many new people at once, and lack of controls made everything worse. The company experienced large losses, inventory control problems, and the departure of loyal customers. This crisis could have been avoided if the management team had pursued less aggressive growth. Sometimes managers should turn down growth opportunities in an expanding market rather than lose control of the operation.

Alternative Forms of Entrepreneurship

This chapter has focused on *independent entrepreneurship*. Alternatives to this form of entrepreneurship are intrapreneurship, spin-offs, and franchising. In general, these alternative forms involve smaller risks than independent entrepreneurship.

From Outsourcing to Franchising: Capitalizing on the Entrepreneurial Spirit

Yorkshire Electricity is an electric utility company located in the U.K. As with many utility companies around the globe, Yorkshire experienced great pressure to reduce costs and increase productivity. Government shareholder pressure resulted in the top management at Yorkshire cutting staff and looking for reengineering options. Maintenance was a major cost in the utility company since 15,000 operational sites were being maintained by a department that couldn't compete with the external marketplace in terms of productivity and cost. The immediate solution appeared to be outsourcing the maintenance function. However, there were many skilled people employed by the utility that were the best in their trade. It did not seem advisable to lose that valuable resource. Instead, the management team developed a novel approach to achieving private sector productivity and costs: They set up a franchise model.

Yorkshire Electricity established an organization called Freedom Maintenance in which people still work for the utility, but as franchisees, not as employees. It took two years to gain the approval of the board of directors and the union. Freedom Maintenance started with 55 franchises in 1996 and now has approximately 500 franchises.

The franchises are responsible for their own tools, vehicles, and materials. The Freedom organization helps out by handling some administrative work, such as invoicing and collection, on behalf of the franchises. The process has created hundreds of new businesses that work independently, but with some assistance from the overall organization. The model has allowed some former Yorkshire employees to exercise their skills along with an entrepreneurial spirit. One franchiser now employs eight people and relies on his former employer for less than 50 percent of his business. The self-employment model has worked well for Yorkshire Electricity. The company has realized a 20 percent savings in maintenance costs since establishing the franchise model. The model has worked so well in the United Kingdom, Freedom is promoting the approach in the electric utility industry in the United States.

Source: B. Mottram, S. Rigby, and A. Webster, "The Freedom to Call Your Own Shots," *Transmission & Distribution World* 55 (January 2003).

Intrapreneurship

The development of new business units within a larger corporate structure in order to deploy the firm's resources to market a new product or service is **intrapreneurship,** or *corporate entrepreneurship.* Some large companies develop cultures that foster innovation and the nurturing of new businesses. The 3M Company maintains a corporate goal that requires over 30 percent of corporate sales to come from products less than four years old. The technical staff is encouraged to devote 15 percent of its time to experimentation in new product designs that are peripheral to the projects they have been assigned to work on. These policies support a culture of innovation that has resulted in a steady stream of internally developed new products at the 3M Company.

When Apple showed the world that there was a large market for personal computers, IBM saw the need to design its own personal computer to challenge the Apple computer. The IBM Personal Computer was developed in a separate business unit located in Florida and isolated from the rest of the company. To build, test, and market launch the IBM PC in only 12 months, the IBM Personal Computer unit used standard electronic components and systems, rather than using all-IBM manufactured components as was typical in the company.

In the 1990s the National Broadcasting Company (NBC), the television network owned by General Electric, launched CNBC, a cable television network that provided financial news 24 hours a day. The launch coincided with the 1990s bull market that generated a large demand for televised financial news. Within a few years CNBC was profitable and successful, attracting a highly desirable audience of wealthy executives and investors.

An advantage of intrapreneurship is that the company provides funding and corporate resources that an independent entrepreneur cannot gather. The intrapreneuring corporate engineer or manager does not have to abandon a corporate career to manage the new venture. On the other hand, a successful *intrapreneur* within a corporation usually does not receive the financial rewards that might be generated by an independent entrepreneurship.

Spin-Offs

Sometimes a new product developed by a corporation does not fit with the company's established products. A group of managers may decide to create a new business for this product rather than forgo the opportunity to market it. A **spin-off** is an independent entrepreneurship that produces a product or service that originated in a large company. Spin-offs are typical of technology companies, which must develop a steady stream of new products to keep up with competitors. Some of the new technologies do not fit with the company's core competencies, providing the opportunity for spin-offs.

spin-off

An independent entrepreneurship that produces a product or service that originated in a large company.

Dippin' Dots franchises sell tiny beads of "flash-frozen" ice cream in many flavors and colors. In January 2003, Dippin' Dots ranked 144th on Entrepreneur Magazine's Franchise 500 list. A Dippin' Dots franchise currently costs $12,500 plus other costs.

Xerox's Palo Alto Research Center (PARC) is a laboratory located in California's Silicon Valley that develops new optical imaging products that fit with the core competencies of Xerox. Occasionally, new technologies that do not fit with other Xerox products are spawned in this research laboratory. Xerox encourages the formation of spin-offs when the technology has commercial potential. In some cases, Xerox forms a partnership with the managers who start the spin-off. For example, when a security product that encrypts messages for cellular phones was developed in the PARC laboratories, Xerox created a spin-off called Semaphore Communications to manufacture and market the device.

Franchises

When a business with an established name and product is sold to additional owners along with the rights to distribute the product, a franchise operation is created. Franchising is particularly prevalent in the retail service sector of the economy, such as in the restaurant, hotel, and retail businesses. McDonald's, Taco Bell, Subway, Quality Inn, Dunkin' Donuts, Radio Shack, and Midas are well-known franchises. Franchising can also occur in unexpected situations. See Management Close-Up 8.d for a description of franchising that has occurred in the public sector.

In franchising, an entrepreneur assumes fewer risks because the franchise can provide: (1) a product or service with an established market and favorable image; (2) management training and assistance in operating the business; (3) economies of scale for advertising and purchasing; (4) operating and structural controls; and (5) financial assistance. The franchising company sells the distribution rights for a limited geographic area to the entrepreneur for a fee plus a share of the revenues.

Sometimes franchising companies fail to provide promised services. The franchise company may oversell franchise rights in a geographic location, making it difficult for an entrepreneur to profit. Such conflicts of interests can result in lengthy courtroom battles.

Innovation

Innovation is a key to long-term success. Exploring and developing new technologies and new ways of doing things is vital to the future viability of an organization.[6] Entrepreneurs often pursue innovative ideas in their new business ventures. For example, entrepreneurs may come up with ideas and pursue them when an organization decides that the time and cost of development are just too great. An example of an entrepreneur who should soon be bringing a new product to market is rock musician Jerry Riopelle. An overview of his innovative product is presented in Management Close-Up 8.e.

HumanBeams: It's Music to My Ears!

THEME: DEALING WITH CHANGE Innovation and entrepreneurship often go together. The two concepts certainly seem to work well for Jerry Riopelle, a rock musician who is also an innovator and entrepreneur. Riopelle has been working for years on a mix of hardware and software that allows people to make music by manipulating laser beams. He calls this innovative product Human-Beams. After about nine years of work on the product and a $600,000 investment, he thinks he is close to production. Perhaps by the time this book is published, Riopelle will have the manufacturing process ready for mass production. He thinks HumanBeams will sell for $700 or less.

The HumanBeams product became reality because of Jerry's musical talent and his understanding of technology. The device involves moving a hand, for example, to break the path of laser beams. The movement is translated by a computer into musical tones. The music produced is goof-proof, it harmonizes, and there are no bad notes.

Source: J. Larson, "Musician Beams with Joy," *The Arizona Republic*, February 8, 2003, pp. D1, D2.

However, as pointed out earlier, entrepreneurship is often about rather modest and incremental change to a product or service, rather than a radical change. Further, larger organizations may embrace and encourage innovation. Thus, we end this chapter with a separate consideration of innovation.

What is an innovation? Fundamentally, it is doing something differently. As Michael Tushman, professor of management at Harvard Business School describes,[7] innovation can involve *radical* or *incremental* change. Radical innovations often make prior technologies obsolete. For example, digital compact discs have all but replaced cassette tapes and require a compact disc player to use them. Alternatively, incremental innovations are generally improvements of existing products that usually do *not* render prior products or technologies obsolete. Examples include smaller cell phones or even Caffeine Free Coke. So while it may be difficult to find cassette tapes in your local record store due to the radical innovation of the CD, both Coke and Caffeine Free Coke can easily be had at your local supermarket.

It is not just the innovation, per se, that is important. An innovator must find a way to implement the idea as a cost-effective or commercially viable product or service. Having ideas without the ability to execute them won't be of much business use to an entrepreneur or to a larger organization. Management Close-Up 8.f presents an innovation that would seem to have great potential. However, the commercial viability of the product has yet to be proven. Skills for Managing 8.3 invites you to take a closer look at the innovation and consider its current status as a potential product.

HUMANBEAMS: CHECKING ON AN ENTREPRENEURIAL INNOVATION

As discussed in Management Close-Up 8.e, Jerry Riopelle is developing a new type of musical instrument called HumanBeams. It doesn't require lengthy practice and it can't make bad notes!

Discussion Questions

1. What are the entrepreneurial characteristics of Jerry Riopelle? What other resources were needed for this innovation to be developed?

2. Assess the market for the HumanBeams innovation. Do you think it will translate into a commercially viable project? Why or why not?

Research Question

1. Locate information on the current state of the HumanBeams project. Is the product being produced? Report your findings to the rest of the class.

TABLE 8.2

Management Tactics to Maximize Innovation—The Five Cs

TACTIC	FOCUS
Capability	People
Culture	Balance
Cash and recognition	Rewards
Customer orientation	Trends
Cut losses	Manage investments

If innovation is a key to long-term success, how can an organization be managed so that innovation is encouraged and maximized? While there are no sure-fire, simple solutions, there are things that can be done that should give innovation a chance to flourish.[8] We refer to these management tactics as the "Five Cs." They are summarized in Table 8.2.

The first management tactic listed in Table 8.2 is capability. *Capability* means having people with the skills and interests needed to generate innovative ideas. People who are smart and open and who like to try new things are more likely to create new ideas.

In addition to having the capability to generate innovation, the organizational environment should foster creativity. In most situations, organizational leaders devote most company resources to current services or products. On the other hand, giving all of the resources to the current business means that the organization may be trapped in the past. What is needed is a *culture* that balances routine work and innovative efforts. The

Electronic Ink: The Next Big Thing?

THEME: DEALING WITH CHANGE E Ink is a Massachusetts Institute of Technology spin-off that, in 2002, received $25 million in fourth-round venture funding from Toppan Printing. What was E Ink working on that merited that kind of investment? Electronic ink—a product that promises fundamental change in how we communicate. Electronic ink is a new way to form characters that can be presented on paper-thin screens. Monitors and handheld devices using electronic ink displays would have screens that are five times brighter and use 90 percent less energy than current displays. Perhaps the most wide ranging application for electronic ink is a new form for books and newspapers.

Just what is electronic ink? It is a plastic sheet in which miniature spheres are suspended in packets of oil. The spheres, about the size of the diameter of a human hair, are either black or white. The two colors of spheres have opposite electrical charges. When given appropriate electrical charges, the white and black spheres will configure to shape letters. The figure below provides further description and a representation of how electronic ink works. Once charged, the spheres maintain the configuration until a new electrical impulse is delivered. E Ink is developing flexible thin-film transistors to provide the electrical charges. The company hopes to be able to manufacture sheets of flexible electronic paper that would mimic the pages of newspapers or books by 2005.

The vision that E Ink hopes to bring to reality is the contents of books and newspapers being delivered electronically. A newspaper subscription could, for example, mean an electronic delivery of the newspaper via a radio fre-

quency receiver attached to the electronic ink pages. The content of the paper would appear on the plastic pages until the new edition of the "paper" was delivered. Note, reading the newspaper or book would not involve scrolling down a monitor and the content would be highly portable, just as with a paper-based product. Further, the electronic paper can be reused indefinitely without cutting down any trees to make paper.

Sources: Adapted from C. T. Heun, "New 'Ink' Veers Display toward the Good Old Look," *Informationweek,* February 11, 2002, p. 18; B. Schmitt, "Growth Signs for New Ink," *ChemicalWeek* 164 (February 27, 2002), p. 46.

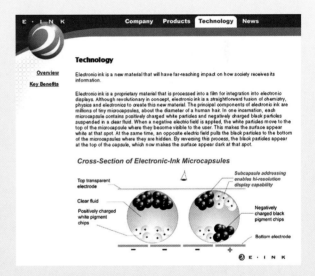

Cross-Section of Electronic-Ink Microcapsules

appropriate *balance* depends upon the industry and on the type of managers in the organization. Whatever the balance point is, the trick is to maintain control and structure within the core process, while encouraging risk taking and experimentation outside of the everyday service or production process. Disney Corporation, for example, insists on a strict script in terms of how visitors are greeted, how rides are operated, and so on. The company also holds a monthly competitive and fun opportunity for any employee to attend and present a new idea.[9] On one side of their operation, the organization may need to limit variation. On the other side,

ELECTRONIC INK: FROM COOL INNOVATION TO COMMERCIAL PRODUCT?

As described in Management Close-Up 8.f, Electronic ink has the potential to replace paper, save trees, and disseminate information immediately. These possible outcomes, among others, as well as the potential market have probably been key to enticing venture capital to E Ink.

technology to signs and Dow Chemical working on plastic light-emitting diodes). Look for current information on these competitors and on E Ink. Do you think the market is differentiated enough that each company will have its own niche or do you think that there will be a competitive struggle for dominance in the market?

Discussion Questions

1. Is electronic paper a radical or incremental change? Defend your judgment.

2. Evaluate the potential market for electronic paper. Do you think it is a commercially viable innovation? Why or why not?

Internet Research Questions

1. The market for electronic paper has some competitors (such as Gyricon media applying the

2. A key to successfully launching a new innovation is protecting the idea from possible competitors. How did E Ink protect the electronic paper technology? Do you think protecting an innovation is a necessary expense?

3. Assess the current status of E Ink. Does the company seem close to making electronic paper a commercial reality? What recommendations, if any, would you make to E Ink?

it needs to be encouraged. It is a question of balance and making sure that people understand when each approach is appropriate.

The third "C" represents the tactic of *cash and recognition*. If you really want to encourage new ideas and creativity, then there should be recognition and reward for those who can deliver. Organizations can offer cash prizes for ideas that are implemented and might even offer stock or other *rewards* to recognize particularly noteworthy innovations. Given incentives, people will quickly recognize that the encouragement to "think outside the box" is more than empty rhetoric.

Customers are another important resource with regard to innovation. Listening to customers can provide a wealth of beneficial information. Critical customers may be the key to identifying improvements or new *trends* in products or services.

The last "C" stands for *cutting losses*. Often individuals or teams become emotionally committed to an innovative idea they have been working on. While this personal investment can increase the effort put into the project, it can also cloud judgment about what is reasonable. A process of checkoffs by people not directly involved in the project can make for an objective decision as to whether to continue investment.

Applications for the Manager   As an entrepreneurship grows, the owner must learn how to manage an increasingly complex enterprise. One of the key components of success is the entrepreneur's ability to delegate responsibilities and duties to others. Many people who start businesses like to be in control. It is not easy for them to learn how to delegate to others. The entrepreneur must free up time for the work he or she is best at doing and set time aside for family and leisure in order to maintain mental and emotional health. An entrepreneur cannot be in all places at once. The inability to delegate can stifle the growth of the firm.

As a firm grows, the entrepreneur must also take on the role of manager. This means no longer managing on an ad hoc basis, but rather being more systematic in dealing with business issues. The entrepreneur will need to develop a formal, consistent, and fair policy for dealing with recurring business issues (such as how to select new employees to hire) so as not to have to "reinvent the wheel" each time an issue arises.

Applications for Managing Teams   Many entrepreneurships are started by founding teams of two or more people. Teams can bring more brain-power and competencies to a new venture, as well as providing psycho-logical support against loneliness, isolation, and stress. Entrepreneurs in teams must learn how to share power and authority with partners and develop ways to settle conflicts. One approach is to set up a board of advisers, such as a group of trusted elders that includes experienced entrepreneurs, who can counsel the partners and provide a neutral sounding board to settle conflicts.

Applications for Individuals   It takes an optimistic person to start a business in light of the evidence that more than half of all new busi-nesses fail. An entrepreneur is the type of individual who always sees the glass as half full, rather than half empty. Those who succeed at entrepre-neurship are self-confident and in fact may be *overconfident*. Overconfi-dence occurs when decision makers have overly optimistic assessments and fail to examine all the available information. An advisory board can provide some perspective and grounding.

When starting a business, it is prudent to keep fixed costs and overhead expenses to a minimum until there is a consistent level and flow of revenue. Some ways to minimize fixed costs include: (1) working out of a home office, rather than signing a lease for a commercial office; (2) using consultants who are paid on the basis of completed projects, rather than hiring employees who are paid salaries; and (3) having customers pay in advance for raw materials, rather than purchasing an inventory of raw materials before a customer has been identified.

After the entrepreneurial examples that opened the chapter, some critical thinking questions were posed regarding entrepreneurial ventures and new business ideas. Now that we have explored the topics of entrepreneurship and innovation, it's time to revisit these introductory questions. First, while there are some personal characteristics, such as an internal locus of control, that are important assets for entrepreneurs, anyone with the motivation can become an entrepreneur. Entrepreneurs need a deep well of motivation, in addition to abilities and personal characteristics relevant to the business they would like to pursue. The source of motivation is often an internal commitment to an idea or process. The practical reality is that motivation often comes from necessity and external obstacles. For example, many people have become entrepreneurs because of being laid off or because of frustration as a member of a large organization.

Second, the risk involved in entrepreneurial effort isn't as great as is typically thought. The initial financial investment of an entrepreneur may be relatively modest. It is later when the business has grown that the entrepreneur may have more dollars at risk. Nonetheless, in terms of psychological risk, the entrepreneur may be putting in an incredible investment at the start of a new venture.

Finally, the basis for a new business idea doesn't have to be radical change. To the contrary, entrepreneurs often capitalize on modest incremental changes to a product or service. Whether an incremental change or a radical innovation, the ideas often come from the particular skills and experiences of the entrepreneur. What may be more important than the particular idea is how it is implemented. The lack of a viable business plan can be the ruin of even a great idea.

Entrepreneurship is the process of creating an enterprise capable of entering new or established markets. An **entrepreneur** is the individual who creates the enterprise that becomes a new entry to the market. Entrepreneurship differs from a small business because many entrepreneurships are small only during the early stage and may grow to become large corporations. A small business is by definition a firm with fewer than 100 employees.

Entrepreneurship is critical to the economic vitality of the United States and other developed countries. Entrepreneurship accounts for a majority of new jobs created in the economy. It is also a major source of innovation. Entrepreneurship provides opportunities for people of diverse backgrounds to improve their economic status and develop interesting careers. Women, minorities, and immigrants face fewer barriers to entrepreneurship than to success in large corporations.

Some of the characteristics associated with successful entrepreneurs are: (1) a high need for achievement; (2) an **internal locus of control** (having strong beliefs that one's innate abilities and efforts will lead to successful outcomes); (3) moderate risk-taking behavior; and (4) self-confidence that translates into the ability to inspire and motivate others. Entrepreneurs depend on negotiation, networking, and leadership skills to manage business ventures.

When starting and managing a new enterprise, entrepreneurs make decisions that will influence the success of the business:

- They develop an idea for the new business based on discovering an unsatisfied need in the market.

- They create a **business plan,** which provides a blueprint for understanding how the business should function and how it will compete in its markets.

- They select **proprietorship, partnership** or **corporation** as the appropriate legal form for the business.

- They determine sources of capital, selecting either **debt financing** or **equity financing.**

- They manage the rate of growth of the business so that the entrepreneurship can take advantage of market opportunities without sacrificing product or service quality.

Entrepreneurship occurs in several different forms including (1) independent entrepreneurship (a new and independent business); (2) **intrapreneurship** (a new business unit developed within a larger corporate structure to enter a market); (3) **spin-off** (an independent entrepreneurship that has its origins in a large corporation); and (4) franchising (a business that is created by purchasing the rights to distribute an established product or service from the franchising company).

Innovation, doing things differently, is a key to long-term success for entrepreneurs, as it is for most businesses, small and large. Management tactics to enhance innovativeness focus on the "Five Cs" of capability, culture, cash and recognition, customers, and cutting losses.

1. How does an entrepreneurial business differ from a small business? What are the similarities?

2. What are the differences between an entrepreneur and a manager?

3. What is the significance of entrepreneurship to the U.S. economy?

4. Identify the important personal characteristics of entrepreneurs. Do you think only people with these characteristics should become entrepreneurs? What problems does this approach present? What alternatives could be used to encourage people to choose an entrepreneurial path?

5. Compare and contrast debt financing and equity financing as ways of starting a new business. Does one have an overall advantage over the other? What situation is more favorable to the use of debt financing? Which situation favors equity financing?

6. Why is growth important to an entrepreneurial business? How can rapid growth be detrimental to it survival?

7. Can an individual be an entrepreneur yet work within a large corporation? Explain your answer.

8. What are the advantages of starting a franchise business (such as a McDonald's) instead of an independent entrepreneurial business? What are the disadvantages?

9. What is the purpose of a business plan for an entrepreneurial effort? Some successful businesses are started without any business plan and operate according to the gut instincts of the entrepreneur. What do you think accounts for the success of businesses that are run "by the seat of the pants" without any formal planning?

10. Describe how you would go about setting up conditions to maximize innovativeness. Put yourself in the place of a manager and use the "Five Cs." How would you assure quality while at the same time encouraging the chaos of experimentation and creativity?

Should an Entrepreneur's Leadership Style Change as the Business Expands?

Knowledge Adventure, Inc. (KA), a California company that produces multimedia "edutainment" software for the child and teen markets, was founded in 1991. The company continues to have great success with its products; it now has sales of more than $35 million and employs about 750 people. It faces stiff competition today, but even giants like Microsoft and Nintendo had a tough time matching the growth speed of Knowledge Adventure.

Knowledge Adventure's founder and chairman, Bill Gross, 35, tried to keep the culture of his company from seeming like a large corporation and becoming "professional." Gross's entrepreneurial style was evident from junior high school, when he sold candy bars from his locker for less than what the cafeteria charged. He put himself through Cal Tech from his high school earnings on a solar power gadget he had invented and marketed in the backs of magazines; while at college he made and sold stereo speakers.

Lotus Development Corp. sued Gross over accounting for Lotus add-on software he created and marketed using Lotus's package design, dropped the suit, and then in 1985 paid him $10 million for a simplified program. After five years developing other products, Bill Gross and his brother Larry started Knowledge Adventure.

Bill Gross was personally involved in making sure that every employee felt the fun and challenge of working in an entrepreneurial company. Gross's goal was to reach $1 billion in sales within 10 years, and he planned to do it by thinking "small."

Gross's leadership style was reflected in the culture of KA. The joke at the company was that every employee had his or her own door—not office, just a $13.99 door purchased by Gross from the local Home Depot. Gross liked to keep things participative and democratic. When the company wanted to relocate, the question of "where" was put to a vote of the employees. After a frenetic month that saw the release of five separate new products, Gross closed the firm down for three days to give all the employees a vacation and treated them and their families to a weekend in Yosemite, planning on Hawaii for the next year.

Was Gross indulgent, or does this style produce results? KA's *Dinosaur Adventure* interactive learning program had the market to itself until Microsoft issued *Jurassic Park*. Within a month Gross had assembled a team that worked three months of all-nighters to upgrade *Dinosaur Adventure* with 3-D technology and more than 30 minutes of new animation. KA regained the number-one position and outsold Microsoft three to one over the Christmas season.

Gross worried about the future, losing a top executive who wanted to implement a more professional "top-down" style. There was increasing pressure to go public. Although many employees would do well financially because they owned stock, Gross felt he was not ready. "The minute we go public, everything changes," he said. More attention would have to be paid to stockholders and less to the employees. That might be bad for business.

In 1995, Gross turned control of the company over to his brother Larry. He had learned that he was better at starting companies than running them. "I love the invention part, but I wasn't paying attention to the details of making a profit," he says. "Had Larry not stepped in and run the company, I don't think it would have survived," says one former board member.

KA was sold to Cendant (CUC) in 1997 for $100 million. Bill Gross now has a new company he started called "idealab!"

Discussion Questions

1. How would you characterize Gross's leadership approach to Knowledge Adventure? What are its benefits? Are there any drawbacks?

2. Would Gross's approach work in a larger firm? Why or why not?

3. What do you think characterizes a "professional" leadership style? Why?

4. Do you believe entrepreneurs should all have similar leadership styles? Why or why not?

Sources: Adapted from M. J. Dollinger, *Entrepreneurship*, New York: Irwin/McGraw-Hill, 1995, p. 442; L. Armstrong, "Knowledge Adventure's Trickiest Game: Success," *Business Week*, April 11, 1994, pp. 48–49; L. Armstrong, "Bill Gross, Online Idea Factory," *Business Week*, June 29, 1998, pp 100–102; www.knowledge adventure.com.

Rapid Growth Short-Circuits Wired Venture's Public Offering Plans

Sometimes unchecked growth can be disruptive to a company's financial plans. Wired Ventures is a San Francisco-based media company that produces *Wired*, a glossy publication that chronicles the issues and spirit of the cybergeneration. In 1996 Wired Ventures shelved its plans for an initial public offering (IPO). Prospective investors were leery of the red ink being generated by the company's far-flung operations, which had lost $35 million during the first half of the year.

Wired Ventures was once perceived as a hot media company. It was valued at $450 million in 1995, but that amount was reduced to around $125 million a year later. The management team got caught in an all-too-familiar quandary: how to manage growth without overstretching resources, overestimating financial returns, or overhyping market potential. As a hot property, Wired had expanded at a heady pace. In addition to *Wired* magazine, it published books, produced a weekly TV show for the MSNBC cable network, produced a British version of *Wired*, and invested heavily in online products. The company could not sustain all that growth on an eroding capital structure and overtaxed executives.

The top executives at Wired Ventures had expected the market to respond positively to its aggressive growth. Instead, investors were critical of management's growth strategy and insisted that Wired Ventures end the red ink and become profitable. Wired was forced to look for alternative sources of capital because an IPO was no longer feasible.

As an epilogue to the decision that is the focus of this case, *Wired* was sold in 1998 to Condé Nast, a large publisher of magazines. In 1999 Wired Ventures was bought by Lycos, a leading Web media company and one of the most visited hubs on the Internet, as part of a bundle of media properties.

Discussion Questions

1. How could rapid growth threaten the survival of Wired Ventures?
2. What are the potential benefits of rapid growth for Wired Ventures?
3. Why do you think investors rejected Wired Ventures's aggressive growth strategy?

Source: Adapted from L. Himmelstein, "Can *Wired* Get Wired Again?" *Business Week*, November 3, 1997, pp. 74–78; www.wired.com.

Running a Sole Proprietorship

The most common form of business ownership in the United States is the sole proprietorship. One such business was L. A. Nicola, a Los Angeles restaurant owned by Larry Nicola. Located away from diners' row, the restaurant attracted clientele for one major reason: great food. As with his later restaurants, Nicola made the menu choices and, in his role as chef, saw that the food was cooked to perfection. He kept on top of new industry trends and knew how to change the menu to reflect the emerging tastes of customers. For example, before health foods became a fad, L. A. Nicola had cut down on sauces and fatty foods and was offering leaner cuisine.

Nicola gets out into his restaurants and works the crowd. He ensures that everything is running smoothly, greets old customers, and welcomes new ones. From his L. A. Nicola venture he went on to open other California restaurants.

What does Nicola like best about being a sole proprietor? He says it is the freedom of choice to do things his own way. If he sees something going wrong, he can correct it. If a customer is not getting proper service, Nicola will intervene and help the waiter out or assign a second waiter to the area. If a customer's food has not been cooked to his or her taste, Nicola can send it back to the kitchen and personally supervise the preparation.

Nicola is not alone in his desire for freedom in running things his own way. In recent years more and more sole proprietorships have been formed by individuals who used to work for other companies and have now broken away and started their own businesses. In the restaurant industry, chefs with an entrepreneurial spirit often first learn the business through experience and then open their own restaurants. Since chefs are usually the people who know the most about restaurants, they have a distinct advantage in starting a new business—the operation cannot succeed without them.

Critical Thinking Questions

1. Why is the sole proprietorship business form so popular with people who want to start a business?

2. What type of liability do sole proprietors have if their business suffers a large loss?

3. If Nicola decided to raise $1 million and expand his restaurant, could he do this as a sole proprietor or would he have to form a partnership or corporation? Explain.

Collaborative Learning Exercise

One of the drawbacks of a proprietorship is that the responsibilities of operating the business are the proprietor's alone. It is difficult to take vacations, and sole proprietors tend to be workaholics who average 61 hours of work per week. Stress, burnout, and neglected families are occupational hazards. Further, there is no one in the business to provide guidance, since the business is owned and operated by one person. The business owner may make a serious blunder in the business strategy and may not become aware of it before it is too late to recover. Meet in a small group to develop tactics that would be useful to entrepreneurs for dealing with these challenges for sole proprietors.

Sources: Adapted from D. F. Kuratko and R. M. Hodgetts, *Entrepreneurship,* 2nd ed., Fort Worth: Dryden Press, 1992, pp. 220–221; R. R. Roha, "Home Alone," *Kiplinger's Personal Finance Magazine,* May 1997, pp. 85–89.

Freedom!

Management Close-Up 8.d focused on the Freedom Maintenance franchise model set up in the U.K. Freedom Franchising Services has a website that further describes the franchising model. Explore the Freedom Franchising website and any related websites regarding this franchise.

1. What services are offered by the Freedom franchises?

2. What is needed to be a Freedom franchise? What skills or other characteristics would a franchise owner need to have in order to be successful?

3. What is the current status of the Freedom Franchise organization?

4. Would you recommend the franchise concept to U.S. electric companies? Why or why not?

5. Could the concept be successfully implemented in other industries?

6. Can you find any information on Freedom applying its franchise model in the United States?

Are You a High Achiever?

The following 10 questions will help you identify your achievement drive. Read the question and circle your answer to each.

1. An instructor in one of your college classes has asked you to vote on three grading options.

   a. Study the course material, take the exams, and receive the grade you earn.

   b. Roll a die and get an A if you roll an odd number and a D if you roll an even number.

   c. Show up for all class lectures, turn in a short term paper, and get a C.

2. How would you describe yourself as a risk taker?

   a. High

   b. Moderate

   c. Low

3. Your boss asks you to take on a new project in addition to the many things you are already doing. What do you say?

   a. I'm already snowed under—I can't handle any more.

   b. Sure, I'm happy to help out—give it to me.

   c. Let me look over my current workload and get back to you tomorrow about whether or not I can take on any more work.

4. Which of these people would you most like to be?

   a. Steve Jobs, founder of Apple Computers.

   b. Lee Iacocca of Chrysler fame.

   c. Roger Smith, former CEO of General Motors.

5. Which game are you most likely to play?

   a. Monopoly

   b. Bingo

   c. Roulette

6. Which approach would you take to become more physically active?

   a. Join a neighborhood team.

   b. Work out on your own.

   c. Join a local health club.

7. Which group do you like to play poker with?

   a. Friends.

   b. High-stake players.

   c. Anyone who can challenge you.

8. Who would you most like to be?

   a. A detective solving a crime.

   b. A politician giving a victory statement.

   c. A millionaire sailing on your yacht.

9. What do you like to do on your evening off?

   a. Visit a friend.

   b. Work on a hobby.

   c. Watch television.

10. Which occupation has the greatest career appeal for you?

    a. Computer salesperson

    b. Corporate accountant

    c. Criminal lawyer

Scoring: Give yourself points for your answers based on the following answer key. Then total your points. The answer key gives an explanation for each question's points.

ANSWER

Question	(a)	(b)	(c)	Scoring Rationale
1.	10	0	2	High achievers take personal responsibility for their actions and do not rely on luck. Points for option *c* assume that the class time saved will be used to study for other classes—otherwise the score for *c* would be a zero.
2.	2	10	2	High achievers are moderate risk takers in important situations.
3.	6	2	10	High achievers like to study a situation before committing themselves to a course of action.
4.	7	10	5	Jobs is a high-achieving individual but is more interested in design and engineering than in goal accomplishment; Iacocca is an extremely high-achieving salesperson/executive; Roger Smith is more driven by the need for power than the need to achieve.
5.	10	0	0	Monopoly allows the high achiever to use his or her skills; bingo and roulette depend on luck.
6.	2	10	6	High achievers would work out alone; a health club offers less individual freedom but allows feedback and guidance from experts.

7.	4	2	10	High achievers like challenge but not high risk (if you are a very good poker player and chose *b*, raise your score on this question from 2 to 10).
8.	10	7	4	High achievers like to accomplish goals, so the detective would have the greatest appeal for them. The politician is more interested in power, and the millionaire is simply enjoying himself or herself.
9.	4	10	4	High achievers prefer to do constructive things to improve themselves, such as working on a hobby.
10.	10	5	10	The computer salesperson and the criminal lawyer have a much higher need to achieve than the corporate accountant.

High achievers = 76–100

Moderate achievers = 50–75

Low achievers = less than 50

Source: Excerpt from *Entrepreneurship: A Contemporary Approach,* 2nd Ed. by Richard M. Hodgetts and Donald F. Kuratko, Copyright © 1992. Reprinted with permission of South-Western, a division of Thomson Learning, www.thomsonrights.com.

The Living Room: Conflict Management in Small Business

Co-owner/manager: Rande Gedaliah, female, early 40's, liberal/hippie-ish
Co-owner/manager: Jonas Goldberg, male, early 40's, liberal/hippie-ish

General Background info:

The Living Room is a small business located in the Boston suburbs. It is set up as a legal partnership. The business is a new spin on the café bookstore, with additions of an active community center and bakery distribution to local restaurants/stores.

Jonas is a freelance writer and stay at home dad with three young children. His wife is a District Attorney. He was looking for a side venture as well as supplemental income. Jonas is kind of a jumpy guy and cannot stand confrontation. When he's nervous he fumbles, says the wrong things, reveals things by mistake, etc.

Rande is a divorced mother of two teenagers and a successful sculptor who needed income with a schedule she could control. Rande is very levelheaded and generally calm, as long as all the balls she's juggling stay in the air.

Rande and Jonas opened "The Living Room"—bookstore, café, and community meeting place—two years ago and have recently expanded the hours/customer flow drastically in an attempt to finally make a decent income. They've gone from weekday evenings only to a 10-hour/day, 6 days/week schedule. They split most of the business duties, share the larger tasks, and each spend a certain number of hours in the café supervising. They are 50-50 partners. They've known each other for years and years—(their parents are family friends)—and have had a generally smooth relationship.

"Documents":

* A detailed list of the various facets of the business with a breakdown and division of specific tasks.

* An itemized list of the conflicts that have transpired over the past month.

- Legal definitions and terms of a Partnership including *termination, transference, rights,* etc.
- General info on each others families—parents are old family friends.

Pre-Viewing Class Questions
1. How should Rande approach Jonas in regards to the current situation?
2. What should Rande's goal be for her discussion with Jonas?
3. Is Jonas justified in thinking that this problem is not as important as his familial commitments?

Scene One: Brain Storm
Location: Back-room coffee break area

Backstory:
Jonas and Rande had agreed completely about increasing business hours drastically about two months ago. But Jonas did not anticipate the impact this would have on his life and is struggling to deal with it.

In the past six weeks Jonas has cancelled meetings at the last minute, missed the Tax Accountant meeting altogether, forgot to do employees weekly payroll twice, and has not brought in a single community event for the month—both are responsible for booking at least three lucrative events/month. Meanwhile, the change in hours is exhausting Rande and Jonas' unreliability is totally stressing her out.

Break for Manager Questions & Analysis

Scene Two: Switch-Hitter
Location: Small Home Office
TWO WEEKS LATER

Two weeks later, things are basically the same. Rande's frustration has increased and she's plain angry with Jonas for not stepping up to his share of the responsibilities. It's always been 50-50; she needs to try new tactics to resolve this conflict—proactive/cooperative/better listening, etc.

Post-Viewing Class Questions
1. How did Jonas' attitude change?
2. What specific things did Rande do to de-stress the situation while still maintaining a business perspective?
3. How well did Rande and Jonas handle this situation? What could or should have been done differently?

Turbulence in the Sky: The Airline Industry in Need of a Survival Strategy

The airline industry is in a major tailspin. It faces internal and external environmental (government, technology, competition, bankruptcy, and labor) problems that threaten its very existence if it does not change the ways in which it does business.

First, the industry has not fully recovered from the September 11, 2001 (9/11), terrorists' attacks despite the federal government's financial support, post-9/11, through $5 billion infusion of cash and some $10 billion in guaranteed loans. Some steep new taxes—a 7.5 percent federal excise tax, a $3.00 tax on each one-way ticket, and a $2.50 tax for the Transportation Security Administration for airport security—have added to the airlines' problems.

Second, technology has had a mixed impact on the airline industry. On the one hand, airline Internet websites have made it much more convenient for a customer to purchase an e(lectronic) ticket and boarding pass. But on the other hand, Internet access and capability have allowed computer savvy passengers to secure discounted airline fares by booking their flights directly through discount brokers such as Travelocity.com at significantly reduced costs resulting in hundreds of millions of dollars of lost revenues.

Third, low-cost competitors such as JetBlue and Southwest, two leading carriers, have become threats to the major airlines. Low-cost carriers own about a 20 percent market share—and their market share is growing rapidly. In fact, some projections indicate that they may double their present market share by 2008. These carriers have also been able to attract more business travelers, the heart of the airline industry, by charging them substantially less money for last-minute business flights, approximately six times less than their larger competitors; they are more cost effective than their competitors. For example, United Airlines' costs are some 140 percent higher than at Southwest, while Continental's costs are double Southwest's; and while United Airlines has a cost of 11 cents

This case was prepared by Joseph C. Santora, who is professor of business at Essex County College, Newark, New Jersey.

per seat mile, Southwest's is 7.4 cents. As a result of its business strategy, a low-cost carrier such as Southwest continues to remain profitable. It has not furloughed employees (some 35,000 work there) since it began operations about 30 years ago. It continues to maintain its fleet of 375 planes, and it is currently worth more than all other airline carriers combined. No wonder the low-cost carriers are beginning to seriously erode their counterparts' market share.

Fourth, the airline industry has been reeling from major financial problems. Eastern Airlines is gone, so is Pan Am, and TWA was absorbed in 2001 by another airline. US Airways and United Airlines have filed for Chapter 11 bankruptcy. To add to the financial misery, the first fiscal quarter of 2003 was not kind to the airlines. US Airways lost some $3 billion versus a $1.7 billion loss for the same time period in 2002, an increased loss of $1.3 billion. If these financial losses continue, one airline executive spokesperson has predicted, "The woes of the U.S. aviation industry will prompt a shakeout that will leave it with just a handful of global carriers."

Fifth, labor costs present a grave financial problem for airlines. Since labor (unions) is exempt from antitrust laws, organized labor can make or break an airline. Labor costs represent approximately 40 percent of airline costs. In 2002, labor costs accounted for approximately half of United Airlines' and American Airlines' revenues. In the last few years, however, labor has made some major financial concessions to save some of the major airline carriers. United Airlines may have gotten a major financial reprieve from a six-year labor agreement that will save the company some $314 million in annual salaries, and possibly another $794 million in salary saving if contract negotiations work out with the International Association of Machinists (IAM), but there is much more work to be done. Northwest Airlines needs approximately $1 billion in wage and benefit concessions by the middle of 2003 to compete with other carriers. Personnel cuts at American Airlines include a reduction of 13,000 or 13 percent of employees, and a payroll savings of 23 percent or $1.8 billion; United Airlines has witnessed a reduction of 17,200 or 20 percent and a $2.5 billion payroll savings. While these concessions may have helped the airline business survive, they may have done irreparable damage to staff morale. According to one source, "Unless management can find a way to motivate these employees and their colleagues, the carriers' woes could drag on even longer."

Sixth, the industry business model of hubs (airports in large cities, e.g., Newark, NJ) and spokes (airports in smaller cities around them, e.g., Buffalo) is passé. Once thought to reduce costs and to allow for more nonstop flights, hubs are now too costly and difficult to manage. Travel has been made "less convenient for the business fliers" by reducing the number of available business flights and by increasing the waiting time for connecting flights at some hubs by an additional 15 minutes. Business travelers are no longer willing to pay higher airline fares for the convenience of hubs. Unfortunately, if the major carriers reduce their number of hubs, they will lose their competitive edge—service—to low-cost carriers, who in turn will benefit from increased business travelers.

Seventh, several recent unanticipated issues have seriously threatened the airline business. The second Gulf War with Iraq has impacted the industry's economic burden with increased fuel costs and fewer airline passengers, and Severe Acute Respiratory Syndrome, commonly known as SARS, a highly infectious and deadly illness, has affected the industry as well. SARS has severely curtailed travel to Asia, particularly to the Chinese cities of Shanghai and Beijing, and to Canada, particularly Toronto, where SARS has registered the highest number of cases. The result has been the losses of millions of dollars to the airline industry. Finally, there are the projected delays in airport expansion plans in San Francisco and Washington, DC; an increase by the five major carriers—United Air, Continental, Northwest, Delta, and US Airways—in the price of tickets to offset some costs; and over the next five years, the number of major airline carriers may decline by one or two carriers.

Clearly, a new management strategy is in order for the major carriers in the airline industry.

Questions

1. Do the major airlines have a strategy?
2. Do a SWOT analysis for the airline industry.
3. Conduct an internal/external audit of the airline industry.
4. What are some entrepreneurial and innovative business strategies the major airline carriers should adopt to avoid extinction?

Sources: M. Ardnt and W. Zellner, "How to Fix the Airlines," *BusinessWeek,* April 14, 2003, pp. 74–76, 78; S. Cary, "UAL Flight Attendants Approve Pact," *Wall Street Journal,* April 30, 2003, p. 2; J. Crawley and D. Schwab, "Airlines' Woe Putting the Squeeze on Airports, Too," *The Star-Ledger,* May 12, 2003, p. 18; C. Daniel, "Shake-Out Will Leave Handful of Big Airlines," *Financial Times,* May 5, 2003, p. 1; D. Leonhardt and M. Maynard, "Troubled Airlines Face Reality: Those Cheap Fares Have a Price," *New York Times,* August 18, 2002 (online); S. McCartney, "Airlines Will Raise Fares, Pocket Security Fees," *Wall Street Journal,* May 13, 2003, p. D3; C. Murphy, "A No-Fly Zone," *Fortune,* April 14, 2003, p. 56; S. Tully, "The Airlines' New Deal," *Fortune,* April 28, 2003, pp. 79–80, 82; S. Tully, "Straighten Up and Fly Right." *Fortune,* February 17, 2003, pp. 66–70; M. W. Walsh, "Northwest Flight Attendants Sue over Wage Concessions," *New York Times,* June 4, 2003 (online); W. Zellner, "Coffee, Tea, or Bile?" *BusinessWeek,* June 2, 2003, pp. 56–57; W. Zellner, with M. Ardnt, "Can Anything Fix the Airlines?" *BusinessWeek,* April 7, 2003, pp. 52–53; W. Zellner, with M. Ardnt, "Holding Steady: As Rivals Sputter Can Southwest Stay on Top?" *BusinessWeek,* February 3, 2003, pp. 66–68.

Organization
Management

A successful organization doesn't just happen! Resources need to be arranged and the right people brought together in order for an organization to function effectively and efficiently. Organizing people in an ineffective way or treating them inappropriately can undermine even the greatest hopes and efforts for effective performance. The manager has responsibility for setting the stage by arranging a structure for the organization and by setting policies and practices that bring together the best skills and efforts of people.

In Part Four we will examine various choices for how an organization might be structured. We will also look at policies and practices for managing people as a means of bringing together and maintaining an effective workforce. People bring with them a variety of skills and experiences and there are many ways in which contributions to the organization can be made. The effective manager can orchestrate the variety of talents in ways that contribute to organizational success. Finally, in this part we will also examine managing diversity in the workplace.

NINE

Managing the Structure and Design of Organizations

chapter 9

After reading this chapter, you should be able to:

- Identify the vertical and horizontal dimensions of organization structure.

- Develop coordination across departments and hierarchical levels.

- Differentiate between authority, responsibility, and accountability.

- Understand the structural characteristics of centralization, span of control, formalization, and chain of command.

- Apply the three basic approaches—functional, divisional, and matrix—to departmentalization.

- Use organization structure and the three basic organization designs—mechanistic, organic, and boundaryless—to achieve strategic goals.

- Anticipate the key strategic events that are likely to trigger a change in the structure and design of an organization.

Nokia Changes Its Structure in order to Get Closer to the Customer

Customer service is one key to success that applies to nearly every situation. In 2002, Nokia, the world's number one maker of mobile phones, reorganized its business to respond to a shifting marketplace. Nokia is based in Finland. While the company has one of the most recognized brand names in the industry, the mobile phone industry had slowed, as Europe, North America, and parts of Asia reached a saturation point. At the close of 2002, there were 405 million handsets in use worldwide.

Because of the slowdown, Nokia CEO Jorma Ollila created a strategy designed to break the company down into nine profit-and-loss centers. Each was charged with finding ways to bolster the company's position in a specific market ranging from the $1,000 smartphones to the $160 barebones handsets. "We had to break up the company in a meaningful way to retain the entrepreneurial thrust we had in the 1990s," Ollila explained.

Each of the nine newly formed business units was placed in charge of product and business development projects in defined market segments. The idea was to allow the company to move faster and be more flexible. The goal was to better serve customers while developing innovative products. The units included groups that focused on various mobile phone products for residential customers in both developed and undeveloped countries. Others concentrated on phones for corporate customers, high technology phones for data processing and video imaging. Another unit was dedicated to camera phones featuring color screens and graphical software. Innovative project unit groups worked on hybrid messaging phone and music players, smart phones with software that act as personal organizers, cordless headset phones, and even a group called "Club Nokia." Club Nokia is an online clearinghouse for technical support information, downloadable ring tones, and other software applications.

To coordinate the units, each utilizes a central research lab for basic technology and product design. As a project moves forward, the products are handed off to a shared operations and logistics group.

Sources: A. Reinhardt, "Nokia's Next Act," *Business Week,* July 1, 2002; Jorma Ollila and Pekka Ala-Pietila, *Nokia Letter to Shareholders,* February 7, 2003, www.nokia.com.

1. *Is there a relationship between the organizational structure that was created by Nokia's leadership team and a changing marketplace? What is that relationship?*

2. *Why was the former structure at Nokia, which clustered all mobile phone products into one large unit, no longer useful for reaching strategic goals? What strategic factors were the most crucial?*

organizing

The management function that determines how the firm's resources are arranged and coordinated; the deployment of resources to achieve strategic goals.

organization structure

The formal system of relationships that determines lines of authority and the tasks assigned to individuals and units.

vertical dimension

The element of who has the authority to make decisions and who supervises which subordinates.

horizontal dimension

The element of dividing work into specific jobs and tasks and assigning jobs into units.

unity of command

The management concept that a subordinate should have only one direct supervisor.

Many strategies and key business decisions have profound effects on the structures and designs of various organizations. A change in strategic direction due to a merger or acquisition or a change in competitive strategy requires the management team to rethink how to deploy company resources. **Organizing** is the deployment of resources to achieve strategic goals, and is reflected in: (1) the organization's division of labor that forms jobs and departments, (2) formal lines of authority, and (3) the mechanisms used for coordinating diverse jobs and roles in the organization.

Organizing follows the formulation of strategy. While strategy indicates *what* needs to be done, organizing shows *how* to do it. This chapter begins by examining the vertical and horizontal dimensions of organization structure. It then examines ways to coordinate organizational units so that they move in the same direction toward meeting organization goals. Finally, it identifies different approaches to organization design.

Skills for Managing 9.1 lists the key skills for managing organizing.

The Vertical Dimension of Organization Structure

Organization structure is a formal system of relationships that determines lines of authority (who reports to whom) and the tasks assigned to individuals and units (who does what task and with which department). The **vertical dimension** of organization structure indicates who has the authority to make decisions and who is expected to supervise which subordinates. The **horizontal dimension** is the basis for dividing work into specific jobs and tasks and assigning those jobs into units such as departments or teams.

Unity of Command

The concept of **unity of command** is based on one of Fayol's 14 principles of management (see Chapter 1): a subordinate should have only one direct supervisor. Multiple bosses may give a subordinate conflicting in-

ORGANIZATION STRUCTURE AND DESIGN

- *Understanding the chain of command.* Some organizations are structured in a hierarchical fashion. In these organizations, employees are expected to respect and follow the chain of command, that is, the directives of top managers. Other organizations are less hierarchical and permit individuals in the lower ranks to initiate and implement ideas without the approval of their bosses.

- *Understanding the dimensions of organization structure.* Some of the factors that affect the design of an organization include size (large or small), emphasis on teams or individuals, degree of change in the work environment, and broad versus narrow spans of supervisory control. By understanding the key dimensions of organization structure, you can get an idea of what it would be like to work in an organization so that you can choose a work environment in which you can make your most valuable contributions.

structions or goals. In unity of command, a decision can be traced back from the subordinates of the manager who made it.

Exceptions to the unity of command principle are sometimes necessary. For example, computer programmers in software firms are often assigned to different projects as the need arises. They are supervised by a project manager who coordinates the people and resources on the project and by a functional manager, the manager of information technology (IT), who supervises the IT department. This violation of the unity of command principle makes it critical for both managers to coordinate goals and priorities to avoid causing confusion.

Authority, Responsibility, and Accountability

Managers, teams, and employees have varying amounts of authority, responsibility, and accountability based on where they are in the vertical structure of the organization. **Authority** is the formal right of a manager to make decisions, give orders, and expect those orders to be carried out. A manager is an agent of the owners of the business. The role of the manager encompasses decision-making authority to manage the workforce, resources, and assets of the business in the owners' best interests. Authority is given to the position of the manager, not the person. It originates at the top of the organization based on the property rights of the owners and flows down the vertical organizational hierarchy from top executives to middle managers to supervisors and operative employees. Consequently, positions at the top of the hierarchy have more authority than positions at lower levels.

authority

The formal right of a manager to make decisions, give orders, and expect the orders to be carried out.

Effective Ways to Organize Your Work as a Manager

MANAGER'S NOTES

How can you conquer the feeling that you don't have enough time to do your job? Here are some suggestions.

1. *Multitask appropriately.* Multitasking—doing two or more things at once—can be helpful when dealing with *things*, not people. For example, talking to a customer on the phone while filling out a performance evaluation for the subordinate who is sitting across the desk from you would not be effective multitasking. While flying on a business trip, respond to e-mail on a laptop, or fill out your expense report on the way home.

2. *Use technology wisely.* Technology can waste time for you or save time. Wait for new versions of software and other equipment to be tested and accepted by the marketplace before switching from tried and true software programs that you already know how to use.

3. *Give yourself thinking time.* Close your door if possible and spend an hour each day working without the interruptions of people, phones, or e-mail. Schedule the most crucial, creative tasks when you have the most energy, and use your down time when you tend to tire to open mail or return phone calls. Keep track of your day—one manager notes in a work journal the key decisions he makes every day, as well as issues he has dealt with. He can then review several days to see what his patterns were and how he can respond more quickly to new issues.

4. *Establish priorities.* Priorities include both urgent and important tasks. Spend as much time as possible doing things that are important but not urgent. Otherwise you will find you have neglected important tasks such as training and learning opportunities (and your skills have become obsolete) because you've only attended to the urgent tasks as you "put out fires." Schedule self-improvement and other learning opportunities as priorities in your weekly or monthly schedule. If you don't, you'll find yourself attending to the less critical but more urgent activities that arise that will preclude improving your skills.

Source: Adapted from S. Covey and R. Merrill, "New Ways to Get Organized at Work," *USA Weekend,* February 6, 1998, p. 18.

---

responsibility

The manager's duty to perform assigned tasks.

Responsibility is the duty to perform assigned tasks. All employees are expected to accept these responsibilities as a condition of employment. Ideally, a manager's responsibilities are matched with the appropriate amount of authority so that the manager is in "control" of the task. The manager may *delegate,* or transfer responsibility to a subordinate or team, but the manager is still in control because the subordinate or team is subject to his or her authority. Managers delegate decision-making authority for some tasks in order to give themselves more time to focus on the most important tasks and decisions. Chapter 6, on decision making, listed the steps that lead to effective delegation skills. Manager's Notes 9.1 provides useful approaches to organizing responsibilities and activities.

Sometimes managers are given responsibility without equal levels of authority. This situation is common in organizations in which managers must work with managers of other units or with customers outside of the organization. For example, the vice president of global learning solutions at Lucent Technologies, a manufacturer of telecommunications equipment, is responsible for disseminating employee development courses to various business units throughout the large corporation. This executive does not have the authority to control whether or how business-unit managers use the training services with their own employees. Instead, the executive must "market" the training courses to various business units in order to effectively fulfill the responsibility of the position.

A manager may delegate responsibilities to subordinates, but he or she remains accountable for the actions of subordinates. Managers hold the ultimate responsibility for tasks they delegate. **Accountability** means that a manager or other employee with authority and responsibility must be able to justify results to a manager at a higher level in the organizational hierarchy. One way managers are held accountable for the performance of their units is in periodic performance appraisals. For example, a **management by objectives (MBO)** program can be used to compare planned goals with achieved results. Employees receive rewards based on meeting or exceeding expected results.

There are two distinct types of authority: line and staff authority. **Line authority** entitles a manager to directly control the work of subordinates by hiring, discharging, evaluating, and rewarding them. It is based on superior–subordinate authority relationships that start at the top of the organization hierarchy and extend to the lowest level. This provides what is called the **chain of command. Line managers** hold positions that contribute directly to the strategic goals of the organization. For example, the line managers of a manufacturing firm include production managers and sales managers who contribute directly to the bottom line.

Staff authority includes giving advice, making recommendations, and offering counsel to line managers and other members of the organization. Staff authority is based on expertise and is not directly related to achieving the strategic goals of the organization. **Staff managers** help line managers achieve bottom-line results, but they contribute only indirectly to outcomes. For example, the accounting, legal, and human resource management staffs of a manufacturing firm provide specialized advice on cost control, federal regulations, and staffing requirements to line managers.

The key to knowing whether a position has line or staff status is the organization's strategic objectives. In an accounting firm, the accountants have line authority since their work directly contributes to the bottom line, whereas accountants in a manufacturing firm are used in an advisory capacity and thus are classified as having staff authority.

An **organization chart** summarizes the lines of authority in an organization. In the organization chart seen in Figure 9.1, authority flows in

accountability

The expectation that the manager must be able to justify results to a manager at a higher level.

management by objectives (MBO)

A goal-setting program for managers and subordinates.

line authority

The manager's control of subordinates by hiring, discharging, evaluating, and rewarding.

chain of command

The superior–subordinate authority relationship.

line managers

The management level that contributes directly to the strategic goals of the organization.

staff authority

Management function of advising, recommending, and counseling line managers.

staff managers

The level of management that directs line managers.

organization chart

A graphic depiction that summarizes the lines of authority in an organization.

FIGURE 9.1

A Formal Organization Chart

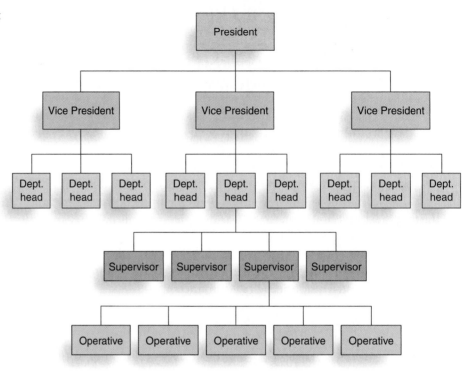

a vertical downward direction starting with the president, who has authority over the vice president, who in turn supervises several department heads. The department heads manage the supervisors, who have authority over the operatives. Each box represents a position in the organization occupied by one person. Each horizontal level of boxes represents a level of authority in the organization.

Span of Control

span of control

The feature of the vertical structure of an organization that outlines the number of subordinates who report to a manager, the number of managers, and the layers of management within the organization.

A critical feature of the vertical structure of an organization is the number of subordinates who report to a manager. This is called the **span of control,** and it determines the number of managers and number of levels of management in an organization. A manager with a small span of control supervises a small number of subordinates (about five or six on average) and can closely monitor the work of each subordinate. Small spans of control are usually associated with many levels of management, which gives rise to a tall vertical organization structure.

A tall vertical structure may have too many levels of management separating front-line employees from top executives. It may cause the organization to perform inefficiently because the company is not being responsive to the needs of customers. When a top executive is required to go through numerous intermediaries to learn what is happening at the operational level of the business, information often gets distorted and poor decisions result.

Larger spans of control (ranging from 10 to 20 or more subordinates) mean more responsibility is pushed to lower levels. A manager with a large span of control may not be able to directly monitor the behavior of all subordinates. However, using management information systems, which provide systematic feedback on employee performance, and work teams, in which monitoring activities are performed by peers on the team, managers can effectively supervise many subordinates.

Large spans of control result in fewer management levels. Executives at well-managed companies such as General Electric and Nucor (one of the most productive steel companies in the world) take pride in having fewer levels separating top management from first-level operative employees who deal with customers or produce the product. A large span of control works best when there are routine tasks, highly trained subordinates, competent managers, similar jobs with comparable performance measures, and subordinates who prefer autonomy.

Centralization and Decentralization

Centralization and decentralization are related to the degree of concentration of decision authority at various levels of the organization. **Centralization** means that decision-making authority is located at the top of the organization hierarchy. Centralized companies can coordinate activities in a consistent way across diverse units or departments of an organization.

centralization

The location of decision authority at the top of the organization hierarchy.

With **decentralization** decision-making authority is pushed to lower levels in the organization. Decentralization is often more effective in rapidly changing environments where it is necessary to be responsive to changing customer needs and tastes. Decentralized decision-making authority spurs innovation and risk taking by allowing individuals to control resources and engage in experimentation without having to obtain the approval of higher authorities.

decentralization

The location of decision authority at lower levels in the organization.

In recent years decentralized decision authority has become relatively common in organizations. Decentralization permits greater utilization of the talents and abilities of managers and teams of employees and makes it possible to be more responsive to the needs of customers. By maintaining a highly decentralized structure, the 3M Corporation has become one of the world's most innovative companies with more than 60,000 diverse products such as Scotch Tape, Post-it Notes, video recording tape, reflective highway signs, and computer storage diskettes. One of the keys to the high rate of innovation at 3M is its 40 autonomous product divisions and other business units that are purposely kept small. Managers of these divisions and units have the authority to run their establishments as they see fit.

Johnson & Johnson's decentralization is at the root of the beginnings of the company. The new bride of a J & J cotton mill worker kept cutting and burning her hand while learning to cook. Her husband came up with makeshift bandages out of the gauze they made at the mill and adhesive tape. Taking his idea to J & J management, and after a few tweaks, the Band-Aid bandage was born. No top down management here—innovation comes from all over the company to this day.

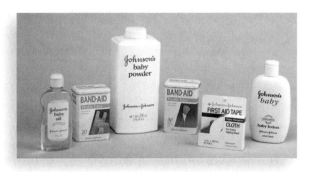

There is a trade-off between centralization and decentralization. Centralization allows management to coordinate the various parts of the organization in a consistent manner. Decentralization provides greater flexibility to respond to change. IBM used a centralized structure for many years because building mainframe computers required the expenditure of vast sums of money and the coordination of units that built and designed hardware and software components. However, IBM moved significantly in the direction of decentralization as its dependence on mainframe computers diminished and as its consulting services began to provide a significant portion of its total revenues. Decentralized decision authority made IBM more flexible and responsive to customers.

Formalization

formalization

The degree of written documentation that is used to direct and control employees.

The degree of written documentation that is used to direct and control employees is the level of **formalization** present. An organization with high formalization provides employees with many documents that specify the "right way" to conduct business with customers or interact with other employees. These documents include policy manuals, job descriptions, procedures, memos, and rule books. A high degree of formalization encourages employees to do their jobs in standardized and predictable ways.

Other organizations choose a low degree of formalization, with few rules and regulations, which encourages employees to improvise. This is especially useful when customer needs and conditions are subject to change. For example, Nordstrom, a retail store that serves affluent customers, has an employee handbook that consists of a single page with one rule: "Use your good judgment in all situations."

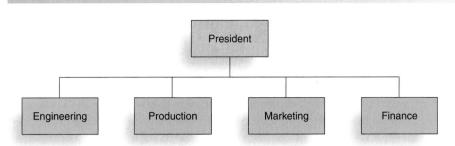

FIGURE 9.2

Functional Departmental
Structure

The Horizontal Dimension
of Organization Structure

The horizontal basis for organizing jobs into units in an organization is called **departmentalization**. The three basic approaches to departmentalization are functional, divisional, and matrix.

Functional Structure

A **functional structure** places similar jobs into departments. For example, the departments in Figure 9.2 are engineering, production, marketing, and finance. The president integrates the activities of these departments so that each department's efforts are aligned with organizational goals and objectives.

The functional approach works best in small to medium-sized companies operating in somewhat stable business environments without a great deal of change and uncertainty. The functional structure has several advantages. Decision authority is centralized at the top of the organization hierarchy. Career paths foster professional identity with the business function. Because this approach permits employees to do specialized tasks, it creates a high degree of efficiency.[1] A functional form of structure causes employees to develop specialized expertise in a functional area of the business, such as finance or marketing.

In a company with a functional form of structure, an employee in the finance department of a telecommunications company, for example, can specialize in providing financial assistance to small-business clients who purchase small phone systems. The employee can advance within the finance department by building a depth and breadth of knowledge in finance and identifying professionally with the field. The individual may be promoted to a position that provides financing to corporate clients who purchase larger, more sophisticated phone systems. The result of serving a variety of clients is that the employee eventually becomes a financial expert.

departmentalization

The horizontal basis for organizing jobs into units in an organization.

functional structure

A departmentalization approach that places similar jobs into departments.

The disadvantages of the functional departmental structure include communication barriers and conflicts between functional departments. It may be difficult to coordinate products and services, which could result in diminished responsiveness to the needs of customers. When employees are assigned to functional departments, they tend to identify with the functional departmental goals rather than with organizational goals or customer needs. This could lead to departmental conflict. Anyone who has called a large corporation looking for service only to be put on hold and transferred several times by indifferent employees has experienced one of the disadvantages of a functional organization.

Engineers who work in an engineering department may provide a "state of the art" technical design that is difficult to manufacture and that contains features that are not desired by the targeted customer. In this case, engineering goals are at odds with production and marketing goals. If the top executive does not have time to manage the conflict among the engineering, marketing, and production departments, the product development cycle may slow down as the departmental managers try to work out their differences. By the time these differences are ironed out the product may be late to market and potential sales revenues are lost.

Divisional Approach

The **divisional approach,** sometimes called the *product approach,* organizes employees into units based on common products, services, or markets. The divisional approach is used when a company produces many products or provides services to different types of markets, such as regional, domestic, and international markets, that require specialized knowledge. In the divisional approach key functional activities are present in each division and are coordinated by a general manager responsible for generating divisional profits.

Figure 9.3 shows a hypothetical computer company structured into three divisions: computer, software, and consulting services. The division structure allows employees to develop expertise in both a function and a line of products or services. A salesperson in the computer division can develop specialized product knowledge in selling computer systems without knowing about software or consulting services. The salesperson is likely to produce more sales revenues by focusing on computer systems rather than trying to sell software and consulting.

General Motors was one of the companies that pioneered the division structure, creating divisions based on its different automobile brands (Chevrolet, Pontiac, Buick, Oldsmobile, and Cadillac). Hewlett-Packard has used the division structure to reinforce its entrepreneurial culture so that employees identify with smaller units within the large company. Hewlett-Packard expects that keeping the divisions small will encourage employees to innovate new products. Large consumer products companies such as PepsiCo, Procter & Gamble, Johnson & Johnson, and Colgate-

FIGURE 9.3

Divisional Organization
Structure

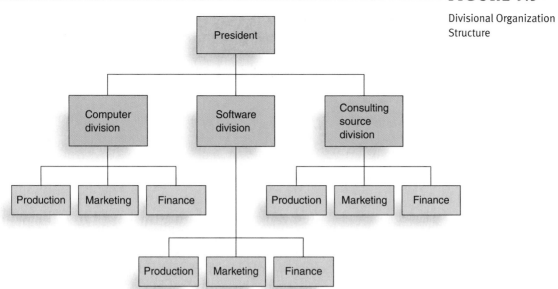

General Motors broke its
corporate structure into
several divisions based on
automobile brands, each with
its own management.

Palmolive also use the division structure to create opportunities for managers to learn the skills of operating a unit of the company from a profit-and-loss perspective. The most successful division managers (judged by the profitability of their divisions) are identified as likely candidates for executive leadership roles.

GEOGRAPHIC-BASED DIVISIONS   A variation of the product-based divisional structure organizes divisions by geographic region. **Geographic-based divisions** allow an organization to focus on customer needs that may vary by geographic region or market. In this approach to organizing, the functional business activities are coordinated by a division manager, who is responsible for products or services provided to a specific area. Figure 9.4 shows the organization of a fast-food company with United

geographic-based divisions

A variation of the product-based departmentalization structure in which divisions are organized by geographic region.

FIGURE 9.4

Geographic-Based
Organization Structure

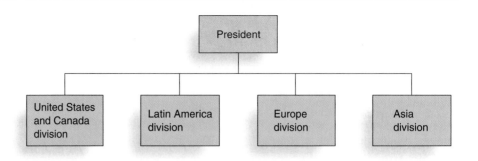

States and Canadian, Latin American, European, and Asian divisions. This structure allows each division manager to satisfy customer tastes and preferences in the region. Thus, American and Canadian menus may focus on hamburgers, a favorite North American food; the menu may add chicken burgers in India, since beef is a forbidden food for many Indians, and noodle soup in China; and the European menu may make wine available to French, Italian, and Spanish customers who customarily drink wine with meals.

CUSTOMER-BASED DIVISIONS Another variation of the product-based divisional structure organizes divisions by particular types of customers or clients. Customer-based divisions allow an organization to focus on customer needs within a basic functional structure. With customer divisions, each department contains employees who perform functional tasks for a specific type of customer. The division manager coordinates the business activities for a specific type of customer. Figure 9.5 shows the organization of a bank that organizes its banking services into divisions that serve personal banking customers, small business banking customers, and corporate banking customers. Each customer division provides a different array of services that are relevant to it. For example, Wells Fargo Bank, a large San Francisco–based commercial bank, has organized its banking services into a customer-based structure.

ADVANTAGES AND DISADVANTAGES OF THE DIVISIONAL APPROACH The divisional approach has several advantages, including:

- Coordination among different business functions.
- Improved and speedier service.
- Accountability for performance.
- Development of general manager and executive skills.[2]

Bringing all the functional areas together to focus on a line of products reduces barriers that inhibit coordination among marketing, finance,

FIGURE 9.5

Customer-Based Organization
Structure

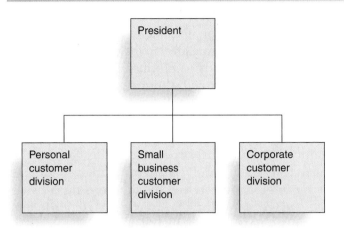

production, and other functions. Employees identify with products and customers rather than with professional business disciplines. This allows the company to provide better quality products and services and employees are more responsive to customers. Division managers have bottom-line profit responsibility, which prepares them to operate larger units or assume higher level corporate responsibilities. In a sense, the division managers are running a smaller company within the company, which motivates them to meet performance goals for the unit.

The disadvantages of the divisional approach include:

- Duplication of resources by two or more departments.
- Reduced specialization in occupation skills.
- Competition among divisions.[3]

The price an organization pays for the better coordination of the functional areas within the division is that some efficiencies are lost due to the duplication of employee roles within divisions. For example, each division may have its own direct sales force, which is more costly to support than a single sales force serving the entire organization. Further, employees operating within the division structure may not be able to specialize in their functional areas to the degree needed to provide specific competencies. Thus, each division may employ one or two human resource management generalists who know a little bit about payroll, benefits, and basic employment policies but are incapable of designing specialized performance appraisal systems for supervisory personnel. Consequently, each division may hire expensive outside consultants to perform this activity. Finally, coordination and cooperation between divisions may be problematic, resulting in further inefficiencies. When divisions compete for corporate resources, office politics may inhibit cooperation or sharing of information between divisions. At General Motors, auto sales gains in the new Saturn division came at the expense of some lost sales in the Chevrolet division. Executives in the Chevrolet division engaged in politics at the corporate level to make sure their Saturn "rival" did not receive corporate funds to produce a proposed Saturn minivan or sport utility vehicle, currently the hottest growth segments in the auto industry.

In general, the divisional structure is best suited to medium to large-size firms with a variety of products in environments with moderate to high levels of uncertainty. The divisional structure provides flexibility to allow an organization to respond to rapidly changing market conditions. However, provisions for integration between the divisions must be developed to take full advantage of the division structure. Methods to integrate across divisions are discussed later in this chapter.

Matrix Approach

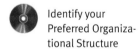

Identify your Preferred Organizational Structure

The **matrix approach** superimposes a divisional structure over a functional structure in order to combine the efficiency of the functional approach with the flexibility and responsiveness to change of the divisional approach. Each employee in a matrix unit reports to two bosses—a functional manager and a product or project manager. This means that there are dual lines of authority in the matrix organization. As seen in Figure 9.6, there is a vertical chain of command for the functions of finance, operations, manufacturing, and sales and marketing. There is a lateral chain of command for the three regions. An engineer who is assigned to work in region A will report to both region manager A and the vice president of engineering applications.

The matrix approach originated in U.S. defense companies so that employees with scarce technical skills could work on one or more projects that were under time pressures for completion. The project manager is responsible for coordinating budgets, personnel, and resources in order to bring the project in on time and within budget. The functional manager is responsible for allocating specialists to projects, making sure their skills are current, and evaluating their performance according to professional standards. The National Aeronautics and Space Administration (NASA) has used matrix structures to assign space scientists to various projects such as weather satellite or space shuttle programs. Dow Corning has used matrix structures to give marketing specialists broader exposure to different products.

The advantages of the matrix approach include:

- Efficient utilization of scarce, expensive specialists.
- Flexibility that facilitates starting new projects and ventures quickly.
- Development of cross-functional skills by employees.

FIGURE 9.6

Matrix Organization Structure

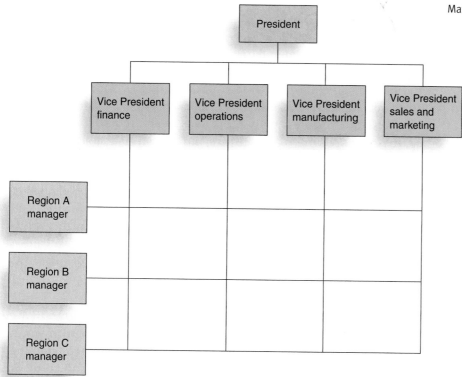

- Increased employee involvement in management decisions affecting project or product assignments.[4]

The key advantage is that flexibility makes it easier to start new projects or business ventures quickly with a minimum of bureaucratic inertia. Further, talented specialists can be utilized more efficiently under this approach.

The disadvantages of the matrix form include:

- Employee frustration and confusion as a result of the dual chain of command.
- Conflict between product and functional managers over deadlines and priorities.
- Too much time spent on coordinating decisions in meetings.[5]

One of the main problems with the matrix structure is that the product manager and functional manager may not agree on priorities or resource allocations, leading to conflict. Employees who have two bosses with different priorities may feel stressed and powerless to please both. The result may be another disadvantage, too much time devoted to meetings to coordinate various agendas and resolve conflicts.

Coordination Mechanisms

No matter whether the functional, divisional, or matrix approach to horizontal structure is selected, each requires **coordination** to link activities so that diverse departments or divisions work in harmony and learn from each other. For example, an innovation in customer service in one division can quickly be diffused throughout the organization so that gains in customer satisfaction spread throughout the entire organization. The Wal-Mart "greeter" who welcomes customers entering the store began as an experiment in one store and spread throughout the organization when customers responded positively to being greeted. Coordination also allows units to align departmental goals with organizational goals so that interdepartmental goal conflicts are avoided or resolved. Coordination mechanisms include meetings, organizationwide reward systems, teams and task forces, liaisons, integrating managers, and the organization's culture.

Meetings

To achieve harmony in pursuing organizational goals, individual employees must "be on the same page" as their leaders and their co-workers. One way to achieve this harmony is to organize a **strategic meeting** to synchronize plans and objectives. Representatives of each unit attend the meeting and participate in the formulation of policies that are designed to align the activities of the various departments. Such meetings may occur at the division level (involving functional managers) or at the corporate level (typically involving division managers). They provide opportunities for face-to-face contact so that managers can learn to trust and collaborate with one another. For example, McGraw-Hill/Irwin, the publisher of this text, holds a marketing strategy meeting twice a year to discuss sales and marketing policies and strategies for marketing its textbooks to colleges. Editorial, production, marketing, and sales managers exchange information about books and ideas for new projects that may serve unmet needs in the market. Chapter 15 examines meetings in greater detail.

Organizationwide Reward Systems

Another approach to coordinating activities of people from different departments is to provide a reward based on organizationwide profits. **Profit-sharing** plans pay a share of the company's profits to the employees in the form of a bonus. In a typical plan, the size of the bonus check is tied to quarterly profits.

Profit sharing creates a "we're in this together" mentality, which nurtures collaboration between departments. As a result of profit shar-

The Wal-Mart "greeter" position is a specialized job that has become a symbol of the firm's commitment to customer service throughout the firm.

ing at Hewlett-Packard, for example, new technologies developed in one division can be shared with other divisions and fashioned into new products. Profit sharing bonuses have averaged around 15 percent of base salaries at Hewlett-Packard. An employee earning an annual salary of $50,000 may earn an additional $8,000 in a typical year. Profit sharing can also be used to encourage cooperation between people at different levels of the hierarchy. For example, pay raises of both union and management personnel at Ford are tied to a profit-sharing plan. The result has been better labor relations and a total absence of work stoppages in recent years.

Task Forces and Teams

One of the keys to an effective workforce is teamwork. A **task force** is a temporary interdepartmental group formed to study an issue and make recommendations. The issue typically has organizationwide implications, and the task force gathers input from different departments. For example, the University of Colorado's diversity task force consists of representatives from all nine colleges. The group provides recommendations on how to make the culture of the university welcoming to people from diverse backgrounds.

A **problem-solving team,** sometimes called a **parallel team,** is a special type of group. A representative group from different departments is formed to solve problems such as quality improvement, workplace safety, and employee grievances. A problem-solving team can operate either on a temporary or a continuing basis. A problem-solving team at Federal Express improved the process of package sorting, providing savings in labor costs. At Ford, problem-solving teams made improvements in the quality of employee work life, which ultimately resulted in improved product quality. For more information, see Chapter 14, "Managing Teams."

task force

A temporary interdepartmental group formed to study an issue and make recommendations.

problem-solving team

A group representing different departments that solves problems; sometimes called a *parallel* team.

liaison role

A management role used to facilitate communications between two or more departments.

A liaison ... es, and department ... ivities continuously coordin... con- ...

brand managers

A management role that coordinates the ongoing activities of branded products.

etween two or more ... t is necessary to continuously coordin... between ...roducts. ...o improve the quality of communication and resolve misunderstandings and conflicts.

A software systems specialist from the information technology (IT) department may be assigned to coordinate contact between the IT and the marketing departments. When the IT department makes a decision involving the purchase of new computer software or decides to get rid of old software, the IT liaison meets with the marketing department to obtain input. Without the IT liaison, the IT experts may unknowingly discard software in the middle of a critical task, or they may purchase software that is not "user friendly" for the marketing people. Liaison roles reduce the likelihood of making decisions that do not represent the interests of other departments.

Integrating Managers

integrating manager

A management position designed to coordinate the work of several different departments: the integrating manager is not a member of any of the departments whose activities are being coordinated.

Many times the job of coordination is assigned to a specific individual. For example, an **integrating manager** position may be created to coordinate the work of several different departments. The integrating manager is not a member of any of the departments whose activities are being coordinated. These managers have job titles such as project manager, product manager, or brand manager. They use negotiation and persuasion skills to influence functional managers to provide resources and to influence employees to be committed and motivated to achieve the product or project goals on time and within budget.

project manager

A management role that coordinates work on a scientific, aerospace, or construction project.

A **project manager** coordinates work on a scientific, aerospace, or construction project. When the Denver International Airport was being built, a project manager coordinated construction in each of five project management areas: site development (earth-moving, grading, and drainage); roadways and on-grade parking (service roads, on-airport roads, and off-airport roads connecting to highways); airfield paving; building design (baggage handling, concourses, terminal, and parking); and utility systems and other facilities (electrical transmission, oil and gas line removal and relocation).

product managers

A management role that coordinates the development of new products.

Matrix organization structures utilize **product managers.** These individuals coordinate the development of new products. They also negotiate with various functional managers for resources (people, finances, technology) and keep the product moving so it can be released to the market on time. The product manager must be a champion for the new product during the budget planning process, so that the product receives the resources needed to finish the project. New products without champions are vulnerable to critics who support diverting resources to areas that offer more immediate cash returns.

Brand managers coordinate the ongoing activities of bra[nd] [con]sumer products such as food, soap and cleaning products, toilet[ries] over-the-counter medicines. A brand manager coordinates the ac[tivities] of marketing, advertising, sales and pricing, production, accounting, [con]trol, packaging, and product research. The brand manager makes sure the work of people in these different functional areas is aligned with the strategy for the product.

Organizational Culture

The system of shared values, assumptions, beliefs, and norms that unite the members of an organization is the company's culture. It reflects employees' views about "the way things are done around here." **Organizational culture** influences people to share values and that translates into a commitment to working together to achieve important goals. Culture gives employees an internal gyroscope that directs them to do things that make the entire organization more effective.[6] The concept of culture as a coordinating mechanism can also be applied to teams, as indicated in Manager's Notes 9.2.

> **organizational culture**
>
> A system of shared values, assumptions, beliefs, and norms that unite the members of an organization.

The culture of Nordstrom, a Seattle-based retail company, encourages employees to provide extraordinary customer service. Employees who have gone the extra mile for customers become company "heroes." Their exploits become part of company lore. New employees are told dozens of stories about Nordstrom employees who have provided heroic customer service. One employee ironed a newly purchased shirt for a customer who needed it for a meeting that afternoon. Another cheerfully gift wrapped a present purchased at the store of a competitor. There was even a Nordstrom employee who warmed customers' cars in the winter while they were shopping. Still another made a last-minute delivery of party clothes to a frantic hostess.[7] Consequently, Nordstrom employees who work in different departments or different outlets feel as though they are a part of something bigger than a department. They all agree that the customer is king and departmental goals are subordinate to serving the customer.

The Walt Disney Company has a strong culture focusing on "making people happy." Disney wants customers in its theme parks to experience "joy," "excitement," "imagination," and "magic." The company carefully selects and hires people who are well groomed and have outgoing and enthusiastic personalities for all jobs, even the most menial. New hires are trained and oriented to the Disney culture and taught to speak a language that reflects the core Disney value of making people happy:

- Employees are "cast members."
- Customers are "guests."
- A crowd is an "audience."
- A work shift is a "performance."

Teams as well as organizations develop cultures that show employees how "things are done on this team." A team's cultural values begin developing when its members first start interacting and help to define acceptable behavior. Three key methods to build and strengthen a culture on your team are listed below.

1. *Exploit critical events.* How you apply core values to a critical event will show team members the importance of that value and when to apply it. For example, innovation may be one of the team's core values. Suppose a team member tries a new approach with a major customer; the new approach is not successful and the team member can't meet expectations as a result. You can use this critical event to deepen the core value of innovation by showing the failure as a valuable learning process that all team members can benefit from. On the other hand, if the failure results in punishment and the rest of the team treats the unsuccessful team member poorly, the team members will be less likely to try new approaches and the core value of innovation will be weakened.

2. *Set the tone early.* Be aware that patterns developed during the formation of the team will continue when the team is performing its job. For example, the team will start establishing its own procedures for making decisions if it needs to resolve conflicts over setting team goals, and this procedure may be difficult to change later. To resolve these early conflicts, the team members may all voice their ideas as part of the decision-making process and slowly build a consensus that the entire team can agree on. When later business decisions need to be made, however, there may not be enough time for consensus decisions, but the team members may balk at a less democratic decision-making approach.

3. *Use symbols, rites, and rituals.* Strengthen the team culture and core values with symbols, rites, and rituals. For example, celebrate the team's achievement of a critical team goal with an awards dinner, where the members can share the satisfaction and show their gratitude to each other. These rituals intensify the team's commitment to high performance so that the ritual can be repeated. They also form a permanent and lasting memory, which becomes a powerful motivator for the members to work together on a new goal.

Source: Adapted from R. L. Daft, *Leadership: Theory and Practice,* Fort Worth: Dryden Press, 1998, pp. 283–284.

- A job is a "part."
- Being on duty is "onstage."
- Being off duty is "backstage."
- A uniform is a "costume."[8]

This language helps employees believe they are part of a special entertainment organization, even if they are just hot dog vendors or "mouse ear" salespeople. Employees develop strong emotional ties with each other. This creates bonds between "cast members" from different Disney departments.

The Walt Disney Company focuses on making people happy, and the firm hires outgoing people for all levels of jobs within the firm.

Unfortunately, many organizations have weak cultures. Weak cultures reflect disagreement about values and goals. In a weak culture employees are likely to focus on narrow departmental or divisional objectives. To turn a weak culture into a strong culture, management can use the other coordinating mechanisms described in this chapter.

Organization Design

The structure of a company must match the firm's strategies in order to operate at peak levels. **Organization design** is the selection of an organization structure that best fits the strategic direction of the business. The three basic organization designs are mechanistic, organic, and boundaryless (see Table 9.1). These designs incorporate the vertical and horizontal structural elements covered earlier in this chapter.

Before the most appropriate design can be selected, management should determine how to best deploy the organization's assets and develop a strategy for the business. (For more information on how organizations develop strategies that improve firm performance, see Chapter 7.) As the strategic direction changes, so do the structural elements that make up the design. The opening vignette of this chapter shows how changes in strategy can affect organization structure and design.

organization design

The selection of an organization structure that best fits the strategic goals of the business.

TABLE 9.1

Mechanistic, Organic, and Boundaryless Designs

MECHANISTIC	ORGANIC	BOUNDARYLESS
Rigid hierarchical relationships	Collaboration (both vertical and horizontal)	Collaboration (vertical and horizontal, as well as customers, suppliers, and competitors)
High formalization	Low formalization	Same as organic
Top-down communication	Informal communication	Same as organic
Centralized decision authority	Decentralized decision authority	Same as organic
Narrowly defined specialized jobs	Broadly defined flexible jobs	Same as organic
Emphasis on individuals working independently	Emphasis on teams	Emphasis on teams that also may cross organization boundaries

Sources: Adapted from S. P. Robbins and M. Coulter, *Management,* 5th ed. Upper Saddle River, NJ: Prentice Hall, 1996, p. 352; L. R. Gomez-Mejia, D. B. Balkin, and R. L. Cardy, *Managing Human Resources,* 3rd ed. Upper Saddle River, NJ: Prentice Hall, 2001, p. 53.

Strategic factors that affect the choices of organization design include:

1. *Organization capabilities.* The activities that the company does best are likely to be retained, while under certain strategic conditions (for example, a cost leadership strategy) the activities that are peripheral to the core mission of the business may be contracted out to more efficient suppliers.

2. *Technology.* The type of technology the firm uses to produce its product or service has an effect on the organization design. For example, an automobile manufacturer using a labor-intensive assembly line technology organizes differently than an oil refinery that uses a capital-intensive production technology.

3. *Organization size.* As organization size increases, so do work specialization and the need to coordinate the work of diverse employees. Large organizations need more coordinating mechanisms than small ones.

4. *Environmental turbulence.* Organizations that operate in turbulent environments require different designs than organizations that operate in more stable environments in which change happens gradually. Turbulent environments are characterized by dynamic change due to market, technological, political, and regulatory or social forces.[9] Under conditions of rapid change, on-the-spot decisions are made, and lower level employees need the authority to make decisions. Decentralized structures that delegate authority to lower-level employees are used in turbulent environ-

ments to enable decisions to be made by those who are closest to the customer or the source of change.[10] An organization with a predictable and stable environment is more likely to have a structure with greater centralization.

Mechanistic Organizations

A **mechanistic organization design** emphasizes vertical control with rigid hierarchical relationships, topdown "command and control" communication channels, centralized decision authority, highly formalized work rules and policies, and specialized, narrowly defined jobs. It is based on many of the classical management principles that were described in Chapter 1. The organization has a tall pyramid shape with numerous levels of management. Managers have small spans of control and closely supervise subordinates.

A mechanistic organization design is best suited to a stable and relatively predictable environment. It depends on managers making decisions and front-line workers executing the decisions by doing repetitive tasks. While industry is moving away from this design, it is still applied in government agencies, labor unions, and some family businesses.

Organic Organizations

A focus on change and flexibility requires a more **organic organization design.** Such a design emphasizes horizontal relationships involving teams, departments, or divisions and provisions to coordinate these lateral units. Organic organizations are relatively decentralized and low in specialization, formalization, and standardization. Employees have more leeway in dealing with changing customer needs or technological challenges. The span of control is larger than in a mechanistic organization, and managers are less inclined to closely supervise subordinates. The organic design has fewer levels of management separating front-line employees from the executives. Its shape is flatter in appearance.

An organic organization design is most effective in turbulent and uncertain environments. Organic designs are beneficial for nurturing creativity and innovation, where employees are more likely to spend their time thinking and planning. Organizations that use organic design include high technology, entertainment and media, financial services, and consumer goods companies. Many entrepreneurships adopt organic designs from inception because management anticipates future growth in a highly uncertain environment. As deregulation has heated up the competitive landscape, public utilities, airlines, and telecommunications companies are also moving toward the use of organic designs.

mechanistic organization design

A management design based on the classical perspective of management, emphasizing vertical control with rigid hierarchical relationships, top-down "command and control" communication channels, centralized decision authority, highly formalized work rules and policies, and specialized, narrowly defined jobs; sometimes called a *bureaucratic design.*

organic organization design

A management design that is focused on change and flexibility, emphasizing horizontal relationships that involve teams, departments, or divisions, and provisions to coordinate these lateral units.

 Mechanistic versus Organic Organizational Structures

Home Box Office (HBO) plays movies and produces programs with adult topics. HBO has benefited from the flexibility and decentralization of an organic design. Its corporate parent, AOL-Time Warner, has given HBO writers creative and artistic freedom of expression. With the organic design, HBO is physically removed from the rest of the AOL-Time Warner corporation, which also contains the larger Warner Brothers operating under the pressure of ratings-driven broadcast schedules.[11] HBO programs, on the other hand, are directly paid for by subscribers. This allows HBO to produce more controversial and cutting-edge television content than is possible under traditional television broadcasting constraints. Partly due to the independence provided within an organic design, HBO programs such as *The Sopranos* and *Sex and the City* have won many Emmy television industry awards for quality. Moreover, HBO has also become a highly profitable business for AOL-Time Warner.

Some organizations have a hybrid design in which mechanistic and organic designs are used in different parts of the organization. For example, McDonald's utilizes a mechanistic design at its Chicago-area headquarters, where corporate functions such as training, marketing, and advertising are centralized. Managers are arranged in a hierarchy with an emphasis on vertical reporting relationships. However, within the geographical regions of McDonald's, the company applies an organic design so that divisions can be more responsive to changing customer tastes.

Boundaryless Organizations

boundaryless organization design

A management design that eliminates internal and external structural boundaries that inhibit employees from collaborating with each other or that inhibit firms from collaborating with customers, suppliers, or competitors.

Recently, a newer form of organizational structure has emerged in response to changing technologies and evolving marketplace relationships. A **boundaryless organization design** eliminates internal and external structural boundaries that inhibit employees from collaborating with each other or that inhibit firms from collaborating with customers, suppliers, or competitors. This design has many of the features of organic design, but it uses a flexible structure that makes it possible to overlap with other organizations so that seamless cooperation between organizations results in better service to the customer. By using teams that span organization boundaries, a boundaryless organization may share employees with a supplier through a joint venture; use its sales force to sell a partner's products; share a patented manufacturing process with a customer through a licensing agreement; or buy a large block of a competitor's stock to gain the right to use the competitor's technology. Such cooperative arrangements enable a boundaryless organization to improve the speed with which it reacts to change and uncertainty in the environment.

One of the first executives to use the boundaryless organization design was Jack Welch, the former CEO of General Electric. Welch was the architect of a bold plan to redesign General Electric, a large, diversified corporation, so that each of its divisions would operate with a minimum

WHERE CAN YOU DO YOUR BEST WORK?

Different types of organization design provide different environments for working and managing. This exercise lets you assess your preferences with respect to different structural dimensions of an organization.

First answer the following questions individually. Then, in groups of four to five people, share your responses with each other. Finally, complete the group discussion questions that appear at the end of the exercise and be ready to share your group's answers with the class.

1. Would you rather work in a large (more than 1,000 employees) or small (fewer than 100 employees) organization? Why?

2. Do you prefer to have frequent (on a daily basis) interactions with your boss, or would you prefer infrequent (once or twice per month) interactions with your boss?

3. Do you prefer to work primarily as part of a team or as an individual?

4. Do you prefer to be a specialist in a company (knowing a lot about a highly specialized function or business process), or do you prefer to be a generalist (having a broad scope of knowledge of different facets of the business, but not specializing in any of them)?

5. Do you prefer a job that is constantly changing and requires continuing training and education to keep pace with change, or do you prefer a job with stable content that lets you develop work routines that are predictable after you master the job skills?

6. Do you prefer working cross-functionally with people you have no line authority to influence, or do you prefer working in vertical relationships with people who are either subordinates or superiors, located up or down the chain of command?

Discussion Questions

1. What are the advantages of working in a mechanistic organization, an organic organization, and a boundaryless organization? You may want to refer to Table 9.1.

2. What are the disadvantages of working in a mechanistic organization, an organic organization, and a boundaryless organization?

3. Do group members agree or disagree that one design is superior to the others for providing the best work environment? Does organization design matter when it comes to choosing a company to work for? Are there certain designs that one should avoid when searching for a job?

4. What conclusions about your career path and goals can you draw from this discussion?

of bureaucracy. Hierarchies were flattened and vertical functional silos were broken down.

- At its locomotive division in Erie, Pennsylvania, GE formed a partnership with a paint supplier to improve the consistency of the paint used on its locomotives. Team members from GE and the paint supplier collaborated to reduce painting time and improve quality.

- GE Capital's Global Consumer Finance business worked with top global retailers such as Wal-Mart to deliver financial services to their customers.

- GE signed a 10-year maintenance agreement with British Airways in 1998. GE and British Airways maintenance crews work together on maintenance and overhaul projects.

Other companies have followed GE's lead. Boundaryless designs have been used to: (1) enter foreign markets, (2) manage the risk of developing new technologies, and (3) pool resources to compete in an industry with high financial entry barriers. For example,

- Airbus Industries utilizes a boundaryless design that consists of a partnership of four firms from France, Germany, England, and Spain that collaborated to market and develop commercial jet aircraft. The group competes with Boeing, the world's leading producer of passenger jets.

- Paramount and Twentieth Century Fox combined to produce, market, and distribute the enormously expensive epic movie *Titanic,* which broke box office records in the late 1990s. The production costs of the movie were higher than any single film company could risk alone.

- Apple Computer, IBM, and Motorola formed a customer–supplier alliance to develop the PowerPC microprocessor used in the Power Macintosh computer.

- Northwest Airlines and KLM (the Dutch national airline) formed a partnership merging air routes and customer sales processes to facilitate better service on international flights.

A type of boundaryless design that has been adopted by many multinational firms in recent years is the network design. The *network design* consists of a series of strategic alliances or relationships that a company develops with suppliers, distributors, or manufacturers in order to produce and market a product. A *strategic alliance* is an agreement between two or more companies to collaborate by sharing or exchanging resources to produce and market a product (see Chapter 2 for more on strategic alliances). For example, Hewlett-Packard and Canon formed a network design to produce laser printers that has endured for over 15 years. Hewlett-Packard provides its computer technologies and know-how which is combined with Canon's knowledge of imaging and laser technology. By sharing the knowledge and technologies, the laser printers that are marketed by Hewlett-Packard own a dominant share of the market. Manager's Notes 9.3 provides some important symptoms to let managers become aware of a malfunctioning organization design.

Redesigning Organizations

As a firm's strategy changes, organization structure and design also change to support the implementation of the new strategy. In a sense, organization design can be considered a continuous work in progress. An

Managers should be aware of symptoms that indicate a malfunctioning organization design. Here are some of the most important. If one or more of these exist, managers are advised to consider making changes to the organization's structure.

- *The organization design focuses employees on work that uses noncritical skills rather than emphasizing the opportunity to use their strength.* The design should provide the opportunity for highly skilled employees to do the work that they do best, rather than being bogged down by less critical tasks of less value. For example, sales and marketing people may be spending too much time attending required staff meetings to coordinate with others on projects within a matrix structure. Disappointing sales results may be the result of using a structure that keeps sales people away from their customers by forcing them to attend regular meetings. The matrix structure may be diverting sales people from making their most valuable contributions to company performance.

- *The organization design has too many levels in the hierarchy.* Too many management levels inhibit the responsiveness of employees in an organization. Consequently they do not serve customers, because they are oversupervised and do not have enough autonomy. Employees' contacts with customers are limited, because they must obtain management approval to take action. Instead, the structure should help them show initiative and adopt standardized procedures in order to please a customer. A good rule to use is to ask if the managers at higher levels are adding value to or taking value away from the business activity. Value is added when they improve quality or consistency. Managers take value away by slowing down the process of giving service to the customer or by taking away the initiative of lower-level employees to better serve customers. By giving additional authority to lower-level employees who have direct contact with customers, organizations provide better service. The executive team may also learn that they need fewer levels of managers to supervise employees.

- *The organization design is not flexible enough to accommodate changes in strategy or the environment.* A well-designed structure should allow the organization to be innovative and adapt to changing circumstances. For example, if a new product takes off unexpectedly and is in high demand in a fast growing market, this market jolt is likely to result in a reallocation of company resources devoted to producing the successful new product. The current organization design should be able to accommodate a decision made to reallocate capital, people, and technology to satisfy the surging demand for the new product. A flexible design, like a tree bending in the wind, should be able to deal with an unexpected jolt from the environment.

Source: Adapted from M. Goold and A. Campbell, "Do You Have a Well-Designed Organization? *Harvard Business Review,* March 2002, pp. 117–124.

The CEOs of Hewlett-Packard and Compaq Computer Corporation, Carly Fiorina and Michael D. Capellas, announce the merger of their two companies to shareholders in 2002.

organization is *redesigned* to enable the firm to more effectively use its technology, assets, and human resources to accomplish strategic goals. The key strategic events that are likely to trigger change in the structure and design of an organization are mergers, acquisitions, and divestitures.

MERGER   When two independent companies agree to combine their assets and form a single organization a **merger** has taken place. In many cases, companies that compete in the same industry merge to create a larger entity with greater economies of scale. Redundant facilities such as corporate headquarters or back-office operations can be disposed of to create a more efficient operation.

There were numerous bank mergers in the 1990s. California-based Wells Fargo and Midwest-based Northwest Banks merged operations and decided to use the Wells Fargo name for the emergent organization. Citicorp, the largest U.S. Bank, merged with Travelers Group, a leading insurance company, to create a global financial giant called Citigroup.

ACQUISITION   An **acquisition** takes place when a firm buys all or part of another business. The acquiring firm may use cash or trade some of its stock to purchase the acquired firm. In the 1980s, many companies acquired businesses in unrelated industries as part of a strategy of diversification, as when Phillip Morris, a tobacco company, acquired Kraft and General Foods.

In the 1990s the dynamic economic opportunities of the Internet gave impetus to strategic acquisitions in the telecommunications industry. In one deal, AT&T, the long distance telephone company, acquired Telecommunications-Inc. (TCI), the largest cable television company. The acquisition was driven by AT&T's strategy to reenter the local phone service market, which it had been forced to abandon in 1984 as a result of a court order. AT&T intended to use TCI's huge wired network of cable TV customers to deliver local phone service. WorldCom, a fast-growing long-distance and Internet provider, went on a buying spree, acquiring many smaller telecommunications companies in order to realize its

merger

The process of integrating two firms.

acquisition

The process of purchasing other firms.

part four   Organization Management

Deverticalizing Sara Lee

THEME: DEALING WITH CHANGE Many large consumer goods companies have embraced outsourcing. For example, Nike doesn't make any shoes. Pillsbury's Green Giant line of canned vegetables are not actually canned by the Minneapolis, Minnesota, food company—Seneca Foods does it for Pillsbury. Outsourcing lets companies concentrate on sales, marketing, and improving their brands while the actual manufacturing of their products is done by other companies.

In 1949 a Chicago baker perfected cheesecakes that kept their quality after being frozen. Charles Lubin, the baker, named his shop after his eight-year-old daughter, Sara Lee. Today Sara Lee is a top multinational corporation whose products are sold in over 140 countries. Globally, the company is first in the packaged meats industry, and it is ranked first in the United States for frozen baked goods, intimate apparel, and socks.

Since 1997, however, Sara Lee has sold or closed more than 100 plants while maintaining its position in its markets. The corporation surprised everyone with its decision to sell its manufacturing operations and outsource the work. The corporation wanted to focus on developing new products and promoting its brands instead of manufacturing them. Senior management called the divestiture action "deverticalizing" the company's organization, with its brands being made by suppliers according to Sara Lee's specifications.

Then-CEO John Bryan believed the firm would grow more quickly by concentrating on the most profitable parts of its various businesses, using "skills and knowledge, and not a whole lot of bricks and mortar." Sara Lee's strategic reshaping, begun in 2000, narrowed the company's structure further to the three units—food and beverage, intimates and underwear, and household products—that made up the company's leading world category positions. Toward that end the company began consolidating and centralizing operations and administrative functions, moving to a smaller number of larger, more focused companies and reducing duplication of common functions—moves that changed its organizational structure while enhancing its core values.

Sources: Adapted from S. Seifert, "Hired Guns," *Office.com*, February 1, 2000, www.office.com; "Selling the Factory," *Alliance Analyst*, January 15, 1998, adapted from "Separate and Lift," *The Economist*, September 20, 1997, p. 69; *Sara Lee Annual Report*, 2000.

growth strategy of becoming a global competitor in the telecommunications industry.

DIVESTITURE   A **divestiture** occurs when an organization sells a business in order to generate cash. The goal is to better deploy the funds elsewhere, or to refocus on a core business which is better understood by management. General Electric divested many business units that did not fit with its boundaryless organization strategy and high performance expectations. GE acquired others (such as the NBC television network) that better fit with the company's strategy. The redesign helped General Electric become a flatter and more competitive company and increased its market value from $12 billion in 1981 to $259 billion in 2003.

Many corporations that increased their size through mergers and acquisitions in the 1970s and 1980s found that the complexity of managing the new business units led to disappointing earnings. In the late 1980s and the 1990s, many corporate divestitures took place, and **downsizing** (a strategy used to reduce the scale and scope of a business to improve its financial performance) became common. Management Close-Up 9.a shows how Sara Lee adopted a strategy of divestiture to add value.

> **divestiture**
>
> The corporate process of selling a business in order to generate cash, which the corporation can better deploy elsewhere, or to refocus on a core business which is better understood by management.

> **downsizing**
>
> A management strategy used to reduce the scale and scope of a business to improve its financial performance.

Applications for the Manager   An organizational structure provides sources other than formal authority for a manager to use to get things done. One source is the recognition of how the resources that a unit or department controls can contribute to organization performance. For example, the chairman of the accounting department in a college of business has cultivated a relationship with several of the big-five accounting firms by supplying them with accountants. In return, the firms make large donations to support faculty research activities at the business school. By controlling this important funding source, the accounting chairman has more influence in the college, which he can use to hire additional clerical and technical support staff or acquire improved facilities for the faculty. Other department heads may have less influence because they have not cultivated generous benefactors.

Another resource provided by the organization that managers can use to get things done is knowledge provided by the informal organization. The *informal organization* is a network of social groups that are formed based on friendships or interests between employees. Most typical, *friendship groups* within an informal organization are groups of employees who meet for lunch, or meet after work for drinks, sports, or other activities. A manager can use the informal organization to solve work-related problems and gather information that may not be available through the formal processes. For example, a manager may learn while playing golf with some company executives who are part of a friendship group that corporate headquarters is about to enact a freeze on hiring new employees within a week. Knowledge of this suspension of hiring may enable the manager to urgently conclude employment negotiations with a desirable employee being recruited and bring the individual on board before the hiring freeze is formally announced.

Applications for Managing Teams   An interesting way to strengthen the culture of a company for members of a team is to organize a ceremony that exemplifies what the team values. Ceremonies reinforce specific values and create bonds among employees by allowing them to celebrate the achievements of the team or of individual team members. These ceremonies celebrate high-performing employees and help build cohesion among team members.

Applications for Individuals   While formal power and influence in an organization are often structured to flow in a top-down direction, this does not mean that you cannot influence your boss by managing your relationship with him or her. You can

- Make yourself indispensable by anticipating your boss's need for support and by providing it without being asked.

- Look for ways to show loyalty by speaking well of your boss to others.

- Develop a trusting relationship by being dependable, consistent, and honest. Do your work well and look for ways to exceed your boss's expectations.

- Keep your boss well informed.

CONCLUDING THOUGHTS

In the introductory vignette at the beginning of the chapter we presented some critical thinking questions related to aspects of organization structure at Nokia. Now that you have had the opportunity to learn about managing organization structure and design in the chapter let's reexamine questions that were raised in the vignette.

First, there is a strong and direct relationship between the new organizational structure at Nokia and the changing marketplace. The change in strategic direction was designed to allow the company to move faster and be more flexible in response to slower demand. The new structure was put in place to enable group leaders to create the best possible products for individual markets. In this case, the organization became more organic and decentralized to meet a changing marketplace.

The reason that the structure of Nokia was no longer working was that the growth rate of the market for mobile phones had slowed down, making additional growth more difficult. Nokia would need to work harder to attract new customers in a slow growth market. In addition, the mobile phone products and services provided by Nokia had become more specialized, requiring more knowledge by sales people to sell and service the products. Consequently, one single telecommunications division within Nokia could not efficiently and effectively market, sell, and provide service to customers at a level of quality that would be equal or superior to that of competitors unless Nokia was reorganized to provide higher-quality service to customers. By organizing into several different divisions based on products, Nokia had sales, marketing, and customer service employees with specialized product knowledge who could better serve customers. Further, each product unit would have profit and loss responsibilities so that Nokia executives could be in greater control of the company's financial resources.

SUMMARY

This chapter is about **organizing,** which is the deployment of resources to achieve strategic goals. The first part of the chapter examines **organization structure,** developing a formal system of relationships that determine lines of authority and the tasks assigned to individuals and units. The **vertical dimension** of organization structure is concerned with who has the authority to make decisions; it involves

- **Unity of command:** each subordinate should have only one supervisor.
- **Authority:** the formal right of a manager to make decisions and give orders that are carried out by others.
- **Responsibility:** the duty to perform a task that has been assigned.
- **Delegation:** a transfer of responsibility to a subordinate or team subject to the authority of the manager.
- **Line authority:** direct control over the work of subordinates.
- **Staff authority:** advising, recommending, and counseling other managers and personnel in the organization.
- **Span of control:** the number of subordinates who directly report to a manager.
- **Centralization:** decision authority concentrated at the top of the organization hierarchy.
- **Decentralization:** decision authority pushed to lower levels in the organizational hierarchy.
- **Formalization:** the amount of written documentation that is used to direct and control employees.

Departmentalization is the horizontal dimension of organization structure, and it involves organizing jobs into units called departments. The **functional structure** of departmentalization assigns people with similar skills to a department such as accounting or marketing. It is highly efficient because it permits employees to do specialized tasks. The **divisional approach** organizes employees into units based on common products, services, or markets. It improves coordination between different business functions and allows for faster service to customers. The **matrix approach** combines the efficiency of the functional approach with the flexibility and responsiveness to change of the divisional approach. The matrix approach greatly facilitates starting new projects and ventures, and it efficiently utilizes the talents of scarce specialists.

As organizations grow and become more complex, there is a greater need for **coordination mechanisms** to link activities between departments. Some key coordination mechanisms include the following:

- **Meetings:** face-to-face gatherings of departmental or division managers to coordinate overarching organizational objectives.
- **Organizationwide reward systems:** rewards that are based on organizationwide results that strengthen collaboration between departments.
- **Task forces:** ad hoc interdepartmental groups that are formed to study a specific problem and make recommendations.
- **Problem-solving teams:** groups representing different departments that solve problems on either a temporary or permanent basis.

- **Liaison role:** a position held by an individual that is used to facilitate communications between two or more departments.

- **Integrating manager:** a manager who is responsible for the success of a project or product and who coordinates the work of people from different departments.

- **Organizational culture:** a system of shared values, assumptions, beliefs, and norms that give the members of an organization a common understanding about "the way things are done around here." A strong culture facilitates collaboration of people from different departments.

Organization design involves selecting an organization structure that best fits the strategic goals of the business. Managers can design organizations that are mechanistic, organic, or boundaryless. **Mechanistic designs** emphasize vertical structure and use top-down "command and control" communication channels with a high level of formalization. **Organic designs** emphasize horizontal relationships involving teams and rely on coordination mechanisms to keep everything under control. There is more flexibility and less formalization in an organic design than in a mechanistic design. **Boundaryless designs** eliminate structural boundaries between organizations and units within them so that employees can develop collaborative relationships with customers, suppliers, and sometimes competitors. While sharing some similarities with the organic design, the boundaryless design uses teams to span organizational boundaries with other firms to more quickly respond to change and uncertainty in the environment.

DISCUSSION QUESTIONS

1. What would it be like to be a department manager in a functional organization structure? In a divisional approach to organization structure? In your comparison discuss responsibilities, skills, competencies, and decision-making authority.

2. How do responsibility, authority, and accountability differ? What happens to responsibility, authority, and accountability when a manager delegates work to a subordinate?

3. What are the advantages and disadvantages of centralization and decentralization? You are the CEO of a diversified food company with four divisions that produce breakfast cereals, cookies, salty snack foods, and fruit juices under different brand names. Give an example of a situation were centralized decision authority would be more effective to use. Give an example where decentralized decision authority would be more effective to use. Justify your answers.

4. What does the term "organizational culture" mean? Explain the difference between strong and weak cultures and list some ways that a company can build a strong culture. Is a weak organization structure purposely planned by management, or does it just happen that way? Explain.

5. What issues or problems would an organization encounter with a matrix structure? Would you like to work in a matrix organization structure? Why or why not?

6. Your organization is organized with functional departments. It has encountered the following problems. What coordinating mechanism would you select to manage each problem? Justify your selection.

   a. The number of workplace accidents has increased greatly in all the departments.

   b. Departments are competing with each other for budgets and other scarce resources, resulting in dysfunctional conflict.

   c. The research, engineering, manufacturing, and marketing departments disagree on product specifications and performance features, and new products are being delivered too late to market as a result.

7. How are teams used in the organic design? What about in the boundaryless design?

8. Does an organization in a turbulent environment require more horizontal relationships than one in a stable environment? Explain.

9. Why does the structure of an organization follow the development of the organization strategy, rather than the strategy following the development of the structure?

10. An entrepreneurial, innovative, and very competitive company is merging with a company that is conservative and hierarchical and that enjoys a monopoly position in the market. The two companies have strong, distinct, and different cultures. What concerns would you have with this merger? How would you suggest the merger be structured?

MANAGEMENT MINICASE 9.1

Should a Company Cooperate with Its Competitor?

One of the more controversial ways in which boundaryless organizations are formed is an alliance between two competitors who join forces to produce a product or deliver a service that neither could produce or market on its own.

One of the most enduring partnerships between competitors is the one between Canon, a large Japanese firm that makes electronic and imaging products, and Hewlett-Packard, the U.S. producer of electronic computers, electronic printers, and integrated circuits. These two rivals joined forces to make laser printers, and the partnership has lasted more than 15 years. Hewlett-Packard combined its computer know-how with Canon's superb laser motors to create Hewlett-Packard's laser printers. Hewlett-Packard and Canon's color printers were first and second, respectively, in the U.S. market, and sales to Hewlett-Packard accounted for 20 percent of Canon's laser printer sales.

Although the two companies worked together to overcome the huge technical challenges in developing inkjet printer technology, they are in head-to-head competition and are intense rivals in other areas. Canon surprised Hewlett-Packard by introducing its own impressive printer software package that helped it grab a big chunk of the U.S. market. This led to a nasty price war that all but wiped out their margins. Each side blamed the other for starting it.

Can the laser printer partnership between Canon and Hewlett-Packard last? Analysts wondered when Hewlett-Packard chose Konica over Canon, which could have provided the component, to make the motors for its color laser printers. Canon executives played down any friction, however, describing their partnership as that of "a typical married couple. We rely on each other, and there is no prospect of divorce." Keeping the marriage healthy hasn't been easy.

Discussion Questions

1. Why did Hewlett-Packard and Canon form an alliance to produce laser printers?

2. In a technology alliance such as the one described in this case, it is typical for each of the partners to provide some employees who collaborate in a team (called a joint venture) that spans the boundaries of both companies. What type of coordination mechanism do you think would be useful for each partner to apply to the team that is developing the laser printers?

3. What problems could threaten the success of the Hewlett-Packard and Canon partnership? Do you agree or disagree that there is value in forming partnerships between competitors? Explain the reason for your opinion.

Sources: Adapted from E. W. Desmond, "Can Canon Keep Clicking?" *Fortune*, February 2, 1998, p. 102; "The Science of Alliance," *The Economist*, April 4, 1998; pp. 69–70; *Canon Annual Report*, 1999; *Hewlett-Packard Annual Report*, 2000.

Restructuring the 3M Company for Growth and Profitability

The 3M Company of 2003 bore a resemblance to the "old IBM" of the 1980s, which was a place of lifetime employment for tinkerers, coddled from postgraduate life to the grave, and who might or might not eventually turn out commercial products. They read the company's weekly newspaper that provided features about cooking classes, stamp collecting, and volunteerism. In other words, life at 3M was cushy and undemanding for its employees.

Complacency begat financial disappointments. Between 1992 and 2002 sales crept ahead at an average of 1.6 percent and profits increased 4.9 percent a year. The 3M Company generated $16 billion in sales in 2002. The 3M Company's product lines focused on industrial and consumer goods such as abrasives, glues, and various types of tapes with adhesive qualities. Starting in 2001, CEO James McNerney formulated a strategy of diversification to refocus 3M on faster-growing markets that could provide better performance in terms of growth and profitability to investors. McNerney used a two-pronged approach to realize these goals. First, he reduced operating expenses by $500 million, mostly by laying off 6,500 of 3M's 75,000 workers. He slashed inventories and accounts receivable by $675 million and trimmed debt. Profitability jumped 38 percent to $2 billion due to these efforts.

Second, CEO McNerney decided to reposition 3M as more of a health care company, building on the health unit's 22 percent of revenue and 27 percent of operating income. Until now, 3M's medical products have been mostly low tech, such as skin patches or inhalers, or service based, including software used to code medical procedures for Medicare reimbursement. Scientists in 3M's laboratories are developing medications to treat respiratory, cardiovascular, skin, and sexually related diseases. The company is an important supplier of materials to repair and replace teeth, and the

CEO wants to branch into such areas as fluoride treatment and products to stem periodontal disease. With the U.S. population aging, the $12 billion restorative dental care market is expected to reach $21.5 billion in 10 years. McNerney is also looking for acquisitions in expanding industries. He recently completed a $680 million acquisition of Corning's precision lens business, which makes parts for projection TVs.

The 3M Company had 148 plants in 60 countries with 53 percent of sales outside the United States. At any given time there were 1,500 products in development. Many never made it further. The company's organization chart was bewildering. Mixing faster-growing businesses with low-tech slowpokes made it impossible to evaluate performance, a frequent complaint from the investment community. McNerney has asked researchers to focus the $1 billion they spend annually on their best ideas, ones that have a sales potential of $100 million or more in annual sales. He is also asking 3M employees to think more like their customers—a novel idea in this organization.

Discussion Questions

1. The CEO at 3M has formulated a new strategy of diversification with increased growth and profitability. In what ways will the new strategy affect the organization structure at 3M? How will it affect the vertical dimension of organization structure? Will it be flatter or taller? How will it affect the horizontal dimension of organization structure? Will 3M need to change the basis for its allocation of departments?

2. The CEO is asking the scientists at the research laboratories at 3M to focus on research projects that could result in $100 million or more annual sales. Will this new policy result in a more centralized or decentralized research and development unit at 3M?

3. With the changes in structure that are likely to follow the diversification strategy that calls for higher performance in terms of growth and profitability, what type of coordination mechanisms do you think will best enable 3M management to link activities between diverse departments or divisions. Do you think that the portfolio of 3M products and services is becoming more diverse or less diverse? Justify your answers.

Source: Adapted from M. Tatge, "Prescription for Growth," *Fortune,* February 17, 2003, pp. 64–66.

INDIVIDUAL/
COLLABORATIVE
LEARNING
CASE 9.1

Changing Company Culture at Gateway

Can a company change its culture without alienating its employees and customers who were committed to the old culture? In 1997 Gateway was a $6 billion business that made and sold personal computers to order directly to consumers, and it was second largest in its market. Based in South Dakota, the company prided itself on its heartland hayseed style and had almost a cult following among computer users. For a while, Gateway's old folksy culture had served it well. The low labor and commercial real estate costs in South Dakota helped Gateway compete as a low-priced direct marketer of personal computers to consumers. In 1998, however, Gateway was about to find out what would happen when it underwent a company makeover of its image and culture.

Growth drove the redesign strategy at Gateway, which wanted to increase the company's revenues and market share. North Sioux City, South Dakota, was too far from the action. The management team decided to move the company's administrative headquarters from North Sioux City to San Diego, California to take advantage of the dynamic high-tech labor pool in California.

Considerable risks accompanied Gateway's growth strategy. With the move to San Diego, Gateway was turning its back on the folksy, Midwestern culture and marketing that defined the company and helped make it a brand name. It changed its name from Gateway 2000 to simply Gateway. Even its trademark Holstein cows featured in its ads were put out to pasture. Only the spots were kept, relegated to the company's logo and shipping boxes of its computers, as the company presented itself as a serious strategic partner for business.

Part of Gateway's new strategy includes repositioning itself in the market by focusing on small businesses and consumers who buy cutting-edge PCs rather than the home computer user of its original market. Gateway also broadened its product lines under a new strategy of providing new products and services. For example, the company began a novel program in which the customers pay one monthly fee for a combination of Internet access and personal computer bundled together at an attractive price. The company moved into retail using the name Gateway Country Stores. Gateway also offered online buying options and gave buyers a purchase program allowing them to trade in their computers every two years to keep up with technology. In addition there are future plans for the Gateway Country Stores to be changed from showrooms into full-fledged technology centers where customers can take courses on downloading music or paying bills electronically and where small businesses can get training and round-the-clock repair services for a monthly fee. But no matter how ambitious a firm's plans, dumping a successful corporate image can turn off its existing customers.

Critical Thinking Questions

1. Why do you think Gateway wants to change its company culture?

2. Some companies take pride in sustaining a culture for many years. (The Walt Disney Company ["imagination"] and McDonald's [fast service, consistent quality, and clean facilities] are two examples.) What are the risks of changing a company culture?

3. Do you think Gateway should try to retain its current culture, which capitalized on its Midwestern, rural location? Why or why not? What opportunities would Gateway forgo by remaining with what has worked in the past?

Collaborative Learning Exercise

With a partner or small group, visualize the new culture of Gateway. How would you describe it? Discuss how Gateway could go about changing its culture. Think in terms of values, rites, rituals, heroes, and stories that people use to describe a company culture. Be prepared to explain your interpretation of Gateway's new culture to the class.

Sources: Adapted from R. O. Crockett, "Gateway Loses the Folksy Shtick," *Business Week,* July 6, 1998, pp. 57–58; *Gateway Annual Report,* 2000, www.gateway.com; A. Weintraub, "Can Gateway Survive in a Smaller Pasture?" *Business Week,* September 10, 2001, p. 48.

Making People Happy on the Web

One company with a strong culture is the Walt Disney Company, which focuses on "making people happy." Explore the Disney website and answer the following questions:

1. What words would you use to describe the Disney website? Does the cultural value of "making people happy" come across on the website? Explain why or why not, with examples.

2. Based on the information provided at Disney's website, what do you think it would be like to work at Disney? Describe the characteristics of a person that you think would "fit" into the Disney culture.

3. Do you see any disadvantages to working at a company that has a strong organization culture such as Disney? Describe what in your opinion may be some disadvantages.

Do You Follow the Chain of Command?

Would you fit into the traditional hierarchical structure of a corporation? Would an organization that puts a low priority on hierarchical relationships be more your style? This exercise can indicate your ability to manage within an organization that expects allegiance to the chain of command.

Consider the following statements and mark each as "True" or "False" to indicate whether you agree or disagree.

_____ 1. When something bothers me at work, I go straight to top management.

_____ 2. The only way to get what you need is to talk to the owner of the company.

_____ 3. If my supervisor behaved in a way that offended me, I would speak directly to his or her boss.

_____ 4. Although I feel comfortable delegating responsibility to my employees. I follow up to make certain they have accomplished the tasks they were assigned.

_____ 5. If I suspected my boss were engaging in unethical behavior, I would speak to someone in the human resources department in strict confidence.

_____ 6. I will not mention a potential promotion to my star employee until I have received approval to do so from upper management.

_____ 7. If I wait for the required approval from human resources to begin interviewing candidates for the new position that is open, it will be months before I can get anyone on board to help with this project. So I am going ahead with the interviews.

_____ 8. If I suspected my boss were having emotional problems, I would speak to his or her best friend, who also works at the company.

_____ 9. If a customer made a special request I did not have the authority to approve, I would politely explain that I'd get back to him or her as soon as possible.

_____ 10. If a friend of mine wanted to apply for a job at my organization, I'd sneak her past human resources to speak with my boss.

Scoring: "True" responses to statements 4, 5, 6 and 9 indicate an ability to follow the chain of command. "True" responses to statements 1–3, 7–8 and 10 indicate an inability to follow the chain of command.

Source: From *Management of Organizations*, by P. M. Wright and R. A. Noe. Copyright © 1996 The McGraw-Hill Companies, Inc. Reprinted with permission.

TEN

Human Resource Management

chapter 10

After reading this chapter, you should be able to:

- Determine appropriate responses to the major changes in the environment that affect human resources.

- Comply with the legal framework governing human resources.

- Develop tactics to implement desired human resource strategies.

- Prepare a staffing program to recruit and select the best applicants.

- Establish orientation, training, and career development programs to enhance employees' contributions to the firm.

- Implement an effective performance appraisal program to capitalize on employee strengths and reduce employee weaknesses.

- Develop a reward system to attract, retain, and motivate employees.

Brewing Success at Starbucks with HR

"How do you build an enduring company? Starbucks is doing it one person at a time. Each person, in every job, throughout the company shares a common vision—a passion for quality." So begins a recent annual report for Starbucks, one of the great business stories of recent history.

Starbucks attributes much of its success to the company's human resource practices. The first guiding principle found in the company's credo is "Provide a great work environment and treat each other with respect and dignity." The 50,000 plus employees of Starbucks are called "barista partners," and hundreds of partners are hired every month. New employees are carefully selected, and experienced employees are often involved in the selection process. Each participates in Starbucks's employee training program during their first six weeks with the company. Employees in the San Francisco area take the classes in a fluorescent-lit training room set up to resemble a Starbucks store, where they learn "calling" ("triple tall nonfat mocha") and making drinks. They learn to make the drinks in an eight-hour marathon of lectures, demonstrations, and hands-on practice. They also learn about Starbucks's obsession with customer service.

By 2003, Starbucks had grown to an astonishing 5,700 outlets, 1,200 of which were located in 27 other countries. By 2006, the plan is to almost double the number of stores to 10,000. Company profits have been climbing about 24 percent per year. And despite the overall market drop during 2000–2003, Starbucks's stock price continued to be at an all-time high, soaring more than 2,200 percent over the past decade, surpassing Wal-Mart, General Electric, PepsiCo, Coca-Cola, Microsoft, and IBM in total return.

Starbucks's turnover rate is about 40 percent of the industry's average. Customer satisfaction is high, and loyal customers don't mind spending $1,400 or more per year at Starbucks. The company replicates its coffee experience in stores from Seattle to the Philippines and adds more than a store per day, every day, in a different spot around the world.

Training is not the only HR program that makes Starbucks a success. The company recognizes its partners' contributions by providing an enhanced benefits program (which includes health insurance and tuition reimbursement), above average wages (about $9 per hour in 2004 including tips), and granting stock options through its "Bean Stock" plan for both full- and part-time employees. As noted by one dedicated partner, "This is the only place that will offer full benefits for 20 hours a week, stock options, and decent pay. Oh, yeah, we get a pound of coffee free each week—how cool is that?" During 2000–2004, Starbucks was the only fast-food company that had made it into Fortune's top 50 of the best companies to work for, and the only one among Fortune's top 10 most admired companies in America.

Sources: J. Reese, "Starbucks: Inside the Coffee Cult," *Fortune,* December 9, 1996, pp. 191–200; S. Branch, "The 100 Best Companies to Work for in America," *Fortune,* January 11, 1999, pp. 118, 122; N. D. Schwartz, "Still Perking after All These Years," *Fortune,* May 24, 1999, pp. 203–210. G. Khermouch, S. Holmes, and M. Ihlwan, "The Best Global Brands," *Business Week,* August 6, 2001, pp. 51–56; S. Holmes, D. Bennett, K. Carlisle, and C. Dawson, "To Keep Up the Growth, It Must Go Global Quickly," *Business Week,* September 9, 2002, pp. 126–138; R. Levering and M. Moskowitz, "100 Best Companies to Work For," *Fortune,* January 20, 2003, pp. 127–150; N. Stein, "America's Most Admired Companies," *Fortune,* March 3, 2003, pp. 81–94; and updates by author obtained from Starbucks's Web page (www.starbucks.com).

CRITICAL THINKING QUESTIONS

1. *How has Starbucks been able to attract, develop, retain, and motivate competent employees in a fast-food industry known for rapid turnover, minimum skills, and little employee commitment?*

2. *Why is effective management of human resources critical to achieving a sustainable competitive advantage?*

The Importance of Human Resource Management

The heart and soul of practically every company is its employees. Human resource issues are crucial at every level of the organization. Even entry-level supervisors play a vital role in HR practices. They are part of the selection process, and then train, coach, and evaluate employees.

The Human Resources Department supports managers in carrying out HR responsibilities. The HR department may conduct a pay survey to determine a salary range for a given position, inform managers about changes in employment law, develop a form to evaluate employees, or determine if applicants meet minimum position requirements. But in the end, it is managers who determine a prospective employee's salary subject to budget constraints, ensure that the law is being applied correctly, assess a subordinate's performance, and make final hiring decisions. For this reason, there is an old saying among HR professionals: "Every manager is a personnel manager."

SKILLS FOR MANAGING HUMAN RESOURCES

- *Congruency skills.* Managers should ensure that human resource programs and practices are attuned to changes in the organization and the environment. The success of HR practices depends on how compatible they are with the firm's overall strategy, the competitive environment, the firm's unique organizational features, and the legal environment. Managers need to anticipate and respond to changes by developing and implementing HR programs that are most appropriate to current and emerging conditions.

- *Hiring skills.* Managers need to hire the right employees at the right time. Putting the wrong person in a job can result in lost productivity. This chapter describes ways to recruit, select, and place the best candidates.

- *Training skills.* Today's business, economic, and technological environments are characterized by rapid change. Employees need to prepare themselves for these job and career changes. This chapter covers training and career developmental activities that will help an organization meet its skill requirements.

- *Performance appraisal skills.* An important part of a manager's job is to provide constructive performance feedback to help employees capitalize on their strengths and improve job performance. This chapter discusses how managers and employees can make effective use of appraisal data as a developmental tool.

- *Pay allocation skills.* Compensation is the payment employees receive in exchange for their labor. Pay is one of the most powerful tools to attract employees from competing firms and to prevent the best employees from leaving. The criteria used to reward employees are likely to affect their behavior. The chapter discusses how managers can make pay allocation decisions that help attract and retain employees and that reinforce behaviors important to the organization.

This chapter describes the human resource skills you will need to help an organization become more productive, comply with legal requirements, and gain or maintain a competitive edge in the marketplace. Skills for Managing 10.1 lists some important skills for managing human resources.

Environment of Human Resources

Managers need to constantly monitor the external environment for opportunities and threats affecting human resources and be prepared to react quickly to these changes. Major environmental considerations include workforce diversity, legislation, globalization, competitive forces, and labor unions.

Workforce Diversity

The U.S. workforce is rapidly becoming more diverse. Company leaders can take advantage of diversity in order to succeed. African Americans,

Asian Americans, Hispanics, and other minorities make up approximately one-third of the U.S. workforce. At least 5 million undocumented workers are also estimated to be working in the United States. In large urban centers where most business activity takes place and corporate headquarters are usually located, the workforce is often 50 percent to 75 percent nonwhite. Women represent almost half of the workforce, and women with children under six years of age are the fastest growing segment. The workforce is aging, includes a larger proportion of disabled employees, and a growing number are openly homosexual.

In 2004, the proportion of the U.S. population that is foreign born reached almost 11 percent. This historic high is more than double what it was in 1970 and a third higher than it was in 1990.[1] Unlike early immigrants who came from Europe, recent immigrants come from every corner of the world.[2] Clear-cut racial distinctions are also blurring as intermarriage of different groups has steadily increased. The resulting large population of biracial children "view the world from the wondrous, troubling perspective of insider/outsider."[3]

Employees and managers need to work effectively with people who are different from them. The HR department is responsible for facilitating this process. Many HR departments organize diversity training workshops for managers and employees to enable them to better relate to customers and one another. Some HR departments hire a manager of diversity who is responsible for dealing with the day-to-day issues of managing a diverse workforce.

Globalization

In order to grow, many firms enter the global marketplace as exporters, overseas manufacturers, or both. Even those that choose to remain in the domestic market are not insulated from foreign competition. Human resources plays a central role in this process. A firm may restructure the top-management team and decentralize operations to meet the global challenge, use cheaper foreign labor to reduce costs, or promote managers with foreign experience and language skills. The HR department can organize international training programs, offer financial incentives for managers to export the company's products, and identify the appropriate mix of foreign (or *expatriate*) and local managers in overseas operations.

Legislation

Over the past 40 years, federal, state, and local governments have passed many laws to protect employees and ensure equal employment opportunity. Company leaders must deal effectively with applicable government regulations. The HR department plays a crucial role by monitoring the le-

TABLE 10.1

Key Legislation Affecting Human Resources

LAW	YEAR	DESCRIPTION
Workers compensation laws	Various	State-by-state laws that establish insurance plans to compensate employees injured on the job
Social Security Act	1935	Payroll tax to fund retirement benefits, disability, and unemployment insurance
Wagner Act	1935	Legitimized labor unions and established the National Labor Relations Board
Fair Labor Standards Act	1938	Established minimum wage and overtime pay
Taft-Hartley Act	1947	Provided protection for employers and limited union power; permitted states to enact right-to-work laws
Landrum-Griffin Act	1959	Protects union members' right to participate in union affairs
Equal Pay Act	1963	Prohibits unequal pay for the same job
Title VII of Civil Rights Act	1964	Prohibits employment decisions based on race, color, religion, sex, or national origin
Executive Order 11246	1965	Same as Title VII, also requires affirmative action
Age Discrimination in Employment Act	1967	Prohibits employment decisions based on age of persons aged 40 or older
Occupational Safety and Health Act	1970	Establishes safety and health standards for organizations to protect employees
Employee Retirement Income Security Act	1974	Regulates the financial stability of employee benefit and pension plans
Vietnam-Era Veterans Readjustment Act	1974	Prohibits federal contracts from discriminating against Vietnam-era veterans
Pregnancy Discrimination Act	1978	Prohibits employers from discriminating against pregnant women
Job Training Partnership Act	1982	Provides block money grants to states to pass on to local governments and private entities that provide on-the-job training
Consolidated Omnibus Budget Reconciliation Act (COBRA)	1985	Requires continued health insurance coverage paid by employee following termination
Immigration Reform and Control Act	1986	Prohibits discrimination based on citizenship status; employers required to document employees' legal work status
Worker Adjustment and Retraining Act (WARN)	1988	Employers required to notify workers of impending layoffs
Drug-Free Workplace Act	1988	Covered employers must implement certain policies to restrict employee drug use
Americans with Disabilities Act (ADA)	1990	Prohibits discrimination based on disability
Civil Rights Act	1991	Amends Title VII; prohibits quotas, allows for monetary punitive damages
Family and Medical Leave Act	1993	Employers required to provide unpaid leave for childbirth, adoption, illness

Source: From *Managing Human Resources* by Gomez-Mejia, et al. Copyright © 2004. Reprinted by permission of Pearson Education, Inc., Upper Saddle River, NJ.

gal environment and developing internal systems such as supervisory training and grievance procedures to avoid costly legal battles. Key legislation and executive orders are summarized in Table 10.1.

Most work-related laws are designed to prevent **discrimination,** the unfair treatment of employees because of personal characteristics that are not job-related. Title VII of the Civil Rights Act of 1964 is considered the most important legislation on this matter. Title VII prohibits firms from basing "compensation, terms, conditions, or privileges of employment"

discrimination

The unfair treatment of employees because of personal characteristics that are not job-related.

TABLE 10.2

Central Provisions of Title VII, Civil Rights Act of 1964

Section 703. (a) It shall be an unlawful employment practice for an employer—

(1) to fail or refuse to hire or to discharge any individual, or otherwise to discriminate against any individual with respect to his compensation, terms, conditions, or privileges of employment, because of such individual's race, color, religion, sex, or national origin, or

(2) to limit, segregate, or classify his employees or applicants for employment in any way which would deprive or tend to deprive any individual of employment opportunities or otherwise adversely affect his status as an employee, because of such individual's race, color, religion, sex, or national origin.

Source: Title VII, *Civil Rights Act of 1964.*

---

protected class

The legal definition of specified groups of people who suffered widespread discrimination in the past and who are given special protection by the judicial system.

affirmative action

A federal government-mandated program that requires corporations to provide opportunities to women and members of minority groups who traditionally had been excluded from good jobs; it aims to accomplish the goal of fair employment by urging employers to make a conscious effort to hire members of protected classes.

disparate treatment

A form of discrimination that occurs when an employer treats an employee differently because of his or her protected class status.

adverse impact

A form of discrimination, also called disparate impact, that occurs when one standard that is applied to all applicants or employees negatively affects a protected class.

on a person's race, color, religion, sex, or national origin. The central provisions of Title VII appear in Table 10.2.

Interpretations of the Civil Rights Act led to a legal definition of a **protected class** of groups of people who suffered widespread discrimination in the past and who are granted special protection by the judicial system. These include African Americans, Asian Americans, Hispanic Americans, Native Americans, and women. **Affirmative action** aims to accomplish the goal of fair employment by urging employers to make a conscious effort to hire members from protected classes. In affirmative action programs, employment decisions are made at least in part on the basis of demographic characteristics such as race, sex, or age. These programs are controversial because some people believe that only "blind" hiring practices are fair and that the programs may result in hiring quotas that hurt people who are not members of protected groups. This, in effect, penalizes them for the errors of their parents and grandparents. A series of Supreme Court decisions indicate that employment decisions cannot be made solely on the basis of protected class status; people should be "essentially equally qualified" on job-relevant factors before protected class status is permitted to play a role. The Supreme Court in a 2003 ruling reaffirmed the notion that protected class status may be considered in retention decisions but prohibited the use of such explicit criteria as quotas or added points in an exam based on a person's race, ethnic status, or gender.

Two forms of discrimination are considered illegal and may result in substantial fines and penalties for employers and/or in a court-imposed affirmative action plan. The first form of discrimination, **disparate treatment,** occurs when an employer treats an employee differently because of his or her protected class status. The second form of discrimination, **adverse impact** (also called *disparate impact*), occurs when the same standard is applied to all applicants or employees but that standard affects a protected class more negatively. For instance, a minimum height requirement for police tends to automatically disqualify more women than men. If a protected class suffers from adverse impact, then the firm may be required to demonstrate that the standards used were job-related and that alternative selection methods were too costly or unreliable.

The Equal Employment Opportunity Commission (EEOC) was created by the Civil Rights Act of 1964 to initiate investigations in response to discrimination complaints. An individual bringing a complaint to court must prove that there is *prima facie* ("on its face") *evidence* of discrimination. In the case of disparate treatment, a plaintiff can establish prima facie discrimination by showing that he or she was at least as qualified for the job as the person who was hired. In the case of an adverse impact lawsuit, the EEOC has established the *four-fifths rule* for prima facie cases. This means that the hiring rate of a protected class should be at least four-fifths of the hiring rate of the majority group. For example, a firm may hire 50 percent of all its white male job applicants but only 25 percent of all African-American male job applicants. Using the four-fifths rule, there is prima facie evidence of discrimination because four-fifths of 50 percent is 40 percent, which exceeds the 25 percent hiring rate for African-American men.

Once a plaintiff has established a prima facie case, the accused organization must demonstrate that illegal discrimination did not occur. This can be difficult to prove. There are three basic defenses that an employer can use:

1. **Job relatedness** is the most compelling defense. Here the firm shows that decisions were made for job-related reasons. The HR department can help demonstrate job relatedness by preparing written documentation to support and explain the decision.

2. The organization may claim a **bona fide occupational qualification (BFOQ),** a personal characteristic that must be present to do the job. An example is the need for a female actor for a woman's part in a movie. This option is severely restricted as a justification to discriminate.

3. The final basis to justify disparate impact is **seniority.** In companies with a well-established seniority system, more senior workers may receive priority, even if this has an adverse impact on protected class members.

As illustrated in Table 10.1, other federal legislation influences HR decisions. For instance, the **Drug-Free Workplace Act** requires employers to implement policies that restrict drug use, and the **Family and Medical Leave Act** requires employers to provide unpaid leave for childbirth, adoption, and illness. In most large firms, the HR department is responsible for keeping track of changes in legislation that affects human resources and for developing steps to comply with various laws. This role is crucial because the law may be enforced differently for each firm. For example, many firms require drug testing of all employees, but some require testing only at the time of hiring or at random times. Organizations must also be flexible to respond to changing circumstances in enforcing the law. For example, the Air Force used to randomly test 65 percent of its

job relatedness

A defense against discrimination claims in which the firm must show that the decision was made for job-related reasons.

bona fide occupational qualification (BFOQ)

A defense against discrimination in which a firm must show that a personal characteristic must be present to do the job.

seniority

A defense against discrimination in which companies with a well-established seniority system can give more senior workers priority, even if this has an adverse impact on protected class members.

Drug-Free Workplace Act

Federal legislation that requires employers to implement policies that restrict drug use.

Family and Medical Leave Act

Federal legislation that requires employers to provide unpaid leave for childbirth, adoption, and illness.

cadets for drug use. The Air Force has recently decided to increase that percentage and do more testing on weekends, because some of the new recreational drugs, such as Ecstasy, pass through the body quickly.[4]

Sexual harassment, a violation of the Civil Rights Act, has become a highly visible issue. There are two forms of sexual harassment. The first involves sexually suggestive remarks, unwanted touching, or any other physical or verbal act that creates what is called a "hostile environment," for either gender. The second type is called *quid pro quo* harassment, in which sexual favors are sought and/or granted in exchange for company rewards, such as pay raises, promotions, or more choice job assignments. To avoid liability, a company must develop an explicit policy against sexual harassment and a system to investigate allegations. Managers must be made aware that this type of behavior will not be tolerated and may result in severe penalties, including termination. They must also be educated about sexual harassment policies, for instance, in special workshops.

Many state and local governments have also passed laws that restrict organizational discretion in the use of human resources. An important law is a limitation on **employment at will,** a longstanding legal doctrine stating that unless there is an employment contract (such as a union contract or an implied contract), both employer and employee are free to end the employment relationship whenever and for whatever reasons they choose. Most states have written employment laws that allow terminated employees to sue if they can show that they have been wrongfully discharged. One common ground is lack of good faith and fair dealing, such as firing a worker shortly before he or she becomes eligible for a retirement plan.

Manager's Notes 10.1 lists some interview questions that, if asked, could be interpreted as violating employment law.

Unions

In 1945, about 35 percent of the labor force belonged to unions. Since then, union membership has been declining steadily, reaching a low of approximately 13 percent in 2004.[5] If the present trend continues, this percentage will drop to approximately 8 percent by 2012. Strong employer challenges to unions, plant closures, international competition, and a shrinking manufacturing sector have all contributed to the decline in union membership. Unions are still influential in some sectors, such as automobile manufacturing; even there, however, unions have been more willing to work closely with management in such areas as quality control, cross-training, and innovative compensation systems to meet global challenges.

U.S. employees generally seek representation from a union for one or more of the following reasons:

- Dissatisfaction with certain aspects of their job (such as poor working conditions or pay that is perceived to be low).

---

sexual harassment

A form of discrimination that is broadly interpreted to include sexually suggestive remarks, unwanted touching, any physical or verbal act that indicates sexual advances or requests sexual favors, a promise of rewards or hidden threats by a supervisor to induce emotional attachment by a subordinate, and a "hostile environment" based on sex.

employment at will

A very old legal doctrine stating that unless there is an employment contract (such as a union contract or an implied contract), both employer and employee are free to end the employment relationship whenever and for whatever reasons they choose.

Nine Don'ts of Interviewing

MANAGER'S NOTES

1. Don't ask applicants if they have children, plan to have children, or have child care arrangements made.

2. Don't ask an applicant's age.

3. Don't ask whether the applicant has a physical or mental disability that would interfere with the job. (Employers can explore the subject of disabilities only after making a job offer that is conditional on the applicant's satisfactory completion of a required physical, medical, or job-skills test.)

4. Don't ask for identifying characteristics, such as height and weight.

5. Don't ask marital status, including asking a female candidate her maiden name.

6. Don't ask applicants about their citizenship.

7. Don't ask applicants about their arrest records (employers may ask whether a candidate has ever been convicted of a crime).

8. Don't ask applicants if they smoke (employers can ask whether applicants are aware of legislative restrictions against smoking and whether they are willing to comply with them).

9. Don't ask applicants if they are HIV-positive or have AIDS.

Source: From *Managing Human Resources* by Gomez-Mejia, et al. Copyright © 2004. Reprinted by permission of Pearson Education, Inc., Upper Saddle River, NJ.

- A belief that as individuals they lack influence with management to make needed changes, and that by working together through concerted action they can put greater pressure on management to make concessions.

- A belief that the union can equalize some of the power between workers and management, so that the company cannot act unilaterally.

- Job insecurity and the conviction that unions can protect workers from arbitrary layoffs by establishing a set of rules that management will abide by. For instance, a unionized firm may stipulate that layoffs will be done in order of seniority.

- The need to establish formal grievance procedures, administered by both the union and management, whereby individual workers can appeal managerial decisions that they believe are unfair.

The agreement between the union and management is written in a document called the **labor contract.** In addition to specifying pay schedules, fringe benefits, cost of living adjustments and the like, the labor contract gives employees specific rights. If an employee believes his or her rights have been violated under the contract, the individual can file a grievance

labor contract

A written agreement negotiated between union and management.

against the company. For instance, an employee who believes that he or she was overlooked for promotion may try to remedy this perceived unfairness by filing a grievance, hoping to be reconsidered for the promotion.

Labor unions were largely unprotected by law in the United States until 1935. Crafted by Congress during the Great Depression, the Wagner Act (1935), also known in union circles as the "Magna Carta of Labor," facilitated the establishment and expansion of unions. The Wagner Act created the National Labor Relations Board (NLRB), which is responsible for supervising union elections through secret ballots by workers. The NLRB also determines whether or not a union or management group has engaged in unfair labor practices. For example, firing union sympathizers is an unfair practice, as is a union's calling for a strike while a labor contract is still in effect. The Wagner Act tried to equalize the power of unions and management. After World War II, however, there was a widespread perception that unions had become too powerful, and in some cases corrupt.

The Taft-Hartley Act (1947) specified a set of unfair labor practices by unions along with the remedies that the National Labor Relations Board may take if the union is found guilty of engaging in those practices. Unfair union practices include causing an employer to pay for services that are not performed (a practice often called *featherbedding*) or refusing to bargain in good faith for a new contract.

Twelve years later, The Landrum-Griffin Act (1959) allowed the federal government, through the Department of Labor, to regulate some union activities. Landrum-Griffin was enacted because a few unions experienced problems with corrupt leadership and had misused union funds. Among other things, Landrum-Griffin requires each union to report its financial activities and the financial interests of its leaders to the Department of Labor.

Labor relations tend to be country specific and reflect the sociocultural and historical milieu of each nation. For instance, in the United States labor relations are characterized by:

- *Business unionism.* Unlike most other countries where unions are ideological and often tend to pursue political goals, U.S. unions focus on "bread and butter" issues such as wages, benefits, and job security.

- *Job-based unionism.* In contrast to unions in many other countries, which tend to be organized according to political persuasion, U.S. unions tend to be organized by the type of job. Truck drivers are often members of the Teamsters Union and many public school teachers are members of the National Education Association. This is in line with the American notion that interest groups represent the desires of particular constituencies.

- *Collective bargaining.* Under the U.S. collective bargaining system the government takes a neutral or nonintervention role, allowing the players to make the rules that govern their particular

business unionism

Unions that focus on "bread and butter" issues such as wages, benefits, and job security.

job-based unionism

Unions that are organized by type of job.

collective bargaining

Negotiations between union and management with little, if any, government involvement.

workplace. In most other countries, the government is closely involved in labor-management relations. For instance, for almost 70 years the Partido Revolucionario Institucional (PRI) governed Mexico, and unions were an integral part of the government machinery.

- *Voluntary contracts.* Because both parties enter into the labor contract voluntarily, in the United States one party can use the legal system to enforce the terms of the contract if the other party does not fulfill its responsibilities. In many other countries, such as Italy and Sweden, working conditions and employee benefits are codified into labor laws. These laws are enforced by the central government and labor unions often put direct pressure on the government to modify legislation affecting workers. General strikes to force the government's hand are common around the world, but unheard of in the United States. Recently, unions in France called for a general strike to force the government to pass a 35-hour working week. Likewise, unions in Spain recently called for a general strike to force the government to pass legislation that would make it costly for firms to lay off workers.

> **voluntary contracts**
>
> Because both parties enter the labor contract freely, one party can use the legal system to enforce the terms of the contract if the other party does not fulfill its responsibilities.

- *Adversarial relations.* U.S. labor laws view management and labor as natural adversaries who want to have a larger share of the firm's profits and who must reach a compromise through collective bargaining. When asked about the objectives of the labor movement, Samuel Gompers (considered the founder of the AFL-CIO) responded with one word: More! For this reason, rules have been put in place so that the pie can be divided peacefully through orderly negotiations. In some other countries, the labor relations system stresses cooperation rather than competition between management and labor. For instance, the German system uses work councils and codetermination to involve workers in decisions at all levels of the organization. Even a companys' board of directors generally will include union members. This would be seen as a conflict of interest in the United States. In Japan, enterprise unions work closely with companies for mutual benefits and the union generally has complete access to the company's financial records.

> **adversarial relations**
>
> U.S. labor laws view management and labor as natural adversaries who want to have a larger share of the firm's profits and who must reach a compromise through collective bargaining.

The Human Resource Management Process

Figure 10.1 introduces the key components of the human resource management process. The input that drives the entire process is **strategic HR planning (SHRP),** which is the development of a vision about where the company wants to be and how it can utilize human resources to get there. By forcing managers to think ahead, SHRP can help a firm identify the

> **strategic HR planning (SHRP)**
>
> The development of a vision about where the company wants to be and how it can use human resources to get there.

FIGURE 10.1

The Human Resource Management Process

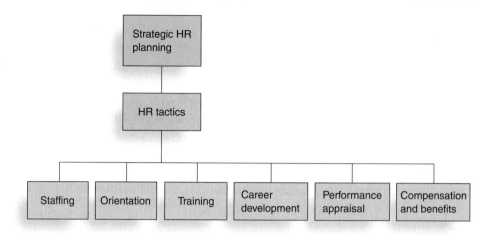

difference between "where we are today" and "where we want to be," and to implement human resource programs (often referred to as **HR tactics**) to achieve its vision.

The ultimate objective of SHRP is creating a *sustained competitive advantage.* A common view held by HR managers is based on the **contingency theory** notion that no HR strategy is "good" or "bad" in and of itself but rather depends on the situation or context in which it is used. According to this approach, the consistency or compatibility between HR strategies and other important aspects of the organization, which is known as *fit,* leads to better performance. The lack of a fit creates inconsistencies that reduce performance. Management Close-Up 10.a shows how HR strategies fit with the overall business strategy of Southwest Airlines.

Human Resource Planning

Human resource planning (HRP) is the process organizational leaders follow to ensure that the company has the right number and the right kinds of people to meet output or service goals. Figure 10.2 summarizes the HRP process. The first step is forecasting **labor demand,** or how many and what type of workers the organization will need in the future. Labor demand is likely to increase as the demand for the company's products increases and to decrease as productivity increases, since fewer labor hours will be needed to produce the same level of output. However, the demand for various types of workers (for example, factory versus clerical) may not increase or decrease at the same rate, so this forecast must be performed for various employee groups.

The second part of the HRP process entails estimating the **labor supply,** or the availability of workers with the required skills to meet the

HR tactics

The implementation of human resource programs to achieve the firm's vision.

contingency theory

The management theory that there is no "one best way" to manage and organize an organization because situational characteristics, called contingencies, differ; also, the view that no HR strategy is "good" or "bad" in and of itself but rather depends on the situation or context in which it is used.

labor demand

The forecast of how many and what type of workers the organization will need in the future.

labor supply

The availability of workers with the required skills to meet the firm's labor demand.

The Formula for Success Equals HR Practices

Southwest Airlines just keeps winning national awards: *Fortune* magazine has rated Southwest one of the top five of America's most-admired companies for six years in a row (1998–2003). The company won the U.S. Department of Transportation's Triple Crown Award (its top major airline award for on-time performance and fewest mishandled baggage reports) five times in a row. Southwest also ranks first in an airline reputation study conducted for *The Wall Street Journal;* and was named best low-fare carrier in *Business Travel Entrepreneur* magazine during 2000. In 2001 Southwest CEO Herbert D. Kelleher, at the helm since 1971, was chosen by *Business Week* as one of the top 25 managers of the year. The most profitable airline in the 1990s, Southwest has one of the lowest operating costs of all major airlines, achieving around seven cents per available seat mile. The airline has been able to offer low-cost fares that routinely beat the competition.

Southwest's HR practices reinforce its high-performance culture in many ways. First, there is a great deal of freedom and responsibility. Employees contribute ideas and take actions that serve customers and improve the organization. More than 120 employees are members of the Corporate Culture Committee, and even more serve on culture committees established in each department and location.

Second, Southwest sustains its culture by hiring people who match the desired employee profile. Recruitment and selection—from pilots and operations staff to administrative support staff—involve a great number of employees. Also, the interview process examines how applicants have handled various past situations and how they would address current situations. The selection team wants applicants to have successful interviews and encourages them to be themselves during the interview process. The team then uses these in-depth interviews to determine the character of the applicant and predicts the degree of fit with the organization. Every hiring decision is both a commitment to the person and a statement about the company's culture.

Third, Southwest strongly supports and emphasizes training at every level of the organization. Employee training goes beyond skill development—they are trained not just to do their jobs, but to "color outside the lines" and to use initiative to fill the gaps in functions, departments, and operations to better serve the customer. The training process reinforces the company's culture of involvement, action, and customer service.

Finally, Southwest integrates employee rewards into the fabric of the organization. The company shares the risks and

Southwest Airlines celebrates its 34th anniversary in 2004. Many trace the firm's success to the unique human resources philosophy that founder Herb Kelleher instilled in the company during his tenure.

rewards of the company's performance through profit-sharing options. Employees can also purchase stock at a discount. More than monetary rewards, however, employee recognition makes working at Southwest special. Every day, somewhere at a Southwest facility, something is being celebrated. An extensive series of special employee recognition programs developed and managed by local committees of employees have titles such as "Together We Make It Great," "Stuck On Service," "Go See Do," "Joe Cool Award," and "Superstars." Employees can win anything from small cash awards, gift certificates, and savings bonds to books, concert tickets, champagne, watches, T-shirts, and flowers—whatever is creative and meaningful to the employee committee.

Southwest's employee satisfaction does not lie in the company's programs but rather in a culture that fosters a process, and the process that fosters a culture. Southwest has created an environment where employees can experiment, make mistakes, learn, and try again. Initiative to better serve the customer is expected, encouraged, and rewarded. There is no question that at Southwest the customer is king and employees are imbued with that idea from the start.

Source: Adapted with permission from T. B. Wilson, *Rewards That Drive High Performance.* New York: American Management Association, 1999, pp. 29–36; "The Top 25 Managers," *Business Week,* January 8, 2003, p. 76; N. Stein, "America's Most Admired Companies," *Fortune,* March 3, 2003, pp. 81–94.

FIGURE 10.2

Human Resource Planning

Source: From *Managing Human Resources* by Gomez-Mejia, et al. Copyright © 2004. Reprinted by permission of Pearson Education, Inc., Upper Saddle River, NJ.

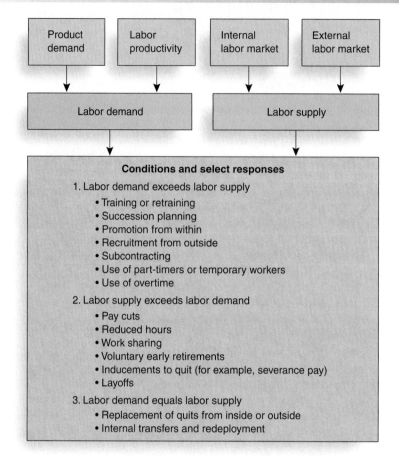

Stages of the Strategic HRM Planning Process

---

skills inventory

A human resource inventory that keeps track of the firm's internal supply of talent by listing employees' education, training, experience, and language abilities; the firm can use this information to identify those eligible for promotion or transfer before trying to fill the position from the external market.

---

firm's labor demand. The labor supply may come from the internal labor market inside the firm or from the external labor market outside the firm. Many firms keep track of the internal supply of talent by generating a human resource inventory called a **skills inventory.** Employees are asked to list their education, training, experience, and language abilities. This information is used to identify those eligible for promotion or transfer before trying to fill the position from the external market. Such a process can reduce recruitment costs and increase employee commitment to the firm.

As shown in Figure 10.2, the HR planning process may lead to very different organizational responses. If labor demand exceeds supply, the firm may invest in training workers, promoting from within, and actively recruiting employees to meet projected needs. On the other hand, if there is an excess labor supply, the HR department may plan cutbacks in the workforce through work sharing, voluntary early retirements, and layoffs.

Through careful planning some firms develop creative means to avoid or minimize layoffs, which are costly in terms of employee morale and loss of human capital. For example, these firms have been able to minimize layoffs during the recent 2001–2004 recession by using alternative ways to save money:

- Hewlett-Packard delayed employee raises for several months and awarded no bonuses for its top executives.

- First Union asked employees to limit the number of color copies they make and restricted first-class travel to red-eye flights.

- Charles Schwab cut salaries for senior executives and gave smaller bonuses to the rank and file. The brokerage firm also rationed travel and entertainment dollars and reviewed advertising contracts.

- Xerox, which has laid off several thousand workers in recent months, grounded corporate jets and cut back on catered food and free coffee to prevent more layoffs.[6]

Staffing Process

Human resource planning guides the staffing process, or the hiring of employees to meet the firm's labor needs. The staffing process has three components: recruitment, selection, and socialization.

RECRUITMENT   Generating a pool of qualified candidates for a particular job is the **recruitment** component of staffing. It requires a **job specification,** which identifies the qualifications necessary for effective job performance. Most firms conduct a **job analysis** in which they systematically gather and organize information about the tasks, duties, and responsibilities of various jobs. While there are many job analysis techniques, virtually all of them lead to a **job description,** which is a formal document that identifies, defines, and describes the duties, responsibilities, and working conditions associated with a job. A properly conducted job analysis ensures that the hiring process is job-related in case of a legal challenge.

Once the qualifications for effective job performance have been identified, the HR department looks for recruitment sources that are most likely to produce the best candidates. Most searches start with current employees, utilizing skill inventories if available. The second major source of recruits is referrals from current employees. Both sources give HR more information about applicants than would going outside. One disadvantage is that the firm may not attract a diverse pool of applicants, creating potential equal employment opportunity (EEO) problems. Other sources of recruits include former employees, advertisements, employment agencies, colleges, and customers. Recruitment over the Internet is becoming more prevalent and occurs at broad job search engines such as Monster.com, which includes all types of positions. Specialized job search

recruitment

The process of generating a pool of qualified candidates for a particular job.

job specification

The knowledge, skills, and abilities needed to successfully perform the job.

job analysis

The systematic gathering and organizing of information about the tasks, duties, and responsibilities of various jobs.

job description

A formal document that identifies, defines, and describes the duties, responsibilities, and working conditions.

FIGURE 10.3

Performance Consequences
of Selection Decision

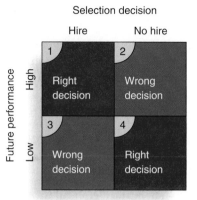

engines such as Dice.com target information technology professionals; Dice.com is advertised as "a high-traffic job board with over 350,000 IT professionals searching every week."[7]

One way to increase recruitment effectiveness is a *realistic* **job preview** in which potential applicants are provided with honest information about the positive and negative aspects of the job. It can reduce selection expenses because individuals can "self-select" into or out of positions based on realistic job information.

SELECTION An effective recruitment effort should create a pool of qualified applicants. As the word implies, **selection** is the screening process used to decide which individuals to hire. The ultimate objective is to hire people who will perform well based on the criteria the firm uses to evaluate employees. No selection process is foolproof. Some hires will turn out to be mistakes and other candidates who would have made good employees may be rejected. An organization with a high proportion of individuals who fall into these categories, as shown in Figure 10.3, is likely to see much lower job performance on average than an organization that consistently makes the right hiring decisions.

Valid and reliable selection techniques help reduce the proportion of errors and increase the proportion of correct hiring decisions. **Validity** is how well a technique used to assess candidates is related to performance in the job. A technique that is not job-related is useless and, as noted earlier, is also illegal if it results in discrimination. In fact, documenting validity is essential to a legal defense of job discrimination.

Validity can be demonstrated in two ways. **Content validity** means that the selection process represents the actual activities or knowledge required to successfully perform the job. Many firms require applicants to perform tasks similar to those they will carry out on the job if hired. For in-

---

job preview

Information about the positive and negative aspects of the job that is provided to potential applicants.

selection

The screening process used to decide which job applicant to hire.

validity

The measurement of how well a technique used to assess candidates is related to performance in the job.

content validity

The measurement that the selection process represents the actual activities or knowledge required to successfully perform the job.

part four Organization Management

TABLE 10.3

Quality of Selection Tools as Predictors

TOOL	POSITION			
	SENIOR MANAGEMENT	MIDDLE AND LOWER MANAGEMENT	COMPLEX NONMANAGERIAL	ROUTINE OPERATIVE
Application form	2	2	2	2
Written tests	1	1	2	3
Work samples	—	—	4	4
Assessment center	5	5	—	—
Interviews	4	3	2	2
Verifying application data	3	3	3	3
Reference checks	1	1	1	1
Physical exam	1	1	1	2

Note: Validity scale is 5 at the highest and 1 as the lowest.

Source: From *Management* by Robbins. Copyright © 2003. Reprinted by permission of Pearson Education, Inc. Upper Saddle River, NJ.

stance, if a minimum requirement for a job is possession of a valid pilot's license, a flight simulator may be used to select the best pilot. **Empirical validity** means that there is statistical evidence that the selection method distinguishes between higher and lower performing employees. For instance, a selection method that consistently predicts which individuals fall into boxes 1 and 4 in Figure 10.3 would have high empirical validity. Lack of empirical validity means that the selection method cannot predict who is going to be a better or worse performer.

empirical validity

Statistical evidence that the selection method distinguishes between higher and lower performing employees.

RELIABILITY   It is important to measure the consistency or **reliability** of results of the selection method. For instance, if multiple interviewers reach entirely different conclusions about each job applicant, the method is not reliable. Or if test scores for the same applicant vary dramatically from one day to the next, the test is not reliable. In other words, reliability is an indicator of how much random error there is in the measure being used. Lack of reliability is equivalent to a speed indicator on a car that is 10 to 30 miles per hour above or below the actual speed. Because the reading is unreliable, the position of the speed needle is not helpful in assessing how fast the car is traveling.

reliability

The consistency of results from the selection method.

Reliability and Validity

SELECTION TOOLS AS PREDICTORS OF JOB PERFORMANCE

An organization may use a variety of selection tools to screen out applicants and attempt to increase the proportion of good performers, as shown in Manager's Notes 10.2. The quality of different selection tools as predictors of performance is shown in Table 10.3.

If properly conducted, interviews can provide useful information and help select the best candidates. Skills box 10.2 provides an exercise

- *Application forms* are used almost universally. They provide information that shows whether the candidate meets minimum qualification requirements as identified in the job analysis. Firms can also use information from application forms to determine whether the applicant would qualify for other openings when they occur. A *biodata form* asks a series of specific questions about the candidate's background, experiences, and preferences. Biodata have been found to have moderate validity in predicting job performance.

- *Letters of recommendation* typically are very positive—most people are reluctant to put negative information in writing. Their value thus is limited as a predictor of future performance, but they still may be helpful, particularly in finding a job match for the employer.

- *Ability tests* measure a wide range of abilities, from manual dexterity to verbal skills. *Cognitive ability tests* measure reasoning skills in a particular area, such as math or writing, and may be a good predictor of job performance. *General cognitive ability* tests measure general intelligence or ability to learn. Ability tests can be valid, but they may also be culturally biased and result in a disproportionate number of minorities being rejected.

- *Performance simulation tests* attempt to mimic the job experience and are based on actual job behaviors or *work samples*. These tests are particularly helpful for hiring managers. An *assessment center* is a set of simulated tasks, such as making business decisions with limited information. *In-basket exercises* provide memos, reports, requests, data, and messages for candidates to work through. Candidates can then be evaluated by the quality of their decisions and of their process. Performance simulation tests are highly predictive for managerial jobs and may identify hidden strengths and weaknesses.

- *Personality tests* are used to measure enduring traits, such as extroversion, that can affect how applicants relate to others and their basic outlook on life.

- *Psychological tests* gauge an individual's values, motivation, attitudes, and so on. These tests ask questions such as, "To what extent do you agree that luck plays a key role for success in life?" These types of tests are used to select employees who presumably are

to sharpen your interviewing skills by applying a set of good interviewing practices.

Interviews are the most often used screening tool, but they, too, have a variety of problems, which are shown in Table 10.4.

To avoid some of these shortcomings, many organizations are turning to a particular type of interviewing technique known as the *situational* or *behavioral interview*. This type of interview requires that the applicant role-play a particular situation—for instance, calming down an irate customer. As can be seen in Management Close-Up 10.b, behavioral interviews seem to do a much better job of predicting future performance than other selection methods. On the other hand, when professionally conducted with the help of a consultant, these interviews can be rather exmore motivated, more open to new experiences, and more capable of working independently without close supervision. The validity and reliability of a particular test or situation may not have been established, however, and the firm must be careful not to delve into applicants' personal lives.

- *Honesty tests* are growing in use among retail chains, banks, and other service-sector companies to screen out applicants who may steal from the employer.

- *Interviews* are the most frequently used selection technique. Ironically, the interview is often unreliable and a poor predictor of job performance. Interviews are subject to many overt and subtle biases, but they can be a useful selection device. Excellent guides are available to help managers be objective during the interview process and keep it job-related. For example, the National Federation of Independent Business and the Atlantic Legal Foundation recently developed a handbook on federal employment laws, including a list of questions managers should never ask in job interviews.

- *Physical exams* once were widely used, but their use has declined. Employers cannot discriminate on the basis of disability. Furthermore, social attitudes toward the disabled have changed dramatically in recent years. Employers are more willing to hire employees with overt physical problems that are easily spotted in a cursory physical exam. The cost of physical exams has increased enormously, and employer health insurance programs such as health maintenance organizations typically do not exclude prior conditions that may be uncovered during a physical examination.

Sources: C. J. Russell et al., "Predictive Validity of Biodata Items Generated from Retrospective Life Experience Essays," *Journal of Applied Psychology* 75 (1990): 569–580; P. M. Muchinsky, "The Use of Reference Reports in Personnel Selection," *Journal of Occupational Psychology* 52 (1979): 287–297; M. G. Damodt, D. A. Bryan, and A. J. Whitcomb, "Predicting Performance with Letters of Recommendation," *Public Personnel Management* 22 (1993): 81–90; J. E. Hunter, "Cognitive Ability, Cognitive Aptitudes, Job Knowledge, and Job Performance," *Journal of Vocational Behavior* 29 (1986): 340–362; G. M. McEvoy and R. W. Beatty, "Assessment Centers and Subordinate Appraisal of Managers," *Personnel Psychology* 42 (1989): 37–52; L. R. Gomez-Mejia, D. B. Balkin, and R. Cardy, *Managing Human Resources,* Upper Saddle River, NJ: Prentice Hall, 2004; www.nfib.com/legal.

pensive, costing between $245 and $500 per interview. Yet, the investment may be worthwhile for many critical positions. Skills for Managing 10.3 asks you to practice developing and conducting this type of interview.

Another recent trend in personnel selection in the United States is allowing the applicant to display his or her skills by performing certain jobs, often for little or no pay. The performance is used as the basis for hiring instead of written paper-and-pencil exams or other types of tests. Management Close-Up 10.c provides an example in which New York State proposes the use of a so-called "Public Service Alternative Bar Exam" for prospective lawyers, with support of the American Bar Association. The argument behind such a proposal is that a multiple-choice bar exam does not truly capture the essence of what a lawyer does on the

INTERVIEWING SKILLS

The objective of the interview is to elicit information from applicants so that the company can choose the applicant who is best qualified to perform the tasks the job requires. This exercise helps you develop interviewing skills for selection purposes.

In this exercise, an interviewer for a large retail store is on campus to recruit students for management trainee jobs after graduation. There are several job openings. The exercise proceeds through the following steps:

1. The class is divided into pairs of students. One student in each pair will act as interviewer and the other will play the role of applicant. The applicant should create a curriculum vitae (either real or fictitious) before class and provide a copy to the interviewer.

2. The interviewer from each pair interviews the applicant for 10 minutes in front of the entire class.

3. The class rates each pair using the interviewer skills checklist. For each item in the checklist, assign a rating of 0 (very poor) to 10 (outstanding).

4. At the end of each interview, the class discusses how effective it was by answering the discussion questions at the end of this exercise.

Interview Skills Checklist

Rate each of the following skills demonstrated by the interviewer on a 0 (very poor) to 10 (outstanding) scale. Maximum = 100.

_____ Was the interviewer prepared? (Lack of preparation is the most common, and costly, mistake interviewers make. Use the interviewee's résumé to create an interview agenda and review it before the interview.)

_____ Did the interviewer put the applicant at ease? (Few things are more unsettling to an applicant than being ushered into an office and waiting for the interviewer to be ready. Greet applicants, and put them at ease with some pleasant small talk before moving on to the interview questions.)

_____ Did the interviewer make snap judgments or treat the applicant as a stereotype? (Stereotyping is bad for the manager and bad for the company. Curb your tendency to rush to judgment. Always keep in mind that you are dealing with an individual, not a type.)

_____ Did the interviewer ask results-oriented questions? (Ask questions that will uncover not only what the job candidate has done but also what the results of the person's actions have been.)

job. This selection practice is routine in some countries. For instance, German firms have long relied on apprenticeships (roughly similar to what are called "internships" in the Untied States) to make hiring decisions; the firm only keeps those who performed well during the trial period.

Orientation

An *orientation program* helps new employees to learn more about the company and what is expected of them in the job. The program should also be designed to help reduce the initial anxiety of the transition into the

____ Did the interviewer allow the applicant to pause? (Many interviewers jump in during any pause in the dialogue to discuss their own views on management and the company. The applicant may be absorbing information before forming a question or comment, which the interviewer should wait for.)

____ Did the interviewer stick to job-related issues? (The interviewer's questions should be directly relevant to the tasks the employee is expected to carry out in the future.)

____ Did the interviewer avoid questions that may increase the risk of being sued for discrimination in hiring? (Litigious questions include queries about children, disabilities, age, and maiden name, as well as seemingly innocent questions such as, "Are you originally from this area?" which may be misused or misinterpreted.)

____ Did the interviewer ask simulated questions? (These are questions that try to elicit from candidates how they would respond to particular work situations.)

____ Did the interviewer establish two-way communication? (The applicant should be given a chance to ask questions about the job, the company, and the long-term career prospects within the company.)

____ Did the interviewer close definitively? (Don't let the session drift on until both parties begin to flounder about or lose interest; don't close it abruptly when interrupted by a phone call or a colleague. Plan a time limit and bring the interview to a natural close rather than letting an outside event terminate the conversation prematurely.)

Discussion Questions

1. Assess the effectiveness of the interviewing approach used by various interviewers. How well did the applicants handle the questions raised by the interviewers?

2. Use the skills checklist total to determine whether a particular interviewer was better than others. Did one applicant handle the interview questions better than the others?

company. An orientation program should also familiarize employees with coworkers and provide the opportunity to systematically learn about work rules, personnel policies, benefits, equipment, location of the copy room, as well as how to get supplies.

Several studies show that most people find starting a new job to be stressful. Stress may be compounded by other changes in a person's life, such as having lost a previous job, going through a divorce, or moving into a new town. One important function of orientation is to help employees cope with stress. John Wanous, a well-known researcher, suggests using the Realistic Orientation Programs for New Employee Stress,

TABLE 10.4

Common Problems with Selection Interviews

1. Interviewers may not agree on their assessment of a candidate—their evaluation thus may say more about the interviewers than their subject.

2. The interviewer may form an overall impression of the applicant in the first two or three minutes of the interview. Snap decisions reduce the validity of the interview, because judgments are made based on very limited information.

3. Interviewers may hold a stereotype of the ideal candidates and give lower assessments to individuals who don't fit it.

4. The interview may proceed haphazardly depending on the applicant's response to open-ended questions, such as "Where would you like to be 10 years from now?" and "Tell me about yourself." The applicant's answers may trigger questions different from those asked of other candidates, with different information thus available for evaluating them.

5. The interviewer may view more favorably those candidates who are like himself or herself in terms of background, attitudes, gender, ethnicity, and so on.

6. The order in which applicants are interviewed may affect the evaluation.

7. What an interviewer perceives as negative information, such as an applicant revealing an upcoming marriage to someone who works in a different state, may outweigh the positive information.

8. The interviewer's style may affect the applicant's responses. For instance, an aggressive interviewer may intimidate an individual who is shy, even if this trait is not job-related.

9. The interviewer may not make careful written notes of the information provided by the applicant and may just have a global perception of the applicant after the interview has concluded.

Source: From *Managing Human Resources* by Gomez-Mejia, et al. Copyright © 2004. Reprinted by permission of Pearson Education, Inc., Upper Saddle River, NJ.

or ROPES, which provides realistic information about the job and the organization, gives general support and reassurance, demonstrates coping skills, and identifies potential stressors. This program helps employees become fully functional more quickly and reduces turnover.[8]

Employee Training

Training is a planned effort to provide employees with specific skills to improve their performance. Effective training can also improve morale and increase an organization's potential. Poor, inappropriate, or inadequate training can be a source of frustration for everyone involved. Unfortunately, training programs often are affected by passing fads. For example, many firms in the late 1990s sent key employees to newly developed e-commerce programs that were offered in business schools at Carnegie-Mellon in Pittsburgh, Old Dominion in Norfolk, Virginia, Stanford in Palo Alto, and dozens of other colleges and universities. By 1999, these schools were earning at least $24.3 million in revenue from such courses. In 2001, many of the programs were struggling and companies

The Interview as Most of Us Know It Is Fast Disappearing

THEME: DEALING WITH CHANGE At one time, Microsoft and McKinsey reveled in subjecting job candidates to mind-crunching strategy sessions as part of the selection process. If that seems rough, imagine an interview in which no amount of research or grilling of insiders would help. Instead, all you can do is eat a healthy breakfast, pick out your favorite suit, and hope for the best. In the new interview, they're not just testing what you know. They're also testing who you are.

This new technique is called a situational interview. Such interviews are quickly becoming common in the job-seeking world. In the post-Enron culture of caution, corporations are heeding an obvious insight: a gold-plated résumé and winning personality are about as accurate in determining job performances as Wall Street analysts are in picking stocks. Now, with shareholder security, hiring slowdowns, and expense-slashing, no manager can afford to hire the wrong person. Companies ranging from J. P. Morgan Chase to General Electric Co.—and hundreds more—are switching to these new methods. And no wonder. Whereas the conventional interview has been found to be only 7 percent accurate in predicting job performance, situational interviews deliver a rating of 54 percent—the most of any interviewing tool. (See the accompanying table.)

The situational interview is replacing the traditional interview because it more accurately identifies how people will behave in real on-the-job situations.

SELECTION APPROACH	ACCURACY IN PREDICTING PERFORMANCE
Standard interview—The sit-down affair with management or personnel	7%
Resume analysis—Quasi-scientific résumé sifting	37
Work sample test—Pen-and-paper skills tests	44
Assessment center—Lengthy, off-site skills/personality workup	44
Behavioral interview—Candidates role-play in mock scenarios	54

The situational technique's superiority stems from the ability to trip up even the most savvy of interviewees. Every applicant must display a healthy dose of occupational know-how, but at the same time a behavioral and ethical backbone plays a major role—one that can't be easily feigned. For example, a prospective analyst at a Wall Street bank might have to face a customer with an account discrepancy. The situation is not happening on paper, but in real time—with managers and experts watching nearby. The interviewer plays the role of an irate customer on the phone who is angry about money lost when a trade wasn't executed on time, an obvious mistake on the banker's part.

Interviewers watch each candidate's reactions as well as how they process the complex account information, their ability to calm the client down, what their body language says, and which words they choose. "These are very vivid re-creations. There's no time to put on an act," says Ron Garonzik, who heads assessment-services practices at human-resources consultant Hay Group. In this instance, not being honest about the mistake or showing anger or frustration—no matter how glowing your résumé—means you're out.

Source: Adapted from J. Merritt, "Improve the Interview," *Business Week,* February 3, 2003, p. 63.

CREATE AND CONDUCT YOUR OWN BEHAVIORAL INTERVIEW

Going back to Management Close-Up 10.b, assume that you are part of a team of four managers asked to develop a situational or behavioral interview for the following positions:

- Customer representative
- First-line supervisor of a clerical pool
- Human resource director
- Marketing director

Once you develop a behavioral or situational interview for each, you are asked to role-play one or two interviews for each position. The instructor will then assign students to serve as interviewees. At the end of the exercise, the entire class will discuss the effectiveness of the behavioral interview.

---

needs assessment

A training tool that is used to determine whether training is needed.

development and conduct of training phase

A stage in the training process that ensures training will solve an organizational problem or need; this step is critical to ensuring that training will be beneficial to the organization.

on-the-job training (OJT)

Training that takes place in the actual work setting under the guidance of an experienced worker, supervisor, or trainer.

off-the-job training

Training that takes place away from the employment site.

doubted their value as Internet business faltered. Companies also suspected that e-commerce training, instead of being something new or unique, was really a principles-of-marketing course in a different format.[9] As of 2004 there is renewed interest in Internet-based training but there is greater sensitivity as to when it might be appropriate (for instance, a step-by-step technical training course) and when it might not (for instance, human relations training for supervisors).

For a training program to be effective, it must encompass the entire training process, which consists of three major phases. As shown in Figure 10.4, the first phase is **needs assessment,** a determination of whether training is needed. This requires an examination of the organization's plans to expand, diversify into new products, establish an overseas joint venture, or undertake other activities that may require employees with additional skills.

Next is the **development and conduct of training phase.** Making sure that training solves an organizational problem or need is critical to ensuring that it will be beneficial to the company. The first major decision is the location of the training. **On-the-job training (OJT)** takes place in the actual work setting under the guidance of an experienced worker, supervisor, or trainer. Job rotation, apprenticeships, and internships are all forms of on-the-job training. **Off-the-job training** takes place away from the employment site. Common examples are formal courses, simulations, and role playing. One major advantage of off-the-job training is that employees can concentrate on the training without the interruptions that are likely to occur on the job, which facilitates learning and retention. A variety of presentation techniques and approaches may be used for off-the-job training:

Bye-Bye Bar Exam?

THEME: CUSTOMER FOCUS No prospective lawyer looks forward to the bar exam—the months of preparation, the dreaded bar course, and nail-biting anticipation. The test itself consists of two grueling days of multiple-choice agony. For law grads in New York state there may soon be a way to avoid the multi-state portion of the ordeal: the Public Service Alternative Bar Exam. If adopted, the two-year pilot will offer 200 selected law graduates the opportunity to be admitted into the legal profession by working within the state court system. If that happens, New York will be the first state to have such a method of bar admission. The policy would then be likely to be followed by other states.

Instead of taking the existing paper-and-pencil multiple-choice exam, law graduates electing the alternative would work full time for three months in New York's civil courts. They would assist judges in legal research, write opinions, help unrepresented litigants, and conduct mediations. Graduates would then be assessed both by their court supervisors and by independent outside evaluators. These individuals would make judgments concerning each candidate's level of skills, and if they are sufficient for admission to the profession. The proposal is supported by the Legal Education and Admission to the Bar committees of the Association of the Bar of the City of New York and the New York State Bar Association. "The pilot proposed here is not seen as a substitute for, or as a replacement of, the current exam but, rather, simply as another way in which an applicant's competence might be assessed," says Lawrence Grosberg, chairman of the city bar's admission committee.

According to Grosberg, the proposal addresses a recurring criticism of the current bar examination, namely, that it fails to assess many of the skills universally acknowledged as central to the competent practice of law. The real test is whether a lawyer can effectively defend his or her clients. This cannot be accurately assessed using the bar exam. Moreover, critics of the current exam complain that it has a disparate impact on minority applicants which is unrelated to the ability to practice law.

"The legal profession already lacks racial diversity in an increasingly diverse society," says Kristin Booth Glen, dean of City University of New York School of Law and a member of the state bar's admission committee.

"Meanwhile," she says, "the current bar exam precludes or delays qualified minority applicants from entering the legal profession. The Public Service Alternative Bar Exam is an employment test that is manifestly related to the job of being a lawyer." In a city such as New York, where minorities are in the majority, this is a critical issue. Many believe the alternative exam will better serve the customer base of city and state.

Once graduates pass the alternative exam and are admitted to practice law, they will be required to provide 150 hours of pro bono work in the courts over three years. According to those who back the proposal, this will help the overburdened court system by infusing it with 200 lawyers providing 30,000 pro bono hours. Furthermore, many clients believe that proving your worth on the firing line is more important than passing a paper-and-pencil test. Most of the information tested by the bar exam does not need to be memorized, as it is easily available in legal manuals that lawyers can refer to.

Source: Adapted from V. Rinkin, "Bye-Bye, Bar Exam?" *ABA Journal*, February 2003, p. 16.

- *Slides* and *videotapes* are relatively inexpensive. They can be an excellent way to stimulate discussion and raise questions. An HR representative should be available to offer more detailed explanations.

- *Computer-assisted instruction (CAI)* lets trainees learn at their own pace—the computer is always available and never becomes tired, bored, or irritable. CAI programs will limit flexibility in that the computer cannot answer questions that have not been

FIGURE 10.4

The Training Process

Source: From *Managing Human Resources* by Gomez-Mejia, et al. Copyright © 2004. Reprinted by permission of Pearson Education, Inc., Upper Saddle River, NJ.

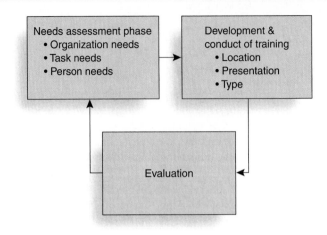

preprogrammed, and some employees may not be comfortable or well versed in using computers effectively.

Training Methods

- *Classroom lectures* provide specific information and raise issues for group discussion, facilitating problem solving. However, people may forget what they learn in a lecture unless they practice it.

- *Simulations* duplicate tasks or activities normally encountered on the job. Firms use simulations when the information to be mastered is complex, the equipment used on the job is expensive, and the costs of making the wrong decision are high.

- *Virtual reality* provides three-dimensional electronic environments for tasks that require rehearsal and practice or the visualization of objects and processes where many factors need to be monitored simultaneously.

- *Vestibule training* provides training on the same equipment the employees will use at work. They can learn how to use the equipment without disrupting ongoing operations at the workplace.

- *Cross-functional training* trains employees to work effectively with employees in other areas. Two commonly used forms of cross-functional training are *team training,* which helps employees learn to work effectively in groups, and *brainstorming,* which helps employees learn creative problem solving by encouraging them to generate ideas openly, without the fear of judgment.

evaluation

The organization's reexamination of whether training is providing the expected benefits and meeting the identified needs.

On-the-job training is more appropriate in certain situations. Manager's Notes 10.3 lists some situations when OJT should be used.

The final phase of the training process is **evaluation.** From time to time, an organization should reexamine training methods to determine whether they provide the expected benefits and meet the needs identified in phase I. Effectiveness may be measured in monetary terms (e.g., dollars saved by

When To Use OJT

Ask these questions when deciding whether on-the-job training should be undertaken. If your answer is "yes," the training generally should be done on the job.

1. Is participatory learning necessary?

2. Is one-on-one training called for?

3. Does only a small group of employees need training?

4. Is the cost of training the employees away from the job more than the benefit expected from the training?

5. Is the training not appropriate for a classroom setting?

6. Are safety factors and equipment requirements not available away from the job site?

7. Does the training have to be done immediately?

8. Does the training have to be done to meet new safety requirements that have just been implemented?

9. Is disrupting ongoing work by pulling employees away from the job too costly?

10. Is the training designed for an infrequently performed task?

11. Does the employee have to meet defined standards to obtain certification or qualification?

12. Is the equipment needed for training too large to move or not moveable?

13. Is the equipment needed for training too fragile or carefully calibrated to move?

14. Are the materials required for training also part of the overall job site?

15. Are the training procedures or equipment too dangerous to use off site?

16. Does the training involve sensitive information that must be kept in a secure environment?

Source: From C. A. Mullaney and L. D. Trask, "Show Them the Ropes," *Technical & Skills Training*, October 1992, pp. 8–11. Reprinted with permission.

reducing the number of defects) or nonmonetary terms (e.g., fewer employee complaints). The most important consideration is that the evaluation criteria should reflect the needs that the training was supposed to address.

In recent years, many companies have introduced ethics training programs or require that prospective hires, particularly middle- and top-level executives, show evidence that they have undergone such training. This is clearly one of the most rapidly growing areas in executive training programs, whether conducted in-house or by educational institutions. For instance, one such program requires that the trainee actually visit with executives who are in prison to learn firsthand what landed them there (see Management Close-Up 10.d, "Teaching Ethics to Executives in Prison").

Teaching Ethics to Executives in Prison

THEME: ETHICS Enron's chief financial officer. Tyco's chief corporate counsel. The assistant to Martha Stewart's stockbroker. The world of white-collar crime hasn't seen a red-carpet perp walk of this caliber since the junk-bond scandal of the 1980s.

At the University of Maryland's Robert H. Smith School of business, instructors are capitalizing on this scamming streak, hoping that offering executive students a little face time with corporate jailbirds will prevent future instances of corporate fraud. The school launched the Smith Executive Ethics Certificate Program, which is an intense four-day course in business ethics geared specifically to company managers, officers, and directors. The curriculum, which can be customized by a company enrolling its executives, includes the predictable B-school menu of case studies and seminars, plus an unorthodox twist: a visit to a federal penitentiary. But it's no spectator tour; executives actually meet with inmates serving time for business crimes and learn about the choices that caused them to end up in jail.

"There's nothing subtle about it," says William N. Shepherd, a former Miami prosecutor who was a driving force behind the program. "It brings it home to the students in the class and gets them thinking, 'Am I doing things that can put me in prison?' "

Prison visits have been an important component of the Smith School's MBA curriculum since 1996. Shepherd, now in private practice with a law firm in West Palm Beach, Florida, became involved with the school after reading about the MBA-level visits in a legal magazine and volunteering his expertise as a prosecutor. He is the co-academic director of the new executive ethics course.

The first group of about 20 executives recently made the trip to the federal correctional institution at Cumberland, Maryland. Associate Dean Scott Koerwer, Director of Executive Education, says he believes the visit had the greatest impact on the more experienced managers. "They

have more of an understanding of what a prisoner is talking about when he says his wife left him and his kids have ostracized him," he says.

Although the executive students are taken to a minimum-security facility, they soon realize it's not an experience to be minimized. There are no walls topped with concertina wire or armed guards in towers, but prisoners are at the mercy of their jailers. These officials decide everything from roommate assignments (rooms often are shared with street-level drug dealers, says Shepherd) to when prisoners will eat and sleep.

"Prison isn't just about being behind bars; it's about losing privilege, about having boundaries that remove you from society," says Koerwer. "Your life is controlled—it is no longer your own."

The motivations of the inmates who speak to the executive students vary from breaking up the monotony to wanting to make a difference, says Shepherd. He notes that the messages are hauntingly similar: "It's not a single horrible act, it is a slippery slope. They get in the habit of doing things just on the other side of the line because they want to close the big deal or save the company money. Then they find they've been doing it for a year or two."

Kirby D. Behre, a Washington, D.C., lawyer and coauthor of Federal Sentencing for Business Crimes, says ethics programs like that offered by Smith are likely to become more critical. He notes that regulations such as the Sarbanes-Oxley Act (discussed in Chapter 7) mandate tougher corporate sentences.

"The visit to Cumberland helps to dispel the myth that only those who personally gain from corporate crime go to jail," Behre says. "The clear trend is for corporate officers to be held criminally accountable for crimes that benefit the company by misleading the public."

Source: Adapted from J. B. Davis, "Corporate Crime Fighter," *ABA Journal,* February 2003, p. 26.

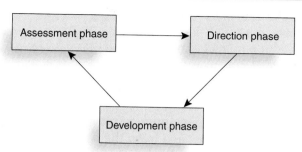

FIGURE 10.5

The Career Development Process

Source: From *Managing Human Resources* by Gomez-Mejia, et al. Copyright © 2004. Reprinted by permission of Pearson Education, Inc., Upper Saddle River, NJ.

Career Development

Career development is a long-term effort in which the organization helps employees utilize their full potential. It is not a one-shot training program or a series of workshops. Instead there are three major phases—assessment, direction, and development—as shown in Figure 10.5.

ASSESSMENT   The **assessment phase** involves helping employees choose career paths that are realistically attainable and fit with the employee's temperament and personality. The assessment phase includes determining what obstacles they need to overcome to succeed. Some companies use a combination of tools to accomplish this, including performance appraisal data from supervisors, psychological tests, assessment centers, interest inventories, and skill inventories.

DIRECTION   The next phase, the **direction phase,** includes determining the steps employees must take to reach their career goals. Appropriate direction requires understanding of the *sequence* of jobs employees are expected to fill over time—that is, identifying jobs that are logically connected and that offer increasing responsibility. A job analysis may provide a sound basis for creating a logical career path so that skills learned on a job prepare the employee for the next higher level of responsibility. The **career path** presents the steps and a plausible time frame for accomplishing them.

Firms use a variety of approaches to assist employees in the direction phase, including:

- *Promotability forecasts,* judgments by managers about the advancement potential of subordinates.
- *Succession planning,* the identification and development of replacements for jobs that are expected to open up.
- *Individual career counseling,* one-on-one sessions to examine the person's present and possible next career stages.

 Career Planning Based on Brain Dominance and Thinking Styles Inventory

assessment phase

A career development step in which employees are helped to choose personally fitting career paths that are realistically attainable and to determine any obstacles they need to overcome to succeed.

direction phase

The step in career development that involves determining the steps employees must take to reach their career goals.

career path

The steps for advancement to a career goal and a plausible time frame for accomplishing them.

- *Job posting systems*, in which all vacancies are listed on a bulletin board, in a company newsletter, or in a phone recording or computer system.
- *Career resource centers*, where career development materials such as workbooks, tapes, and texts are located in a central location, such as the HR department.

DEVELOPMENT   The final phase, the **development phase,** outlines actions designed to help the employee grow and learn the necessary skills to move along the desired career paths. Some common programs include:

- **Mentoring,** or the developmental activities carried out by more seasoned employees to help those who are learning the ropes. Mentoring takes many forms, including role modeling, sharing contacts, bouncing ideas, advising, and giving general support. It may be formal or informal. Most firms expect senior employees, particularly those in managerial positions, to act as mentors.
- **Coaching,** which is the ongoing, mostly spontaneous, meetings between managers and employees to discuss career goals, roadblocks, and opportunities.
- **Job rotation** is a formal program in which employees are assigned to different jobs to expand their skills base and to learn more about various parts of the organization.
- **Tuition assistance programs,** which support the employee's education and development by covering the cost of tuition and other fees for seminars, workshops, and continuing education programs.

Performance Appraisal

One of the keys to both individual and organizational success is providing quality feedback about individual performance. Performance appraisals have three important objectives. First, they open two-way communication channels so that supervisors may convey to employees what is expected of them and employees have an opportunity to tell supervisors what is on their minds. Second, they provide constructive feedback to employees so that positive steps may be taken to capitalize on strengths and reduce weaknesses; performance appraisal is an integral part of the career development process. Finally, a performance appraisal helps the manager decide who should be paid more based on individual contributions. The numerous techniques that measure performance can be classified by the type of judgment required (relative or absolute). They can also be classified by the focus of the measure (trait, behavior, or outcome).

---

development phase

A career development step in which actions are designed to help the employee grow and learn the necessary skills to move along the desired career path.

mentoring

Developmental activities carried out by more seasoned employees to help those who are learning the ropes.

 Mentoring

coaching

Ongoing, mostly spontaneous, meetings between managers and their employees to discuss career goals, roadblocks, and available opportunities.

job rotation

A formal program in which employees are assigned to different jobs to expand their skills base and to learn more about various parts of the organization.

tuition assistance programs

Support by the firm for employees' education and development by covering the cost of tuition and other fees for seminars, workshops, and continuing education programs.

JUDGMENT APPROACHES TO PERFORMANCE APPRAISAL Performance appraisals may use relative judgment or absolute judgment approaches.

In **relative judgments,** employees are compared to one another. Supervisors may be asked to rank subordinates from best to worst, or they may be asked to create a *forced distribution* by classifying a given percentage of employees into various groups, such as exceptional, standard, room for improvement, and not adequate.

The advantage of the relative judgment approach is it requires supervisors to make difficult choices. Supervisors who want their subordinates to like them typically prefer to rate most as excellent, which may not be valid. The relative judgment approach has serious disadvantages, however. Performance distributions may vary among units: the performance of a person at the top in one unit may rank at the bottom of another. These systems can force managers to make unrealistic performance distinctions, which creates dissatisfaction in the workforce. They may also reduce cooperation among workers, which will have a negative impact on the performance of the entire unit.

Appraisal methods using **absolute judgments** evaluate the performance of employees against performance standards, and not in comparison to other employees. There are several advantages to this approach. The evaluation data are comparable from one unit to another. Employees are more likely to cooperate with one another since individual ratings that are high are not a threat to the other workers. From a developmental perspective, the supervisor can provide more constructive feedback since the evaluation is centered on job requirements. Absolute judgments are also easier to defend legally than relative judgments; the firm can show that each employee's evaluation is based on performance dimensions that measure success on the job.

Absolute judgments are based on the performance appraisal interview, which also provides a manager the opportunity to help employees deal with behavioral problems that make them less effective. An estimated 19 million U.S. citizens suffer from depression each year, and most receive no treatment.[10] The regularly scheduled appraisal interview may provide the supervisor with a mechanism to help depressed employees seek professional help without the employees feeling that they are being singled out.

MEASUREMENT APPROACHES TO PERFORMANCE APPRAISAL

Performance appraisals may also be based on focus of the measures approaches. These appraisals assess different aspects of employee characteristics and focus on specific data.

Trait appraisal instruments evaluate employees based on characteristics that tend to be consistent and enduring, such as decisiveness,

relative judgments

A performance appraisal approach in which employees are compared to one another.

absolute judgments

A performance appraisal approach in which the performance of employees is evaluated against performance standards, and not in comparison to each other.

trait appraisal instruments

Performance appraisal tools that evaluate employees based on consistent and enduring worker characteristics.

reliability, energy, and loyalty. Because people routinely make trait judgments about others, they can be a powerful way of describing people. This type of appraisal instrument also has several disadvantages, such as ambiguity (what does it take to be loyal?) and propensity for conscious or unconscious bias (the supervisor may feel that women are more emotional than men and therefore rate the trait differently). It is also difficult to defend legally, given that assessment of traits focuses attention on the person rather than on job performance.

Behavioral appraisal instruments assess certain employee behaviors, such as coming to work on time, completing assignments within stipulated guidelines, and getting along with coworkers. A *behavioral observation scale* is one type of behavioral appraisal instrument in which various behaviors are listed and supervisors record the frequency of their occurrence.

Behavioral anchored rating scales assess the effectiveness of the employee's performance using specific examples of good or bad behaviors at work, often referred to as *critical incidents*). The main advantage of this approach is that it is closely focused on concrete aspects of job performance. Employees may more clearly understand why they received a particular rating and what they need to do to improve their performance. This approach is easier to defend legally. One drawback to using this approach is that the instrument is expensive to develop. They become more difficult to apply in companies with a wide variety of jobs, especially if those jobs frequently change.

Outcome appraisal instruments measure results, such as sales volume, the number of units produced, and meeting deadlines. Setting quantitative measures of performance for most jobs is subjective. The most prevalent outcome-oriented approach focuses on goals agreed to by the employee and supervisor. Management by objectives (MBO) is one technique widely used for this purpose (see the planning chapter, Chapter 5, for a more extensive description of these programs). In MBO programs, employees and supervisors agree on a set of goals to be accomplished for a particular period. Performance is then assessed at the end of the period by comparing actual achievement against the agreed-upon goals. This approach provides clear direction to employees, reduces subjectivity, and allows individual goals to be established (for instance, objectives for new workers may be less challenging than those set for senior employees). As we saw in Chapter 5, MBO also has drawbacks in that it can be manipulated—employees and managers may set conservative goals to lessen the risk of not reaching the target. Some aspects of a job that are difficult to measure quantitatively, such as cooperating with other units or departments, may not be made part of the evaluation and thus may be ignored by the employee.[11]

behavioral appraisal instruments

Performance appraisal tools that assess certain employee behaviors, such as coming to work on time.

behavioral anchored rating scales

Performance appraisal tools that assess the effectiveness of the employee's performance using specific examples of good or bad behaviors at work.

outcome appraisal instruments

Performance appraisal tools that measure workers' results, such as sales volume, number of units produced, and meeting deadlines.

 Potential Errors in the Rating Process

Compensation

The three key objectives of any compensation system should be to attract high-quality workers from the labor market, retain the best employees the

PERFORMANCE APPRAISAL FEEDBACK SKILLS

Constructive feedback is critical to effective performance management, with evaluative communication directed at the employee's performance and not at the person. Skills in providing feedback can help you uncover reasons for a performance problem and create an effective solution and performance improvement. This exercise, which helps you develop feedback skills, begins with the following steps:

1. The class is divided into pairs of students. One student in each pair will act as supervisor and the other will play the role of the employee.

2. Each student pair will meet outside class to prepare and discuss a performance problem, based on any personal work experiences, experiences heard from other people, or personal observation.

3. In front of the class, the supervisor and employee in each pair discuss the performance problem for 10 minutes. The class rates each of the supervisor–employee pairs using the performance feedback skills checklist. For each item in the checklist, students in class will assign a rating of 0 (very poor) to 10 (outstanding).

4. At the end of each pair's meeting in front of the class, the class discusses the feedback approaches used and then answers the discussion questions at the end of this exercise.

Performance Feedback Skills Checklist

Rate each of the following skills demonstrated by the supervisor–employee pair from 0 (very poor) to 10 (outstanding). Maximum = 100.

_____ Did the pair present perceptions, reactions, and opinions as such and not as facts?

_____ Did the pair refer to the problem relative to performance, behavior, or outcomes, not to the individual as a person?

_____ Did the pair provide feedback in terms of specific, observable behavior, not general behavior?

_____ Did the pair talk in terms of established criteria, probable outcomes, or possible improvement, as opposed to being good or bad?

_____ Did the pair discuss performance and the specific behaviors that appear to be contributing to or limiting full effectiveness?

_____ Did the pair avoid overload terms (for example, _crabby, mess-up, rip-off,_ or _stupid_) that can produce emotional reactions and defensiveness?

_____ Did the pair concentrate on things that the employee or supervisor can control, and focus on ways the employee can use the feedback to improve performance?

_____ Did the pair react defensively or emotionally rather than trying to convince, reason, or supply additional information?

_____ Did the pair give each other feedback in a manner that communicates acceptance of the employee as a worthwhile person and of that person's right to be an individual?

_____ Was feedback tied to specific development plans that could capitalize on strengths and minimize performance weaknesses?

Discussion Questions

1. Describe the feedback approach used by various supervisors. Was there an approach that you felt was particularly effective or ineffective? Why?

2. Use the checklist to determine if a particular pair was more effective than others. If there is significant disagreement in the class, discuss the reasons why.

FIGURE 10.6

Components of Total Compensation

Source: From *Managing Human Resources* by Gomez-Mejia, et al. Copyright © 2004. Reprinted by permission of Pearson Education, Inc., Upper Saddle River, NJ.

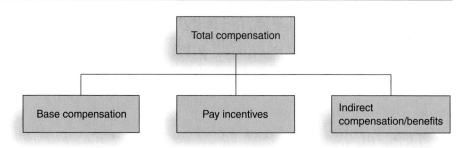

Offering additional compensation can be profitable to the firm in the long run, such as Boeing's bonus to its employees for their work in meeting a major deadline.

base compensation

The fixed amount of money the employee expects to receive in a paycheck weekly or monthly or as an hourly wage.

pay incentives

Compensation that rewards employees for good performance, including variable pay and merit pay.

benefits

A compensation component that accounts for almost 40 percent of the typical total compensation package and includes health insurance, pension plans, unemployment insurance, vacations, sick leave, and the like.

company already has, and motivate employees to work harder and to help the company achieve its strategic goals.

As illustrated in Figure 10.6, an employee's total compensation package is made up of three components. The first is **base compensation,** or the fixed amount of money the employee expects to receive in a weekly or monthly paycheck or as an hourly wage. The second is **pay incentives,** or the compensation that rewards employees for high performance. Incentives may be based on employees' own contributions or the performance of the team, business unit, or entire company. They are generally paid out as a percentage of base compensation. Pay incentives are often referred to as *variable pay* because the amount is contingent on or varies according to changes in performance. Incentive plans include one-time-only bonuses, pay raises (*merit pay* increases), profit sharing, and company stock or stock options. For instance, 19,000 engineers and technical workers at Boeing each recently received a $1,000 bonus after meeting a deadline for delivery of Boeing's 491st commercial jetliner.[12] The third component of total compensation is **benefits,** or *indirect compensation,* which accounts for almost 40 percent of the typical total compensation package. Benefits include health insurance, pension plans, unemployment insurance, vacations, and sick leave.

Compensation is a major cost for most firms. Labor costs may be as high as 60 percent in some manufacturing environments and even higher in service organizations. For instance, personnel costs reach 80 percent of the total budget of the U.S. Postal Service. This means that how well compensation dollars are allocated is likely to have a significant effect on firm performance. The design of the compensation system should fit with the firm's strategic objectives, the firm's unique characteristics, and the company's environment. Pay should also exhibit internal equity and external equity, and match employee contributions.

FIT WITH THE FIRM'S STRATEGIC OBJECTIVES The reward system should help implement the firm's strategy. A firm trying to expand its market share may pay the sales force on commission in order to generate more sales, while a firm trying to create customer loyalty in a narrow market segment may pay the sales force primarily on salary to focus on existing customers as well as on new business. This requires strong collaboration between top executives, who are responsible for strategy formulation, and the HR department, which designs the compensation program.

Compensation practices that best support the firm's business strategy are called **strategic compensation.** For instance, Ford, a pioneer in quality improvements since the 1980s, made it a core of its business strategy and summarizes it in its motto: "Quality Is Job One." A rash of quality-related problems surfaced in 2000, however, culminating with the recall of Firestone tires used in Ford vehicles and safety concerns with Ford Explorer. To prevent these problems from recurring, Ford executives' bonuses were tied to improving customer satisfaction more quickly than its rivals in the industry, based on consumer surveys and other data.[13]

FIT WITH THE FIRM'S UNIQUE CHARACTERISTICS AND ENVIRONMENT Company leaders must consider the organization's needs along with the firm's environment when designing a compensation program. A labor-intensive company with a highly unstable demand for products may provide more incentives and less in base pay to reduce financial risks, because base pay requires a fixed financial commitment.

What is important to one firm may be almost irrelevant to another. A high-tech firm that provides generous compensation to managerial and marketing personnel and underpays its research and development staff may lose the ability to innovate because competitors have stolen the company's best talent. On the other hand, a manufacturing firm producing a standard commodity that has changed little over the years, such as coat hangers, may not need to pay a premium for innovative talent.

INTERNAL EQUITY The perceived fairness of the pay structure within a firm is termed **internal equity.** A common procedure called **job evaluation** is intended to provide a rational, orderly, and systematic judgment of how important each job is to the firm. The key input to job

strategic compensation

Compensation practices that best support the firm's business strategy.

internal equity

The perceived fairness of the pay structure within a firm.

job evaluation

A rational, orderly, and systematic judgment of how important each job is to the firm and how each job should be compensated.

TABLE 10.5

Determining Pay Structure Using a Job-Based Approach

GRADE	JOB TITLE	NUMBER OF POSITIONS	HOURLY PAY
6	Chef	2	$21.50–32.50
5	Manager	1	12.50–22.00
5	Sous chef	1	12.50–22.00
4	Assistant manager	2	8.50–13.00
4	Lead cook	2	8.50–13.00
4	Office manager	1	8.50–13.00
3	General cook	5	7.50–9.00
3	Short-order cook	2	7.50–9.00
3	Assistant to lead cook	2	7.50–9.00
3	Clerk	1	7.50–9.00
2	Server	45	7.00–8.00
2	Hostess	4	7.00–8.00
2	Cashier	4	7.00–8.00
1	Kitchen helper	2	6.50–7.25
1	Dishwasher	3	6.50–7.25
1	Janitor	2	6.50–7.25
1	Busser	6	6.50–7.25
1	Security guard	2	6.50–7.25

Source: From *Managing Human Resources* by Gomez-Mejia, et al. Copyright © 2004. Reprinted by permission of Pearson Education, Inc., Upper Saddle River, NJ.

compensable factors

A set of evaluation criteria used in job evaluation.

evaluation is the job analysis, which was discussed earlier. Most firms use committees (which may include manager, employees, consultants, and union members) to examine the job analysis data to make that judgment. After applying a set of evaluation criteria called **compensable factors,** such as responsibility, educational requirements, and problem-solving potential, the committee develops a hierarchy of jobs in terms of their relative importance. To simplify matters, some firms group jobs into grade levels, where jobs at higher grade levels are considered to be more important than those at lower levels. Table 10.5 is an example of the pay structure of a large restaurant that uses grade levels.

external equity

The perceived fairness of the compensation employees receive relative to what other companies pay for similar work.

EXTERNAL EQUITY The perceived fairness of the compensation employees receive relative to what other companies pay for similar work is termed **external equity.** HR departments often use market surveys to study external equity. An organization may conduct its own salary surveys, but most purchase commercially available surveys. Information about these surveys may be obtained over the Internet. HR.com offers timely information on compensation and benefit surveys available to employers. The purpose of these surveys in most job-based compensation systems is to determine pay ranges for each grade level.

EMPLOYEE CONTRIBUTIONS One important element of an employee's level of contribution to the company is the job he or she holds.

As discussed earlier, employees with more responsible positions generally contribute more to the organization, which is why they get paid more. Another key factor is how effectively employees perform their tasks. To attract, retain, and motivate high performers and to be fair to all workers, a company should reward employees based on their relative levels of performance.

Most firms reward employees based on their individual contributions. Companies may use piece rates, special awards, stock, bonuses, and merit pay. Merit pay increases, which are based on the supervisor ratings of employee performance and normally given once a year, are by far the most popular and are used by almost all companies.

APPLICATIONS: MANAGEMENT IS EVERYONE'S BUSINESS

Applications for the Manager   Many if not most management problems are a result of poor human resource practices. Indicators that something is wrong with HR practices include inability to recruit top talent, loss of key employees to competitors, costly lawsuits, internal conflicts that sap the organization's time and energy, low innovation by employees afraid of taking risks or with outdated skills, and little concern for quality. By diagnosing the cause of these problems, managers may be able to design and implement appropriate HR programs in collaboration with the HR department or external consultants to help the firm gain or maintain an edge against its competitors.

Applications for Managing Teams   Employees working in teams often take over HR functions that have traditionally come under the purview of supervisors. For instance, peers may evaluate each other, allocate rewards, decide who should be on the team, interview candidates, and organize their own work flow. The firm needs to provide adequate support so that teams are able to perform these HR functions. Ultimately, the firm is responsible for the team's actions. For instance, the firm is liable for discriminatory practices or sexual harassment within teams even if managers do not condone such practices.

Application for Individuals   Whether you are a manager or an employee, to a large extent your success depends on your ability to take advantage of the HR opportunities the firm offers. You need to use appraisal feedback constructively, take courses to keep your skills up to date, learn the important criteria for promotion and pay allocation decisions, and join teams that best complement your interests. In the end, it is your responsibility to make the "right moves" to position yourself well. What it takes to succeed may vary by firm; successful individuals learn how to identify this and act accordingly.

Thinking back to the introductory vignette and the questions raised at the beginning of this chapter, Starbucks became successful in large measure because of the quality of company employees. *Fortune Magazine* stated it simply in 2003, when the magazine chose Starbucks as one of America's most admired companies: "Starbucks employees are always friendly." This is probably a reflection of the employees' belief that they are treated with dignity and that the company has been able to select, train, and compensate its workers in such a way that they are willing to give 100 percent to help the company succeed. If Starbucks does better, so will its employees, because they are part owners of the firm. In the end, nothing will make a company more successful than carefully selecting and placing the right people for the right jobs, ensuring that employees learn their jobs well, seeing to it that they will all have futures in the company, and making them believe that they are treated fairly when it comes to compensating them for their efforts.

All managers are responsible for making human resource decisions. The human resource department provides the necessary support so that managers can hire the best talent, train employees, assess performance, and reward contributions. The business strategy of the firm should guide human resource strategies, which in turn provide the basis for HR programs to effectively implement those strategies. The environment is constantly changing, and managers must deal with the changes to be effective. Some of these changes are related to demographics, globalization, and legislation.

It is necessary to forecast human resource needs based on the firm's future strategic goals. The firm may have to retain employees, hire new employees, or reduce the workforce. One of the key human resource decisions for most firms is staffing—deciding whom to hire. Firms can greatly improve the quality of the workforce by generating a good pool of applicants and by developing selection programs that are job-related and capable of predicting who is most likely to be a good performer.

Once employees are hired, it is important to provide them with tools to succeed. The orientation program can ease the entry of employees into the company so that they become fully functioning in the shortest time possible. Training provides employees with specific skills to enhance their job performance. Career development offers long-term growth so that employees can use their abilities to the maximum during their employment with the firm.

The performance appraisal system can help identify employee weaknesses that should improve through training and career development as well as strengths that may be channeled to better utilize the employee's talents. The appraisal system may also provide important input to reward employees based on their relative contributions. The compensation system allocates pay based on the importance of the job and how well employees perform their assignments. A well-designed compensation system should also reward people for supporting the strategic goals of the company and should strive to maintain parity with labor market pay to prevent the best performers from being lured by competing firms.

1. Many firms today subcontract to external consultants part of the work that traditionally was conducted in the HR department. Why do you think this is happening?

2. What do you foresee as the major forces affecting human resources in the future? Do you see those forces as threats or opportunities for firms? Why?

3. A cynic might argue that most firms do not hire employees following the practices outlined in this chapter (job analysis, realistic job previews, and the like), but they still manage to have an effective workforce. Some go even further and argue that those practices tend to create an expensive bureaucracy with doubtful benefits. Do you agree? Why or why not?

4. Going back to Management Close-Up 10.c, do you believe that an experience-based requirement for lawyers is a more valid and reliable accreditation tool than passing a multiple-choice bar exam? Why or why not?

5. Should a firm use an objective or a subjective performance appraisal system? What factors determine which type of system a company should use? Explain.

6. The practice of using pay incentives as a proportion of total compensation has grown rapidly in recent years. This is even happening in Japan, long accustomed to pay linked to years of service. For instance, Nissan recently "violated

most of the taboos of Japanese business" by introducing a new compensation system that rewards merit, not seniority, and a stock-option plan that ties employees' financial fortunes to Nissan's stock price.[14] What do you think accounts for this trend? In your opinion, is this a positive or a negative development? Why?

7. Going back to Management Close-Up 10.d, do you believe that ethics can be learned in a training program such as that illustrated in this Close-Up? Why or why not?

Should a Company Pay More to Bilingual Employees?

Callers to Southwestern Bell directory assistance who don't speak English are routed to bilingual operators. Maggie Morales, one of those operators, finds her job a lot tougher since she is expected to be able to provide directory assistance in two languages. Moving back and forth between languages takes time, and she can't always meet the company's target of providing assistance in two and a half seconds or less.

It's not that she minds the extra work, but she and many of her colleagues want to be paid more for using their language skills. After all, higher-ranking jobs pay a premium for people who can communicate in more than one language. Corporate recruitment of bilingual workers has increased as companies move to market to U.S. residents who speak another language as their first language (which in 2004 represents approximately 15 percent of the population, and in some areas may reach two to three times this percentage).

Paying higher wages for Morales's level, however, is perceived by management as going against the principle of "pay the job, not the person." Would other skills deserve more money, too? "What if someone wants more because he's the star on a winning company softball team and argues he's created great marketing exposure for the company?" asked a labor lawyer. "Employers can't afford to let compensation take that route."

Some companies pay language premiums for positions such as Morales's. Operators who are required to speak another language more than half the time on the job earn a 10 percent bonus at MCI Communications Corp. The company finds the bonus reduces turnover and is good for community relations. For certain positions fluency in a second language is a requirement: an Office Depot in Hollywood, Florida, wanted French speakers who could communicate with French Canadians in Florida during the winter; bilingual Delta Air Lines flight attendants earn an extra $1.50 per hour for international routes; San Francisco brokers who serve Mandarin and Cantonese customers of Charles Schwab & Co. are paid more because they are in greater demand.

Standard Microsystems Corp. of Hauppauge, New York, came to a different conclusion. Although its two Spanish-speaking technical-support staffers might earn a premium elsewhere, the company worried that any bonus paid to the two workers, who are members of a minority group, might be seen as favoring an ethnic group, which is forbidden under federal law, and could jeopardize the company's work as a government contractor.

Discussion Questions

1. Should firms pay a premium for bilingual employees? How can a firm do this without creating perceptions of inequity among employees who speak only English?

2. What do you recommend to a firm that feels it needs to pay more to attract and retain bilingual employees but is afraid to violate federal antidiscrimination laws?

Sources: "Bilingual Employees Are Seeking More Pay, And Many Now Get It," *The Wall Street Journal,* November 13, 1996, p. A6; L. Lee, "Speaking the Customer's Language—Literally," *Business Week,* September 25, 2000, p. 178; J. Norman, "Cultural Savvy Goes a Long Way in Sales," *Arizona Republic,* January 16, 2001, p. D2; D. Foust et al., "The Changing Heartland," *Business Week,* September 9, 2002, pp. 80–82; and B. Newman, "For Ill Immigrants, Doctors' Orders Get Lost in Translation," *Wall Street Journal,* January 9, 2003, p. A-1.

A Case of Sexual Harassment?

Even though sexual harassment is very difficult to prove, most people believe it happens. Suzanne Porter joined McKinsey & Co. after earning an MBA. She had sought the associate position at the elite consulting operation. During her seven years consulting for the company in Texas, she was blatantly sexually harassed by some of the firm's partners, according to Porter. Her outstanding performance reviews notwithstanding, she was not nominated for a partner position and was therefore forced out of the firm, as are all associates who don't move up.

Porter claims McKinsey assured her that she was on the partnership track. By the time she left, she was a senior engagement manager, the highest rank below partner. McKinsey acknowledges promoting Porter and giving her bonuses, but the company claims her performance and her total compensation were substandard, she had difficulty working with others, required a high degree of supervision, lacked analytical rigor, and reached conclusions with insufficient data.

Porter alleges that she endured frequent sexual advances at the firm: one partner told her that it gave him an orgasm to hug her, and a married partner made sexual advances to her during an assignment in Japan. Porter did not complain, however, because she wanted to make partner. "If you talk to your partners about it, you feed yourself to the wolves." McKinsey says its investigation of the Japan incident showed it never happened.

In another case, Robert Hammer was the Minneapolis-based manager for a headhunting firm. New employees were warned about his outgoing sexual behavior. An account executive sued Hammer and the company, accusing him of grabbing her posterior, trying to kiss her, and making sexual statements. The attorney for the account executive feels Hammer was kept on because he was productive and made money for the company.

Hammer's attorney denied the allegations and maintained he had a strong personality, which people either loved or hated, but he wasn't a lecher. Hammer's company settled the suit by the account executive for $1.3 million but denies any wrongdoing.

A third case involved one of the securities industry's highest-ranking women, Karen Nelson Hackett. Hackett was a floor governor at the New York Stock Exchange and had worked for the exchange for 30 years. In 2001, she alleged in an affidavit filed against ING (a unit of Dutch financial services giant ING Group NV) that for three years she and other women were "verbally harassed," "forcibly kissed," and "constantly received inappropriate comments about a desire to have sex" by several ING officials.

A fourth case involved Luthansa Airlines and Subway sandwich shops. In 2003, the United Auto Workers (UAW) decided to fight these companies to protest alleged sexual abuses. About 200 female employees, mostly illegal aliens, claimed with support from the UAW that top managers engaged in sex abuse such as threatening to fire them or turn them or family members in to U.S. immigration authorities if they didn't submit to sex.

Discussion Questions

1. If you were an executive, what would you do to prevent sexual harassment from occurring? What would you do if such allegations were made?

2. Based on the information given, does McKinsey have sufficient grounds to claim that Suzanne Porter was fired for job-related reasons? Why or why not?

3. Some people believe that widely publicized harassment allegations such as the ones described here may hurt women's career opportunities because senior mentors (who are likely to be males) may shy away from working closely with a member of the opposite sex. Do you agree? Why or why not?

Sources: "Sexual Harassment at McKinsey?" *Business Week,* December 9, 1996, p. 44; B. Morris, "Addicted to Sex" *Fortune,* May 10, 1999, pp. 68–74; K. Kelly, "Floor Governor at Big Board Claims Sex Bias at ING Barings," *The Wall Street Journal,* January 11, 2001, p. C1; and S. Prasso, "The UAW Answers a Cry for Help," *Business Week,* February 18, 2003, p. 8.

INDIVIDUAL/ COLLABORATIVE LEARNING CASE 10.1

Online Degree Programs Surge, but Do They Pass Hiring Tests?

Guerin Moorman won't receive his online degree from Capella University until next year. He is anxious to see how employers will perceive his credential when he graduates—particularly if the economy doesn't pick up.

"I don't get much feedback on how much [an online degree] is valued," says the 35-year-old Moorman, who lives in Spokane, Washington, and is getting a bachelor's of science degree in information technology from the Minneapolis institution. "But now that employers have the cream of the crop, it'll be interesting to see what happens."

The number of online and other distance learning programs has ballooned during the past few years. There are an estimated 350,000 students enrolled in fully online degree programs. If these trends continue, by the year 2010, more than 1 million people will receive degrees online. Even elite institutions that previously eschewed distance learning courses are starting to offer these options—for instance, Harvard University, University of California at Berkeley, Stanford, and Duke.

In spite of the popularity of such degrees, it is clear some employers still have doubts about them. Recruiters say figuring out how deep those doubts run is complicated. Job seekers who have taken online classes at traditional institutions tend to fudge the distinction on their résumés. Also, many individuals who pursue online degrees already are employed and are merely looking to increase their pay or get promoted to higher positions.

Numerous recruiters and hiring managers are openly skeptical. "Some recruiting managers say that the online degree doesn't weigh as heavily as the more traditional degrees," says Michael Brennan, manager of corporate learning and performance research at IDC Inc., a Framingham, Massachusetts, marketing intelligence and consulting firm. "That has been the challenge of online degree programs either launched by schools or in the process of being developed. They haven't built up the brand equity to warrant the accolades."

On the other hand, Richard Douglas, who studies nontraditional forms of higher education in Vienna, Virginia, recently surveyed 267 human resources professionals and found most don't spend too much time dissecting degrees. "There isn't a lot of checking going on, so [online degree earners] don't experience any more resistance than any other graduate would," he adds.

Critical Thinking Questions

1. If you were a manager of a firm considering two entry level applicants, one with a traditional degree from a well-known school and another one with an online degree from an ivy league school, which one would you prefer to hire, assuming that the grades and curriculum are similar? Explain.

2. Why do you think that "brick and mortar" universities are entering full-fledged into the distance learning market, a market niche that until very recently was filled by vocational-type programs and so called "diploma mill" institutions? Explain.

3. For what types of training do you believe that online programs are most and least effective? Explain.

Collaborative Learning Exercise

Form groups of four students and role-play a task force put together by a human resource director of a large Fortune 500 company which hires approximately 5,000 new employees a year. Offer the director recommendations about how to interpret the educational credentials of applicants who have received their degrees online and approaches that may be used to determine when the traditional and online degrees may be considered equal.

Source: Adapted from L. Dunham, "Online-Degree Programs Surge but Do They Pass Hiring Tests?" *Wall Street Journal,* January 28, 2003, p. B-8.

Help on the Web

HR.com provides extensive and current information, updated almost daily, on all facets of human resource management, including compensation and benefits, staffing, legal issues, training and development, and labor relations. Explore the website and answer the following questions.

1. How can you use this information to become more effective as a manager? As a team member? In managing your own work? Explain.

2. What specific examples can you draw from this website that illustrate how this information may be beneficial to you in these different roles?

www.hr.com

ELEVEN

Managing Employee Diversity

chapter 11

After reading this chapter, you should be able to:

- Monitor labor force trends and their implications.

- Recognize the advantages and challenges of diversity in the workforce.

- Resolve the unique problems and issues confronted by different employee groups.

- Capitalize on employee diversity as a source of competitive advantage.

- Develop and implement human resource management programs that best utilize the talents of a diverse employee population.

Employee Diversity Equals Corporate Success

Shoney's and Denny's (whose corporate name is Advantica) are two firms that recovered from legal problems stemming from their unfair treatment of minorities to be named to the top five on *Fortune's* list of "best companies for minorities."

About a decade ago Shoney's paid $132.8 million to 20,000 employees and rejected job applicants to settle a class action lawsuit. Jesse Spaulding, a regional director of operations for Captain D's, a seafood chain owned by Shoney's, said the company's all-white "buddy system" method of hiring and promotion "left people of color by the wayside, because there were no people of color in higher positions who could make decisions on promotions."

From this low point, Shoney's has turned its employment policies around to the extent that it has been ranked in *Fortune's* top 50 of "best companies for minorities" for almost every year that the magazine has published the list. Spaulding, whose own career at Shoney's had stalled for 10 years before the company turned its policies around, today is helping to shape the new, multiethnic workplace. He recently hired a new area director whose former bosses would have promoted him only in a nonwhite area.

Leaders from both Denny's and Shoney's understand that a firm's good intentions aren't enough. Management jobs, measurable goals, and incentives to reach those goals are what make the difference, to both employees and the corporation.

By hiring and promoting multicultural employees, corporations discover a new source of talent and new business. Jennifer Kannar, 44, is a Hong Kong–raised product manager at UPS. Her idea for a bilingual support center for Korean-American entrepreneurs in Southern California was approved by UPS and has now expanded to include Vietnamese, Chinese, and Japanese businesses. Ludyn Campos, a native of Guatemala, learned English with the help of his employer and rose from housekeeper to chief engineer at a Marriott Residence Inn. Dora Abreu is a Dominican-American programmer at Lucent; while growing up in Queens, New York, she poured her energy into math and earned two master's degrees.

It is clear that both employees and firms benefit from hiring, promoting, and retaining a talented multicultural workforce. While difficult to quantify, effective management of diversity has a profound impact on the bottom line of firms in many key sectors such as high technology, services, manufacturing, and construction. One of America's most innovative firms, Microsoft, heavily depends on software developers from an East Indian background, who represent about 20 percent of Microsoft's workforce in the United States. Top hospitality chains such as Wyndham, Marriott, Hyatt, and Hilton have an approximate minority representation of 60 percent of company employees. The United States is the envy of the world in attracting the best talent from many lands. For instance, in 2004 approximately 600,000 overseas students attend U.S. colleges and universities, 40 percent of PhDs in computer science go to foreigners, more than a third of research assistants in academic labs are foreigners, and almost a third of all American Nobel prizes to date have been awarded to naturalized Americans. The working population is likely to become even more diverse in the future, not only in the United States but also across most of the industrialized world. This chapter deals with the challenges and opportunities posed by these demographic trends.

Source: Adapted from Stephanie V. Mehta, "What Minority Employees Really Want," *Fortune,* July 10, 2000, p. 180; and *Fortune's* "Best Companies for Minorities," www.fortune.com/diversity (2003); C. Arnst, "How the War on Terror Is Damaging the Brain Pool," *Business Week,* May 15, 2003, p. 73.

CRITICAL THINKING QUESTIONS

1. *Why do most executives believe that effective management of diversity is critical to business success?*

2. *What are the most difficult challenges firms face in managing employee diversity? What can they do to deal with those challenges?*

The Meaning of Diversity

diversity

The wide spectrum of individual and group differences.

Appreciating and Valuing Diversity

The term **diversity** is used to describe a wide spectrum of differences between people. On an individual level, a person's sexual preference, disability status, or many other characteristics may cause the individual to be perceived as different. Groups of individuals share characteristics that distinguish them from other groups. Some of the characteristics, such as race, age, and gender, cannot be controlled by the individuals involved. Others, such as occupation, political party membership, and religion, may be changed through conscious choice and deliberate effort.

The crucial fact to bear in mind about diversity, however, is that although the attitudes, life interests, expectations, and norms of behavior of groups may differ on average, the differences between groups are smaller than the differences within groups. Classifying people into such typologies as black or white, male or female, and gay or straight often leads to false stereotypes because it incorrectly assumes that group averages or characteristics apply to every individual in the group.

FIGURE 11.1

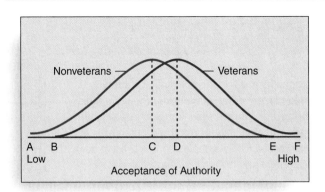

Group versus Individual Differences on Acceptance of Authoritarian Leadership

Source: From *Managing Human Resources,* by Gomez-Mejia, et al., copyright © 2004. Reprinted by permission of Pearson Education, Inc., Upper Saddle River, NJ.

In Figure 11.1 the curve for veterans shows that people who have been in the armed forces tend to be more accepting of an authoritarian management style than nonveterans. However, the figure does not prove that a particular veteran is more accepting of an authoritarian management style than a particular nonveteran. About half the veterans—those below point D on the curve—are less accepting of authoritarianism, and there is a great deal of overlap between veterans and nonveterans on this trait. This is true of almost all psychological traits.[1] In other words, only a relatively small amount of employee diversity is explained by group membership. This is an important point to keep in mind. While managers need to be alert to diversity in their employees, the effective manager views employees as individuals, not as members of a particular group.

Currently, American-born white males constitute only 15 percent of new entrants to the workforce. The rest are women, immigrants, and minorities. Women now represent about half of the workforce, and nonwhites comprise about a third of the working population. In many parts of the country, the numbers are even more striking. Almost a third of New York residents are foreign-born, Miami is two-thirds Hispanic, San Francisco is one-third Asian, and 80 percent of Detroit residents are African Americans. The Hispanic community in the United States is increasing by 1.7 million a year. In seven of the largest states (including California, Texas, Florida, and New York) 20 percent or more of the population speaks a foreign language at home; in an additional 16 states, the proportion of non-native English speakers exceeds 10 percent.

In this chapter, you will be able to develop some skills that will positively affect your ability to relate to employees of different backgrounds, as shown in Manager's Notes 11.1.

Advantages of Employee Diversity

A firm can derive many benefits from a heterogeneous workforce. First, however, company leaders must help employees avoid misunderstandings, ill feelings, and marginalization of those who do not fit into the

Skills for Managing Employee Diversity

- *Interpersonal flexibility skills.* To be a successful manager in the twenty-first century requires that you work effectively with people who are different from you. The labor force is becoming more diverse in terms of ethnicity, race, gender, sexual orientation, disability, and the like. Managers can develop an appreciation and respect for these differences and make better use of the organization's human resources. They can use these skills to deal effectively with some of the key challenges brought about by this increased workforce diversity.

- *Heterogeneous team skills.* Groups composed of people from different backgrounds can be more innovative by bringing a multiplicity of points of views to bear on a problem. By being skillful in managing heterogeneous teams, firms can use employee diversity to their advantage. Managers need diversity skills to improve organizational functioning by stimulating greater creativity, better problem solving, and greater system flexibility. Diversity skills are also essential to avoid the potential downside of diversity such as garbled communications, conflict, and resentment.

dominant groups. Some of the most important potential benefits of diversity are better market access, global competitiveness, greater creativity, and improved team performance.

MARKET ACCESS   A diverse employee base allows a firm to tap into profitable markets. Utilizing employees who are attuned to these markets gives the firm a competitive edge. Women, older Americans, African Americans, Hispanics, and Asian Americans have more buying power than in the past. They expect businesses to provide products and services that meet their needs. As Deborah Yarborough, a manager at Silicon Graphics, points out, if they "don't feel respected and listened to, they will take their business elsewhere."[2]

Many companies have successfully tapped into diverse markets. Hispanic, Asian, and female community development officers from First Community Bank Boston present seminars to diverse communities in order to develop market opportunities. The bank also provides translation, advertising, an 800 line for people who do not speak English well, and modification of loan application procedures to make them less threatening to non-Anglo groups.[3] As described in Management Close-Up 11.a, other banks are targeting services to minority groups. These companies are able to develop those market niches to attain a sustainable competitive advantage. Avon has a workforce that is almost a third minority. The marketing team at Avon discovered a niche in an industry

How Banks Meet the Needs of Minority Customers and Make Money in the Process

Black Banks Are Racing to Reach the $1 Billion Deposit Milestone

James E. Young has a dream. He wants Atlanta's Citizens Trust Bank to become the first black-owned bank with $1 billion in assets. Since 1997, Citizens' assets have more than doubled to $276 million, making it the nation's third largest African-American bank. At this pace, Young, the president and CEO, figures he'll reach the mountaintop by decade's end—or sooner—with an acquisition or two. "We're servicing some of the wealthiest black neighborhoods in the country," he says.

Citizens isn't the only black bank racing to hit the $1 billion mark. "It's our industry's Holy Grail," says Deborah C. Wright, president and CEO of New York's Carver Bancorp Inc., with $425 million in assets. Carver was the largest black bank until it lost the title last year to Boston's OneUnited Bank, which boasts celebrity investors including athlete Earvin "Magic" Johnson and entertainer Janet Jackson.

The fuel for the race to become the first billionaire bank is the rapidly rising wealth of African Americans. Growing deposits at the country's 31 black banks are turning this once small niche into the fastest growing segment of the industry. To capitalize on this trend, a new breed of black bankers focuses on meeting the needs of the black community. "Customers are always pleasantly surprised that they can talk directly to me, the president of the bank, when they have a complaint," says Young.

Money Also Talks in Spanish

Until recently, the financial institutions of choice or necessity for many of the nation's 40 million Hispanics had been the sort of check-cashing storefronts that charge fees of as much as 20 percent to wire money back home. Now the situation is changing. Banks and brokerage firms are scrambling to cater to this fast-growing group in order to grab a slice of the $580 billion in purchasing power it represents. Marketing to the fast growing ethnic population "might be the single biggest opportunity for growth in the consumer space," says Kenneth D. Lewis, chief executive of Bank of America Corp. In early December, the company paid $1.6 billion for a 24.9 percent stake in Mexico's Santander Central Hispano as part of this broader strategy.

The Bank of America Corp. is not alone. Multilingual ATMs, tellers, and phone reps are increasingly common. Wells Fargo & Co. and BB&T Corp. now accept Mexican ID cards from undocumented workers to open certain accounts. Citigroup, which recently paid $12.5 billion for Banamex, a leading Mexican bank, now offers a Banamex credit card in the United States. Merrill Lynch & Co. and FleetBoston Financial Corps.'s Quick & Reilly Inc., among others, are also trying to attract Spanish-speaking brokers and customers.

For Korean Banks, Truly a Golden State

Korean-American banks represent some of the fastest growing and most profitable financial institutions in the nation. There are now nine in Southern California, and five are traded on NASDAQ. During the past four years, their assets have doubled, to more than $5 billion. The five NASDAQ-listed Korean banks earned an annualized 18 percent return on equity through the third quarter of last year, versus 13 percent by similarly sized banks nationwide. The banks are bolstered by a large influx of South Koreans. The Korean immigrant population climbed 35 percent during the past decade, triple the rate for the population as a whole. About 250,000 of the country's 1 million Korean Americans live in Southern California. Koreans are the most entrepreneurial of all U.S. ethnic groups, with one business for every eight people. Although they account for just 0.4 percent of the U.S. population, Koreans control 11 percent of the nation's grocery stores and as much as a third of its dry cleaners—small businesses that are often hungry for loans. And more than half of these businesses have accounts at Korean-American banks.

Sources: Adapted from C. Haddad, "Eyes on the 1 Billion Dollar Prize," *Business Week*, April 7, 2003 p. 72; D. Foust, "For Banks, Money Also Talks in Spanish," *Business Week*, January 13, 2003, pp. 110–111; and C. Palmeri, "For Korean Banks, Truly a Golden State," *Business Week*, February 13, 2003, p. 62.

Fannie Mae, the nation's largest mortgage finance operation, is headed by Franklin Raines, CEO, who became the first black CEO of a Fortune 500 company. The company is committed to hiring, promoting, and retaining minority employees.

that had been largely ignored: the beauty needs of women of color. The company introduced a highly profitable cosmetic line for black women in 1999 that is run by an African-American female executive.[4] At both American Express Co. and Merrill Lynch & Co., African-American female employees attempt to attract black investors by holding workshops and networking receptions in such venues as African-American museums. Within two years of launching the program, 68 percent of new business at American Express has come from African-American clients.[5] Upon the advice of several older employees approaching retirement, in 2003 Motorola decided to romance the rapidly growing over-55 market by making phones with features that aging consumers like, such as a zoom function to bump up the font size on the tiny screen and internal speakers that can be connected to hearing aids.[6]

INTERNATIONAL COMPETITION   As discussed in Chapter 2, success increasingly depends on a firm's ability to compete on an international stage. A growing number of U.S. firms have established joint ventures with foreign companies, and many workers are employed by foreign companies and work for foreign managers. Japanese cars are produced in Kentucky, Swedish pharmaceuticals are made in Italy, and U.S. software is developed in India. Phillip Morris and Intel operate in more then 200 countries and employees speak more than 100 languages.

Firms with employee diversity in their home offices are likely to display the cultural sensitivity, understanding, and awareness that will help them succeed in the global arena. An observer has noted that "there is a growing consensus that U.S. managers are more . . . able to adapt to other cultures and environments than managers from other countries. Experts suspect that's because U.S. managers grow up leading a more diverse workforce at home."[7]

Bank of America has taken advantage of its employee diversity in a global context. The organization does business in 37 countries, and the California customer call center staff speaks more than 13 languages. This is possible because 32 million Americans speak a language other than English at home, and 8.6 million of them live in California.[8] Similarly, the Du Pont Company uses its 100-plus ethnic and gender networks as a source of internal resource for global access. As a senior manager explains, "Network members have provided important insights regarding ethnic markets here in the United States as well as in other regions of the world. For example, the company recently test marketed a new hosiery fiber with women in its Asian network. In addition, African American networks helped our agricultural products business build a closer relationship with black farmers in South Africa, a major customer base for Du Pont."[9]

MULTIPLICITY OF POINTS OF VIEW   People from different backgrounds bring a variety of experiences, skills, abilities, and information to bear on the tasks at hand. This allows them to examine issues and problems from different angles. Research on group dynamics suggests that groups with members from a variety of backgrounds are likely to come up with more ideas and solutions than groups whose members are homogeneous.[10] Diversity is an important source of innovation that helps fuel creativity and improve a firm's competitive position in the marketplace. For example, "diverse groups of employees conceptualized product development, manufacturing and the marketing strategies" for Saturn Corporation.[11] American-born physicists are in the minority at Bell Laboratories, and the first language of biochemists at Schering-Plough's research labs is less likely to be English than Korean, Hindi, Chinese, Japanese, German, Russian, Vietnamese, or Spanish. Effective management of diversity has helped these firms become highly successful in their efforts to be innovative.

TEAM PERFORMANCE   Groups consisting of people with different personality types, attitudes, ethnicity, and gender also make better decisions. A diverse team may be able to find better solutions because of the divergent thinking processes characteristic of a more diverse group of people. Diversity minimizes the phenomenon called groupthink, in which a homogeneous group agrees on a mistaken solution because members share a similar mindset. The presence of team members who view the problem differently may stimulate others in the team to discover novel approaches that they would not have considered, thereby leading to better decisions. Moreover, diverse group members may learn from, emulate, and internalize the different strengths of other team members. This allows the team to conceptualize problems in a more comprehensive manner, avoiding simplistic solutions that may prove to be unsatisfactory.

The Challenges of Diversity

Potential problems can emerge when there is increasing employee diversity. These problems include pressures toward homogenization, lower cohesiveness, interpersonal conflict and tension, and confusing employee diversity with affirmative action. Firms must effectively manage these challenges in order to derive the benefits noted above.

PRESSURES TOWARD HOMOGENIZATION   There is a natural tendency for organizations to become demographically homogeneous because people are attracted to others they believe are similar to themselves. Indeed, as employee diversity increases, individuals segregate into groups composed of people like themselves, and dissimilar coworkers may feel pressure to leave the organization. Turnover of dissimilar employees tends to produce a **monoculture** within the firm, causing the organization to become more homogeneous. As a firm becomes more monocultural, the job satisfaction of minority employees and women decreases, which translates into higher resignation rates. On average, at all organizational levels and among all age groups, the turnover rate of minorities is 40 percent higher than that of whites, and the turnover rate of women is more than twice that of men.[12]

Dissimilar employees who stay may be segregated within the firm and kept out of the mainstream. **Ethnocentrism** may become prevalent among various groups of employees, meaning that they believe that their way of doing things, their values, and their norms are inherently superior to those of other groups and cultures. To the extent that managers are white males, their values, beliefs, motivations, and attitudes may prevent dissimilar employees from being promoted, because they do not look, act, and think in what are considered appropriate ways for individuals who aspire to responsible managerial positions. Although the exclusion of women and minorities may not be malicious or deliberate, ethnocentrism at the top makes it difficult for dissimilar groups to participate at all organizational levels. This creates a **glass ceiling,** an intangible barrier that prevents women and minorities from rising to the upper levels. Only about 3 percent of senior executives in Fortune 500 firms are women.

The prevalence of segregated groups may also lead to **segmented communication** channels within the firm. This means that communication flows are far greater within groups than between groups. For example, one study indicates that a surprising amount of communication occurs only among individuals of the same sex and ethnic status. This was found to be true among all professional groups and at all organizational levels, even at the executive level where there are few women and minorities.[13] When employee viewpoints and ideas remain confined to employees' own groups, it is difficult to establish common ground across various groups. Unfortunately, this also means that dissimilar employees may not be attuned to mainstream communication networks or be able to share their unique experiences with the rest of the company.

monoculture

The homogeneous organizational culture that results from turnover of dissimilar employees.

ethnocentrism

A belief that may become prevalent among majority-group employees, meaning that they believe that their way of doing things, their values, and their norms are inherently superior to those of other groups and cultures.

glass ceiling

The intangible barrier that prevents women and minorities from rising to the upper levels in business.

segmented communication

Flows of information within the firm that are far greater within groups than between groups.

A diverse workforce is a key component of highly regarded firms.

LOWER COHESIVENESS   A measure of how emotionally close group members are and how supportive they are of each other is the degree of **cohesiveness.** Diversity may lead to a fragmented workforce with little cohesion. In the extreme, it may lead to a lack of commonality of organizational values and goals. Taylor Cox, a respected academic and consultant on diversity issues, noted that "a core of similarity among group members is desirable. Members must share some common values and norms to promote coherent actions on organizational goals. The need for heterogeneity, to promote problem solving and innovation, must be balanced with the need for organizational coherence and unity of action to provide competitive advantage."[14]

INTERPERSONAL CONFLICT AND TENSION   As organizations become more diverse, mistrust, lack of understanding, and lack of mutual respect may lead to decreasing cooperation among employees and poor integration of individuals who are supposed to work closely with each other. Diversity may also cause stress and interpersonal friction, making it difficult to reach agreement on issues. In extreme cases, open conflict and other problems may ensue.

CONFUSING EMPLOYEE DIVERSITY WITH AFFIRMATIVE ACTION
As we discussed in the preceding chapter, **affirmative action** is a government-mandated program that requires corporations to provide opportunities to women and members of minority groups who traditionally had been excluded from good jobs. Introduced more than 35 years ago, affirmative action programs are controversial. Some members of groups not covered by the programs have complained that affirmative action programs lead to "reverse discrimination," in which opportunity is denied to majority-group members. There is also a belief that affirmative action programs lead to lower self-esteem among beneficiaries by creating the perception that they received undeserved special treatment.

cohesiveness

The emotional closeness group members feel toward each other and how supportive they are of each other.

 Comparing Affirmative Action, Valuing Diversity, and Managing Diversity

affirmative action

A federal government-mandated program that requires corporations to provide opportunities to women and members of minority groups who traditionally had been excluded from good jobs; it aims to accomplish the goal of fair employment by urging employers to make a conscious effort to hire members of protected classes.

It would be difficult to prove what the real effect of affirmative action has been. It is clear that women and minorities have had more advancement opportunities since the programs were implemented. For instance, the percentage of women managers increased from 27 percent to 43 percent between 1981 and 2004. The number of African-American officials, managers, technicians, and skilled craftspeople has tripled since the mid-1960s, while the number in clerical positions has quadrupled and the number in professional jobs has doubled. In 2004, 14 Hispanics occupied top executive spots among Fortune 1000 companies. Three black executives were listed as CEOs in the Fortune 500 (www.fortune.com/sections). At some of the largest blue-chip firms the progress has been remarkable. For instance, almost half of the 50 highest paid employees at Xerox in 2004 are minorities, and a third of board members at General Motors are minorities.

Unlike affirmative action, a *diversity program* recognizes that, as a *de facto* consequence of demographic changes in the workforce, organizations need to employ women and minorities in order to succeed. Whereas affirmative action is a political solution to societal ills, diversity is a human resource program that focuses on performance and competence to ensure equal opportunities in a manner blind to ethnicity and sex. Unfortunately, some employees, particularly white males, believe that diversity is simply another name for affirmative action. A survey found that twice as many white men as women and minorities believe that promotions of women and minorities are a result of affirmative action.[15]

Diversity programs present four related challenges to HR managers and companies. First, white males may view a program as a threat to their own opportunities for advancement. When white male executives develop a cynical view of diversity management, the program is unlikely to provide competitive advantage to the firm. Second, the perception of special treatment may undermine the formal procedures, policies, and enforcement mechanisms of the diversity program. Third, women and minorities in positions of authority may not receive as much respect from their subordinates and colleagues as do white men. Finally, the organization may not reap the benefits of employee diversity described earlier.

It is probably true that a generation ago many business leaders launched affirmative action programs somewhat begrudgingly. Government pressure and the fear of losing costly class action suits were probably their primary motives. Today, there is strong support for the idea that creating an environment of inclusion of diverse groups is a competitive business necessity. See Management Close-Up 11.b, "Diversity at the Forefront," for an example of this change in thinking. Business leaders are quick to stress that diversity policies are not intended to encourage what may be perceived as preferential quotas for particular groups.[16] Rather, the intent is to provide opportunities to employees of different backgrounds. Nevertheless, debate on these issues is likely to continue for years to come. Most Americans, including a majority of women and minority group members, reject quotas that set aside a proportion of job

Diversity at the Forefront: Successful Business Leaders See Diversity with a Wider Angle of Vision

- "Creating an environment of inclusion for our associates, guests, and suppliers isn't just the right thing to do, it is the core business," says Barry Stemlicht, chairman and CEO, Starwood Hotels and Resorts.

- "Differing opinions give our problems a broader appeal, attracting a larger customer base," says Dieter Zetsch, president and CEO, Daimler Chrysler Corporation. "It is evident from the positive turn-around the company is making today," says Zetsch, "that our diversity has been critical to achieving our short-term goals and will be essential to ensuring our long-term profitability."

- "We must promote diversity and inclusion to attract and retain the best talent, to maintain meaningful client relationships, to win continuously in the marketplace," says Dennis Nally, chairman and CEO of PricewaterhouseCoopers, LLP.

- "Diversity is all about economic investment, market outreach, business results," says Rick Priory, chairman, president and CEO, Duke Energy. "The creative mind power of our team is Duke Energy's greatest competitive advantage," he explains, "and we increase the advantage every time we expand our thinking."

- "The accountability for diversity starts with me," says Bill Harrison, CEO, JPMorganChase. "That's why I head our firmwide diversity council." By continuing to involve employees at all levels and in all locations, concludes Harrison, "we will continue capitalizing on the internal and external opportunities that come from an inclusive, diverse organization."

- "How do corporations build, celebrate and nurture diversity?" According to Ann Mulcahy, Xerox Corporation's chairman and CEO, "You earn it. You stick to it. Most important, you treat it not as something nice to do but as a business imperative."

- "It's my responsibility to establish values, set the cultural tone and keep diversity in front of employees," says Ivan G. Seidenberg, CEO, Verizon Communications.

- "We're a diverse company from our employees, to our supplier base, to the markets we serve," says Daniel Carp, CEO, Eastman Kodak. "Kodak has established a Global Diversity Office and has created a multicultural Marketing Center. Success today demands the best ideas, from the broadest spectrum of people, working together," Carp says.

- "We would not be able to group our business globally if we didn't open ourselves up to the perspectives of others," says Douglas N. Daft, chairman and CEO, Coca-Cola Company. To this end, Coca-Cola has launched an $800 million investment to increase minority and women-owned supplier spending within five years.

Source: Adapted from "Diversity at the Forefront: Visionary Leaders See Results," *Business Week,* special section, www.businessweek.com (2003).

openings for "protected classes".[17] At the same time, most successful firms hold managers accountable for achieving diversity goals.[18]

Diversity Today

The U.S. workforce has been a mosaic of diverse cultures at least since the 1880s. When large contingents of immigrants arrived from southern Europe, Poland, Ireland, and Russia, they were considered outsiders because they had different customs, did not speak English, and were not Protestants. Immigrants from Asia and from eastern and southern Europe were largely excluded under the Immigration Act of 1929 because they were considered intellectually inferior based on their performance on standardized tests during Army recruitment drives in World War I. Women were largely missing from the workforce except in elementary-school teaching, nursing, and sewing. Most clerical administrative work was performed by men. Many of the largest companies considered hiring southern Europeans, Catholics, Jews, and Irish to be a poor business practice.

Throughout successive generations, many ethnic barriers eroded, and the diverse European groups entered the mainstream. This created the myth of the "American melting pot," a belief that the United States was a country of immigrants and that diverse groups would assimilate and blend into the American culture over time. However, "in real life many ethnic and most racial groups retained their identities—but they did not express them at work. Employees often abandoned most of their ethnic and cultural distinctions while at work to keep their jobs and get ahead. Many Europeans came to the United States, Americanized their names, perfected their English, and tried to enter the mainstream as quickly as possible."[19]

Today the prevalent thinking is that rather than making everyone fit a common corporate mold, organizations should support, nurture, and utilize people's differences in a way that both respects employees' unique perspectives and promotes a shared vision. If a firm is going to succeed, company leaders must learn to manage a diverse workforce.

A good place to start is to be cognizant of the unique perspectives, problems, and issues of various groups. It is important to keep two things in mind. First, as discussed earlier, characteristics overlap between any two groups. Second, employees have multiple identities, some of which are more strongly felt at different moments in their lives and in different contexts. For instance, a female black Hispanic engineer from Cuba who is 50 years old and disabled may identify most strongly with women under some circumstances and with Cubans under others.

Each person's self-concept reflects a web of identities: sex, race, ethnic origins, place of birth, religion, age, sexual orientation, occupation, socioeconomic status, and so on. Seeing individuals in terms of multiple identities permits a better appreciation of their personalities in more subtle, less stereotypical, and ultimately more realistic ways. Many of the social and legal barriers that have kept ethnic groups apart have come down because there are millions of people with mixed identities. For this reason, the Census Bureau now allows Americans to classify themselves into multiple racial categories. The evidence seems to suggest that airtight racial distinctions are slowly disappearing. Currently, approximately one-fourth of blacks and more than half of Hispanics marry people outside their racial or ethnic group.[20] At the same time, specific employee groups have concerns that still remain. The following is a presentation of

COUNTERACTING GROUP STEREOTYPES

Members of different groups may possess negative stereotypes of each other and are likely to experience difficulty in communicating and working together well. One of the simplest and most powerful ways to counteract this difficulty can be simply to ask the two groups to articulate and share their stereotypes with each other and then jointly identify ways to move beyond them.

1. The class forms two groups—women and men, whites and people of color, or any two groups. Before the next class, each member of each group completes the following statements with as many responses as necessary:

   a. I see myself as _____.

   b. I see members of the other group as _____.

   c. I think the other group sees members of my group as _____.

2. In the next class, the two groups form and meet in separate spaces. Each group completes the following statements with as many answers as necessary, recording the answers below and also posting them on newsprint, a blackboard, or transparencies to share with others:

   a. We see ourselves as _____.

   b. We see members of the other group as _____.

   c. We think the other group sees us as _____.

3. The two groups return to the classroom and share their answers, clarifying them as necessary for the other group's understanding. One member of each group records the answers:

   a. Members of the other group see themselves as _____.

   b. Members of the other group see us as _____.

   c. Members of the other group think we see them as _____.

4. The two groups jointly complete the following statement with as many answers as necessary:

   a. We can communicate and work better with each other by _____.

Source: From G. N. Powell, *Gender and Diversity in the Workplace,* copyright © 1996 by Sage Publications, Inc. Reprinted by permission of Sage Publications, Inc.

some of these groups' concerns. They should be considered carefully as general trends rather than the stereotyping of every member of the category. The Skills for Managing box 11.1 will help you counteract negative stereotypes that often exist between groups of people who perceive themselves to be different.

African Americans

African Americans constitute 11.3 percent of the population and 11.8 percent of the workforce in the United States. Prior to the Civil War, most African Americans were enslaved. Since then this group has suffered the most blatant forms of discrimination. Discrimination has resulted in poverty, segregated housing, fewer educational opportunities, and severe underrepresentation in managerial and professional jobs.

Until the 1960s, it was legal in the United States to segregate African Americans, and create company policies that automatically eliminated them from employee selection and promotion decisions. Prestigious universities refused to admit them, creating a vicious cycle of low educational achievement, little opportunity for career advancement, and little chance to enter professional, technical, and managerial jobs. Institutionalized racism is now illegal, but it is still present in the corporate world. In the mid-1990s, African-American employees at Texaco reported being passed over for promotions, and senior executives reacted to their race-discrimination lawsuits with vulgar racial epithets. Although the company claimed that racist attitudes were not the norm, "outside experts on diversity say they reflect a climate of widespread racism within the oil industry."[21] Shell Oil Co. and BP Oil also faced racial bias suits in the late 1990s.

Unfortunately, many whites do not realize that bigotry against blacks in the workplace is still a serious problem. For instance, one survey showed that half as many whites as blacks believe that there is a lack of fair treatment in promotion decisions. The discrepancy between white and minority perceptions of equal opportunity in the workplace was larger among African Americans than among any other ethnic group surveyed, including Hispanics and Asian Americans.[22] Bias is not always intentional; unintentional bias has been reported at numerous companies, including Amtrak, Coca-Cola, and the New Jersey State Police.

Asian Americans

Asian Americans make up 3.6 percent of the U.S. population. People designated as Asian Americans include a wide variety of races, ethnic groups, and nationalities including people of Japanese, Chinese, Korean, Indian, and Pakistani descent. Asian Americans are well-represented in technical fields, but despite high educational achievements, they are severely underrepresented in managerial positions and seldom make it to the upper echelons. Those Asians who head high-tech companies are often the founders of the companies. Asian Americans have been held back by the stereotype that they are too reserved to lead others and that they have limited verbal skills. Other characterizations of Asians as hardworking and deferential can end up relegating them to roles as corporate workhorses—not leaders—and keep them segregated in technical areas. Asian Americans are also subject to bigotry; in the mid-1990s, 40 percent of African Americans and Hispanics and almost a third of whites saw Asian Americans as "unscrupulous, crafty, and devious in business."[23] The perception that Asian Americans are already successful paradoxically makes some managers insensitive to their needs and problems.

Disabled Americans

Approximately 43 million Americans suffer from some form of disability; of them, 15 million are employed. People with disabilities are subject to unwarranted discrimination when supervisors resist hiring them for fear that they require special equipment, training, and support. They may also be perceived as being less capable and less flexible than able-bodied employees. Once hired, coworkers may feel uncomfortable around them, making disabled employees feel isolated or patronized so that they are unable to fully integrate into a work group.

In fact, accommodating disabled employees is less expensive than people think. One estimate is that accommodations average between $200 and $500 per employee.[24] Disabled employees are also less prone to absenteeism and turnover than other employees.[25]

Some progress has been made over time in the hiring of disabled people. The National Organization on Disability/Harris Survey of Americans with Disabilities reports that in 2003 56 percent of this group was gainfully employed, compared to 46 percent in 1986 (www.fortune.com/sections). However, this same survey indicates that there are many more disabled people (two out of three) who are unemployed but would prefer to be working. One promising development is the use of telecommuting to increase employment of people with disabilities. In 2003, the Equal Employment Opportunity Commission (EEOC) issued a set of guidelines to encourage the hiring of disabled employees on a telecommuting basis (see www.eeoc.gov/fact/telework.html). According to the EEOC Chair Cari Dominguez, "for some people with disabilities, telework may actually be the difference between having the opportunity to be among an employer's best and brightest workers and not working at all".[26]

Foreign-Born Americans

It is estimated that 10 percent of Americans are foreign born. The statistics are not reliable, because they do not account for at least 7 million undocumented immigrants. About 820,000 immigrants enter the United States legally every year.[27]

Immigrants tend to be relatively young, ambitious, and upwardly mobile. Some business sectors view them as a remedy for the relatively small generation of native-born Americans now entering their thirties. Immigrants form 250,000 new households every year, fueling demand for the services of builders, brokers, bankers, and department stores, among other businesses. In Los Angeles, about a quarter of home buyers aged 25 to 44 are foreign born. More than two-thirds of California's population growth in the past 15 years can be attributed to immigrants. New York State would have lost population were it not for 475,000 newcomers.

As noted in the introductory vignette, the United States is still the land of opportunity for most of the world. At any given time, there are more than half a million foreign students in American universities. A high proportion of them choose to remain in the United States after graduation, particularly those majoring in engineering and technical fields, where they often outnumber native-born Americans.

The United States has had a love–hate relationship with immigrants for much of its history. Periodically, immigrants are denounced for taking jobs away from native-born citizens and for not assimilating into the proverbial American melting pot. Established immigrants have worried that they might have to compete with new immigrants for jobs. Such beliefs have generally been unfounded, but they have often resulted in restrictive legislation. They also expose the foreign born to resentment and discrimination, complicating other factors, such as language, culture, and race, that create barriers to their full participation at work.

Nonetheless, the United States continues to provide upward mobility for people coming to its shores. One study revealed that the earnings of the more than 25 million immigrants who arrived since the mid-1970s had reached the average income of the native-born population within 15 years of arrival. Also, the poverty rate of those who are in the country for 15 to 20 years is lower than that of people born in the United States.[28]

Another study suggests that most foreign-born immigrants do not create an economic threat to those who are native born. According to 2002 figures, the income differential between a household led by a foreign-born and a native-born resident in the United States is only about 12 percent ($36 thousand versus $41 thousand dollars annually). This is amazingly low considering the additional hurdles an immigrant faces in learning a new language, adapting to a new culture, coping with employment discrimination, and so on.[29]

It is important to note that large-scale immigration is not the exclusive province of the United States. World migration has increased dramatically during the past 25 years in many parts of the planet.[30] All one has to do is to stroll through the streets of Paris, Vancouver, Amsterdam, Johannesburg, London, Madrid, Kuwait, or San Jose to see the mix of people from different nationalities who live and work there, often with dubious legal status. (Manager's Close-Up 11.c describes this issue in further detail.) While the United States has always been a nation of immigrants, firms in many other countries are now having to adapt to such demographic changes rather abruptly.

Hispanic Americans

Nearly 28 million people, or one in ten Americans, consider themselves to be of Hispanic origin. This figure, which is based on census data, is probably a conservative estimate. Many Hispanics are afraid to identify

How International Migrants Are Conquering the World

Growing employee diversity is not just a U.S. phenomenon. It is a global trend. Currently, hundreds of millions of people live outside the country of their birth. This is more than the number of people who immigrated in the entire history of humanity. Immigration is now the major contributor to demographic change in many developed countries. In the United States, according to the latest U.S. Census Bureau projections, the population will grow by 129 million, but if immigration stops it would only rise by 54 million.

The United States is not alone. From 1996–2003, the United States received 27 percent of the world's international migrants yet Western Europe received almost as many (21 percent). If it were not for immigration, Europe would lose about 26 million people over the next 50 years. While less publicized, large-scale migration is also occurring within Africa. Some movement occurs between South Africa and its neighbors. Also, more than half of the workforce in Kuwait comes from neighboring countries. Others migrate between Hong Kong and mainland China. In the Caribbean, at least a million illegal Haitians live in the Dominican Republic. In Central America there are at least 1 million Nicaraguans in Costa Rica, or about 20 percent of the population. In South America, there has been heavy migration from Colombia to Venezuela and from Paraguay to Argentina during the past 20 years. Governments around the planet have not been able to stem this tide. Labor moves toward areas with better wages and employment conditions, and employers are willing to hire migrants in order to reduce costs. It has been common for governments during the last few years to pass restrictive immigration legislation. For instance, Hong Kong has passed very strict laws on border controls with mainland China and has made it extremely difficult for mainland Chinese to obtain permanent resident status. At the same time, these same governments tend to look the other way when it comes to implementation, because in most countries immigrants perform the kinds of jobs and tasks that natives would rather not. Eventually this will reshape many of the notions that we currently have about race as people from different backgrounds commingle. In the meantime, company leaders must find ways to manage this growing diversity more effectively.

Source: Adapted from L. R. Gomez-Mejia, D. B. Balkin, R. Cardy, *Managing Human Resources.* Upper Saddle River, NJ: Pearson Education Inc., 2004.

One in ten Americans is of Hispanic origin.

themselves for fear of the Immigration and Naturalization Service and a general distrust of the government. For instance, a Hispanic family with two undocumented parents and five children born in the United States (who are Americans by law) may understandably choose not to report their ethnicity. A widely quoted figure is that the actual number is closer to 40 million and in some areas such as California, New York, southern Texas, and southern Florida, the proportion reaches close to one-fourth of the population.[31]

According to census figures, roughly 60 percent of Hispanics have roots in Mexico, 12 percent in Puerto Rico, and 5 percent in Cuba. Fifty-eight counties in the United States have a Hispanic majority. The largest number of Mexican Americans (2.6 million) live in Los Angeles County. The largest concentration of Puerto Ricans (900,000) live in the five boroughs of New York City. Dade County, Florida, where Miami is located, has the most Cuban Americans (600,000). The portion of the U.S. economy that is Hispanic is bigger than the gross national product of most Spanish-speaking countries, with 772,000 Hispanic-owned firms.[32]

"Hispanic" is not a term for a race but a label encompassing a wide variety of groups. It includes American Indians of the Southwest, whose homelands became Spanish colonies more than three centuries ago and who adopted Spanish surnames and customs, as well as immigrants from Spain, Mexico, Guatemala, Argentina, Cuba, and other Central and South American countries. At least 70 million Latin Americans are of European descent, 25 million are of African descent (mostly from the Spanish Antilles and the Caribbean basin), 10 million or so are of Asian descent from various countries, 60 million are Native Americans, and a high proportion are individuals of mixed ethnic background. Hispanic groups are diverse within their own countries as well as within the United States in terms of race, history, and economic status. What they have in common are the Spanish language, which Hispanic families tend to maintain across generations, the Catholic religion, which plays a key role in people's lives and values, and a high regard for extended family. Hispanic people tend to be family-oriented. Some cultural attributes, such as humor, a more laid-back style, chivalry, and freedom to express emotions, may also be present.

Language and skin color can pose problems for Hispanics in the workplace, particularly for recent immigrants. Many Hispanic immigrants come from an agrarian background and have limited formal education. Value differences may also cause problems. "Some Latinos see non-Latino North Americans as unemotional, insensitive, self-centered, rigid, and ambitious to the point where they live to work rather than the other way around."[33] For their part, non-Hispanics often complain that Hispanics' "punctuality, absenteeism, planning, and scheduling can be a lot more loose than one would expect."[34] Clearly these negative stereotypes do not apply to most people of either group.

Homosexuals

Estimates of the percentage of the population that is homosexual vary between 1 and 10 percent. Homosexuals are sometimes referred to as an "invisible minority" because an individual's status is not obvious unless the person declares his or her sexual orientation. Unlike race, gender, national origin, age, and disability, there is no federal antidiscrimination law protecting homosexuals, and only a handful of states offer such protection at the state level. The military has a controversial "don't ask, don't tell" policy that allows dismissal from the military only if an individual discloses his or her homosexuality.

Understandably, most gays and lesbians keep their homosexuality secret for fear of jeopardizing their careers. Declared homosexuals may face intolerance and scorn from coworkers, bosses, and even clients. However, company attitudes are changing in a way that was unthinkable even a decade ago. For instance, General Motors of Canada, Hewlett-Packard, Intel, American Express, IBM, and the Walt Disney Company now make health benefits available to same-sex partners of employees. Likewise, public policy regarding homosexuals is likely to become more tolerant in the future. For instance, starting in 2005 the state of California grants state-registered domestic partners all of the same rights, protections, benefits, obligations, and duties as married spouses.

Older Workers

The U.S. workforce is growing older each year. The average age of the workforce is expected to reach 40 by the year 2006, and the proportion of employees between 50 and 65 is currently increasing at twice the rate of the overall population. Negative stereotypes of older workers as being inflexible, resistant to learning new skills, and coasting until retirement are pervasive.

Contrary to stereotypes, older workers, particularly those in jobs requiring little physical exertion, function as well as they did 20 or 30 years earlier. They also have more wisdom and seasoned judgment. Many successful companies have implemented programs to share the knowledge and wisdom of older workers with younger employees through mentoring. In the words of an HR consultant, "these companies are striking gold in a silver mine by leveraging senior workers as knowledge champions".[35] Because the service sector has been growing more rapidly than manufacturing, physical strength and health are less important for successful performance than they were in the past. Nevertheless, older workers often suffer from discrimination in hiring and promotion decisions. Also, unlike countries in which the wisdom of older people is respected, the input of older workers in U.S. firms is often not accorded the consideration it deserves. Another serious problem older workers encounter is the rising cost of health insurance and the increasing reluctance of firms to provide any sort of job-based coverage (see Management Close-Up

Old, Ill, and Uninsured

THEME: ETHICS Only about one-third of U.S. seniors now enjoy any sort of job-based coverage, about half of what it was 20 years earlier. This underinsured population is set to balloon dramatically. As retiring baby-boomers lose their company coverage, they will have to buy their own medical insurance or live without it. Overall, they can expect to pay as much as $100,000 in health care costs from the day they retire until they die, new studies show. Unfortunately most employees have no idea just how large their new health care burden will be.

In the private sector, everyone is now vulnerable, including unionized workers, who traditionally had the most protection. For example, General Motors Corp. pays $5 billion per year for health care. Two-thirds of that sum is for GM's 450,000 retirees. GM has already sharply cut retiree benefits for workers hired after 1992. In labor negotiations between the United Auto Workers and the Big Three, the battle over company efforts to slash those costs even more has reached center stage. AFL-CIO officials expect the issue to be critical in labor talks across the country.

Retirees "are the first place employers look for big savings," says Richard Banks, the federation's collective bargaining chief.

Even companies that are not abolishing coverage are shifting costs to retirees. In 1993, when new accounting rules required public companies to disclose their liabilities for future retiree health costs, many corporations capped annual payouts for former workers. About half have hit those caps in 2004, effectively forcing retirees to pay for rising expenses. Many older workers feel that this is unfair and that companies are trying to save money at their expense. They believe they are an easy target for cost-cutting after many years of devoted service. Because older workers have little if any leverage (it is more difficult for them to get a comparable job elsewhere), firms are tempted to cut back on those expenditures, justifying it on the basis of escalating insurance costs.

Source: Adapted from H. Gleckman, "Old, Ill, and Uninsured," *Business Week,* April 7, 2003, pp. 78–79.

11.d, "Old, Ill, and Uninsured"). The United States is the only industrialized country that does not offer public health insurance. This lack of coverage can be catastrophic to elderly workers.

Religious Diversity

Many, if not most, Americans trace their roots to immigrants who fled religious persecution and wars in Europe. Apart from those of the Jewish faith, the United States has been traditionally and overwhelmingly Christian. In recent years, however, there has been a growing non-Christian minority, with approximately 4 million Americans now professing Islamic, Hindu, Taoist, or other non-Christian beliefs. This went largely unnoticed until America's tolerance toward people of different religious backgrounds was severely tested by 9/11. A recent survey by the Society for Human Resource Management (SHRM) revealed that so-called "ethnic religions" such as Islam now come just after race and gender in American perceptions of "otherness" (reported in "Talking to Diversity Experts," 2003, www.fortune.com/sections). Security fears due to terrorist threats have led to many complaints of "racial profiling" and discrimination by Arab Americans, as well as those who may be confused as

Muslims, such as some people of East Indian descent (see Management Minicase 11.2 at the close of the chapter).

Lobnia Ismail, a diversity expert who has appeared frequently on national media, speaks from personal experience. She has seen an increase in tensions and incidents of discrimination directed toward employees because of their faith, particularly when there is an identifiable garment associated with certain religious beliefs. Born and raised in the United States, Ismail asks her audiences to examine their attitudes. "When you think of America and think of your coworkers and customers, do you think of me, a Muslim who chooses to wear a scarf on her hair as a reflection of piety and modesty?" she asks. "It is un-American to exclude or discriminate against anyone, especially your coworkers or an entire faith or group, based on the acts of extremists. September 11 was a test for our corporations and for each of us. Will we stand by our diversity mission statements and policies to maintain an inclusive, respectful workplace that values everyone and not just some? Are we 'walking the talk'?" (cited in "Talking to Diversity Experts," 2003, www.fortune.com/section). Many firms are now developing policies concerning tolerance for religious diversity. These policies cover such issues as permissible garments at work, religious holidays, potential harassment or ridicule based on one's faith, and the display of religious symbols on company premises.

Women

As noted earlier, the labor force is half female, and 40 percent of the U.S. workforce consists of families in which both spouses are working. Women face several problems at work. Those who want families may be seen as not being committed to their careers. Firms in the United States, unlike much of the industrialized world, are not required by law to provide maternity leave. Women continue to have primary responsibility for child rearing and most household duties. Only a tiny percentage of firms offer day care, job sharing, and reduced hours for employees with young children. This situation causes many women in their twenties and thirties to withdraw from the workforce or curtail their work-related activities at crucial times in their careers.

The glass ceiling makes it hard for women to move beyond a certain level in the corporate hierarchy. Women have limited access to the "old boys' network," the informal relationships that exist among managers and executives in which much important communication occurs. Significant decisions, such as who will be promoted, are often made through loose coalitions that are part of this informal network.

Women face sexual harassment at work far more often than men. Unwanted sexual advances, even if they are not overt, may cause women to quit their jobs. When a woman refuses, resists, or challenges such pressures, she often jeopardizes her future with the department or company. Sexual harassment is discussed in more detail in Chapter 10.

Women must frequently choose between their careers and their families.

FIGURE 11.2

Men and Women, Divided by Language

Source: Adapted from R. D. Bucher, *Diversity Consciousness* (Upper Saddle River, NJ: Prentice Hall, 2000), p. 130.

Deborah Tannen is a professor of linguistics, the science of language. In her research, Tannen has focused on the different communication styles of men and women. She has written extensively on this subject. Her books, entitled *You Just Don't Understand, That's Not What I Meant,* and *Talking from 9 to 5,* offer examples of gender differences:

- Men tend to engage in report talk, women in rapport talk. Report talk is a way of showing one's knowledge and skill. Rapport talk allows one to share with others and develop relationships.
- When making requests, women tend to be indirect. A female supervisor might ask: "Could you do this by 5 PM?" Something more direct and to the point is more typical of a male supervisor: "This needs to be done by 5 PM."
- Women have a greater information focus. They do not hesitate to ask questions in order to understand something. Men have more of an image focus. Even though men may be unclear about an issue, they may forgo asking questions, to preserve their image or reputation.
- Women often say "I'm sorry" to express concern about something. Men, on the other hand, may interpret this to mean that women are accepting blame or responsibility. This is not at all what women have in mind.
- People tend to judge men for what they say and do. Women are often judged by how they look and dress.
- For women, tears may be a way of expressing valid emotions. For men, they are a sign of weakness and immaturity.

Tannen makes the point that these differences do not apply to all men or women in all situations. By realizing that differences such as these may exist, we lessen the chances of miscommunication and conflict.

Finally, men and women may have somewhat different communication styles. They may attach a meaning that is different from the one that a person of the opposite sex intended to convey (see Figure 11.2). This increases the odds of miscommunication and conflict. Since more men are in powerful positions than women, this works against a woman's upward advancement. Skills for Managing 11.2 is designed to compare and contrast different communication styles by gender.

Building on Diversity

Organizations can choose from a number of strategies for improving the management of diversity. Several of these are discussed next.

Top Management Commitment

Lower-level managers and employees are unlikely to take diversity seriously if they believe that senior executives are not giving the management of diversity a high priority. Some CEOs take active and visible roles in diversity management, attending multiple meetings on diversity issues, while others merely make an internal announcement about the program. At Sara Lee, top executives played a major role in a three-day conference on diversity, launching several diversity initiatives. Similarly, the top nine officers of Bank of America attended a three-day off-site meeting on how to improve the management of diversity. The meeting involved all of the bank branches and was attended by a cross-section of employees from various geographic areas, job levels, racial groups, ages, and sexual orientations. Attendees examined the following issues:

1. How can we develop all employees so that they are ready for opportunities that arise in the company?
2. How can we be sure that minorities and women gain access to better jobs, as they become available?
3. How can we make sure that we give minorities and women opportunities without discriminating against white men?
4. How can we show all employees that we value their contributions?
5. How can we change attitudes of both employees and customers?
6. Will the same approach work for new employees and those with many years of service?[36]

Linking Diversity Initiatives to Business Strategies and Objectives

If diversity management is perceived only as a program emanating from the Human Resource Department with lip service support from top management, it is unlikely to be effective. Announcing a diversity program without giving it corporate support could give employees the impression that the company is simply going through the motions, which would be counterproductive. This was alleged to be the situation at Texaco in 1996

COMMUNICATION STYLES

Communication styles, which are based on our childhood communication experiences, accepted norms about appropriate and inappropriate workplace topics, and our relationship with the people we are speaking with, influence our responses in the workplace. How do both personal and situational influences affect how we communicate with others at work?

For each situation, choose the response that indicates how you would respond in the given situation. Discuss your answers in class.

1. You, Bill, and Lorie are coworkers. Your company gives an annual scholarship to graduate school, consisting of full tuition and expenses plus half of the employee's salary while in school. Bill and Lorie graduated with high honors from their respective colleges at the same time and have been working in the same department in your company ever since. They are great assets to the company. Both want to apply for the scholarship. Lorie has asked you for your opinion about the merits of her competing with Bill for the scholarship. You reply:

   a. It will be interesting to see who they pick.

   b. I don't think you should get your hopes up—who knows how they will pick the winner?

   c. Lorie, you have been getting great reviews. You are definitely a great applicant for it.

2. You are the vice president of sales for your firm. Susan, one of your employees, has been with the company for a year and usually performs well. She has just lost a major account with one of the firm's largest customers because of her lack of preparation and initiative during the account renewal stage. She has asked to discuss the situation with you and starts out with, "I want to explain what happened . . ." You reply:

   a. Susan, I can't understand what happened. You really didn't do your job.

   b. Yes, I think we need to figure out how to prevent this kind of thing in the future. What happened? This isn't like you.

   c. Okay.

3. You are the top operating officer at your company. Sid, the corporate travel manager, has been with the company for only a year but has a solid record of accomplishment. He makes a presentation to senior management about how to save on corporate travel expenses. He provides a good analysis of why a controversial change in travel policy makes sense and wants approval to make the change. You reply:

   a. Thank you, Sid, for your recommendations. We'll get back to you.

   b. It sounds like you ought to move ahead with this and make it happen! You've done a good job here.

   c. Let's not do anything until all of you have had a chance to review the proposed change with your departments. There may be other implications we haven't thought of. Sid, don't do anything further on this for now.

4. Your coworker Michelle has just been caught drinking on the job. There are rumors that Michelle is having family problems and knows that her job is on the line. You want to help Michelle but aren't quite sure how to go about it. Michelle returns to her desk saying, "I don't know what I'm going to do." She seems to want to talk. You reply:

   a. The boss looks mad, that's for sure.

   b. I don't know, but you'd better get your act together fast or you'll be in big trouble.

   c. Michelle, maybe you should call the Employee Assistance Program and get some professional help.

5. You are the manager of a department at your company. You run into Virginia, one of your subordinates, at the coffee machine and extend a greeting. You and Virginia walk back to the office area together, chatting about the weather, news headlines, and so on. All of a sudden, Virginia starts talking rather explicitly about how hard she and her husband have been trying to have children, stating, "I'm 37 and the clock is ticking." You reply:

   a. I can tell this is very important to you. Would you like to come into my office and discuss it further?

   b. That seems to be a common problem these days.

   c. I feel this is too personal a subject for me to be involved with. Why don't we get back to work?

6. You are a middle-level manager at the same level as Sal, who is writing a report for his boss. He always seems to wait until the last minute to do his work. Sal must compile information from a number of departments within the organization for this report. He can research the required information himself or can obtain it from department heads like you. He asks, "Would you be able to provide me with the information I need by tomorrow? I would really appreciate your help. It would save me lots of time." You reply:

   a. Sal, are you trying to pawn your work off again?

   b. Sure, it's no problem for me to put that information together for you. I'll have it to you tomorrow.

   c. I'll see what I can do.

7. You and Joe are middle-level managers in separate departments of the same organization. You are newer to the company than Joe, who works in one of the more influential departments and is friendly with several of the vice presidents. One evening, you and Joe have a short, humorous conversation about the day's events, and Joe asks, "Are you in a hurry to get home? Do you want to go for a drink?" You reply:

   a. Sure, it will give us a good chance to talk.

   b. Sorry, I've gotta get going. See you tomorrow.

   c. That sounds like fun, but I've really got to work late tonight at home.

8. You are the risk manager for your company. Mary Anderson is the senior sales rep for a major insurance company. She seems overly aggressive, but maybe she's just an ambitious sales type. She is trying to close a sale with you for property insurance, which would be a large piece of new business for her. You like the deal but aren't so sure about Mary, who says, "What more can I say? You've heard our proposal. Our price and service are competitive, and you have received good feedback on us from other customers." You reply:

   a. Thank you for your proposal. I'll put it on the Insurance Committee's Friday agenda.

   b. Well, that may be true, but I don't care for the pressure you're exerting to close this deal. You'll just have to wait until our Insurance Committee meets on Friday.

   c. Well, I like the program you've laid out, and your company's reputation is solid. You've certainly presented a strong case. I'm going to recommend approval to the Insurance Committee on Friday.

9. You are the immediate supervisor to Robert and Diane, both software specialists with promising careers in your company. They have been married to each other for eight years. After their first child was born, they decided there was still an economic advantage with both of them working,

and Diane returned to her job soon after. Their second child was born a year ago, and now they feel they will be better off if one of them stays home and takes care of the children rather than paying for day-care. Robert tells you that they have discussed this matter and that he will stay home with the children. You reply:

a. If you decide to come back later, this is really going to hurt your career in the long term.

b. Robert, you are a valuable worker, and it will be hard to replace you. Please let me know when you are ready to return to work, and we will be glad to have you back.

c. Okay—I'll advertise your position in Sunday's paper.

10. You are the head of a procurement department for a major corporation. You sometimes seek advice on contract clauses from an outside consulting service because of the complexity of federal regulations. One clause in a large contract currently being negotiated has been giving you particular concern. Although you have discussed it several times with Madeline, one of the outside consultants, the consulting service recently reorganized, and Mike has been put in charge of your account. You ask Mike his opinion about the clause, and he tells you, "I have looked this clause over thoroughly. Based on the available data, I have no objection to inserting it in the contract." His opinion is completely opposite to Madeline's previous analysis. You reply:

a. It sounds like you have a different opinion than Madeline did. Could you explain your reasoning in a little more detail so that I can understand why?

b. Thanks for your opinion.

c. That's not the way Madeline saw it. Why don't you talk to her and get her reasoning. I don't see how your opinion could be so different from hers.

Source: Deborah Tannen, *You Just Don't Understand: Women and Men in Conversation.* New York: William Morrow, 1990. The authors have devised this exercise based on insights gleaned from reading Deborah Tannen's book.

before the firm had to make drastic moves in response to the public scandal mentioned earlier in the chapter.

Employee diversity objectives should be key components of corporate mission statements and company strategies. Companies whose leaders have incorporated management of diversity into their mission statements include Inland Steel, FMC Corporation, Digital Equipment Corporation, and NASA. Hewlett-Packard has a comprehensive diversity model that considers external and internal forces and that includes corporate objectives and diversity goals and objectives. FMC has produced a *Diversity Handbook for Managers,* with guidelines and examples to create a tight link among business strategy, human resources strategy, and the management of diversity. Topics covered include new management orientation, diversity briefings for senior management, networking groups, developmental assignments, linking diversity performance to other corporate objectives, and benchmarking with other companies.

Management Responsibility and Accountability

People tend to invest time and effort in things that are measured and rewarded. "Diversity is not likely to become part of management and employee priorities without real accountability for specific objectives."[37] General Electric, Inland Steel, Hewlett-Packard, and other companies hold their managers accountable for employee diversity by making it part of their performance appraisals and merit pay. Some companies link a significant amount of a manager's financial reward to effective handling of diversity issues. For example, one-fifth of managers' annual bonuses at Harvard Pilgrim Health Care is directly tied to meeting measurable diversity objectives.

Firms use a variety of accountability tools to ensure the implementation of diversity strategies. These include written and verbal **360-degree feedback** (multirater feedback from peers, suppliers, other levels of management, and internal and external customers), employee surveys, performance appraisals, and self-evaluations. General Electric has managers assess their own performance on key diversity practices, including recruitment objectives, support of work/life balance programs, and involvement in outreach programs.

360-degree feedback
Multirater feedback from peers, suppliers, other levels of management, and internal and external customers.

Diversity Audits

Before launching a new diversity initiative or designing an intervention to fit a situation, it is important to ascertain why things are the way they are, which things should stay the way they are, and which should be changed. A diversity audit can help reveal possible sources of bias, and the indicators or factors used in the audit can also be used to measure whether corrective actions have the desired effects. For instance, if the percentage of women who quit each year in a particular division is twice as high of that of men, this could indicate that there is a problem that should be examined further.

Developmental Activities

Besides measuring and rewarding diversity efforts, companies also offer developmental opportunities to managers and employees to improve diversity management. The most common activities are diversity training, senior mentoring, apprenticeships, and diversity learning labs.

DIVERSITY TRAINING   Many programs can improve awareness of diversity issues. Managers and employees should learn about specific cultural and gender differences to help them respond in the workplace. At the information services company EDS, for example, employees attend diversity awareness workshops that focus on working together with people of different race, sex, religion, age, and social status, people with disabilities, and the like. Besides improving customer satisfaction with the company, these workshops have increased the pool of applicants for the company.[38] However, any firm using diversity training programs needs to be very careful that these are not perceived as a medium to reinforce stereotypes or as an opportunity to vent hostility toward a particular group, such as white males.

SENIOR MENTORING   Some firms have implemented senior mentoring programs in which managers and senior employees are encouraged to identify women and minorities with promising careers. The mentor is responsible for coaching the employee, offering a nurturing environment, and facilitating the employee's career progress. Marriott, for instance, has made senior mentoring available to disabled employees for many years. Honeywell and 3M team up experienced executives with young women and minorities to give them advice on career strategies and corporate politics. General Electric recently introduced a buddy system to assist new employees with their transition to GE.

APPRENTICESHIPS   Apprenticeship programs groom prospective employees before they are hired on a permanent basis. For instance, General Electric provides scholarships and internships to minority students, many of whom become a permanent part of GE's workforce at a later date.

DIVERSITY LEARNING LABS   Diversity learning labs improve knowledge and insight about market niches of diverse client populations. American Express has established 15 diversity learning labs that "receive concentrated funding, resource and training support from the region and corporate office. They are focused on diverse segments in the African-American, gay and lesbian, Hispanic, and women's market. The labs are not only experiencing increased diverse client acquisition but are also surfacing key learning such as strong project management experience in diverse segments."[39]

Encouraging Diversity Networks

The corporate environment can be insensitive, cold, or even hostile to the needs of many women and minorities. Support groups offer a nurturing environment to employees who otherwise may feel excluded from the corporate mainstream or lost in a bureaucracy run by people dissimilar to them. Companies with support groups for women, homosexuals, and/or racial and ethnic minorities include Allstate, Avon, Digital Equipment, and Xerox. Du Pont is reported to have more than 100 such networks. Apple headquarters in Cupertino, California, has a Jewish cultural group, a gay/lesbian group, and women's groups.

Microsoft has a large number of support groups representing a variety of constituencies, such as Attention Deficit Disorder, Deaf and Hard of

By providing child care for its employees' families, a family-friendly firm typically benefits from both increased employee morale and decreased absenteeism.

Hearing, Single Parents, and Working Parents, in addition to various ethnic groups.[40] Despite their potential value in promoting diversity, it is important to make sure that these support groups do not become "self-contained units" that separate particular kinds of employees from the rest. This inadvertently creates conflict and a "we versus them" mentality.

Company leaders may actively encourage or even require employees, particularly those in responsible professional and managerial positions, to become part of international teams. The growing global economy and increasingly diverse customers and markets justify such added expenses as travel, long-distance calls, and extra time. Intel Business Practices Network makes use of global teams. "Teams are multicultural/multifunctional, often involving people across three to five geographies—domestically and internationally. . . . The global team approach has paid off in a short time to market innovative ideas and product design."[41]

Accommodating Family Needs

Although 8.7 million single mothers and 1.4 million single fathers are in the workforce, as are more than half of women with young children, most companies are not family-friendly. Men as well as women find it difficult to balance family and career. Being responsible for child care results in less opportunity for advancement for employees of both sexes.

This is starting to change. Many executives now realize that the benefits of accommodating employees' family needs can exceed the cost and inconvenience. Family-friendly policies expand the pool of applicants so that the firm can recruit better employees, improve morale, and reduce turnover and absenteeism. Because workers have fewer worries and distractions, they can concentrate on their jobs and better use their talents.

Some of the options available to organizations to help employees handle family and career simultaneously include:

1. Day care assistance—for instance, Merck and Campbell Soup have day care centers at the workplace. One company, Massachusetts-based Bright Horizons Family Solutions, runs round-the-clock child care facilities for Toyota in Kentucky and S. C. Johnson in Wisconsin and two Ford Motor Co./United Auto Workers Family Service Learning Centers, and is currently developing child care facilities for 11 more firms.[42]

2. Flexible work schedules and arrangements.

3. Compressed work weeks—for example, working four 10-hour days instead of five 8-hour days.

4. Job sharing—two part-time workers share one full-time job. A survey of more than 1,000 companies in 2002 by consulting firm Hewitt Associates indicates that 28 percent of the organizations surveyed offer job sharing, up from just 12 percent in 1990.[43]

5. Telecommuting—full- or part-time employees work at home, maintaining their connection to the office via fax, phone, and computer.

6. Care assistance for elderly dependents.

7. Paid time off to care for family members who are ill.

8. Paid parental leave.

9. Keeping relocations to a minimum.

10. Giving a high priority to finding a position for a spouse within the company.

11. Providing job search assistance to relocated spouses.

Applications for the Manager   Today's labor force is highly diverse. If effectively managed, this diversity can provide the organization with a powerful competitive edge. It can foster creativity, improve problem solving, provide greater flexibility, and make a firm more attractive to a broad labor market. But if diversity is not effectively managed, there may be misunderstandings and poor communication, which have negative effects on productivity and teamwork.

Applications for Managing Teams   Despite management's best intentions, employee diversity may lead to interpersonal problems within and between teams unless all employee groups learn to work effectively with one another in a climate of mutual respect. Interpersonal friction can lead to open conflict, chaos, mistrust, lack of respect, and overt or subtle discrimination by those who control organizational resources. If groups become segregated, the problem-solving and innovation benefits of diversity will be reduced or lost.

Applications for Individuals   It is important to learn to work with people who are different from you. Employees who can relate effectively with members of other groups are more likely to be noticed by management and placed in positions of responsibility. One of the most fundamental management skills is the ability to get work done through others. Even those who are not interested in a managerial role will benefit from relating well to people of diverse backgrounds; support from peers will make their work easier to accomplish.

CONCLUDING THOUGHTS

At the beginning of this chapter, we asked why most executives believe that effective management of diversity is critical to organizational success. Besides the moral argument that it is the right thing to do, most executives believe that effective management of diversity is "all business" and that it represents a pragmatic response to demographic changes. These executives argue that effective management of diversity is good as well as necessary for business because (1) changes in technology and competition make diverse thinking a necessity; (2) minorities make up a majority of the labor market in many parts of the country, and, to be competitive, firms need to retain and motivate minority employees; and (3) companies are wooing customers from all corners of the globe, and they need the help of executives who can function in different cultures.

A major challenge organizations face is how to balance the need for greater workforce diversity with the perception that this diversity comes at the expense of the dominant group. In other words, it is important to actively support employee diversity in such a way that everyone sees it as a win–win situation. Managers should devote considerable time and resources to ensure that diversity efforts are inclusive rather than exclusive, and that employees come to appreciate and respect the contributions of other employees who may not be or look like them.

The U.S. workforce is increasingly diverse in terms of gender, race, ethnicity, expressed sexual orientation, age, and so on. Firms can manage employee diversity effectively, and do it better than competitors. The benefits of employee diversity include better access to differentiated markets, greater competitiveness on a global scale, more creative problem solving within the firm, and enhanced team performance. Challenges such as pressures to induce dissimilar employees to leave the firm, segregating them, limiting communication flow, and preventing career advancement must be overcome. When diverse employees come together, a firm's cohesiveness may diminish while interpersonal conflict and tension intensify. Some people believe that employee diversity is the same thing as affirmative action, and that both give minorities and women special treatment.

African Americans, Asian Americans, the disabled, the foreign born, homosexuals, Hispanics, older workers, those who hold different religious views, and women face unique problems in the workplace, and firms need to take their problems into account to improve the management of diversity. However, managers should avoid making inferences about a specific individual based on demographic group characteristics because there is a great deal of overlap between groups on most psychological traits.

Firms that improve the management of diversity can better meet such challenges as lower cohesiveness and enjoy such benefits as greater creativity and better team performance. Improving the utilization of employee diversity includes obtaining top-management commitment, linking diversity initiatives to business strategies and objectives, holding managers responsible for diversity results, conducting diversity audits, implementing a variety of developmental activities, fostering the establishment of employee diversity networks, and offering family-friendly programs to help employees accommodate work and family life.

SUMMARY

DISCUSSION QUESTIONS

1. The term "employee diversity" was not used until the late 1980s, but a dozen years later it had become one of the most recognizable concepts of corporate America. Why do you think this happened?

2. In your opinion, what are some of the dangers involved when a company develops human resource programs targeted for particular employee groups? When are such programs necessary? How would you avoid the accompanying risks that you have identified?

3. If you were a senior manager of a firm, would you attempt to form teams composed of diverse employees? If so, why would you do it, and how would you do it?

4. Of all the challenges of diversity discussed in this chapter, which do you think is the most serious? Explain why.

5. What do you see as the connection between affirmative action and the management of employee diversity? How are they similar? How are they different?

6. How would you know whether your firm was doing a good or a bad job of managing employee diversity? What type of data would you need to answer this question?

7. Of all the initiatives for improving the management of diversity discussed in this chapter, which do you consider the most important? Why?

A Big-Brand Job and More Money Are Not Enough

In spite of being able to command big starting salaries at prestigious firms, some MBA graduates want something different. They're considering broader work and life issues beyond the high salaries.

Sean McDuffy, with an MBA from Wharton, had different priorities. "I think about settling down and starting a family," he said. He accepted a position at Goldman Sachs at least partly because as a trader at the firm, he would work about 10 to 20 fewer hours than if he had taken a job at a consulting firm. Another Wharton grad, Stephen Shoff, said, "Sure, I'd like to make a lot of cash, but I can't believe how important the whole work/life balance is to me now that I'm approaching 30."

New perks, such as the low-cost day-care services offered by Merck, come into the students' decision. The company finds that acceptance of job offers is 25 percent higher as a result. "Firms know they have to adjust," said Tom Fernandez, assistant dean at Columbia University's business school. "We've even heard of small consulting firms limiting their travel days."

Several studies suggest that high-powered jobs still do not allow for work/life balance, which may drive away talented employees, particularly women. A recent study by Harvard Business School professor Myra Hart found that of the women graduates from the classes of 1981, 1986, and 1991, only 38 percent were still working full time in 2002. The B-school's alumni bulletin summed it up with an illustration of a briefcase-toting executive rushing out of her office. The sign on the door read: "Back in Five Minutes," with "Minutes" crossed out and replaced with "Years".[44]

Something similar is happening at Stanford University's Graduate School of Business. MBA Program Director Sharon Hoffman says the ranks of the stay-at-home have swollen so much that she invented a term for them: stopouts. "Women are realizing it's impossible for a human being to have it all," say Hoffman. "You can have it sequentially but not concurrently".[45]

This phenomenon is not only happening to women. Now that one in three women are outearning their husbands, the number of stay-at-home dads has soared 70 percent since 1990, to 1.7 million (Conlin et al., 2002; Conlin, 2003).

Discussion Questions

1. The number of firms with formal "family-friendly" work policies is relatively small. Why do you think this is the case? What may cause these firms to change?

2. Do you think there is any downside to firms' offers of family-friendly services or benefits? What effect do such policies have on employees who don't need them?

Sources: Adapted with permission from S. Branch, "MBAs Are Hot Again and They Know It," *Fortune,* April 14, 1997, pp. 155–157; "100 Best Companies to Work For," *Fortune,* January 9, 2003; M. Conlin et al., "Mommy Is Really Home from Work," *Business Week,* November 25, 2002, pp. 101–104; and M. Conlin, "Look Who's Bringing Home More Bacon," *Business Week,* January 27, 2003, p. 85.

Stereotypes Have a Long History

Racial or ethnic prejudice takes many forms. German Americans were often discriminated against during World War I, Japanese Americans were put into concentration camps during World War II, African Americans are often targeted by police for routine traffic violations, and Hispanic Americans often have to deal with immigration raids. Within five months of the terrorist attacks of September 11, 2001, there was a 150 percent increase in the number of "biases incidents" reported by the police against Arabs, Muslims, and others who may look like them, such as some East Indians. The American-Arab Anti-Discrimination Committee logged more than 440 hate crimes and cases of discrimination and harassment against Arabs and Muslims within two months of Sept. 11. Such claims again increased following the Gulf War II, in 2003.

Racial or ethnic prejudice is generally based on crude stereotypes that are as old as mankind itself. The earliest records of stereotyping are Egyptian hieroglyphs about Assyrians and Babylonians. The Lydian tablets (from present day Izmir), which are just being translated, speak harshly of piratical seamen called Achaeans (Greek). Or think of the Old Testament and the Israelite stereotyping of Phillistines. The Greeks standardized all aliens as "barbarians" because they couldn't speak Greek but went "baa-baa," like sheep. The Scots and the French have, through history, been England's favorite stereotype targets. The Scots have been seen as "wild" ever since their James VI became James I of England in 1603 and brought south thousands of thuggish Scots on the make. Suspicion of France has been rampant ever since the Norman Conquest.

A common threat with stereotyping is that particular groups make themselves feel better by looking down on other tribes and tittering at their expense. The English mock the "stupid" Irish, who in turn make jokes about the Western Irish Paddies, seen to be doltish bumpkins. East Coast Americans look down on Kansans or the Appalachian mountain dwellers. There are also French attitudes toward "boorish" Germans and German attitudes toward "backward" Turks. Old European attitudes, which speak of cruelty and too much lust, are still directed at people from the Orient.

The Pilgrim Fathers sailed West, dreamed of a better world. Unfortunately, once they arrived, they stereotyped the original inhabitants as savages. Even Shakespeare had his stock images. His Frenchmen are invariably silly, his Italians reliably treacherous. But although he never went abroad, he had the imagination to create a heroic Moor, and heroic Romans and Danes.

Discussion Questions

1. Stereotypes often play an important role in how people react to others. Even when managers and employees may not explicitly admit it to themselves or others, widely held stereotypes may lead to discrimination against certain groups. Why does this happen? How can this have a negative effect on the business? What can company executives do to deal with this problem? Explain.

2. Security concerns have grown enormously important since 9/11 and Gulf War II in 2003. These concerns are kept alive through frequent warnings by the federal government. Given that it is impossible to keep an eye on everybody, there is the real possibility that only "high risk" groups such as Arab Americans or those who look foreign are explicitly targeted for close monitoring. This of course would make them feel ostracized for acts they had

nothing to do with. What should a firm do to deal with this situation, particularly in "high risk" industries such as airlines, power plants, and military contractors?

3. If you were a person who might fit a certain stereotype, what would you personally do at work to prevent being a target of prejudice? And if you thought you had been such a target, what would you do to defend yourself? Explain.

Source: Adapted from T. Varadarajan, "At Last! It Is OK to Bash Away with Stereotypes," *Wall Street Journal,* February 21, 2003, p. W-15.

INDIVIDUAL/ COLLABORATIVE LEARNING CASE 11.1

No Way to Treat a Lady?

When Melissa J. Howard started as a department manager at a New Castle, Indiana, Wal-Mart store in 1992, she had high hopes for a long career. She rose steadily to assistant store manager in 1993 and to store manager five years later. After moving to a new super center in 1998, she says, her career hit the proverbial glass ceiling.

Howard was shocked to learn that two new co-managers at the store—both men, with no experience at Wal-Mart Stores Inc.—were making $15,000 more a year than her $70,000 salary and bonus. Then a new district manager arrived, also a man, and soon told her flat out that she belonged at home with her child, she recalls. Howard, the only female manager at the 10 stores in his district, complained to higher-ups with no results. After her new boss pressured her to take a demotion, to co-manager at a store 60 miles away, she finally quit. "I was crushed. That was my dream just taken away," says Howard, 35, who now has a customer service job at about half her former pay in Indianapolis. Wal-Mart declines to comment on her allegations.

Howard's story is one of hundreds of similar tales marshaled by plaintiffs' lawyers in a huge sex discrimination suit filed against the world's largest retailer in a California court. As part of the discovery process, Wal-Mart has had to turn over an unprecedented amount of data on its entire U.S. workforce. In 2003, the plaintiffs released a trio of studies based in part on Wal-Mart data covering 4 million employees. The analyses paint a stark picture of pervasive differences between the treatment of men and women at every level of the company (see the accompanying table). According to experts hired by the plaintiffs, men dominate the higher-paying store management jobs, while women perform more than 90 percent of the $14,000-a-year cashier jobs.

Women also earn less than men in the same jobs, the report shows. Even after accounting for seniority, store location and other factors, a study showed that women earned from 5 percent to 15 percent less than men during the most recent five-year period. Even within the same hourly and salaried job classifications, women earned less. As further evidence of the glass ceiling, plaintiffs point to data showing that about 65 percent of Wal-Mart's 896,000 hourly workers were women, but only 33 percent of its 35,000 managers were women.

Plaintiffs' Evidence in Wal-Mart Case
Shows Men Earning More at Nearly Every Level

JOB	NUMBER OF EMPLOYEES*	PERCENTAGE OF WOMEN	AVERAGE ANNUAL EARNINGS†	
			MALE SALARIES	FEMALE SALARIES
Regional VP	39	10%	$419,400	$279,800
District manager	508	10	239,500	177,100
Store manager	3,241	14	105,700	89,300
Assistant manager	18,731	36	39,800	37,300
Management trainee	1,203	41	23,200	22,400
Department head	63,747	78	23,500	21,700
Sales associate	100,003	68	16,500	15,100
Cashier	50,987	93	14,500	13,800

*Full-time.
†Including bonuses.

Critical Thinking Questions

1. Do you think the numbers used by the plaintiffs provide strong evidence of discrimination by Wal-Mart? If not, what additional evidence would you need? Explain.

2. According to an expert witness hired by the plaintiffs, sociologist William T. Bielby of the University of California at Santa Clara, there were "significant deficiencies" when he looked at Wal-Mart's diversity policies, concluding that "the normally highly centralized company gives local managers wide discretion to make promotions and compensation decisions, with little oversight. Inconsistent job postings and diversity goals with little or no link to pay or promotions were other problems." What diversity policies would you implement to deal with these problems?

3. Some people argue that overt discrimination is a thing of the past and that a company trying to make money has no reason to discriminate. Do you agree? Explain.

Collaborative Learning Exercise

Divide your class into groups of five. Some "pro" groups will play the role of those who argue that Wal-Mart has engaged in discriminatory practices and will request remedies to make Wal-Mart equally fair to men and women. Other "con" groups will represent the company's perspective on the issue. The arguments of both "pro" and "con" groups are to be presented in class. One group should play the role of a jury or an objective external consulting team to assess the merits of the arguments made by the "pro" and "con" groups and to give their assessment.

Source: Adapted from W. Zellner, "No Way to Treat a Lady," *Business Week,* March 3, 2003, pp. 63–66.

Managing Employee Diversity

Choose four or five of the companies listed in *Fortune*'s "America's Best Companies for Minorities," published annually (www.fortune.com). Search the Internet for information about them. Use the companies' websites and other sites. Use this information to answer the following questions:

1. What advantages have accrued to the firms as a result of their effective management of employee diversity?

2. Are there common approaches to managing employee diversity among the companies you've chosen? What strategies are unique to any of the companies? What reasons, such as industry, geographical location, size, and history, might lie behind these unique strategies?

3. Could other firms apply the diversity-related policies and practices used by the firms you've chosen? Why or why not?

4. *Fortune* rates the firms "the best" in their diversity efforts following specified criteria which are noted in the published annual report. What criteria would you use to evaluate a company's diversity efforts? How would you rate the firms you've chosen to investigate based on your criteria?

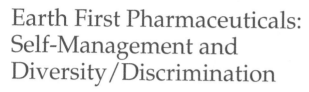

Earth First Pharmaceuticals: Self-Management and Diversity/Discrimination

PART FOUR

Senior supervisor, research: Syl Tang, female, mid 30s. Asian American
Vaccines manager: Dr. Daniel Simmons, male, late 30s, African American
Natural resources manager: Dr. Robert Franklin, male, early 40s, American

General Background info:
Earth First Pharmaceuticals is an enormous company with two essentially isolated branches—research and production. These employees are in the research branch.

Tang supervises eight different teams, with Simmons and Franklin leading two of them. All three characters have been working at Earth First, in their current roles, for over seven years. None of them have any particular bond with one another, Tang knowing each of them a little better, but only in the context of her role as supervisor.

The office has a serious scientific vibe to it—people are very absorbed and committed to their research and their projects. Although people in the lab are friendly, they are not particularly intimate—the environment isn't conducive for such casualness/chatting. There are some small groups of people who have become friends but do their socializing outside of the lab. The only group socializing that occurs is at occasional lunchtime celebrations for birthdays, babies, and weddings, which are very welcomed exceptions.

"Documents":

- Company profile.
- Brief overview of the collaborative project.

Pre-Viewing Class Questions

1. How can Tang successfully prepare for the meeting?
2. How can Tang maintain confidentiality while still addressing the concerns being presented by the 2 employees?
3. What should Tang do to maintain control of the meeting?

Scene One: Big News
Location: Syl Tang's office

Backstory:

Syl has been the supervisor for seven years and is highly respected and regarded. Her teams often cross-collaborate on special projects—each team has a specialized field of expertise. The teams are quite large, totaling over 100 people. With such a large department, Syl has less one-on-one contact with the employees than she would like.

Simmons and Franklin have not worked together often, just on one or two short-term projects. They are currently collaborating on a high-pressure project, heading down the homestretch. Nothing out of the ordinary has happened at the office for a while. Tang is compiling her end of the month reports, without much stress or pressure. Simmons and Franklin are at the stage of their joint project where they are separately recording the joint findings as it pertains to their field of expertise.

Simmons is gay and just started planning a commitment ceremony with his partner of four years. Simmons has never made any declaration in the office about being homosexual—some people know, some don't.

Break for Manager Questions & Analysis

Scene Two: Clash Course
Location: Syl's office

A new meeting has been scheduled to discuss the project facts. However, Simmons now conveys he has a bone to pick with Franklin because of his feelings toward him. Simmons continually speaks of "discrimination."

Post-Viewing Class Questions

1. How effective was Tang's methodology in diffusing the situation?

2. How can she help ensure that the issues discussed during the meetings will remain private and confidential?

3. What can Tang do to ward off Simmons' threatened discrimination suit?

integrated case

Unilever and Gender Diversity

A few years ago, Unilever, a multinational British/Dutch corporation that manufacturers hundreds of products from Dove soap to Lipton tea, realized that there was a noticeable absence of women from its top senior management ranks during a planning meeting for an outdoor leadership development program. The only senior woman manager invited to attend the program opted not to participate. Apparently Unilever co-CEO Niall FitzGerald was very troubled by this situation and commented, "My God, how can we have put so much work into gender diversity and I see no reflection of it in the top leadership?" He believed that gender diversity brought with it a strong degree of innovation and talent and a real understanding of ways in which the company could better promote its products since women consumers purchased approximately 80 percent of company products.

Unilever appears committed to diversity as a corporate strategy. Its UK Web page includes a major statement on diversity as part of its top six key issues (diversity, sustainable development, food safety, gene modification technology, science and innovation, and single currency). Its corporate statement reflects the importance of diversity. "We believe that the success of Unilever (UK) is a living testament of the importance of embracing diversity. The richer the mix of skills and cultures in a company, the greater the range of input, views and experiences. These inputs in turn generate more ideas, more challenges to traditional thinking, and more angles with which to approach any problem."

Unilever has operations in 150 countries; it employs more than 260,000 staff that speak nearly 200 languages; and leadership (the top 200) represent more than 30 nationalities. The last 10 years have been a boom for the advancement of women into managerial positions at Unilever: an 18 percent increase in women managers and a 14 percent increase in senior women managers. Fitzgerald believes that the increase in gender diversity numbers at these managerial levels is a vast improvement, albeit too small and too slow an increase. Despite the fact that both men and women are recruited equally to work for the company, he wondered why

This case was prepared by Joseph C. Santora, who is professor of business at Essex County College, Newark, New Jersey.

there were too few women at the higher ranks. To ensure that women reached higher positions in the company, Unilever had developed and implemented a number of policy strategies to retain women managers which included part-time staffing and career breaks. And while the issue of the "glass-ceiling," where a woman cannot break through to a top management position, unfortunately does still exist at many corporations, it poses a slightly less significant problem at Unilever.

The statement on its Web page reads: "Respecting individuality means challenging traditional assumptions and embracing alternative ways of working. 'Flexibility and Delivery' become the key in working patterns, career paths, and benefits. At the same time, a readiness to listen instills a readiness to talk and gives everyone confidence that their views will be respected." Unilever addressed the gender diversity issues by conducting research through focus group sessions that led to three major findings from focus group participants. First, women do not want to pay the price associated with top jobs; that is, they dislike the travel component that accompanies such positions and they do not want to be on call 24/7. Second, they view the cultural environment at the company as "very male, [and] aggressive." Third, for many reasons, they do not want to uproot themselves and their families, like military leaders, to conduct a tour of duty every four years in another country. And without international work experience, a prerequisite for breaking through to the top, chances are remote that they will be promoted to top-level managerial positions.

In addition to these revelations, about three years ago, Unilever learned that it lost valuable personnel—about 30 percent of women who took a career break from the company never returned to work. Since attrition translated into corporate loss from a personnel investment perspective, the company wanted to find out the causes of the attrition. Current management research lists several reasons women "drop out" from their workplace. About 70 percent of mothers with young children work. For many of these women, there is a limited infrastructure that supports them with accessible quality childcare. Maternity leaves are often limited and neither the women nor their husbands can juggle the stresses of work and childrearing, so many women stop to raise their children and in some cases do not return to work. Second, some women who have honed their managerial skills have opted to pursue careers as entrepreneurs by creating start-up companies or by joining small businesses. And while some of these general reasons may be related to the attrition problem of Unilever, co-CEO FitzGerald learned through informal research that a prominent reason for attrition in his company was that women "opted to work for other companies to avoid comparison with male colleagues who had moved ahead of them in career terms."

FitzGerald has taken on the issue of gender diversity at Unilever. Things are beginning to improve at the company; however, there is some concern that FitzGerald's passion about this issue may be too closely aligned with him. What will happen to this issue when he is no longer leading the charge at Unilever? Will the issue of gender diversity become part of the company's agenda? The company is committed to those who work for the company and "to *how* they work in the organization."

Questions

1. Discuss some strategies for improving diversity in the workplace.
2. What retention strategies should Unilever devise and implement to retain women managers?
3. Can women be serious contenders for top management positions without mentors? Without international work experience in other countries?
4. What impact does the departure of women managers from Unilever have on corporate organizational structures?

Sources: C. Arnst, "Women Work: The Support System Doesn't," *BusinessWeek* November 4, 2002, p. 46; M. Conlin, "Mommy Is Really Home from Work," *BusinessWeek* November 25, 2002, pp. 101–102, 104; A. Maitland, "Unilever Hits the Glass Ceiling from Above," *Financial Times,* June 17, 2003, p. 10; R. J. Phillips, "So That's What Women Want," *BusinessWeek Online,* October 11, 2001; http.//www.unilever.co.uk.

5

Leadership in Management

Designing an appropriate organizational structure and bringing together a workforce with the needed talent doesn't guarantee an effectively performing organization. People need to understand and identify with a vision for the organization and they need to see a link between their performance and the outcomes they obtain. Further, employees often work in a team context and team dynamics need to be managed so that performance is facilitated, not inhibited. In other words, effective management involves more than simply determining what needs to be done and finding the talent to do it. How things are done and conveyed to the workforce is critical to obtaining effective performance.

In Part Five we will examine the tools that managers can use to motivate employees. We will also consider approaches to being an effective leader and why integrity in leadership is critical to maintaining an effective and ethical organization. We will also consider managing people in a team context and how to effectively communicate with others in the organization. In sum, in this part we will examine the process, or the "how," of effective management.

5

Motivation

chapter 12

After reading this chapter, you should be able to:

- Understand the basic approaches to motivation.
- Use goal setting to increase employee effort.
- Improve performance and solve worker performance problems by applying various motivation models.
- Use reinforcement principles to achieve higher performance.
- Differentiate between motivation and other possible influences on performance.

Getting the Job Done: Oil Drilling in the Ocean

Rick Fox was an asset leader for Ursa, which was one of Shell Oil Company's largest deepwater projects in the Gulf of Mexico. The project was not going well. Oil drilling problems had delayed construction on a $1.45 billion platform by six months. This delay cost the company $250 million. Fox knew that if the project wasn't turned around, the result would be major damage to his career and the careers of his peers.

Consequently, Fox had to give serious and honest consideration to his performance problems. He quickly realized that he and his crew found it safer to stay in a comfort zone by negotiating lower-risk performance goals. Fox discovered upon reflecting on it that, in goal setting with senior management, he routinely negotiated for easily attained and safe performance goals. Likewise, Fox faced the fact that his own crew negotiated with him for more readily attained goals. But it wasn't just to make things easier. The heart of the issue was that they didn't want to set goals that went beyond their own areas of responsibility. In other words, if a goal meant counting on each other, that was too scary. It was far safer to commit to goals over which they had personal control than to look at the big picture.

Fox held a meeting with his team leaders. He told them that in his opinion the problems they faced stemmed from their focus on their individual tasks instead of working from a vision of the entire project being owned by the team. He intended to replace their separate, individual goals with an emphasis on teamwork and mutual responsibility. Fox then brainstormed with the group most responsible for the bottleneck at the time. Together, they identified ways to compress their work schedules, along with everyone else's. One of the principal ways to accelerate the project timeline was to shift construction of the drilling platform from an offshore operation to Caracas Bay, Cuaca. There, they would be able to work safely, even through hurricane season. Still, the new site was unknown and the possibility of difficult living and working conditions created concern. In spite of these risks, the crew believed that accelerating the project completion schedule by four months was possible—certainly not easy, but doable. Fox shared the new goal with everyone on his crew and emphasized that it was difficult but achievable.

In these meetings, Fox insisted on everyone's trying to recognize potential barriers to success. He asked his employees to describe what was standing in the way of achieving their performance goals. Again, it turned out that many limitations were internal and were posed by the person rather than by the environment or the goal itself. They realized that not working together and supporting each other had limited performance. The move to Caracas Bay seemed like a winner to everyone, and they all agreed to the accelerated work schedule.

In the end, getting everyone on board to pursue the team goal resulted in a saving to Shell of $40 million due to the shortened completion time; decreased operating costs of 50 percent; and production improvement of 43 percent (12 million barrels). The lesson in these and other achievements is that by coming together the work crew raised their collective performance. Obviously, the capacity to perform was present all along. By emphasizing team effort and a broader vision, Fox helped motivate his workers, which unleashed their potential to achieve key company objectives.

Source: K. Saposnick, "Achieving Breakthrough Business Results through Personal Change: An Interview with Rick Fox," *Pegasus Communications* (2001), http://www.pegasuscom.com/levpoints/foxint.html, accessed February 26, 2003.

CRITICAL THINKING QUESTIONS

1. *Why did Shell's Ursa crew accept the new difficult goal when accepting it could have resulted in failure?*

2. *Previously this same crew would not negotiate for goals that were this difficult to achieve. Why not?*

3. *Is the key to motivation simply setting goals? What else might be important?*

Motivation: An Overview

Motivation is seen by an increasing number of organizations as a key consideration when it comes to company success. Today's competitive environment requires a workforce that is motivated and committed to reaching work-related goals. This chapter focuses on two central questions: First, what motivates people, and second, how can you keep employees engaged and enthusiastic about their work? In the following sections we will consider the answers to these questions by examining two categories of theories about motivation: content and process. **Content theories of motivation** seek to understand *what underlies and drives motivation* in order to effectively motivate people. The **process theories of motivation** seek to understand what steps can be taken *to improve and maintain motivation.*

Before reviewing specific theories and concepts concerning motivation, it may be worthwhile to consider the theories and the concept of motivation more broadly and explain their value. First, it is not that some theories are right and some are wrong. Rather, no single theory captures everything of importance or applies in all situations. Having a broad understanding and the ability to apply various models can give you a much more versatile set of tools with which to manage motivation. Second, the motivation theories, or models, as with most theories, can seem academic, but they have great *applied value*. The models can help you understand motivation, what affects it, and, therefore, how to effectively manage motivation. The models give you frameworks for organizing and thinking through motivation problems.

We may not be consciously aware of it, but models often guide how we assess situations and what actions we take. For example, our personal beliefs can lead us to make assumptions and act in certain ways, even though we may not be aware of our internal models. What accounts for your friend not doing well on a midterm exam? Does the fault lie with the test, the instructor, or with your friend? Was the test too hard, the material not adequately covered by the instructor, or did the friend not study or lack the needed ability? Your personal beliefs will lead you, perhaps without conscious awareness, to conclusions about the source of the poor grade and what may solve it. Similarly, your beliefs about motivation can guide your understanding of a workplace motivation issue and lead you to choosing particular ways to manage the issue.

Finally, while motivation is an internal and unseen force, it is useful to recognize two basic types of motivation: intrinsic and extrinsic. **Intrinsic motivation** comes from the personal satisfaction of the work itself while **extrinsic motivation** comes from the rewards that are linked to job performance, such as a paycheck. An example of intrinsic motivation could be someone volunteering in community efforts, such as helping feed and clothe the homeless. The motivation for doing this is not the explicit rewards linked to the task because the involvement is voluntary. In other words, it is not about the money. Rather, community involvement is typically driven by the task itself: the experience and personal satisfaction of helping others and the knowledge that your efforts can help make a meaningful and positive difference. In contrast, a summer job at a local restaurant is probably something done more for extrinsic than intrinsic reasons. For instance, car payments and money for school may be reasons for working at the summer job. In other words, it's all about the money! The summer job itself may even be something that is disliked, such as strenuous manual labor, busing tables, etc. Yet, there is motivation to perform the job because of the monetary rewards that it is linked to. If someone asked why a student was working at the summer job, the answer would most likely emphasize the money, not characteristics of the job that were positive and satisfying. In most work situations, however, today's workers are seldom driven solely by extrinsic

intrinsic motivation

Motivation that comes from the personal satisfaction of the work itself.

extrinsic motivation

Motivation that comes from the rewards that are linked to job performance, such as a paycheck.

rewards. Today's workers want to derive meaning and satisfaction from their work, not only money.

All these factors are important to keep in mind as we seek to understand what underlies and drives motivation (content theories) and how to improve and maintain motivation (process theories).

Content View of Motivation

People's needs are the content that drives or energizes their efforts. Content theories attempt to look inside people and better understand what energizes action. Fundamentally, all of these theories share a common emphasis on *needs* as the origin of motivation. They conclude that if there were no needs, there would be little basis for energizing any activity. Understanding the needs that motivate people can be a valuable aid to managers. If you know the needs of your workers, you can align organizational characteristics and rewards to meet the needs when employees achieve organization goals. Knowing the needs that drive your workers can help you to provide the types of outcomes and work settings that those workers will find rewarding and satisfying.

Maslow's hierarchy of needs

The theory that people tend to satisfy their needs in a specified order, from the most to the least basic.

MASLOW'S HIERARCHY OF NEEDS According to Abraham Maslow, people experience needs in a specified order, from the simple physical needs to complex psychological needs, as shown in Figure 12.1. In ascending order, the needs are:

- *Physiological needs,* such as food and shelter.
- *Safety or security needs,* such as danger avoidance, a steady job, and a healthy work environment.
- *Social needs,* such as friendships, supervisory support, a sense of belonging, and affection.
- *Esteem needs,* such as personal pride, a positive self-concept, and status.
- *Self-actualization,* or the desire to use one's potential to the maximum.

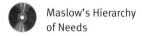

Maslow's Hierarchy of Needs

Maslow argues that each lower level need has to be satisfied before the next higher level need becomes salient or motivating.[1] For instance, a hungry person is highly motivated to do whatever it takes to secure food, even taking actions that jeopardize safety, such as accepting a dangerous job or stealing the food. A person who is deprived of nourishment is not likely to be overly concerned with social status.

One central management implication of Maslow's hierarchy is that providing additional rewards to meet a need will motivate a person only if the need has not already been satisfied. Also, when lower level needs are not satisfied, providing for higher levels will not motivate people. According to Maslow, the only need that can never be fully sat-

part five Leadership in Management

FIGURE 12.1

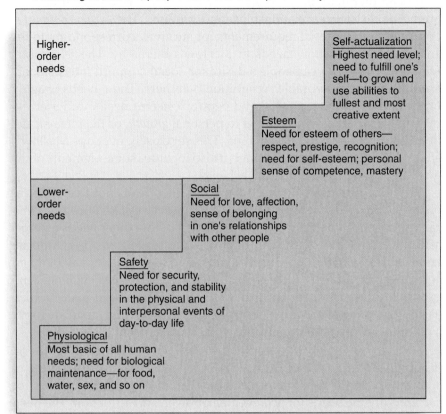

According to Maslow, people have and attempt to satisfy five basic needs.

Higher-
order
needs

Lower-
order
needs

Self-actualization
Highest need level;
need to fulfill one's
self—to grow and
use abilities to
fullest and most
creative extent

Esteem
Need for esteem of others—
respect, prestige, recognition;
need for self-esteem; personal
sense of competence, mastery

Social
Need for love, affection,
sense of belonging
in one's relationships
with other people

Safety
Need for security,
protection, and stability
in the physical and
interpersonal events of
day-to-day life

Physiological
Most basic of all human
needs; need for biological
maintenance—for food,
water, sex, and so on

Maslow's Hierarchy of Needs
Theory

Source: From *Fundamentals of
Management,* by J. H. Donnelly,
et al. Copyright © 1998 The
McGraw-Hill Companies, Inc.
Reprinted with permission.

isfied is *self-actualization*, which is at the top of the hierarchy. People can keep developing and learning as long as they have the opportunity to do so. Interesting and challenging work will continue to promote personal growth.

On the whole, there is only questionable empirical research support for the notion that needs operate in the precise sequence that the steps imply. However, there is general agreement about two important points: (1) a dominant or salient need will motivate people more than a less important or weaker need, and (2) managers should strive to provide employees with opportunities for self-actualization, since personal growth is likely to keep them interested in learning and developing their talents over time. Rewards associated with lower level needs (e.g., higher pay) only go so far in motivating people unless the work itself is stimulating and exciting. In other words, extrinsic motivation is not sufficient for the long haul. People want more from work than a paycheck or a bonus. They also want personal growth and meaningfulness in their jobs.

ALDERFER'S ERG THEORY

ALDERFER'S ERG THEORY   Clayton Alderfer revised Maslow's theory to make the needs and the sequence of needs less rigid. Alderfer's revised need hierarchy is called **ERG theory,** referring to three groups of core needs: existence, relationships, and growth.[2] The *existence group* is concerned with material requirements for survival, corresponding to the physiological and safety needs in Maslow's hierarchy. The *relationship group* of needs involves people's desire for social support, interpersonal relationships, and favorable recognition by others. These needs roughly correspond to Maslow's social and ego (or esteem) needs. Alderfer describes a third set of needs related to personal *growth,* or the intrinsic desire to use and develop one's talents. This set closely overlaps Maslow's self-actualization category, although it also includes some elements of the ego category such as the drive to achieve.

The key difference between these two theories is not that Alderfer collapses five needs to three. Rather, Alderfer does not assume a rigid hierarchy in which one need has to be satisfied before other needs emerge. Instead all three categories can operate simultaneously. Also, Alderfer claims that if a higher order need is not being met, people may demand more rewards to satisfy lower level needs. Cross-cultural evidence suggest that Alderfer's more flexible view of needs is more realistic than Maslow's perspective. For instance, workers in Spain and Japan are likely to place social needs before physiological requirements.

MCCLELLAND'S NEEDS   David McClelland also identified a set of important needs that serve as motives.[3] The most important needs for managers are the needs for achievement, power, and affiliation. The **need for achievement** is a drive to accomplish things, in which the individual receives great satisfaction from personal attainment and goal completion. Most U.S. managers believe that the need for achievement is important to success, and visible signs that a person is achievement-oriented are important in upward movement within organizations. Ironically, some research suggests that effective general managers do not typically have a high need to achieve because people with high achievement needs are more interested in personal gains than in helping others do well.[4] Instead, high achievers tend to be more successful at entrepreneurial activities such as running their own businesses, launching new projects, or leading self-contained units within a large firm. McClelland claims that people can be trained to increase the need for achievement.

The **need for affiliation** is the desire to be liked by others, to receive social approval, and to establish close interpersonal relationships. Research suggests that a low need for affiliation is associated with managerial success.[5] This is so because an important part of the manager's job is to make tough decisions that will displease some people.

The **need for power** is the desire to influence or control other people. Managers have a strong drive to have an effect, to be in charge, and to compete against others. To the extent that an individual does not want

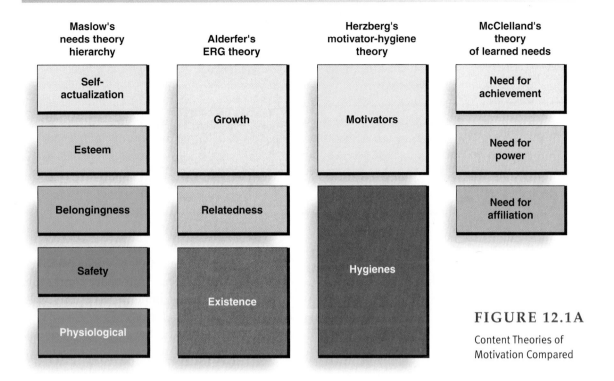

Maslow's needs theory hierarchy	Alderfer's ERG theory	Herzberg's motivator-hygiene theory	McClelland's theory of learned needs
Self-actualization	Growth	Motivators	Need for achievement
Esteem			Need for power
Belongingness	Relatedness	Hygienes	Need for affiliation
Safety	Existence		
Physiological			

FIGURE 12.1A

Content Theories of Motivation Compared

power purely for the pursuit of personal goals and does not place prestige and influence ahead of effective performance, the strength of this need is an important predictor of success in managerial jobs.

One particularly controversial part of this theory is that a high need for achievement in a national population is necessary to launch and sustain a high level of economic development. However, empirical data suggest that a high achievement need is not universal among industrialized nations.[6] For instance, security is a more important motivator among many Greek and Japanese managers, and social needs are often paramount in Scandinavian countries. In most Latin countries, an important part of achievement is the ability to reward friends and families, practices that may be viewed as corrupt in Anglo-American countries. The point is that needs and their importance vary significantly from one society to another.

HERZBERG'S TWO-FACTOR THEORY   Two-factor theory focuses on characteristics that motivate and reduce motivation at work.[7] Frederick Herzberg developed this theory based on interviews with workers regarding what led them to be satisfied and motivated at work and what resulted in being dissatisfied and unmotivated. His key findings, and the heart of two-factor theory, is that two separate sets of characteristics affect motivation and, thus, employee performance.

FIGURE 12.2

Herzberg's Two-Factor Theory

Source: From J. M. Ivancevich, P. Lorenzi, S. J. Skinner, and P. B. Crosby, *Management: Quality and Competitiveness*, McGraw-Hill/Irwin, 1997. Reprinted with permission of J. M. Ivancevich.

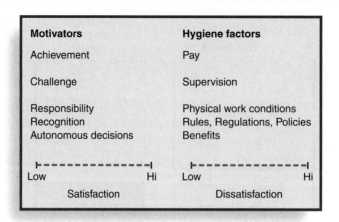

The first set, which Herzberg labeled *hygiene factors,* corresponds to the lower level needs in Maslow's theory. Hygiene factors are contextual or extrinsic aspects of jobs such as salaries, fringe benefits, company policies, working conditions, and interpersonal relations with coworkers and supervisors. They can cause dissatisfaction if they are inadequately met. Unfortunately hygiene factors also *do not* motivate people to do a good job.

To achieve higher levels of worker effort, first the hygiene factors must be well managed. Next, the key is to provide workers with *motivators,* or intrinsic rewards derived from the work itself, that provide continuous stimulation to strive for the best possible performance level, as shown in Figure 12.2. According to Herzberg, such motivators include the nature of the work, responsibility for a task well done, feedback and recognition, opportunities for personal growth and learning, and feelings of achievement derived from task completion. Herzberg contends that these motivators increase job satisfaction, and that removing dissatisfying characteristics from a job does not necessarily make the job satisfying.

The notion that the two sets of factors are distinct and the statement that only intrinsic factors motivate people are controversial. A raise is an extrinsic reward, or a hygiene factor, and it may also be a strong form of recognition (an intrinsic reward, or a motivator factor). Although the pure form of the theory has not been supported by most studies, Herzberg's work has been widely read. Many managers believe that the theory is a helpful method for analyzing motivational problems at work. It reminds managers that intrinsic rewards are too often ignored.

Process View of Motivation

A second approach to motivation revolves around the study of the processes that lead to changes in behavior. These process models provide a map of what determines a person's level of motivation. The question is,

To motivate and reward its employees, IKEA stores worldwide held a one-time Big Thank You Bonus Day to usher in the new millennium. The entire day's sales were awarded to the company's 44,000 employees.

regardless of the content of a need for a person, how is that motive transformed into performance? The process that changes an internal state to a behavior or activity is the focus of these models.

GOAL-SETTING THEORY Hundreds of studies demonstrate that people are more motivated when there are concrete objectives or targets to achieve.[8] These studies suggest that three important aspects of goals energize people to try harder. First, employees must believe that the goals are good. That is, they should "buy into" the goals. One effective way to increase goal acceptability is to have employees and supervisors jointly set the goals in a participative fashion. Second, the targets set should challenge people to "stretch" their abilities, but they should also be realistic. Unattainable goals frustrate and demoralize employees. Third, goals should be specific, quantifiable, and measurable to give people clear direction on how to focus their efforts so they can concentrate on meeting or exceeding the established targets.

Assessing How Personality Type Impacts Goal-Setting Skills

Goal setting must be carefully done. In most jobs, successful performance depends on the accomplishment of intangible tasks or duties that cannot be quantified or translated into a neat set of targets or objectives. The evaluation and reward system should be flexible enough to prevent employees from single-mindedly focusing on the achievement of measurable performance objectives at the expense of other key elements of the job. Consider the following goal-setting failures:

1. In the late 1980s, several airlines experienced deteriorating customer relations and a large number of no-shows when their sales representatives' pay was based on the number of bookings.

WORKING WITH OTHERS

This exercise is based on Herzberg's motivation–hygiene theory. Begin by completing the following questionnaire. Then meet in groups of three to five to discuss your responses and to answer the questions at the end of the exercise. Rate the following 12 job factors according to how important each is to you by checking the corresponding number.

	Very Important	Somewhat Important			Not Important
	5	4	3	2	1
1. An interesting job	—	—	—	—	—
2. A good boss	—	—	—	—	—
3. Recognition and appreciation for the work I do	—	—	—	—	—
4. The opportunity for advancement	—	—	—	—	—
5. A satisfying personal life	—	—	—	—	—
6. A prestigious or status job	—	—	—	—	—
7. Job responsibility	—	—	—	—	—
8. Good working conditions	—	—	—	—	—
9. Sensible company rules, regulations, procedures, and policies.	—	—	—	—	—
10. The opportunity to grow through learning new things	—	—	—	—	—
11. A job I can do well and succeed at	—	—	—	—	—
12. Job security	—	—	—	—	—

2. In a midwestern state, paying snowplow operators on a per-mile basis resulted in many roads packed with snow and ice because it was easier to cover more miles and get paid more by disengaging the snow-removal equipment.

3. In some academic departments, faculty may be poor teachers because pay, promotion, and tenure are based only on having research published in leading journals.

4. Top executives are frequently accused of maximizing short-term gains to trigger larger annual bonuses at the expense of long-term performance.

Scoring: Mark your rating of each of the above factors next to its number below.

Hygiene factors score	Motivator factors score
2. ___	1. ___
5. ___	3. ___
6. ___	4. ___
8. ___	7. ___
9. ___	10. ___
12. ___	11. ___
Total points ___	**Total points** ___

Add up each column. Are hygiene factors or motivator factors more important to you?

Discussion Questions

1. How similar are your scores?

2. How close did your group's results come to those found by Herzberg?

3. What motivational implications did your group arrive at based on your analysis?

Source: From *Human Relations in Organizations: A Skill Building Approach*, 2nd ed. by R. Lussier. Copyright © 1993 The McGraw-Hill Companies, Inc. Reprinted with permission.

One well-known approach to implementing goal theory is management by objectives (MBO). In an MBO system, employees and supervisors agree on a set of measurable goals to be accomplished within a certain amount of time. MBO allows the firm to implement overall organizational objectives by breaking these down into specific objectives assigned to different units and individuals in the firm. As depicted in Figure 12.3, the objectives for the entire firm "cascade down" to the divisional, departmental, and individual levels.

Management by objectives has several advantages. First, it results in a hierarchy of objectives that links specific objectives with each succeeding organizational level. Second, each person knows exactly what is

FIGURE 12.3

Cascading Objectives

Source: From *Organizational Behavior* 7th ed., by Robbins. Copyright © 1996. Reprinted by permission of Pearson Education, Inc., Upper Saddle River, NJ.

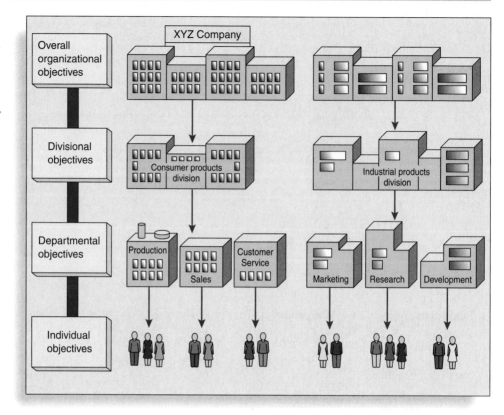

expected of him or her. This makes it easier to evaluate and reward employee contributions by comparing them to agreed-on goals. Third, because employees and managers jointly participate in the goal-setting process, MBO facilitates the flow of work-related information from the bottom up as well as the top down.

One drawback of MBO has already been discussed: in many jobs the most important tasks cannot be easily quantified. By emphasizing what can be measured, an MBO system may cause people to lose sight of crucial behaviors that have no clear metrics, such as being patient and friendly with customers. Another drawback is that MBO systems may encourage people to play it safe by choosing less challenging goals that are more easily attainable. This risk-reduction strategy makes sense from the employee's perspective if job security and organizational rewards are contingent on the achievement of agreed-on goals.

Another issue to consider is, "Where do goals come from?" Goal setting is a proven motivational technique, but who should define the goals that employees are working toward? Skills for Managing 12.2 examines the customer as the source that should drive performance goals.

LINKING MOTIVATION TO THE CUSTOMER

Motivation is often thought of as working harder, but to what end? Exactly what should be maximized? Where do performance expectations come from? Are they meaningful to the workers? Performance goals often reflect company expectations, but goals based on customer expectations can have an immediate impact on a business. Goals or performance expectations that are customer driven can increase motivation because of the link workers can see between their efforts and a meaningful outcome: customer satisfaction. Goals that lack meaningfulness create a sure-fire recipe for loss of motivation and failure.

Discussion Questions

1. How could you develop performance expectations from the customer perspective? Identify the major steps you would take to develop customer-based performance goals.

2. Do you think customer-driven performance goals will inspire increased motivation? Why or why not?

3. What else might be needed in addition to customer-based goals that would maximize performance?

4. Are there potential drawbacks to focusing solely on customer-based goals? For example, employees might work hard to satisfy customer-based goals, but ignore other aspects of the job that don't directly involve customers. Identify any other potential problems with customer-based performance goals. How could you reduce or eliminate those problems?

EQUITY THEORY At work, people develop beliefs about the fairness of the rewards they receive relative to their contributions.[9] **Equity theory** suggests that people's perceptions of fairness depend on their personal assessment of outcomes and inputs. *Outcomes* are rewards such as recognition, promotions, and pay. *Inputs* are contributions such as effort, education, and special skills. Employees have a general expectation that the outcomes or rewards they receive will be proportionate to the inputs they provide. People make this judgment not in an absolute sense but by using others as a reference point. A comparison person may be a coworker inside the firm or a friend who works for a different company. The relationship is summarized by the ratio:

$$\frac{\text{Personal outcomes}}{\text{Inputs}} \quad \text{versus} \quad \frac{\text{Others' outcomes}}{\text{Inputs}}$$

Fairness is achieved when the ratios are equivalent. Ratios that are not equivalent produce a psychological state called *cognitive dissonance,* which creates dissatisfaction and results in attempts to bring the ratios back into balance.

People who perceive that they are being inequitably treated can use one of four methods to attempt to change the ratios, or they can mentally

equity theory

The view that people develop beliefs about the fairness of the rewards they receive relative to their contributions.

FIGURE 12.4

Types of Reinforcement
Conditions

Source: From J. M. Ivancevich,
P. Lorenzi, S. J. Skinner, and
P. B. Crosby, *Management:
Quality and Competitiveness,*
McGraw-Hill/Irwin, 1997.
Reprinted with permission of
J. M. Ivancevich.

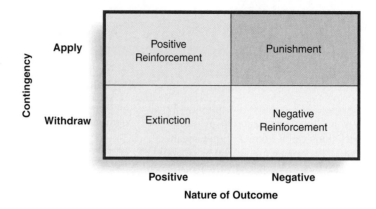

reassess the situation and decide that it is equitable after all. One option is to reduce inputs by cutting back on the level of effort, and if the imbalance becomes too great, to leave the firm. A second option is to influence the outcomes. For instance, the employee may document what he or she has accomplished to persuade the boss to provide a raise or a promotion. Third, a person can decrease others' outcomes. For instance, a dissatisfied employee may spread rumors about people in order to reduce their outcomes. Finally, a person who feels that he or she is getting more than deserved may increase effort levels to reduce the dissatisfaction resulting from guilt.

Equity theory contains two important concepts. First, motivation largely depends on a perception of fairness in the exchange process between what the person contributes and what the person receives. Second, people are constantly comparing themselves to others. The way they see their input–outcome exchange relative to others affects their behaviors.

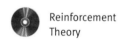
Reinforcement
Theory

REINFORCEMENT THEORY One clearly established principle in the social sciences is called the *law of effect,* which was formalized by psychologist Edward Thorndike. The law of effect states that behaviors are encouraged or discouraged depending on the consequences which follow.[10] Four key consequences, as seen in Figure 12.4, are:

positive reinforcement

A pleasurable stimulus or
reward following a desired
behavior that induces
people to continue the
behavior.

1. **Positive reinforcement** is a pleasurable stimulus or reward following a desired behavior that induces people to continue the behavior. For instance, people are likely to spend more time in the office if they feel it will help them earn promotions even though it may not increase their overall productivity. One common use of positive reinforcement in the workplace is performance contingent pay, such as merit pay and bonuses. Performance contingent rewards can be powerful motivators but, as illustrated in Management Close-Up 12.a and examined in Skills For Managing 12.3,

Motivation and the Disappearing Carrot

THEME: ETHICS Bonuses. Merit pay. Money tied to performance. The idea of making some portion of pay contingent on performance has long been a key motivational tool of Western management. Performance-contingent pay is meant to provide an incentive to workers. The practice is certainly consistent with reinforcement and expectancy theories in which money is the reinforcer. The merit pay system points out exactly how task performance is instrumental to getting a reward. There are also volumes of studies of white lab rats which demonstrate that contingent reinforcement works as a great motivator. Rats, however, do not know what performance contingency plan they are on and whether the terms of it might have been violated. Lab rats can't charge unfairness or file lawsuits. Employees, on the other hand, do have the capacity to examine the provisions of their merit pay plan and draw conclusions about whether or not what they received in bonus pay was fair.

The experience of Cory White, a senior manager, provides an all-too-real example of how the effective motivation principle of performance contingent rewards can go awry. White worked for Idea Integration Corporation, an e-business consulting unit of MPS Group Inc. He managed the PeopleSoft consulting practice. Similar to his staff, White was on a plan in which he would be paid bonuses based on meeting performance goals, including revenue targets and business development. Under White's management, the PeopleSoft practice grew 22 percent and profitability increased 211 percent in the second quarter of 2001. However, Mr. White did not receive a bonus that quarter or for any quarter in 2001. By his calculation, he had accumulated $120,620 in unpaid bonuses and an additional $53,000 for stock options that were promised but never granted. Idea Integration Corporation claims that the problem with White is an isolated event, but White claims the organization had a pattern of not paying bonuses. White left Idea Integration in 2002 and filed a suit against his former employer for fraud and breach of employment contract—an outcome far different from the positive motivation outcome that would be hoped for with the use of performance-contingent pay.

White's case may not be an isolated incident. Six other employees of Idea Integration claimed similar experiences and state that their incentive plans were changed after they earned most or all of the bonuses. The proverbial carrot was there, but they weren't allowed to reach it.

Source: T. Reason, "Incentive Confrontation: A Bitter Dispute over Bonuses Highlights the Hazards of Incentive Pay," *CEO: The Magazine for Senior Financial Executives* 19 (2003), pp. 46–51.

---

these same practices can be the source of problems if they don't work the way people think they should.

2. **Negative reinforcement** is the removal of unpleasant conditions following desired behavior, resulting in an increase in the frequency of that behavior. For instance, a worker may be subjected to close scrutiny and loud direction from an authoritarian foreman. However, the boss may remove this negative condition once the worker demonstrates that he/she can correctly perform the task.

3. **Punishment** is an aversive or unpleasant consequence following an undesired behavior. This leads to a decrease in that behavior. However, the avoidance of undesired behaviors through punishment does not mean that people will engage in desired behaviors. For instance, a boss who yells at people for being late may provoke employees to show little initiative to try their best once they clock

negative reinforcement

The removal of unpleasant consequences associated with a desired behavior, resulting in an increase in the frequency of that behavior.

punishment

An aversive or unpleasant consequence following undesired behavior.

CONSIDERING THE DISAPPEARING CARROT: MANAGEMENT DISCRETION OR UNETHICAL PRACTICE

Performance-contingent pay is often a powerful motivation tool. Unfortunately, as illustrated in Management Close-Up 12.a, it can also cause problems. Management may reserve the right to change the terms of an incentive pay plan, but should such terms be changed? From an employee's perspective, changing terms is tantamount to changing the rules in the middle of the game. As described in Management Close-Up 12.a, the change in terms may even involve removing the bonus. From the employee perspective, the organization received the benefit of his/her efforts, but the employee didn't receive the benefit that was used as a motivator.

Discussion Questions

As teams, consider the following issues and provide a summary of your conclusions to the rest of the class.

1. Idea Integration justifies the change in bonus pay plans on the basis of overall company performance. Specifically, even though the PeopleSoft portion of the operation was doing well, Idea, as a whole, was losing money. However, overall company performance was not part of the incentive plan and some of the affected workers argue that including overall company performance is changing the terms of the contract.

   a. Should organizations have the right to unilaterally change the terms of incentive plans? If so, under what conditions?

   b. What do you think the long-term impact of changing incentive plan terms might be? For example, what might be the impact on motivation, trust, and the culture of the organization?

   c. Why might an organization choose to change incentive plan terms, possibly even refusing to pay bonuses that have already been earned? Do these benefits outweigh the costs?

2. Consider the practice of Idea Integration of eliminating or reducing bonuses. Select a motivation model covered in this chapter and describe how you would expect motivation to be affected by the practice.

3. Design an incentive plan that you think would not have to be altered. Is there a trade-off? For example, are the performance goals in your plan directly under the control of the worker, or are they fairly broad? What do you think would be the impact on motivation?

---

in. In fact, they may resent the boss and try to get even whenever they can. The threat of punishment for undesired behaviors may be more effective than the actual use of punishment because punishment decreases undesirable behaviors only temporarily and may create anger and resentment, which hurt communication and undermine goodwill and personal initiative. Management Close-Up 12.b and Skills for Managing 12.4 explore the negative approach to motivation.

Crack the Whip!

THEME: ETHICS As vice president of a New Jersey auto dealership, Charles Park doesn't always throw things at his workers. He had, however, been known to do it occasionally. In one instance, when he was a manager at an auto dealership, he was confronted with a consistently low level of performance of one of his auto salesmen. Park had a discussion with the salesman but nothing improved. The salesman was older and treated Park as a son. Out of frustration, Park threw a binder at him. Either ironically or because of Park's action, the salesperson actually sold a couple of cars that day. Doling out this form of negative treatment is not the way to treat employees. Park, however, contends that ". . . if you do it once in a while, it works." Even if the statement is correct, being violent with employees invites trouble.

Jeff Leafy, a sales executive at a Washington, D.C., software company, had a promising young salesperson on his staff. He thought she had the capacity to become a superstar in sales, but her productivity had been declining. Leafy decided to get her attention with a little negative feedback in the attempt to kickstart her back toward the right performance path. He firmly told her that she needed to pick up the pace if she expected to move up with the company. Of course, this message was threatening and negative in just its content, but it was also likely delivered in a fairly bombastic and loud manner. His speech ended up pushing the salesperson over the edge and she wound up in a fetal position on his office floor by the conclusion of the interac-

Even though negative treatment works sometimes, it frequently backfires.

tion. The company attorney came to his office and ambulance personnel took the salesperson to the hospital. Unbeknownst to Leafy, the salesperson was going through a period of particular difficulty in her personal life. Leafy's negative approach only made the problem worse.

Source: J. Chang, "Cracking the Whip: In a Perfect World, Sales Managers Would Use Only Positive Incentives to Get the Best Performance from Their Teams. But in Less-than-Ideal Situations, Is There a Time and Place for Negative Motivation?" *Sales & Marketing Management* 155 (2003), pp. 24–27.

---

4. **Extinction** is withholding of a positive consequence following desired behavior. Eventually, faced with never being reinforced following a behavior (that used to be followed by a reward), the frequency of the behavior will decrease to the point where it disappears, or is extinguished. For example, a worker may have been rewarded on the basis of quantity. However, the emphasis in the organization may have shifted to quality. Out of habit, the worker may, for a while, still focus on quantity of production. Behaving in ways to maximize quantity, maybe sometimes at the expense of quality, will soon extinguish when the worker realizes that the behavior is no longer rewarded.

extinction

Withholding of a positive consequence following desired behavior.

SPARE THE WHIP, SPOIL THE EMPLOYEE?

A negative approach to motivation was addressed in Management Close-Up 12.a. While most reinforcement efforts suggest that it is much better to focus on positive reinforcement than on punishment, there is no doubt that some managers make use of threats, yelling, and other forms of negative feedback.

1. Why do you think punishment should not be used as a motivation technique?

2. Would you use punishment in the workplace? Under what conditions?

3. Compare the effectiveness of punishment and positive approaches to motivation in the short term and in the long term. What are your conclusions?

4. How would you feel about your workplace and organization if it used a great deal of punishment?

5. Are there alternatives to negative approaches to motivation? Describe.

 Reinforcing Performance

Some companies use an elaborate system of rewards. For example, Honeywell IT implemented a "multitier reward program" in 2001. Features of Honeywell's program include the following:

- Each quarter, each employee can award a $10 gift certificate to up to four employees who are perceived as doing a good job, helping out, and so on.

- Honeywell chooses three employees who used the certificates in a quarter to receive $50 gift certificates.

- Team leaders can award up to $200 to either individuals or teams based on five different criteria, such as leadership, commitment, and customer focus.

- Employees can nominate individuals or teams for quarterly organizational awards for excellence in the same categories. A committee reviews the nominations to select those that went significantly above and beyond.

Reinforcement theory indicates that managers should link desirable outcomes (such as pay raises or promotion) to the behaviors they want to encourage. They should also try to reduce undesirable outcomes associated with the behaviors they wish people to exhibit. For instance, providing day care facilities may prompt more women to accept jobs that require frequent travel and unpredictable schedules.

It is important to recognize that, based on reinforcement theory, motivation does not reside in the worker. Rather, motivation is in the con-

Honeywell uses reinforcement to elicit desired behaviors from employees.

tingencies that exist between behaviors and rewards. From the reinforcement theory perspective, whether someone is motivated is simply a handy but inaccurate reference. Motivation exists in the contingencies between behaviors and outcomes and there is no need to make any inferences about what is going on inside of the person. Thus, from the reinforcement theory perspective, motivation is largely, if not entirely, due to the contingencies set up by management. Thus, managers should link carefully selected rewards to the behaviors they desire. In essence, the goal is to concentrate on behaviors rather than private employee feelings, thoughts, or "motives."

EXPECTANCY THEORY One of the most widely accepted explanations of motivation is Victor Vroom's **expectancy theory.**[11] According to this theory, the strength to act in a particular way depends on people's beliefs that their actions will produce outcomes they find valuable and attractive. For instance, employees work harder if they believe that hard work will lead to better performance appraisals and promotion. Fundamentally, expectancy theory is a model about choice. That is, the amount of effort that is put forth on a task is something that people choose. As illustrated in Figure 12.5, that choice is based on three critical factors:

- *Expectancy:* The link between effort and performance on a task. It is the belief that a given level of effort will lead to success on the task.

> **expectancy theory**
>
> The view that having the strength to act in a particular way depends on people's beliefs that their actions will produce outcomes they find valuable and attractive.

FIGURE 12.5

Expectancy Theory of
Motivation

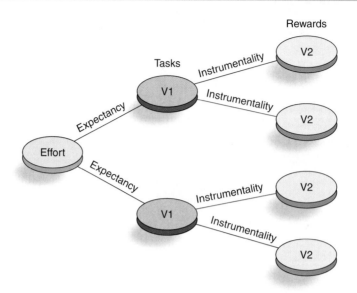

- *Instrumentality:* The perceived link between task performance and rewards.

- *Valence:* The value placed on task performances and rewards.
  V2: The value placed on rewards.
  V1: The value placed on task performance. It is a function of the links (instrumentalities) seen between task performance and rewards, and the value placed on those rewards.

While the expectancy model might appear complex at first, it is a fairly simple and rational model. The basic statement made by the model is:

> The effort put forth on a task will be determined by the value the person places on the task and on the belief that he or she can perform the task.

That's the essence of the expectancy model! In other words, the model states that people will be motivated to perform well on a task only if the reward has value to them and if they believe they can be successful. Does task performance have value to your workers? Do they believe they can succeed? According to the expectancy model, these are critical questions and the answers will determine the level of motivation of workers.

The question of whether the person believes they can succeed is the expectancy link in the model. The expectancy link may be stronger for some people than for others simply because they have greater self-confidence. In addition, expectancy levels would likely be influenced by ability levels and the degree of training on performing the task. If someone hasn't been trained on a task and feels that he or she does not have the skills needed to adequately perform the task, his or her expectancy level would be expected to be low. Another set of factors that can influence expectancy levels, and probably the most important factors in the typical work situation, are situational constraints on performance. *Situational constraints*, or system factors, are barriers to performance. For example, a worker may feel that the materials aren't of sufficient quality or that tools are inadequate for the job. Other system barriers perceived by a worker might include insufficient time, conflicting demands, uncooperative co-workers, or unsupportive management, among others.

The question of whether task performance has value has to do with valence and instrumentality. Workers will place a high value on succeeding at a task if they see a strong link (instrumentality) between task performance and rewards that they desire. Workers might not see a strong tie between performance and rewards because, for example, they think that managers distribute rewards based on politics, not performance. Further, the rewards that good task performance leads to may not always be viewed so positively by all workers. For example, rewards such as more travel and increased authority and responsibility may be viewed as negative, rather than positive, outcomes by some workers. According to the expectancy model, in order for task performance to have a positive value, workers need to see positive outcomes and a strong link between their task performance and those rewards.

Expectancy theory helps explain why some people merely do the minimum necessary to get by while others seem to put all they have into their jobs. First, expectancy theory recognizes that there is no universal way to motivate people, because personal beliefs and perceptions play a major role in how people see the linkage of effort, performance, and outcomes, and the attractiveness of those outcomes. These beliefs may be influenced by the organization (for instance, through training and incentive programs), but factors such as family background, culture, educational level, and personality are likely to play a role. Second, many employees may not give a maximum effort because they don't think it will be properly assessed by the organization. For instance, supervisors often don't differentiate high from low performers or may include personal factors in their evaluations (see Chapter 10). Third, organizations are often afraid to reward people based on performance because measuring performance is difficult and because people disagree about the accuracy of the performance assessment, particularly when it is not favorable. Finally, rewards that are individualized are more motivating. Not all employees want the same thing. A working mother may place a high value on a flexible work schedule and may work harder to obtain flexibility. The hope of a better retirement package may induce a 55-year-old to be a key contributor at a time when other people are slowing down. Unfortunately, many managers are limited in the rewards they can provide, and few organizations allow rewards to be tailored to meet individual needs. Manager's Notes 12.1 presents a calendar of person motivators that could be used in most situations.

Motivation by the Month

Often it's the little things that add up and make more of a difference than the big things. Motivation is no exception. While incentive plans and goals are critically important, it can be at the level of day-to-day activity that managers have the opportunity to change the culture regarding motivation. Personal steps that a manager takes to recognize and motivate performance can be more meaningful and energizing to people than an impersonal reward system with rules set up by the organization. Below are some personal motivation ideas for each month of a year. This calendar is simply a starting point. You may decide to create your own motivation calendar.

- **January**
  Hold a performance contest and give prizes. For example, give a $50 gift certificate for the salesperson who makes the most in sales in a two-hour period.

- **February**
  Ask your top performer to lead a training session for the staff.

- **March**
  Ask a member of your staff to anonymously suggest what he or she would do differently as manager.

- **April**
  Walk around the work area and distribute prizes such as T-shirts, mugs, or cash to those you catch doing positive things.

- **May**
  Take the top performer to lunch and invite your boss to go along.

- **June**
  Ask your staff for anonymous input on obstacles that inhibit performance and how they might be eliminated.

- **July**
  Pair your top person with someone who is having performance problems. Provide lunch on the day they work together.

- **August**
  Write a personal thank-you note to each of your workers recognizing them for their efforts.

- **September**
  Start a wall of fame on which accomplishments of your staff (letters from customers, recognition, awards, etc.) are posted.

- **October**
  Take the worker you know least to lunch. Ask the employee about his or her long-term career goals. Commit to helping the employee reach those goals.

- **November**
  Provide a long weekend to your staff after they hit a major performance target.

- **December**
  Designate one day as "work at home" day and encourage people to do shopping and other holiday activities with the time they save commuting.

Source: "Little Carrots, Big Results," *Sales & Marketing Management* 155 (2003), p. 36.

Motivation by Design

Are there ways to structure jobs to maximize motivation? This basic issue is the focus of a field of study called job design. Job design is the structure of work such that performance and worker satisfaction are maximized. Chapter 9 focused on organizational structure and job design. In this chapter we will address only the aspects of job design that are associated with motivation.

Job Enlargement

Jobs often become specialized, narrow, and routine. Job enlargement tries to reverse this trend. Job enlargement combines tasks into a larger job. The intent of job enlargement is to make a job more varied and interesting by expanding the scope of the job. A single task may quickly become repetitive and boring, but being responsible for more tasks can make the work more interesting. Job enlargement can have a positive effect on motivation and performance if the enlarged job makes a meaningful whole. However, if the job enlargement simply consists of separate routine and unrelated tasks, the enlarged set of tasks will have no greater meaning than the separate tasks. In this case, the enlarged job quickly becomes routine and repetitive, albeit consisting of more tasks than before.

Job Rotation

Job rotation is another approach designed to reduce boredom and monotony. Job rotation moves workers from one task to another, thus increasing the overall complexity and variety of the job. For example, General Electric has a rotation program for entry-level human resource management staff,[12] in which participants might shift from labor relations, to compensation, to staffing, and then to other functions such as auditing and finance. GE found that the rotation program can take some people out of their comfort zones, but even that is viewed as positive. The program provides participants with a broader understanding of the business as well as building connections across the organization. In addition to these benefits, job rotation can also be useful for lowering accident and injury rates.[13] Continuously performing one task can lead to boredom and fatigue, which can then lead to accidents or other injuries, such as muscle strains. Job rotation lowers this risk by introducing variety and changing the worker's activities.

Job Enrichment

Job enrichment involves giving employees greater opportunity to plan, organize, and control portions of their jobs. The intent of the enrichment

General Electric's job rotation program helps Human Resources staff understand the entire organization.

approach to job design is to provide employees with greater involvement in their work, improved meaningfulness of the work, and a greater sense of accomplishment. Job enrichment is not meant to be simply giving people more work. It is giving people greater responsibility and more work that requires a higher level of knowledge and skill.[14] Skills for Managing 12.5 presents the job design concept of a cell as a means to introduce job enrichment as well as gain greater efficiency.

Job Characteristics Model

job characteristics model

According to this model, the way jobs are designed produces critical psychological states which in turn affect key personal and work-related outcomes.

The **job characteristics model,** summarized in Figure 12.6, proposes a view of the relationship between job design and employee motivation. According to this model, the way jobs are designed (for instance, variety of skills required, autonomy, and feedback) produces critical psychological states (such as experienced meaningfulness of the work), which in turn affect key personal and work-related outcomes.[15]

The outcomes include high internal drive to succeed, attention to quality, satisfaction with the work itself, and low rates of absenteeism and turnover. For these outcomes to occur, employees must feel that their jobs are meaningful, that they can accept personal responsibility for a job well done, and that they receive accurate feedback that tells them how well they do their jobs. The job characteristics model refers to these conditions as *psychological states* and indicates that these states are more likely to be present when jobs are designed so that employees utilize a greater

JOB ENRICHMENT AND EFFICIENCY: TAKING THE MANUFACTURING CELL TO THE OFFICE

Many organizations in the manufacturing sector have focused on improving the structures of company factories so that production is completed as efficiently and effectively as possible. One of the techniques used in these improvement efforts has been the manufacturing cell. A manufacturing cell puts together people and equipment that are involved with similar parts of products. The approach of creating these "families" has worked well in the manufacturing environment. The manufacturing cell does away with separate departments for functions such as design, manufacturing, production planning, sales, and finance. Instead, people involved in similar products are put together in a cell and communication, efficiency, lead times, and production can all be improved. The cell design may also be applied to office operations.

Office cells group together people that are involved in handling or producing the same information. While people may be in separate functions, they may all process the same paperwork. Putting all of these people together can eliminate department-to-department handoffs that can take time and introduce errors in communication. For example, Ingersoll Cutting Tool Company created an office cell to handle special customer orders. Before creation of the cell, the special orders went through 12 departments and it took as long as four weeks before an order made its way to the factory floor. The office cell included two workers whose jobs were enriched and included multifunctional duties. After implementing the cell design, the average time to process the special orders decreased from 10 days to 2 days. Similarly, a Finnish manufacturer, Ahlstrom, utilized the cell design to combine different functions. The organization created three office cells with each focusing on a geographic region. The cell design collapsed 10 separate operations into 5 broader jobs. The team of workers in each cell created their own guidelines and operating procedures. The result? After implementation of the cell design, the average time to process an order fell from one week to one day.

Discussion Questions

The following items can be addressed individually or in small groups. The major conclusions can then be shared with the rest of the class.

1. Diagram a traditional organizational design in which people are separated into functions or departments. Use shapes to convey your conception (boxes, arrows, etc.).

2. Diagram a cell design.

3. Distinguish between the two designs. What makes them different? Is one way of designing work better than another? Why? Which design do you think you would rather work in? Why?

4. How do you think it would be best to structure work so that it is motivating and done efficiently? Diagram your suggested design.

5. Shifting to a cell design can be a significant workplace change. How would you implement this change?

Internet Research Questions

1. Can you find examples of organizations that have put the cell design in part of their operation? How has it worked?

2. Are there other examples of designing work that, either through job enrichment or some other means, are meant to improve motivation and performance? Describe these alternative designs.

Source: Adapted from N. L. Hyer and U. Wemnerlow, "The Office That Lean Built: Applying Cellular Thinking to Administrative Work," *IIE Solutions* 34 (2002), pp. 37–42.

FIGURE 12.6

Job Characteristics Model

Source: © 1975 by the Regents of the University of California. Reprinted from the *California Management Review,* vol. 17 no. 4, by permission of The Regents.

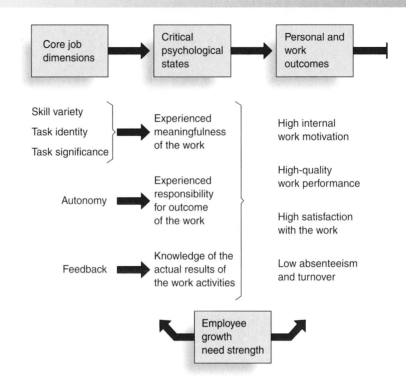

variety of skills; are responsible for completion of a whole, identifiable piece of work; have an opportunity to perform tasks that have a positive effect on the lives of others; enjoy autonomy and discretion in decision making; and can learn where they stand by receiving accurate information about job performance. Providing all five of these core dimensions in a single job results in *job enrichment,* which allows a person to grow and develop.

A supportive leadership style is necessary for job enrichment to work. The leadership notion of *empowerment* (see Chapter 13) is consistent with the idea that enriched jobs created conditions most likely to motivate employees to achieve favorable results. Management Close-Up 12.c shows how Wal-Mart has used enriched jobs to empower employees. Managers who empower employees give them greater responsibility, freedom, and influence to set performance standards, reducing the need to monitor and control their behavior through close supervision.

management close-up

I'm Proud of What I've Made Myself Into

In the midst of shoppers, three dozen employees get together in a suburban St. Louis Wal-Mart for the motivating pep talk that management holds every morning. The store manager gives them the good news that the men's department sales have increased almost 20 percent over the previous year, and the employees break into boisterous applause. Nancy Handley, the 27-year-old manager for the men's department, is thrilled. She is the one who makes sure that enough stock is available to customers, that sales items are marked for shoppers, and that the clothes are presented attractively. Handley works more hours at her Wal-Mart job than she would in a manufacturing position and earns less per hour. A widow with a seven-year-old child, Handley finds the recognition and responsibility that come with her job give her more satisfaction. "I'm proud of who I've made myself into, and the department I've created," she says.

Although Handley's day includes running around to keep clothes hung up and folded as well as being sure prices are marked clearly, she doesn't find her job mindless. It is up to her to decide things such as how many shirts, socks, and undershorts the store should stock. She also has some control over pricing and displays, and she secretly checks on the competition to see what their prices are.

"I used to be scared of having such responsibility," she says, and she doesn't always order the right thing. One year, for example, the St. Louis Rams mittens she ordered didn't sell well; she hadn't realized that most men don't wear mittens. "Nowadays, I make pretty good decisions," she adds.

Wal-Mart's treatment of workers and managers as partners—all employees are called "associates"—has meant that almost all attempts at unionization at the company have failed. Handley herself might be expected to embrace unionization considering that many members of her family belong to unions. Not so—for Wal-Mart, with its responsive and accessible managers, she feels unionization would be "useless" and sees no need to "pay someone to argue for me."

Sources: Adapted from L. Lee, "I Am Proud of What I Have Made Myself Into—What I Have Created," *The Wall Street Journal,* August 28, 1997, p. B1; S. Chandler, "Stumbling Sears Seeks to Launch Second Revolution," *Arizona Republic,* October 17, 1999, p. D1; T. Arango, "Weekly Sales on Plan at Wal-Mart, Below Plan at J. C. Penney," *The Street.Com,* January 29, 2001.

APPLICATIONS: MANAGEMENT IS EVERYONE'S BUSINESS

Applications for the Manager Effective managers understand the factors that influence motivation and use them as levers to energize employees toward organizational goals. These managers know that effective motivation requires much more sophistication than simply kicking workers harder to get more out of them. Instead, long-term effectiveness requires managers to consider the needs and perceptions of workers as well as characteristics of the work environment. The ability to apply motivation theories to the workplace in order to analyze and solve motivation difficulties can help any manager improve performance.

Applications for Managing Teams A critical issue in team motivation is how the team is structured. Are team members all in the same department or function? It is possible that cross-functional teams can make work more varied, interesting, and motivating. Related to this issue is the question of the extent to which the team members are simply a collection of individuals versus being a cohesive team. If the team is given responsibility for a project or area, they can move beyond their individual concerns and be motivated to contribute to the common goal. When a team is truly organized to accomplish a common goal, the work is much more meaningful and energizing.

Applications for Individuals Motivation isn't just something for managers to address in their dealings with employees. After all, motivation is something that happens inside an individual. Others can see the results of our motivation levels, but the force that energizes us is inside ourselves. Who better, then, to understand and manage your motivation than you? As individual performers, we should understand our own needs. What drives us and makes us happy? What kind of work environment energizes us? Once the answers to those questions are answered, you will have a good idea of the type of organizational environment and rewards that would be the best in terms of fit and motivation. It is also helpful to clearly understand the motivation process in the work environment. For instance, a lack of motivation could be due to barriers to performing adequately. In other words, what is influencing your expectancy level and what can you do about it? Similarly, it is important to clarify and manage your personal instrumentalities and valences. There may be strong instrumentalities and great rewards offered in the workplace, but you will need to clarify what they are. It is also possible to help manage your own motivation by making a reward, such as a short trip or vacation, contingent on achieving a goal. The theories of motivation provide a wealth of ideas for managing your own motivation levels.

CONCLUDING THOUGHTS

At the opening of the chapter we considered the performance of the Ursa deepwater crew and posed some critical thinking questions regarding motivation. Now that you have seen the basic approaches to motivation, revisit those introductory questions. First, difficult goals bring challenge and can demand greater effort. If workers understand the importance of a goal, they can commit to achieving it, even though it may be difficult. As described in the section on goal setting, unattainable goals can frustrate employees, but difficult goals can lead workers to stretch their capabilities and rise to the challenge.

Second, workers may not take on difficult goals because they don't accept them or believe that their attainment is that important. Goal acceptance can be related to how the goal is introduced. For example, if a goal is simply unilaterally handed to the workers there is no involvement of the workers in considering the goal. Further, there is little understanding of why the goal is important. In the case of the Ursa deepwater crew, the goal of completing the project four months early was discussed with the crew and they determined that they thought it could be done and committed to the goal. They also all understood that performance of this task was important enough that it would affect their careers. In addition to commitment to the goal, a key aspect of the increased performance potential of the Ursa crew was that they began to see themselves as and to operate as a team whose members complemented and assisted each other, rather than being a collection of separate and independent functions. As with the essence of the cell design discussed in this chapter, the Ursa crew began to act as a team with a common allegiance to the project instead of to their function. The crew members could then think more broadly and act cooperatively in trying to reach a common goal.

The key to motivation involves much more than simply setting goals. In the Ursa crew example, in addition to setting the goal, the crew had to believe that if they put forth the effort, attaining the goal was possible. In expectancy theory terms, the crew had a high expectancy that their effort could translate into adequate performance. In order to achieve the expectancy, the situational constraint of separate functions acting independently had to be overcome. Likewise, the crew members wouldn't have been motivated if they didn't see a link between their performance and rewards that they valued. In expectancy theory terms, attaining the goal had to be seen as instrumental to achieving other outcomes which the crew valued. Beyond these perceptions that the expectancy model identifies as crucial, the work process should be designed so that it is meaningful and motivating. As the Ursa example demonstrates, shifting to a framework in which the team is a unit working toward a common purpose can provide meaning to the work and unleash great motivation potential. As noted in this chapter, other factors, such as needs and equity perceptions, can be crucial determinants of motivation. Effective motivation of people requires broader consideration and skill than simply applying one motivation model to work performance.

SUMMARY

Effort due to external contingencies can be categorized as *extrinsic motivation* while effort due more to internal factors can be categorized as *intrinsic motivation.* The degree to which workers put forth effort in the workplace is often a combination of both types of motivation.

There are several theories, or models, of motivation. The *content theories* focus on the types of needs that can energize people and drive their performance. These include *Maslow's Hierarchy of Needs, Aldefer's ERG Theory, McClelland's Need Theory,* and *Herzberg's Two-Factor Theory.*

The process models of motivation examine how various factors or perceptions influence the level of a worker's motivation. *Goal-setting theory* proposes that people are more motivated when concrete objectives are present. *Reinforcement theory* focuses on the contingencies, or links, between desired behaviors and rewards. *Equity theory* emphasizes the importance of perceptions of fairness in determining motivation. Finally, *expectancy theory* underscores the importance of the belief that you can perform a task and the value you place on the reward which is linked to task performance as critical determinants of motivation.

Motivation can also be influenced by the way in which work is structured. The job design approaches to motivation described in this chapter include *job enlargement, job rotation,* and *job enrichment.* The *job characteristics model* provides an overview of how job design characteristics can influence employee motivation.

DISCUSSION QUESTIONS

1. Use the expectancy model framework to analyze factors which might influence motivation. Specifically, what might influence expectancy levels? Likewise, what might influence instrumentality linkages and valences?

2. Given your answers to question 1, what could be done to improve the levels of expectancy, instrumentality, and valence?

3. Why might someone be motivated to perform poorly or to be a disruptive or negative influence in the workplace? Use the motivation models to analyze the issue. What could be done to improve such a situation?

4. Consider a time when you were highly motivated to do your best at something (such as a particular task, a job, a course). Based on the theories discussed in this chapter, analyze what made you feel that way. Would the same motivation affect you in a different situation?

5. Some people argue that employees are either highly motivated or they are not, and there is little the firm can do to change that predisposition. Do you agree? Why or why not?

6. If you were forced to choose, which of the motivational theories discussed in this chapter do you think is most likely to account for employee motivation? Explain your rationale.

7. On average, U.S. workers spend about 20 percent more time at work and devote less time to leisure in comparison with other industrialized countries such as Japan, Great Britain, France, and Germany. This gap seems to be increasing.[16] How would you explain this phenomenon? Support your answer in light of the material discussed in this chapter.

Does Money Motivate?

Silicon Valley's stock-option culture, in which employees earn stock and can cash in when their company succeeds, made many people rich in return for taking the risk of working for a start-up company. Ten years ago Mark Saul took his MBA from Harvard to a $47,000-a-year job in Silicon Valley. His classmates, going to work on Wall Street and for elite consulting firms, "thought I had a hole in my head," Saul said. Ten years later, after stints at four start-ups, he's a multimillionaire—at 35. Heather Beach took a pay cut four years ago to join software maker Siebel Systems as its office manager; her options are now worth more than $1 million.

Stock options and their potential for huge financial reward have become a major motivator firms can use to get their employees to work harder. Matt Ward's San Francisco consulting firm, WestWard Pay Strategies, designs stock plans for tech companies. Ward says, "Silicon Valley is the economic engine of the world, and options are the fuel."

Stock options became big news in 1986, when some big-name firms first went public, including Oracle, Sun Microsystems, Silicon Graphics, Adobe Systems, Informix—and Microsoft. Already hugely successful, Microsoft didn't need the money from going public. It had to go public so its employees could take advantage of the stock and stock options they'd been given over the company's 11-year lifetime. Options have driven Microsoft's compensation system and finances ever since. In the first three months of 1997, for example, employees realized $32,000 each from their stock options—and another $1 million per employee was outstanding.

Corporate executives in other industries and areas are also starting to use stock options as a motivational tool. Growth companies like Home Depot and Starbucks provide them, as do Warner-Lambert, Citicorp, and Merrill Lynch. General Mills gives options to almost 10,000 employees, and 800 managers can and do choose even bigger options over pay raises. By 2000, there were at least 15 times more employees receiving stock options than a decade earlier.

The idea behind options is very simple: to link employees' and managers' fortunes to those of the firm, for better—and for worse. During the 1990s, millions of employees benefited greatly from stock options. Relatively few options-holders thought about how much risk they were taking. By 2001, an estimated 52 percent of employees' options had lost 10 percent or more of their value, and 11 percent of employees holding stock options realized that they had become worthless. For instance, Xerox employees holding stock saw its value plummet almost 90 percent in less than a year.

Discussion Questions

1. Do you believe that stock options motivate employees to work harder? Should employees be held responsible for factors beyond their control, such as fluctuations in stock prices? Answer this question in light of the motivational theories presented in this chapter.

2. Some people argue that stock options provide an effective mechanism to foster self-leadership within the firm. Do you agree? Why or why not?

3. Which employee needs in Maslow's hierarchy or Alderfer's ERG theory, if any, are met through stock-option plans? Explain your answer.

Sources: Adapted from J. Fox, "The Next Best Thing to Free Money," *Fortune,* July 7, 1997, pp. 52–62; R. Kanetsar and J. Stern, "Get Rich.Com," *Time,* September 27, 1999, pp. 65–78; D. Sparks, "Options Put Grants in a Jam," *Business Week,* January 15, 2001, pp. 68–69; L. Lavelle, "Undermining Pay for Performance," *Business Week,* January 15, 2001, pp. 70–71; G. Smith, "Are High-Tech Stocks Headed for More Turmoil?" *Business Week,* February 5, 2001, p. 50; M. Mandel, "The New Economy's Cruel Math," *Business Week,* February 5, 2001, pp. 42–43.

The Give and Take of Motivation: Give Them What They Need and Take Away the Obstacles

Motivation often involves more than simply pushing someone harder. Motivation can be critically influenced by (1) ability and (2) the presence of situational constraints.

Ability

If a worker doesn't believe that he or she has the ability to adequately perform a task, motivation will surely suffer. An industry consultant points out that the key to workers having the ability they need is training. The emphasis must be on more than formal training sessions. People need the kinds of hands-on experience that gives them the confidence they need to succeed. From employee orientation to learning details about products and services offered by the organization, knowledge can fan the flames of motivation since employees know they have the information they need to perform the job.

Employees should all be familiar with the products or services offered and with the work processes. While this statement may seem obvious, consider the last time you looked for a product or service, only to find that the salesperson really couldn't help. Perhaps there was only one person who had expertise in the area you were looking at (and, of course, that person wasn't available at the time)—or maybe you even found that you knew more than the salesperson. Similarly, not all employees are equally familiar with work processes. For example, some workers may not completely understand or be comfortable with a computerized order process or a phone system.

What happens when there is lack of knowledge of products or services or of work processes? The worker can't have, in expectancy model terms, a high level of expectancy. Even if he or she tries hard, if the individual does not have the knowledge needed, it is impossible to perform well. Poor knowledge can, however, motivate workers to avoid what they don't know. They will try to avoid areas of the operation which make them uncomfortable. These workers are behaving out of fear that their deficiencies will be uncovered. Unfortunately, this doesn't lead to maximum performance. Both workers and the organization are worse off as a result.

Constraints

Motivation to perform can also be influenced by the presence of situational constraints. For example, the red tape of bureaucracy and unnecessary time and steps to get the job done often act as obstacles to job performance. When enough obstacles pile up, workers see that performance is hopelessly constrained by the system. Motivation to improve performance can be quickly choked out by red tape and other obstacles. This problem won't be solved by rousing motivational speeches or by offering training and incentives. Solving this type of motivational problem requires removing the obstacles to performance that are in the work system.

Discussion Questions

1. One way to improve worker knowledge and ability to perform is to institute a "shadow" program. In a shadow program, a less experienced or poorer performing worker is assigned to an effective worker. The shadow program might last a day or a week, depending on the complexity of the job and how quickly the necessary information can be absorbed. The inexperienced or poorer performing worker follows the experienced worker, observing and working alongside him/her. The shadow program gives workers familiarity, experience, and tips on how to effectively perform the job.

a. Assess a shadow program. Do you think it is a good way to eliminate lack of ability as an obstacle to job performance? Why or why not?

b. What other techniques or approaches might work to improve worker knowledge of products/services and work processes? Which do you think would be most cost effective?

2. Pick a job with which you are familiar. Are there unnecessary bureaucratic obstacles that can hinder performance? Describe.

3. What could be done to eliminate or reduce bureaucratic obstacles?

4. Bureaucratic obstacles are just one example of obstacles that weaken motivation. Generate examples of other obstacles. Provide your recommendations for how each of them could be eliminated or reduced.

5. While adequate ability and lack of obstacles are key to maximizing motivation, they certainly aren't the only important factors. What other factors do you think are key to maximizing motivation?

Sources: Adapted from H. Darlington, "People—Your Most Important Asset," *Supply House Times* 45 (2002), pp. 113–114; E. Spragins, "Unmasking Your Motivations," *Fortune Small Business* 12 (2002), pp. 86–87.

Motivating Low-Wage Workers

Mini Maid Inc., a chain of more than 100 franchises in 24 states offering residential maid service, is owned by Leone Ackerly. In the 24 years since she started the firm, Ackerly has developed a philosophy of mutual respect that motivates a low-wage workforce and improves customer service and productivity.

Most Mini Maid employees are women who grew up on welfare, according to Ackerly. They typically are in their twenties and have little education or skills; many have been abused. Ackerly learned that many of her workers felt they were not respected, but when given respect, they changed for the better. Ackerly doesn't care that previous employers looked down on her workers. Even though most of them start working at Mini Maid just for the paychecks, "We ask them to look at us as their partners in a team effort. We tell them, 'this is what we give you; this is what you give us.' Right off the bat, the new employee feels that she is an important part of our company. What happens at this point is that they begin to listen."

Ackerly checks applicants' backgrounds before hiring them—a police record or history of drug use means they won't be offered a job. She presses charges against any maid caught stealing. She expects her employees to be punctual, clean and neat, and polite, and she gives them discipline, standards, and structure.

She has found that fair and honest dealings with employees are returned in kind. If they respect their manager, they do a better job representing the company. Ackerly provides workers with an attendance bonus each pay period for coming to work every day, on time, and in uniform. The extra motivation and reward encourage good work habits. The results go beyond the job. Over the years, Ackerly's workers have learned to apply the concept of mutual respect to their family lives.

Besides respect, low-wage workers need to feel recognized, says consultant Rosalind Jeffries. The self-esteem of a low-wage worker typically is very low, and the pat on the back and expression of thanks go a long way as motivators. Fine Host

Corp., a food service in Greenwich, Connecticut, hires contract workers to bus tables and cook and serve food, and has found that recognition is key to keeping them motivated. Fine Host president and CEO Richard Kerley understands that the employees are the ones who can drive customers away, and he knows that recognition is relatively easy to give. "Though there may be economic restraints on what we pay them, there are no restraints on the recognition we give them." His company gives employee awards and puts their names on company buildings in recognition of good work. Also, the employees receive framed certificates when they complete training courses. Kerley believes companies like his must show people they are appreciated.

Irving Edwards is CEO of All Metro Health Care in Lynbrook, New York, a company that employs home health aides. The company sponsors an award for caregiver of the year and occasionally sponsors essay contests for its workers, complete with prizes. Gifts such as watches and blenders are given to employees when they score high in a quarterly training game. Health aides who are asked to work on holidays know the company will serve them food at the office, too.

ServiceMaster, with more than 20,000 housecleaning and lawn care workers, found one way that its employees would have more take-home pay and earned employee loyalty in return. Many of its employees do not have checking accounts and had to pay a fee to check-cashing services in order to cash their paychecks. ServiceMaster provides a company-sponsored bank account and ATM cards. For $1 a month, employees can have their paychecks deposited every week and they can then withdraw money with ATM cards, bypassing the expensive check-cashing services. For example, Araceli Perez is a ServiceMaster employee in Santa Clara, California, who saves $15 to $20 a month by no longer having to pay check cashers.

Critical Thinking Questions

1. How would you describe the motivational techniques used by these firms in light of the theories discussed in this chapter? Explain.

2. One critic argues that a growing trend is for firms to try to motivate workers the "cheap way"—a pat on the back or an inexpensive certificate—but that these actions make employees more cynical rather than more highly motivated? Do you agree with this assessment? Why or why not?

3. Do you believe that workers can be motivated for the long haul with nonfinancial rewards that appeal to their self-esteem? Why or why not?

Collaborative Learning Exercise

Students form groups of four or five and assume the role of manager for Mini Maid. The task is to outline a short speech to be given to new employees that explains "what we give you, and what you give us." Special attention should be paid to ways to sustain motivation. Post or display completed outlines and compare.

Sources: Adapted from R. Maynard, "How to Motivate Low Wage Workers," *Nation's Business*, May 1997, pp. 35–40; "The Pay Is in the Bank," *Business Week*, January 29, 2001, p. 10.

part five Leadership in Management

The Disappearing Carrot Revisited

INTERNET
EXERCISE 12.1

Cory White was introduced in Management Close-Up 12.a in a discussion of an incentive plan that didn't work out at Idea Integration Corporation.

1. Locate information about Cory White's lawsuit alleging fraud and breach of employment contract. What has happened in regard to his claim?

2. Can you find other claims concerning unfair incentive pay plans involving other organizations? Describe the basics of these claims.

3. Do you think Cory White achieved a fair outcome? Why or why not?

THIRTEEN

Leadership

chapter 13

After reading this chapter, you should be able to:

- Distinguish between management and leadership.
- Recognize how leaders use different power bases to exercise influence.
- Differentiate effective from ineffective leaders.
- Identify and apply the major theories of leadership.
- Identify organizational characteristics that determine the need for and importance of leadership.
- Strengthen the values and ethics of an organization through leadership.

Leadership: Many Paths to Success . . . and Failure

Nissan Motors was near bankruptcy in the 1990s. The company's turnaround has been principally credited to the skillful leadership of Carlos Ghosn.[1] Ghosn was educated as an engineer in France. He worked for Renault, quickly rising to an executive level position. Renault acquired Nissan in the 1990s, but the operations and brands of the two organizations have been kept separate. Ghosn was sent to Japan and charged with turning around Nissan and remaking it into a profitable automaker. How did Ghosn succeed? First, he broke down barriers and brought people together, despite their differences in functional training and in business styles. He brought them together to focus on what would make the company successful. In other words, he had enough courage and focus on achieving success that he jumped in and broke cultural barriers. He interacted with employees and listened to their ideas about how performance could be improved. Ghosn also challenged traditional Japanese business relationships that hindered performance and profitability. Under Ghosn's direction, some plants were closed while others were opened, costs were cut, and automobiles were redesigned.

It took confidence, tenacity, and vision to achieve a successful turnaround. Ghosn saved the company from bankruptcy by taking on the organization's culture as well as Japanese traditions. He involved people, listened to what they had to say, and helped Nissan workers to create a new vision for the company.

It would be impossible for Microsoft Chairman and CEO Bill Gates to stay on top of every issue in every business unit or subsidiary. Instead, his leadership is based on providing strategy and direction so that the firm can move quickly enough to stay in step. Companies that operate from a central authority and ignore the individual are shortsighted, according to Gates, who sees a parallel in NASA's original design of a manned space capsule. The capsule was designed without manual guidance systems under the assumption that the central aviation system would fly the spacecraft, not the astronauts. The U.S. astronauts were veteran combat and test pilots. They soon voiced concerns that the aviation systems would fail. NASA capitulated and added back-up manual controls that would allow the astronauts to fly the space capsule manually. The astronauts were right. Several of the individual astronauts took over and flew the spacecraft when the central aviation system failed. Indeed, the first landing on the moon would have failed if only the central authority, and not the individual, had the power.

Nissan Motors CEO Carlos Ghosn broke cultural barriers t[o] help Nissan turn around successfully.

Being "one of the world's boldest thinkers" wasn't enough for Compaq CEO Eckhard Pfeiffer (pictured above) who was honored as such by the University of Houston in May 1999. A week later, Pfeiffer was fired by Compaq's board. Pfeiffer's stiff leadership style did not mesh with Compaq's culture and the needs of its employees. Former Compaq chief strategist Robert Stearns described the atmosphere at Compaq: "It felt like we were the Olympic dream team of the PC industry, but over a period of about three years, most of the real players were either forced out or left in disgust." When key personnel were hired by competing companies, Pfeiffer reacted defensively, saying, "I delegated authority and responsibility to a point that exceeded some people's ability to fully live up to that expectation."

When Pfeiffer offered executive perks at the company that had always had an egalitarian culture, feelings of inequity quickly grew among the employees, who felt that the rewards reinforced the wrong things. For example, even though reserved parking spaces had never been assigned, Pfeiffer built an executive parking garage. He repeatedly remodeled the executive floor and he restricted access to it. Although Pfeiffer talked constantly about Compaq being number one, he lost touch with employees. The Compaq board reacted to the large but unprofitable company Pfeiffer was in charge of by asking him to resign.

Sources: D. Magee, *Turnaround: How Carlos Ghosn Rescued Nissan* (New York: Harper Business/Harper Collins, 2003); B. Schlender, "e-Business According to Gates," *Fortune,* April 12, 1999, pp. 75–80; D. Kirkpatrick, "Eckhard's Fall, but the PC Rocks On," *Fortune,* May 24, 1999, pp. 153–161; C. Edwards, P. Burrows, and J. Greene, "Microsoft and Intel: Moving In On PC Makers' Turf," *Business Week,* January 15, 2001, p. 41.

1. *What makes someone a good, or even great, leader?*

2. *How much of a difference does leadership make? Can one person really make that much of a difference?*

3. *Is there one leadership type that works best?*

4. *Ethics in organizations has recently become a focal topic. What can leaders do to avoid ethical problems in their organizations?*

There is an increasing realization that leadership can determine a firm's long-term performance prospects. This chapter examines what makes a person an effective leader and how managers can make a difference and bring about improved performance and effective change in organizations. As the opening examples indicate, there are a variety of approaches to leadership. Sometimes they lead to success and sometimes to failure. Leaders can employ different styles and still be successful. Further, a leadership approach that is successful in one situation may not succeed in other situations. In this chapter we will identify the major theories of leadership and explore the models of effective leadership that each of these theories lead to. The intent is to describe the skills needed to lead people to accomplish organizational objectives and help them use their talents effectively.

What Makes an Effective Leader?

Almost everyone agrees that strong leadership is necessary to ensure organizational success. At the same time, there is no simple, universally agreed upon definition of *effective leadership.* Some think that such personal characteristics as charisma, perseverance, and strong communication skills cause people to follow a leader. Thomas Watson of IBM, Alfred Sloan of General Motors, and former presidents Ronald Reagan and John F. Kennedy are seen by many as the embodiment of these traits. Others think of effective leadership as "being at the right place at the right time," where there is a fit between the leader's message and the situation. In the business community, Lee Iaccoca's authoritarian, brassy, and opinionated style contributed to his image as a savior of bankrupt Chrysler Corporation in the early 1980s. After Chrysler became the U.S. auto company that

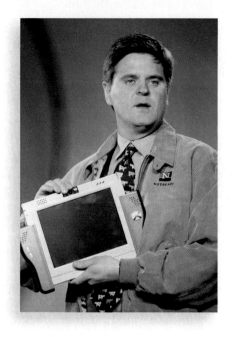

Former AOL Time Warner's CEO Stephen Case built the firm to 17 million subscribers with his "consistent and unwavering" vision.

Assessing Your Leader-Member Exchange

earned the most profit per vehicle, these same attributes were seen by many as egotistical, capricious, and unresponsive to the needs of employees and consumers. Ironically, in 2001 many Chrysler employees, union members, and investors wished Iaccoca would come back from retirement—Chrysler had lost a whopping $1.7 billion during a six-month period and expected to lay off more than 26,000 employees from 2001 through 2003, almost a quarter of its workforce.[2]

One essential aspect of effective leadership is the ability to influence other people. A leader should have vision—ideas or objectives that clarify to others where they should be headed. The vision may be ill conceived, inaccurate, or selfish, or it may identify opportunities that others have failed to see. Although it can take years to assess whether the vision is "good" or "bad," without vision there is little hope of energizing people to act. The leader must "sell" the vision by articulating it in a compelling and persuasive manner that inspires people to overcome obstacles and keep moving toward the ideal future. The leader encourages followers to establish appropriate implementation activities to support the accomplishment of the vision and to induce them to use their personal initiative and talents in achieving the vision. Stephen M. Case, former AOL Time Warner's CEO, noted, "In the end, a vision without the ability to execute is probably a hallucination."[3]

Management versus Leadership

Not all leaders are managers; not all managers are leaders. According to one observer, "Management is about coping with complexity. Good man-

FIGURE 13.1

Management and Leadership
Separate and Combined
Roles

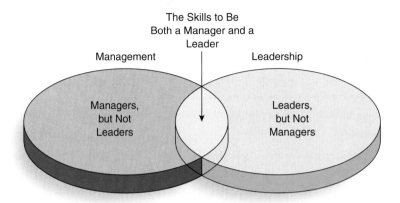

The Skills to Be
Both a Manager and a
Leader

Management | Leadership

Managers,
but Not
Leaders

Leaders,
but Not
Managers

TABLE 13.1

Typical Characteristics of Effective Management and Leadership

MANAGEMENT CHARACTERISTICS	LEADERSHIP CHARACTERISTICS
Control	Inspiration
Implementation	Strategy
Narrow	Breadth
Consistency	Change
Measurement	Establish Direction
Get the Job Done	Changing What the Job Is

agement brings about order and consistency by drawing up formal plans, designing rigid organizational structures, and monitoring results against the plans.[4] In other words, the role of management is in the area of implementation and control. In contrast, leadership involves developing a vision and inspiring people to achieve that vision.[5] Leadership often requires altering the status quo and getting people to commit to the strategy. Management is most likely to be oriented toward maintaining the status quo along with monitoring and measuring to make sure that the right things are getting done in the trenches.

The distinction between leadership and management is more than semantics. It is important to understand the distinction so that the appropriate role can be applied in each situation. While there is a distinction between leadership and management, the two roles are not mutually exclusive. As graphically depicted in Figure 13.1, leadership and management can be overlapping roles. For many people, however, the separate personal characteristics and skills needed for each role mean that they can be effective at either managing or leading, but not both. Table 13.1 summarizes some of the typical contrasts between leadership and

 Do You Have What
It Takes to be a
Leader?

Simon Woodruff, the founder of the Yo Sushi! chain of Japanese restaurants, was honored as Entrepreneur of the Year in 1999. He recently shared the following principles as being keys to his leadership success.

- Act as if you know what you're doing.
- Copy successful people and remember that successful people aren't successful all of the time. You fail a lot in order to succeed.
- When influencing others, the trick isn't to get them to say "yes," just not to say "no."
- Hire revolutionaries.
- Emphasize coaching and mentoring instead of objectives and reviews to drive performance.
- You never get there. Being in the process of working toward your vision is the best it gets.

Source: Adapted from L. Carpenter, "Inspirational Leadership," *Management Services* 46 (2002), pp. 34–36.

management and spells out the skills and characteristics needed for each. Managers who balance both sets of characteristics can enact either role in an organization. Successful business careers and wider choices and opportunities are often the result of having a combination of these characteristics. Sometimes, management skills aren't important while leadership is, and vice versa. Still the capacity to be both a manager and a leader can increase your value and effectiveness in an organization. Taking steps to develop skills in each of these areas can lead to a long-term payoff in your career. Manager's Notes 13.1 presents the principles one CEO identifies as keys to his effective leadership.

While management can be differentiated from leadership, most management positions provide opportunities to engage in leadership. Table 13.2 presents leadership practices that managers can typically engage in.

 Sources of Power

POWER   Managers and leaders can influence other people through their use of power. For a manager, one source of power comes from the position in the organization. Many leaders, however, have the power to influence others more as a function of who they are than because of their positions. For example, people might follow the orders of a manager because he/she has the authority to reward and punish workers. On the other hand, people might follow a leader because they find him/her to be inspirational and charismatic. In a well-known work on power, J. French and B. Raven proposed five ways in which people may be induced to follow a leader (or manager):[6]

TABLE 13.2

Practices Associated with Leadership by Managers

Planning and organizing	Determining long-term objectives and strategies; allocating resources according to priorities; determining how to use personnel and resources efficiently to accomplish a task or project; determining how to improve coordination, productivity, and effectiveness
Problem solving	Identifying work-related problems; analyzing problems in a systematic but timely manner to determine causes and find solutions; acting decisively to implement solutions and resolve crises
Clarifying	Assigning work; providing direction in how to do the work; communicating a clear understanding of job responsibilities, task objectives, priorities, deadlines, and performance expectations
Informing	Disseminating relevant information about decisions, plans, and activities to people who need the information to do their work
Monitoring	Gathering information about work activities and external conditions affecting the work; checking on the progress and quality of the work; evaluating the performance of individuals and the effectiveness of the organizational unit
Motivating	Using influence techniques that appeal to logic or emotion to generate enthusiasm for the work, commitment to task objectives, and compliance with requests for cooperation, resources, or assistance; setting an example of proper behavior
Consulting	Checking with people before making changes that affect them; encouraging participation in decision making; allowing others to influence decisions
Recognizing	Providing praise and recognition for effective performance, significant achievements, and special contributions
Supporting	Acting friendly and considerate; being patient and helpful; showing sympathy and support when someone is upset or anxious
Managing conflict and team building	Facilitating the constructive resolution of conflict; encouraging cooperation, teamwork, and identification with the organizational unit
Networking	Socializing informally; developing contacts with people outside of the immediate work unit who are a source of information and support; maintaining contacts through periodic visits, telephone calls, correspondence, and attendance at meetings and social events
Delegating	Allowing subordinates to have substantial responsibility and discretion in carrying out work activities; giving them authority to make important decisions
Developing and mentoring	Providing coaching and career counseling; doing things to facilitate a subordinate's skill acquisition and career advancement
Rewarding	Providing tangible rewards such as a pay increase or promotion for effective performance and demonstrated competence by a subordinates

Source: From Garry Yukl and David Van Fleet, "Theory and Research on Leadership in Organizations," *Handbook of Industrial and Organizational Psychology,* 1992, Vol. 3, pp. 149–197, L. M. Hough and M. D. Dunnette (eds.). Reprinted with permission of the authors.

1. **Coercive power** is based on fear that the leader/manager may cause people harm unless they support him or her. Intimidation and anxiety may induce people to go along with the actions, attitudes, or directives of a superior even if they disagree. Even if a leader does not use overt threats, the possibility of retaliation such as a poor recommendation to a prospective employer may induce compliance.

2. **Reward power** means that the leader/manager can provide something that other people value so that they trade their support for the rewards. Rewards may be financial (such as promotion with higher pay) or psychological (such as greater status from being perceived as close to the leader).

coercive power

Power based on the fear that the leader may cause people harm unless they support him or her.

reward power

Power derived from the belief that the leader can provide something that other people value so that they trade their support for the rewards.

legitimate power

The legal or formal authority to make decisions subject to certain constraints.

expert power

Power deriving from the leader's valued knowledge or skills, which other people recognize as worthy of respect.

referent power

Power derived from the satisfaction people receive from identifying themselves with the leader.

3. **Legitimate power** comes from the legal or formal authority to make decisions subject to certain constraints. For instance, in most universities the chair of an academic department has the legitimate power to write an annual evaluation of each faculty member to be used to allocate merit pay, assign teaching schedules, and establish differential teaching loads. Few department chairs have the legitimate power to hire or terminate full-time faculty without approval from others.

4. **Expert power** derives from the leader's/manager's unique knowledge or skills, which other people recognize as worthy of respect.

5. **Referent power** is based on the satisfaction people receive from identifying themselves with the leader/manager. They are willing to grant power to the leader because they see him or her as a role model.

These power bases are not independent. Employees may comply with the wishes of a person they admire (referent power) who is a division head (legitimate power) with formal authority to promote (reward power) or terminate employees (coercive power) and who has expertise about a particular product line (expert power). Leaders typically prefer to emphasize some of these sources of power more than others. For instance, some supervisors motivate subordinates by serving as an example (referent power) even if they have the authority to induce compliance through punishment (coercive power) or financial incentives (reward power).

Leadership Theories

Over the years there have been many attempts to understand what makes a leader effective. Can leadership skills be learned or are people just "born" with them? These and other questions have led to the development of a variety of leadership theories. There is probably not one theory that is the best and most accurate. Still, much can be learned about being an effective leader from an understanding of all of the theories. These leadership theories can be roughly divided into the categories of (1) person, (2) situation, (3) dispersed, and (4) exchange. Theories in the person category note the characteristics and behaviors of effective leaders. Situational theories emphasize that what makes for effective leadership depends on the situation. Leadership theories in the dispersed category suggest that leadership comes from sources other than an individual leader. Finally, the exchange theories view leadership from the perspective of relationships with others. Examples of leadership theories in each of these categories appear next.

Person-Based Theories

TRAIT THEORY   What sets Napoleon Bonaparte, Franklin Delano Roosevelt, Mohandas Gandhi, Cesar Chavez, and Nelson Mandela apart from the crowd? When we think about leaders, certain traits or personal characteristics may come to mind, such as self-confidence, determination, and communication skills. Researchers have tried to create a personality profile or set of characteristics that distinguishes leaders from nonleaders. It has become clear, however, that personality traits do not tell the whole story of what makes for an effective leader. Certainly, factors such as the needs of followers, cultural norms, prior group history, and other situational variables come into play. Nevertheless, cumulative research suggests that certain traits, most of which can be learned, increase the likelihood of being an effective leader, although they don't guarantee it. These include ambition; energy; the motivation or desire to lead; intelligence; integrity, or high correspondence between actions and words; a "can-do attitude," or self-confidence; the ability to grasp and interpret large amounts of information; and the flexibility to adapt to the needs and goals of others.[7]

The trait approach never resulted in a list of personality characteristics present in all effective leaders. This led to a loss of popularity of the trait approach to leadership in the 1960s. There has recently, however, been more attention directed at the importance of the personal characteristics of leaders. A major survey of managers in the 1980s revealed that 87 percent identified honesty as a trait associated with effective leadership.[8] Honesty was a trait leaders admired more than competence, being inspirational, and intelligence. The importance of honesty has been underscored by the recent ethical scandals involving the top leadership of organizations such as Enron and WorldCom. Management Close-Up 13.a presents a summary of some of the recent corporate ethical scandals that have changed the importance that many people place on integrity in leadership.

The promise of the trait approach is to provide a profile of the effective leader. This profile can then serve as a map to people who aspire to be leaders and guide their efforts to be effective in the leadership role. However, traits are usually considered fairly fixed characteristics of people that may be difficult to learn or change. On the other hand, behaviors are more under the direct control of people and can be more easily changed than traits. Thus, leadership theorists began turning their attention from inferring internal and unseen traits to observable leader behaviors. We next consider the behaviorally based approach to leadership.

Ethical Poverty at the Top: High Profile Cases

THEME: ETHICS   Executives being led away in handcuffs. CEOs taking the fifth amendment when being questioned by U.S. senators. These are not images that promote faith in business leaders. Unfortunately, incidents involving the lack of integrity, unethical behaviors, and corruption of business leaders have become all too common. Here are summaries of some recent ethical scandals.

- Enron, once a giant in the energy industry, filed for bankruptcy at the end of 2001. That year, Kenneth Lay, then CEO of Enron, received $152.7 million in payments and stock. The company collapsed after a $1 billion loss. Enron's management and accounting leaders had inflated profit numbers by $600 million and hidden debts and exaggerated revenues in order to continue to attract investors. This allowed Lay and other top executives to continue to receive and sell the lucrative Enron stock. Lay's compensation in the year that the company collapsed was 11,000 times the amount of severance paid to the approximately 4,000 workers who were laid off as a result of the collapse. Lay invoked the fifth amendment and declined to answer questions in a congressional hearing regarding improprieties at Enron. He and other former Enron executives are facing a variety of fraud charges. The court cases are still continuing.

Also, the Arthur Anderson accounting firm was convicted in a Texas court in June 2002 for obstruction of justice in the Enron case. Enron was a client of Arthur Anderson and paid approximately $27 million per year in consulting fees and a similar amount in auditing fees. Arthur Anderson's leaders claimed that Enron withheld vital information, but was still found guilty of obstruction for shredding Enron documents.

- Bernard Ebbers was the CEO of WorldCom, a telecommunications firm. Ebbers borrowed $408 million from the company, but the company improperly accounted for $9 billion and was forced into bankruptcy. Ebbers had pledged company stock as collateral, but the shares became worthless after the collapse of the company. Investors and former workers with little money in their retirement funds were left to compare their financial outcomes with that of Ebbers.

- John J. Rigas was the CEO of Adelphia Communications until his indictment for stealing billions from the organization. Rigas is suspected of conspiring with four other executives to take money from the company.

Sources: J. Biskupic, "Why It's Tough to Indict CEOs," *USA Today,* July 24, 2002, pp. A1, A2; B. Foss, "Corporate Image: Greed, Deceit, Handcuffs," *The Arizona Republic,* December 30, 2002, p. D4.

In May 2002, members of Enron's board of directors were questioned by the U.S. Senate. Their CEO at the time, Kenneth Lay, chose to invoke the fifth amendment.

FIGURE 13.2

Initiating Structure by Consideration Matrix

BEHAVIORAL THEORIES Behavioral theories attempt to identify what good leaders do. Broadly speaking, these theories either map out the behavioral dimensions of leadership or describe leadership styles.

Behavioral Dimensions Two classic studies were conducted at Ohio State University and the University of Michigan in the 1940s and 1950s. The studies revealed two dimensions that summarize how subordinates describe most leadership behaviors.[9] The first dimension is the concern that the leader has for the feelings, needs, personal interest, problems, and well-being of followers. This dimension was called **consideration** at Ohio State and *employee-oriented behaviors* at the University of Michigan. The second dimension, which refers to activities designed to accomplish group goals, including organizing tasks, assigning responsibilities, and establishing performance standards, was labeled **initiating structure** at Ohio State and *production-oriented behaviors* at the University of Michigan. The consideration and initiating structure dimensions are often portrayed using a simple 2×2 matrix, as presented in Figure 13.2.

Using these two dimensions, researchers R. R. Blake and J. S. Mouton developed a tool to classify managers based on leadership behaviors in a model called the **managerial grid**.[10] As illustrated in Figure 13.3, the vertical axis of the managerial grid is a scale of 1 to 9 for concern for people, and the horizontal axis is a scale of 1 to 9 for production. Presumably, the "ideal" behaviors fall in the 9,9 quadrant. Leaders who are high on concern for production and high on concern for people tend to achieve optimal subordinate performance and satisfaction. Simply stated, the most effective managers relate well to their followers and can efficiently delineate what needs to be done. The managerial grid is used by practitioners and management trainers because of its simplicity and intuitive appeal.

consideration

The behavioral dimensions of leadership involving the concern that the leader has for the feelings, needs, personal interest, problems, and well-being of followers; also called employee-oriented behaviors.

initiating structure

The behavioral dimension of leadership that refers to activities designed to accomplish group goals, including organizing tasks, assigning responsibilities, and establishing performance standards; also called production-oriented behaviors.

managerial grid

A system of classifying managers based on leadership behaviors.

FIGURE 13.3

The Managerial (Leadership) Grid

Source: From *Grid Solutions*, by Robert R. Blake and Anne Adams McCanse (formerly *The Managerial Grid Figure* by Robert R. Blake and Jane S. Mouton), Houston: Gulf Publishing Company, p. 29. Copyright 1991 by Scientific Methods, Inc. Reproduced by permission of Grid International, Inc.

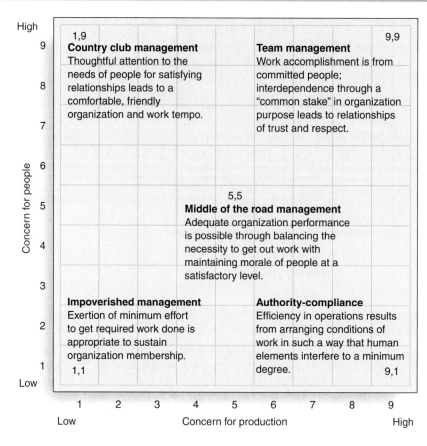

Leadership Style   A classic study defined two behavioral leadership styles or decision-making approaches: the autocratic style and the democratic style.[11] Leaders using the *autocratic* style make decisions on their own and announce them as a done deal. A *democratic* leader actively tries to solicit the input of subordinates, often requiring consensus or a majority vote before making a final decision. This early study suggested that a democratic style resulted in higher subordinate satisfaction with the leader but that an autocratic approach resulted in somewhat higher performance. The performance advantage associated with an autocratic style tends to disappear when the leader is not present to monitor subordinates. A *laissez-faire* style, in which a leader avoids making decisions, results in both low satisfaction and low performance.

Situational Theories

Subsequent research on leadership questioned the "one best way" approach suggested by the behavioral theories. A situational, or "it depends," approach began to replace the simplistic view that a particular set of behaviors or decision-making style separates good from bad leaders. The key point of the situational approach is that leadership success depends on the fit between the leader's behavior and decision-making style and the requirements of the situation. One author illustrated how leadership effectiveness was dependent on the situation as follows:

> *Bob Knight, the men's head basketball coach at Indiana University, consistently uses an intense, task-oriented leadership style that intimidates players, officials, the media, and university administrators. But his style works with the Indiana teams he recruits. Knight has one of the most impressive win–loss records of any active major college basketball coach. But would this same style work if Bob Knight was counsel-general of the United Nations or project manager for a group of Ph.D. software designers at Microsoft? Probably not![12]*

Bob Knight's leadership style ultimately resulted in his being asked to resign by the university in 2000 because of numerous complaints about his behavior, indicating that the fit between him and the university was no longer acceptable.

Several theorists have attempted to isolate critical situational factors that affect leadership effectiveness. The resulting theories include Fiedler's contingency model and the path–goal model.

FIEDLER'S CONTINGENCY MODEL According to Fiedler, three aspects of a situation determine which leader behavior or style is most suitable:[13]

- *Leader–member relations:* The extent to which the leader is well liked and enjoys the trust, support, and respect of subordinates.

- *Task structure:* The extent to which the leader delineates which "what, how, and why" work tasks are performed.

- *Position power:* The degree to which the leader has the authority to reward and punish subordinates.

 Fiedler's Contingency Model

According to Fiedler, the better the leader–member relations, the more highly structured the job, and the stronger the position power, the more control or influence a leader enjoys.

Fiedler identified two major leadership styles. **Task-oriented leadership** emphasizes work accomplishments and performance results; **relationship-oriented leadership** focuses on maintaining good interpersonal relationships. Fiedler contends that task-oriented leaders are more effective in situations that are either highly favorable or highly unfavorable. The most favorable situations are categories I, II, and III in Figure 13.4 where at least two of the three determinants noted above are positive, and the most unfavorable situation is category VIII, where all three determinants are negative. For situations in the middle categories, which are of moderate difficulty, a relationship-oriented leader performs better.

task-oriented leadership

A leadership style that emphasizes work accomplishments and performance results.

relationship-oriented leadership

A leadership style that focuses on maintaining good interpersonal relationships.

FIGURE 13.4

Fiedler's Contingency Model of Leadership

Source: From *Organizational Behavior,* 7th ed., by Robbins. Copyright © 1996. Reprinted by permission of Pearson Education, Inc., Upper Saddle River, NJ.

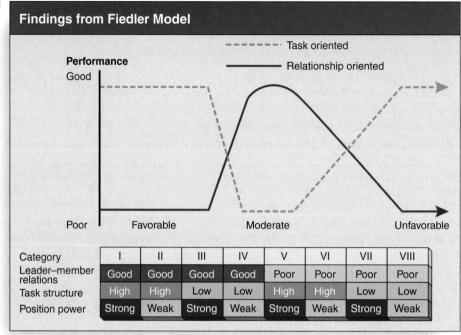

As a whole, there is some empirical evidence for this model.[14] However, the implication that a leader must be assigned to a situation that suits his or her style makes the model somewhat problematic, because it implies that leaders cannot change their styles. The emphasis on a fit between the leader and the situation makes it difficult to translate the theory into practice. Work environments change often, and there is no easy way to assess on an ongoing basis how good the leader–member relations are, how structured the task is, and how much position power the leader actually enjoys.

Despite these warnings, this contingency model provides a useful analytical tool to better understand when and why particular leadership styles appear to be most effective. Management Close-Up 13.b addresses the contrast in leadership styles and their effectiveness within the same company as the favorableness of the situation changes.

PATH–GOAL THEORY Another contingency model of leadership that has gained wide acceptance and enjoys substantial empirical support was developed by Robert House. **Path–goal theory** focuses on how leaders influence subordinate perceptions of work goals and paths to achieve those goals.[15] The crux of the theory is that it is the leader's job to help followers achieve their goals and to influence followers to ensure that their goals are consistent with the overall objectives of the group or organization.

path–goal theory

A contingency model of leadership that focuses on how leaders influence subordinates' perceptions of work goals and the path to achieve those goals.

PeopleSoft People Styles

THEME: DEALING WITH CHANGE The rise and fall of corporate software maker PeopleSoft Inc. is a tale of two personalities. David A. Duffield, the founder and chief executive for 11 years, built a friendly culture for employees and customers alike that was almost legendary. At the company's open and airy Pleasanton, California, offices, Duffield wore sweaters, used "DAD" as his e-mail signature (note that this happens to be his initials), and sponsored an employee rock band called the Raving Daves. Customers were asked for their opinions on features that forthcoming PeopleSoft products should have. Duffield's personable style helped make PeopleSoft a darling of Wall Street.

In 1999, however, the market for giant corporate software packages that could handle everything from employee benefits to tracking inventory fell apart. Although Duffield had created a friendly culture and was very well liked, he wasn't able to manage PeopleSoft through this downturn in its market. Duffield remains as chairman of PeopleSoft, but a different leadership style was needed.

Craig A. Conway, PeopleSoft CEO since September 1999, is the antithesis of touchy-feely. He is using his tough-guy style to keep PeopleSoft viable and see it through. Nicknamed the Clint Eastwood of the industry, Conway had free rein to overhaul the company, and overhaul he did. Half of PeopleSoft's top 12 executives left the company within six months of Conway's appointment. Customers who were late in paying were sent reminder notices, even though they had never been asked to pay their bills on time under Duffield. Conway cringes at referring to employees as "people people."

Says Conway: "I wanted to bring some discipline to the organization." He's been successful. One observer commented, "Conway may not have a cuddly personality, but he gets results." After the company's long slump, revenues and profits rose 116 percent over the 18 months of his leadership.

Source: J. Kerstetter, "PeopleSoft's Hard Guy," *Business Week*, January 15, 2001, pp. 76–79.

The theory specifies four leadership behaviors, as shown in Figure 13.5. A *directive leader* establishes expectations for followers, determines targets to attain, organizes tasks, sets deadlines and schedules, and closely monitors progress. These behaviors are similar to the initiating structure and the autocratic styles discussed earlier. For instance, Thomas M. Siebel is the brash CEO of Siebel Systems Inc., a Silicon Valley maker of software used to manage customer relations. Siebel is almost obsessed with inspecting everything to make sure it is done right. His philosophy is, "No software gets written until customers weigh in. Outside consultants routinely poll clients on their satisfaction, and [employee] compensation is heavily based on those reports." Siebel's direct approach is unusual for Silicon Valley, but his firm has a third of the market for customer-management software, a market Siebel shares with Oracle.[16]

A *supportive leader* is warm and friendly and shows concern about the problems and needs of subordinates. This is the same as consideration. A *participative leader* actively elicits subordinate input and opinions and uses them when making decisions that affect the group. This is similar to a democratic leadership style. A classic example of a highly successful participative leader was William Hewlett, the Silicon Valley and computer-age pioneer who cofounded Hewlett-Packard in a garage in

 Path-Goal Theory

David Packard (left) and William Hewlett, co-founders of Hewlett-Packard, in an early photo.

FIGURE 13.5

The Path–Goal Framework

Source: From *Management of Organizations,* by P. M. Wright and R. A. Noe. Copyright © 1996 The McGraw-Hill Companies, Inc. Reprinted with permission.

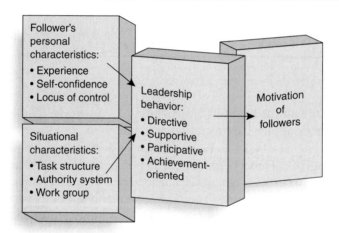

1938. Shortly before his death in 2001 at age 87, he said that he was proudest of his personal relationship and camaraderie with employees. One observer recalled, "Despite his position and wealth, Hewlett delighted in working side-by-side with employees or playing penny-ante poker with them."[17]

An *achievement-oriented leader* is primarily concerned with motivating people by setting challenging goals, coaching subordinates to perform at the highest level, and rewarding those who meet or exceed their targets. House believes that leaders are flexible enough to exhibit all four of these behaviors and that their effectiveness depends on their ability to use the behavior appropriate to the particular circumstances.

Path–goal theory proposes two key factors that determine which leadership behaviors are most appropriate. The first, the **situational context,** refers to factors outside the control of the subordinate, such as the tasks defining the job, the formal authority system of the organization, and the work group. The second, the personal characteristics of the follower, are the attributes of the subordinate such as experience and perceived ability or self-confidence. Effectiveness is defined in terms of the performance of subordinates and the extent to which followers perceive a leader's behavior as increasing their present or future satisfaction. A leader's behavior is more effective if it is congruent with the situation and the personal characteristics of subordinates.

situational context

The factors that are outside the control of the subordinate such as the tasks defining the job, the formal authority system of the organization, and the work group.

Many propositions have been derived from this theory and have been supported empirically. Based on personal characteristics of followers, the following leadership styles are effective:

- Subordinates who are highly authoritarian prefer a directive leadership style because to them this commands respect.

- Subordinates who believe they control their own destinies are more satisfied with a participative leadership style because it gives them more opportunity to influence decisions that affect their lives. Those who believe their destiny is in the hands of others prefer a more directive style.

- Supportive and participative leaders improve satisfaction and enhance group performance of subordinates with high perceived ability who don't wish to be told what to do and those with considerable experience who are capable of offering valuable input.

Based on fit with the situational context, the effective leadership styles are as follows:

- Directive leadership improves followers' satisfaction when the tasks are ambiguous and stressful because it helps clarify the situation.

- Supportive leadership increases subordinate satisfaction when the tasks are clearly structured and laid out. Employees see directive leader behavior as patronizing or insulting when they already understand what needs to get done.

- Achievement-oriented leadership increases subordinates' satisfaction and group productivity when the organization can provide rewards contingent on the performance of the group.

The situational contingency theories described in this section suggest that the leader's style that will be most effective depends on the situation. Thus, situational factors determine the effectiveness of a leader's actions. The situational and contingency theories assume that the source of leadership is the leader. Other approaches emphasize sources of leadership besides the leader. These approaches to leadership are labeled "dispersed" and are considered next.

Dispersed Theories

Leadership can sometimes come from sources other than the leader of the organization, which is the main point of the dispersed approach. Leadership can come from various aspects of the system in an organization, or it can come from the workers themselves. These two possibilities are the focus of the substitute leadership and self-leadership theories, respectively.

SUBSTITUTE LEADERSHIP Substitute leadership theory might be considered the opposite of the person-based approach to leadership. The person-based approach emphasizes the importance of a leader's traits and behavioral style. The substitute leadership theory downplays the importance of the leader and emphasizes characteristics of the situation. Substitute leadership theory is based on the idea that, at least in some situations, leadership is not only ineffective, it is irrelevant. People tend to romanticize leadership and attribute more importance to leaders than may actually be merited.[18] Substitute leadership theory takes the contrary perspective and emphasizes the importance of the situation.

Substitute leadership theory attempts to identify workplace characteristics that can substitute for leadership or neutralize efforts made by a leader. For example, if workers are highly trained and professional, a leader will likely not be needed or have that much impact. In that situation, the workers know what needs to be done and will follow through and perform their function. On the negative side, an inflexible organizational culture may operate to neutralize any attempts to bring change to the organization.

Substitute leadership theory reminds us of the importance of situational factors. Depending on the situation, leaders may make less difference than they think they might. Further, wise leaders can capitalize on substitutes for leadership, putting in place, for example, a highly trained and cohesive workforce so that consistent leader presence and direction isn't needed. However, can putting in place even extensive system upgrades ever totally substitute for effective leadership? Management Close-Up 13.c looks at business ethics and takes the position that it can be both the person and the system that are important for performance. Skill Builder 13.1 also considers ethical performance and addresses whether situational factors can really replace leadership.

SELF-LEADERSHIP **Self-leadership** stresses the individual responsibility of employees to develop their own work priorities aligned with organizational goals. The manager is a facilitator who enhances the self-leadership capabilities of subordinates, encouraging them to develop self-control skills. As summarized in Table 13.3, this leadership approach

self-leadership

Leadership that stresses the individual responsibility of employees to develop their own work priorities aligned with organizational goals; the manager is a facilitator who enhances the self-leadership capabilities of subordinates, encouraging them to develop self-control skills.

Business Ethics: It Takes Leadership and a System

THEME: ETHICS Several recent corporate scandals have led to distrust of business and heightened the perception that business people are crooks. How can an organization assure that honesty and integrity permeate its people and operations? It is now more important than ever that organizations demonstrate to investors and customers that integrity and honesty are their top priorities. The following are examples of organizations that are noted for their strong ethics with leaders who promote and maintain the company's ethical reputation.

Set the Example

Ethical standards have to be established and implemented from the top. Gary Kelly, CEO of Southwest Airlines, takes the position that integrity is revealed in how you deal with customers, vendors, buyers, and employees. In other words, what really matters are the behaviors of leaders, not what they say in speeches and policies. As a leader, if your behavior indicates lack of ethical standards or you condone unethical behavior, you cause irreparable damage to your credibility. Interestingly, Southwest Airlines does not rely on manuals containing layers of policies and procedures to instill and maintain integrity. They rely on a strong culture and trust employees to do the right thing.

Establish a System

Leadership is important for setting the example of high ethical standards. At the same time, simply setting a good example isn't necessarily sufficient to convey the importance of ethical conduct and to maintain it. FedEx uses multiple media of communication such as e-mail, fax, and voice mail, to emphasize integrity. Gene Bastedo, vice president of internal audit at FedEx, also states that the company emphasizes that it will not tolerate impropriety of any kind. If there is any wrongdoing, swift action is taken. Unethical or inappropriate behavior is not tolerated regardless of the dollars involved. Two employees at FedEx recently learned that the company is serious about its strong stance on ethics. The individuals were found to be embezzling and were promptly fired and turned over to authorities for prosecution.

Darden Restaurants Inc., the largest casual dining restaurant in the United States, provides written rules for how employees should conduct themselves. The chain includes over 1,200 restaurants and has developed specific guidelines ranging from acceptance of gifts to dealing with financial information.

Microchip Technology Inc. is also pursuing a written code of conduct for its employees. It is a young, fast-growth company that has relied on a brief statement of ethics that was a part of its original guiding principles. However, the organization is finding that it needs more specifics and clarification of how these ethical values apply to everyday activities. The company is now working on developing a written code of conduct.

In sum, driving ethics through an organization requires leadership that exemplifies those standards. Setting an example is not enough. Clear specification of values and expected conduct can take the form of various communications and policy and procedure statements. These systems can act as leadership substitutes to help develop and maintain the desired ethical performance of the organization.

Source: D. Blank, "A Matter of Ethics: In Organizations Where Honesty and Integrity Rule, It Is Easy for Employees to Resist the Many Temptations Today's Business World Offers," *Internal Auditor* 60 (2003), pp. 26+.

---

is far more decentralized than traditional leadership, which focuses on the supervisor as the pivotal figure.

There are two important mechanisms to foster self-leadership within the firm. The first is **empowerment,** or the process of transferring control of individual work behavior from the supervisor to the employee. Employees must be provided with skills, tools, support, and information

empowerment

The process of transferring control of individual work behavior from the supervisor to the employee.

LEADERSHIP AND ETHICAL EXCELLENCE: OBEDIENCE OR INTERNALIZED VALUES?

The ethical scandals that rocked corporate America, including the high-profile Enron and WorldCom cases (see Management Close-Up 13.a), resulted in a tightening of accounting standards and greater governmental oversight of corporate finances. The purpose for these additional rules and controls is to assure that organizations function ethically. Such controls and reporting requirements can serve as substitutes for leadership and may provide the structure and incentives needed to assure ethical behavior. Controls, policies, and procedures are tools that can help guide ethical conduct, but like all tools, they have limits.

Guidelines cannot make us honest nor can they provide us with integrity. They can lay out a path to follow. They can also be ignored, circumvented, or undermined. Even if there is no unethical intent, what happens when a worker confronts a situation that isn't exactly covered by the guidelines? What will a worker do when there may be great temptation and possibility of personal gain and no one is observing? Harry Jansen Kraemer, CEO of Baxter International Inc., a global health care company, points out that workers in every corner of the world make ethical decisions in the course of conducting business. Kraemer notes that you simply cannot be everywhere looking over every employee's shoulder. The only way to be sure that workers try to make the right decisions and take the right actions is to know that each of them has the right values. It is not enough to provide external rules to be followed. The only way to be sure about ethical conduct is to know that the workers share the same values that guide conduct.

Discussion Questions

1. Do you think guidelines are sufficient to assure ethical conduct in a business. Why or why not?

2. As a business leader, which would you rather have, ethical conduct due to obedience or due to internalized values? Why?

3. How can a leader instill the desired values in the workplace? That is, how could culture based on those values be developed?

4. Consider the following matrix.

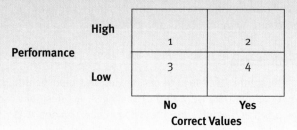

Assume that there are workers in each of these four cells. What do you think should be done about workers who perform their jobs but really don't embrace the ethical values of the organization (cell 1)? What do you think should be done about workers who aren't performing so well, but have the right values (cell 4)? Defend your answers.

Research Questions

1. Identify organizations that have suffered some sort of ethical scandal. Does it appear that the ethical problems are due to a lack of guidelines or due to a lack of shared ethical values?

2. Identify organizations that are noted for their high level of ethical conduct. What appears to most account for their positive ethical performance, the use of specific guidelines or the development of common ethical values?

3. How would you recommend an organization go about improving its ethical performance? Specifically, what steps should be taken to improve and maintain ethical conduct of its employees?

Source: H. M. J. Kraemer, "Doing the Right Thing: Values-Based Leadership Is Not an Oxymoron in Corporate America," *Vital Speeches of the Day* 69 (2003), p. 243+.

TABLE 13.3

Characteristics of Traditional and Self-Managing Behaviors

TRADITIONAL LEADER BEHAVIORS	SELF-MANAGING LEADER BEHAVIORS
Organization. Structures own and subordinates' work	Encourages self-reward
Domination. Restricts or limits the discretion of individuals or groups	Encourages self-observation
Production. Sets standards for task performance	Encourages self-goal setting
Recognition. Expresses approval or disapproval of behavior	Encourages self-criticism
Integration. Promotes group cohesion and reduces group conflict	Encourages self-rehearsal
Communication. Provides, seeks, and exchanges information with group members	Acts as a role model by exhibiting appropriate behavior Fosters the development of a culture that nourishes and supports self-leadership

Source: From J. M. Ivancevich, P. Lorenzi, S. J. Skinner, and P. B. Crosby, *Management: Quality and Competitiveness,* McGraw-Hill/Irwin, 1997. Reprinted with permission of J. M. Ivancevich.

so that authority and responsibility can be successfully delegated to them. The second key vehicle is **role modeling,** whereby managers serve as examples of the behaviors they would like employees to emulate. Role modeling is more likely to be effective if workers can see a link between adopting the desired behaviors and positive outcomes, such as higher pay, a promotion, and public recognition.

The dispersed approaches to leadership emphasize leadership that comes from sources other than the leader. Other perspectives emphasize that leadership is an interaction and the source of leadership comes from the relationships that are developed between a leader and his/her workers. We next turn to the exchange approach to leadership.

Exchange Theories

The exchange perspective on leadership emphasizes the importance of the relationship between a leader and employees. It is the exchange, the nature of the relationship, that underlies a leader's ability to direct and be effective. The following are some of the major leadership theories that fit in the exchange theory category.

TRANSACTIONAL AND TRANSFORMATIONAL LEADERSHIP Most classical leadership theories are concerned with **transactional leaders,** who use legitimate, coercive, or reward powers to elicit obedience. Transactional leaders do not generate passion and excitement, and they do not empower or inspire individuals to transcend their own self-interest for the good of the organization. **Transformational leaders,** on the other hand,

> **role modeling**
>
> The leadership mechanism in which managers serve as examples of the behaviors they would like employees to emulate.

> **transactional leaders**
>
> Leaders who use legitimate, coercive, or reward powers to elicit obedience and attempt to instill in followers the ability to question standard modes of operation.

> **transformational leaders**
>
> Leaders who revitalize organizations by instilling in followers the ability to question standard modes of operation.

TABLE 13.4

Characteristics of Transactional and Transformational Leaders

TRANSACTIONAL LEADER	TRANSFORMATIONAL LEADER
Contingent reward. Contracts exchange of rewards for effort, promises rewards for good performance, recognizes accomplishments	*Charisma.* Provides vision and sense of mission, instills pride, gains respect and trust
Management by exception (active). Watches and searches for deviations from rules and standards, takes corrective action	*Inspiration.* Communicates high expectations, uses symbols to focus efforts, expresses important purposes in simple ways
Management by exception (passive). Intervenes only if standards are not met	*Intellectual stimulation.* Promotes intelligence, rationality, and careful problem solving
Laissez-faire. Abdicates responsibilities, avoids making decisions	*Individualized consideration.* Gives personal attention, treats each employee individually, coaches, advises

Source: Reprinted from *Organizational Dynamics,* Winter 1990, B. M. Bass et al., "Transactional to Transformational Leadership: Learning to Share the Vision," p. 22. Copyright © 1990, with permission from Elsevier Science.

attempt to instill in followers the ability to question standard modes of operation. They are capable of revitalizing organizations by tapping people's reservoir of creativity. While transformational leaders are charismatic, they also inspire people, provide them with intellectual stimulation, and give followers individualized consideration. Table 13.4 compares the characteristics of transactional and transformational leaders. Skills for Managing 13.2 presents an example of how a well-known leader was able to reframe issues and enact change in her organization.

In addition to articulating a vision and communicating that vision to subordinates, transformational leaders build trust by being dependable, consistent, and persevering. "They do not feel self-important or complacent: rather, they recognize their personal strength, compensate for their weaknesses, nurture their skills and continually develop their talents, and know how to learn from failure. They strive for success rather than merely trying to avoid failure."[19] Overall, transformational leadership is more likely than transactional leadership to reduce turnover rates, increase productivity, and improve employee satisfaction.[20]

Recent work indicates that transformational leadership has a positive impact on performance by lowering frustration and increasing optimism.[21] In other words, it is not characteristics of transformational leaders, per se, that have a direct influence on performance in an organization. Rather, it is the influence on levels of worker frustration and optimism that, in turn, leads to improved performance.

TRANSFORMATION: IT'S HOW YOU FRAME THE CHANGE

Carly Fiorina joined Hewlett-Packard Company in 1999. Now she is one of the best known female CEOs in the United States. One of the most difficult and publicized events in her tenure as CEO at H-P involved a merger with Compaq Computer Corporation. Fiorina was convinced of the merits of the merger but needed the backing of the board. If she didn't get it, her position as leader might be seriously eroded. While some board members were supportive of the merger, others were neutral or wary. How did she convince them? Fiorina explained the strategy of H-P to the directors and presented evidence of how the merger made economic sense. In the end, however, some directors were not persuaded. A dinner followed Fiorina's presentation and she discovered that a few of the board members were still not convinced. So, if strategic plans, facts, and even a fancy meal wouldn't sway the board members, what did?

After the dinner, Fiorina handed each director a single sheet of paper. Each sheet had the following three questions on it:

1. Do you think the information-technology industry needs to consolidate and, if so, is it better to be a consolidator or a consolidatee?

2. How important is it to our strategic goals to be number 1 or number 2 in our chief product categories?

3. Can we achieve our strategic goals without something drastic?

With a single sheet of paper and three questions, Carly Fiorina had reframed the issue. She had taken the merger decision out of the domain of politics, power struggles, and personality clashes and stated the decision as a strategic choice. Cast this way, the choice was obvious. Anyone aligned with H-P would prefer to see it as a consolidator, a market leader, and needing to do something to stay competitive. Fiorina didn't try to convince or cajole. She framed the decision as a strategic issue and the merger went forward.

Source: Adapted from G. Anders, "Carly Fiorina, Up Close—How Shrewd Strategic Moves in Grueling Proxy Battle Let H-P Chief Take Control," *Wall Street Journal,* Eastern Edition, January 13, 2003, p. B1+.

Discussion Questions

1. Why do you think Fiorina's tactic of the three questions was successful?

2. Would you classify this example as portraying transformational leadership? Why or why not?

3. What other approaches could be used to engage people and commit them to change in an organization? Are there other ways that leaders could transform an organization?

Research Questions

1. Locate information about Carly Fiorina. How would you capture her leadership style—transformational or other approaches as well? Share your information and judgments with the rest of the class.

2. What is the current status of Fiorina's leadership? Do you think she is effective or having difficulty as a leader? Why? Share your findings and judgments with the rest of the class.

AUTHENTIC LEADERSHIP Authentic leadership theory[22] is an approach that emphasizes the importance of a positive directive force, particularly in an environment of increasing complexity, change, and uncertainty. Authentic leadership is a recent development that is meant to go beyond transformational leadership. Transformational leadership may be viewed as instrumental leadership. That is, the task of the leader is to facilitate the attainment of organizational goals through the effective leadership of the workforce. The transformational leader may embrace certain values and ways of doing things because they are instrumental in obtaining desired performance outcomes.

In contrast, authentic leadership emphasizes a terminal value approach. An authentic leader is true to his/her values and portrays those values and positively influences employees. The primary goal is not portraying whatever facade of values or emotions that might facilitate achieving a performance goal. Rather, the authentic leader provides a positive influence and role model in the organization. Management Close-Up 13.d presents a tool that authentic leaders can use to effectively convey their values. While authentic leadership theory will likely be further developed, we next provide a description of the authentic leadership approach as it currently exists.

Authentic leadership theory suggests that effective leaders are guided by doing what is right for constituents, not their own self-interests. Authentic leaders focus on making a positive difference and on developing others to be leaders. What may best describe the authentic leader is the profile of characteristics of authentic leadership, as summarized in Table 13.5.

As shown in the list of authentic leadership characteristics, the emphasis of authentic leadership is on people and making a positive difference. Trust, credibility, integrity, and inspiration can be far more powerful for motivating performance than can coercion and deceit. Authentic leadership places values and integrity at the forefront of effective leadership, the kind of leadership model that is crucial in the wake of various legal and ethical scandals in organizations.

Assessing Emotional Intelligence

Leadership and Emotional Intelligence

emotional intelligence

The attributes of self-awareness, impulse control, persistence, confidence, self-motivation, empathy, social deftness, trustworthiness, adaptability and a talent for collaboration.

In two groundbreaking bestsellers, psychologist Daniel Goleman drew on a wealth of research to argue that successful leaders demonstrate **emotional intelligence.** This includes self-awareness, impulse control, persistence, confidence, self-motivation, empathy, social deftness, trustworthiness, adaptability, and a talent for collaboration.[23] "Effective leaders have a knack for articulating a mission or a goal and knowing how to bring everyone on board to get it accomplished. Can you take the pulse of a group, understand its unspoken currents of thought and concerns,

Tell Us a Story

THEME: CUSTOMER DRIVEN Rational arguments, statistics, and facts are often the tools of a manager. However, effective leaders may know what recent research has revealed: storytelling is much more convincing and memorable than facts. For example, Mary Contratto, CEO of Little Company, a health care organization, believes storytelling is a leadership skill. She tells the story to employees in the organization of how a trainer at a gym assigned to her 13-year-old son became an emergency room nurse. Contratto and the trainer were discussing her son's goals when Contratto learned that the trainer had given up on being a nurse and was about to switch occupations. The CEO was able to provide the support and motivation that was needed. The trainer is now a dedicated nurse. Contratto shares the story to convey to employees that each of them can make a difference. They can be recruiters and promoters for the organization when interacting in their communities.

Contratto also encourages employees to share their stories of best and worst service. The organization emphasizes service as a critical aspect of the company's mission. They plan to use stories to make real the importance of service to patients, the families of patients, and doctors. Stories can engage employees and be far more effective than a statement that service is part of the mission. Storytelling is memorable, effectively conveys values, and feels more authentic.

Source: Adapted from B. Kaufman, "Stories That Sell, Stories That Tell: Effective Storytelling Can Strengthen an Organization's Bonds with All of Its Stakeholders," *Journal of Business Strategy* 24 (2003), p. 11+.

TABLE 13.5

Profile of Authentic Leadership Characteristics

CHARACTERISTIC	DESCRIPTION
1. Value Driven	Motivated by doing what's right and belief that everyone has something positive to contribute.
2. No Gap between Internal Values and Actions	Authentic leader understands his/her own core values and projects them with consistency.
3. Transparent	Open about weaknesses and open to suggestions for improvements and changes in direction.
4. Influence by Inspiration	Authentic leaders portray confidence, hope, and resiliency.
5. Developmental Focus	Authentic leaders view development of people as important as task accomplishment.
6. Moral Capacity	Authentic leader can judge unclear issues and dilemmas. They may change their mind, but not to shift with popular opinion, but to be consistent with their values and current analysis.

and communicate with people in terms they can understand and embrace? That is great leadership. And it takes huge intelligence."[24] Often people who are promoted on the basis of technical ability fail in their new jobs. The problem is that they lack the emotional competencies needed to lead others.

Manager's Checkup 13.2 at the end of the chapter lists 25 questions that assess emotional intelligence. The maximum score is 100. According to Goleman, a score below 70 indicates a problem, but "if your total is somewhere in the basement, don't despair: EQ [emotional quotient] is not unimprovable. Emotional intelligence can be learned, and in fact we are each building it, in varying degrees, throughout life. EQ is nothing more or less than a collection of tools that we can sharpen to help ensure our own survival."[25]

APPLICATIONS: MANAGEMENT IS EVERYONE'S BUSINESS

Applications for the Manager   The leadership models described in this chapter should be used by managers to improve effectiveness. Managers should identify the theories that best fit them and their situations. Each may be used to devise a personal leadership style. Some situations call for a strong person to guide the organization through a major change. In others, the layout and complexity of the organization calls for a dispersed leadership approach. Uncertainties and difficult times may best match authentic leadership. Managers should decide upon the leadership approach that works the best. Applying the leadership theories covered here can help you succeed at both managing and leading. Quality leaders are noticed in organizations. Both management and leadership skills can be positive for employees and the organization; they will also bode well for your own career.

Applications for Managing Teams   Team effectiveness requires more than simply identifying and dividing tasks among team members. Effective teams have a shared vision and sense of common purpose that comes from leaders. Leadership may, in part or in whole, come from inside the team itself. The increasing prevalence of empowerment and self-leadership underscores the importance of team members understanding and developing leadership skills.

Applications for Individuals   Employees are more likely to succeed if they can manage themselves without relying on others to motivate them and define their tasks. Employees can become self-leaders by finding opportunities in their work environment, showing initiative, encouraging others to do their best, and generating enthusiasm for the tasks at hand. Individuals can apply these leadership theories to their work environments and improve performance, as well their potential for advancement.

At the beginning of this chapter, some critical thinking questions were posed. After covering some of the basics of leadership, we now return to these issues. First, there is no standard set of characteristics that make for a great leader. A variety of personalities have developed into great leaders. There are also a variety of situational demands and constraints. Great leadership is more likely to occur when the characteristics of a person fit the situation. The person-based leadership approaches outline the characteristics of the leader that make a difference. However, situational theories indicate that company circumstances are important as well.

Second, leadership can make a critical difference. As noted at the beginning of this chapter, without Carlos Ghosn at the helm, it is possible that Nissan Motors might not even exist. However, there does seem to be a tendency to focus on a leader and attribute greater causal significance to him/her than is merited. As discussed in the description of substitute leadership, it is possible to overly romanticize the role of a leader. The best leaders realize that they can't be in all places at all times. Instead, they rely on their people being aligned with the interests of the organization and on effective systems being in place.

The issue of leadership style was raised in the chapter. As with personal characteristics, no one style always works best. A style may resonate or be a better natural fit than others for a leader. Some situations may call for an autocratic style or a task-oriented leader. Other situations may be better suited to a leader with a more people-oriented style. Thus, any given style is not always the best.

Finally, ethics are a central issue when considering leadership. A leader must make ethics a central concern of the organization and not just rhetoric that can be ignored. Going beyond "ethics as window dressing" means the leader communicates the importance of ethical conduct, acts as a role model, and assures that everyone in the organization shares ethical values. Ethical conduct doesn't just happen, nor can it always be assured through compliance. People need to understand and align themselves with the values of integrity and ethics and know what those values mean in terms of actual behaviors. Leaders can make a positive ethical difference, but it takes an active and concerted effort.

The various leadership theories provide a variety of models to follow. No one approach is best for every situation. The approach that is best must be guided by what fits you and the work situation. However, it is clear that the themes of our text—ethics, being customer driven, and change—are all key concerns of today's business leaders.

In this chapter we examined the major theories of leadership as well as an emerging theory. The theories emphasize either the person, the situation, a dispersed approach, or an exchange. The *person approach* includes the *trait* and *behavioral theories*. The *situational and contingency approach* includes *Fiedler's Contingency Model* and *Path–Goal Theory*. The *dispersed leadership* theories that were described are *substitute leadership* and *self-leadership*. *Exchange theories* include *transformational leadership* and the emerging theory of *authentic leadership*.

1. Do you agree that managers and leaders are different kinds of people? Why or why not?

2. Some people argue that organizations need to put in place mechanisms to prevent informal leaders from imposing their own agenda on others. Do you agree? Why or why not?

3. Think about some people you have met who are excellent leaders and some who have been entrusted with a leadership position yet are highly ineffective. Use the theories discussed in this chapter to analyze what made those individuals effective or ineffective as leaders.

4. Develop your own leadership theory. It can be a combination of the approaches covered in this chapter or you can bring in something entirely new. Why do you think your approach is an effective way to lead?

5. When are the substitutes for leadership most important. Is the need for substitutes decreasing or increasing in today's work environments? Why?

6. How much of a difference do you think a leader can make? Explain your judgment.

7. Differentiate between the major types of leadership theories (person, situation, and so on). Which type do you think offers the best approach?

8. Are there instances when each of the major types of leadership theories would be best? Can you identify the type of situation that would call for each type of leadership approach?

Put It on the Card: What's Your Leadership Message?

Lee Enterprises, Inc., is led by Mary Junck, the company's first woman CEO. Lee owns 44 daily newspapers in 18 states and more than 175 weekly newspapers, shoppers, and specialty publications. The company also has book-publishing, commercial printing, and online operations. Junck took the helm in 1999. The organization sold all of its TV stations that year and has since seen its revenues soar 58.9 percent and its daily circulation increase by 75 percent. By all measures, the organization is doing very well. What accounts for this positive performance?

When asked about what drives the continued high performance at Lee, many employees point to a tool developed by Mary Junck—a card about the size of a business card. Officially known as the "Priorities Card," the card succinctly lists Junck's most important goals. Some of the goals are:

- Growing revenue—creatively and rapidly.
- On-time delivery—meet deadlines and get it there on time.
- Focus coverage on real people.
- Strong local news.

The goals of the Priorities Card are simple and everyone in the organization has one. Greg Veon, a vice president at Lee, says that he always carries a Priorities Card with him. The card brings priorities into focus for everyone in the organization. Kathleen Rutledge, an editor for Lee, points out that the card puts things in black and white, which she finds to be supportive and comforting. For example, including "strong local news" in the set of goals makes a priority that may have always been implicit into an explicit priority.

Discussion Questions

1. The Priorities Card is a very simple tool. Why do you think it is effective?
2. What leadership theory would best capture the Priorities Card approach?
3. Other organizations use cards as well. Find examples of these cards. Are they different from Junck's approach?
4. Would you use a priorities card if you were a leader in an organization? Why or why not?
5. If you were a leader in an organization, what goals would you list on a priorities card?

Adapted from: Anonymous, "All a Matter of Priorities," *Editor & Publisher*, February 10, 2003.

Where Having Fun Really Pays

Garrett Brown, 32, a desktop support specialist for DWL Inc., recently spent the day in simulated dogfights in a World War II Spitfire replica. Even better, he gets an extra $1,000 each year to do it.

DWL is a privately held Toronto customer-relationship management consulting firm founded in the late 1990s, with clients such as Body Shop International and National Life Insurance. Being sure people have fun is part of DWL's day-to-day management. Top executives believe encouraging fun helps morale and retention among the 300 employees, and the company is spending about $500,000 a year on this belief. The company offers $1,000 annually to each employee to do something fun. Trips and cruises are common uses for the money. One employee surprised his father with a trip to a favorite fishing camp. Another bought a guitar, and still another signed up for cooking lessons.

At year's end, the company posts photos of the activities—the more colorful, the better. Sometimes the photograph tells it all. For example, one employee's wife coaches high school girls' volleyball. The employee used his money to tag along on one of his wife's trips to the Caribbean with the girls. His photo of 15 volleyball players carrying him on the beach impressed the panel of five employees voting on who had the most fun during the year.

The winner is awarded $5,000 for next year's activity; two runners-up each receive $2,000. Last year's winner used the money for his avocation: video art. Though he enjoys producing videos, there isn't much local interest in it, so the employee used the money to produce a video and travel to its showing in Amsterdam.

Mark Mighton, VP of Sales Operations, invented the program and earned the informal title of Director of Fun. He reviews the employees' applications for the annual grant, which are usually informal e-mails. About 90 percent of the applications are accepted immediately; the other 10 percent usually are approved on the second try. The typical reason for rejection is that the idea didn't involve having enough fun— a new TV, a mortgage payment, a new bathroom sink, and anything job-related will be rejected. Mighton sets an example with his own choices—in 2001, his African safari was paid for in part by the fun fund.

Justin La Fayette, DWL's CEO and founder, wants everyone to participate to keep work in perspective and to offset the "north of 50-plus, 60-plus hours a week for extended periods" so many employees put in. He sees the fun fund as a way of keeping work and leisure balanced and believes that it is a key factor in the 98 percent retention rate the company boasts as well as a powerful employee motivator. Workers themselves make decisions on how they can best contribute to the company's success and are rewarded both by jobs that are more exciting and by the opportunity and the means to enjoy their time outside the office.

Discussion Questions

1. Based on the material you read in this chapter, how would you characterize the leadership approach used by DWL Inc.'s top management? Explain.

2. Do you think that the leadership style at DWL Inc. would be successful in most situations? Why or why not? If not, explain under what situations it may work better.

3. The focus on fun in some organizations, such as DWL and Southwest Airlines, may seem paradoxical. The more the focus is on fun the greater the performance seems to be. How would you explain this paradox?

Source: D. R. Khurallah, "Where Having Fun Really Pays," *Information Week,* January 15, 2001, p. 87.

Leaders: Made, Not Born

Leadership positions are often given to people whose performance stands out. Unfortunately some high performers do not have the skills needed to be effective leaders. While some people might appear to be natural leaders, for most people, leadership requires learning a key set of skills. Organizations take a variety of approaches to developing leadership skills.

Targeted Training

Training is aimed at people recently promoted to leadership positions. The management team at Appleton Papers, a manufacturing company in Appleton, Wisconsin, saw too many untrained new supervisors making costly mistakes. The HR department implemented a new supervisor training program in 2002 that focuses on communication, interpersonal, and performance management skills. Company leaders believe the training has returned many multiples of its cost.

Not all such training is equally effective. It is not just an issue of covering content, but how the content is covered. Small nibbles are often better than a big bite. For example, offering brief sessions focused on an aspect of effective leadership provides new leaders the opportunity to practice and apply the skill in the workplace. A month-long full-time leadership course, on the other hand, can be overwhelming. Trainees can have difficulty remembering all of the content.

Training for new leaders may not always be immediately available. Southwest Airlines counters this problem by providing new supervisors with an on-the-job survival guide. The guide is customized to each position and is available online to all new supervisors.

Leadership training isn't just needed by new supervisors. Mid- and upper-level managers sometimes need to improve their leadership skills. General Physics, a training and development company headquartered in Elkridge, Maryland, noted the need for leadership improvement in its operations. According to one of the directors at General Physics, there were difficulties in communication networks, establishing goals, empowerment, and managing performance. In an attempt to make a targeted and positive change in their level of leadership skills, management at General Physics instituted a leadership boot camp. Participants in the boot camp included managers who had been identified as having some difficulty on a leadership skill through a 360-degree evaluation program. Officers of the organization were also included as participants and were expected to learn the materials and act as role models following the program.

The boot camp was meant to both convey material and shock and grab people, thereby convincing them of the importance of effective leadership. The boot camp included an overnight stay, a 5:30 A.M. wake-up call, physical exercise, a gruff presentation by "Sergeant Death," and training activities that continued until 10:00 P.M. The boot camp was effective at General Physics. People proudly hung their boot camp diplomas on their walls and dog tags were made into key fobs. Most importantly, a follow-up study revealed a 17–25 percent improvement in leadership competencies. General Physics now requires the boot camp experience for anyone promoted to a supervisory position.

Diffuse Training

Leadership skills can be important for anyone in an organization. A person may not be in a formal leadership position, but need leadership skills as part of a team or project. In these situations, leadership skills are helpful to everyone. Unisys Corporation, an information technology company headquartered in Pennsylvania, takes a broad-based approach to leadership training. Employees from all ranks are encouraged to take advantage of the program. The goal of Unisys is not to develop 25 key leaders, but to develop 2,500 leaders throughout the organization. Larry Weinback, CEO of Unisys, started the program and acts as its dean. He is a champion for the program and a frequent class speaker. He contends that the leadership training program has had a powerful impact on the Unisys culture.

Critical Thinking Questions

1. Do you think that effective leadership can be learned, or are some people simply born to it?

2. Which approach to leadership training would you recommend, targeted or diffuse? Why?

3. What advantages are there to the diffuse approach? What costs are associated with this approach? Do you think the benefits would be worth the cost?

Collaborative Learning Exercise

Form groups of four or five students. The task for each team is to develop the basics of a leadership training program. Specifically: (*a*) What leadership competencies would you focus on? (You might research the topic of leadership competencies to generate a comprehensive list to choose from.) (*b*) What criteria would you use to identify program participants? That is, who would be selected to attend the training? (*c*) Would your program be targeted or diffuse? Share the essentials of your program with the rest of the class.

Sources: Adapted from K. Tyler, "Sink-or-Swim Attitude Strands New Managers," *HRMagazine* 48 (2003), pp. 78–83; J. Ronan, "A Boot to the System: How Does a Training Company Shake Up Its Leadership Style? It Marches the Managers Off to Boot Camp," *T & D* 57 (2003), p. 38+; S. F. Gale, "Building Leaders at All Levels," *Workforce* 81 (2002), pp. 82–85.

Leading the Pack

In January of each year *Business Week* identifies top managers and entrepreneurs as exemplary leaders and justifies its choices. Visit the *Business Week* website (www.businessweek.com) and enter "Top 25 Managers" as a search term to access articles from the January issue. Use the results of your search to answer the following questions:

1. Develop a list of 3–10 characteristics that these people have in common.

2. How do differences in leadership style contribute to success?

3. How did the firm's context or situation affect the leadership style among *Business Week*'s top leaders?

Power and Influence

This exercise can help you discover your attitudes toward different kinds of power and influence. Each student should complete the worksheets independently and then meet in groups of three to five students to discuss their answers. Each group also should answer the questions at the end of the exercise and then report their ideas to the entire class.

A. Power Worksheet
Following are some statements about power. Indicate how you feel about each of the statements by circling the corresponding number.

	Strongly Disagree	Disagree	Neutral	Agree	Strongly Agree
1. Winning is everything.	1	2	3	4	5
2. Nice guys finish last.	1	2	3	4	5
3. There can only be one winner.	1	2	3	4	5
4. There's a sucker born every minute.	1	2	3	4	5
5. You can't completely trust anyone.	1	2	3	4	5
6. All power rests at the end of the gun.	1	2	3	4	5
7. Power seekers are greedy and can't be trusted.	1	2	3	4	5
8. Power corrupts; absolute power corrupts absolutely.	1	2	3	4	5
9. You get as much power as you pay for.	1	2	3	4	5

B. Influence Worksheet

1. On the following table, list the first names of people who influenced you during the past week or so according to the kind of power that person used. If a person used multiple power bases, put the name next to all that apply. Indicate whether the influence was positive (+) or negative (−).

Social Power Base	Name	(+) or (−)
Coercive	_____	_____
Reward	_____	_____
Legitimate	_____	_____
Expert	_____	_____
Referent	_____	_____

2. Answer yes or no to the following questions about the list in question 1.

   a. Is anyone listed next to several power bases with + after his or her name?

   b. Is anyone listed next to several power bases with − after his or her name?

    c. Do most of the people marked + fall under the same power bases?

    d. Do most of the people marked − fall under the same power bases?

3. From your answers to questions 1 and 2, list which social power bases you found to be positive (+) and which you found to be negative (−). Do you prefer to use those power bases you listed under + when you try to influence people? Do you actually use them?

C. Power and Influence Worksheet

Use the table in the influence worksheet to identify the person having the strongest positive influence on you (Person 1) and the person having the strongest negative influence (Person 2). These persons' names usually appear most frequently in the worksheet.

For each statement that follows, circle the number that indicates how you think Person 1 would respond to it. In a different color, circle the number that indicates how you think Person 2 would respond to it.

		Strongly Disagree	Disagree	Neutral	Agree	Strongly Agree
10.	Winning is everything.	1	2	3	4	5
11.	Nice guys finish last.	1	2	3	4	5
12.	There can only be one winner.	1	2	3	4	5
13.	There's a sucker born every minute.	1	2	3	4	5
14.	You can't completely trust anyone.	1	2	3	4	5
15.	All power rests at the end of the gun.	1	2	3	4	5
16.	Power seekers are greedy and can't be trusted.	1	2	3	4	5
17.	Power corrupts; absolute power corrupts absolutely.	1	2	3	4	5
18.	You get as much power as you pay for.	1	2	3	4	5

Compare your responses in Part A to those in Part C. Do you more closely resemble Person 1 or Person 2? Do you prefer to use the kinds of power that person uses. Which kinds of power do you use most frequently? Which do you use least frequently? When do you feel you have the greatest power? When do you have the least power? How do these answers compare to what you found in Part B?

Source: Excerpt from *The Managerial Experience: Cases, Exercises, and Readings,* 4th ed., by Arthur G. Bedeian, Lawrence R. Jauch, Sally A. Coltrin, and William F. Glueck. Copyright © 1986 by The Dryden Press, reprinted by permission of the publisher.

What's Your EQ at Work?

Quiz

Answering the following 25 questions will allow you to rate your social skills and self-awareness.

EQ, the social equivalent of IQ, is complex, in no small part because it depends on some pretty slippery variables—including your innate compatibility, or lack thereof, with the people who happen to be your coworkers.

To get an idea of your emotional quotient (EQ) in a work situation, estimate how you rate in the eyes of your peers, bosses, and subordinates on each of the following traits, on a scale of one to four, with four representing strong agreement, and one, strong disagreement.

_____ I usually stay composed, positive, and unflappable even in trying moments.

_____ I can think clearly and stay focused on the task at hand under pressure.

_____ I am able to admit my own mistakes.

_____ I usually or always meet commitments and keep promises.

_____ I hold myself accountable for meeting my goals.

_____ I'm organized and careful in my work.

_____ I regularly seek out fresh ideas from a wide variety of sources.

_____ I'm good at generating new ideas.

_____ I can smoothly handle multiple demands and changing priorities.

_____ I'm results-oriented, with a strong drive to meet my objectives.

_____ I like to set challenging goals and take calculated risks to reach them.

_____ I'm always trying to learn how to improve my performance, including asking advice from people younger than I am.

_____ I readily make sacrifices to meet an important organizational goal.

_____ The company's mission is something I understand and can identify with.

_____ The values of my team—or of our division or department, or the company—influence my decisions and clarify the choices I make.

_____ I actively seek out opportunities to further the overall goals of the organization and enlist others to help me.

_____ I pursue goals beyond what's required or expected of me in my current job.

_____ Obstacles and setbacks may delay me a little, but they don't stop me.

_____ Cutting through red tape and bending outdated rules are sometimes necessary.

_____ I seek fresh perspectives, even if that means trying something totally new.

_____ My impulses or distressing emotions don't often get the best of me at work.

_____ I can change tactics quickly when circumstances change.

_____ Pursuing new information is my best bet for cutting down on uncertainty and finding ways to do things better.

_____ I usually don't attribute setbacks to a personal flaw (mine or someone else's).

_____ I operate from an expectation of success rather than a fear of failure.

A score below 70 indicates a problem.

Source: D. Goleman (appearing as part of interview) "Success Secret: A High Emotional EQ," by A. Fisher, *Fortune,* October 28, 1998, p. 298. Copyright © Daniel Goleman. Reprinted with permission.

FOURTEEN

Managing Teams

chapter 14

After reading this chapter, you should be able to:

- Translate the benefits teams provide into competitive advantages.

- Manage the different types of teams—self-managed, parallel, project, and virtual.

- Track the stages of team development that occur over the life of a project and help the team perform effectively.

- Recognize the key roles that team members must play to ensure high performance.

- Develop skills to detect and control team performance problems.

- Manage team conflict through negotiation.

Teamwork at Toyota and Boeing

A customer who purchases a new car at Boulder Toyota, in Boulder, Colorado, is assigned to one of three customer service teams responsible for the car. Each of these teams consists of: (1) a service manager, who deals directly with the customer and solves any problems; (2) an assistant service manager, who keeps records about the car on a computer database; (3) a technical team leader, who manages the technicians; and (4) several team technicians working together to provide mechanical service. Each time a customer brings a car to Boulder Toyota for maintenance, the customer is greeted by the same service manager along with the same mechanics who work on the car. The result is committed relationships between customers and service teams, which leads to better service. The management team at Boulder Toyota believes that a customer who has positive service experiences is more likely to buy another vehicle there. The company's motto is, "Exceeding the expectations of our customers and the community."

The executives at Boeing Company's Airlift and Tanker Programs formed employee teams when they wanted to revitalize the company's environment. Boeing employees elect their own team leaders and "interview prospective employees, looking especially for culture fit and attitude," says Amy Gillespie, HR specialist at Boeing. Team development moves through four stages: formation; learning the basics of teamwork; moving toward decision making and understanding their measures; and beginning to interact with customers and set their own goals. When one of the company's supervisors began educating team members about performance measures, the teams "began looking at metrics and measures and charts, which had previously been intimidating. Their performance really kicked in when they took responsibility for these things."

Source: C. Joinson, "Teams at Work," *HR Magazine,* May 1999, www.shrm.com.

www.boeing.com

575

Many U.S. companies that employ knowledge workers are increasingly using teams to fully engage and empower workers to take advantage of their specialized knowledge. As more work is being performed by teams, the ability to manage them has become an increasingly important skill. This chapter examines the management of teams, beginning with the reasons companies use teams and the different types and design aspects of teams. Key topics include the behavioral issues that must be identified and administered, problems that need to be addressed along with ways to deal with them, and the critical skills needed to effectively manage teams such as those outlined in Skills for Managing 14.1.

The Benefits of Teams

In this new millennium, many tasks are far too complex to be completed by a single individual. As a result, the success of various teams and groups directly affects the success of the overall organization.

team

A small number of people with complementary skills who are committed to a common purpose, a set of performance goals, and an approach for which they hold themselves mutually accountable.

A **team** is a small number of people with complementary skills who are committed to a common purpose, a set of performance goals, and an approach for which they hold themselves mutually accountable. Team members interact with each other on a regular basis. A team can be as small as two people, such as a telephone company's sales team, composed of a customer service representative and a customer service engineer. Larger teams may be responsible for taking charge of core business processes such as order fulfillment, customer service, or procurement of raw materials and supplies. When the size of a team exceeds 25 members the individuals have difficulty interacting intensively. The range of team size for high-performing teams is between 5 and 12 members. This range in size allows for teams to be large enough to take advantage of the different skills of members and small enough to provide a feeling of community and cohesion between the team members.[1]

SKILLS FOR MANAGING TEAMS

- *Conflict management skills.* Conflict is a natural part of the growth and development of a team. Team members need to be able to recognize the difference between functional conflict, which stimulates team performance, and dysfunctional conflict, which can undermine effectiveness. Different situations call for different approaches to managing conflict.
- *Negotiation skills.* The *win–win* approach to negotiation is a way to develop a solution that satisfies the needs of both parties. This type of negotiation is particularly effective when it is important to

maintain long-term relationships, which is the case with teams.

- *Skills for handling difficult team members.* In cases in which a team member is preventing the team from performing to potential, it is crucial to deal with and motivate the difficult person. Two types of difficult people you are likely to encounter on a team are the "free rider," who tries to get away with doing as little work as possible, and the "nonconforming high performer," who performs well as an individual but does not work well with other people.

Teams share performance goals. Individuals on teams are mutually responsible for end results. The teams at the Toyota dealership discussed in the opening vignette are responsible for customer satisfaction. If one mechanic is negligent, all team members are responsible for and affected by the dissatisfaction of the customer.

A quality team environment produces **synergy,** which allows individuals to blend complementary skills and talents to produce a product that is more valuable than the sum of the individual contributions. This can energize and motivate individuals to perform at consistently high levels.

A **work group** differs from a team. Members of a work group are held accountable for individual work, but they are not responsible for the output of the entire group. For example, a group of accountants in an accounting firm may meet occasionally to discuss auditing procedures. Still, each accountant works individually with clients, and the firm holds the accountant responsible only for that work. The accountants are part of a group, not a team.

Table 14.1 lists the differences between a team and a work group. Team members hold themselves mutually accountable for team goals, and leadership responsibilities are shared among the members of the team. They openly discuss goals and procedures with each other until they reach a consensus. A work group is more likely to have a strong, directive leader who seeks input from group members and then delegates work to various individuals to complete.

synergy

Allows individuals to blend complementary skills and talents to produce a product that is more valuable than the sum of the individual contributions.

work group

Members of a group who are held accountable for individual work, but they are not responsible for the output of the entire group.

TABLE 14.1

Not All Groups Are Teams

CHARACTERISTIC	WORKING GROUP	TEAM
Leadership	Strong, clearly focused leader	Shared leadership roles
Accountability	Individual	Individual and mutual
Purpose	Same as the broader organizational mission	Team purpose that the team itself delivers
Work products	Individual	Collective
Meeting style	Efficient	Open-ended discussion, active problem-solving
Performance measurement	Indirectly, by its influence on others (e.g., financial performance of the business)	Directly, by collective work products
Decision-making process	Discusses, decides, and delegates	Discusses, decides, and does real work together

Source: Reprinted by permission of *Harvard Business Review.* Excerpt from "The Discipline of Teams," by J. R. Katzenbach and D. K. Smith, March–April 1993. Copyright © 1993 by the President and Fellows of Harvard College. All rights reserved.

Effectively managing teams makes it possible for companies to achieve important strategic business objectives, which may result in competitive advantages. The benefits of using teams include lower costs and higher productivity, quality improvements, speed, and innovation. Each is described in further detail next.

Costs and Productivity

When a company delegates management work to teams, team members do many of the things that were formerly carried out by the supervisor, and the organization needs fewer supervisors. Companies can save on the labor cost of surplus supervisors and middle managers. In addition, cross-training team members to have a broad set of competencies allows a significant reduction of the total number of employees required.

Before organizing its auto assembly plants into teams, Ford Motor Company hired more skilled production workers than needed in order to have substitutes available. Using teams meant that cross-trained workers were available to cover for absent employees, making the plants more productive. This allowed Ford to abandon the practice of stockpiling employees.

Quality Improvements

The responsibility for quality now rests with team members who assemble the product or provide the service rather than on an inspector who judges quality after the product is completed. This self-inspection, or "do it right the first time," approach to quality has several advantages. It saves the company money on defective products and wasted raw materials. It can also greatly reduce the labor cost of hiring quality specialists who inspect the work of others.

Quality management experts such as W. Edwards Deming recommend using teams that include employees who deal directly with customers. The goal is to achieve continuous quality improvements.[2] "Small wins" in quality delight customers. These new work methods and practices can be rapidly disseminated throughout the company by quality teams that inform other organizational members about them. Levi Strauss, the manufacturer of casual clothing, used teams to reduce defects in its clothing by 25 percent. The Saturn division of General Motors used self-managed teams to achieve one of the highest levels of customer satisfaction of any U.S. auto manufacturer.[3]

Speed

The responsiveness of a company to the needs of the customer is a vital area of concern. Improved speed reduces the time it takes to fill a customer order. It can shorten the time required to develop a new product. Speed can also improve the responsiveness of a company, such as how quickly an electric company restores service when a power transmission line is downed in a severe storm.

Teams can reduce the time needed to respond to customers. When teams are organized around important business processes, the time to complete the processes can be greatly reduced. A **business process** is a value-adding, value-creating activity such as product development or order fulfillment. Teams reduce barriers between departments that slow the flow of work. An example of such a barrier is the handoff from a bank loan officer to a credit analyst who then lets the paperwork sit for many days before examining the creditworthiness of the customer.

business process

A value-adding, value-creating activity such as product development or order fulfillment.

Many companies have taken advantage of improved speed. Kodak cut product development process time in half by using concurrent engineering teams composed of employees with cross-functional skills. Motorola used multiskilled production teams to manufacture a custom paging device within two hours of placement of an order. Southwest Airlines turns around an aircraft from landing to takeoff in 20 minutes by using customer service teams to unload, service, and load the aircraft. This is one-third the time it takes competitors to load and unload planes.

Innovation

The ability to create new products and services can be enhanced with the use of teams. Teams allow companies to innovate more quickly. In high-technology industries, being first to market with a unique or improved product provides a powerful competitive advantage. A cross-functional team composed of people who have knowledge of the market, technologists, and experts in production reduces the cycle time for product development. It is no coincidence that companies known for innovation such as Microsoft and Hewlett-Packard intensively utilize teams in their product development processes. Moreover, recent research reveals that teams composed of members with diverse work experience backgrounds are more innovative and more likely to share information than teams composed of people with similar kinds of work experience.[4]

When engineers at Boeing designed its innovative 777 aircraft, the company's management group relied exclusively on more than 200 teams to design and build major components of the plant. The teams included representatives from nearly every function, including customers and suppliers. They made it possible for the company to build the aircraft right the first time and not incur the cost of altering the configuration after the fact.

Management Close-Up 14.a explains how AES Corporation employs teams to achieve and sustain a position as a leading power company.

Types of Teams

Just as a mechanic looks for the right tool to do a job, management must identify the right type of team to complete a task or project. The four types of teams normally found in organizations are self-managed teams, project teams, parallel teams, and virtual teams. Each differs in terms of duration (a few months or less compared to several years or more) and the amount of time members are expected to commit to the activities of the team (full-time or part-time). Figure 14.1 shows where each of these teams fits in terms of duration and time commitment.

Self-Managed Teams

self-managed team (SMT)

Sometimes called a *process team*, a group that is responsible for producing an entire product, component, or service.

A **self-managed team (SMT),** which is sometimes called a *process team,* is responsible for producing an entire product, component, or service. These teams are formalized as part of the organization's structure. Employees are assigned to them on a full-time basis and they have a longer duration. SMTs utilize employees whose jobs are similar but who may have different levels of skill. Team members combine skills to produce an important organizational outcome, such as an automobile engine (production process) or the installation of a computer system for a customer (customer service process).

Self-managed teams have authority to make many decisions traditionally reserved for supervisors or managers. For example, team members at General Motors's Saturn facility in Spring Hill, Tennessee,

Teams Give AES Corporation a Competitive Advantage

THEME: CUSTOMER FOCUSED   The AES Corporation is a successful global developer and operator of electric power and steam plants. Company sales are more than $8.6 billion per year and AES has over $33 billion in corporate assets across 28 countries. The company has never formed corporate departments or assigned officers to oversee project finance, operations, purchasing, human resources, or public relations. Instead, these functions are handled at the plant level, where plant managers assign them to volunteer teams.

The front-line employees on teams at AES develop expertise in domains such as finance. They also receive the responsibility and authority to carry out required tasks. While mistakes are sometimes made while learning, the overall results are impressive. The AES team structure saves on management costs because the company has only five managerial levels. This allows AES to optimize the time of specialized staff members such as financial experts. For example, when the company developed a $400 million plant in Cumberland, Maryland, a team of just 10 people obtained more than 36 separate permit approvals and negotiated the complex financing, including tax-exempt bonds and contracts with 10 different lenders. Normally, projects of this scope require hundreds of employees, each with narrow and specific tasks to perform. The savings, increased speed, and flexibility of the AES team-based approach are

AES volunteer teams perform tasks that might normally be handled by traditional departments.

clear and constitute a key source of the company's competitive advantage.

Sources: "AES Corporation: The Global Power Company," www.aes.com (2003); J. Pfeffer, *The Human Equation: Building Profits by Putting People First.* Boston: Harvard Business School Press, 1998, p. 77.

FIGURE 14.1

Team Characteristics

Source: Based on material from *Compensation for Teams: How to Design and Implement Team-Based Reward Programs* by Steven E. Gross. Copyright © 1995 The Hay Group, Inc. Adapted with the permission of the publisher, AMACOM Books, a division of American Management Association International, New York, NY. All rights reserved. http://www.amacombooks.org.

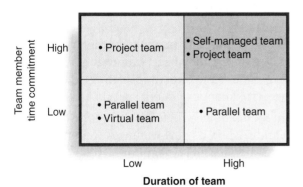

Saturn retains a high level of customer satisfaction by using self-managed teams.

schedule work, hire new team members, select appropriate work methods, manage budgets, schedule delivery of raw materials, and maintain quality standards for the work output. There are no supervisors. Each team literally manages itself. Other SMTs utilize a supervisor or manager to direct the work, but this supervisor is a coach rather than a traditional boss who tells subordinates what to do. The SMT or process team concept requires empowerment in order to engage each worker's best mental and physical efforts.

SMT members need to be trained in a variety of skills to become fully functional. These include:

1. *Technical skills.* Team members must be cross-trained to rotate between different tasks or workstations. Cross-training team members offers the SMT greater flexibility to provide speed, efficiency, and quality.

2. *Management skills.* Members of the SMT have the authority to make management decisions. Therefore, they need training in such skills as budgeting, scheduling, time management, planning, goal setting, and judging the performance of peers.

3. *Interpersonal skills.* Team members need effective interpersonal skills to form the team and sustain its performance. They must be able to communicate ideas persuasively, negotiate when there are differences of opinion, and manage conflict when emotions are

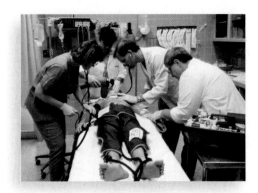

Emergency room staff are highly trained to work quickly and closely together to save lives.

aroused over important differences in goals. Two important interpersonal skills necessary for all types of teams, conflict management and negotiation, are examined later in this chapter.

Project Teams

A **project team** works on a specific project that has a beginning and an end. Team members work full-time until the project is complete and then disband to work on other projects, possibly with different team members. A project team is composed of members from different functions (such as marketing, production, and finance) or different technical disciplines (such as biology, chemistry, and mathematics). Members collaborate to complete the project. A key criterion for judging project team performance is meeting or exceeding deadlines or important milestones leading to completion.

Project teams have many uses. The Mobil energy company used project teams to reengineer key business processes in order to bring employees closer to the customer. At Massachusetts General Hospital in Boston, the trauma center uses a project team composed of doctors, nurses, interns, and technicians to treat accident victims. The speed at which the trauma center team can respond to the patient's medical condition can make the difference in saving a life. Management Close-Up 14.b describes how Hewlett-Packard reined in the company's team concept so that decisions could be made more quickly.

<aside>
project team

A group that works on a specific project that has a beginning and an end.
</aside>

Parallel Teams

Parallel teams are sometimes called *problem-solving teams* or *special-purpose teams.* These teams focus on a problem or issue that requires only part-time commitment from team members. The employee spends a few hours per week with the parallel team. The remainder of the time is spent

<aside>
parallel teams

Sometimes called *problem-solving teams* or *special purpose teams*, groups that focus on a problem or issue that requires only part-time commitment from team members.
</aside>

Taming Teamwork at Hewlett-Packard

When Kathy Wheeler left Hewlett-Packard for Apple Computer in 1992, the engineer-turned-manager looked forward to being responsible for a product team and enjoying the salary increase offered by Apple. Fourteen months later she was back at Hewlett-Packard despite Apple's efforts to keep her. Comfortable with Hewlett-Packard's teamwork values of collaboration and consensus seeking, Wheeler was unhappy with Apple's culture of individual heroes and slick user interfaces instead of teamwork. The "evangelists" who touted Apple products to the outside world seemed more valued than the most skilled engineers.

A commitment to decision by consensus can be a disadvantage in fast-moving markets, as Hewlett-Packard CEO Carly Fiorina—the first woman to head a Dow 30 company—discovered when she took the post in 1999. Founders Bill Hewlett and David Packard had established what was known as the Hewlett-Packard Way, with its renowned emphasis on teamwork and respect for coworkers. The bureaucratic, consensus-style culture that resulted put the company at a sharp disadvantage in the Internet-speed era, where new products have to be developed and produced quickly for a company to remain competitive. On the other hand, the elements that have made the company a U.S. icon—its deep engineering roots and its good, old-fashioned dependability—are irreplaceable.

The team concept at Hewlett-Packard was out of control. With 130 different product groups, the bureaucracy was becoming overwhelming. When four managers from retailer Best Buy Co. wanted some computer products, 50 HP employees visited to push their units' wares, says a former executive. "I left HP because I did not want to spend 80 percent of my time managing internal bureaucracy anymore," says Jeffrey L. Cooke, who once had to clear an operational change with 37 different internal committees. When researcher Ira P. Goldstein showed former CEO Lew Platt a prototype Web browser—two years before Netscape Communications Corp. became the first Internet superstar with its Navigator browser—he was told to have the company's computer division review it, and the browser never made it to the market.

After two years of falling sales and inconsistent profits brought on by the Asian economic crisis, plummeting computer prices, and painful product delays, Hewlett-Packard had already made the company more nimble by giving CEO-like authority to four divisional heads. A group of maverick engineers and marketers had sprung up in the high-end computing unit, promising to catapult HP into the Internet fray. In the resulting New Enterprise Group, "one of the sa-

Hewlett-Packard CEO, Carly Fiorina.

cred cows we killed was every individual's ability to influence decisions," says Nicholas J. Earle, chief marketing officer for HP's Enterprise Computing Solutions Division, who presented the new, not-so-democratic rules. "HP was like a herd of 46,000 wildebeest. Everyone knows we're there, but we were just meandering around."

One of Fiorina's main goals is applying the maverick spirit in the New Enterprise Group to HP's mammoth organization and bringing the team concept under control without losing the HP culture. To cope with the economic slowdown that struck nearly all technology companies in 2001, Fiorina unveiled a plan that asked all workers—from administrative assistants to senior executives—to volunteer for pay cuts and unpaid vacation. Workers could also choose to maintain their current salaries and not take any unpaid leaves without penalty, which many management professors and psychologists assumed that most people would choose. According to HP, however, 86 percent of HP's workforce chose the pay cuts and unpaid vacation.

Management believes the high participation rate relates to the firm's corporate culture. Other companies would find it difficult to implement a similar voluntary cost-cutting campaign, said corporate consultant and psychologist Art Resnikoff. "It's contrary to the survival of the fittest theory, but it's not contrary to HP's corporate culture," Resnikoff said. "There really is a sense of collaboration that oozes through: collaboration, working together, this attitude that 'if we keep each other happy, we'll in the long run be profitable because we won't have turnover and we will have consistency.'"

Sources: M. Siegel, "The Perils of Culture Conflict," *Fortune,* November 11, 1998, p. 257; P. Burrows. "HP's Carly Fiorina: The Boss," *Business Week,* August 2, 1999; R. Konrad, "Layoffs May Spoil HP Workers' Allegiance," CNET News.com, July 26, 2001.

working as an individual contributor in a functional department such as accounting. The parallel team does not alter the structure of the organization. Instead, a team is formed to solve a specific problem. When the problem is solved the team is likely to be disbanded. The team may be of short or long duration.

Parallel teams can make important contributions to organizations. *Suggestion teams* offer work method improvements or find new ways to please and delight customers. *Safety teams* reduce accidents and such common work maladies as back injuries or repetitive motion strain. *Selection committees* recruit and select job applicants for professional organizations such as law, accounting, or consulting firms. *Grievance committees* settle employee relations problems.

American Airlines involves nearly the entire workforce in parallel teams. Its 3,500 seven-person suggestion teams have proposed better ways to satisfy customers and save money for the company. In one three-month period, these suggestion teams developed 1,600 suggestions that were adopted, resulting in more than $20 million in cost-saving or revenue-generating improvements.

Virtual Teams

In order to take advantage of interactive computer technologies such as the Internet, groupware (software that permits people at different computer workstations to collaborate on a project simultaneously), and computer-based videoconferencing to enable distant people to work together, **virtual teams** may be formed. These teams are similar to problem-solving teams in that they require only a part-time commitment from team members. Virtual team members interact electronically, rather than engaging in face-to-face interaction typical of problem-solving teams.

Virtual teams permit organizations to link individuals who would otherwise be unable to work together. The most talented technical staff can work on problems that require their special skills. This can be a strategic advantage. Accenture, a global firm that provides information technology (IT) consulting services, can deploy a top IT consultant in the Chicago office and Accenture colleagues from the London and Amsterdam offices to work for a client in Belgium. Using the virtual team saves valuable time and the costs of travel, lodging, and downtime.

Virtual teams also make it possible for companies to cross organizational boundaries by linking customers, suppliers, and business partners to improve the quality and increase the speed with which a new product or service is brought to the market. For example, textbook authors who are university professors form a virtual team with the publishing company's editors and self-employed specialists who design the book and create the graphics.

virtual teams

Groups that use interactive computer technologies such as the Internet, groupware (software that permits people at different computer workstations to collaborate on a project simultaneously), and computer-based videoconferencing to work together regardless of distance.

Managing Team Performance

Team performance requires vigilant management. Teams do not always perform effectively, possibly because of a lack of team spirit, a disruptive team member, or a lack of commitment to team goals. Factors that need to be taken into account in managing effective team performance are the stages of team development, the roles of team members and leaders, and team member behaviors.

Stages of Team Development

Before a team can get started, planning and organizing must take place so that all members understand their roles and how they contribute to achieving team objectives. There are five stages of development: forming, storming, norming, performing, and adjourning.[5] These stages occur in sequence, although they may occur rapidly when a team is under strong time pressure.[6]

FORMING   When team members meet for the first time to get acquainted and discuss expectations the group is in the **forming stage.** Basic ground rules are established: What is the purpose of the team? How often will it meet? Should everybody expect to participate?

It is important for team members to begin to develop social bonds during the forming stage. Team leaders may organize a social activity to help members interact and build relationships.

STORMING   Team members voice differences about team goals and procedures during the **storming stage.** Differences may involve goal priorities, the allocation of team resources, fair work procedures, role expectations, or the selection of a team leader. These are important issues. All team members must be comfortable with the decisions before the team can perform its task.

Conflict is a normal part of team development. It should be out in the open and not suppressed. Coalitions often form during the storming stage. These subgroups may compete for dominance in setting the team agenda. Such conflict must be managed so that the team can move forward. If it is not properly managed, conflict can halt team development, leading to failure. Team leaders play an important role by defusing the negative aspects of conflict and tapping creative energies so that harmony and cohesion are achieved.

NORMING   Conflict resolution and agreement over team goals and values emerge in the **norming stage.** Team members finally understand their roles and establish closer relationships, intensifying the cohesion and interdependence of members. At this point, the members begin to de-

forming stage

The first stage of team development, which brings the team members together so they can get acquainted and discuss their expectations.

storming stage

A stage in team development in which team members voice differences about team goals and procedures.

norming stage

A stage in team development that is characterized by resolution of conflict and agreement over team goals and values.

velop a team identity rather than seeing themselves as individuals. The team is in agreement about how to deal with and sanction members who violate important team rules and procedures.

PERFORMING The **performing stage** is characterized by a focus on the performance of the tasks delegated to the team. Team members collaborate to capture synergies between individuals with complementary skills. When situations change and new tasks and priorities emerge, the team adjusts its tactics. When the team receives critical feedback, it has the flexibility to learn from mistakes and make improvements.

> **performing stage**
>
> A stage of team development that is characterized by a focus on the performance of the tasks delegated to the team.

The performance stage of team development can be viewed as the payoff of the investment of time and effort by team members. Forcing a team to perform before it has its house in order (by skipping some stages or spending too little time on the earlier stages) is likely to result in a malfunctioning group that is unable to achieve performance expectations.

ADJOURNING Teams that are designed to disband reach the **adjourning stage** in which the team has completed its work. Team members feel satisfaction about the completion of the team's goals, but they are also anxious about possible new assignments and about separating from friends they made while on the team.

> **adjourning stage**
>
> A stage of team development in which teams complete their work and disband, if designed to do so.

It is a good idea to have a ceremony to celebrate the end of the project or mission when the adjourning stage is reached, especially if the team's work was successful. Team members benefit from feedback on lessons learned that they can apply to future assignments. Teams and outstanding contributors can be recognized in various ways:

1. When a team completed an important project, the owner of Five Star Speakers, a training company in Kansas, closed the office for a half day and took the entire staff to a movie and to a restaurant for coffee afterward.

2. After a team successfully achieved an important deadline at The Gap, headquartered in San Bruno, California, the manager gave a gift certificate for a facial or massage at a spa to each team member.

3. Team members at Naval Publications and Forms Center in Philadelphia preserve the memory of a completed team project with a specially designed pin.[7]

Roles of Team Members

Roles are expectations regarding how team members should act in given situations. Effective team performance requires the enactment of two roles, the task-facilitating role and the relationship-building role. It is difficult to enact both of these roles equally. Most team members emphasize one or the other.

> **roles**
>
> Expectations regarding how team members should act in given situations.

The **task-facilitating role** places a priority on helping the team accomplish its task goals such as improving quality, satisfying customers, or developing new ideas. Some of the ways team members enact the task-facilitating role include:

1. *Direction giving:* Identifying ways to achieve goals and providing goal clarification.
2. *Information seeking:* Asking questions, identifying knowledge gaps, and requesting other members' opinions.
3. *Information giving:* Providing facts and data, offering judgments.
4. *Coordinating:* Pulling ideas together and helping others understand team members' suggestions and opinions.
5. *Summarizing:* Combining ideas made by team members and drawing conclusions.

The **relationship-building role** focuses on sustaining harmony between team members. This role facilitates improved interpersonal relationships and sustains team morale. The relationship-building role involves:

1. *Supporting:* Praising team members' ideas and recognizing their contributions.
2. *Harmonizing:* Mediating the differences between team members and identifying compromises.
3. *Tension relieving:* Using humor to put others at ease.
4. *Energizing:* Exuding enthusiasm and good spirits to motivate others.
5. *Facilitating:* Acting as a catalyst to smooth interactions between individuals who have difficulty communicating with each other.

Team Roles Preference Scale

Both the task-facilitating and relationship-building roles must be enacted. Some team players must focus on team objectives while others concentrate on maintaining team morale. If they do not, the team is likely to perform inadequately. If all members select the task-facilitating role, for example, the team will not develop past the norming stage because it will not get past the interpersonal conflicts that arise at this point of development.

The Role of the Team Leader

Most teams have leaders who help the teams progress through the stages of development and reach their objectives. Leaders help teams balance task-facilitating and relationship-building roles. They also deal with individuals who cause problems, such as people who dominate discussions, take unrealistic positions, or are so critical they stifle creativity. Their style of leadership is typically similar to that of a coach who:

Effective Ways to Enact the Role of Team Leader

How can a team leader positively influence team processes and outcomes?

- *Take care of team members.* Set an example of how you want team members to treat one another and customers. If the leader is self-focused, the resulting negative example for other team members will make the team less effective. Be a strong advocate for team members with management when it is justified, even when it may mean taking the heat for their mistakes or the mistakes of the team as a whole. Your loyalty to the team members will be paid back when they need to make personal sacrifices to reach team goals in high-pressure situations.

- *Communicate with team members.* Effective team leaders are good communicators. Including the entire team in the communication loop by letting team members know what other managers want them to know. Listen to the concerns of team members as well, and communicate their ideas or comments to higher level managers who can respond to these concerns by making changes. Facilitate good feedback and participation from all team members so that effective team decisions can be made.

- *Share power with the team.* Effective team leaders embrace the concept of teamwork in deeds as well as words. Share the power, information, and responsibility with the team members. Have faith in their decisions, even when they might not be the ones you would have made.

- *Learn to relax and admit your ignorance.* Team leaders aren't expected to know everything, and they cannot always be in control. Overcome the fear of looking vulnerable by not knowing the answer to a question—leaders who admit and learn from mistakes earn the respect of team members faster than those who act as if they were always in control. Being open and vulnerable also serves to build trust and improve team relationships. Team members will respond by opening up to each other, which will strengthen team members' bonds with each other.

Source: R. L. Daft, *The Leadership Experience*, 2nd ed. Cincinnati, OH: South-Western, 2002, pp. 363–366.

(1) provides feedback to team members ("I like how you answered that customer question"); (2) expresses a shared vision for the team ("Let's see if we can make zero defects for the entire week"); and (3) supports team members ("Tell me what resources you need to achieve our goal, and I will find them for you"). Manager's Notes 14.1 lists ways to be a successful team leader.

Some teams are led by supervisors or managers, who are expected to adjust their leadership style to work effectively with a team composed of subordinates. Parallel teams and project teams are likely to have a manager or supervisor in the role of the team leader. Other teams, especially self-managed teams, may have leaders selected from the ranks. This "lead

TABLE 14.2

Team Leaders at Saturn and Chrysler

TEAM CHARACTERISTIC	SATURN	CHRYSLER
Size	6–15 members	20–25 members
Election of leader	Yes	Yes
Term of leader	3 years	1 year
Premium pay of leader	None	$0.50/hour
Supervisor	None	Yes

Source: From H. Shaiken, S. Lopez, and I. Mankita. "Two Routes to Team Production: Saturn and Chrysler Compared," *Industrial Relations* 36 (1997), pp. 17–45. Copyright © 1997 Blackwell Publishers. Reprinted with permission.

employee" may be chosen by peers or by management. Some teams are "leaderless," generally those composed of highly motivated and experienced employees. In a sense, all team members are leaders on a leaderless team. Each of the four musicians who make up the Tokyo String Quartet, one of the world's finest chamber music ensembles, is a skilled virtuoso soloist, and the quarter operates more or less as a leaderless team. The automobile manufacturing plants at both Saturn and Chrysler use self-managed teams in their manufacturing process. Table 14.2 lists the similarities and differences of these teams. In particular, the self-managed teams at Saturn do not have a direct supervisor, while at Chrysler a supervisor acts as a "facilitator" or coach.

Behavioral Dimensions of Effective Teams

Members of effective teams share several behavioral characteristics. They are cohesive with each other, select high performance norms, cooperate, exhibit interdependence, and trust one another.

COHESIVENESS   The extent to which members feel a high degree of camaraderie, team spirit, and sense of unity is the degree of **team cohesiveness.** Individuals who are part of a cohesive team are concerned about the welfare of teammates as well as the team as a whole. When teams lack cohesion, individuals are less likely to enjoy meetings or social events and to work toward team goals. Members of teams that display cohesiveness are more likely to communicate with and influence each other. This is particularly beneficial when members have a strong attachment to high team performance.

There are ways to positively influence team cohesiveness:

1. Provide ample opportunities for team members to interact with each other during the early stages of team development. Social activities such as ice breaker exercises help stimulate interaction.

---

team cohesiveness

The extent to which members feel a high degree of camaraderie, team spirit, and sense of unity.

Navy SEALs are Highly Cohesive and Effective Teams

THEME: DEALING WITH CHANGE Some examples of high-performing teams occur outside the world of business in fields such as sports, medicine, and the military. The U.S. Navy SEALs are an elite team of individuals in the military who perform dangerous missions for the Navy. For example, one team of Navy SEALs went behind enemy lines recently to rescue Private Jessica Lynch who was captured during the war between the United States and Iraq in 2003. Other teams of Navy SEALs advanced on Taliban strongholds in Afghanistan during the 2001 war and called in devastating jet bomber firepower that blasted enemy troop concentrations.

While the first four weeks of Navy SEAL training is grueling, they pale in comparison with the fifth week known as hell week. During hell week, recruits swim many miles in cold water in the Pacific Ocean, they row rubber boats for hours on end, they run obstacle courses over and over, they perform grueling calisthenics using 300-pound logs, and they sustain personal insults from train-ers. During the entire hell week, recruits sleep perhaps four hours.

About 30 percent of the recruits drop out during the five-day, hell-week experience. This commitment is needed because hell week is followed by months of rigorous underwater training, weapons training, explosives training, parachute training, and a six-month probationary period. The ultimate success rate for recruits is about 30 percent.

Highly cohesive teamwork is essential because SEALs never operate on their own and team members identify totally with the group. Navy SEALs will never leave the battlefield if a fallen SEAL remains. The SEALs show us that rigorous training and a strong sense of cohesion among team members can produce highly effective outcomes.

Sources: J. Morse, B. Bennett, S. Donnelley, and M. Hequet, "Saving Private Jessica," *Time,* April 14, 2003, pp. 66–67; S. Foster, *Managing Quality,* Upper Saddle River, NJ: Prentice Hall, 2001, pp. 333–334; K. Labich and E. Davies, "Elite Teams Get the Job Done," *Fortune,* February 19, 1996, pp. 90–98.

2. Ensure that all team members have a voice in determining team goals. When the goals are attractive to all members, individuals are more motivated to participate in activities that intensify team cohesion.

3. Celebrate successful team outcomes with rewards for team members or recognize outstanding individual contributions to the team with an awards ceremony. These celebrations build team spirit.[8]

A good example of a highly cohesive team is given in Management Close-Up 14.c, which examines the rigorous training experienced by the Navy SEALs, an elite military unit.

NORMS   The shared beliefs that regulate the behavior of team members are its **team norms.** They represent the values and aspirations of the members and are likely to be formed during the forming and norming stages of development. Teams enforce norms with rewards and sanctions.

It is important for teams to develop and enforce norms to govern the behavior of employees who avoid doing their fair share of the work. When a team is cohesive but has weak performance norms, members are

team norms

Shared beliefs that regulate the behavior of team members.

likely to tolerate loafers rather than confront them, making failure more likely. A cohesive team with high performance norms has low tolerance for poor performance and is more likely to be effective. A shirker will feel that all team members are monitoring his or her behavior just as a supervisor would, making it uncomfortable to resist improving performance.

One way to ensure that team members have high performance norms is to select high-performing individuals as members of the team. Students in a management course that required team projects took this approach when they asked their professor to let them form their own teams so they could avoid conflicts with students who expected the rest of the team to do most of the work.

Team performance norms vary according to the mission of the team. At Microsoft, teams of software developers expect to work 80 or more hours a week to complete projects on time. A software developer insisting on a 40-hour weekly schedule would not last very long at Microsoft. Team performance norms influence quantity, quality, attendance at meetings, and open discussion of topics. Teams prohibit taking phone calls at meetings. And norms indicate that the team is more important than any individual, so it is better to be a team player than a star.[9]

COOPERATION   The willingness to share information and help others reflects the level of **cooperation** in the group. Team members who help achieve goals exhibit useful cooperative behaviors. These behaviors are sometimes at odds with **competitive behaviors,** which view other people as rivals for a limited pool of resources and focus on individual goals, noncollaboration with other employees, and the withholding of information. It is up to the team to nurture cooperative behavior by enforcing norms that reward cooperation and sanction competitive behavior. Rewarding team outcomes can help raise the level of interdependence among team members.

INTERDEPENDENCE   The extent to which team members depend on each other for resources, information, assistance, or mutual support to accomplish their tasks[10] is the degree of **interdependence** present. Tasks that involve teams of musicians giving an orchestral concert or actors giving a theatrical performance require a high degree of interaction and exchange—consequently these tasks are highly interdependent. On the other hand, tasks that involve a dock team unloading boxes of fresh fruit from a large trailer truck require lower levels of interaction, exchange, and interdependence. Three types of interdependence affect teams: pooled, sequential, and reciprocal.

Pooled interdependence is found in teams requiring the lowest amount of reliance on other members. Team members have significant aspects of their jobs where they are relatively independent from one another. With pooled interdependence, team members share some common resources such as fax and copy machines, clerical supplies, and secretar-

cooperative behavior

Team behavior that is manifested in members' willingness to share information and help others.

competitive behavior

Team behavior that views other people as rivals for a limited pool of resources and focuses on individual goals, noncollaboration, and the withholding of information.

interdependence

The extent that team members depend on each other for resources, information, assistance, or mutual support to accomplish their tasks.

pooled interdependence

Team behavior where team members share common resources such as fax and copy machines, supplies, and secretarial support, but most of the work is performed independently.

ial support, but most of the work is performed independently. Real estate agents in the same branch office may share office space, supplies, copy and fax machines, and the same clerical person, but nonetheless do most of their selling activities independently. Teamwork still matters when pooled interdependence is present. Anyone who has experienced an urgent need to copy an important document for a customer and found the copy machine in a state of disrepair due to the harsh treatment it received from the last user will attest to the need for teamwork.

Sequential interdependence is a series of hand-offs of work flow between team members in which the output of one team member becomes the input of the next team member, and so forth. Each team member in the sequence of exchanges depends on all previous team members to do their portion of the work correctly or else the entire team performance falls short of expectations. For example, automobile insurance companies often organize claims adjustment processes as a sequence of steps acted on by different claims specialists. An insurance team handles an automobile accident claim starting first with the insurance agent who collects accident information from the customer. The agent hands the accident claim over to the accident investigator who inspects the damage to the car and writes a claims report. Finally the case is sent to an accident claims adjuster who coordinates the claims of other parties involved in the accident and determines the payout to the customer. A mistake assessing the damage to the car by the accident investigator diminishes the performance of the entire claims adjustment team, because either an over- or underpayment will be made.

The greatest amount of interdependence, **reciprocal interdependence,** occurs when team members interact intensively back and forth with each other. The output of team member X becomes the input of team member Y, and the output of team member Y returns as the input to team member X. This series of reciprocal exchanges of work between team members continues until the work is judged to meet performance standards. Projects involving research and scientific work are often organized with teams that are characterized by reciprocal interdependence. Software development teams consist of: (1) software design experts that create the computer code, (2) software testing experts that test the software for bugs that reduce the reliability of the software, and (3) technical writers that create technical manuals that explain to customers how to use all the different applications that are built into the software. Software designers, testers, and writers are reciprocally interdependent, as can be demonstrated when software bugs are discovered by testers. The presence of a software bug is a flaw in the code which results in a need to make a modification to the code by the designers. The software code modification may in turn result in the need for revisions to be made to the computer user manual by the technical writers. Each time a software bug is located, this cycle of change is repeated until all the bugs are eliminated.

sequential interdependence

A series of hand-offs of work flow between team members in which output of one team member becomes the input of the next team member, and so forth.

reciprocal interdependence

The greatest amount of interdependence that occurs when team members interact intensively back and forth with each other until their work is judged to meet performance standards.

TRUST Team members are mutually accountable. If one member makes a serious error, it reflects on the performance and reputation of all team members. **Trust** is the willingness of one person to increase his or her vulnerability to the actions of another person whose behavior he or she cannot control.

All teams require trust between members. Self-managed teams require the highest degree of trust. Supervision of a self-managed team is performed by team members who are mutually vulnerable. They evaluate, reward, and even discipline each other. When trust is present, there is a much greater likelihood that team members will cooperate to complete critical tasks.

Trust can be created among team members by:

1. *Communicating openly.* At team meetings and in face-to-face conversations, strive to be open and honest. Share thoughts and feelings with team members when they relate to the business of the team.

2. *Sharing credit with others.* Do not take credit for more than your fair share of the team's success. Be generous with praise and recognition for the contributions of other teams.

3. *Reciprocating help from teammates.* Look for ways to help teammates, and reciprocate goodwill so teammates feel that their efforts are appreciated.

4. *Avoiding acting purely out of self-interest.* Find ways to align your needs with the interests of the team and other team members.

Team Performance Problems

Several problems within teams make it difficult to succeed. Trust and cooperation are absent or weak in malfunctioning teams and performance suffers. Managers and team members must try to determine the cause of poor team performance and implement changes to improve it. Manager's Notes 14.2 identifies typical team performance problems a manager can expect to encounter. Three of the most challenging problems are free riders, the nonconforming high performer, and the lack of rewards for teamwork.

Free Riders

Individuals who find it rational to withhold effort and provide minimum input to the team in exchange for a full share of the rewards are known as **free riders,** which is also called *social loafing* or *shirking.* It takes place because individuals can hide behind the collective effort of the team and get "lost in the crowd." When free riders are tolerated, other members may reduce their efforts ("Why should I work hard when free riders profit at my expense?") and team productivity suffers as a result.

Threats to Effective Team Performance

1. *Free riders.* Free riders do not participate in team efforts, but they expect to take credit for team success and receive a full share of team rewards. Free riders can quickly reduce team morale and productivity if their behavior is tolerated.

2. *Dysfunctional team conflict.* Teams can become dysfunctional if some members take a personal dislike to others or engage in political maneuvers and games. Factions within the team that compete for power by rewarding friends and punishing enemies are often the result. Infighting among these factions redirects team energies to political goals of the factions rather than the performance goals of the team and the organization.

3. *Groupthink.* Groupthink is a malady that happens when the team is intolerant of a healthy diversity of opinions—teams come to value agreement and consensus and avoid the functional conflict over real differences that can positively influence the team's performance. Groupthink undermines the purpose of most teams: the combination of people with different skills and experiences to create something more valuable than what the individual could have accomplished alone.

4. *Self-management opposition.* Team members may not want to be self-managed. Some teams are composed of individuals who prefer to have leaders direct and inspire them and who prefer less involvement in the actual decision making. Teams that desire a strong leader but who are forced to become self-managing typically will not be successful.

5. *Insecure supervisors.* Many team initiatives are derailed by supervisors and managers who feel threatened by any proposed change. Some supervisors may feel that self-managed teams reduce their status when the teams take on some of the supervisor's responsibilities. These supervisors may resist and undermine the success of self-managed teams. Unless supervisors have a reason to support teams, they may meet this approach with strong resistance.

6. *Disruptive high performers.* A high-performing team member may demand special treatment and treat other team members disrespectfully. Disruptive high performers often cost the team more in terms of cohesiveness and total outcome than their special talents warrant.

7. *Lack of teamwork rewards.* An organization that expects people to work productively in teams might nevertheless reward employees based on their individual contributions. This bias toward individual performance rather than team performance reinforces competition among team members to be seen as individual achievers rather than cooperative workers. It creates strong disincentives for teamwork to take place.

Sources: Adapted from A. Sinclair, "The Tyranny of Team Ideology," *Organization Studies* 13 (1992): 611–626; L. R. Gomez-Mejia and D. B. Balkin, *Compensation, Organizational Strategy, and Firm Performance.* Cincinnati: South-Western, 1992.

Free riders take advantage of the difficulty managers face in separating out each team member's contribution to the overall outcome. Fortunately, there are a number of ways to deal with free riders before they undermine team morale. The best approach is to make it difficult for individuals to profit from free riding:

- Empower team members to have control over the recruitment and selection of new members. Front-line employees have more opportunities than managers to observe coworkers and know their work habits.

- Empower team members to have a voice in evaluating and disciplining peers who are not performing up to expectations. This makes it more difficult for free riders to loaf without consequences. For example, Unisys, a computer information systems company, requires that performance reviews be carried out by the team leader and three peers chosen by the employee. A poor evaluation may result in a diminished team bonus for the poorly performing member.

- Ensure that high performance norms are established early in the life of the team so that each member clearly understands performance expectations. Social controls, such as shunning those who violate performance norms, are more effective at eliminating free riding than monitoring by the supervisor. Managers can influence the development of norms by articulating a shared vision and mission that captures the imagination of the team and that spells out the expectation that each individual must provide a high level of effort.

The Nonconforming High Performer

nonconforming high performer

A team member who is individualistic and whose presence is disruptive to the team.

Teams have procedures to deal with poor performers and individuals who violate a norm. These include disciplining the offending party through peer group pressure and giving the individual strongly worded critical feedback during a performance evaluation. A greater challenge is dealing with a high-performing team member who is individualistic and whose presence is disruptive to the team.

Sports teams and the entertainment industries have many examples of high-performing individuals with outsized egos who expect star treatment. Allen Iverson, an all-star guard on the Philadelphia 76ers professional basketball team and the league's most valuable player in 2000–2001, has been a difficult player to manage. Despite being an excellent player in games, Iverson had missed team practices as well as flights to games with team members. He also recorded songs that are disrespectful to women. Iverson's behavior had a negative impact on the team's morale, his coach, and the team's fans. In the 1990s, television actresses Roseanne, of the "Roseanne" show, and Brett Butler, the star of

Big screen star Russell Crowe has had many well-documented confrontations, yet his star continues to rise.

"Grace Under Fire," drove out a succession of writers and producers. The executive producers for these popular programs, Marcy Carsey and Tom Werner, were sometimes criticized for caving in to the stars' demands and for being inhospitable to writers. Carsey and Werner brushed aside the criticism. Such stars "have a lot on the line," says Carsey. "And any kind of nervousness, insecurity on their part is totally natural and very healthy."[11]

Must high performers conform and be treated like everybody else on the team or be asked to leave? The answer is, "it depends." Japanese corporations have a motto that "the head that sticks out gets pounded," which means that there is little tolerance for nonconforming behavior on Japanese teams. Those who ignore norms cause other members of the team to lose face, the personal dignity that is vitally important in Japanese culture. The United States has a more individualistic culture and is more tolerant of quirky behavior, even on teams.[12]

Sometimes it is better to channel the star's creative energies into the work of the team. A high performer who deserves special recognition should receive it. Some high performers simply want recognition for their contributions. Sports has most valuable player awards, and film has the Oscars. There's no reason why a business cannot have a recognition event for high contributors to team success.

Some teams are less cohesive and more individualistic than others. These teams can better tolerate a nonconformist. Nonconforming high performers can succeed on problem-solving teams, virtual teams, and project teams where the intensity of team interactions is low compared to self-managed teams. A nonconformist is less likely to upset other team members on a virtual team because they are interacting via computer terminal, while an egotistical team member may quickly get on the nerves of others on a self-managed team because there are many more opportunities for face-to-face interactions.

Lack of Rewards for Teamwork

A problem common to many organizations that utilize teams is that there are few if any rewards for teams that meet or exceed performance goals. These same organizations provide merit pay and other rewards for individual performance. When the only rewards are for individual performance, employees are likely to compete with each other for the incentive pay. This undermines the willingness to collaborate and team cohesiveness. For example, scientists at the National Institute of Standards and Technology (NIST), a U.S. government research laboratory, are expected to work on project teams with scientists from different disciplines. However, the main reward is merit pay, which rewards individual scientific contributions such as publishing research in leading scientific journals or making presentations at prestigious scientific conferences. Managers determine which scientists receive merit pay by comparing all the scientists and ranking them. These same managers have found it difficult to motivate the scientists to work on team projects that produce results for the good of the laboratory.

The lesson is that teamwork must be rewarded to strengthen and sustain team effort. Rewards can be monetary (such as a team bonus) or nonmonetary (such as a recognition). Other ways to reward teamwork include:

- Develop a "reward and recognition" committee that has a budget to recognize outstanding team performance with monetary or nonmonetary rewards that are meaningful to the team members. The committee should be composed of representatives from various teams and managers. It should design team reward policies and then administer rewards to deserving teams.

- Involving customers in the team reward process. For example, customers could nominate a team for a cash bonus or recognition reward. Xerox recognizes its customer service teams in this way.

- Using team rewards to complement pay policies that reward employees for their work as individuals. Team-based pay does not have to replace merit pay. Employees will be less likely to neglect their team responsibilities because they will be motivated to focus their best efforts on both individual and team goals in order to realize their total potential earnings.[13]

Team Management Skills

Teams must advance through stages where conflict and differences between members are normal. If members get stuck on important issues because of conflict, the team fails to achieve its potential, and performance suffers. Two management skills—conflict management and negotiation—are critical for team members and team leaders.

Conflict Management Skills

Conflict arises when members disagree over team policies, goals, or the motives and values of other team members. People are always going to have differences of opinion. Conflict is a normal part of the work of teams. But if conflict is not managed effectively, team members will focus on the dispute rather than on team performance. The first step in managing conflict is determining whether the conflict is functional or dysfunctional.

FUNCTIONAL CONFLICT   There are times when conflict stimulates team and organizational performance. As suggested in Figure 14.2, moderate levels of conflict can have a positive influence on the team and the organization, because:

- *Creativity is stimulated.* Various positions can be contrasted when team members advocate differing approaches to achieving a goal. The debate can engage each member to express an opinion and even come up with a creative compromise that was not obvious until the conflict put the issues into perspective. Teams in creative fields such as advertising or consulting rely on the tensions embedded in conflict to develop innovative solutions for clients.

- *Poor solutions are avoided.* People often become emotionally attached to their ideas. Disagreements over a goal or a decision alternative may lead to conflict. If the conflict is over an issue that affects team performance, the conflict is functional. When team members feel free to openly express their opinions and disagree with others, poor choices are avoided.

- *Team members are energized.* Conflict excites and arouses individuals. Moderate conflict can energize people to exert more effort toward team goals. Debates are an excellent way to motivate students to learn about a topic in economics such as capitalism or markets. When students take sides in a highly charged debate, their motivation to learn about the topic increases.

Styles of Handling Conflict

FIGURE 14.2

Intensity of Conflict and Organizational Outcomes

Source: From L. David Brown, *Managing Conflict at Organizational Interfaces*, 1983. Reprinted with permission of L. David Brown.

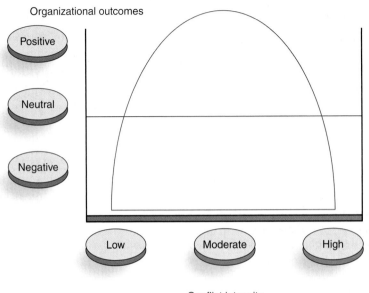

Organizational outcomes

Positive

Neutral

Negative

Low   Moderate   High

Conflict intensity

---

dysfunctional conflict

Conflict that has a negative effect on team and organizational performance.

DYSFUNCTIONAL CONFLICT   Some forms of conflict have negative effects on team and organizational performance. This occurs when the intensity of the conflict is high, which is disruptive to team performance, or when the intensity is too low, which results in lack of stimulation. Dysfunctional conflict can be caused by:

- Competition for scarce resources such as pay, promotions, or equipment.
- Clashing personalities or styles resulting in bad chemistry between people on a team.
- Incompatible value systems that create conflict about, for instance, the relative importance of work, family, and leisure.
- Role ambiguities in which individuals enact their team roles in ways that are not expected by other team members.
- Time pressures due to unrealistic deadlines.
- Goal differences that result in team members working for different outcomes.

groupthink

Team behavior that occurs when members prefer to avoid conflict rather than tolerate a healthy diversity of opinions.

Managers Notebook 14.2 introduced the idea of **groupthink,** which occurs when team members prefer to avoid conflict rather than tolerate a healthy diversity of opinions. This results in traditional and conservative decisions which are likely to be unsatisfactory. It is important to find ways to manage groupthink as well as other forms of dysfunctional conflict.

People tend to have different conflict management styles, based on placing different emphasis on concern for their own needs and concern

NEGOTIATION FOR A PAY RAISE

This exercise applies win–win negotiation skills in a business situation that is common to many managers and employees—negotiating a pay raise.

Many managers are faced with the situation where one of the employees under their supervision asks for an increase in pay. The negotiation can be sensitive. The manager and employee are likely to be in a long-term employment relationship, and if one party "wins" at the expense of the other in the context of negotiation, it could strain their working relationship. A win–win negotiation style seems to be most appropriate for this situation.

Instructions: Find one partner to work with in this exercise. One person takes the role of the employee seeking a pay raise, and the partner takes the role of the manager. Together, explore ways to turn a request for a pay raise into a win–win negotiation where the outcome is a settlement that is satisfactory to each party. Following are the constraints of the negotiation situation:

1. The manager must follow the salary guidelines provided by the policy and cannot make a special exception for this employee.

2. The employee has already received a pay raise this year but feels it is inadequate and is not due for another pay raise until next year.

3. The manager wants to preserve the motivation of this employee, who is a good performer in the unit.

Discuss how you and your partner would approach the salary negotiation and answer the following questions.

Discussion Questions

1. How should the employee frame the request for a pay raise to the manager to get a more favorable outcome? What kind of information should the employee focus on?

2. How should the manager frame the answer to the request to the employee to get a more favorable outcome? What kind of information should the manager focus on?

3. What are the areas of agreement between the two parties? What are the areas of disagreement between the two parties?

4. What are some possible solutions that would be acceptable to both parties?

---

for the needs of others. The various styles of conflict management include integrating, obliging, dominating, avoiding, and compromising. Each is appropriate in different situations. It helps to have a repertoire of conflict management styles to draw upon.

The **integrating style,** or *problem-solving style,* is used when the manager or team member can frame the issue as a problem and encourage the parties to identify the problem, examine alternatives, and agree on a satisfactory solution. The solution depends on the negotiating skills of the parties. This style enables each party to achieve its interests. The integrating style provides effective long-term solutions to conflicts, enabling the parties to come to a consensus and get on with the work. It is also time-consuming and does not work when immediate conflict resolution is needed.

integrating style

Conflict resolution demonstrated by framing the issue as a problem and encouraging the interested parties to identify the problem, examine alternatives, and agree on a solution.

An **obliging style,** or *smoothing style,* may be used when the party managing the conflict is willing to neglect his or her own needs in order to accommodate the needs of the other party. The individual decides to smooth over the conflict and focus on similarities with the other party. This style creates a win for the other party and a loss for the individual making the accommodation. It provides a short-term resolution to conflict, but the solution may give rise to resentment that may later cause a new conflict.

A **dominating style,** or *forcing style,* may be used when the manager or team member acts in an assertive and forceful way and persuades the other party to abandon his or her objectives. The dominating style is a top-down approach to managing conflict. When time is critical and there is an emergency, this style may be the most effective way to proceed. When a verbally aggressive team member uses it to intimidate another team member during a discussion of values, the style is inappropriate and intensifies rather than mitigates conflict.

An **avoiding style** is used when the individual decides it is better to avoid the conflict rather than deal with it. It can be effective when the issues are trivial and avoiding can be used to buy time. The avoiding style will be ineffective when applied to more serious issues. If all team members have a tendency to use the avoiding style, the team is highly likely to suffer from groupthink and lag in performance.

A **compromising style** may be used when the manager or team member makes some concessions to the other party and the other party is willing to reciprocate. When this happens, a give-and-take resolution is reached. The compromising style requires the parties be able to "split the difference" over the issues in dispute. This style may be effective when resources can be shared. It may be inappropriate when values or principles are the source of the conflict. In some cases, compromise results in a solution that is of low quality and unacceptable to all team members.

APPLYING THE PROBLEM-SOLVING STYLE OF CONFLICT MANAGEMENT   The problem-solving style of conflict management offers the best opportunity for both parties in a dispute to achieve their interests. It can be used when the parties are willing to communicate openly and disclose their interests to each other. They must be able to explore different ways to reach mutually satisfying solutions. In many cases, the interests of a party may be different than that party's stated position. While a party's stated position may focus on competition over a limited resource or opportunity that each party wants, a party's interest may be reached by other means. For example, an employee's stated position in a conflict over her work schedule with a manager could be to avoid working overtime hours in order to be able to coach her daughter's soccer team which plays games late in the afternoon. The employee's interest, which is to spend time with her daughter in the late afternoon, may be achieved with a more flexible work schedule, allowing her to do some of the work at home, which may also satisfy her manager's need for overtime work to be performed.

The problem-solving approach to conflict management should convene with a meeting at the right time and place when both parties are feeling motivated to resolve the conflict. After the problem-solving discussion between the parties gets under way, there may be times when one or both parties become angry or frustrated with each other. Time out may need to be taken at these points to allow the parties to cool down. Later, after the cooling-off period, discussions can resume until a workable resolution is achieved.

Becky, an advertising account executive, used the problem-solving style of conflict resolution with her team. Becky managed an account team at a busy advertising agency. The team worked hard and played hard. In return Becky was flexible about time off for team members. Recently, Becky felt that they were prioritizing their social lives above meeting work deadlines. Having stayed late to finalize urgent jobs for clients, she felt angry that tasks had been left for her to complete. Becky called a team meeting and calmly and assertively stated how she felt about the team's behavior. She explained that in taking on their work, her own work had not been completed on time, putting potential new business at risk. Becky asked the team for ideas to solve the problem. They all agreed that with privileges on time off came responsibilities for seeing jobs through. The result of this problem-solving discussion with the team was that Becky was able to complete her work and rely on her team to take their responsibilities seriously. Becky was able to resolve the conflict because she was able to state how her team's behavior had affected her. She explained what she wanted to happen instead and was willing to explore ideas to overcome the problem with her team.[14]

Unfortunately the willingness of both parties in a conflict to communicate openly is not always present, and this is needed for the problem-solving style to be effective. For example, at times parties in a conflict may not want to reveal their interests to each other because they have hidden agendas. The hidden agendas may be to "get even" with the other party because of real or imagined causes attributed to the other person. Problem solving in this case is pointless, because one or both of the parties are not willing to cooperate to solve the problem. In this hidden agenda situation, a different conflict management style such as the avoiding approach will be more appropriate.

SELECTING A CONFLICT MANAGEMENT STYLE   A useful approach to selecting a conflict management style is to examine the conflict situation according to the chart presented in Figure 14.3. The figure matches a person's combined level of assertiveness and cooperativeness to one of the five conflict management styles: problem solving, smoothing, dominating, avoiding, and compromising. Assertiveness means a person is willing to satisfy his or her own concerns. Cooperativeness occurs when a person attempts to satisfy the other party's concerns. Since conflict management is a dynamic process, a party that behaves in an uncooperative fashion is likely to be treated the same way by the other party.

FIGURE 14.3

Five Conflict-Handling Styles

Source: Adapted from K. Thomas, "Conflict and Conflict Management," in *Handbook of Industrial and Organizational Behavior,* ed. M. D. Dunnette. New York: John Wiley, 1976, p. 900.

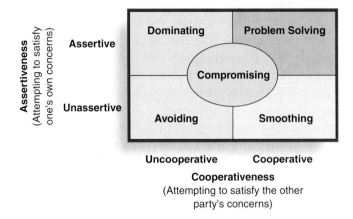

Therefore, styles that depend on cooperativeness such as the problem-solving and smoothing styles cannot be used. The mutual uncooperativeness enacted by the parties would result in the use of either the dominating or avoiding styles of conflict management. An assertive party will select the dominating style while a less assertive party will select the avoiding style.

When the parties strive to be cooperative with each other, they can select the problem-solving or smoothing styles, but not the dominating or avoiding styles. The problem-solving style provides the most promising opportunity to reach long-term solutions because both party's concerns are likely to be met. However, if a party in the conflict does not behave in an assertive way the smoothing style may be selected to reach a resolution. Smoothing solutions may provide a short-term conflict resolution for the unassertive party, but it will not be satisfying to this party in the long term since one's concerns were not satisfied. Finally, if the parties in the conflict are only moderately assertive and cooperative as shown in Figure 14.3, a compromising style of conflict management is selected. In the compromising style the parties have moderate concern for their own interests and those of the other party. Compromises can be effective in some situations and not in others, since the compromise produces solutions that partially satisfy the concerns of each party but do not fully satisfy the concerns of either party.

Negotiation Skills

Negotiation skills are used in situations where people attempt to exchange goods and services and to find a fair price or solution. The problem-solving style of conflict management relies heavily on negotiating skills. Negotiation skills can also be used in negotiating a raise, settling on the price of a house, or agreeing on a fair procedure to allocate overtime hours.

One of the most useful negotiation skills is the **win–win style** of negotiation which is also referred to as *integrative bargaining*. The win–win negotiating style requires the parties to convert a potential conflict into a problem-solving process in which each party seeks to identify common, shared, or joint goals. In a sense, each party is looking for solutions that are good for everyone. This is particularly important when they are involved in a long-term working relationship.

To make use of the win–win negotiating style:

1. Prepare for negotiation by understanding your own needs and strengths and weaknesses. Determine your own bottom line.

2. Attempt to understand the other party's real needs and objectives. Engage in a dialogue in which both parties disclose their true preferences and priorities, rather than disguise and manipulate them.

3. Emphasize the commonalities and minimize the differences between the parties. Reframe goals as part of a larger collaborative goal. For example, the team goal of providing customer satisfaction is a common goal on which both parties agree, although they may differ on specific approaches to achieve it.

4. Search for solutions that meet both parties' goals and objectives. When parties are combative or competitive, they are more likely to focus on their own objectives and ignore those of the other party. A win–win negotiation is successful only when the needs of both parties are met.

5. Focus on building a relationship in a negotiation rather than making a one-time deal.[15]

One other style of negotiation that can be used in limited situations is the **win–lose style** of negotiation, sometimes referred to as *distributive bargaining*. The win–lose negotiating style is typically used when there is a single issue that consists of a fixed amount of resources in which one party attempts to gain at the expense of the other. Therefore, the win–lose negotiation is concerned with who will receive the most beneficial distribution of a fixed amount of goods. A negotiation between a buyer and seller of a used car may take the form of a win–lose negotiation regarding the car's price. The seller is interested in obtaining the highest price and the buyer is interested in obtaining the lowest price for the car.

Win–lose negotiating styles have limited applications on teams because team members are mutually accountable and interdependent on each other to achieve their common goals. Moreover, parties involved in a win–lose negotiation are most likely to use the dominating style of conflict management. Successful win–lose negotiation outcomes depend on each's party's ability to impose its will and convince its opponent that the costs of disagreement with the other person's terms are high. The party that can impose the highest costs of disagreement to one's position achieves the most concessions from the opposing party.

win–win style

Negotiating style requiring all interested parties to convert a potential conflict into a problem-solving process in which each party seeks to identify common, shared, or joint goals.

win–lose style

Negotiating style used when there is a single issue that consists of a fixed amount of resources in which one party attempts to gain at the expense of the other.

Behaviors typical of a win–lose style include deception, exaggerating one's strengths, threats, bluffs, and withholding information that would be helpful to the other party. A job applicant who is desperate for a job may enter into a win–lose negotiation with an employer who may use his ability to impose high costs (the threat of no job offer) on the job applicant and pressure her to take a job offer at a much lower salary than she wants. As this example shows, success in win–lose negotiation depends on the ability of each party to take advantage of and exploit the weaknesses of the other party. Win–lose negotiating styles should be used sparingly and only in exceptional circumstances. Most management processes require developing effective, collaborative, long-term relationships between employees, customers, and other parties. These relationships will be impaired when win–lose negotiating styles are used. The party that "loses" the negotiation is not likely to have positive feelings toward the "winner."

Finally, there are three common mistakes that inexperienced negotiators should be aware of and try to avoid making:

- *Do not assume that a negotiation must always result in a settlement.* When a person assumes that a negotiation must result in a settlement, the other party can take advantage by threatening to end the negotiations. This can result in unnecessary concessions being made to facilitate a settlement. It is a better practice to enter a negotiation with a resistance point in mind. The resistance point represents one's minimum acceptable position for a settlement. If the other party refuses to at least meet your resistance point in negotiations then it is better to walk away and end the negotiations.

- *Avoid becoming fixated on one particular issue in the negotiation.* Some issues are easier to settle than others in a negotiation. If the parties get stuck on an issue and find their positions frozen and lacking a settlement, it is best to move on. Settle other issues that are less difficult to agree on. In many cases the goodwill that is established between the parties when they can resolve the easier issues provides the momentum that enables the parties to collaborate and finalize the difficult issues that remain.

- *Do not assume that the other party has all the power due to greater levels of experience.* If you assume that you are powerless in a negotiation, there is a good chance you will act as if that assumption were true. You will be less apt to reach your goals. In truth, each party to a negotiation has some power—otherwise the negotiation would not take place. People negotiate because each party perceives that its counterpart controls something that it wants in an exchange. By being aware of both your interests and those of the other party, you can negotiate more confidently and increase your chances of reaching a satisfying settlement.

Applications for the Manager   When determining how many people should be on a team, keep the team small. When a team is larger than 15 people, it becomes difficult to develop common purpose, goals, approach, and mutual accountability. It is also easier for individuals to shirk their duties on a large team without being noticed. Rather than have one large team of 24 employees, it is preferable to have two smaller ones of 12 people.

When assigning people to work on a team, select the right mix of people with complementary skills. People with the appropriate technical skills are needed to do the actual work of the team. People with administrative skills are needed to organize and schedule work and to document useful information and make it accessible to other team members. People with quality interpersonal skills are required to sustain group cohesion and harmony. If a team is composed of individuals who are competent in only one of these skills, the team is not likely to reach its potential.

Applications for Managing Teams   It takes time for a team to earn the right to manage itself. It is not realistic to expect a team to start out with the ability to manage itself. In most cases, a team should first be given a few responsibilities, with more responsibilities added as the team proves itself capable of handling them.

Not all groups of people are capable of functioning as a team. Sometimes the chemistry between people is wrong, the team malfunctions, and it may be best to disband the team and reassign the people to different teams. One indicator of a troubled team is getting stuck in the development process and being unable to reach the performance stage in an acceptable amount of time.

Applications for Individuals   It is important to know how to cope with disruptive team members. The general rule is to avoid embarrassing or intimidating participants regardless of their disruptive behavior. It is best to use supportive communication and collaborative conflict management approaches. For example, if a member habitually arrives late and interrupts team meetings, announce an odd starting time (9:43 A.M.) for the meeting to emphasize the need for promptness, and establish a "latecomer kitty" for refreshments. A way to handle the "silent distracter" who reads newspapers, rolls the eyes, and fidgets while other people are speaking is to ask the person questions and draw him or her into the conversation.

After the introductory vignette at the beginning of the chapter we presented some critical thinking questions related to the use of teams at Toyota automobile dealerships and Boeing Airlift and Tanker Programs. Now that you have had the opportunity to learn about managing teams in the chapter, study the questions that were raised in the opening vignette. First, the customer service teams at the Toyota dealership are likely to provide better service to the customer because the customer will always work with the same service manager and team of mechanics each time the car is left at the dealership for service. The special needs of the customer's car will be better known to the service manager and the other team members due to their familiarity with the care from previous service visits. The service team will be more committed to providing quality service to the customer. A long-term relationship will develop between the customer and the service team. When the customer has a problem with the service that is provided, instead of asking for help from an unknown person, the customer can work with a service manager whom he or she knows and trusts.

The type of team that most closely matches the teams described at Boeing's Airlift and Tanker Programs is a self-managed team. The teams were given the responsibility to: (1) elect their own team leaders, (2) set their own goals, (3) develop measures for monitoring and judging their performance, and (4) interview new team members. These responsibilities provided strong indicators that the team is self-managed because they all represent the kinds of responsibilities that could be delegated to self-managed teams.

SUMMARY

A **team** is a small number of people with complementary skills committed to a common purpose, set of performance goals, and approach for which they hold themselves mutually accountable. The benefits of using teams include lower costs and higher productivity, quality improvements, speed, and innovation.

Teams can be classified according to the expected duration of the team and the time commitment that team members can be expected to provide. Based on these two factors, the types of teams include the **self-managed team** responsible for producing an entire product, component, or service; the **project team,** which works on a project until completion and then disbands; the **parallel team,** which works on a particular problem that requires only part-time commitment; and the **virtual team** in which team members collaborate via computer.

There are five stages in the development of teams. The first is the **forming** stage, when people get acquainted and establish ground rules. Second is the **storming** stage, when team members discuss differences in goals, priorities, and values and strive to manage conflicts over these issues. Third is the **norming** stage, characterized by resolution of important differences in goals and values and the establishment of norms governing the behavior of team members. The norms enable the team to sanction individuals who violate important team rules and procedures. Fourth is the **performing** stage, where the team focuses on performing its important tasks. The last is the **adjourning** stage which results in disbanding of the team when the team's purpose is completed.

Effective team performance requires team members to play different roles to enable the team to realize its potential. The **task-facilitating** role puts a priority on helping the team accomplish its task goals. Other team members enact the **relationship-building** role, which focuses on sustaining harmony between people on the team. The team leader helps the team strike a balance between the task-facilitating and relationship-building roles and deal with deviant individuals who frustrate the team's ability to perform effectively.

One of the challenges of managing teams is dealing with problems that can undermine the focus of the team. Three of the most challenging issues are **free riders,** who take credit for team efforts while providing minimal work; **nonconforming high performers,** who perform well as individuals but are difficult to work with in collaborative endeavors; and lack of rewards for teamwork in contrast to individual performance.

DISCUSSION QUESTIONS

1. Based on your personal experiences, what do you think are the advantages of teams? Which situations in a business are most likely to be most favorable for teams to perform effectively?

2. Again drawing on your own personal experiences, indicate what you think are the disadvantages of using teams. Which situations in a business are least suitable for team performance?

3. What is the role of the team leader? Should teams always have leaders? When might it be reasonable for a team to purposely leave out the role of team leader?

4. How do teams deal with individuals who violate important norms, for example, by engaging in negative conflict? Which do you think is a more effective way to sustain team performance: (a) the use of peer group pressure or (b) a supervisor who monitors and controls the behavior of team members?

5. Suppose you are working on a class project with five students, and one of the team members never shows up for your weekly meetings. Soon your project is due to be turned in to the professor. You and other team members are getting concerned about this "free rider." How should the team deal with this problem?

6. Suppose you are on a project team similar to the one in question 5. One of the team members is very abrasive—using foul language and having a negative attitude—and is highly critical of the work of all the other team members, including you. This person also has an A (3.95) grade point average and wants to do the whole project alone and is willing to turn it in to the professor and share the credit with the whole team. The team is divided about how to respond to this offer, because this team member could quite possibly achieve a better grade on the project than the team. How should the team deal with this individual?

7. Can too little conflict be a problem for a team? What are the effects on team performance of little or no conflict? In cases where there is an absence of functional conflict, how can conflict be stimulated? Which role(s) are most likely to stimulate the conflict?

8. Many contingent (temporary and part-time) employees are used in the workplace today. Do you think a team composed of a mix of full-time and contingent employees can work together effectively? What problems might be encountered in this mix? Which type of team (parallel, project, self-managed, or virtual) is most likely to experience an adverse effect on performance when full-time and contingent employees are both present?

Are Teams Worth It?

Giving employees more say over their jobs will likely boost workplace morale. It may not, however, increase productivity, according to a recently published National Bureau of Economic Research study.

The study surveyed executives at 373 companies, including manufacturing, service, and retail. The researchers discovered that employee participation in decision making had increased greatly in recent years. Management practices to foster this involvement included soliciting input from employees in designing compensation packages, creating self-managed teams, and setting up worker committees to analyze quality problems.

In 1983, the 373 companies each had an average of 1.5 such programs in place; by 1993, they averaged 6. Although only 20 percent of the companies surveyed their employees about their job conditions in 1983, some 74 percent did so by 1993.

The study also surveyed 2,408 employees and found that 34 percent of employees whose companies had programs involving them in decision making were very satisfied with the level of influence they exercised over their work lives. In companies without these programs, only 19 percent showed the same level of satisfaction. Those involved in decision making were more trusting of their employees and felt greater loyalty to them, with management relations rated better than average. Workers in nonunion companies were also less inclined than other workers to favor union representation. The employees surveyed believed the programs had been effective in improving productivity or quality.

The study results, however, revealed no difference in terms of sales per employee between companies with large percentages of workers in employee-involvement programs and companies with little commitment to them. Although the study didn't look at the programs in terms of turnover and absenteeism, it could be assumed that the happier employees will be less likely to quit and have lower rates of absenteeism. This would save the company money. Even if this assumption is true, the cost of setting up and running employee-involvement programs may offset savings in turnover and absenteeism, says Morris M. Kleiner, a labor economist at the University of Minnesota, who wrote the study with Richard B. Freeman, a Harvard economist, and Cheri Ostroff, a professor and expert in organizational management at Columbia University's Teachers College.

The researchers certainly do not suggest that companies do away with these programs. Even if productivity isn't increased, it isn't harmed, and the workforce is happier. Their involvement breeds contentment. "Employees tend to like it," Kleiner says. "They would be upset if these programs were done away with."

Discussion Questions

1. The study described in this case suggests that the use of teams, a popular way to empower employees at the workplace, does not necessarily lead to any higher levels of sales per employee than at companies that do not use teams. What conclusions, if any, can you draw from this finding?

2. What positive outcomes to the companies in this study would you expect the use of teams to provide? Explain your reasoning.

3. Describe a situation where it might be better not to use teams at all, and perhaps to do away with teams.

Source: P. Mendels, "Is Breeding Contentment Worth the Investment?" *Business Week*, January 10, 2001.

Whole Foods: Using Teamwork as a Recipe for Success

Whole Foods Inc. is the nation's number one chain of natural foods supermarkets. The company has more than 143 stores under the names of Whole Foods Market, Bread & Circus, Bread of Life, Fresh Fields, Merchant of Vino, and Wellspring Grocery. These stores are complete supermarkets with an emphasis on organically grown produce, fresh-baked bread, wholesome deli foods, and other health-food products. Conspicuously absent at Whole Foods stores are soft drinks in plastic containers, coupon dispensers for laundry detergent, salted potato chips, sugared cereals, and other high-sugar or high-fat products.

In the turbulent supermarket industry, Whole Foods has created a new approach to managing its employees—an approach based on teamwork and employee empowerment. Each Whole Foods store is an autonomous profit center composed of an average of 10 self-managed teams. A separate team operates each of the departments of the store, such as produce, canned goods, or the bakery. Each team has a team leader and specific team goals. The teams function as autonomous units. Members meet monthly to share information, exchange stories, solve problems, and talk about how to improve performance. The team leaders in each store form additional teams. Store leaders in each geographical region are a team and the leaders of each of the company's six regions are a team.

Why teams? Two primary benefits result from the company's emphasis on teamwork. First, teams promote cooperation among the store's employees. The teamwork approach facilitates a strong sense of community. This fosters pride and discipline in the work ethic of employees. An example of this is found in Whole Foods' hiring practices. The teams, rather than the store managers, have the power to approve new hires for full-time jobs. The store leaders provide the initial screening, but it takes a two-thirds vote of the team, after what is usually a 30-day trial period, for the candidate to become a full-time employee. This type of approval helps a team bond, which in turn facilitates a cooperative atmosphere. Another example of the ways in which teamwork promotes cooperation is evident in Whole Foods' team meetings. Each team holds a team meeting at least once a month. There is no rank at the team meetings. Everyone is given an equal opportunity to contribute to the discussion.

The second benefit that Whole Foods realizes from its emphasis on teamwork is an increased competitive spirit among its employees. The individual teams, stores, and regions of the company compete against each other in terms of quality, service, and profitability. The results of these competitions determine employee bonuses, recognition, and promotions. To facilitate competition, the company is extraordinarily open in terms of team performance measures. At a Bread & Circus store in Wellesley, Massachusetts, a sheet posted next to the time clock lists the previous day's sales broken down by team. A separate sheet lists the sales numbers for the same day the previous year. This information is used by the teams to determine "what it will take" to be the top team for the store during a particular week. This type of competition also exists at the store level. Near the same time clock, a weekly fax is posted listing the sales of each store in the New England region broken down by team with comparisons to the same week the previous year. One note of caution has emerged from these experiences: Competition between teams can become too intense. The company had to "tone down" the intensity of the competition between teams and stores on a few occasions.

The overall results of Whole Foods' management practices have been encouraging. The company has grown from one store in 1980 to 143 stores in 2003. The profitability of the company has been strong. In 2002 Whole Foods Inc. reported $2.69 billion of sales with $85 million net income, which was a 25 percent increase in net income over the previous year. This is a strong level of performance in the competitive grocery store industry, in which low profit margins are common. Whole Foods' decision to use teamwork as a "recipe for success" represents a novel and innovative approach to management.

Discussion Questions

1. Do you think Whole Foods' emphasis on teamwork could be applied to other companies in the grocery store industry such as Safeway, Kroger, or Albertson's? Why or why not? Do you think it would make a difference if the company's employees were represented by a union?

2. What are your thoughts about the Whole Foods practice of sharing team performance data with all company employees? Do you think that this practice risks creating an "overly competitive" spirit among the firm's teams and employees? Explain your answer.

Sources: Adapted from S. T. Foster, *Managing Quality*, Upper Saddle River, NJ: Prentice Hall, 2001, pp. 346–347; "Whole Foods Market," www.wholefoodsmarket.com/company/, 2003.

Managing Rewards for Teams

The following are three different reward situations you may encounter as a manager or a team member. Think about the type of reward and how it should be administered in each of these situations.

Parallel teams at Colorado General Hospital. Colorado General Hospital is a large hospital in Denver, Colorado. Employees are organized into traditional departments based on medical services: emergency room, intensive care, surgery, and so on. Support services include building maintenance, food services, and administration. Employees work in departments as individuals reporting to functional line managers. They are also placed on parallel teams or committees, such as the quality committee, safety committee, and the public relations committee. Employees spend about two hours per week on committee assignments and can expect to be a member of the committee for a two-year period before being replaced by new members. The output of the committees can be very significant, such as productivity-enhancing suggestions that result in labor or materials savings to the hospital.

Process teams at Universal Insurance. Universal Insurance provides automobile, property, and casualty insurance to its customers. The company recently underwent a major reengineering effort. The firm was restructured into core business processes, including claims administration, new product development, marketing services, and financial investment, focusing on processes that add value to the needs of the customer. Information systems technology software is applied to each process, requiring employees to learn new application software (and periodic software upgrades) that enhance employee productivity. The company has a strong culture that values quality and applies customer satisfaction as a criterion for success. Employees are given permanent assignments to self-managed process teams that are responsible for providing a core business process.

Project teams at Speedy Software. Speedy Software is a Seattle, Washington, software company that provides applications software that operates on the Internet. The market for this software is highly competitive. New products are released every year and upgrades on existing software appear even more frequently. If the company misses announced product release dates, the potential for lost profits is substantial because market share can quickly be captured by competitors who are first to market with software with better features. Therefore, time to market is a critical factor for company success. The software engineers are organized into different project teams according to the type of software product. Engineers may work on a project very intensively for a period of 6 to 24 months and then can be reassigned to a new product. Sometimes project priorities change and a talented software designer may be shifted to a hot project before the other product is completed.

Critical Thinking Questions

1. In each of the team reward situations, what size reward, measured in dollars, do you think is most appropriate? For example, should any of the teams receive a substantial reward (worth thousands of dollars)? What about more frequent small rewards ($25–$100)? In which situations would monetary rewards work most effectively? What about nonmonetary rewards, such as tickets to a sports event or dinner for two at a nice restaurant?

2. What should be the criteria for the team reward in each of the three situations? Justify your choice.

3. Should team members each receive equal amounts of the reward, or should the reward be based on each individual member's contribution to the team? Should team members who leave in the middle of a project or reward period (for example, during the middle of the fiscal year) be eligible for a full share of the team reward? How should newcomers to the team be rewarded?

Collaborative Learning Exercise

The instructor organizes the class into five- or six-member teams, each assigned to one of the team reward situations. The team develops a policy for rewarding teams in its situation which includes the following: eligibility to receive reward, basis of dividing the reward between team members, size of reward, the frequency of giving the reward to the team, and performance criteria for the reward. The teams present their policies to the class and compare the policies. The class and the instructor develop a list of conclusions that represents the best practices for providing rewards to teams.

INTERNET EXERCISE 14.1

www.saturn.com:97/ company/employment/ team_jobs/

General Motors' Saturn Division Thrives on Teamwork

This chapter discussed how employees in the Saturn Division of General Motors work together on self-managed teams to assemble cars. Visit the Saturn website for information on other team jobs at Saturn. Read the descriptions of the various team jobs at Saturn and then answer the following questions:

1. What does the word "team" represent at Saturn? For example, does it symbolize an important aspect of the Saturn culture? If so, what might that be?

2. In your opinion, what kind of team do the Saturn engineers most closely resemble—self-managed, project, parallel, or virtual? Explain your answer.

3. What kind of team do you think that Saturn sales, service, and marketing teams are likely to be—self-managed, project, parallel, or virtual? For example, the service parts team works closely with retailers that sell the auto parts, and the marketing team works closely with advertising agencies to tell the Saturn story to customers. Explain your answer.

MANAGER'S CHECKUP 14.1

What Is Your Primary Conflict-Handling Style?

For each of the 15 items, indicate how often you rely on that tactic by circling the appropriate number.

Conflict-Handling Tactics	Rarely				Always
1. I argue my case with my coworkers to show the merits of my position.	1	2	3	4	5
2. I negotiate with my coworkers so that a compromise can be reached.	1	2	3	4	5
3. I try to satisfy the expectations of my coworkers.	1	2	3	4	5

Conflict-Handling Tactics	Rarely				Always

4. I try to investigate an issue with my coworkers to find a solution acceptable to us.

      1   2   3   4   5

5. I am firm in pursuing my side of the issue.

      1   2   3   4   5

6. I attempt to avoid being "put on the spot" and try to keep my conflict with my coworkers to myself.

      1   2   3   4   5

7. I hold on to my solution to a problem.

      1   2   3   4   5

8. I use "give and take" so that a compromise can be made.

      1   2   3   4   5

9. I exchange accurate information with my coworkers to solve a problem together.

      1   2   3   4   5

10. I avoid open discussion of my differences with my coworkers.

      1   2   3   4   5

11. I accommodate the wishes of my coworkers.

      1   2   3   4   5

12. I try to bring all our concerns out in the open so that the issues can be resolved in the best way possible.

      1   2   3   4   5

13. I propose a middle ground for breaking deadlocks.

      1   2   3   4   5

14. I go along with the suggestions of my coworkers.

      1   2   3   4   5

15. I try to keep my disagreements with my coworkers to myself in order to avoid hard feelings.

      1   2   3   4   5

Scoring

Integrating		Obliging		Dominating		Avoiding		Compromising	
Item	Score	Item	Score	Item	Score	Item	Score	Item	Score
4	___	3	___	1	___	6	___	2	___
9	___	11	___	5	___	10	___	8	___
12	___	14	___	7	___	15	___	13	___
Total	___	Total	___	Total	___	Total	___	Total	___

Your primary conflict-handling style is _____

(The category with the highest total.)

Your backup conflict-handling style is _____

(The category with the second highest total.)

Source: *Academy of Management Journal* by M. A. Hahim. Copyright © 1983 by Academy of Management. Reproduced with permission of Academy of Management via Copyright Clearance Center.

FIFTEEN

Managing Communication

chapter 15

After reading this chapter, you should be able to:

- Understand the communication process.

- Eliminate barriers that distort the meaning of information.

- Analyze basic patterns of organizational communication.

- Develop the skills needed to organize and run effective meetings.

- Master electronic forms of communication and know when to use them.

- Work with an organization's informal communication system.

- Improve assertive communication, presentation, nonverbal, and listening skills.

Communication Challenges at High-Flying Boeing

Philip M. Condit's relaxed and insightful manner belies his position as chairman and chief executive officer for Boeing, the leader in building commercial aircraft and one of the most successful companies in the world. He spearheaded the development of the company's 777 aircraft by making sure all employees understood the project from the beginning all the way to its unveiling in 1995. Condit began by holding a general orientation meeting to communicate the goals for the new plane to all Boeing employees. The company set up hundreds of employee teams representing each facet of the project. Face-to-face communication among the teams helped identify potential problems early, when they could be solved much more easily. The engineers responsible for the design of the 777 worked closely with production and operations people in the manufacturing process. The final product was acclaimed by the airlines, pilots, and passengers.

When Boeing's executives decided to modify the company's approach to manufacturing aircraft and reduce the size of the workforce by a third, Condit's formidable communication skills again came into play. Following Boeing's low stock prices in the late 1990s and the resulting shareholder concerns, Condit offered a strategic plan designed to improve the company's financial performance. A fundamental step was changing Boeing from its paternalistic culture to one that emphasized high performance in the workplace. For the strategic plan to be successful, the commercial aviation division would be reduced by 48,000 employees over a two-year period.

Implementing the reduction in the workforce was a feat of leadership and communication skills. Condit used his relaxed approach to work successfully with the company's highly unionized workforce to achieve the necessary reduction, and in the process was able to set Boeing investors' minds at ease.

CEO Condit and Boeing in 2001 faced a new threat from Airbus, its chief competitor, which has engineered the world's largest passenger jet. The Airbus A380 can carry 200 more passengers than a fully loaded Boeing 747 and is expected to be in operation by 2005. Airbus's announcement of commitments from several airlines to build 62 of the planes and its conspicuous success at the 2001 Paris Air

Show meant that Boeing no longer had a monopoly on supplying jumbo passenger jets to airlines. Condit's skills as a communicator will be needed to mobilize Boeing's workforce as the company risks billions of dollars in developing not only new products like its new, super-efficient jet liner, but also airplane Internet access and a satellite-based air traffic management system. Condit's new message is that Boeing technology will reshape the flying experience.

Sources: K. Labich, "Boeing Finally Hatches a Plan," *Fortune,* March 1, 1999, pp. 100–106; M. McDermott, "Boeing's Modern Approach," *Profiles,* September 1996, pp. 41–44; S. Holmes, "Diverging Plans at the Paris Air Show," *Business Week,* June 22, 2001; L. Zuckerman, "Boeing Plays a Serial Wild Card," *New York Times,* June 17, 2001, section 3, p. 1; "Boeing Selects Leaders for New Commercial Airplane Development Plan," www.boeing.com/news/releases, January 29, 2003.

CRITICAL THINKING QUESTIONS

1. *CEO Condit used face-to-face communication with the project teams that were developing the new Boeing 777 airplane in order to identify potential problems early. What are the advantages of face-to-face communication between the Boeing CEO and the project teams in this situation? Are there any disadvantages?*

2. *CEO Condit also gave a general orientation to all of Boeing's employees in order to communicate the goals for the new 777 airplane. Why do you think he wanted all of Boeing's employees to know some basic details about this new aircraft? What form or forms of communication do you recommend that Condit use to speak to all the Boeing employees about the new product? Give reasons for your choice.*

Communication is the glue that holds social organizations together. This chapter begins with a simple model of communication between two people. We then explain why it is important for the communication process to be managed to avoid misunderstandings. Next, the ways communication processes operate in organizations are described. Effective methods to manage different forms of communication in organizations and useful communication skills are also provided. This chapter will help you learn and develop skills to improve your ability to communicate with other employees, as outlined in Skills for Managing 15.1.

communication

A process that involves the transmission of meaningful information from one party to another through the use of shared symbols.

The Process of Communication

Communication is a process that involves the transmission of meaningful information from one party to another through the use of shared symbols.

SKILLS FOR MANAGING COMMUNICATION

- *Assertive communication skills.* Assertive communication skills enable you to communicate in ways that meet your needs while at the same time respecting the needs and rights of others. Developing assertive communication skills allows you to send a message directly to other people while avoiding many barriers that may distort the message. A manager who can communicate a request for assistance assertively to an employee is more likely to motivate the employee to provide the needed support.

- *Presentation skills.* Presentation skills help you inform or persuade customers or other employees. Because there is limited time to communicate with a client or an executive, having strong presentation skills allows you to make the best case for your ideas.

- *Nonverbal communication skills.* Nonverbal communication skills are invaluable for understanding the emotional state of the people you are dealing with. An employee who can understand the boss's nonverbal messages will know when it is a good time to ask for a pay raise. Lack of ability to understand nonverbal communication makes it more difficult for managers to know whether a strategy or policy is working according to plan.

- *Listening skills.* Listening skills are as important as verbal communication skills because they help employees and managers frame messages to meet the needs of the intended audience. Employees who possess listening skills are more effective at forming positive working relationships with other team members. Managers with listening skills are better able to understand and counsel subordinates.

Communication is successful when meaning is understood. Two forms of information are sent and received in communication: facts and feelings.

Facts are bits of information that can be objectively measured or described, such as the retail price of a new product, the cost of raw materials, the defect rate of a manufacturing process or the number of employees who quit during a year. Facts can be communicated verbally or in written documents and can also be transformed into digital symbols and stored in computer databases. **Knowledge workers** are employees who manage information and make it available to decision makers in the organization. They are the most common type of worker in the twenty-first century organization, and they depend on the process of communication to obtain appropriate information to do their jobs effectively.

Feelings are an individual's emotional responses to decisions made or actions taken by other people. Although feelings can be communicated verbally or in written documents, they are more likely to be communicated as nonverbal facial expressions, tone of voice, or body postures. To be effective, managers and employees must know how to interpret the feelings of others. Since managers achieve results through the actions of employees, it is important for them to take emotional reactions into consideration. During periods of downsizing, for example, workers interpret

facts

Bits of information that can be objectively measured or described, such as the retail price of a new product, the cost of raw materials, the defect rate of a manufacturing process, or the number of employees who quit during a year.

knowledge workers

Employees who manage information and make it available to decision makers in the organization.

feelings

An individual's emotional responses to decisions made or actions taken by other people.

excessive executive compensation as disloyalty on the company's part. Boeing CEO Phil Condit declined to accept his bonus in the wake of lay-off announcements affecting tens of thousands of Boeing workers, as discussed at the beginning of this chapter. Actions such as Condit's communicate loyalty to a firm's employees.

Organizations require diverse communication channels to facilitate communication among employees, managers, and customers. When messages with strong emotional content are to be received and understood, these channels must allow for face-to-face communication. Despite advances in computer technology that have created powerful ways to store, retrieve, and manipulate information, company leaders must still make provisions for communication on an interpersonal basis in order to develop trust and cohesion among organization members.

A Model of Communication

Figure 15.1 is a simple model of the communication process. Although the model illustrates communication between two people, it also applies to more complex communication situations. As the figure indicates, communication begins with a **sender,** who has a message for the **receiver.** The sender *encodes* the message and selects a **communication channel** that will deliver it to the receiver. Encoding is selecting appropriate symbols such as written words, numbers, digital symbols, sounds, or body language that can be correctly *decoded* by the receiver. The sender must anticipate the decoding skills of the receiver. For example, when a businessperson from the Netherlands does business with a U.S. executive, it is likely that all conversations and documents will be in English, because most Americans do not speak or understand Dutch, the language of the Netherlands, whereas the Dutch businessperson is very likely to speak English.

The communication channel influences the quantity and quality of information that is conveyed to the receiver. Communication channels include face-to-face conversations, group meetings, memos, policy manuals, e-mail, voice mail, videotapes, and computer printouts. Factors that influence the choice of a communication channel include the complexity of the message, the time available to compose and distribute it, the size and proximity of the audience, and the skill of the sender in using various channels. For example, some professors rely on traditional blackboard lectures because they do not have enough preparation time to create multimedia overheads.

For communication to be effective, the receiver must be able to decode the message and understand its true meaning. **Decoding** means translating the symbolic verbal, written, or visual symbols into an undistorted, clear message. The receiver may misinterpret the message if unable to decode it, perhaps because the receiver does not have the necessary skills in language or culture. For example, a U.S. buyer may insist on a written contract before agreeing to do business with a Mexican

sender

Individual or party that initiates communication with another individual or party.

receiver

Individual or party that receives message from sender.

communication channel

Influences the quantity and quality of information that is conveyed to the receiver. Channels of communication include face-to-face conversations, group meetings, memos, policy manuals, e-mail, voice mail.

decoding

Translating the symbolic verbal, written, or visual symbols into an undistorted, clear message.

FIGURE 15.1

The Communication Process

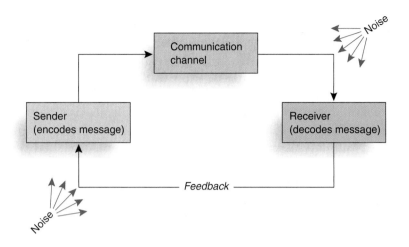

supplier. However, in Mexico, business deals are based on oral agreement, and contracts represent a lack of good faith. There are cultural differences within the United States. A simple example is the fast-talking New York sales representative who is trying to sell life insurance to a potential client in Monroe, Louisiana. The New Yorker may interpret the slower speech of the southerner as unsophisticated and less intelligent. The southerner may interpret the New Yorker's accent and fast speech as rude and untrustworthy. Other decoding problems include the use of technical jargon and the ambiguity of English words with multiple meanings. A communication channel that is rich in information, with opportunities for visual as well as verbal cues, provides a context to help the receiver select the appropriate meaning of a word with several different meanings. On the other hand, lean communication channels provide a limited context from which to select the true meaning of an ambiguously worded message.

Important messages should include opportunities for feedback from the receiver. **Feedback** allows the sender to make sure the true meaning is received. For example, if a company decides to change the basis of sales representatives' pay from salary to straight commission, communicating the change to the sales team at a face-to-face meeting is more effective than sending a memo or e-mail message because there are more opportunities for feedback and clarification. Many management problems can be avoided by using communication channels with feedback, especially when individuals are likely to feel strongly about the content of the message.

Channels that provide for feedback are called **two-way communications,** because they allow the sender and receiver to interact. Communication channels that provide no opportunity for feedback are **one-way communications.** Although interactive communication is ideal, it is not

feedback

Information received back from the receiver, which allows the sender to make sure the true meaning is received.

two-way communications

Communication channels that provide for feedback.

one-way communications

Communication channels that provide no opportunity for feedback.

always possible when information must be disseminated to many employees in a short period of time. IBM informs employees about the promotions of top executives in its corporate newsletter (a one-way communication channel). However, the sales force is informed about new products at a sales meeting (a two-way communication channel). As this example suggests, two-way communication channels are required for important and complex information.

Another important condition of effective communication is overcoming noise. **Noise** is anything that interferes with sending or receiving the message. Noise can distort the true meaning of the message. Sources of noise include the sender (whose accent may be difficult to understand); the communication channel (if the telecommunications system lacks bandwidth, an Internet message may be slow and frustrating); the receiver (who may have poor vision and be unable to read a memo); and the environment (time pressures may reduce availability to listen to a message). A manager at the Houston distribution center of Baxter International, a medical and health products company, receives more than 60 voice mail messages a day from customers and employees. Having many customers to satisfy and employees to supervise makes it difficult for the manager to respond to all messages promptly. However, by using some of the communication options in the voice mail system, the manager can respond to queries that require only short, direct answers.

noise

Anything that can interfere with sending or receiving a message.

Barriers to Effective Communication

The model of communication presented in Figure 15.1 suggests that barriers can disrupt the accurate transmission of information. These barriers take different forms:

Barriers to Effective Communication

1. *Sender barrier.* The sender may send a message to an audience that is not interested in the content of the message.

2. *Encoding barrier.* The sender uses a vocabulary that is too technical for the audience.

3. *Communication channel barrier.* The sender selects a communication channel that is too lean to provide the richness of information receivers need to decode the message. For example, a written memo is inadequate for explaining a change in the employee retirement plan.

4. *Decoding barrier.* The receiver does not have the decoding skills necessary to understand the message. For example, poor reading skills can prevent employees from using manuals and other reference materials.

5. *Receiver barrier.* The receiver is too busy focusing on other things to be able to accurately listen to and understand the verbal or nonverbal content of the message.

6. *Feedback barrier.* The organization has few formal communication channels with feedback loops to give lower echelon employees the opportunity to communicate their true feelings about policies.

7. *Noise barrier.* The receiver does not understand how to use time-saving features of e-mail and voice mail, resulting in message overload and unacceptable delays in responding to messages of customers and coworkers.

8. *Perception barriers.* Perception barriers occur when two individuals experience the same message differently because their mental images of the message are not identical. A receiver will fit a message into an existing pattern of experiences to make sense out of it. Sometimes the message becomes distorted during this sense-making process. One type of perception barrier is **selective perception,** whereby the receiver focuses on the parts of the message that are most salient to his or her interests and ignores other parts that are viewed as not relevant. For example, an employee interested in a job vacancy may use selective perception to discount the fact that the job requires more work experience than the employee currently has accumulated. The result is a personal disappointment when the employee is not chosen for the job.

   Another important type of perceptual barrier is **prejudgment,** which involves making incorrect assumptions about a person due to membership in a group (based on age, race, gender or ethnicity) or about a thing (such as performance evaluation) based on earlier positive or negative experiences. For example, a manager who has a negative earlier experience with an older employee may generalize this experience to other old people. The manager may become resistant to hiring an older job applicant even if positive information is available, because the manager has already negatively prejudged the applicant. It is important to be aware of these perceptual barriers and avoid them. Prejudging older people (over 40 years of age) negatively is an illegal practice that can have costly legal implications.

Large, complex organizations are likely to have many barriers. These barriers can be managed by using various management practices. Senders should be educated about the necessity of learning the background of intended audiences and should gain firsthand familiarity with audiences prior to initiating communication. All members of the organization should be trained in the effective use of communication technologies to manage the flow of information. There should be a diverse mix of communication channels from lean (memos or policy manuals) to rich (videoconference and multimedia) so that senders can match the channel to the complexity of the message. The management team must make sure employees have appropriate communication skills. Key skills include

selective perception

Type of perception barrier whereby the receiver focuses on the parts of the message that are most salient to his or her interests and ignores other parts that are not relevant.

prejudgment

Type of perceptual barrier which involves making incorrect assumptions about a person due to membership in a group or about a thing based on earlier positive or negative experiences.

listening, public speaking, and nonverbal communication skills. HR departments can either screen applicants for evidence of these skills or provide on-the-job training programs which give employees opportunities to practice and improve their communication skills.

Patterns of Organizational Communications

Communication patterns in organizations are complex. Possible barriers to organizational communication include: (1) differences in employee status and power, such as communication between a subordinate and a supervisor; (2) diversity, such as cross-gender communication; and (3) differences in interests, such as a manufacturing unit focused on quality and efficiency of output and an engineering unit focused on executing a technically elegant design that may be difficult to manufacture. Organizational communication patterns operate downward, upward, and horizontally. Each direction poses specific management challenges.

Downward Communication

downward communication

Sending a message from a high position in the organization to an individual or group lower in the hierarchy.

Downward communication frequently occurs between managers and subordinates, when the manager provides direction, feedback, and critical information to help subordinates perform at expected levels. Examples include employee performance evaluations, job descriptions, orientation of new employees, praise and recognition, company business strategies and goals, and company policies and procedures.

Upward Communication

upward communication

Sending a message from a position lower in the hierarchy to a receiver higher in the hierarchy.

In **upward communication,** a message is sent from a position lower in the hierarchy to a receiver higher in the hierarchy. It lets managers know how individuals, teams, and units of the company are performing. When performance deviates from expected standards, managers can make corrective adjustments.

One of the most important components of upward communication is feedback to managers about employee feelings about company policies. Organizations are likely to have barriers that filter information from subordinates before it is received by managers. Employees are well aware of the tendency to punish the bearer of bad news. It is also considered disloyal for employees to take a problem "over the head" of the boss to a higher echelon manager. Therefore, it is necessary to design special communication channels that encourage employees to express their true feelings or provide unfiltered information. Hewlett-Packard has an open-door policy that encourages employees to bring problems to any manager in the company and requires managers to resolve problems within a specified period of time. Toyota is well-known for effectively using employee sug-

Companies such as Toyota use employee suggestions to improve the quality of their products and processes.

gestion systems to improve product and process quality. Besides suggestions, upward communication includes employee grievances, information about the unethical behavior of managers, accounting information, and information about the defect rate of the product.

Horizontal Communication

When a sender and a receiver are at a similar level in the organization **horizontal communication** takes place. This includes communications between team members, between different teams, and between employees in different units, such as when a safety specialist and a quality control inspector discuss proposed changes in the manufacturing process. Horizontal communication is becoming increasingly important in organizations because it involves collaboration between employees with different skills and competencies. The vignette at the beginning of this chapter described how important this type of communication was to the development of the Boeing 777 airplane. A high proportion of communications between knowledge workers consists of horizontal communication in which information is shared.

> **horizontal communication**
>
> Communication between a sender and a receiver at a similar level in the organization.

Downsizing and reengineering have resulted in slimmer organizations with fewer levels and a greater emphasis on teams. Horizontal communication plays an important role in this environment. Interactive electronic communication technologies such as e-mail greatly facilitate horizontal communication by making it possible to establish learning communities and virtual teams of employees who work together even when separated geographically. Other examples of horizontal communication are peer performance, cross-functional new product development team meetings, self-managed work team meetings, suggestion committee meetings, and diversity task forces.

How to Provide Constructive Feedback to Others

Here are some useful suggestions about giving constructive feedback to peers or subordinates.

1. *Focus your feedback on specific behaviors* that were successful or that were unsuccessful. You will help motivate the employee to continue the successful behaviors and to improve the unsuccessful ones. Instead of saying "You did a great job on this project," tell the employee, "Your careful checking and rechecking caught several errors."

2. *Keep personality traits out of your feedback* by focusing on "what" rather than "who." Specify what results the person achieved or failed to achieve. Instead of saying "You don't work hard enough," tell the employee, "You used outdated figures in your report."

3. *Investigate whether the employee had control over the results* before giving feedback about unsuccessful behaviors. For example, the employee who used outdated figures in a report may have been given them by corporate headquarters and had no way of knowing they were outdated. Ask questions of the employee to find out whether unsuccessful behavior is something the employee can control. Be very cautious before offering negative feedback.

4. *Feedback should be given as soon as possible;* don't save up your feedback about both successful and unsuccessful behaviors for an end-of-the-quarter meeting, for example. Feedback given shortly after an event occurs is the most effective at changing or sustaining an employee's behaviors.

5. *Ensure privacy when giving feedback about negative behaviors;* giving it in public will cause a reaction against you by any observers. *Feedback about positive behaviors can be given in public* to recognize an employee's success. It can help motivate the employee and others.

Source: Adapted from S. P. Robbins and P. L. Hunsaker, *Training in Interpersonal Skills,* 2nd ed., Upper Saddle River, NJ: Prentice Hall, 1996, pp. 73–75.

Managers and team members should have the ability to give feedback to subordinates or peers. Feedback may be communicated either horizontally (from peer to peer) or vertically (from supervisor to subordinate). All employees need feedback to improve their skills. Positive feedback lets them know they are progressing toward their goals and can be used to strengthen behaviors that are already learned. Negative feedback tells employees which behaviors should be modified to improve performance. Tips for providing feedback can be found in Manager's Notes 15.1.

Managing Organizational Communications

Organizations can improve the quality of communications by providing a diverse mix of lean to rich communication channels that provide

FIGURE 15.2

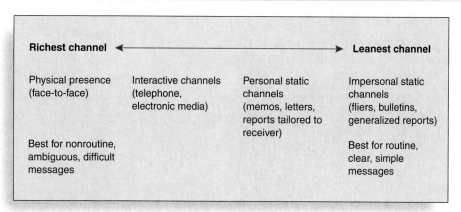

Communication Channels
Ranked by Information
Richness

Sources: Robert H. Lengel and
Richard L. Daft, "The Selection of
Communication Media as an
Executive Skill," *Academy of
Management Executive* 2 (August
1988): 225–232; and Richard L.
Daft and Robert H. Lengel,
"Organizational Information
Requirements, Media Richness,
and Structural Design,"
Managerial Science 32 (May
1986): 554–572.

opportunities to communicate in upward, downward, and horizontal directions. Managers and employees must be trained to use the communication channels appropriately. Because communication technologies are rapidly changing, upgrading the communication skills of employees should be considered a process of continuous improvement.

Communication channels vary according to **information richness,** the potential information-carrying capacity of data. Rich communication channels provide opportunities for feedback, provide a full range of visual and audio information, and personalize the message for the receiver. Rich communications channels are best for nonroutine, ambiguous, and difficult messages. Face-to-face communication provides the richest channel of communication, as displayed in Figure 15.2. Lean communication channels provide no opportunity for feedback, have a limited mix of information, and are impersonal. A mass-produced bulletin or flier is an example of a lean communication channel.

> **information richness**
>
> The potential information-carrying capacity of data.

Face-to-Face Communication

Rich information content is possible in face-to-face communication, because there is a high level of interactivity between the sender and the receiver. Job interviews are likely to be done face-to-face. One of the most important types of face-to-face communication is the meeting.

Meetings, or gatherings of organizational members, are held to inform and train participants, solve problems, monitor and coordinate activities, delegate tasks, and create social bonds between diverse organization members. *Staff meetings* allow managers to coordinate activities with subordinates. *Corporate or business-unit meetings* address strategic issues and involve executives who formulate long-range goals. *Task force meetings* are held to discuss goals that affect a broad range of employees such as diversity in the workplace or safety. *Team meetings* are used to coordinate the work activities of members of a self-managed

Face-to-face communications, such as meetings, provide an opportunity for feedback and personalized messages for receivers.

team, including performance goals, training new members, scheduling work, and suggesting improvements in work methods. The application of multimedia technologies that transmit video, voice, and text over satellite networks have made face-to-face meetings with globally dispersed people possible.

Managers can spend as much as 60 percent to 80 percent of their time in meetings. A sales manager is likely to hold regular meetings with sales representatives, attend management meetings with other sales managers, and participate in committee meetings with marketing, advertising, and promotion employees on new product development or brand management. Employees who are asked to spend more time in team-based work units require periodic meetings to form a consensus on how the team should conduct its activities. Meetings can waste time and become frustrating. It is important to manage them effectively. Manager's Notes 15.2 lists techniques to run a meeting effectively.

Written Communication

Choosing the Best Communication Medium

Written communication includes memos, policy manuals, employee handbooks, company newsletters, bulletin boards, letters, and fliers. Written documents have an advantage over face-to-face communication, because messages can be revised, stored and made available when needed, and disseminated in identical copies so the same message is received by all. Written communication can be personalized for a small audience or written in a generic style that accommodates a larger audience. The limitations of

Managing Productive Meetings

Here are some steps you can take to make meetings more productive:

1. *Ask yourself if it's important even to schedule a meeting.* If you can handle the issue with an e-mail or a memo instead, don't schedule a meeting.

2. *Schedule the meeting for an appropriate place.* Be sure the room is large enough for the participants and that they can all hear each other and the speaker. Be careful to limit the number of meeting participants to only individuals who have a good reason to attend and who are able to make contributions to the goals of the meeting.

3. *Create an agenda for the meeting* including topics and time limits, and distribute it ahead of time. The meeting participants will be able to plan their own contributions. Keeping the meeting to the agenda will ensure that all topics are covered. Plan to take careful notes during the meeting as each topic is covered.

4. *Establish rules for participation.* All participants need to have an opportunity to contribute; determine an order so that a few participants don't dominate the meeting.

5. *Follow the agenda's time limits* for each topic. Keep an eye on the clock; if a topic exceeds its allotted time, you should return to it later and go on to the next topic.

6. *Leave some open time* for topics that may not have been included on the agenda. If discussion of additional topics is expected to take more time, add them to the next meeting's agenda instead.

7. *End the meeting with a plan of action.* Discuss the steps that will be taken as a result of the meeting. Distribute a written report of the meeting and the steps to be taken based on your notes.

Sources: Adapted from R. Volkema and F. Niederman, "Planning and Managing Organizational Meetings: An Empirical Analysis of Written and Oral Communication," *Journal of Business Communication* 33 (July 1996): 275–293; E. A. Michaels, "Business Meetings," *Small Business Reports*, February 1989, pp. 82–88.

written communication are that there are no provisions for feedback, and the sender may not be certain if the message was received, read, and/or understood. Two popular forms of written communication are memos and company newsletters.

MEMOS   Short business messages that provide information to employees are sent in memos. They can be used to inform employees about the agenda, time, and place of a meeting; to schedule work; or to describe a change in an employment policy. A memo should be brief and to the point. Also,

- Make sure that the heading indicates: (1) the intended audience; (2) the subject of the memo; (3) the name of the sender; and (4) the date that the memo was written.

- Revise and edit the memo to eliminate misspellings and poor grammar. Make sure the message is clear and unambiguous. If the sender catches an error after the memo is distributed, it may be necessary to send a follow-up memo to tell the audience to disregard the previous memo. This can annoy receivers.

- Add the names of people who need to be aware of the communication to a copy list at the end of the memo. Copied individuals may not be the focus of the memo, but they need to know about it. For example, the controller who schedules a meeting of staff accountants to discuss a new way to expense research and development costs may copy the vice president of finance.

- Avoid sending memos to people who do not need to know about the content. Employees should not waste time reading memos that are not important.

COMPANY NEWSLETTERS   Many companies have short monthly or quarterly publications designed to keep employees informed of important events, meetings, and transitions and to provide inspirational stories about employee and team contributions to the business. Newsletters help foster community spirit by keeping everybody informed about what others are doing. Desktop publishing software has made the production of newsletters feasible for even the smallest companies.

A newsletter can be a one-way or interactive form of communication depending on the goals established by management. In the one-way form, a newsletter is an official downward communication from management to inform employees about company policies, procedures, and other information. In its two-way form, the newsletter is a communication channel for all directions of communication (upward, downward, and horizontal), allowing each member of the workplace to voice opinions and contribute stories of interest. Large corporations are likely to have several newsletters, with the corporate-level news from headquarters presented in a one-way version and business-unit or plant newsletters containing employee input.

Electronic Communication

Advances in electronic technology make interactive communication possible between senders and receivers, even when they are separated by physical distance and busy schedules. Electronic communication channels vary in the richness of the information that is transmitted and can include text, voice, graphics, or video. Two important forms of electronic communication are voice mail and e-mail.

VOICE MAIL   A detailed audio message that is recorded electronically and can be played back when convenient is a voice mail. Employees can play back all messages at once and answer them in a concentrated block of time so that redundant "telephone tag" calls can be avoided. Voice mail also allows a sender to set up a menu of responses to commonly asked questions, which saves additional time. Routine calls can be routed to a recorded message, and more attention can be paid to callers with non-routine questions. Vanguard, one of the largest U.S. mutual fund companies, uses a voice mail menu to answer commonly asked questions about investments. Each customer has a special code to obtain daily mutual fund account balances and market prices of funds and to make financial transactions.

Voice mail is not always used effectively. Many organizations, including such government offices as the Social Security Administration, present a long menu of options that waste the caller's time. Some people use voice mail to screen phone calls, avoiding callers they do not want to talk to. Screening too many calls can annoy customers and block internal company communication. The following suggestions can help managers use voice mail appropriately:

- Update your personal greeting regularly. Let callers know when they can expect your return call.

- Include information in the greeting about how to reach a coworker who can help callers if you are unavailable or if the call is urgent.

- Try to answer your phone while at your desk. Use the voice recording only for good reasons, such as being in the middle of an important meeting with a colleague.

- Check messages regularly and return calls promptly.

- Set the message capacity for one or two minutes to discourage callers from leaving overly verbose messages. For long conversations other communication channels are preferable to voice mail.[1]

ELECTRONIC MAIL **E-mail** allows employees to communicate via written messages through personal computer terminals linked to a network. It is a fast way to distribute important business results to a large number of employees. Virtual teams of employees can work simultaneously on a document even though they may be separated geographically using e-mail attachments. E-mail is often used to exchange information (such as coordinating project activities and scheduling meetings), for social reasons (such as keeping in touch with colleagues), and to post general information that can be of use to many employees (for example, the time and place of the company picnic). The use of e-mail creates an upward communication channel for employees to gain access to executives who previously may have been inaccessible to them. For example, Bill Gates, the chairman of Microsoft, makes his e-mail address known to all Microsoft employees. He reserves several hours each day to send and reply to messages.

e-mail

Electronic mail via computers.

Despite its advantages, e-mail creates challenging problems. It can contribute to information overload; numerous e-mail messages are sent to large lists of people when the message may be of interest to only a few. E-mail should not be considered private. Recent court decisions state that U.S. companies have a right to monitor the e-mail of employees.

When using e-mail,

- Scan the subject heading at the beginning of the message. If the topic is of no interest to you, delete the message without reading it.
- Create electronic files to store important messages so they can be quickly retrieved when needed.
- Set up electronic lists of people who should receive the same message. For example, the project team leader should set up a list of all team members and send messages to the list rather than to each individual member.
- Assume that your e-mail will be read by management. Use other communication channels for private or controversial messages.
- Protect sensitive documents with encryption software so that private information is not accessible to hackers or other unintended receivers.
- Use e-mail to transmit factual information, and avoid using it to criticize colleagues or to communicate messages with content that will cause strong emotional reactions from the receiver.
- Avoid sending messages written in all-capitals, which is like screaming.[2]

Internet

A computer network with multimedia communication capabilities, allowing a combination of text, voice, graphics, and video to be sent to a receiver; a network of networks, connecting hundreds of thousands of corporate, educational, and research computer networks around the world.

The **Internet** is a computer network with multimedia communication capabilities. A combination of text, voice, graphics, and video can be sent to a receiver over the Web. Companies' sites on the World Wide Web are places where potential customers can learn about products and services and place orders. The use of the Internet makes it possible for companies to serve international customers. Many universities advertise MBA programs on their websites to attract international students. Electronic commerce over the Internet has created many new business opportunities. Amazon.com sells books and other merchandise over the Internet. Charles Schwab, the discount broker, lets customers buy and sell stocks online. Management Close-Up 15.a describes how the Krispy Kreme Company uses its Web portal, an Internet-based communication device, to display valuable information to the managers of the franchise stores so they can more accurately forecast and produce fresh doughnuts for their customers.

grapevine

Informal communication that takes place at the workplace.

Informal Communication

Informal communication, sometimes referred to as the **grapevine,** is used when there are gaps in or barriers to formal communication and employ-

*Krispy Kreme's Web Portal Makes Franchises
More Profitable*

THEME: CUSTOMER FOCUS It turns out that a combination of doughnuts and Internet can be highly profitable. Krispy Kreme is a national doughnut franchise with headquarters in Winston-Salem, North Carolina. The wildly popular Krispy Kreme doughnuts are sold in 278 locations in the United States and Canada. The company sells over 2.7 billion of these sweet treats each year. Each franchise store makes between 4,000 and 10,000 doughnuts per day. Managers must have all the necessary tools to keep the 24 hour production process running smoothly. One of the critical tools that the Krispy Kreme Company uses is a customized Web portal, mykrispykreme.com. It is an Internet-based communication device used to take the guesswork out of managing a doughnut franchise. Local owners are able to connect directly with Krispy Kreme Company headquarters.

When a franchise manager logs on, the opening screen offers weather news, because people buy more doughnuts and coffee when the weather turns. These weather updates have paid big dividends to the franchises by allowing managers to better forecast the number of doughnuts to make, says Frank Hood, the company's chief information officer. Ordering supplies and doughnut mix is performed online, eliminating costly errors. The Web portal even has a virtual help desk. Need to know how to calibrate a coffee grinder? Fix a fryer? It's all there, with streaming video and audio and

By using information from its Web portal, franchise store managers at Krispy Kreme can run the doughnut machines more efficiently to meet the daily demand of customers.

graphics on what to do. The videos called "Hot Topics" are available 24 hours a day. Owners have seen healthy increases in store profitability since the Web portal has become available to them.

Source: Adapted form C. Skipp, "Hot Bytes, by the Dozen: Krispy Kreme's Web Portal Keeps Franchises Humming," *Newsweek*, April 28, 2003, p. 42.

ees do not receive information they desire. It takes place at the water cooler or in the hallway, in the company cafeteria, in employees' offices, in the parking lot, in restaurants, and at trade shows. Job opportunities, who is being considered for a big promotion, the likelihood of downsizing, the features of a competitor's new product, and the unethical behavior of a manager are typical topics on the grapevine.

Informal communication can be a source of creative ideas. Sun Microsystems, a Silicon Valley manufacturer of computer workstations, schedules occasional Friday afternoon parties so that technical employees can visit with business-oriented employees. Ideas for new products sometimes start out as informal conversations over a beer.

Some gossip and rumors are harmful to employee morale. If employees fear that the company will soon downsize, rumors that exaggerate the true state of affairs are likely to be exchanged. This makes employees fearful of losing their jobs and negatively affects company performance. Negative rumors that disrupt employee motivation must be managed with other forms of communication.

management by wandering around (MBWA)

Dropping in unannounced at a work site and engaging employees in spontaneous conversations.

One effective way to manage rumors and misinformation is **management by wandering around (MBWA),** dropping in unannounced at a work site and engaging employees in spontaneous conversations. MBWA can improve the level of trust between employees and management by opening up new channels of communication. Sam Walton, the founder of Wal-Mart, visited stores weekly and used MBWA to learn what front-line employees were thinking about and to see if they needed help with problems. General managers at Hewlett-Packard use MBWA to develop personal rapport with all the employees in their business units. Business units at HP contain fewer than 500 employees, to facilitate informal communication. MBWA permits the general manager to deal with potentially harmful rumors before they spread. It also helps sustain an entrepreneurial company culture that allows HP to be an innovator and technology leader. Management Close-Up 15.b shows how companies can utilize different types of communication to develop a trusting work environment with open communications.

Communication Skills

One of the best ways to ensure effective communication is to provide opportunities for employees to develop communication skills. Skill in sending and receiving messages greatly reduces the possibility that a distorted message will be transmitted. Four key communication skills are assertive communication skills, presentation skills, nonverbal communication skills, and listening skills.

Assertive Communication Skills

Assertive communication skills enable an individual to communicate in ways that meet her or his own needs while at the same time respecting the needs and rights of others. A person who displays these skills states exactly what is wanted or needed from individuals being targeted for the message. The communicator holds himself or herself personally accountable for meeting needs. At the same time, the individual respects the needs of others and does not intrude or act childishly or manipulatively. Speaking calmly, directly, and confidently without instilling fear or anger in the other person is being assertive. The goal is to respond directly and outwardly to a problem.

A person who communicates assertively sticks to the facts, and does not communicate in a critical, subjective way. Assertive communication involves giving facts, feedback or information that makes clear the com-

How Companies Communicate to Build Trust

THEME: ETHICS Open communication is essential to building trust between employees and management, which leads in turn to improved sharing of information—upward, downward, and horizontally. Following are some methods that companies have used in creating a trusting environment with open communication:

1. *Communicating across borders*. Ciba Specialty Chemicals uses a satellite conference meeting to distribute its quarterly results to 5,000 employees in 14 corporate regions around the world. Employees of the specialty chemical firm can fax questions back to the board during the meeting.

2. *Using focus groups and teams to understand and resolve employee concerns*. S. C. Johnson & Son, the household cleaning goods company, holds employee focus groups and forms teams to discover and resolve issues that concern employees. The company, which employs 12,500 people around the world, also has business councils for special interest groups within the company, such as minorities, that meet and present their concerns to management.

3. *Sharing company information in meetings*. Family-owned industrial valve and seal manufacturer A. W. Chesterton holds quarterly meetings with its employees, and CEO Jim Chesterton answers questions. The company's departments, divisions, and subsidiaries also meet regularly and exchange information openly.

4. *Using a bulletin board for suggestions*. Dana Corporation employees are encouraged to post two suggestions a month on the company's bulletin board. Other workers add comments to them, and 80 percent of them are then implemented or acted on. The suggestions help the industrial manufacturer understand employee concerns and also provide valuable input for improving quality.

Source: Adapted from J. C. McCune, "That Elusive Thing Called Trust," *Management Review*, July/August 1998, pp. 10–16.

---

municator's wishes, needs, wants, beliefs, or feelings. Here are some examples of speaking directly in a factual manner:[3]

- "I would like you here by eight o'clock."
- "I am quite pleased with the way the situation has been resolved."

Assertive communication includes obtaining honest feedback from others. The individual will ask direct questions or make direct statements to find out the other person's views, needs, wants, and feelings to make sure there is no misunderstanding between the two parties. Here are some examples of ways to receive direct feedback:

- "What would you prefer to do?"
- "I would like to hear your views on this."
- "What are the pros and cons on this idea from your point of view?"

There are several less effective communication styles that people use in the workplace. This is because the communicator is either indirect or is not mindful of the needs of others or of her or his own needs. These dysfunctional communication styles include: (1) passive, (2) aggressive, and (3) passive-aggressive communication.[4] An individual who engages in **passive communication skills** does not let others know directly what he or she wants or needs. A passive communicator hopes that his or her needs will be met without asking. Others are expected to figure out what is needed, and, if they fail, the passive communicator becomes resentful and pouts. Passive communicators often worry about what others think about them. They do not disclose their feelings or needs for fear of offending others. Not surprisingly, passive communicators are often frustrated and moody, making them difficult to work with.

An **aggressive communication** style is a forceful approach to communicate with others which expresses dominance and even anger. An aggressive communicator ignores the needs and rights of others, and loudly proclaims what he or she wants. The aggressive communicator may coerce others by using threatening words until he or she gets what is wanted. The individual who uses this style intimidates others. The cost is damage to relationships with others, who are not likely to trust an aggressive communicator. In the long run, others begin to resent and avoid the aggressive communicator.

A **passive-aggressive communication** style avoids giving direct responses to others' requests or feedback. Instead the passive-aggressive communicator tries to "get even" with others later for real or imagined injustices. This individual fears giving direct feedback to others for the same reasons that the passive communicator does. On the other hand, the passive-aggressive communicator uses sarcasm, sniping, and indirect criticism to express anger and aggression. Often the passive-aggressive communicator manipulates others by playing on their fears or insecurities to obtain what is wanted or needed. Needless to say, passive-aggressive communication is dishonest and does not foster positive working relationships.

If a person becomes aware of a tendency to communicate in one of these three dysfunctional styles, he or she should learn and practice honest, assertive communication skills.

Presentation Skills

Presentation skills are critical in almost every job. Salespeople must present products in convincing ways to potential clients. Engineers need to present ideas persuasively to the managers who control funding. Managers must present performance results to executives, and team members may need to present ideas for quality improvement at staff meetings. Managers and team leaders often need to persuade the team or employees to do something or to accept a new policy. Basic guidelines for developing effective presentation skills include the following:

passive communication

Style of communication whereby individual does not let others know directly what he or she wants or needs.

aggressive communication

A forceful style of communication with others that expresses dominance and even anger. The needs and wants of others are ignored.

passive-aggressive communication

Style of communication whereby individual avoids giving direct responses to other's requests or feedback.

 What is Your Communication Style Under Stress?

- *Prepare objectives* for your presentation. Know what you want the audience to do. Do you want them to buy a product? Invest in a new technology? Implement a new policy that controls travel expenses?

- *Organize the presentation* into several key ideas, no more than five, that will persuade the audience to act in the way you want them to. Organize your ideas in a logical sequence based on the relative importance of each idea. Use a mix of information to support your ideas, including publications, statistics, quotes from famous people, and personal anecdotes that you share with the audience.

- *Structure the presentation* into three parts: introduction, body, and conclusion. The *introduction* tells the audience what the presentation is about and what benefits they should get out of it. It should begin with a good opening, such as a story or declarative statement that grabs the audience's attention and sustains it through the rest of the presentation. The *body* is the main message and idea of the presentation. The *conclusion* summarizes the key takeaway points that the speaker wants to emphasize so that the audience will be persuaded to act.

- *Tailor the presentation* to the needs of the audience. Find out in advance who will be attending the meeting, anticipate the motivations and interests of the audience, and design the presentation to meet some of those needs and interests.

- *Establish your credibility* if the audience is not familiar with your credentials. An effective leader will introduce the speaker to establish the speaker's credentials.

- *Speak in a responsive and conversational style* that engages listeners. Nobody wants to hear a speaker read aloud or make a programmed presentation that sounds like it was memorized. Treat the audience as if you developed the presentation just for their benefit.

- *Use visual aids* such as overhead slides, charts, exhibits, or colorful posters that reinforce the verbal message. Computer programs that combine text, graphics, and color to make overhead slices are a basic part of the professional's toolkit.

- *Practice your presentation skills,* which, as all performance skills, improve with effort and practice. Look for opportunities to make presentations and receive feedback. Making a presentation to a school group or a social organization or teaching a class is a good way to get additional experience.

- *Restate the key ideas* you want the audience to remember when concluding the presentation. Summarize the objectives and purpose of the talk. End the presentation with an audience appeal for action if appropriate. Also, it is always a good idea to leave some extra time at the end of the presentation for answering questions. This lets the speaker clarify any misunderstandings that members of the audience may have had concerning the message the speaker wants them to receive.

Nonverbal Communication Skills

nonverbal communication

The sending and decoding of messages with emotional content. Important dimensions include body movements and gestures, eye contact, touch, facial expressions, physical closeness, and tone of voice.

Effective communication involves more than words. **Nonverbal communication** is sending and decoding messages with emotional content. Friendliness, respect, acceptance, rejection, dominance, submissiveness, anger, fear, and humor are conveyed primarily by nonverbal signals. When the verbal and nonverbal messages disagree, the receiver is likely to discount the verbal message and believe the nonverbal message. For example, a sender who verbally promises to act in good faith but does not make eye contact and keeps glancing at a wristwatch is indicating lack of respect for the receiver. Important dimensions of nonverbal communication include body movements and gestures, eye contact, touch, facial expressions, physical closeness, and tone of voice.

BODY MOVEMENTS AND GESTURES   Posture can indicate attentiveness or lack of interest in a conversation. In a job interview, an interviewee should lean slightly forward to indicate that he or she is attentive to the interviewer. Gestures can add or detract from the verbal message. Hand gestures help emphasize points, but fidgeting sends the message that the speaker is nervous and lacks confidence. Different cultures place different meanings on gestures. In the United States, holding the thumb and first finger in a circle means OK. In Brazil it is an insult and may provoke a fight.

EYE CONTACT   Attentiveness or lack of interest on the part of the sender or receiver in face-to-face communication is conveyed by eye contact. In business communication, it is important for both parties to make some eye contact, but prolonged eye contact may be interpreted as aggressiveness or inappropriate intimacy. Use eye contact carefully in business conversations.

TOUCH   A firm handshake is an enthusiastic greeting, but a weak handshake sends a negative signal, indicating low enthusiasm. Touch signals liking, acceptance, and friendship. Even more than eye contact, touch should be used sparingly in business situations. Unwanted touching in the U.S. workplace is a form of sexual harassment. Some other cultures are more permissive about touching. For example, in France it is not uncommon for employees who are good friends to greet each other with a kiss on the cheek.

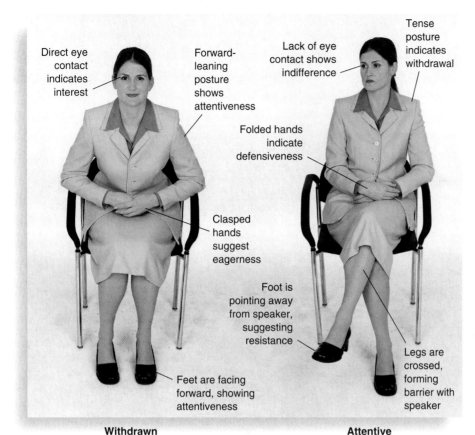

Direct eye contact indicates interest

Forward-leaning posture shows attentiveness

Lack of eye contact shows indifference

Tense posture indicates withdrawal

Folded hands indicate defensiveness

Clasped hands suggest eagerness

Foot is pointing away from speaker, suggesting resistance

Legs are crossed, forming barrier with speaker

Feet are facing forward, showing attentiveness

Withdrawn

Attentive

By having a forward leaning posture and making direct eye contact with a speaker (photo on far left), one conveys attentiveness to the other person.

FACIAL EXPRESSIONS Emotions such as happiness, satisfaction, anger, fear, and confusion are signaled by facial expressions. A confused look is feedback that the verbal message was not clearly received. Smiling conveys happiness and warmth. Along with the handshake, a smile is probably one of the most effective ways to establish a positive connection with a new acquaintance.

PHYSICAL DISTANCE Individuals regulate the physical distance between themselves and others, reserving the smallest distance (from touching to two feet away) for close, intimate friends and family, and the greatest distance (4 to 12 feet) for business and casual social acquaintances.[5] Violating an individual's expectations of an appropriate social distance causes discomfort and high probability of a miscommunication.

Physical distance expectations vary between cultures. Some cultures permit closer physical distances than others. Venezuelans have much smaller distance zones for business acquaintances than U.S. workers and might consider it rude if one backs away. A public speaker who understands how to use physical distance can create a strong bond with the

NONVERBAL COMMUNICATION

Most nonverbal communication deals with feelings. Although feelings may be hidden, they are typically very potent. This exercise illustrates common nonverbal signals and explores their potency compared to verbal communication.

Form groups of four to five students. Each team works together as follows.

1. Each member of the group writes down three feelings ("happy," "irritated," and so on).

2. Each group member takes a turn trying to communicate nonverbally one of the feelings to the rest of the group. After about a minute, group members guess at the feeling. After each person's turn, he or she records how many group members guessed the correct feeling.

3. The entire class then reviews the overall level of accuracy and briefly discusses the typical accuracy of nonverbal communication.

4. In the small groups, again, step 2 is repeated except that while the person is giving the nonverbal message, he or she also gives a different verbal message. (The verbal message need not be opposite to the nonverbal, but it must be different.)

5. The entire class group discusses the difference between the two nonverbal communication approaches.

Discussion Questions

1. How accurately were people able to understand the first round of nonverbal signals? Were more subtle or less common feelings harder to identify?

2. What happened to the level of accuracy when a different verbal signal was present?

3. When you see this happen in a real situation—different verbal and nonverbal messages are sent—which are you most likely to believe? Why?

Source: From *Organizational Behavior* by Sashkin and Morris. Copyright © 1984. Reprinted by permission of Pearson Education, Inc., Upper Saddle River, NJ.

---

audience. Oprah Winfrey, the television talk show host, bonds with her audience by reducing physical distance and going into the audience to speak with audience members up close.

TONE OF VOICE   Emotions such as attentiveness, friendliness, anger, or fear are transmitted by the tone in a voice. Aspects of the tone of voice that communicate different emotional states include pitch, loudness, speed, clarity of speech, and inflection. In a business setting, it is important to communicate confidence in order to establish credibility. Therefore, it is a good practice to speak clearly, emphasize key words, and use variable speed and inflection at appropriate times to keep the audience interested. Avoid talking in a monotone, which conveys lack of interest to the audience and reduces their motivation to listen.

Oprah Winfrey's strong verbal communication skills are enhanced by her use of nonverbal communication, including touch and facial expression, with her audiences.

Listening Skills

Listening is a fundamental communication skill for understanding both the verbal content and the underlying feelings embedded in the message. Listening is an active, not a passive, activity. It requires the listener to be involved in the communication process. The listener should try to avoid judging the speaker or the message being given. Instead, the listener should focus attention on trying to understand the content of the message. An active listener indicates both verbally and nonverbally that he or she is engaged in the conversation. When the speaker is communicating a feeling, the listener can restate what the speaker is expressing, asking for confirmation. The speaker will either confirm the impression or clarify it. In either case, the speaker will be encouraged to continue the conversation. Also, by using nonverbal indicators of listening—making eye contact, nodding the head, and leaning forward, for example—the listener is encouraging the speaker to continue. Lack of feedback from the listener can discourage the speaker from sharing opinions or feelings. Passively listening may unintentionally short-circuit a conversation.

When listening to another person, the speaker's tone of voice often discloses his or her emotional state, which helps the listener understand the feelings behind the words. Aspects of the speaker's tone of voice to listen for include the pitch, loudness, and speed of the verbal message. By decoding the meaning of the speaker's tone of voice, the listener can provide feedback to the speaker that can improve the quality of communication between the two parties. Here are some examples of how to interpret and respond to a speaker's tone of voice.

- If a speaker's pitch of voice is high and strained, it indicates feelings of nervousness. A calm, reassuring response from the listener encourages the speaker to proceed speaking. On the other hand, a quick, jerky response from the listener may cut the speaker short and disrupt the speaker's train of thought. Speaking in a lower pitch that is unstrained indicates the speaker is feeling confident and has emotional composure.

- If the speaker's tone of voice is shaky and hesitant with numerous pauses, it indicates a lack of confidence and doubt. By maintaining eye contact and offering reassuring gestures such as nodding one's head, the listener encourages the speaker to go on and complete the message.

- When the speaker's voice is too loud, or on the other hand the speaker mumbles the words quietly, the listener will have difficulty understanding the message. In either case the listener has a duty to ask the speaker to reduce or increase the voice volume depending on the situation. If the speaker's voice is too loud, the listener should calmly ask the speaker to reduce the volume to a more comfortable level. This should be done in a nonjudgmental way. If the speaker speaks too softly and mumbles, making it difficult to hear the words, the listener should ask the speaker to increase the volume. In both instances the focus should be on conveying the desire to understand the speaker.

Listening is an invaluable skill for managers. By actively listening to another individual, the manager shows empathy for and understanding of the speaker's perspective, even if it is different from the manager's own position. This is critical when managers negotiate with each other or with customers to find solutions acceptable to both parties. Employees or other managers are unlikely to bring problems to managers who have weak listening skills. This is likely to undermine a manager's credibility and limit effectiveness. Manager's Notes 15.3 presents specific ways to improve active listening skills.

Guidelines for Active Listening

You can show a speaker you are actively listening to the ideas and feelings that are being communicated by observing the following dos and don'ts.

Do create a supportive atmosphere.

Do listen for feelings as well as words.

Do note cues, such as gestures, tone of voice, and body posture.

Do occasionally test for understanding by asking, "Is this what you mean?"

Do demonstrate acceptance and understanding verbally and nonverbally.

Do ask exploratory, open-ended questions.

Don't try to change the other's views.

Don't solve the problem for the speaker.

Don't give advice, no matter how obvious the solution may seem.

Don't pass judgment.

Don't explain or interpret others' behavior.

Don't give false reassurances.

Don't attack if the speaker is hostile to you (try to understand the source of any anger).

Don't ask questions about the "why" of feelings.

Source: From *Effective Behavior in Organizations,* by Cohen, et al. Copyright © 1976 The McGraw-Hill Companies, Inc. Reprinted with permission.

APPLICATIONS: MANAGEMENT IS EVERYONE'S BUSINESS

Applications for the Manager When dealing with an employee who has an issue that is emotional in nature, use quality listening skills. First, seek to understand the nature of the problem and the perspective of the employee before passing judgment or telling the employee what you think about the issue. Hear the employee out. Use listening skills to understand the issue from the employee's perspective. This will help you develop a mutually beneficial solution.

If it is necessary to give negative feedback, make sure that the behavior being criticized is one the employee is able to control. There is little value in communicating a shortcoming to a person if he or she has no control over it. For example, a dyslexic employee might have difficulty writing memos that are free from spelling errors. Rather than criticizing the dyslexic employee's spelling skills, the manager could encourage the employee to use the spell-checking function on a computer before distributing written memos. The dyslexic employee is better able to control using the spell-checking function on the computer than to correctly spell all of the words in a written message.

Applications for Managing Teams   If you are part of a virtual team that coordinates work over a computer network, it is important to schedule periodic face-to-face meetings in order to build team spirit and trust. Without trust, there can be misunderstandings and teams are likely to be short-lived. With trust, team members are willing to give people who do not meet expected task demands the benefit of the doubt, and members can depend on each other to get the job done right.

Make sure individual team members and the team as a whole receive performance feedback. This allows the team to monitor its performance and steadily find ways to improve. Giving team members customer feedback is helpful.

Applications for Individuals   Look for ways to practice presentation skills by speaking to different audiences. Volunteer to present your team's accomplishments to other organization members at meetings. Join a professional organization and volunteer to give a presentation on a topic that members want to learn more about.

Find ways to enhance your credibility so that people want to listen to what you have to say. Act with integrity around other employees, making sure your actions are consistent with your verbal messages. For example, making promises you fail to keep undermines your credibility, and people become less interested in what you tell them.

CONCLUDING THOUGHTS

After the introductory vignette at the beginning of the chapter we presented some critical thinking questions related to aspects of communication at Boeing. Now that you have had the opportunity to learn about managing communication in the chapter, review the questions that were raised in the vignette. First, the advantage of using face-to-face communication between the Boeing CEO and the project teams during the development of the company's 777 aircraft is that it provides the richest communication channel. Both facts and feelings can be accurately transmitted with face-to-face communication. Moreover, the CEO, using face-to-face communication with the project teams, obtains direct information from the employees instead of information that is filtered through different levels of management. If the CEO had obtained information from written reports provided by subordinate managers, it might not have been as useful or accurate. Subordinates who gather and interpret information for the boss often downplay the negative and have a tendency to play up the positive facts as a way to be viewed in a favorable light by superiors in the organization.

One of the disadvantages of face-to-face communication is that it is inefficient and time consuming. The CEO would need extra time to learn how all the project teams are faring on the development of the new Boeing aircraft. Another disadvantage is that the Boeing employees may try to focus on impressing the CEO with favorable information rather than disclosing problems that are keeping the projects from reaching their planned targets. Nonetheless, by randomly sampling representative projects teams for face-to-face communication, and by communicating openly and honestly, CEO Condit should be able to gather useful information for planning purposes by taking advantage of his strong communication skills.

Condit communicated a general orientation to all employees about the company's 777 aircraft in order to provide them with a sense of mission and purposefulness. They could then better understand how their contributions fit into the overall goals and direction of the company. The investment in a new aircraft such as the 777 was a gamble costing the company billions of dollars. The CEO believed that the employees deserved to know how important this new product would be for their shared success. One possible form of communication that the CEO could select would be a live cable television broadcast sent to all Boeing sites simultaneously. The live broadcast speech gives employees a shared experience during an important and historical event. An alternative would be a series of live speeches scheduled at various Boeing aircraft plants over a period of several days. Speaking directly to the employees either with a video broadcast or by giving a speech means the CEO is using rich communication channels. Employees who hear directly from the CEO are more likely to be motivated to embrace the 777 aircraft development project than if they were given a written text message in the form of a memo or e-mail from the CEO.

SUMMARY Communication is a process that involves the transmission of information from one party to another through the use of shared symbols. The information may take the form of facts, objective information, or feelings. Communication includes a sender and a receiver. The sender encodes the message in symbols and the receiver must decode the message to receive the intended meaning.

The sender selects a communication channel that can vary from rich to lean in terms of the amount of content that can be transmitted. Communication channels include face-to-face conversations, written memos, videotapes, or voice mail. Communication channels that provide feedback should be utilized when the content of the message is complex and important. Noise may interfere with the receiver's ability to accurately decode the message. Communication channels with feedback provisions can reduce the threat of noise-distorted messages.

Patterns of organizational communication include **downward communication,** in which the sender is at a high level in the organization and the receiver is at a lower level; **upward communication,** in which the sender is at a lower level in the organization than the receiver; and **horizontal communication,** in which sender and receiver are at similar levels. Differences in employee status and power, diversity, and self-interest create communication barriers that must be managed for effective organizational communication to take place.

All members of organizations need basic communication skills to be effective in their jobs. Some key communication skills are assertive communication skills, presentation skills, nonverbal communication skills, and listening skills.

DISCUSSION QUESTIONS

1. Why is it important for a communication channel to have provisions for feedback? Can you think of a situation in which it may be useful to have communication without any provisions for feedback? Describe this situation.

2. What communication barriers could distort the communication between you and your professor? What are some approaches you could use to overcome these communication barriers?

3. Why are organizations today placing a greater emphasis on horizontal communications?

4. Is e-mail superior to older forms of electronic communications such as the telephone or voice mail? What are the advantages of e-mail? What are the disadvantages of e-mail? How can we manage a large volume of e-mail messages so that we are not spending too much time responding to messages each day?

5. Assume you are a manager and you overhear two employees exchanging harmful gossip about the personal life of another employee. Why do employees gossip and spread rumors about each other? How can this type of informal communication be managed? How would you handle this situation?

6. As a team leader, suppose one of the employees on your team has poor listening skills and continuously interrupts others who are speaking, becoming a source of frustration for the other team members. How would you improve this situation?

7. Research shows that in a job interview, the interviewer is likely to be strongly influenced by first impressions of the interviewee. In many cases a decision is made within the first minute of the interview. Assuming you want to make a positive impression in a job interview, how would you communicate nonverbally to create a favorable impression?

8. What is the role of communication in the management of diversity? Which type of communication channels enable diverse employees to feel respected and supported in an organization?

9. What is the difference between communicating assertively and communicating aggressively?

MANAGEMENT
MINICASE 15.1

Should Employees Be Required to Communicate Only in English?

When many different languages are spoken in a workplace, communication among employees becomes more difficult. To overcome this difficulty, some U.S. companies have made the use of English mandatory. These policies have caused a great deal of controversy in that some believe that employees have the right to communicate in their own language.

The rationale given for the English-only mandate is that it makes the workplace more productive by facilitating communication. It also keeps the workplace safer because rules are standardized. Another reason some companies offer is that speaking a language that not everyone understands makes those who do not understand it feel isolated.

Those who disagree with such mandates feel just as strongly that workers should communicate in the language they are most comfortable with. They believe that forcing everyone to speak English downplays employee diversity and makes employees feel unrespected.

As long as company rules do not discriminate against a particular race or nationality, companies are not violating any federal law. The Equal Employment Opportunity Commission permits the English-only workplace rule only if the policy is a business necessity; otherwise, employers may be in violation of Title VII of the Civil Rights Act. In one landmark case, a company called Spun Steak implemented an English-only policy after several workers complained of harassment and being insulted by other workers in a language they could not understand. The company's policy allowed its workers to deviate from the English-only rule during breaks but urged its workers not to insult others in their native tongue. The court upheld the company's right to implement its policy.

In San Francisco, on the other hand, chef Jean Alberti is teaching himself Spanish to be able to keep up with his kitchen crew of mostly Spanish-speaking employees. He fears his operations will suffer if he can't communicate with his staff.

Discussion Questions

1. Do you think English-only rules are an overly harsh way of creating a common focus among employees? Are there better ways to encourage employees to communicate effectively with each other and with customers?

2. You are managing a fast-food restaurant with an English-only rule that is enforced at all times based on business necessity. The majority of the employees under your supervision are recent immigrants who speak only Spanish. How could you manage the workforce under the English-only policy without offending the Spanish-speaking employees?

Sources: Adapted from T. Brady, "The Downside of Diversity," *HR Focus*, August 1996, pp. 22–23; R. L. Brady, "English-Only Rules Draw Controversy," *HR Focus*, June 1996, p. 20; J. Yabroff, "Habla Español?" *San Francisco Chronicle*, April 21, 2000.

MANAGEMENT MINICASE 15.2

Actions Speak Louder than Words All around the World

"He wouldn't look me in the eye. I found it disconcerting that he kept looking all over the room but rarely at me," said Barbara Walters after her interview with Libya's Colonel Muamar el-Qaddafi. Like many people in the United States, Walters was associating eye contact with trustworthiness, so when Qaddafi did not make eye contact, she felt uncomfortable. In fact, Qaddafi was paying Walters a compliment. In Libya, *not* looking conveys respect. Looking straight at a woman is considered nearly as serious as physical assault.

Nonverbal communication varies widely between cultures and even between subcultures. The differences strongly affect communication in the workplace. Whether you are trying to communicate with a new Asian-American assistant, the Swedish managers who recently bought your company, the young African-American college student who won a summer internship with your firm, or representatives from the French company you hope will buy your firm's new designs, your efforts will depend as much on physical cues as on verbal ones. Most Americans aren't usually aware of their own nonverbal behaviors. They have trouble understanding the body language of people from other cultures. The list of differences is endless:

- In Thailand it is rude to place your arm over the back of a chair in which another person is sitting.
- Finnish female students are horrified by Arab girls who want to walk hand in hand with them.
- Canadian listeners nod to signal agreement.
- Japanese listeners nod to indicate only that they have understood.
- British listeners stare at the speaker, blinking their eyes to indicate understanding.
- People in the United States are taught that it's impolite to stare.
- Saudis accept foreigners in Western business attire but are offended by tight-fitting clothing and by short sleeves.
- Spaniards indicate a receptive friendly handshake by clasping the other person's forearm to form a double handshake.
- Canadians consider touching any part of the arm above the hand intrusive, except in intimate relationships.

It may take years to understand nonverbal communication in other cultures, but there are resources to help you prepare. Books and seminars on cultural differences are readily available, as are motion pictures showing a wide range of cultures. You can always rent videos of films and TV shows from other countries. Examining the illustrations in news and business magazines can give you an idea of expected business dress and personal space. Finally, remaining flexible and interacting with people from other cultures who are visiting or living in your country will go a long way toward lowering the barriers presented by nonverbal communication.

Discussion Questions

1. Explain how watching a movie from another country might help you prepare to correctly interpret nonverbal behavior from that culture.

2. Assume that one of your co-workers is originally from Saudi Arabia. You like him, and the two of you work well together. However, he stands so close when you speak with him that it makes you very uncomfortable. How would you communicate your discomfort to this co-worker?

Source: Adapted from C. Bovée and J. Thill, *Business Communication Today,* 6th ed. Upper Saddle River, NJ: Prentice Hall, 2000, p. 38.

Selecting the Most Effective Form of Communication

INDIVIDUAL/
COLLABORATIVE
LEARNING
CASE 15.1

You are a sales representative for a leading pharmaceutical company, which produces a full range of drugs for medical treatments to patients. You communicate on a regular basis with other sales representatives within and outside your sales region, the sales manager and the district manager, and many clients within your sales territory who are primarily physicians and directors of managed care health organizations. Since you work primarily out of an office in your home, you must depend heavily on electronic communication to stay in touch with customers, colleagues, and management. Here is some information about e-mail, voice mail, and fax to help you select the most appropriate electronic communication channel.

E-mail has the following advantages:

It is fast and inexpensive and provides easy access to others.

It facilitates communication with busy executives and managers.

It provides documented evidence that a message was received.

It is less intrusive than other forms of communication. Recipients can respond when time permits.

Senders can communicate with large numbers of people quickly and simultaneously.

It facilitates global communication where time zones create communication barriers.

E-mail also has disadvantages:

Not all offices have e-mail.

Some people are uncomfortable or inexperienced with e-mail.

It may be awkward to use when the message contains emotional content or when a relationship of trust has not yet been established between the parties.

It is not suitable for private or confidential messages.

Here are some tips for users of e-mail:

Check e-mail three or four times per day.

Assume e-mail is not private.

Check spelling and grammar, because e-mail represents you and your organization.

Voice mail has the following advantages:

It is the most personal form of electronic communication.

It allows the receiver to give a quick response.

Your voice can convey sincerity that the written word cannot. It can ease a problematic situation.

Voice mail also has disadvantages:

It can be frustrating to listen to a long prerecorded message with a menu of choices that may not apply to the caller's needs.

It cannot replace a handwritten thank-you note.

Here are some tips for using voice mail:

Anticipate that you may be leaving a recorded message. Before you make the call, prepare what you want to say and avoid rambling.

Avoid leaving the same message several times.

The greeting you prepare on your own voice mail should communicate your availability and tell the caller how to reach a live person in case of an emergency.

Avoid cute and humorous greetings.

Fax has the following advantages:

It quickly delivers a close approximation to original documents.

It is useful when a relationship is new or formal.

It is sometimes important to use stationery with the company name on the letterhead.

It is useful when a document requires a signature.

Fax also has disadvantages:

Many people share fax machines and waiting is sometimes necessary.

Confidential information may be disclosed because faxes can rarely be sent privately.

Faxes sometimes get lost.

Here are some tips for users of fax machines:

Always use a cover sheet that has your fax and telephone numbers.

Avoid reading other employees' faxes.

Critical Thinking Questions

1. You want to let the sales manager know which clients you will be visiting within your territory next week. Which communication channel would you select and why?

2. One of your clients complained about a late delivery of a shipment of drugs that was promised by a certain date. You must provide a response to the problem. Which communication channel would you select and why?

3. You will be attending the annual sales convention at Las Vegas, and while there you want to meet a colleague who works in the Australian subsidiary of your firm who will also attend the meeting. Which communication channel would you select to set up your meeting in advance and why?

Collaborative Learning Exercise

With a partner or small group, rank e-mail, voice mail, and fax from best to worst according to the following characteristics: richness of information, ease of use, availability, level of privacy, and speed of communication. Did everyone in your group agree on the rankings? What accounts for any differences in your rankings of these communication channels?

Source: Adapted from B. Pachter, "Tips for Technological Correctness," *HR Focus*, November 1996, p. 21.

Whole Foods, Whole Philosophy

Visit the website of Whole Foods Market, click on the "company" button, and explore the "whole company philosophy" section, including the "core values," "quality goals," and "declaration of interdependence" sections of the company philosophy. Then answer the following questions:

1. What message does the Whole Foods Market company philosophy communicate to the consumer about the food products it sells?

2. What message does the Whole Foods Market company philosophy communicate to employees and job applicants about the work environment at the company?

3. Do the graphic and visual images on the website communicate the same or a different message to you as the text (the words) describing the company philosophy?

4. Suppose the text gave a different message to the reader than the visual images do. Which message would most likely be received by the reader? Explain your answer.

INTERNET EXERCISE 15.1

www.wholefoodsmarket.com

Listening Self-Inventory

How good are you at listening? Consider the following statements and check yes or no next to each. Be as truthful as you can in light of your behavior in the last few meetings or gatherings you attended.

	Yes	No
1. I frequently attempt to listen to several conversations at the same time.	____	____
2. I like people only to give me the facts and then let me make my own interpretation.	____	____
3. I sometimes pretend to pay attention to people.	____	____
4. I consider myself a good judge of nonverbal communications.	____	____
5. I usually know what another person is going to say before he or she says it.	____	____
6. I usually end conversations that don't interest me by diverting my attention from the speaker.	____	____
7. I frequently nod, frown, or whatever to let the speaker know how I feel about what he or she is saying.	____	____
8. I usually respond immediately when someone has finished talking.	____	____
9. I evaluate what is being said while it is being said.	____	____
10. I usually formulate a response while the other person is still talking.	____	____

	Yes	No

11. The speaker's "delivery" style frequently keeps me from listening to content. ____ ____

12. I usually ask people to clarify what they have said rather than guess at the meaning. ____ ____

13. I make a concerted effort to understand other people's points of view. ____ ____

14. I frequently hear what I expect to hear rather than what is said. ____ ____

15. Most people feel that I have understood their point of view when we disagree. ____ ____

Scoring: The correct answers according to communication theory are as follows: "No" for questions 1, 2, 3, 5, 6, 7, 8, 9, 10, 11, 14. "Yes" for questions 4, 12, 13, 15. If you missed only one or two questions, you strongly approve of your own listening habits, and you are on the right track to becoming an effective listener in your role as manager. If you missed three or four questions, you have uncovered some doubts about your listening effectiveness, and your knowledge of how to listen has some gaps. If you missed five or more questions, you probably are not satisfied with the way you listen, and your friends and coworkers may not feel you are a good listener either. Work on improving your active listening skills.

Source: From *Supervisory Management*, by Florence M. Stone. January 1989. Copyright © 1989 American Management Association/Amacom. Reproduced with permission of American Management Association/ Amacom via Copyright Clearance Center.

Wolinsky & Williams: Teamwork

Account manager: Joe Tanney, male, 20s, Caucasian
VP account management: Simon Mahoney, male, 40s, Caucasian
Account manager: Cheng Jing, male, 30s, Asian
Account manager: Rosa Denson, female, 30s Hispanic

General Background info:
Wolinsky & Williams, Inc. is a very large international architecture firm with over 400 employees and six offices throughout the world. They specialize in office parks and corporate high rises, with 35 years of success. They have moved into region after region—today they have or are constructing buildings in over 35 cities in nine countries.

Tanney has been with Wolinsky & Williams for six years—he started as an assistant while he was still completing his degree. He has been an account manager for a little over a year now and is thrilled, excited, diligent, motivated, and up for any challenge—a real go-getter.

Simon has been with the company for over fifteen years and although he still does a great job, he is quite jaded and tired—tired of everything really. He's running on autopilot most of the time, following his routine, doing no more, no less. He unfortunately has lost passion for his company and the work and is reluctant to do anything outside of his routine.

Cheng has been an account manager for two years, but has always wanted to be a designer—he's finishing another degree right now and has been promised a position in the design department as soon as he gets his master's degree. Needless to say, his heart is not in account management.

Rosa transferred to this office from the Dallas office about three years ago. She is generally enthusiastic and does great work, but is very susceptible to distraction—mostly from her personal life, whether it is difficulties with her in-laws, her husband, her own mother—they always get the best of her to the point where she can hardly think or talk of anything else.

"Documents":

- Company profile.
- Project information—general tasks, steps, overarching ideas.
- Joe's memos about the proposal.

Pre-Viewing Class Questions

1. How should Joe proceed with this meeting and its agenda?

2. What skills must he possess in order to have a productive outcome from the meeting?

3. How important is it for Joe to clearly identify the many facets to be discussed/resolved?

Scene One: "Not Me" Syndrome
Location: Conference room

Backstory:

W & W has been expanding by leaps and bounds over the past eight years or so. The growth has been spectacular and hurried—they have not always taken the time to implement change in the most efficient fashion nor have they opened new offices with any sense of continuity of process or corporate culture. Business has been steadying off/plateauing for about eight months now and senior management has decided to take this opportunity to assess efficiencies and practices and make the necessary improvements across the board.

These four account managers have been asked to get together by senior management to generate a proposal for streamlining the antiquated blueprint generation process. Each office is at different stages of computerization, with different teams preferring different technologies for particular tasks. This makes everything more complex—from collaboration to revisions to cost and time management, etc.

The team has been attempting to meet for a couple of weeks and was never able to agree on a date. They all agreed to start generating ideas and breaking down the tasks in the meantime—nobody has done it except Joe, who has created a very thorough analysis of the project. This is their first meeting—they need to plan a course of action, assign tasks, and set deadlines. Simon is the manager with the most seniority and everyone, including senior management, has assumed he would lead the team.

Break for Manager Questions & Analysis
Scene Two: End of the Road
Location: Same conference room
Some time has elapsed and the next meeting is about to commence. Nobody has kept a single deadline or shared a single memo except Joe.

Post-Viewing Class Questions

1. How effective was Joe's leadership during the meetings?

2. How could the meetings have been conducted in a more formal/structured manner?

3. What hidden agendas may be present within the meeting participants?

Leadership Challenges for Bill Ford

On June 16, 2003, the Ford Motor Company celebrated its 100th anniversary. A few months later, the company was expected to produce its 300 millionth vehicle. After more than two decades of a non-Ford family member as a president/CEO, a Ford family member has once again been selected to drive the company in the 21st century. In 2001, 46-year-old William Clay Ford, the great-grandson of Henry Ford, the founder of the second largest automobile manufacturer in the world, was named president and CEO of the company. He is only the third Ford family member since his grandfather to serve as president/CEO, and the first since Henry Ford II (his uncle) served as CEO in 1979. Bill Ford, as he likes to be called, has all the right pedigrees to lead the company: He is a "blue blood" Ford, and he is a graduate of two top universities—Princeton (undergraduate degree) and Massachusetts Institute of Technology (MIT) (graduate degree in management).

Prior to his appointment as president/CEO, Bill Ford spent some 23 years at the company in various capacities. In 1979, he served as a product planning analyst; in 1988, he was elected to serve on the company's board of directors; in 1995, he was elected chairperson of the financial committee, board of directors; and in 1999, he was elected chairperson of the board of directors. Serving as a member of a board of directors and setting policy is much different than serving as president/CEO and implementing policy. In his role as the president/CEO Bill Ford now answers directly to the board. This new position is in stark contrast to his former role as chairperson of the board, where he held the previous president/CEO accountable. Some critics have been quick to remark that on paper Bill Ford's corporate experiences do not suggest his meriting a position as a president/CEO at one of the Big 3 automobile manufacturers. Instead, they suggest that his lack of actual practical executive experience, coupled with his lack of the management functions (e.g., finance, manufacturing), makes leading a complex company such as Ford a very difficult task for him. They quietly whisper that all his previous work experiences at Ford were part of a master plan that prepared and trained

This case was prepared by Joseph C. Santora, who is professor of business at Essex County College, Newark, New Jersey.

him to become the president/CEO at Ford. (The Ford family owns some 40 percent of the company stock and Bill Ford receives some $4 million in dividends from company stock personally.)

On the other hand, Bill Ford has demonstrated good leadership and managerial skills—he is "an excellent communicator and [has] had a well of trust and affection from many of [his] constituents." As a board leader he did not recluse himself in his office waiting for events to unfold mysteriously. He took an active role and received high marks for his handling of a tragic 1999 company situation. In his role as board chair, he traveled to the company's River Rouge Complex in Dearborn, Michigan, when an explosion stopped production, killed one employee, and injured 30 other employees (five of whom died several days later). He was quite visible and spent considerable time with the families of the injured extending his condolences.

Unlike many other major company executives who seek short-term accomplishments to satisfy their boards of directors, he has taken the long-term view for the nearly 100-year-old company. Despite his relatively thin executive-level experience, he seems to have developed his own style of leadership that separates him from many of his contemporaries. His reputation is both pro-union and pro-employee. He believes in the value of all stakeholders (e.g., dealers, workers, and suppliers). He demonstrated leadership skills—both communicative and inspirational—in a recent speech to Ford workers. He sounded almost Churchillian when he sounded a metaphorical call to arms:

> I'm asking you to work hard. Keep the big picture in mind. Think about what really matters. Do that and nothing else. We've come back from devastation many times in our history. We're going to do it again. On the eve of our 100th anniversary, the stage is set for a dramatic return to greatness. We started the job; now let's finish it.

According to many sources, he also possesses good listener skills and appears less autocratic than Jacques Nasser, his predecessor (the immediate past president who was ousted from office because of quality and morale problems).

Problems

Mid-management experience, board of director exposure, degrees from world-class universities, and a caring long-term vision for a company do not necessarily make for a good leader; but indeed they do help. Yet, Bill Ford will undoubtedly face many major challenges that will test his leadership capabilities and mettle.

He faces four major immediate nagging problems. First, the top management team (TMT) is new, recently assembled, and problematic for several reasons. None has worked with him for any length of time. Their appointment to senior-level positions has been a result of corporate reorganizations and retirements. Teamwork among members of Ford's new TMT—Nick Scheele, chief operating officer (COO, Jaguar), James Padilla, executive vice president (North America), and David Thursfield, head of Europe PAG purchasing—has been described as extremely problematical. These men are highly competitive, jockey for position, and fight among themselves, although Bill Ford had instructed them to work together without criticizing each other, especially in public. In addition, the company faces contract negotiations with the United Auto Workers (UAW) in the summer of 2003. The TMT will certainly need solidarity to deal with the impending contract discussions.

Second, there is the issue of profits. The war in Iraq and its aftermath, fears of recession, foreign competition, and an incentive price war have all contributed to the decline in automobile sales, resulting in higher inventories. U.S. automobile sales are some 5 percent below normal at a comparable point in time. In 2002, Ford lost more than $550 million. In order to sell cars in such an economic climate, Ford, like other automotive companies, has had to offer incentives that have added to its financial losses. The company is also struggling to recapture its lost market share—a 4 percent decline from 25 to 21 percent in the last four years, an average loss of 1 percent annually.

Third, there is a good deal of street talk about high debt level and the possibility of bankruptcy. Ford has lost more than $6 billion in the last few years; its stock has taken a dramatic freefall to approximately $9.00 a share (as of May 2003); its pension fund is not funded adequately; and its massive retiree medical liabilities amount to some $23 billion. To date, health benefits costs have exceeded 2002 by some 20 percent. In addition, Ford's luxury car business, the Premier Automotive Group (PAG) (Volvo, Land Rover, Lincoln Continental, and Jaguar) has lost nearly $90 million in the first quarter of 2003. Ford Credit is saddled with more than $160 billion of debt and there is some speculation in the financial community that Ford may approach junk bond status by summer 2003. If these financial problems persist, the company may be forced to delay producing its new models and hold off on its desire to modernize factories—undoubtedly these factors will add financial hardships for the company and will reduce its ability to rebound.

Fourth, in the operational area, there are issues of automobile quality as a result of manufacturing cars in outdated factories. There are some defects in new models and engineering designs are considered careless. To add insult to injury, the April 2003 issue of *Consumer Reports* placed Ford last in the reliability category.

Ford does have its share of troubles. Given these complex corporate problems, can Bill Ford rescue the company from the possible brink of disaster?

Questions

1. What can Bill Ford do to help the members of the top management team (TMT) work together?

2. What would you do if you were Bill Ford?

3. What would motivate Bill Ford to become president/CEO of Ford Motor Company?

4. Discuss Bill Ford's leadership style. Compare his style of leadership as chairperson of the board and president/CEO. Has it changed? Should it change? Why? Why not?

5. Should Bill Ford have become president/CEO by virtue of his family name?

Sources: C. Isidore, "Nasser Out as Ford CEO," http://money.cnn.com/2001/10/30/CEOS/ford (2001); K. Kerwin, "Can Ford Pull Out of Its Skid?" *Business Week,* March 31, 2003, pp. 70–72; B. Morris, "Can Ford Save Ford?" *Fortune,* November 18, 2002, pp. 52–57, 60–62; A. Taylor III, "Getting Ford in Gear: CEO Bill Ford Must Cut Costs and Stop Feuds and Turn His Company Around," *Fortune,* May 12, 2003, pp. 102–106; http://www.automuseum.com/forddate.html.

Operations
and
Information
Systems
Management

6

6

Establishing and adhering to standards is critical for safety and customer satisfaction. Regardless of the talent and motivation in an organization, errors can occur and performance can only be as good as the information it is based on. To assure continued high performance and survivability of the organization, managers need to be able to determine what should be done and whether their decisions are being adequately executed. Responsible management requires standards, good information, and the means to quickly bring any deviant performance back to the standard level.

In Part Six we will examine how managers can assure that performance meets expectations. We will consider how managers can control performance and whether the focus of control efforts should be on people or systems. We will also consider how production processes can be assessed and deviations from standards eliminated. The old adage that knowledge is power is now more true than ever. We will, therefore, look at how information can be utilized for effective management.

SIXTEEN

Management Control

chapter 16

After reading this chapter, you should be able to:

- Understand the importance of control systems.
- Distinguish between system- and person-based control systems.
- Distinguish between process- and outcome-based control systems.
- Evaluate various control approaches.
- Understand why measurement is necessary for control.
- Develop measures that support effective control systems.
- Develop and implement a balanced scorecard.

All You Have Is Your Reputation: Control It or Lose It

Numico, a multinational company employing 29,000 people, learned the importance of control over product quality. Numico produces baby and clinical food. The company's Olivarit baby food is a widely recognized brand in the Netherlands, and Numico enjoyed an impeccable reputation. Then, in 1993, residue from a detergent was found in some baby food jars. Millions of units of Olivarit were recalled. The direct cost of the recall was millions of dollars. However, the indirect costs were potentially staggering, since the recall tarnished the image of the Olivarit brand, making it more vulnerable to competitors. Numico received approximately 17,000 phone calls from concerned parents following the recall announcement.

The incident served as a wake-up call. Even though it was later demonstrated in court that the source of the contamination was a meat supplier and that there was no substantive threat to public health, the company's image remained tarnished. Nonetheless, Numico realized that without adequate control over quality the company's survival could be at risk.

The result was a renewed focus on food safety and quality control beginning with an investigation of what had happened in the recall ordeal. It turned out that the Dutch Food Safety Department had warned Numico of possible contamination months before the recall. Unfortunately, these warnings sat on the desk of a Process and Quality Control Manager. The executive board terminated the employee, but the top managers knew this was only a retroactive remedy. What was really needed was a system to prevent another incident of contamination, consequent recall, and the loss of consumer confidence.

Numico saw the need for a uniform approach to production and food safety standards. There were 42 Numico factories worldwide, and each differed in terms of production processes and safety standards. While each factory is viewed as primarily responsible for its own product quality and safety, Numico needed a more centralized and uniform approach. The company centralized its food safety department in Germany. The reaction of the rest of the organization, however, was not overly positive. A number of Numico employees were concerned that the centralized department would simply be an internal police force. Further, they worried that the uniform standards they were to develop would simply become a whip with which to beat production.

The central safety department set about the task of developing uniform standards by inviting input from production managers from various facilities. Numico's management team took the position that unilaterally developing and then imposing standards on the organization would not work. Instead, they took a participative approach to developing the standards. Further, the standards included detailed information about problems faced by production in some facilities and the process used to resolve these problems. In other words, the standards were not rules which would be used to hammer everyone into compliance; they were a source of case studies that could be used to help improve quality and safety. In sum, the central safety department overcame initial skepticism by emphasizing involvement and by going beyond rules and using the standards as a source for learning and problem solving.

The uniform standards were built around five domains, or "pillars." They include supply chain control, general manufacturing processes, good hygiene practices, documentation, and quality control. These pillars and their associated standards cover the entire manufacturing process, from incoming materials to storage of the finished product. The standards developed around the pillars go beyond national requirements, providing Numico a margin that minimizes any chances of another recall.

Standards, no matter how carefully constructed, can become outdated. The uniform standards at Numico are anything but static—they are designed to be dynamic and to evolve. A committee including central safety department members and production managers continually update the standards. Regular meetings are held to discuss current food safety issues. They also distribute a food safety newsletter to every facility in the organization.

The standards developed at Numico were only part of what was needed to prevent quality and safety problems. The management team needed to be certain that the standards were actually followed. Compliance was assured through the use of two control tools.

First, the central safety department now annually inspects all factories, distribution centers, and suppliers. These inspections last three to four days and focus on critical points within the production process. The central safety department then sends an inspection report back to production personnel and factory management. If there is deviation from Numico's standards, the report is also sent to higher level management. In that case, factory managers are required to identify improvements that will solve the problem. The central safety department then checks to make sure that the improvements have been implemented.

As a second control tool, the central safety department continuously monitors the quality of raw materials and finished products. The monitoring reports are provided to upper management and are used to identify possible threats to high quality and safety.

If a product is found to not meet a standard, production and top management at the factory are immediately informed. Then, the factory manager, the central safety department, and production management define an action plan. Depending on the situation, possible actions include disposing of contaminated stock, temporarily halting production, or a recall.

Numico also scores each factory in terms of quality and food safety. These scores determine the annual winner of a food safety award. The factory that won the award in 2002 was the Netherlands factory where the 1993 recall took place.

Source: "Better Safe than Sorry: The House That Numico Built." *Food Engineering & Ingredients* 28 (2003), p. 15+.

CRITICAL THINKING QUESTIONS

1. *The recall event provided Numico the motivation to put centralized control systems in place. Do you think organizations can be as effective at assuring quality and safety without such a wake-up call?*

2. *The central safety department is external to the factories, yet controls company production processes. Wouldn't it be better to have this control internal to the factories?*

3. *The two control tools used by Numico include an annual review of the production process and the continuous monitoring of the quality of input and output. Wouldn't it be best to have continuous monitoring of all facets of production?*

Control is an important management function. Control ensures that standards are met, errors are limited, quality is acceptable, products are safe, and the company is performing at the highest possible level. When control is missing or inadequate, management cannot know if standards are being adhered to or if outcomes are acceptable or safe. Inadequate controls lead to poor or unsafe products, shoddy service, or, as in the introductory feature on Numico, recall of a product along with substantial direct and indirect costs. One key management role is making sure that the process and outcomes of the business meet expected standards. Without having data that provides this assurance, management is hoping for the best but really can't know or promise a customer what they will get in terms of a product or service.

In this chapter we examine the concept of management control. The major management control tools are reviewed and a variety of issues regarding control are examined. Several questions are considered, such as: What should be the focus of control efforts—people or the system? What steps are needed for effective control? Is there a downside to control, and can it be eliminated/minimized? First, however, this chapter begins with a consideration of the nature of management control.

What Is Management Control?

control

The process of comparing performance to standards and taking corrective action.

Control is the process of comparing performance to standards and taking corrective action, if needed. In other words, control involves measurement and regulation. It is the means by which management assures that desired objectives are being achieved.

Control is closely associated with the management function of planning. People often refer to "planning and control" in one phrase, as if the two were almost one function. Control complements planning because it is the means by which management assesses whether or not plans are being appropriately carried out. Corrective actions get the organization back on track and help managers achieve their intended goals.

There are a variety of ways to categorize the various types of control approaches. Figure 16.1 is a framework of management approaches to control. As depicted in the figure, control approaches can be categorized according to two factors: type and focus. The type factor is divided into formal and informal approaches to control. Formal control systems consist of written rules. They specify explicitly and in detail the processes, standards, and steps to be followed. In contrast, informal control relies on unwritten expectations regarding performance. For example, work groups are likely to develop norms for performance. Employees who fail to perform at those levels receive quick and certain feedback that they need to improve. Even though they are unwritten, informal controls can be a powerful source for regulating performance.

The focus factor refers to whether a control tool is directed at the outcome or the process. An outcome approach focuses on the results of a business process, such as number of units sold, amount of market share, or financial outcomes, such as profits. In contrast, a process approach focuses on how the work is actually performed. A process control tool centers on the steps involved in a process and the standards that should be followed in carrying out these steps.

The framework in Figure 16.1 will be used to organize our discussion of management control techniques. Remember that the framework may oversimplify the reality of control as it is practiced in organizations. First, both factors (type and focus) are, in reality, more of a matter of gradation than of a choice between two levels. For example, an organization may employ a control strategy that is in the range of informal to formal. Second, and related, the control techniques are not necessarily "pure." That is, an organization may employ multiple control approaches, some

part six Operations and Information Systems Management

FIGURE 16.1

Control Approaches as a
Function of Type and Focus

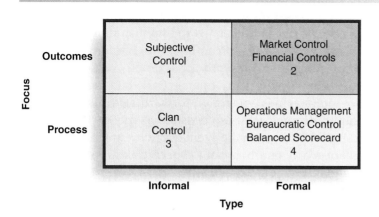

of which may be more formal and others more informal, and some more focused on process and others on outcomes. Nonetheless, in most organizations, there is a primary, or dominant, approach to control.[1] Company executives may use control techniques that focus on both process and outcomes, but outcome control may clearly be the primary focus, while process is only a secondary concern. With these caveats in mind, control techniques from each of the four cells of the framework are examined next.

Informal and Outcome-Focused Control

An informal approach and a focus on outcomes is a combination labeled in Figure 16.1 in cell 1 as **"subjective control."** These are controls that are not guided by objective standards. Rather, outcomes are subjectively considered and actions are taken based on those assessments. For example, a company may rely on feedback from customers regarding the quality of their products or services. If no complaints are heard, it is assumed that things are fine. When given a complaint, the company will try to satisfy the customer. The subjective control approach does not typically utilize explicit standards or a standard process for adjusting outcomes. Instead, the approach employs more global, or broad-based, assessments, such as "Are you satisfied with the product?" or "Are there any problems?" if there is any assessment at all. When assessments are not systematic, customers are asked different questions in different ways. The subjective approach also does not specify how deviations from an acceptable level of performance (whatever it is or however that may be defined by individual customers) should be handled. For example, if quality is claimed not to be acceptable, the organizational leaders may try to do something, but what should be done isn't specified beforehand.

subjective control

Informal approach based
on global assessment of
outcomes.

The subjective control approach is common, particularly in smaller businesses and in service settings. Smaller and start-up organizations may not have the time or resources needed to establish more systematic control systems. In service settings, it can be more difficult to establish standards. In manufacturing settings, products can be exactly measured to determine if they are within quality tolerances. While measuring the quality of a service interaction is not straightforward, it is possible to systematically measure outcomes. It is also possible to specify various corrective steps that should be taken in the event quality is not achieved. The subjective control approach simply is not as specific about corrective actions, as compared to other methods of control.

The subjective control approach might be summed up with the description that "We aren't really sure how we are doing, but we hope you like our diligent efforts." Control efforts in this approach might be considered as an example of management-by-exception. That is, if there is a complaint, action will be taken. Otherwise, management approaches the issue of control based on the old adage, "no news is good news." The subjective control approach is not a professionally acceptable or effective management control technique; however, it is common. You may have encountered this approach in any number of situations.

Formal and Process-Focused Control

Another set of control techniques, found in cell 4 of Figure 16.1, are formal and focus on the process. These approaches are probably the most widely known and used. They occur when the focus is on the work process and impose established standards, or rules, for how this process should be carried out. Operations management and, in particular, the quality approach, are examples of a formal and process-focused approach. Remember, however, that operations management is not simply a control technique; it is a means for increasing efficiency and effectiveness in production processes. Since Chapter 17 is devoted to a consideration of operations management, it is not covered here. The following are some well-known and newer emerging control approaches from the formal and process-focused category.

Bureaucratic Control

bureaucratic control

A formal control approach involving a cycle of (1) establishing standards, (2) performance measurement, (3) identifying gaps, and (4) corrective action.

Bureaucratic control is likely what most people think of when they think of management control. Bureaucratic control techniques are characterized by written guidelines or controls. While these standards can apply to outcomes, bureaucratic controls routinely focus on work processes. Bureaucratic control techniques apply standards to assess performance and apply corrective actions to regulate performance and bring it back to the level of the standards. The focus of bureaucratic control techniques is to detect discrepancies between performance and standards and to take systematic action to remove any deficiencies.

THE CONTROL PROCESS   Bureaucratic control techniques are composed of a cycle of steps, including (1) establishing standards; (2) performance measurement; (3) identifying gaps; and (4) corrective action. Each step is considered next.

Establishing Standards   Standards are the benchmarks against which performance is compared. Standards can take a variety of forms and be derived from a variety of sources. For example, standards could take the form of goals or could consist of professional guidelines or legal or financial procedures. Standards can also be based on statistical analysis and what is considered to be acceptable variance in performance (see the discussion of the quality approach in Chapter 17). Standards can also be derived from the practice of benchmarking, examining the performance of other organizations. No matter how standards are derived and whatever types they are, they form the requirements of the job. The standards are the criteria against which performance will be compared.

Categories of Managerial Control

A critical issue is how the standards are developed. While it can be relatively quick and easy to take a top-down approach and unilaterally develop standards, this approach may not work well in practice. A participative approach to creating standards takes longer but yields standards that are understood by everyone. When employees participate in creating standards, they are likely to be more committed to the standards and will work harder to achieve the desired results. Consider the approach used by Numico, the company described in the introduction to this chapter. Numico purposefully took a participative approach to developing standards. The involvement paid off with standards that are understood and pursued across the organization.

Performance Measurement   Levels of performance can be assessed in a variety of ways. The data used to determine performance levels can be classified as objective or subjective. Objective performance data includes measures such as number of pieces produced, amount of downtime, amount of waste, time to complete a task, and so on. The advantage of objective data is that it is typically free from error and bias.

Subjective performance data includes measures that involve human judgment. A supervisor's judgment of overall performance levels, a worker's judgment of the quality of materials, or a manager's assessment of the safety level of the work environment are all subjective assessments. The subjective nature of the data reflects the fact that it involves human judgment, thus opening the door to possible error and/or bias. However, subjective data is not constructed out of thin air—it is based on the work environment, albeit as perceived and assessed by people. These perceptions and assessments can sometimes make for subjective data that is superior to objective performance data. Consider, for instance, objective data that lists the number of accidents in a plant. For a given time period, there may be no accidents and the lack of mishaps might lead top management to conclude that the operation is safe. At the same time, subjective data from supervisors or employees might tell a much different but more accurate story. Supervisors might judge the work environment as too cluttered and conclude that the work practices of many workers emphasize speed over safety. In other words, the environment might be an accident waiting to happen. Management control based on objective data may completely fail to recognize how hazardous the work environment might be. Objective data by itself often fails to tell the whole story—it is often deficient. Subjective data can sometimes provide a more complete picture.

Whether performance data is subjective or objective in nature, it is important that adequate measures be devised and data collected. An old adage states that if you don't measure it, you can't manage it. Skills for Managing 16.1 looks at the importance of performance measurement in the domain of personal hygiene and food safety.

Identifying Gaps After developing standards and performance measures, the next step in the control cycle is to compare the two in order to identify any deficiencies. This step points out gaps between actual and intended performance levels. At times the task is not quite as simple as it may seem. It is important to recognize that there is always some amount of variation in any process, and not every deviation from a standard is meaningful. In other words, the problem in identifying gaps is determining how big a difference makes a difference. Figure 16.2 presents a control chart, a tool commonly used in the quality approach (see Chapter 17). The control chart is helpful for determining whether deviations are meaningful gaps between performance and standards.

As presented in Figure 16.2, control charts include upper and lower control limits. Where these limits are set depends upon how variable a process is and how important deviations are to quality or safety. It is common to set control limits at the levels of 2 standard deviations above or below the average performance level. Consider the performance levels depicted in the example control chart as representing the amount of time taken by each of three teams to respond to calls for service. Team 2 tends to perform the best, with response times even quicker than the standard. Team 3 tends to have the slowest response times, but all teams exhibit appreciable variance on this performance measure. Are any of the deviations from the prescribed or preferred level of meaningful size? The answer, according to the control chart approach, is "no."

The upper and lower control limits on a control chart set the limits of acceptable, or normal, variation. Deviations from standard levels that fall within those limits are simply normal variation. To treat those deviations as a meaningful gap in performance is making the proverbial

"DID YOU WASH YOUR HANDS?"

Handwashing is recognized as one of the most effective ways to reduce the occurrence of foodborne illness. Unfortunately, people in the foodservice industry estimate that handwashing frequency is about half of what it should be, even in schools and hospitals. This subjective estimate is about as good as the performance data gets. In most organizations, many things get measured, but handwashing is seldom one of them. This lack of objective measurement may be coming to an end.

Various models of handwashing stations are being developed to improve and better manage this simple but important activity. One model uses scanning technology to identify each employee who washes his or her hands. The system even includes a minimum scrub time in the handwashing process.

Are you washing your hands as often as needed?

Discussion Questions

1. Do you think that objective measurement of handwashing is important to a food safety control system? Or do you think subjective self-report (yes—I washed my hands!) is sufficient? Explain your answer.

2. Measurement is needed to manage. However, simply measuring something can also convey its importance. Do you think this will work for handwashing? If not, what else could be done to increase handwashing frequency?

3. How could the scanning technology be used to not only record but also reward frequent handwashers? Do you think the motivational component could be important to a food safety control system? Explain.

Research Questions

1. To what extent does lack of handwashing seem to be implicated in episodes of foodborne illness? Is there any data that you can find that provides some assessment of the extent to which lack of handwashing is a problem?

2. Can you find information on technology being applied to measure handwashing frequency? Do you think technology and objective measurement are the solution to handwashing problems? Why or why not?

Source: J. Mann, "Handwashing: Technology Adds a Measure of Management," *Foodservice Equipment & Supplies* 56 (2003), p. 39+.

FIGURE 16.2

The Control Chart:
Determining if Deviations Are
Meaningful Gaps

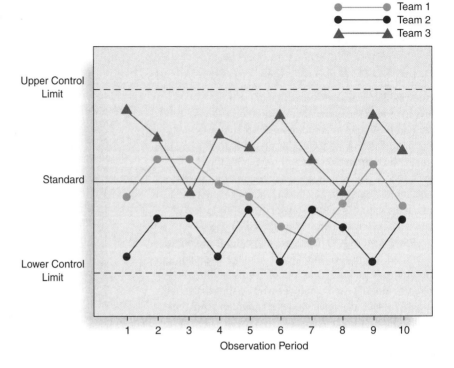

mountain out of a molehill. Deviations that fall outside the range defined by the control limits are, however, meaningful gaps between performance and the expected levels of performance.

Corrective Action   The final step in the control process is taking corrective action. Based on the previous step, what should management do? One option is to do nothing. Doing nothing is appropriate, and actually preferable, when no meaningful gaps in performance are found. If management takes action based on deviations that are within the acceptable range, meaningful performance improvement will not occur. Quite the contrary, management intervention when performance is within the range of the control limits may actually lead to increased variance in performance.[2] For example, a poor performance episode, but one that is within the acceptable range, might lead a vigilant manager to take action. Depending on the situation and the type of performance being examined (perhaps response time, as in our example, or the amount of sales, amount of waste, etc.), a manager might focus on motivating workers and tell them they need to work harder or decide to provide additional training. The manager might also look for ways to change the work situation, methods for arranging tools or materials, or advertising programs. The problem is that these interventions are not called for based on the control limits. The changes may upset normal work processes and end up increasing variability in performance. Taking no action can be the best approach, particularly when deviations from a standard are not of meaningful size.

When deviations from a standard are meaningful gaps in performance, a manager should take action. If corrective action is appropriate but isn't taken, the control process becomes simply a measurement exercise. The question is, what corrective action should be taken? While performance is typically thought of as the focus of corrective actions, there is another possibility; the standards themselves. When performance levels are systematically and significantly better or worse than the standard level, it is possible that the problem lies with the criteria and not with the performance. The standards may be too easy or unduly harsh. This means the problem lies with the standards, not with performance.

Managers must first be certain that the standards are reasonable and defensible. Then, management action can be directed at performance. The goal of the action is to improve performance and eliminate the gap from the standard level. But how best to do that? To say that action should be directed at performance still begs the question of what actions should really be taken. What should a manager do?

Simply stated, corrective actions need to be directed at the cause(s) of the deficiencies. Corrective actions directed at aspects of the performance system that aren't the cause of the problem will fail to correct anything meaningful. For example, directing action to employees to motivate them to work harder will not remove a deficiency if the cause is poor materials or supplies. Manager's Notes 16.1 presents general categories of factors that may be causes of accidents. While the examples are focused on safety, the categories of person and system causes are generic and can be applied to any type of performance.

The cause(s) of performance deficiencies need to be carefully identified so that corrective action can be effective and lead to improvement. Taking action without first carefully determining the cause of the deficiency can easily lead to workers questioning the quality of management and can erode respect for the manager. Analyzing performance deficiencies with a framework such as the one presented in Manager's Notes 16.1 can help assure that corrective actions are appropriate and effective.

TYPES OF BUREAUCRATIC CONTROL   There are three basic types of control that managers can exercise: feedforward control, concurrent control, and feedback control. These types of bureaucratic control are summarized in Figure 16.3.

Feedforward Control   Feedforward, or preliminary, control is designed to prevent problems before they occur. Preventive maintenance on aircraft is an example of control that is meant to avoid problems. Rules and procedures must be strictly followed in aircraft maintenance to maximize

Possible Causes of Accidents

Maintaining safety and eliminating accidents is an important management issue. Control of accidents requires an understanding of the causes so that corrective actions can be directed at the source of the problem.

Listed below are categories of possible causes of accidents and examples of each. The categories and examples can be a useful starting place for identifying the causes of performance problems.

Person Factors

Unsafe behavior and accidents can occur due to characteristics of the worker. The following are examples.

PERSONAL BELIEFS AND FEELINGS

- Employee didn't believe accident would occur to them.
- Employee liked working fast and showing off or pretending to know it all.
- Employee was distracted because of personal problems.

PHYSICAL AND MENTAL CHARACTERISTICS

- Employee was in poor physical condition.
- Employee was fatigued.
- Employee was mentally unfocused.
- Employee used drugs or alcohol.
- Employee did not remember rule or procedure.

SOCIAL CHARACTERISTICS

- Peer pressure caused employee to work unsafely.
- Horseplay occurred among the employees.

safety and reduce the chances of an accident. Feedforward control is also represented by rules and procedures that are to be followed so that ethical and performance problems are minimized. When an organization estimates market demand for a product and examines whether or not sufficient supplies of materials are available and adequate production capacity exists to meet demand, feedforward control is being used.[3] Management Close-Up 16.a presents an example of a company that restructured the production process to more efficiently meet market demand. Feedforward

System Factors

System issues and accidents also arise because of the work situation. The following are examples of system characteristics that can lead to unsafe practices and accidents.

PHYSICAL WORK ENVIRONMENT

- Tasks are complex or difficult.
- The work environment is stressful (e.g., noisy, hot, dusty, etc.).
- Tasks are repetitive and boring.
- Lighting or ventilation is insufficient.

EQUIPMENT

- Inappropriate or defective equipment provided to employees.
- Confusing displays or controls.
- Poor tool or workstation design resulting in awkward positions or movement.

MANAGEMENT

- Lack of clear policy, rules, or procedures.
- Poor hiring or placement of employees.
- Inadequate inspections.
- Failure to correct hazards.
- Rules not enforced.
- Poor safety communication; safety not adequately promoted.
- Safe behavior not reinforced.

Source: D. Hartshorn, "Solving Accident Investigation Problems: Thorough Accident Investigations Can Be One of the Most Valuable Exercises That Companies Undertake, Yet Too Few Have Policies and Programs in Place to Carry Them Out," *Occupational Hazards* 65 (2003), p. 56+.

control can also be based on models of past work processes. This approach has been used at a sophisticated level to predict and control various characteristics of chemical reactions used in the energy industry.[4] The same principles can be applied to other areas of business. Models can be developed to predict demand for a product or service by taking into account factors such as seasonal and cyclical economic conditions. The resulting prediction is then used to determine the amount of supplies and staffing levels that are needed.

FIGURE 16.3

Types of Control

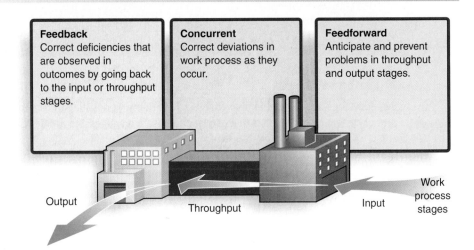

Feedback
Correct deficiencies that are observed in outcomes by going back to the input or throughput stages.

Concurrent
Correct deviations in work process as they occur.

Feedforward
Anticipate and prevent problems in throughput and output stages.

Output

Throughput

Input

Work process stages

The advantage of feedforward control: Preventive maintenance is better than accident analysis!

Concurrent Control Concurrent control takes place as the work process is being carried out. A simple but effective form of concurrent control is supervisory oversight of the work process. A knowledgeable manager observes the work process and quickly corrects problems as they occur. Advances in information technology have dramatically increased the possibilities for concurrent control. For example, remote and

Medtronic: Moving to a Pull-Based System

Medtronic Inc.'s Xomed plant is located outside Jacksonville, Florida. The plant produces medical devices for ear, nose, and throat surgery and for ophthalmology. Between mid-2000 and the end of 2002, the production lead time decreased from 253 days to 129 days and productivity (measured as annual sales per employee) increased 40 percent. How did Medtronic do it?

The Xomed plant was the typical production facility, with production occurring in batches. Customers would receive orders depending on what batches were being run, how many, and in what order. Plant management set a goal to become more flexible and lean so that production would be more responsive to customer requests. A technique called value-stream mapping was used to make the production process more efficient and responsive to market demand.

Value-stream mapping is the process of documenting the process flow from suppliers through to the delivery of final products to customers (in Xomed's case, doctors, hospitals, and surgery centers). In the Xomed system, this included the flow of physical components as well as the flow of information. The mapping helped management identify bottlenecks and waste. It also helped them to change their view of production from batches prepared on separate "islands" to a stream of connected processes.

The improvements that the mapping process made were dramatic, such as a 40 percent reduction in production lead time. Further, weekly production meetings and production plans are now a thing of the past. Now, a doc-

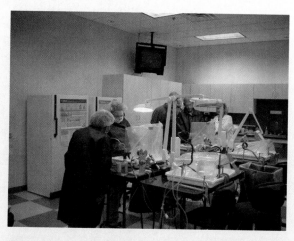

Medtronic's Xomed plant implemented value-stream mapping and has improved its ability to deliver its products on time.

tor's order that pulls a product from the finished goods inventory sends a signal to the production process. Even for intricate surgical tools and devices the plant's on-time delivery rate (based on the date the customer requested) is 96 percent. Management of Xomed now boasts that the production process has become flexible, fluid, and pull-based, being driven by customers rather than capacity.

Source: J. S. McClenahen, "Mapping Manufacturing: Remarkable Results at Medtronic's Medical-Devices Plant Flow from Value-Stream Mapping," *Industry Week* 251 (2002), p. 62+.

real-time access to production and budgetary data allow managers to take concurrent control over processes that were not previously possible. Further, new technologies provide the opportunity for concurrent control to be carried out automatically. Wyandot, Inc., is an example of a company that has embraced technology as an aid to concurrent control of the production process. Wyandot, located in Marion, Ohio, enjoys approximately $100 million in annual sales of its tortilla chips, corn chips, corn snacks, and caramel corn.[5] The company produces 2,000 pounds of corn chips per hour and 5,000 pounds of tortilla chips per hour. The baking and frying processes are central to Wyandot's business.

Wyandot's cooking processes are carefully and automatically controlled with sensors and computers.

Consequently, the management team developed automated concurrent controls over the processes. Sensors are used to constantly measure the temperature at the fryer inlet and outlet. This data results in an automatic adjustment that maintains the optimal temperature. Similar controls are used throughout the production process, based on the 156 miles of wire that run through the facility and connect everything to two computer systems.

Feedback Control Feedback control occurs after a process has been completed. Feedback control uses data from past performance to improve future performance. Timeliness is a serious concern with feedback. The longer feedback is delayed, the less useful it becomes. A long delay makes it more difficult to identify the causes of performance problems. Further, the delay may have allowed poor service to continue or defective or unsafe products to be made and distributed. Delay in feedback is often not helpful to workers. People want feedback. Feedback can be motivational if provided in a timely fashion. Feedback that is not timely is less helpful, because workers are already focused on different tasks or projects. Motivation and performance can be improved with feedback, but only if it is timely. Management Close-Up 16.b presents a real-life example of delayed feedback that proved to be costly to a company. Skills For Managing 16.2 further explores this situation and considers control techniques that could be implemented that would prevent the problem or provide more timely performance measures.

Employee Theft: Feedback from an Annual Inventory Just Doesn't Cut It as a Control System

THEME: ETHICS The location is a large East Coast distribution center that will remain anonymous. The manager of the facility was confident that the annual inventory would come out fine. However, the inventory report revealed a loss of $800,000. The manager told the corporate office that he simply did not believe the report. Another complete inventory was scheduled for 90 days later. That report confirmed the loss and showed that additional losses had occurred since the prior inventory. The manager thought it was impossible to have $1 million dollars of inventory walk out the door without him knowing about it. What was going on? Corporate headquarters instructed the manager to bring in assistance. A team of security experts was retained.

What the security experts found was, in short, employee theft. There were control systems in place, but they had been circumvented or were not effective. The following describes how theft was taking place.

A truck driver signed in at the distribution center and backed his truck up to the appropriate door. There he counted the cases of product to assure that he had the correct amount. The driver was just going through the motions because his accomplice, an employee at the distribution center, had already called him by cell phone and told him 12 extra cases of inventory would be included in the load. The truck driver told the forklift driver that the load was correct

and to put it on the truck. The trucker was waved through a gate by a security guard who wrote down the license plate number of the truck. The guard looked at the load, but didn't know how much product the trucker had when he arrived or how much he should be leaving with. After leaving the facility, the trucker dropped off the $9,000 worth of goods at a rented storage facility. The items had already been negotiated to be sold for 30 percent of their value. A few days later, the trucker returned to the distribution center and shared the proceeds with the shipping employee. The security team brought in by the manager found that this pair of thieves had repeated the scam more than 50 times in 16 months, accruing an inventory loss of $1 million.

The general manager of the facility had always assumed that the company's inventory was well protected. The facility had 24-hour guard service and a state-of-the art perimeter alarm system, and more than two dozen closed-circuit television cameras constantly videotaped the facility. Obviously, these employees had found a way to get around the safeguards. While the inventory feedback came too late to prevent the $1 million loss, at least the problem was finally brought to light. Management was then able to work on control systems that were more effective.

Source: B. Brandman, "How $1.2 Million of Inventory Vanished into Thin Air," *Transportation & Distribution* 42 (2001), p. 31+.

The Balanced Scorecard

The **balanced scorecard**[6] is a technique designed to control and improve performance in the four areas of: (1) customer service, (2) learning and growth, (3) finance, and (4) internal business processes. While bureaucratic control typically focuses on how internal business processes are carried out, the balanced scorecard takes a much broader approach. An important function of the scorecard is to link strategy to action.[7] For instance, strategic direction can be used to derive goals for each of the four areas of the scorecard. While the balanced scorecard takes into account a broad range of factors, it is included here as an example of a formal technique focused on the work process. The reason for this is because the broad and future-oriented approach of the scorecard is meant to influence behaviors and actions on a day-to-day basis. In other words, it

balanced scorecard

A technique designed to control and improve
(1) customer service,
(2) learning and growth,
(3) finance, and
(4) internal business processes

EMPLOYEE THEFT: GOING BEYOND FEEDBACK CONTROL

As described in Management Close-Up 16.b, employee theft was a serious problem at a distribution center. The following is additional information gathered by the security team.

- The alarm system was not fully operational. Several motion detectors were blocked by inventory or had been repositioned to point at the ceiling. Magnetic contacts on two doors were found to be deliberately defeated so that the alarm would not operate.

- Closed-circuit cameras provided broad views of the docks and storage areas, but details of the number of cases being shipped or received couldn't be seen clearly on the videotape. Further, no one monitored the camera system or reviewed the videotape.

- Security guards made routine patrols and were instructed to keep an eye out for anything. However, security guards couldn't detect the kind of collusion that was going on between employees and truckers.

Discussion Questions

1. A number of theft control systems were not working or had been deliberately defeated. Aside from trying to steal from an employer, why else might employees take steps to defeat alarm systems?

2. Given your response to the previous question, how would you recommend this company go about developing more effective theft control procedures? Would a participative approach be useful? Why or why not?

3. Alarm and tracking systems offer concurrent control. How could this company take steps toward preventing the theft problem, not just detecting it and then dealing with it? (Hint: Could background checks on new hires be helpful for prevention? Explain.)

Research Question

Locate security recommendations (a number of companies offer security suggestions on their websites). Can you classify these suggestions as either feedforward, concurrent, or feedback control techniques? Which approach do you think is best for purposes of controlling theft? Why?

is typically the work process, priorities, and how things are done that remain the focus of the balanced scorecard.

Figure 16.4 presents a basic framework that is commonly used for balanced scorecards. Balanced scorecards can, however, take a variety of forms. Some scorecards use different weights to reflect the importance or priority of each of the four domains of finance, customers, business process, and learning and growth. Scorecards generally share the focus on these four areas as well as specify goals, targets, or standards in each area. The balanced scorecard directs activities in various strategic directions and then provides a means of control by assessing performance attained

FIGURE 16.4

A General Balanced Scorecard
Format

	Objectives	Measures	Targets	Initiatives
Financial What we need to do to succeed financially				
Customer What we need to do to excel at customer service				
Internal Business Processes What we need to do to have world class processes				
Learning and Growth What we need to do to change and increase our potential and effectiveness				

in each of the four areas against the stated standards or goals. Figure 16.5 presents an example of a portion of a balanced scorecard from Southwest Airlines. As shown in the Southwest Airlines scorecard, the approach can be applied to an entire organization. Balanced scorecards can also be at the level of units, teams, and individuals.

The balanced scorecard has become a widely used management tool. Many organizations have implemented some version of the approach. As originally conceived, it should be possible to implement the balanced scorecard in 16 weeks. However, a number of managers have found that time frame to be difficult.[8] Manager's Notes 16.2 presents suggestions for quickly and effectively implementing a balanced scorecard approach.

Bureaucratic control typically focuses directly on the work process and directly regulates how the process is carried out. The balanced scorecard takes a broad look at the directions and priorities of the organization. However, the thrust of the technique is to regulate actions taken in the workplace. The initiatives in the balanced scorecard identify the process, or how the objectives will be achieved. The process embodied in these initiatives may not be part of the balanced scorecard, but these guidelines and standards are likely in the bureaucratic controls that are in place for those initiatives. There are formal approaches to control that focus on

FIGURE 16.5

Southwest Airlines Scorecard

Source: Adapted from G. H. Anthes, "Balanced Scorecard," *Computerworld* 37 (2003), p. 34+.

Area	Objectives	Measures	Targets	Initiatives
Customer	On-time flights Lowest prices	FAA on-time annual meeting	No. 1	Quality management
		Customer ranking (survey)	No. 1	Customer loyalty program
Internal	Fast ground turnaround	Time on ground	30 minutes	Cycle-time optimization program
		On-time departures	90%	
Learning	Ground-crew alignment with company goals	% ground-crew shareholders	Year 1: 70% Year 3: 90%	Employee stock option plan
		% ground-crew trained	Year 5: 100%	Ground-crew training

outcomes, not the process that might be used to achieve those outcomes. The following section reviews outcomes-focused control, the techniques in cell 2 of Figure 16.1.

Formal and Outcome-Focused Control

Formal and outcome-focused control techniques regulate performance by applying standards or guidelines to the outcomes of a process. The details of how a work process should be carried out are not the concern of this approach to control. Rather, outcomes are regulated and processes must then be adapted to achieve or comply with the requirements. Here are some of the more well-known approaches to formal outcome-focused control.

Market Control

Market control is the use of indicators of market values as standards for regulating performance. For example, an organization may use profits as the means for evaluating the performance of a business unit. Poor profit levels may result in corrective actions, from various improvement efforts to closing or selling the unit. Market control does not necessarily rely on financial measures of value in a market. For example, the dean of a business school at a university uses market control when assessing the performance of the doctoral programs of the various departments. Specifically, allocation of budget dollars is driven, in part, by how many doc-

Implementation Suggestions for the Balanced Scorecard: Get It Done!

Get Top Management Commitment

If the balanced scorecard is to be successfully driven through the organization in a timely fashion, there must be top management support. Start with a half-day workshop on the balanced scorecard for top management and anyone who would need to lead the implementation initiative. If top management isn't sold on the concept, implementation is bound to flounder.

Focus on the Priorities

Identify the key priorities and measures in the organization. It may be effective to have two levels of balanced scorecards: (1) a governance level that includes 5 or 6 high-level measures and (2) a management level that includes up to 20 priority areas and measures.

Select a Small Team

Pick 2–4 committed and fearless leaders who won't procrastinate and can implement the scorecard approach.

Don't Get Too Flashy

A number of organizations are offering specialized software for the development of balanced scorecards. However, most data needed to set up an initial scorecard framework should already be readily available in-house. Investment in expensive consulting and software shouldn't be needed!

Balanced Scorecards Are an Art, Not a Science

There is no one best way. Things can always be changed or improved later on. Don't let perfectionism derail implementation of a value-added system.

Source: D. Parmenter, "Balanced Scorecard," *Accountancy Ireland* 35 (2003), pp. 14–17.

toral students the department places and the quality of the jobs they take. Those departments whose doctoral students get jobs at the best places are rewarded with larger budgets.

Financial Controls

Financial controls use various monetary measures to regulate performance. While market controls rely on external measures of the value of products or services, financial controls focus on internal monetary values, largely regarding revenues and expenses in the organization. A business unit could, for example, be doing very well in terms of the market value of its products or services, but may not be in good financial health internally. This outcome can occur due to mismanagement of funds, poor investments, and other problems. A thorough consideration of the various financial control techniques is beyond the scope of this chapter. However, some of the basic financial control approaches will be considered, beginning with the most common financial control approach—the budget.

BUDGETARY CONTROL   Budgets are used to specify amounts to be expended for various activities or events. Budgets are frequently stated in monetary terms, but they can take other forms. A production budget might specify the number of units to be produced and a labor budget might specify the number of hours of labor that will be available along with dollar amounts. Normally, however, budgets are stated in monetary terms. Whatever the unit of measurement, budgets provide quantitative measures. These measures provide the yardstick by which performance can be judged. Further, budgeting allows management to control and allocate its resources. Without budgetary control, the best of business ventures can easily run into financial trouble and even bankruptcy.

Budgeting helps managers control and predict costs. Recently, there has been a growing amount of criticism directed at the practice of budgetary control. These critics suggest that budgets amount to "managing by the numbers" and do not allow the flexibility needed to pursue other potentially valuable options. For example, a business opportunity may arise that is promising and fits with the strategic direction of an organization. However, if the budget is fixed, there may be no resources available to pursue the opportunity. The fixed and limiting nature of budgets can simultaneously be both an advantage and a disadvantage.

FINANCIAL STATEMENTS   In addition to budgets, financial statements are also tools that are used to assess and control the financial health of an organization. Two of the most commonly used are balance sheets and profit and loss statements.

Balance Sheets   The balance sheet provides a financial picture of an organization by listing assets and liabilities at a particular point in time. The balance sheet is a "snapshot" of how an organization is doing in financial terms.

Profit and Loss Statements   A profit and loss statement provides a listing of income and expenses over time. A profit and loss statement may cover a period of years and offers a picture of trends in the organization.

Balance sheets and profit and loss statements can be used to identify problem areas and take corrective actions, if needed. The overall performance of an organization or business unit can be summarized and evaluated using data from financial statements. The data can be combined to create key financial ratios that reflect various aspects of bottom-line, financial performance.

FINANCIAL RATIOS   Financial ratios provide a quick overall check of company performance. Many types of financial ratios are available. For example, *liquidity ratios* reflect an organization's ability to pay short-term debt. *Leverage ratios* reflect the amount of funds available in an organization from shareholders and creditors. *Profitability ratios* indicate the amount of financial return from an investment, with return on investment (ROI) as probably the most widely recognized example of a profitability ratio. There are standards, or at least rules of thumb, regarding acceptable ranges for the financial ratios. The values of the financial ratios relative to the standard levels or the change in the ratios over time can help management to assess and control the business. Financial information, such as profit levels and return on investment, is commonly after-the-fact information that is averaged over the work process. However, Management Close-Up 16.c describes how some innovative organizations are pushing financial outcome control into the work process.

ACTIVITY-BASED COSTING   Activity-based costing is another financial control technique. Traditional accounting approaches separate costs into discrete functional categories, such as purchasing, human resources, and maintenance. Activity-based costing, in contrast, associates costs associated with tasks that are performed. As an example, consider the costs that might be associated with producing a particular product. Costs are traditionally divided into categories such as labor salary, labor fringe benefit, supplies, and fixed costs. However, costs could also be calculated for tasks such as receiving and processing sales orders, expediting supplies, expediting production, distribution of finished products, and resolving errors and problems. The latter way of breaking out costs is much more useful for management. It is difficult to control or lower fixed costs. It is much easier to try to manage costs associated with the various tasks that are part of the production process. That is the reason for organizations to be attracted to the use of activity-based costing.

Formal control measures regulate performance by applying standards to outcomes. In other words, this approach to control is the application of external standards to which people in the organization need to comply. In the case of outcome-focused control techniques, the standards have to do with financial or market-based measures. With process-focused control approaches, the standards have to do with how work is carried out. In either case, formal control mechanisms rely on imposing

Profit Velocity: Financial Control Meets the Work Process

THEME: CHANGE Profit is a straightforward measure, as represented by the function:

$$Profit = Revenues - Expenses$$

In many organizations, profits are often taken at face value. If profits are up, everything is good. If profits are down, it's time to cut costs. That's about as sophisticated as it gets in many organizations. However, competitive pressures are pushing organizations to find new ways to maximize financial outcomes. New technologies now provide the means for financial data to be introduced into the work process itself. One emerging approach is called "profit velocity."

To understand the concept of profit velocity, consider the example of Ondeo Nalco, an Illinois-based maker of water treatment chemicals. The company is using software to track the velocity with which product flows through key production and supply-chain bottlenecks. Factors such as product price, rate of production, the amount of scrap, and others are all considered. The sales force can then take the information and push sales of products that maximize profits. Profit isn't necessarily maximized by selling the highest-priced or most complex products. It may be that those products have the highest error rates and greatest amounts of waste. In essence, the profit velocity approach shows the sales force that they could be maximizing revenues but are getting nowhere on profits if they are pushing the wrong products.

In addition to marketing implications, Ondeo Nalco has applied the profit velocity concept into the work process itself. The approach highlights the areas that must be closely managed or improved if profits are to be maximized. Further, the company has gotten to the point where a line operator knows that turning a screw on a variable feed pump to the right would mean making $780 per hour while turning it to the left would mean profit would go down to $650 per hour. The approach makes profit a highly visible and real concept on the plant floor. It gives workers a direct sense of impact and ownership in the organization.

U.S. Steel is another company that uses software and the profit velocity concept to guide production and sales. The profit velocity measure has given everyone in the organization a common metric to work with. Normally, production people often want to produce quantity while the sales force wants to maximize revenues. Instead, profit velocity provides the information both sides need to maximize profits. The focus for production becomes making products that maximize profits, not just making more product. For sales, the focus becomes selling products that maximize profits, not just revenues.

Source: D. Drickhammer, "Goosing the Bottom Line," *Industry Week* 251 (2002), pp. 24–28.

external standards and putting in place the possibility of corrective actions to assure compliance with those standards. However, there may be situations in which internalizing standards would result in better performance control. These are found in another approach to control.

Informal and Process-Focused Control

Informal and process-focused control emphasizes an implicit sense and common understanding of how things should be done. This control approach does not rely on explicit guidelines and standards. Instead, it assumes that people have an internal set of standards that will appropriately guide how they do their jobs. This approach has been termed clan control. (See again Figure 16.1, cell 3.)

Clan Control

Reliance on corporate culture and the norms it develops as an informal means for regulating the work process is **clan control.** In essence, with clan control, employees control themselves. A strong culture can influence performance levels and how work is carried out. Chapter 4 was devoted to a consideration of culture and how to develop or change the culture of an organization. It is recommended that you revisit that chapter for details concerning culture and how it can control behaviors in organizations.

> **clan control**
> Culture-based control.

Culture-based control offers an advantage of not overspecifying how a work process should be performed. The reason for this being an advantage, at least in many of today's organization settings, is the degree to which work environments are dynamic and driven by customer service. Change in many work environments has become the norm. Given this dynamic nature, explicit guidelines and standards might be obsolete by the time they are put in place. Likewise, a customer-driven strategy means that the work process can't be overly structured. Discovering customer needs and finding ways to best satisfy customers are difficult, and change from one customer to the next. Given today's dynamic and customer-focused work environments, an internalized means of control is more effective. Culture may not specify operational details, but it can provide a clear set of values that guide workers, even when explicit rules or standards are not available.

What Is Management Control (Revisited)?

This chapter began with a description of control as principally involving measurement and regulation. While the *process* of control is clear in this description, what should be the *content* of its focus? In other words, control should involve the measurement and regulation of *what?* Specifically, should control efforts be directed at people, systems, or some other aspect of the company?

People versus Systems

Control mechanisms are, fundamentally, directed at performance. However, the question remains as to what is the best way to improve and control performance, with measures and corrective actions focused on people or systems? This question is simple to state but it is an issue fundamental to management philosophy. The traditional Western management approach has been to assume that workers are the critical factor in determining performance. Thus, motivational programs and close supervision are viewed as the best ways to control and improve performance. In contrast, the quality perspective has emphasized the importance of the system as a determinant of performance. Thus, quality advocates emphasize control over systems as key to performance improvement. This issue is not easily resolved. It is safe to say that in most situations, both person and system factors make a difference when it comes to performance. But where should control efforts be directed?

There are differing opinions on this issue,[9] but we recommend that control efforts be focused on systems and on performance, rather than on people. Focusing on people can result in resistance and negative reactions, problems commonly associated with control efforts. For example, workers may not like the increased monitoring or reporting required by the control system. They may resist and find fault with the system if they don't see it as improving, or somehow necessary to, performance. If they feel that the control system is overly intrusive (for example, involves unneeded videotaping of back office operations), they may do their best to undermine the control system.

Control is a necessary management function. It is important to focus on both performance and the system. Focusing external control on people conveys the message that management distrusts them. Focusing control efforts on performance and system characteristics and involving and empowering workers can convey that management views workers as partners in the effort to maximize performance. How the control system is developed and implemented is also critical. Referring back to the chapter's introductory Numico example, remember that a participative approach in the design of a control system brought people on board and reduced their resistance to the control system.

Applications for the Manager   Control over the actions and outcomes in the workplace is a central management responsibility. Effective control mechanisms can not only improve performance, but, also make the role of management much less stressful. Knowing how the organization is performing, including whether or not quality, quantity, or financial aspects are in line with expectations, provides a solid basis for managing the process. Measurement is a key component of effective control. However, control involves more than simply measurement. Managers go beyond measurement to take corrective action, which is part and parcel of an effective control system. As a manager, you will need to understand the control systems used in an organization as well as whether your own philosophy regarding control fits with the organization's approach.

Applications for Managing Teams   Many teams of workers now find themselves empowered and with responsibility for control over work processes. Knowledge of control systems is important for team members. It is important to carefully choose the type of control system, formal or informal, and whether it is focused on process or outcomes. As a practical matter, there are often multiple control systems in operation, and teams are no exception. Teams of workers often employ formal and process-focused control in regard to performance of the production process. However, team roles and contributions to team efforts are often controlled with the culture and norms that develop and characterize the team. Understanding how these control mechanisms can work is to the benefit of all of the team members.

Applications for Individuals   As individuals, we are often subject to a variety of control mechanisms. For example, security checks in an organization, completing various types of paperwork, quality and quantity checks, and providing interim reports are all examples of various control efforts that employees encounter. It is easy to view these control efforts as intrusive and useless exercises. However, understanding of control mechanisms can clarify why they are needed and how they contribute to the effectiveness of the organization. Further, many of the control techniques discussed in this chapter can be applied to your own work. For example, there is no reason why the balanced scorecard, or other techniques, couldn't be used to manage your own work efforts and career.

CONCLUDING THOUGHTS

The introductory section of this chapter posed some critical thinking issues regarding management control. Now that you have seen these approaches to control, revisit those introductory questions. First, organizations often put control systems in place because of a problem with quality or safety. However, effective managers know that control is not an option to be employed only if it is needed. Control is central to effective management. If managers clearly understand the role of control, it won't take a wake-up call to motivate them to put control systems in place.

Second, the location of control authority is an important consideration. In the Numico example, a separate facility is ultimately responsible for control. There are two characteristics to recognize in regard to this example. One, individual facilities still had their own control systems. It is not as if a separate and distant location was the sole source of control. Two, food safety is a critical concern for consumers and a separate facility for assuring quality conveys independence in the quality control process. In sum, internal control systems should be in place. However, an external oversight and control system can be useful, particularly when it is important to convey that control is impartial and independent of production or sales pressures.

Finally, the extent of monitoring that is needed must be decided on a case-by-case basis. In general, however, if there is continuous monitoring of inputs (for example, quality of raw materials) and outputs (quality of finished products), there is probably little need for continuous monitoring of the work process. The reason for this is twofold. First, the work process is not independent of the inputs and outputs. That is, if the quality of raw materials and of finished products is acceptable, these characteristics would imply that the work process is acceptable. Second, constant monitoring and assessment by an external agent could easily be viewed by workers as intrusive or a sign of management distrust.

Management control is the process of comparing performance to standards and taking corrective actions that might be needed to remove deficiencies. Control complements planning, because it is the means by which management can assess whether plans are being carried out effectively.

Control techniques can be categorized according to their type (formal or informal) and their focus (process or outcome). **Subjective control** results when an informal approach is taken to controlling outcomes. Subjective control usually employs global measures and reactive management actions. Although common, it is not an effective control technique.

Formal and process-focused control techniques include operations management, bureaucratic control, and the balanced scorecard. **Bureaucratic control** consists of a cycle of control steps which includes: (1) establishing standards, (2) measuring performance, (3) identifying gaps, and (4) taking corrective actions. How standards are developed can have an important influence on their acceptance. A participative approach can be helpful for gaining acceptance of standards. Performance measures can include both subjective and objective data. When identifying gaps, it is important to focus on only those deficiencies that are meaningful. Finally, corrective actions can only be effective when they address the causes of performance problems. Bureaucratic control can involve feedforward, concurrent, or feedback control.

The **balanced scorecard** approach brings into consideration four perspectives in the control of performance: (1) customer service, (2) learning and growth, (3) finance, and (4) internal business processes. Initiatives, targets, and measures are identified for each of these four areas.

Formal and outcome-focused control techniques include *market control* and *financial controls*. Market control is based on the value placed on a product or service by the market. Financial controls include budgeting control, financial statements, financial ratios, and activity-based costing.

Finally, **clan control** is an informal and process-focused control technique. Clan control is based on the culture and social norms that emerge in a workplace. This form of control is internalized, rather than being externally imposed.

Control is a necessary management function. How a control system is developed and implemented determines how effective it is. Taking a participative approach to development and focusing on performance and system characteristics can improve employee acceptance of the system and reduce resistance and negative reactions.

1. What are the four categories of control techniques? Which of the four categories do you think is the best approach? Why?

2. Differentiate among feedforward, concurrent, and feedback control. Can you provide an example of each?

3. Standards are critical to control efforts. How do you think they should be developed?

4. Identifying gaps between performance and standard levels is an important step in the bureaucratic control process. Describe situations in which it is not beneficial to take corrective action in response to every gap.

5. Describe the balanced scorecard approach. It does not offer tight operational guidelines or standards, so what advantage(s) does it offer? Would you recommend using it? Why or why not?

6. Differentiate between market and financial controls. In what type of organizational situations do you think each approach would be best to use? Describe.

7. What is clan control? Under what organizational circumstances do you think it would be an effective control technique?

8. Do you think control efforts should be directed at people or at systems? Why?

Standards for Quality Control: Don't Forget the Customer!

Control systems are often developed from an internal and functional perspective. For example, production may develop standards regarding product features and quality based on common practice and guidelines in the industry. However, these standards and features may be irrelevant to customers. The same disconnect can occur in the services sector. For example, the police department of a large metropolitan area had a self-imposed standard of responding to a burglary call within 5 minutes. However, they treated cases of missing children as a standard missing person case and took no action for 24 hours. Focus groups with citizens quickly revealed that the standards did not translate into effective performance from the public's perspective. Citizens really didn't care about timeliness in response to a burglary since it had already occurred. A police response within the day would be nice, but a dramatic and quick response just wasn't needed or useful. On the other hand, citizens wanted an immediate and serious response to a missing child case. As a result of listening to constituents, the police department dropped its 5 minute standard for burglaries. In addition, it will now call out police officers on bikes, cars, and even helicopters in response to cases of missing children.

A number of organizations check on their service levels by collecting customer feedback. Of course, it is best to integrate the customer perspective into the development of standards right from the start. For example, the development of quality standards for Motel 6 and Red Roof Inn included customer focus groups across the country.

Discussion Questions

1. Does including the customer perspective reduce the control of management over work processes or outcomes? Explain.

2. Do you think customer feedback is a sufficient way to involve the voice of the customer in setting standards?

3. Other than focus groups, can you think of other ways to include customers in the development of standards?

4. Are there other ways in which customers could effectively be included in a control system? For example, would it be worthwhile to include customers in the performance measurement step? What about in other steps?

Sources: R. L. Cardy, *Performance Management: Concepts, Skills, and Exercises,* Armonk, NY: M. E. Sharpe, 2004; R. A. Nozar, "Guest's Input Helps Develop Standards," *Hotel and Motel Management* 216 (2001), p. 36+.

Outcomes or Process?

A focus on measuring and managing the process is a common approach to control. As discussed in this chapter, process-focused control typically involves strict guidelines and detailed procedures to follow. Some organizations, however, are discovering that focusing on outcomes can offer advantages over a process focus. For example, Drew, a water treatment company, shifted to an outcome-based control system to regulate chemical levels. Specifically, the common approach to regulating chemicals in water treatment focuses on measuring the flow of chemicals themselves. Drew moved to a system in which chemical levels are regulated by monitoring their effects. Such a system reduces the use of corrosion control chemicals by monitoring the occurrence of the corrosion effect. The result can be less chemical usage and a less negative environmental impact.

Water can't talk back or resist control efforts, but people can! Some hotels are finding that focusing on outcomes rather than process can be an effective approach to controlling energy usage. A process approach to energy usage might involve providing requests and guidelines to hotel guests regarding heat, cooling, and lighting levels. Some guests may not appreciate such requests and resist complying. Instead, it is possible to use an outcome-based approach to managing energy usage in a hotel or similar building, such as the control approach employed by WebGen Systems. WebGen is an energy management company that offers an Internet-based energy management system. The system tracks energy usage over time, considers weather, energy price, and current levels of energy consumption. Based on this information, specific adjustments are automatically made to the hotel's energy management system. For example, the system might adjust the temperature of water in a chiller or slightly raise the temperature level in a ballroom.

Discussion Questions

1. When do you think process control is the preferred control approach? Explain.

2. Is outcome-based control the best approach in a service setting? Why or why not?

3. What disadvantages might there be to outcome-based control? Do you think they outweigh the potential advantages?

Sources: B. Schmitt, "Water Treatment: Pouring on the Service," *Chemical Week* 164 (2001), p. 20+; "Mission: Maintain Satisfaction: Smart Implementation plus the Right System Add Up to Happy Guests," *Hotel & Motel Management* 218 (2003), p. M7+.

Profit vs. Equity: Beyond Short-Term Financial Performance

Making profits is a critical focus of business. Without sufficient profits, the business will fail. Maximizing profits is the goal of most business efforts. It is no surprise, then, that management commonly focuses attention and control efforts on profit levels. Take, for instance, a grocery store that is focused on profits and utilizes control mechanisms to maximize them. Part of a profit control system could involve measuring financial aspects of various areas of the business. Measurements could be broken down to the level of profitability per item. Consequently, a grocery store manager might decide to eliminate less profitable items, resulting in relatively immediate improvement in the profitability of the store.

As a contrasting approach, consider the same grocery store from the customer's perspective. Why does a customer continue to do business with a particular grocery store? There is a three-part answer that can be summed up with one concept: customer equity. Customer equity is the overall and long-term return that a customer receives from doing business with an organization. There are three components to customer equity: value equity, brand equity, and retention equity. Value equity has to do with the objective benefits and costs involved in dealing with the organization. For example, how convenient is the store's location and what are the prices and quality levels at the store? Brand equity is the more intangible and emotional aspects of the store. For example, does the store offer a sense of community or identification for the customer? Finally, retention equity is the benefits a customer receives from continuing to

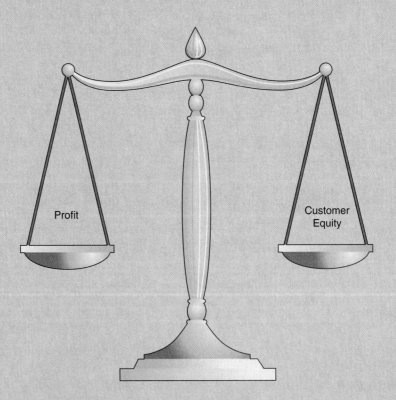

Profit or Customer Equity: Choice or Balance?

do business with an organization. So, why would a customer continue to do business with a grocery store? The answer would be because of positive levels of value, brand, and retention equities. Taking less profitable products off the shelves reduces convenience and may cause the customer to look elsewhere for the three forms of equity.

Critical Thinking Questions

1. Take the profit control approach. What other steps would you recommend in addition to retaining or deleting items based on profit levels?

2. Based on the customer equity approach, identify measures for each type of equity. How would you collect the data?

3. What actions could you take as a manager to maximize the levels of each of the three components of customer equity?

Collaborative Learning Exercises

1. Divide into opposing teams taking either the profit or customer equity approach as the focus for management control efforts. Profits are needed, but profits can't be made without customers. Is there a clear winner or other resolution to the debate?

2. Is there a way to combine or balance the profit and customer equity perspectives or are they opposed management control choices? With your team members, develop a control system that combines or balances the two perspectives. Share your system and ideas with the rest of the class.

Source: R. T. Rust, V. A. Zeithaml, and K. N. Lemon, *Driving Customer Equity.* New York: Free Press, 2000.

Balanced Scorecard: State of the Art

The balanced scorecard has quickly become a popular management control technique. It is being used in a variety of settings, from manufacturing to services, and from nonprofit to profit organizations. Research the status of the balanced scorecard on the Internet. You will find numerous sites devoted to the topic.

1. Does the balanced scorecard appear to be maintaining its popularity?

2. As originally conceived, scorecards included four factors. Are additional factors being used? If so, what are they? Do you think they are useful?

3. What do you think accounts for the popularity of the balanced scorecard approach?

4. Can you find examples of balanced scorecards used by companies? If so, share them with the rest of the class.

INTERNET EXERCISE 16.1

SEVENTEEN

Operations Management

chapter 17

After reading this chapter, you should be able to:

- Define operations management and its three stages: inputs, transformation, and disposition.

- Describe how operations management ensures supplies of inputs and an efficient production system.

- Use the tools of operations management, including Gantt charts, PERT networks, and statistical process tools.

- Explain the role quality management plays in the operations management process.

- Understand and apply the principles of quality management, kaizen, just-in-time manufacturing, and kanban to the production process.

Kaizening in Iowa

In the early 1990s Pella Corporation, a family-owned maker of windows and doors with all operations in Iowa, needed help. Sales were flat, but even more worrisome was the company's declining market share. Pella was losing ground in retail home centers and to Andersen, which was closing in on Pella's reputation as the quality line of windows.

In 1993 Pella decided to implement *kaizen,* the process of continuous improvement developed in Japan. Those first kaizen sessions have been followed by 1,000 more, held throughout the company. By following the basic philosophy—use what the company has, get everybody involved, and make some change for the better without worrying about a perfect overall solution—everything changed. Relationships with suppliers and dealers improved, the breadth of the company's product line grew, and innovations in manufacturing methods, even building its first plant outside Iowa, created dramatic new levels of efficiency and effectiveness. Annual sales are estimated to have at least tripled since 1991.

Pella's kaizen implementation involved forming teams, either made up of members of one department or production cell or including people from various parts of the company. The team's five-day schedule begins with everybody thinking about the problem and how to attack it on Monday; coming up with some tentative solutions Tuesday and getting the equipment or procedure in place that night; starting and tweaking the new arrangement on Wednesday; proving it on Thursday; and on Friday, presenting what's actually been done. At that point "you sit there and say, whew," said Mel Haught, one of the executives who initiated the process.

Pella made major changes in its supply chain of dealer-distributors that sell most of its products. Previously, the company had supplied basic windows to the dealers, who typically modified them extensively. The resulting price markup made the already expensive window less competitive. Dealers also had to carry a great deal of inventory because Pella frequently missed delivery dates. Now the company takes less than half the time to deliver windows. Pella builds them to order on the production line, including all modifications, and almost 100 percent of orders are shipped on time. Dealers

have reduced their markups since they now need smaller inventories, fewer people, and less storage space.

From its basic product, Pella now offers several lines divided by market segment. One line is sold to the big home centers which were formerly competitors. The company's independent dealers and company stores handle the rest. Pella continues to treat employees well, providing generous bonus and profit-sharing plans and avoiding layoffs.

Pella sees no end to the kaizen process. The management team believes there will always be new people, new products, and new vendors to educate, and something can always be improved. Says Gary Christensen, Pella's president and CEO: "Every year, the product has got to be better."

Source: P. Siekman, "Glass Act: How a Window-Maker Rebuilt Itself," *Fortune,* November 13, 2000, p. 384.

CRITICAL THINKING QUESTIONS

1. *Do you think the kaizen process employed by Pella could work without employees being empowered? Explain.*

2. *A common phrase is "If it ain't broke, don't fix it." However, quality approaches, and kaizen in particular, suggest that "the process can always be improved." In your opinion, which approach to managing the operations in an organization is better? Why?*

3. *Is there a downside to continuously making adjustments to improve a process?*

4. *What workforce skills are needed to make a quality improvement program, such as Pella's, work effectively?*

The heart and soul of many business operations is the production process. As witnessed in the Pella company example, a new technique, such as kaizen, can greatly improve a firm's ability to deliver high quality products at a lower cost in a shorter amount of time. This chapter describes operations management methods for controlling production inputs and production processes. Many of the skills which are needed have been described in previous chapters. Manager's Notes 17.1 summarizes these skills.

What Is Operations Management?

Many organizations, both for-profit and not-for-profit, provide a product—whether a good, a service, or both. General Motors provides automobiles to its dealers, libraries provide books, and online databases provide information. **Operations management** is the process an organization uses to obtain the materials or ideas, the process of transforming them into the product, and the process of providing the final product to a user. Operations management principles can be applied to a variety of departments within an organization. Typically, however, operations management refers to the firm's main product.

Operations management is closely tied to strategic management (Chapter 7), to planning (Chapter 5), and to information systems management (Chapter 18). Information systems today are also closely linked to the firm's operations, as will be noted in Chapter 18.

operations management

The process an organization uses to obtain the materials or ideas, the process of transforming them into the product, and the process of providing the final product to a user.

Three Stages of Operations

Operations management consists of three stages, as shown in Figure 17.1:

1. Acquiring inputs (the materials or ideas).
2. Controlling the conversion processes (transforming the materials or ideas into the organization's products).
3. Delivering the output (providing the organization's product to the user).

Although these stages are listed separately, they are highly interrelated. The inputs a firm acquires are influenced by the production process that is available as well as by refinements based on the customers'

FIGURE 17.1

The Operations Management Process

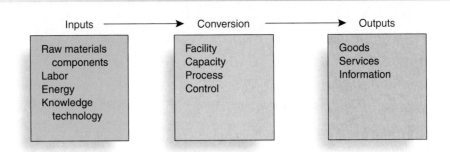

feedback. The production process is influenced by the type of inputs, such as skilled labor, that are available. Finally, the disposition of the product is influenced by the cost of production: What market can it be priced to? And how will the good or service be distributed and delivered to customers?

Planning

planning

The management function that assesses the management environment to set future objectives and map out activities necessary to achieve those objectives.

The foundation of operations management is **planning.** Planning typically begins with identifying the organization's customers and their needs. Market research helps company leaders target specific groups for its product. By determining the need for a product, managers can plan for the level of resources needed, the time involved, and the objectives that the operations management process must achieve. Managing the planning process was described in detail in Chapter 5.

Strategic Planning

Several types of strategic management decisions are part of operations management. After determining the need for the product and the market the firm wishes to target, organizational leaders must first determine if they want to make or buy their product. As discussed in Chapter 9, outsourcing allows a firm to concentrate on marketing and new product development.

make–buy analysis

An operations management tool used to help make the decision as to whether to produce an item or to purchase it.

A **make–buy analysis** is a tool operations managers use to help make this decision. The process begins with an assessment of whether the firm will lose or gain a competitive advantage by outsourcing the product or some aspects of the production process. Sara Lee found that outsourcing its manufacturing improved its competitive advantage. If outsourcing will hurt a firm's competitive advantage, the firm will continue making the product internally regardless of cost savings that may be obtained from outsourcing. Other factors in a make–buy analysis are the suitability of the product for outsourcing, the reasons for outsourcing, and the cost. The cost of buying the product may be less than the cost to the firm of equipment purchase and maintenance, labor and other inputs, inventory costs, administrative overhead, and so on.

part six Operations and Information Systems Management

Too Little of a Good Thing

THEME: CUSTOMER FOCUS
Immunex Corporation has a winner in its drug Enbrel, used to treat rheumatoid arthritis. The drug beat its optimistic 2000 sales projection by almost a third, and it has become the fastest growing biological drug in history. Unfortunately, Enbrel became the largest supply shortage story in the history of prescription drugs.

Patients inject it to counteract the pain, swelling, and joint damage caused by the disease. The manufacturing process is complicated and time-consuming, however, using massive 10,000-liter tanks in sterile manufacturing plants. In spite of these quantities, the demand for Enbrel is so great that Immunex can't make enough of it. After a year on the market, it was obvious that demand would sooner or later outstrip supply. In March 2002, Immunex sent letters to doctors and to patients who were currently taking Enbrel that a shortage of two to three weeks might occur. Enbrel is a maintenance drug, not a cure. Thus, within about a month without the drug, arthritis symptoms typically return. in May 2002, the company again sent out letters informing doctors that the shortage might last longer than anticipated. In the meantime, there were approximately 20,000 people who were placed on a waiting list to receive the drug.

Enbrel's unexpected success created an overwhelming supply shortage in the drug industry. The drug was being rationed as patients across the United States were demanding it. When it wasn't available, doctors prescribed an alternative drug that required a doctor to administer it and a rigid medical regimen.

Enbrel's supply shortage left Immunex vulnerable to potential competitors. The company constructed a new plant in Greenwich, Rhode Island, that doubled its capacity for manufacturing Enbrel, and another plant is planned in Ireland to meet European demand. In a surprise letter to physicians in December 2002, Immunex announced that all patients on the waiting list would have access to Enbrel. Perhaps capacity had finally caught up with demand. However, lost sales and the loyalty of doctors and patients may never be regained.

Sources: D. Shook, "Immunex' Supply-Side Cliffhanger," *Business Week,* February 8, 2001; "Delays for Enbrel Continue," www.psoriasis.org/news/news/2002/20020524_enbrel.php, accessed May 20, 2003; "Alert! Enbrel Supply Shortage," http://arthritiscentral.com/enbrel/, accessed May 20, 2003.

Once a decision has been made to make the product, the operations manager must consider capacity, facilities, process, and layout. **Capacity** is the firm's ability to produce the product during a given period. Creating capacity that exceeds the amount of products that can be sold is inefficient because unused capacity wastes the firm's resources. Not having enough capacity to meet demand also works against the firm, as described in Management Close-Up 17.a.

Operations management decisions also involve **facilities,** the design and location of an operation. Location decisions are based on factors such as the availability and cost of labor and energy as well as how close to suppliers or customers the facility needs to be.

Process decisions are also made regarding how a product or service will be produced. Operations managers evaluate the available production methods to see how efficiently they can achieve the operating objectives. Closely tied to process decisions are those regarding **facilities layout design:** What is the best physical arrangement for the facility that will allow for efficient production?

capacity

The firm's ability to produce the product during a given period.

facilities

The design and location of an operation.

process

How a product or service will be produced.

facilities layout design

The physical arrangement for the facility that will allow for efficient production.

Availability of labor and potential customers are important considerations in the facilities location for retail firms. By locating in areas with ample labor and a large customer population base, firms such as Best Buy keep labor costs down and sales volume high.

Once the strategic planning decisions have been made to lay the framework for producing the firm's goods or services, more focused planning must be completed for each stage of the operation.

Acquiring Inputs

inputs

The supplies needed to create a product, which can include materials, energy, information, management, technology, facilities, and labor.

An organization requires a sufficient supply of inputs to create various products. **Inputs** include materials, energy, information, management, technology, facilities, and labor. Individual organizations have different types of inputs. Sarnamotive Blue Water, Inc., supplies plastic products and components to the automotive industry. Sarnamotive's inputs include chemicals, natural resources, and technology. Inputs for General Motors include materials in the form of the finished products from its suppliers as well as energy, information, and so on. Dealers that sell General Motors cars have the finished automobiles as their most important input.

Managers oversee not only the selection of inputs and suppliers, but also the availability of the needed quantity of inputs, the quality of the inputs, the ability of suppliers to meet delivery dates, and the reliability of the suppliers. Obtaining supplies from foreign sources sometimes offers great dollar savings. Manager's Notes 17.2 suggests that there also can be substantial risk and difficulty in finding out if the supplies you are getting are really what you think they are. To manage inputs, operations managers continually monitor both performance and costs.

Getting What You Pay For?

Continued economic pressure has pushed manufacturers to search for ways to reduce operational costs. One way is to find a lower-cost supplier of materials. While many organizations looked to Mexico for lower-cost parts, China has the lowest labor costs in the world. It is expected that the number of components made in China for export will dramatically increase in the next five years. Unfortunately, organizational leaders eager to take advantage of the cost savings are finding that the materials they receive may not be what they think they are. Specifically, some may be generic knockoffs of parts that are made using lower quality standards. In short, these are counterfeit parts that may not work well.

In the electronics industry, parts that look like those made by reputable manufacturers can be made poorly by a Chinese manufacturer and then identified with the reputable manufacturer's label. These counterfeit parts are then sold to brokerage houses and distributed. Recently, an electronics customer in Florida ordered 400,000 capacitors only to discover that they were counterfeits made in China labeled with a reputable manufacturer's name. The Chinese government is finally taking increasing responsibility for limiting the occurrence of counterfeiting; however, the problem is not likely to disappear soon. Here are some steps you can take to lower the possibility that your supply of materials will be tainted by low-quality counterfeits.

- *Get an agent.* Find a person in the local area who can separate the good from the questionable suppliers.

- *Ask those who know.* If you are already doing business with a reliable Chinese supplier for one type of part, that organization may know of other reliable suppliers for other types of material you need.

- *Go through an independent distributor.* A distributor may be a third party between you and the source of manufactured material. This distributor can filter poor quality or counterfeit parts. If the distributor has been in the local area for long, the company probably has established relationships with reliable manufacturers.

- *Don't put all of your supply eggs in one basket.* As a measure of insurance, avoid obtaining all of your parts from one place. If it does turn out that there is a problem with the part, you won't be entirely dependent on that source.

Source: "How to Spot Counterfeit Parts: Caveat Emptor, or Buyer Beware, Is Appropriate Advice for Buyers Sourcing in China," *Purchasing* 131 (2002), p. 31+.

Materials Requirements Planning

A product's inputs are based on its design. **Materials requirements planning (MRP)** is the process of analyzing the design to determine the materials and parts that it requires in the production process. This information is then used for purchasing, inventorying, and planning. The MRP process increasingly is tied into the firm's information technology capabilities. MRP computer applications are discussed in Chapter 18.

> **materials requirements planning (MRP)**
>
> The process of analyzing a design to determine the materials and parts that it requires in the production process.

While an MRP process may typically evoke images of a high technology environment and product, the process can be successfully used in low-tech situations. Consider, for example, the humble product of prepared horseradish. Silver Springs Gardens is one of the manufacturers involved in annually turning 24 million pounds of raw horseradish into 6 million gallons of prepared horseradish.[1] The company has multiple plants. Each plant traditionally had planners who determined production schedules. These planners considered account sales demand and stock on hand to manually create production orders. Transfers of materials between plants were discussed via phone. Only after the orders were placed and negotiations were complete would the requirements for raw materials be known. Unfortunately, this process often took so long that the purchasing department did not have enough time to obtain needed materials. The manufacturer often faced having to inform customers that the company was temporarily out of stock. Silver Springs Gardens has resolved the problem and become more efficient by implementing MRP software. The software checks sales orders and stock levels automatically. It then generates production schedules and orders raw materials. The company has been able to reduce inventory levels as efficiency increased. Thus, even mundane processes can benefit from an MRP system.

Inventory

Most manufacturing operations require a stock of raw materials, inputs, and component parts on hand. Optimum **inventory** levels may be set when capacity decisions are made; the quantity of products to be created determines the amount of inventory the firm maintains. **Reordering systems** are used to help keep inventory levels more or less constant. In *fixed-point reordering systems,* the operations manager determines a minimum level of inventory; once this level is reached, inputs are reordered. In *fixed-interval reordering systems,* reordering is based on time—the operations manager determines that supplies need to be reordered every two months, for example. Just-in-time inventory levels are discussed later in this chapter.

inventory

The stock of raw materials, inputs, and component parts that the firm keeps on hand.

reordering systems

The process used to help keep inventory levels more or less constant.

The Conversion Process

The second major stage of operations management is the **conversion process**—taking the product's inputs and converting them to the final product. The operations manager designs and controls the production system which should create high-quality, low-cost products that customers are willing to buy or use. An effective conversion process lowers the cost of creating the product or creates a better product for the same cost. Many software tools are available to help with the design and implementation of the conversion process; these are discussed in Chapter 18.

conversion process

The operations management stage in which the product's inputs are converted to the final product.

TABLE 17.1

Process Analysis Information

STEP	ORDER	RELATION TO OTHER STEPS	TIME
A. Get permit	1	None	4 weeks
B. Order equipment	1	None	1 week
C. Paint interior	2	None	2 weeks
D. Install electrical fixtures	3	Following C	1 week
E. Install floors	4	Following C	1 week
F. Install equipment	5	Following B, E	1 week
G. Test equipment	6	Following F	1 week

Designing the Process

The conversion process typically involves several steps that may occur either at the same time or in sequence. The process will be designed to accommodate these activities. For complex operations, the conversion process is designed in subparts. An aggregate plan shows the process for the entire operation, but each subpart requires individual analysis and design. Each subpart's schedule is taken into account in a master schedule.

In designing the process, the operations manager should be careful to avoid overlooking less critical steps. Critical steps may depend on what are perceived as less important areas, but if they are not planned for, the entire process may be delayed.

Process design begins with an analysis of the general operation and identifying:

- Every major step.
- The order that the steps must take.
- The flow of the steps from start to finish, including their relationship to each other.
- The amount of time each individual step requires.

Table 17.1 shows how this information is used to set up a new bakery's baking facility. If each step were done in order, the bakery would take 11 weeks to open. Because some of the steps can be done concurrently, however, the time can be shortened to 5 weeks.

Several tools are available to help analyze the steps needed to determine an efficient sequence and also to monitor the process. Three of the best known tools are a Gantt chart, a load chart, and a PERT network.

GANTT CHARTS　Developed by Henry Gantt in the early 1900s, **Gantt charts** provide a visual sequence of the process steps. A Gantt chart using the information in Table 17.1 appears in Figure 17.2.

Gantt charts

A visual sequence of the process steps used in planning, scheduling, and monitoring production.

FIGURE 17.2

A Gantt Chart

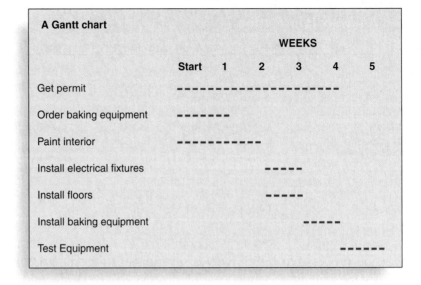

A Gantt chart

	WEEKS					
	Start	1	2	3	4	5
Get permit						
Order baking equipment						
Paint interior						
Install electrical fixtures						
Install floors						
Install baking equipment						
Test Equipment						

Project Planning

load chart

A type of Gantt chart that is based on departments or specific resources that are used in the process.

program evaluation and review technique (PERT) network

A tool for analyzing the conversion process.

facilities layout

The grouping and organization of equipment and employees.

Facilities Layout

LOAD CHARTS Another way to analyze the process is with a load chart. A **load chart** is a type of Gantt chart that is based on departments or specific resources, used in the process. Instead of the tasks listed in Figure 17.2, the load chart would list the people involved in each step and the time frame for their involvement, as seen in Figure 17.3.

PERT NETWORKS Another way to analyze the process, especially complex projects, is with a **program evaluation and review technique (PERT) network.** This technique was developed in the 1950s, when the work of thousands of contractors and government agencies needed to be coordinated for the Polaris submarine weapons system. A PERT network is illustrated in Figure 17.4.

FACILITIES LAYOUT Once the major steps have been identified, the design of the actual work area is created. **Facilities layout**—the grouping and organization of equipment and employees—affects the efficiency of the production system. Workstations are arranged based on product layout, process layout, or fixed-position layout schemes.

Functions in a *product layout* are organized so that each function is performed in a fixed sequence. Employees and equipment stay in one place, or workstation, as the product moves through the system. Mass production (assembly) lines are one type of product layout system. These systems have become efficient for relatively small levels of production, but traditionally they were used for large production runs.

In *process layout,* each workstation is relatively self-contained. The product moves to the workstation needed to perform the next operation, which may not be in sequence. Process layouts are often used to create

FIGURE 17.3

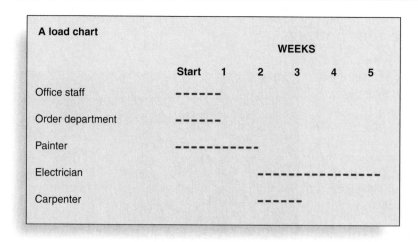

FIGURE 17.4

A PERT Network

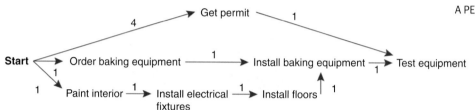

custom-made products because they offer flexibility to make product changes. This layout does reduce efficiency, making it more expensive.

In a *fixed-position layout,* remote workstations assemble the product's components, which then are brought to the production area for final assembly. Fixed-position layouts are used for complex products that are difficult to assemble and for large products that are not easily moved, such as aircraft.

FLEXIBLE MANUFACTURING   When changes are made to a product, time spent in setting up and reconfiguring the workstations is lost if the process must shut down during setup, increasing the cost and reducing efficiency. It is possible to design the process using principles of **flexible manufacturing,** which are operations management techniques that help reduce the setup costs associated with the production system. Computer-aided design, engineering, and manufacturing tools make the work process more flexible. For example, when a change in a component is needed, a computer program, not the machinery, might be modified, greatly reducing the time the machinery is not available for production and enabling more types of product to be created. Management Close-Up 17.b provides a closer look at one company's efforts to emphasize flexibility in manufacturing.

flexible manufacturing

Operations management techniques that help reduce the setup costs associated with the production system.

Getting Your Bearings

Since mid-2000, the United States has experienced a manufacturing recession resulting in the loss of 2.1 million jobs. Some manufacturers coped with the difficult times by shifting operations to other countries with lower labor costs. At the same time, some U.S.-based manufacturers have not only survived but increased their competitiveness by emphasizing world-class quality and flexibility. Timken Company, a $3.9 billion maker of industrial bearings headquartered in Canton, Ohio, provides a prime example.

Timken made investments in building a sophisticated plant in the United States. This action came at a time when many of Timken's manufacturing competitors were shifting operations to lower-cost overseas facilities. The plant, located in Asheboro, North Carolina, is a model of flexibility in the production of small batches of goods without having to refit machine tools in between runs of different products. One of the keys to the flexibility of the production function is the library the company has developed featuring digital three-dimensional models of components. The models can be used as the design for a production run and can be tweaked for various custom features, when needed. The design is then sent out to networked machine tools. This process used to take half a day when refitting had to be done manually. Now, depending on the extent of modifications needed, the process takes 15 to 30 minutes. At the company's Asheboro plant, Timken can go from work order to finished part in four hours, a process that used to take six to eight weeks.

Timken Company increased flexibility at their Asheboro, North Carolina, plant by using a library of digital three-dimensional models of components.

Source: A. Aston and M. Arndt, "The Flexible Factory: Leaning Heavily on Technology, Some U.S. Plants Stay Competitive with Offshore Rivals," *Business Week,* May 5, 2003, pp. 90–91.

Flexible manufacturing also involves physical layout. A Y-shaped layout, for example, is often more amenable to flexible manufacturing than a straight-line layout. While one arm of the Y is being reconfigured, processes along the other two arms can continue. In a spiral layout, workers can easily physically turn to help with other steps to keep the work flow even.

Another consideration in flexible manufacturing is how employees work. Some firms use self-managed work teams to produce an entire product or component. Team members learn all the tasks in the production process, move from job to job, and fill in for each other, thereby creating a great deal of flexibility. Team members schedule work, order materials, and hire new staff for the team. Productivity and efficiency typically increase, and the supervisor position can often be eliminated, streamlining the hierarchy.

Monitoring the Process

Operations management is a continuous function. Once the process has been designed and implemented, the systems need to be monitored and improved. *Benchmarks* that set levels of production and costs are strategic management decisions. These benchmarks are used to evaluate the production process in a number of ways.

In **acceptance sampling,** a sample of materials or products is measured against the benchmark. Based on the results of this measurement, the entire run is either accepted or rejected.

Statistical process control uses quantitative methods and procedures to evaluate transformation operations and to detect and eliminate deviations. This type of control is in wide use today. Manager's Notes 17.3 lists several statistical process tools. By using statistical data about the process, operations managers can pinpoint problems and find solutions that address the problem. They can also see areas of improvement that will often circumvent a problem. By making the operations process more efficient, managers can also improve the firm's financial performance in most cases. Later in this chapter, systems for improving operations management quality are described in greater detail.

Another important goal of operations management is increasing the efficiency of the production process beyond the benchmarks. For example, if operations management can determine how to use fewer inputs or processes in the production system, the efficiency of the system will be improved and the operations will be more productive. Two methods are typically used to determine productivity: total factor productivity and partial factor productivity.

Total factor productivity measures how well an organization utilizes all company resources, such as capital, labor, materials, or energy, to produce its outputs, according to the equation:

$$\frac{\text{Outputs}}{\text{All inputs}} = \text{Total factor productivity}$$

For total factor productivity to be valid, managers must convert all inputs to a common unit. Because inputs are typically initially measured in different units (labor may be measured in hours, materials in tons, energy in joules, for example), converting these units to their dollar cost allows them to be added.

Partial productivity measures the contribution of a single input, such as labor or materials, to the final product. The efficiency of materials would be expressed as:

$$\frac{\text{Outputs}}{\text{Materials}} = \text{Materials productivity}$$

The measurement of the partial productivity of labor is often used to compare the efficiency of firms within an industry.

acceptance sampling

An operations management monitoring tool in which a sample of materials or products is measured against a benchmark.

statistical process control

An operations management monitoring tool that uses quantitative methods and procedures to evaluate transformation operations and to detect and eliminate deviations.

total factor productivity

The measurement of how well an organization utilizes all of its resources, such as capital, labor, materials, or energy, to produce its outputs.

partial productivity

The measurement of the contribution of a single input, such as labor or materials, to the final product.

Check Sheets   Check sheets are quantity-based forms, where a check mark is made for a particular attribute. Check sheets can provide data when the attribute is tracked by time, location, or some other variable—to pinpoint workstations or processes that produce more or less than the average or that have fewer defects, for example.

Pareto Analysis   The concept behind Pareto analysis is that 20 percent of an operation results in 80 percent of the gap between expected and actual performance. Pareto analysis involves specifying the causes of a problem and assigning a value (such as dollars or time) to each cause based on its contribution to the problem in order to determine the causes that have the most negative effects on the operation.

Process Flow Analysis   Process flow analysis is a method of graphically representing the activities in a process, the exact tasks of these activities, and their organization or structure within the process. By diagramming the process, managers can identify variations and disruptions.

Cause-and-Effect Diagrams   Also called *fishbone diagrams* and *Ishikawa charts,* cause-and-effect diagrams are a mechanism for identifying potential causes of problems and tracing back through interrelationships to identify the root causes. The main cause of a problem typically is a function of other causes, which can be identified by breaking the main cause down by area.

Process Capability Measures   Certain specifications (S) can be defined as acceptable levels of variations, with a lower and upper limit set. By also setting acceptable variation in the process (P), the actual performance we can evaluate the actual performance statistically as

$$C_P = \frac{\text{Specification width}}{\text{Process width}} = \frac{S}{P}$$

As the process variation narrows, the specification typically improves.

Control Charts   Control charts plot data collected over time across a set of limits for the upper and lower boundaries of acceptable performance. Points outside the acceptable limits indicate a problem that needs to be solved to improve the operation.

Source: Adapted form S. Melnyk and D. Denzler, *Operations Management.* New York: McGraw-Hill/Irwin, 1996.

Operations management is typically focused on the production process. The operations management approach can also be applied to monitoring and managing finances. Management Close-Up 17.c reviews the use of operations management to assure ethical financial performance and to make financial falsification more difficult.

Disposition of the Product

The end result of the firm's operations process is the product, whether it is a good or a service. Other areas of the firm, including marketing

SERVICE OPERATIONS MANAGEMENT

Form small groups of four or five students. Each group will choose a local service industry establishment, such as the public library, a video rental establishment, a dry cleaner, or a hand car wash. The establishment can be a for-profit or a not-for-profit firm. Before class, research the establishment—if possible, observe the organization in action.

1. Describe the service organization that you selected.

2. Define the target customers of that organization and what you think they value most.

3. List inputs that the service requires.

4. List the business processes that the organization uses to create its service.

5. Create a PERT network showing the business process from inputs through delivery of the service. Create a network for each process if the firm's activities require more than one process.

In class, meet with your group and share your results. Compare the PERT networks each member has created. Refine the network to show an efficient process for providing the service. Each group should then present its findings to the class.

---

and sales, usually bear the responsibility for finding the user of the firm's product; actual delivery of the product may fall to customer service. Operations management, however, includes the customer-fulfillment process.

Customer fulfillment begins when an order is received, sometimes long before the firm's product will be delivered. An **order review/release (ORR) activity** is used to evaluate and track the order through the process, from creating order documentation, to material checking, capacity evaluation, and load leveling (releasing orders so that the workload is evenly distributed).

The final step of the customer-fulfillment process in operations management is the order disposition. The order must be checked to verify that it is complete. Records of labor hours, material amounts, and any problems in the production process are finalized so that the cost of producing the order can be arrived at and made available for pricing purposes.

order review/ release (ORR) activity

An operations management tool that is used to evaluate and track the order through the process, including creating order documentation, material checking, capacity evaluation, and load leveling (releasing orders so that the work load is evenly distributed).

Managing Quality

During World War II, intense development in machinery and processes took place in U.S. factories to produce goods for the war effort and to use inputs more efficiently for manufacturing domestic goods. Innovations in the production process in the United States stagnated after the war,

Ethical Financial Performance and Operations Management

THEME: ETHICS Shady financial dealings at companies such as Enron and WorldCom have led to an erosion of consumer confidence in the ethics of business. While the government is enacting changes in an attempt to bring about greater openness and accuracy in how companies manage their finances, proactive action at a company level can help assure that finances are managed ethically. The operations management approach and its common measures can be used in the finance domain. Although typically associated with the production process, operations management can help monitor and improve financial processes in organizations.

An important starting point for operations management is the development of standards. Applied to finance, these standards consist of various financial ratios that take into consideration the unique characteristics of the organization. Past performance of the organization provides a baseline standard against which variations are compared. In addition, benchmarking provides financial standards based on similar types of organizations.

Once standards are developed, measurements must be taken to see how the process compares with these standards. As noted in the section on the quality approach to operations management, workers are often empowered to take their own measurements of the production process. In regard to the financial process, it is interesting to note that empowerment and open information sharing is much less common. At WorldCom, for instance, federal prosecutors have alleged that with more than 60,000 employees, a group of approximately six officers and staff were able to inappropriately reallocate nearly $4 billion in expenses. Management prerogative and concerns over proprietary information being leaked to competitors may lead members of an organization to avoid sharing financial information. However, there must be some access to data so that measures can be taken and, at the same time, confidential data remains confidential.

Finally, the measurements must be fed back and, if needed, corrective steps taken. For example, General Electric uses online dashboards which senior managers can use to assess aspects of operations and finance. The dashboard concept can include limits and color coding (such as green, red, and yellow to represent financial conditions which are fine, in trouble, or should be attended to). (See the end-of-chapter minicase on visual operations management for more consideration of communicating with shapes and colors.)

With the above type of processes in place, problems can be anticipated or identified. Further, the open measurement and feedback approach makes unethical financial dealings less likely.

Source: D. M. Faltin and F. W. Faltin, "Toe the Line: No More World-Coms," *Quality Progress* 36 (2003), pp. 29–35.

---

however. W. Edwards Deming, considered the father of quality management, taught Japanese firms how to use statistics to measure and improve quality—but U.S. firms had rejected his ideas. By the 1970s, firms in other countries had begun using computers to integrate manufacturing operations with strategic planning. The resulting products were better as they were being continually improved, and they became cheaper as the production process became more efficient. Their U.S. counterparts had been overtaken both in productivity and profitability.

The impact of quality improvement efforts in other countries on the U.S. economy was dramatic. Managers in the United States were forced to look hard at their operations. They began to take a second look at Deming's teachings and other means of improving quality. Quality management became an important issue to many firms by the middle of the 1980s. Company leaders began seeking a more efficient production process to lower production costs and ultimately increase profitability.

Top management must make improvement in productivity a strategic objective of the firm. Managers from different areas of the firm must work together to increase efficiency. Many of the steps to improve quality and efficiency cut across departmental boundaries.

Quality management techniques are not limited to operations management. Chapter 5 mentioned the role of total quality management and the six-sigma objective in GE's planning process, and Chapters 1 and 14 discuss Deming's principles. It is in the operations management area, however, that a quality philosophy is essential to the success of the firm. Identifying and implementing production improvements fall to operations management. Quality management, kaizen, just-in-time, and process reengineering are four methods of managing quality.

The Quality Management Approach

One of the main objectives of operations management should be to make the production sequence as effective as possible. Just what "effectiveness" means and how it can be achieved are critical issues. Traditionally, Western management approached production from the perspective of internal standards (often quantity produced), a focus on workers, and independent quality inspection. In contrast, the quality management philosophy approaches production from the perspective of external standards driven by customers, a focus on the system, and the belief that quality is integral to the work process.[2] Therefore, quality management becomes customer driven. It is the customer who is the source of standards for defining quality. The quality approach underscores the importance of the system in determining performance. Traditional Western management focuses on employee motivation and ability levels, whereas a quality approach emphasizes characteristics of the production system as the major influence on quality outcomes. Further, quality management emphasizes the empowerment of workers and their responsibility for the quality of the outcomes of work processes. Thus, workers in an organization, guided by a quality philosophy, are often responsible for inspecting the quality of their own work. In contrast, a traditional Western management approach typically keeps quality inspections separate, performed by separate personnel. According to Deming, inspection as a separate function puts fear into workers. He believed the work process was better if workers were responsible for their own work processes and the quality of outputs.

The quality management philosophy resulted in the development of a program called Total Quality Management. **Total quality management (TQM)** is based on the belief that all of an organization's activities should be focused on improving its product. TQM has been described as "a total

total quality management (TQM)

An organizationwide management approach that focuses on quality as an overarching goal. The basis of this approach is the understanding that all employees and organizational units should be working harmoniously to satisfy the customer.

commitment to quality and attitude expressed by everybody's involvement in the process of continuous improvement of products and services, through the use of innovative scientific methods."[3] One focus of TQM is on the use of SPC tools. Thus, a TQM program often emphasizes training workers in the use of SPC tools and then empowering workers to use the tools to measure the quality of work processes and the effectiveness of attempts to improve quality. While the TQM acronym virtually stands for every quality management perspective, Deming never espoused the use of the term. He believed that quality will be meaningfully improved by managers who understand the quality philosophy, not by applying a stand-alone, set program of steps. Recently TQM has become less visible, but not because quality is less important. To the contrary, quality continues to be critically important to the survival and competitiveness of organizations. Quality is now commonly viewed as simply part of the operation of an organization. That is, quality is often "baked in" to the management process, rather than treated as a separate element of the production recipe.

Four interrelated steps make up the quality approach according to Deming: plan, do, check, and act (also called the *PDCA cycle* or the *Deming wheel*). These processes are ongoing and will result in total quality management. At each step in the cycle, firms must focus on customer needs, emphasize participation and teamwork of all involved in the firm's activities (suppliers, employees, and customers), and establish an organizational climate of continuous improvement by all employees.

MANAGEMENT AND THE QUALITY PHILOSOPHY   Deming's 14 points for management, as discussed in Chapters 1 and 14, provide the underlying management structure for the quality process. They define the tenets that make up the philosophy. Operations management also draws from Deming's theory of variance. Deming believed that variance causes unpredictability, which increases uncertainty and reduces control. Variations from standard work flows and activities can be seen as a major source of operations management problems. Correcting these variances by using quality principles to find and correct their source is one form of continuous improvement.

Common causes of ongoing variances that operations management should correct include weak designs, scheduling errors, chronic equipment problems, and inaccurate documentation. Individual employees can correct specific problems as part of their responsibilities, such as alerting their supervisor to late deliveries and suggesting ways to improve scheduling.

EMPLOYEES AND QUALITY   Operations managers must be certain employees understand that the quality approach means each worker is responsible for improving quality. They must also be willing to act on any suggestions or problems that employees identify. **Quality circles**—groups of employees who meet regularly to discuss ways to increase quality—were a useful means of finding sources of and solutions to poor quality.

quality circles

Groups of employees who meet regularly to discuss ways to increase quality.

As with TQM, there are now fewer references to quality circles since quality is integrated into the responsibilities of employees and teams of employees.

Goals should be set for each employee so that management can evaluate how well each has achieved these goals. When individual quality goals are met, employees should be recognized and rewarded.

CUSTOMERS AND TQM Customers ultimately decide what constitutes quality through purchasing decisions. Other departments may identify what customers want as well as what the firm actually is providing to them. Operations management can focus on improving the **quality gap**—the difference between what customers want and what they actually get from the company. By consistently monitoring the production process, as discussed earlier in this chapter, managers can determine if improvements are taking place.

SUPPLIERS AND QUALITY From a quality perspective, suppliers are regarded as partners with the firm. Poor quality in a product is often caused by poor quality in its inputs. The problem may be traced to the quality of the supplier's materials. On the other hand, it may be a function of the design and the materials the supplier was requested to provide. Involving suppliers during the design and production process takes advantage of their expertise in the materials that are available and any qualifications for using them.

Suppliers who are perceived (and perceive themselves) as partners with the firm will be proactive in solving problems. Operations managers should work to develop cooperative, long-term relationships with suppliers.

In addition to partnerships, many organizations are employing established standards and asking their suppliers to also adhere to those same standards. The International Organization for Standardization (ISO) is the world's largest developer of standards. It is a network of national standards institutes from 146 countries. ISO develops technical standards that guide, for example, production and distribution. The purpose of these standards is to make the development, manufacture, and supply of products and services safer, more efficient, and cleaner. In addition, the standardization is meant to make international trade easier and fairer. There are numerous ISO guidelines and standards. The ISO 9000 family of standards focuses on quality management in organizations. The ISO 1400 family of standards focuses on environmental management so that organizations minimize harmful impacts on the environment. While exploring the details of these standards is beyond the scope of this discussion, you can find more information about ISO standards at the ISO website (www.iso.ch/iso/en/ISOOnline.frontpage).

QUALITY AND THE PRODUCTION PROCESS Operations management uses quality techniques to focus on the production process. Products that can be manufactured with fewer components, for example, can

The quality framework is often thought of in the context of producing goods. The approach applies equally well to organizations providing services. The following characteristics were recently found to be most related to cost-effective performance in a large service organization.

- The extent to which the employee is satisfied with the internal processes of the organization.
- The extent to which the organization emphasizes doing things right the first time.
- The extent to which the structure of the organization makes it easy to focus on process improvement.
- A continuous learning culture.
- A multi-skill work environment providing clear knowledge of expectations.
- Task autonomy.
- Job satisfaction.
- Organizational commitment to the employee.
- Few restrictions to innovation.
- Rapid technology assimilation.

Source: C . Kontoghiorghes, "Examining the Association between Quality and Productivity Performance in a Service Organization," *The Quality Management Journal* 10 (2003), pp. 32–42.

be assembled more quickly and with fewer steps and typically have fewer defects. The quality of the product improves, the wasted labor spent in making and dealing with defective products decreases, and the firm's profitability is improved. While quality management is often associated with producing goods, the approach can also be applied to providing services. Manager's Notes 17.4 summarizes recent findings regarding quality indicators that were most important in service settings.

As discussed in Chapter 8, one way to combat defects is by adhering to the six-sigma philosophy. Sigma is a statistical measurement of defects in parts per million. Four sigma, where most firms operate, equals 6,210 defects per million. Five sigma equals 233 defects per million, which is considerably improved over four sigma. Six sigma, however, is the ultimate goal, where defects occur at the rate of 1 per 3.4 million—a product or process that is 99.999666 percent defect-free.

kaizen

The Japanese process of continuous improvement in the organization's production system from numerous small, incremental improvements in production processes.

Kaizen (Continuous Improvement) and Efficiency

Another quality management technique is kaizen, the approach used by Pella, the firm discussed at the beginning of this chapter. **Kaizen** is the Japanese term for the need for continuous improvement in the organization's production system from numerous small, incremental improve-

TABLE 17.2

Implementing Kaizen

MAINTENANCE

- Question current practices without making excuses or justifying them.
- Question everything five times to identify the root causes of waste and to come up with solutions.

KAIZEN

- Discard conventional ideas and methods in finding causes and devising solutions.
- Remember that kaizen ideas are limitless.
- Think positively of how to accomplish something, not negatively about why it can't be done.
- Focus wisdom on the kaizen process and solutions, not money.
- Understand that undergoing hardship increases wisdom.
- The wisdom of ten people is more valuable than the knowledge of one.

INNOVATION

- Begin implementing solutions right away—don't wait until the solutions have been perfected.
- Correct mistakes immediately, as they occur, before they can cause further problems.

Source: The Kaizen Institute, www.kaizen-institute.com.

ments in production processes. The principles of kaizen were introduced in 1985 by Masaaki Imai.[4] According to these principles, process should be dealt with in three steps: maintenance, kaizen, innovation.

The maintenance step is the status quo of the process—how it is done. Kaizen is the interim step of identifying small ways to improve maintenance. Innovation is the resulting changes to the process. After the process is modified, the innovated process then becomes the new status quo and the kaizen process begins again. Table 17.2 lists suggestions from the Kaizen Institute for implementing kaizen in an organization. The kaizen principle of continuous improvement is now incorporated into the ISO 9000 standards and is a part of most quality improvement efforts. Thus, as with TQM, kaizen may not be readily visible in organizations, because it is integrated into organizational operations, rather than standing out as a separate program.

One of the main principles of kaizen is reducing waste in materials, inventory, production steps, and activities that don't add value, such as moving parts from one machine to another. According to the Kaizen Institute, every second that is spent in adding value to a product is offset by 1,000 seconds of activities that add no value.[5] Sources of waste include inefficient facilities layouts. Implementing flexible manufacturing systems and facilities layouts is consistent with the kaizen approach. Another waste-reduction technique is using a limited number of suppliers, which enables the organization to control inputs. Just-in-time manufacturing, discussed next, is another method of operations management that firms use as part of their quality efforts.

Computerized cash register transactions at Wal-Mart automatically trigger inventory restocking by the firm's suppliers. Wal-Mart's computer database is second only to the Pentagon's in capacity.

Just-In-Time Systems

just-in-time (JIT)

The concept behind creating the firm's product in the least amount of time.

The concept of creating the firm's product in the least amount of time led to another operations management approach. The goal of a **just-in-time (JIT)** system is improving the firm's profitability. Managers develop a smooth, integrated production process in which steps are performed just as subsequent steps require them, from inputs and the conversion process through disposition of the product.

Like TQM and kaizen, JIT is implemented at the strategic level rather than the operations management level. Product design, employee compensation, accounting, and sales are all affected by JIT. Under JIT, product design can be as up to date as possible, because the production process won't begin until orders are received. Inventory levels can be more easily modified. On the other hand, product design must be finished when it is needed in the JIT production process or the cost of the product will increase.

In a JIT system, the firm's inventory of inputs—the raw materials, components, labor, and energy that the firm has available—are kept at the lowest level possible. Inputs arrive at the organization when, not before, they are needed. Close relationships with suppliers are critical to JIT inventory systems. Wal-Mart generates its inventory reorders with a computer network that receives data as each purchase is scanned at the checkout counter. When inventory levels for the product reach a predetermined level, information about the number of replacement items needed and where to send them is sent to the suppliers' computers. Suppliers agree to use this method of managing inventory and almost become Wal-Mart's warehouses, as the suppliers must maintain enough inventory to fill Wal-Mart's orders on demand.

Kanban's Creator

Kanban was developed during the 1960s by Taichi Ohno, a Toyota mechanical engineer. The assembly shop he managed at Toyota produced component parts for the company's assembly lines. Huge quantities of component parts were produced at one time and stored in a warehouse until needed. Ohno realized that defective parts would not be discovered until they were needed in the assembly process, which could be months after they were produced. By the time the defect was discovered, a large stockpile of defective parts would have to be scrapped, creating enormous waste. It would often be impossible to determine why the defect had occurred, so that correcting it would be very difficult.

Ohno began improving the system. He was able to set up shop equipment so that it could be reconfigured in minutes instead of hours, thus making production of small batches of components economically feasible: because less time was spent setting up the equipment, fewer components needed to be made to recapture the cost. Smaller batches meant components could be sent to the assembly line just as they were needed. The components were sent in wheeled containers that came to be known as *kanbans*. After the assembly line emptied the kanban it was sent back to the assembly shop, signaling that the shop should produce another batch of components.

Ohno's system reduced inventory warehousing needs and made identifying and resolving defects in the components much easier. Toyota adopted it throughout the company, and the once nearly bankrupt Toyota became the third-largest automobile maker in the world, behind General Motors and Ford.

Source: G. R. Jones, J. M. George, and C. W. L. Hill, *Contemporary Management,* 2nd ed., New York: McGraw-Hill/Irwin, 2000. p. 657.

JIT inventory systems are valuable in several ways. They save on warehouse space and labor, and financial resources are not tied up in inputs waiting to be used. They also play a major role in identifying production errors. Since inputs are received and put into the production process immediately, any defects in them quickly become apparent and replacements are sent by the firm's suppliers. Because orders are processed only after they are received, products are produced in small batches. Consequently, problems in the production process can be remedied before another batch goes through.

KANBAN   A form of JIT systems called kanban originated in Japan. **Kanban,** from the Japanese word for "card" or "sign," uses cards to generate inventory. Inputs are shipped to manufacturers in containers with a card in a side pocket. Upon receipt, the card is removed and returned to the supplier. The supplier then sends more inputs based on a predetermined schedule so that they will arrive just when the preceding shipment is used up. The origins of kanban are discussed in Manager's Notes 17.5.

kanban

A form of JIT systems originated in Japan that uses cards to generate inventory; from the Japanese word for "card" or "sign."

KEEP ON TRUCK'N?

JIT has allowed many U.S. organizations to streamline operations by making production processes as efficient as possible. JIT means less warehouse and manufacturing space, since the product can be shipped or used as soon as it is produced or received. However, new security rules scheduled to take effect at the end of 2003 may impact JIT programs for firms that include Mexico and Canada in supply chains.

U.S. Customs has proposed that cargo information be supplied to customs four hours prior to loading goods to be shipped by truck. This four-hour notice may not seem like much of a delay in the shipping process, but it is enough to be a serious concern for managers in a number of organizations. As stated by a Sony executive at a facility located in Tijuana, Mexico, in many cases, the truck has already crossed the border within the four-hour period from when it was produced on the line! The executive pointed out that Sony relies on JIT and no longer stages or warehouses goods produced in the company's Mexican manufacturing facilities. Sony has approximately 100 trucks making runs back and forth across the U.S.–Mexican border. This operation is dynamic and fast moving. Sony is just one of many such organizations that count on an uninterrupted supply line between its U.S. facilities and those across the border. The concern is that even a four-hour notification will have a negative impact because an order can be received, filled, and across the border in a shorter amount of time. These new security regulations will end up raising the cost of delivered goods and have a negative impact on the economy.

Discussion Questions

1. Assess the magnitude of the four-hour rule. Do you think the problem is as great as the Sony representative portrays it? Why or why not?

2. One possible adaptation to the rule would be to stage, or warehouse, stock in the Mexican facilities. The stock could be held long enough to satisfy the four-hour rule. Why do the organizations that have invested in their JIT programs not like this solution?

3. Are there solutions, other than warehousing products, that you can identify?

Research Question

At the time of this writing, U.S. Customs had been holding discussions with shippers and carriers trying to work out implementation of the new rule (specified under Section 343 (a) of the Trade Act of 2002, as amended by the Maritime Port Security Act of 2002). Can you find information about how the new rule has been implemented? Is it working effectively?

Source: "JIT Just Won't Be the Same: Security Rules Could Affect Cross Border Trade," *World Trade* 16 (May 2003), p. 28.

DRAWBACKS TO JIT   Some organizations utilize a modified JIT system because one major drawback of JIT is that having just enough inventory leaves the firm without a buffer. Thus, it becomes difficult to cover problems that sometimes arise, such as unexpected orders or labor disputes involving the firm's suppliers. Warehouse employees are forced to carefully monitor supplies to continue to be able to meet JIT deadlines with quality parts. Skills for Managing 17.2 explores a JIT issue associated with increased security in our nation.

Another problem is keeping the labor supply stable. Unexpected demand means a firm must either increase its staff or pay overtime wage scales to meet order deadlines, since no inventory of products is available under a JIT system. The additional labor costs typically must be absorbed by the firm, cutting into profit margins.

A related problem is maintaining production equipment and other factors when demand is higher than expected. The firm's resources typically are focused on filling orders and not on maintenance of machines. Company employees may also not be able to take advantage of training opportunities to keep their skills up to date, another form of maintenance. Delaying maintenance for both equipment and skills puts the firm at a competitive disadvantage later.

Other Quality Management Systems

There are many exciting new ways to enhance quality in organizations. Whereas JIT systems are based on each area supplying materials or services to other areas for them to be built upon, and kaizen and TQM effect change in ongoing small increments over time, process reengineering is a new and different technique. Also, enterprise resource planning, or ERP, is an information technology form of quality management. Both process engineering and ERP are relatively new approaches for improving processes.

PROCESS REENGINEERING A more dramatic approach to quality includes changing the entire production process rather than making incremental adjustments. In **process reengineering,** the firm is viewed as a complete process—a series of activities that produce the products and services necessary to fulfill the firm's mission. Therefore the objective is to change the entire process at one time. Process reengineering came on the scene in 1993.

process reengineering

A method of changing the entire production process rather than making incremental changes.

Process reengineering focuses on processes rather than individual activities. Its goal, like that of the other quality management techniques, is to reduce waste and improve the firm's profitability. Process reengineering involves fundamentally rethinking and radically redesigning the entire process, including cutting out steps that aren't needed and reducing paperwork. The result should be improvements in cost, quality, timeliness, and service as a whole. Information technology, which has become an important part of process reengineering, is discussed in Chapter 18.

The management team at Ford reengineered company procurement process when they discovered that their strategic business partner, Mazda, had five people in its accounts payable department while Ford had 500 people in its U.S. accounts payable department. As a result of the reengineering, a buyer in Ford's purchasing department now enters purchase orders into an online database and, at the same time, they are sent to the supplier. Upon receipt, the goods are verified against the online database. If they are acceptable, the database is updated and payment to the supplier is automatically authorized rather than the authorization being granted by the accounts payable department. If the goods are not acceptable against the online database, they are returned to the supplier.

As a result of this process reengineering, Ford greatly reduced the size of the company's accounts payable department. The unproductive activities of the accounting staff and the operations employees in maintaining records and verifying deliveries manually were also eliminated. This reengineering effort increased the efficiency of the entire organization.[6]

APPLICATIONS: MANAGEMENT IS EVERYONE'S BUSINESS

Applications for the Manager   The supply of materials, the production process, and the outputs of that process are central management issues. With the advent of quality thinking and at the same time unprecedented competitive pressures, operations management is no longer just a separate function. Quality-centered management of operations is the key to remaining competitive and possibly the survival of the organization. Effective managers understand and utilize the concepts and techniques of operations management.

Applications for Managing Teams   Operations management has increasingly become part of the responsibility of teams. The quality philosophy brings with it empowerment of workers and a team approach. Thus, team members need the technical skills involved in measurement and evaluation. They also need interpersonal skills so that the team structure facilitates rather than gets in the way of improving production processes.

Applications for Individuals   Operations are composed of individual efforts. Individual workers must understand the objectives of the organization and how they are adding value to the process. Errors, waste, and poor productivity are simply not acceptable in today's competitive market. While measurement and improvement efforts might take place at a team level, it is ultimately individuals that make the difference in performance.

In the introductory section that focused on Pella Corporation, several critical thinking issues were posed. Now that you have read about the basics of operations management, it is time to revisit those issues. First, quality improvement efforts require the involvement and responsibility of those closest to the work—the workers! The workers can best understand and measure improvements in the work process. Without empowering the workers to make quality-related decisions, it is difficult to imagine how a quality program would get very far.

Second, continuous improvement might be considered the mantra of the quality approach. In today's competitive environment, taking the approach of "if it ain't broke, don't fix it" quickly results in the loss of competitive position. Other organizations will not be complacent and will continue to look for ways to do something faster, better, or more inexpensively. The fact that a process works is no reason for complacency. There is always room for improvement.

Third, remember that constantly adjusting a process can have a negative impact. If adjustments to a process become a preoccupation, they can distract attention from actually getting the work done and achieving key organizational outcomes. Further, constant adjustment, particularly when variance is within acceptable limits, can actually increase variance. As an example, consider resighting a gun every time you shoot it. The constant adjustment would likely decrease your accuracy and cause greater variance in your shots.

Finally, to be successful, quality improvement efforts require a variety of worker skills. Workers will need more than technical knowledge, such as information about statistical process control techniques. They must also be able to work effectively in teams and have good interpersonal skills so that problems can be identified and improvements can be evaluated.

Every organization produces or provides a product or service to customers by transforming inputs (raw materials or ideas) into outputs (goods and services) that have value. This transformation is achieved through effective **operations management,** which is the design, operation, and control of any aspect of a production system that transforms inputs into finished goods and services. A production system is the system that an organization uses to acquire inputs, convert the inputs to outputs, and dispose of the outputs.

Operations managers are responsible for managing an organization's production system. They do what is needed to transform inputs into outputs. Their job is to manage the three stages of production—**acquisition of inputs, control of conversion processes,** and disposal of goods and services. They must determine where operating improvements might be made to increase quality, efficiency, and responsiveness to customers, giving an organization a competitive advantage.

Achieving superior responsiveness to customers through quality and efficiency often requires a profound shift in management operations and in the culture of an organization. It can also involve the use of techniques such as **quality management, just-in-time** inventory systems, **kaizen,** and **process reengineering.** None of these systems is a panacea. Making these techniques work within an organization poses a challenge calling for hard work and years of persistence by the sponsoring managers.

DISCUSSION QUESTIONS

1. Why do you think Deming's work was more widely accepted by Japanese firms than by U.S. firms?

2. Why is the supplier relationship so important in operations management? What problems do you think might occur for the firm if it used too many suppliers? Too few? Do you think being an exclusive supplier for a firm is advantageous for the supplier?

3. How do you think an Internet provider might structure its operations management for its product, which is a service rather than a good? Describe what you think would be the inputs, transformation process, and disposition of its service.

4. Why is the concept of reducing waste so important to quality management systems?

5. Why do you think statistical tools are important in a total quality management organization?

6. Can a service industry use just-in-time principles? Explain your answer.

7. In what circumstances do you think a firm would choose process reengineering to improve its operations management? When might it choose the kaizen process?

Quality Improvement for the Small Shop

World class quality is usually associated with very large organizations, such as Toyota or Harley Davidson. Today, however, many smaller organizations are successfully applying the quality approach with limited budgets. Consider the example of Sunset Manufacturing, a family-owned 35-person business in Tualatin, Oregon.

Sunset may be a small machine shop, but the owners have the objective of performing at a world class level. Sunset's customers were increasingly focused on cost reduction and quality. As a result, Sunset established teams of people focused on kaizen, being lean (doing more with less), and six sigma. They held a number of "events" in which there was a concentrated focus on an area of operation. One event examined ways to reduce setup times by standardizing components and reorganizing tool storage. As a result, average tool setup times went from 3.5 hours to 36 minutes, an impressive 83 percent improvement. This and other similar events resulted in a 75 percent reduction in scrap associated with setup procedures.

Discussion Questions

1. What obstacles does a smaller business face in trying to implement quality improvement efforts?

2. How could the obstacles identified in question 1 be reduced or eliminated?

3. What additional steps would you recommend to Sunset in their quest to perform at a world class level?

4. Do you think that "events" are the best approach to improving quality? Why or why not? What other approaches would you recommend?

Source: G. Connor, "Benefiting from Six Sigma," *Manufacturing Engineering* 130 (2003), pp. 53–59.

Visualize It!

Organizational processes can often be made more efficient and safer by using visual operations management (VOM). VOM is the use of visual aids to communicate messages in an organization. Symbols have the advantage of conveying a message quickly (consider how quickly you can respond to a stop sign) and they can also overcome language barriers.

VOM helps make the workplace understandable to new employees and visitors. The practice leads to improved safety as well as greater efficiency in operations. Recently, an organization instituted visual production control with a simple three-color board placed behind expensive stock. Because of the expense, the employer didn't want to carry too much of the material. On the other hand, the employer could not afford to run out of the material, which would shut down the production line. When the material was in the green level on the board, employees knew there was sufficient inventory. When the level went down to yellow, that signaled it was time to order more of the material. At the red level, the supplier of the material was to be contacted to expedite an order. Further, as the warehouse managers worked with suppliers to implement just-in-time practices, they lowered the heights of the colored boxes to correspond to lower levels of required inventory.

As another example of VOM, a four-page set of written instructions at an organization was reduced to an easy-to-follow one-page diagram. The single sheet was laminated and posted in the relevant work area. This made instructions more accessible and easier to understand for everyone.

Discussion Questions

1. VOM can involve signs, markings on floors or walls, etc. Have you seen VOM at work in organizations? Describe.

2. What kind of visual communication could be used to increase productivity?

3. What kind of visual communication could be used to improve safety?

4. A visual guide may oversimplify and not convey all of the important nuances of a process. Do you think this is a reason for not using VOM? Why or why not?

Source: G. Stocker, "Use Symbols instead of Words," *Quality Progress* 35 (2003), pp. 68–72.

INDIVIDUAL/ COLLABORATIVE LEARNING CASE 17.1

It's All about Variance

The quality approach is fundamentally about understanding and reducing the variance involved in a process. Limiting variation is the key to reducing the number of bad parts and having a more stable, predictable manufacturing output. In the service sector, lowering variance in processes can also reduce mistakes with customers and produce a smoother and more satisfying purchasing process. Limiting variance in a service setting can also be a difficult task.

Consider some of the variance that occurs in health care. People arriving at a hospital emergency room have no way of knowing how busy the hospital is or how long their visit may last. Some people may be lucky and arrive when other patients aren't there and be ready to leave, depending on treatment needed, in a matter of minutes. Others may wait for hours. The variance in this process is, in part, due to the variance in the arrival times of patients.

There are certainly many other sources of variance in health care. A community hospital in California experienced difficulty with variation in the surgery center. The hospital staff had developed a same-day surgery center that was quite successful, but scheduling soon became a serious problem. A process improvement committee was formed and discovered that part of the scheduling problem was due to surgeons who did not arrive on time for 7:30 A.M. surgeries. Further investigation revealed that patients sometimes did not arrive on time for their surgeries either, thereby compounding the problem. Also, some operating rooms were not set up and ready for early morning surgeries. In sum, scheduling variations in this case were found to involve the doctors, the patients, and other facility employees.

Critical Thinking Questions

1. Why is variance a concern in a health care or service setting?

2. Simulations and statistical models demonstrate that random variation in service delivery times can produce longer wait times than fixed wait times. That is, even if patients arrive at random times, the average duration of their

stay will be less if the treatment times could be fixed. How could you make treatment times less variable?

3. Variance in arrival times is less under control of a hospital than variance in treatment times. Nonetheless, reducing this variance may be possible. How could you reduce variance in arrival times?

Collaborative Learning Exercise

Consider the example of the same-day surgery center. There are at least three sources of variance contributing to scheduling problems and delays. Understanding the sources of variance is only part of the management battle. What to do about the variance is the next critical issue. As a team, address each of the sources of variance. Identify ways to reduce, if not eliminate, the variance due to each source. What would be the benefits of reducing variance due to these sources? Share your suggestions and conclusions with the rest of the class.

Source: C. E. Noon, C. T. Hankins, and M. J. Cote, "Understanding the Impact of Variation in the Delivery of Healthcare Services," *Journal of Healthcare Management* 48 (2003), p. 82+.

Andersen Windows

Pella Windows, discussed in the chapter opening vignette, started implementing kaizen in the early 1990s to regain its competitive edge. Visit the website of one of Pella's competitors, Andersen Windows, and read Andersen's timeline in the corporation section of the site. Then answer the following questions:

1. How did Andersen use effective operations management in its first 10 years?

2. Although Andersen may not have instituted a kaizen program, identify some examples of quality management techniques the company has used over the years.

3. What quality management principles can you see at work in the timeline?

INTERNET EXERCISE 17.1

www.andersenwindows.com

EIGHTEEN

Managing Information Systems

chapter 18

After reading this chapter, you should be able to:

- Understand the difference between data and information, and how to use each to achieve organizational goals.

- Integrate the components of a firm's information technology.

- Compare different types of networks, including local area networks, intranets, extranets, and the Internet.

- Understand the role of software and how it changes business operations.

- Discuss the ethical issues involved with the use of computer technology.

- Understand how productivity, efficiency, and responsiveness to customers can be improved with information technology.

IBM Gets Connected

By 1995, when IBM started its Internet division, start-up dot-com firms were already blazing the Web. The IBM view of the Internet was a little different. CEO Louis V. Gerstner Jr. saw it not as a tool for browsing and posting content, but as a venue for business-to-business e-commerce. He believed that every physical transaction in the world would eventually be augmented or replaced by a digital transaction. Moreover, for an e-commerce operation to be effective, a firm must integrate the same Web technology into the information technology infrastructure that runs its business process. Transactions made on the Internet would need to become part of the firm's systems for logistics, fulfillment, credit, manufacturing, and accounts receivable/accounts payable.

IBM invested $300 million in a new Internet division and changed the way it operated—after all, how could the people at IBM claim to be experts if their own operations weren't integrated? A universal design database maintained by IBM's engineers now allows them to collaborate quickly and easily with its contract manufacturers early in the design process. Inventory control has also changed. Under the old system, planning for supplies was conducted manually. Employees separated bills of materials into individual orders and had to carry extra inventory to be able to fulfill them on time. With new technology in place, the order process automatically plans for supplies and notifies suppliers when parts need to be delivered to IBM factories. The new approach saved the firm 25 percent of its inventory costs.

IBM made the company's 12,000 suppliers part of a network. The suppliers input data about all the materials they use to create components for IBM, including the prices they pay for the materials and their own suppliers. The result is a huge database that includes information about every component in IBM's machines. The company's marketing department is able to use data-mining software to sort through the data. They might find that the same chip is used or can be used in several machines, qualifying the firm for a volume discount. If suppliers are paying more for the same chips that IBM buys, IBM's management team makes sure the price is lowered for those suppliers—and requires these suppliers to pass the savings along to IBM.

IBM's distributors are also part of the network, using it to send new orders to IBM and to check their status.

In 2002 CEO Louis V. Gerstner Jr. retired and was succeeded by Sam Palmisano. By 2003 IBM was in the midst of rapidly transforming itself from a hardware company into a service business with 40 percent of its revenues and half of its profits coming from providing services to diverse customers. Interestingly enough, CEO Palmisano was the chief of IBM's services business prior to succeeding Gerstner to attain the top job.

Sources: I. Sager, "Big Blue Gets Wired," *Business Week,* April 3, 2000; S. E. Ante. "The Second Coming of Software," *Business Week Online,* June 19, 2000; "Q&A with Lou Gerstner," *Business Week,* December 2, 1999; B. Schlender, "How Big Blue Is Turning Geeks into Gold," *Fortune,* June 9, 2003.

CRITICAL THINKING QUESTIONS

1. *How did IBM apply the data-mining software to lower its manufacturing costs?*

2. *In what ways does the application of technology on the Internet provide IBM with the ability to improve the performance of its inventory control process?*

Information is like glue and it is like gasoline. It is like glue, because information systems hold together all company operations. It is like gasoline, because information fuels innovation and change. When IBM decided to change its management information systems to take advantage of new technology, the company's business processes were integrated with the information system. This chapter looks at information systems from two perspectives: how the firm's information systems and information technology are part of management and how management information systems are used by managers. Skills for Managing 18.1 lists the skill managers use in managing information systems.

Managing Information

Information systems in some form existed long before today's technology was even dreamed of. The use of automated information processing became common at the end of the nineteenth century. In 1890, statistician Herman Hollerith designed the Punch Card Tabulating System to record that year's U.S. census. Census takers created the database with cards and punched holes in them that corresponded to answers to 240 questions. The collected data were then tabulated using electric current. The 1880 census, which had been performed by hand, took seven years to tabulate.

MANAGEMENT SKILLS FOR INFORMATION SYSTEMS MANAGEMENT

- *Analytical skills.* Managers need to be able to gather, synthesize, and compare data about their firms and about the options available to them.

- *Organization skills.* Data alone are rarely useful. Managers need to be able to make sense of information by organizing data to facilitate analysis and comparison. Organization skills are also essential in determining how to control data distribution.

- *Flexibility and innovation skills.* Managers must be able to be flexible in adapting standard business practices to new information technologies. Because information systems and technology are fast changing, looking for new ways of doing things is essential to being a proactive manager.

Hollerith was able to complete the 1890 census in only 12 weeks, saving $5 million for the U.S. Census Bureau.[1] Hollerith then began a data-tabulating firm, which merged with two other firms in 1911. The resulting firm was renamed International Business Machines in 1924, and Hollerith became known as the father of information processing.

By the 1960s, with the advent of affordable information technology, information systems experienced dramatic changes.[2] They have continued to evolve as technology developed. Management of information systems and technology has evolved as well. Today's systems allow greater use of information throughout the firm. They also generate new challenges in organizing, analyzing, and protecting information. The study of the design, implementation, management, and use of information technology applications in organizations is known as MIS, or management information systems.

A management information system provides access to important information used in many of the management activities presented in previous chapters of this text. These include the planning process (Chapter 5), decision making (Chapter 6), human resource management (Chapter 10), communication (Chapter 15), control (Chapter 16), and operations management (Chapter 17). The planning process, for example, requires an economic forecast which depends on the availability of historical cost and revenue information. These items may be retrieved and manipulated using a management information system.

Herman Hollerith's electric tabulating machine, first used in the 1890 U.S. census, reduced the time required to process census data from seven years to twelve weeks.

Data and Information

The term **data** refers to raw facts, such as the number of items sold or the number of hours worked in a department. By itself data can be useful at a rudimentary level. For instance, a retail clothing store can determine which style of jeans was the best seller based on data. By gathering and analyzing additional data about the jeans, however, the company can use the resulting information to determine past trends in sales, make forecasts about future sales, determine the profit margin, and make marketing decisions. The term **information** refers to data that have been gathered and converted into a meaningful context.

For information to be useful in decision making, it must be of high quality, timely, relevant, and comprehensive. The *quality* of information is determined by its accuracy and reliability. If the information that is provided to or by a firm is inaccurate or unreliable, it is likely to cause errors or to be ignored. *Timely* information is essential for decision making. Decisions about purchasing commodities, for example, that are based on market conditions may be costly if out-of-date information is used. *Relevant* information is also essential. A firm that markets products to foreign countries needs country-specific information that takes cultural differences into account; otherwise the information will be irrelevant. *Comprehensive* information contains the complete data set necessary to make a decision.

Information that is outdated or unclear can lead to poor decisions. When Firestone tires on Ford Explorers were linked to fatal accidents, Ford CEO Jacques Nasser defended his company's actions by claiming that Ford acted as quickly as possible to replace tires once its data supported a U.S. tire recall in August 2000. The firm had already recalled tires in other countries beginning a year earlier, based on Ford's analysis of property claims data from Bridgestone/Firestone. Had data been available to support an earlier U.S. recall, some lives might have been saved and Ford's reputation would not have been damaged.[3]

Ultimately in 2001 Ford decided to replace 13 million tires on Ford Explorers, costing the company $3 billion. Moreover, Ford CEO Jacques Nasser was fired in 2001 and replaced by Bill Ford, great-grandson of Henry Ford, the company's founder.[4]

Databases and Data Warehousing

When Herman Hollerith tabulated the answers to 240 questions for the 1890 census, the result was a database, although the term *database* was unheard of at the time. **Databases** are programs that assign multiple characteristics to data and allow users to sort the data by characteristic. Databases are the heart of information systems.

Databases can be relatively small and specialized, such as those used for accounting systems and payroll records. These databases often are not designed for sharing among a firm's management. The database users typically create computer-generated *reports* for management purposes. These reports are customized to contain only the data that management needs for decision making. The advantage of these databases is that access to them is usually restricted, so that sensitive or confidential information is available to only a limited number of people.

Data warehouses are, in essence, massive databases containing almost all of the information about a firm's operations. Chapter 17 describes how Wal-Mart manages its inventory using information about every item sold. Founder Sam Walton often said, "People think we got big by putting big stores in small towns. Really we got big by replacing inventory with information."[5] In 1999 Wal-Mart's computer system received 8.4 million updates every minute from the checkout scanners. All of this information is stored in the firm's data warehouse, which can hold up to 12 terabytes of data (more than 12,000 gigabytes). Multiple users have controlled access to both retrieving and entering data in data warehouses. Wal-Mart's customers, for example, can access the firm's online shopping site to retrieve information on items in stock. In purchasing items using the site, customers are entering data into the data warehouse.

Many other large firms in other industries use data warehouses. Package delivery firms, such as FedEx and UPS, use data warehouses that contain data about millions of packages shipped daily. Customers can access these firms' online sites to track packages and to request services. Government agencies maintain data warehouses, as do large manufacturers such as automakers. As data warehouse technology becomes more common, smaller firms will also be able to use data warehousing.

The Internet is, in essence, a type of data warehouse. Information from millions of sources is available to Internet users. Information that is publicly available on Internet websites can be retrieved. At the same time, the ability to change a website's content is controlled and in most cases limited.

databases

Computer programs that assign multiple characteristics to data and allow users to sort the data by characteristic.

data warehouses

Massive databases that contain almost all of the information about a firm's operations.

Data Mining

data mining

The process of determining the relevant factors in the accumulated data to extract the data that are important to the user.

The amount of data contained in data warehouses is overwhelming. Finding useful data is the goal of data-mining software. **Data mining** is the process of determining the relevant factors in the accumulated data to extract the data that is important to the user. Automakers use data-mining software to find patterns among car buyers. They need to know which models buyers prefer in order to tailor marketing and production decisions accordingly.

Software applications use complex decision-making processes to find and analyze data, based on the user's input. A means of data mining for information on the Internet is the search engine, such as Yahoo! and Lycos. As with the data-mining software applications, the more refined the Internet search, the more likely it is that the user will receive relevant data.

The objective of data mining is to extract patterns, trends, and rules from data warehouses to evaluate (predict or score) proposed business strategies. This, in turn, improves competitiveness and profits and helps transform business processes. Data mining is used extensively in marketing to improve customer retention; cross-selling opportunities; market, channel and pricing analysis; and customer segmentation analysis.[6]

Applications of data mining are plentiful. Credit card issuers and insurers use data mining to identify subtle patterns within thousands of customer transactions to identify fraud, often as it happens. Bell Canada uses data mining to identify patterns, group customers with similar characteristics, and create predictive target models to determine which customers should receive a particular offer for telephone service.[7] Some examples of how data mining reveals customer motives for purchasing products are provided in Management Close-Up 18.a.

Information Technology

technology

The means of transforming inputs into products.

Technology is the means of transforming inputs into products. The roots of improvements in technology began when steam power and electricity became available. Railroads were created as a result of steam power. Herman Hollerith's census tabulation system revolutionized data processing because it used electricity. Today, the term *technology* is mostly associated with computer-driven equipment and processes.

Information technology includes six basic data-processing operations: capturing, transmitting, storing, retrieving, manipulating, and displaying data. These different functions of information technology can be seen in a grocery store's customer checkout system:[8]

1. It *captures* data using the bar code.
2. It *transmits* data to a computer that looks up the item's price and description.
3. It *stores* information about the item for calculating the bill.

Data Mining Yields Valuable Customer Information

THEME: CUSTOMER FOCUS Data mining is a new technology that yields valuable and surprising information about customer habits as well as the reasons why people use certain products. Data mining is the process of conducting computer-based searches through mountains of corporate transaction data. The goal is to develop useful information about both product purchases and consumer groups. A recent increase in data warehouses, a drop in secondary storage prices, and a plethora of consumer data from the Internet have come together in a way that makes data mining a value-adding activity.

SAS Institute is one of many organizations offering advanced tools to support data-mining efforts. SAS's Enterprise Miner provides an integrated suite of data-mining tools for businesses seeking to conduct comprehensive analyses of customer data. These tools can help uncover previously unknown patterns of data that reveal customers' buying habits and provide a greater understanding of underlying motivation.

Some basic rules are useful to make sense out of the data-mining analysis.

1. Keep data close to the customer. Data directly from the customer will be more recent and of higher quality.

2. Understand your customer. The more you know about your customers, the more likely you are to determine motives for their behavior.

3. Use past behavior to predict future actions. There are various statistical techniques that can be used to project expected actions.

4. Rely on your team. Turning information into business value takes teamwork and discipline.

New insights into marketing efforts can be obtained by using data-mining tools. For example, men who are sent out to buy diapers between 6 and 8 P.M. are also likely to pick up a six-pack of beer. Analysts have also discovered that although senior citizens buy hip hop music CDs by such artists as Snoop Doggy Dogg and Limp Bizkit, an effort to sell concert tickets at retirement homes would probably fail. Instead, a targeted marketing campaign emphasizing discounted music might sell more to senior citizens on fixed incomes buying presents for their grandchildren.

Source: Adapted from Ralph M. Stair and George W. Reynolds, *Fundamentals of Information Systems*. Boston: Thompson Learning, 2001, p. 122.

---

4. It *retrieves* price and description information from the computer.

5. It *manipulates* the information when it adds up the bill.

6. It *displays* information when it shows each price it calculates and prints the receipt.

Table 18.1 defines the six functions of information technology and shows some technologies that focus on each of them.

The relationship between the technology and various processes has also changed. New processes are being developed because of available new technology, rather than the other way around, and change may be forced on a firm. IBM's decision to implement an Internet division, as discussed at the beginning of the chapter, ultimately changed the way it did business. As IBM CEO Gerstner explained,

> When you bring your company to the Web, when you truly integrate business processes to the Web, you expose—to yourself and ultimately your

TABLE 18.1

Six Functions of Information Technology

FUNCTION	DEFINITION	EXAMPLES OF DEVICES OR TECHNOLOGIES USED TO PERFORM THIS FUNCTION
Capture	Obtain a representation of information in a form permitting it to be transmitted or stored	Keyboard, bar code scanner, document scanner, sound recorder, video camera, voice recognition software
Transmit	Move information from one place to another	Broadcast radio, broadcast television, via regional transmitters, cable TV, satellite broadcasts, telephone networks, data transmission networks, for moving business data, fiber optic cable, fax machine, electronic mail, voice mail, Internet
Store	Move information to a specific place for later retrieval	Paper, computer tape, floppy disk, hard disk, optical disk, CD-ROM, flash memory
Retrieve	Find the specific information that is currently needed	Paper, computer tape, floppy disk, hard disk, optical disk, CD-ROM, flash memory
Manipulate	Create new information from existing information through summarizing, sorting, rearranging, reformatting, or other types of calculations	Computer (plus software)
Display	Show information to a person	Laser printer, computer screen

Source: Adapted from S. Alter, *Information Systems: Foundation of E-Business,* 4th ed. Upper Saddle River, NJ: Prentice Hall, 2002, p. 23.

customers—all of the inefficiency that comes from silos or decentralized organizations. Banks are a great example: mortgage departments, credit-card departments, home-loan departments. Now, when a customer comes to you on the Web, they're expecting to be able to move across those departments. They're expecting to see a common look and feel. They don't want to see pricing presented in different ways. They don't want to be bounced from department to department.[9]

Technology has improved operations management, including productivity, efficiency, and customer responsiveness. A firm's information technology may incorporate its operations technology. Information technology includes equipment, networks, and software.

Managers of information systems and information technology need to establish policies for use of the firm's information technology. Misguided employee use can lead to hardware and software damage. Employee use of computers for unethical or illegal purposes puts the firm at risk, as can damaging e-mail. Manager's Notes 18.1 lists some general guidelines.

Equipment

Computer-based information technology began with the advent of mainframe computers in the 1950s. These machines allowed industry to automate information storage and retrieval for the first time. By 1964 individual workstations were linked to a firm's mainframe, allowing individuals to share information stored on the mainframe. The development of floppy disks in 1971 allowed users to share information easily with each other. In the early 1980s stand-alone personal computers were introduced to business. Soon these computers were being linked together within a firm as a *local-area network (LAN)* in which users could share information among themselves without using a mainframe. Network technology converts data to on or off signals, in contrast to analog technology, which sends signals in virtually infinite increments. *Servers* were designed to store information for users linked to them, which allowed the development of data warehouses. The Internet provided a means for computers to connect outside a LAN using telephone lines.

As information became more easily shared, the equipment became more powerful. Microprocessors, such as Intel's Pentium and Apple's G4, are able to make complex calculations almost instantaneously. Internet connections moved beyond standard telephone lines to broadband and DSL, allowing data to be transmitted even more quickly.

Since the Apple II ignited the personal computer revolution in the 1970s, computing power has doubled approximately every 18 months or less. The Power Mac G4 pictured here is Apple Computer's latest offering.

Computers no longer have to have a physical connection to a network. Wireless networking allows users to access and provide information using the same technology as cellular and digital telephones. A signal is sent to a satellite or central location and then bounced to its destination. Wireless systems currently have some drawbacks, which no doubt will soon be resolved. Currently, if a wireless data transmission signal is lost even momentarily, the transmission ends and incomplete data may have been transmitted. Security and privacy of information transmitted using wireless technology may also be compromised.

Computer Networks

As noted earlier, a LAN is a type of computer network. Other types of networks employed by firms include the Internet, extranets, and intranets. Firms use networks in many ways, including for e-business. **E-business,** also called e-commerce, is the process of conducting business transactions using online resources.

Information posted on networks is a form of intellectual property and can be covered under copyright law. A link to the firm's copyright statement must be provided on every screen of the site. Individuals should be cautious about posting information from other sources covered by copyright. Making this type of information generally available without permission can leave a firm liable to lawsuits and damages.

THE INTERNET The Internet and the World Wide Web (one of the services on the Internet) revolutionized information sharing. For the first time, data could be shared in real time as text, voice, graphics, and video among anyone with access to the Internet. The **Internet** is a network of networks, connecting hundreds of thousands of corporate, educational,

e-business

The process of conducting business transactions using online resources; also called *e-commerce*.

Internet

A computer network that is a network of networks, connecting hundreds of thousands of corporate, educational, and research computer networks around the world.

An example of an extranet.

and research sites around the world. The Internet features several communication and information sharing capabilities:

- Electronic mail (e-mail) provides for communication of text messages and file attachments between computers.

- Telnet enables users to connect to other computers and interact with them as if the originating computers were directly connected to the remote computers.

- File-transfer protocol (FTP) sites are intermediate sites that are used to move files and data from one computer to another.

- The World Wide Web (the Web) employs the Internet's standards and protocols to allow users to get and contribute text, documents, images, and many other things.

EXTRANETS   When a company is able to link employees, suppliers, customers, and other key business partners in an electronic online environment for business communications, an **extranet,** or wide-area network, is created.[10] This network allows a firm's customers and suppliers to connect, through the Internet, to certain internal computer-based systems. Some extranets cannot be accessed by the general public. Access to these sites may be controlled by the firm by requiring registration or by issuing user names and passwords.

extranets

Also called *wide-area networks*, networks that link a company's employees, suppliers, customers, and other key business partners in an electronic online environment for business communications.

INTRANETS Private or semiprivate internal networks are called **intranets.** Unlike LANs, intranets use the infrastructure and standards of the Internet and the Web. An intranet site is typically a website with areas within it for employee use.

An intranet allows an organization's employees to communicate with each other and to access company information and databases using desktop or laptop computers. Access to intranets typically is limited to a firm's employees, and access to restricted data can further be limited to certain employees.[11] One of the advantages of an intranet is that employees can work at remote locations and still be connected to the firm.

Companies use intranets for many purposes. Managers must consider several factors before designing and implementing an intranet, as shown in Skills for Managing 18.2.

When using intranets or extranets the computer department should be careful about allowing access to sensitive information. Network security is discussed later in this chapter. Information thieves can find other ways to access a firm's computer, as described in Management Close-Up 18.b.

Software

Software developments have profound implications for firms. Time and cost savings from implementing software that can drive processes have enabled employees to work more efficiently. Labor can sometimes be replaced by technology, freeing employees to focus on more challenging tasks. Information technology advances have also eliminated many positions and squeezed middle managers out of many organizations. Legal software, for example, is used to create standard contracts, wills, trusts, incorporations, and partnerships and perform other routine activities. Accounting and tax software are used for routine functions that had been performed by accountants. Medical software transforms information about symptoms and test results into a possible diagnosis for a doctor to consider. Computer-aided design (CAD) software can be used to graphically display and manipulate a product or component, making manual drafting virtually obsolete. New software affects almost every position within a firm.[12]

Operating system software tells the computer hardware how to run. *Applications* software is developed for a specific task. *Artificial intelligence (AI)* software can perform tasks such as searching through data and e-mail. Firms also use *speech recognition* software, which allows customers to speak numbers when placing orders over the telephone.

Almost every firm has software for accounting and word processing. The functions of each type, although specialized, are sometimes usable in other applications; a document created in an accounting program, for example, can often be inserted within a word processing document. Computer experts have also been able to integrate software systems so that data generated by one area of the firm can be linked to other areas,

BUILDING AN INTRANET

Form groups of four to five students. Each group will choose a medium-sized firm and design an intranet for the firm. Prepare a report for the firm's board of directors with a plan for the intranet, covering the following steps:

1. Define the firm's needs.

   a. How will you determine the users? What departments need access to the intranet? What individuals in those departments would need access?

   b. What content will be shared?

   c. How is the information going to be accessed and used?

2. Research some programs that firms use for Web development and recommend an intranet program.

   a. Do you need a flexible program?

   b. Is a standard program that has been in existence appropriate or should a new program be used?

   c. Can remote users easily access the program with standard computers?

3. Plan for testing the program and how you will measure the result.

   a. Who will be involved in the testing?

   b. What kind of feedback do you need from the testers?

   c. How will you incorporate the results into the program?

4. Prepare for the implementation.

   a. What information will you supply in advance of the implementation?

   b. How will you schedule the implementation?

   c. What kind of training will be necessary and who will provide it?

5. Follow up the ongoing use of the intranet.

   a. How will you measure the use of the system— who is using it and what information are they accessing?

   b. How will you provide information to different levels of user about the success of the intranet?

   c. How will you approach the need to update the intranet in terms of content and structure?

Each group will present its plan to the class, which will evaluate the plan.

Group Evaluation

1. Would access to the intranet allow information to fall into the hands of competitors? Can it be amended by users who might have information to contribute?

2. Does the group's intranet program allow for the site to be updated as technology changes?

3. Did the testing consider all potential users or just the users identified in step 1? Did the group get information about frequency of use, speed of access, appropriateness of content? Did the group plan to get all feedback before changing the program?

4. Did the group plan to send out regular reports about the intranet's implementation? How early would this information begin? Was an effort planned to get respected staff members to "buy into" the program? Did the group consider how to include updating information in the program's implementation?

5. Did the group monitor frequency of use? Did it plan to measure the type of information that is being accessed and how often? Did it plan for changing access based on its findings?

Source: Intranet Design Magazine, March 21, 2001, http://idm.internet.com.

Information Theft

THEME: ETHICS
The Internet has made information available to the public but it has also provided information thieves access to high-level material. In September 2000, Qualcomm's founder and CEO Irwin Jacobs gave a talk on the wireless universe to journalists at a meeting in California. He illustrated his speech with a PowerPoint presentation from his laptop computer. Afterwards, he left the computer on the podium and moved several feet away to talk with a group of people. During that short discussion, his computer was taken.

Local police viewed the theft of the $4,000 computer as a commonplace occurrence, but the potential cost to the firm was much higher. The information stored on the computer had been saved at the firm's headquarters, but that fact brought little relief to the firm. The information on the hard drive could have been valuable to foreign governments, since Qualcomm was then negotiating to provide service to the People's Republic of China. Even more worrisome, however, was the possibility that other parties would be able to use information stored on the computer to figure out Jacobs's password, thus allowing access to the firm's main computers. Whether that happened may never be known.

It's bad enough, said Graham Titterington, senior analyst for technology consultants Ovum Ltd. in London, that senior executives carry sensitive information on a laptop, but if that laptop enables others to break into the firm's main computers, "that's the biggest possible security hole in the company's fence."

Sources: Peter Key, "Media Confab Includes Act of Brazen Thievery," *Philadelphia Business Journal*, September 29, 2000; Steve Barth, "Post-Industrial Espionage," *Knowledge Management Magazine*, March 2001, www.kmmag.com.

---

such as the operations management functions described in Chapter 17 and Wal-Mart's data warehouses.

One form of integrated software has been implemented by many large firms. **Enterprise resource planning (ERP) software** combines all of a firm's computerized functions into a single, integrated software program that runs off a single database. This allows various departments to easily share information and communicate with each other. ERP combined with the Internet is the basis of these firms' e-business. Large manufacturing firms were the original target market for ERP. Recently other types of organizations have implemented it as well.

Company leaders decide to implement ERP for three main reasons:

- To integrate financial data by providing one set of numbers for the company's finance department, sales department, and individual business units.

- To standardize manufacturing processes, especially so that a firm with multiple business units can save time, increase productivity, and reduce staff.

- To standardize human resources information with a unified, simple method for tracking employee time and communicating about benefits and services.

The main suppliers of ERP software and support are Baan, People-Soft, and SAP. The software differs, but the processes share basic character-

---

enterprise resource planning (ERP) software

A computer program that combines all of a firm's computerized functions into a single, integrated software program that runs off a single database, allowing various departments to easily share information and communicate with each other.

istics. For example, the typical method for processing an order before a firm implements ERP involves several steps: (1) the customer sends in the order; (2) the customer service representative sends the order to the accounting department, which checks the customer's credit history and sends the order to the production floor; (3) the production floor sends the order to the inventory department, which supplies the inventory (and may need to order it) back to the production floor; (4) after production is complete, the order is sent to the shipping department, which schedules the shipment and sends the order to the customer and the paperwork to the accounting department for billing. If the customer has questions about the order at any time, he or she contacts the customer service representative, who may need to go through several layers to find out what happened to the order.

After implementing ERP, the company's order process is quite different, as the following typical path shows. The customer service representative may still take the order, or the order may be made online by the customer, who can then immediately see when the order will be filled and how much it will cost. The customer service representative will immediately be able to see the customer's credit rating and order history, the company's inventory levels, and the shipping dock's trucking schedule. Once the order is put into the system, everyone else in the company can see the new order. When one department finishes with the order it is automatically routed via the ERP system to the next department. To find out where the order is at any point, the customer can log into the ERP system and track it down. The order process moves through the organization, resulting in orders being delivered faster and with fewer errors. Other major business processes, such as employee benefits or financial reporting, are also performed with ERP software, because the data that support them are now available (for example, the number of hours spent by an employee on a particular project is in the database, allowing payroll functions to be integrated).

Chapter 17 describes how process reengineering and ERP are used for quality management. As with process reengineering, adopting ERP programs requires a major commitment by the firm, from the CEO down. All of the firm's processes are integrated at one time, which means changing how employees work. Planning and training can take one to three years before an ERP program is implemented. The cost of ERP is substantial—one survey showed the average total cost of implementing it at $15 million—and the cost and time savings it can provide may not be apparent immediately.

Not all implementations of ERP are successful, as illustrated in Management Close-Up 18.c. FoxMeyer's experience with ERP, which was relatively new in 1994, shows that company leaders should proceed with caution in implementing software changes. Some software analysts believe that niche vendors of Web applications will take over ERP's e-commerce functions, and that it will be possible to implement some of ERP's functions without needing to revamp the entire operation.

Did ERP Sink FoxMeyer?

THEME: DEALING WITH CHANGE The FoxMeyer Corporation was one of the largest U.S. wholesale drug distribution companies, with more than $5 billion in annual revenues, when it decided in 1994 to implement SAP's ERP system to improve its productivity. FoxMeyer paid Arthur Andersen, the accounting and consulting firm, $30 million to oversee the project.

By 1997, after two and a half years of effort and an additional $100 million investment in the project, the company could process only 2.4 percent of the overnight orders that it previously had been able to process—and even those had information errors. The computer system would shut down constantly for anywhere from a few minutes to several hours at a time. Also, the equipment froze frequently, and even when the system was running, it was slow.

Having retooled and integrated all of its central business functions from inventory management to accounts processing, FoxMeyer was crippled. The company fell into bankruptcy and was acquired for a mere $80 million. Its trustees are blaming the ERP implementation for its business failure and have filed a combined $100 million in lawsuits against the system suppliers and Andersen Consulting. The firm charges that Accenture had billed itself as the world's leading installer of SAP but "delivered only ruin." (Andersen Consulting has recently changed its name to Accenture.)

One of FoxMeyer's trustees claims that Accenture used the firm as a "guinea pig" for training its own employees in SAP. According to the lawsuit, Accenture consultants realized that SAP's systems could not handle the job soon after they started work, but instead of alerting FoxMeyer, moved its implementation up to protect its fees. A hearing on the lawsuit is pending.

Sources: Scott Buckhout, Edward Frey, and Joseph Nemec Jr., "Making ERP Succeed: Turning Fear into Promise," *Strategy and Business*, Second Quarter, 1999, www.strategy-business.com; Peg Brickley, "Defunct Outfit Blames IT Firm," *Philadelphia Business Journal*, November 13, 1998.

Information Ethics and Security

There are many types of temptation when computer networks are being utilized. Each computer system entails some management issues regarding ethics and security.

Computer Ethics

computer ethics
The analysis of the nature and social impact of computer technology and the development of policies for its appropriate use.

Management needs to be concerned about ethical uses of information. **Computer ethics** is the analysis of the nature and social impact of computer technology and the development of policies for its appropriate use.[13] Use of computers has created some unique problems that foster the need for development of ethics policies:

- Computer-generated errors are unlike human error.
- Computers are able to communicate over great distances at low cost.
- Computers can store, copy, erase, retrieve, transmit, and manipulate huge amounts of information quickly and cheaply.

- Computers can depersonalize originators, users, and subjects of programs and data.
- Computers can use data created for one purpose for another purpose for long periods of time.[14]

An emerging ethical issue is employee use of computers for personal business or entertainment while on company time. Employees who browse the Internet and use it to play video games or engage in chat room activities with virtual friends are stealing work time from their employers. The computer should only be a tool for work activities. Further, employees who use company-owned computers (which are more likely to have broadband connections) to exchange personal music or video files with friends waste valuable storage space on music and video files that gobble up large chunks of computer memory. This slows the speed of the computer system to respond to the commands of users who are trying to serve customers. Thus, unrestricted employee use of a company's computer system could reduce the quality of services provided to customers, with negative implications to the bottom line.

While many company leaders take a flexible approach based on trust in regard to permitting employees to use the computer for nonwork interests, others are more restrictive. It is possible to monitor employee use of computers and sanction those who violate policies limiting the nonwork use of the computer. Companies that restrict the use of the computer to work activities should notify employees in advance. Workers should understand how the policy works and how it is enforced. Employers who monitor employee computer use without notifying employees in advance risk creating a less trusting work environment, which could in turn negatively affect morale.

Figure 18.1 lists 10 commandments of computer ethics that provide guidance in ethical situations.

Security

Another primary consideration in managing information systems and information technology is information security. While the Internet makes information readily available, it may also allow unwanted parties a gateway to the firm. Companies can implement information security in several ways.

User names and passwords are one way to restrict access to information on a network. Sensitive or financial information transmitted using networks can be *encrypted,* using software that scrambles the data before it is sent and then unscrambles it when it is received. Companies also use firewalls to protect sensitive or proprietary information available on a network. A **firewall** is a combination of computer hardware and software that controls access to and transmission of data contained in a network.[15]

firewall

A combination of computer hardware and software that controls access to and transmission of data and information contained in a network.

FIGURE 18.1

Ten Commandments for
Computer Ethics

Source: Copyright © 1991
Computer Ethics Institute. Author
Dr. Ramon C. Barquin.

Ten Commandments for Computer Ethics

1. Thou shalt not use a computer to harm other people.

2. Thou shalt not interfere with other people's computer work.

3. Thou shalt not snoop around in other people's files.

4. Thou shalt not use a computer to steal.

5. Thou shalt not use a computer to bear false witness.

6. Thou shalt not use or copy software for which you have not paid.

7. Thou shalt not use other people's computer resources without authorization.

8. Thou shalt not appropriate other people's intellectual output.

9. Thou shalt think about the social consequences of the program you write.

10. Thou shalt use a computer in ways that show consideration and respect.

Information systems are also at risk for computer viruses. The computer team should establish policies regarding downloading documents and other files from networks or e-mails. They should also provide tools for detecting and eliminating viruses.

Company leaders must be aware that almost any security system can be breached. New viruses are created and disseminated without warning. Security measures designed to prevent unauthorized access are not perfect. Even Microsoft periodically finds that hackers have broken into its systems.[16] Managers who are in charge of information systems that include sensitive data must be extremely vigilant in changing and updating security measures as often as is practical.

Sometimes it is employees, not hackers, who are at fault for compromising the security of sensitive information. For example, medical information covering a person's health history and use of pharmaceutical products is regulated by the Health Insurance Portability and Accountability Act (HIPPA), which requires that health care institutions, pharmaceuticals firms, and insurers use secure computer systems to protect the accessibility to health information. In a recent case, Eli Lilly, a drug maker, was accused of violating customer privacy when employees accidentally revealed the e-mail addresses of 669 patients who were taking the antidepressant Prozac. The company settled out of court with the Federal Trade Commission and agreed to improve its security procedures.[17] In other cases, security systems are breached because passwords can be

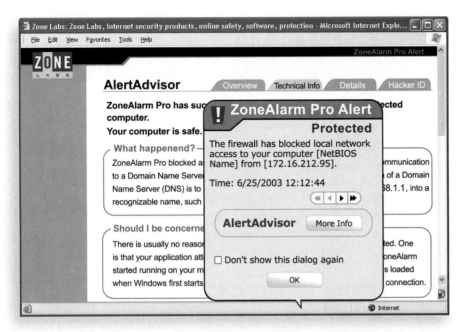

Firewalls prevent unregistered users from accessing computer files. They may also advise when information being transmitted may be accessible by other parties.

easily guessed or tricked out of employees. In 2002, an associate dean at Princeton University was removed from his post after admitting he used easily guessed passwords to access a student admissions site set up by Yale University. A survey of 500 corporations taken that year by the Computer Security Institute revealed that 80 percent of the companies reported that they had been broken into, resulting in combined losses of $455 million.[18] Manager's Notes 18.2 shows some points to consider in order to create a more secure computer system.

Information Systems

Information systems combine computers and other hardware, software such as data-mining tools, and human resources to manipulate data into usable information. Newer systems use computers with so-called business intelligence to analyze information.[19] Several types of information systems are used in firms.

Operations Information Systems

An operations information system maintains records and supports operations and decisions at a nonstrategic level. These systems may actually be part of a firm's management information system, or they may stand alone.

Process control systems are used to monitor and run machinery and other equipment. A process control system can warn an operator that a

process control systems

An operations information system that monitors and runs machinery and other equipment.

Ways to Protect Computer Security

Maintaining effective computer security includes quality technology and carefully crafted management policies. Here are some key elements to consider:

- **Secure the perimeter.** Build a secure perimeter around your company's computers by installing three components: a firewall, virtual private network (VPN) software for remote access, and virus detectors on your mail server. Mail should be the only non-VPN traffic that is allowed to cross the perimeter inbound (firewall settings allow you to do this).

- **Lock down computers.** Install antivirus and personal firewall software on all laptops, desktops, and servers. These are inexpensive and are available at most computer stores. Turn off unneeded functionality on all machines (a computer security service provider can do this).

- **Communicate and enforce policies.** Make sure that everyone in the company is aware that they should not run unapproved network applications: P2P file sharing (for example, many popular music-sharing services), instant messaging, and the like. Have the information technology (IT) staff monitor security bulletins from vendors for the products you are using. Finally, have a checklist ready so that when employees leave, the IT staff can immediately deactivate their passwords and VPN access.

Source: Adapted from R. D. Austin and C. A. Darby, "The Myth of Secure Computing," *Harvard Business Review,* June 2003, p. 124.

---

office automation systems

An operations information system used to maintain and publish information for an organization.

transaction-processing systems

An operations information system used to maintain data about transactions, such as inventory, sales, and purchase of supplies.

expert system

An advanced information system that uses human knowledge captured in a computer to solve problems that normally require human expertise.

machine is overheating, for example, or can control the speed of a conveyor belt. **Office automation systems** are used to maintain and publish information for an organization. For example, e-mail and other electronic communication systems can disseminate information throughout the firm, to a company's customers, and to the public.

Transaction-processing systems are used to maintain data about transactions, such as inventory, sales, and purchase of supplies. Information from transaction-processing systems can be used for billing customers and managing a firm's payroll. Many supermarkets have transaction-processing systems connected to cash registers. These systems record data about items sold and payments received. Data from transaction-processing systems can be used in making management decisions.

Other Types of Information Systems

Besides operations information systems and management information systems, some advanced information systems are being developed. Expert systems are the most sophisticated information systems available. An **expert system** uses human knowledge captured in a computer to solve problems that normally require human expertise. Expert systems are a variant of artificial intelligence. They take specialized knowledge about a particular problem, apply qualitative reasoning, explain the solution, and learn from the experience.[20]

Neural network systems are another type of information system. This computer software imitates brain cells and the systems can distinguish patterns and trends by correlating hundreds of variables. They can perform many operations simultaneously, recognizing patterns, making associations, generalizing about problems they haven't seen before, and learning through experience.

Management Information Systems

Not all information systems are management information systems. A **management information system (MIS)** is an information system that provides information to managers to help make decisions. Although MIS programs traditionally have supported strategic management, all types of management use them today. An operations manager needs data about past operations to compare against present results to determine if business processes can be improved. Marketing managers need information to make decisions about pricing, distribution channels, and promotions.

> **management information system (MIS)**
>
> An information system (MIS) that provides information to managers to use in making decisions.

Types of Management Information Systems

There are several types of MIS available in business today. *Information reporting systems* provide specific types of information for making structured decisions. *Decision support systems* give users decision models to manipulate data to project possible alternative outcomes to decisions. *Group decision support systems* allow members of a group to interact with each other using computers to share information and solutions.

Executive information systems provide information to facilitate strategic decision making. These systems provide software that analyzes large amounts of data to clearly present timely information. They typically provide quick access to both internal and external sources of information.

A *human resource information system* (HRIS) is designed to collect, store, analyze, and retrieve data concerning an organization's human resources. Information that is collected and stored in the HRIS may include an employee's current rate of pay, pay history at the organization, the current status of the employee's benefits eligibility and usage, as well as a skills inventory that maintains records of the skills the employee has mastered. These can all be added to a performance management record that keeps a running account of the history of each employee's performance reviews while at the organization. It is important to protect the integrity and security of the HRIS, so that unauthorized users cannot gain access to sensitive employee data.

Effect of Management Information Systems on the Firm

Advances in MIS and technology continue to have profound effects on organizations and managers in organizations. Information technology is helping managers to coordinate and control the activities of their organizations, as well as helping them to make better decisions.

Modern computer-based information systems have become central components of many organizations' structures. Effective information systems are one source of a competitive advantage.

ORGANIZATIONAL STRUCTURE   The development of computer-based information systems presents alternatives to the traditional vertical organizational hierarchy in existence since the 1850s.[21] By providing managers with high-quality, timely, relevant, and relatively complete information, management information systems have reduced the need for tall management hierarchies. **Horizontal information flows** are now viable, supplanting the flow of information from one department up through management layers and then back down to another department through other layers. The rapid development of mainframe–server–client computing configuration and organizationwide computer networks, including e-mail systems, file sharing, and intranets makes this possible. Management decisions can be reached with fewer layers of staff, as departments are now able to share information directly with each other.

Advanced information systems can also reduce the number of employees needed to perform many organizational activities. Managers can use this breakdown of barriers between departments to increase productivity and improve performance by employees.

COMPETITIVE ADVANTAGE   The goal of increasing a competitive advantage has been behind the development and use of management information systems in many companies. With improved decision making based on the information available through a management information system, a manager can help the organization enhance its competitive position. The flattened organizational structure also increases an organization's efficiency and therefore its competitive advantage.

Computer networks also help marketing departments to become more responsive to customers. Managers are using management information systems to improve customer service by identifying areas where customer service can be personalized and where customer product support can be improved. Firms can also customize product offerings without incurring any extra costs.

Another competitive advantage area that MIS enhances is market entry. Using an MIS, a manager can identify markets that previously had been perceived as unapproachable. The firm's information technology also enables the firm to enter into joint ventures, partnerships, and strategic alliances; use new distribution channels; and sell goods globally.

One of the most significant sources of a competitive advantage has been the addition of **e-commerce** to a company's operations. E-commerce combines the Internet with management information systems and transaction-processing systems to create powerful new ways of doing business. The result is a new competitive advantage that emerges from generating value for the customer. E-commerce involves any business transaction executed electronically by parties such as companies (*business-to-business*) and companies and consumers (*business-to-consumer*).[22] Here are a few examples of how e-commerce created a competitive advantage.

e-commerce

Any business transaction executed electronically by companies or consumers.

- Amazon.com, an electronic retailer of books, applied business-to-consumer e-commerce to sell books electronically over the Internet directly to customers. Amazon's website offers an electronic list of 3 million books, 20 times larger than that of the largest bricks-and-mortar retail store. The site features book reviews, customized book recommendations, and direct shipping of books to the customer's home. These value-enhanced customer services were not provided by the traditional book-retailing outlets.[23]

- Cisco Systems, the maker of Internet routers and other telecommunications equipment, saved $350 million in paperwork and transaction costs in the first year of its business-to-business e-commerce operation. Cisco Systems put its procurement operation online. This cut purchase order fulfillment times in half and produced dramatic savings in material and labor costs.[24]

Implementing Management Information Systems

Before implementing a management information system, managers need to consider the organization's principal goals and what types of information managers need to be able to measure how well they are moving toward achieving those goals. Managers also need to investigate what sources of information might be available to measure and improve the firm's efficiency, quality, innovation, and responsiveness to customers.

The firm's current MIS should be evaluated to determine the accuracy, reliability, timeliness, and relevance of the information provided. Also, the current system should be compared to the firm's competitors and others in the industry.

Technological Change

After determining that a change in the firm's MIS is warranted, managers need to convince employees to support the change by demonstrating how it will benefit them. Formal training programs and appropriate backup support must be incorporated in advance of the system's implementation. Employees at all levels should be involved in a continuing discussion of how best to exploit information technology to create a competitive advantage.

Managers also need to take other factors into account. Consistent technological standards should be used so that the system is accessible to various types of computer operating systems. Making the technology more user-friendly, especially to managers who have little or no prior computer experience, lessens resistance to the new MIS. Remember, some managers may perceive the new MIS as a threat to their authority and job security. The potential breakdown of department barriers by a new MIS may reduce managers' responsibility. Some may be tempted to thwart it by diverting resources from the project, working against the goals of the project, slowing its momentum, and neglecting it.

Finally, managers who use MIS should carefully consider the human element. Quantifiable information, as provided by an MIS, is not the only information involved in the firm's success. Electronic communication should supplement—not replace—face-to-face interactions. It is important to create policies and procedures that ensure continuing interaction among users of the firm's information systems.

Seven factors influence the successful implementation of information systems, as listed in Table 18.2.

TABLE 18.2

Factors for Successful MIS Implementation

1. *User involvement.* Involve users in the design process. They can create an accurate picture of current work flows, costs, and time requirements for various functions as well as pinpointing potential problems. They will also understand why changes are being made and can prepare for them.
2. *Management support.* Strong visible support from higher management is essential.
3. *Time and cost evaluations.* Prepare realistic evaluations of the time and cost of implementing the system and weigh them against not implementing it.
4. *Phased implementation.* Introduce the system in gradual phases, which will allow problems that arise to be resolved before they affect later phases. Train employees in the new system before they begin using it. This training will ensure that they will have time to adjust to it and will reduce their resistance to the change.
5. *Thorough testing.* Test the hardware and software in terms of individual modules, sets of modules as the system is assembled, and the entire system before it becomes fully operational. Test for likely errors and try to anticipate unlikely errors. Involve users in the debugging process.
6. *Training and documentation.* Provide hands-on training and complete procedural documentation for the users so that they can understand the limitations and capabilities of the system.
7. *System backup.* Backup procedures and access to a backup computer system will enable employees to continue working while problems are evaluated and solved.

APPLICATIONS: MANAGEMENT IS EVERYONE'S BUSINESS

Applications for the Manager   The difficult challenges of managing information technology make it tempting for a manager to hand the job over to someone else in an outsourcing arrangement. In fact, outsourcing the information technology (IT) function to companies such as Accenture, IBM, or EDS is a growing business. Senior managers negotiate contracts with these IT service providers to run their entire IT functions. At a minimum, these providers are often able to provide IT capabilities for a lower cost and with fewer glitches than companies were able to provide for themselves.

The outcomes from these outsourcing relationships have, in many cases, resulted in dissatisfaction. This may occur especially when a company's business needs change. Service providers with standard packages of services may offer IT capabilities that are not flexible enough to meet changing requirements. They are often not responsive to problems as they arise. In addition, the relationship with the IT service provider often requires substantial investments of money and time, which entrenches the supplier, making it difficult to exit this relationship. The company becomes vulnerable if the service provider fails to meet its contractual obligations. Therefore, managers should analyze very carefully both the pros and cons before agreeing to enter an IT outsourcing relationship. The key is to be aware of the trade-offs between owning the IT function or giving up control of it to an outside party.[25]

Applications for Managing Teams   IT has given teams powerful new tools to collaborate with each other on projects even when team members are physically separated from each other. *Groupware* software supports collaborative efforts among group members, such as scheduling meetings, holding meetings, collaborating on projects, and sharing documents. This means teams can be more productive with less downtime despite conflicting demands placed on each team member's work schedule to work on other tasks.

Applications for Individuals   Individual employees in companies use IT services daily to communicate with e-mail and to use business applications software such as word processing, graphics, and spreadsheet programs to perform their work assignments. They also browse the Internet to search for information and perform tasks such as purchasing an airline ticket for business travel. These business applications tools are in a continuous state of change as more functions are added to the software. For the individual, this requires a constant updating of personal computer skills to master the upgraded versions of the software and to learn new software applications that are adopted by the company. Given such a dynamic work environment, it is an excellent idea to take some time to cultivate a constructive work relationship with the IT person who serves as a liaison with your department. This relationship could be critical for you to obtain responsive support when there is a computer network malfunction that affects your ability to access the computer software needed to complete an important task. By managing your relationship with the IT person, this individual will understand your computing needs and your work priorities. You are more likely to get better service than if you neglect forming a relationship with the IT person and simply expect service to be magically delivered to you instantly every time the computer system is malfunctioning.

After the introductory vignette at the beginning of the chapter we presented some critical thinking questions related to understanding how IBM uses information technology to improve business processes and cost effectiveness. Now that you have had the opportunity to learn about managing information systems in the chapter, examine again the questions that were raised in the vignette. First, IBM applied its data-mining software to a data warehouse it collected, which is a huge database that includes data on every component IBM uses in its machines as well as data from all 12,000 suppliers that indicate prices for their own materials they use to make components. The data-mining software sorts through the database and identifies patterns, trends, and relationships from the data that suggest ways to improve and transform business processes. Data analysts may discover that the same component is used in several different products, qualifying for a volume discount. IBM can then use its massive buying power to negotiate lower prices from the supplier of the component to other IBM suppliers. This, in turn, results in cost savings for IBM.

IBM applied technology on the Internet as a means to develop a business-to-business e-commerce approach to improve the efficiency of the company's inventory control system. The supply inventory at IBM previously was operated on a manual basis with an exchange of paper documents that would be sent and filed for supplies as they were needed. Using this approach forced IBM to maintain large inventories of supplies to cover for time lags between the time when new supplies were ordered and when they were delivered. Under the new inventory control system using the Internet and order-fulfillment software, expert systems embedded in the software determine when the inventory of each component will be exhausted and automatically order new components in advance of when they are needed so as to arrive on a just-in-time basis. By automating the purchasing process, leaner inventories can be maintained. As a result, IBM needs less capital for inventories, and the capital that is freed up can be used for more productive investments.

SUMMARY

Information systems analyze data to create information. **Data** are raw facts that are useful on a rudimentary level. **Information** is created by gathering and analyzing different types of data to perceive patterns and relationships. Information systems help transform data into information for many purposes, including operations, communications, and management.

Databases are computer software programs that are used to store and manipulate data. **Data warehouses** are enormous databases that hold all of a firm's data. Firms use **data mining** to extract data stored in data warehouses. Data-mining programs can be used to detect patterns and relationships using complex decision-making processes. Internet search engines employ a low-level form of data mining to find data from websites.

For information to be useful, it must be of high quality, timely, relevant, and comprehensive. Information that does not meet these criteria is less useful at best and may lead to poor decisions.

Information systems are supported by information technology. Technology has come to mean computer-driven equipment and processes. Information technology includes equipment, networks, and software. As information technology develops, it may drive changes in business processes, rather than the other way around.

The use of computer-based information technology in business began in the 1950s with mainframe computers; during the 1980s stand-alone personal computers became the standard business tool. These machines were first linked together to allow efficient sharing of information. Networks, developed to allow computers to link with each other and with central computer servers, include **local-area networks, intranets,** and **extranets.** The **Internet** is another type of network that links networks together.

Businesses use operating system software, applications software, artificial intelligence (AI) software, and operations management software. **Enterprise resource planning (ERP)** software combines all of the firm's computerized functions into a single, integrated program that runs from a single database.

Managers must also consider information **ethics** and security in their information systems. Computer ethics is the analysis of the impact of computer technology on society and developing policies for its appropriate use. Because a firm's information systems are vulnerable to unauthorized access, managers must also be vigilant in protecting the firm's sensitive information.

Information systems combine computers and other hardware, software, and human resources to manipulate data. A firm may use operations information systems, transaction-processing systems, expert systems, and neural network systems. A **management information system (MIS)** is a specialized information system that provides information to managers to use in making decisions. The development of management information systems has affected organizational hierarchies. The layers of middle management staff can be reduced, giving the firm a competitive advantage in becoming more efficient; the firm can be more responsive to its customers; and managers can use the MIS to identify and refine markets for the firm's product.

1. How do data affect information? What steps would you take to ensure that available data meet the major criteria for useful information (high quality, timeliness, relevance, and comprehensiveness)?

2. How do databases differ from data warehouses? Why would a firm choose to maintain databases instead of a data warehouse?

3. What factors do you think a firm would have considered in the early 1980s in deciding whether to provide mainframe computer terminals or to provide stand-alone personal computers for its employees to use?

4. What type of network would you recommend for a small manufacturing business with nationally based representatives and customers? What would you recommend for a retail operation with a single large store? Why?

5. Why is an enterprise resource planning system most appropriate for a manufacturing firm? Would you try to incorporate existing business processes into an ERP system, or would you suggest changing the processes? What benefits and disadvantages do you see in each alternative? Explain.

6. Do you think that computer ethics issues, such as protecting individuals' privacy, are important? Should computer network users expect that their information will be protected? Explain your answers.

7. How should a company balance the benefits of making its information accessible to customers and suppliers against the drawback of unauthorized users possibly gaining access to it? Do you think firms can be overly cautious about protecting information? Explain.

8. Why do strategic managers need different types of information systems than other managers? Why would strategic managers need to meet with others, face to face, if they can get information electronically?

Who Wants to Pretend to Be a Millionaire?

Identity theft has been a federal crime since 1998. 2,000 complaints are made to the Federal Trade Commission each week. In early spring 2001, a New York restaurant busboy took the concept of identity theft to a new level. Abraham Adballah, 32, was charged with accomplice Michael Pugliese in a scheme to steal millions from such figures as Steven Spielberg, Martha Stewart, Oprah Winfrey, and George Lucas—not at gunpoint, not with sophisticated computer skills, but with a library computer and cell phones.

Abdallah, a high school dropout with four prior arrests, used *Forbes* magazine's list of the 400 richest people in the United States to identify targets. He apparently was able to get information about the private finances of more than half of them. When police arrested him, they found a copy of the magazine with his targets' home addresses, bank account numbers, account balances, and even their mothers' maiden names, often used as account passwords or for identity verification, written in the margins. He also had credit card information on more than 500 people across the country.

Using computers at a library, Web-enabled cell phones, and virtual voicemail, he duped major credit reporting companies such as Equifax into providing detailed credit reports on his victims. With this information, he gained access to credit cards and accounts at brokerage houses such as Goldman Sachs, Bear Stearns, and Merrill Lynch. Soon he was forging bank stationery, deploying multiple messengers to escape detection, and running around with a credit card in Steven Spielberg's name. When Merrill Lynch executives got an e-mail request to transfer $10 million from one account to an account in Australia, they contacted their client because the transfer was for more than was available. When the executives found that the client had not made the requests, it looked at the accounts of other well-known clients, found similar requests, and contacted police.

The Internet has made identity theft, from stealing others' credit card numbers to creating new identities, much easier than ever before. Websites sell Social Security numbers, addresses, birthdays, and other personal data that will then allow someone to obtain another person's driver's license number, birth certificate, security clearance, and even a college degree. The irony is that although it makes so much personal data available to steal, the Internet allows criminals to work anonymously. After assuming the new identity, the thief can quickly use the new identity for profit on the Internet. Most of the time identity theft isn't discovered until the victim receives a credit card bill.

Sites sell forms for driver's licenses, birth certificates, student IDs, permits to carry concealed weapons, and bartender cards. About 30 percent of the false ID documents seized in Florida in 2000 were obtained on the Internet. Until recently, the cost of identity theft was borne by credit card companies, but now online retailers are being hit hard—without an imprint of the card and the signature of the buyer, they cannot hold the card issuer responsible.

Although Abdallah was still working as a busboy at a restaurant in Brooklyn when he was arrested, authorities believe he has millions of dollars in offshore bank accounts and that he owns several buildings. "He's the best I ever faced," said New York detective Michael Fabozzi.

Discussion Questions

1. Think about your identification: your name, your Social Security number, date of birth, and address. If someone else were using your identity, how would you prove that you are who you say you are?

2. How would you prove that someone else was using your credit cards?

3. Do you think firms should be liable for losses caused by fraud such as Abdallah's? How might they safeguard themselves?

Sources: "Hacker Uses Forbes List to Steal," Associated Press, March 20, 2001; Sharon Walsh, "Oprah, Call Your Broker," *TheStandard.com*, March 27, 2001; Jenny Lyn Bader, "Paranoid Lately? You May Have Good Reason," *New York Times*, March 24, 2000.

Data Drives Dell

Dell Computer Corporation is considered a company that fully understands the customer service dimension of e-commerce, given its success at online selling. But when Dell started its website in the early 1990s, it simply wanted to provide effective technical support to its existing customers. "Initially, Dell.com had no commerce capability," recalls Manish Mehta, director of online support.

By 1997, although customers could order computers online from Dell, their orders were handled the old-fashioned way once received: the firm's procurement staff would decide what components were needed and contact the firm's suppliers by e-mail, phone, or fax to deliver them. To integrate its business processes, including order fulfillment, the company initiated an enterprise resource planning system. After two years and more than $200 million had been spent on the project, the foundering project was publicly canceled.

CEO Michael Dell then asked the firm's supply-chain group why they weren't "eating their own dog food" by using the latest Web techniques. "We had made some pretty fantastic progress on [the sales side] and were lagging in procurement, and I was goading our team to get with the program," Dell recalls. The firm reinvented procurement and manufacturing processes to create a combined system/process solution. By the end of 1999, 43 percent of the company's total revenue—$40 million a day—came from sales over the Internet. People such as Ford CEO Jacques Nasser and Eastman Chemical CEO Ernie Deavenport were asking Michael Dell for guidance.

At least 90 percent of Dell's suppliers are connected to the company's system. They can see what parts Dell needs today and how many the company expects to use in the coming weeks. Cameras broadcast bottlenecks via the Internet. Shipping is also integrated, often completed only 15 hours after the customer places the order. The system maintains data for each step of the process.

As a result, it is easy to look up how long it took to ship a product after receiving an order, if a product caused a problem, whether the problem was fixed with a phone call, and how long the phone call lasted. If service is necessary at the customer's site, the service representative's arrival time and the length of the visit are tracked. Customers can use Dell's website to research products, design their own computers and systems, and order parts. All of this information is captured as well, so Dell's marketing team can learn customer buying patterns, replacement needs, and strategy shifts. They can almost read their customers' minds.

Customer data also reveal the ultimate fact about Dell's largest customers—exactly how profitable they are to Dell—and Dell in turn can tailor its treatment of these customers. Someone who buys servers and storage from Dell may be offered a special package that includes PCs and portables.

At the company's annual employee meeting in 1999, Michael Dell told his staff their goal for the coming year: to be "the premier Internet partner for customers around the world."

Discussion Questions

1. What kind of information would Michael Dell need from the firm's information systems to make strategic decisions? How would you ensure it met the four standards for information (high quality, timely, relevant, and comprehensive)?

2. How could an information technology firm such as Dell not be able to successfully implement an ERP system?

3. Do you think a firm needs the level of data that systems such as Dell's maintain? What criteria would you use to make sure the data are up to date?

Sources: David Rocks, "Dell's Second Web Revolution," *Business Week Online,* September 18, 2000; Brent Schlender, "Their Reign Is Over," *Fortune,* October 16, 2000; Betsy Morris, "Can Michael Dell Escape the Box?" *Fortune,* October 16, 2000; John H. Sheridan, "Dell Courts Customer's Online," *Industry Week* 249, no. 7 (April 3, 2000): 23.

INDIVIDUAL/ COLLABORATIVE LEARNING CASE 18.1

Hunting for Hackers to Help with Hacking

Breaking into networks has become a useful tool for illegally cutting corners. In October 2000, Microsoft discovered that someone had been breaking into the firm's network and looking at its source code of products under development. Other documents that may have been vulnerable included contracts, e-mail, and other components. Microsoft officials had little doubt that this break-in was an act of industrial espionage. Not surprisingly, Microsoft's security team is one of the best, with huge resources and incentives to maintain the integrity of the firm's information channels. If Microsoft can't keep its secrets secret, who can?

The United States is expected to need an additional 50,000 to 75,000 information-security professionals in the next few years. Computer-security professionals' salaries have leapt 50 percent in the past 12 months. Hetal Patel, an associate at PPS Information Systems Staffing in Baltimore, is a headhunter for information-security specialists. Even with the huge increase in salaries, there aren't enough people out there interested in this work, however, so companies are trying to improve their information-security defenses internally. These efforts create business for firewall engineers, intrusion-detection specialists, and programmers with expertise in cryptography algorithms. "It's very tough to find the engineers because there is so much competition," Patel says.

The small number of U.S. academic programs with an information-security emphasis graduate only 200 people annually, and only 14 universities are considered to provide information-security expertise by the National Security Agency. The International Information Systems Security Certifications Consortium, Inc., has issued only 3,000 certificates over the past four years. Most certification programs teach one particular type of equipment, while university programs teach the principles underlying everything. Understanding security principles has become more important for security experts, with complex technologies mixing multiple protocols and devices. Twenty-five years ago, firms had one operating system and one security product for it. New technologies and cross-platform operations create new headaches. And on-the-job training is essential.

Security experts feel that until the field gains academic status, as computer science did in the 1960s and 1970s, and receives money for academic programs, information security will continue to be threatened.

Critical Thinking Questions

1. Is it possible to create a security system to protect computer networks? Explain your answer.

part six Operations and Information Systems Management

2. How do you think hackers can gain access to systems as well protected as Microsoft's? Does it follow that companies with virtually all of their operations and information online would be expected to have the expertise to protect themselves?

3. How would you safeguard a firm's information from former employees—especially those who were responsible for its security?

Collaborative Learning Exercise

Your firm, DataStore, has recently found that its online databases have been broken into. Two members of your group have been assigned the responsibility for upgrading the firm's information security. They must outline the firm's security needs by detailing the firm's existing information technology, access to information, safeguards, and maintenance, and then provide the outline to two security firms, made up of the other members of the group. One firm can provide security based on an academic background, and the other must develop its security system from hands-on work only. Each security firm creates and presents a proposal that includes what it would do and why it should be chosen, and the DataStore staff must decide which to use.

Sources: Alex Salkever, "Security Net," *Business Week*, November 28, 2000; Steve Barth, "Post-Industrial Espionage," *Knowledge Management Magazine*, March 2001.

Computer Privacy

Many firms that do business online have made privacy a key issue. Visit the websites of several firms, such as those listed and others of your choice, and answer the following questions:

1. Did the firm's website include information about maintaining visitors' privacy? Did it spell out how information about you would be used?

2. Now visit http://nclnet.org/essentials/ and click the areas found there. Would you incorporate the safeguards from this consumer site into a privacy policy?

3. What kind of customer information do you feel firms have the right to know?

INTERNET
EXERCISE 18.1

www.irs.gov
www.abercrombie.com
www.amazon.com

How Effectively Do You Use Technology?

Technology is all around you. Assess your comfort level to see whether you can use it effectively. Mark "T" for true or "F" for false next to each of the following statements.

_____ 1. I am comfortable using a computer for familiar tasks, but I do not explore its functions or new uses.

_____ 2. I trust technology to take care of almost everything.

_____ 3. I think it is important to update my information technology knowledge and skills continually by taking training courses and subscribing to relevant journals.

_____ 4. If part of my job were automated, I could increase my creative output.

_____ 5. There are so many features in our new communications system that I am afraid I won't be able to learn them all.

_____ 6. I have access to a computer network, but I depend on one of my colleagues to obtain information from it for me.

_____ 7. The use of enterprise resource planning (ERP) software could greatly improve my productivity.

_____ 8. I don't like the idea of sharing all the information I obtained through computer databases.

_____ 9. If we had an extranet, I would try to find new ways to develop linkages with suppliers, customers, and other key business partners.

_____ 10. Not all technology is an improvement; it is important to choose technology that is appropriate for our organization.

Scoring: "True" responses to statements 3, 4, 7, 9, and 10 indicate the most effective use of technology.

Source: Adapted from Patrick M. Wright and Raymond A. Noe, _Management of Organizations._ Chicago: Irwin, 1996, p. 846.

TechBox: Conflict Management: Hierarchies and Personalities

Managing supervisor of production: Patrick Bennett, male, late 20s. African-American

Vice president of operations: Sam Adelson, male, late 50s, Caucasian

Director of product management: Lucinda Bergen, female, mid-50s, Hispanic American

Vice president of distribution: Morgan Baines, male, mid-40s, Caucasian

General Background info:

TechBox produces a specialized computer chip for a large client base of high-end computer companies such as Dell, IBM, and Compaq. Within the TechBox compound are the manufacturing factories and the corporate headquarters.

Patrick Bennett is the new hotshot manager overseeing the production of the main component of the chip. He has started to implement a computerized tracking system to increase quality control and workflow. He supervises a floor of fifty workers. Patrick has been working at Tech-Box for two years and has been widely praised for numerous successes and improvements on the factory floor—improvements with very positive financial results. He is young and motivated, possessing a unique comprehension of production/engineering knowledge and management sensibilities. He is greatly admired by his team and generally received well by top senior management.

Sam Adelson has worked his way up from the mailroom. He does not embrace change and is skeptical of young hot shots and young people in general. He also does not embrace computerized system enhancements, which is odd for a man in high tech. In a nutshell, he's stodgy, grumpy, and difficult.

Lucinda Bergen is the only female executive at TechBox. She is generally compassionate, understanding, and easy going, but is quick to defend her position within the company and overassert herself when she feels confronted. She is very comfortable with young, talented people and has instituted many technological systems for workflow improvement within her own department.

Morgan Baines is the class clown and jokester of the company. He's hyper, making wisecracks/goofball stuff. He speaks without thinking—

supports, attacks, and withdraws without rhyme or reason. Everyone always has the impression that he's on their side; the kind of guy who agrees with the last person who spoke. He's been around very many years, successfully overseeing product distribution—between wisecracks.

"Documents":

- A simple description of the product.
- A semi-detailed history of Patrick's performance.
- A simple explanation of the new system and its implementation.

Pre-Viewing Class Questions

1. How should Patrick approach this meeting and its agenda?
2. What information should Patrick be prepared to provide to the meeting members?
3. How can Patrick gain leadership of the meeting?

Scene One: Mixed Signals

Location: TechBox conference room

Backstory:

Three months ago, Patrick was given the go ahead to implement a computerized tracking system on the factory floor with the expectations that it would raise quality control and workflow by a significant percentage. The team spends an enormous amount of time revising/fixing chips after they fail QC testing—mostly due to lack of information. There would be a serious review of the project after the first phase is complete—that is now.

Patrick is called to a meeting with three top executives. The tracking system project is very costly and has not been proven, although the company was gung-ho, knowing their competitors were using all sorts of computerized systems in their production facilities. Patrick has spent a little time writing a report, but is feeling generally confident—everybody's been really excited about the tracking system and implementation is going as planned.

Break for Manager Questions & Analysis

Scene Two: Tides Turn

Location: TechBox conference room

The second meeting is at hand. For the past week and since the first meeting, Patrick has managed to rally the troops and prepare his information more precisely. Patrick is nervous and needs to convince these three execs, who are rarely on the same page, to let him complete the project.

Post-Viewing Class Questions

1. How effective was Patrick's new approach during the second meeting?
2. What specific things could Patrick have done to alleviate the tenseness/confusion during the meetings?
3. How well did Patrick ultimately handle this situation? What could or should have been done differently?

Lack of Controls at HealthSouth

In 1984 Richard Scrushy founded HealthSouth, the largest health care provider in the United States. Two years later, he brought the company public. The mission of the company was "to create a transition environment between the hospital and home that provides both outpatient rehabilitation services and financial incentive." Its initial facility, and outpatient rehabilitation center, was located in Little Rock, Arkansas. HealthSouth, now headquartered in Birmingham, Alabama, approaches health care using a model of integrated services by providing a variety of outpatient (diagnostic, surgical, and rehabilitation) and inpatient (rehabilitation) services through some 1,700 rehabilitation hospitals and acute-care medical centers, outpatient surgeries, and rehabilitation and diagnostic imaging centers located throughout the United States (in all 50 states) and facilities in Australia, Canada, Puerto Rico, Saudi Arabia, and the United Kingdom. It employs some 135,000 medical and business professionals (approximately 50,000) and referring physicians (approximately 85,000), and it has provided sports medicine care to superstar athletes such as Roger Clemens (baseball), Michael Jordan (basketball), and Terry Bradshaw (football). The company has also been a leading contributor to the community at large; it has donated millions of dollars and thousands of hours to community causes. Over the years, its largess has helped to support nonprofit organizations such as the American Lung Association, the American Red Cross, the American Stroke Association, the Arthritis Foundation, the National Multiple Sclerosis Society, the Spinal Cord Injury Foundation, and the United Way.

Trouble in the Accounting Department

In January 2003, an anonymous source posted a warning about Health-South on Yahoo! On February 13, 2003, this source, known only as Junior, posted the following message on Yahoo!: "What I know about the accounting at HRC will be the blow that will bring HRC to its knees." Several minutes later, Junior posted another message: "what is going on at HRC . . . if discovered by the right people will bring change to the

This case was prepared by Joseph C. Santora, who is professor of business at Essex County College, Newark, New Jersey.

accounting department at HRC if not the entire company." On March 19, 2003, the Securities and Exchange Commission (SEC) filed a civil lawsuit against the company and chairperson and CEO Scrushy accusing "massive accounting fraud." Earnings were allegedly overstated by more than $1 billion over four years. Both the SEC and Department of Justice (DoJ) are investigating the accuracy of financial statements that the company previously filed and which the public should no longer view as reliable.

Junior, a 31-year-old company employee, began working for Health-South in 1997. In 2001, while working in the accounting department, he became aware of some problems related to the accounting principles and operations of the company. He believed that accounting department personnel were "falsifying assets on the balance sheet." The accounting "problem" was created when entering expenses between $500 and $4,999. It seems that Ernst & Young LLP, the external auditors for HealthSouth, only concerned itself with expenditures of $5,000 and up when reviewing accounting ledgers. Junior told his supervisor, a vice president in the accounting department, of his concern. He learned that his supervisor "falsified an invoice" and would use one invoice "to cover up the large accounting frauds." Junior felt compelled to take action so he e-mailed Ernst & Young LLP to discuss one aspect of the accounting problem; his warnings listed on Yahoo! were similarly rejected by some online readers as simply the rantings of a disgruntled employee. Junior did not notify the SEC, since he assumed that Ernst & Young LLP would follow up on the information he provided them.

Deception

HealthSouth had an excellent financial track record. It had met Wall Street earnings expectations for the past decade. Meeting estimates was no easy feat and CEO Scrushy allegedly ordered employees to inflate company earnings. The 12 or so employees who participated in the deception and accounting fraud were members of an elite group dubbed the "little family." Scrushy, a University of Alabama graduate, had systematically recruited many HealthSouth employees from Alabama and rewarded them well as employees. "Family" members were well paid, given stock options and airplane rides on the company's airplane fleet, and some were even fortunate enough to take pleasure trips on Scrushy's private yacht.

In some cases, employees believed "that some of the improper accounting changes they helped make would be needed only for one quarter and that senior executives would 'fix it' later." Moreover, these employees were given verbal assurances by CFO William T. Owens that only senior-level company officials would be held responsible since they would be the ones who signed the financial documents. However, not all employees felt a total degree of comfort with the alleged accounting fraud. Some of them thought that they would be physically harmed if they revealed the alleged fraud. One executive felt so uncomfortable about the alleged fraud that he "left the accounting department to become chief information officer."

At the end of each quarter, Scrushy, the CFO, and selected senior executives would receive the company's actual operating results from the assistant controller. This group would meet to select an appropriate earnings per share to satisfy the financial numbers set by the Wall Street analysts. Once that was done, the assistant controller and the "family" would meet and discuss the earnings per share and then employ accounting "tricks" by inflating certain items to ensure that the company's balance sheet was allegedly inflated by about $1 billion. Things began to unravel rapidly in February 2003, when the FBI began investigating insider stock trading and soon top-level executives got caught with their "hands in the proverbial cookie jar."

Interim Controls

Effective March 19, 2003, Richard Scrushy, chief executive officer (CEO) and chairperson, and William T. Owens, chief financial officer (CFO), two top HealthSouth executives, were placed on administrative leave. The company appointed Robert P. May, a board of directors member, acting CEO, and Joel C. Gordon, another board of directors member, as acting board chair of HealthSouth, as an interim solution to the leadership vacuum created by the departure of the top executives. Chairperson Gordon issued a strong statement regarding the board's position on the matter: "The Board is committed to cooperating with the governmental investigation. We are going to dig out of these problems and take every available step to restore corporate credibility. During this process, we will maintain our commitment to providing outstanding patient care."

The directors of the company have set a number of controls in place. First, the audit committee replaced Ernst & Young LLP as the independent auditors of the company. Second, Alvarez & Marsal, Inc., a turnaround advisory firm, was hired to manage the finances and administration of the company. Byron P. Marsal, a founding managing director of HealthSouth, was appointed chief restructuring officer (CRO). He and his staff have implemented "measures to stabilize the company's operation, conserve its cash and reduce costs, including evaluating the sale of non-core assets, without disrupting patient care services." Third, PriceWaterhouseCoopers, an international accounting firm, was hired to provide "forensic auditing services" to investigate all allegations pertaining to SEC investigations. Finally, the company appointed Skadden, Arps, Slate, Meagher & Flom LLP, the tony Washington, DC, law firm that represents many Fortune 250 companies as well as government organizations, "to serve as lead coordinating counsel on both corporate and litigation matters."

On March 24, 2003, Chairperson Gordon issued the following statement on the company's website: "HealthSouth is committed to fully investigating and resolving all issues relating to its financial reporting, and will take appropriate actions against any employee found to have committed any fraud or wrongdoings."

On March 26, 2003, CFO Owens, who was placed on administrative leave from the company, pleaded guilty to financial fraud as did 11 other company executives including five former CFOs and six former executives who provided authorities with specific details of the alleged accounting fraud linking an additional $1 billion+. HealthSouth, a company which rose like the phoenix from a one-facility site and whose stock sold for a high of $30.56 on the New York Stock Exchange (NYSE) in 1998, fell just as precipitously. Stock was worth only pennies. On March 31, 2003, the board of directors took another corrective action when it fired founder and CEO/Chairperson Richard Scrushy.

Questions

1. What should the company have done to ensure that auditing controls were in place?

2. Is the implementation of current controls a case of too much too late?

3. What controls should the new top management team set in motion at HealthSouth?

4. How did the "family" get executives from various company levels to comply with the alleged accounting fraud?

5. How was the accounting situation kept quiet for several years?

Sources: http://www.healthsouth.com; C. Mollenkamp, "Accountant Tried in Vain to Expose HealthSouth Fraud," *Wall Street Journal,* May 20, 2003, pp. 1, 13; C. Terhune, C. Mollenkamp, A. Carrns, with D. Solomon, contributor, "Inside Alleged Fraud at HealthSouth, a 'Family' Plot," April 3, 2003, pp. 1, 12.

a

absolute judgments   A performance appraisal approach in which the performance of employees is evaluated against performance standards, and not in comparison to each other.

academy culture   A type of organization culture that seeks to hire people with specialties and technical mastery who will be confined to a set of jobs within a particular function and will be rewarded by long-term association and a slow, steady climb up the organization ladder.

acceptance sampling   An operations management monitoring tool in which a sample of materials or products is measured against a benchmark.

accommodation strategy   A means of dealing with stakeholder groups when a firm decides to accept social responsibility for its business decisions after pressure has been exerted by stakeholder groups.

accountability   The expectation that the manager or other employee with authority and responsibility must be able to justify results to a manager at a higher level in the organizational hierarchy.

acquisition   The process of purchasing other firms.

actions   The specific steps the firm intends to take to achieve the desired objectives.

adjourning stage   A stage of team development in which teams complete their work and disband, if designed to do so.

administrative management   The management approach that examines an organization from the perspective of the managers and executives responsible for coordinating the activities of diverse groups and units across the entire organization.

adversarial relations   U.S. labor laws view management and labor as natural adversaries who want to have a larger share of the firm's profits and who must reach a compromise through collective bargaining.

adverse impact   A form of discrimination, also called *disparate impact*, that occurs when one standard that is applied to all applicants or employees negatively affects a protected class.

affirmative action   A federal government-mandated program that requires corporations to provide opportunities to women and members of minority groups who traditionally had been excluded from good jobs; it aims to accomplish the goal of fair employment by urging employers to make a conscious effort to hire members of protected classes.

aggressive communication   A forceful style of communication with others that expresses dominance and even anger. The needs and wants of others are ignored.

assessing   Evaluating the environmental data received to accurately specify the implications for the firm.

assessment phase   A career development step in which employees are helped to choose personally fitting career paths that are realistically attainable and to determine any obstacles they need to overcome to succeed.

attribution theory   The idea that the major function of the leader is to be blamed or given credit for a bad or a good situation, even if the leader has little or no control over the factors that led to the results.

authority   The formal right of a manager to make decisions, give orders, and expect the orders to be carried out.

avoiding style   Conflict resolution used when the individual decides it is better to avoid the conflict rather than to deal with it.

b

bankruptcy   A legal procedure that distributes company assets to creditors and protects the debtor from unfair demands of creditors when the debtor fails to make scheduled loan repayments.

base compensation   The fixed amount of money the employee expects to receive in a paycheck weekly or monthly or as an hourly wage.

baseball team culture   The fast-paced, competitive, high-risk form of corporate culture typically found in organizations in rapidly changing environments, with short product life cycles, with high-risk decision making, and dependent on continuous innovation for survival.

behavioral anchored rating scales   Performance appraisal tools that assess the effectiveness of the employee's performance using specific examples of good or bad behaviors at work.

behavioral appraisal instruments   Performance appraisal tools that assess certain employee behaviors, such as coming to work on time, completing assignments within stipulated guidelines, and getting along with coworkers.

behavioral perspective   The management view that knowledge of the psychological and social processes of human behavior can result in improvements in productivity and work satisfaction.

benchmarking   A strategic management approach that assesses capabilities by comparing the firm's activities or functions with those of other firms.

benefits   A compensation component that accounts for almost 40 percent of the typical total compensation package and includes health insurance, pension plans, unemployment insurance, vacations, sick leave, and the like.

bona fide occupational qualification (BFOQ)   A defense against discrimination in which a firm must show that a personal characteristic must be present to do the job.

bottom-up change   Organizational change that originates with employees.

boundaryless organization design   A management design that eliminates internal and external structural boundaries that inhibit employees from collaborating with each other or that inhibit firms from collaborating with customers, suppliers, or competitors.

brainstorming   A technique to generate creative ideas for solving problems by reducing critical and judgmental reactions to ideas from group members.

brand managers   A management role that coordinates the ongoing activities of marketing branded consumer products.

budgeting   Controlling and allocating the firm's funds; *variable budgeting* allows for deviations between planned output and actual output by considering the fact that variable costs depend on the level of output, whereas fixed costs do not; *moving budgeting* creates a tentative budget for a fixed period of time and then revises and updates it on a periodic basis to take changes into account.

bureaucratic management   The management approach that examines the entire organization as a rational entity, using impersonal rules and procedures for decision making.

business ethics: *See* Ethics.

business network   A firm's alliances formed with other businesses to achieve mutually beneficial goals.

business plan   The business's blueprint that maps out its business strategy for entering markets and that explains the business to potential investors.

business process   A value-adding, value-creating activity such as product development or order fulfillment.

business unionism   Unions that focus on "bread and butter" issues such as wages, benefits, and job security.

c

capacity   The firm's ability to produce the product during a given period.

career path   The steps and a plausible time frame for accomplishing them for advancement to a career goal.

centralization   The location of decision authority at the top of the organization hierarchy.

certainty   The condition when all the information needed to make a decision is available.

chain of command The superior-subordinate authority relationship that starts at the top of the organization hierarchy and extends to the lowest levels.

change agents People who act as catalysts and assume responsibility for managing change.

charismatic leader A leader who can engender a strong emotional attachment from followers; charisma is associated with admiration, trust, and a willingness to believe what the leader says.

civil law The legal system that relies on a comprehensive set of rules that form part of a highly structured code; enforcement and interpretation of laws are made in reference to this code.

classical perspective The management perspective formed during the nineteenth and early twentieth centuries, with the evolution of the factory system and the formation of modern corporations, to meet the challenges of managing large, complex organizations.

club culture A form of organizational culture that seeks people who are loyal, committed to one organization, and need to fit into a group and rewards them with job security, promotion from within, and slow progress.

coaching Ongoing, mostly spontaneous, meetings between managers and their employees to discuss career goals, roadblocks, and available opportunities.

coalitions Political alliances between managers who agree on goals and priorities.

code of ethics A formal statement of the company's ethics and values that is designed to guide employee conduct in a variety of business situations.

coercive power Power based on the fear that the leader may cause people harm unless they support him or her.

cohesiveness The emotional closeness group members feel toward each other and how supportive they are of each other.

collective bargaining Negotiations between union and management with little, if any, government involvement.

common law The legal system in which precedents based on past court decisions play a key role in interpreting the meaning and intent of legal statutes.

communication A process that involves the transmission of meaningful information from one party to another through the use of shared symbols.

communication channel Influences the quantity and quality of information that is conveyed to the receiver. Channels of communication include face-to-face conversations, group meetings, memos, policy manuals, e-mail, voice mail.

compensable factors A set of evaluation criteria used in job evaluation.

competitive behavior Team behavior that views other people as rivals for a limited pool of resources and focuses on individual goals, noncollaboration, and the withholding of information.

competitive dynamic The actions and counteractions of firms that compete in a particular industry segment.

compromising style Conflict resolution used when the manager or team member makes some concessions to the other party and the other party is willing to reciprocate.

computer ethics The analysis of the nature and social impact of computer technology and the development of policies for its appropriate use.

concentration strategy A form of diversification strategy that focuses on a single business operating in a single industry segment.

concentric diversification strategy A form of diversification strategy in which the firm expands by creating or acquiring new businesses related to the firm's core business.

conduct of training phase A stage in the training process that ensures training will solve an organizational problem or need; this step is critical to ensuring that training will be beneficial to the organization.

confrontation strategy One means a firm may use to deal with a stakeholder group whose goals are perceived to threaten company performance; the firm may use the courts, engage in public relations, or lobby against legislation.

conglomerate diversification A form of diversification strategy that involves managing a portfolio of businesses that are unrelated to each other.

consideration The behavioral dimension of leadership involving the concern that the leader has for the feelings, needs, personal interest, problems, and well-being of followers; also called *employee-oriented behaviors.*

content validity The measurement that the selection process represents the actual activities or knowledge required to successfully perform the job.

contingency theory The management theory that there is no "one best way" to manage and organize an organization because situational characteristics, called contingencies, differ; also, the view that no HR strategy is "good" or "bad" in and of itself but rather depends on the situation or context in which it is used.

controlling The management function that measures performance, compares it to objectives, implements necessary changes, and monitors progress.

conversion process The operations management stage in which the product's inputs are converted to the final product.

cooperative behavior Team behavior that is manifested in members' willingness to share information and help others.

cooperative strategies Establishing partnerships or strategic alliances with other firms.

coordination Linking activities so that diverse departments or divisions work in harmony and learn from each other.

core beliefs A firm's principles that are widely shared, that operate unconsciously, and that are considered nonnegotiable.

corporate credo A formal statement focusing on principles and beliefs, indicating the company's responsibility to its stakeholders.

corporate-level strategy The corporation's overall plan concerning the number of businesses the corporation holds, the variety of markets or industries it serves, and the distribution of resources among those businesses.

corporate social responsibility The belief that corporations have a responsibility to conduct their affairs ethically and to be judged by the same standards as people.

corporation A form of business that is a legal entity separate from the individuals who own it.

cost leadership strategy Providing products and services that are less expensive than those of competitors.

cultural symbols The acts, events, or objects that communicate organizational values, used by management to convey and sustain shared meaning among employees.

culture shock The reaction when exposed to other cultures (social structure, religion, language, and historical background) with different norms, customs, and expectation.

d

damage control strategy A means a firm may use to deal with a stakeholder group when it decides that it may have made mistakes and wants to improve its relationship with the stakeholders and to elevate its public image.

data Raw facts, such as the number of items sold or the number of hours worked in a department.

data mining The process of determining the relevant factors in the accumulated data to extract the data that are important to the user.

data warehouses Massive databases that contain almost all of the information about a firm's operations.

databases Computer programs that assign multiple characteristics to data and allow users to sort the data by characteristic.

debt financing A means of obtaining financial resources that involves obtaining a commercial loan and setting up a plan to repay the principal and interest.

decentralization The location of decision authority at lower levels in the organization.

decision acceptance The aspect of decision making that is based on people's feelings; decision acceptance happens when people who are affected by a decision like it.

decision making The process of identifying problems and opportunities and resolving them.

decision quality The aspect of decision making that is based on such facts as costs, revenues, and product design specifications.

decision scope The effect and time horizon of the decision.

decoding Translating the symbolic verbal, written, or visual symbols into an undistorted, clear message.

delegation The transfer of decision-making authority from a manager to a subordinate or a team at a lower level in the organization.

Delphi technique A decision-making technique in which group members are presented with a problem and complete an anonymous questionnaire soliciting solutions; the results are tabulated, summarized, and returned to the group members, and each is asked again for solutions; the process continues until a consensus decision is reached.

departmentalization The horizontal basis for organizing jobs into units in an organization.

development phase A career development step in which actions are designed to help the employee grow and learn the necessary skills to move along the desired career path.

devil's advocate The role of criticizing and challenging decision alternatives that are agreed on by other members of the group, to induce creative conflict and possibly alternative, better solutions.

differentiation strategy Delivering products and services that customers perceive as unique.

direction phase The step in career development that involves determining the steps employees must take to reach their career goals.

discrimination The unfair treatment of employees because of personal characteristics that are not job-related.

disparate treatment A form of discrimination that occurs when an employer treats an employee differently because of his or her protected class status.

diversification strategy A firm's strategic plan to create and manage a mix of businesses owned by the firm.

diversity The wide spectrum of individual and group differences.

divestiture The corporate process of selling a business in order to generate cash, which the corporation can better deploy elsewhere, or to refocus on its core related businesses, which are better understood by management.

division of labor The production process in which each worker repeats one step over and over, achieving greater efficiencies in the use of time and knowledge; also, the formal assignment of authority and responsibility to job holders.

divisional approach A departmentalization approach, sometimes called the product approach, that organizes employees into units based on common products, services, or markets.

dominating style Conflict resolution used when the manager or team member acts assertively and forcefully and persuades the other party to abandon his or her objectives.

downsizing A management strategy used to reduce the scale and scope of a business to improve its financial performance.

downward communication Sending a message from a high position in the organization to an individual or group lower in the hierarchy.

Drug-Free Workplace Act Federal legislation that requires employers to implement policies that restrict drug use.

dysfunctional conflict Conflict that has a negative effect on team and organizational performance.

e

e-business The process of conducting business transactions using online resources; also called *e-commerce*.

e-commerce Any business transaction executed electronically by companies or consumers.

e-mail Electronic mail.

emotional intelligence The attributes of self-awareness, impulse control, persistence, confidence, self-motivation, empathy, social deftness, trustworthiness, adaptability, and a talent for collaboration.

empirical validity Statistical evidence that the selection method distinguishes between higher and lower performing employees.

employment at will A very old legal doctrine stating that unless there is an employment contract (such as a union contract or an implied contract), both employer and employee are free to end the employment relationship whenever and for whatever reasons they choose.

empowerment The process of transferring control of individual work behavior from the supervisor to the employee.

encounter stage The stage of socialization at which the individual begins to compare expectations about the firm's culture with reality.

enterprise resource planning (ERP) software A computer program that combines all of a firm's computerized functions into a single, integrated software program that runs off a single database, allowing various departments to easily share information and communicate with each other.

entrepreneur An individual who creates an enterprise that becomes a new entry to a market.

entrepreneurship The process of creating a business enterprise capable of entering new or established markets by deploying resources and people in a unique way to develop a new organization.

equity financing A means of obtaining financial resources that involves the sale of part of the ownership of the business to investors.

equity theory The view that people develop beliefs about the fairness of the rewards they receive relative to their contributions.

ERG theory A theory of needs based on three core groups: existence, relationships, and growth (ERG).

espoused values The aspects of corporate culture that are not readily observed but instead can be perceived from the way managers and employees explain and justify their actions and decisions.

ethical policy statements A firm's formal guidelines that provide specific formulas for employees' ethical conduct.

ethical structure The procedures and the division or department within a company that promotes and advocates ethical behavior.

ethics Principles that explain what is good and right and what is bad and wrong and that prescribe a code of behavior based on these definitions. Business ethics provide standards or guidelines for the conduct and decision making of employees and managers.

ethics training A means of providing employees and managers practice in handling ethical dilemmas that they are likely to experience.

ethnocentric approach   An approach to managing an international subsidiary that involves filling top management and other key positions with people from the home country (expatriates).

ethnocentrism   A belief that may become prevalent among majority-group employees, meaning that they believe that their way of doing things, their values, and their norms are inherently superior to those of other groups and cultures.

evaluation   The organization's reexamination of whether training is providing the expected benefits and meeting the identified needs.

expectancy theory   The view that having the strength to act in a particular way depends on people's beliefs that their actions will produce outcomes they find valuable and attractive.

expert power   Power deriving from the leader's unique knowledge or skills, which other people recognize as worthy of respect.

expert system   An advanced information system that uses human knowledge captured in a computer to solve problems that normally require human expertise.

exporting   A means of entering new markets by sending products to other countries and retaining production facilities within domestic borders.

external equity   The perceived fairness of the compensation employees receive relative to what other companies pay for similar work.

external locus of control   A strong belief that luck, fate, or other factors control one's progress, causing feelings of helplessness and decreasing intensity of goal-seeking efforts in the face of failure.

extranets   Also called *wide-area networks,* networks that link a company's employees, suppliers, customers, and other key business partners in an electronic online environment for business communications.

extrinsic motivation   Motivation that comes from the rewards that are linked to job performance, such as a paycheck.

f

facilities   The design and location of an operations facility.

facilities layout   The grouping and organization of equipment and employees.

facilities layout design   The physical arrangement for the facility that will allow for efficient production.

facts   Bits of information that can be objectively measured or described, such as the retail price of a new product, the cost of raw materials, the defect rate of a manufacturing process, or the number of employees who quit during a year.

Family and Medical Leave Act   Federal legislation that requires employers to provide unpaid leave for childbirth, adoption, and illness.

feedback   Information received back from the receiver, which allows the sender to clarify the message if its true meaning is not received.

feelings   An individual's emotional responses to decisions made or actions taken by other people.

firewall   A combination of computer hardware and software that controls access to and transmission of data and information contained in a network.

first-mover advantage   The important advantage enjoyed by firms that recognize a market's potential before others do and thus typically outperform firms that are late entrants.

flexible manufacturing   Operations management techniques that help reduce the setup costs associated with the production system.

force-field analysis   A model of organizational change that states that two sets of opposing forces are at equilibrium before a change takes place and puts at disequilibrium to make change come about the driving forces, which are pushing for change, and the restraining forces, which are opposed to change.

forecasting   Predicting what is likely to happen in the future, the intensity of the anticipated event, its importance to the firm, and the pace or time frame in which it may occur.

formal planning   A system designed to deliberately identify objectives and to structure the major tasks of the organization to accomplish them.

formalization   The degree to which written documentation is used to direct and control employees.

forming stage   The first stage of team development, which brings the team members together for the first time so they can get acquainted and discuss their expectations.

fortress culture   An organization culture with the primary goal of surviving and reversing business problems, including economic decline and hostile competitors.

franchising   A means of entering new markets similar to licensing, mainly used by service companies, in which the franchisee pays a fee for using the brand name and agrees to strictly follow the standards and abide by the rules set by the franchise.

free riders   Individuals who find it rational to withhold their effort and provide minimum input to the team in exchange for a full share of the rewards.

functional analysis   A strategic management approach that establishes organizational capabilities for each of the major functional areas of the business.

functional conflict   Conflict that stimulates team and organizational performance.

functional structure   A departmentalization approach that clusters people with similar skills in a department.

g

Gantt charts   A visual sequence of the process steps used in planning, scheduling, and monitoring production.

General Agreement on Tariffs and Trade (GATT)   A treaty signed by 120 nations to lower trade barriers for manufactured goods and services. In 1993, the GATT negotiations in Uruguay, known as the Uruguay Round, created the World Trade Organization to ensure compliance by member nations.

geocentric approach   An approach to managing an international subsidiary in which nationality is deliberately downplayed, and the firm actively searches on a worldwide or regional basis for the best people to fill key positions.

geographic-based divisions   A variation of the product-based departmentalization structure in which divisions are organized by geographic region.

glass ceiling   The intangible barrier that prevents women and minorities from rising to the upper levels in business.

global shift   A term used to characterize the effects of changes in the competitive landscape prompted by worldwide competition.

grapevine   Informal communication that takes place at the workplace.

groupthink   Team behavior that occurs when members prefer to avoid conflict rather than tolerate a healthy diversity of opinions.

groupthink   Valuing social harmony over doing a thorough job.

h

Hawthorne effect   The finding that paying special attention to employees motivates them to put greater effort into their jobs (from the Hawthorne management studies, performed from 1924 through 1932 at Western Electric Company's plant near Chicago).

horizontal communication   Communication between a sender and a receiver at a similar level in the organization.

horizontal dimension   The organizational structure element that is the basis for dividing work into specific jobs and tasks and assigning jobs into units such as departments or teams.

horizontal information flows   The flow of information from one department up through management layers and then back down to another department through other layers.

HR tactics   The implementation of human resource programs to achieve the firm's vision.

human relations approach   A management approach that views the relationships between employees and supervisors as the most salient aspect of management.

i

illusion of control   The tendency for decision makers to be overconfident of their ability to control activities and events.

implementation guidelines   The planning step that shows how the intended actions will be carried out.

individualism   The degree to which a society values personal goals, autonomy, and privacy over group loyalty, commitment to group norms, involvement in collective activities, social cohesiveness, and intense socialization; ethical decisions based on individualism promote individual self-interest as long as it does not harm others.

information   Data that have been gathered and converted into a meaningful context.

information richness   The potential information-carrying capacity of data.

initiating structure   The behavioral dimension of leadership that refers to activities designed to accomplish group goals, including organizing tasks, assigning responsibilities, and establishing performance standards; also called *production-oriented behaviors*.

inputs   The supplies needed to create a product, which can include materials, energy, information, management, technology, facilities, and labor.

intangible resources   Resources that are difficult to quantify and include in a balance sheet, which often provide the firm with the strongest competitive advantage.

integrating manager   A management position designed to coordinate the work of several different departments; the integrating manager is not a member of any of the departments whose activities are being coordinated.

integrating style Conflict resolution demonstrated by framing the issue as a problem and encouraging the interested parties to identify the problem, examine alternatives, and agree on a solution.

internal equity The perceived fairness of the pay structure within a firm.

internal locus of control A strong belief in one's own ability to succeed, so that one accepts responsibility for outcomes and tries harder after making mistakes.

Internet A computer network with multimedia communication capabilities, allowing a combination of text, voice, graphics, and video to be sent to a receiver; a network of networks, connecting hundreds of thousands of corporate, educational, and research computer networks around the world.

intranets Private or semiprivate internal networks.

intrapreneurship A form of business organization in which new business units are developed within a larger corporate structure in order to deploy the firm's resources to market a new product or service; also called *corporate entrepreneurship.*

intrinsic motivation Motivation that comes from the personal satisfaction of the work itself.

intrinsic reward design theory The perspective that a potent motivator for work is the intangible reward people derive from performing well in a job they find interesting, challenging, and intriguing and that provides an opportunity for continued learning.

inventory The stock of raw materials, inputs, and component parts that the firm keeps on hand.

j

job analysis The systematic gathering and organizing of information about the tasks, duties, and responsibilities of various jobs.

job-based unionism Unions that are organized by type of job.

job characteristics model According to this model, the way jobs are designed produces critical psychological states which in turn affect key personal and work-related outcomes.**job description** A formal document that identifies, defines, and describes the duties, responsibilities, and working conditions.

job evaluation A rational, orderly, and systematic judgment of how important each job is to the firm and how each job should be compensated.

job preview Information about positive and negative aspects of the job that is provided to potential applicants.

job relatedness A defense against discrimination claims in which the firm must show that the decision was made for job-related reasons.

job rotation A formal program in which employees are assigned to different jobs to expand their skills base and to learn more about various parts of the organization.

job specification The knowledge, skills, and abilities needed to successfully perform the job.

joint venture A means of entering new markets where two or more independent firms agree to establish a separate firm; the firms normally own equivalent shares of the joint venture and contribute a corresponding proportion of the management team.

justice approach An approach to decision making based on treating all people fairly and consistently when making business decisions.

just-in-time (JIT) The concept behind creating the firm's product in the least amount of time.

k

kaizen The Japanese process of continuous improvement in the organization's production system from numerous small, incremental improvements in production processes.

kanban A form of JIT system originated in Japan that uses cards to generate inventory; from the Japanese word for "card" or "sign."

knowledge workers Employees who manage information and make it available to decision makers in the organization.

l

labor contract A written agreement negotiated between union and management.

labor demand The forecast of how many and what type of workers the organization will need in the future.

labor supply The availability of workers with the required skills to meet the firm's labor demand.

leadership substitute view The leadership theory that contends that people overestimate the effect of leaders even when leader behaviors are irrelevant, so organizations need to develop mechanisms to replace or substitute the influence role assigned to leaders.

leading The management function that energizes people to contribute their best individually and in cooperation with other people.

learning organization The management approach based on an organization anticipating change faster than its counterparts to have an advantage in the market over its competitors.

legitimate power The legal or formal authority to make decisions subject to certain constraints.

liaison role A management role used to facilitate communications between two or more departments.

licensing A means of entering new markets, primarily used by manufacturing firms, by transferring the rights to produce and sell products overseas to a foreign firm. In return, the licensing company receives a negotiated fee, normally in the form of a royalty.

line authority The control by a manager of the work of subordinates by hiring, discharging, evaluating, and rewarding them.

line managers The level of management positions that contribute directly to the strategic goals of the organization.

load chart A type of Gantt chart that is based on departments or specific resources that are used in the process.

long-term/short-term orientation The extent to which values are oriented toward the future (saving, persistence) as opposed to the past or present (respect for tradition, fulfilling social obligations).

m

make–buy analysis An operations management tool used to help make the decision as to whether to produce an item or to purchase it.

management by objectives (MBO) A performance appraisal strategy in which employees and supervisors agree on a set of goals to be accomplished for a particular period; performance is then assessed at the end of the period by comparing actual achievement against the agreed-on goals.

management by wandering around (MBWA) Dropping in unannounced at a work site and engaging employees in spontaneous conversations.

management information system (MIS) An information system that provides information to managers to use in making decisions.

managerial grid A system of classifying managers based on leadership behaviors.

masculinity/femininity The degree to which a society views assertive or "masculine" behavior as important to success and encourages rigidly stereotyped gender roles.

Maslow's hierarchy of needs The theory that people tend to satisfy their needs in a specified order, from the most to the least basic.

materials requirements planning (MRP) The process of analyzing a design to determine the materials and parts that it requires in the production process.

matrix approach A departmentalization approach that superimposes a divisional structure over a functional structure in order to combine the efficiency of the functional approach with the flexibility and responsiveness to change of the divisional approach.

mechanistic organization design A management design based on the classical perspective of management, emphasizing vertical control with rigid hierarchical relationships, top-down "command and control" communication channels, centralized decision authority, highly formalized work rules and policies, and specialized, narrowly defined jobs; sometimes called a *bureaucratic design.*

mentoring Developmental activities carried out by more seasoned employees to help those who are learning the ropes.

merger The process of integrating two firms.

metamorphosis stage The stage of socialization at which the employee is induced to bring his or her values and ways of doing things closer to those of the organization.

monitoring Observing environmental changes on a continuous basis to determine whether a clear trend is emerging.

monoculture The homogeneous organizational culture that results from turnover of dissimilar employees.

Muslim law The legal system based on religious Muslim beliefs that regulates behavior; strict interpretation and enforcement varies significantly from country to country.

n

need for achievement A strong drive to accomplish things, in which the individual receives great satisfaction from personal attainment and goal completion.

need for affiliation A strong desire to be liked by others, to receive social approval, and to establish close interpersonal relationships.

need for power The desire to influence or control other people.

needs assessment A training tool that is used to determine whether training is needed.

negative reinforcement   The removal of unpleasant consequences associated with a desired behavior, resulting in an increase in the frequency of that behavior.

noise   Anything that can interfere with sending or receiving a message.

nominal group technique (NGT)   A decision-making technique that helps a group generate and select solutions while letting group members think independently; group members are given the problem and each presents one solution without discussion, then all solutions are discussed, evaluated, and ranked to determine the best alternative.

nonconforming high performer   A team member who is very individualistic and whose presence is disruptive to the team.

nonprogrammed decision   The process of identifying and solving a problem when a situation is unique and there are no previously established routines or procedures that can be used as guides.

nonverbal communication   The sending and decoding of messages with emotional content. Important dimensions include body movements and gestures, eye contact, touch, facial expressions, physical closeness, and tone of voice.

norming stage   A stage in team development that is characterized by resolution of conflict and agreement over team goals and values.

O

objectives   The goals or targets that the firm wishes to accomplish within a stated amount of time.

obliging style   Conflict resolution demonstrated when the party managing the conflict is willing to neglect his or her own needs in order to accommodate the needs of the other party.

office automation systems   An operations information system used to maintain and publish information for an organization.

off-the-job training   Training that takes place away from the employment site.

one-way communications   Communication channels that provide no opportunity for feedback.

on-the-job training (OJT)   Training that takes place in the actual work setting under the guidance of an experienced worker, supervisor, or trainer.

operational action plan   A management plan normally created by line managers and employees directly responsible for carrying out certain tasks or activities.

operational decisions   Decisions with a short time perspective, generally less than a year, and that often are measured on a daily or weekly basis.

operational managers   The firm's lower-level managers who supervise the operations of the organization.

operations management   The process an organization uses to obtain the materials or ideas for the product it provides, the process of transforming them into the product, and the process of providing the final product to a user.

opportunistic planning   A type of planning that involves programmatic actions triggered by unforeseen circumstances; it can coexist with formal planning and can help the formal plan function more smoothly.

optimizing   Selecting the best alternative from among multiple criteria.

order review/release (ORR) activity   An operations management tool that is used to evaluate and track the order through the process, including creating order documentation, material checking, capacity evaluation, and load leveling (releasing orders so that the work load is evenly distributed).

organic organization design   A management design that is focused on change and flexibility, emphasizing horizontal relationships that involve teams, departments, or divisions, and provisions to coordinate these lateral units.

organization chart   A graphic depiction that helps summarize the lines of authority in an organization.

organization design   The selection of an organization structure that best fits the strategic goals of the business.

organization politics   The exercise of power in an organization to control resources and influence policy.

organization structure   The formal system of relationships that determines lines of authority (who reports to whom) and the tasks assigned to individuals and units (who does what task and with which department).

organizational culture   A system of shared values, assumptions, beliefs, and norms that unite the members of an organization.

organizing   The management function that determines how the firm's human, financial, physical, informational, and technical resources are arranged and coordinated to perform tasks to achieve desired goals; the deployment of resources to achieve strategic goals.

outcome appraisal instruments   Performance appraisal tools that measure workers' results, such as sales volume, number of units produced, and deadlines met.

owners   The parties that have invested a portion of their wealth in shares of company stock and have a financial stake in the enterprise.

p

parallel teams   Sometimes called *problem-solving teams* or *special-purpose teams*, groups that focus on a problem or issue that requires only part-time commitment from team members.

partial productivity   The measurement of the contribution of a single input, such as labor or materials, to the final product.

partnership   A form of business that is an association of two or more persons acting as co-owners of a business.

passive-aggressive communication   Style of communication whereby individual avoids giving direct responses to other's requests or feedback.

passive communication   Style of communication whereby individual does not let others know directly what he or she wants or needs.

path-goal theory   A contingency model of leadership that focuses on how leaders influence subordinates' perceptions of work goals and the path to achieve those goals.

pay incentives   Compensation that rewards employees for good performance, including variable pay and merit pay.

performing stage   A stage of team development that is characterized by a focus on the performance of the tasks delegated to the team.

personal network   The relationships between an entrepreneur and other parties, including other entrepreneurs, suppliers, creditors, investors, friends, former colleagues, and others.

planning   The management function that assesses the management environment to set future objectives and map out activities necessary to achieve those objectives.

polycentric approach   An approach to managing an international subsidiary in which subsidiaries are managed and staffed by personnel from the host country (local nationals).

pooled interdependence   Team behavior where team members share common resources such as fax and copy machines, supplies, and secretarial support, but most of the work is performed independently.

portfolio analysis   An approach to classify the processes of a diversified company within a single framework or taxonomy.

positive reinforcement   A pleasurable stimulus or reward following a desired behavior that induces people to continue the behavior.

postheroic leadership perspective   The view that most top executives, no matter how good they are, are limited in what they can do to solve problems, so that leadership responsibilities are spread throughout the firm.

power distance   The extent to which individuals expect a hierarchical structure that emphasizes status differences between subordinates and superiors.

prearrival   The first stage of socialization, encompassing the values, attitudes, biases, and expectations the employee brings to the organization when first hired.

prejudgment   Type of perceptual barrier which involves making incorrect assumptions about a person due to membership in a group or about a thing based on earlier positive or negative experiences.

proactive management   A management style in which problems are anticipated before they become pervasive and time is set aside on both a daily and weekly basis to plan goals and priorities.

proactive strategy   A means of dealing with stakeholders when a firm determines that it wants to go beyond stakeholder expectations.

problem-solving team   A group representing different departments that solves problems; sometimes called a *parallel team*.

process   The way a product or service will be produced.

process control systems   An operations information system that monitors and runs machinery and other equipment.

process reengineering   A method of changing the entire production process rather than making incremental changes.

product managers   A management role that coordinates the development of new products.

profit sharing   Providing a share of a company's profits to the employees in the form of a bonus.

program evaluation and review technique (PERT) network   A tool for analyzing the conversion process.

programmed decision   Identifying a problem and matching the problem with established routines and procedures for resolving it.

project manager   A management role that coordinates work on a scientific, aerospace, or construction project.

project team   A group that works on a specific project that has a beginning and an end.

proprietorship   A form of business that is owned by one person.

protected class   The legal definition of specified groups of people who suffered widespread discrimination in the past and who are given special protection by the judicial system.

public offerings   A means of raising capital by the sale of securities in public markets such as the New York Stock Exchange and NASDAQ.

punishment   An aversive or unpleasant consequence following undesired behavior.

q

quality circles   Groups of employees who meet regularly to discuss ways to increase quality.

quality gap   The difference between what customers want and what they actually get from the company.

r

reactive management   The management style of responding to the most urgent problem first when not enough time is available.

receiver   Individual or party that receives message from sender.

reciprocal interdependence   The greatest amount of interdependence that occurs when team members interact intensively back and forth with each other until their work is judged to meet performance standards.

recruitment   The process of generating a pool of qualified candidates for a particular job.

referent power   Power derived from the satisfaction people receive by identifying themselves with the leader.

relationship-building role   The team-member role that focuses on sustaining harmony between team members.

relationship-oriented leadership   A leadership style that focuses on maintaining good interpersonal relationships.

relative judgments   A performance appraisal approach in which employees are compared to one another.

reliability   The consistency of results from the selection method.

reordering systems   The process used to help keep inventory levels more or less constant.

resource allocation   The planning step that determines where the resources will come from (for instance, borrowing versus internally generated funds) and how the resources will be deployed to achieve the agreed-on objectives.

resource-based view   A strategic management viewpoint that basing business strategy on what the firm is capable of doing provides a more sustainable competitive advantage than basing it on external opportunities.

responsibility   The manager's duty to perform an assigned task.

reward power   Power derived from the belief that the leader can provide something that other people value so that they trade their support for the rewards.

rights approach   A means of making decisions based on the belief that each person has fundamental human rights that should be respected and protected.

risk   The level of uncertainty as to the outcome of a management decision.

role modeling   The leadership mechanism in which managers serve as examples of behaviors they would like employees to emulate.

roles   Expectations regarding how team members should act in given situations.

s

satisficing   Selecting the first alternative solution that meets a minimum criterion.

scanning   The analysis of general environmental factors that may directly or indirectly be relevant to the firm's future.

scientific management   A management method that applies the principles of the scientific method to the management process: determining the one best way to do a job and sharing the rewards with the workers.

segmented communication   Flows of information within the firm that are far greater within groups than between groups.

selection   The screening process used to decide which job applicant to hire.

selective perception   Type of perception barrier whereby the receiver focuses on the parts of the message that are most salient to his or her interests and ignores other parts that are not relevant.

self-leadership   Leadership that stresses the individual responsibility of employees to develop their own work priorities aligned with organizational goals; the manager is a facilitator who enhances the self-leadership capabilities of subordinates, encouraging them to develop self-control skills.

self-managed team (SMT)   Sometimes called a *process team,* a group that is responsible for producing an entire product, component, or service.

sender   Individual or party that initiates communication with another individual or party.

seniority   A defense against discrimination in which companies with a well-established seniority system can give more senior workers priority, even if this has an adverse impact on protected class members.

sequential interdependence   A series of hand-offs of work flow between team members in which output of one team member becomes the input of the next team member, and so forth.

sexual harassment   A form of discrimination that is broadly interpreted to include sexually suggestive remarks, unwanted touching, any physical or verbal act that indicates sexual advances or requests sexual favors, a promise of rewards or hidden threats by a supervisor to induce emotional attachment by a subordinate, and a "hostile environment" based on sex.

situational context   The factors that are outside the control of the subordinate such as the tasks defining the job, the formal authority system of the organization, and the work group.

six sigma   A quality standard that is equivalent to generating fewer than 3.4 defects per million manufacturing or service operations.

skills inventory   A human resource inventory that keeps track of the firm's internal supply of talent by listing employees' education, training, experience, and language abilities; the firm can use this information to identify those eligible for promotion or transfer before trying to fill the position from the external market.

small business   Any business that is independently owned and operated, that is small in size, and that is not dominant in its markets.

socialization   The process of internalizing or taking organizational values as one's own.

span of control   The feature of the vertical structure of an organization that outlines the number of subordinates who report to a manager, the number of managers, and the layers of management within the organization.

spin-off   An independent entrepreneurship that produces a product or service that originated in a large company.

staff authority   Management function of advising, recommending, and counseling line managers and others in the organization; it provides specialized expertise and is not directly related to achieving the strategic goals of the organization.

staff managers   The level of management that helps line managers achieve bottom-line results while only indirectly contributing to the outcome.

stakeholders   The groups or individuals who have an interest in the performance of the enterprise and how it uses its resources, including employees, customers, and shareholders.

statistical process control   An operations management monitoring tool that uses quantitative methods and procedures to evaluate transformation operations and to detect and eliminate deviations.

storming stage   A stage in team development in which team members voice their differences about team goals and procedures.

storyboarding   A variation of brainstorming in which group members jot down ideas on cards and then can shuffle, rewrite, or even eliminate cards to examine complex processes.

strategic action plans   Management plans based on macro approaches for analyzing organizational features, resources, and the environment and establishing long-term corporatewide action programs to accomplish the stated objectives in light of that analysis.

strategic alliances   Cooperative arrangements between competitors or potential competitors from different countries, possibly to establish a formal joint venture or collaboration between firms on specific projects.

strategic compensation   Compensation practices that best support the firm's business strategy.

strategic decisions   Decisions that have a long-term perspective of two to five years and affect the entire organization.

strategic HR planning (SHRP)   The development of a vision about where the company wants to be and how it can use human resources to get there.

strategic intent   The firm's internally focused definition of how the firm intends to use its resources, capabilities, and core competencies to win competitive battles.

strategic managers   The firm's senior executives who are responsible for overall management.

strategic meeting   Bringing people from different departments or divisions together to synchronize plans and objectives and to coordinate activities.

strategic mission   The firm's externally focused definition of what it plans to produce and market, utilizing its internally based core competence.

strategizing   The management skill of focusing on the firm's key objectives and on the internal and external environments and responding in an appropriate and timely fashion.

strategy formulation   The design of an approach to achieve the firm's mission.

SWOT (strengths-weaknesses-opportunities-threats) analysis   A strategic management tool to evaluate the firm, which is accomplished by identifying its strengths and weaknesses, identifying its opportunities and threats, and cross-matching strengths with opportunities, weaknesses with threats, strengths with threats, and weaknesses with opportunities.

synergy   Allows individuals to blend complementary skills and talents to produce a product that is more valuable than the sum of the individual contributions.

systems theory   A modern management theory that views the organization as a system of interrelated parts that function in a holistic way to achieve a common purpose.

t

tactical action plans   Management action plans at the division or department level that indicate what activities must be performed, when they must be completed, and what resources will be needed at the division or departmental level to complete the portions of the strategic action plan that fall under the purview of that particular organizational subunit.

tactical decisions   Decisions that have a short-term perspective of one year or less and focus on subunits of the organization, such as departments or project teams.

tactical managers   The firm's management staff who are responsible for translating the general goals and plan developed by strategic managers into specific objectives and activities.

tangible resources   Assets that can be quantified and observed, including financial resources, physical assets, and manpower.

task force   A temporary interdepartmental group formed to study an issue and make recommendations.

task-facilitating role   The team-member role with the priority of helping the team accomplish its task goals.

task-oriented leadership   A leadership style that emphasizes work accomplishments and performance results.

team   A small number of people with complementary skills who are committed to a common purpose, a set of performance goals, and an approach for which they hold themselves mutually accountable.

team cohesiveness   The extent to which members feel a high degree of camaraderie, team spirit, and sense of unity.

team norms   Shared beliefs that regulate the behavior of team members.

technology   The means of transforming inputs into products.

Theory X   A negative perspective on human behavior.

Theory Y   A positive perspective on human behavior.

third-country nationals   Citizens of countries other than the host nation or the firm's home country.

360-degree feedback   Multirater feedback from peers, suppliers, other levels of management, and internal and external customers.

three-step model   A model of organizational change that features the three steps of unfreezing (melting the resistance to change), change (the departure from the status quo; also called movement or transformation), and refreezing (making new practices part of the employees' routine activities).

top-down change   Organizational change that is initiated by managers.

total factor productivity   The measurement of how well an organization utilizes all of its resources, such as capital, labor, materials, or energy, to produce its outputs.

total quality management (TQM)   An organization-wide management approach that focuses on quality as an overarching goal. The basis of this approach is the understanding that all employees and organizational units should be working harmoniously to satisfy the customer.

trait appraisal instruments   Performance appraisal tools that evaluate employees based on worker characteristics that tend to be consistent and enduring, such as decisiveness, reliability, energy, and loyalty.

transactional leaders   Leaders who use legitimate, coercive, or reward powers to elicit obedience and attempt to instill in followers the ability to question standard modes of operation.

transaction-processing systems   An operations information system used to maintain data about transactions, such as inventory, sales, and purchase of supplies.

transformational leaders   Leaders who revitalize organizations by instilling in followers the ability to question standard modes of operation.

transformational leadership   A leadership style characterized by the ability to bring about significant change in an organization, such as a change in vision, strategy, or culture.

trust   The willingness of one team member to increase his or her vulnerability to the actions of another person whose behavior he or she cannot control.

tuition assistance programs   Support by the firm for employees' education and development by covering the cost of tuition and other fees for seminars, workshops, and continuing education programs.

turnkey projects A specialized type of exporting in which the firm handles the design, construction, start-up operations, and workforce training of a foreign plant, and a local client is handed the key to a plant that is fully operational.

two-way communications Communication channels that provide for feedback.

U

uncertainty The condition when incomplete information is available and must be used to make a management decision.

uncertainty avoidance The extent to which a society places a high value on reducing risk and instability.

unity of command The management concept that a subordinate should have only one direct supervisor, and a decision can be traced back through subordinates to the manager who originated it.

upward communication Sending a message from a position lower in the hierarchy to a receiver higher in the hierarchy.

utilitarianism A means of making decisions based on what is good for the greatest number of people.

V

validity The measurement of how well a technique used to assess candidates is related to performance in the job.

value-chain analysis Strategic management analysis that breaks the firm down into a sequential series of activities and attempts to identify the value-added of each activity.

venture capitalists Financial investors who specialize in making loans to entrepreneurships that have the potential for rapid growth but are in high-risk situations with few assets and would therefore not qualify for commercial bank loans.

vertical dimension The organization structure element that indicates who has the authority to make decisions and who is expected to supervise which subordinates.

vertical integration strategy A form of diversification strategy in which a firm integrates vertically by acquiring businesses that are supply channels or distributors to the primary business; producing its own inputs is backward integration, and distributing its own outputs is forward integration.

virtual teams Groups that use interactive computer technologies such as the Internet, groupware (software that permits people at different computer workstations to collaborate on a project simultaneously), and computer-based videoconferencing to work together regardless of distance.

visible culture The aspects of culture that an observer can hear, feel, or see.

voluntary contracts Because both parties enter the labor contract freely, one party can use the legal system to enforce the terms of the contract if the other party does not fulfill its responsibilities.

W

whistleblower policies A method by which employees who disclose their employer's illegal, immoral, or illegitimate practices can be protected; companies with whistleblower policies rely on whistleblowers to report unethical activities to the ethics officer or committee, which will then gather facts and investigate the situation in a fair and impartial way.

wholly owned subsidiaries A means of entering new markets in which a firm fully owns its subsidiary in foreign countries.

win–win style Negotiating style requiring all interested parties to convert a potential conflict into a problem-solving process in which each party seeks to identify common, shared, or joint goals.

win–lose style Negotiating style used when there is a single issue that consists of a fixed amount of resources in which one party attempts to gain at the expense of the other.

work group Members of a group who are held accountable for individual work, but they are not responsible for the output of the entire group.

World Trade Organization (WTO) *See* General Agreement on Tariffs and Trade (GATT).

Chapter 1

1. G. R. Jones, J. M. George, and C. W. Hill, *Contemporary Management.* New York: McGraw-Hill/Irwin, 2000, p. 42.
2. L. R. Gomez-Mejia, D. B. Balkin, and R. Candy, *Managing Human Resources.* Englewood Cliffs, NJ: Prentice Hall, 2004.
3. Harris, 1915.
4. J. Heizer and B. Render, *Production and Operations Management.* Englewood Cliffs, NJ: Prentice Hall, 1996, p. 650.
5. G. R. Jones, J. M. George, and C. W. Hill, *Contemporary Management.* New York: McGraw-Hill/Irwin, 2000, p. 54.
6. C. I. Barnard, *The Functions of the Executive.* Cambridge, MA: Harvard University Press, 1938, p. 65.

Chapter 2

1. G. de Jonquieres, "Foreign Direct Investment Worldwide Figures to Reach $430 Billion," *Financial Times,* November 11, 1998, p. 6; D. I. Oyama, "World Watch," *The Wall Street Journal,* June 1, 1999, p. A16.
2. C. W. Hill, *International Business.* New York: McGraw-Hill/Irwin, 2000.
3. World Trade Organization, *International Trade Trends and Statistics.* Geneva: WTO, 1998; see the special issue of *Business Week* on globalization, February 3, 2003.
4. "The Global 500," *Fortune,* August 7, 1995, pp. 130–131.
5. Hudson, R. L. (2003, January 24). Europe's great expectations. *Wall Street Journal,* A-10.
6. Naik, G., V., Karp, J., Millman, J., Fassiti, F., & Slater, J. (2003, January 24). Global baby bust. *Wall Street Journal,* B-1.
7. T. Raithel, "Panel to Look at Changes Brought by Toyota," *Evansville Courier and Press,* July 2, 1999, pp. 3–4.
8. Hill, C. (2003). *International business.* New York: McGraw-Hill/Irwin.
9. Hill, *International Business,* p. 6.
10. S. N. Mehta, "Enterprise: Small Companies Look to Cultivate Foreign Businesses," *The Wall Street Journal,* July 7, 1994, p. B-2.
11. Hill, *International Business,* p. 11.
12. J. H. Donnelly, J. Gibson, and J. M. Ivancevich, *Fundamentals of Management.* Burr Ridge, IL: Irwin, 1995, p. 67.
13. D. A. Ball, McCulloch, W. H., Frantz, P. L., Geringer, J. M., & Minor, M. S. (2002). *International business: The challenge of global competition.* New York: McGraw-Hill.
14. R. S. Greenberger, and C. S. Smith, "CD Piracy Flourishes in China," *The Wall Street Journal,* April 28, 1997, p. A1.
15. J. Darling and D. Nauss, "Stall in the Fast Lane," *Los Angeles Times,* February 19, 1995, p. 1.
16. G. Hofstede, *Culture's Consequences: International Differences in Work Related Values.* Beverly Hills, CA: Sage, 1984, p. 21.
17. Ibid.
18. Wild, J., Wild, K. C., & Han, J. C. (2002). *International business.* Englewood Cliffs, NJ: Prentice Hall.
19. Taylor, A. (2003, January 20). Got 300,000? *Fortune,* 118–125.
20. Wild et al., p. 372.
21. Hill, C. (2003).
22. R. Miller, P. Coy, C. Tierney, and D. Fairlamb, "Good News! The Dollar is Down," *Business Week,* May 26, 2003, pp. 36–39.
23. B. Bremner, Z. Schiller, T. Smart, and W. Holstein, "Keiretsu Connections," *Business Week,* July 22, 1996, pp. 52–53.
24. Ibid., p. 2.
25. Hill, *International Business,* p. 412.
26. R. Cohen, "For Coke, World Is Its Oyster," *The New York Times,* November 21, 1991, pp. D1, D5.
27. P. Oster, "Why Japan's Execs Travel Better," *Business Week,* November 1993, p. 68.
28. L. Grant, "That Overseas Job Could Derail Your Career," *Fortune,* April 14, 1997, p. 166.
29. Ibid.
30. G. Koretz, "A Woman's Place Is . . . ," *Business Week,* September 13, 1999, p. 28; H. Lancaster, "To Get Shipped Abroad, Women Must Overcome Prejudice at Home," *The Wall Street Journal,* July 29,

1989, p. B1; M. L. Wilson, "She Got the Last Laugh When Colleagues Bet She Would Fail in Japan," *The Wall Street Journal*, July 16, 1999, p. B1.

31. G. Koretz, "Where Expats Spend the Most." *Business Week*, June 25, 2001, p. 30.

Chapter 3

1. M. Jackson, "50% of Workers Commit Unethical Acts, Survey Says," *Boulder Daily Camera*, May 12, 1997, p. 1B; "Business Ethics: Doing Well by Doing Good," *The Economist*, April 22, 2000, pp. 65–67.

2. F. D. Sturdivant and H. Vernon-Wortzel, *Business and Society*, 4th ed. Burr Ridge, IL: Irwin, 1990.

3. P. E. Murphy, "Creating Ethical Corporate Structures," *Sloan Management Review* 30 (Winter 1989): 81–89.

4. Eli Lilly & Company, Guidelines of Company Policy, 1990.

5. General Dynamics, Standards of Business Ethics and Conduct, 1988.

6. JD Edwards & Company, Corporate Ideals and Values, 1993.

7. M. Gundlach, S. Douglas, and M. Martinko, "The Decision to Blow the Whistle: A Social Information Processing Framework," *Academy of Management Review* 28 (2003): 107–123.

8. T. M. Dworkin and J. P. Near, "A Better Statutory Approach to Whistle Blowing," *Business Ethics Quarterly* 7, no. 1 (1997): 1–16.

9. Ibid.

10. P. Dwyer and D. Carney, "Year of the Whistleblower," *Business Week*, December 16, 2002, pp. 107–110.

11. W. Zellner, "The Whistleblower: A Hero—and a Smoking-Gun Letter," *Business Week*, January 28, 2002, pp. 34–35.

12. M. Sashkin and K. J. Kiser, *Putting Total Quality Management to Work* (San Francisco: Berrett-Koehler, 1993).

13. I. Sager, "Tech's Kickback Culture," *Business Week*, February 10, 2003, pp. 74–77.

14. A. Park, "Family Feuds Don't Get Nastier than This," *Business Week*, February 10, 2003, pp. 62–63.

15. *Global Corruption Report 2003*, www.globalcorruptionreport.org.

16. "Pharmaceuticals: Pushing Pills," *The Economist*, February 15, 2003, p. 61.

17. D. B. Turban and D. W. Greening. "Corporate Social Performance and Organizational Attractiveness to Prospective Employees," *Academy of Management Journal* 40 (1997): 658–672; J. B. McGuire, A. Sundgren and T. Schneeweis, "Corporate Social Responsibility and Firm Financial Performance," *Academy of Management Journal* 27 (1988): 42–56; P. L. Cochran and R. A. Wood, "Corporate Social Responsibility and Financial Performance," *Academy of Management Journal* 31 (1984): 854–872.

18. S. V. Brull, "For All That Tobacco Money, Don't Stint on the Smoking War," *Business Week*, May 10, 1999, p. 40; D. Noonan, "Lighting into Big Tobacco," *Newsweek*, July 24, 2000, pp. 30–31.

19. D. Driscoll, "The Dow Corning Case: First, Kill All the Lawyers," *Business and Society Review* 100 (June 1998): 57–63.

20. A. B. Carroll, *Business and Society*, 3rd ed. Cincinnati, OH: SouthWestern Publishing, 1996.

21. J. Greenwald, "Let's Make a Deal," *Time*, March 22, 1989, pp. 84–86.

22. B. McLean, "Why Enron Went Bust," *Fortune*, December 24, 2001, pp. 58–68; and W. Zellner and S. Forest, "The Fall of Enron," *Business Week*, December 17, 2001, pp. 30–36.

23. N. Munk, "How Levi Trashed a Great American Brand," *Fortune*, April 12, 1999, pp. 82–90.

24. C. Schulaka, "Profiting with Nonprofits," *Boulder Daily Camera*, July 14, 1997, pp. 1D, 12D–13D.

25. "Boeing v. Airbus," *Economist*, July 26, 1997, pp. 59–61.

26. A. B. Carroll, *Business and Society*, 3rd ed. Cincinnati, OH: SouthWestern Publishing, 1996.

27. J. H. Jackson, R. L. Miller, and S. G. Miller, *Business and Society Today* (St. Paul, MN: West Publishing, 1997).

28. N. C. Roberts and P. J. King, "The Stakeholder Audit Goes Public," *Organizational Dynamics*, Winter 1989, pp. 63–79.

29. R. Will, "Corporations with a Conscience," *Business and Society Review*, Spring 1995, pp. 17–20.

30. D. A. Whetton and K. S. Cameron, *Developing Management Skills*, 3rd ed. (New York: HarperCollins, 1995).

Chapter 4

1. Larson, L. (2002). A new attitude: Changing organizational culture. *Trustee*, 55, 8–14.

2. M. Conlin, "Workers, Surf at Your Own Risk," *Business Week*, June 12, 2000, p. 106.

3. M. Arndt and A. Berstein, "From Milestone to Milestone," *Business Week*, March 20, 2000, p. 122.

4. Gifford, B. D., Zammuto, R. F., Goodman, E. A., & Hill, K. (2002). The relationship between hospital unit culture and nurse's quality of work life. *Journal of Healthcare Management*, 47, 13–21.

5. J. Rossant, "Old World, New Mandate," *Business Week*, January 31, 2000, p. 92.

6. R. L. Cardy. HRM and the virtual workplace: Some concluding observations and future directions. In R. L. Heneman & D. B. Greenberger Eds., *Human Resource Management in Virtual Organizations*. (Greenwich, CT: Information Age Publishing, 2002).

7. S. Robbins, "Organizational Behavior (Englewood Cliffs, NJ: Prentice Hall, 2001), p. 693.

8. Jeffrey Pfeffer, quoted in J. Hamilton, "The Panic over Hiring," *Business Week*, April 3, 2000, p. 131.

9. P. M. Wright and R. A. Noe, *Management of Organizations* (Burr Ridge, IL: Irwin, 1996), p. 185.

10. A. Nahavandi and A. R. Malekzadeh, *Organizational Behavior: The Person–Organization Fit* (Englewood Cliffs, NJ: Prentice Hall, 1999), p. 95.

11. Enderle, R. (2002). Personal communication, November, 27.

12. Roznowski, D. (1999, August 19). Johnson Control employees help to reduce cost, waste, and increase safety quality through team rally event. *PR Newswire Association*.

13. Heneman, R. L., Fisher, M. M., & Dixon, K. E. (2001). Reward and organizational systems alignment: An expert system. *Compensation and Benefits Review*, 33, 18–29.

14. C. Hymowitz, "Which Culture Fits You?" *The Wall Street Journal*, July 13, 1989, p B1.

15. R. E. Quinn & J. Rohrbaugh. A spatial model of effectiveness criteria: Toward a competing values approach to organizational analysis. *Management Science, 1983, 23,* 363–377.

16. Gifford et al. 2002.

17. Cardy, 2002.

18. P. Mornell, "Nothing Endures but Change," *Inc,* July 2000, pp. 131–132.

19. Trebilcock, B. (2002). The shadow knows. *Logistics Management & Distribution Report, 41,* 39.

20. E. E. Lawler, Managing change. *Executive Excellence, 2002, 19,* 17–18.

21. K. Lewin, *Field Theory in Social Science: Selected Theoretical Papers* (New York: Harper & Brothers, 1951).

22. "Change Management: An Inside Job," *The Economist,* July 15, 2000, p. 61.

Chapter 5

1. D. Stipp, "Why Pfizer Is So Hot," *Fortune,* May 11, 1998, p. 88.

2. J. Muller, J. Green, and C. Tierney, "Chrysler's Rescue Team," *Business Week,* January 15, 2001, pp. 48–50.

3. L. Grant, "Why Kodak Still Isn't Fixed," *Fortune,* May 11, 1998, pp. 179–181.

4. J. A. Byrne, "How Jack Welch Runs GE," *Business Week,* June 8, 1998, pp. 90–110; E. Brown, "America's Most Admired Companies," *Fortune,* March 1, 1999, pp. 68–76.

5. S. A. Snell, Control theory in strategic human resource management: The mediating effect of administrative information. *Academy of Management Journal,* June 1992, *35,* 293.

6. C. O. O'Reilly, Corporations, culture and commitment: Motivation and social control in organizations. *California Management Review,* Summer, 1992.

7. *Business Week,* September 17, 1985. Special feature issue on planning.

8. "The Year of the Dot.Bomb," *Business Week,* January 15, 2001, p. 10; www.dotcomfailures.com, www.company.com.forrester research, *Business Week.*

9. E. H. Burack, *Creative Human Resource Planning and Applications* (Englewood Cliffs, NJ: Prentice Hall, 1988).

10. D. Eisenberg, "Power to the People," *Time,* 2001, pp. 46–47.

11. D. Welch, "Detroit's Big Steeds Are Losing Traction," *Time,* 2001, pp. 37–40.

12. "FedEx, Post Office Combine Deliveries," *The Arizona Republic,* January 12, 2001, p. D1.

13. Byrne, "How Jack Welch Runs GE," p. 95.

14. A. Barrett, DuPont tries to unclog a pipeline. *Business Week,* 2003, January 27, pp. 103–104.

15. "FedEx, Post Office Combine," p. D7, Altavista Co.

16. T. Satterfield. "From Performance Management to Performance Leadership." *Worldatwork* 2003, first quarter, *Journal,* pp. 15–20.

17. D. W. Jarrell, *Human Resource Planning* (Englewood Cliffs, NJ: Prentice Hall, 1993), p. 73.

18. P. Tsao, "Reports of Cancer's Imminent Death Were an Exaggeration," *Business Week,* June 8, 1998, p. 13.

19. J. Muller, "Thinking out of the Cereal Box," January 15, 2001, pp. 54–55.

20. M. L. Tushman and C. A. O'Reilly III, *Winning through Innovation* (Boston: Harvard Business School Press, 1997).

21. Ibid.

22. Ibid.

23. Ibid.

24. Ibid.

Chapter 6

1. C. M. Pearson and J. A. Clair, "Reframing Organizational Crisis," *Academy of Management Review* 23 (1998): 59–76.

2. N. R. Maier, *Psychology in Industrial Organizations,* 4th ed. (Boston: Houghton Mifflin, 1973).

3. A. A. Thompson and A. J. Strickland, (1998). *Strategic Management: Concepts and Cases,* 10th ed. New York: Irwin/McGraw-Hill.

4. S. P. Robbins and M. Coulter, *Management,* 5th ed. (Upper Saddle River, NJ: Prentice Hall, 1996), pp. 196–197.

5. H. A. Simon, *Models of Man* (New York: Wiley, 1957).

6. M. D. Cohen, J. G. March, and J. P. Olsen, "The Garbage Can Model of Organizational Choice," *Administrative Science Quarterly* 17 (1972): 1–25.

7. R. H. Hall, *Organizations* (Upper Saddle River, NJ: Prentice Hall, 1999).

8. A. L. Delbecq, A. H. Van de Ven, and D. H. Gustafson, *Group Techniques for Program Planning* (Glenview, IL: Scott, Foresman, 1975).

9. R. E. Quinn, S. R. Faerman, M. P. Thompson, and M. R. McGrath, *Becoming a Master Manager,* 2nd ed. (New York: John Wiley & Sons, 1996).

Chapter 7

1. www.ford.com, accessed August 1, 2003.

2. *Business Week,* January 12, 1998: 154–60; www.american express.com.

3. J. Revell, (2002, October 28). GM's slow leak. *Fortune,* pp. 105–110.

4. *San Jose Mercury News,* 1998, Gates is Too Busy To Define Government. Story appearing in *Arizona Republic,* E1.

5. J. Unseem, (2003, March 3). One nation under Wal-Mart. *Fortune,* p. 65.

6. N. Stein, (2003, March 3). America's most admired companies. *Fortune,* pp. 81–98.

7. D. Carney, Uncle Sam's trustbusters: Outgunned and outmoded. *Business Week,* (2002, November 18), pp. 44–45.

8. S. Hamm, J. Greene, & A. Reinhardt, (2002, November 18). What is a rival to do now? *Business Week,* pp. 44–46.

9. M. E. Porter, *Competitive Advantage* (New York: Free Press, 1990).

10. W. Echikson, "Designers Climb onto the Virtual Catwalk," *Business Week,* October 11, 1999, pp. 164–166.

11. R. A. D'Aveni, "Coping with Hypercompetition: Utilizing the New 75's Framework," *Academy of Management Executive* 9, no. 3 (1995): 54.

12. M. S. Hunt, *Competition in the Major Home Appliance Industry* (Cambridge, MA: Harvard University Press, 1972).

13. M. A. Hitt, R. D. Ireland, and R. E. Hoskisson, *Strategic Management* (New York: Irwin/McGraw-Hill, 2001).
14. R. M. Grant, *Contemporary Strategy Analysis* (Malden, MA: Blackwell, 1998), p. 129.
15. Stein, 2003, p. 81–98.
16. G. Khermouch, S. Holmes, and M. Ihlwan, "The Best Global Brands". *Business Week,* 2001, August 6, pp. 51–55.
17. U. Kher, "The Workhorse of Genomic Medicine," Time, January 15, 2001, p. 62.
18. Michael Hitt, R. Duane Ireland, and Robert E. Hoskisson, *Strategic Management: Competitiveness and Globalization* (Cincinnati, OH: South-Western Publishing, 1999), p. 26.
19. Stein, 2003, p. 81–98.
20. Kunii, I. M. (2002, September 16). Making Canon click. *Business Week,* pp. 40–42.
21. Grant, R. M. (2001). *Contemporary strategic analysis.* Malden, MA: Blackwell.
22. K. Hughes and C. Oughton, "Diversification, Multimarket Contact, and Profitability," *Economics* 60 (1993): 203–224; C. W. L. Hill, "Diversification and Economic Performance: Bringing Structure and Corporate Management Back into the Picture," in R. P. Rumelt et al. (Eds.), *Fundamental Issues in Strategy* (Boston: Harvard Business School Press, 1994), pp. 297–321.
23. "Upfront". *Business Week,* 2001, August 6, p. 7.
24. Adapted from *Business Week,* January 12, 1998, p. 12; www.mnba.com.
25. Hitt, Ireland, and Hoskisson, *Strategic Management,* p. 347.
26. Hitt, Ireland, and Hoskisson, *Strategic Management: Competitiveness and Globalization,* p. 28.
27. Ibid., p. 383.

Chapter 8

1. U.S. Small Business Administration, 2000 (www.sba.com).

Chapter 9

1. D. Robey and C. A. Sayles, *Designing Organizations* (Burr Ridge, IL: Irwin, 1994).
2. Ibid.
3. Ibid.
4. R. C. Ford and W. A. Randolph, "Cross-Functional Structures: A Review and Integration of Matrix Organization and Project Management," *Journal of Management* 18 (1992): 267–294.
5. R. L. Daft, *Management,* 4th ed. (Fort Worth: Dryden Press, 1997).
6. K. A. Frank and K. Fahrback, "Organization Culture as a Complex System: Balance and Information Models of Influence and Selection," *Organization Science* 10 (1999): 253–277.
7. J. C. Collins and J. I. Porras, *Built to Last: Successful Habits of Visionary Companies* (New York: Harper Business, 1994), p. 117.
8. Ibid., p. 128.
9. M. S. Kraatz and E. J. Zaja, "How Organizational Resources Affect Strategic Change and Performance in Turbulent Environments: Theory and Evidence," *Organization Science* 12(2001): 632–657.

10. G. R. Jones, *Organizational Theory,* 2nd ed. (Reading, MA: Addison-Wesley, 1998).
11. *Economist,* "How to Manage a Dream Factory," January 18, 2003, pp. 73–75.

Chapter 10

1. "USA Today Snapshots," *USA Today,* January 17, 2001, p. 1A.
2. D. Gonzalez, "World's Cultures Converge in State," *The Arizona Republic,* January 8, 2001, p. A1.
3. Rebecca Walker, *Black, White and Jewish: Autobiography of a Shifting Self* (New York: Riverhead Books, 2001).
4. T. Kenworthy, "Air Force Academy Hit by Drug Scandal," *USA Today,* January 16, 2001, p. 3A.
5. "Companies Try Creative Cutbacks: Managers Hope to Avoid Drastic Step of Layoffs." *USA Today,* January 8, 2001, p. D1.
6. www.latestandgreatest5@hrpomotions.com.
7. J. P. Wanous, *Organizational Entry,* 2nd ed. (Reading, MA: Addison-Wesley, 1992).
8. S. Armour, "Degrees in e-Commerce Seem Less Dazzling," January 16, 2001, p. B1.
9. F. Golden, "Probing the Chemistry of the Brain," *Time,* January 15, 2001, p. 55.
10. L. M. Gomez-Mejia, D. B. Balkin, and R. Cardy, *Managing Human Resources* (Englewood Cliffs, NJ: Prentice Hall, 2001).
11. "Boeing Engineers to Get Bonuses," *USA Today,* January 8, 2001, p. A3.
12. G. L. White, "Ford Admits Last Year's Quality Snafus," *The Wall Street Journal,* January 12, 2001, p. A3.
13. T. Larimer, "Rebirth of the Z," *Time,* January 15, 2001, pp. 42–44.

Chapter 11

1. L. R. Gomez-Mejia, D. B. Balkin, and R. Cardy, *Managing Human Resources.* (Englewood Cliffs, NJ: Prentice Hall, 2001).
2. M. L. Wheeler, "Capitalizing on Diversity," *Business Week,* December 14, 1998, special advertising section.
3. Ibid.
4. G. Colvin, "50 Best Companies for Asians, Blacks, and Hispanics," *Fortune,* July 19, 1999, pp. 52–59.
5. R. O. Crockett, "African-Americans Get the Investing Bug," *Business Week,* May 24, 1999, p. 39.
6. Prystay, C., & Ellison, S. (2003, February 27). Time for marketers to grow up? *Wall Street Journal,* p. B-1.
7. D. Jones, "U.S. Managers Earn Global Credentials," *USA Today,* February 26, 1997, p. A1.
8. M. L. Wheeler, "Diversity: Making the Business Case," *Business Week,* December 9, 1996, special advertising section.
9. Ibid.
10. V. I. Sessa, S. E. Jackson, and D. T. Rapini, "Workforce Diversity: The Good, and Bad, and the Reality." In G. Ferris, S. D. Rosen, and D. T. Barnum (Eds.), *Handbook of Human Resource Management* (Cambridge, MA: Blackwell, 1995), pp. 263–282.
11. Wheeler, "Diversity."

12. T. H. Cox and S. Blake, "Managing Cultural Diversity: Implications for Organizational Competitiveness," *Academy of Management Executive* 5, no. 3 (1991): 45–46.

13. M. C. Fine, P. L. Johnson, and S. M. Ryan, "Cultural Diversity in the Workplace," *Public Personnel Management* 19, no. 3 (1990): 305–319.

14. Wheeler, "Diversity."

15. Fine, Johnson, and Ryan, "Cultural Diversity in the Workplace."

16. Crockett, R. O. (2003, January 27). *Business Week*, p. 96.

17. H. Fineman, & T. Lipper, (2003, January 23). Spinning race. *Newsweek* pp. 27–38.

18. C. Hastings, (2003, April). Engaging in a growing workforce. *Workspan*, pp. 35–39.

19. T. S. Bateman and S. A. Snell, *Management: Building Competitive Advantage*, 4th ed. (Burr Ridge, IL: Irwin, 1999), p. 320.

20. L. R. Gomez-Mejia, D. B. Balkin, & R. Cardy, (2004). *Managing Human Resources.* Englewood Cliffs, NJ: Prentice Hall.

21. M. France and T. Smart, "The Ugly Talk on the Texaco Tape," *Business Week,* November 18, 1996, p. 58.

22. "Research National Phone Poll," *Chattanooga Times,* March 4, 1994, p. 1.

23. Ibid.; Stephanie Mehta, "What Minority Employees Really Want," *Fortune,* July 10, 2000, p. 180.

24. L. Koss-Feder, "Spurred by the Americans with Disabilities Act, More Firms Take On Those Ready, Willing and Able to Work," *Time,* January 25, 1999, p. 82.

25. Briefs (1993, Feb. 22). *Workforce Strategies,* 4, no.2, (February 22, 1993): WS-12.

26. Y. Armendariz, (2003, February 10). Disabled workers can telecommute. *Arizona Republic,* p. D-3.

27. R. Alonso-Zaldivar, (2003, February 1). Immigrants at 7 million, revised INS report says. *Arizona Republic* p. A–5.

28. L. Koss-Feder, "Spurred by the Americans with Disabilities Act, More Firms Take On Those Ready, Willing and Able to Work," p. 82.

29. J. Kanman, & H. Rozenberg, (2002, February 7). Survey looks at residents with recent foreign roots. *Arizona Republic,* p. A–8.

30. Doyle, R. (2002, February). Assembling the future. *Scientific American,* p. 30.

31. Gomez-Mejia, Cardy, and Balkin, *Managing Human Resources.*

32. R. Mendosa, "The $152 Billion Engine," *Hispanic Business,* October 1996, pp. 28–29; R. Mendosa, "A Downward Count," *Hispanic Business,* October 1996, p. 18.

33. Gomez-Mejia, Cardy, and Balkin, *Managing Human Resources.*

34. E. Banach, "Today's Supply of Entry Level Workers Reflect Diversity," *Savings Institution,* September 1990, p. 74.

35. D. S. Fellows, (2001). Striking gold in a silver mine: Leveraging senior workers as knowledge champions. *Worldatwork Journal, 10*(4), 1–12.

36. Wheeler, "Diversity."

37. Ibid.

38. Ibid.

39. Ibid.

40. Gomez-Mejia, Cardy, and Balkin, Managing *Human Resources.*

41. Wheeler, "Diversity."

42. Ashton, A. (2002, February). Around-the-clock child care. *Working Women,* p. 14.

43. Newman, A. M. (2002, February). Fair shares. *Working Women,* pp. 64–71.

44. Conlin, M., Merrill, J., & Himelstein, L. (2002, November 25). Mommy is really home from work. *Business Week,* pp. 101–104.

45. Ibid.

Chapter 12

1. A. H. Maslow, "A Theory of Human Motivation," *Psychological Review,* July 1943, pp. 370–396.

2. C. Alderfer, *Existence, Relatedness, and Growth: Human Needs in Organizational Settings* (Glencoe, IL: Free Press, 1972).

3. D. McClelland, *The Achieving Society* (New York: Van Nostrand Reinhold, 1961).

4. R. E. Boyatzis, "The Need for Close Relationships and the Manager's Job," in D. A. Kolls, I. M. Rubin, and J. M. McIntyre (eds.), *Organizational Psychology: Readings on Human Behavior in Organizations,* 4th ed. (Englewood Cliffs, NJ: Prentice Hall, 1984).

5. D. C. McClelland and R. Boyatzis, "Leadership Motive Pattern and Long-Term Success in Management," *Journal of Applied Psychology* 67 (1982): 737–743.

6. N. Adler, *International Dimensions of Organizational Behavior,* 3rd ed. (Cincinnati, OH: South-Western Publishing Co., 1997); G. Hofstede, *Culture's Consequences: International Differences in Work Related Values* (Beverly Hills, CA: Sage, 1980).

7. F. Herzberg, (2003). One more time: How do you motivate employees? *Harvard Business Review, 81,* 87–96.

8. P. C. Early, T. Connolly, and G. Ekegren, "Goals, Strategy Development, and Task Performance: Some Limits on the Efficacy of Goal Setting," *Journal of Applied Psychology* 74 (1989): 24–33; C. E. Shalley, "Effects of Productivity Goals, Creativity Goals, and Personal Discretion on Individual Creativity," *Journal of Applied Psychology* 76 (1991): 179–185. Most of these studies are based on the pioneering work of E. Locke, "Toward a Theory of Task Motivation and Incentives," *Organizational Behavior and Human Performance* 3 (1968): 157–189. For practitioner perspective, see J. W. Marcum, "Out with Motivation, in with Engagement," *National Productivity Review* 19, no. 4 (Autumn 2000): 57–60.

9. J. S. Adams, "Inequity in Social Exchanges," in L. Berkowitz (ed.), *Advances in Experimental Social Psychology* (New York: Academic Press, 1965), pp. 267–300; S. Ronen, "Equity Perception in Multiple Comparisons: A Field Study," *Human Relations,* April, 1986, pp. 333–346; T. P. Summers and A. S. DeNisi, "In Search of Adam's Other: Reexamination of Referents Used in the Evaluation of Pay," *Human Relations,* June 1990, pp. 495–511.

10. E. L. Thorndike, *The Fundamentals of Learning* (New York: AMS Press, 1971).

11. V. H. Vroom, *Work and Motivation* (New York: John Wiley & Sons, 1964); H. J. Arnold, "A Test of the Multiplicative

Hypothesis of Expectancy-Valence Theories of Work Motivation," *Academy of Management Journal,* April 1981, pp. 128–141.

12. R. Grossman, (2003). Putting in rotation: Experts say job rotation programs are best way to gain a broad view of the business, yet HR often leaves itself out of the loop. *HRMagazine, 48,* 50+.

13. D. Abbott, (2003). Stress and strain. *The Safety & Health Practitioner, 21,* 34+.

14. T. Pollack, (2002). Three ways to motivate people. *Automotive Design & Production, 114,* 10.

15. J. R. Hackman, G. Oldham, R. Janson, and K. Purdy, "A New Strategy for Job Enrichment," *California Management Review* 16 (1975): 57–71.

16. M. Memmotl, "Reich Knows High Cost of 'Success': He Paid It," *USA Today,* January 8, 2001, p. A1.

Chapter 13

1. D. Magee, (2003). *Turnaround: How Carlos Ghosn rescued Nissan.* New York: Harper Business/Harper Collins.

2. J. R. Healey, "Chrysler Again Runs Low on Financial Fuel," *USA Today,* January 30, 2001, p. 1B; D. Goodman, "Can Chrysler Survive?" *Arizona Republic,* January 30, 2001, p. D1.

3. J. E. Garten, "The Mind of the CEO," *Business Week,* February 5, 2001, p. 107.

4. S. P. Robbins, *Organizational Behavior,* 7th ed. (Englewood Cliffs, NJ: Prentice Hall, 1999), p. 413.

5. W. Adamchick, (2003). Elliot Institute must distinguish leadership from management. *Nation's Restaurant News, 37,* p. 36.

6. J. French and B. Raven, "The Bases of Social Power," in D. Cartwright (ed.), *Studies in Social Power* (Ann Arbor, MI: Institute for Social Research, 1959).

7. R. G. Lord, C. C. DeVader, and G. M. Alleger, "A Meta-analysis of the Relation between Personality Traits and Leadership Perceptions," *Journal of Applied Psychology* 71, no. 3 (1986): 402–410; D. A. Kenny and S. J. Zaccaro, "An Estimate of the Variance due to Traits in Leadership," *Journal of Applied Psychology* 68, no. 4 (1983): 678–685; D. A. Kenny and B. W. Hallmark, "Rotation Designs in Leadership Research," *Leadership Quarterly* 3, no. 1 (1992): 25–41; J. L. Denis, "Becoming a Leader in a Complex Organization," *Journal of Management Studies* 37, no. 8 (2000): 1063–1099; B. O'Reilly, "What It Takes to Start a Startup," *Fortune,* June 7, 1999, pp. 135–139; "The Top 25 Managers of the Year," *Business Week,* January 8, 2001, pp. 60–79.

8. J. M. Kouzes, & B. Z. Posner, (1990, July–August). The credibility factor: What followers expect from their leaders. *Business Credit,* p. 92.

9. S. Kerr, C. A. Schriesheim, C. J. Murphy, and R. M. Stogdill, "Toward a Contingency Theory of Leadership Based upon the Consideration and Initiating Structure Literature," *Organizational Behavior and Human Performance,* August 1974, pp. 62–82; and R. Kahn and D. Katz, "Leadership Practices in Relation to Productivity and Morale," in D. Cartwright and A. Sander (eds.), *Group*

Dynamics: Research and Theory (Elmsford, NY: Row, Peterson, 1960).

10. R. R. Blake and J. S. Mouton, *The Managerial Grid* (Houston: Gulf, 1964).

11. R. White and R. Lippit, *Autocracy and Democracy: An Experimental Inquiry* (New York: Harper & Brothers, 1960).

12. Robbins, *Organizational Behavior,* p. 419.

13. F. E. Fiedler, *A Theory of Leadership Effectiveness* (New York: McGraw-Hill, 1967): F. E. Fiedler, "Validation and Extension of the Contingency Model of Leadership Effectiveness," *Psychological Bulletin* 76 (1971): 128–148.

14. L. H. Peter, D. D. Hartke, and J. T. Pohlmann, "Fiedler's Contingency Theory of Leadership: An Application of the Meta-analysis Procedures of Schmidt and Hunter," *Psychological Bulletin,* March 1985, pp. 274–285; and C. A. Schriesheim, B. J. Tepper, and L. A. Tetrault, "Least Preferred Co-worker Score Situational Control, and Leadership Effectiveness: A Meta-analysis of Contingency Model Performance Predictions," *Journal of Applied Psychology,* August 1994, pp. 562–573.

15. R. J. House, "A Path Goal Theory of Leader Effectiveness," *Administrative Science Quarterly* 16 (1971): 321–338; R. J. House and T. R. Michell, "Path Goal Theory of Leadership," *Journal of Contemporary Business* 3 (1974): 81–97; R. House, "Weber and the Neo-charismatic Paradigm," *Leadership Quarterly* 10, no. 4 (2000): 15–26; R. House, P. J. Hanges, A. Quintanilla, P. W. Dorfman, M. W. Dickson, M. Javidan, et al., *Advances in Global Leadership* (Greenwich, CT: JAI Press, 1999), pp. 100–185.

16. "The Top 25 Managers," *Business Week,* January 8, 2001, pp. 60–80.

17. "Pioneer Hewlett Dies at 87," *Arizona Republic,* January 13, 2001.

18. J. R. Meindl, & S. B. Ehrlick, (1987). The romance of leadership and the evaluation of organizational performance. *Academy of Management Journal, 30,* 91–109.

19. T. Bateman and S. Snell, *Management: Building Competitive Advantage,* 4th ed. (New York: Irwin/McGraw-Hill, 2000).

20. B. M. Bass and B. J. Avolio, "Developing Transformational Leadership: 1992 and Beyond," *Journal of European Industrial Training,* January 1990, p. 23; B. Bass, B. Avolio, and L. Goodheim, "Biography in the Assessment of Transformational Leadership at the World Class Level," *Journal of Management* 13 (1987): 7–20.

21. J. R. McColl-Kennedy, & R. D. Anderson, (2002). Impact of leadership style and emotions on subordinate performance. *Leadership Quarterly, 13,* 545–559.

22. F. Luthans, & B. Avolio, (2003). Authentic leadership: A positive developmental approach. In K. S. Cameron, J. E. Dutton, & R. E. Quinn (Eds.), *Positive Organizational Scholarship.* San Francisco: Berett-Koehler.

23. D. Goleman, *Emotional Intelligence* (New York: Bantam Books, 1995); D. Goleman, *Working with Emotional Intelligence* (New York: Bantam Books, 2000). See also Hay Group Emotional Intelligence (EI) Services (2001). This website offers a chance to ask Daniel Goleman questions and to become an accredited EI practitioner (see ei.haygroup.com).

24. Goleman, *Working with Emotional Intelligence,* p. 297.

25. Ibid., p. 299.

Chapter 14

1. R. L. Daft, *The Leadership Experience,* 2nd ed. (Cincinnati, OH: South-Western, 2002), p. 367.
2. W. E. Deming, *Out of the Crisis* (Cambridge, MA: MIT Press, 1986).
3. M. Sashkin and K. J. Kiser, *Putting Total Quality Management to Work* (San Francisco: Barrett-Koehler Publishers, 1993).
4. J. Bunderson and K. Sutcliffe, "Comparing Alternative Conceptualizations of Functional Diversity in Management Teams: Process and Performance Effects," *Academy of Management Journal* 45 (2002): 875–893; K. Bantel and S. Jackson, "Top Management and Innovations in Banking: Does the Demography of the Top Team Make a Difference?" *Strategic Management Journal* 10 (1989): 107–124.
5. C. J. Gersick, "Time and Transition in Work Teams: Toward a New Model of Group Development," *Academy of Management Journal* 31 (1988): 9–41.
6. A. Chang, P. Bordia, and J. Duck, "Punctuated Equilibrium and Linear Progression: Toward a New Understanding of Group Development," *Academy of Management Journal* 46 (2003): 106–117.
7. B. Nelson, *1001 Ways to Reward Employees* (New York: Workman Publishing, 1994).
8. W. H. Weiss, "Teams and Teamwork," *Supervision* 59, no. 7 (1999): 9–11.
9. J. R. Katzenbach and D. K. Smith, "The Discipline of Teams," *Harvard Business Review,* March–April 1993, pp. 111–120.
10. Daft, *The Leadership Experience,* p. 368.
11. I. Berkow, "A Superstar, Iverson, Isn't a Role Model," *The New York Times,* February 2, 2001, p. C15; R. Zoglin, "Carsey and Werner, Last of the Mom-and-Pop Producers, Have a Hot Hand This Fall," *Time,* September 23, 1996.
12. T. Raz, "*Taming the Savage Genius: The Delicate Art of Managing Employees Who Are Way, Way Smarter than You,*" *Inc.,* May 2003, pp. 33–35.
13. D. B. Balkin, S. Dolan, and K. Forgues, "Rewards for Team Contributions to Quality," *Journal of Compensation and Benefits* 13, no. 1 (1997): 41–46.
14. C. Osborne, *Dealing with Difficult People* (London: DK, 2001), p. 61.
15. J. Wecker, "Powers of Persuasion," *Fortune,* October 12, 1998, pp. 161–164; R. Lewicki and J. Litterer, *Negotiation* (Burr Ridge, IL: Irwin, 1985).

Chapter 15

1. D. Weeks, "Voice Mail: Blessing or Curse?" *World Traveler,* February 1995, pp. 51–54.
2. M. Conlin, "Watch What You Put in That Office E-Mail," *Business Week,* September 30, 2002, pp. 114–115.
3. C. Osborn, *Dealing with Difficult People* (London: DK, 2001).
4. C. Price, *Assertive Communication* (Boulder, CO: Career Track, 1994).
5. M. Munter, "Cross-Cultural Communication for Managers," *Business Horizons,* May–June 1993, pp. 69–78.

Chapter 16

1. B. J. Jaworski, V. Stathakopolous, & S. Krishnan, (1993). Control combinations in marketing: Conceptual framework and empirical evidence. *Journal of Marketing, 57,* pp. 57–69.
2. W. E. Deming, (1986). Out of the crisis. Cambridge, MA: Center for Advanced Engineering Study.
3. D. A. Huffman, (1998). Feedforward, not feedback. *Beverage World, 117,* p. 170+.
4. B. Pelletier, & V. VanDoren, (2003). Advanced Control saves energy. *Control Engineering, 50,* pp. 41–44.
5. Better safe than sorry: The house that Numico built, *Food Engineering & Ingredients, 28* (2003). p. 15+.
6. R. Kaplan, & D. Norton, (1992, January–February). The balanced scorecard: Measures that drive performance. *Harvard Business Review,* pp. 71–79.
7. G. H. Anthes, Balanced scorecard. *Computerworld, 37,* (2003). p. 34+.
8. D. Parmenter, (2003). Balanced scorecard. *Accountancy Ireland, 35,* 14–17.

Chapter 17

1. M. Gupta, A. Adams, & L. Raho, Traditional management, quality management, and constraints management: Perceptions of ASQ members. *The Quality Management Journal, 10,* 2003, pp. 25–37.
2. A. Kumar. Software takes the sting out of horseradish production: System automatically ages ingredient and end-item lots ensuring stock won't be wasted. *Food Engineering, 75,* 2003, p. 78+.
3. N. Logothetis, *Managing for Total Quality* (Hertfordshire, UK: Prentice Hall International, 1992), p. 5.
4. M. Imai, *Kaizen: The Key to Japan's Competitive Success* (New York: Random House, 1986).
5. R. Gourlay, "Back to Basics on the Factory Floor," *Financial Times,* January 4, 1994, p. 12.
6. M. Hammer and J. Champy, *Reengineering the Corporation* (New York: Harper Business, 1993), p. 35.

Chapter 18

1. Geoffrey Austrian, *Herman Hollerith: Forgotten Giant of Information Processing* (New York: Columbia University Press, 1982).
2. Gareth R. Jones, Jennifer M. George, and Charles W. L. Hill, *Contemporary Management,* 2nd ed. (New York: McGraw-Hill/Irwin, 2000), pp. 624–625.
3. Jeffrey McCracken, "More Deaths Tied to Tires," *Detroit Free Press,* September 2, 2000.
4. H. Stoffer, "Explorer Ruling Helps Ford, but Legal Woes Remain," *Automotive News,* February 18, 2002; M. Miles, "Firestone, Ford Feud," *Tire Business,* December 17, 2001.
5. Wal-Mart, *Annual Report,* 1999.
6. R. M. Stair and G. W. Reynolds, *Fundamentals of Information Systems.* (Boston: Thompson Learning, 2001), p. 113.
7. Ibid.
8. S. Alter, *Information Systems: Foundation of E-Business,* 4th ed. (Upper Saddle River, NJ: Prentice Hall, 2002), p. 22.

9. "Q&A with Lou Gerstner," *Business Week,* December 2, 1999.

10. R. H. Baker, *Extranets: The Complete Sourcebook* (New York: McGraw-Hill, 1997).

11. J. Stone Gonzalez. *The 21st Century Intranet* (Upper Saddle River, NJ: Prentice Hall, 1998).

12. P. E. Ross, "Software as Career Threat," *Forbes,* May 22, 1995, pp. 240–246.

13. J. Weckert and D. Adeney, *Computer and Information Ethics* (Westport, CT: Greenwood Press, 1997).

14. Don Hellriegel, Susan E. Jackson, and John W. Slocum, *Management,* 8th ed. (Cincinnati: South-Western Publishing, 1999).

15. P. Lashin, *Extranet Design and Implementation* (Alameda, CA: Sybex, 1997).

16. Steve Barth, "Post-Industrial Espionage," *Knowledge Management Magazine,* March, 2001.

17. "A Survey of Digital Security," *Economist,* October 26, 2002, p. 4.

18. F. Keenan, "You're Only as Good as Your Password," *Business Week,* September 2, 2002, pp. 77–80.

19. IBM timetable, www.ibm.com.

20. E. Rich, *Artificial Intelligence* (New York: McGraw-Hill, 1983).

21. A. D. Chandler, *The Visible Hand* (Cambridge, MA: Harvard University Press, 1977).

22. Stair and Reynolds, *Fundamentals,* p. 11.

23. P. Evans, and T. S. Wurster, *Blown to Bits: How the New Economics of Information Transforms Strategy* (Boston: Harvard Business School Press, 2000) pp. 60–61.

24. Stair and Reynolds, *Fundamentals,* p. 174.

25. J. W. Ross, and P. Weill, "Six Decisions Your IT People Shouldn't Make," *Harvard Business Review,* November 2002, p. 88.

Chapter 1

Barnard, C. I. (1938). *The functions of the executive.* Cambridge, MA: Harvard University Press.

Barnes, B. (2003, January 3). The new face of air rage. *Wall Street Journal,* W-1.

Bartol, K. M., & Martin, D. C. (1998). *Management* (3rd ed.). New York: McGraw-Hill/Irwin.

Bateman, T. S., & Snell, S. A. (1999). *Management* (3rd ed.). New York: McGraw-Hill/Irwin.

Boulding, K. E. (1956). General systems theory: The skeleton of science. *Management Science, 2,* 197–208.

Burns, T., & Stalker, B. M. (1961). *The management of innovation.* London, UK: Tavistock Publications.

Cohen, W. M., & Levinthal, D. A. (1990). Absorptive capacity: A new perspective on learning and innovation. *Administrative Science Quarterly, 35,* 128–152.

Daft, R. L. (2000). *Management* (4th ed.). Forth Worth: Dryden Press.

Dean, J. W., & Bowen, D. E. (1994). Management theory and total quality: Improving research and practice through theory development. *Academy of Management Review, 19,* 392–418.

Deming, W. E. (1986). *Out of the crisis.* Cambridge, MA: MIT Center for Advanced Engineering Study.

Donaldson, L. (1996). The normal science of structural contingency theory. In S. Clegg & C. Hardy (Eds.), *Handbook of organization studies* (pp. 57–76). Thousand Oaks, CA: Sage Publishing.

Duncan, W. J. (1989). *Great ideas in management.* San Francisco: Jossey-Bass.

Farnham, A. (1997, July 21). The man who changed work forever. *Fortune,* p. 114.

Fast, N. (1982). The Lincoln Electric Company. In F. K. Foulkes (Ed.), *Human resources management.* Englewood Cliffs, NJ: Prentice Hall.

Feder, B. J. (1995, September 5). Rethinking a model incentive plan. *The New York Times,* section 1, p. 33.

Foust, D. (2003, January 27). What worked at GE isn't working at Home Depot. *Business Week, 40.*

Gomez-Mejia, L. R., Balkin, D. B., & Cardy, R. (2004). *Managing human resources.* Englewood Cliffs, NJ: Prentice Hall.

Gomez-Mejia, L. R., Balkin, D. B., & Cardy, R. L. (2001). *Managing human resources* (2nd ed.). Upper Saddle River, NJ: Prentice Hall.

Hamel, G., & Prahalad, C. K. (1994). *Competing for the future.* Boston: Harvard Business School Press.

Hammer, M., & Champy, J. (1993). *Reengineering the corporation.* New York: Harper Business.

Heizer, J., & Render, B. (1996). *Production and operations management.* Englewood Cliffs, NJ: Prentice Hall.

Huber, G. P. (1991). Organizational learning: The contributing processes and the literatures. *Organization Science, 2,* 88–115.

Hyde, P. (2003, January 22). Timesizing: Less work and more pay. What a crazy idea? www.timesizing.com.

Jackson, J. H., Morgan, C. P., & Paolillo, J. G. (1986). *Organization theory* (3rd ed.). Englewood Cliffs, NJ: Prentice Hall.

Jay, A. (1970). *Management and Machiavelli.* New York: Harper & Row.

Jones, G. R., George, J. M., & Hill, C. W. (2000). *Contemporary management.* New York: Irwin/McGraw-Hill.

Jones, G. R., George, J. M., & Hill, C. W. (2001). *Contemporary management.* New York: McGraw-Hill/Irwin.

Kast, F. E., & Rosenweig, J. E. (1972). General systems theory: Applications for organization and management. *Academy of Management Journal, 15,* 447–465.

Lawrence, P. R., & Lorsch, J. W. (1967). *Organization and environment.* Boston: Graduate School of Business Administration, Harvard University.

Maslow, A. H. (1954). *Motivation and personality.* New York: Harper & Row.

McGregor, D. (1960). *The human side of enterprise.* New York: McGraw-Hill.

Prasad, E. R., Prasad, V. S., & Satyanarayana, P. *Administrative thinkers.* New Delhi, India: Sterling Publishers.

Ripley, A., & Sieger, M. (2003, January 6). The special agent. *Time*, 34–30.

Roethlisberger, F., & Dickson, W. (1939). *Management and the worker: An account of a research program conducted by the Western Electric Company, Hawthorne Works, Chicago.* New York: John Wiley & Sons.

Schiller, Z. (1996, January 22). A model incentive plan gets caught in a vise. *Business Week*, p. 89.

Schlosser, J. (2003, February 3) Uphill battle. *Fortune*, 64.

Sharplin, A., & Seeger, J. (1998). The Lincoln Electric Company, 1996. In A. A. Thompson, & A. J. Strickland (Eds.), *Strategic management* (10th ed.). New York: McGraw-Hill/Irwin.

Sheldrake, J. (1996). *Management theory.* London, UK: International Thompson Business Press.

Smith, A. (1937). *The wealth of nations.* New York: Modern Library.

Spencer, B. A. (1994). Models of organization and total quality management: A comparison and critical evaluation. *Academy of Management Review, 19*, 446–471.

Tzu, S. (1963). *The art of war.* Oxford, UK: Oxford University Press.

Chapter 2

Agarwal, S. (1994). Socio-cultural distance and the choice of joint ventures: A contingency perspective. *Journal of International Marketing, 2*, 63–80.

Allen, J. L. (1999). *Student atlas of economic growth* (p. 50). New York: Dushkin/McGraw-Hill.

Barkema, H. G., Bell, J. H., & Pennings, J. M. (1996). Foreign entry, cultural barriers, and learning. *Strategic Management Journal, 17*, 151–166.

Barlett, C. A., & Ghoshal, S. (2000). *Transnational management.* New York: McGraw-Hill/Irwin.

Beamish, P. W., Morrison, A. J., & Rosenzweig, P. M. (2000). *International management.* New York: Irwin/McGraw-Hill.

Berstein, A. (1998, November 8). A floor under foreign factories. *Business Week*, pp. 128–130.

Bremner, B., Schiller, Z., Smart, T., & Holstein, W. (1996, July 22). Keiretsu connections. *Business Week*, pp. 52–53.

Brenner, B. (1999, June 14). Don't kill all the lawyers, send them to Japan. *Business Week*, pp. 66–67.

Brown, E. (1999, March 1). America's most admired companies. *Fortune*, p. 68.

Burgers, W., Hill, C. W. L., & Kim, W. C. (1993). Alliances in the global auto industry. *Strategic Management Journal, 14*, 419–432.

Business Week (2003, February 3). Special issue on globalization.

Byrne, J. (1999, October 4). The search of the young and gifted. *Business Week*, pp. 108–119.

Chang, L. (1999, May 7). A dream project turned nightmare. *Wall Street Journal Europe*, p. 10.

Cohen, R. (1991, November 21). For Coke, world is its oyster. *The New York Times*, pp. D1, D5.

Collins, S. M. (1998). *Export, imports, and the American worker.* Washington, DC: Brooking Institute.

Cooper, J. C., & Madigan, K. C. (1999, October 4). So much for that safety valve. *Business Week*, pp. 31–32.

Darling, J., & Nauss, D. (1995, February 19). Stall in the fast lane. *Los Angeles Times*, p. 1.

Dawes, P. L., Patterson, P. G., & Lee, D. Y. (1996). Internal and external buying center membership in high technology business markets. *Journal of High Technology Management Research, 7*, 15–26.

De Jonquieres, G. (1998, November 11). Foreign direct investment worldwide figures to reach $430 billion. *Financial Times*, p. 6.

De La Torre, J., Doz, Y., & Devinney, T. (2000). *Managing the global corporation.* New York: McGraw-Hill/Irwin.

Deresky, H. (1997). *International management.* Reading, MA: Addison-Wesley.

Dickson, M. (1998, October 16). All those expectations aside, many firms are finding the Internet invaluable in pursuing international trade. *Los Angeles Times*, p. 10.

Donnelly, J. H., Gibson, J., & Ivancevich, J. M. (1995). *Fundamentals of management.* Burr Ridge, IL: Irwin.

The Economist. (1995). Pocket world in figures. London: Penguin Books.

The Economist. (1995, June 24). Who wants to be a giant? pp. 3–4.

Ewing, J. (1999, January 14). Who is running this central bank, anyway? *Business Week*, p. 62.

Fatehi, K. (1996). *International management: A cross cultural and functional perspective.* Upper Saddle River, NJ: Prentice Hall.

Fatsis, S. (1999, April 22). Olympic panel hires firm to fill sponsor shortfall. *The Wall Street Journal*, p. B10.

Ferdows, K. (1997). Making the most of foreign factories. *Harvard Business Review, 75*, 73–88.

Fortune. (1995, August 7). The global 500. pp. 130–131.

Gomez-Mejia, L. R., Balkin, D. B., & Cardy, R. L. (2001). *Managing human resources.* Upper Saddle River, NJ: Prentice Hall.

Gomez-Mejia, L. R., & Palich, L. E. (1997, Second Quarter). Cultural diversity and the performance of multinational firms. *Journal of International Business Studies*, pp. 309–335.

Grant, L. (1997, April 14). That overseas job could derail your career. *Fortune*, p. 166.

Greenberger, R. S., & Smith, C. S. (1997, April 28). CD piracy flourishes in China. *The Wall Street Journal*, p. A1.

Guyon, J. (1999, February 15). Europe's new capitalists. *Fortune*, pp. 104–110.

Hill, C. W., & Jones, G. R. (1995). *Strategic management theory.* Boston: Houghton Mifflin.

Hodgets, R. M., & Luthans, F. (2000). *International management* (2nd ed.). New York: McGraw-Hill.

Hofstede, G. (1984). *Culture consequences: International differences in work related values.* Beverly Hills, CA: Sage.

Kahn, J. (1999, June 7). Wal-Mart goes shopping in Europe. *Fortune*, pp. 105–110.

Kenton, S. B., & Valentine, D. (1997). *Crosstalk.* Upper Saddle River, NJ: Prentice Hall.

Khanna, T., Gulati, R., & Nohria, N. (1998). The dynamics of learning alliances: Competition, cooperation, and relative scope. *Strategic Management Journal, 19*, 193–210.

Kogut, B. (1988). Joint ventures: Theoretical and empirical perspectives. *Strategic Management Journal, 9*, 319–332.

Koretz, G. (1999, September 13). A woman's place is . . . *Business Week*, p. 28.

Kraar, L. (1997, May 12). Behind Samsung's high stakes push into cars. *Fortune*, p. 119.

Kripalani, M., Engardio, P., & Nathans, L. (1998, December 7). Whiz kids: Inside the Indian Institutes of Technology's Star Factory. *Business Week*, pp. 116–120.

Lancaster, H. (1999, July 29). To get shipped abroad, women must overcome prejudice at home. *The Wall Street Journal*, p. B1.

McGeary, J. (1999, September 27). Russia's ruble shakedown. *Business Week*, pp. 54–57.

McQuade, K., & Gomes-Casseres, B. (1995). Xerox and Fuji-Xerox. *Harvard Business School Case 9-391*, p. 156.

Mehta, S. N. (1994, July 7). Enterprise: Small companies look to cultivate foreign businesses. *The Wall Street Journal*, p. B2.

Mendenhall, M., Punnett, B. J., & Ricks, D. (1995). *Global management*. Cambridge, MA: Blackwell Publishers.

Murray, S. (1999, June 22). Europe's MBA programs attract Americans: Demand for global view gets students across Atlantic. *Wall Street Journal Europe*, pp. 4–5.

Oster, P. (1993, November). Why Japan's execs travel better. *Business Week*, p. 68.

Palich, L. E., & Gomez-Mejia, L. R. (1999). A theory of global strategy and firm efficiencies: Considering the effects of cultural diversity. *Journal of Management, 25*(4), 587–606.

Punnett, B. J., & Ricks, D. A. (1997). *International Business*. Cambridge, MA: Blackwell Publishers.

Rheem, H. (1997). Logistics: A trend continues. *Harvard Business Review, 75*, 8.

Schellhardt, T. D. (1999, June 1). Your career matters: Asian women flock to U.S. for MBAs. *The Wall Street Journal*, p. B10.

Serwer, A. E. (1994, October 17). McDonald's conquers the world. *Fortune*, pp. 103–116.

Siekman, P. (1999, January 11). Bosch wants to build more of your car. *Fortune*, pp. 143–147.

Smith, G., & Malkin, E. (1998, December 21). Mexican makeover. *Business Week*, pp. 50–52.

Stein, N. (2003, January 20). No way out. *Fortune*, 102–108.

Stevenson, M. (2003, January 20). Mexican farmers renew NAFTA protests. Associated Press International, story appearing in *Yahoo! News*, www.yahoo.com.

Sullivan, R. (1999, January 25). How the Olympics were bought. *Time*, pp. 38–41.

Tran, K. T. L., & Johnson, K. (1999, September 30). Nike barred by Spanish court from use of name on sports apparel sold there. *The Wall Street Journal*, p. B24.

Vitzhum, C. (1999, July 20). Global strategy powers Endesa's power moves. *Wall Street Journal Europe*, pp. 4–6.

Wild, J. J., Wild, K. L., & Han, J. C. Y. (2000). *International Business*. Upper Saddle River, NJ: Prentice Hall.

Williams, F. (1994, April 15). Trade round like this may never be seen again. *Financial Times*, p. 8.

Wilson, M. L. (1999, July 16). She got the last laugh when colleagues bet she would fail in Japan. *The Wall Street Journal*, p. B1.

World Bank (1996). *World development report*. New York: Oxford University Press.

World Trade Organization. (1998). *International Trade Trends and Statistics*. Geneva: WTO.

Chapter 3

Brull, S. V. (1999, May 10). For all that tobacco money, don't stint on the smoking war. *Business Week*, p. 40.

Byrne, J. (1988, February 15). Businesses are signing up for ethics 101. *Business Week*, pp. 56–57.

Carroll, A. B. (1996). *Business and society* (3rd ed.). Cincinnati: OH: South-Western Publishing.

Cochran, P. L., & Wood, R. A. (1984). Corporate social responsibility and financial performance. *Academy of Management Journal, 31*, 854–872.

Donaldson, T., & Preston, L. E. (1995). The stakeholder theory of the corporation: Concepts, evidence, and implications. *Academy of Management Review, 20*, 65–91.

Driscoll, D. (1998, June). The Dow Corning case: First, kill all the lawyers. *Business and Society Review, 100*, 57–63.

Driscoll, D. (1998, March). Business ethics and compliance: What management is doing and why. *Business and Society Review, 99*, 33–51.

Dworkin, T. M., & Near, J. P. (1997). A better statutory approach to whistle blowing. *Business Ethics Quarterly, 7*(1), 1–16.

Dwyer, P., & Carney, D. (2002, December 16). Year of the whistleblower, *Business Week*, pp. 107–110.

Economist. (1997, July 26). Boeing v. Airbus, pp. 59–61.

The Economist. (2003, February 15). Pharmaceuticals: Pushing pills, p. 61.

Eli Lilly and Company. (1990). Guidelines of company policy.

Field, D. (1997, August 5). UPS strike stifles shippers. *USA Today*, p. 1A.

Freeman, R. E. (1984). *Strategic management: A stakeholder approach*. Boston: Pitman Publishing.

Frooman, J. (1999). Stakeholder influence strategies. *Academy of Management Review, 24*, 191–205.

Gelman, E. (1985, February 11). A giant under fire: General Dynamics faces numerous charges of fraud. *Newsweek*, pp. 24–25.

General Dynamics. (1988). Standards of business ethics and conduct.

Global corruption report 2003. www.globalcorruptionreport.org.

Greenberg, J. (1990). Organizational justice: Yesterday, today and tomorrow. *Journal of Management, 16*, 399–432.

Greenwald, J. (1989, March 22). Let's make a deal. *Time*, pp. 84–86.

Gundlach, M., Douglas, S., & Martinko, M. (2003). The decision to blow the whistle: A social information processing framework. *Academy of Management Review, 28*, 107–123.

Hanson, A. (1990, July). What employees say about drug testing. *Personnel*, pp. 32–36.

Harrington, S. J. (1991). What corporate America is teaching about ethics. *Academy of Management Executive, 5*(1), 21–30.

Harrison, J. S., & St. John, C. H. (1996). Managing and partnering with external stakeholders. *Academy of Management Executive, 10*(2), 46–59.

Hemphill, T. A. (1994, Summer). Strange bedfellows cozy up for a clean environment. *Business and Society Review*, pp. 38–44.

Henderson, V. E. (1982). The ethical side of enterprise. *Sloan Management Review, 23,* 37–47.

Hoffman, W. M., & Moore, J. M. (1990). *Business ethics* (2nd ed.). New York: McGraw-Hill.

Jackson, J. H., Miller, R. L., & Miller, S. G. (1997). *Business and society today.* St. Paul: West Publishing.

Jackson, M. (1997, May 12). 50% of workers commit unethical acts, survey says. *Boulder Daily Camera,* p. 1B.

JD Edwards & Company. (1993). Corporate ideals and values.

McGuire, J. B., Sundgren, A., & Schneeweis, T. (1988). Corporate social responsibility and firm financial performance. *Academy of Management Journal, 27,* 42–56.

McLean, B. (2001, December 24). Why Enron went bust. *Fortune,* pp. 58–68. Zellner, W., & Forest, S. (2001, December 17). The fall of Enron. *Business Week,* pp. 30–36.

Moore, T. (1982, November 29). The fight to save Tylenol. *Fortune,* pp. 48–49.

Munk, N. (1999, April 12). How Levi's trashed a great American brand. *Fortune,* pp. 82–90.

Murphy, P. E. (1989). Creating ethical corporate structures. *Sloan Management Review, 30,* 81–89.

Near, J. P., & Miceli, M. P. (1985). Organizational dissidence: The case of whistleblowing. *Journal of Business Ethics, 4,* 1–16.

Park, A. (2003, February 10). Family feuds don't get nastier than this. *Business Week,* pp. 62–63.

Robbins, S. P., & Coulter, M. (1996). *Management* (5th ed.). Upper Saddle River, NJ: Prentice Hall.

Roberts, N. C., & King, P. J. (1989, Winter). The stakeholder audit goes public. *Organizational Dynamics,* pp. 63–79.

Sager, I. (2003, February 10). Tech's kickback culture. *Business Week,* pp. 74–77.

Sashkin, M., & Kiser, K. J. (1993). *Putting total quality management to work.* San Francisco: Berrett-Koehler.

Savage, G. T., Nix, T. W., Whitehead, C. J., & Blair, J. D. (1991). Strategies for assessing and managing organizational stakeholders. *Academy of Management Executive, 5*(2), 61–75.

Schulaka, C. (1997, July 14). Profiting with nonprofits. *Boulder Daily Camera,* pp. 1D, 12D–13D.

Sherman, S. (1997, May 12). Levi's: As ye sew, so shall ye reap. *Fortune,* pp. 104–116.

Sturdivant, F. D., & Vernon-Wortzel, H. (1990). *Business and society* (4th ed.). Homewood, IL: Irwin.

Trevino, L. K., & Nelson, K. A. (1995). *Managing business ethics.* New York: John Wiley & Sons.

Turban, D. B., & Greening, D. W. (1997). Corporate social performance and organizational attractiveness to prospective employees. *Academy of Management Journal, 40,* 658–672.

Weaver, G. R., Trevino, L. K., & Cochran, P. L. (1999). Corporate ethics programs as control systems: Influence of executive commitment and environmental factors. *Academy of Management Journal, 42,* 41–57.

Whetton, D. A., & Cameron, K. S. (1995). *Developing management skills* (3rd ed.). New York: HarperCollins.

Will, R. (1995, Spring). Corporations with a conscience. *Business and Society Review,* pp. 17–20.

Zellner, W. (2002, January 28). The whistleblower: A hero—and a smoking-gun letter. *Business Week,* pp. 34–35.

Chapter 4

Arndt, M., & Berstein, A. (2000, March 20). From milestone to millstone. *Business Week,* pp. 120–122.

Baker, S. (2000, April 10). Telefonica: Takeover escape artist? *Business Week,* pp. 58–60.

Barlow, W., Hatch, D., & Murphy, B. (1996, April). Employer denies jobs to smoker applicants. *Personnel Journal,* p. 142.

Bateman, T., & Snell, S. (1999). *Management: Building competitive advantage.* New York: McGraw-Hill/Irwin.

Bernstein, A. (1997, August 25). This package is a heavy one for the Teamsters. *Business Week,* pp. 40–41.

Business Week. (2000, May 15). The e.biz: Masters of the Web world, p. 25.

Conlin, M. (2000, June 12). Workers, surf at your own risk. *Business Week,* pp. 105–106.

Crockett, R. O. (2000, April 17). A new company called Motorola. *Business Week,* pp. 86–91.

Crockett, R., & Rosenbush, S. (2000, February 7). Doug Daft isn't sugarcoating things. *Business Week,* pp. 36–38.

Currie, A. (2000, February). Merrill's internet conversion. *Euromoney,* p. 10.

Daft. R. L. (1997). *Management* (4th ed.). Fort Worth: Dryden Press.

Daft, R. L. (2000). *Management* (5th ed.). Fort Worth: Dryden Press.

Davidson, J. (2002). Overcoming resistance to change. *Public Management, 84,* 20–23.

Deal, T. E., & Kennedy, A. A. (1982). *Corporate cultures: The rites and rituals of corporate life.* Reading, MA: Addison-Wesley.

Deresky, H. L. (2000). *International management: Managing across borders and cultures.* Englewood Cliffs, NJ: Prentice Hall.

Economist. (1999, October 23). Good scores or else, p. 28.

Economist. (2000, July 15). Change management: An inside job, p. 61.

Gale, S. F. (2002). For ERP success, create a culture change. *Workforce,* September, 88–94.

George, J., & Jones, G. (1999). *Understanding and managing organizational behavior.* Reading, MA: Addison-Wesley.

Gomez-Mejia, L. R., Balkin, D. B., & Cardy, R. (2001). *Managing human resources.* Englewood Cliffs, NJ: Prentice Hall.

Gomez-Mejia, L. R., & Welbourne, T. (1991). Compensation strategies in a global context. *Human Resource Planning, 14*(1), 38.

Greenwald, J. (2000, February 28). Lloyd's of London falling down. *Time,* pp. 54–58.

Griffin, R. W., & Pustay, M. W. (1998). *International business: A managerial perspective.* Reading, MA: Addison-Wesley.

Hamilton, J. (2000, April 3). The panic over hiring. *Business Week,* pp. 130–131.

Hamm, S., & Kripalani, M. (2000, March 6). Software's tough guy. *Business Week,* pp. 131–136.

Hof, R. D., Green, H., & Brady, D. (2000, February 21). An eagle eye on customers. *Business Week,* pp. 67–81.

Hymowitz, C. (1989, July 13). Which culture fits you? *The Wall Street Journal,* p. B1.

Jones, G. R., George, J. M., & Hill, C. W. L. (2001). *Contemporary management* (2nd ed.). New York: McGraw-Hill/Irwin.

Kerwin, K. (2000, September 4). Fighting to stay on the road: Firestone's woes have dragged in Ford too. *Business Week,* p. 44.

Kerwin, K., Burrows, P., & Foust, D. (2000, February 21). Workers of the world, logon. *Business Week,* pp. 52–53.

Kiger, P. J. (2002). Axciom rebuilds from scratch. *Workforce, 81,* 52–55.

Kotter, J. P., & Heskett, J. L. (1992). *Corporate culture and performance.* New York: Free Press.

Kotter, J. P., & Schlesinger, L. A. (1979, March–April). Choosing strategies for change. *Harvard Business Review,* pp. 106–114.

Lewin, K. (1951). *Field theory in social science: Selected theoretical papers.* New York: Harper & Brothers.

Lewis, L. K., & Seibold, D. R. (1993). Innovation modification during intra-organizational adoption. *Academy of Management Review, 10*(2), 322–354.

Makri, M., Lane, P., & Gomez-Mejia, L. R. (2000). *Patent quality, firm performance, and CEO pay in high and low technology firms.* Unpublished manuscript, Management Department, Arizona State University.

Mandel, M. J. (2000, January 3). The new economy. It works in America. Will it go global? *Business Week,* pp. 24–28.

Mandel, R. (2000, April 3). Up front. *Business Week,* pp. 8–9.

Mitchell, M. A., & Yates, D. (2002). How to use your organizational culture as a competitive tool. *Nonprofit World, 20,* 33–34.

Moorhead, G., & Griffin, R. W. (2001). *Organizational behavior.* New York: Houghton Mifflin.

Mornell, P. (2000, July). Nothing endures but change. *Inc,* pp. 131–132.

Morris, B., & Sellers, P. (2000, January 10). What really happened at Coke. *Fortune,* pp. 114–117.

Nahavandi, A., & Malekzadeh, A. R. (1999). *Organizational behavior: The person–organization fit.* Englewood Cliffs, NJ: Prentice Hall.

O'Reilly, C. A., & Chatman, J. A. (1996). Culture as social control: Corporations, cults, and commitment. In B. Staw & L. L. Cummings (Eds.), *Research in Organizational Behavior, 18,* 157–200.

Peek, R. (2000, March). Jump-starting electronic books. *Information Today,* pp. 46–48.

Pettigrew, A. M. (1979). On studying organizational cultures. *Administrative Science Quarterly, 24,* 570–582.

Pfeffer, J., & Veiga, J. F. (1999). Putting people first for organizational success. *Academy of Management Executive, 13*(2), 38.

Quinn, R., Faerman, S., Thompson, M., & McGrath, M. (1996). *Becoming a master manager* (2nd ed.). New York: John Wiley & Sons.

Reingold, J., Stepanek, M., & Brady, D. (2000, February 14). The boom. *Business Week,* pp. 100–118.

Reinhardt, A. (2000, January 31). I have left a few dead bodies. *Business Week,* pp. 69–70.

Robbins, S. (2001). *Organizational behavior.* Englewood Cliffs, NJ: Prentice Hall.

Rossant, J. (2000, January 31). Old world, new mandate. *Business Week,* pp. 92–93.

Schein, E. H. (1983). The role of the founder in creating organizational culture. *Organizational Dynamics, 12,* 13–28.

Terpstra, V., & David, K. (1991). *The cultural environment of international business.* Cincinnati: South-Western Publishing.

Trice, H. M., & Beyer, J. M. (1993). *The cultures of work organizations.* Englewood Cliffs, NJ: Prentice Hall.

Van Maanen, J. V. (1975). Police socialization: A longitudinal examination of job attitudes in an urban police department. *Administrative Science Quarterly, 20,* 207–228.

Wall Street Journal. (2000, May 26). General Motors Corp.: Saturn unit of General Motors is laying off about 490 workers, p. B10.

Watson, T. (2002). Goodnight, sweet prince. *Canadian Business, 75,* 77–78.

Welch, D. (2000, February 21). Running rings around Saturn. *Business Week,* pp. 114–117.

Wilkins, A., & Ouchi, W. G. (1983, September). Efficient cultures: Exploring the relationship between cultures and organizational performance. *Administrative Science Quarterly,* pp. 468–481.

Wiscombe, J. (2002). CEO takes HR to prime time. *Workforce, 81,* 10.

Wright, P. M., & Noe, R. A. (1996). *Management of organizations.* Burr Ridge, IL: Irwin.

Chapter 5

Ahmed, N. V., Montagno, R. V., & Frienze, R. J. (1998). Organizational performance and environmental consciousness: An empirical study. *Management Decision, 36*(2), 57–63.

Ang, J. S., & Chua, J. H. (1979, April). Long range planning in large United States corporations: A survey. *Long Range Planning, 12*(2), 99–102.

Applebaum, S. H., & Hughes, B. (1998). Ingratiation as a political tactic. *Management Planning, 36*(2), 85–96.

Barkdoll, G., & Bosin M. R. (1997, August). Targeted planning: A paradigm for public service. *Management Planning,* pp. 529–540.

Barrett, A., Carey, J., & Brull, S. (1999, May 3). Bitter medicine ahead for drug companies. *Business Week,* p. 50.

Barrett, P. (1998, June 8). Hot war over herbal remedies. *Business Week,* p. 42.

Brown, E. (1999, March 1). America's most admired companies. *Fortune,* pp. 68–76.

Brown, E. (1999, May 24). 9 ways to win on the web. *Fortune,* pp. 112–118.

Burack, E. H. (1988). *Creative human resource planning and applications.* Englewood Cliffs, NJ: Prentice Hall.

Burack, E. H., Hochwarter, W., & Mathys, N. J. (1997). The new management development paradigm. *Human Resource Planning, 20*(1), 14–22.

Burrows, P. (1999, September 20). The big squeeze in the pc market. *Business Week,* p. 40.

Business Week. (1985, September 17). Special issue on planning.

Bylinsky, G. (1999, July 5). Hot new technologies. *Fortune,* pp. 168–176.

Byrne, J. A. (1998, June 8). How Jack Welch runs GE. *Business Week,* pp. 90–110.

Byrne, J. A. (2003, February 17). Leaders are made, not born. *Business Week,* p. 16.

Byrne, J. (1999, October 4). The search for the young and gifted. *Business Week,* pp. 108–112.

Byrnes, N., & Judge, P. L. (1999, June 28). Internet anxiety. *Business Week,* pp. 79–88.

Churchill, N. (1984, July–August). Budgeting choice: Planning vs. control. *Harvard Business Review,* pp. 150–164.

Cox, A., & Thompson, I. (1998). On the appropriateness of benchmarking. *Journal of General Management, 23*(3) 1–21.

Cravens, D. W., Greenley, G., Piercy, N. F., & Slater, S. (1997, August). Integrating contemporary strategic management perspectives. *Management Planning,* pp. 493–507.

Crockett, R. O. (1999, June 21). Motorola is ringing again. *Business Week,* p. 40.

Crockett, R. O. (1999, August 30). Why Motorola should hang up on iridium. *Business Week,* p. 46.

Donnelly, J. H., Gibson, J. L., & Ivancevich, J. M. (1998). *Fundamentals of management.* New York: McGraw-Hill/Irwin.

Einhorn, B. (1999, October 4). Big brother and the e-revolution. *Business Week,* pp. 132–136.

Ernst, R., & Ross, D. N. (1993). The Delta force approach to balancing long run performance. *Business Horizons,* pp. 4–9.

Faust, D., Smith, G., & Rocks, D. (1999, May 3). Man on the spot. *Business Week,* pp. 142–147.

Genentech Inc. website www.gene.com.

Gomez-Mejia, L. R., & Balkin, D. B. (1992). *Compensation, organizational strategy, and firm performance.* Cincinnati, OH: South-Western Publishing.

Gorman, P., & Thomas, H. (1997, August). Strategy at the leading edge: The theory and practice of competence-based competition. *Management Planning,* pp. 615–628.

Grant, L. (1998, May 11). Why Kodak still isn't fixed. *Fortune,* pp. 179–181.

Greising, D. (1998, April 13). I would like the world to buy a coke: The life and leadership of Robert Goizueta. *Business Week,* pp. 70–76.

Grundy, T. (1997). Human resource management: A strategic approach. *Management Planning,* pp. 507–518.

Grundy, T. (1998). How are corporate strategy and human resources strategy linked? *Journal of General Management, 23*(3), 49–73.

Gurley, W. J. (1999, March 15). How the net is changing competition. *Fortune,* p. 168.

Hanm, S. (1999, April 5). Netscapes storm the valley. *Business Week,* p. 104.

Hax, A., & Majluf, N. S. (1996). *The strategy concept and process.* Upper Saddle River, NJ: Prentice Hall.

Hay, M., & Williamson, P. (1997, October). Good strategy: The view from below. *Management Planning,* pp. 661–665.

Hitt, M. A., Ireland, D. R., & Hoskisson, R. E. (1998). *Strategic management: Competitiveness and globalization.* St. Paul, MN: West Publishing Company.

Hof, R. D. (1999, October 4). A new era of bright hopes and terrible fears. *Business Week,* pp. 84–98.

Holland, K. (1998, May 4). China slams a door in Amway's face. *Business Week,* p. 54.

Hoskisson, R. E., Hitt, M. A., Wan, W. P., & Yui, D. (1999). Theory and research in strategic management. *Journal of Management,* pp. 417–456.

Jarrell, D. W. (1993). *Human resource planning.* Englewood Cliffs, NJ: Prentice Hall.

Kaplan, R. S., & Norton, D. P. (1993, September–October). Putting the balanced scorecard to work. *Harvard Business Review,* pp. 134–147.

Kripalani, M., & Clifford, M. L. (2003, February 10). Finally, Coke gets it right. *Business Week,* p. 47.

Kudia, R. J. (1979). The components of strategic planning. *Long Range Planning, 11*(6), 48–52.

Kumar, P. (1978). Long range planning practices by U.S. companies. *Managerial Planning, 26*(4), 31–33.

Kunii, I. M. Thorton, E., & Rae-Dupree, J. (1999, March 22). Sony's shake. *Business Week,* p. 52.

Labich, K. (1999, March 1). Boeing finally hatches a plan. *Fortune,* pp. 101–106.

Light, L. (1998, May 25). Litigation: The choice of a generation. *Business Week,* p. 42.

Makridakis, S., Wheelwright, S., & McGee, V. (1982). *Forecasting methods and applications.* New York: John Wiley & Sons.

Mandel, M. J. (1999, October 4). The internet economy. *Business Week,* pp. 72–77.

McKay, B., & Vranica, S. (2003, January 9). Cracking the China market. *Wall Street Journal,* pp. B1–B2.

Munk, N. (1999, June 21). Title flight. *Fortune,* pp. 84–86.

Narisetti, R. (1998, March 12). How IBM turned around its ailing PC division. *The Wall Street Journal,* p. B1.

O'Connor, R. V. (1986). *Corporate guides to long range planning* (Conference Board Report No. 687). New York: Conference Board.

Odiorne, G. S. (1987, July/August). Measuring the unmeasurable: Setting standards for management performance. *Business Horizons,* pp. 69–75.

Overholt, M. H. (1997). Flexible organizations: Using organizational design as a competitive advantage. *Human Resource Planning, 20*(1), 22–23.

Pearson, G. (1986). Business strategy should not be bureaucratic. *Accountancy, 97*(1112), 109–112.

Port, O. (1999, October 4). Customers move into the driver's seat. *Business Week,* pp. 103–110.

Preble, J. F. (1992). Environmental scanning for strategic control. *Journal of Managerial Issues, 4,* 254–268.

Prestowitz, C. (1998, May 11). Asia's flawed fundamentals. *Fortune,* p. 52.

Reingold, J., & Brody, D. (1999, September 20). Brain drain. *Business Week,* pp. 113–122.

Revell, J. (2003, February 3). Can Home Depot get its groove back? "*Fortune,* pp. 110–112.

Sager, I. (1999, June 21). Big Blue at your service. *Business Week,* pp. 130–131.

Sager, I., Burrow, P., & Reinhardt, A. (1998, May 25). Back to the future at Apple. *Business Week,* pp. 56–58.

Sandersen, S. M. (1998). New approaches to strategy: New ways of thinking for the millennium. *Management Decision, 36*(1), 9–14.

Schlange, L. E., & Juttner, V. (1997, October). Helping managers to identify the key strategic issues. *Management Planning,* pp. 777–787.

Stepanek, M. (1999, June 7). Closed, gone to the net. *Business Week,* pp. 113–116.

Stipp, D. (1998, May 11). Why Pfizer is so hot. *Fortune,* p. 88.

Thurlby, B. (1998). Competitive forces are also subject to change. *Managerial Decisions, 36*(1), 19–25.

Tosi, H. L., Katz, J. P., & Gomez-Mejia, L. R. (1997). Disaggregating the agency contract: The effects of monitoring, incentive alignment, and term in office on agent decision making. *Academy of Management Journal, 40,* 584–602.

Tsao, P. (1998, June 8). Reports of cancer's imminent death were an exaggeration. *Business Week,* p. 13.

Tushman, M. L., & O'Reilly, C. A., III (1997). *Winning through innovation.* Boston: Harvard Business School Press.

USA Today. (1998, June, 1). Godzilla rampage slows, p. D1.

Weir, D., & Smallman, C. (1998). *Management Decision, 36*(1), 43–50.

Wright, P. M., & Noe, R. A. (1999). *Management of organizations.* New York: McGraw-Hill/Irwin.

Chapter 6

Bateman, T. S., & Snell, S. A. (1996). *Management* (3rd ed.). Burr Ridge, IL: Irwin.

Benartzi, S., & Thaler, R. H. (1999). Risk aversion or myopia? Choices in repeated gambles and retirement investments. *Management Science, 45,* 364–381.

Bowen, J., & Qui, Q. (1992). Satisficing when buying information. *Organizational Behavior and Human Decision Process, 51,* 471–481.

Carter, B. (1997, December 26). Seinfeld says it's over, and it's no joke for NBC. *The New York Times,* pp. A1, A15.

Cohen, M. D., March, J. G., & Olsen, J. P. (1972). The garbage can model of organizational choice. *Administration Science Quarterly, 17,* 1–25.

Conlon, D. E., & Garland, H. (1993). The role of project completion information in resource allocation decisions. *Academy of Management Journal, 36,* 401–413.

Covey, S. R. (1989). *The 7 habits of highly effective people.* New York: Simon & Schuster.

Daft, R. L. (1997). *Management* (4th ed.). Fort Worth: Dryden Press.

Daft, R. L. (1999). *Leadership: Theory and practice.* Fort Worth: Dryden Press.

Dean, J. W., & Evans, J. R. (1994). *Total quality.* St. Paul, MN: West Publishing.

Delbecq, A. L., Van de Ven, A. H., & Gustafson, D. H. (1975). *Group techniques for program planning.* Glenview, IL: Scott, Foresman.

Eisenhardt, K. M. (1988). Agency and institutional theory explanations: The case of retail sales compensation. *Academy of Management Journal, 31,* 488–511.

Grove, A. (1996). *Only the paranoid survive.* New York: Currency Doubleday.

Hall, R. H. (1999). *Organizations.* Upper Saddle River, NJ: Prentice Hall.

Hom, P. W., & Griffeth, R. W. (1995). *Employee turnover.* Cincinnati, OH: South-Western Publishing.

Howard, R. (1988). Decision analysis: Practice and promise. *Management Science, 34,* 679–695.

Huey, J. (1997, December 29). In search of Roberto's secret formula. *Fortune,* pp. 230–234.

Jackson, J. A., Kloeber, J. M., Ralson, B. E., & Deckro, R. F. (1999). Selecting a portfolio of technologies: An application of decision analysis. *Decision Sciences, 30,* 217–238.

Jones, G. R., George, J. M., & Hill, C. W. (1998). *Contemporary management.* New York: McGraw-Hill/Irwin.

Kiley, T. (1993, January). The idea makers. *Technology Review,* pp. 33–40.

Kreitner, R., & Kinicki, A. (1995). *Organizational behavior* (3rd ed.). Burr Ridge, IL: Irwin.

Leana, R. R. (1986). Predictors and consequences of delegation. *Academy of Management Journal, 29,* 754–774.

Mackenzie, R. A. (1972). *The time trap.* New York: McGraw-Hill.

McNamara, G., & Bromily, P. (1999). Risk and return in organizational decision making. *Academy of Management Journal, 42,* 330–339.

Maier, N. R. (1973). *Psychology in industrial organizations* (4th ed.). Boston: Houghton Mifflin.

March, J. G., & Simon, H. A. (1958). *Organizations.* New York: John Wiley & Sons.

Mealiea, L. W., & Latham, G. P. (1996). *Skills for managerial success.* Burr Ridge, IL: Irwin.

Pearson, C. M., & Clair, J. A. (1998). Reframing organizational crisis. *Academy of Management Review, 23,* 59–76.

Quinn, R. E., Faerman, S. R., Thompson, M. P., & McGrath, M. R. (1996). *Becoming a master manager* (2nd ed.). New York: John Wiley & Sons.

Rimer, S. (1996, March 6). A hometown feels less like home. *The New York Times,* pp. A1, A8, A9.

Robbins, S. P., & Coulter, M. (1996). *Management* (5th ed.). Upper Saddle River, NJ: Prentice Hall.

Simon, H. A. (1957). *Models of man.* New York: Wiley.

Sitkin, S. B., & Pablo, A. L. (1992). Reconceptualizing the determinants of risk behavior. *Academy of Management Review, 17,* 9–38.

Sitkin, S. B., & Weingart, L. R. (1995). Determinants of risky decision making behavior: A test of the mediating role of risk perceptions and risk propensity. *Academy of Management Journal, 38,* 1573–1592.

Stoner, J. (1968). Risk and cautious shifts in group decisions. *Journal of Experimental and Social Psychology, 4,* 442–459.

Thompson, A. A., & Strickland, A. J. (1998). *Strategic management: Concepts and cases* (10th ed.). New York: McGraw-Hill/Irwin.

Thompson, R. (1993, July). An employee's view of empowerment. *HR Focus,* pp. 14–15.

Vroom, V. H., & Jago, A. G. (1988). *The new leadership: Managing participation in organizations.* Englewood Cliffs, NJ: Prentice Hall.

Waller, M. J. (1999). The timing of adaptive group responses to nonroutine events. *Academy of Management Journal, 42,* 127–137.

Whyte, G. (1989). Groupthink reconsidered. *Academy of Management Review, 14,* 40–56.

Wright, P. M., & Noe, R. A. (1996). The management of organizations. Burr Ridge, IL: Irwin.

Wu, G. (1999). Nonlinear decision weights in choice under uncertainty. *Management Science, 45,* 74–85.

Chapter 7

Afuah, A. (1998). *Innovation management.* New York: Oxford University Press.

Amato, I. (1999, June 7). Industrializing the search for new drugs. *Fortune,* pp. 110–118.

Armstrong, L. (1999, March 22). Amgen nurses itself back to health. *Fortune*, pp. 76–78.

Associated Press. (1996, February 7). Southwest Airlines earns triple crown award again. *Arizona Republic*, p. A15.

Barney, J. B. (1995). Looking inside for competitive advantage. *Academy of Management Executive*, 9(4), 59–60.

Barney, J. B., & Hoskisson, R. (1990). Strategic groups: Untested assertions and research proposals. *Managerial and Decision Economics, 11*, 198–208.

Barret, P. (1999, May 3). Bitter medicine ahead for drug companies. *Business Week*, p. 50.

Bergh, D. (1995). Size and relatedness of units sold: An agency theory and resource based perspective. *Strategic Management Journal, 16*, 221–229.

Bettis, R., & Hitt, M. A. (1995, Summer). The new competitive landscape [Special Issue]. *Strategic Management Journal, 16*, 7–19.

Brody, D. (1999, April 2). Xerox. *Business Week*, pp. 93–94.

Brown, E. (1999, March 1). America's most admired companies. *Fortune*, pp. 68–75.

Brown, E. (1999, May 24). 9 ways to win on the web. *Fortune*, pp. 112–120.

Brush, T. A. (1996). Predicted change in operational synergy and post acquisition performance of acquired businesses. *Strategic Management Journal, 17*, 1–24.

Burrows, P. (1999, September 20). The big squeeze in the PC market. *Business Week*, pp. 40–41.

Business Week. (1998, January 12), p. 32.

Business Week. (1998, January 12). The 25 top managers of the year, pp. 54–60.

Bylinsky, G. (2000, June 26). Hot new technologies for American factories. *Fortune*, p. 288.

Byrnes, N. (1999, June 28). Internet anxiety. *Business Week*, pp. 79–86.

Campbell, A., Goold, M., & Alexander, M. (1995). Corporate strategy: The question for parenting advantage. *Harvard Business Review*, 73(2), 120–132.

Campbell, A., & Luchs, K. (1998). *Core competency-based strategy*. London, UK: International Thompson Business Press.

Charkham, J. (1994). *Keeping good company: A study of corporate governance in five countries*. New York: Oxford University Press.

Clarkson, M. B. E. (1995). A stakeholder framework for analyzing and evaluating corporate social performance. *Academy of Management Review, 20*, 92–117.

Colvin, G. (1998, November 23). How Rubbermaid managed to fail. *Fortune*, pp. 32–36.

Crockett, R. O. (1999, June 21). Motorola is ringing again. *Business Week*, pp. 40–42.

Crockett, R. O. (1999, August 30). Why Motorola should hang up on iridium. *Business Week*, pp. 46–47.

D'Aveni, R. A. (1995). Coping with hypercompetition: Utilizing the new 75's framework. *Academy of Management Executive*, 9(3), 54.

Davis, J. B. (2003, February). Sorting out Sarbanes-Oxley. *ABA Journal*, pp. 44–50.

Desmond, E. W. (1998, February 2). Can Canon keep clicking? *Fortune*, pp. 98–107.

Dessler, G. (2000). *Human resource management*. Englewood Cliffs, NJ: Prentice Hall.

DeWit, R., & Meyer, R. (1998). *Strategy: Process, content, context*. London, UK: International Thompson Business Press.

Donaldson, T., & Preston, L. E. (1995). The stakeholder theory of the corporation: Concepts, evidence, and implications. *Academy of Management Review, 20*, 65–91.

Echikson, W. (1999, October 11). Designers climb onto the virtual catwalk. *Business Week*, pp. 164–166.

Einhorn, B. (1999, February 15). Foreign rivals vs. the Chinese: If you can't beat them. *Business Week*, p. 78.

Eisenhardt, K., & Zbaracki, M. (1992, Winter). Strategic decision making [Special Issue]. *Strategic Management Journal, 13*, 17–37.

Fahey, L., & Narayanan, V. K. (1986). *Macroenvironmental analysis for strategic management*. St. Paul, MN: West Publishing Co.

Fine, C. H. (1999, March 29). The ultimate core competency. *Fortune*, pp. 144–149.

Fineman, H., & Lipper, T. (2003, January 27). Spinning race. *Business Week*, pp. 25–30.

Finkelstein, S., & Hambrick, D. C. (1996). *Strategic leadership: Top executives and their effects on organizations*. St. Paul, MN: West Publishing Co.

Fisher, A. B. (1996, March 6). Corporate reputations. *Fortune*, pp. 90–93.

Flynn, J., Carey, J., & Crockett, R. (1998, January 26). A fierce downdraft at Boeing. *Business Week*, pp. 34–35.

Foust, D. (2002, September 9). The changing heartland. *Business Week*, pp. 80–83.

Galbraith, J. R. (1995). *Designing organizations*. San Francisco: Jossey-Bass.

Genus, A. (1998). *Managing change: Perspective and practice*. London, UK: International Thompson Business Press.

Gibney, F. (1999, March 1). Nissan calls a low. *Time*, p. 48.

Godfrey, P. C., & Hill, C. W. L. (1995). The problem of unobservables in strategic management research. *Strategic Management Journal, 16*, 519–533.

Gomez, P. (1998). *Value management*. London, UK: International Thompson Business Press.

Gomez-Mejia, L. R., Balkin, D. B., & Cardy, R. (2001). *Managing human resources*. Englewood Cliffs, NJ: Prentice Hall.

Goold, M., & Luchs, K. (1993). Why diversify? Four decades of management thinking. *Academy of Management Executive*, 7(3), 7–25.

Greene, J. (2003, March 3). The Lenux uprising. *Business Week*, pp. 78–86.

Hall, R. H. (1996). *Organizations: Structures, processes, outcomes*. Englewood Cliffs, NJ: Prentice Hall.

Hamel, G., & Prahalad, C. K. (1993). Strategy as stretch and leverage. *Harvard Business Review*, 71(2), 75–84.

Hamel, G., & Prahalad, C. K. (1994). *Competing for the future*. Boston: Harvard Business School.

Hamm, S. (1999, April 5). Netscapees storm the valley. *Business Week*, pp. 104–105.

Hill, C. H. (2000). *International business*. New York: McGraw-Hill/Irwin.

Hill, C. W. L. (1994). Diversification and economic performance: Bringing structure and corporate management back into the picture. In R. P. Rumelt et al. (Eds.), *Fundamental issues in strategy* (pp. 297–321). Boston: Harvard Business School Press.

Hitt, M. A., & Ireland, R. D. (1986). Relationships among corporate level distinctive competencies, diversification strategy, corporate structure, and performance. *Journal of Management Studies, 23,* 401–416.

Hitt, M. A., Ireland, R. D., & Hoskisson, R. E. (2001). *Strategic management.* New York: McGraw-Hill/Irwin.

Hitt, M. A., Park, D., Hardee, C., & Tyler, B. B. (1995). Understanding strategic intent in the global market place. *Academy of Management Executive, 9*(2), 12–19.

Holstein, W. J. (2002, October 14). Canon takes aim at Xerox. *Fortune,* pp. 215–220.

Hoskisson, R. E., Hitt, M. A., Wan, W. P., & Yui, D. (1999). Theory and research in strategic management. *Journal of Management,* pp. 417–456.

Hughes, J., Ralf, M., & Michels, W. (1998). *Transform your supply chain.* London, UK: International Thompson Business Press.

Hughes, K., & Oughton, C. (1993). Diversification, multimarket contact, and profitability. *Economics, 60,* 203–224.

Hunt, M. S. (1972). *Competition in the major home appliance industry.* Cambridge, MA: Harvard University Press.

Ireland, D., & Hitt, M. A. (1999). Achieving and maintaining strategic competitiveness in the 21st century: The role of strategic leadership. *Academy of Management Executive, 13*(1), 43–58.

Jenison, D. B., & Sitkin, S. B. (1986). Corporate acquisitions: A process perspective. *Academy of Management Review, 11,* 145–163.

Jones, T. M. (1995). Instrumental stakeholder theory: A synthesis of ethics and economics. *Academy of Management Review, 20,* 404–437.

Kahn, J. (1999, June 7). Wal-Mart goes shopping in Europe. *Fortune,* pp. 105–110.

Kelm, K. M., Narayanan, V. K., & Pinches, G. E. (1995). Shareholder value creation during R&D innovation and commercialization stages. *Academy of Management Journal, 38,* 770–780.

Kerwin, K., & Ewing, J. (1999, September 27). Nasser: Ford be nimble. *Business Week,* pp. 42–43.

Kosnik, R., & Chatterjee, S. (1997). *Corporate governance.* St. Paul, MN: West Publishing Co.

Kotha, S., & Nair, A. P. (1995). Strategy and environment as determinants of performance: Evidence from the Japanese machine tool industry. *Strategic Management Journal, 16,* 497–518.

Kumii, I. M. (1999, March 22). Sony's shake up. *Business Week,* pp. 52–54.

Labich, K. (1999, March 1). Boeing finally hatches a plan. *Fortune,* pp. 101–106.

Lado, A. A., Boyd, N. G., & Wright, P. (1992). A competency based model of sustainable advantage: Toward a conceptual integration. *Journal of Management, 18,* 77–91.

McGahan, A. M. (1994). Industry structure and competitive advantage. *Harvard Business Review, 72*(5), 115–124.

McGrath, R. G., MacMillan, I. C., & Venkataraman, S. (1995). Defining and developing competence: A strategic process paradigm. *Strategic Management Journal, 16,* 251–275.

Meznar, M. B., & Nigh, D. (1995). Buffer or bridge? Environmental and organizational determinants of public affairs activities in American firms. *Academy of Management Journal, 38,* 975–996.

Monks, R. A. G., & Minow, N. (1995). *Corporate governance.* Cambridge, MA: Blackwell Business.

Montgomery, C. A. (1994). Corporate diversification. *Journal of Economic Perspectives, 8,* 163–178.

Munk, N. (1999, June 21). Title fight. *Fortune,* pp. 84–94.

Naughton, K. (1999, January 25). The global six. *Business Week,* pp. 68–76.

Nerf, R. (1991, December 9). Guess who is selling Barbies in Japan now? *Business Week,* pp. 72–76.

Peteraf, M. A. (1993). The cornerstone of competitive strategy: A resource based view. *Strategic Management Journal, 14,* 179–191.

Petrick, J. A., Scherer, R. F., Brodzinski, J. D., Quinn, J. F., & Ainina, M. F. (1999). Global leadership skills and reputational capital: Intangible resources for sustainable competitive advantage. *Academy of Management Executive, 13*(1), 58–70.

Pfeffer, J. (1994). *Competitive advantage through people: Unleashing the power of the workforce.* Boston: Harvard Business School Press.

Porter, M. E. (1990). *Competitive advantage.* New York: Free Press.

Porter, M. E. (1994). Toward a dynamic theory of strategy. In R. P. Rumelt, D. E. Schendel, & D. J. Teece (Eds.), *Fundamental issues in strategy.* Boston: Harvard University Press.

Pound, J. (1995). The promise of the governed corporation. *Harvard Business Review, 73*(2), 90.

Prahalad, C. K., & Hamel, G. (1990). The core competence of the organization. *Harvard Business Review, 68*(3), 79–91.

Preble, J. F. (1992). Environmental scanning for strategic control. *Journal of Managerial Issues, 4,* 254–268.

Price, R. (1996). Technology and strategic advantage. *California Management Review, 38*(3), 38–56.

Reed, S. (1999, February 22). Busting up Sweden Inc. *Business Week,* pp. 52–53.

Reger, R. K., & Huffs, A. S. (1993). Strategic groups: A cognitive perspective. *Strategic Management Journal, 14,* 103–123.

Rogers, B. (1998). *Seize the future for your business.* London, UK: International Thompson Business Press.

Sager, I. (1999, June 21). Big Blue at your service. *Business Week,* pp. 131–136.

San Jose Mercury News. (1998). Gates too busy to define government. [story appearing in *Arizona Republic,* E1].

Schendler, B. (1999, April 12). Sony's new game. *Fortune,* pp. 30–31.

Schrivastava, P. (1995). Ecocentric management for a risk society. *Academy of Management Review, 20,* 119.

Sherman, S. (1995, November 13). Stretch goals: The dark side of asking for miracles. *Fortune,* pp. 231–232.

Siekman, P. (1999, April 26). Where build-to-order works best. *Fortune,* p. 160.

Sirois, C. (1995, August 25). Unifi, Inc. *Value Pine,* p. 1640.

Sparks, D. (1999, October 25). Partners. *Business Week,* pp. 106–107.

Stiles, T. (1995). Collaboration for competitive advantage. *Long Range Planning, 28,* 109–112.

Symonds, W. C. (1999, April 5). Looking to lose just a few more pounds. *Business Week,* pp. 64–70.

Taylor, A., III. (1995, September 18). Ford's really B16 leap at the future: It's risky, it's worthy, and it may work. *Fortune,* pp. 134–144.

Taylor A., III. (1999, January 11). The Germans take charge. *Fortune,* pp. 92–96.

Taylor, A., III. (1999, April 26). Why Dupont is trading oil for corn. *Fortune,* pp. 154–160.

Time Magazine (2003, February 24). Milestones, p. 16.

Veale, J. (1999, August 30). How Daewoo ran itself off the road. *Business Week,* pp. 48–49.

Vlasic, B., & Naughton, K. (1997, September 22). The small car wars are back. *Business Week,* pp. 40–42.

Weber, J. (1999, June 14). As the world restructures. *Business Week,* pp. 150–152.

Wiles, R. (2003, February 18). Manage your money, control your future. *The Arizona Republic,* p. D-1.

www.ford.com (accessed August 1, 2003).

Zellner, W. (1999, February 8). Southwest's new direction. *Business Week,* pp. 58–59.

Zhang, H. (1995). Wealth effects of U.S. bank takeovers. *Applied Financial Economics, 5,* 329–336.

Chapter 8

Barrett, C. (2003, January 27). Good times and bad: Innovation is key. *Information Week,* p. 20.

Cassidy, M. (2003, December 5). Creative marketing: The mouse tap. *Detroit Free Press,* www.freep.com/money/tech/mice5_20021205.htm, accessed February 19, 2003.

Cherwitz, R. A., & Sullivan, C. A. (2002). Intellectual entrepreneurship: A vision for graduate education. *Change, 34,* 23–28.

Eckberg, J. (2002, October 14). Innovation spells success. *Cincinnati Enquirer,* p. B6.

Heun, C. T. (2002, February 11). New "ink" veers display toward the good old look. *Informationweek,* p. 18.

Hopkins, J. (2003, February 24). Start-up succeeding study says. *The Arizona Republic,* p. D1.

Kunze, R. J. (2001). The dark side of multilevel marketing: Appeals to the symbolically incomplete. Dissertation at Arizona State University.

Larson, J. (2003, pp. D1, D2). Musician beams with joy. *The Arizona Republic.*

Lindsay, N., & Craig, J. (2002). A framework for understanding opportunity recognition: Entrepreneurs versus private equity financiers. *Journal of Private Equity, 6,* 13–24.

Mottram, B., Rigby, S., & Webster, A. (2003, January). The freedom to call your own shots. *Transmission & Distribution World, 55.*

National Commission on Entrepreneurship (2001). Five myths about entrepreneurs: Understanding how businesses start and grow. www.ncoe.org, accessed February 19, 2003.

Pellet, J. (2002). Leading creative charge. *Chief Executive, 1,* 6–11.

Raz, T. (2003, January). The 10 secrets of a master networker, *Inc. Magazine,* pp. 90–99.

Schmitt, B. (2002, February). Growth signs for new "ink." *Chemical Week, 164,* 46.

Small Business Administration (2002). Small business by the numbers. www.sba.gov/advo/stats/, accessed April 6, 2003 (see "Small Business Frequently Asked Questions").

The White House (2003). "Taking action to strengthen small business." www.whitehouse.gov/infocus/smallbusiness/, accessed April 6, 2003.

Armstrong, L. (1997, May 26). Powerwave technologies: Pump up the volume. *Business Week,* p. 102.

Barker, E. (1999, June). Maker of rugged PCs crumbles in IPO bid. *Inc,* p. 25.

Baron, R. A. (1998). Cognitive mechanisms in entrepreneurship: Why and when entrepreneurs think differently than other people. *Journal of Business Venturing, 13,* 275–294.

Berringer, B. R., & Bluedorn, A. C. (1999). The relationship between corporate entrepreneurship and strategic management. *Strategic Management Journal, 20,* 421–444.

Bildner, J. (1995, July). Hitting the wall. *Inc,* pp. 21–22.

Bruno, A. V., Leidecker, J. K., & Harder, J. W. (1987, March–April). Why firms fail. *Business Horizons,* pp. 50–58.

Bruno, A. V., & Tyebjee, T. (1985). The entrepreneur's search for capital. *Journal of Business Venturing, 1,* 61–74.

Burgelman, R. A. (1983). Corporate entrepreneurship and strategic management: Insights from a process study. *Management Science, 29,* 1349–1364.

Burgelman, R. A., Maidique, M. A., & Wheelwright, S. G. (1996). *Strategic management of technology and innovation* (2nd ed.). Burr Ridge, IL: Irwin.

Busenitz, L. A., & Barney, J. B. (1997). Differences between entrepreneurs and managers in large organizations: Biases and heuristics in strategic decision-making. *Journal of Business Venturing, 12,* 9–30.

Buttner, E. H., & Moore, D. P. (1997). Women's organizational exodus to entrepreneurship: Self-reported motivations and correlated with success. *Journal of Small Business Management, 34*(4), 1–13.

Callan, C., & Warshaw, M. (1995, September). The 25 best business schools for entrepreneurs. *Success,* pp. 37–54.

Carland, J., Hoy, F., Boulton, W., & Carland, J. (1984). Differentiating entrepreneurs from small business owners: A conceptualization. *Academy of Management Review, 9,* 354–359.

Covin, J. G., Slevin, D. P., & Covin, T. J. (1990). Content and performance of growth-seeking strategies: A comparison of small firms in high- and low-technology industries. *Journal of Business Venturing, 5,* 391–412.

DeCastro, J. D. (1997, March). When firms disappear have they really failed? *Colorado Business Review,* p. 3.

Dollinger, M. J. (1995). *Entrepreneurship.* New York: McGraw-Hill/Irwin.

Dubini, P., & Aldrich, H. (1991). Personal and extended networks are central to the entrepreneurial process. *Journal of Business Venturing, 6,* 305–313.

Economist. (1993, July 10). Barefoot into PARC, p. 68.

Fisher, R., & Ury, W. (1983). *Getting to yes.* New York: Penguin Books.

Gartner, W. B. (1985). A conceptual framework for describing the phenomena of new venture creation. *Academy of Management Review, 10,* 696–706.

Gartner, W. B. (1989). Who is an entrepreneur? Is the wrong question. *Entrepreneurship Theory and Practice, 13*, 47–64.

Gersick, C. J. (1994). Pacing strategic change: The case of a new venture. *Academy of Management Journal, 37*, 9–45.

Gomez-Mejia, L. R., Balkin, D. B., & Welbourne, T. (1990). Influence of venture capitalists on high tech management. *Journal of High Technology Management Research, 1*, 90–106.

Hambrick, D. C., & Crozier, L. M. (1985). Stumblers and stars in the management of rapid growth. *Journal of Business Venturing, 1*, 31–45.

Hamel, G., Doz, Y., & Prahalad, C. K. (1989, January–February). Collaborate with your competitors—and win. *Harvard Business Review*, pp. 133–139.

Himelstein, L. (1998, September 7). Yahoo! The company, the strategy the stock. *Business Week*, pp. 66–76.

Hisrich, R. D., & Peters, M. P. (1998). *Entrepreneurship* (4th ed.). New York: McGraw-Hill/Irwin.

Hof, R. D. (1998, December 14). Amazon.com: The wild world of e-commerce. *Business Week*, pp. 106–119.

Hofman, M. (1997, August). Desperation capital. *Inc*, pp. 54–57.

Jones, G. R., & Butler, J. E. (1992). Managing internal corporate entrepreneurship: An agency theory perspective. *Journal of Management, 18*, 733–749.

Kazanjian, R. K. (1988). Relation of dominant problems to stages of growth in technology-based new ventures. *Academy of Management Journal, 31*, 257–279.

Kotter, J., & Sathe, V. (1978). Problems of human resource management in rapidly growing companies. *California Management Review, 21*(2), 29–36.

Kuratko, D. F., & Hodgetts, R. M. (1992). *Entrepreneurship* (2nd ed.). Fort Worth: Dryden Press.

Lesley, E., & Mallory, M. (1993, November 29). Inside the black business network. *Business Week*, p. 70.

Lumpkin, G. T. (1996). Clarifying the entrepreneurial orientation construct and linking it to performance. *Academy of Management Review, 21*, 135–172.

McNamee, M. (1997, September 1). Good news from small biz. *Business Week*, p. 24.

Megginson, W. L., Boyd, M. J., Scott, C. R., & Megginson, L. C. (1997). *Small business management* (2nd ed.). Burr Ridge, IL: Irwin.

Meyer, G. D., & Dean, T. J. (1995, July). Why entrepreneurs fail. *Colorado Business Review*, pp. 3–4.

O'Reilly, B. (1999, June 7). What it takes to start a startup. *Fortune*, pp. 135–140.

Pinchot, G. (1985). *Intrapreneuring*. New York: Harper & Row.

Russo, J. E., & Schoemaker, P. J. (1992). Managing overconfidence. *Sloan Management Review, 33*(2), 7–17.

Schlender, B. (1997, July 7). Cool companies. *Fortune*, pp. 84–110.

Statistical Abstracts of the United States. (1994). Washington, DC: U.S. Government Printing Office.

Stewart, W. H., Watson, W. E., Carland, J. C., & Carland, J. W. (1999). A proclivity for entrepreneurship: A comparison of entrepreneurs, small business owners, and corporate managers. *Journal of Business Venturing, 14*, 189–214.

Timmons, J. A. (1994). *New venture creation* (4th ed.). New York: McGraw-Hill/Irwin.

Usdansky, M. L. (1991, August 2). Asian businesses big winners in '80s. *USA Today*, p. 1A.

Useem, J. (1998, August). Partners on the edge. *Inc*, pp. 52–64.

Vincent, V. C. (1996). Decision-making policies among Mexican-American small business entrepreneurs. *Journal of Small Business Management, 34*(4), 1–13.

Williams, D. L. (1999). Why do entrepreneurs become franchisees? An empirical analysis of organizational choice. *Journal of Business Venturing, 14*, 103–124.

Chapter 9

Bartol, K. M., & Martin, D. C. (1998). *Management* (3rd ed.). New York: McGraw-Hill.

Budros, A. (1999). A conceptual framework for analyzing why organizations downsize. *Organization Science, 10*, 69–82.

Burns, T., & Stalker, G. (1961). *The management of innovation*. London, UK: Tavistock Institute.

Burrows, P. (1999, August 12). The boss: Carly Fiorina's challenge will be to propel staid Hewlett-Packard into the Internet age without sacrificing the very things that have made it great. *Business Week*, pp. 76–84.

Byrne, J. A. (1998, June 8). Jack: A close-up look at how America's #1 manager views GE. *Business Week*, pp. 40–51.

Caroll, P. (1993). *Big blues: The unmaking of IBM*. New York: Crown Publishers.

Clark, K., & Wheelwright, S. (1992). Organizing and leading "heavyweight" development teams. *California Management Review, 34*(2), 9–28.

Cobb, A. T. (1980). Informal influence in the formal organization: Perceived sources of power among work unit peers. *Academy of Management Journal, 23*, 55–61.

Collins, J. C., & Porras, J. I. (1994). *Built to last: Successful habits of visionary companies*. New York: Harper Business.

Crockett, R. O. (1998, May 4). How Motorola lost its way. *Business Week*, pp. 140–148.

Crockett, R. O. (1999, June 21). Motorola is ringing again. *Business Week*, p. 40.

Daft, R. L. (1983). *Organization theory and design*. St. Paul, MN: West Publishing Company.

Daft, R. L. (1997). *Management* (4th ed.). Fort Worth: Dryden Press.

Daft, R. L. (1999). *Leadership: Theory and practice*. Fort Worth: Dryden Press.

Deal, T. E., & Kennedy, A. A. (1982). *Corporate cultures*. Reading, MA: Addison-Wesley.

Duncan, R. (1979, Winter). What is the right organization structure? Decision tree analysis provides the answer. *Organizational Dynamics*, pp. 59–80.

Economist. (1997, April 5). Conglomorates on trial, p. 59.

Economist. (1998, May 9). A new kind of car company, pp. 61–62.

Economist. (1999, January 9). How to merge: After the deal, pp. 21–23.

Economist (2003, January 18). How to manage a dream factory, pp. 73–75.

Fama, E. F. (1980). Agency problems and the theory of the firm. *Journal of Political Economy, 88*, 288–307.

Fama, E. F., & Jensen, M. L. (1983). Separation of ownership and control. *Journal of Law and Economics, 26*, 301–325.

Ford, R. C., & Randolph, W. A. (1992). Cross-functional structures: A review and integration of matrix organization and project management. *Journal of Management, 18,* 267–294.

Frank, K. A., & Fahrbach, K. (1999). Organization culture as a complex system: Balance and information models of influence and selection. *Organization Science, 10,* 253–277.

Freedman, A. M. (1988, October 20). Phillip Morris's bid for Kraft could limit product innovation. *The Wall Street Journal,* p. A1.

Garten, J. (1998, July 20). Daimler has to steer the Chrysler merger. *Business Week,* p. 20.

Glasgall, W. (1998, April 20). Citigroup: Just the start? *Business Week,* pp. 34–40.

Gomez-Mejia, L. R., Balkin, D. B., & Cardy, R. L. (1998). *Managing human resources* (2nd ed.). Upper Saddle River, NJ: Prentice Hall.

Gooding, R., & Wagner, J. (1985). A meta-analytic review of the relationship between size and performance: The productivity and efficiency of organizations and their subunits. *Administrative Science Quarterly, 30,* 462–481.

Hatch, M. J. (1997). *Organization theory.* Oxford, UK: Oxford University Press.

Hodge, B. J., & Anthony, W. P. (1979). *Organization theory.* Boston: Allyn and Bacon.

Hoskisson, R. E., & Hitt, M. A. (1994). *Downscoping: How to tame the diversified firm.* New York: Oxford University Press.

Jones, G. R. (1998). *Organizational theory* (2nd ed.). Reading, MA: Addison-Wesley.

Kirkpatrick, D. (1996, November 25). They're all copying Compaq. *Fortune,* pp. 28–32.

Kochan, T. A., & Osterman, P. (1994). *The mutual gains enterprise.* Boston: Harvard Business School Press.

Kraatz, M. S., & Zajac, E. J. (2001). How organizational resources affect strategic change and performance in turbulent environments: Theory and evidence. *Organization Science, 12,* 632–657.

Kruse, D. L. (1993). *Profit sharing.* Kalamazoo, MI: W. E. Upjohn Institute for Employment Research.

Larson, E. W., & Gobeli, D. H. (1987, Summer). Matrix management: Contradictions and insights. *California Management Review,* pp. 126–138.

Larsson, R., & Finkelstein, S. (1999). Integrating strategic, organizational, and human resource perspectives on mergers and acquisitions: A case survey of synergy realization. *Organization Science, 10,* 1–26.

Lawler, E. E. (1992). *The ultimate advantage.* San Francisco: Jossey-Bass.

McWilliams, G. (1998, February 9). Power play: How the Compaq–Digital deal will reshape the entire world of computers. *Business Week,* pp. 90–97.

Meyer, M. (1998, July 6). The call of the wired. *Newsweek,* pp. 44–47.

Miller, A. (1998). *Strategic management* (3rd ed.). New York: McGraw-Hill/Irwin.

Miller, C., Glick, W., Wang, Y., & Huber, G. (1991). Understanding technology-structural relationships: Theory development and meta-analytic theory testing. *Academy of Management Journal, 34,* 370–399.

Mintzberg, H. (1979). *Structuring organizations.* Englewood Cliffs, NJ: Prentice Hall.

Montealegre, R., Nelson, J., Knoop, C., & Applegate, L. (1996). *BAE Automated Systems (A): Denver International Airport baggage-handling system.* Boston: Harvard Business School Publishing.

Moore, M. T. (1992, April 10). Hourly workers apply training in problem solving. *USA Today,* p. C1.

Murphy, K. R., & Cleveland, J. N. (1995). *Understanding performance appraisal.* Thousand Oaks, CA: Sage Publications.

Quinn, R. E., Faerman, S. R., Thompson, M. P., & McGrath, M. R. (1996). *Becoming a manager* (2nd ed.). New York: John Wiley & Sons.

Rebello, K. (1994, March 7). A juicy apple? *Business Week,* pp. 88–90.

Robbins, S. P., & Coulter, M. (1996). *Management* (5th ed.). Upper Saddle River, NJ: Prentice Hall.

Robey, D., & Sayles, C. A. (1994). *Designing organizations.* Burr Ridge, IL: Irwin.

Silverman, G. (1999, August 16). Citigroup: So much for 50–50. *Business Week,* p. 80.

Smart, T. (1996, October 28). Jack Welch's encore. *Business Week,* pp. 155–160.

Smircich, L. (1983). Concepts of culture and organizational analysis. *Administrative Science Quarterly, 28,* 339–358.

Van Fleet, D., & Bedeian, A. (1977). A history of the span of management. *Academy of Management Review, 2,* 356–372.

Whetton, D. A., & Cameron, K. S. (1995). *Developing management skills* (3rd ed.). New York: HarperCollins.

Wright, P. M., & Noe, R. A. (1996). *Management of organizations.* Burr Ridge, IL: Irwin.

Chapter 10

Alpern, D. M. (1995, July). Why women are divided on affirmative action. *Working Woman,* p. 18.

Arizona Republic. (1997, January 25). Supermarket chain settles sex bias suit, p. E1.

Bernardin, H. J., & Cooke, D. K. (1993). Validity of an honesty test in predicting theft among convenience store employees. *Academy of Management Journal, 36,* 1097–1108.

BNA's Employee Relations Weekly. (1993, September 13). EEOC meets new, higher burden of proof in race bias case in California court, pp. 11, 991.

Branch, S. (1999, January 11). The 100 best companies to work for in America. *Fortune,* p. 118.

Burack, E. H. (1988). *Creative human resource planning and applications.* Englewood Cliffs, NJ: Prentice Hall.

Bureau of Labor Statistics. (1999). *Employment and earnings* (Tables 44 and 45). Washington, DC: Government Printing Office.

Carrell, M. R., & Heavrin, C. (1998). *Labor relations and collective bargaining.* Upper Saddle River, NJ: Prentice Hall.

Cowan T. R. (1989). Drugs and the workplace. *Public Personnel Management, 16,* 313–322.

Damodt, M. G., Bryan, D. A., & Whitcomb, A. J. (1993). Predicting performance with letters of recommendation. *Public Personnel Management, 22,* 81–90.

Dessler, G. (2000). *Human resource management.* Upper Saddle River, NJ: Prentice Hall.

Eisenberg, D. (1999, August 16). We are for hire, just click. *Time,* pp. 46–50.

Filipzak, B. (1993, October). Training budgets boom. *Training*, pp. 37–44.

Fitzgerald, W. (1992). Training versus development. *Training and Development*, pp. 46–81.

Foust, D., Grow, B., & Pascual, M. M. (2002, September 9). The changing heartland. *Business Week*, pp. 80–82.

Goldstein, I. C. (1986). Training in organizations: Needs assessment, development, and evaluation (2nd ed.). Monterey, CA: Brooks/Cole.

Gomez-Mejia, L. R., & Balkin, D. B. (1992). *Compensation, organizational strategy, and firm performance*. Cincinnati, OH: South-Western Publishing.

Gomez-Mejia, L. R., Balkin, D. B., & Cardy, R. (2001). *Managing human resources*. Englewood Cliffs, NJ: Prentice Hall.

Griggs v. Duke Power Co., 401 U.S. 424 (1971).

Gunsch, D. (1993, September). Comprehensive college entry strengthens NCR's recruitment. *Personnel Journal*, pp. 58–62.

Henderson, R. I. (1997). *Compensation management* (7th ed.). Upper Saddle River, NJ: Prentice Hall.

Hill, C. W. C. (2000). *International business*. New York: McGraw-Hill/Irwin.

Hogan, R. (1991). Personality and personality measurement. In M. D. Dunnette & L. M. Hough (Eds.), *Handbook of industrial and organization psychology* (2nd ed., vol. 1). Palo Alto, CA: Consulting Psychologists.

Holmes, S., Bennett, D., Carlisle, K., & Dawson, C. (2002, September 9). To keep up the growth, it must go global quickly. *Business Week*, pp. 126–138.

HR News. (1994, February). No beard rule found to have disparate impact, p. 17.

Hunter, J. E. (1986). Cognitive ability, cognitive aptitudes, job knowledge, and job performance. *Journal of Vocational Behavior, 29*, 340–362.

Kasindorf, M. (1999, September 10). Hispanics and blacks find their futures entangled. *USA Today*, p. 21A.

Koretz, G. (1996, December 2). College majors that really pay. *Business Week*, p. 34.

Levering, R., & Moskowitz, M. (2003, January 20). 100 best companies to work for. *Fortune*, pp. 127–150.

Longnecker, B. M., Petersen, B., & Hitt, R. (1999). Long-term incentives: How private companies can compete with public companies. *Compensation and Benefits Review, 31*(1), 44–53.

Lopez, J. A. (1993, October 6). Firms force job seekers to jump through hoops. *The Wall Street Journal*, pp. B1, B6.

Mandel, M. J. (1996, October 28). The high risk society: Coping with uncertainty. *Business Week*, pp. 86–94.

McDonough, D. C. (1999, April 26). A fair workplace? Not everywhere. *Business Week*, p. 6.

McEvoy, G. M., & Beatty, R. W. (1989). Assessment centers and subordinate appraisal of managers. *Personnel Psychology, 42*, 37–52.

Milkovich, G. T., & Newman, J. M. (1999). *Compensation* (6th ed.). New York: McGraw-Hill/Irwin.

Muchinsky, P. M. (1979). The use of reference reports in personnel selection. *Journal of Occupational Psychology, 52*, 287–297.

Murphy, K. R. (1993). *Honesty in the workplace*. Belmont, CA: Brooks/Cole.

Murphy, N. J. (1993). Performance measurement and appraisal. *Employment Relations Today*, pp. 47–62.

Newman, B. (2003, January 9). For ill immigrants, doctors' orders get lost in translation. *Wall Street Journal*, p. A-1.

Prasso, S. (2003, February 18). The UAW answers a cry for help. *Business Week*, p. 8.

Ray, H. H., & Altmansberger, H. N. (1999). Introducing goal sharing in a public sector organization. *Compensation and Benefits Review, 31*(3), 40–45.

Reese, J. (1996, December 9). Starbucks: Inside the coffee cult. *Fortune*, pp. 191–200.

Reinhardt, A., & Holf, R. D. (1999, October 4). The search for the young and gifted. *Business Week*, pp. 108–112.

Russell, C. J., Mattson, J., Devlin, S. E., & Atwater, D. (1990). Predictive validity of biodata items generated from retrospective life experience essays. *Journal of Applied Psychology, 75*, 569–580.

Rynes, S. L. (1991). Recruitment, job choice, and post hire consequences. *Handbook of industrial and organizational psychology* (2nd ed., Vol. 2, pp. 399–344).

Schwartz, N. D. (1999, May 24). Still perking after all these years. *Fortune*, pp. 203–210.

Stein, N. (2003, March 3). America's most admired companies. *Fortune*, pp. 81–94. *Time Magazine* (2003, March 10). Numbers, p. 17.

Symons, J. L. (1995, May–June). Is affirmative action in America's interest? *Executive Female*, p. 52.

Useem, J. (1999, May 24). Read this before you put your résumé on line. *Fortune*, p. 290.

Useem, J. (1999, July 5). Getting a job on line. *Fortune*, p. 69.

Walker, J. (1992). *Human resource management strategy*. New York: McGraw-Hill.

Wanous, J. P. (1992). *Organizational entry* (2nd ed.). Reading, MA: Addison-Wesley.

Wessel, D. (1989, September 7). Evidence is skimpy that drug testing works, but employers embrace the practice. *The Wall Street Journal*, p. B1.

Wright, P., Licthenfels, P., & Pursell, E. D. (1989). The structure interview: Additional studies and a meta-analysis. *Journal of Occupational Psychology, 6*, 191–199.

Chapter 11

Allport, G. W., & Odbert, H. S. (1993). Trait names: A psycholexical study. *Psychological Monographs, 47*, 171–220.

Arvey, R. D., Ross, A., Ostgoard, D., & Raghuram, S. (1996). The implications of a diverse labor market on human resource planning. In E. E. Kossek & S. A. Lobel (Eds.), *Managing Diversity*. Malden, MA: Blackwell Publishers.

Baba, M. (1995). The cultural economy of the corporation: Explaining diversity in work group responses to organizational transformation. *Journal of Applied Behavioral Science, 31*(2), 202–233.

Baird, J. E., & Bradley, P. H. (1979, June). Styles of management and communication: A comparative study of men and women. *Communication Monographs, 46*, 104–110.

Baker, L. (1995). Racism in professional settings: Forms of address as clues to power relations. *Journal of Applied Behavioral Science, 31*(2), 186–201.

Banach, E. (1990, September). Today's supply of entry level workers reflect diversity. *Savings Institution,* pp. 74–75.

Bantel, K. A., & Jackson, S. E. (1989). Top management and innovation in banking: Does the composition of the top team make a difference? *Strategic Management Journal, 10,* 107–124.

Bateman, T. S., & Snell, S. A. (1999). *Management: Building competitive advantage* (4th ed.). New York: McGraw-Hill/Irwin.

Branigin, W. (1998, August 7). Patent office looks like U.S. future: Agency celebrates multicultural mix. *The Washington Post,* p. A23.

Briefs (1993, February 22). *Workforce strategies, 4*(2), ws12.

Carlson, M. (1999, September 20). Sexual harassment, Chapter 999. *Business Week,* p. 45.

Colvin, G. (1999, July 19). 50 best companies for Asian, Blacks, and Hispanics. *Fortune,* pp. 52–59.

Conlin, M. (2003, January 27). Look who's bringing home more bacon. *Business Week,* p. 85.

Cox, T. H., & Blake, S. (1991). Managing cultural diversity: Implications for organizational competitiveness. *Academy of Management Executive, 5*(3), 45–46.

Crockett, R. O. (1999, May 24). African-Americans get the investing bug. *Business Week,* p. 39.

Daft, R. (2000). *Management.* Fort Worth: Dryden Press.

Dass, P., & Parker, B. (1996). Diversity: A strategic issue. In E. E. Kossek & S. A. Lobel (Eds.), *Managing Diversity.* Malden, MA.: Blackwell Publishers.

Dass, P., & Parker, B. (1999). Strategies for managing human resource diversity: From resistance to learning. *Academy of Management Executive, 13*(2), 68–80.

Deogum, N. (1999, May 20). Coke was told in '95 of need for diversity. *The Wall Street Journal,* p. A3.

Drummond, T. (1999, June 14). It is not just in New Jersey. *Time,* p. 61.

Fisher, A. (1998, October 12). Women need at least one mentor and one pantsuit. *Fortune,* p. 208.

Fortune. (1999, April 26). The bus company that stopped pretending it was an airline, p. 48.

Fine, M. C., Johnson, P. L., & Ryan, S. M. (1990). Cultural diversity in the workplace. *Public Personnel Management, 19*(3), 305–319.

Finkelstein, L. M., Burke, M., & Raju, N. S. (1995). Age discrimination in simulated employment contexts: An integrative analysis. *Journal of Applied Psychology, 80*(6), 652–663.

France, M., & Smart, T. (1996, November 18). The ugly talk on the Texaco tape. *Business Week,* p. 58.

Fritsch, P., & Sullivan, A. (1996, November 8). Texaco's new chairman navigates PR crisis. *The Wall Street Journal,* p. B1.

Gentile, M. C. (1996). Managerial excellence through diversity. Burr Ridge IL: Irwin.

Gleckman, H. (2003, April 7). Old, ill, and uninsured. *Business Week,* p. 78.

Gleick, E. (1996, November 25). Scandal in the military. *Time,* pp. 28–31.

Gonzalez, D. (2001, February 19). "Illegal workers fueled new economy." *Arizona Republic,* A-1.

Gomez-Mejia, L. R., Balkin, D. B., & Cardy, R. (2001). *Managing human resources.* Englewood Cliffs, NJ: Prentice Hall.

Hogan-Garcia, M. (1995). An anthropological approach to multicultural diversity training. *Journal of Applied Behavioral Science, 31*(4), 490–505.

Ibarra, H. (1992). Homophily and differential returns. *Administrative Science Quarterly, 37,* 422–447.

Ibarra, H. (1993). Personal networks of women and minorities in management. *Academy of Management Review, 18,* 57–87.

Ibarra, H. (1995). Race, opportunities, and diversity of social circles in managerial networks. *Academy of Management Journal, 38*(23), 673–703.

Jackson, S. E., May, K., & Whitney, K. (1994). Diversity in decision making teams. In R. A. Guzzo & E. Salas (Eds.), *Team decision making effectiveness in organizations.* San Francisco: Jossey-Bass.

Jones, D. (1997, February 26). U.S. managers earn global credentials. *USA Today,* p. A1.

Jordan, A. (1995). Managing diversity: Translating anthropological insight for organization studies. *Journal of Applied Behavioral Science, 31*(2), 124–140.

Kossek, E. E. (1996). Managing diversity as a vehicle for culture change. In E. E. Kossek & S. A. Lobel (Eds.), *Managing diversity.* Malden, MA: Blackwell Publishers.

Lancaster, H. (1996, November 5). Should managers tell colleagues that they are gay. *The Wall Street Journal,* p. B1.

Lavelle, L. (2001, April 21). "For female CEOs it is stingy at the top." *Business Week,* 70–71

Lobel, S. A., & Kossek, E. E. (1996). Human resource strategies to support diversity in work and personal life styles. In E. E. Kossek & S. A. Lobel (Eds.), *Managing diversity.* Malden, MA: Blackwell Publishers.

Loden, M., & Rosener, J. B. (1991). *Workforce America.* Burr Ridge, IL: Irwin.

Magnusson, P. (2001, April 9). "The border is more porous than you think." *Business Week,* 94.

Malachalaba, D. (1999, July 2). Amtrack to pay $8 million and change practices to settle racial-bias suit. *The Wall Street Journal,* p. B8.

McCleod, P. L., & Lobel, S. A. (1992). The effects of ethnic diversity on idea generation in small groups. Paper presented at the annual meetings of the Academy of Management, Las Vegas, August.

McDonough, D. C. (1999, April 26). A fair workplace? Not everywhere. *Business Week,* p. 6.

McNamee, M. (1998, August 17). First hired, first fired? *Business Week,* p. 22.

Mehta, S. (1996, November 11). More women quit lucrative jobs to start their own business. *The Wall Street Journal,* p. A1.

Mendosa, R. (1996, October). The $152 billion engine. *Hispanic Business,* pp. 28–29.

Mendosa, R. (1996, October). A downward count? *Hispanic Business,* p. 18.

Merrill, D. (2001, March 30). "Census 2000: Counting America." *USA Today,* 10-A.

Merritt, J. (2001, June 18). "Big strides at black B-schools." *Business Week,* 136.

Miller, L. (1995). Two aspects of Japanese and American co-worker interaction. *Journal of Applied Behavioral Science, 31*(2), 141–161.

Mitteldstadt, M. (1997, February 8). Illegals in U.S. at 5 million, INS reports. *The Arizona Republic*, p. A1.

Morris, B. (1997, March 17). Is your family wrecking your career? *Fortune*, pp. 71–87.

Morris, K. (1998, November 23) You've come a short way, baby. *Business Week*, pp. 82–86.

Muir, J. G. (1993, March 31). Homosexuals and the 10% fallacy. *The Wall Street Journal*, p. A13.

Munk, N. (1999, February 1). Finished at forty. *Fortune*, pp. 50–64.

Newman, B. (2003, January 9). For ill immigrants, doctors' orders get lost in translation. *Wall Street Journal*, pp. A1, A8.

Reeves-Ellington, R. (1995). Organizing for global effectiveness. *Human Organization, 54*(3), 249–262.

Reingold, J., & Brody, D. (1999, September 20). Brain drain. *Business Week*, pp. 113–122.

Research National Phone Poll (1994, March 4). *Chattanooga Time*, p. 1.

Ricks, T. E. (1996, November 11). Army is facing inquiries and battle over policies as sex scandal widens. *The Wall Street Journal*, p. B9.

Romano, C. (1993, October). All aboard? The composition of the boardroom is changing—albeit slowly. *Management Review*, p. 5.

Rynes, S., & Rosen, B. (1995). A field survey of factors affecting the adoption and perceived success of diversity training. *Personnel Psychology, 48*, 247–259.

Schrage, M. (1999, May 24). Digital day care. *Fortune*, p. 294.

Sessa, V. I., Jackson, S. E., & Rapini, D. T. (1995). Workforce diversity: The good, the bad, and the reality. In G. Ferris, S. D. Rosen, & D. T. Barnum (Eds.), *Handbook of human resource management* (pp. 263–282). Cambridge, MA: Blackwell Publishers.

Stodghill, R. (1996, November 25). Get serious about diversity training. *Business Week*, p. 39.

U.S. News and World Report. (1996, October 21). Hispanics in the U.S., p. 30.

Weber, J. (1988, June 6). Social issues: The disabled. *Business Week*, p. 140.

Wheeler, M. L. (1996, December 9). Diversity: Making the business case. *Business Week*, special advertising section.

Wheeler, M. L. (1998, December 14). Capitalizing on diversity. *Business Week*, special advertising section.

White, J. E. (1999, August 23). Affirmative actions Alamo. *Time*, p. 48.

White, J. R. (1996, November 25). Texaco's high octane racism problems. *Time*, p. 33.

Wood, W. (1987). Meta-analytic review of sex differences in group performance. *Psychological Bulletin, 102*, 53–71.

Wynter, L. (1999, January 6). Business and race. *The Wall Street Journal*, p. B1.

Wysocki, B. (1996, October 10). Influx of immigrants adds new vitality to housing market. *The Wall Street Journal*, p. A1.

Yakura, E. K. (1996). EEO law and managing diversity. In E. E. Kossek & S. A. Lobel (Eds.), *Managing diversity*. Malden, MA: Blackwell Publishers.

Yang, C., Therese, A., Browder, S., & Cuneo, A. (1996, November 11). Lessons: How Marriott keeps good help—even at $7.40 an hour. *Business Week*, pp. 105–115.

Chapter 12

Adams, J. S. (1965). Inequity in social exchanges. In L. Berkowitz (Ed.), *Advances in experimental social psychology* (pp. 267–300). New York: Academic Press.

Adler, N. (1997). *International dimensions of organizational behavior* (3rd ed.). Cincinnati, OH: South-Western Publishing.

Alderfer, C. (1972). *Existence, relatedness, and growth: Human needs in organizational settings*. Glencoe, IL: Free Press.

Arnold, H. J. (1981, April). A test of the multiplicative hypothesis of expectancy-valence theories of work motivation. *Academy of Management Journal*, pp. 128–141.

Bass, B., Avolio, B., & Goodheim, L. (1987). Biography in the assessment of transformational leadership at the world class level. *Journal of Management, 13*, 7–20.

Bass, B. M. (1985). *Leadership and performance beyond expectations*. New York: Free Press.

Bass, B. M. (1990). *Bass and Stogdill's handbook of leadership: Theory, research and managerial application* (3rd ed.). New York: Free Press.

Bass, B. M., & Avolio, B. J. (1990, January). Developing transformational leadership: 1992 and beyond. *Journal of European Industrial Training*, p. 23.

Bennis, W., & Nanus, B. (1985). *Leaders: The strategies for taking charge*. New York: Harper & Row.

Blake, R. R., & Mouton, J. S. (1964). *The managerial grid*. Houston: Gulf.

Boyatzis, R. E. (1984). The need for close relationships and the manager's job. In D. A. Kolls, I. M. Rubin, & J. M. McIntyre (Eds.), *Organizational psychology: Readings on human behavior in organizations* (4th ed.). Englewood Cliffs, NJ: Prentice Hall.

Brooker, K. (1999, April 26). Can Procter and Gamble change its culture, protect its market share, and find the next Tide? *Fortune*, pp. 146–153.

Burns, J. M. (1978). *Leadership*. New York: Harper & Row.

Business Week. (2001, January 8). The top 25 managers, pp. 60–81.

Business Week. (2001, January 22). Can Texan Marjorie Scardino transform Britain's Pearson into a global media colossus? pp. 78–88.

Byrne, J. A. (1998, July 6). How Al Dunlap self-destructed. *Business Week*, pp. 58–64.

Carvell, T. (1998, September 28). By the way . . . your staff. *Fortune*, pp. 200–206.

Chandler, S. (1999, October 17). Stumbling Sears seeks to launch 2nd revolution. *Arizona Republic*, p. D1

Chang, J. (2003). Cracking the whip: In a perfect world, sales managers would use only positive incentives to get the best performance from their teams. But in less-than-ideal situations, is there a time and place for negative motivation? *Sales & Marketing Management, 155*, 24+.

Charan, R., & Colvin, G. (1999, June 21). Why CEOs fail. *Fortune*, pp. 69–78.

Colvin, G. (1999, May 24). How to be a great CEO. *Fortune*, pp. 104–110.

Conger, J. A., & Kanungo, R. A. (1987). Toward a behavioral theory of charismatic leadership in organizational settings. *Academy of Management Review, 12,* 637–647.

Crockett, R. O. (2001, January 22). Motorola can't seem to get out of its own way. *Business Week,* p. 72.

Darlington, H. (2002). People—your most important asset. *Supply House Times, 45,* 113–114.

Dickson, G. W., & DeSanctis, G. (Eds.). (2001). *Information technology and the future enterprise: New models for managers.* Upper Saddle River, NJ: Prentice Hall.

Early, P. C., Connolly, T., & Ekegren, G. (1989). Goals, strategy development, and task performance: Some limits on the efficacy of goal setting. *Journal of Applied Psychology, 74,* 24–33.

Fiedler, F. E. (1967). *A theory of leadership effectiveness.* New York: McGraw-Hill.

Fiedler, F. E. (1971). Validation and extension of the contingency model of leadership effectiveness. *Psychological Bulletin, 76,* 128–148.

Fisher, A. (1998, October 26). Success secret: A high emotional IQ. *Fortune,* pp. 295–298.

Foust, D., Smith, G., & Rocks, D. (1999, May 3). Man on the spot. *Business Week,* pp. 142–152.

French, J., & Raven, B. (1959). The bases of social power. In D. Cartwright (Ed.), *Studies in social power.* Ann Arbor, MI: Institute for Social Research.

Garten, J. E. (2001). *The mind of the CEO.* New York: Basic Books/Perseus Publishing.

Gomez-Mejia, L. R., & Balkin, D. B. (1992). *Compensation, organizational strategy and firm performance.* Cincinnati, OH: South-Western Publishing.

Gomez-Mejia, L. R., Welbourne, T., & Wiseman, R. (2000). The role of risk sharing and risk taking under gainsharing. *Academy of Management Review, 25*(3), 492–509.

Guyon, J. (1999, March 29). Getting the bugs out at VW. *Fortune,* pp. 96–99.

Hackman, J. R., Oldham, G., Janson, R., & Purdy, K. (1975). A new strategy for job enrichment. *California Management Review, 16,* 57–71.

Hamm, S., Sager, I, & Burrowns, P. (1999, July 26). The lion in winter. *Business Week,* pp. 108–120.

Hofstede, G. (1980). *Culture's consequences: International differences in work related values.* Beverly Hills, CA: Sage.

House, R. J. (1971). A path goal theory of leader effectiveness. *Administrative Science Quarterly, 16,* 321–338.

House, R. J., & Aditya, R. (1997). The social scientific study of leadership: Quo vadis? *Journal of Management, 23*(3), 409–475.

House, R. J., & Michell, T. R. (1974). Path goal theory of leadership. *Journal of Contemporary Business, 3,* 81–97.

House, R. J., Shane, S., & Herold, D. (1996). Rumors of the death of dispositional theory and research in organizational behavior are greatly exaggerated. *Academy of Management Review, 21*(1), 203–224.

Huey, J. (1994, February 21). The new post-heroic leadership. *Fortune,* pp. 42–50.

Hyer, N. L., & Wemmerlow, U. (2002). The office that lean built: Applying cellular thinking to administrative work. *IIE Solutions, 34,* 37–2.

Ivancevich, J. M., Lorenzi, P., Skinner, S. J., & Crosby, P. B. (1997). *Management: Quality and competitiveness.* Burr Ridge, IL: Irwin.

Jones, G. R., George, J. M., & Hill, C. W. (2001). *Contemporary management.* New York: McGraw-Hill/Irwin.

Kahn, R., & Katz, D. (1960). Leadership practices in relation to productivity and morale. In D. Cartwright & A. Sander (Eds.), *Group dynamics: Research and theory.* Elmsford, NY: Row, Peterson.

Kenny, D. A., & Hallmark, B. W. (1992). Rotation designs in leadership research. *Leadership Quarterly, 3*(1), 25–41.

Kenny, D. A., & Zaccaro, S. J. (1983). An estimate of the variance due to traits in leadership. *Journal of Applied Psychology, 68*(4), 678–685.

Kerr, S., Schriesheim, C. A., Murphy, C. J., & Stogdill, R. M. (1974, August). Toward a contingency theory of leadership based upon the consideration and initiating structure literature. *Organizational Behavior and Human Performance,* pp. 62–82.

King, W. A., & Zeithaml, C. P. (2001). Competencies and firm performance. *Strategic Management Journal, 22*(1), 75–87.

Kirpatrick, D. (1999, May 24). Eckhard's fall, but the PC rocks on. *Fortune,* pp. 153–161.

Kulik, C. T., & Ambrose, M. L. (1992). Personal and situational determinants of referent choice. *Academy of Management Review, 17,* 212–237.

Kupfer, A. (1999, April 26). Mike Armstrong's AT&T. *Fortune,* pp. 82–86.

Le Pine, J. A., & Dyne, L. V. (2001). Peer responses to low performers: An attributional model of helping in the context of groups. *Academy of Management Review,* pp. 67–85.

Locke, E. (1968). Toward a theory of task motivation and incentives. *Organizational Behavior and Human Performance, 3,* 157–189.

Lord, R. G., DeVader, C. C., & Alleger, G. M. (1986). A meta-analysis of the relation between personality traits and leadership perceptions. *Journal of Applied Psychology, 71*(3), 402–410.

Manz, C., & Sims, H. P. (1990). *Superleadership.* New York: Berkeley.

Maslow, A. H. (1943, July). A theory of human motivation. *Psychological Review,* pp. 370–396.

McClelland, D. (1961). *The achieving society.* New York: Van Nostrand Reinhold.

McClelland, D. C., & Boyatzis, R. (1982). Leadership motive pattern and long-term success in management. *Journal of Applied Psychology, 67,* 737–743.

McClelland, D. C., & Winter, D. C. (1969). *Motivating economic achievement.* New York: Free Press.

McGregor, D. (1960). *The human side of enterprise.* New York: McGraw-Hill.

Mischel, W. (1973). Toward a cognitive social learning reconceptualization of personality. *Psychological Review, 80,* 252–283.

Muller, J. (2001, January 15). Thinking out of the cereal box. *Business Week,* pp. 54–70.

Munk, N. (1999, April 12). How Levi's trashed a great American brand. *Fortune,* pp. 83–88.

O'Reilly, B. (1999, June 7). What it takes to start a startup. *Fortune,* pp. 135–139.

Osterloh, M., & Frey, B. S. (2000). Motivation, knowledge transfer, and organizational forms. *Organization Science, 11*(5), 538–551.

Palmer, B. (1999, June 21). Hasbro's new action figure. *Fortune*, pp. 189–192.

Reason, T. (2003). Incentive confrontation: A bitter dispute over bonuses highlights the hazards of incentive pay. *CEO: The Magazine for Senior Financial Executives, 19*, 46–51.

Robbins, S. P. (1999). *Organizational behavior* (7th ed.). Englewood Cliffs, NJ: Prentice Hall.

Ronen, S. (1986, April). Equity perception in multiple comparisons: A field study. *Human Relations*, pp. 333–346.

Rosenbush, S. (2001, February 5). Armstrong's last stand. *Business Week*, pp. 88–91.

Sales & Marketing Management, 155 (2003). Little carrots, big results, p. 36.

Saposnick, K. (2001). Achieving breakthrough business results through personal change: An interview with Rick Fox. Pegasus Communications, accessed February 26, 2003 at http://www.pegasuscom.com/levpoints/foxint.html.

Schlender, B. (1999, Arpil 12). E-business according to Gates. *Fortune*, pp. 75–80.

Schurenberg, E. (1999, May 24). The fly boys. *Fortune*, pp. 236–240.

Schwab, D. P., & Cummings, L. L. (1970, October). Theories of performance and satisfaction: A review. *Industrial Relations*, pp. 403–430.

Shalley, C. E. (1991). Effects of productivity goals, creativity goals, and personal discretion on individual creativity. *Journal of Applied Psychology, 76*, 179–185.

Shellenbarger, S. (1997, March 19). Investors seem attracted to firms with happy employees. *The Wall Street Journal*, p. B1.

Shipper, F., & Manz, C. C. (1992, Winter). Employee self-management without formally designated teams: An alternative road to empowerment. *Organizational Dynamics*, pp. 48–61.

Simonton, D. K. (1987). Presidential inflexibility and veto behavior: Two individual situational interactions. *Journal of Personality, 55*(1), 1–18.

Spragins, E. (2002). Unmasking your motivations. *Fortune Small Business, 12*, 86+.

Stogdill, R. M. (1948). Personal factors associated with leadership: A survey of the literature. *Journal of Psychology, 25*, 35–71.

Stogdill, R. M. (1974). *Handbook of leadership: A survey of theory and research*. New York: Free Press.

Stogdill, R. M., & Coons, A. E. (1957). *Leader behavior: Its description and measurement*. Columbus, OH: Ohio State University Press.

Summers, T. P., & DeNisi, A. S. (1990, June). In search of Adam's other: Reexamination of referents used in the evaluation of pay. *Human Relations*, pp. 495–511.

Symonds, W., Smith, G., & Judge, P. (1999, June 21). Fisher's photo finish. *Business Week*, pp. 34–36.

Vroom, V. H. (1964). *Work and motivation*, New York: John Wiley & Sons.

Wahba, M., & Birdwell, L. (1975). Maslow reconsidered: A review of the need hierarchy theory. *Organizational Behavior and Human Performance, 15*(2), 212–240

Weiss, H. (1977). Subordinate imitation of supervisor behavior: The role of modeling in organizational socialization. *Organizational Behavior and Human Performance, 19*, 89–105.

White, R., & Lippit, R. (1960). *Autocracy and democracy: An experimental inquiry*. New York: Harper & Brothers.

Zellner, W. (1999, August 16). Earth to herb: Pick a co-pilot. *Business Week*, pp. 70–73.

Chapter 13

All a matter of priorities. (2003, February 10). *Editor and Publisher*.

Anders, G. (2003, January 13). Carly Fiorina, up close—How shrewd strategic moves in grueling proxy battle let H-P chief take control. *Wall Street Journal*, Eastern Edition, p. B1.

Blank, D. (2003). A matter of ethics: In organizations where honesty and integrity rule, it is easy for employees to resist the many temptations today's business world offers. *Internal Auditor, 60*, 26.

Biskupic, J. (2002), July 24). Why it's tough to indict CEOs. *USA Today*, pp. A1, A2.

Carpenter, L. (2002). Inspirational leadership. *Management Services, 46*, 34–36.

Foss, B. (2002, December 30). Corporate image: Greed, deceit, handcuffs, *The Arizona Republic*, p. D4.

Gale, S. F. (2002). Building leaders at all levels. *Workforce, 81*, 82–85.

Kaufman, B. (2003). Stories that sell, stories that tell: Effective storytelling can strengthen an organization's bonds with all of its stakeholders. *Journal of Business Strategy, 24*, 11.

Kraemer, H. M. J. (2003). Doing the right thing: Values-based leadership is not an oxymoron in corporate America. *Vital Speeches of the Day, 69*, 243.

Ronan, J. (2003). A boot to the system: How does a training company shake up its leadership style? It marches its managers off to boot camp. *T & D, 57*, 38.

Tyler, K. (2003). Sink-or-swim attitude strands new managers. *HRMagazine, 48*, 78–83.

Chapter 14

Albanese, R. E., & Van Fleet, D. D. (1985). Rational behavior in groups: The free-riding tendency. *Academy of Management Review, 10*, 244–255.

Balkin, D. B., Dolan, S., & Forgues, K. (1997). Rewards for team contributions to quality. *Journal of Compensation and Benefits, 13*(1), 41–46.

Banker, R. A., Field, J. M., Schroeder, R. G., & Sinha, K. K. (1996). Impact of work teams on manufacturing performance: A longitudinal field study. *Academy of Management Journal, 42*, 58–74.

Bantel, K., and Jackson, S. (1989). Top management and innovations in banking: Does the demography of the top team make a difference? *Strategic Management Journal, 10*, 107–124.

Bunderson, J., & Sutcliffe, K. (2002). Comparing alternative conceptualizations of functional diversity in management teams: Process and performance effects. *Academy of Management Journal, 45*, 875–893.

Carbonara, P. (1997, March). Fire me. I dare you! *Inc*, pp. 58–64.

Caudron, S. (1993, December). Are self-directed teams right for your company? *Personnel Journal*, pp. 76–84.

Chang, A., Bordia, P., & Dune, J. (2003). Punctuated equilibrium and linear progression: Toward a new understanding of group development. *Academy of Management Journal, 4*, 106–117.

Cohen, S. G., & Bailey, D. E. (1997). What makes teams work: Group effectiveness research from the shop floor to the executive suite. *Journal of Management, 23*, 239–290.

Daft, R. L. (2002). *The leadership experience* (2nd ed.). Cincinnati, OH: South-Western.

Daly, R. E., & Nicoll, D. (1997). Accelerating a team's developmental process. *OD Practitioner, 24*(1), 20–28.

Deming, W. E. (1986). *Out of the crisis.* Cambridge, MA: MIT Press.

Denton, D. K. (1992). Multi-skilled teams replace old work systems. *HR Magazine, 37*, 48–56.

Dumaine, B. (1990, May 7). Who needs a boss? *Fortune*, pp. 52–60.

Dumaine, B. (1994, September 5). The trouble with teams. *Fortune*, pp. 86–92.

Fisher, R., & Ury, W. (1981). *Getting to yes: Negotiating agreement without giving in.* New York: Penguin Books.

Geber, B. (1992, June). Saturn's grand experiment. *Training*, pp. 27–35.

Gersick, C. J. (1988). Time and transition in work teams: Toward a new model of group development. *Academy of Management Journal, 31*, 9–41.

Gross, S. E. (1995). *Compensation for teams.* New York: American Management Association.

Hammer, M., & Champy, J. (1993). *Reengineering the corporation.* New York: HarperCollins.

Hammer, M., & Champy, J. (1994, April). Avoiding the hottest new management cure. *Inc*, pp. 25–26.

Hosmer, L. T. (1995). Trust: The connecting link between organizational theory and philosophical ethics. *Academy of Management Review, 20*, 379–403.

Jones, G. R., & George, J. M. (1998). The experience and evolution of trust: Implications for cooperation and teamwork. *Academy of Management Review, 23*, 531–546.

Katzenbach, J. R., & Smith, D. K. (1993, March–April). The discipline of teams. *Harvard Business Review*, pp. 111–120.

Kets De Vries, M. F. (1999, Winter). High performance teams: Lessons from the pygmies. *Organizational Dynamics*, pp. 66–77.

Kidwell, R. E., & Bennett, N. (1993). Employee propensity to withhold effort: A conceptual model to intersect three avenues of research. *Academy of Management Review, 18*, 429–456.

Kirkman, B. L., & Rosen, B. (1999). Beyond self-management: Antecedents and consequences of team empowerment. *Academy of Management Journal, 42*, 58–74.

Kreitner, R., & Kinicki, A. (1995). *Organizational behavior* (3rd ed.). Burr Ridge, IL: Irwin.

Labich, K. (1996, February 16). Elite teams get the job done. *Fortune*, pp. 90–99.

Lawler, E. E. (1992). *The ultimate advantage.* San Francisco: Jossey-Bass.

Lewicki, R., & Litterer, J. (1985). *Negotiation.* Burr Ridge, IL: Irwin.

Maidique, M. A., & Hayes, R. H. (1984). The art of high-technology management. *Sloan Management Review, 25*, 18–31.

Mayer, R. C., Davis, J. H., & Schoorman, F. D. (1995). An integrative model of organizational trust. *Academy of Management Review, 20*, 709–734.

Montemayor, E. F. (1995, Summer). A model for aligning teamwork and pay. *ACA Journal*, pp. 18–25.

Nelson, B. (1994). *1001 ways to reward employees.* New York: Workman Publishing.

O'Lone, R. (1991, June 3). 777 revolutionizes Boeing aircraft development process. *Aviation Week and Space Technology*, pp. 34–36.

Osborne, C. (2001). *Dealing with difficult people.* London: DK.

Phillips, J. M. (1999). Antecedents of leader utilization of staff input in decision-making teams. *Organizational Behavior and Human Decision Processes, 77*, 215–242.

Rahim, M. A. (1983). A measure of styles of handling interpersonal conflict. *Academy of Management Journal, 26*, 368–376.

Raz, T. (2003, May). Taming the Savage Genius: The delicate art of managing employees who are way, way smarter than you. *Inc.*, pp. 33–35.

Sashkin, M., & Kiser, K. J. (1993). *Putting total quality management to work.* San Francisco: Barrett-Koehler.

Shaiken, H., Lopez, S., & Mankita, I. (1997). Two routes to team production: Saturn and Chrysler compared. *Industrial Relations, 36*, 17–45.

Shaw, M. (1981). *Group dynamics: The psychology of small group behavior.* New York: Harper.

Steers, R. M. (1984). *Introduction to organizational behavior.* Glenview, IL: Scott, Foresman.

Tjosvold, D. (1993). *Learning to manage conflict: Getting people to work together cooperatively.* New York: Lexington Books.

Townsend, A., M., DeMarie, S. M., & Hendrickson, A. R. (1996, September). Are you ready for virtual teams? *HR Magazine*, pp. 123–126.

Wageman, R. (1995). Interdependence and group effectiveness. *Administrative Science Quarterly, 40*, 145–180.

Wall, J. A. (1985). *Negotiation: Theory and practice.* Glenview, IL: Scott, Foresman.

Wecker, J. (1998, October 12). Powers of Persuasion. *Fortune*, pp. 161–164.

Weiss, W. H. (1999). Teams and teamwork. *Supervision, 59*(7), 9–11.

Whetton, D. A., & Cameron, K. S. (1995). *Developing management skills* (3rd ed.). New York: HarperCollins.

Zand, D. E. (1972). Trust and managerial problem solving. *Administrative Science Quarterly, 17*, 229–239.

Chapter 15

Conlin, M. (2002, September 30). Watch What You Put in That Office E-Mail. *Business Week*, pp. 114–115.

Creighton, J. L. (1998, January). The cybermeeting's about to begin. *Management Review*, pp. 29–31.

Daft, R. L. & Lengel, R. H. (1986). Organizational information requirements, media richness, and structural design. *Managerial Science, 32*, 554–572.

Falcone, P. (1998, October). Communication breakdown. *HR Focus*, p. 8.

Greengrad, S. (1998, September). 10 ways to protect intranet data. *Workforce*, pp. 78–81.

Knapp, M. (1980). *Essentials of nonverbal communication.* New York: Holt, Rinehart and Winston.

Labich, K. (1999, March 1). Boeing finally hatches a plan. *Fortune*, pp. 100–106.

McCune, J. C. (1998, July/August). That elusive thing called trust. *Management Review*, pp. 10–16.

McDermott, M. (1996, September). Boeing's modern approach. *Profiles*, pp. 41–44.

Munter, M. (1993, May–June). Cross-cultural communication for managers. *Business Horizons*, pp. 69–78.

Osborn, C. (2001). *Dealing with Difficult People.* London: DK.

Pearl, J. (1993, July). The E-mail quandry. *Management Review*, p. 3.

Price, C. (1994). *Assertive Communication.* Boulder, CO: Career Track.

Rice, R. E. (1991). Task analyzability, use of new media, and effectiveness: A multi-site exploration of media richness. *Organization Science, 2,* 475–500.

Robbins, S. P., & Hunsaker, P. L. (1996). *Training in interpersonal skills* (2nd ed.). Upper Saddle River, NJ: Prentice Hall.

Rogers, E., & Allbritton, M. (1995, April). Interactive communications technologies in business organizations. *Journal of Business Communication, 32,* 177–195.

Sullivan, C. (1995, January). Preferences for electronic mail in organizational communication tasks. *Journal of Business Communication, 32,* 49–64.

Thumma, S. A. (1998, July). E-mail zaps the workplace. *HR Focus*, p. 9.

Townsend, A., DeMarie, S., & Hendrickson, A. (1996, September). Are you ready for virtual teams? *HR Magazine*, pp. 123–126.

Volkema, R., & Niederman, F. (1996, July). Planning and managing organizational meetings: An empirical analysis of written and oral communication. *Journal of Business Communication*, pp. 275–293.

Weeks, D. (1995, February). Voice mail: Blessing or curse? *World Traveler*, pp. 51–54.

Chapter 16

Blessings in disguise, *Snack, Food & Wholesale Bakery, 92* (2003). p. 18.

Brandman, B. (2001). How $1.2 Million of Inventory Vanished into Thin Air. *Transportation & Distribution, 42,* p. 31+.

Cardy, R. L. (2004). *Performance management: Concepts, skills, and exercises.* Armonk, NY: M. E. Sharpe.

Drickhammer, D. (2002). Goosing the bottom line. *Industry Week, 251,* pp. 24–28.

Godfrey, G., Dale, B., Marchington, M., & Wilkinson, A. (1997). Control: A contested concept in TQM research. *International Journal of Operations & Production Management, 17,* pp. 558–573.

Hartshorn, D. (2003). Solving accident investigation problems: Thorough accident investigations can be one of the most valuable exercises that companies undertake, yet too few have policies and programs in place to carry them out. *Occupational Hazards, 65,* p. 56+.

Libby, T., & Lindsay, M. (2003a). Budgeting—an unnecessary evil: A European idea to drop budgeting altogether is starting to find receptive ears in North America. *CMA Management, 77,* p. 30+.

Libby, T., & Lindsay, M. (2003b). Budgeting—an unnecessary evil, part two: How the BPRT envisions a world without traditional budgeting. *CMA management, 77,* p. 28+.

Mann, J. (2003). Handwashing: Technology adds a measure of management. *Foodservice Equipment & Supplies, 56,* p. 39+.

McClenahen, J. S. (2002). Mapping manufacturing: Remarkable results at Medtronic's medical-devices plant flow from value-stream mapping. *Industry Week, 251,* p. 62+.

Mission: Maintain satisfaction: Smart implementation plus the right system add up to happy guests, *Hotel & Motel Management, 218* (2003). p. M7.

Nozar, R. A. (2001). Guest's input helps develop standards. *Hotel and Motel Management, 216,* p. 36+.

Rust, R. T., Zeithaml, V. A., & Lemon, K. N. (2000). *Driving customer equity.* New York: Free Press.

Schmitt, V. (2001). Water treatment: Pouring on the service. *Chemical Week, 164,* p. 20+.

Chapter 17

Aston, A., & Arndt, M. (2003, May 5). The flexible factory: Leaning heavily on technology, some U.S. plants stay competitive with offshore rivals. *Business Week*, pp. 90–91.

Bickens, J., & Elliott, B. B. (1997). *Operations management: An active learning approach.* Cambridge, MA: Blackwell.

Braganza, A., & Myers, A. (1998). *Business process redesign: A view from the inside.* Boston: Thomson.

Bremner, B. (2000, May 23). Nissan's Ghosn: Can he bring back Japan's samurai spirit? *Business Week.*

Connor, G. (2003). Benefiting form six sigma. *Manufacturing Engineering, 130,* pp. 53–59.

D'Aveni, R. (1994). *Hypercompetition.* New York: Free Press.

Deming, W. E. (1986). *Out of the crisis.* Cambridge, MA: MIT Press.

Deming, W. E. (1981–1982, Winter). Improvement of quality and production through action by management. *National Productivity Review, 1,* 12–22.

Deming, W. E. (1986). Out of the crisis. Cambridge, MA: Center for Advanced Engineering Study.

Faltin, D. M., & Faltin, F. W. (2003). Toe the line: No more Worldcoms. *Quality Progress, 36,* pp. 29–35.

Gabor, A. (1990). *The man who discovered quality.* New York: Times Books.

Galuszka, P. (1999, November 8). Just-in-time manufacturing is working overtime. *Business Week.*

Garvin, D. (1988). *Managing quality: The strategic and competitive edge.* New York: Free Press.

Garvin, D. (1984, Fall). What does product quality really mean? *Sloan Management Review, 26,* 24–25.

Gourlay, R. (1994, January 4). Back to basics on the factory floor. *Financial Times*, p. 12.

Hammer, M., & Champy, J. (1993). *Reengineering the corporation.* New York: Harper Business.

How to spot counterfeit parts: Caveat emptor, or buyer beware, is appropriate advice for buyers sourcing in China, (2002). *Purchasing, 131,* p. 31+.

Imai, M. (1986). *Kaizen: The key to Japan's competitive success.* New York: Random House.

JIT just won't be the same: Security rules could affect cross border trade, (2003, May). *World Trade, 16,* p. 28.

Jones, G. R., George, J. M., & Hill, C. W. L. (2000). *Contemporary management,* 2nd ed. New York: McGraw-Hill/Irwin.

The Kaizen Institute. www.kaizen-institute.com.

Kontoghiorghes, C. (2003). Examining the association between quality and productivity performance in a service organization. *The Quality Management Journal, 10,* pp. 32–42.

Krajewski, L. L., & Ritzman, L. R. (2001). *Operations management: Strategy and analysis,* 6th ed. Upper Saddle River, NJ: Prentice Hall.

Logothetis, N. (1992). *Managing for total quality.* Hertfordshire, UK: Prentice Hall International.

Markland, R. E., Vickery, S. K., & Davis, R. A. (1998). *Operations management: Concepts in manufacturing and service,* 2nd ed. Cincinnati: South-Western Publishing.

Melnyk, S., & Denzler, D. (1996). *Operations management.* New York: McGraw-Hill/Irwin.

Noon, C. E., Hankings, C. T., & Cote, M. J. (2003). Understanding the impact of variation in the delivery of healthcare services. *Journal of Healthcare Management, 48,* p. 82+.

Porter, M. E. (1985). *Competitive advantage.* New York: Free Press.

Powell, T. C. (1995, January). Total quality management as competitive advantage: A review and empirical study. *Strategic Management Journal,* pp. 15–37.

Russell, R. S., & Taylor, B. W. (2000). *Operations management.* Upper Saddle River, NJ: Prentice Hall.

Skinner, W. (1969, May/June). Manufacturing—Missing link in corporate strategy. *Harvard Business Review,* pp. 136–145.

Slack, N. (1997). *The Blackwell encyclopedia of operations management.* Cambridge, MA: Blackwell.

Stevenson, W. (2001). *Operations management,* 7th ed. New York: McGraw-Hill.

Stocker, G. (2003). Use symbols instead of words. *Quality Progress, 35,* pp. 68–72.

Taiichi, O. (1990). *Toyota production system.* Cambridge, MA: Productivity Press.

Young, S. M. (1992, October). A framework for successful adoption and performance of Japanese manufacturing practices in the United States. *Academy of Management Review, 17,* 677–701.

Chapter 18

Alter, S. (2002). *Information systems: Foundations of e-business* (4th ed.). Upper Saddle River, NJ: Prentice Hall.

Ante, S. E. (2000, June 19). The second coming of software. *Businessweek Online.*

A survey of digital security, *Economist* (2002, October 26). p. 4.

Austrian, G. (1982). *Herman Hollerith: Forgotten giant of information processing.* New York: Columbia University Press.

Baker, R. H. (1997). *Extranets: The complete sourcebook.* New York: McGraw-Hill.

Black, J. (2001, April 26). Tracking customers while preserving their anonymity. *Business Week.*

Buckhout, S., Frey, E., & Nemec, J. (1999, second quarter). Making ERP succeed: Turning fear into promise. *Strategy and Business.*

Cate, F. H. (1997). *Privacy in the information age.* Washington, DC: Brookings Institute.

Chandler, A. D. (1977). *The visible hand.* Cambridge, MA: Harvard University Press.

Cortada, W. J. (1997). *Best practices in information technology: How corporations get the most value from exploiting their digital investments.* Upper Saddle River, NJ: Prentice Hall.

Davis, G. B. (1997). *The Blackwell encyclopedic dictionary of management information systems.* Cambridge, MA: Blackwell.

Evans, P., & Wurster, T. S. (2000). *Blown to bits: How the new economics of information transforms strategy.* Boston: Harvard Business School Press.

Gilster, P. (1997). *Digital literacy.* New York: John Wiley & Sons.

Gonzalez, J. S. (1998). *The 21st century intranet.* Upper Saddle River, NJ: Prentice Hall.

Hallows, J. E. (1997). *Information systems project management: How to deliver functions and value in information technology projects.* New York: AMACOM.

Hellriegel, D., Jackson, S. E., & Slocum, J. W. (1999). *Management,* 8th ed. Cincinnati, OH South-Western Publishing.

Jones, G. R., George, J. M. & Hill, C. W. L. (2000). *Contemporary management,* 2nd ed. New York: McGraw-Hill/Irwin.

Keenan, F. (2002, September 2). You're only as good as your password. *Business Week,* pp. 77–80.

Lashin, P., & Rich, E. (1983). *Artificial intelligence.* New York: McGraw-Hill.

Luconi, F. L., Malone, T. W., & Morton, M. S. S. (1996, Summer). Expert systems: The next challenge for managers. *Sloan Management Review.*

Miles, M. (2001, December 17). Firestone, Ford feud. *Tire Business.*

Pinsonneault, A., & Kraemer, K. L. (1993, September). The impact of information technology on middle managers. *MIS Quarterly,* 271–292.

Ross, J. W., & Weill, P. (2002, November). Six decisions your IT people shouldn't make. *Harvard Business Review,* p. 88.

Ross, P. E. (1995, May 22). Software as career threat. *Forbes,* 240–246.

Stair, R. M., & Reynolds, G. W. (2001). *Fundamentals of information systems.* Boston: Thompson Learning.

Stoffer, H. (2002, February 18). Explorer ruling helps Ford, but legal woes remain. *Automotive News.*

Teresko, J. (1999, February 19). Information rich, knowledge poor. *Industry Week.*

Watson, H. J., Houdeshel, G., & Rainer, R. K. (1997). *Building executive information systems and other support applications.* New York: John Wiley & Sons.

Weckert, J., & Adeney, D. (1997). *Computer and information ethics.* Westport, CT: Greenwood.

Chapter 13

P13.1, AP/Wide World Photos; P13.2, AP/Wide World Photos; P13.3, AP/Wide World Photos; P13.4, AP/Wide World Photos; P13.5, Hewlett Packard/Getty Images

Chapter 14

P14.1, Matthew Neal McVay/Stock, Boston, LLC; P14.2, AP/Wide World Photos; P14.3, Pablo Bartholomew/Getty Images; P14.4, © James Shaffer/Photo Edit; P14.5, © Getty Images; P14.6, AP/Wide World Photos

Chapter 15

P15.1, AP/Wide World Photos; P15.2, © Fujifotos/The Image Works; P15.3, Ryan McVay/Getty Images; P15.4, AP/Wide World Photos; P15.5a, © Dorling Kindersley Ltd.; P15.5b, © Dorling Kindersley Ltd.; P15.6, © Getty Images

Chapter 16

P16.1, Photo Courtesy of Numico; P16.2, © RF/Corbis; P16.3, Matthew J. Decker/Getty Images; P16.4, Photo courtesy of Medtronic Powered Surgical Solutions; P16.5, Photo compliments of Wyandot, Inc., Marion, Ohio

Chapter 17

P17.1, Courtesy of Pella® Windows & Doors; P17.2, AP/Wide World Photos; P17.3, © The Timken Company, P17.4, © Jose Carillo/Photo Edit

Chapter 18

P18.1, "Courtesy of International Business Machines Corporation. Unauthorized use not permitted."; P18.2, © Hulton Archives/Getty Images; P18.3, AP/Wide World Photos; P18.5, © 1999-2003 Zone Labs, Inc., 1060 Howard Street, San Francisco, CA 94103 USA. All rights reserved.

Company Index

A

A. T. Kearney Inc., 117–118
A. W. Chesterton, 635
AACC, 80
ABB AG, 93
Accenture, 744
Adelphia Communications, 548
Adobe Systems, 533
Adolph Coors Company, 205
Adopt-a-Road, 127
Adopt-a-School, 132
Advantica, 457
AES Corporation, 580, 581
Aetna, 233
Affymetrix, Inc., 301
Airbus Industries, 128, 398
Air France, 122
All Metro Health Care, 536
Allstate, 484
Altavista, 214
Amazon.com, 12, 13, 165, 632, 751
American Airlines, 128, 147, 296, 368
American Apparel Manufacturers
        Association (AAMA), 87
American Bar Association, 431
American Express Co., 67, 125,
        277–278, 462, 475
Amtrak, 470
Amway, 206
Andersen Consulting, 744
Andersen Windows, 697, 727
Andersen Worldwide, 106
Anheuser-Busch, 121
AOL-Time Warner, 396, 542
Apple Computer, 168–169, 208, 211,
        332, 348, 398, 484, 584, 738
Appleton Papers, 569

Arthur Andersen, 8, 548
Atari, 330
AT&T, 163, 296, 316, 400
Austin McGregor International, 137
Avon, 460, 462, 484
Axciom, 163, 164

B

Baan, 742
Babson University, 339
Baker Electronics, 139–140
Banamex, 461
Bank of America Corp., 57, 461, 463, 479
Barnes & Noble, 12–13, 165
Baxter International Inc., 558
Baylor Institute for Immunology
        Research, 149
BB&T Corp., 461
Bell Atlantic North, 233
Bell Canada, 734
Bell Laboratories, 463
Ben & Jerry's Ice Cream, 122, 123
Berg Electronics, 55
Best Buy, 702
Black & Decker, 298
Black Enterprise, 333
Blockbuster, 199–200, 270
Bluefly Inc., 288
BMW, 298
Boeing Co., 95–96, 128, 201, 233, 286,
        290, 446, 575, 580, 617–618,
        620, 625, 645
BP Oil, 190, 470
Bridgestone/Firestone, 173, 732

C

Cablevision Systems Corporation, 12
Campbell Soup, 205

ICL, 305
IDC Inc., 455
Idea Integration Corporation, 517
IKEA, 511
Immunex Corporation, 701
Informix, 533
Infosys Technologies Ltd., 57
ING Group NV, 453–454
Inland Steel, 482, 483
Intel, 67, 156, 218, 239–241, 271–272, 298, 305, 331, 345, 462, 475, 485
International Information Systems Security Certifications Consortium, 760
Intuit, 290

J

J. Bildner & Sons Inc., 347
J. D. Edwards and Company, 108
J. D. Power & Associates, 279
J. P. Morgan Chase, 435, 467
JetBlue, 367
Jockey International, 87
Johnson Controls, 155
Johnson & Johnson, 107, 108, 382

K

Kaisen Institute, 717
Kellogg, 223–224
Kentucky Fried Chicken, 73
Kidz Mouse, 340
KLM, 398
Knowledge Adventure, Inc. (KA), 358–359
Konica, 406
Kraft, 400
Krispy Kreme Company, 632, 633

L

L. A. Nicola, 360–361
Leeds School of Business (University of Colorado), 258–259

Lehman Brothers, 154
Levi Strauss and Co., 60, 101–102, 119, 122, 134, 140
Lillian Vernon Corp., 327
Lincoln Electric Company, 5, 36
Little Company, 563
Li Tung International, 94
Liz Claiborne, 88
L'Oreal, 129
Loxley, 182
Lucent Technologies, 55, 377
Luftansa Airlines, 454
Lycos, 360

M

Marine Corps, 150
Marks & Spencer, 298, 301
Marriott International, 484
Mary Kay Cosmetics Company, 154, 155
Mass. General Hospital, 583
MasterCard, 278
Matsushita, 76, 109, 110
Mattel, 62–63, 292
Maytag, 314
Mazda, 293, 721
McDonald's Corp., 60, 64, 73, 77, 78, 125, 131, 138, 207, 287, 291, 349, 396
McGraw-Hill/Irwin, 388
MCI Communications Corp., 452
McKinsey & Co., 314, 435, 453
Meals on Wheels, 127
Medtek, 225
Medtronic Inc., 155, 677
Mercedes Benz, 94
Merck, 132
Mercy Health System, 176
Merrill Lynch & Co., 164–165, 168, 315, 461, 462, 533
Microchip Technology Inc., 557
Microsoft Corporation, 33, 67, 127–128, 154, 282, 291, 292, 301, 305, 331, 345, 435, 484, 533, 580, 631–632, 746, 760
Midas, 349
Miles Press, 55
Mini Maid Inc., 535
Mitsubishi-Caterpillar, 79

Mitsui-General Electric, 79
Morgan Stanley Dean Witter, 154
Motorola, 23, 73, 74, 88, 94, 158, 298, 398, 462

N

NASDAQ, 345
National Aeronautics and Space Administration (NASA), 235, 256, 386, 482, 539
National Broadcasting Company (NBC), 164, 165, 184, 315, 348
National Council of Churches, 129
National Education Association (NEA), 129
National Hispanic Scholarship Fund, 132
National Organization for Women (NOW), 129
National Security Agency, 760
Nestlé, 300
Netscape Communication Corp., 290
New Jersey State Police, 470
New York Stock Exchange, 345
Nike, 88, 94, 401
Nissan Motors, 279, 539–540, 565
Nokia, 74, 249, 301, 373
Nordstrom, 280, 391
Northwest Airlines, 147, 369, 398
Northwest Banks, 400
Nucor, 379
Numico, 663–665, 669, 690

O

Oak Industries, 205
Office Depot, 452
Ondeo Nalco, 686
OneUnited Bank, 461
Oracle, 533, 553
Ovum Ltd., 742

Name Index

A

Abbott, D., 525
Abreu, D., 457
Ackerly, L., 535
Adamchick, W., 543
Adams, A., 713
Adballah, A., 757–758
Ala-Pietila, P., 373
Alderfer, C., 508
Alfonzo, J. P. P., 191
Alter, S., 736
Anders, G., 561
Anderson, R. D., 560
Ante, S. E., 730
Anthes, G. H., 679, 682
Antioco, J., 270
Arango, T., 529
Ardnt, M., 369
Armstrong, L., 359
Arndt, M., 210, 708
Arnst, C., 499
Aston, A., 708
Austin, R. D., 748
Avolio, B., 562

B

Bader, J. L., 758
Balfour, F., 67
Balkin, D. B., 20, 431, 468, 473
Banks, R., 476
Barnard, C. I., 32
Barnes, B., 31
Barnett, A., 213, 296
Barrett, C., 7, 210, 349
Barth, S., 742, 761
Bass, B. M., 560
Bastedo, G., 557
Bateman, I., 280
Bateman, T. S., 9
Beach, H., 533
Beatty, R. W., 431
Becker, E., 34
Bedeian, A. G., 572
Behre, K. D., 440
Bennett, D., 414
Berardino, J., 106

Berstein, A., 52, 233
Betita, K., 67
Bildner, J. L., 347
Biskupic, J., 548
Blake, R. R., 549, 550
Blank, A., 327
Blank, D., 557
Borrus, A., 319
Brady, R. L., 648
Brady, T., 648
Bram, J., 245
Branch, S., 414, 490
Brandman, B., 679
Branson, R., 71, 330
Brennan, M., 454–455
Brickley, P., 744
Brim, R., 52
Brody, D., 233
Bronfman, E., 254
Brown, G., 568
Bryan, D. A., 431
Bryan, J., 401
Buckhout, S., 744
Burrows, P., 540
Bush, G. W., 289
Bushnell, N., 330
Bussman, V., 279
Byrne, J. A., 196

C

Cameron, K. S., 261
Campbell, A., 399
Campos, L., 457
Capell, K., 63
Cardy, R., 20, 149, 163, 431, 468, 473, 692
Carlisle, K., 414
Carlson, G., 176
Carlton, J., 211
Carney, D., 290
Carp, D., 322, 467
Carpenter, L., 544
Carrns, A., 768
Carty, D., 223
Cary, S., 369
Case, S., 542
Cassidy, M., 340
Catan, T., 191
Cawley, C. M., 316
Chaffin, J., 191
Chandler, S., 529

Chang, J., 519
Chenault, K., 278
Cherwitz, R. A., 328
Chesterton, J., 635
Chiang, E., 94
Christensen, G., 698
Clifford, M. L., 196
Cohen, A., 643
Cohen, B., 123
Coltrin, S. A., 572
Condit, P. M., 617, 618, 620
Conlin, M., 490, 499
Connor, G., 725
Contratto, M., 563
Convis, G., 51
Conway, C. A., 553
Coplan, J. H., 55
Cote, M. J., 727
Couette, Y., 123
Covey, S., 376
Cox, T., 465
Craig, J., 329
Crandall, R., 296
Crawley, J., 369
Crockett, R. O., 10, 74, 319, 409, 466
Cropper, C., 139
Crosby, P., 21
Crosby, P. B., 510, 559
Curameng, S., 94

D

Daft, D., 10, 467
Daft, R. L., 115, 175, 183, 252, 257, 392
Dale, B., 688
Daley, W., 55
Damodt, M. G., 431
Daniel, C., 369
Darby, C. A., 748
Darlington, H., 535
Davidson, D., 41
Davidson, J., 167
Davis, J. B., 316, 440
Dawley, H., 63
Dawson, C., 414
Deavenport, E., 759
Dell, M., 327, 334, 335, 759
Deming, W. E., 21–23, 579, 672, 712–714
Denzler, D., 710

Subject Index

A

Ability, 534
Ability tests, 430
Absolute judgments, 443
Academy culture, 160–161
Acceptance sampling, 709
Accidents, 674–675
Accommodation, 131
Accountability, 316
Achievement need, 508
Acquisitions, 313, 400–401
Action plans
  operational, 220–221
  strategic, 217
  tactical, 217–220
Actions, 197
Activity-based costing, 685–686
Administrative management,
  25–26
Adverse impact, 418
Affiliation need, 508
Affirmative action, 418, 465–467
African Americans
  affirmative action and, 466
  discrimination against, 469–470
  financial institutions catering
    to, 461, 462
Aggressive communication, 636
Alliances, strategic, 78–79, 317,
  398
Analysis
  of environment, 286–293, 306
  functional, 302
  value-chain, 302–303
Application forms, 430
Apprenticeships, 484
Artificial intelligence (AI), 740
The Art of War (Sun Tzu), 15
Asian Americans, 470
Asia Pacific Economic
    Cooperation (APEC), 60
Assertive communication skills,
  619, 634–636
Assessment, 285–286
Assessment center, 430
Assessment phase, of career
    development, 441
Association of Southeast Asian
    Nations (ASEAN), 60

Authentic leadership theory, 562,
  563
Authority, 223, 375
Autocratic leaders, 550

B

Backward integration, 312
Balanced scorecard
  explanation of, 679–680
  framework used for, 680, 681
  implementation suggestions
    for, 683
  use of, 681–682, 695
Balance sheets, 684
Bankruptcy, 345
Barriers to entry, 294–295
Baseball team culture, 160
Base compensation, 446
Behavioral anchored rating scales,
  444
Behavioral appraisal instruments,
  444
Behavioral interviews, 430
Behavioral perspective
  explanation of, 26
  Follett and, 27
  Hawthorne studies and, 28–29
  human relations and, 29–31
Behavioral theories of leadership,
  549–550
Benchmarks
  explanation of, 304–305
  production and cost, 709
Benefits, 446. *See also*
    Compensation
Biodata forms, 430
Body movement, 638
Bona fide occupational
    qualification (BFOQ), 419
Boston Consulting Group's
    Growth-Share Matrix,
    310–312
Bottom-up change, 174
Boundaryless organizations
  explanation of, 396–398
  formation of, 406
Bounded rationality, 253
Brainstorming, 257–258
Brand managers, 391
Break-even analysis, 20
Bribery, 188–191

Budgeting
  control through, 684
  explanation of, 218
  techniques for, 218–220
Bureaucratic control
  explanation of, 668–669
  steps in, 669–670, 672–673
  types of, 673–678
Bureaucratic management,
  23–25
Business environment. *See*
    Environment
Business ethics. *See also* Ethics
  approaches to, 104–106
  computer, 744–746
  decision making related to, 113
  employee training in, 109, 439,
    440
  explanation of, 102–104
  for international managers,
    86–87, 94–95
  leadership and, 557, 558, 565
  management of, 109–111
  recent financial scandals and,
    548, 558
Business-level strategy, 313–315
Business network, 336–337
Business plans, 340–342
Business process, 579
Business-unit meetings, 627

C

Call centers, international, 67
Canada, 55
Capacity, 701
Career counseling, 441
Career development
  for international managers,
    84–85
  phases of, 441–442
Career path, 441–442
Career Resource Centers, 442
Cause-and-effect diagrams, 710
Centralization, 379–380
Ceremonies, 154–155
Certainty, 242
Chain of command, 377
Change, 7. *See also* Organizational
    change
Check sheets, 710
Child care, 485, 486

recent financial scandals and, 548, 558, 712

whistleblower policies and, 111–112

Ethics committees, 110

Ethics officers, 109

Ethics training, 109

Ethnocentric approach to global management, 82

Ethnocentrism, 464

European Union (EU), 58–60

Exchange rate, 65

Exchange theories of leadership, 559–560, 562

Executive information systems, 749

Expectancy theory, 521–523

Expert systems, 748–749

Exporting, 75–76

Export power, 546

External environment. *See also* Environment

assessing and, 285–286

explanation of, 282

forecasting and, 284–285

monitoring and, 284

scanning and, 282, 284

External equity, 448

External locus of control, 333–334

Extinction, 518–520

Extranets, 739

Extrinsic motivation, 505

Exxon Valdez, 120

Eye contact, 638

F

Face-to-face communication

explanation of, 627–628

use of, 645

Facial expressions, 639

Facilities

layout design of, 701

layout of employees and equipment and, 706–707

operations management decisions related to, 701

Facts, 619

Family accommodations, 485–486

Family and Medical Leave Act, 419

Faxes, 650

Feedback

barriers to, 623

explanation of, 32, 621

providing constructive, 626

Feedback control, 678

Feedforward control, 673–675

Feelings, 619–620

File-transfer protocol (FTP), 739

Financial controls

approaches to, 684–686

explanation of, 683–684

Financial institutions, 461

Financial ratios, 685

Financial resources, 344–346

Financial statements, 684–685

Firewalls, 745, 747

First-mover advantage

in China, 73, 74

explanation of, 71

Fixed-interval reordering systems, 704

Fixed-point reordering systems, 704

Fixed-position layout, 707

Flexible manufacturing, 707–708

Flexible work weeks, 486

Force-field analysis, 172–173

Forecasts, 205–206, 284–285

Foreign Corruption Practices Act (FCPA), 190

Foreign countries. *See also* Globalization; International business; *specific countries*

choosing to enter, 68, 70–73

mode of entry in, 75–82

scale of involvement in, 74–75

when to enter, 71, 73

Formalization, 380

Formal planning, 210, 211

Formal planning process

implementation and, 222–226

objective setting in, 212–217

operational action plans and, 220–221

organizational change and, 226–228

organizational control systems and, 226

strategic action plans and, 217

tactical action plans and, 217–220

Fortress cultures, 161

Forward integration, 312

Four-fifths rule, 419

Franchising

example of, 350

explanation of, 77, 349

Friendship groups, 402

Functional analysis, 302

Functional structure, 381–382

The Functions of the Executive (Barnard), 32

G

Gantt charts, 705–706

Garbage can model, 254

Gender roles, 68, 69. *See also* Women

General Agreement on Tariffs and Trade (GATT), 58

General cognitive ability tests, 430

General systems theory, 32–33

Geocentric approach to global management, 82

Geographic-based divisions, 383–384

Germany, 53–54, 66

Gestures, 638

Gifts, 117–118

Glass ceiling, 464, 477

Global business. *See* International business

Globalization. *See also* International business

drug manufacturers and, 234

effects of, 7, 292–293

human resources management and, 416

Global shift, 52–53. *See also* International business

Global teams, 485

Goal-setting theory, 511–514

Governments, 125

Grapevine, 632–634

Group decision making

benefits and drawbacks of, 254–255

management of, 256–259

Group decision support systems, 749

Groups

friendship, 402

managing homogeneous, 460

stereotypes of, 469

technological advances and, 61–62

trade barriers and, 57–58

trends in world output and world trade and, 53–54

International Convention for the Protection of Industrial Property (Paris Union), 66

International management careers, 97–99

International managers
approaches for, 82
career development for, 84–85
compensation for, 85–86
ethics and social responsibility for, 86–87
reasons for failure in, 84
selection criteria for, 83
skills for, 87
training of, 83, 85

International Organization for Standardization (ISO), 715

International strategy, 313

Internet
barriers to entry and, 295
as data warehouse, 733
information theft and, 742, 757–758
initial views of, 12–13
international business and, 62
overview of, 632, 738–739

Interpersonal roles, 11–12

Interpersonal skills, 13, 14

Intranets, 739–740

Intrapreneurship, 348

Intrinsic motivation, 505

Intuit QuickBase, 221, 222

Inventory, 704

Investments, socially responsible, 128

ISO 1400, 715

ISO 9000, 715

J

Japan
business ethics in, 110
economic growth in, 54
profile of, 72–73

Job analysis, 427

Job characteristics model, 526, 528

Job descriptions
explanation of, 427
trends in, 39

Job enlargement, 525

Job enrichment
efficiency and, 527
motivation and, 525–526, 528

Job interviews
developing skills for conducting, 432–433
explanation of, 430–431
situational, 430, 435

Job performance, 429–432

Job posting systems, 442

Job preview, 428

Job relatedness, 419

Job rotation
explanation of, 442
motivation and, 525

Job searches, 137

Job sharing, 486

Job specification, 427

Joint ventures
explanation of, 78
with foreign companies, 462

Justice approach, 105–106

Just-in-time (JIT) systems
application of, 720
drawbacks to, 720–721
explanation of, 718–719
kanban and, 719

K

Kaizen
application of, 697–698, 727
explanation of, 716–717

Kanban, 719

Kickbacks, 110, 118

Knowledge workers, 619

Korean Americans, 461

L

Labor contracts, 421–422

Labor demand, 424

Labor supply, 424, 426

Labor unions
agreements between management and, 421–422
explanation of, 420–421
functions of, 422–423

Laissez-faire leaders, 550

Landrum-Griffin Act, 422

Language, 155–156

Leadership
early views of, 16
elements of successful, 541–542
emotional intelligence and, 562–564
ethics and, 557, 558, 565
explanation of, 11
management vs., 542–546
organizational culture and, 156
relationship-oriented, 551
self-, 556–557
strategic, 317
substitute, 556
task-oriented, 551
transactional, 559
transformational, 559–560, 562

Leadership style
decision making and, 256, 550
entrepreneurs and, 338, 358–359
organizational culture and, 156

Leadership theories
behavioral, 549–550
categories of, 546
dispersed, 556–557, 559
exchange, 559–560, 562, 563
person-based, 547
situational, 550–555

Learning organizations, 35

Legal environment
analysis of, 289–291
monitoring, 416–417

Legal risk, 65

Legal systems, 65

Legends, 155

Legitimate power, 546

Letters of recommendation, 430

Leverage ratios, 685

Liaison roles, 390

Licensing, 76–77

Line authority, 377

Line managers, 377

Liquidity ratios, 685

Outcomes, strategic, 279–280, 318, 319
Outsourcing, 401

P

Parallel teams, 389, 583, 585
Pareto analysis, 710
Partial productivity, 709
Partnerships
    advantages and disadvantages of, 344
    explanation of, 343
Passive-aggressive communication, 636
Passive communication, 636
Path-goal theory, 552–555
Pay incentives. *See* Compensation
PDCA cycle, 714
Perception barriers, 623
Performance
    objective, 669–670
    subjective, 669–670
Performance appraisals
    ethical issues related to, 114–115
    explanation of, 442
    feedback skills for, 445
    focus of the measures approaches to, 443–444
    judgment approaches to, 443
Performance measures
    explanation of, 669–670
    identifying gaps between standards and, 670, 672
Performance simulation tests, 430
Performance standard setting, 202–203
Personality tests, 430
Personal network, 336
Personal space, 639–640
Persuasion, 223–224
PERT networks, 706, 707
Philippines, 67
Physical distance, 639–640
Physical exams, 431
Pioneering costs, 71
Planning
    benefits of, 198–204
    contingency, 204, 205
    explanation of, 10, 197–198

formal, 210–228
    keys to successful, 208–210
    as operations management function, 700
    opportunistic, 210–212
    organizational change and, 209–210
    pitfalls of, 204–208, 233
Planning process
    implementation and, 222–226
    objective setting in, 212–217
    operational action plans and, 220–221
    organizational change and, 226–228
    organizational control systems and, 226
    strategic action plans and, 217
    tactical action plans and, 217–220
Policy statements, 107–108
Political forces, 289–291
Political risk, 64
Politics, organization, 251
Polycentric approach to global management, 82
Portfolio analysis
    Boston Consulting Group's Growth-Share Matrix, 310–312
    explanation of, 309
    McKinsey-General Electric Portfolio Analysis Matrix, 309–310
Positive reinforcement, 516–517
Power
    leadership and, 544–546
    need for, 508–509
    types of, 545, 546
Power distance, 66, 69
Prearrival stage of socialization, 150
Prejudgment, 623
Presentation skills, 636–638
Prima facie evidence, 419
The Prince (Machiavelli), 16
Proactive managers, 260
Proactive strategy, 131–132
Problem solving, 224–226. *See also* Decision making
Problem-solving teams, 389, 583, 585
Procedural justice, 105

Process
    operations management decisions related to, 701
    steps in monitoring, 709–710
Process capability measures, 710
Process control systems, 747–748
Process flow analysis, 710
Process layout, 706–707
Process reengineering, 721–722
Product approach. *See* Divisional approach
Production, globalized, 60–61
Production-oriented behaviors, 549
Productivity, 709
Product layout, 706
Product managers, 390
Products, 610–611
Profit
    equity vs., 694–695
    explanation of, 686
Profitability ratios, 685
Profit and loss statements, 684–685
Profit-sharing plans, 388–389
Profit velocity, 686
Program evaluation and review technique (PERT) network, 706, 707
Programmability, 241–242
Programmed decisions, 241
Project management, 221
Project managers, 390
Project teams, 583
Promotability forecasts, 441
Proprietorships, 343
Protected class, 418
Psychological tests, 430–431
Public offerings, 345–346
Public Service Alternative Bar Exam, 431, 437
Punch Card Tabulating System, 730
Punishment, 517–518

Q

Quality
    employees and, 714–715
    production process and, 715–716

suppliers and, 715
teams and, 578–579
Quality circles, 714–715
Quality control standards, 692
Quality Is Free (Crosby), 21
Quality management
approach to, 713–716
background of, 711–713
explanation of, 21–23
just-in-time systems and, 718–721
kaizen and efficiency and, 716–717
process reengineering and, 721–722
Quality planning, 204
Quantitative management, 20–21
Quid pro quo harassment, 420

R

Rationality, bounded, 253
Reactive managers, 260
Realistic Orientation Programs for New Employee Stress (ROPES), 433–434
Receiver barriers, 622
Recruitment, 427–428
Referent power, 546
Reinforcement theory, 516–521
Relative judgments, 443
Reliability, 429
Religious diversity, 476–477
Reordering systems, 704
Reputation, 300–301
Resource allocators, 12
Resource-based view, 297
Resources
allocation of, 12, 197
financial, 344–346
intangible, 299–301
tangible, 299
Responsibility, 376–377
Reward power, 545
Reward systems, 388–389, 520
Rights approach, 105
Risk
decision making and, 242–243
economic, 65
of entrepreneurial ventures, 330, 356

legal, 65
political, 64
Rituals, 154–155, 392
Role models, 559
Romance, in workplace, 116–117

S

Sarbanes-Oxley Act of 2002, 316
Satisficing, 248
Satisficing model, 253
Scalar chain of command, 26
Scanning, 282, 284
Scientific management
effect of, 18–19
explanation of, 6, 17–18
shortcomings of, 19–20
Securities and Exchange Commission (SEC), 45, 121
Segmented communication, 464
Selective perception, 623
Self-actualization, 506, 507
Self-leadership, 556–557
Self-managed teams (SMTs), 580, 582–583
Sender barriers, 622
Seniority, 419
Servers, 737
Sexual harassment
case example of, 453
explanation of, 420
in workplace, 477
Sherman Antitrust Act, 290, 291
Sigma, 716
Simulations, 438
Single-use plans, 223
Situational constraints, 523
Situational context, 555
Situational interviews, 430, 435
Situational theory of leadership, 550–551
Skills inventory, 426
Small businesses. *See also* Entrepreneurship
entrepreneurial ventures vs., 330–331
explanation of, 330–331
minority and female-owned, 332
statistics for, 331–332

Smith Executive Ethics Certificate Program (University of Maryland), 440
Social activists, 128–129
Socialization, 150–151
Social responsibility
benefits and costs of, 119–122, 124
explanation of, 119
for international managers, 86–87
Sociocultural conditions, 291–292
Software
data-mining, 734, 735
developments in, 740
enterprise resource planning, 40, 183–184, 743, 744
Span of control, 378–379
SPC tools, 714
Specialization of labor, 23–24
Speech recognition software, 740
Spin-offs, 348–349
Staff authority, 377
Staffing. *See* Employee staffing
Staff managers, 377
Staff meetings, 627
Stakeholders
community as, 126–127
competitors as, 127–128
customers as, 126
employees as, 125
explanation of, 123–124, 318
governments as, 125
in immigration issues, 319
owners as, 124–125
social activist groups as, 128–129
strategies for managing, 129–132
Standard operating procedures (SOPs), 222–223
Standards
explanation of, 669
identifying gaps between performance measures and, 670, 672
Standing plans, 222
Star Model, 170–172
Statistical process control, 709, 710
Stereotypes. *See also* Discrimination
background of, 491
counteracting, 369

of Hispanics, 474
of older workers, 475
Stock options, 533
Storyboarding, 258
Storytelling, 563
Strategic action plans, 217
Strategic alliances
    explanation of, 78–79, 398
    functions of, 317
Strategic decisions, 244
Strategic groups, 297
Strategic HR planning (SHRP),
    423–424
Strategic intent, 305
Strategic management. *See also*
    Management
    analysis of firm's capabilities
        and, 301–305
    business-level strategy and,
        313–315
    corporate-level strategy and,
        308–313
    environment analysis and,
        281–282, 284–286
    explanation of, 8, 9
    internal environment and,
        297–299
    operations management
        decisions and, 700–702
    overview of, 276–280
    resource types and, 299–301
    scope of external analysis and,
        286–297
    strategic formulation and, 308
    strategic intent and mission
        and, 305–307
    strategic outcomes and,
        318–319
    strategy implementation and,
        315–318
Strategic meetings, 388
Strategic mission, 305–307
Strategic outcomes, 279–280, 318,
    319
Strategizing, 14
Strategy formulation
    business-level, 313–315
    corporate-level, 308–313
    explanation of, 308
Strategy implementation
    cooperative strategies and,
        316–317

corporate entrepreneurship
    and innovation and,
    317–318
explanation of, 315–316
human resources and, 317
leadership and, 317
organizational structure and
    controls and, 316
Stress
    starting new job as source of,
        433
    workplace practices and, 31
Subjective control, 667–668
Subjective performance, 669–670
Substitute leadership, 556
Subsystems, 33
Succession planning, 441
Suppliers, 295, 715
Support groups, 484–485
SWOT analysis, 280–282
Synergy, 33
Systems theory, 32–33

T

Tactical action plans, 217–220
Tactical decisions, 244
Tactical managers, 8, 9
Taft-Hartley Act, 422
Targeted training, 569
Tariffs, 57–58, 60
Task force meetings, 627
Task forces, 389
Taxation, 66
Team management skills, 577
Team meetings, 627–628
Teams
    behavioral dimensions of,
        590–594
    conflict management and,
        599–604
    costs of, 578
    cross-disciplinary, 9
    cross-functional, 8, 580
    culture of, 392
    diversity and, 460, 463
    ethical climate of, 115
    function of, 389, 576–578
    global, 485
    to help implement change, 178

innovation and, 579–580
leadership and, 588–590
negotiation skills and,
    604–606
parallel, 389, 583, 585
performance problems of,
    594–598
problem-solving, 389, 583, 585
productivity of, 578
project, 583
quality improvements by,
    578–579
response speed of, 579
roles for members of, 587–588
self-managed, 580, 582–583
stages of development for,
    586–587
virtual, 585
work groups vs., 577, 578
Teamsters Union, 125
Technology. *See also* Electronic
    communication;
    Information systems;
    Information technology;
    Internet; Software
    analysis of, 292, 295, 301
    globalization and, 61–62
    impact of, 734
Telecommuting, 471, 486
Telnet, 739
Terrorism, 476, 477
Theft
    employee, 678
    identity, 757–758
    information, 742, 757–758, 760
Theory X, 30
Theory Y, 30–31
Third-country nationals, 82
360–degree feedback, 483
Three-step model of
    organizational change,
    172
Time management, 260–261
Time orientation, 68
Top-down change, 173–174
Total factor productivity, 709
Total Quality Control
    (Feigenbaum), 21
Total quality management (TQM)
    customers and, 715
    explanation of, 21–23, 168,
        713–714